PrincetonReview.com

THE BEST 300
BUSINESS SCHOOLS

2011 EDITION

Nedda Gilbert
and the Staff
of The Princeton Review

Random House, Inc.
New York

The Princeton Review, Inc.
111 Speen Street, Suite 550
Framingham, MA 01701
E-mail: bookeditor@review.com

© 2010 by The Princeton Review, Inc.

All rights reserved under International and Pan-American Copyright
Conventions. Published in the United States by Random House, Inc., New York,
and simultaneously in Canada by Random House of Canada Limited, Toronto.

All rankings, ratings, and listings are intellectual property of The Princeton
Review, Inc. No rankings, ratings, listings, or other proprietary information in
this book may be repurposed, abridged, excerpted, combined with other data,
or altered for reproduction in any way without express permission of TPR.

ISBN: 978-0-375-42790-9

Senior VP, Publisher: Robert Franek
Production: Best Content Solutions, LLC
Editor: Laura Braswell
Production Editor: Kristen O'Toole
Account Manager: David Soto

Printed in the United States of America on partially recycled paper.

9 8 7 6 5 4 3 2 1

2011 Edition

ACKNOWLEDGMENTS

This book absolutely would not have been possible without the help of my husband, Paul. With each edition of this guide, his insights and support have been invaluable—this book continues to be as much his as it is mine. That said, I also need to thank my daughter, Kaela, and her little sister, Lexi, for enduring all the time I have spent immersed in this project.

A big thanks goes to Tom Meltzer and Anna Weinberg for their smart and savvy profile writing. The following people were also instrumental in the completion of this book: Scott Harris, Laura Braswell, David Soto, Ben Zelevansky, Andrea Kornstein, Ann DeWitt, Abe Koogler, Kristen O'Toole and Adrinda Kelly for putting all the pieces together; the sales staff at The Princeton Review, Josh Escott; Robert Franek and Young Shin, as well as Alicia Ernst, for giving me the chance to write this book; and to the folks at Random House, who helped this project reach fruition.

Thanks go to Kristin Hansen (Tuck '01) and Matt Camp (Tuck '02), and to Ramona Payne and all the folks at The Diversity Pipeline Alliance. I am also grateful for the unique insights provided by Cathy Crane-Moley, Stanford Graduate School of Business, Class of '92; Patricia Melnikoff and Chiara Perry, Harvard Business School, Class of '92; Caroline Grossman, University of Chicago Graduate School of Business, Class of '03; Sara Weiss, MIT Sloan School of Management, Class of '04; and Stephen Hazelton, MIT Sloan School of Management, Class of '05. Thanks are also due to the business school folks who went far out of their way to provide essential information. They continue to make this book relevant and vital.

Linda Baldwin, Director of Admissions, The Anderson School, UCLA

Derek Bolton, Assistant Dean and Director of Admissions, Stanford University School of Business

Eileen Chang, former Associate Director of Admissions, Harvard Business School

Allan Friedman, Executive Director of Communications and Public Relations, University of Chicago

Wendy Hansen, Associate Director of Admissions, Stanford Business School

Stacey Kole, Deputy Dean for the full-time MBA Program and Clinical Professor of Economics, University of Chicago Graduate School of Business

Steven Lubrano, Assistant Dean and Director of the MBA Program, Tuck School of Business

Rose Martinelli, Director of Admissions and Financial Aid, The University of Chicago

Jon McLaughlin, Assistant MBA Admissions Director, Sloan School of Management, MIT

Julia Min, Executive Director of MBA Admissions, UC—Berkeley, Haas School of Business

Jeanne Wilt, Assistant Dean of Admissions and Career Development, University of Michigan

Linda Meehan, Assistant Dean for Admissions, Columbia University

CONTENTS

INTRODUCTION

A RETURN TO OUR ROOTS

Over the past 16 years, The Princeton Review has annually published a guide to business schools. For the early editions of the guide, we collected opinion surveys from thousands of students at a select group of graduate business schools as well as school statistics from school administrators that include enrollment and demographic figures, tuition, and the average GMAT scores of entering students. We used the students' opinions to craft descriptive narratives of the schools they attended and reported the statistics in the sidebars of those narrative profiles.

For the 2001–2004 editions of this guide, we discontinued collecting opinion surveys from students and writing narrative descriptions of the schools; instead we focused solely on collecting and reporting school statistics. While we were able to report statistics for many more business schools in the new format (the last [2000] edition of the guide with narrative descriptions profiled only 80 schools, and the first edition of the statistics-only guide profiled 372 schools), we learned over the next few years that readers are interested in more than just school-reported statistics. They want to read what the experts—current graduate business school students—have to say about the experiences of today's graduate business student. They want from-the-horse's-mouth accounts of what's great (*and* what's not) at each school.

So, in 2005, we decided to reintroduce the student survey-driven descriptive narrative, offering students a more intimate look at the inner workings of each school, and we've continued with this approach ever since.

We also brought back several top 10 lists that rank the profiled schools according to various metrics (more on the rankings later). You'll find these rankings in Part II of this book.

Taken together, we believe that these candid student opinions, school statistics, and rankings provide a unique and helpful resource to help you decide what business schools to apply to. But let us stress that we hope that this book will not be the *only* resource you turn to when making this expensive (both in terms of time and treasure) decision to enter a graduate business program. Do additional research on the Internet and in newspapers, magazines, and other periodicals. Talk to Admissions Officers and current students at the programs that interest you. If at all possible, visit the campuses you are seriously considering. But treat the advice of all these resources (including ours) as you would treat advice from anyone regarding any situation: as input that reflects the values and opinions of others as you *form your own opinion*.

TWO TYPES OF ENTRIES

For each of the 432 business programs in this book, you will find one of two possible types of entries: a two-page profile with lots of descriptive text and statistics, or a straight statistical listing. Our descriptive profiles are driven primarily by 1) comments business students provide in response to open-ended questions on our student survey, and 2) our own statistical analysis of student responses to the many multiple-choice questions on the survey. While many business students complete a survey unsolicited by us at http://survey.review.com, in the vast majority of cases we rely on business school administrators to get the word out about our survey to their students. In the ideal scenario, the business school administration sends a Princeton Review-authored e-mail to all business students with an embedded link to our survey website (again, http://survey.review.com). If for some reason there are restrictions that prevent the administration from contacting the entire graduate business school student body on behalf of an outside party, they often help us find other ways to notify students of the fact that we are seeking their opinions, such as advertising in business student publications or posting on business student community websites. In almost all cases, when the administration is cooperative, we are able to collect opinions from a sufficient number of students to produce an accurate descriptive profile and ratings of its business school.

There is a group of business school administrators, however, that doesn't agree with us that current business school student opinions presented in descriptive profile and rankings formats are useful to prospective business school students. Administrators at the many AACSB-accredited business schools not appearing with two-page descriptive profiles are a part of this group. They either ignored our multiple attempts to contact them in order to request their assistance in notifying their students about our survey, or they simply refused to work with us at all. While we would like to be able to write a descriptive profile each of these many schools anyway, we won't do so with minimal business student opinion.

So if you are a prospective business school student and would like to read current business student opinion about schools that do not appear with a two-page descriptive profile, contact the schools and communicate this desire to them. (We include contact information in each of the business school data listings.) If you are a current business student at one of the many AACSB-accredited business schools without a two-page descriptive profile, please don't send us angry letters; instead, go to http://survey.review.com, complete a survey about your school, and tell all of your fellow students to do the same.

You will find statistics for business schools whose administrators were willing to report their school statistics to us but unwilling to allow us to survey their students under the school's name in the section of the book entitled "Business School Data Listings."

One more thing to note about the different entries: The majority of our various rankings lists are based wholly or partly on student feedback to our survey. Only one top 10 ranking, The Toughest to Get Into, is based on school-reported statistics alone. So while *any* of the 432 programs listed in the book may appear on that list, *only those schools with two-page descriptive profiles will appear on all other rankings lists.*

BUT SOME THINGS NEVER CHANGE

Admission to the business school of your choice, especially if your choice is among the most selective programs, will require your absolute best shot. One way to improve your chances is to make sure you apply to schools that are a good fit—and the comments provided by students in our descriptive profiles will provide more insight into the personality of each school than does its glossy view book.

In addition, you'll find plenty of useful information in Part I of this book on how to get in to business school and what to expect once you arrive. You'll find out what criteria are used to evaluate applicants and who decides your fate. You will also hear directly from admissions officers on what dooms an application and how to ace the interview. We've even interviewed deans at several of the top schools to share with you their take on recent events, including trends in business, b-school applications, recruitment, and placement.

Again, it is our hope that you will consult our profiles as a resource when choosing a list of schools that suit your academic and social needs, and that our advice is helpful to you during the application process. Good luck!

HOW WE PRODUCE THIS BOOK

In August 1999, we published *The Best 80 Business Schools, 2000 Edition*. By the time the 2001 edition of the guide was published, we had shifted our focus from student opinion-driven profiles of a select number of schools to more data-driven profiles of every graduate business school accredited by the AACSB. Although we continue to present readers with data from 300 accredited graduate b-school programs, we have reintroduced the student survey-based descriptive profile. In order to clarify our position, intent, and methodology, we've created a series of questions and answers regarding the collection of data and the production of our descriptive profiles.

How do we choose which b-schools to survey and profile? And why do some competitive schools have only a data listing?

Any business school that is AACSB-accredited and offers a Master of Business Administration degree may have a data listing included in the book, as long as that school provides us with a sufficient amount of school-specific data. In addition, this year we offered each of those accredited schools in which the primary language of instruction is English an opportunity to assist us in collecting online business student surveys.

Some schools were unable to solicit surveys from their students via e-mail due to restrictive privacy policies; others simply chose not to participate. Schools that declined to work with us to survey their students remain in the book, although they do not have a descriptive profile. A school with only a data listing does not suggest that the school is less competitive or compelling; we only separated these profile types into two sections for easier reference. If you're not sure where to find information on a school in which you're interested, you can refer to our alphabetical b-school listing in the back of the book.

There is no fee to be included in this book. If you're an administrator at an accredited business school and would like to have your school included, please send an e-mail to surveysupport@review.com.

What's the AACSB, and by what standards are schools accredited?

The AACSB stands for the Association to Advance Collegiate Schools of Business. In April 2003, the AACSB made some significant changes to its standards for accreditation. In fact, the actual number of standards went from 41 to 21. Some of the changes in accreditation included a shift from requiring a certain number of full-time faculty members with doctorates to a focus on teacher participation. Schools may employ more part-time faculty members if they are actively involved in the students' business education. The onus of both the development of a unique curriculum and the evaluation of the success of that curriculum will fall on each b-school, and schools will be reviewed by the association every five years instead of every ten. As a result of the changes in accreditation standards, a number of schools have been newly accredited or reaccredited.

How were the student surveys collected?

Back in Fall 2005, we contacted Admissions Officers at all accredited graduate b-schools and requested that they help us survey their students by distributing our Princeton Review–authored survey message to the student body via e-mail. The survey message explained the purpose of the survey and contained a link to our online business student survey. We had a phenomenal response from students—at least ten percent of full-time students responded at almost all institutions we surveyed; at many schools, we scored responses from as many as one-third or one-half of the student body—and nearly all students in a few cases.

The surveys are made up of 78 multiple-choice questions and 7 free-response questions, covering 5 sections: About Yourself, Students, Academics, Careers, and Quality of Life. Students may complete the secure online survey at any time and may save their survey responses, returning later, until the survey is complete and ready for submission. Students sign in to the online survey using their school-issued .edu e-mail address to ensure that their response is attributed to the correct school, and the respondent certifies before submission that he or she is indeed a current student enrolled in said program. In addition, an automated message is sent to this address once the student has submitted the survey, and they must click on a link in the e-mail message in order to validate their survey. We also offered a paper version of the survey to a few schools that were unable to e-mail their students regarding our online survey.

We use the resulting responses to craft descriptive profiles that are representative of the respondents' feelings toward the b-school they attend. Although well-written and/or humorous comments are especially appreciated, they would never be used unless they best stated what numerous students have told us.

What about the ranking lists and ratings?

When we decided to bring the student opinion-driven resources back into the fold, we updated our online survey and reconsidered all ranking lists. You will find that only a few of the rankings in this year's book resemble our b-school rankings of yesteryear. We've done our best to include only those topics most vital to success in business school, and we have added a few brand new lists that you will find timely and relevant.

We offer several ranking lists on a variety of considerations, from academic experience to career expectations, to the atmosphere for women and minority students. It must be noted, however, that none of these lists purport to rank the business schools by their overall quality. Nor should any combination of the categories we've chosen be construed as representing the raw ingredients for such a ranking. We have made no attempt to gauge the "prestige" of these schools, and we wonder whether we could accurately do so even if we tried. What we have done, however, is presented a number of lists using information from two very large databases—one of statistical information collected from business schools and another of subjective data gathered via our survey of 11,000 business students at 300 AACSB-accredited business schools. We do believe that there is a right business school for you, and that our rankings, when used in conjunction with our profile of each school, will help you select the best schools to apply to.

Since the 2009 edition of this book, we have included "Best Classroom Experience" list, based on students' answers to survey questions concerning their professors' teaching ability and recognition in the field, the integration of new business trends and practices into course offerings, and the level of student engagement in the classroom.

What do the schools have to say about all this?

Our contact at each school is kept abreast of the profile's status throughout the production process. After establishing a contact through whom we are able to reach online student respondents, we get to work writing our profiles and crunching the data. Once this information has been poured into profile pages, we send a copy of the school's profile to our contact via e-mail. We request that the administrator review the data and comments included in the profile, and we invite their corrections to any inaccurate data, or text that may be misrepresentative of overall student opinion. With their suggestions in hand, we revisit survey responses and investigate any such claims of inaccuracy.

We are aware that a general distaste for rankings permeates the business school community, and that top schools have recently backed down from providing the data necessary for such calculations. We agree that overall rankings that purport to decide the "best" overall school are not so helpful to students, and that they may be tainted by the agendas of school administrators hoping to advance their schools' reputations, without taking the necessary measures to actually improve the quality of the school. This is why the meat of our book is the schools' descriptive profiles, which are meant to showcase each school's unique personality. The ranking lists are simply used as reference tools for students looking for a particular attribute in a prospective b-school. We don't claim to be the final word on what school has the best MBA program in the country—that's nearly impossible to determine. We simply relay the messages that the students at each school are sending us, and we are clear about how our rankings are determined.

HOW THIS BOOK IS ORGANIZED

This book is packed with information about business schools, and we want to make sure you know how to find what you're looking for. So here's a breakdown of how this book is organized.

Part I is comprised of several chapters that give you an idea of what to expect at business school and tell you how to put together a winning application.

Part II has our b-school ranking lists. Of the ten lists, six are based entirely on student survey responses; one is based solely on institutionally reported data, while four others are based on a combination of survey responses and statistical information. Along with each list, you will find information about which survey questions or statistical factors were used to calculate the rankings.

Part III contains profiles of all AACSB-accredited graduate schools with MBA programs divided into two sections: those with descriptive profiles based on student surveys, and those with only a statistical listing.

Please see the sample descriptive profile below.

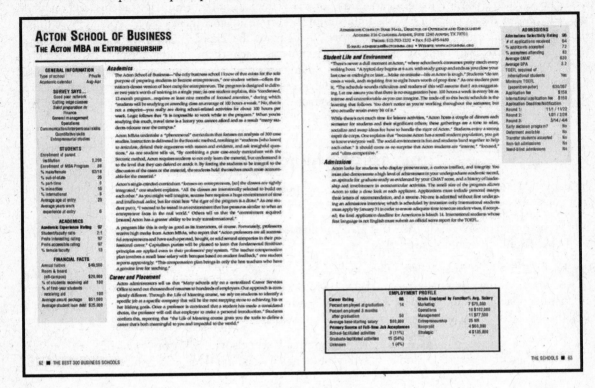

Each two-page spread is made up of eight major components. At the top of each page, you'll find the name of the business school, along with the name of an admissions contact and his or her address, phone number, fax number, if applicable, and e-mail address. This section also includes the b-school's website address. There are two sidebars (the narrow columns on the outer edge of each page) that contain information reported by the schools through the Business Data Set (BDS) and some student survey data as well. The Survey Says information reflects aspects of the school about which students feel the strongest; there are nine different possible results. We also offer an Employment Profile for each school, which is made up of statistical information from the BDS. The main body of the profile contains descriptive text discussing Academics, Placement and Recruiting, Student/Campus Life, and Admissions. Each description is based on student survey responses and may call upon statistical data where necessary.

The Sidebars

All information in the sidebars falls under the following categories: General Information, Academics, Financial Facts, and Admissions. Please note that not every category will appear for every school; in some cases the information is not reported or not applicable. These are the same data fields that are reported for those schools listed in Part III-B: Business School Data Listings, save for four of the five ratings, which appear only in the descriptive profiles.

Here is what each sidebar heading tells you.

General Information

Type of school

Public or private school.

Affiliation

Any religious order with which the school is affiliated.

Academic Calendar

Whether the school schedule runs according to trimesters, semesters, quarters, or another calendar type like a 4-1-4 (4-month semester, 1-month interim term, 4-month semester).

Survey Says

Survey Says gives you an at-a-glance look at what students are most in agreement about at their school. You'll find up to six results per school. Three will reflect the top three subject areas as indicated by responses to the following question:

How well has your school prepared you in the following areas:

Marketing

Finance

Accounting

General management

Operations

Teamwork

Communication/Interpersonal skills

Presentation skills

Quantitative skills

Computer skills

Doing business in a global economy

Entrepreneurial studies

In addition, Survey Says may include (up to) three things from the following list that students were most in agreement about:

- Students like Hometown, State. Based on level of agreement with the statement, "I like the town where my school is located."

- Friendly students. Based on level of agreement with the statement, "Your business school classmates are friendly."

- Good social scene. Based on level of agreement with the statement, "Your business school classmates have active social lives."

- Good peer network. Based on level of agreement with the statement, "Your business school classmates are the type of people you want to network with after graduation."

- Cutting-edge classes. Based on responses to the question, "How well has your school integrated new business trends and practices into course offerings?"

- Helpful alumni. Based on responses to the question, "How helpful have alumni been in assisting you in your job search?"

- Happy students. Based on level of agreement with the statement, "Overall, I am happy here."

- Smart classrooms. Based on level of agreement with the statement, "Classroom facilities are equipped with computer/multimedia resources."

Students

Enrollment of parent institution

Total number of undergraduate and graduate students enrolled in parent institution program.

Enrollment of MBA program

Total number of students enrolled in MBA programs at the business school, including both full- and part-time programs.

"% male/female" through "% international"

Items based on demographic information about full-time b-school students as reported by the schools

Average age at entry

The average age of incoming first-year MBA students.

Average years work experience at entry

The average years of work experience for incoming first-year MBA students.

Academics

Academic Experience Rating

This rating measures the quality of the learning environment. Each school is given a score between 60 and 99. Factors taken into consideration include GMAT scores and undergraduate grades of enrolled students; percent accepted; percent enrolled; student/faculty ratio; and student survey questions pertaining to faculty, fellow students, and realization of academic expectations. This rating is intended to be used only to compare those schools within this edition of the book whose students completed our business student survey.

Please note that if a 60* Academic Experience Rating appears for any school, it means that the school didn't report all the rating's underlying data points by our deadline, so we were unable to calculate an accurate rating. In such cases, the reader is advised to follow up with the school about specific measures this rating takes into account.

Please also note that many foreign institutions use a grading system that is different from the standard U.S. GPA; as a result, we approximated their Admissions Selectivity and Academic Ratings, indicating this with a † following the rating.

Student/Faculty Ratio

The ratio of full-time graduate instructional faculty members to all enrolled MBA students.

Professors Interesting Rating

Based on the answers given by students to the survey question, "Overall, how good are your professors as teachers?" Ratings fall between 60 and 99. This rating is intended to be used to compare those schools within this edition of the book whose students completed our business student survey.

Professors Accessible Rating

Based on the answers given by students to the survey question, "How accessible are your professors outside of the classroom?" Ratings fall between 60 and 99. This rating is intended to be used to compare those schools within this edition of the book whose students completed our business student survey.

% female faculty

Percent of graduate business faculty in the 2008–2009 academic year who were women.

% minority faculty

Percent of graduate business faculty in the 2008–2009 academic year who were members of minority groups.

Joint Degrees

A list of joint degrees offered by the business school. See Decoding Degrees on page 745 for the full name of each degree.

Prominent Alumni

School administrators may submit the name, title, and company of up to five prominent alumni.

Financial Facts

Please note that we rely on foreign institutions to convert financial figures into U.S. dollars. Please check with any foreign schools you are considering for up-to-date figures and conversion rates.

"Tuition (in-state/out-of-state)" and "Fees (in-state/out-of-state)"

In-state and out-of-state tuition and fees per academic year. At state-supported public schools, in-state tuition and fees are likely to be significantly lower than out-of-state expenses.

Books and supplies

Estimated cost of books and supplies for one academic year.

Room and board

Cost of room and board on campus per academic year, and estimate of off-campus living expenses for this time period.

"% of students receiving aid" through "% of students receiving grants"

Percent of students receiving aid, then specifically those receiving grants and loans. These numbers reflect the percentage of all enrolled MBA students that receive financial aid, regardless of whether or not they applied for financial aid or for specific aid types. Likewise, the second figure, "% of first year students receiving aid" takes into account all first-year MBA students, regardless of whether they applied for financial aid or specific aid types.

Average award package

For students who received financial aid, this is the average award amount.

Average grant

For students who received grants, this is the average amount of grant money awarded.

Average student loan debt

The average dollar amount of outstanding educational MBA loans per graduate (class of 2009) at the time of graduation.

Admissions

Admissions Selectivity Rating

This rating measures the competitiveness of the school's admissions. Factors taken into consideration include the average GMAT score and undergraduate GPA of the first-year class, the percent of students accepted, and the percent of applicants who are accepted and ultimately enroll. No student survey data is used in this calculation. Ratings fall between 60 and 99. This rating is intended to be used to compare all schools within this edition of the book, regardless of whether their students completed our business student survey.

Please note that if a 60* Admissions Selectivity Rating appears for any school, it means that the school did not report all of the rating's underlying data points by our deadline, so we were unable to calculate an accurate rating. In such cases, the reader is advised to follow up with the school about specific measures this rating takes into account.

Please also note that many foreign institutions use a grading system that is different from the standard U.S. GPA; as a result, we approximated their Admissions Selectivity and Academic Ratings, indicating this with a † next to the rating.

of applications received

The total number of applications received for any and all MBA programs at the school.

% applicants accepted

The percentage of applicants to which the school offered admission.

% acceptees attending

Of those accepted students, the percentage of those who enrolled.

Average GMAT

The average GMAT score for the first-year class.

Average GPA

The average undergraduate GPA of the first year class, reported on a four-point scale.

TOEFL required of international applicants?

For those international students interested in applying, the b-school reports whether the Test of English as a Foreign Language (TOEFL) is required.

Minimum TOEFL (paper/computer/web)

The minimum TOEFL score necessary for consideration. We list acceptable scores for both the paper and computer versions of the test.

Application fee

The amount it costs to file an application with the school.

International Application Fee

The amount it costs an international student to file an application with the school if it is different from the cost of the regular application.

"Application deadline" and "Regular notification"

This regular application deadline reflects the date by which all materials must be postmarked; the notification date tells you when you can expect to hear back.

"Early decision program" and "ED deadline/notification"

If a school offers an early decision option, we'll tell you when early decision apps are due to be postmarked, and when you'll be notified of the school's decision.

"Deferment available?" and "Maximum length of deferment"

Some schools allow accepted students to defer enrollment for a year or more, while others require students who postpone attendance to reapply.

Transfer students accepted?

Whether or not students are accepted from other MBA programs.

Transfer Application Policy

Lets you know how transfer applications are reviewed and how many credits will be allowed to transfer from another program.

Non-fall admissions?

Some business schools may allow students to matriculate at the beginning of each semester, while for others, the invitation to attend stipulates that fall attendance is mandatory.

Need-blind admissions?

Whether or not the school considers applications without regard to the candidate's financial need.

Applicants also look at

The school reports that students applying to their school are also known to apply to a short list of other schools.

EMPLOYMENT PROFILE
Career Rating

Taking into account both student survey responses and statistical data, this rating measures the confidence students have in their school's ability to lead them to fruitful employment opportunities, as well as the school's own record of having done so. Factors taken into consideration include statistics on the average starting salary and percent of students employed at graduation from the Business Data Set and comments from the student survey, assessing the efforts of the placement office, the quality of recruiting companies, level of preparation, and opportunities for off-campus projects, internships, and mentorships. Ratings fall between 60 and 99. This rating is intended to be used to compare only those schools within this edition of the book whose students completed our business student survey.

* Please note that if a 60* Career Rating appears for any school, it means that the school did not report all of the rating's underlying data points by our deadline, so we were unable to calculate an accurate rating. In such cases, the reader is advised to follow up with the school about the specific attributes this rating takes into account.

% grads employed within three months of graduation

This reflects the percentage of MBA grads who earned a job within three months of graduation.

Average starting salary

Average starting salary of all 2009 graduates.

Primary source of full-time job acceptances

This reflects the percentage of full-time job acceptances that are the result of school-facilitated, graduate-facilitated, or unknown activities.

Grads employed by field %: avg. salary

Reflects the distribution of 2009 graduates across many different industries and the average starting salary for each field.

Top five employers hiring grads

Reflects the top five employers who hired 2009 job seeking full-time MBA graduates, and the number of students they hired.

DESCRIPTIVE PROFILE

Each school's descriptive profile is made up of four sections which highlight those qualities that characterize the school as a unique institution. *Academics* covers students' opinions on the quality of professors, curriculum, special or noteworthy programs, the administration, and anything else academic in nature. *Career and Placement* deals with the school's efforts to secure internships and jobs for its current students and graduates; information about alumni assistance and popular recruiters of MBAs at the school may also be included. In *Student Life and Environment*, you'll find out how students balance work and play and whether they find it manageable to do so; often, you'll also find reviews of the school's facilities as well. Finally, the *Admissions* section describes what the Admissions Committee is looking for in potential students.

All quotes in these sections are taken from students' responses to our survey. We choose quotes that were consistent with the overall survey results.

PART III-B: BUSINESS SCHOOL DATA LISTINGS

This section contains all of the statistical info that is presented in the sidebars of the descriptive profile. Each school in this section will include an Admissions Selectivity rating but will not include the other three ratings, the Survey Says section, or a descriptive profile.

PART IV: SCHOOL SAYS

Part IV offers more detailed information about particular business schools authored by the schools themselves. The business schools included in this section pay a small fee for this space. These schools also have descriptive profiles or data listings in Part III.

EVERYTHING ELSE

Following Part IV, we offer a small section of profiles of b-schools who may pay a small fee for inclusion. Next is a section entitled *Decoding Degrees* that will help you make sense of the myriad degree abbreviations you'll see listed in the book. You'll then find the indexes—alphabetical by school name, and then by location. Finally, you'll have an opportunity to learn more about our author, Nedda Gilbert.

Enjoy and good luck!

PART I
ALL ABOUT BUSINESS SCHOOL

Chapter 1

This Isn't Your Father's (or Mother's) B-School Anymore

THE NEW MBA CLASS: FEWER, YOUNGER, AND WORKING WHILE THEY LEARN

The MBA has always been seen as a golden passport; the trip ticket to romance and riches. The destination: career acceleration, power networks and recruiters, elite employers, and, of course, generous paychecks.

But not everyone wants to make the trip. Several factors will always impact on the popularity of the MBA: 1) the state of the economy—interest in getting the MBA has generally waxed and waned with economic times; 2) trends and favorable or unfavorable press—in the 1980s, a rash of insider trading scandals in which MBAs were ensnared made the degree look smarmy and other graduate programs, notably law and medicine, look more appealing; 3) the immediacy of good professional opportunities—the collapse of the dot-com boom, followed by the severe retrenchment of traditional MBA destinations (such as investment banks and consulting firms) in a depressed economy, has left many current MBAs stranded; and 4) recruiter demand for newly minted MBAs—do employers see the skill sets of today's MBAs bringing measurable value to their companies?

B-SCHOOL: INTEREST AND APPLICATIONS ON UPSWING

After three straight years of declining applications, the numbers increased in 2006, and application volume continues to climb or remain steady at many schools. Almost 70% of full-time MBA programs participating in the 2009 GMAC Application Trends Survey saw application levels rise in 2007. Part-time programs are still reporting a modest increase in volume, and flexible MBA programs continue to attract more students, reporting a 66 percent increase in volume overall. Among executive MBA programs, applications are down almost half from the previous year.

YOUNGER MINDS

Although growing applicant pools may make admission seem more competitive, there are now some unrecognized opportunities for candidates with less than the traditional two to four years of work experience to make a strong case for admittance.

Admissions officers at large benchmark schools such as Stanford say that this trend pre-dates the economic downturn. Derek Bolton, director of admissions at Stanford notes, "The pendulum has gone too far in one direction in terms of the number of younger candidates applying to b-school. It has not kept pace with the overall pace of applicants. We want more young applicants applying. The goal is to bring the average age down in the next couple of years."

"What's driving this is the willingness on the part of the b-schools to not be rigidly fixed on what's right for someone. We may not always be the best judge of when the best time is for a candidate to go to b-school," continues Bolton.

Wharton's former Director of Admissions Rose Martinelli observed "a shift in that we became more tuned in to when students are ready in their leadership, professional, and personal development. We see so many nontraditional students that we don't want to have rules on when they can apply. We don't want to miss out on fabulous applicants because they don't think they can get in."

"When the applicant pool continues to get older and older, then we're closing out younger applicants who are on a fast track." Martinelli continues, "Why should we wait? Why should they wait? We want to catch the human element in the application process."

This perspective continues to hold true. As University of Chicago's Stacey Kole sums up, "The pendulum had swung too far in terms of the type of student who should be admitted and when. Now schools are correcting that and experimenting, taking less experienced candidates. We believe that this experimentation is a good thing."

There may be more to the story, too. Because they may be less likely to be in committed relationships or have families, younger students are more active, generous alumni, and b-schools can't afford to ignore the market that these younger students represent. Despite the heightened competition, candidates with less experience are increasingly being deemed worthy of a coveted b-school acceptance.

The Draw of The Part-Time Program

Ironically, even as the economy appears to be recovering, many young adults are choosing to brave a newly robust job market over immersing themselves in the uncertainty—not to mention the high costs—of a graduate program in business or even law. Because part-time education programs continue to attract applicants, pundits say that the future of b-school may lie in programs that offer more flexible part-time opportunities, allowing students to get the degree without making a full-time commitment. In fact, Stacey Kole, Deputy Dean for the full-time MBA Program and Clinical Professor of Economics, University of Chicago Graduate School of Business states, "There is this tendency to think of the MBA as a full-time-only product. But schools like Chicago offer MBA programs in the evening, on weekends, and in executive program formats. For us, whether the student matriculates in our part-time or full-time program, the process is exactly the same. Ours is the same degree, only delivered in full-time, part-time, and weekend formats with different scheduling options. Chicago GSB offers individuals interested in an MBA considerable flexibility in how they pursue their education."

Kole continues, "Part-time and executive programs are now providing more of the outside-the-classroom, extracurricular experience that did not exist 10 years ago. For example, they are offering student-led clubs, speakers, and recruiter events that historically were the exclusive domain of full-time programs. This is one explanation for why part-time programs are looking like better substitutes for a full-time program."

Payback Time

The MBA, particularly at the top schools, continues to pay out high dividends to grads. Although salaries for U.S. alumni are still higher than those paid to their European counterparts, the gap is closing rapidly. That's a hefty return on investment. But the degree doesn't come with any promises. The world of business requires some risk, as many MBA wannabes found out several years go: You can enter a business school program at the height of the economy only to graduate when things are dismal. But you can also enter b-school at low tide then watch as the job market swells and employers are fighting over the newest and brightest MBA grads, including you. Indeed, the current economic climate has many MBA students and grads concerned about their job prospects, however, it's important to realize that with these financial challenges come opportunities for innovative and dedicated individuals.

MBA CONCENTRATIONS

The MBA has changed a lot over the years. Once upon a time, it was enough to simply earn your degree and enter the working world a more knowledgeable and employable individual for it. Nowadays, business represents an increasingly multi-faceted and diverse world, meaning that MBA students can't be jacks-of-all-trades—they need areas of specialization. When looking at potential business schools, it's imperative to know if they offer the concentration you're keen on. To help you decide what your concentration might be, we've added these helpful indexes to the back of our book (see page 767) along with brief explanations of what each entails below.

ACCOUNTING

As an accounting specialist, you'll become an expert in the gathering and interpretation of financial data, and the ways in which that data can affect a company.

ENTREPRENEURSHIP

A concentration in entrepreneurship offers you the chance to develop real business savvy, network with potential collaborators and investors, and try out new ideas with fewer risks than you'll encounter in the real world.

FINANCE

The finance concentration is about money: how to make it, manage it, and make more of it. A specialization in finance will prepare you to make smart financial decisions for individuals, institutions, and companies.

HEALTHCARE ADMINISTRATION

This specialization will teach you how the nation's healthcare system works, as well as the challenges facing healthcare organizations—from government agencies to hospitals to biotech, pharmaceutical, and medical technology companies.

HUMAN RESOURCES MANAGEMENT

In this concentration, you'll learn how to maximize human output in a business environment, from understanding individual behavior to designing effective management structures, training programs, and compensation schemes.

INTERNATIONAL MANAGEMENT

A concentration in international management will prepare you to succeed in today's global business environment. Many programs actually require students to spend a semester overseas, working at a company or studying at a partner university.

LEADERSHIP

This concentration is designed to help students develop skills that are essential to success in any field: critical thinking, problem-solving, communicating, negotiating, and acting ethically in professional situations.

MARKETING

Marketing professionals anticipate consumer demands, help to create products and services that consumers want, attract consumers to that product or service, and retain consumers over the long haul. They also have their hand in pricing and distribution; figuring out what products should cost and how they'll get to customers.

NON-PROFIT MANAGEMENT

Running a non-profit requires many of the same skills needed to run a business: raising capital, managing organization for maximum cost efficiency, and effectively delivering a service to your "clients."

SUPPLY CHAIN MANAGEMENT

A specialization in supply chain management will prepare you to create and manage the entire selling process for any company with a good or service to vend. In a world of global suppliers and tight profit margins, effective supply chain management can mean the difference between profitability and bankruptcy.

FOREIGN MBA STUDENTS: THE NEW REALITY

Opportunities to study or work abroad during an MBA program are considered highly relevant. Likewise, international enrollment at U.S. business schools has always been a priority. At some schools, the percentage of foreign students has been sky-high, anywhere from 30 to 40 percent. Of course, that was before the new screening and tracking processes for international applicants went into effect.

Previously, our position was clear: International students represent a win-win proposition for both U.S. business schools and the foreign industries that send them here. American business schools prize the global perspective and diversity international students bring into the classroom and community; foreign businesses operating in a global economy desire expertise in U.S. business practices which are becoming the international standard.

Unfortunately, due to international security issues, this informal but critical partnership faces greater challenges. These have come primarily in the form of increased scrutiny. Foreign students must slog through tougher rules and procedures for obtaining and maintaining a visa under the United States Citizenship and Immigration Services (USCIS). And many foreign students feel that even if they are successful in obtaining a student visa, they will face an even tougher battle after they graduate: trying to get a work visa. That puts them back at square one. Though armed with an American MBA, they often find themselves looking for work in their home country—a scenario from which they may originally have wanted a professional out.

FOREIGN STUDENTS: GETTING IN

As of January 2003, U.S. institutions must comply with the Student and Exchange Visitor Information System, or SEVIS, which tracks foreign students and exchange visitors, as well as some foreign professors. While there is hope that SEVIS will prevent potential terrorists from slipping through the cracks, critics fear that the intensified scrutiny drives away many foreign applicants. The system causes major delays in obtaining a student visa and leaving or reentering the country. In addition, compliance with SEVIS requires the staff of international student offices to perform a great deal of data entry, detracting from the face-time advisors can spend with foreign students.

For the foreseeable future, students wishing to obtain a visa will not be able to escape the shadow of world events, but they should not be deterred. Most business schools stand firm on their commitment to foreign applicants throughout the entire process.

In fact, Don Martin, Director of Admissions at the University of Chicago notes that the number of international students enrolled at UChicago has remained constant. Martin says, "We have made no change in terms of our desire and commitment to enroll foreign students. This world will never go back to what it was before it became a global village. For the sake of diversity and the perspective international students bring to the table, or for understanding foreign business culture, we need to have people who represent that world in every sense."

Martin does agree that for foreign MBA students intending to study on American soil, "The journey of enrolling them is going to be more challenging. A part of that is tied into the changes the U.S. government has imposed on getting visas. Some applicants will need to take another year for the paperwork." But most notably, he sees different forces at play in the shrinking foreign MBA market, namely, the competition U.S. schools are feeling from business schools abroad. Martin continues, "The issue influencing more international business students away from U.S. business schools is the large amount of European, Australian, and Latin American business schools that heretofore I would not have thought would have had as much pull as they did. These business schools have become more visible and prominent. They are being ranked by the large news organizations and magazines. So I would say American business schools still want international students, but the ability to recruit and draw them here to us will be difficult against this new competition."

To those applying for a visa, Wharton's former Director of Admissions Rose Martinelli offers this advice: "Emphasize plans to return home, [not] plans to immigrate to the United States." If a visa is denied, many schools will defer admission and hold that student's spot until the visa is obtained. "It may take a little longer for students from some countries to get their visas. But decisions here are not made based on whether they got a visa or not. Decisions are made based on what they'll do at our school and on the contributions they'll make," sums up Martinelli.

Of course, all this is subject to change, perhaps even by the time of this book's publication. Non-U.S. citizens should visit the USCIS website (www.uscis.gov) for the latest information on student visas.

FOREIGN STUDENTS: GETTING A JOB

Just when a foreign student is ready to reap the rewards of his or her hard-won business degree, he or she hits another roadblock. And this one's a brick wall: an unforgiving and limited job market fueled not just by wartime security, but also a new nationalism.

Historically, foreign students have always had a tougher time than their American counterparts in trying to get that first job out of b-school. That's because of the hassle of sponsoring a foreigner on a visa, rigid immigration rules, and other cultural and relocation issues. Nonetheless, for grads of the top schools, there has always been a pot of gold waiting at the end of that long journey. That pot of gold has meant the opportunity to embark on an entirely new career and life—to be sponsored by a U.S. company, on U.S. soil, with post-MBA pay scales that supersede those of their home countries and launch them on a high-earnings career path.

In recent years, the environment in the United States has changed, and the home-field advantage of American MBAs is even greater. Simply put, U.S. companies have been reluctant to offer a foreign MBA a plush job over an American MBA who is equally talented and qualified, especially in a depressed market. The result is that foreign hires have been more limited to hard-to-fill positions, to employment in their locations abroad, or to positions in the student's home country. Some MBA recruiters won't even offer an international student an interview.

As for companies shrinking their foreign MBA hires down to bare bones, as we've said many times before, and Don Martin concurs, where you go to school matters. He explains, "Some companies have changed their hiring strategies. Fewer overall international students are being hired, but not at our school. Companies typically will drop down from their list of 10 schools they go to, to a much smaller number of programs. In a high percentage, we've remained on their lists. We are seeing 90 percent of our international students placed in internships and going on to full-time hires."

The result of the shrinking job market for most foreign students is that business schools have begun to cut back on the number of applicants admitted, and this has made it even tougher to get accepted. Many schools have begun to be upfront about the limited career opportunities on U.S. soil for foreigners. Indeed, this will soon be compounded by a reduction of more than 50 percent in the number of work visas the government issues annually to employees sponsored by their company.

But as the economy improves and MBA hiring begins to rebound, it is possible that recruiters, particularly Wall Street and the top-flight consulting firms, will once again open their doors to whomever is most qualified, foreign or not. History, it should be remembered, shows us that the top jobs always go to the most capable applicants. This next cycle should be no different than the preceding cycles. Talent still rules.

In the meantime, buyers beware: An MBA is not the passport to riches it once was for foreign applicants. International students should think twice about the costs of pursuing a degree that may only deliver them back into the hands of their home countries saddled with the expense, but not the benefit, of an American MBA education.

THE CONTINUING RELEVANCE OF BUSINESS SCHOOL

The MBA is such an attractive option because it *does* confer huge value on the recipient. Business schools know how to keep pace with the rapidly changing face of business. After all, that's *their* business, so you're never really out of the game. In fact, if you look at the nation's top business programs, you'll find exciting innovations in curriculum that reflect all that's new and relevant. This includes unique opportunities for teamwork, internships, and laboratory simulations that replicate real-world, real-time business scenarios.

The integration of these real-world experiences into the basics produces better-trained, more well-rounded managers, as graduates are more adept at discerning the correlation between principle and reality. Even so, programs and students in search of business knowledge that is more widely applicable and more relevant long-term has caused a strong return to fundamentals.

BACKPEDALING TO THE BASICS

Many top schools are reviving the old classics: It's back to basics. Both schools and students now have enough of a perspective to look back at the frenzy of the last business cycle and understand that enduring values are rooted in a solid foundation. Gone is the frothy demand for trendy courses on e-commerce and other hype-driven topics. Just five years ago, a class at Stanford on the principles of Internet marketing was oversubscribed. Last year, only a few people signed up for it.

So here's a sampler of the back-to-basics you'll get at b-school: An in-depth immersion in all of the key functional areas of an organization: marketing, management, sales, finance, operations, logistics, and so on. You'll look at these areas across dozens of industries and organizational types, from start-ups to Fortune 500 companies.

The renewed focus on basics doesn't mean that you'll find yourself shorted on current trends and events. Expect plenty of case study debate on corporate governance and the Enron debacle, and expect the themes of global perspective and technological competence to permeate many programs. You'll also find classes and seminars on leadership gaining popularity. "We're seeing a resurgence of leadership courses as students seek out professions and business models that are other-oriented," notes Stanford's Bolton. "This may be a new generation. But these are students who look at business as a positive force in the world, a more noble calling."

SURVIVOR POWER

Once you have your MBA, you can expect to hit the ground running. You'll start off your post b-school career with a load of contacts that you will periodically leverage over your career. Many graduates use the degree to embark on entirely new career paths than those that brought them to the school; consultants become bankers, entrepreneurs become consultants, marketers become financiers, and so on. The MBA has and will continue to be a terrific opportunity to reinvent oneself.

"An MBA is unlike any other professional degree because the breadth of knowledge poises you for a multitude of career choices," says Julia Min, Assistant Dean of MBA Admissions for NYU Stern School of Business. "You can be an investment banker, yet two years from that point, segue into nonprofit work. You can move from banking to corporate finance, to a venture-capital proposition, to ultimately having an entrepreneurial experience. So it's a credential that allows you the flexibility to explore different industries; it's a long-term investment that will give you the tools to transition if you want to."

"What's wonderful about the MBA is that it provides fundamental skills that you can use whenever and wherever you need them," champions Martinelli. "I'm a cheerleader for the nontraditional because I feel the MBA is such a fundamental tool. It offers an ability to enter the business world and link passion with functionality."

"For example, for folks who want to go into public service or nonprofit, even the arts industry, they're very narrow fields. You need the passion and vision to be successful in them. But often credibility is undermined when you don't understand the business world's perspective," states Martinelli.

"You've got to know that industry if you're going to make it viable for the future. But you have to be able to know how to talk to the business world in order to get those investments to make it happen. And that's one of the reasons why an MBA is so valuable. It bestows credibility in the marketplace and helps us maintain these organizations in a world that doesn't often respect passion over the bottom line," she continues.

Despite the nation's current financial woes, MBA grads still have plenty of prospects. Hundreds of companies continue to visit and recruit from business school campuses, with today's MBA candidates receiving two job offers on average. Recruiters exist in a symbiotic relationship with business schools. Employers like to maintain a strong presence on campus—even during an economic downturn—so that they'll have their top picks of MBA talent when the good times return. Thus, MBA programs remain one of the most effective means to get oneself in front of recruiters and senior managers from the most desirable companies. And while that may not grant you "immunity" from an economy characterized by up and downs, it will absolutely improve your survivor power.

COMPETITION HAS EASED UP

With an economic recovery seemingly underway, the chance to dive into any number of secure, well-paying jobs will lure a percentage of professionals away from the MBA. After years of struggling through economic hardship, a decent paycheck from the pocket of a much improved labor market may seem the best bet. There's no doubt that risk-averse individuals would prefer the stability of a secure job to what might-be, could-be, or should-be two years down the road—even with an MBA in hand. This may keep the applicant pool smaller.

Additionally, the continued decrease in the number of foreign applicants, who at many schools comprised more than 20 percent of students, will keep applications down, too. Other factors include the fact that there are currently smaller percentages of people in the country who are in the typical age bracket of business school applicants. Lastly, the increased interest in flexible and part-time MBA programs may continue to drive the decline in full-time business school applications.

What does all of this mean? Basically this: If you have a handsome application and you plan on applying to the most competitive programs this year, you may find yourself met with welcoming arms.

AS THE SONG GOES...MONEY, MONEY, MONEY, MONEY...

But don't go buying the flashy car to go with that flashy degree quite yet. It needs to be said that, after several years of a slump, there could actually be a surge in this upcoming applicant pool that would correspond with improvements in the economy. Recruiters are once again canvassing the top business schools as hiring slowly returns to healthy levels. At programs like Chicago, Harvard, and Stanford, six-figure salaries and signing bonuses of $15,000-plus are still the norm. That's why it's important to remember that the MBA from the right school can deliver an immediate and hefty return on investment. According to the Graduate Management Admission Council Global MBA Graduate Survey of 2009, respondents reported an annual (mean) salary of approximately $60,000 before entering business school and a (mean) salary of almost $80,000 in their first job out. Amid a healthy recruiting environment built on strong employer confidence in the economy, the average new MBA with a job offer in hand will earn $79,271 during the first year of employment.

Another trend worth noting: Although applications are down overall at b-schools, that doesn't mean the quality of applicants has suffered. Notes Chicago's Kole, "Our applications are of high quality, and applicants appear to be quite focused with regard to why they seek an advanced degree. Whether they are career switchers or planning to resume their career path, those applicants who present a compelling story for why they want to be here leave a stronger impression with the admissions committee."

Top schools are always going to have people knocking at their doors. The possibility that business school applications in general could once again rise means you'll still want to be competitive. The long application process starts with developing a solid application strategy and applying to a diverse portfolio of schools.

LET US HELP YOU DECIDE

There are many factors to consider when deciding whether or not to pursue an MBA, and we'll help you make that decision in the following chapters. We'll also tell you a bit about each school in our profiles and prepare you to do further research on the schools on your list. We've worked hard to provide you with thorough information on every aspect of the MBA, but you don't have to take our word for it—see for yourself. Stanford's Bolton advises future applicants, "Start early. Visit as many schools as you can, because it's very hard to differentiate among programs from websites, books, and marketing materials. You need to get a feeling from walking down the halls."

After you decide to go, finding the right program can be extremely difficult. Bolton explains, "Applicants really have to dig beneath the programs they're looking at to determine what's going to make them happy. A lot of people wind up going to the wrong school. A lot of external factors contribute to that. People shouldn't worry about justifying the decision to others, but to themselves."

MAKING THE DECISION TO GO

The next step for you may be b-school. Indeed, armed with an MBA you may journey far. But the success of your trip and the direction you take will depend on knowing exactly why you're going to b-school and just what you'll be getting out of it.

The most critical questions you need to ask yourself are the following: Do you really want a career in business? What do you want the MBA to do for you? Are you looking to gain credibility, accelerate your development, or move into a new job or industry? Perhaps you're looking to start your own business, in which case entrepreneurial study will be important.

Knowing what you want doesn't just affect your decision to go, it also affects your candidacy; admissions committees favor applicants who have clear goals and objectives. Moreover, once at school, students who know what they want make the most of their two years. If you're uncertain about your goals, opportunities for career development—such as networking, mentoring, student clubs, and recruiter events—are squandered.

You also need to find a school that fits your individual needs. Consider the personal and financial costs. This may be the single biggest investment of your life. How much salary will you forego by leaving the workforce? What will the tuition be? How will you pay for it? If you have a family, spouse, or significant other, how will getting your MBA affect them?

If you do have a spouse, you may choose a program that involves partners in campus life. If status is your top priority, you should simply choose the most prestigious school you can get into.

The MBA presents many opportunities but no guarantees. As with any opportunity, you must make the most of it. Whether you go to a first-tier school or to a part-time program close to home, you'll acquire the skills that can jump-start your career. But your success will have more to do with you than with the piece of paper your MBA is printed on.

Chapter 2

Blackberrys and Power Lunches: What Does an MBA Offer?

NUTS-AND-BOLTS BUSINESS SKILLS

Graduate business schools teach the applied science of business. The best business schools combine the latest academic theories with pragmatic concepts, hands-on experience, and real-world solutions.

B-schools also teach the analytical skills used to make complicated business decisions. You learn how to define the critical issues, apply analytical techniques, develop the criteria for decisions, and make decisions after evaluating their impact on other variables.

After two years, you're ready to market a box of cereal. Or prepare a valuation of the cereal company's worth. You'll speak the language of business. You'll know the tools of the trade. Your expertise will extend to many areas and industries. In short, you will have acquired the skills that open doors.

ACCESS TO RECRUITERS, ENTRÉE TO NEW FIELDS

Applicants tend to place great emphasis on "incoming" and "outgoing" statistics. First they ask, "Will I get in?" Then they ask, "Will I get a job?"

Obviously, the first is largely dependent on how selective the school is and the quality of your credentials. The latter question can almost assuredly be answered in the positive, "Yes, you will."

But the real question is: How many—and what kind—of offers will you receive? Again, that is dependent on the appeal of the school to recruiters (what companies recruit on campus and how often is a readily available statistic you can get from each school) and the particular industry you elect to pursue. For example, investment banks and consulting firms are always going to come to the schools for formal recruiting periods, whereas more off-the-beaten-path choices will possibly require you to go off campus in search of opportunity.

It's Good to Be Wanted, It's Great to Be Paid

As we reported in Chapter 1, the average return on investment for business school grads in 2009 was an impressive 38 percent increase in annual salary. According to the Graduate Management Council, the before and after picture looks something like this: Average entering salary: roughly $60,000. Average first job out of school salary: $79,271. Presumably, starting salaries will continue to increase as the economy improves.

The majority of top grads receive a generous relocation package too. Indeed, if you were fortunate enough to have spent the summer between your first and second year at a consulting company, then you will, in all likelihood, also receive a "rebate" on your tuition. These companies often pick up a student's second-year tuition bill. The best package, however, goes to those MBA students who worked at the firm before b-school. These lucky capitalists often get their whole tuition paid for.

GETTING THE MBA FOR THE LONG RUN

Despite its potential value, going to business school still requires you to take a bit of a gamble. Leaner years make business school a riskier proposition. The nation appears to be heading out of what has been a lingering recession, but economic factors are always unpredictable. Furthermore, the world has witnessed great political turmoil. All of these factors can quickly and negatively impact the job market for newly minted MBAs.

So as you make plans to go to b-school, you need to accept that there is some risk that the labor market won't greet you with open arms at graduation. Consider the plight of current MBAs: when they entered b-school, the economy was roaring ahead. The immediate future looked exceptionally bright. Most MBAs probably thought that once they got in, they had it made, and they looked forward to generous starting salaries and bonuses. Few probably anticipated that tough times could hit so dramatically.

But that's just the point. Good times and bad times cycle in and out. Many economic experts agree that the economy is starting to look up and the markets will continue to improve. This means traditional hirers of MBAs, such as the investment banks and consulting firms, may once again be wooing many a b-school grad. Still, it's hard to know when all of the recruiters who typically hire MBAs will feel comfortable again about bringing their hiring levels back up to what they were before the downturn.

The best way to consider the value of the degree is by focusing on its long-lasting benefits. "When people come here for their MBA, they talk about retooling for their life. They think about the long term and recognize that there are some short term hurdles," says Rose Martinelli, former director of admissions at the Wharton School. "Just out of business school, this is the very first job in a long career. This is really about building blocks and going for the long run. You may have to work harder to find a job now, but building your career is a lifelong process." The MBA gives you the tools, networking, and polish to meaningfully enhance your long-term prospects and earning potential.

"There is real opportunity here. The opportunity right now is to pursue your passion and perhaps not your wallet," continues Martinelli. "We're seeing more of an equalization in salary. Those high-paying jobs in finance, investment banking, and consulting are fewer and harder to find. So here you have an opportunity for a job with a true learning experience rather than one that just pays a lot. More people are going into nonprofit and government and making contributions back to the community."

BRAND POWER COUNTS

Of course, there is great variability with placement rates and starting salaries among schools. The MBA does not swap your tuition bill for a guarantee that you'll get rich quick. As we've noted, it is at the best schools—those that have the greatest prestige and global recognition—where the strongest recovery is taking place. It's brand power at work. Even in an uncertain economy, top schools will continue to produce in-demand MBAs for the marketplace.

Branded schools tend to have an extensive history with big recruiting companies because the schools are a steady source of exceptional talent. As the economy stabilizes and hiring creeps up again, recruiters are naturally going to orient themselves at the top-brand schools.

At the University of Chicago, Deputy Dean Stacey Kole notes: Hiring activity has really skyrocketed. . . . We had thousands of interviews available for our grads."

At less prominent schools, the picture may not be quite as optimistic. It is important to consider placement rates and the list of companies that typically recruit on campus at any school you are considering.

Getting a Job

For most would-be MBAs, b-school represents a fresh beginning—either in their current profession or in an entirely different industry. Whatever promise the degree holds for you, it's wise to question what the return on your investment will be.

Several factors affect job placement and starting salary. School reputation and ties to industries and employers are important. At the top programs, the lists of recruiters read like a "Who's Who" of American companies. These schools not only attract the greatest volume of recruiters, but consistently get the attention of those companies considered to be "blue chip."

Not to be overlooked are lesser-known, regional schools that often have the strongest relationships with local employers and industries. Some b-schools (many of them state universities) are regarded by both academicians and employers as number one in their respective regions. In other words, as far as the local business community is concerned, these programs offer as much prestige and pull as a nationally ranked program.

Student clubs also play a big part in getting a job because they extend the recruiting efforts at many schools. They host a variety of events that allow you to meet leading business people, so that you can learn about their industries and their specific companies. Most important, these clubs are very effective at bringing in recruiters and other interested parties that do not recruit through traditional mainstream channels. For example, the high-tech, international, and entertainment student clubs provide career opportunities not available through the front door.

Your background and experiences also affect your success in securing a position. Important factors are academic specialization, academic standing, prior work experience, and intangibles such as your personal fit with the company. These days, what you did before b-school is particularly important; it helps establish credibility and gives you an edge in competing for a position in a specific field. For those using b-school to switch careers to a new industry, it's helpful if something on your resume ties your interest to the new profession. It's also smart to secure a summer job in the new area.

Finally, persistence and initiative are critical factors in the job search. Many fast tracks have been narrowed since the beginning of the decade. Increasingly, even at the best schools, finding a job requires off-campus recruiting efforts and ferreting out the hidden jobs.

A RETURN ON YOUR INVESTMENT

Not everyone measures their return on investment from business school with a dollar amount. (See the interview at the end of this chapter as one example.) We've heard many b-school grads explain that the fundamental skills, the network of people, and the proper environment in which to formulate their long-term career path were the most valuable things they wanted to get back from their MBA programs—in doing so, they considered the experience a success, regardless of their starting salary at graduation.

But for those who are anxious to start paying back those school loans, it's important to note that the industry in which you are hired can strongly affect your job prospects. Traditionally heavy hirers such as investment banking and consulting companies continue to lead the salary pack. Historically these sectors have offered the highest starting salaries and sign-on bonuses, with recruiters gravitating to the name-brand schools. At Chicago, Kole notes, "We saw tremendous activity in consulting, investment banking, investment management, and in leadership development programs. We are up in all of these areas, but most significantly in management consulting."

Also impacting your placement outlook is the geographic location of the school. Regional powerhouses such as Rutgers University in New Jersey may hold great sway at nearby, national employers such as Johnson &

Johnson and Warner Lambert/Pfizer, providing graduates of those programs a unique competitive advantage. Although these companies reach out far and wide to recruit everywhere, a homegrown MBA may catch their attention and hold greater appeal.

As always, prioritize your criteria for school selection. Research who the top hirers are at any school you are considering. If you know what field you are interested in, look at how strong a particular business school's track record is in finding jobs for their graduates in that industry. To cement the relationships between school and recruiter, companies often foster a partnership with the school that includes sponsoring academic projects and internships, and hosting school club functions and informational cocktail hour events.

You may indeed be accepted at one of the nation's most prestigious schools, but if they lack real access to the type of industry you desire to work in, you are better off elsewhere.

FRIENDS WHO ARE GOING PLACES, ALUMNI WHO ARE ALREADY THERE

Most students say that the best part about b-school is meeting classmates with whom they share common goals and interests. Many students claim that the "single greatest resource is each other." Not surprisingly, with so many bright and ambitious people cocooned in one place, b-school can be the time of your life. It presents numerous professional and social opportunities. It can be where you find future customers, business partners, and mentors. It can also be where you establish lifelong friendships. After graduation, these classmates form an enduring network of contacts and professional resources.

Alumni are also an important part of the b-school experience. While professors teach business theory and practice, alumni provide insight into the real business world. When you're ready to interview, they can provide advice on how to get hired by the companies recruiting at your school. In some cases, they help you secure the interview and shepherd you through the hiring process.

B-schools love to boast about the influence of their alumni network. To be sure, some are very powerful, but this varies from institution to institution. At the very least, alumni will help you get your foot in the door. A resume sent to an alum at a given company, instead of to "Sir or Madam" in the personnel department, has a much better chance of being noticed and acted on.

After you graduate, the network continues to grow. Regional alumni clubs and alumni publications keep you plugged in to the network with class notes detailing who's doing what, where, and with whom.

Throughout your career, an active alumni relations department can give you continued support. Post-MBA executive education series, fund-raising events, and continued job placement efforts are all resources you can draw on for years to come.

CHAPTER 3
ADMISSIONS

PREPARING TO BE A SUCCESSFUL APPLICANT

GET GOOD GRADES

If you're still in school, concentrate on getting good grades. A high GPA says you've got not only brains but also discipline. It shows the Admissions Committee you have what you need to make it through the program. If you're applying directly from college or have limited job experience, your grades will matter even more. The Admissions Committee will have little else on which to evaluate you.

It's especially important that you do well in courses such as economics, statistics, and calculus. Success in these courses is more meaningful than success in classes like "Monday Night at the Movies" film appreciation. Of course, English is also important; b-schools want students who communicate well.

STRENGTHEN MATH SKILLS

Number-crunching is an inescapable part of b-school. If your work experience has failed to develop your quantitative skills, take an accounting or statistics course for credit at a local college or b-school. If you have a liberal arts background and did poorly in math, or got a low GMAT Math score, this is especially important. Getting a decent grade will go a long way toward convincing the Admissions Committee you can manage the quantitative challenges of the program.

WORK FOR A FEW YEARS—BUT NOT TOO MANY

Business schools have traditionally favored applicants who have worked full-time for several years. There are three primary reasons for this:

1. With experience comes maturity.

2. You're more likely to know what you want out of the program.

3. Your experience enables you to bring real-work perspectives to the classroom. Because business school is designed for you to learn from your classmates, each student's contribution is important.

Until recently, b-schools preferred to admit only those students with two to five years of work experience. The rationale was that at two years you have worked enough to be able to make a solid contribution, while beyond four or five, you might be too advanced in your career to appreciate the program fully. However, as we noted earlier in this book, there is a new trend among top schools toward admitting "younger" applicants—that is, candidates with limited work experience as well as those straight from college.

Depending on the schools to which you're applying and the strength of your resume of accomplishments, you may not need full-time, professional work experience. Of course, there's a catch: The younger you are, the harder you'll have to work to supply supporting evidence for your case as a qualified applicant. Be prepared to convince Admissions Committees that you've already done some incredible things, especially if you're hailing straight from college.

If you've targeted top-flight schools like Wharton, Columbia, or Stanford, applying fresh out of college is still a long shot. While your chances of gaining admission with little work experience have improved, your best shot is still to err on the conservative side and get a year or two of some professional experience under your belt.

If you're not interested in the big league or you plan on attending a local program, the number of years you should work before applying may vary. Research the admissions requirements at your target school. There's no doubt the MBA will jumpstart your career and have long-lasting effects on your business (and perhaps personal) outlook. If you're not ready to face the real world after college, plenty of solid b-schools will welcome you to another two years of academia.

There is one caveat to this advice, however. If your grades are weak, consider working at least three years before applying. The more professional success you have, the greater the likelihood that Admissions Committees will overlook your GPA.

LET YOUR JOB WORK FOR YOU

Many companies encourage employees to go to b-school. Some of these companies have close ties to a favored b-school and produce well-qualified applicants. If their employees are going to the kinds of schools you want to get into, these may be smart places to work.

Other companies, such as investment banks, feature training programs, at the end of which trainees go to b-school or leave the company. These programs hire undergraduates right out of school. They're known for producing solid, highly skilled applicants. Moreover, they're full of well-connected alumni who may write influential letters of recommendation.

Happily, the opposite tactic—working in an industry that generates few applicants—can be equally effective. Admissions Officers look for students from underrepresented professions. Applicants from biotechnology, health care, not-for-profit, and even the Peace Corps are viewed favorably.

One way to set yourself apart is to have had two entirely different professional experiences before business school. For example, if you worked in finance, your next job might be in a different field, like marketing. Supplementing quantitative work with qualitative experiences demonstrates versatility.

Finally, what you do in your job is important. Seek out opportunities to distinguish yourself. Even if your responsibilities are limited, exceed the expectations of the position. B-schools are looking for leaders.

MARCH FROM THE MILITARY

A surprising number of b-school students hail from the military (although the armed forces probably had commanders in mind, not CEOs, when they designed their regimen). Military officers know how to be managers because they've held command positions. And they know how to lead a team under the most difficult of circumstances.

Because most have traveled all over the world, they also know how to work with people from different cultures. As a result, they're ideally suited to learn alongside students with diverse backgrounds and perspectives. B-schools with a global focus are particularly attracted to such experience.

The decision to enlist in the military is a very personal one. However, if you've thought of joining those few good men and women, this may be as effective a means of preparing for b-school as more traditional avenues.

CHECK OUT THOSE ESSAY QUESTIONS NOW

You're worried you don't have interesting stories to tell. Or you just don't know what to write. What do you do?

Ideally, several months before your application is due, you should read the essay questions and begin to think about your answers. Could you describe an ethical dilemma at work? Are you involved in anything outside the office (or classroom)? If not, now is the time to do something about it. While this may seem contrived, it's preferable to sitting down to write the application and finding you have to scrape for or, even worse, manufacture situations.

Use the essay questions as a framework for your personal and professional activities. Look back over your business calendar, and see if you can find some meaty experiences for the essays in your work life. Keep your eyes open for a situation that involves questionable ethics. If all you do is work, work, work, get involved in activities that round out your background. In other words, get a life.

Get involved in community-based activities. Some possibilities are being a big brother/big sister, tutoring in a literacy program, or initiating a green initiative on campus. Demonstrating a concern for others looks good to Admissions Committees, and hey, it's good for your soul, too.

It's also important to seek out leadership experiences. B-schools are looking for individuals who can manage groups. Volunteer to chair a professional committee or run for an office in a club. It's a wide-open world; you can pick from any number of activities. The bottom line is this: The extracurriculars you select can show that you are mature, multifaceted, and appealing.

We don't mean to sound cynical. Obviously, the best applications do nothing more than describe your true, heartfelt interests and show off your sparkling personality. We're not suggesting you try to guess which activity will win the hearts of admissions directors and then mold yourself accordingly. Instead, think of projects and activities you care about, that maybe you haven't gotten around to acting on, and act on them now!

PICK YOUR RECOMMENDERS CAREFULLY

By the time you apply to business school, you shouldn't have to scramble for recommendations. Like the material for your essays, sources for recommendations should be considered long before the application is due.

How do you get great recommendations? Obviously, good work is a prerequisite. Whom you ask is equally important. Bosses who know you well will recommend you on both a personal and professional level. They can provide specific examples of your accomplishments, skills, and character. Additionally, they can convey a high level of interest in your candidacy.

There's also the issue of trust. B-school recommendations are made in confidence; you probably won't see exactly what's been written about you. Choose someone you can trust to deliver the kind of recommendation that will push you over the top. A casual acquaintance may fail you by writing an adequate, yet mostly humdrum letter.

Cultivate relationships that yield glowing recommendations. Former and current professors, employers, clients, and managers are all good choices. An equally impressive recommendation can come from someone who has observed you in a worthwhile extracurricular activity.

We said before you won't see *exactly* what's being written about you, but that doesn't mean you should just hand a blank piece of paper to your recommender. Left to their own devices, recommenders may create a portrait that leaves out your best features. You need to prep them on what to write. Remind them of those projects or activities in which you achieved some success. You might also discuss the total picture of yourself that you are trying to create. The recommendation should reinforce what you're saying about yourself in your essays.

About "big shot" recommendations: Don't bother. Getting some professional athlete who's a friend of your parent's to write you a recommendation will do you no good if he or she doesn't know you very well. Don't try to fudge your application; let people who really know you and your work tell the honest, believable, and impressive truth.

PREPARE FOR THE GRADUATE MANAGEMENT ADMISSION TEST (GMAT)

Most b-schools require you to take the GMAT. The GMAT is now a three-and-a-half-hour computer adaptive test (CAT) with multiple-choice Math and Verbal sections as well as an essay section. It's the kind of test you hate to take and schools love to require.

Why is the GMAT required? B-schools believe it measures your verbal and quantitative skills and predicts success in the MBA program. Some think this is a bunch of hooey, but most schools weigh your GMAT scores heavily in the admissions decision. If nothing else, it gives the school a quantitative tool to use to compare you with other applicants.

The test begins with the Analytical Writing Assessment (AWA) containing two essays questions. In the past, all questions that have appeared on the official GMAT have been drawn from a list of about 150 topics that appear in *The Official Guide to the GMAT* (published by the Educational Testing Service). Review that list and you'll have a pretty good idea of what to expect from the AWA. You will have 30 minutes to write each essay. By the way, you will be required to type your essay at the computer. Depending on how rusty your typing skills are, you may want to consider a bit of practice.

Next comes the multiple-choice section which has two parts: a 75-minute Math section and a 75-minute Verbal section. The Math section includes problem-solving questions (e.g., "Train A leaves Baltimore at 6:32 A.M...") and data-sufficiency questions. Data-sufficiency questions require you to determine whether you have been given enough information to solve a particular math problem. The good news about these types of questions is that you don't actually have to solve the problem; the bad news is that these questions can be very tricky. The Verbal section tests reading skills (reading comprehension), grammar (sentence correction), and logic (critical reasoning).

For those unfamiliar with CAT exams, here's a brief overview of how they work: On multiple-choice sections, the computer starts by asking a question of medium difficulty. If you answer it correctly, the computer asks you a question that is slightly more difficult than the previous question. If you answer incorrectly, the computer asks a slightly easier question next. The test continues this way until you have answered enough questions that it can make an accurate (or so they say) assessment of your performance and assign you a score.

Most people feel they have no control over the GMAT. They dread it as the potential bomb in their application. Relax; you have more control than you think. You can take a test-preparation course to review the Math and Verbal material, learn test-taking strategies, and build your confidence. Test-prep courses can be highly effective. The Princeton Review offers what we think is the best GMAT course available. Even better, it offers two options for online preparation in addition to the traditional classroom course and one-on-one tutoring. Another option is to take a look at our book *Cracking the GMAT CAT*, which reviews all the subjects and covers all the tips you would learn in one of our courses.

How many times should you take the GMAT? More than once if you didn't get your desired score on the first try. But watch out: Multiple scores that fall in the same range make you look unprepared. Don't take the test more than once if you don't expect a decent increase, and don't even think of taking it the first time without serious preparation. Limiting your GMAT attempts to two is best. Three tries are okay if there were unusual circumstances. If you take it more than three times, the Admissions committee will think you have an unhealthy obsession. A final note: If you submit more than one score, most schools will take the highest.

If you don't have math courses on your college transcript or numbers-oriented work experience, it's especially important to get a solid score on the quantitative section. There's a lot of math between you and the MBA.

HOW THE ADMISSIONS CRITERIA ARE WEIGHTED

Although admissions requirements vary among business schools, most rely on the following criteria: GMAT score, college GPA, work experience, your essays, letters of recommendation (academic and/or professional), an interview with an admissions representative, and your extracurriculars. The first four are generally the most heavily weighted. The more competitive the school, the less room there is for weakness in any area. Any component out of sync, such as a weak GMAT score, is potentially harmful.

Happily, the admissions process at business school is one where great emphasis is placed on getting to know you as a person. The essay component is the element that allows the schools to do just that. Your essays can refute weaknesses, fill in gaps, and in general, charmingly persuade an admissions board you've got the right stuff. They are the single most important criteria in business school admissions.

But as we've just said, they're not the only criteria. All pieces of your application must come together to form a cohesive whole. It is the *entire application* that determines whether you win admission.

ANTICIPATE AND COORDINATE

The application process is very time-consuming, so anticipating what you need to accomplish within the admissions time frame is critical. To make the best use of our advice, you should first contact each of the programs on your personal list of schools. Their standards and criteria for admission may vary, and you'll need to follow their specific guidelines. Please note that the less competitive a school is, the more easily you may be able to breeze through (or completely omit) the rigorous requirements we identify as crucial in the application process for the top programs.

In addition, business school applicants are often overwhelmed by how much they have to do to complete not only one, but several applications. Proper management of the process is essential, since there are so many factors to coordinate in each application.

You'll have to prep for the GMAT, then actually take the test, round up some writers for your recommendations, follow up with those chosen to write recommendations, make sure the recommendations are mailed in on time, have your college transcript sent, and finally, write the essays. Of course, some schools require an interview as well. What makes all of this particularly challenging is that many applicants have to do all of this while balancing the demands of a full-time job.

We know that it takes a supreme force of will to complete even one application. As grad school applications go, a top business school's is pretty daunting. So if you don't stay focused on the details and deadlines, you may drop the ball.

There are many common and incredibly embarrassing mistakes you can avoid with prudent early planning. These include allowing your recommenders to miss the deadline, submitting an application full of typos and grammatical errors, sending one school an essay intended for another, or forgetting to change the school name when using the same essay for several applications. Applicants who wind up cramming for the GMAT or squeezing their essay writing into several all-nighters end up seriously shortchanging themselves.

APPLY EARLY

The best advice is to plan early and apply early. The former diminishes the likelihood of an accidental omission or a missed deadline. The latter increases your chances of acceptance.

The filing period ranges anywhere from six to eight months. The earlier you apply, the better your chances. There are a number of reasons for this:

First, there's plenty of space available early on. Many b-schools have rolling admissions, and as the application deadline nears, spaces fill up. The majority of applicants don't apply until the later months because of procrastination or unavoidable delays. As the deadline draws close, the greatest number of applicants compete for the fewest number of spaces.

Second, in the beginning, Admissions Officers have little clue about how selective they can be. They haven't reviewed enough applications to determine the competitiveness of the pool. An early application may be judged more on its own merit than on how it stacks up against others. This is in your favor if the pool turns out to be unusually competitive. Above all, Admissions Officers like to lock their classes in early; they can't be certain they'll get their normal supply of applicants. Admissions decisions may be more generous at this time.

Third, by getting your application in early you're showing a strong interest. The Admissions Committee is likely to view you as someone keen on going to their school.

To be sure, some Admissions Officers report that the first batch of applications tend to be from candidates with strong qualifications, confident of acceptance. In this case, you might not be the very first one on line; but being closer to the front is still better than getting lost in the heap of last-minute hopefuls.

ROUNDS VS. ROLLING ADMISSIONS

Applications are processed in one of two ways: rounds or rolling admissions. Schools that use rounds divide the filing period into three or so timed cycles. Applications are batched into the round in which they are received and reviewed in competition with others in that round. A list of a b-school's round dates can be obtained by contacting its Admissions Office if it employs this method. Applications to schools with rolling admissions are reviewed on an ongoing basis as they are received.

GMAT AND GPA

The GMAT and GPA are used in two ways. First, they're "success indicators" for the academic work you'll have to slog through if admitted—will you have the brainpower to succeed in the program? Second, they're used as benchmarks to compare each applicant to other applicants within the pool. At the more selective schools, you'll need a higher score and average to stay in the game.

Pearson VUE and the American College Testing Program (ACT) administer the GMAT. You'll need to register to take the exam by registering online at www.mba.com. Many applicants take the exam more than once to improve their scores. Test preparation is also an option for boosting your numbers—visit PrincetonReview.com for more information about The Princeton Review's GMAT courses.

Your college transcript is a major factor in the strength of your candidacy. Some schools focus more closely on the junior- and senior-year grades than the overall GPA, and most consider the reputation of your college and the difficulty of your course selections. A transcript loaded with offerings like "Environmental Appreciation" and "The Child in You" won't be valued as highly as one packed with calculus and history classes.

THE ESSAYS

Admissions committees consider the essays the clincher, the swing vote on the admit/deny issue. Essays offer the most substantive information about who you really are. The GMAT and GPA reveal little about you, only that you won't crash and burn. Your work history provides a record of performance and justifies your stated desire to study business. But the essays tie all the pieces of the application together and create a summary of your experiences, skills, background, and beliefs.

The essays do more than give answers to questions. They create thumbnail psychological profiles. Depending on how you answer a question or what you present, you reveal yourself in any number of ways—creative, witty, open-minded, articulate, mature, to name a few. On the other hand, your essay can also reveal a negative side, such as arrogance, sloppiness, or an inability to think and write clearly.

CHECK IT OUT: Most top schools require multiple essays, and our popular book *Business School Essays that Made a Difference* lets you know how to ace them all. Including sample essays from successful applicants with comments from admissions officers on what worked and what didn't, *Business School Essays that Made a Difference* lets you know how to write the essays that will get you admitted. Pick it up at Princetonreview.com/bookstore.

LETTERS OF RECOMMENDATION

Letters of recommendation function as a reality check. Admissions committees expect them to support and reinforce what they're seeing in the rest of your application. When the information doesn't match up with the picture you've painted, it makes you look bad. Because you won't see the recommendation (it's sent in "blind"), you won't even know there's a problem. This can mean the end of your candidacy.

That's why you need to take extreme care in selecting your references.

Scan each application for guidelines on choosing your references—business schools typically request an academic and a professional reference. The academic reference should be someone who can evaluate your performance in an academic environment. It's better to ask an instructor, teacher's aide, or mentor who knew you well than a famous professor who barely knew your name.

The same holds true for your professional reference. Seek out individuals who can evaluate your performance on many levels. The reference will be far more credible. Finding the right person to write your professional reference, however, can be trickier. You may not wish to reveal to your boss early on that you plan on leaving, and if the dynamics of your relationship are not ideal (hey, it happens once in a while), he or she might not make an appropriate reference. If this is the case, seek out a boss at a former job or someone who was your supervisor at your current job but has since moved to another organization. Avoid friends, colleagues, and clients as references unless the school explicitly says it's okay.

Advise your writers on themes and qualities you highlighted in your application. Suggest that they include real-life examples of your performance to illustrate their points. In other words, script the recommendation as best you can. Your boss, even if he or she is your biggest fan, may not know what your recommendation should include.

A great recommendation is rarely enough to save a weak application from doom. But it might push a borderline case over to the "admit" pile. Mediocre recommendations can be damaging; an application that is strong in all other areas now has a weakness, an inconsistency.

A final warning on this topic: Procrastination is common here. Micromanage your references so that each recommendation arrives on time! If need be, provide packaging for an overnight letter, have your reference seal it up, and then ship it out yourself.

THE INTERVIEW

Not all business schools attach equal value to the interview. For some, it's an essential screening tool. For others, it's used to make a final decision on those caught somewhere between "admit" and "reject." Some schools may encourage, but not require, the interview. Others make it informative, with little connection to the admissions decision.

Like the letters of recommendation, an interview may serve as a reality check to reinforce the total picture. It may also be used to fill in the blanks, particularly in borderline cases.

If an interview is offered, take it. In person, you may be a more compelling candidate. You can use the interview to further address weaknesses or bring dull essays to life. Most importantly, you can display the kinds of qualities—enthusiasm, sense of humor, maturity—that can positively sway an admissions decision.

Act quickly to schedule your interview. Admissions Departments often lack the time and staff to interview every candidate who walks through their doors. You don't want your application decision delayed by several months (and placed in a more competitive round or pool) because your interview was scheduled late in the filing period.

A great interview can tip the scale in the "admit" direction. How do you know if it was great? You were calm and focused. You expressed yourself and your ideas clearly. Your interviewer invited you to go rock climbing with him or her the following weekend. (Okay, let's just say you developed a solid personal rapport with the interviewer.)

A mediocre interview may not have much impact, unless your application is hanging on by a thread. In such a case, the person you're talking to (harsh as it may seem) is probably looking for a reason not to admit you, rather than a reason to let you in. If you feel your application may be in that hazy, marginal area, try to be extra-inspired in your interview.

Approach this meeting as you would a job interview. Remember, you're being sized up as a person in all of your dimensions. Here are a few tips to use during the interview.

- Dress and act the part of a professional but avoid being stiff or acting like a stuffed shirt.

- Limit your use of business jargon. Interviewers often hear a lot of the same generic answers. They are more interested in you being your witty, charming, natural self.

- Be personable and talk about your passions, such as hobbies or a recent trip you've taken. The idea is to get the interviewer thinking of you as someone who will contribute greatly to the quality of campus life.

Highlight your achievements and excellence, even in something like gourmet cooking, but avoid stunts, such as pulling out a platter of peppercorn pate sautéed in anchovy sauce.

CHAPTER 4

QUOTAS, RECRUITMENT, AND DIVERSITY

B-schools don't have to operate under quotas—governmental or otherwise. However, they probably try harder than most corporations to recruit diverse groups of people. Just as the modern business world has become global and multicultural, so too have b-schools. They must not only teach diversity in the classroom but also make it a reality in their campus population and, if possible, faculty.

Schools that have a diverse student body tend to be proud of it. They tout their success in profiles that demographically slice and dice the previous year's class by gender, race, and geographic and international residency. Prospective students can review this data and compare the diversity of the schools they've applied to.

However, such diversity doesn't come naturally from the demographics of the applicant pool. Admissions Committees have to work hard at it. In some cases, enrollment is encouraged with generous financial aid packages and scholarships.

While they don't have quotas per se, they do target groups for admission, seeking a demographic balance in many areas. Have they admitted enough women, minorities, foreign students, marketing strategists, and liberal arts majors? Are different parts of the country represented?

As we've said before, the best b-schools tend to attract top talent, students, and recruiters to their campus. Women and minorities are the most sought-after groups targeted for admission. So it's no surprise that programs that report higher-than-average female and minority enrollments tend to be among the very best.

AN INITIATIVE FOR MINORITIES

Some schools report higher minority enrollments than others, so our advice is consistent: You need to thoroughly research the program you've set your sights on. Consider your goals. Do you simply want to attend the most prestigious program? How will social factors impact your goals and experiences on campus?

Most business schools aspire to diversify their programs. It's the number of minorities applying to business school that has remained consistently low. An initiative of the Graduate Management Admissions Council called The Diversity Pipeline Alliance (DiversityPipeline.org) was formed to reverse this trend and increase the number of underrepresented minorities pursuing a business career. Much like the initiative for women, this organization plans a powerful marketing campaign with a pro-business career message for minority students from middle school to graduate school. It offers information on current opportunities for mentorships, internships, and financial assistance and provides an impressive roster of member organizations, services, and educational opportunities.

Minority enrollment at business schools is still quite low, so in all likelihood, you will not experience the dramatic upward shift in b-school demographics in the near future that initiatives like the Diversity Pipeline Alliance hope to influence. However, by recognizing the disparity between the minority presence in the U.S. and minority involvement in business education and practice, we are working toward a solution.

As you make up your mind about where you want to go for b-school, know that the scenario is positive and that new infrastructures exist to support your business career.

FEMALE APPEAL: BUSINESS SCHOOLS GET UP TO SPEED

If you've toured the campus and classrooms of a business school, you may have noticed something: On average, roughly 70 percent of any given MBA program's students are male. While this may make a nice pool of dating prospects for the women who are enrolled, it's not something business schools are happy with—far from it! In fact, it's something they are working to change as quickly as they can.

Beyond showing significantly higher application volume, MBA programs of all types are seeing female applications increase. About 64 percent of full-time MBA programs have seen applications from women rise since 2006; the figure is 47 percent for part-time-programs and 50 percent for executive programs. While these numbers may not match the 50 percent male-to-female ratio of other graduate programs, closing the b-school gender gap is only a matter of time.

School Initiatives

How can we be sure that female enrollment will continue to increase? One reason is that getting women enthused about a career in business is a sky-high priority at business schools across the country these days. To wit, many business schools have launched their own women-only outreach and recruiting events. Columbia University hosts an annual "Women in Business" conference that brings together more than 700 alumnae, business leaders, students and prospective students to network and share ideas on achieving success in the marketplace. Linda Meehan, Assistant Dean for Admissions at Columbia Business School, knows that this outreach is working because "applicants walk away wowed by the extraordinary experience of being surrounded by so many intelligent, passionate and successful women." Events like these aim to dispel myths, discuss the perceived lack of role models, and help women make informed decisions.

Stanford's events, says Wendy Hansen, Associate Director of Admissions at the Stanford Business School, "focus on the educational experience, but also on the unique types of issues women have, such as: how does getting the MBA fit in with having a family or having a spouse? How do I make this experience fit in with my life?" Julia Min, Executive Director of Admissions at UC Berkeley's Haas School of Business, says attendees often find comfort in numbers. "Seeing such a large presence of women is empowering. They realize they're not in this alone, that there are other women around like them."

If all this sounds like good public relations, it is. Schools want to get the word out: MBAs offer women viable opportunities. But if the business schools are talking the talk, they're also walking the walk. There's nothing superficial about this campaign. Bit by bit, the MBA landscape for women is changing.

Opportunities begin even before the first day of class. At Stanford, admitted women are treated to one-on-one admit-lunches with female alumni. Once an admit gets to campus, they find MBA life is chock-full of student-run women and management programs, support groups, retreats, executive conferences, mentoring programs, and other dedicated resources for women only.

For many years now, most business programs have had an on-campus Partners Club for spouses and significant others—a benefit to both female and male students. Newcomers to the business-school scene include groups like The Parents Club and Biz Kids where students can find family-oriented classmates and activities. Columbia University's Mother's Network is an initiative that provides a formal support network for new, current and future b-school moms. Perhaps the most symbolic gesture of the increasing influence of women in business school is Stanford's provision of a private nursing room for MBA moms and their babies in its main classroom facility.

MORE FLEXIBILITY AND MAKING IT WORK

Of course, there's still room for improvement. A continuing problem at business schools is a lack of course work and case study material featuring women leaders. Likewise, there is an absence of female professors on the academic front.

Apart from these lingering issues, business schools continue to tackle the particular challenges female students face. For many women, the late starting age can be a turn-off. But even here, there are new options and opportunities to consider.

If you're stressed out from trying to have it all and have written off getting an MBA, new early-initiative programs might make you pause and reconsider your decision. Harvard and Stanford have developed an early career track that aims to minimize the impact of the biological clock on a prospective applicant's decision to pursue an MBA. Other schools are likely to follow suit.

The early career track offers a solution that is as simple as it is practical: Admit women (and men) to the MBA program either straight out of college or with just a few years of work experience. Business schools hope that the option to attain their MBA early on in their careers will prompt more women to apply to their programs. With a bigger window to accomplish their professional goals, more women will turn to the MBA as a viable option that won't require them to sacrifice their personal lives.

Beginning a business career earlier eliminates the immediate problem of timing. But what happens down the road? While it helps to remove one timing issue, it can't indefinitely postpone the balancing act that shadows many women's careers. It's hard to rationalize the opportunity costs of the MBA knowing that the investment might be forsaken when tough choices have to be made.

Business schools blame misconceptions about the utility of the MBA for women's reticence on this front. They feel that many women underestimate the broad reach of the degree. The MBA is not just for hard-core careers like banking and finance, but is also useful in not-for-profit work, less high-stress industries such as consumer goods, and leadership positions in a wide range of fields.

Further, says Hansen, "There is a tremendous amount of flexibility in a general management degree. The MBA positions you much more effectively to make an impact wherever you fall at different points in your life. It gives you the tools and framework to apply those skills at different levels and in different intensities. For example, women can rise to a partner level or a senior leadership position and then scale back to a different role within the organization. They can also scale back to part-time work." In other words, the investment doesn't have to be forsaken; it might instead be redirected.

There's no doubt the return on investment (that's ROI in business speak) for the MBA is high. Six-figure salaries and sign-on bonuses that pay you back for the cost of your MBA tuition are hard to beat (and unlike medical, veterinary, and law school grads, you won't have malpractice premiums eating into your take-home pay). If you've thought business school might be right for you, keep investigating—you might be right.

WHERE ARE THE WOMEN IN MBA PROGRAMS?

Are you a professional woman in her mid-to-late twenties? Do you see graduate school in your future? During these tough times, you might envision yourself back on campus sooner rather than later. Downturns do tend to fuel grad school applications. After all, what better place to wait out the economy and avoid the gaping pit of joblessness?

Grad school can be a cure-all for many ills: It can jump-start or redirect a stubbornly off-track career; it can give you a place to hang out while you figure out what you want to be when you grow up (law school, a three-year degree, offers an even longer alternative); and it can transform your personal life as you vault into a new career. Even in uncertain times there is certainty in knowing that after two years in school you can emerge reborn as a professional with a spanking new identity, prescribed career track, and a solid alumni network.

Despite the huge appeal of graduate school, be it as an escape from bad times or as your true, chosen path, MBA programs have remained a problematic choice for many women. Female enrollment at law, medical, and veterinary schools now hovers at, or near, the 50 percent mark. So what's up with business schools? Why has female enrollment at business schools stagnated at about 30 percent?

Even during the best of times, business schools have struggled to attract women. Is this due to the unique challenges women face in building and sustaining their careers over a lifetime of choices, both professional and personal, or is there another reason? Clearly an MBA presents many opportunities, but, for women, will these opportunities upset their already delicate balancing acts?

THINKING OF FAMILY

Let's start with biology—as in biological clocks. Since a prerequisite for admission to many business programs is prior work experience, first-year business school students are typically a bit older than their law or med school counterparts. In fact, the average age for entering full-time MBA students is 28. This means that by the time graduation rolls around, MBA students are heading into their thirties—a prime time for marriage and children. For some women, that timing couldn't be worse.

Newly minted MBAs in their early thirties are just starting to reap the rewards of their business school investments by scoring brand new, mid-to-senior level jobs. With these jobs come ever-greater demands and time pressures. But, for many, the pressure to have a personal life is just as great. Those kinds of competing priorities are the very headaches women hope to avoid. Making matters worse, MBA jobs at the senior level can vault women into a culture that may still be dominated by old-school thinking (translation: men) and a culture that may be less tolerant of efforts to balance work commitments with family.

These dilemmas begin long before business school graduation. Again, because MBA students tend to be older, many women have to factor a partner or child into their graduate school decision, especially if it involves relinquishing a paycheck and/or relocation. Many of these women encounter a potential double standard: Husbands and boyfriends, especially those with careers, are often less willing to relocate on their female partner's behalf than vice versa.

NO URGENT MATTER

Another reason business school enrollment for women may be low is that an MBA is not a barrier to entry nor is it a requirement for success in business. In addition, it isn't a rite of passage in many fields that appeal to high numbers of women: marketing, publishing, fashion, and teaching. By contrast, notes Eileen Chang, former Associate Director of Admissions at the Harvard Business School, "If your objective is to be a lawyer or doctor, you simply can't practice without the requisite degree. Business school is fundamentally different because the career path is one where the MBA can put you on any number of tracks—be it banking, accounting, or management—but doesn't require a credential." Between the lack of a required degree for entering business and the late starting age to enter a program, some women perceive a high opportunity cost for the MBA.

FEAR OF MATH?

Why more women aren't pursuing an MBA is a question that business schools have been asking themselves for years. Some hard answers came in the form of a recent study by the University of Michigan's Business School Center for the Education of Women and the Catalyst Foundation. The following issues were identified as key deterrents to business school for women: the MBA is still seen as a male domain; there is a lack of support from employers; a lack of career opportunity and flexibility; a lack of access to powerful business networks and role models; and a perception that b-school is overloaded with math.

According to many schools, math fears are just that—fears. Chang observes, "Maybe historically, math was considered a hurdle. But we see so many women who have strong skills coming from fields that are quantitative, such as banking and engineering, that I think the math fears are almost a myth. But this is a myth we want to work against. We want applicants to know they can handle the math."

Julia Min, Executive Director of Admissions at UC Berkeley's Haas School of Business, concurs, "The math phobia may be unfounded to a certain degree, and still it's a perception that has been long-lasting. Women [enter business school] and perform extremely well."

If you're frightened by math, you need to know that a business school education does require a basic command of the subject. "You do need to be comfortable with numbers," advises Wendy Hansen, Associate Director of Admissions at the Stanford Business School. "The strongest MBA programs are going to be rigorous in math. Knowing how to influence and lead an organization requires understanding the language of business, which includes accounting and finance."

Still, prospective MBAs with a math phobia need not panic; most programs will work with students who lack the necessary math background. "At Stanford, we have a pre-term program of courses before classes begin to get students up to speed," says Hansen, "We also encourage people to take quantitative courses before they come to our school to develop their skills."

If your math fears are not so easily assuaged, concerns about a persistent Old Boys Network might be. As Hansen notes, "Women may say, I don't see the masses of female role models doing what I want to do. That is going to change slowly. But it is going to change. We have to reach a point where those in school reach a place where they are out in the world having an impact."

OUR ADVICE

Look at the number of female MBA students attending your targeted school and evaluate whether you would feel comfortable there. Research the number and range of student organizations for women and speak with female MBAs about school life.

CHAPTER 5

MONEY MATTERS

HOW MUCH WILL IT COST?

THE TRUTH

To say that business school is an expensive endeavor is an understatement. In fact, to really gauge how expensive business school is, you need to look not only at your tuition costs and living expenses, but also at the opportunity cost of foregoing a salary for the length of your program. Think about it: You'll have a net outflow of money.

But keep in mind that, unlike law school or medical school, business school is just a two-year program. Once those two years are over, you can expect to reap the rewards of your increased market value. Unfortunately, business school differs from law school and medical school in a much less desirable way as well—there are serious limitations on the amount of money available through scholarships and grants. Most business school students seeking financial aid will be limited to loans, and lots of them.

Try not to get too upset about borrowing the money for business school; think of it as an investment in yourself. But, like all investments, it should be carefully thought out and discussed with everyone (spouse, partner, etc.) concerned. This is especially important for those of you considering business school. You need a law degree to practice law, and a medical degree to practice medicine, but a business degree is not required to work in business. That said, certain professional opportunities may be tougher to pursue without an MBA on your resume.

THE COST OF B-SCHOOL

So get out some paper, a pencil, and a calculator, and figure out how much it will cost you to attend school. What should you include? Your opportunity cost (lost income) and your cost of attending b-school (tuition and fees). One more thing: For a more accurate assessment of your investment, you should figure taxes into the equation by dividing tuition cost by 0.65 (this assumes taxes of about 35 percent). Why? Because in order to pay tuition of $25,000, you would have to make a pre-tax income of about $38,500. If you are lucky enough to have a source of aid that does not require repayment, such as a grant, scholarship, or wealthy benefactor, subtract that amount from the cost of attending b-school.

For example, if you currently make $50,000 and plan to attend a business school that costs $25,000 per year, your investment would be approximately $177,000.

$(50,000 \times 2) + [(25,000 \times 2)/.65] = 177,000$

Now say you receive an annual grant of $5,000. Your investment would now be approximately $161,500.

$(50,000 \times 2) + [(20,000 \times 2)/.65] = 161,500$

How Long Will It Take You to Recoup Your Investment?

To estimate this figure, you first need to estimate your expected salary increase post-MBA. Check out the average starting salaries for graduates of the programs you are looking at and adjust upward/downward based on the industry you plan to enter. Subtract your current salary from your expected salary and you'll get your expected salary increase.

Once you complete the step above, divide your investment (tuition and fees plus lost income) by your expected salary increase, and then add 2 (the length of a full-time MBA program). If you are contemplating a one-year MBA program, just add 1.

Going back to the example above, if your pre-MBA salary is $50,000 and you expect to make $75,000 when you graduate, your expected salary increase is $25,000 (a 50 percent increase). Let's assume you did not receive a grant and that your investment will be about $177,000.

$$(177,000/25,000) + 2 = 9.08$$

It will take you approximately nine years to earn back your investment.

Keep in mind, these are approximations and don't take into account annual raises, inflation, and so on. But it is interesting, isn't it?

While business school is an expensive proposition, the financial rewards of having your MBA can be immensely lucrative as we discussed before. You won't be forced into bankruptcy if you finance it correctly. There are tried-and-true ways to reduce your initial costs, finance the costs on the horizon, and manage the debt you'll leave school with—all without selling your soul to the highest bidder.

Comparison Shopping

While cost shouldn't be the first thing on your mind when you are choosing a school, depending on your goals in getting an MBA, it might be fairly high on your list. Private schools aren't the only business schools. Many state schools have fantastic reputations. Regional schools may be more generous with financial aid. Tuition costs will vary widely between public and private schools, especially if you qualify as an in-state student. Keep in mind, however, that salary gains tend to be less dramatic at more regional schools.

HOW DO I FUND MY MBA?

The short answer: loans. Unless your company is underwriting your MBA, or you're able to pay your way in cash, you'll be financing your two years of business school through a portfolio of loans. Loans typically come in one of two forms: federal and private. Only a few of you will be lucky enough to qualify for, and get, grants and scholarships.

Anyone with reasonably good credit, regardless of financial need, can borrow money for business school. If you have financial need, you will probably be eligible for some type of financial aid if you meet the following basic qualifications:

- You are a United States citizen or a permanent U.S. resident.

- You are registered for Selective Service if you are a male, or you have documentation to prove that you are exempt.

- You are not in default on student loans already.

- You don't have a horrendous credit history.

International applicants to business school should take note: Most U.S. business schools will require all international students to pay in full or show proof that they will be able to pay the entire cost of the MBA prior to beginning the MBA program.

FEDERAL LOANS

The federal government funds federal loan programs. Federal loans are usually the "first resort" for borrowers because many are subsidized by the federal government and offer generous interest rates. Some do not begin charging you interest until after you complete your degree. Most federal loans are need-based, but some higher interest federal loans are available regardless of financial circumstances. Your business school's Financial Aid Office will determine what your need is, if any.

PRIVATE LOANS

Private loans are funded by banks, foundations, corporations, and other associations. A number of private loans are targeted to aid particular segments of the population. You may have to do some investigating to identify private loans for which you might qualify. As always, contact your law school's Financial Aid Office to learn more.

ALTERNATIVE SOURCES OF FUNDING

We've already mentioned these in one form or other, but they are worthy of a bit more attention.

The first alternative is sponsorship of your employer or educational reimbursement. Not all companies treat this the same way, but if you are able to get your employer to kick in a portion of the cost, you are better off than before. But beware, this benefit also comes with strings attached. Most companies that pay for your MBA will require a commitment of several years upon graduation. If you renege, you could be liable for the full cost of your education. Others will require that you attend business school part-time, which you may or may not want to do. Often, part-time students are unable to participate in on-campus recruiting and networking efforts to the same extent as full-time students.

Educational reimbursement can come in another form as well. Some companies will provide sign-on bonuses to new MBAs that will cover the cost of a year's tuition. This is a fantastic development from the years of a robust economy, but it is by no means a guarantee during tougher times. Don't assume that you will have this option open to you just because it has been a common occurrence in past years.

The other "alternative" source of funding is a financial gift from family or another source. Either you have a resource that is willing and able to fund all or part of your MBA, or you don't. If you do, be thankful.

APPLYING FOR FINANCIAL AID

In order to become eligible for financial aid of any kind, you will need to complete the Free Application for Federal Student Aid, also known as the FAFSA. You complete and submit this form after January 1 of the year in which you plan to enter business school. You should aim to complete and submit this form as soon as possible after the first of the year to avoid any potential delays. The FAFSA is available from a school's Financial Aid Office. You can also download the form directly from the website of the U.S. Department of Education at FAFSA.ed.gov. A third option is to use the FAFSA Express software (also downloadable from the website) and transmit the application electronically.

It is important to note that the form requires information from your federal income tax returns. Plan to file your taxes early that year.

In addition to the FAFSA form, most schools will have their own financial aid form that you will be required to complete and submit. These often have their own deadlines, so it is wise to keep careful track of all the forms you must complete and all their respective deadlines. Yes, it's a lot of paperwork, but get over it. You'll be much happier when the tuition bill arrives.

LOAN SPECIFICS

GUIDE TO FEDERAL LOANS
Stafford Loans

Stafford loans require you to complete the FAFSA form in order to qualify. These are very desirable loans because they offer low-interest rates capped at 8.25 percent and are federally guaranteed. There is a limit to how much you can borrow in this program. The maximum amount per year you may borrow as a graduate student is $18,500; $10,000 of which must be unsubsidized loans. The maximum amount you may borrow in total is $138,500 (only $65,500 of this may be in subsidized loans). The aggregate amount includes any Stafford loans you may have from your undergraduate or other graduate studies.

Stafford loans come in two types: subsidized and unsubsidized. Subsidized loans are need-based as determined by your business school. They do not accrue interest while you are in school or in an authorized deferment period (such as the first six months after graduation). This cost is picked up by the government (hence the name "subsidized"). Repayment begins at that time. Unsubsidized loans are not need-based and do charge interest from the time of disbursement to the time of full repayment. You can pay the interest while you are in school or opt for capitalization, in which case the interest is added to the principal. You will pay more in the long run if you choose capitalization. Interest payments may be tax deductible, so be sure to check. The standard repayment period for both is 10 years.

You will pay a small origination and guarantee fee for each loan, but this is not an out-of-pocket expense. It is simply deducted from the loan amount. Some schools will allow you to borrow the money under the Stafford program directly from them, while others will require you to borrow from a bank. For more information on federal loans, call the Federal Student Aid Information Center at 800-433-3243.

Perkins Loans

Perkins loans are available to graduate students who demonstrate exceptional financial need. The financial aid office will determine your eligibility for a Perkins Loan. If you qualify for a Perkins Loan as part of your financial aid package, take it. The loans are made by the schools and are repaid to the schools, although the federal government provides a large portion of the funds. You can borrow up to $6,000 for each year of graduate study up to a total of $40,000 (this includes any money borrowed under this program during undergraduate study). The interest rates on this loan are low, usually 5 percent. There are no fees attached. The grace period is nine months upon graduation.

PRIVATE/COMMERCIAL LOANS

This is expensive territory. Not only are interest rates high, but terms are also quite different from those found with federal loans. You may not be able to defer payment of interest or principal until after graduation. Origination and guarantee fees are also much higher since these loans are unsecured. After all, banks and other specialized lenders exist to loan money to folks like you, and unlike the federal government, want to make money doing it. If you go this route, shop around diligently. Think of it as good practice for your post-MBA executive career.

SCHOLARSHIPS AND GRANTS

The usual sources for this type of funding are alumni groups and civic organizations. This funding is limited, and actual awards tend to be small. Even if you benefited from generous scholarship funding as an undergraduate, it would be unwise to assume you'll have the same experience as a graduate student. But do investigate. You never know what's out there. Schools will frequently list any scholarships and grants that are available at the back of their financial aid catalog.

FOR MORE INFORMATION

Find out more about your financing options for business school education at PrincetonReview.com.

CHAPTER 6
WHAT B-SCHOOL IS REALLY LIKE

AN ACADEMIC PERSPECTIVE

The objective of all MBA programs is to prepare students for a professional career in business. One business school puts it this way:

Graduates should be all of the following:

1. Able to think and reason independently, creatively, and analytically.

2. Skilled in the use of quantitative techniques.

3. Literate in the use of software applications as management tools.

4. Knowledgeable about the world's management issues and problems.

5. Willing to work in and successfully cope with conditions of uncertainty, risk, and change.

6. Astute decision makers.

7. Ethically and socially responsible.

8. Able to manage in an increasingly global environment.

9. Proficient in utilizing technology as a mode of doing business.

Sound like a tall order? Possibly. But this level of expectation is what business school is all about.

Nearly all MBA programs feature a core curriculum that focuses on the major disciplines of business: finance, management, accounting, marketing, manufacturing, decision sciences, economics, and organizational behavior. Unless your school allows you to place out of them, these courses are mandatory. Core courses provide broad functional knowledge in one discipline. To illustrate, a core marketing course covers pricing, segmentation, communications, product-line planning, and implementation. Electives provide a narrow focus that deepen the area of study. For example, a marketing elective might be entirely devoted to pricing.

Students sometimes question the need for such a comprehensive core program, but the functional areas of a real business are not parallel lines. All departments of a business affect each other every day. For example, an MBA in a manufacturing job might be asked by a financial controller why the company's product has become unprofitable to produce. Without an understanding of how product costs are accounted for, this MBA wouldn't know how to respond to a critical and legitimate request.

At most schools, the first term or year is devoted to a rigid core curriculum. Some schools allow first-years to take core courses side by side with electives. Still others have come up with an entirely new way of covering the basics, integrating the core courses into one cross-functional learning experience, which may also include sessions on topics such as globalization, ethics, and managing diversity. Half-year to year-long courses are team-taught by professors who will see you through all disciplines.

TEACHING METHODOLOGY

Business schools employ two basic teaching methods: case study and lecture. Usually, they employ some combination of the two. The most popular is the case study approach. Students are presented with either real or hypothetical business scenarios and are asked to analyze them. This method provides concrete situations (rather than abstractions) that require mastery of a wide range of skills. Students often find case studies exciting because they can engage in spirited discussions about possible solutions to given business problems and because they get an opportunity to apply newly acquired business knowledge.

On the other hand, lecturing is a teaching method in which—you guessed it—the professor speaks to the class and the class listens. The efficacy of the lecture method depends entirely on the professor. If the professor is compelling, you'll probably get a lot out of the class. If the professor is boring, you probably won't listen, which isn't necessarily a big deal since many professors make their class notes available online.

THE CLASSROOM EXPERIENCE

Professors teaching case methodology often begin class with a "cold call." A randomly selected student opens the class with an analysis of the case and makes recommendations for solutions. The cold call forces you to be prepared and to think on your feet.

No doubt, a cold call can be intimidating. But unlike law school, b-school professors don't use the Socratic Method to torture you, testing your thinking with a pounding cross-examination. They're training managers, not trial lawyers. At worst, particularly if you're unprepared, a professor will abruptly dismiss your contribution.

Alternatively, professors ask for a volunteer to open a case, particularly someone who has had real industry experience with the issues. After the opening, the discussion is broadened to include the whole class. Everyone tries to get in a good comment, particularly if class participation counts heavily toward the grade. "Chip shots"—unenlightened, just-say-anything-to-get-credit comments—are common. So are "air hogs," students who go on and on because they like nothing more than to hear themselves pontificate.

Depending on the school, class discussions can degenerate into wars of ego rather than ideas. But for the most part, debates are kept constructive and civilized. Students are competitive, but not offensively so, and learn to make their points succinctly and persuasively.

A GLOSSARY OF INSIDER LINGO

B-school students, graduates, and professors—like most close-knit, somewhat solipsistic groups—seem to speak their own weird language. Here's a sampler of MBA jargon (with English translations):

Admissions Mistake: How each student perceives him or herself until getting first-year grades back from midterms.

Air Hogs: Students who monopolize classroom discussion and love to hear themselves speak.

B2B: "Business to Business"—a company that sells not to retail consumers, but to other enterprises. With the renewed focus on more traditional industries, this now stands for "Back to Basics."

B2C: "Business to Consumer"—a company that sells primarily to individual retail consumers. As with the above joke about B2B, business students occasionally say this really means "Back to Consulting."

Back of the Envelope: A quick analysis of numbers, as if scribbled on the back of an envelope.

Benchmarking: Comparing a company to others in the industry.

Burn Rate: Amount of cash a money-losing company consumes during a period of time.

Case Study Method: Popular teaching method that uses real-life business cases for analysis.

Cold Call: Unexpected, often dreaded request by the professor to open a case discussion.

Chip Shot: Vacant and often cheesy comments used not to truly benefit class discussion, but rather to get credit for participation.

Cycle Time: How fast you can turn something around.

Deliverable: Your end product.

Four Ps: Elements of a marketing strategy: Price, Promotion, Place, Product.

Fume Date: Date the company will run out of cash reserves.

Functional Areas: The basic disciplines of business (e.g., finance, marketing, R&D).

HP12-C: A calculator that works nothing like a regular one, used by finance types when they don't have Excel handy.

Lingo Bingo: A furtive game of Bingo whereby he who "wins" must work a decided upon, often trite phrase (see "chip shot") into the class discussion. For example: "I didn't actually read the case last night, but the protagonist is *two beers short of a six-pack*." The winner also earns a prize and the admiration of classmates.

Low Hanging Fruit: Tasks or goals that are easiest to achieve (consultant jargon).

Monitize: To turn an idea into a moneymaking scheme.

Net Net: End result.

Power Nap: Quick, intense, in-class recharge for the continually sleep-deprived.

Power Tool: Someone who does all the work and sits in the front row of the class with his or her hand up.

Pre-enrollment Courses: Commonly known as MBA summer camp—quantitative courses to get the numerically challenged up to speed.

Pro Forma: Financial presentation of hypothetical events, such as projected earnings.

Quant Jock: A numerical athlete who is happiest crunching numbers.

Rule of Three: You should not talk more than three times in any given class, but you should participate at least once over the course of three classes.

Run the Numbers: Analyze quantitatively.

Shrimp Boy: A student who comes to a corporate event just to scarf down the food.

Skydeck: Refers to the back row of the classroom, usually when it's amphitheater style.

Slice and Dice: Running all kinds of quantitative analysis on a set of numbers.

Soft Skills: Conflict resolution, teamwork, negotiation, oral and written communication.

Take-aways: The key points of a lecture or meeting that participants should remember.

The Five Forces: Michael Porter's model for analyzing the strategic attractiveness of an industry.

Three Cs: The primary forces considered in marketing: Customer, Competition, Company.

Value-Based Decision Making: Values and ethics as part of the practice of business.

YOUR FIRST YEAR

The first six months of b-school can be daunting. You're unfamiliar with the subjects. There's a tremendous amount of work to do. And when you least have the skills to do so, there's pressure to stay with the pack. All of this produces anxiety and a tendency to overprepare. Eventually, students learn shortcuts and settle into a routine, but until then, much of the first year is just plain tough. The programs usually pack more learning into the first term than they do into each of the remaining terms. For the schools to teach the core curriculum (which accounts for as much as 70 percent of learning) in a limited time, an intensive pace is considered necessary. Much of the second year will be spent on gaining proficiency in your area of expertise and on searching for a job.

The good news is that the schools recognize how tough the first year can be. During the early part of the program, they anchor students socially by placing them in small sections, sometimes called "cohorts." You take many or all of your classes with your section-mates. Sectioning encourages the formation of personal and working relationships and can help make a large program feel like a school within a school.

Because so much has to be accomplished in so little time, getting an MBA is like living in fast-forward. This is especially true of the job search. No sooner are you in the program than recruiters for summer jobs show up, which tends to divert students from their studies. First-years aggressively pursue summer positions, which are linked with the promise of a permanent job offer if the summer goes well. At some schools, the recruiting period begins as early as October, at others in January or February.

A DAY IN THE LIFE

MATT CAMP, FIRST YEAR
Tuck School of Business, Dartmouth College

7:00 A.M.: Get dressed. Out of the door by 7:45 A.M. to head to the campus dining hall for breakfast. If I have time, I'll grab the *Financial Times* and *The Wall Street Journal* and gloss over the front page. Today, I have an informal get-to-know-you-better meeting with a marketing professor over breakfast.

8:30 A.M.: Core class in Corporate Finance. Grab any seat in a tiered classroom set-up. I'm usually in the middle toward the side. If possible, the front row stays empty.

10:00 A.M.: Go to e-mail kiosk on campus and check messages. Hang out or do a quick run to the library to read more of the *Times*.

10:30 A.M.: Macroeconomics lecture/case study class. Again, no assigned seating. Expect cold calls on case. Cold calls are not terrifying. Professors are supportive, not out to embarrass you. Class discussion is lively, with a mix of people offering their views.

Noon: Back to the cafeteria. Tuck may be one of the few schools where everyone eats together at the same place. There isn't much in town, and you're tight on time, so it doesn't make sense to go back home or elsewhere. It's crowded, so I look for friends, but basically grab a seat anywhere at one of the large tables that seat six to seven. Professors, administrators, and students all eat at the same place. Food is above-average.

1:15 P.M.: Classes are over for the day. From this point, I begin to start homework; there's a lot of work to do. I can go to a study room on campus, but they get booked up pretty quickly for groups, so I head to the library. The majority of the people are doing work for tomorrow. It's rare to have someone working on a project that's due the following week. It's pretty much day-to-day.

4:00 P.M.: I head off to one of the scheduled sports I've signed up for. Today it's soccer, played about one mile from campus. I drive; friends hitch a ride with me. This is a big international scene, mostly men, but there's a small group of women too. It's definitely a game we play hard, but in a very congenial way.

6:00 P.M.: Head back to campus. I'm hungry. It's off to the dining hall again. Most first-years live in dorms, so home cooking is not an option. Almost all second-years live off-campus, so they head back for a home-cooked meal. Cafeteria is not crowded; I may eat alone.

7:00 P.M.: Head home for a quick shower and change. The night is just beginning.

7:30 P.M.: Meet with study group at school to flesh out rest of work that needs to be done in preparation for tomorrow's classes.

11:00 P.M.: Students and their wives/husbands or partners head out to play ice hockey at one of the two rinks here. Wives/husbands and partners play. There are different games going on for different skill levels. It's a lot of fun.

Midnight: Time to go and celebrate either a hard game or a sore butt, but everyone goes to get some wings and a beer. There are only two bars on campus, and they close at 1:00 A.M. so we head to one of them.

1:00 A.M.: After the bar closes, people head home.

1:15 A.M.: Exhausted, I go to bed. No TV. I've forgotten what that is.

YOUR SECOND YEAR

Relax, the second year is easier. By now, students know what's important and what's not. Second-years work more efficiently than first-years. Academic anxiety is no longer a factor. Having mastered the broad-based core curriculum, students now enjoy taking electives and developing an area of specialization.

Anxiety in the second year has more to do with the arduous task of finding a job. For some lucky students, a summer position has yielded a full-time offer. But even those students often go through the whole recruiting grind anyway because they don't want to cut off any opportunities prematurely.

Most MBAs leave school with a full-time offer. Sometimes it's their only offer. Sometimes it's not their dream job, which may be why most grads change jobs after just two years. One student summed up the whole two-year academic/recruiting process like this: "The first-year students collapse in the winter quarter because of on-campus recruiting. The second-years collapse academically in the first quarter of their second year because it's so competitive to get a good job. And when a second-year does get a job, he or she forgets about class entirely. That's why pass/fail was invented."

A DAY IN THE LIFE

KRISTIN HANSEN, SECOND-YEAR
Tuck School of Business, Dartmouth College

9:00 A.M.: Wake-up (my first class is at 10:30 A.M.) and finish work for Monday classes.

10:15 A.M.: Ride my bike to campus for 10:30 A.M. class.

10:30 A.M.: Head to International Economics class, an elective. I have only three classes this semester, my last. Prior to this I had four and a half classes each term. I front-loaded so I would have a light last semester. Grab a yogurt and juice on way in. Eat in class. We discuss a currency crisis case.

Noon: Head to study room to plug my personal computer into one of the many networked connections on campus to check e-mail. Finish work for next class.

1:00 P.M.: Grab a quick lunch in the dining hall. Will bring it to eat during class.

1:15 P.M.: Managerial Decision Making class, another elective. Today is the very last class that second-years will have at Tuck; we're off to graduation! Our professor brings in strawberries and champagne to celebrate. We all hang out and toast each other. This obviously doesn't happen everyday, but this is just the kind of thing a Tuck professor would do.

2:45 P.M.: I'm one of four Tuck social chairpersons, so I use this time to send e-mails to my co-chairs about the upcoming chili cook-off and farm party. Then I send a message to the school regarding other social events for the weekend. I get an e-mail from the New York office of CS First Boston, with whom I've accepted a job offer, with a calendar of the dates for my private client-services training.

3:00 P.M.: Go for a run, swim, or bike ride.

5:00 P.M.: Head home to shower and change. Usually I'd make dinner at home and eat, but tonight, I'm heading out to a social event. So I relax a bit and do an hour of preparation for the next day. On Monday, Tuesday, and Wednesday nights, the workload is heavier.

7:00 P.M.: Off to a Turkey Fry Dinner. This is a meal that will be prepared by my two economics professors. They donated this "dinner" for the charity student auction. Friends of mine bid on it and won. Each of eight bidders gets to bring a guest, and I'm one of the guests. The professors are hosting this at one of their homes. Basically, they're taking three large turkeys and fry-o-lating them.

8:30 P.M.: We all head out to an open mic night, led by the same two economics professors that hosted the Turkey Fry. It's held at a local bar. Anyone in the audience can get onstage and perform. I'm a member of the Tuck band, so I get up on stage with my acoustic guitar and play various folk and bluegrass songs. This is a great warm-up for the open mic night at Tuck.

10:45 P.M.: We head out for Pub Night in downtown Hanover.

1:00 A.M.: The bar closes, so we head to "The End Zone," one of the second-year houses close to campus. All the second-year houses are named; these are names that have been passed down from generation to generation. On a typical Thursday night at Tuck, a small number of students will stay out until 3:00 A.M. I'm usually one of them.

3:00 A.M.: I walk home. My house, called "Girls in the Hood," is just a ten-minute stroll away. I may grab a 3:00 A.M. snack. Then, I quickly fall asleep, exhausted.

Life Outside of Class

Business school is more than academics and a big-bucks job. A spirited community provides ample opportunity for social interaction, extracurricular activity, and career development.

Much of campus life revolves around student-run clubs. There are groups for just about every career interest and social need—from MBAs for a Greener America to the Small Business Club. There's even a group for significant others on most campuses. The clubs are a great way to meet classmates with similar interests and to get in on the social scene. They might have a reputation for throwing the best black-tie balls, pizza-and-keg events, and professional mixers. During orientation week, these clubs aggressively market themselves to first-years.

Various socially responsible projects are also popular on campus. An emphasis on volunteer work is part of the overall trend toward good citizenship. Perhaps to counter the greed of the 1980s, "giving back" is the b-school style of the moment. There is usually a wide range of options—from tutoring in an inner-city school to working in a soup kitchen to renovating public buildings.

Still another way to get involved is to work on a school committee. Here you might serve on a task force designed to improve student quality of life, 0r you might work in the admissions office and interview prospective students.

For those with more creative urges there are always the old standbys: extracurriculars such as the school paper, yearbook, or school play. At some schools, the latter is a dramatization of "b-school follies" and is a highlight of the year. Like the student clubs, these are a great way to get to know your fellow students.

Finally, you can play on intramural sports teams or attend the numerous informal get-togethers, dinner parties, and group trips. There are also plenty of regularly scheduled pub nights, just in case you thought your beer-guzzling days were over.

Most former MBA students say that going to b-school was the best decision they ever made. That's primarily because of nonacademic experiences. Make the most of your classes, but take the time to get involved and enjoy yourself.

PART II
SCHOOLS RANKED BY CATEGORY

On the following pages you will find eleven top 10 lists of business schools ranked according to various metrics. As we noted earlier, none of these lists purports to rank the business schools by their overall quality. Nor should any combination of the categories we've chosen be construed as representing the raw ingredients for such a ranking. We have made no attempt to gauge the "prestige" of these schools, and we wonder whether we could accurately do so even if we tried. What we have done, however, is presented a number of lists using information from two very large databases—one of statistical information collected from business schools, and another of subjective data gathered via our survey of 19,000 business students at 300 business schools.

Ten of the ranking lists are based partly or wholly on opinions collected through our business student survey. The only schools that may appear in these lists are the 300 business schools from which we were able to collect a sufficient number of student surveys to accurately represent the student experience in our various ratings and descriptive profiles.

One of the rankings, "Toughest to Get Into," incorporates *only* admissions statistics reported to us by the business schools. Therefore, any business school appearing in this edition of the guide, whether we collected student surveys from it or not, may appear on this list.

Under the title of each list is an explanation of what criteria the ranking is based on. For explanations of many of the individual rankings components, turn to the "How This Book is Organized" section, on page 5.

It's worth repeating: There is no one best business school in America. There is a best business school for you. By using these rankings in conjunction with the descriptive profiles and data listings in subsequent sections of this book, we hope that you will begin to identify the attributes of a business school that are important to you, as well as those schools that can best help you to achieve your personal and professional goals.

Please note that in an effort to avoid comparing apples to oranges, we have not placed any international business schools on any of our rankings lists.

The top schools in each category appear in descending order.

TOUGHEST TO GET INTO
BASED ON THE ADMISSIONS SELECTIVITY RATING (SEE PAGE 11 FOR EXPLANATION)

1. Stanford University
2. Harvard University
3. University of California—Berkeley
4. Columbia University
5. Massachusetts Institute of Technology
6. University of Pennsylvania
7. Yale University
8. Dartmouth College
9. New York University
10. Cornell University

BEST CAREER PROSPECTS
BASED ON THE CAREER RATING (SEE PAGE 13 FOR EXPLANATION)

1. Harvard University
2. Stanford University
3. Northwestern University
4. Georgetown University
5. University of Pennsylvania
6. University of Virginia
7. University of Michigan—Ann Arbor
8. Duke University
9. University of California—Berkeley
10. Carnegie Mellon University

BEST CLASSROOM EXPERIENCE
BASED ON STUDENT ASSESSMENT OF PROFESSORS' TEACHING ABILITIES AND RECOGNITION IN THEIR FIELDS, THE INTEGRATION OF NEW BUSINESS TRENDS AND PRACTICES IN THE CURRICULA, AND THE INTELLECTUAL LEVEL OF CLASSMATES' CONTRIBUTIONS IN COURSE DISCUSSIONS

1. Cornell University
2. University of California—Berkeley
3. Acton School of Business
4. Harvard University
5. University of Pennsylvania
6. University of Virginia
7. Yale University
8. University of Notre Dame
9. Vanderbilt University
10. Indiana University—Bloomington

BEST PROFESSORS
BASED ON THE PROFESSORS INTERESTING AND PROFESSORS ACCESSIBLE RATINGS (SEE PAGES 9 AND 10 FOR EXPLANATIONS)

1. University of Virginia
2. University of California—Berkeley
3. The University of Texas at Austin
4. Harvard University
5. University of Michigan—Ann Arbor
6. Rice University
7. Brigham Young University
8. Indiana University—Bloomington
9. College of William and Mary
10. Cornell University

MOST COMPETITIVE STUDENTS

Based on student assessment of how competitive classmates are, how heavy the workload is, and the perceived academic pressure

1. Vanderbilt University
2. University of Pennsylvania
3. Acton School of Business
4. Brigham Young University
5. Southern Methodist University
6. Texas A & M University—College Station
7. University of Miami
8. University of Mississippi
9. University of Arkansas—Fayetteville
10. Texas Christian University (TCU)

MOST FAMILY FRIENDLY

Based on student assessment of: how happy married students are, how many students have children, how helpful the business school is to students with children, and how much the school does for the spouses of students

1. Brigham Young University
2. Dartmouth College
3. Indiana University—Bloomington
4. Harvard University
5. College of William and Mary
6. Cornell University
7. University of Notre Dame
8. University of Utah
9. Northwestern University
10. Pennsylvania State University

BEST CAMPUS ENVIRONMENT

Based on student assessment of the safety, attractiveness and location of the school

1. University of California—Los Angeles
2. University of Washington
3. The University of Iowa
4. University of San Diego
5. University of Virginia
6. Cal Poly State University at San Luis Obispo
7. Stanford University
8. American University
9. Ithaca College
10. Claremont Graduate University

BEST CAMPUS FACILITIES

Based on student assessment of the quality of classroom, library and gym facilities

1. Bentley University
2. University of Virginia
3. Baylor University
4. Harvard University
5. Elon University
6. University of Georgia
7. West Virginia University
8. University of Wisconsin—Madison
9. Georgia Institute of Technology
10. The Ohio State University

BEST ADMINISTERED

BASED ON STUDENT ASSESSMENT OF HOW SMOOTHLY THE SCHOOL IS RUN, AND THE
EASE WITH WHICH STUDENTS CAN GET INTO REQUIRED AND POPULAR COURSES

1. Bentley University
2. University of Virginia
3. Baylor University
4. Harvard University
5. Elon University
6. University of Georgia
7. West Virginia University
8. University of Wisconsin—Madison
9. Georgia Institute of Technology
10. The Ohio State University

GREATEST OPPORTUNITY FOR MINORITY STUDENTS

BASED ON THE PERCENT OF STUDENTS FROM MINORITIES, THE PERCENT OF FACULTY
FROM MINORITIES, AND STUDENT ASSESSMENT OF RESOURCES FOR MINORITY STUDENTS,
HOW SUPPORTIVE THE CULTURE IS OF MINORITY STUDENTS, AND WHETHER FELLOW
STUDENTS ARE ETHNICALLY AND RACIALLY DIVERSE

1. Bentley University
2. University of Virginia
3. Baylor University
4. Harvard University
5. Elon University
6. University of Georgia
7. West Virginia University
8. University of Wisconsin—Madison
9. Georgia Institute of Technology
10. The Ohio State University

GREATEST OPPORTUNITY FOR WOMEN

BASED ON THE PERCENT OF STUDENTS WHO ARE FEMALE, THE PERCENT OF FACULTY WHO
ARE FEMALE, AND STUDENT ASSESSMENT OF: RESOURCES FOR FEMALE STUDENTS, HOW
SUPPORTIVE THE CULTURE IS OF FEMALE STUDENTS, WHETHER THE BUSINESS SCHOOL
OFFERS COURSEWORK FOR WOMEN ENTREPRENEURS, AND WHETHER CASE STUDY
MATERIALS FOR CLASSES PROPORTIONATELY REFLECT WOMEN IN BUSINESS

1. Bentley University
2. University of Virginia
3. Baylor University
4. Harvard University
5. Elon University
6. University of Georgia
7. West Virginia University
8. University of Wisconsin—Madison
9. Georgia Institute of Technology
10. The Ohio State University

PART III-A
BUSINESS SCHOOL
DESCRIPTIVE PROFILES

ACTON SCHOOL OF BUSINESS
THE ACTON MBA IN ENTREPRENEURSHIP

GENERAL INFORMATION
Type of school	Private
Academic calendar	Aug–Apr

SURVEY SAYS...
Good peer network
Cutting-edge classes
Solid preparation in:
Finance
General management
Operations
Communication/interpersonal skills
Quantitative skills
Entrepreneurial studies

STUDENTS
Enrollment of parent institution	2,200
Enrollment of MBA Program	38
% male/female	82/18
% out-of-state	26
% part-time	0
% minorities	16
% international	8
Average age at entry	29
Average years work experience at entry	6

ACADEMICS
Academic Experience Rating	**97**
Student/faculty ratio	2:1
Profs interesting rating	97
Profs accessible rating	97
% female faculty	13

FINANCIAL FACTS
Annual tuition	$49,500
Room & board (off-campus)	$20,000
% of students receiving aid	100
% of first-year students receiving aid	100
Average award package	$51,500
Average student loan debt	$25,000

Academics

The Acton School of Business—"the only business school I know of that exists for the sole purpose of preparing students to become entrepreneurs," one student writes—offers the nation's closest version of boot camp for entrepreneurs. The program is designed to deliver two year's worth of training in a single year; as one student explains, this "condensed, 12-month program...requires at least nine months of focused attention," during which "students will be studying or attending class an average of 100 hours a week." No, that is not a misprint—you really are doing school-related activities for about 100 hours per week. Logic follows that "It is impossible to work while in the program." When you're studying this much, travel time is a luxury you cannot afford and as a result "many students relocate near the campus."

Acton MBAs undertake a "phenomenal" curriculum that focuses on analysis of 300 case studies. Instruction is delivered in the Socratic method, resulting in "students [who learn] to articulate, defend their arguments with reason and evidence, and ask insightful questions." As one student tells us, "By combining a pure case-study curriculum with the Socratic method, Acton requires students to not only learn the material, but understand it to the level that they can defend or attack it. By forcing the students to be integral to the discussion of the cases or the material, the students hold themselves much more accountable for the material."

Acton's single-minded curriculum "focuses on entrepreneurs, [so] the classes are tightly integrated," one student explains. "All the classes are intentionally selected to build on each other." As you might well imagine, success here requires a huge commitment of time and intellectual ardor, but for most here "the rigor of the program is a draw." As one student put it, "I wanted to be tested in an environment that has pressures similar to what an entrepreneur faces in the real world." Others tell us that the "commitment required [means] Acton has a greater ability to be truly transformational."

A program like this is only as good as its instructors, of course. Fortunately, professors receive high marks from Acton MBAs, who report that "Acton professors are all successful entrepreneurs and have each operated, bought, or sold several companies in their professional career." Capitalism purists will be pleased to learn that fundamental Smithian principles are applied even in their professors' pay system. "The teacher compensation plan involves a small base salary with bonuses based on student feedback," one student reports approvingly. "This compensation plan brings in only the best teachers who have a genuine love for teaching."

Career and Placement

Acton administrators tell us that "Many schools rely on a centralized Career Services Office to send out thousands of resumes to hundreds of employers. Our approach is completely different. Through the Life of Meaning course, we rely on students to identify a specific job at a specific company that will be the next stepping stone to achieving his or her lifelong goals. Once a professor is convinced that a student has made a considered choice, the professor will call that employer to make a personal introduction." Students confirm this, reporting that "the Life of Meaning course gives you the tools to define a career that's both meaningful to you and impactful to the world."

ADMISSIONS CONTACT: SUSIE HALL, DIRECTOR OF OUTREACH AND ENROLLMENT
ADDRESS: 816 CONGRESS AVENUE, SUITE 1240 AUSTIN, TX 78701
PHONE: 512-703-1232 • FAX: 512-495-9480
E-MAIL: ADMISSIONS@ACTONMBA.ORG • WEBSITE: WWW.ACTONMBA.ORG

Student Life and Environment

"There's never a dull moment at Acton," where schoolwork consumes pretty much every waking hour. "A typical day begins at 6 A.M. with study group and ends as you close your last case at midnight or later....Make no mistake—life at Acton is tough." Students "do ten cases a week, each requiring five to eight hours worth of prep time." As one student puts it, "The schedule sounds ridiculous and readers of this will assume that I am exaggerating. Let me assure you that there is no exaggeration here. One hundred hours a week is every bit as intense and uncomfortable as you can imagine. The trade-off to this hectic schedule is the learning that follows. You don't notice as you're working throughout the semester, but you actually retain every bit of it."

While there's not much time for leisure activities, "Acton hosts a couple of dinners each semester for students and their significant others; these gatherings are a time to relax, socialize and swap ideas for how to handle the rigor of Acton." Students enjoy a strong esprit de corps. One explains that "because Acton has a small student population, you get to know everyone well. The social environment is fun and students band together to help each other." It should come as no surprise that Acton students are "intense," "focused," and "ultra-competitive."

Admissions

Acton looks for students who display perseverance, a curious intellect, and integrity. You must also demonstrate a high level of achievement in your undergraduate academic record, an aptitude for graduate study as evidenced by your GMAT score, and a history of leadership and involvement in extracurricular activities. The small size of the program allows Acton to take a close look at each applicant. Applications must include personal essays, three letters of recommendation, and a resume. No one is admitted without first undergoing an admissions interview, which is scheduled by invitation only. International students must apply by January 31 in order to ensure adequate time to secure student visas, if accepted; the final application deadline for Americans is March 14. International students whose first language is not English must submit an official score report for the TOEFL.

ADMISSIONS	
Admissions Selectivity Rating	98
# of applications received	64
% applicants accepted	72
% acceptees attending	83
Average GMAT	630
Average GPA	3.2
TOEFL required of international students	Yes
Minimum TOEFL (paper/computer)	630/267
Application fee	$150
International application fee	$150
Application Deadline/Notification	
Round 1:	11/1 / 11/22
Round 2:	1/31 / 2/28
Round 3:	3/14 / 4/4
Early decision program?	No
Deferment available	No
Transfer students accepted	No
Non-fall admissions	No
Need-blind admissions	No

EMPLOYMENT PROFILE				
Career Rating	88	Grads Employed by Function	%	Avg. Salary
Percent employed at graduation	14	Marketing	7	$75,000
Percent employed 3 months after graduation	50	Operations	18	$102,000
		Management	11	$77,500
Average base starting salary	$80,000	Entrepreneurship	25	NR
Primary Source of Full-time Job Acceptances		Nonprofit	4	$60,000
School-facilitated activities	3 (11%)	Strategic	4	$135,000
Graduate-facilitated activities	15 (54%)			
Unknown	1 (4%)			

ALFRED UNIVERSITY
COLLEGE OF BUSINESS

GENERAL INFORMATION
Type of school	Private

SURVEY SAYS...
Good social scene
Cutting-edge classes
Solid preparation in:
Accounting

ACADEMICS
Academic Experience Rating	**78**
Student/faculty ratio	2:1
Profs interesting rating	61
Profs accessible rating	69
% female faculty	26
% minority faculty	50

FINANCIAL FACTS
Annual tuition	$34,294
Fees	$880
Cost of books	$1,000
Room & board	
(on/off-campus)	$10,000/$8,000
% of students receiving aid	70
% of first-year students	
receiving aid	90
% of students receiving loans	85
% of students receiving grants	90
Average award package	$17,147
Average grant	$12,860

Academics

If you're looking for an "intimate environment" for your MBA experience, Alfred University is well worth a look. This program serves a population of 17 graduate students. The result is a program with a "family atmosphere" where everyone is "really friendly and willing to help." As one student told us, "The greatest strength of Alfred University is its size. The classes are between 10 and 20 people, and the interaction is incredible. One really feels a part of the class discussions." The school is especially strong in entrepreneurial studies, an area abetted by the university's Center for Family Business and Entrepreneurial Leadership, a research center.

Professors at Alfred have the time to go the extra mile for students, and they "work hard to make sure you understand what they are teaching, but they also expect you to do your share of the work." Students also appreciate that "professors here are very diverse and have experiences [in other countries] ranging from Japan to Tunisia." With no crowd to fight, Alfred students have a better chance to shine (though keep in mind this also means there's no anonymity for anyone—"Show up to class prepared and hand your work in on time," advises one student). Another writes, "One professor liked a paper I wrote for his class. He offered to co-author another paper with me and pursue getting it published. These opportunities are so valuable to me and something I would never have expected." And this sense of support and enterprise doesn't end in the classroom. As one student explains, "MBA students at Alfred receive great amounts of attention not only from faculty but also from business school staff. The Assistant Dean keeps a close eye on all of us to make sure we're getting everything we need: from bindings for term papers to a listening ear [for our] concerns."

Of course, a small school can only offer students so much. Some students find that there are "few academic options within the program," "too few courses," and "limited electives." Even so, they regard their MBA experience as extremely "positive." They approve of the school's "active learning" strategies, which emphasize teamwork, case studies, simulations, and field experience (usually gained through an internship). "As a result, I have found the program challenging, rewarding, and enriching," explains one student.

Career and Placement

All Alfred students receive career services through the Robert R. McComsey Career Development Center. The office provides one-on-one counseling sessions; workshops in interviewing, resume writing, and networking; a career library with online and conventional print resources; and annual job fairs. The school also boasts a 100 percent placement rate for its MBAs. Students point out, however, that Alfred's remote location complicates their search for jobs and internships. Many agree that "Alfred is a small community" and that "outside internships and projects are more difficult to obtain due to the university's rural location." However, over the past few years the administration had worked "to expand local, as well as international, opportunities with particular focus on MBA students," and as such, many find that the school currently "does very well in providing big city opportunities."

Prominent employers of Alfred MBAs include Alstom, AOL Communications, Avantt Consulting, Met Life/New England Financial, General Electric Company, Eli Lilly and Company, Citynet, Corning, Dresser Rand, Nestlé, NYSEG, Toro Energy, and Wal-Mart.

ADMISSIONS CONTACT: COREY FECTEAU, GRADUATE ADMISSIONS
ADDRESS: OFFICE OF GRADUATE ADMISSIONS, ALUMNI HALL, SAXON DRIVE ALFRED, NY 14802
PHONE: 800-541-9229 • FAX: 607-871-2198
E-MAIL: GRADINQUIRY@ALFRED.EDU • WEBSITE: HTTP://BUSINESS.ALFRED.EDU/

Student Life and Environment

Alfred, New York, is a quiet, rural town with few distractions, and accordingly, student life centers on campus. The university is a community of about 2,000 students, including 210 business undergrads and 20 MBAs, making it large enough to support all manner of activity. The "wide variety of clubs and organizations offer great opportunity for individual growth" and if you want a club "All you have to do is ask." One student explains, "Alfred's clubs and activities are astounding. Diverse clubs and organizations regularly attend student senate to discuss concerns that are circulating the student population."

Alfred's infrastructure includes "plenty of computers and good Internet bandwidth"; however, "The recreational facilities aren't the best, and the library needs help." Fortunately, a "large renovation and expansion project" is underway, which could be "the largest project for the university within the last few decades." The renovations are expected to "address shortcomings of the university, greatly enhance the campus, and benefit students." Also, while the "huge" dorms get glowing reviews, "Housing is really poor off campus."

Alfred's 16 Division III intercollegiate teams provide entertainment, as does the popular intramural sports program. The school's divisions of music, theater, and dance frequently hold performances. Alfred also has an active visual-arts community; it houses one of the best ceramic arts programs in the country. The "peaceful and safe" village of Alfred has a year-round population of 1,000 and surrounding towns are not much larger. These "secluded" surroundings lessen "the chances of distractions from studies," though when students need a break from the books, Rochester is only 80 miles away, with Buffalo only a little farther down the road—provided you have four-wheel drive in the winter.

Admissions

Applicants must provide the school with official copies of undergraduate transcripts, GMAT scores, TOEFL scores (for international students whose first language is not English), a personal statement, and letters of recommendation (preferably from former employers or professors). Previous work experience is not required, and an interview, while always recommended, is optional.

ADMISSIONS

Admissions Selectivity Rating	75
TOEFL required of international students	Yes
Minimum TOEFL (paper/computer)	590/243
Application fee	$60
International application fee	$60
Regular application deadline	5/1
Early decision program?	No
Deferment available	Yes
Maximum length of deferment	2 years
Transfer students accepted	Yes
Transfer application policy: Transfer a maximum of 6 credit hours from a comparable program.	
Non-fall admissions	Yes
Need-blind admissions	Yes

AMERICAN UNIVERSITY
KOGOD SCHOOL OF BUSINESS

GENERAL INFORMATION

Type of school	Private
Affiliation	Methodist
Academic calendar	Semester

SURVEY SAYS...

Students love Washington, D.C.
Solid preparation in:
Accounting
Doing business in a global economy

STUDENTS

Enrollment of parent institution	12,186
Enrollment of MBA Program	270
% male/female	57/43
% part-time	45
Average age at entry	28
Average years work experience at entry	4.5

ACADEMICS

Academic Experience Rating	**86**
Profs interesting rating	85
Profs accessible rating	87
% female faculty	22

Joint Degrees

JD/MBA—4 years; MBA/MA in
International Affairs—3 years;
LLM/MBA—2 years

Prominent Alumni

Marvin Shanken, Chairman, M.
Shaken Communications; Loretta
Sanchez, United States Congress;
David Blumenthal, Senior Vice
President and COO, Lion Brand Yarn
Com; Mark Murphy, CEO and
President of the Green Bay Packers

Academics

The "small and friendly" MBA program at American University's Kogod School of Business offers a "solid academic program" that, like its namesake (Robert P. Kogod, Charles E. Smith Co.), excels in the area of real estate. American's Washington, D.C. location is ideally situated for a curricular focus on international matters, and the school exploits that opportunity well, interjecting "an international perspective in class discussions that is second to none. Almost all classes integrate an international component."

Kogod's strengths extend far beyond real estate and international business, however. The school boasts a finance faculty that is "internationally recognized for their research. They are great instructors too." Students praise the commercial banking career track offered here and love the fact that the program "allows you to concentrate in two areas of expertise," which "lets you design your own MBA" and "is a great advantage in the job market." Kogod now has concentrations in accounting, consulting, entrepreneurship, finance, global emerging markets, leadership, strategic human capital management, marketing, and real estate. In addition, students can design their own major. Kogod recently "created the first LLM/MBA in the country, which is an excellent way to combine international law studies and business."

Kogod's pedagogical approach embraces a mixture of case studies and theory, combined with plenty of group work that acts as good practice for the real world. Professors "have a great reputation and have done interesting research." They are also easy to contact because of an "open-door policy." Faculty members "bring a lot of academic and professional experience" to the program—another plus. "We have former investment bankers, former consultants, former CFOs, and lifelong academics," brags one student. Small class sizes "give Kogod an advantage over the other D.C. schools like Georgetown and GW. I know everyone by name, and that's a nice feeling." As a result, the program "feels like being in a big family. Everyone knows you and does their best to help you."

Kogod's D.C. address "creates many opportunities for networking, internships, etc." As one student puts it, "The D.C. location gives Kogod a huge advantage. There are so many more opportunities to pursue when you are in a big city. It also helps Kogod draw "international students from very diverse countries," enhancing in-class and networking experiences. Perhaps best of all, this is a school that "is in the middle of overhauling its curriculum." In addition, the school recently completed a 21,000 square foot expansion which opened in 2009. The expansion which included 7 new class rooms, 3 student lounges, a financial services and information technology lab, a career center suite, a behavioral research lab, a mini-computer lab, and several breakout rooms. With these changes, one MBA predicts that "I think there will be some great changes" in the school's near future.

Career and Placement

Career Services at Kogod "does a great job in involving alumni in school life. There are lots of networking opportunities . . . [and] lots of on-site visits with direct interactions with alumni, both young and more experienced." A Wall Street trip includes visits to "all the major financial institutions with alumni as tour guides and a session for Q & A's and recruiting procedures and tips, concluded by an alumni networking dinner." Career Services Counselors also provide "constant information about new jobs/internship opportunities in the D.C. area and beyond."

Companies that have recently hired Kogod MBAs include: America Online, BearingPoint, Booz Allen Hamilton, Citigroup, Deloitte Touche Tohmatsu, Discovery Communications, Ernst & Young, Exxon Mobil, Fannie Mae, Freddie Mac, The Gallup Organization,

Goldman Sachs, IBM, Johnson & Johnson, JPMorgan, Lehman Brothers, Marriott International, MetLife, MSN, PricewaterhouseCoopers, Raytheon, U.S. Bank, the U.S. Government Accountability Office, the U.S. Securities and Exchange Commission, the U.S. Senate, and Unisys.

Student Life and Environment

The atmosphere in the Kogod MBA program "is low key, friendly, and accessible," with "a great learning environment. The students are all very friendly and socialize together regularly. The professors are very approachable and friendly, and have some impressive resumes. The academics are tough and the program is effective but not cut-throat." Kogod offers "many clubs and organizations in different fields," and students report that "involvement is highly encouraged."

Some here feel that "the program is not as social as others, and this is due in large part to the fact that the school is located in a relatively upscale neighborhood, and there are few restaurants or bars in the immediate area. Also, students tend to live all over Washington, D.C.," so "Getting large groups together can be difficult. However K-LAB provides co-curricular programs for grad students and students at Kogod are very involved with intramural sports. "Further, most agree that D.C. is one of the most exciting and fun cities in the country." As an added bonus, "There is so much work in D.C. that making $100K a year is almost automatic if you connect with the right government-related job."

Students here represent a variety of backgrounds. "I come from a military background," says one MBA, "and I really enjoy mingling and working with people from nonprofits, other government agencies, small companies, and large companies." The population includes a substantial international contingent.

Admissions

The Kogod Admissions Office requires the following from all applicants: a completed online application form; a personal statement of purpose in pursuing the MBA; a current resume; two letters of recommendation; an official transcript from all attended undergraduate and graduate institutions; and an official GMAT score report. International applicants whose first language is not English must also submit an official score report for other the TOEFL or the IELTS. An interview is required of all applicants.

FINANCIAL FACTS

Annual tuition	$28,226
Fees	$430
Room & board	
(on/off-campus)	$20,000/$20,000
% of first-year students	
receiving aid	54
Average award package	$31,105

ADMISSIONS

Admissions Selectivity Rating	83
# of applications received	544
% applicants accepted	53
% acceptees attending	34
Average GMAT	585
Range of GMAT	490–715
Average GPA	3.2
TOEFL required of	
international students	Yes
Minimum TOEFL (paper)	600
Application fee	$100
International application fee	$100
Application Deadline	
Round 1:	2/1
Round 2:	4/14
Early decision program?	No
Deferment available	Yes
Maximum length	
of deferment	1 year
Transfer students accepted	Yes
Non-fall admissions	Yes
Need-blind admissions	Yes

EMPLOYMENT PROFILE

Career Rating	83	**Grads Employed by Function% Avg. Salary**	
Percent employed at graduation	37	Marketing	1 NR
Percent employed 3 months		Consulting	13 $83,385
after graduation	18	Management	3 $63,333
Average base starting salary	$75,129	Finance	7 $73,925
Primary Source of Full-time Job Acceptances		HR	1 NR
School-facilitated activities	13 (46%)	MIS	1 NR
Graduate-facilitated activities	8 (29%)	**Top 5 Employers Hiring Grads**	
Unknown	7 (25%)	Bearing Point (3), IBM (3), Watkins, Meegan, Drury (1)	

APPALACHIAN STATE UNIVERSITY
WALKER COLLEGE OF BUSINESS

GENERAL INFORMATION
Type of school   Public
Academic calendar   Semester

SURVEY SAYS...
Good social scene
Happy students
Solid preparation in:
Accounting
Presentation skills
Doing business in a global economy

STUDENTS
Enrollment of parent
  institution   16,610
Enrollment of MBA Program   18
% male/female   65/35
% out-of-state   11
% part-time   25
% international   11
Average age at entry   28
Average years work experience
  at entry   5

ACADEMICS
Academic Experience Rating   79
Student/faculty ratio   20:1
Profs interesting rating   83
Profs accessible rating   83
% female faculty   20

Academics

Nested in the Blue Ridge Mountains of North Carolina, the Walker College of Business at Appalachian State University offers a small, efficient, and affordable MBA program to a largely local student population. For many, the fast-paced course schedule is a major benefit of this program. Here, the entire MBA—including an optional internship—can be completed in "only one year." (Prospective students should note that the one-year program is designed for students with an undergraduate degree in business. Before matriculation, the MBA requires up to 31 hours of prerequisite coursework.) Despite its speedy schedule, the MBA covers all functional areas of business, including accounting, economics, finance, management, marketing, operations, and information systems. In addition to the core curriculum, students have the option of tailoring their education through a concentration in one of three fields: sustainable business, international business, or general management. There is a focus on international business throughout the curriculum, which helps students "gain the knowledge [they] will need to compete in today's global economy." Of particular note, all students participate in an International Seminar in the last semester of the MBA, which includes a trip overseas. Recent programs took students around China to cities including Beijing, Nanjing, Shanghai and Hong Kong. While the program is scarcely large enough to support more variety, students feel, "the MBA program needs to add a computer information systems option" to the current offerings.

For full-time students, the schedule is rigorous and "the days are pretty packed." Throughout the program, "students spend about two hours in class each day, Monday through Thursday," while their afternoons are "spent working on group projects, homework, and or actually working at a job." Fortunately, the full-time MBA program is very small, with just over 20 students per class (in fact, the entering class size is capped at 24). The result is a caring, student-oriented atmosphere, and plenty of personal attention. Offering guidance and support, "The school has a great administration that is willing to work with the students in order to help the students achieve their goals." In addition, "The professors, on the whole, are easy to get along with and are always willing to help the students." Academically, the program is strong, but the teachers can be hit or miss. A student admits, "There have been some professors who have challenged me and were at the caliber that I expected, but there were also some who I felt were inadequate to be teaching graduate-level classes." Overall, Walker "teachers are knowledgeable and excited for students to learn."

In addition to the campus-based MBA program, ASU offers a part-time off-site MBA at a satellite facility in Hickory, North Carolina. In content, this program is similar to the Boone MBA, yet students learn through various delivery formats, including interactive audio-video sessions and web-based instruction, as well as in-person lectures from ASU faculty. No matter where you choose to study, the icing on the cake is the program's "low cost." This public school maintains a "very reasonable" tuition price, while also offering "scholarship and assistantship" programs, which can lower the price tag even further.

ADMISSIONS CONTACT: ANNA BASNIGHT, ADMISSIONS CONTACT
ADDRESS: ASU BOX 32068 BOONE, NC 28608-2068
PHONE: 828-262-2130 • FAX: 828-262-2709
E-MAIL: BASNIGHTAL@APPSTATE.EDU • WEBSITE: WWW.MBA.APPSTATE.EDU

Career and Placement

While the MBA program does not have its own career office, there is a career counselor assigned to the business school, who can help with career planning and placement. In addition, the Career Development Center on the Appalachian State University campus serves the entire undergraduate and graduate student body, as well as ASU alumni. The Career Development Center assists students with cover letter and resume revisions, personalized career counseling, mock interviews, and myriad online resources. In addition, the Career Development Center organizes networking events and "career fairs that bring in companies that have positions all over the U.S. and around the world." With a strong local reputation, ASU "does well with helping the students find a job," but nothing's perfect and "there are still improvements that can be made."

Student Life and Environment

Located on a "beautiful campus" in Boone, North Carolina, "Life is fabulous" at ASU. On this pleasant, hilltop campus, "Students hang out as a collective most times and crime rates are relatively low." Not to mention, this Southern city boasts "terrific weather" and great outdoor activities, including hiking and fishing. MBA classes take place in Raleigh Hall, which boasts wireless Internet and graduate student lounges. On the larger campus, students have access to study labs and a large library system.

Bringing a positive attitude to the classroom, ASU students "are willing to learn, as well as willing to begin friendships that have lasted the length of the program." While the accelerated schedule keeps them busy, "Students find time to attend sporting events, concerts, and many other extra curricular activities. All of the students also find time to hang out with one another and with their friends." While there are some local student hangouts, students say "nightlife could be a little better," in Boone. Most students, however, feel that "Being in a small town has been wonderful for my school experience." A current student writes, "In general, I wouldn't have chosen anywhere else to go."

Admissions

Appalachian State University's small MBA program only enrolls about 20 to 25 students each year. Prospective students are evaluated based on their GMAT score, three letters of recommendation, undergraduate academic performance, and current resume. To be eligible for the program, students must have completed a series of prerequisite courses in marketing, finance, accounting, management information systems, economics, law, and calculus with a grade point average of B or better. Professional work experience is not required.

FINANCIAL FACTS

Annual tuition (in-state/ out-of-state)	$3,474/$16,491
Fees	$2,180
Cost of books	$1,200
Room & board (on/off-campus)	$4,400/$7,200
Average grant	$1,000

ADMISSIONS

Admissions Selectivity Rating	76
# of applications received	33
% applicants accepted	67
% acceptees attending	64
Average GMAT	542
Range of GMAT	460–620
Average GPA	3.46
TOEFL required of international students	Yes
Minimum TOEFL (paper/computer)	550/233
Application fee	$45
International application fee	$45
Regular application deadline	3/1
Regular notification	3/31
Early decision program?	No
Deferment available	Yes
Maximum length of deferment	1 year
Transfer students accepted	Yes
Transfer application policy: Up to six hours of graduate credit may be transferred for equivalent courses completed with at least grade of B.	
Non-fall admissions	Yes
Need-blind admissions	Yes

ARIZONA STATE UNIVERSITY
W.P. CAREY SCHOOL OF BUSINESS

GENERAL INFORMATION
Type of school	Public
Academic calendar	Trimester

SURVEY SAYS...
Friendly students
Good peer network
Cutting-edge classes
Happy students
Solid preparation in:
General management
Teamwork

STUDENTS
Enrollment of parent institution	68,064
Enrollment of MBA Program	1,328
% male/female	76/24
% out-of-state	71
% part-time	87
% minorities	5
% international	29
Average age at entry	28
Average years work experience at entry	4.5

ACADEMICS
Academic Experience Rating	**90**
Student/faculty ratio	25:1
Profs interesting rating	84
Profs accessible rating	85
% female faculty	24
% minority faculty	25

Joint Degrees
Two year programs: W. P. Carey MBA/Master of Science in Information Management, W. P. Carey MBA/Master of Accountancy, W. P. Carey MBA/Master of Taxation, W. P. Carey MBA/Master of Health Sector Management. Three to four year programs: W. P. Carey MBA/Juris Doctorate, W. P. Carey MBA/Master of Architecture.

Academics

The W.P. Carey School of Business at Arizona State offers an "excellent value for its cost," a leading distance-learning MBA program, and a "growing reputation not only in the Southwest, but also throughout the country." Depending on your professional experience and educational goals, W.P. Carey offers several MBA options: a full-time program, an accelerated evening program, a fast-paced Executive MBA, and a flexible online MBA. Both full-time and part-time programs combine core course work in business fundamentals with advanced electives in specialized topics. For those with focused educational goals, the curriculum allows for "specialization courses to be taken in the first year," as well as the "option to pursue a dual degree within the same two years as the MBA." Many students come to ASU for its "high-ranked supply chain management program," while others note that the "corporate finance course work is [among] the best in the country." Students can further tailor their MBA experience through international elective courses (usually scheduled during breaks in the academic calendar) and summer internships.

Arizona State is rated among the best distance-learning MBAs in the country, and with good reason; Students in this program say it's a "stellar experience." Unlike the full-time and part-time programs, online students take "one class at a time, but compressed into only six weeks each." In many ways, this schedule "works very well for working professionals because you don't have to try to balance between competing classes, just drink from the fire hose." Students feel connected to campus, and have access to "customized modules with professors available live through chat and email." Especially noteworthy is the "outstanding" student services program run by dedicated staff members who always "keep students informed of upcoming events and requirements and assist with any academic or related needs." Administration is a breeze, and online students "are registered for classes and sent books automatically" each semester.

No matter what program you choose, W.P. Carey professors are "recognized leaders in their fields and often provide expert opinion[s] to newspapers, journals, and congress." While not every professor gets top marks in the classroom, the majority are "are passionate, current, and very open to discussion." A current student assures, "If a professor is not a leader in his or her field, you can be sure that he is an exceptional educator." In ASU's on-campus programs, "class size ranges around 25 people" and professors "are very accessible and willing to work with students to help improve their experience." In addition, "The school is committed to including students in the planning and decision-making processes. Student input is sought out on nearly all major decisions." Patently student-friendly, "The dean knows most students by first name and keeps an open door policy."

Career and Placement

Students in the ASU's full-time program must complete a required Career Leadership course in their first year, which focuses on career development and preparation. In addition, every student must complete a summer internship between the first and second year of the MBA. Moreover, students are pleased to report that career management counselors "take a very aggressive approach to the job hunt and they are incredibly helpful." On campus, "recruiting is amazing," and "The Career Management Center regularly accepts challenges to build relationships with companies that even one student is interested in." Within three months of graduation, about 80 to 90 percent of full-time students have accepted employment, with students reporting a base salary between $50,000 and $125,000, plus signing bonuses ranging from $2,000 to $37,000. Part-time and online students have access

ADMISSIONS CONTACT: RUDY PINO, DIRECTOR, ADMISSIONS, W. 'P. CAREY MBA
ADDRESS: P.O. BOX 874906 TEMPE, AZ 85287-4906
PHONE: 480-965-3332 • FAX: 480-965-8569
E-MAIL: WPCAREYMBA@ASU.EDU • WEBSITE: WPCAREY.ASU.EDU/MBA

to the career services website and may schedule individual counseling sessions. They may also participate in the On-Campus Recruitment Program, but must first attend the school's Boot Camp course, which teaches students how to use ASU's eRecruiting system and prepare for campus interviews.

Student Life and Environment

A near-perfect place to live and learn, ASU boasts a comfortable campus, friendly people, and even better weather. On the pretty Southwestern campus, "The facilities are great," including a "graduate suite where all the students from the different graduate programs at the school spend most of their time." There's also a "gym, library, wireless Internet, and off-campus housing minutes away from school." With such "beautiful" weather to work with, "the campus offers several options to maintain a balanced life of school, family, work," including "plenty of outdoor activities." Through ASU's many student clubs and organizations, students "are encouraged to get involved in activities for professional, social and community development." Within the business school, "Students are always mingling, which opens up…networking opportunities." "Whatever reputation ASU has as a party school does not translate to the graduate program," though "Thursday night is a casual happy hour for all students." A student adds, "The small class sizes enhance the ability to develop close-knit relationships with other classmates. I am married and my wife is highly involved in MBA activities."

Admissions

When making an admissions decision, Arizona State considers your resume, work experience, essays, academic transcript, GMAT score, letters of recommendation and personal interview. Admissions requirements vary by program. In recent years, full-time students had an average undergraduate GPA of 3.3 and an average GMAT score of 673, with a large percentage of students coming from the West and Southwest. In the evening program, the average GMAT score was 577 and the average undergraduate GPA was 3.25. In the online program, the average GMAT score was 583 and students had an average 7.8 years work experience.

Prominent Alumni

Craig Weatherup, Chairman, The Pepsi Bottling Group (retired); Steve Marriott, Vice President of Corp. Marketing, Marriott Hotels; Chris Cookson, President, Technologies, Sony Pictures; Peter Ruppe, VP & GM, Men's Training & Fitness, Nike; Jack Furst, Partner, Hicks, Muse, Tate & Furst, Inc.

FINANCIAL FACTS

Annual tuition (in-state/ out-of-state)	$7,127/$20,321
Fees	$12,848
Cost of books	$2,300
Room & board	$10,660
% of students receiving aid	78
% of first-year students receiving aid	81
% of students receiving loans	56
% of students receiving grants	63
Average award package	$25,801
Average grant	$12,890
Average student loan debt	$42,581

ADMISSIONS

Admissions Selectivity Rating	96
# of applications received	671
% applicants accepted	27
% acceptees attending	50
Average GMAT	673
Range of GMAT	650–700
Average GPA	3.33
TOEFL required of international students	Yes
Minimum TOEFL (paper/computer)	600/250
Application fee	$70
International application fee	$90
Application Deadline/Notification	
Round 1:	10/18 / 12/18
Round 2:	12/13 / 2/26
Round 3:	2/14 / 4/16
Round 4:	4/4 / 6/4
Early decision program?	No
Deferment available	Yes
Maximum length of deferment	1 year
Transfer students accepted	No
Non-fall admissions	Yes
Need-blind admissions	Yes

EMPLOYMENT PROFILE

Career Rating	87	**Grads Employed by Function% Avg. Salary**	
Percent employed at graduation	61	Marketing	15 $70,600
Percent employed 3 months after graduation	78	Operations	55 $89,888
		Consulting	2 NR
Average base starting salary	$85,013	Management	9 $83,200
Primary Source of Full-time Job Acceptances		Finance	13 $83,333
School-facilitated activities	33 (61%)	MIS	4 NR
Graduate-facilitated activities	18 (33%)	**Top 5 Employers Hiring Grads**	
		Chevron (4), Intel (2), Apple (2), Bank of America (2), Mattel (2)	

AUBURN UNIVERSITY
COLLEGE OF BUSINESS

GENERAL INFORMATION
Type of school   Public
Academic calendar   Semester

SURVEY SAYS...
Good social scene
Solid preparation in:
Marketing

STUDENTS
Enrollment of parent institution	23,332
Enrollment of MBA Program	450
% male/female	63/37
% out-of-state	71
% part-time	80
% minorities	10
% international	29
Average age at entry	26
Average years work experience at entry	2

ACADEMICS
Academic Experience Rating	**79**
Student/faculty ratio	29:1
Profs interesting rating	87
Profs accessible rating	83
% female faculty	20
% minority faculty	5

Joint Degrees
Dual degree programs with Industrial and Systems Engineering (MISE) and with Information Systems (MMIS). These dual programs are 54 credit hours and are available to both our on campus and distance learning students. Other dual degree options are available on a case-by-case basis with approval of the AU Graduate School.

Academics

Whether you're seeking a traditional on-campus MBA experience or the opportunity to earn your graduate degree from the comfort of your own home, Auburn University can accommodate you. The school offers three curriculum models: an on-campus MBA; the Graduate Outreach Program, which allows students to fulfill most of the obligations toward their degrees remotely (students must attend one five-day case analysis during their final fall semester, but otherwise never need to visit campus); and two Executive MBA programs (one a general EMBA, the other geared specifically to the needs of physicians), which require five one-week residencies over a two-year period, with the larger portion of instruction coming via Internet and DVD technologies. The distance program offers concentrations in finance, management information systems, technology management, marketing, and operations management. The full-time program offers all of these plus concentrations in agribusiness, healthcare administration, human resources management, sports management, and supply chain management. The EMBA offers specialization in technology management and healthcare management.

Students in the on-campus program praise "the great sense of community" here, with "plenty of team building and leadership education. The "very team-based" approach to learning means "you will walk away with the ability to work effectively with anyone," especially "given the diversity of the classes in terms of ethnicity and academic background." Another part of the MBA program that contributes to the close-knit nature of each class is the integrated international trip. Students learn through visiting companies and schools in other countries in an effort to expand the students' understanding of, and appreciation for, the global nature of world business. The selection of specific trips is based on academic interest areas, as each group travels to a different geographic region. Recent trip destinations include China/Korea, Italy/France/Switzerland and Germany/Hungary. Among the many academic disciplines covered here, students say that supply chain management, and finance are standouts. Auburn professors "are really helpful" and "very approachable," but many feel that "some could foster more innovative teaching approaches." Administrators earn high marks for "knowing every random question about the program you can think up." As one MBA observes, "With such a small MBA class, the administration can provide plenty of attention."

Career and Placement

Auburn's newly created Office of Professional and Career Development (OPCD), which is located in 5,400 square feet of newly renovated office and meeting space on the first floor of the College of Business building, provides career counseling, professional development and employee relations services for the MBA programs. The office provides one-on-one career coaching, seminars, workshops, an extensive career library and a multitude of technology resources to assist students. An emphasis has been placed on adding video technologies to enhance student readiness as well as to enhance employer development efforts. The OPCD also organized career expos, company information sessions and on campus recruiting events. The creation of this new team and the build out of the new space and technology is in direct response to student feedback. In the past Auburn MBAs have seen room for improvement in career placement, telling us the school "needs to actively create better business fairs and get names out to more companies... While it is good for many people if they want to stay local, it's hard to get your name out to specific companies and certainly ones that are out of the South" under current conditions. Employers most likely to hire Auburn MBAs include eBay, Aflac, Regions Bank, BB&T, Home Depot, WalMart, Proctor & Gamble, and IBM; the school also maintains "working

ADMISSIONS CONTACT: MS. KATIE BROCK, INTERIM DIRECTOR MBA ADMISSIONS
ADDRESS: 415 W. MAGNOLIA AVENUE, SUITE 503 LOWDER BUSINESS BUILDING
AUBURN UNIVERSITY, AL 36849 • PHONE: 334-844-4060 • FAX: 334-844-2964
E-MAIL: MBADMIS@AUBURN.EDU • WEBSITE: WWW.MBA.BUSINESS.AUBURN.EDU

relationships" with such employers as Dell, Eli Lilly, Ernst & Young, KPMG, and Deloitte. One in five graduates winds up in finance and accounting; operations and production, consulting, and MIS each claim about 17 percent of the graduating class.

Student Life and Environment

Auburn's MBA program draws "a great group from across the U.S. and across the globe" with "a strong presence of diverse nationalities, including students from China, Thailand, India, Mali, Curacao, Guam, and Belgium." Some complain that too many students, both American and international, lack sufficient work experience, "which lessens their contributions in class," but they are otherwise satisfied with their peers. One tells us that "The Auburn MBA program has done a wonderful job at promoting cohesion among students. We feel like a family and are there to pull each other through. No matter what your views and characteristics are, you are accepted with an open mind."

Football occupies center stage in the life of the Auburn campus. "The football team brings about being part of something bigger than yourself," one student explains, while another simply observes that "The tailgating is the best." The surrounding town, though small, "is great for being social. Between the football games and the bars, we hang out a lot as an entire class. If anything, the social life sometimes gets in the way of school life because it's hard to turn down such a fun time." It's all business during the daytime, however, when most full-timers "come up to the student lounge in the business building to either do work or to socialize. It is a healthy environment that encourages fellowship." Part-timers are, of course, less engaged in campus life.

Admissions

All applicants to the Auburn MBA program must submit official transcripts for all postsecondary academic work, an official GMAT score report, three letters of recommendation, a completed application to the Graduate School, and a completed application to the MBA program. All applicants to the on campus program are required to go through an interview process. For students who live some distance from the university, Skype and phone interviews are also available. Although work experience is not required for admission into the on campus program, it is encouraged and students who have less than 2 years of work experience are required to do a summer internship as a part of their degree. International students whose first language is not English must also submit TOEFL scores. Undergraduate-level competency in accounting, calculus, finance, macro- and microeconomics, management, marketing, and statistics are all prerequisites to starting the Auburn MBA program. Students lacking appropriate undergraduate credentials may purchase the corresponding courses on CD and must subsequently pass a competency exam in each course (administered by the university, by CLEP, or, for military candidates, through the DANTES system) prior to commencing work on the MBA. In an effort to boost the population of under represented students, Auburn makes recruiting trips all over the U.S. and the world, as well as participates in special on-campus events with students from minority campuses.

Prominent Alumni

Mohamed Mansour, CEO, Mansour Group in Egypt; Joanne P. McCallie, Head Coach, Michigan State U. Women's Basketball; Wendell Starke, Past President of INVESCO; General Michael E. Ryan (ret.), Chief of Staff of the U.S. Air Force; Tee Green, President/CEO, Greenway Medical Technologies.

FINANCIAL FACTS

Annual tuition (in-state/ out-of-state)	$6,972/$19,452
Fees	$430
Cost of books	$1,200
Room & board (off-campus)	$10,746
% of students receiving aid	95
% of first-year students receiving aid	81
% of students receiving grants	30
Average award package	$6,115
Average grant	$1,200
Average student loan debt	$14,665

ADMISSIONS

Admissions Selectivity Rating	89
# of applications received	104
% applicants accepted	55
% acceptees attending	49
Average GMAT	643
Range of GMAT	590–690
Average GPA	3.4
TOEFL required of international students	Yes
Minimum TOEFL (paper/computer)	550/213
Application fee	$50
International application fee	$60
Regular application deadline	3/1
Early decision program?	Yes
ED Deadline	11/1
Deferment available	Yes
Maximum length of deferment	1 year
Transfer students accepted	Yes
Transfer application policy: AACSB schools only. Case-by-case basis and accepted in lieu of elective courses only. Limit of 12 credit hours.	
Non-fall admissions	No
Need-blind admissions	Yes

AUBURN UNIVERSITY—MONTGOMERY
SCHOOL OF BUSINESS

GENERAL INFORMATION

Type of school	Public

SURVEY SAYS...
Friendly students
Solid preparation in:
Communication/interpersonal skills
Presentation skills
Quantitative skills

STUDENTS

Enrollment of parent institution	5,287
Enrollment of MBA Program	197
% male/female	60/40
% out-of-state	21
% part-time	57
% minorities	28
% international	12
Average age at entry	27

ACADEMICS

Academic Experience Rating	71
Student/faculty ratio	20:1
Profs interesting rating	83
Profs accessible rating	79
% female faculty	25
% minority faculty	10

Academics

The AACSB-accredited MBA program at Auburn University Montgomery is "a great place to get your MBA at night," according to the program's locally-based student body. Students here also appreciate the "affordable" tuition as well as the school's "reputation for academic excellence" and "instructors who bring real-life business experiences to the classroom" and "have connections in the business world." The program is designed for part-time students; in fact, any student wishing to exceed a course load of nine hours per semester must first receive approval from the dean of the School of Business.

The MBA program at AUM is divided into three parts. The first is called the Basic Program, consisting of 11 half-term courses covering business concepts typically taught at the undergraduate level (accounting, management, marketing, business law, microeconomics, macroeconomics, operations management, statistics, MIS, and finance). Students who can demonstrate sufficient background in these areas may petition to be exempted from some or all of these requirements. The second part of the program is the Business Core, a seven-course set of classes covering such integrative concepts as managerial applications of accounting information and synergistic organizational strategy (the latter is a capstone course), as well as such essential functions as marketing, data analysis, and managing personnel. The program concludes with either three or four electives, depending on whether the student chooses a General MBA or a specialization. Specializations are offered in accounting, contract management, economics, finance, global business management, information systems, management of information technology, management, and marketing. Students earning a GPA below 3.25 must pass comprehensive exams at the end of the program in order to graduate. The program must be finished within five years of starting.

AUM MBAs brag that "Professors are extremely knowledgeable, helpful, and outstanding in their areas," and that they also "understand that most of the evening students are fully employed and try to incorporate their day-to-day activities" into the curriculum. Most here "would like to see the use of more technology in the classroom" and complain that the school needs "all classrooms to be enabled with things like wireless internet access." Classrooms could also be improved by making them "resemble the real world, i.e. u-shaped seating"; at the very least, the school "needs to upgrade classroom furniture to make it feel less like a high school/junior high," students tell us.

Career and Placement

The Career Development Center (CDC) at AUM serves all university students and alumni. The office maintains a library of career-related material, including documents tracking salary and hiring trends around the region, state, country, and world. Career counseling services are available, as are job fairs and seminars and workshops in interviewing, job hunting, resume, and cover-letter writing. The office arranges internships and recruiting events for qualifying MBA students.

ADMISSIONS CONTACT: SHARON JONES, ADMISSION SPECIALIST
ADDRESS: P. O. BOX 244023 MONTGOMERY, AL 36124-4023
PHONE: 334-244-3623 • FAX: 334-244-3927
E-MAIL: VJONES1@AUM.EDU • WEBSITE: WWW.AUM.EDU

Student Life and Environment

AUM MBAs are "mostly working students between their mid-20s and mid-30s in age, with some being older." Most "work full time and go to school at night" and, despite their busy schedules, find a way to remain "extremely focused on their class work and understanding of the material" while also being "extremely helpful, kind, open for conversation, and willing to do whatever it takes to see that everyone in class is successful." They "don't seem to have any specific clubs or organizations available to them, especially in the evening hours," but most agree that their extracurricular schedule wouldn't allow them time to participate.

Montgomery is a midsize southern city well known for its integral part in the civil rights movement. The population of the city is about evenly split between whites and blacks, with small Hispanic, Native American, and Asian populations accounting for a small minority. The city is home to the Alabama Shakespeare Festival, a year-round enterprise that mounts a dozen or more productions and attracts over 300,000 visitors annually. Another major attraction is the minor-league baseball Montgomery Biscuits, the AA affiliate of the Tampa Bay Devil Rays. And no Montgomery summer is complete without Jubilee CityFest, a three-day outdoor festival that in recent years has attracted such headlining musical acts as Taylor Swift, Erykah Badu, the Goo Goo Dolls, Ludacris, and Vince Gill.

Admissions

Applicants to the AUM MBA program must submit official transcripts for all previous post-secondary academic work, official GMAT score reports, and a completed application form. The screening committee may request an interview, typically in the case of borderline candidates; otherwise, interviews are not required. International applicants must meet all of the above requirements and must also provide certified English translations of any academic transcripts in a foreign language and a course-by-course evaluation of undergraduate work "by a recognized, expert service in the field of foreign credential evaluations and international admissions." Applicants whose first language is not English must submit TOEFL scores. Candidates may be admitted conditionally pending completion of prerequisite undergraduate-level classes in business.

FINANCIAL FACTS

Cost of books	$1,500
% of students receiving aid	60
% of first-year students receiving aid	65
% of students receiving loans	45
% of students receiving grants	15
Average award package	$17,894

ADMISSIONS

Admissions Selectivity Rating	62
# of applications received	96
% applicants accepted	98
% acceptees attending	70
Average GMAT	473
Average GPA	2.92
TOEFL required of international students	Yes
Minimum TOEFL (paper)	500
Application fee	$25
Early decision program?	No
Deferment available	No
Transfer students accepted	No
Non-fall admissions	Yes
Need-blind admissions	Yes

AUGUSTA STATE UNIVERSITY
COLLEGE OF BUSINESS ADMINISTRATION

GENERAL INFORMATION

Type of school	Public
Academic calendar	Trimester

SURVEY SAYS...
Solid preparation in:
Accounting
General management

STUDENTS

Enrollment of parent institution	6,689
Enrollment of MBA Program	116
% male/female	62/38
% out-of-state	16
% part-time	65
% minorities	22
% international	14
Average age at entry	28
Average years work experience at entry	5

ACADEMICS

Academic Experience Rating	**75**
Student/faculty ratio	20:1
Profs interesting rating	85
Profs accessible rating	86
% female faculty	7
% minority faculty	1

Academics

Convenience and cost are the two main reasons students cite for choosing the MBA program at Augusta State University. Many students here tell us that they attended the school as undergraduates and saw no reason to leave.

At ASU's MBA program, "Personal attention and career development are a given. Students have to actively work at not being known by the administration and faculty of the Business School." Service is key; despite its relatively small MBA enrollment, "ASU has a dedicated educational professional to usher graduate students through the program." One student notes, "The school is the perfect size. It is small enough to allow for more personal relations between the student and the teacher but is big enough to enjoy all the aspects of attending a college." A "low teacher/student ratio" and "professors who are approachable and willing to help students" are among the other perks of attending. ASU works hard to accommodate its students' schedules by offering "almost every needed subject in the program" during the fall and spring semesters.

MBAs at ASU must complete a 12-course sequence that includes 2 electives and 10 required courses in human resources management, marketing, finance, accounting, economics, production management, leadership, management information systems, business research methods, and an integrating course in strategic management. Students tell us that the school has traditionally been recognized for strengths for economics, finance, and accounting, as well as in "certain quantitative-based courses like market research." In addition, ASU has taken steps in order to better prepare the students for information-based knowledge. Those steps include "recently naming an information technology professor to chair the program."

Career and Placement

The ASU Career Center serves all undergraduates and graduate students at the university. Services are geared primarily toward undergraduates, in part because the school's graduate divisions are so small and in part because many graduate students—including many MBAs—attend while continuing in jobs they intend to keep post-graduation. The office sponsors an annual Career Fair and offers the standard battery of career services: job posting, counseling, mock interviews, on-campus recruiting, and more.

Student Life and Environment

Most ASU MBAs "work full-time during the day and attend classes at night," which means they have limited time to devote to extracurricular activities. Students tell us that "many professors acknowledge the average students' work/demand schedule and design their courses to allow students to catch up on the weekends." MBAs also appreciate how the small-school environment creates "the opportunity to get to know the students and faculty on a greater than superficial level," an opportunity students take advantage of by "congregating in a small centralized area of the building before classes." With so many chances to bond with peers and professors, it's no wonder students tell us that "the school feels like a family."

Full-time students—consisting primarily of international students and undergraduates proceeding directly from their BA program to the MBA—tell us that "there is an active campus life at ASU even though few students actually live on campus. There are so many groups to be involved with and [there are] always activities going on. The school spirit at ASU is so alive, and the students there really love their campus. Most of the MBA students are graduates of ASU, so I believe they feel the same as well." Clubs "are very active on campus." Phi Beta Lambda is one of the major ones for business students.

ADMISSIONS CONTACT: MIYOKO JACKSON, DEGREE PROGRAM SPECIALIST
ADDRESS: HUILL COLLEGE OF BUSINESS MBA OFFICE, 2500 WALTON WAY AUGUSTA, GA 30904-2200
PHONE: 706-737-1565 • FAX: 706-667-4064
E-MAIL: MBAINFO@AUG.EDU • WEBSITE: WWW.AUG.EDU/COBA

MBAs tell us that the school has worked hard to beautify and improve this campus, which, they note, "was an arsenal during the Civil War. The school has done a great job of keeping that heritage intact" while simultaneously adding such assets as a " beautiful new student center" that "provides study areas, gym equipment, billiards, and a host of other activities for students that help to release school stress." Commuters warn that "parking is limited during morning hours, but afternoon and evening parking is very good."

The ASU student body is "broadly diverse in age, occupation, race, and educational background, but [they are] uniformly goal oriented, serious, and competitive, [while also] capable or working in a team environment." Students seem to appreciate this diversity. One student says, "I have come in contact with people from many different cultures, and it gives me a different outlook on business." Even though there are "so many international students," most "seem to be regular people with careers who have felt a need to improve themselves."

Admissions

Applicants to the Hull College of Business MBA program must submit all of the following: official transcripts for all undergraduate and graduate work; an official score report for the GMAT (test score can be no more than 5 years old); and a completed application form. In addition, international students whose first language is not English must submit an official score for the TOEFL and a financial responsibility statement. International transcripts must be submitted via Educational Credential Evaluators, Inc., a company that matches international course work to its American equivalent. The Admissions Committee looks for students with significant and diverse work experience, varied educational backgrounds, and sound academic achievement. Incoming students must be able to run word processing, spreadsheet, and database programs.

FINANCIAL FACTS

Annual tuition (in-state/ out-of-state)	$2,700/$10,800
Fees	$910
Cost of books	$500
Room & board	$9,501

ADMISSIONS

Admissions Selectivity Rating	76
# of applications received	51
% applicants accepted	90
% acceptees attending	71
Average GMAT	517
Range of GMAT	450–710
Average GPA	3.11
TOEFL required of international students	Yes
Minimum TOEFL (paper/computer)	550/213
Application fee	$30
International application fee	$30
Early decision program?	No
Deferment available	Yes
Maximum length of deferment	1 year
Transfer students accepted	Yes
Transfer application policy: Must meet regular MBA admission standards. Up to nine semester credit hours from a regionally accredited institution may be accepted for transfer.	
Non-fall admissions	Yes
Need-blind admissions	No

BABSON COLLEGE
F. W. OLIN GRADUATE SCHOOL OF BUSINESS

GENERAL INFORMATION

Type of school	Private
Academic calendar	Semester

SURVEY SAYS...

Cutting-edge classes
Solid preparation in:
Doing business in a global economy
Entrepreneurial studies

STUDENTS

Enrollment of parent institution	3,445
Enrollment of MBA Program	1,485
% male/female	66/34
% out-of-state	58
% part-time	73
% minorities	5
% international	39
Average age at entry	28
Average years work experience at entry	5

ACADEMICS

Academic Experience Rating	**89**
Student/faculty ratio	13:1
Profs interesting rating	88
Profs accessible rating	88
% female faculty	23
% minority faculty	12

Prominent Alumni

William Green, Chairman and CEO, Accenture; Deborah McLaughlin, Vice Chancellor, Administration & Finance, UMASS Dartmouth; Akio Toyoda, President, Toyota Motor Corporation; William Teuber, Vice Chairman, EMC Corporation; James Poss, Founder, President and CEO, Big Belly Solar.

Academics

Boston's Babson College was ranked number one for entrepreneurship in the annual Princeton Review/*Entrepreneur* magazine MBA ranking in both 2008 and 2009. Students concur, saying "entrepreneurship is everywhere" and "innovation is the status quo." Geared toward students who are "highly inquisitive" and "obsessed with finding opportunities," this unique MBA program takes a distinctly "holistic approach to business." In the core curriculum, each class "is part of a one-year program that integrates each and every reading, case study, and problem set." In fact, "Professors will frequently reference cases and discussions from other courses, so you can tell that they've worked hard at making cross-curriculum learning work." At the same time, creative thinking is the focus and "every professor teaches with an entrepreneurial angle," no matter what the topic. A student adds, "Whether you are continuing on in a corporate job or starting your own company, entrepreneurial thought and action is taught at all levels, providing us with a unique business perspective." "The workload, especially in the first year, is extreme." Fortunately, "The professors genuinely care about what you learn and getting to know and assist you in your endeavors." With so much focus on entrepreneurship, students appreciate that "there isn't pressure to choose a concentration." "Students take what they are interested in."

Babson strives to stay cutting edge, and every year, there are "new course offerings tailored to emerging business trends, such as social networking." "Professors bring new, innovate ideas to our classes. They are up on the latest news, from financial disasters to the newest innovative product or technology solution." In addition to classroom experiences, "The out-of-class opportunities are limitless and the experiential learning [opportunities] are the keys to success here." "Babson's student consulting projects are held in such high regard in the Boston [area]," and offer extensive real-world experience. Learning to work with a diverse set of colleagues is another cornerstone of the Babson experience. Throughout the curriculum, "Babson is all about group work! These team exercises are the most grueling part of the experience, but are also incredibly informative." A diverse class, "More than a third of the full-time MBA students are international, and the breadth of work experience across industries and countries adds significantly to the classroom discussions."

For older students with significant business experience, the "flexible program for working adults (Fast-Track)" gets top marks for its "convenient online delivery format plus face-to-face meetings that allow you to continue working full time." As a current Fast-Track student explains, the program "allows me to continue as CFO of the company, traveling extensively around the world and still be able to work on a[n] MBA degree." On the whole, Babson is effectively managed and highly student focused. A case in point, "The dean regularly walks the halls and makes conversation with students, and he also holds lunches with students just to see how things are going." Through him and others, students say their concerns are addressed, and "problems are solved almost immediately."

Career and Placement

Babson weaves career preparation into the curriculum through numerous experiential learning projects. For example, the "first-year consulting project gives [students] hands-on experience with a real company" while "networking at events" on campus helps students make contacts in different business industries. Although "the tough market makes it difficult" to place every student, "The career center has been through an overhaul, and their staff works overtime for its students to help them get the jobs they want." While the career center offers mentoring programs, campus recruiting, and personal counseling, some students feel, "it would be nice to see more alumni networking events" as well.

ADMISSIONS CONTACT: BARBARA SELMO, DIRECTOR OF GRADUATE ADMISSIONS
ADDRESS: OLIN HALL BABSON PARK (WELLESLEY), MA 02457-0310
PHONE: 781-239-5591 • FAX: 781-239-4194
E-MAIL: MBAADMISSION@BABSON.EDU • WEBSITE: WWW.BABSON.EDU/MBA

During the past five years, between 72 and 95 percent of Olin's graduating class had a job or was self-employed within three months of graduation. In recent years, students have been hired or recruited by diverse companies, including American Express, Bank of America, Boston Celtics, The Boston Globe, Boston Properties, Deloitte & Touche LLP, JP Morgan Chase, Liz Claiborne, McKinsey & Company, Microsoft Corporation, Philips Medical Systems, and Toshiba Corporation.

Student Life and Environment

Attracting students who are "highly self-motivated, creative, and friendly," "Babson has a really friendly and team-oriented dynamic." Here, "People really work together and spend a lot of time doing homework and studying in groups." Most part-timers have full-time jobs while attending school, and therefore, "part-time students are known to have a more transient experience than the full timers" at Babson. Even so, their "sense of community is strong," and many evening students "arrive early and dine together in Olin over friendly conversation." Babson also has a reputation for being supportive of women; In fact, "Every full-time first-year female student gets matched up with a 'Mama' who provides advice and touches base throughout the school year to make sure we're surviving."

For MBA candidates, "Olin Hall is the hub of the graduate school and is where 95 percent of classes and activities take place." Here, you'll find, "club events, networking events, and social events almost every night of the week." Babson is located in a "very safe, upper-class neighborhood," just 25 minutes from downtown Boston. Nearby, "the restaurants in Wellesley and Needham are great," and "There are also two pubs on campus for a regular social evening or for networking events." Despite the "very heavy academic workload," students say, "Every weekend you'll have something fun to do, from going skiing to party[ing] in the city."

Admissions

Babson operates several rounds of admission for each graduate program—evening, Fast-Track, and traditional MBAs. You'll have the best chance of acceptance if you apply early in the admissions cycle. There is no minimum GMAT score required for admission, though the average score for accepted applicants ranges between 590 and 660 each year. All programs require an admissions interview.

FINANCIAL FACTS

Annual tuition	$46,000
Cost of books	$1,200
Room & board	$15,728
% of students receiving aid	72
% of first-year students receiving aid	72
% of students receiving loans	48
% of students receiving grants	57
Average award package	$19,715
Average grant	$17,442
Average student loan debt	$61,237

ADMISSIONS

Admissions Selectivity Rating	88
# of applications received	722
% applicants accepted	43
% acceptees attending	53
Average GMAT	625
Range of GMAT	590–660
Average GPA	3.17
TOEFL required of international students	Yes
Minimum TOEFL (paper/computer)	600/250
Application fee	$100
International application fee	$100
Application Deadline/Notification	
Round 1:	11/15 / 1/15
Round 2:	1/15 / 3/30
Round 3:	3/15 / 4/30
Round 4:	4/15 / 5/15
Early decision program?	No
Deferment available	Yes
Maximum length of deferment	1 year
Transfer students accepted	Yes
Transfer application policy: We accept transfer credit from AACSB accredited programs into our Evening MBA program.	
Non-fall admissions	Yes
Need-blind admissions	Yes

EMPLOYMENT PROFILE

Career Rating	**94**	**Grads Employed by Function% Avg. Salary**	
Percent employed at graduation	48	Marketing	19 $74,133
Percent employed 3 months after graduation	72	Operations	4 $75,336
		Consulting	11 $96,916
Average base starting salary	$78,234	Management	15 $71,284
Primary Source of Full-time Job Acceptances		Finance	20 $80,138
School-facilitated activities	73 (62%)	Entrepreneurship	29 NR
Graduate-facilitated activities	27 (23%)	**Top 5 Employers Hiring Grads**	
Unknown	18 (15%)	EMC (5), National Grid (4), Johnson and Johnson (3), Vertex Pharmaceuticals (2), Raytheon (2)	

BARRY UNIVERSITY
ANDREAS SCHOOL OF BUSINESS

GENERAL INFORMATION
Type of school | Private
Affiliation | Roman Catholic
Academic calendar | All year

SURVEY SAYS...
Friendly students
Solid preparation in:
Communication/interpersonal skills
Doing business in a global economy

STUDENTS
Enrollment of parent
  institution | 8,581
Enrollment of MBA Program | 140
% male/female | 52/48
% part-time | 73
% minorities | 60
% international | 39
Average years work experience
  at entry | 4

ACADEMICS
Academic Experience Rating | **79**
Student/faculty ratio | 13:1
Profs interesting rating | 78
Profs accessible rating | 77
% female faculty | 42
% minority faculty | 42

Joint Degrees
Master of Science in Sport
Management/MBA, 57 credits;
Master of Science in Nursing/MBA,
69 credits; Doctor of Podiatric
Medicine/MBA, 205 credits.

Prominent Alumni
Gary Spulak, President, Embraer
Aircraft of North America; Gregory
Greene, Senior VP, Strategy, Ryder
Systems; John Primeau, President,
Valley Bank; Arthur Snyder,
President, Indiana Institute of
Technology; Craig Lemasters,
President & CEO, Assurant
Solutions.

Academics

Besides offering all of the advantages of a small, private school, the Andreas School of Business at Barry University manages to offer a surprising number of custom-tailored options to meet the needs and goals of its student body. Part-timers, who make up about two-thirds of the student body, can choose between evening classes or the Saturday MBA program. All MBA courses are taught by full-time faculty who hold terminal degrees. Full-time students can complete their program of study at the main campus. All students can opt for dual degrees in nursing, podiatry, and sports management. The last is an especially popular option, cited by a number of MBAs as their primary reason for choosing Barry. Besides a general MBA, Andreas also offers a full complement of areas of specialization, with options including accounting, finance, general business, international business, management, and marketing. Besides the MBA, the School of Business also offers a Master of Science in Accounting (MSA) and a Master of Science in Management (MSM).

All told, Barry provides choices that are typically available only at larger universities. Yet this program is relatively pint-size, to the great advantage of its MBAs. One such MBA explains, "Because the business school is small, you get the benefit of personalized attention. The administrators and class coordinators know your name, and professors can always make time for you to visit them." Another agrees, "No other school would give you such personal attention. Several of my classes have had fewer than 10 students, and the professor tailors the material to fit our schedules and individual ambitions. And because there's such close contact, it's easy to build relationships with professors. I even was able to collaborate with one professor on writing a business case that will appear in a textbook supplement."

Andreas classes "are designed to challenge students in several ways. One is the explanation of theories; others include the implementation of practical assignments or case studies." In keeping with the school's Catholic world view, many courses "promote social responsibility." The school's religious affiliation also helps it attract international students, whose presence "truly prepares students for working with many different types of people in many different contexts."

Career and Placement

School of Business administrators and the university's Career Services Center maintain close working relationships with local, state, and national companies. One student in the past indicated, "While job placement efforts could certainly be improved, I, like most Barry MBAs, have a job already, so I'm not really worried about the post-graduation job hunt, and that might be why Barry doesn't bring more companies to campus and be more aggressive in job placement. But for those students who do need to find work after school, Barry isn't equipped to be the kind of resource they really need." Additionally, international students are among those who feel most strongly that these services must be improved. The Andreas School has also partnered with the following firms and companies: Burger King Corporation, Microsoft Latin America, Franklin Templeton, KPMG International, FBI, JM Family Enterprises, Robert Half International, Northwestern Mutual, Morgan Stanley, MTV Networks Latin America, Assurant, and Ryder.

ADMISSIONS CONTACT: GUSTAVO CORDEIRO, DIRECTOR OF ALUMNI AND EXTERNAL RELATIONS
ADDRESS: GRADUATE ADMISSIONS, 11300 NE 2ND AVENUE MIAMI SHORES, FL 33161
PHONE: (305) 899-3100 • FAX: (305) 892-6412
E-MAIL: ADMISSIONS@MAIL.BARRY.EDU • WEBSITE: WWW.BARRY.EDU/BUSINESS

Student Life and Environment

For MBA students, Barry is "mostly a commuter school, so most MBA students are on campus in the evenings or weekends. As a result, there is not much extracurricular life. Not that that's necessarily a bad thing; as one student observes, "Barry is tranquil and laid-back, the ideal place for a person who would get overwhelmed by a high-stress, backstabbing MBA program. The MBA school is also made for people already working full time." The school offers "limited clubs" and didn't even have a graduate business association until students took the initiative to form one. Those who truly desire a higher level of involvement can find it here, though. One student explains, "I have made myself get involved. I am a former student-athlete; currently a residence assistant as well as a graduate assistant. So my life has been great here. There is potential for everyone if you look for it."

"There is a vast cultural diversity within the university" and the MBA program at Barry. "It is delightful to see the peace that exists among classmates." Students "are very willing to help one another. There are always study groups, and in every class all students have each others' phone numbers, e-mails, etc. so that we can discuss the class when we need to." One MBA notes, "Learning in a cohort group has been the number one reason my MBA experience at Barry has been so successful. We've bonded as classmates, collaborated on projects, and built friendships that will extend beyond our MBA studies. In general, Barry MBA students are culturally diverse, unfailingly nice, and, since most work full-time while going to school, eager to use their degree to move up the career ladder."

Barry is located in Miami Shores, a central location offering easy access to the entire Miami metropolitan area. The area surrounding the campus offers access to the beach, and plenty of shopping, dining, and housing.

Admissions

The Admissions Committee at Barry University School of Business looks closely at the following components of the application: undergraduate GPA; GMAT scores (in lieu of the GMAT, we also accept the GRE, LSAT, or the MCAT); quality of undergraduate curriculum; personal essay; resume; two letters of reference supporting the resume; and TOEFL scores (for non-native English speakers). The GMAT requirement may be waived for applicants with substantial managerial experience. All of the following are prerequisites to MBA study: 6 credit hours of introductory accounting; 6 credit hours of macro and microeconomics; 3 credit hours of algebra or precalculus; 3 credit hours of statistics; 3 credit hours of introductory computer skills; 3 credit hours of operations management; and 3 credit hours of marketing. Students may demonstrate competency in any of these areas through undergraduate work or through non-credit workshops offered by the Andreas School.

FI...

Annual tuiti...	
Cost of books	
Room & board	
% of students receiv...	
% of first-year students... receiving aid	
% of students receiving loan...	
% of students receiving grants	
Average award package	$19,8...
Average grant	$4,544
Average student loan debt	$25,634

ADMISSIONS

Admissions Selectivity Rating	82
Average GMAT	476
Range of GMAT	390–720
TOEFL required of international students	Yes
Minimum TOEFL (paper/computer)	550/213
Application fee	$30
International application fee	$30
Early decision program?	No
Deferment available	Yes
Maximum length of deferment	1 year
Transfer students accepted	Yes
Transfer application policy: Up to six transfer credits.	
Non-fall admissions	Yes
Need-blind admissions	Yes

EMPLOYMENT PROFILE

Career Rating	70	Top 5 Employers Hiring Grads
		Assurant, Florida Power and Light, Grant Thorton, PricewaterhouseCoopers, Ryder

NANCIAL FACTS

$15,210
$1,500
$13,000
70

72
46
37

RSITY
BUSINESS

Academics

Baylor University, a popular Southern institution located halfway between Dallas and Austin, appeals to those looking for "a small program" with "a cozy atmosphere" and "a lot of emphasis on ethics." With both a concentration and a dual degree program in healthcare administration, Baylor is also a strong draw for those looking to make their mark in the nation's transforming healthcare sector. By one student's tally, one-third of the full-time students at Hankamer were studying healthcare administration in 2009-2010. Those students have high praise for the program, asserting that "it will be ranked among the top programs" soon. "Hospital CEOs speak to our class approximately nine times per semester," writes one student, extolling the "incredible healthcare administration speaker series." The program includes a placement experience during which students "work directly with a CEO and become an actual hospital administrator for seven months."

There's more than healthcare to Baylor, though. MBAs call the strategy and organizational behavior courses here "some of the best in the country." Students also tell us that the program provides "the freedom and opportunity to engage in any activity that would benefit your personal development." "Whether it's spending an entire day with Warren Buffett, working in China for a semester with top global firms, traveling to Austin every Friday to learn and explore capital investment analysis, or going to a local prison to decrease the recidivism rate by going over business plans with inmates, you can do it at Baylor," one student writes. Another cites an MBA class devoted to inter-program case competition, for which Baylor not only offers a course but also pays participants' cost of participation, including "room, entry fee, flight, etc." (The team took third prize at the competition hosted by George Washington University in 2010.) Business education neophytes praise the Integrated Management Seminar, "a semester specifically designed for non-business undergrads to provide a fabulous foundation before the core MBA program begins."

Career and Placement

Baylor employs career placement professionals who work exclusively with the school's approximately 90 MBA students as well as with alumni. Students tell us that "The career professionals are planning to take the case to businesses more aggressively than bringing the businesses to Baylor (although...some of that will [still] take place)." Students say this strategy makes sense considering that "Baylor is not competing right now with Texas, Rice, and SMU" when it comes to on-campus recruiting, in part due to the small size of the program. Some complain that "The [placement office's] focus is on Texas, and if you're not looking in Texas, good luck!"

Employers who most frequently hire Baylor MBAs include: Accenture, American Express, Anadarko Petroleum, Bank of America, Baptist Health Center, Bearing Point, CITGO, CNA Insurance, Comerica, Community Bank And Trust, ConocoPhillips, Deloitte & Touche, Echostar Communications, Edward Jones, Ernst & Young, ExxonMobil, FBI, First City Financial, First Preference Mortgage, Hatteras Yachts, H.E.B. Grocery Company, Intecap, Internal Revenue Service, Johnson & Johnson, JP Morgan Chase Bank, Keller Williams, Kersher Trading, KPMG, Merck, Microsoft, Middleton, Burns & Davis, Occidental Services, Inc., Perot Systems, Perryman Consulting, PricewaterhouseCoopers, Protiviti, Quala-T, Steak 'n Shake Operations, Inc., Sterling Bank, Sungard Consulting, TXU, Texas Farm Bureau, U.S. Department of Labor, UBS Financial Services, Inc., and Wal-Mart.

...udents
Good peer network
Smart classrooms
Solid preparation in:
Communication/interpersonal skills
Presentation skills

STUDENTS

Enrollment of parent institution	14,614
Enrollment of MBA Program	99
% male/female	77/23
% part-time	0
% minorities	11
% international	15
Average age at entry	25
Average years work experience at entry	2

ACADEMICS

Academic Experience Rating	**85**
Student/faculty ratio	14:1
Profs interesting rating	79
Profs accessible rating	88
% female faculty	20
% minority faculty	2

Joint Degrees

MBA/MSIS is 2 years; MBA/Master of Engineering and MBA/MS in Computer Science are both 3 years for both degrees; JD/MBA and JD/MTax are 4 years for both degrees.

ADMISSIONS CONTACT: JOANNA ITURBE, ADMISSIONS COORDINATOR
ADDRESS: ONE BEAR PLACE #98013, 1311 S. 5TH STREET WACO, TX 76798-8013
PHONE: 254-710-3718 • FAX: 254-710-1066
E-MAIL: MBA_INFO@BAYLOR.EDU • WEBSITE: WWW.BAYLOR.EDU/MBA

Student Life and Environment

"Student life in the MBA program is excellent," with "ample opportunity to meet interesting business leaders outside of the classroom, attend case competitions, and participate in intramural sports. Additionally, many students find that there is a healthy work-life balance at Baylor's MBA program." The university "gives free tickets to all sporting events for graduate students, which is a big deal in the Big 12 Conference, and that includes football and basketball games. Business school students often attend the games together." Some students say Baylor is "a conservative Baptist school" that "does not encourage...drinking or partying," so those unaccustomed to a more conservative setting may find the extracurricular scene here "limited."

The Baylor campus features "several resources available for use [by] graduate students only, including a graduate lounge and breakout rooms with access restricted to grad students, which facilitates the ease of group work." When there are "breaks during the day, students usually hang out in the graduate lounge playing ping pong or talking and catching up on each other's weekend."

Admissions

Those seeking admission to Baylor's Hankamer School of Business must submit the following materials: a completed application (online application preferred); two letters of recommendation from individuals who know you professionally and can assess your skills and potential; official undergraduate transcripts (international students who attended a non-English-speaking school must provide professionally translated and interpreted academic records); a GMAT score report; a current resume; and personal essays detailing qualifications, experiences, and objectives in pursuing a Hankamer MBA. International students whose first language is not English must also submit a score report for the TOEFL or the IELS. Hankamer processes applications on a rolling basis; candidates are notified of their admission status as soon as a decision is made.

FINANCIAL FACTS

Annual tuition	$26,966
Fees	$3,028
Cost of books	$4,000
Room & board	$10,000
% of students receiving aid	75
% of first-year students receiving aid	75

ADMISSIONS

Admissions Selectivity Rating	87
# of applications received	134
% applicants accepted	51
% acceptees attending	72
Average GMAT	614
Range of GMAT	580–650
Average GPA	3.38
TOEFL required of international students	No
Minimum TOEFL (paper/computer)	600/250
Application fee	$50
International application fee	$50
Application Deadline/Notification	
Round 1:	11/15 / 12/1
Round 2:	2/15 / 3/1
Round 3:	4/15 / 5/1
Round 4:	6/15 / 7/1
Early decision program?	Yes
Deferment available	Yes
Maximum length of deferment	1 year
Transfer students accepted	Yes
Transfer application policy:	

A student who has been admitted to a graduate program at another university, and who desires admission to Baylor, must present a transcript that presents the student's active, satisfactory work toward the same degree. Only 6 hours may be transferred into the MBA program.

Non-fall admissions	Yes
Need-blind admissions	Yes

EMPLOYMENT PROFILE

		Grads Employed by Function	%	Avg. Salary
Career Rating	87			
Percent employed at graduation	74	Marketing	5	$40,000
Percent employed 3 months after graduation	93	Operations	15	$71,029
		Consulting	15	$61,667
Average base starting salary	$65,186	Management	45	$61,292
Primary Source of Full-time Job Acceptances				
School-facilitated activities	1 (3%)			
Graduate-facilitated activities	18 (47%)			
Unknown	19 (50%)			

BELLARMINE UNIVERSITY
W. FIELDING RUBEL SCHOOL OF BUSINESS

GENERAL INFORMATION

Type of school	Private
Affiliation	Roman Catholic

SURVEY SAYS...

Friendly students
Cutting-edge classes
Solid preparation in:
Teamwork
Communication/interpersonal skills
Presentation skills

STUDENTS

Enrollment of parent institution	3,090
Enrollment of MBA Program	206
% male/female	54/46
% part-time	53
% minorities	14
% international	1
Average age at entry	29

ACADEMICS

Academic Experience Rating	**71**
Profs interesting rating	83
Profs accessible rating	77
% female faculty	33
% minority faculty	7

Prominent Alumni

Joseph P. Clayton, In 2001, was the CEO and now is the Chairman of the Board of Directors, Sirius Satellite Radio. Dr. James Heck, Inventor of the drug, Cancidas. Honored by the National Science Foundation for research. Susan M. Ivey, Chairman, President/CEO Reynolds American Inc. Angela Mason, Co-founder of ITS Services. Sold in 2003, with over 600 employees. One of America's top Aftrican-American Enterprises; Leonard P. Spalding, Retired, CEO Chase Mutual funds Corp/Retired, Pres. & CEO Vista Capital Management.

Academics

If you think "team-based learning is the way to go," check out Bellarmine University's distinctive MBA program, which emphasizes collaboration, networking, and small, discussion-oriented classes. Bellarmine's program is cohort-based, which means students work with the same group of classmates throughout the MBA curriculum. A current student elaborates, "We are organized into groups at the beginning of the program and work together on each project throughout the entire program. We learn to work together as a team and work through our problems. It's an incredible experience." Another student writes, "Bellarmine's program is unique in that you learn and grow from your interaction with the other students. There is so much to learn from their experiences and insight that you aren't focused on solely what the professors are doing [and] saying, but pulling from what the class is sharing."

Given the school's focus on peer-to-peer interaction, Bellarmine professors are "more like facilitators" than lecturers. Small, discussion-based classes are a hallmark of the program, and the "teacher to student ratio is very low." You won't have to clamor to get your voice heard at Bellarmine; "small class sizes lead to more personal attention. Professors know and remember details of students from several years ago and keep up with many of them on a regular basis." A current student raves, "The faculty and staff are some of the best people I've met and should be commended for the job they do each and every day. They are all very dedicated to the success of the program." Bellarmine distinguishes itself further by teaching all material through case study and with a cross-disciplinary focus, rather than relying on traditional lecture, so Bellarmine graduates are trained to think in real-world scenarios. The result is a memorable and surprisingly exciting education. A student details, "Each class was a new experience. If I had to miss a class, I felt I would lose an important topic for discussion."

Another undeniable benefit to this small school is that there is "virtually no red tape" and "the administration is wonderful and could not make the admission and registration process any easier." Rather than getting the run-around, students say their "questions are answered promptly and accurately the first time asked." For working professionals, Bellarmine also offers weekend and weeknight MBA programs. A part-time student reports, "The layout of the program and the balance of classes is exactly what I needed to keep the stress level down and balance my work load. I wouldn't change anything about the experience; the faculty and staff have been amazing."

Career and Placement

As the only AACSB-accredited private school in Kentucky, Bellarmine students have a leg up in the local job market. On campus, the Bellarmine University Career Center serves students and alumni, offering resume preparation services, mock interviews, and an online job database. The Career Center also hosts campus recruiting and several career fairs.

Many of the school's part-time students plan to stay with their current employer after graduation, using the skills from their MBA to help move up the corporate ladder. To that end, the school is very successful. A current student enthuses, "I am easily able to complete tasks that I was incapable of before starting the MBA program. The program has improved my skills at work. I am now a candidate for one of the top positions within my company." For those who are looking to start their career after graduation, recent Bellarmine University graduates have taken jobs at AIG, Abercrombie and Fitch, Deloitte & Touche, Ernst and Young, GE Industrial, Sherwin Williams, U.S. Bank, Wells Fargo, and William M. Mercer Company.

ADMISSIONS CONTACT: DR. SARA YOUNT, DEAN OF GRADUATE ADMISSIONS
ADDRESS: 2001 NEWBURG ROAD LOUISVILLE, KY 40205
PHONE: (502) 452-8258 • FAX: (502) 452-8002
E-MAIL: GRADADMISSIONS@BELLARMINE.EDU • WEBSITE: WWW.BELLARMINE.EDU

Student Life and Environment

While they may study in the library from time to time, the Bellarmine business program caters to commuters and "no graduate students live on campus." Therefore, campus life is limited to class and study groups. Unfortunately, the school offers "a lot of activities for undergrads, but few for grad students—even fewer (if any) aimed at families." Still, students appreciate the school's convenient and peaceful location in Louisville's Highlands neighborhood, just a few minutes drive from downtown.

A local crowd, the school's student population is a nice mix of students who are "finishing up their undergrad" (the school allows business undergraduates to complete a BS and an MBA over five years though shared credits) as well as older, working students, some with families. While they are all in business school so as to promote their career, the vibe is "laid-back and friendly," as most of Bellarmine's levelheaded students are "very focused on balanced work/life and less about improving promotion chances at work."

Admissions

To apply to Bellarmine, students must submit undergraduate transcripts, GMAT scores, two letters of recommendation, and two personal essays describing their career goals and experience. As Bellarmine's program is largely interactive, students' qualitative skills are weighed alongside their quantitative abilities. While many MBA students have a professional and academic background in business or accounting, the campus also draws students from a range of areas, including non-profit and government organizations, health care, and humanities.

ADMISSIONS	
Admissions Selectivity Rating	66
# of applications received	80
% applicants accepted	91
% acceptees attending	79
Average GMAT	501
Range of GMAT	430–570
Average GPA	3.2
TOEFL required of international students	Yes
Minimum TOEFL (paper/computer)	550/213
Application fee	$25
International application fee	$25
Early decision program?	No
Deferment available	Yes
Maximum length of deferment	5 years
Transfer students accepted	Yes
Transfer application policy: Accept up to 12 graduate credits from an accredited university.	
Non-fall admissions	Yes
Need-blind admissions	No

BELMONT UNIVERSITY
THE JACK C. MASSEY GRADUATE SCHOOL OF BUSINESS

GENERAL INFORMATION
Type of school   Private
Affiliation   Christian
      (Nondenominational)
Academic calendar   Trimester

SURVEY SAYS...
Students love Nashville, TN
Good peer network
Cutting-edge classes
Solid preparation in:
Doing business in a global economy

STUDENTS
Enrollment of parent institution	5,424
Enrollment of MBA Program	154
% male/female	93/7
% part-time	91
% minorities	14
Average age at entry	28
Average years work experience at entry	6

ACADEMICS
Academic Experience Rating	**80**
Student/faculty ratio	6:1
Profs interesting rating	87
Profs accessible rating	89
% female faculty	34
% minority faculty	2

Joint Degrees
Dual MBA/MACC, 2.5 to 3 years.

Academics

For Nashville-area professionals looking to jump-start their career, Belmont University's graduate business programs offer a "great value." The professional MBA for working adults—Belmont's flagship program—offers a "great classroom-based education that is flexible enough for a working student." With all classes held at night, most Belmont students are juggling career and studies; fortunately, "educators understand [students'] work/life demands" and "are consistently flexible when [students need] to balance work and life with academics." Belmont's core curriculum covers a wide breadth of business areas, including basics like finance, business law, and technology, as well as more innovative topics in entrepreneurship and leadership. Neither highly qualitative nor quantitative, "The program is balanced between verbal, interpersonal, and mathematical reasoning abilities." Overall, the program is challenging, and "The pace is so fast that sometimes we are not able to cover some subjects in enough detail." If you do want to delve into details, the MBA offers the "flexibility to customize [your] degree" through areas of concentration in accounting, entrepreneurship, finance, general business, healthcare, marketing, or music business. Of particular note, every Belmont student must also participate in an international trip as a requirement of graduation; destinations range from Istanbul to Seoul to Amsterdam.

Working professionals want to learn skills they can apply in the workplace, and Belmont caters to that goal. Here, "The classes are focused on real world topics" and "the learning style is hands-on." In the classroom, "the program is largely case-based, encouraging students to use critical thinking skills and sharpen interpersonal skills," and across disciplines, "The professors encourage classroom discussion." The faculty further promotes Belmont's practical perspective by bringing their extensive business experience to the classroom. Like the students, most Belmont professors are "working professionals and therefore experts in the field they are teaching." At this friendly school, faculty members "give great practical advice" and are "truly interested in helping students learn and grow."

At Belmont, classes are uniformly small, with about 20 students in the average classroom. Students love the mix of big-name resources and intimate atmosphere, saying "Belmont has the feel of a small school with the professors and reputation of a top university." A student adds, "It is big enough to offer amenities and benefits of a large school, but small enough to still be a tight-knit group." On this community-oriented campus, "Fellow students, the professors, and the school staff seem to sincerely care about me and each other."

Career and Placement

The Massey College of Business Career Development Center serves undergraduate and graduate business students through individualized career coaching, interview training, resume preparation, and job and internship listings. After graduation, the vast majority of Massey graduates (about 85 percent) stay in the Middle Tennessee area, contributing to the school's strong alumni network in greater Nashville. While praising their school's deep ties in the region, students feel that "Belmont could improve more in getting more companies to recruit their students" and by drawing new employers from some of Nashville's overlooked industries, such as healthcare. In recent years, companies that have hired graduates of the Massey College of Business Administration, include BellSouth, Dell, Deloitte & Touche, Enterprise Rent-a-Car, Ernst & Young, Pfizer, Morgan Stanley Smith Barney, Marriott, Sony/ATV, and WebMD.

ADMISSIONS CONTACT: TONYA HOLLIN, ADMISSIONS ASSISTANT
ADDRESS: 1900 BELMONT BOULEVARD NASHVILLE, TN 37212
PHONE: 615-460-6480 • FAX: 615-460-6353
E-MAIL: MASSEYADMISSIONS@BELMONT.EDU • WEBSITE: MASSEY.BELMONT.EDU

Belmont MBA candidates are predominantly working professionals, and many aren't looking for a new position after graduation (rather, they are hoping to assume new responsibilities at their existing job with the help of an MBA.) However, should they someday be looking to make a change, Massey graduates can count on lifelong loyalty: All alumni have access to services offered through Center for Career Development including a job posting site, career counseling, and various online tools.

Student Life and Environment

With its evening course schedule, accommodating staff, and practical approach to business, Belmont attracts many "young professionals up on current events and looking to advance their careers." At this school, "people are smart and hard workers, and have big, diverse goals [in] life," offering great opportunities to network in different industries. Between students, "the culture is professional but fun without being too rigid," and, though there is a mix of cultures and viewpoints, "Everyone feels comfortable and gets to express their personal views." "There are numerous activities and clubs to take part in" through the business school, including honor societies and volunteer work. Even if they don't participate in campus activities, "everyone is still very social and friendly," and networking opportunities abound. A student explains, "Courses are structured with many group work requirements, which somewhat supercedes the need for student activity groups, as we are all meeting together regularly."

Located on 75 acres in southeast Nashville, Belmont University has a "great urban location" and a comfortable campus environment, boasting modern classrooms and "beautiful flower gardens." Although most Belmont MBA students don't have extra time to take advantage of the resources on campus, they do appreciate the school's "convenient location." At the same time, Belmont has a growing reputation, and students say it's time to "significantly update some of [its] facilities and technologies to keep up with the expansion."

Admissions

To apply to Massey, students must submit an application, an undergraduate transcript, GMAT scores, a current resume, and at least two professional recommendations. In recent years, the average Belmont MBA candidate was about 28 years old, had over six years of professional work experience, and scored around 532 on the GMAT. To be eligible for the program, students must have an undergraduate degree in any field. For those without a degree in business, Belmont will help a student determine which basic business courses they should take before matriculation.

FINANCIAL FACTS

Annual tuition	$40,290
Fees	$670
% of students receiving aid	67
% of first-year students receiving aid	67
% of students receiving loans	54
% of students receiving grants	22
Average award package	$15,173
Average grant	$4,805
Average student loan debt	$21,206

ADMISSIONS

Admissions Selectivity Rating	68
# of applications received	50
% applicants accepted	96
% acceptees attending	88
Average GMAT	532
Range of GMAT	470–600
Average GPA	3.09
TOEFL required of international students	Yes
Minimum TOEFL (paper/computer)	550/213
Application fee	$50
International application fee	$50
Regular application deadline	7/1
Early decision program?	No
Deferment available	Yes
Maximum length of deferment	1 year
Transfer students accepted	Yes
Transfer application policy: Application process is the same for all students. May transfer up to 6 hours from an accredited university.	
Non-fall admissions	Yes
Need-blind admissions	Yes

BENTLEY UNIVERSITY
MCCALLUM GRADUATE SCHOOL OF BUSINESS

GENERAL INFORMATION
Type of school	Private
Academic calendar	Semester

SURVEY SAYS...
Cutting-edge classes
Happy students
Smart classrooms
Solid preparation in:
Teamwork
Computer skills
Doing business in a global economy

STUDENTS
Enrollment of parent institution	3,616
Enrollment of MBA Program	558
% male/female	60/40
% out-of-state	22
% part-time	71
% minorities	2
% international	40
Average age at entry	25
Average years work experience at entry	2

ACADEMICS
Academic Experience Rating	**83**
Student/faculty ratio	11:1
Profs interesting rating	82
Profs accessible rating	78
% female faculty	37
% minority faculty	11

Joint Degrees
Dual Degrees are available.

Prominent Alumni
Joseph Antonellis, MBA '82 Vice Chairman, State Street Corp., Board of Directors, Boston Financial Data Services; Juergen Rottler, MBA '91 EVP, Oracle Customer Service, Oracle Corporation; Dale A. Boch, MBA '83 President, Management Developers, Inc., Thomas R. Venables, MBA '85, President and CEO, Benjamin Franklin Bank; Ed Lafferty, MBA '96, General Partner & CFO, Saturn Asset Management.

Academics

Students in the McCallum MBA program at Bentley University brag that their program combines "the most modern technology available" with "real-world work experience" to provide "the best mix of price, location, and quality." Bentley's impressive resources include a 3,500-square-foot facility complete with a trading floor with two Trans-Lux data walls, 60 work stations, an adjacent business suite, and a marketing center that features numerous state-of-the-art research and analysis labs. "Some [of the technology] is accessible from home, too," a boon to the school's many commuting part-timers.

McCallum's cutting-edge approach extends to its academics. Students pursue "the most unique and interesting concentrations" in addition to "all the traditional areas of study." Unique offerings include Human Factors in Information Design, Quantitative Methods for Business Decisions, and Marketing Analytics, programs that students argue "are in line with what is needed in the real world." Bentley's "accounting program is the best around," excelling in both general accounting and taxation. Information technology, unsurprisingly, is also an area of strength.

McCallum's many part-time students appreciate the program's flexibility ("You can take two courses in one night, and there are some online offerings," a student explains), but warn that "it is hard to connect with other students" because "there are no real cohorts." The full-time program, in contrast, "is comparatively small and becomes tight-knit over the two-year course." For all students, the program is "intense," but fortunately "The professors and administration are very helpful." One student points out that "many workshops and information sessions exist outside of class," and as a result students enjoy "a very engaging academic experience." MBAs also appreciate that "professors teach course work in a practical manner. I always leave feeling like I have something I can use the next day."

Career and Placement

Bentley's Nathan R. Miller Center for Career Services (CCS) "offers a great deal of support in finding career opportunities" for the school's MBAs. Career Advisors receive a strong assist from Bentley's solid "reputation among Boston-area employers" as well as from professors who "use their networks" to help their students. Students here also benefit from the Job Search Skills (JSS), a program designed to help them better position themselves in the battle for top jobs. JSS programs vary by area of concentration, meaning students receive plenty of field-specific assistance. The CSS provides lifetime service to alumni, another huge plus.

Top employers of Bentley MBAs include: Boston Scientific, Converse Inc., Couidien, Deloitte Consulting, Federal Reserve Bank of Boston, Ernst & Young, Fidelity Investments, EMC, Genzyme Corporation, JPMorgan Chase & Company, KPMG, Morgan Stanley, PricewaterhouseCoopers, Microsoft, National Grid USA, Nuance Communications, Raytheon, Staples, and State Street Corporation.

ADMISSIONS CONTACT: SHARON HILL, ASSISTANT DEAN, DIRECTOR OF GRADUATE ADMISSIONS
ADDRESS: 175 FOREST STREET WALTHAM, MA 02452
PHONE: 781-891-2108 • FAX: 781-891-2464
E-MAIL: BENTLEYGRADUATEADMISSIONS@BENTLEY.EDU • WEBSITE: WWW.BENTLEY.EDU

Student Life and Environment

The majority of Bentley MBA students attend the part-time evening program. The full-time program, is comprised of 10 percent of the student body. Bentley typically draws "academically capable people with many diverse backgrounds," although some here "wish there were fewer people coming straight out of a four-year program," even though such students "are still surprisingly able to contribute to conversations. However, they lack a certain perspective."

Bentley MBAs enjoy "a beautiful campus and buildings." Grad classes "are concentrated in a couple of buildings near each other," a blessing during the cold Massachusetts winters. So too are the "shuttles around campus." Even so, some feel that the space dedicated to graduate students needs to be expanded. One writes that the school "should have more options for dining on campus and more places suitable for graduate students to study either individual[ly] or in groups." Most part-time students must balance "a heavy course load" with work and family responsibilities, leaving little or no time for extracurricular and other campus activities. Those not so burdened report that "Campus activities are in abundance, from professional to entertainment. There is usually at least one club or association hosting an event open to the whole school body" at any time. Campus organizations "cater to different educational paths and cultures," with a number representing various international student constituencies.

Off-campus entertainment is also readily accessible, as Bentley is located in Waltham, a mere 10 miles from downtown Boston. Both Boston and Cambridge are easily accessible by train. The school also runs a regular shuttle between the Bentley campus and Harvard Square.

Admissions

Applicants to the Bentley MBA program must submit all of the following materials to the Admissions Committee: a completed application form; official copies of all transcripts for all post secondary academic work; an official GMAT score report; two letters of recommendation; essays (topics detailed in application); and a resume. Applicants to the full-time MBA program or the MS + MBA program must sit for an interview; interviews are optional for all other applicants. In addition to all of the above, international applicants must also submit an international student data form and confirmation of financial resources; a copy of their passport name page; and TOEFL score. International applicants are strongly encouraged to use a transcript evaluation service. Bentley admissions officers pride themselves on personalizing the admissions process by looking at the whole person when making admissions decisions. Work experience is strongly preferred but not required.

FINANCIAL FACTS

Annual tuition	$32,780
Fees	$404
Cost of books	$1,150
Room & board	$13,780
% of students receiving aid	51
% of first-year students receiving aid	87
% of students receiving loans	32
% of students receiving grants	29
Average award package	$16,733
Average grant	$12,203

ADMISSIONS

Admissions Selectivity Rating	**81**
# of applications received	463
% applicants accepted	63
% acceptees attending	58
Average GMAT	590
Range of GMAT	550–630
Average GPA	3.54
TOEFL required of international students	Yes
Minimum TOEFL (paper/computer)	600/250
Application fee	$50
International application fee	$50
Application Deadline/Notification	
Round 1:	12/1 / 1/15
Round 2:	1/20 / 3/15
Round 3:	3/15 / 5/1
Early decision program?	Yes
ED Deadline/Notification	12/1 / 1/15
Deferment available	Yes
Maximum length of deferment	1 year
Transfer students accepted	No
Non-fall admissions	Yes
Need-blind admissions	Yes

EMPLOYMENT PROFILE

		Grads Employed by Function	% Avg. Salary
Career Rating	92		
Percent employed at graduation	42	Marketing	12 NR
Percent employed 3 months		Consulting	12 NR
after graduation	75	Finance	12 NR
Average base starting salary	$73,056	MIS	47 $70,750
Primary Source of Full-time Job Acceptances		**Top 5 Employers Hiring Grads**	
School-facilitated activities	9 (50%)	Deloitte (1), Fidelity Investments (1), Morgan	
Graduate-facilitated activities	9 (50%)	Stanley (1), KPMG (1)	

BERRY COLLEGE
CAMPBELL SCHOOL OF BUSINESS

GENERAL INFORMATION
Type of school	Private
Academic calendar	August–July

SURVEY SAYS...
Friendly students
Solid preparation in:
General management
Teamwork
Communication/interpersonal skills

STUDENTS
Enrollment of parent institution	1,922
Enrollment of MBA Program	32
% part-time	94
Average age at entry	27
Average years work experience at entry	8

ACADEMICS
Academic Experience Rating	**74**
Student/faculty ratio	12:1
Profs interesting rating	81
Profs accessible rating	85
% female faculty	29

Academics

Berry College is a small private school, located on a beautiful and expansive wooded campus in Rome, Georgia. This setting provides a unique backdrop for the Campbell School of Business, which unites a savvy MBA curriculum with a friendly and intimate atmosphere. Within the greater Rome area, Berry College is a "convenient and reputable" choice for an MBA, with all classes offered in the evenings (classes meet one night per week throughout the fall, spring, and summer terms.) Located fewer than 100 miles from Atlanta and Chattanooga, the program is designed for working professionals, as well as early-career students. For full-time students, the school offers the opportunity to take on a graduate assistantship position, which offsets the cost of tuition in exchange for hours worked on campus.

Along with the master of education, the MBA is one of two graduate programs offered at Berry, and the atmosphere reflects the intimate atmosphere of the undergraduate college. With a low enrollment, the "small class sizes and the relationships students have with professors" are the best parts of their educational experience. Here, professors "are always willing to help and seem happy to be there, teaching the courses." Bringing strong educational and professional backgrounds to the program, "the faculty at Berry [is] surprisingly accomplished," and students note a "professional commitment to academic excellence" throughout the faculty and staff. An interactive environment, students are encouraged to participate in class discussions, and those who have already entered the workforce often "have interesting stories and work experience to contribute to class." While the benefits are manifold, the low enrollment also has some drawbacks. For example, course scheduling can be difficult because "The school does not offer all required classes at all times. Just once every two years." In addition, the elective offerings are more limited at Berry than at larger institutions; some feel it would be a benefit to have "more classes, more options" within the MBA curriculum.

Overseen by a competent administration, "the school is run well," and the curriculum is well-designed, emphasizing a holistic approach to business. The MBA begins with a series of proficiency requirements in accounting, marketing, statistics, economics, finance, and management—but these can be waived for students who have an undergraduate degree in business. Thereafter, all students must complete 21 credit hours of core courses and nine credit hours of business electives (students may also earn course credit for internships), which cover a range of topics including written and oral communication skills, leadership, and ethics. Typically, students complete the program in two years, though the college allows up to six years of study.

Career and Placement

The Berry College Career Center offers career counseling, resume and cover letter assistance, online job boards, and an online database of job tips and resources. These services are open to all undergraduates and graduate students, as well as alumni (alumni may even request login information to access online job boards); however, the Career Center's efforts are principally aimed at the undergraduate community.

Graduates of the Campbell School of Business, students have taken jobs with companies including CFA, Georgia Pacific, Walton Communications, Industrial Developments International, Wiser Wealth Management, and Anheuser Busch. While the school has a strong reputation in the region, students admit that, "Berry College could improve in connecting its grad students with jobs outside of the Rome metropolitan and Atlanta areas."

ADMISSIONS CONTACT: DR. GARY WATERS, ASSOCIATE VP OF ENROLLMENT MANAGEMENT
ADDRESS: 2277 MARTHA BERRY HWY NW, PO BOX 490159 MOUNT BERRY, GA 30149-0159
PHONE: 1.800.BERRY.GA • FAX: 706.290.2178
E-MAIL: ADMISSIONS@BERRY.EDU • WEBSITE: BERRY.EDU

Student Life and Environment

Taking a cue from Berry's pastoral campus environment, Berry students are "friendly and down-to-earth," yet also take their studies seriously. At Berry, students "work hard all day and work hard during their classes," and many are "goal-oriented" and "driven." A tribute to the Berry College's pleasant atmosphere and academic excellence, many MBA candidates are returning Berry students who also received their undergraduate degree from the school. In fact, many come to the graduate program directly after college. Therefore, "the majority of students are fairly young and inexperienced," with limited experience in the real world. As a result, the older, working students who "come from outside of the school add a great deal of value" to the program.

Berry is located on an enormous wooded campus (one of the world's biggest) on the outskirts of Rome, Georgia. If you would like to get involved in extracurricular pursuits, "the school has a great campus with many activities to participate in," and "there is always an activity or cultural event" at school. At the same time, students observe, "The graduate program isn't as active in the school community but the opportunity is there if the student wanted to be involved." Even so, "gym and library facility access is fully granted" to graduate students, and many take advantage of these resources.

Admissions

To apply to Berry College's MBA program, students must submit undergraduate transcripts, two letters of reference, official GMAT scores, a current resume, and a 500-word goals statement. To be eligible for the program, students must have a GMAT score of at least 400; an undergraduate GPA of 3.0 or better is preferred. To be considered for a position, students should submit their application materials at least 30 days before the start of a new semester.

ADMISSIONS

Admissions Selectivity Rating	67
# of applications received	20
% applicants accepted	90
% acceptees attending	89
Average GPA	3.06
TOEFL required of international students	Yes
Minimum TOEFL (paper/computer)	550/213
Regular application deadline	7/15
Early decision program?	No
Deferment available	Yes
Maximum length of deferment	1 semester
Transfer students accepted	Yes

Transfer application policy:
The curriculum committee may grant transfer credit for appropriate graduate-level course work completed at other AACSB-accredited institutions to a maximum of two 3-semester-hour courses, for a total of 6 semester hours. Transfer credit is not granted for Strategies of World-Class Organizations (BUS 685).

Non-fall admissions	Yes
Need-blind admissions	No

BOSTON COLLEGE
CARROLL SCHOOL OF MANAGEMENT

GENERAL INFORMATION
Type of school	Private
Affiliation	Roman Catholic/Jesuit
Academic calendar	Semester

SURVEY SAYS...
Students love Chestnut Hill, MA
Friendly students
Good social scene
Good peer network
Solid preparation in:
Finance
General management
Teamwork

STUDENTS
Enrollment of parent institution	14,623
Enrollment of MBA Program	697
% male/female	65/35
% part-time	71
% minorities	12
% international	23
Average age at entry	27
Average years work experience at entry	4

ACADEMICS
Academic Experience Rating	**89**
Student/faculty ratio	13:1
Profs interesting rating	83
Profs accessible rating	84
% female faculty	34
% minority faculty	14

Joint Degrees
MBA/MSF, 24 months; MBA/MSA, 24 months; MBA/JD, 48 months; MBA/MSW, 3 yrs; MBA/MSN, 36–48 months; MBA/MEd, 36 months; MBA/MS Biology, Chemistry, Geology, Geophysics, 36 months; MBA/MA Math, Slavic Studies, Russian, Linguistics, 36 months; MBA/MA Pastoral Studies, 36 months.

Academics

Boston College's Carroll School of Management prides itself on fostering a sense of community among students, and matriculants agree that networking and collaboration are among the MBA program's greatest strengths. At this medium-sized school, group work is encouraged and "100-person cohorts mean the whole class has a strong network by [the] end of the two-year term." Thanks to the "small, intimate class sizes," students really get to know each other, and everyone has a chance to "bring valuable experience into the classroom." With its "outstanding reputation" in the Northeast, BC can easily attract "big name professors," with "some even flying in from NYC each week for class." Here, "The teachers are engaged senior faculty who are passionate about their field and who are continually researching and actively contributing to that field." Despite their lofty credentials, Carroll School of Management "professors really seem to care about the students' well-being" and "are willing to take the time to get to know the students." Administrators are likewise student-oriented: "You are definitely not just a number at this school; they really take care of their students."

Offering a "well-balanced" MBA, the Carroll School of Management "clearly put[s] a lot of intelligent effort into coordinating classes, projects, and external company involvement," resulting in a program that helps students "develop skills and experience directly applicable to real world challenges we will face." While theory is stressed, adjunct and full-time faculty also "bring in their experience from their workplace" and students praise the "courses organized by the Center of Investment Management and Research at Boston College, which [are] taught by experts with significant industry experience." Academically, "the focus at BC is on finance," and coursework that is "analytically rigorous and challenging." The environment is ideal for students seeking careers in asset management and investment; however, students with other interests would like the school to "provide more non-finance electives," and to encourage more creative and entrepreneurial thinking.

To complement the classroom experience, co-curricular opportunities and internships are abundant. In the second semester of their first year, MBA students complete a local consulting project with a corporation, nonprofit organization, or government office. Students also get a taste of the real world through overseas programs, participation in clubs and extracurricular activities, and the required business plan project. A student enthuses, "Between the TechTrek West course and the summer international programs (IME and ICP), Carroll graduate students are provided with unique opportunities to engage with and learn from business leaders throughout the world." Back on campus, the Manager's Studio brings top executives to speak to Carroll students; many say they're "amazed with the caliber of speakers" invited to address the business school.

Career and Placement

A thoroughly Bostonian institution, "BC has a very powerful alumni network," which is a "huge strength during the hiring process." On campus, there are plenty of resources for job seekers, including "a separate full-time career placement team for the MBA program itself," staffed by professionals who are "just as dedicated and skilled as the rest of the faculty and administration." Working with local employers, the Career Center continually draws upon "the school's relationship with the Boston business community," especially its "close ties with the asset management industry" and "strong reputation in finance." Despite their deep roots in the local region, some students opine that "The counselors are ill-equipped to help students who are looking outside the Boston area."

ADMISSIONS CONTACT: SHELLEY BURT, DIRECTOR OF GRADUATE ENROLLMENT
ADDRESS: FULTON HALL 315, 140 COMMONWEALTH AVENUE CHESTNUT HILL, MA 02467-3808
PHONE: 617-552-3920 • FAX: 617-552-8078
E-MAIL: BCMBA@BC.EDU • WEBSITE: WWW.BC.EDU/MBA

Last year's graduating class had an average total compensation (salary plus signing bonuses) of over $98,000. Financial services was the most popular field, drawing more than 30 percent of graduates, followed by consumer products (16 percent), and consulting (13 percent). Over the past few years, hiring companies include AT&T Corp, Boston Blazers, CIGNA Corporation, Comcast Corporation, Deutsche Bank, Ernst & Young LLP, Federal Reserve Bank of Boston, Fidelity Investments, GE Healthcare, PepsiCo, Inc, Putnam LLC, and Unilever.

Student Life and Environment

Students at the Carroll School of Management are "friendly, welcoming, and respectful," and bring a "good mix of social, political and professional backgrounds" to campus. Most "take class seriously" and are "driven for success," yet they are "not at all the hypercompetitive student that is the typical MBA stereotype." On the contrary, BC's MBA students are a social bunch, who "appreciate work-life balance" and "love to interact outside of class." In the full-time program, "everyone spends time together socially", and many students like to "go out every Thursday night for drinks (the entire program is invited)." Even part-time students say, "You feel connected to the school with communications and opportunities made quite clear."

Students love BC's "idyllic campus, located in [an] affluent suburb right near Boston." In fact, many students say they chose the Carroll School of Management for its excellent location, telling us that, "Boston is a great city to live in, and we try to take advantage of it as much as possible." On the weekends, students might "explore Boston, visit a museum, or try to find an adventure outdoors."

Admissions

When you ask Boston College students what makes their MBA program special, many will tell you: It's the people. Indeed, BC's admissions department prides itself on selecting a diverse, cooperative, and accomplished student body, seeking students with a potential for success academically and in leadership roles. In recent years, incoming graduate business students at Boston College had an average GMAT score of about 663 and an average undergraduate GPA of 3.4. Though only two years of work experience is recommended before entering the program, the average student had 4.4 years of professional experience before beginning their MBA.

Prominent Alumni

John Fisher, '71, President & CEO, Saucony; Norman Chambers, '82, President & COO of NCIS Building Systems, Inc.; Paul LaCamera, '83, President & GM, WCVB-TV, Channel 5; Alexis Sarkissian, '91, CEO Vivid Collection; Ronald Logue, '74, Chairman & CEO, State Street Corporation.

FINANCIAL FACTS

Annual tuition	$34,160
Fees	$150
Cost of books	$1,500
Room & board (on/off-campus)	$18,390/$18,390
% of students receiving aid	82
% of students receiving grants	82
Average award package	$33,750
Average grant	$16,539
Average student loan debt	$52,408

ADMISSIONS

Admissions Selectivity Rating	94
# of applications received	980
% applicants accepted	29
% acceptees attending	38
Average GMAT	663
Range of GMAT	630–700
Average GPA	3.4
TOEFL required of international students	Yes
Minimum TOEFL (paper/computer)	600/250
Application fee	$100
International application fee	$100
Application Deadline/Notification	
Round 1:	11/15 / 1/15
Round 2:	1/15 / 3/15
Round 3:	3/15 / 5/1
Round 4:	4/15 / 6/1
Early decision program?	No
Deferment available	No
Transfer students accepted	Yes
Transfer application policy: 4 courses are accepted (with a grade of B or higher) from other AACSB MBA Programs.	
Non-fall admissions	No
Need-blind admissions	Yes

EMPLOYMENT PROFILE

Career Rating	92	Grads Employed by Function	% Avg. Salary
Percent employed at graduation	52	Marketing	16 $78,455
Percent employed 3 months after graduation	82	Operations	3 $81,677
		Consulting	3 $106,667
Average base starting salary	$90,387	Management	5 $92,400
Primary Source of Full-time Job Acceptances		Finance	25 $91,867
School-facilitated activities	42 (67%)	HR	2 NR
Graduate-facilitated activities	21 (33%)	MIS	1 NR

Top 5 Employers Hiring Grads
Fidelity Investments (7), Ernst & Young (2), Cigna (2), Johnson & Johnson (2), Staples (2)

BOSTON UNIVERSITY
SCHOOL OF MANAGEMENT

GENERAL INFORMATION

Type of school	Private
Academic calendar	Semester

SURVEY SAYS...

Students love Boston, MA
Good peer network
Happy students
Solid preparation in:
Teamwork

STUDENTS

Enrollment of parent institution	32,485
Enrollment of MBA Program	1,030
% male/female	59/41
% part-time	68
% minorities	18
% international	35
Average age at entry	28
Average years work experience at entry	5

ACADEMICS

Academic Experience Rating	89
Student/faculty ratio	20:1
Profs interesting rating	85
Profs accessible rating	85
% female faculty	23

Joint Degrees

MS/MBA (dual degree MS in Information Systems and traditional MBA), 84 credits in 21 months; MBA/MS Television Management; MBA/MA International Relations; MBA/MS Manufacturing Engineering; MBA/MA Economics; MBA/MA Medical Sciences, 80 credits; MBA/JD, 116 credits; MBA/MPH, 85 credits; MBA/MD, 114 credits.

Academics

"Fusing the art, science, and technology of business," Boston University's MBA programs provide a well-rounded and well-respected business education, which can be effectively tailored to each student's career goals and interests. In the first year, BU's "well-planned cohort curriculum" promotes "integration across multiple curricula to teach not only independent subjects but also how they interact with one another." You'll get "a good mix between case [study] discussion and lecture" in the classroom, and "There is a heavy emphasis on teamwork and presentation skills." In fact, "intensive group projects" are a part of every class, and students insist that "When you leave this program, you definitely know how to manage people and their personalities." The program is challenging, and "The workload is very tough, especially the first semester." A full-time student admits, "Everyone pulls at least one all-nighter and people who are from the area joke about never seeing their other friends anymore." Part-timers are no less challenged, though they assure us that, "Teachers are understanding of our busy schedule[s] and cater their assignments appropriately."

The ability to tailor your education is an important aspect of the BU MBA, which distinguishes itself through various specialty degrees and concentrations. Currently, the business school confers 10 dual degrees—such as the MS/MBA in public and nonprofit management—as well as numerous elective concentrations, like a "well-regarded health sector management concentration." The school's "great electives" include special programs like the international field seminars. In addition, students praise the "breadth of course offerings" within the business school, as well as in the larger university (business students can cross-register in related departments, like international relations.)

Boston University has no trouble attracting top-notch faculty to its MBA program. "The accomplishments and abilities of the professors are nothing short of astounding. Many of them [are] Ivy League PhDs with decades of teaching experience." However, there is "a good mix of career academics and individuals with real world experience" on the teaching staff at BU, with many Boston-area professionals who "provide great insight about different industries." Best of all, "All classes are taught by faculty (most tenured, some PT professionals) and never by TAs."

Outside the classroom, BU professors are "very outgoing, always willing to help, and even willing to come out with our class for a drink every now and then." Similarly supportive, "The administration helps coordinate a lot of activities...plan for classes, and is very responsive to students' concerns." When planning your business school curriculum, "academic advisors are always available to help." "The school administration is really open to feedback. Each year the new class has new changes that are implemented based upon feedback collected from the previous year."

Career and Placement

At BU, the Feld Career Center begins working with students during their very first week on campus, and career advisors offer individual counseling, resume critiques, mock interviews, and recruiting events throughout the year. Students say, "the Career Center does a great job networking and attracting many companies to BU," and evening students enjoy "the same Career Center fairs/services open to full-time and part-time students." Students say "The school really does healthcare and IT well. A lot of the big companies in those fields recruit here." However, students admit that, "outside those fields it gets a little more difficult" to find an excellent job.

ADMISSIONS CONTACT: HAYDEN ESTRADA, ASSISTANT DEAN FOR GRADUATE ADMISSIONS
ADDRESS: 595 COMMONWEALTH AVENUE BOSTON, MA 02215
PHONE: 617-353-2670 • FAX: 617-353-7368
E-MAIL: MBA@BU.EDU • WEBSITE: MANAGEMENT.BU.EDU

With its stellar Boston location, BU students "have great access to the city and its resources, as well as the alumni base here." In recent years, 90 to 95 percent of BU graduates had a job within three months of graduation. Companies recruiting at BU include Adobe, AT&T, Chevron, Hewlett Packard, Fidelity, New Balance, Philips Healthcare, and Staples.

Student Life and Environment

One major benefit of Boston University's MBA program is that you will instantly begin building a local network with your talented classmates. The admissions department makes a point of admitting an interesting and accomplished student body, and "The class is extremely diverse with both international and domestic students from around the nation. While the intellect of my fellow classmates was a little intimidating at first, everyone is very friendly which makes networking effortless." The emphasis on group work promotes bonds between students. A current student enthuses, "I absolutely loved the students on my team and my cohort is very cohesive and social!"

At the clean and modern BU business school, "Each classroom is designed beautifully and provides the latest technologies." A hub of social and cultural opportunities, the Boston University campus is located "right in the middle of the city," within easy walking distance to countless attractions. Part-time, full-time, married, single, working, or otherwise, "Everyone finds time to bond and go out for appetizers or drinks before or after classes, which makes for a very friendly and social environment." "A different student club hosts Thirsty Thursday each week where everyone gathers together at a bar for relaxing and socializing." Even if you take classes in the evening, you can also share in the fun. A current student tells us, "The activities provided for evening students are fun and engaging, and we are provided all the same opportunities as full-time students."

Admissions

Admissions to BU's MBA programs are highly competitive, with only 30 percent of applicants receiving an offer of admission each year. For the full-time program, the mean GMAT score for last year's entering class was 680 with an 80 percent mid-range of 610 to 740. In the evening program, the GMAT mid-range was 530 to 710, and students had an average of five years of work experience.

Prominent Alumni

Christine Poon, Vice Chairman, Pharmacy Group, Johnson & Johnson; Millard S. Drexler, Chairman and CEO, J. Crew Group, Inc.; Edward J. Zander, Chairman, Motorola; Walter Skowronski, President, Boeing Capital; Donald McGrath, Chairman & CEO, Bank of the West.

FINANCIAL FACTS

Annual tuition	$37,910
Fees	$486
Cost of books	$1,574
Room & board	$11,808
% of students receiving aid	96
% of first-year students receiving aid	97
% of students receiving loans	56
% of students receiving grants	81
Average award package	$28,330
Average grant	$20,589

ADMISSIONS

Admissions Selectivity Rating	93
# of applications received	1,617
% applicants accepted	38
% acceptees attending	50
Average GMAT	680
Range of GMAT	610–740
Average GPA	3.36
TOEFL required of international students	Yes
Minimum TOEFL (paper/computer)	600/250
Application fee	$125
International application fee	$125
Regular application deadline	3/15
Regular notification	5/1
Application Deadline/Notification	
Round 1:	11/15 / 1/1
Round 2:	1/15 / 3/1
Round 3:	3/15 / 5/1
Early decision program?	No
Deferment available	No
Transfer students accepted	Yes
Transfer application policy: Classes must be from AACSB-accredited institution.	
Non-fall admissions	Yes
Need-blind admissions	Yes

Applicants Also Look At

Boston College, Harvard University, Massachussettts Institute of Technology, New York University

EMPLOYMENT PROFILE

Career Rating	97	Grads Employed by Function	% Avg. Salary
Percent employed at graduation	74	Marketing	9 $90,444
Percent employed 3 months after graduation	90	Operations	2 $75,000
		Consulting	5 $85,257
Average base starting salary	$93,725	Management	9 $103,111
Primary Source of Full-time Job Acceptances		Finance	8 $91,750
School-facilitated activities	41 (46%)	MIS	2 $80,000
Graduate-facilitated activities	29 (33%)	Nonprofit	1 $85,000
Unknown	19 (21%)	**Top 5 Employers Hiring Grads**	
		Bank of America (5), Philips (5), AT&T (2), Thermofisher Sceintific (2), Staples (2)	

BOWLING GREEN STATE UNIVERSITY
COLLEGE OF BUSINESS ADMINISTRATION

GENERAL INFORMATION

Type of school	Public
Academic calendar	Semester

SURVEY SAYS...

Cutting-edge classes
Solid preparation in:
Doing business in a global economy

STUDENTS

Enrollment of parent institution	21,071
Enrollment of MBA Program	141
% male/female	56/44
% out-of-state	7
% part-time	51
% minorities	7
% international	44
Average age at entry	25
Average years work experience at entry	5

ACADEMICS

Academic Experience Rating	88
Profs interesting rating	81
Profs accessible rating	82
% female faculty	28
% minority faculty	38

Joint Degrees

MBA (full-time) with specialization in Accounting or Finance, 18 months.

Prominent Alumni

William Ingram, CEO, White Castle Systems; Cheryl Krueger, Founder, Cheryl and Company; David May, President, S.C. Johnson and Company; Richard Stephens, President (retired) Cooper Tire and Rubber Company; Mary Minnick, Former President of Marketing, Coca-Cola.

Academics

Whether you choose to enter the full-time, part-time, or Executive MBA program at Bowling Green State University you will experience efficient, practical, instruction at a great value. Offering a crash course in business, Bowling Green's full-time MBA "is only 12 months long," and is comprised of a series of foundation, core, and capstone courses. Tuition is reasonable and, for many students, graduate assistantships can cover "the cost of tuition, and [pay] an additional living stipend." Given the program's accelerated time frame, low cost, and scholarship options, students say, "It is probably [a] much better bang for the buck than most two-year programs (even at Ivy League schools.)" Similarly, the school's 23-month Professional MBA is "perfect for busy, working professionals." Designed for students with a minimum of three years in the workforce, "The location and times are extremely convenient and the cost is very reasonable," making it an affordable way to boost your career prospects in Bowling Green.

While convenience and value are large part of the equation, students assure us that practicality isn't the only reason they chose BGSU. For many, the school's small size and community atmosphere is a major draw. Here, the administration is accessible, and the school is "very well-run and very user-friendly." A current student shares: "I have had a very positive experience working with everyone in the college from the secretaries to the dean." Thanks to uniformly small class sizes, students are "encouraged to work with our fellow students through group projects and presentations." A current student adds, "We have a well-rounded cohort and the class spends a lot of time debating all kinds of issues relating to the material." No matter which program you enter, you'll benefit from friendly professors, who "share a love and enthusiasm for teaching as well as helping their students to [achieve] success." Providing both rigor and support, "The program is challenging (as it should be), but the professors are encouraging, treat us as professionals, and make themselves available outside of class and office hours to aid in our success." Successful in the real world—not just the ivory tower—Bowling Green's "knowledgeable and friendly" faculty "consistently incorporate[s] useful information and real-life scenarios into their instruction, making each class valuable to my future career." A student in the Professional MBA program agrees: "Even though I've been working for over 25 years, I have taken away a good deal of information to apply on the job." Despite the strength of the curriculum, some would like the school to offer "more areas of specialization" (currently, BGSU offers three areas of concentration in accounting, finance, and organizational studies), or incorporate internship experiences into the curriculum.

In addition to the full-time and part-time programs at Bowling Green, the Executive MBA Program gets top marks from seasoned professionals, who say "the course work is very challenging and stimulating" and "professors are extremely knowledgeable and friendly." To make everything smooth and simple, "All course registration and book purchases are handled by the staff for the Executive MBA program, easing the burden on working professionals." While EMBA students "only spend Friday, Saturday and Sunday on campus once a month," they say, "Subjects are taught on task and time is used wisely."

ADMISSIONS CONTACT: BRIAN CHILDS, ASS'T. DIRECTOR
ADDRESS: 369 BUSINESS ADMINISTRATION BUILDING, BOWLING GREEN, OH 43403
PHONE: 419-372-2488 • FAX: 419-372-2875
E-MAIL: MBA-INFO@BGSU.EDU • WEBSITE: WWW.BGSUMBA.COM

Career and Placement

Most students in the Professional and Executive MBA programs are already working full time when they begin the program at Bowling Green, and therefore, many are not actively seeking employment. For full-time students, career planning is woven into the curriculum at Bowling Green State University through practical courses in leadership, technology, and other applied skills, as well as a series of professional development seminars. Through the business school, students may also contact career development specialists to help them with their job search.

In addition to the assistance they receive within the business school, the Bowling Green State University Career Center assists the undergraduate and graduate community with their job search through career counseling, job and internship fairs, campus recruiting and career development workshops.

Student Life and Environment

For Professional MBA students, "Classes are not held on the main campus, but rather at a newly renovated, state-of-the-art complex that is approximately 25 miles north of the main campus." This facility is "convenient, well-maintained," and offers "full access to all technology (wireless web access, software, printers, etc.) to ensure success." Even though they attend school off-site, part-time students say, "The administration office does a good job of keeping us informed of what is happening on campus." Unfortunately, most part-time students agree that between "working full time and going to school two nights a week, plus homework and reading, there is no time left for other club activities."

On the main campus, "The business school has made great strides in improving facilities," though some would like the school to improve the "building appearance and technology amenities" in the classrooms. Full-time students benefit from "an active student body" and "a diverse array of activities on campus such as sporting events that we can access for free." On campus and in the surrounding town, there are "a lot of students to socialize with." On that note, students say Bowling Green "is very much a college town, with a good bar scene" and an affordable cost of living.

Admissions

To apply to BGSU's graduate business programs, students must submit an application form, an official undergraduate transcript, GMAT scores, a resume, and two professional recommendations. The school also requests a personal statement, outlining the applicant's objectives in pursuing an MBA and explaining how they might contribute to the program. In some cases, applicants to the Executive MBA who have extensive work experience (10 years or more) may be exempt from submitting GMAT scores.

FINANCIAL FACTS

Annual tuition	$15,252
Fees (in-state/ out-of-state)	$1,672/$12,634
Cost of books	$1,500
Room & board (off-campus)	$6,000
% of students receiving aid	50
% of first-year students receiving aid	45
% of students receiving loans	35
% of students receiving grants	40
Average award package	$16,924
Average grant	$13,000

ADMISSIONS

Admissions Selectivity Rating	89
# of applications received	200
% applicants accepted	31
% acceptees attending	77
Average GMAT	571
Range of GMAT	530–618
Average GPA	3.41
TOEFL required of international students	Yes
Minimum TOEFL (paper/computer)	550/213
Application fee	$30
International application fee	$30
Regular application deadline	3/15
Early decision program?	No
Deferment available	Yes
Maximum length of deferment	1 year
Transfer students accepted	Yes
Transfer application policy: Students in the MBA programs (full-time, professional, and executive) are limited to a maximum of six graduate credit hours of transfer credit from AACSB accredited institutions.	
Non-fall admissions	Yes
Need-blind admissions	Yes

BRANDEIS UNIVERSITY
BRANDEIS INTERNATIONAL BUSINESS SCHOOL

GENERAL INFORMATION

Type of school	Private
Affiliation	nonsectarian Jewish-sponsored college
Academic calendar	Semester

SURVEY SAYS...
Cutting-edge classes
Solid preparation in:
Finance
Teamwork
Quantitative skills
Doing business in a global economy

STUDENTS

Enrollment of MBA Program	64

ACADEMICS

Academic Experience Rating	**73**
Student/faculty ratio	8:1
Profs interesting rating	94
Profs accessible rating	88
% female faculty	43
% minority faculty	33

Academics

While many MBA programs offer a few international business classes, at the International Business School (IBS) at Brandeis University, "globalization and economic interdependence is at the core of the program." Renowned for its finance and economics departments, IBS students receive a "well-rounded global business education with great quantitative skills." Professors are "widely known in their fields and have both academic and professional experiences," and classes are a "good mixture between case study method and lecture-based method." Outside the classroom, "the MBA program requires all students to have spent time working abroad before they can graduate" and basic proficiency in a language other than English is also required. A truly international environment, the school's academic focus is reflected in its students, who hail from "different backgrounds and more than 50 countries." Says a current student, "I learned a lot about different cultures and enjoyed different perspectives which prepared me for a career in a multinational environment."

In addition to the IBS, Brandeis's Heller School for Social Policy and Management operates the Heller MBA in Non-Profit Management. This distinctive program has a unique "focus on 'managing for a social mission,' which combines the rigors of a traditional MBA program with an emphasis on mission-based organizations and companies." In addition to coursework in finance and accounting, organizational and operations management, and social justice, students incorporate practical experience through case studies and consulting projects. Students can tailor this 16-month program through elective coursework, including "courses at other Boston area schools for subjects that are not offered at Heller."

Students in both Brandeis business programs say the academic experience is "outstanding." Professors are "leaders in their field, and many have come from industry, so have vast experience which they are very eager to share with students." Fortunately, "the school has a good faculty/student ratio that facilitates easy access and personal touch with professors and staff." Plus, the "small class sizes also give you the opportunity to participate in class discussions more often, which highly contributes to your communication skills and self-confidence." "The curriculum can be very demanding and intense," requiring "endless projects, homework, and exams." Even so, the academic experience is rewarding and enjoyable. A student adds, "Class is challenging, but professors get us laughing and thinking at the same time."

Career and Placement

The IBS Career Center helps students through every step of the job search process, offering career counseling, mock interviews, resume and cover letter preparation, campus career fairs, and an updated list of open positions. If you want individualized career assistance, you're in luck; "at IBS you definitely enjoy personal attention from the career services." Two-thirds of Brandeis students take jobs in the United States after graduation. However, for those who'd like to work abroad, "this relatively young school makes itself visible to employers throughout the globe." In recent years, Brandeis students went on to jobs at Citibank, Morgan Stanley, Nomura Research, Rice Group, Standard and Poor's, Smith Barney, United Airlines, EMC, State Street, and UBS Warburg. Twenty-five percent of students took jobs in international banking and 20 percent in asset management.

ADMISSIONS CONTACT: HOLLY L. CHASE, ASSISTANT DEAN OF ADMISSIONS AND FINANCIAL AID
ADDRESS: 415 SOUTH STREET, MS 032 WALTHAM, MA 02454
PHONE: (781) 736-2252 • FAX: (781) 736-2263
E-MAIL: ADMISSION@LEMBERG.BRANDEIS.EDU • WEBSITE: WWW.BRANDEIS.EDU/GLOBAL

Heller MBA candidates also benefit from extensive professional support through the Heller School's Career Services office. About 77 percent of Heller MBA graduates take jobs at non-profit organizations, such as AIDS Action Committee or Environmental Defense, with another 17 percent taking positions in the public sector. Of the three percent of Heller graduates who take a job in a for-profit company, many choose a position that relates to their socially-minded degree.

Student Life and Environment

Diversity is the name of the game at Brandeis's progressive business programs, which attract students "from a range of backgrounds. One may have worked as a physician in India, the other in air traffic control." A student adds, "Not only are there students from 60 different countries, but the unique environment fosters camaraderie between the different ethnic groups and nationalities. There is no such thing as the "American crowd" and "international crowd." It's just one big cluster of people from all corners of the globe." On campus, Brandeis offers "a great deal of activities and events so that everyone, regardless of their interests, is represented. In addition to the events run by our Student Services office, we have a number of clubs, some more professionally focused such as the Marketing Club [and the] International Business Women Club, and others that are more activity focused, such as the Golf Club or the Soccer Club." Socially, students gather for "golf Saturdays, karaoke nights, international night, ice skating, bowling nights, pot luck dinners, semi-formal and formal dances, and many other events at the university scale and also around the Boston area." At the end of the school day, "a bunch of us will often go out and grab a beer together in downtown Waltham."

What's more, with Boston just 30 minutes away, "students can take the free school shuttle to downtown areas" where they can "enjoy the memorable Bostonian experience."

Admissions

Typical Brandeis MBA students are between 24 and 28 years old and had an undergraduate GPA of about 3.3. The school looks for GMAT scores in the 600s, and requires at least two years of professional work experience before entering the program. In addition to test scores and official undergraduate transcripts, students must submit three letters of recommendation and a current resume.

FINANCIAL FACTS

Annual tuition	$38,974
Cost of books	$1,000
Room & board	$14,000
% of students receiving aid	80
% of first-year students receiving aid	80
% of students receiving loans	25
% of students receiving grants	75
Average award package	$30,000
Average grant	$15,000

ADMISSIONS

Admissions Selectivity Rating	**60***
TOEFL required of international students	Yes
Minimum TOEFL (paper/computer)	600/250
Application fee	$55
International application fee	$55
Early decision program?	Yes
ED Deadline/ Notification	11/15 / 12/15
Deferment available	Yes
Maximum length of deferment	1 year
Transfer students accepted	Yes
Transfer application policy: We will accept transfer credit by waiving required courses.	
Non-fall admissions	No
Need-blind admissions	No

BRIGHAM YOUNG UNIVERSITY
MARRIOTT SCHOOL OF MANAGEMENT

GENERAL INFORMATION
Type of school	Private
Affiliation	Church of Jesus Christ
	of Latter-day Saints
Academic calendar	2 Semester

SURVEY SAYS...
Friendly students
Good peer network
Happy students
Solid preparation in:
Finance
Teamwork

STUDENTS
Enrollment of parent	
institution	32,955
Enrollment of MBA Program	316
% male/female	84/16
% out-of-state	52
% minorities	10
% international	13
Average age at entry	29
Average years work experience	
at entry	4

ACADEMICS
Academic Experience Rating	**94**
Student/faculty ratio	2:1
Profs interesting rating	95
Profs accessible rating	86
% female faculty	14
% minority faculty	1

Joint Degrees
MBA/JD, 4 years; MBA/MS, IPD
Program with Engineering
Department, 3 years; MAcc/JD, 4
years; MPA/JD, 4 years.

Prominent Alumni
Andrea Thomas, Senior VP, Private
Brands, Wal-mart; D. Fraser
Bullock, Founder/Managing Director,
Sorenson Capital; Robert Parsons,
Executive VP & CFO, Exclusive
Resorts; David W. Checketts, Chair,
Sports Capital Partners; Bill P.
Benac Sr., Senior VP & CFO,
American Rail Car Industries.

Academics

Brigham Young University, the educational Mecca of the Church of Jesus Christ of Latter-Day Saints (commonly referred to as 'the Mormon Church'), "is truly a hidden gem," according to its students, who point out that "BYU consistently ranks near the top of the nation in return on investment." That distinction results from a combination of factors: low tuition, excellent quality of instruction, and an "incomparable alumni network."

Unsurprisingly (given its church affiliation), "BYU stresses ethics in business," a fact that appeals to the school's predominantly LDS student body. One student points out the program's "emphasis on social change and corporate social responsibility. Many of the students have lived or worked in third-world countries and have a strong desire to give back and improve the world around them." Students also love that the BYU MBA is "a smaller program that enables students to have working relationships with faculty and opportunities to do more than in larger programs," but "is large enough to have a good network while small enough for the network to have a family-like feel. We are a very tight-knit group in the BYU MBA program," especially important since "much of the coursework is done in groups" here.

BYU "has a fantastic reputation for accounting, corporate finance, and human resources," and "the marketing program has also grown to become a strength" and is now one of the fastest growing and high-profile majors" on campus, with its "students getting internships and job offers at top CPG, technology, and retail companies." The school's organizational behavior and human resources program "is superior," with recruitment "beginning one month into class. There are many excellent companies who come to campus in October. Excellent companies came and left here empty-handed because students had so many options. Also, it's an HR track in an MBA program, which exposes us to both HR and business, and companies really value that." BYU professors "typically had experience teaching at Harvard, Stanford or Wharton, where they earned awards for their teaching quality. I believe they chose BYU for the same reason that I did: The culture can't be duplicated elsewhere."

Career and Placement

Career services at Marriott are provided by the Steven and Georgia White Business Career Center, which school materials describe as "the focal point for the school's placement, internship, and field study efforts." Facilities include a reference library, interview rooms, a large presentation room, 17 interview rooms, and an eRecruiting system. School materials identify nearly 100 companies that recruit at the Marriott School. Students praise the "top-notch career placement people" and the "committed and talented alumni network."

School promotional materials list the following recruiting companies that visit the BYU campus: 3M, American Express, Amgen, Bain & Company, BMW, Caterpillar, Centex, Cisco, Citigroup, DaimlerChrysler, Dell, Deutsche Bank, Eli Lilly, FedEx, Ford Motor Company, General Electric, Goldman Sachs, Honeywell, JP Morgan, Lockheed Martin, Nike, NBC, PepsiCo, Rolex, Union Pacific, Vanguard Group, Wal-Mart, and Zions Bank. About one-quarter of BYU MBAs enter the finance and accounting sector; about one in six takes a job in human resources. Students tell us, "We are starting to compete in the private equity and venture capital field really well."

ADMISSIONS CONTACT: YVETTE ANDERSON, MBA PROGRAM ADMISSION COORDINATOR
ADDRESS: W437D, TANNER BUILDING PROVO, UT 84602
PHONE: 801-422-3500 • FAX: 801-422-0513
E-MAIL: MBA@BYU.EDU • WEBSITE: MBA.BYU.EDU

Student Life and Environment

BYU's commitment to its MBA program can be seen in the recent completion of an extensive expansion project. The newly erected Tanner Building addition—a four-story, approximately 76,000-square-foot structure built directly west of the existing building—has added about 50 percent more space and includes: tiered case rooms, flat classrooms, team study areas, open study areas, MBA program offices, faculty offices, conference rooms, and a New York-style deli.

Life on the BYU campus presents "many opportunities to socialize and network with other classmates. For example, one of our fellow students is a chocolate expert, so we are having a gourmet chocolate tasting event. In addition, almost every week there is a cultural awareness mixer or an opportunity to hear from well-known guest speakers. So far, we've heard from the CEO of Citigroup, the whistleblower from Enron, and many more very recognizable business leaders." Extracurricular life also includes "a plethora of opportunities to enter case competitions. Local companies partner with the school to sponsor web analytics competition, business plan competition, social change competition, and venture capital competition." Students' spouses and families receive excellent support at BYU; writes one MBA, "The Spouses Association takes care of the needs of spouses, creates baby sitting and playgroup, organizes dinners to be brought to families after childbirth."

Admissions

A completed application to the Marriott MBA program includes an application form, personal essays, an official GMAT score report, official transcripts for all post-secondary academic work, three letters of recommendation (one academic, two professional), an honor code commitment form, and a personal statement of intent. An interview is required; the school contacts applicants who have cleared initial screening to set up an interview appointment. International students must submit all of the above and must also provide financial disclosure forms and, if appropriate, TOEFL scores. Full-time post-undergraduate professional experience is highly recommended but not required; those lacking such experience are expected to demonstrate other outstanding qualifications through testing, undergraduate work, etc. Personal attributes are also considered. While students need not belong to the Church of Jesus Christ of Latter-Day Saints, "an understanding of and a commitment to support the church's mission are necessary."

FINANCIAL FACTS

Annual tuition	$9,980
Cost of books	$1,850
Room & board	$8,400
% of students receiving aid	92
% of first-year students receiving aid	97
% of students receiving loans	49
% of students receiving grants	80
Average award package	$5,650
Average grant	$3,564
Average student loan debt	$24,129

ADMISSIONS

Admissions Selectivity Rating	91
# of applications received	478
% applicants accepted	51
% acceptees attending	68
Average GMAT	673
Range of GMAT	640–700
Average GPA	3.54
TOEFL required of international students	Yes
Minimum TOEFL (paper/computer)	590/240
Application fee	$50
International application fee	$50
Application Deadline/Notification	
Round 1:	12/1 / 2/1
Round 2:	1/15 / 3/15
Round 3:	3/1 / 5/1
Round 4:	5/1 / 7/1
Early decision program?	Yes
ED Deadline/Notification	1/15 / 3/15
Deferment available	Yes
Maximum length of deferment	2 years
Transfer students accepted	Yes
Transfer application policy: 15 credit hours of approved graduate-level courses, no pass/fail grades, and a minimum grade of B.	
Non-fall admissions	No
Need-blind admissions	Yes

EMPLOYMENT PROFILE

		Grads Employed by Function	% Avg. Salary
Career Rating	93		
Percent employed at graduation	67	Marketing	23 $87,074
Percent employed 3 months after graduation	78	Operations	10 $85,375
		Consulting	1 NR
Average base starting salary	$88,958	Management	10 $77,125
Primary Source of Full-time Job Acceptances		Finance	29 $85,308
School-facilitated activities	65 (66%)	HR	18 $89,467
Graduate-facilitated activities	26 (26%)	**Top 5 Employers Hiring Grads**	
Unknown	8 (8%)	Hewlett-Packard (7), Ensign Group (6), Intel (5), Cisco (5), Proctor & Gamble (4)	

BROCK UNIVERSITY
FACULTY OF BUSINESS

GENERAL INFORMATION
Type of school   Public
Academic calendar   Semester

SURVEY SAYS...
Solid preparation in:
Accounting
Teamwork
Communication/interpersonal skills
Presentation skills

STUDENTS
Enrollment of parent institution	17,000
Enrollment of MBA Program	64
% male/female	70/30
% part-time	34
% international	8
Average age at entry	26
Average years work experience at entry	4

ACADEMICS
Academic Experience Rating	**83**
Student/faculty ratio	1:1
Profs interesting rating	82
Profs accessible rating	86
% female faculty	24

Academics

Boasting "an excellent reputation for its business degree, especially in accounting," Ontario's Brock University offers "a great learning environment with many opportunities" to a youngish student body. Because it's a relatively new program, the Brock MBA is especially open to innovation; students praise the curriculum for "encouraging fresh ideas" and the faculty for its "innovative approaches to teaching."

MBAs also love Brock's "small class sizes, which enable professors to recognize students' strengths and weaknesses and permit students to approach professors when they need help. It is a relaxed learning environment" in which "an atmosphere of trust between students and school personnel" prevails. Brock profs "are knowledgeable and well-respected in their fields" and "do an exceptional job of presenting the material in an attention-grabbing style." Students appreciate how their instructors "always have time to talk outside of class and are extremely helpful."

The Brock MBA includes a sequence of required courses and an option for specialization in one of four "streams": accounting, finance, human resource management, and marketing. Students may also opt for a general MBA. Students may choose to replace up to three of their specialization courses with independent research projects; such projects are subject to the approval of the dean and the MBA Committee. Students may attend on a full-time or part-time basis. The full-time degree can be completed in two years; the part-time degree must be completed within six years. Part-timers who adhere to the suggested schedule—two courses during each of the Fall and Winter terms, one course during the Spring term—can finish the program in four years.

Career and Placement

The Faculty of Business at Brock University maintains a Business Career Development Office to serve all undergraduates and graduates enrolled at the faculty. The office manages the Graduate Recruitment Program for MBA students; through this program, students have access to employer information sessions and on-campus interviews. A Career Expo in the fall brings employers to campus for recruiting purposes. The office also offers resume review, interviewing and job search workshops, online job search tools, and assistance with international job placement. Brock offers a co-op MBA to students who are at the university for at least two semesters of study (beginning in the fall term) and who maintain at least a 75 average in the program. Co-op provides access to additional workshops, seminars, and a speaker series in addition to co-op placement. The program is open to international students.

Student Life and Environment

Brock's student body "is extremely diverse," with "many international students [who arrive] through the International Student Program and through exchanges." Students also bring "a diverse set of experiences" to the program: "Some students come to the program with many years of experience, while others bring a more academic perspective to the program." Some feel the balance needs to shift in this area, reporting that "way too many students have no work experience and are straight out of undergrad." Everyone agrees that "some here, especially the part-time students, have great work experience and input to contribute."

ADMISSIONS CONTACT: ANDREA JOHNSON, GRADUATE RECRUITMENT OFFICER
ADDRESS: TARO HALL, 500 GLENRIDGE AVENUE ST. CATHARINES, ON L2S 3A1 CANADA
PHONE: 1-888-528-0746 • FAX: 905-688-4286
E-MAIL: MBA@BROCKU.CA • WEBSITE: WWW.BROCKU.CA/BUSINESS

Brock's student-run Graduate Business Council "does an excellent job of giving us opportunities to connect outside of the classroom. They organize pub nights and socials as well as organize us to compete in business case competitions." Campus amenities include "state-of-the-art" gymnasiums, fitness centers, an Olympic size swimming pool, squash and tennis courts, outdoor fields, and a hiking trail system that runs through campus and beyond, leading to the Niagara Escarpment. Students report that school facilities "are great for athletics, food, and study areas."

Hometown St. Catharines, located a mere 12 miles from Niagara Falls and just 70 miles from Toronto, "has a great lifestyle," with "tons of trendy nightclubs in St. Catharines and Niagara Falls." Students describe the overall vibe as "easy-going" with "not too much hustle and bustle," which they ascribe to "the nature of being located in St. Catharines." The city is accommodating enough that "many students spend a lot of time off campus."

Admissions

Admission to the MBA program at Brock is based on five main criteria. The quality of one's undergraduate education is most important; Brock seeks students with at least a 3.0 undergraduate GPA. A minimum GMAT score of 550 is required, as are three letters of recommendation from professors and/or supervisors at work; a personal statement; and a resume. Applications are assessed holistically; strength in one area may be sufficient to compensate for weaknesses elsewhere, according to the school's website. Professional experience, though preferred, is not required. Those whose first language is not English must demonstrate English proficiency through the TOEFL or TWE; students with TOEFL scores between 570 and 620 may be admitted conditionally pending completion of an ELS program).

FINANCIAL FACTS

Annual tuition (in-state/ out-of-state)	$9,170/$18,340
Fees	$450
Cost of books	$1,000
Room & board (on/off-campus)	$8,800/$7,050

ADMISSIONS

Admissions Selectivity Rating	85
# of applications received	159
% applicants accepted	45
% acceptees attending	70
Average GMAT	600
Range of GMAT	550–700
Average GPA	3.4
TOEFL required of international students	Yes
Minimum TOEFL (paper/computer)	620/260
Application fee	$105
International application fee	$105
Regular application deadline	8/1
Early decision program?	No
Deferment available	Yes
Maximum length of deferment	1 year
Transfer students accepted	Yes
Transfer application policy:	
All transfer applications must submit the same documentation as regular applicants. Their transcripts are assessed for transfer credits (up to 10) during the admissions review process.	
Non-fall admissions	Yes
Need-blind admissions	Yes

EMPLOYMENT PROFILE

Career Rating	86
Percent employed at graduation	60
Percent employed 3 months after graduation	93
Average base starting salary	$70,000

BRYANT UNIVERSITY
GRADUATE SCHOOL OF BUSINESS

GENERAL INFORMATION
Type of school	Private
Academic calendar	Semester

SURVEY SAYS...
Solid preparation in:
General management
Teamwork
Communication/interpersonal skills
Presentation skills

STUDENTS
Enrollment of parent institution	3,598
Enrollment of MBA Program	180
% male/female	64/36
% out-of-state	41
% part-time	78
% minorities	10
% international	13
Part-Time MBA Program	
Average age at entry	27
Average years work experience at entry	5
Full-Time MBA Program	
Average age at entry	23
Average years work experience at entry	1

ACADEMICS
Academic Experience Rating	**78**
Student/faculty ratio	26:1
Profs interesting rating	83
Profs accessible rating	82
% female faculty	26
% minority faculty	30

Prominent Alumni
David M. Beirne '85, Gen. Partner, Benchmark Capital Partners; WSharon Garavel '85, VP of Operations & Quality, GE Capital Solutions; Thomas Hewitt '68, CEO, Interstate Hotels and Resorts; Joseph Puishys '80, President, Honeywell Environmental & Combustion Controls; Kristian P. Moor '81, President and CEO, Chartis Insurance.

Academics

Bryant University's MBA program is "designed with working professionals in mind," according to the school, and students report that the school definitely lives up to this reputation. The "structured part-time program [makes] it easy to balance the rigors of graduate study with the reality of maintaining a full-time job," one student explains.

The part-time MBA at Bryant is structured as a cohort program, "where students are accepted to the school as a class and move through the entire program together." Students complete all core courses as part of a single team (although "some professors allow teams to change members") before "becoming separated in electives." Most students find the cohort system a huge plus, saying it promotes "a lower dropout rate, better student interaction, and deeper relationships and networks with students." One writes, "The cohort approach is excellent. I have built great relationships with my fellow students, and teachers are in tune with where classes stand in the learning process, making the flow from semester to semester seamless."

Bryant recently added a full-time one-year program. The first class graduated in 2010, and some members say of their experience, " Being the first year there were some kinks, but they have tried to put together a program that is not only academically beneficial but also gives us some real-world exposure."

Students note that "Bryant has a very good reputation" in the region. Professors "have industry experience, they are not only theoretical or academic," and most "are enthusiastic...the passion they exude filters throughout the class." Administrators "are very open and approachable. We recently voted on electives, and there is one that wasn't selected. Instead of being stuck, the dean is setting aside time to consider how we might be able to add the course. I've been very pleased that this type of response has been the norm [for] any issues that arise and not just a glowing example." Academically, "the environment is challenging, yet fair and well-supported. It is a great investment." As one student sums up, "Overall Bryant is probably the best value MBA in New England outside of Cambridge/Boston. The campus is very clean and safe, the professors are all gray hairs with decades of experience in the real world, and the library and gym facilities are exceptional."

Career and Placement

The Amica Center for Career Education serves the undergraduate students, graduate students, and alumni of Bryant University. The office provides counseling services, assessment instruments, and workshops on resume writing, interviewing, and job-search skills. The Center maintains a career services library and facilitates contact with alumni through the school's Alumni Career Network. It should be noted that the Bryant MBA is designed for working professionals, many of whom are looking to improve their positions with their current employers rather than seeking new jobs. The school draws students from a number of local employers, including Amgen, Amica Mutual Insurance, Citizens Bank, Davol, Fidelity Investments, Gilbane Building Company, Perot Systems, Rogers Corporation, Stanley Bostich, Tyco Healthcare, and Zebra Technologies.

ADMISSIONS CONTACT: KRISTOPHER SULLIVAN, ASSISTANT DEAN OF THE GRADUATE SCHOOL
ADDRESS: 1150 DOUGLAS PIKE SMITHFIELD, RI 02917-1284
PHONE: 401-232-6230 • FAX: 401-232-6494
E-MAIL: GRADPROG@BRYANT.EDU • WEBSITE: WWW.BRYANT.EDU

Student Life and Environment

Located in "a safe rural setting," Bryant's campus is "beautiful and inviting, not too big but not too small." "All the buildings and grounds are maintained impeccably," one student repots. The campus is also "on the cutting edge of technology," with "every room completely equipped." Bryant has an active undergraduate campus life, but opinion is mixed on the extent to which Bryant MBAs take advantage. Some students observe that "Students in the graduate program are very removed from the undergraduate programs and students. For the most part, graduate students are not involved in campus life, although attendance is high at 'graduate only' events. Most graduate students do not get involved with campus organizations," though all this may change in coming years as the full-time, one-year MBA program expands. On the other hand, a student in the one-year program notes that "Life at Bryant is very community-focused. The school tries to involve all students in all activities, such as on-campus presenters, homecoming activities, etc."

Though the extent of graduate student involvement on campus might be up for debate, the on-campus diversity is not. There's "a really strong multicultural element" at Bryant. In the part-time program, "students range in age from early 20s to late 50s," and many have "more than 10 years of business experience. The diversity of professional backgrounds brings an added element to the class, as we have many engineers in the program." Students tend to be "competitive" and "like to challenge one another to promote and foster positive results. It's a very team-orientated program."

Admissions

Applicants to graduate programs at Bryant University must provide the Admissions Department with the following materials: a completed application form; a personal statement of objectives (no less than 500 words long); a current resume; one letter of recommendation from a professional who can evaluate your skills and potential; official transcripts for all previous undergraduate and graduate work (regardless of whether it resulted in a degree); and an official GMAT score report. In addition to the above, international students must also provide a statement of finances, professional translation and interpretation of any foreign language transcripts, and, for those whose first language is not English and who did not earn an undergraduate degree from an English-speaking institution, an official TOEFL score report. An interview is "strongly encouraged."

FINANCIAL FACTS

Annual tuition	$29,880
Cost of books	$1,200
Room & board	$13,200
% of students receiving aid	33
% of first-year students receiving aid	56
% of students receiving loans	33
% of students receiving grants	3
Average award package	$21,518
Average grant	$22,528
Average student loan debt	$21,414

ADMISSIONS

Admissions Selectivity Rating	71
# of applications received	80
% applicants accepted	73
% acceptees attending	69
Average GMAT	523
Range of GMAT	465–570
Average GPA	3.07
TOEFL required of international students	Yes
Minimum TOEFL (paper/computer)	580/237
Application fee	$80
International application fee	$80
Regular application deadline	7/15
Early decision program?	No
Deferment available	Yes
Maximum length of deferment	1 year
Transfer students accepted	Yes
Transfer application policy: Transfer credits are limited to two courses taken within the last 3 years with a grade of B (3.0) or better from an AACSB-International accredited master's program.	
Non-fall admissions	Yes
Need-blind admissions	Yes

BUTLER UNIVERSITY
COLLEGE OF BUSINESS ADMINISTRATION

GENERAL INFORMATION

Type of school	Private
Academic calendar	Semester

SURVEY SAYS...

Students love Indianapolis, IN
Good peer network
Solid preparation in:
Doing business in a global economy

STUDENTS

Enrollment of parent institution	4,438
Enrollment of MBA Program	270
% male/female	70/30
% part-time	93
% international	6
Average age at entry	29
Average years work experience at entry	7

ACADEMICS

Academic Experience Rating	87
Student/faculty ratio	20:1
Profs interesting rating	85
Profs accessible rating	88
% female faculty	20
% minority faculty	12

Joint Degrees

PharmD/MBA, 6 years full-time to completion.

Academics

At Butler, an MBA student may major in finance, international business, leadership, or marketing. There is also a combined program leading to both a Doctor of Pharmacy and an MBA. All students must take a core curriculum, which begins with what's known as the Gateway Experience, a day-long immersion in the activities of a local business followed by an evening of analysis by the students. Students "love how this school works with local businesses to enhance experiential learning and to also provide a sort of 'symbiotic' relationship." The students "help the businesses by offering solutions to their current problems, and they also help us learn by providing us with actual business problems." That practical exercise gets students thinking about scenarios that will show up in future courses such as ethics, financial management, managerial finance, and related subjects, which account for about half the credits needed for the degree. The students then move into areas of specialization and finish things off with what's known as a Capstone Experience, which is somewhat of an extended version of the Gateway Experience they encountered at the beginning of the program. It addresses more complex issues and allows the student to make good use of the knowledge gained during the program.

"Flexibility" is a definite key word when in comes to describing the MBA program at Butler. "It is not a lockstep program, meaning that if I missed a class, I would not have to wait an entire year to retake it," one student explains. "The approach that the school takes at understanding that the part-time MBA students have lives outside of the classroom" is a strength of the program, students say, and "I travel frequently for my job, and I have yet to encounter a professor who has not attempted to help ensure I would be caught up when I return," adds another. Classes are offered on evenings and weekends, and though some students would like to see the schedule of classes expanded, they uniformly praise the quality of teaching that goes on in them. "The professors at Butler are excellent. They make themselves available to their students and truly enjoy interaction in the classroom," and "Professors have demonstrated mastery of their subject as well as an ability to relate theory of a subject to real-world situations," students say.

Throughout the program students find that the emphasis is on "high-quality and high-value, in-class lessons, and great real-world learning." Many courses are taught by professors in conjunction with business leaders, and the case studies and problems students work on in class are most often real-world business issues. "Incorporation of practical business cases and scenarios in conjunction with the course work" is a hallmark of the program, as are "up-to-date, relevant [classroom] activities and problems" and "small class size, so that one can really get to know the other students and the professors."

ADMISSIONS CONTACT: STEPHANIE JUDGE, DIRECTOR OF MARKETING
ADDRESS: COLLEGE OF BUSINESS, 4600 SUNSET AVENUE INDIANAPOLIS, IN 46208-3485
PHONE: 317-940-9221 • FAX: 317-940-9455
E-MAIL: MBA@BUTLER.EDU • WEBSITE: WWW.BUTLERMBA.COM

Career and Placement

Most of Butler's MBA students are employed while completing the degree. Some students feel that "since almost all students are already working full-time, there is little emphasis on new career opportunities," remarking that Career Services seem to be geared toward undergraduates. However, being located in Indianapolis, a city ranked in the "Top 10 Best Places for Business and Careers" in a ranking of the 200 largest metropolitan areas in the United States by *Forbes*, helps with prospects. "There are thousands of top companies right in our backyard," students point out. "Many local companies have allowed students to participate in hands-on business simulations, and prominent business leaders have come to campus to speak and network." Butler's "regional reputation with business and community leaders and the number of very successful alumni working in the region" are also strong points for those who are job hunting.

Eli Lilly and Company, Roche, M&I Bank, Regions Bank, Firestone, and the NCAA are among those who employ Butler's MBA graduates.

Student Life and Environment

MBA students love Butler's small-school atmosphere and personal touch. "Butler is a beautiful campus. Although I live off campus, I am always surprised by how many students are around participating in various on-campus activities," notes one student. "My classes include students from different ethnic, cultural, social, and religious backgrounds. This leads to great discussions on the wide varieties of experiences we have had in our careers." "Everyone on campus is engaging and helpful. Because of the small campus and class size, you get to know a number of peers, professors and administration well," others say. Students find the workload moderate, the administration responsive, and their fellow students friendly and focused. Noting that "the school is small enough to have a personal touch," "You can easily get the help and support that you need." Some would like better child care support and more opportunities to involve spouses in their academic lives, but they like the attention both faculty and staff pay to the needs of working students with families. "Most are busy with careers just like I am, but that gives us common ground to support each other in balancing work, school, and life," one student says.

Admissions

The Admissions Committee for the MBA program at Butler weighs an applicant's undergraduate GPA, GMAT score, letters of recommendation, and work experience most heavily. Though most students are from the Midwest, residency is not a factor that Butler, a private institution, takes into account, and it also does not consider a student's extracurricular activities. In 2008 the average GPA of recently admitted students was 3.33/4.0, and their GMAT score ranged from 560–650. Most students had 7 or more years of work experience.

FINANCIAL FACTS

Annual tuition	$9,000
Cost of books	$800
Room & board (on-campus)	$8,530

ADMISSIONS

Admissions Selectivity Rating	**87**
# of applications received	142
% applicants accepted	63
% acceptees attending	57
Average GMAT	600
Range of GMAT	560–650
Average GPA	3.33
TOEFL required of international students	Yes
Minimum TOEFL (paper/computer)	550/213
Regular application deadline	7/1
Regular notification	7/10
Early decision program?	No
Deferment available	Yes
Maximum length of deferment	1 year
Transfer students accepted	Yes
Transfer application policy: Up to 9 credit hours, pending approval.	
Non-fall admissions	Yes
Need-blind admissions	No

CALIFORNIA POLYTECHNIC STATE UNIVERSITY—SAN LUIS OBISPO
ORFALEA COLLEGE OF BUSINESS

GENERAL INFORMATION
Type of school	Public
Academic calendar	Quarter

SURVEY SAYS...
Students love San Luis Obispo, CA
Good social scene

STUDENTS
Enrollment of parent institution	19,777
Enrollment of MBA Program	119
% male/female	69/31
% out-of-state	23
% part-time	15
% minorities	7
% international	5
Average age at entry	26
Average years work experience at entry	3

ACADEMICS
Academic Experience Rating	**78**
Student/faculty ratio	25:1
Profs interesting rating	74
Profs accessible rating	87
% female faculty	20
% minority faculty	15

Joint Degrees
Master of Business Administration/ Master of Science in Engineering Management (MBA/MS). Master of Business Administration/Master of Science in Computer Science (MBA/MS). Master of Business Administration/Master of Science in Electrical Engineering (MBA/MS). Master of Business Administration/Master of Science in Mechanical Engineering (MBA/MS). Master of Business Administration/Master of Science in Industrial and Technical Studies (MBA/MS). Master of Business Administration/Master of Science in Industrial Engineering (MBA/MS). Master of Business Administration/Master of Science in Civil and Environmental Engineering (MBA/MS).

Academics

Poised at the intersection of business and technology, California Polytechnic State University's graduate business programs are a great choice for students with a background in applied science or architecture. As a state school, Cal Poly is "less expensive" than comparable private institutions, yet its AACSB-accredited business programs are rigorous, current, and intimate, enrolling fewer than 50 students each year. The MBA comprises 60 to 64 total credits for graduation; depending on your schedule, availability, and academic goals, students have "the option for one- or two-year completion" of the MBA, with an academic focus in general management, agribusiness, or graphic communication document systems management. The chance to complete a specialized MBA in just one year—even without an undergraduate degree in business—is a huge advantage to this program. At the same time, students must be prepared to work hard: not only is coursework challenging and accelerated, "the program requires students [to] maintain a 3.0 GPA" throughout. For working students who want to pursue a degree part-time, or for those who'd like to explore concurrent employment or internship opportunities, Cal Poly also allows students to take fewer than the full-time 16 units per quarter, through a secondary MBA track.

For many, the major benefit of Cal Poly is its strength in technical fields, which students can exploit through technology-oriented electives, or through formal dual degree programs with other academic departments. Of particular note, the school offers joint MS and MBA degrees in engineering management and engineering fields (including aerospace, civil and environmental, computer science, and more). Almost 40 percent of current MBA candidates are concurrently enrolled in a master's program, telling us that, "the dual degree program is fantastic" at Cal Poly. A current student adds, "The MBA/EMP dual degree program they offer was exactly the type of program that I was looking for, and Cal Poly has a tremendous reputation in the world of engineering."

A hallmark of the Cal Poly MBA program is the "learning-by-doing teaching style," which encourages students to develop applicable skills through coursework. To that end, classes and assignments include teamwork, case studies, and presentations. Additionally, the "international business course"—a unique offering within an accelerated program—gives students the opportunity to study a foreign economy and business practices during a two-week trip overseas. In recent years, the program took students to India and China. Students can also tailor their education by pursuing research projects in conjunction with Cal Poly faculty, or by competing with other business students in national case study and strategy competitions. When it comes to Cal Poly's faculty and administration, it's a mixed bag. Here, "There are some professors that are outstanding, and some that are good in their field, but not good at teaching." A student summarizes, "It's a cliché, but the more effort you put into the program, the more you will get out of the program."

Career and Placement

At Cal Poly, Career Services hosts career fairs and networking events for the entire school community. They also offer career preparation assistance, including resume revisions and interview skills workshops. While graduate students are free to participate in these offerings, "the career services are more geared towards undergrad" at Cal Poly. Fortunately, the school boasts an excellent reputation and strong ties to the local community. Even without extensive assistance, around 85 percent of Cal Poly students have accepted a job offer by graduation; three months out, 100 percent of MBA alumni are employed.

Top employers of Cal Poly MBA graduates include Northrup Grumman, Raytheon, Rantec, General Dynamics, Sun MicroSystems, Deloitte Consulting, Qualcomm, IBM, Agilent Technology, Amgen Inc., Lawrence Livermore Labs, Pacific Gas & Electric, USDA, Dept of Veterans Affairs, KPMG, Pratt & Whitney, Morgan Stanley, Boston Scientific, PriceWaterhouseCoopers, Sandia National Lab, Lam Research, Columbia Sportswear, Adelaida Cellars. The mean base salary for MBA graduates is $100,000.

Student Life and Environment

Life is good at Cal Poly. Located on a hilltop overlooking San Luis Obispo, "the college campus is gorgeous" and the surrounding town is beautiful, friendly, and student-oriented. No wonder many students say "the location" is among the Cal Poly's greatest assets. Graduate students have access to the school's excellent recreation center, health center, and library, and they may even choose to live on campus. Within the business school, the Graduate Students in Business Association (GSBA) organizes social gatherings for students and faculty, as well as fundraisers and professional development events.

Cal Poly offers just a few graduate programs; therefore "the undergrads overwhelmingly outnumber the graduate students" on campus. Fortunately, "the Graduate School of Business students have their own Room/Lounge with a fridge, microwave, tables, computers, and whiteboards"—a nice enclave for the more mature crowd. At Cal Poly, most MBA candidates are "young, career-driven" professionals, principally from technical or engineering backgrounds.

Admissions

To be eligible for admission to Cal Poly's Orfalea College of Business graduate programs, students must possess an undergraduate degree from an accredited university, and a competitive undergraduate GPA and GMAT scores. For accepted applicants, the mid-80 percent GPA range was 2.8 to 3.75; for GMAT scores, the mid-80 percent range was 580 to 750. To be eligible for dual degree programs, students must meet the eligibility requirements for both programs.

Prominent Alumni

Robert Rowell, President, Golden State Warriors; Linda Ozawa Olds, Founder, Jamba Juice; Bill Swanson, Chairman & CEO, Raytheon Company; Burt Rutan, Pres., Scaled Composites, designer SpaceShipOne; Gary Bloom, CEO, Veritas.

FINANCIAL FACTS

Annual tuition (in-state/ out-of-state)	$13,870/$23,790
Fees	$2,869
Cost of books	$1,638
Room & board	$8,793
% of students receiving aid	45
% of first-year students receiving aid	25
% of students receiving loans	45
% of students receiving grants	5
Average award package	$11,634
Average grant	$2,176

ADMISSIONS

Admissions Selectivity Rating	95
# of applications received	243
% applicants accepted	59
% acceptees attending	84
Average GMAT	615
Range of GMAT	580–750
Average GPA	3.28
TOEFL required of international students	Yes
Minimum TOEFL (paper/computer)	550/213
Application fee	$55
International application fee	$55
Regular application deadline	7/1
Early decision program?	No
Deferment available	No
Transfer students accepted	Yes
Transfer application policy: Maximum of 8 units transfer.	
Non-fall admissions	No
Need-blind admissions	Yes

EMPLOYMENT PROFILE	
Career Rating	96
Percent employed at graduation	85
Percent employed 3 months after graduation	100
Average base starting salary	$100,000

CALIFORNIA STATE POLYTECHNIC UNIVERSITY—POMONA
COLLEGE OF BUSINESS ADMINISTRATION

GENERAL INFORMATION
Type of school   Public

SURVEY SAYS...
Solid preparation in:
General management
Teamwork
Communication/interpersonal skills
Presentation skills
Computer skills

ACADEMICS
Academic Experience Rating   **67**
Profs interesting rating   83
Profs accessible rating   74

Academics

The College of Business Administration at California Poly Pomona parlays the university's strengths in engineering and technology into a unique MSBA in Information Systems Auditing, a program that prepares students for careers in computer forensics and information systems security. "It's a nationally-recognized program," students here remind us while insisting we feature it prominently in the school's profile. Consider it done.

Cal Poly also offers a more conventional MBA program, with concentrations available in accounting, finance, marketing, operations management, human resources, hospitality management, entrepreneurship, information management, and international business. Even in its more conventional pursuits, however, the school forges a unique tack. A Cal Poly MBA, students inform us, is a "hands on MBA" with "a technical emphasis" that encourages a "learning-by-doing philosophy." One student explains: "Very few professors will stand in the front of the room and lecture for four hours. Classes are very interactive and students are provided with plenty of opportunities to present their opinions and put learning points to use." Students also report that "All classes require students to work on group projects, which prepares you well to work in teams in real world." Cal Poly also offers a Professional MBA at its Metro in Downtown Los Angeles (minimum two years' supervisory work experience mandatory for entry).

Cal Poly is "one of the few state universities using the quarter system," which "makes things fly by. When you are starting the quarter, you already have to start studying for midterms; when mid-quarter arrives, you already have to start seeking for affordable books for the next quarter." Fortunately, the program has "exceptional instructors" who "are mostly young (in their forties) and provide access to modern management principles and practices while at the same timing give information about classical management principles." Good instruction helps ease the academic burden some, but students warn that many here "reduce their work responsibilities to cope with the heavy course load. It's not an easy place for full-time/part-time working professionals."

Career and Placement

Career services for MBAs here are provided by the Cal Poly Pomona Career Center (CPPCC), a central office serving all undergraduate and graduate students at the university. The CPPCC provides all standard counseling and placement services. Many students do not even use the service; they already have jobs that they hope to advance in by earning a graduate degree. One who does complains unequivocally: "The career placement is terrible at Cal Poly for MBA students. Ninety-five percent of companies come in looking for engineers, accountants and some hospitality, and most are only interested in undergrads for entry-level positions. I'm considering crashing a UCI career day just to get referrals." Employers who frequently recruit at Cal Poly include: Bank of America, Boeing, Deloitte, Disneyland Resort, Ernst and Young LLP, IBM, Kaiser Permanente, KPMG International, Merrill Lynch, PricewaterhouseCoopers, Proctor & Gamble, Southern California Edison, and Wells Fargo Bank.

ADMISSIONS CONTACT: SANDRA ROHR, ADMINISTRATIVE SUPPORT COORDINATOR
ADDRESS: GRADUATE BUSINESS PROGRAM, 3801 WEST TEMPLE AVENUE POMONA, CA 91768
PHONE: 909-869-2363 • FAX: 909-869-4559
E-MAIL: GBA@CSUPOMNA.EDU • WEBSITE: CBA.CSUPOMONA.EDU/CBA/

Student Life and Environment

The Cal Poly student body consists of "smart working professionals" who are "very diverse both ethnically and professionally." Their professions "range anywhere from human resources managers to information technology managers to production line managers," and "several *Fortune* 500 companies" are represented here. Academically, the group includes "students who graduated with degrees in engineering, psychology, liberal arts, science, etc." The quality of students has "a significant impact on the class [because they] have plenty of experience to draw from" and "have a lot to say about the subjects that we are learning." Students "raise the bar [for each other] by being very competitive in studies and overall creativity and innovation."

Because most students are "full-time workers and commuters to classes," they typically "do not get too involved with on-campus activities." "MBA students here are more focused on their careers and families then on being connected to the school," one student explains. That's too bad, because the Cal Poly Pomona campus is "beautiful. It's nestled in between mountains and is full of trees," and students tell us that makes it a "good place to study and lead a stress-free life." Perhaps things will change in the years to come; some here already detect a campus that is "transferring from a commuter school to a school with a lot of campus activities. All of the events are getting bigger and better. The exposure of the campus is being seen in the size and popularity of the events."

Admissions

Cal Poly Pomona operates on a quarterly academic schedule; the school accepts MBA applications for each quarter. All of the following components of the application are carefully considered: complete postsecondary academic record as reflected in official transcripts; GMAT scores (must be no more than five years old); two letters of recommendation from current or former employers; and a resume. Applicants who attended an undergraduate institution at which English is not the primary language of instruction must provide official TOEFL scores. Applicants must meet the following criteria to be considered for admission: an overall undergraduate GPA of at least 3.0; a minimum GMAT score of 450; and, if required, TOEFL scores of at least 580 on the paper-and-pencil test, 237 on the computer-based test, or 92 on the Internet-based test. Meeting minimum requirements does not guarantee admission to the program.

ADMISSIONS

Admissions Selectivity Rating	**60***
TOEFL required of international students	Yes
Minimum TOEFL (paper/computer)	580/237
Application fee	$55
International application fee	$55
Application Deadline/Notification	
Round 1:	6/15 / 8/1
Round 2:	10/1 / 10/31
Round 3:	12/1 / 1/30
Round 4:	3/1 / 3/30
Early decision program?	No
Deferment available	No
Transfer students accepted	Yes
Transfer application policy: Candidates must meet our admission criteria.	
Non-fall admissions	Yes
Need-blind admissions	Yes

CALIFORNIA STATE UNIVERSITY—CHICO
COLLEGE OF BUSINESS

GENERAL INFORMATION
Type of school   Public
Academic calendar   Semester

SURVEY SAYS...
Students love Chico, CA

STUDENTS
Enrollment of parent institution	17,132
Enrollment of MBA Program	64
% male/female	67/33
% part-time	44
% minorities	58
% international	56
Average age at entry	25
Average years work experience at entry	7

ACADEMICS
Academic Experience Rating	74
Student/faculty ratio	22:1
Profs interesting rating	80
Profs accessible rating	78
% female faculty	30
% minority faculty	20

Prominent Alumni
Tim Sandford, Senior Director of Global Procurement, Siemens; Prabhakar Kalavacheria, Partner, KPMG, LLP. Member, International Accounting Standards Board; David Hodson, Entrepreneur Co-Founder and CTO of iPrint Technologies;

Academics

With a "unique combination of excellent and caring professors, a well-run program, and a great environment," the College of Business at California State University—Chico well serves the needs of its part-time and full-time MBA student populations. Students tout the school's convenient location, strong regional reputation, and affordable tuition in citing their reasons for choosing the school.

The Chico MBA requires students to complete 30 credit hours of graduate-level courses. The core curriculum consumes 24 credit hours; the remaining six are devoted to electives. Students may take all their electives in one discipline to earn a degree with a concentration in accounting, finance, human resources, management information systems, marketing, or supply chain management; or, they may take electives in a variety of disciplines to earn a general management degree. Students lacking undergraduate coursework in business and management may be required to complete up to 27 credit hours of foundation coursework prior to commencing the MBA. Students can complete the MBA program in 18 months or less by attending on a full-time basis; all students must complete the program within five years of commencing. A Professional MBA (PMBA) program is also available. PMBA classes meet on Saturdays only; students complete the PMBA in 24 months.

Students here appreciate the program's emphasis on group projects. One tells us: "Nearly every class has teamwork. This truly prepares you for the real working world" and helps students develop "people and presentation skills and good verbal and written communication skills." They also approve of the curriculum's focus on "developing practical skills that make graduates effective," calling the Chico MBA "a great hands-on education system." Professors here "are caring and have both practical and academic knowledge" and "are willing to back up students in regard to group-related problems. There is a great support system in this MBA program." On the downside, some here feel that "the program could be improved by making it more rigorous, or at least by requiring a higher level of commitment from the students."

Career and Placement

MBA career-planning activities at Cal State Chico are handled by the Office of Career Planning and Placement, which, according to the school's website, "engages in various recruitment, retention, graduation, and placement activities to support its diverse student population." About one in five Chico MBAs works in government after receiving the MBA; one in ten is employed in the financial services sector. Operations and production, consulting, and finance and accounting each claim about 20 percent of Chico MBAs. Students report that the MBA program "does a great job of placing graduates in jobs." Top employers of Chico MBAs include Accenture, Bearing Point, Capgemini, Chevron, Deloitte & Touche, Ernst & Young, IBM, KPMG, and SAP.

ADMISSIONS CONTACT: GRADUATE SCHOOL ADMISSIONS,
ADDRESS: 400 WEST FRIST STREET CHICO, CA 95928-0722
PHONE: 530-898-6880 • FAX: 530-898-6889
E-MAIL: MBA@CSUCHICO.EDU • WEBSITE: WWW.CSUCHICO.EDU/COB/

Student Life and Environment

Cal State Chico is situated on a "charming campus in a great town with a huge park." Chico itself is "a wonderful community with enough diversity to make it interesting, but small enough to make the lifestyle warm and comfortable." The combined result of these factors is "a friendly environment" for MBAs. One student speculates the Chico "has more entrepreneurs per capita than any other US city, which means a creative and business-supportive environment." Top employers in the area include Enloe Medical Center, the county and city governments, the university, TriCounty Banks, Sierra Nevada Brewery, and SunGard Bi-Tech.

The Cal State Chico campus offers "quite a bit of activities and performances," but few MBAs have the time for such diversions. As one explains, "Generally, MBA classes are during evenings, so there's really not much time for us to be involved in.... During the daytime, there's quite a bit of things going on, but for us who hold full-time jobs, we don't really have time and energy for it."

Chico attracts a youngish student body; reports one MBA, "Most of my fellow students are younger and unmarried. They are friendly and nice to work with but only half have work experience that adds value to the program." The "team-oriented" program requires students to be "cooperative and friendly," and most here are "wonderful and hardworking, although there are a few slackers." Students note "a large disparity between the international students, students who came directly from their undergraduate studies, and those students who have been working for several years."

Admissions

Applicants may be admitted to the Chico MBA program under the 'Conditionally Classified' status if they (1) have earned a satisfactory undergraduate GPA (at least 2.75 for the final 60 semester hours of undergraduate work or comparable grades in a more recently undertaken graduate program); (2) have received acceptable GMAT or GRE scores (at least 50th percentile in math and verbal portions); and (3) have demonstrated aptitude in business and management through academic and/or career achievement. Applicants must provide the Admissions Committee with official transcripts for all undergraduate and graduate work; an official score report for the GMAT or GRE; letters of recommendation; a personal statement of purpose; and a resume. Two years of work experience is recommended but not required. Students advance from "Conditionally Classified" status to "Classified Status" once they have completed (or placed out of) the non-degree "common body of knowledge" prerequisites to the MBA program. Finally, students are reclassified as degree candidates once they have successfully completed at least nine credit hours toward the MBA degree.

FINANCIAL FACTS

Annual tuition (in-state/ out-of-state)	$4,716/$10,818

ADMISSIONS

Admissions Selectivity Rating	76
# of applications received	62
% applicants accepted	47
% acceptees attending	48
Average GMAT	550
Range of GMAT	480–640
Average GPA	3.22
TOEFL required of international students	Yes
Minimum TOEFL (paper/computer)	550/213
Application fee	$55
International application fee	$55
Regular application deadline	4/1
Early decision program?	No
Deferment available	No
Transfer students accepted	Yes
Transfer application policy: A maximum of 9 Semester units of post-baccalaureate transfer and/or CSU Chico Open University course-work may be included in a master's degree program, provided that the courses are from an AACSB accredited institution.	
Non-fall admissions	Yes
Need-blind admissions	No

EMPLOYMENT PROFILE

Career Rating	86	Grads Employed by Function	% Avg.	Salary
Percent employed at graduation	85	Marketing	10	NR
Percent employed 3 months after graduation	85	Consulting	17	NR
		Management	17	NR
Average base starting salary	$60,000	Finance	10	NR
Primary Source of Full-time Job Acceptances		HR	10	NR
School-facilitated activities	7 (27%)	MIS	36	NR
Unknown	26 (73%)	**Top 5 Employers Hiring Grads**		
		Chevron USA, CapGemini, IBM, Deloitte, KPMG		

CALIFORNIA STATE UNIVERSITY—EAST BAY
COLLEGE OF BUSINESS AND ECONOMICS

GENERAL INFORMATION
Type of school	Public
Academic calendar	Quarter

SURVEY SAYS...
Happy students
Solid preparation in:
Quantitative skills
Computer skills

STUDENTS
Enrollment of parent institution	14,749
Enrollment of MBA Program	338
% part-time	100
Average age at entry	28
Average years work experience at entry	3

ACADEMICS
Academic Experience Rating	**72**
Student/faculty ratio	28:1
Profs interesting rating	83
Profs accessible rating	75
% female faculty	16
% minority faculty	47

Prominent Alumni
Mark Mastov, Founder of 24 Hour Fitness; Bill Lockyer, State Treasurer of California; Mike Abary, Senior VP, Sony IT Products Division; Mahla Shagfi, Senior VP and Regional Director, Union Bank of California; Judy Belk, Senior VP Rockefeller Philanthropy Advisors.

Academics

A cost-effective public school in the San Francisco Bay Area, California State University East Bay offers an MBA program that is "the perfect blend of affordability and expediency." "Perfectly suited for working adults," the "flexible schedule options" and evening classes make the program convenient for professionals who live and work in the San Francisco Bay Area. In fact, "The vast majority of our students also work full time and the school makes it easy to integrate a course load into their life." While working professionals predominate in the MBA class, CSUEB attracts students from "various experience levels." Those with more time to devote to their studies can "finish the program in one year." To top off the return on investment, CSUEB's low in-state tuition cost is "significantly less than other schools in the area." Fortunately, the low cost does not translate into hassles and red tape; the business school is well-run. A student reassures us, "I have found the administration within the business school to be much more organized and accommodating than within the university as a whole. I get answers quickly and access to information when I need it."

The MBA curriculum is divided into proficiency requirements, fundamental courses, core courses, and option courses. Proficiency requirements can be waived if a student has completed equivalent coursework in these areas; however, students are not required to complete the proficiency courses before applying to the program. In addition, students must complete a course in Globalization, Innovation, and Sustainability, as well as a capstone experience, which usually takes the form of a a real-life project experiential learning. One of the benefits of a CSUEB degree is that students have the opportunity to focus on their education on one of a range of business specialties, including entrepreneurship, finance, human resources and organizational behavior, information technology management, marketing management, international business, or operations and supply chain management.

CSUEB maintains a strong "reputation in the area," and the administration has been steering the school on a steady course of improvement. While the teaching staff can be "hit or miss, with some excellent and some terrible" professors, the school has recently "brought in new talented teachers" to the program. In the school's MBA program, as well as their graduate programs in economics and taxation, you'll find "Great professors who have first hand knowledge of the outside business world." Fellow students also contribute to the learning experience through their "interesting and very diverse working experience that enable valuable contribution in class discussions."

Career and Placement

Academic Advising and Career Education at CSUEB serves the school's undergraduate and graduate community. The AACE organizes job fairs and other campus recruiting events, while also offering counseling services aimed specifically at graduate students. While the school lacks a dedicated MBA career office, there are plenty of resources for MBA candidates. A current student attests, "I was able to get advice on transitioning into a new field (Finance from Retail), access to an almost overwhelming number of positions to apply for, and access to a wide field of employers. I was able to secure interviews with 10 different employers, multiple offers, and a position in my new field paying significantly more than my previous position as a tenured manager—all through my campus career development center." According to the Academic Advising and Career Education's Success Report, graduate students from the College of Business and Economics had a salary range of $20,000 to $150,000, with an average salary of $73,250.

Student Life and Environment

Located in the Oakland suburb of Hayward, California, CSUEB is enviably positioned near both San Francisco and the Silicon Valley. Drawing a largely local population, CSUEB is "generally a commuter school" for both undergraduates and graduate students. At the same time, students report that the school "has been slowly growing to change its identity," incorporating more student life and activities into campus culture. At the same time, most busy business students commute to school while working full-time, and, therefore, they do not always have the opportunity to participate in any extracurricular activities or take advantage of the campus. Nonetheless, attending CSUEB is comfortable and convenient, and "the Valley Business center is excellent."

Drawing its student population from the San Francisco Bay Area, as well as internationally, diversity is a mainstay of the CSUEB experience. Within the business school, you'll meet "lots of international students" from "diverse backgrounds," which, in the classroom, translates into an "excellent experience for a global economy." Students say, "CSU East Bay is exceptionally diverse and it is difficult to pigeonhole the students—they are young, old, of all races and ethnicities, from all kinds of industries, and many of them are married, with children."

Admissions

To be considered for admission at California State University East Bay, students must score in the 20th percentile of the GMAT in both the verbal and quantitative sections. Students must also have a GPA of at least 2.5 for all upper division undergraduate coursework as well as minimum index score of 1050 (Upper Division GPAx 200) + total GMAT score. Exceptions to these minimum requirements are rarely made.

FINANCIAL FACTS

Annual tuition	$5,952
Fees	$9,183
Cost of books	$1,734
Room & board (on/ off-campus)	$11,043/$12,078
% of students receiving aid	30
% of first-year students receiving aid	28
% of students receiving loans	23
% of students receiving grants	22
Average award package	$13,890
Average grant	$5,124
Average student loan debt	$20,928

ADMISSIONS

Admissions Selectivity Rating	**72**
# of applications received	286
% applicants accepted	65
% acceptees attending	58
Average GMAT	557
Range of GMAT	520–600
Average GPA	3.1
TOEFL required of international students	Yes
Minimum TOEFL (paper/computer)	550/213
Application fee	$55
International application fee	$55
Regular application deadline	6/30
Regular notification	8/30
Early decision program?	No
Deferment available	No
Transfer students accepted	Yes
Transfer application policy: With the approval of the director of the program students can transfer up to 13 quarterly units (from AACSB accredited schools)	
Non-fall admissions	No
Need-blind admissions	No

CALIFORNIA STATE UNIVERSITY—FRESNO
CRAIG SCHOOL OF BUSINESS

GENERAL INFORMATION
Type of school	Public
Academic calendar	Rotating-spring and fall starts

SURVEY SAYS...
Solid preparation in:
General management
Doing business in a global economy

STUDENTS
Enrollment of parent institution	19,416
Enrollment of MBA Program	128
% part-time	100
Average age at entry	30

ACADEMICS
Academic Experience Rating	**89**
Student/faculty ratio	20:1
Profs interesting rating	90
Profs accessible rating	79
% female faculty	30
% minority faculty	18

Academics

A "low price and high quality education" make the Craig MBA at California State University Fresno "a great value" for its predominantly regionally-based student body. One MBA calls it "an amazing deal," explaining that "The cost of the program is extremely reasonable, course times are tailored to full-time working students, and the cost of living is low. For students with children and families, CSUF provides an excellent opportunity to complete the coursework while living at a high standard of living, sending their children to top-notch, schools and not wasting hours commuting."

Craig has developed "a good overall MBA program" that provides "a solid foundation," students tell us. MBAs here benefit from "real-world business training" through "real-world case studies and projects" and "heavy involvement in the community. [The program is] very close to the community and many local businesses." Professors complement this aspect of the program; most "are either actively involved in research, consulting, or full-time management roles in the industries in which they teach. Many of the professors are frequently called upon by companies throughout the region for special consulting projects." The curriculum also provides "a solid ethical foundation" that students appreciate and "keeps up with current events in the business world and integrates them into the curriculum," another plus.

Craig offers both a conventional MBA (three-hour weekday evening sessions, Monday through Thursday) and a cohort-based Executive MBA (full-day sessions on Saturdays prefaced by several intensive Wednesday through Saturday foundation sessions at the start of the first term). In both, "Expectations for the classes are clear and teachers push students to reach these expectations." Instructors "are very demanding, expecting nothing but focus and excellence from the students," but "are also very personable and accommodating to assist students toward learning and excelling in the program." A few "come only slightly prepared and use textbook-provided PowerPoint presentations like a crutch," but students are pleased with the overall quality of instruction. Craig's busy students also appreciate that "the program is run like a well-operated business," with a staff that "takes care of the details, allowing the students to focus on school."

Career and Placement

Craig MBAs do not enjoy a dedicated Career Services Office. Instead, a university-wide office that serves both undergraduates and graduate students handles all MBA-related internship and placement services. The office provides a number of recruiting events and other support services, but few are designed to serve the unique needs of MBAs. An MBA Student Association offers additional services, organizing events that "connect MBA students with alumni, faculty, and local community, and business leaders" in order to "build a professional network and lay the foundation for friendships that will last a lifetime." Most Craig students are part-time students with full-time jobs (many attend at their employers' expense), reducing the need for MBA-specific career service.

Student Life and Environment

The Craig MBA "is very well suited to full-time professionals" who "come to class straight from work at an 8 to 5 job," catering to their desire to get on and off campus with maximum benefit and minimum hassle. "Although strictly 'social' activities sponsored by the program are limited, evening and weekend group project work among students is frequent," so students do interact outside the classroom fairly regularly. For those so inclined, "There are many different organizations doing things on campus all the time: movies, meetings, discussions, etc." as well as "clubs for almost every interest" and "many activities [primarily] for MBA students."

Overall, however, "campus life is not great" at Fresno State, because "Most students live off campus, so the campus is dead on the weekends and after 7 P.M. Everyone also commutes by car because public transportation is horrible, just city buses with limited routes." As one student puts it, "The campus life is horrible outside of sports events, because no one has a reason to be on campus on the weekends or in the evenings. If they could improve this, the college experience at Fresno State would be equal to any other large high quality college."

Students in the Executive MBA program typically visit the campus on weekends only, and their extracurricular involvement in negligible. The program "is made up of students who live as far as 150 miles away. It is a diverse group of students who have excelled in other areas of their lives, especially in their careers. Students are professionals returning to gain business academic resources to continue to further their careers or enter the world of being an entrepreneur." The conventional MBA program is also largely populated with busy professionals; "The majority hold full-time jobs and more than half are married. They are intelligent and focused on excelling in the program."

Admissions

Applicants to the Craig MBA program must submit the following materials: official GMAT score report (minimum score of 550 with ranking at or above the first quartile on verbal and mathematics portions); a completed online application; two letters of recommendation; a statement of purpose/essay; and official transcripts for all post-secondary academic work. International non-English-speaking students who did not graduate from an English language institution must also submit an official TOEFL score report. Admissions decisions are based primarily on GMAT scores and academic performance over the last 60 semester credits of undergraduate work; applicants must have earned at least a 2.5 GPA over that period to merit consideration. Work experience, demonstrated management potential, and the applicant's statement of purpose are also considered.

FINANCIAL FACTS

Annual tuition (in-state/ out-of-state)	$5,610/$14,170

ADMISSIONS

Admissions Selectivity Rating	88
# of applications received	153
% applicants accepted	42
Average GMAT	601
Range of GMAT	500–770
Average GPA	3.4
TOEFL required of international students	Yes
Minimum TOEFL (paper/computer)	550/213
Application fee	$55
International application fee	$55
Application Deadline/Notification	
Round 1:	4/1 / NR
Round 2:	11/1 / NR
Early decision program?	No
Deferment available	Yes
Maximum length of deferment	1 year
Transfer students accepted	Yes
Transfer application policy: Transfer must be from and AACSB accredited school, 9 units may be transfer on an approved basis and applicant must meet standard admittance requirements (same as a new applicant).	
Non-fall admissions	Yes
Need-blind admissions	No

CALIFORNIA STATE UNIVERSITY—FULLERTON
MIHAYLO COLLEGE OF BUSINESS AND ECONOMICS

GENERAL INFORMATION
Type of school   Public
Academic calendar   Semester

SURVEY SAYS...
Solid preparation in:
General management
Teamwork
Computer skills

STUDENTS
Enrollment of parent
  institution   27,408
Enrollment of MBA Program   414
% part-time   75
% international   25
Average age at entry   26

ACADEMICS
Academic Experience Rating   77
Student/faculty ratio   19:1
Profs interesting rating   84
Profs accessible rating   87
% female faculty   25
% minority faculty   33

Prominent Alumni
Steve Charton, President and CEO, Hospitality; Kevin Costner, Businessman and Actor; Steve G. Mihaylo, President & CEO, Telecommunications; Jim Woods, Chairman Emeritus & CEO (Retired), Aerospace; Richard Davis, President, CEO & Chairman, Banking.

Academics

California State University—Fullerton offers a part-time MBA program featuring "flexible schedules," a "location in the vibrant Orange County economy," and a "low tuition that allows me to pay for my education without going into a large degree of debt." In this last regard it differs from its neighbor and competitor UCLA. Students here feel that, despite the difference in price, both schools share "the prestige of being a major source of a highly educated workforce in California."

MBA students at Cal Fullerton must complete between 11 and 15 courses, depending on their academic background in business disciplines. Ten core courses cover fundamental principles; some cover basics (e.g., financial accounting, microeconomics) and others take an interdisciplinary approach (e.g., legal and ethical environment in business, management information in the corporate environment). Students with undergraduate degrees in business or extensive professional experience may be able to place out of some core courses. Students may devote four courses to developing a concentration (five if they chose international business). Concentrations are available in accounting, economics, business intelligence, entrepreneurship, finance, information systems, international business, management, management science, marketing, risk management and insurance. A general degree is also available.

Students praise the school's "teaching philosophy, which is underpinned with both practical and theoretical applications" and love "the amount of attention that is given to each student." "It's great that each professor has not only learned my name, but has gotten to know me individually in the classroom," one student says, "I feel that most all professors are very receptive to providing assistance and guidance related to students' professional work experience and are happy to support positive opportunities for students." Some here feel that the program could be more challenging, telling us that "building more rigor in would help." Others, while noting, "The workload is not overly heavy," tell us that they "feel as though we are learning quite a lot."

Career and Placement

Cal State Fullerton Career Planning and Placement Center provides career services to MBAs at both the Fullerton and Irvine campus locations. Services include walk-in counseling, interview tips, resume review, and job databases. Students may continue to utilize these facilities for up to one year after they graduate for a $25 fee. While some here report that there are "a lot of career events organized," others complain that "due to the lack of institutional funding and a small administrative staff, students are not provided enough opportunity to network among local professionals and entities." Employers who most frequently hire Cal Fullerton MBAs include Ernst and Young, LLP, KPMG, The Home Depot, Mercury Insurance, Pacific Life, and Target.

ADMISSIONS CONTACT: PRE-ADMISSION ADVISOR, PRE-ADMISSION ADVISOR
ADDRESS: PO BOX 6848 FULLERTON, CA 92834-6848
PHONE: 657-278-3622 • FAX: 657-278-7101
E-MAIL: MBA@FULLERTON.EDU • WEBSITE: BUSINESS.FULLERTON.EDU/GRADUATEPROGRAMS

Student Life and Environment

"CSUF is a commuter school" with "small class sizes that provide a sense of community in the program," but most here "usually just go to class and go home." Those who can stick around for extracurriculars will find a "very diverse" campus life among "over 37,000" other students, "which makes for a very busy campus." There are plenty of business-related activities, including "15 clubs and organizations…and job fairs with what feels like countless employers looking to hire students," but these are targeted almost exclusively to the undergraduate population. The MBA program does do a good job of "supporting a lot of students from abroad."

Fullerton nurtures a campus culture that is "relaxed yet serious enough to get to work when necessary." "Buildings are located close enough to each other so that students from other schools can talk to each other," one student says. While MBAs have complained in the past about classroom resources, a new facility opened in August 2008 to address those concerns.

Most students here are "full-time working professionals who contribute greatly to the program. They have a great deal of work experience, are very competitive, and provide great insights during class discussions." They're an older group who are "very outspoken," but whose professional experience justifies their being so. The student body also includes "a good portion of foreign exchange students."

Admissions

Cal State Fullerton requires the following of all applicants to its MBA program: an "acceptable bachelor's degree from an appropriately accredited institution," with a minimum GPA of 2.5 for the final two years of undergraduate work; two sets of transcripts for all undergraduate and graduate academic work; GMAT scores reflecting placement in the top 50 percent on the verbal, analytical, and quantitative sections of the exam; a completed background sheet that includes a summary of academic and professional experience and a personal statement of purpose; updated professional resume, up to three letters of recommendation from employers or professors; and demonstrated proficiency in calculus, statistical analysis, and introductory-level computer programming. International students whose first language is not English must score a minimum 570 on the TOEFL paper-and-pencil exam, 230 on the computer-based exam, or 88 on the iBT. Applications are accepted for the fall and spring semesters and are processed on a rolling basis. Programs can fill prior to the application deadline, so applying as early as possible is highly recommended.

FINANCIAL FACTS

Annual tuition (in-state/ out-of-state)	$8,742/$15,438
Fees	$636
Cost of books	$3,900
Room & board (on/off-campus)	$8,772/$11,124
Average award package	$4,000
Average grant	$4,000

ADMISSIONS

Admissions Selectivity Rating	85
# of applications received	543
% applicants accepted	36
% acceptees attending	52
Average GMAT	553
Range of GMAT	490–600
Average GPA	3.31
TOEFL required of international students	Yes
Minimum TOEFL (paper/computer)	570/230
Application fee	$55
International application fee	$55
Regular application deadline	5/31
Early decision program?	No
Deferment available	No
Transfer students accepted	Yes
Transfer application policy: Students must apply as a new student and courses will be evaluted. Students may transfer in up to 9 units.	
Non-fall admissions	Yes
Need-blind admissions	Yes

CALIFORNIA STATE UNIVERSITY—LONG BEACH
COLLEGE OF BUSINESS ADMINISTRATION

GENERAL INFORMATION

Type of school	Public
Academic calendar	Semester

SURVEY SAYS...
Solid preparation in:
Marketing
Accounting
General management

STUDENTS

Enrollment of parent institution	36,800
Enrollment of MBA Program	367
% male/female	58/42
% out-of-state	1
% part-time	70
% minorities	15
% international	30
Average age at entry	29
Average years work experience at entry	5

ACADEMICS

Academic Experience Rating	80
Student/faculty ratio	25:1
Profs interesting rating	92
Profs accessible rating	87

Joint Degrees
The MFA/MBA is a three year, full time program (including two summer sessions) offered jointly between the Theatre Arts Department and the Graduate School of Business.

Academics

For practically minded business students, CSU Long Beach offers three affordable and efficient MBA options: the Fully Employed MBA, the Self-Paced Evening MBA, and the one-year Accelerated MBA. Catering to working adults in the Southern California region, these "focused, fast-paced, and competitive" programs are specially designed to help students balance professional and personal commitments while pursuing their educations. To that end, the programs are highly successful, offering a convenient and user-friendly educational experience. A current student explains, "The ease and inclusiveness of the school are exemplary. Every professor or administrator is highly accessible, and I have no problems at all getting into needed classes." Another adds, "The FEMBA program is specifically targeted to busy professionals, holding classes exclusively on Saturdays. The program administration goes out of their way to make sure we are getting everything we need." Indeed, CSU Long Beach runs smoothly from top to bottom, and "there is good communication with the administration to make suggestions for changes and improvement."

Like administrators, CSU faculty is "closely connected with [the students], and they are extremely helpful." Bringing both real-world and academic expertise to the classroom, "professors are well-versed and have a strong command of the subjects they teach." In addition, the diversity of the "required coursework gives a balanced exposure to different business areas." Interaction is highly encouraged and "student-driven class activities" form the backbone of the educational experience. In fact, be prepared for "as many as three to five major group projects per semester." As a result, your classmates at CSULB will also be your teachers. Drawing a range of students from the region, graduate students at CSU are "very diverse in work experience, culture, backgrounds, and motivation." What's more, the school boasts "a large percentage of international students that are able to contribute a lot of different perspectives to the program. With the move towards a global business world, making these connections during the program are a big bonus." Most importantly, when it comes to group work, "all of the students that survived the program are smart, creative, team players, and committed to doing the best that they can each and every quarter."

Career and Placement

Students at the College of Business Administration are served by the MBA Career Management Services, which maintains an MBA job board and hosts on-campus recruiting events in a variety of business disciplines. The services also maintains contact with the school's alumni and maintains an up-to-date online job database for MBA students. In addition, students may choose to attend special workshops and seminars to assist in career development, or participate in one of the many large, campus-wide career fairs hosted by CSULB's Career Development Center. Many big companies have visited campus in recent years, including Alaska Airlines, Accountants Incorporated, American Capital Group, California National Bank, CVS/Carmark Pharmacy, First Investors, Kelly Scientific Resources, Ameriprise Financial, Boeing, Northrop Grumman, and Comerica Bank, among others.

ADMISSIONS CONTACT: MARINA FREEMAN, GRADUATE PROGRAMS ADMISSIONS MANAGER
ADDRESS: 1250 BELLFLOWER BOULEVARD LONG BEACH, CA 90840-8501
PHONE: 562-985-5565 • FAX: 562-985-5590
E-MAIL: MBA@CSULB.EDU • WEBSITE: WWW.CSULB.EDU/COLLEGES/CBA/MBA

Student Life and Environment

A safe, cooperative, and pleasant campus atmosphere creates an appealing backdrop for CSULB's MBA programs. A current student explains, "The campus is very casual, and the students are very nice and friendly. It is like a second home, and I feel comfortable and safe in the environment." Since CSULB's graduate programs are designed for working adults, it's no surprise that "most students are part time, working during the day and coming to school at night. The majority of MBA students are only on campus three to six hours per week." However, those who would like to augment their coursework with a bit of extracurricular stimulation should not despair: "There are opportunities to participate in seminars and other social events with the MBA Association" and "there's a strong nucleus, which mingles off-campus throughout the semester." No matter what your background, you'll feel at home at this large public school community, which draws students who "range from open-minded thinkers to engineers who like to think by the rules."

Admissions

Admissions criteria vary at CSU, depending on the program to which you are applying. In recent years, students entering the full-time, accelerated MBA had an average GMAT score of 520, an average GPA of 3.2, and an average age of 26. Evening MBA and Fully-Employed MBA candidates entered with a GMAT score of 555 and 536, respectively.

FINANCIAL FACTS

Annual tuition	$7,896
Fees (in-state/ out-of-state)	$3,758/$7,826

ADMISSIONS

Admissions Selectivity Rating	81
# of applications received	320
% applicants accepted	50
% acceptees attending	168
Average GMAT	555
Range of GMAT	460–670
Average GPA	3.24
TOEFL required of international students	Yes
Minimum TOEFL (paper/computer)	550/213
Application fee	$55
International application fee	$55
Regular application deadline	3/30
Regular notification	5/1
Early decision program?	No
Deferment available	Yes
Maximum length of deferment	1 semester
Transfer students accepted	Yes
Transfer application policy: Must meet our admissions criteria	
Non-fall admissions	Yes
Need-blind admissions	Yes

CALIFORNIA STATE UNIVERSITY—NORTHRIDGE
COLLEGE OF BUSINESS AND ECONOMICS

GENERAL INFORMATION

Type of school	Public
Academic calendar	Semester

SURVEY SAYS...

Solid preparation in:
Marketing
General management
Teamwork
Communication/interpersonal skills
Presentation skills
Quantitative skills

STUDENTS

Enrollment of parent institution	33,000
Enrollment of MBA Program	195
% male/female	56/44
% out-of-state	19
% part-time	84
% international	11
Average age at entry	28
Average years work experience at entry	5

ACADEMICS

Academic Experience Rating	**82**
Student/faculty ratio	22:1
Profs interesting rating	81
Profs accessible rating	73
% female faculty	18
% minority faculty	6

Academics

"California State University—Northridge's greatest strengths are its diverse student population, its understanding of the educational needs of the surrounding community, and its commitment to students' educations," MBAs in this "affordable" Los Angeles graduate program tell us. Students, predominantly full-time employees attending the school in evenings in order to improve their promotability, appreciate that the program is "inexpensive and designed to get you through your degree quickly." They also benefit from the fact that "CSUN has a great reputation for producing great MBA graduates. The school is well-respected in the area as well as [in] the defense industry."

CSUN's MBA program offers electives in accounting, economics, entertainment, finance, information systems, international business, management, and marketing. MBAs enjoy "an open work environment" in which "fellow students are not extremely competitive, which creates a good learning environment." They also respect how the program's leaders are "driven to expand the curriculum to be state-of-the-art while also adding value to the degree by recognizing alums' and students' accomplishment on a regular basis. There is a passion for business at this school that I did not expect." This passion permeates the classroom, where "teachers are friendly and excited about what they do," although students warn: "The quality of the professors has a wide variety. Some are great, extremely effective, and impactful; others are not engaging, don't seem interested in teaching, and are not effective."

CSUN stresses a "relevant curriculum" through such innovations as its entertainment industry concentration. The program is "self-directed," meaning that students have some flexibility in sequencing their coursework. While students agree: "For the money, it can't be beat," they also recognize some shortcomings inherent to state funding. One wishes that "the state would stop cutting the budget so much." Others concede that the program "lacks some of the extras that private and better-funded schools enjoy" and yearn for such perks as "an option to travel abroad as a culminating experience project—many of us work for multinational companies" and "more extensive use of online collaborative learning in a global business-related framework." The MBA program is adding an international trip in spring 2011.

Career and Placement

The Career Center at California State University—Northridge serves the entire undergraduate and graduate student population. Counselors there offer workshops in interviewing, resume-writing, and job search strategies. The office arranges on-campus interviews and alumni meet-and-greets, and it also maintains a database of job listings. Students tell us: "There are monthly speakers from the community who are business leaders. They are informative about what to expect in future job pursuits." Professors, likewise, can be a useful source of job leads and advice. In addition, the school has added an MBA Career Services Program and an MBA internship program. The vast majority of MBAs here are not actively looking to leave their current employers, so the school's lack of career resources is not a major inconvenience to them.

ADMISSIONS CONTACT: DEBORAH COURS, PH.D., DIRECTOR OF GRADUATE PROGRAMS
ADDRESS: NORTHRIDGE, CA 91330-8380
PHONE: 818-677-2467 • FAX: 818-677-3188
E-MAIL: MBA@CSUN.EDU • WEBSITE: CSUN.EDU/MBA

Student Life and Environment

"CSUN is a commuter school, so many people live outside campus" and "don't spend much time here." A typical student describes the routine: "I attend class twice per week for lectures and communicate via conference calls or weekend meetings with fellow students. It's a fairly typical commuter college experience." Even those who only visit for classes appreciate the campus's "easy access to cafes and restaurants for when you don't have time to stop for dinner" and recognize that "the campus has made good efforts to make space available in the library and other buildings for students to meet when they are required to do group work." Those who choose to immerse themselves in campus life tell us that the experience is "exceptional. The school has a tremendous amount of student-related activities and accommodations. As an alumnus of CSUN's undergraduate program, I am very proud to be a member of the community."

CSUN MBAs are "inquisitive and genuine for the most part, and looking for new career paths or networking opportunities. Many intend to continue working where they are after graduation." They tend to be "laid-back and open-minded—i.e., not brutally competitive—which is perfect for the mid-career person looking to enhance his skill set." They are also "very encouraging to each other. We have study groups and are always willing to help each other. Everyone has different backgrounds, and we're able to learn from each others' experiences."

Admissions

Admission to the CSUN MBA program is competitive. Applicants are expected to have achieved a minimum GPA of 3.0 during their final two years (60 semester credits/90 quarter credits) of undergraduate work and to reach at least the 50th percentile rank on all sections of the GMAT. A minimum of two years post-undergraduate professional experience is acceptable, although three to five years is the preferred length. Applicants whose native language is not English must earn a minimum score of 213 on the computer-based TOEFL. CSUN requires all students without an undergraduate business degree (or equivalent coursework) to complete five foundation courses. These can be completed in an accelerated one year pre-MBA certificate program, but are not required prior to admission.

FINANCIAL FACTS

Annual tuition (in-state)	$6,236
Cost of books	$1,300
Room & board (off-campus)	$12,414

ADMISSIONS

Admissions Selectivity Rating	89
# of applications received	340
% applicants accepted	24
% acceptees attending	71
Average GMAT	588
Range of GMAT	460–710
Average GPA	3.3
TOEFL required of international students	Yes
Minimum TOEFL (paper/computer)	550/213
Application fee	$55
International application fee	$55
Regular application deadline	5/1
Early decision program?	No
Deferment available	No
Transfer students accepted	Yes
Transfer application policy: 9 units max transfer credit	
Non-fall admissions	Yes
Need-blind admissions	Yes

CALIFORNIA STATE UNIVERSITY—SAN BERNARDINO
COLLEGE OF BUSINESS AND PUBLIC ADMINISTRATION

GENERAL INFORMATION

Type of school	Public
Academic calendar	September to June

SURVEY SAYS...
Friendly students
Good social scene
Good peer network
Cutting-edge classes
Smart classrooms

STUDENTS

Enrollment of parent institution	17,852
Enrollment of MBA Program	349
% male/female	54/46
% out-of-state	1
% part-time	45
% minorities	23
% international	32
Average age at entry	29
Average years work experience at entry	5

ACADEMICS

Academic Experience Rating	**78**
Student/faculty ratio	13:1
Profs interesting rating	78
Profs accessible rating	67
% female faculty	17
% minority faculty	10

Prominent Alumni
Yuzo Tobisaka, President Mitsubishi Corporate; Larry Sharp, CEO Arrowhead Credit Union; Dr. Gnana Dev, Medical Director of Sugery—Arrowhead Hospital; Yusuf Akcayoglu, President of TAV Construction—Turkey/Dubai; Kerrick Bubb, KWB Wealth Manager.

Academics

Students tell us that the College of Business and Public Administration at California State University—San Bernardino offers "a good mix of practical and theoretical business applications and concepts" in a program that delivers in a variety of disciplines, all "at a very good price." According to those we surveyed, the program is the perfect size, "small enough that you can build relationships with the professors and administration, but also big enough to give students some independence and freedom to do things on their own."

Entrepreneurship leads the pack here. The program is well supported by the CBPA's Inland Empire Center for Entrepreneurship, a research center that promotes entrepreneurship in the surrounding area. Operations management is also reportedly strong. Students here may pursue either a part-time or full-time MBA with one of eight concentrations: accounting, entrepreneurship, finance, information assurance and security, mgmt, information management, management, marketing, and operations management/supply chain management. While a few feel that "it would be nice if the school had a general MBA option, rather than having to select a major," most see no problem with the current system.

San Bernardino operates on a quarterly schedule, meaning that the term flies by quickly. The curricular emphasis "is practical and exposes you to real-world experiences." One student offers this example: "For my MBA project, l did a marketing plan for a company in Palm Springs called Crystal Pure drinking water. They manufacture water-purifying machines, and from the plan we developed they realized $1.6 million in sales within six months. Their websites had many hits from customers around the world. Professors "are seasoned in their fields of study and provide real-world application for what we learn. We don't just read about business, we create it, and we grow it."

Career and Placement

As of spring 2010, CSUSB opened a new Graduate Career Services Center solely designed to serve MBA/MSA students and alumni, which provides career services, international advising, graduate internships, alumni programs and exit interviews. Students have access to workshops on interview skills, resume writing and job search methods. Students can also schedule mock interviews, phone appointments or private appointments. Some students wish that the school "would build stronger relationships with local companies," while others note that "there really isn't a demand for MBA graduates in San Bernardino County." However, many agree, "The teachers are always there to help when you need them . . . and are very willing to help in getting jobs or career advice," and faculty "bring their students in touch with prospective employers outside the classroom."

Employers likely to hire CSUSB MBAs include Arrowhead Credit Union, GE Transportation, Enterprise Rent-a-Car, American Express Financial, ESRI, Internal Revenue Service, the Central Intelligence Agency, Target, Arthur Anderson, FEMA, Wells Fargo, and almost all the regional accounting firms, banks, and credit unions.

Student Life and Environment

The CSUSB MBA program "has students from all over the world who make class discussions interesting and make one grow an appreciation of different cultures." MBAs here "are encouraged to do research and be involved in community activities," and the school offers "leadership development programs and faculty research seminars where students are also invited. This prepares students for future leadership roles in society." The degree to which students can take advantage of these opportunities varies; a sizeable portion of the student body is part-time, typically pursuing a degree in addition to full-time employment.

The CSUSB campus "provides the latest technology for the students and an extremely comfortable setting." All students enjoy "plenty of places to relax and the scenery (the campus recently received an excellence award for its facilities management)." A recently completed student union includes "a new cutting-edge recreational sports facility," and students tell us, "The Fullerton Art Museum is also a great leisure escape." Conveniently, "Everything is within walking distance, and you get to know familiar faces because the campus is not as large as other CSUs."

Admissions

Applicants to the CSUSB MBA program must first apply for admission to the university, which requires a baccalaureate with a GPA of at least 2.5 for the final two years of undergraduate work. Students clearing this hurdle may then apply for admission to the MBA program. Applicants must submit two sets of official transcripts for all post-secondary academic work; an official GMAT score report; and a personal statement. Three letters of recommendation are recommended but are technically optional. International students must additionally provide an Affidavit of Financial Support and TOEFL scores (minimum score 550 paper, 213 computer, 79 Internet). The minimum requirement for admission to the program is a formula score of 1050 under the formula ((undergraduate GPA x 200) + GMAT score), with a minimum GMAT score of 470 (along with a minimum score of 10% on both the verbal and quantitative sections) and a minimum GPA of 2.5. No student may begin MBA work without having earned at least a C grade in the following undergraduate courses or their equivalent at another accredited institution: financial accounting I and II; microeconomics; macroeconomics; business finance; corporate finance; information management; business law; management and organization behavior; expository writing for administration; strategic management; marketing principles; business statistics; and principles of supply chain management.

FINANCIAL FACTS

Fees	$11,040
Cost of books	$2,400
Room & board	
(on/off-campus)	$19,000/$21,000
% of students receiving aid	66
% of first-year students receiving aid	66
% of students receiving loans	66
% of students receiving grants	2
Average award package	$18,500
Average grant	$20,000
Average student loan debt	$28,800

ADMISSIONS

Admissions Selectivity Rating	72
# of applications received	278
% applicants accepted	66
% acceptees attending	50
Average GMAT	529
Range of GMAT	470–640
Average GPA	3.2
TOEFL required of international students	Yes
Minimum TOEFL (paper/computer)	550/213
Application fee	$55
International application fee	$55
Regular application deadline	7/1
Regular notification	8/1
Application Deadline/Notification	
Round 1:	4/1 / 5/1
Round 2:	5/1 / 6/1
Round 3:	6/1 / 7/1
Round 4:	7/1 / 8/1
Early decision program?	Yes
Deferment available	No
Transfer students accepted	Yes
Transfer application policy:	
Only three approved graduate courses may be transferred into our MBA Program from approved U.S. universities.	
Non-fall admissions	Yes
Need-blind admissions	No

EMPLOYMENT PROFILE

Career Rating	73	**Top 5 Employers Hiring Grads**
		Arrowhead Credit Union, Target, Enterprise, ESRI, IRS

CARNEGIE MELLON UNIVERSITY
TEPPER SCHOOL OF BUSINESS

GENERAL INFORMATION
Type of school	Private
Academic calendar	Mini-semester

SURVEY SAYS...
Smart classrooms
Solid preparation in:
Operations
Quantitative skills

STUDENTS
Enrollment of parent institution	11,084
Enrollment of MBA Program	753
% male/female	79/21
% part-time	53
% minorities	28
% international	23
Average age at entry	28
Average years work experience at entry	5

ACADEMICS
Academic Experience Rating	98
Student/faculty ratio	5:1
Profs interesting rating	88
Profs accessible rating	89
% female faculty	14
% minority faculty	1

Joint Degrees
Computational Finance & MBA (Dual, 2.5 years); Software Engineering & MBA (Dual, 2.5 years); Law & MBA (Dual, 3–4 years); Software Engineering & MBA (Dual, 2 years); Environmental Engineering & MBA (Dual, 2 years); Civil Engineering & MBA (Dua, 2 years). MBA/Public Policy (Heinz) (2.5 years, Dual).

Prominent Alumni
David A. Tepper, CEO & Founder, Appaloosa Management; David Coulter, Managing Director & Sr. Adv., Warburg Pincus LLC; Lewis Hay III, President & CEO FPL Group; Yoshiaki Fujimori, President & CEO of GE Japan; Pamela Zilly, Sr. Managing Dir., The Blackstone Group.

Academics

Situated near downtown Pittsburgh, Carnegie Mellon's Tepper School of Business is "recognized by employers as the best quantitative MBA program in the country." Students are drawn to this school because of its "excellent quantitative reputation and core competencies in technology and entrepreneurship." One student captures the unique strengths of the school by describing it as "a small start-up with a tight-knit family, unparalleled intellect and bleeding-edge coursework that's going to change the game. Tepper channels and exemplifies the best reasons why you really want an MBA: genuinely relevant skills—not fluff—that sharpen your blade and make you lethal in the business world." The school's approach can also be neatly summarized by its "Tepper 3C Philosophy: Content, Commitment, Community."

The program works "on a mini-system" in which the "students have new classes every seven weeks" and partake in a program that is "fast-paced, yet flexible, and prepares one for the grind of professional life." Students praise how "The school goes out of its way to put business students together with engineering and design students." One student also notes that "Ethics is woven into almost every class, whether we talk about making certain OTC swap contracts in international finance or decide upon sustainable practices in operations." There is general agreement that "The small atmosphere at Tepper makes for an intimate learning environment plus a highly customizable experience." At the same time, several students point out that "although the school is small in class size...[s]tudy spaces and meeting rooms are hard to come by."

The school's many assets include its "outstanding professors who teach from their own research" and "are very passionate about teaching and mentoring students. They make themselves available to students at any time not only for classes, but for career advice." In addition to a supportive faculty, students observe that "The administration is very responsive. Recently, they have deployed the 'Think Big' feedback mechanism which allows students to offer instant suggestions for immediately improving aspects of the program."

Career and Placement

Students are generally pleased with Tepper's "excellent job placement record" as well as its "wonderful recruiting relationship with technology companies from around the world." The key to the school's success in recruiting and placement is its devoted alumni network. "Alumni from Tepper feel strongly about the school and are very bonded and willing to help current students—this especially is something that Career Services has been able to exploit to help students in a very difficult job market." Offering an illustrative example, one student explained that "as internship recruiting started up and so many companies pulled back their recruiting, administration, faculty, and students utilized their connections in a concerted effort to provide internship recruiting opportunities which yielded another 100 percent placement of the 2010 class in the midst of a recession." Despite this excellent track record, students point out the need for improvement. "Being that Tepper is in Pittsburgh, PA, it seems hard to have companies on the West Coast (aside from Amazon.com) recruit at Tepper." Others feel that "recruiting is a little too concentrated in a few areas, namely operations research, IT consulting, and quantitative finance," and that although "the quality of companies is high (Amazon, McKinsey, Microsoft, etc.), and the salaries offered are competitive, the variety of employers and roles is not yet where it should be."

ADMISSIONS CONTACT: LAURIE STEWART, EXECUTIVE DIRECTOR OF MASTERS ADMISSIONS
ADDRESS: TEPPER SCHOOL OF BUSINESS, 5000 FORBES AVENUE PITTSBURGH, PA 15213
PHONE: 412-268-2272 • FAX: 412-268-4209
E-MAIL: MBA-ADMISSIONS@ANDREW.CMU.EDU • WEBSITE: WWW.TEPPER.CMU.EDU

Student Life and Environment

The city of Pittsburgh is "affordable, and jam-packed with cultural attractions and an endless supply of nooks and crannies to explore." Because of the lack of "on-campus housing, almost all business students live in two surrounding neighborhoods. There is a collection of bars/restaurants/shopping in these areas so you feel very connected to your classmates both on campus and at home." Despite the challenging schedule and workload, "there are a good number of opportunities to socialize with classmates," especially because "Tepper has many great traditions—from our weekly satire magazine, to our bi-weekly B**rs social event hosted by clubs and companies." During the B**rs events, "students are able to eat and drink for free, as well as socialize with classmates and their spouses."

Tepper attracts students who "tend to be very down-to-earth and humble" and who make up the "friendliest, most community-oriented group of MBAs you can imagine." According to one particularly enamored student, "If Tepper could bottle and sell the skills of my cohort, it would be the greatest business tool since the calculator." However, one student offers a slightly different viewpoint and cautions that most of the students "come from technical backgrounds, and so it is not an overwhelming amount of natural social butterflies."

Admissions

Applicants to the Tepper School of Business must submit an online application, three essays, unofficial transcripts of all academic work, GMAT scores, a current resume, and a comprehensive employment record. Applicants who are non-native speakers of English must also submit a TOEFL score report. The school encourages applicants to focus "more on the range, rather than the mean when reviewing class profile factors" and reports that "half of our students have GMAT scores below the median." While many of its students come from an engineering or science background, the school encourages candidates from diverse academic backgrounds and disciplines to apply.

FINANCIAL FACTS

Annual tuition	$49,200
Fees	$418
Cost of books	$1,300
Room & board	$15,000
% of students receiving aid	74
% of students receiving grants	74
Average award package	$41,181
Average grant	$12,790
Average student loan debt	$75,240

ADMISSIONS

Admissions Selectivity Rating	97
# of applications received	1,425
% applicants accepted	28
% acceptees attending	39
Average GMAT	690
Average GPA	3.35
TOEFL required of international students	Yes
Minimum TOEFL (paper/computer)	600/250
Application fee	$100
International application fee	$100
Application Deadline/Notification	
Round 1:	10/27 / 12/19
Round 2:	1/5 / 3/16
Round 3:	3/9 / 5/4
Round 4:	4/27 / 6/1
Early decision program?	No
Deferment available	No
Transfer students accepted	No
Non-fall admissions	No
Need-blind admissions	Yes

EMPLOYMENT PROFILE

		Grads Employed by Function	% Avg. Salary
Career Rating	98	Marketing	17 $101,773
Percent employed at graduation	86	Operations	2 $97,500
Percent employed 3 months after graduation	96	Consulting	22 $118,062
Average base starting salary	$103,012	Management	17 $97,681
Primary Source of Full-time Job Acceptances		Finance	38 $95,697
School-facilitated activities	102 (80%)	MIS	2 $82,500
Graduate-facilitated activities	23 (18%)	Strategic	5 $90,300
Unknown	3 (2%)	**Top 5 Employers Hiring Grads**	

Top 5 Employers Hiring Grads
McKinsey & Company (7), Deloitte Touche Tomatsu (7), Amazon.com (6), Thermo Fisher Scientific (5), H. J. Heinz Company (5)

CASE WESTERN RESERVE UNIVERSITY
WEATHERHEAD SCHOOL OF MANAGEMENT

GENERAL INFORMATION
Type of school   Private
Academic calendar   Semester

SURVEY SAYS...
Good social scene
Cutting-edge classes
Smart classrooms
Solid preparation in:
General management
Teamwork
Communication/interpersonal skills

STUDENTS
Enrollment of parent
  institution   10,052
Enrollment of MBA Program   435
% male/female   60/40
% out-of-state   65
% part-time   61
% minorities   10
% international   46
Average age at entry   26
Average years work experience
  at entry   3.25

ACADEMICS
Academic Experience Rating   82
Student/faculty ratio   12:1
Profs interesting rating   88
Profs accessible rating   93
% female faculty   14
% minority faculty   15

Joint Degrees
MBA/JD, 4 yrs; MD/MBA, 5 yrs.

Prominent Alumni
Chuck Fowler, CEO and President,
Fairmount Minerals; Dave
Cooperrider, PhD, Business as an
Agent of World Benefit; Joseph
Sabatini, Managing Director, JP
Morgan; Linda Rae, COO Keithley
Instruments; Don Gallagher,
President, Cleveland Cliffs.

Academics

The MBA candidates who attend the Weatherhead School of Management at Case Western Reserve University are drawn to its "innovative and well-designed courses," its "emphasis on sustainability and design," and its "extensive scholarship program." The school's MBA program "integrates Case's Design, Sustainability, and Organizational Behavior cases, all of which are top-ranked in the world" and offers a "wonderful learning environment that encompasses real-world application in projects with real companies and real issues to solve." One student enthuses that "The academic experience has been outstanding, professors are accessible and know you by name, and the small class size is conducive to excellent and thought-provoking class discussions."

In the fall of 2009, the school implemented a new "integrated" curriculum with decidedly mixed results. Some students opine that "The integrated curriculum really makes the classes fit together and make sense." They also appreciate that "the program was just redesigned to account for the recent changes in business following the current financial crisis" and that the "administration is working diligently to design a program that meets the needs of today's employers." On the opposite side of the fence are the students who argue that "while the concept is great the execution has been rocky." and that there was "a lack of coordination with planning the curriculum." They complain that the administration has been "very rigid, and at times [is] not willing to listen to the students" and that "academic changes tend to be very top-down and heavy-handed without seeming consideration for the student [point of view]."

While students may differ in their opinions of the administration and curriculum, the one thing they all seem to agree on is that "The professors are some of the greatest assets the school has to offer." "Not only are they world-renowned, but they make a point to get to know the students by name and make themselves available to us." "The professors are demanding but excellent purveyors of knowledge" and "some professors even go so far as to schedule special review sessions before exams." Students also tout the school's Dean as an asset especially after having undergone several years of turnover in that position. "The current Dean has been at Weatherhead for several years now and he offers incredible leadership for the school. He is very dynamic and inspiring."

Career and Placement

When it comes to recruiting and job placement, Weatherhead students deal with the stark reality that "unfortunately Cleveland is not a business capital of the world and it is difficult to bring in global/national firms here." They acknowledge that "part of the problem with a regional school is that it has difficulty attracting employers outside the region." Students reveal, "The career and placement center has brought in many companies, but has not always been clear on what they're looking for." One student suggests that there is also a need to leverage "the efforts of the professors to get good jobs to the students" while another recommends "more focus on jobs from student clubs, [and] more recruiters on campus."

On a brighter note, the school does offer "a class integrated into the program to [ensure] that all students are getting a good foundation in interviewing skills." In addition, "there are several companies that have shown interest and there is a strong alumni base.... *Fortune* 500 companies hiring at WSOM include Johnson & Johnson, 3M, Invacare, McKinsey, Kraft, Cleveland Clinic, Cliffs Natural Resources, RJ Reynolds, [and] Wells Fargo." According to one student, "there is a lot of private equity and banking in Cleveland, and many students have had internships in New York in finance."

Student Life and Environment

The Weatherhead School offers its students "plenty of opportunities to socialize on campus with Dean-sponsored luncheons and happy hours." On campus there is also "a common lounge where students can socialize or do team work and this area is highly utilized. The student clubs are very active and have made significant strides in club events this year." Many students also praise their school's "strong sense of community" and express that "learning cohort teams are quite high-functioning because there is a lot of support given to them by the faculty." The small class size also lends itself to "many opportunities to take on leadership roles through clubs, team and group work, case competitions, and other activities."

Weatherhead seems to attract "three types of students: international students who bring a unique flavor to the school; professional students who came here after working for a number of years; and students who came here after undergraduate or a few years out of school." The large number of international students "presents great opportunities to learn about how people from different cultures approach problems and communication."

Admissions

Applicants to Weatherhead's MBA program must submit an online application, application fee, transcripts for every degree completed before matriculating, an official GMAT or GRE score report, two personal essays, two letters of recommendation and a resume. International students must also submit an official TOEFL, IELTS or PTE score unless they graduated from an institution in which English was the main language of instruction.

FINANCIAL FACTS

Annual tuition	$39,600
Fees	$1,320
Cost of books	$1,524
Room & board (off-campus)	$17,730
% of students receiving aid	92
% of first-year students receiving aid	92
% of students receiving loans	36
% of students receiving grants	92
Average award package	$24,520
Average grant	$19,072
Average student loan debt	$25,970

ADMISSIONS

Admissions Selectivity Rating	84
# of applications received	352
% applicants accepted	62
% acceptees attending	48
Average GMAT	614
Range of GMAT	580–650
Average GPA	3.25
TOEFL required of international students	Yes
Minimum TOEFL (paper/computer)	100/600
Application fee	$100
International application fee	$100
Regular application deadline	3/1
Regular notification	4/10
Application Deadline/Notification	
Round 1:	12/1 / 1/31
Round 2:	1/15 / 3/1
Round 3:	3/1 / 4/10
Round 4:	3/1 / 7/1
Early decision program?	No
Deferment available	Yes
Transfer students accepted	Yes
Transfer application policy: Maximum number of transferable credits is 6 Semester hours from an AASCB-accredited program.	
Non-fall admissions	Yes
Need-blind admissions	Yes

EMPLOYMENT PROFILE

Career Rating	85	Grads Employed by Function	% Avg. Salary
Percent employed at graduation	33	Marketing	11 NR
Percent employed 3 months after graduation	53	Operations	7 NR
		Consulting	8 NR
Average base starting salary	$80,023	Management	11 $79,333
Primary Source of Full-time Job Acceptances		Finance	27 $58,750
School-facilitated activities	11 (42%)	**Top 5 Employers Hiring Grads**	
Graduate-facilitated activities	3 (12%)	Cleveland Clinic Foundation (1), Mckinsey (1),	
Unknown	12 (46%)	IBM (1), Gallup (1), Rockwell Automation (1)	

CENTRAL MICHIGAN UNIVERSITY
COLLEGE OF BUSINESS ADMINISTRATION

GENERAL INFORMATION

Type of school	Public
Academic calendar	Semester

SURVEY SAYS...

Solid preparation in:
General management
Teamwork
Communication/interpersonal skills
Quantitative skills
Doing business in a global economy

STUDENTS

Enrollment of parent institution	
Enrollment of MBA Program	113
% male/female	64/36
% out-of-state	34
% part-time	49
% international	34
Average age at entry	28
Average years work experience at entry	3

ACADEMICS

Academic Experience Rating	76
Student/faculty ratio	23:1
Profs interesting rating	82
Profs accessible rating	87
% female faculty	20
% minority faculty	10

Prominent Alumni

Roger L. Kesseler, Retired, VP & Controller, The Dow Chemical Company; Jerry D. Campbell, Pres. & CEO, Community National Bank of the South; Michael Fred O'Donnell, Retired, Managing Director, Protiviti Inc.; Robert I. Noe, CEO, 1 Sync; Michael J. Bowen, Chairman & CEO, Westwood Development Group.

Academics

Central Michigan University offers a comprehensive MBA program with a focus on general management. Students appreciate the fact that "The program is affordable, and offers flexible scheduling though weekend classes and night classes." CMU's "well-structured...flexible" curriculum begins with a set of foundational and core courses, taught in a series of quick, eight-week terms. While the core is "very broad," students can later pursue a concentration in one of many fields, including accounting, business economics, general management, management consulting, and management information systems. Emphasizing real-world business skills, CMU "allows students to learn through practical applications of techniques," including case studies, simulations, and consulting projects. "Faculty is the greatest strength" here. Well-versed in contemporary business topics, "The graduate level professors in the business school contribute well-researched concepts with real-world practices to provide students with a relevant, practical skill set."

CMU offers the complete full-time MBA on its main campus in Mount Pleasant, as well as at its auxiliary facilities in Midland, Michigan. "All MBA classes are in the evenings [and] some on weekends," which makes the program a "great fit for full-time employees." At the same time, the program is appropriate for early career professionals who want to make a move into management positions, and many complete the program on a full-time basis. No matter what your previous professional preparation, the small class size "fosters communication through insightful dialogue between students and faculty" and "really allow[s] students to become more involved in the learning process." In most classes, "Students are willing to engage in thoughtful conversation and challenge the view points of both other students and faculty." With a low graduate enrollment and a patently "friendly atmosphere," CMU's environment is student-centered and supportive. While the workload in some classes can be "very heavy," the teaching staff is "down-to-earth and easy to talk to," comprised of caring professors who "truly want what's best for the student." Similarly, "The administration at CMU is very competent and willing to help with an open-door policy to its students."

Career and Placement

Thanks to the school's flexible schedule and convenient evening classes, a large percentage of CMU students are working professionals—many of whom may not be looking for a new position after graduation. For those starting a new career (or those who want to make a career change), Central Michigan University's MBA program is designed to prepare students for a position in management, with numerous real world and practical experiences woven into the curriculum.

The university Career Services department maintains a job vacancy bulletin and hosts campus career fairs; however, students in the MBA program say the school could improve if they "spread more awareness of their programs." With such a strong academic program, students admit that, "CMU could improve how they market themselves as a business school. The quality of the MBA program is an aspect they should take greater steps to express to the nation."

ADMISSIONS CONTACT: PAMELA STAMBERSKY, MBA ADVISOR
ADDRESS: 252 ABSC-GRAWN HALL MOUNT PLEASANT, MI 48859
PHONE: (989) 774-3150 • FAX: (989) 774-1320
E-MAIL: MBA@CMICH.EDU • WEBSITE: WWW.CBA.CMICH.EDU

FINANCIAL FACTS

Annual tuition (in-state/	
out-of-state)	$13,303/$23,746
Cost of books	$1,600
Room & board	$7,947

ADMISSIONS

Admissions Selectivity Rating	**71**
# of applications received	93
% applicants accepted	86
% acceptees attending	89
Average GMAT	513
Average GPA	3.59
TOEFL required of	
international students	Yes
Minimum TOEFL	
(paper/computer)	550/213
Application fee	$35
International application fee	$45
Early decision program?	No
Deferment available	Yes
Maximum length	
of deferment	1 semester
Transfer students accepted	Yes
Transfer application policy:	
Limit of 12 credit hours from an	
accredited institution	
Non-fall admissions	Yes
Need-blind admissions	No

Student Life and Environment

Attracting a mix of "international students, professionals, and full-time students," you might be "surprised at the diversity" on CMU's small, Midwestern campus. "There are a lot of foreign students and it is so cool to get to know people from around the world. You see many of the same faces as you move through the program so you are able to get to know people and make good friendships and networking connections." Across the board, students are "driven and striving for success in the program" and "willing to lend a hand."

"There is definitely a small-class, small-school feel" at CMU. The campus is "intimate, friendly, [and] safe," and "it is very easy to feel comfortable and welcome here." "People are very friendly, and good team players." While academics (and professional life) keep students on the go, there is more to CMU than classes and homework. "There are a multitude of clubs and activities for students to join," both through the business school, as well as the university at large. Juggling work and school, some part-timers don't have time to participate in extracurricular activities; others take full advantage of the school's lively atmosphere. A current MBA agrees, "As a married graduate student with a full-time career, I still find CMU to be engaging both in the classroom and on campus in general. There are plenty of student organizations, activities, and professional networking opportunities to take advantage of."

Most part-time students commute to school, while many full-time students live on campus. Unfortunately, campus residents without a car can feel a bit stranded. Happily, the CMU campus provides the necessary amenities, with "plenty of facilities like computer labs, libraries, [and a] student activity center." As its name implies, Mount Pleasant makes a nice backdrop to campus life; "The campus is located in a safe town, so students can freely walk around the beautiful campus and enjoy themselves." During the summer, students also enjoy "kayaking down the Chippewa River, bicycle trails, and events such as home shows and boat shows that are hosted on campus."

Admissions

To calculate a students' eligibility for admission, Central Michigan University multiplies their undergraduate GPA by 200, then adds that number to their GMAT score. Using this calculation, prospective students must achieve at least 1050 points to be considered for admission. Additionally, students cannot be admitted if their GMAT score is below 450, no matter what their GPA. International students must submit TOEFL scores; however, students with TOEFL scores that fall short of that minimum requirement may take additional English classes while they begin the MBA program.

CHAPMAN UNIVERSITY
THE GEORGE L. ARGYROS SCHOOL OF BUSINESS AND ECONOMICS

GENERAL INFORMATION
Type of school	Private
Affiliation	Disciples of Christ
Academic calendar	Semester

SURVEY SAYS...
Students love Orange, CA
Happy students
Smart classrooms
Solid preparation in:
Accounting

STUDENTS
Enrollment of parent institution	6,398
Enrollment of MBA Program	278
% male/female	65/35
% out-of-state	8
% part-time	66
% minorities	5
% international	25
Average age at entry	25
Average years work experience at entry	2

ACADEMICS
Academic Experience Rating	**87**
Student/faculty ratio	22:1
Profs interesting rating	90
Profs accessible rating	86
% female faculty	19
% minority faculty	8

Joint Degrees
JD/MBA, 4 years; MBA/MFA, 3 years; MBA/MS in Food Science, 2.5 years.

Prominent Alumni
The Honorable George Argyros, CEO Arnel and Affiliates; The Honorable Loretta Sanchez, Member of U.S. Congress; David Bonior, Former Member of U.S. Congress; Steve Lavin, Sports Analyst; Michael Bell, Tony Award Nominee.

Academics

Armed with "a great reputation," an "outstanding entrepreneurial program," and "a great location right in the middle of Orange County, which makes it relatively easy for commuters to get to and makes plenty of entertainment and activities available to people on campus," Chapman University has a lot to offer the predominantly part-time student body in its MBA program. Some students will even go so far to project that Chapman will one day "be one of the best b-schools in the nation" and that they "are a part of something that is going to be very special."

Chapman's evening MBA program—which can be completed on either a part-time or full-time basis—loads students up with core requirements; 33 of the 52 credits necessary for graduation are devoted to the core here. "Small class sizes and excellent resources" complement "a very personal program" that allows students to "interact with the faculty in a better way." Full-time students also love the program's 16-month duration, which, while sometimes imposing a challenging pace, is "very good" at delivering a quick return on time invested. The school adds that "Students in the Argyros School of Business and Economics can take advantage of the classes, seminars, and scholarly opportunities afforded by our research centers: The Ralph W. Leatherby Center for Entrepreneurship and Ethics, The Walter Schmidt Center for International Business, the A. Gary Anderson Center for Economic Research," and the Larry C. Hoag for Real Estate and Finance. Chapman also offers an Executive MBA program.

Chapman currently offers electives in accounting, corporate governance, entrepreneurship, finance, human resources, international business, management, marketing, investments, creativity and innovation, and taxation. Students report: "Entrepreneurship is currently strong and growing. It offers many opportunities for students and most of all accepts any suggestions for further expansion." Students also brag: "The school has great connections and sponsors within the community. This leads to outstanding opportunities for networking as well as learning from standout professionals not employed by the university."

Career and Placement

Chapman's MBA Career Management Center is "fast becoming a first-rate resource for emerging business leaders seeking a leg up on the job market," students report, telling us that "direct access to career counseling, alumni job referrals, and 20/20 interviews have vaulted the program to a new level." Furthermore, "The online portal provides job listings for full-time, part-time, and internship opportunities, as well as subscription access to Vault's career search resources." This service is further strengthened by "an increasing focus on networking" and a "great director and terrific staff that do a lot to communicate the availability of resources." "The business school as a whole is recognizing networking as key to the success of the schools reputation, which ties directly to the success of its students," a student notes. Students generally agree that "Chapman's career management services are a vital link for students in their pursuit of greater career opportunities" and that the office is "one of the strongest parts of the program."

ADMISSIONS CONTACT: DEBRA GONDA, ASSOCIATE DIRECTOR
ADDRESS: BECKMAN HALL, ONE UNIVERSITY DR., ORANGE, CA 92866
PHONE: 714-997-6745 • FAX: 714-532-6081
E-MAIL: GONDA@CHAPMAN.EDU • WEBSITE: WWW.CHAPMAN.EDU/ARGYROS

Student Life and Environment

Among the highlights of the Chapman MBA program are the Distinguished Speaker series and Dinner for 8 programs, both of which provide exposure to high-powered business figures and networking opportunities. As one student explains, "Tonight the Dinner for 8 is being hosted by billionaire and former ambassador George Agyros. We have had various executives of multi-billion dollar companies speak at the Distinguished Speaker series, including the CEO of Allergan, David Pyott. Their talks were inspiring and delivered in an intimate venue." More networking opportunities present themselves because "there are many alumni that are very involved with the program and willing to give back to current MBAs." "Whether they are asked to host a dinner or be a distinguished speaker, alumni are able and willing to help if given the opportunity."

Chapman MBAs enjoy a friendly environment in which they "rarely have issues finding someone to answer questions or help solve problems." "Chapman is what a University should be: a place that shapes people into outstanding business professionals." Students tend to be "on the young side" with quite a few "fresh out of undergrad" but also a good crowd of "hard-working professionals with great insights." Together these two groups create "a combination that results in a great balance."

Admissions

The admissions office factors "academic performance, leadership ability, work experience, and communication skills" into each of it decisions. The school requires a minimum GPA of 2.5 for the applicants' final two years' worth of undergraduate credits (either the final 60 semester credits or the final 90 quarter credits). All applications must include an official GMAT score report, sealed copies of official transcripts for all post-secondary academic work, two letters of recommendation "from individuals familiar with the applicant's academic or professional abilities," and a completed application with a personal statement "explaining why the applicant is interested in pursuing a graduate degree at Chapman." Two years of business-related work experience is preferred. International applicants "whose native language is not English must submit results of the Test of English as a Foreign Language (TOEFL) or International English Language Testing System (IELTS). TOEFL scores must be a minimum of 550 (paper-based), 213 (computer-based), or 80 (Internet-based) and must have been taken within two years of the date of application for admission to Chapman."

FINANCIAL FACTS

Annual tuition	$34,320
Cost of books	$1,200
Room & board	$16,200
% of students receiving aid	69
% of students receiving loans	41
% of students receiving grants	52
Average award package	$20,583
Average grant	$12,844

ADMISSIONS

Admissions Selectivity Rating	88
# of applications received	100
% applicants accepted	49
% acceptees attending	76
Average GMAT	620
Range of GMAT	580–650
Average GPA	3.26
TOEFL required of international students	Yes
Minimum TOEFL (paper/computer)	550/216
Application fee	$60
International application fee	$60
Application Deadline/Notification	
Round 1:	1/27 / 3/17
Round 2:	3/3 / 4/21
Round 3:	4/14 / 6/2
Early decision program?	No
Deferment available	Yes
Maximum length of deferment	1 year
Transfer students accepted	Yes
Transfer application policy: Transfer up to six units of course work	
Non-fall admissions	No
Need-blind admissions	Yes

EMPLOYMENT PROFILE

Career Rating	82	Grads Employed by Function	% Avg. Salary
Percent employed at graduation	35	Marketing	22 NR
Percent employed 3 months after graduation	45	Management	33 $70,667
		Finance	22 NR
Average base starting salary	$66,222	**Top 5 Employers Hiring Grads**	
Primary Source of Full-time Job Acceptances		Hurley, Janes Capital Partners, Southern	
School-facilitated activities	1 (11%)	California Edison, Coca-Cola North America,	
Graduate-facilitated activities	8 (89%)	Kaiser Permanente	

THE CHINESE UNIVERSITY OF HONG KONG
FACULTY OF BUSINESS ADMINISTRATION

GENERAL INFORMATION
Type of school   Public

SURVEY SAYS...
Friendly students
Good social scene
Good peer network
Smart classrooms

STUDENTS
Enrollment of parent institution	18,642
Enrollment of MBA Program	366
% male/female	64/36
% part-time	81
% international	77
Average age at entry	28
Average years work experience at entry	5

ACADEMICS
Academic Experience Rating	81
Profs interesting rating	69
Profs accessible rating	68
% female faculty	21

Joint Degrees
JD/MBA program in Hong Kong (3 years full-time or 5 years part-time); Dual Degree Program between CUHK and HEC, France (18 months); Dual Degree Program between CUHK and University of Texas at Austin, USA (21 months).

Prominent Alumni
Mr. Lawrence Yee, Managing Director, GC, Dun & Bradstreet (HK) Ltd.; Mr. Henry Yan, Managing Director, UBS AG; Mr. Antony Hung, Manaing Director, Merrill Lynch (Asia Pacific) Ltd; Mr. Jackson Cheung, Cheif Executive, Societe Generale Asia Ltd.; Ms. Lau, Bing Ying, Managing Director, Kimberly-Clark (HK) Ltd.

Academics

In 1966, The Chinese University of Hong Kong became the first school in China to offer a full-time MBA program. Today, the university boasts one of the most reputable business schools in Asia and the Pacific, attracting students for its "international recognition, good academic reputation, and diverse teacher and student pools." A great entryway for those seeking a professional position in Hong Kong, the school boasts a "strong alumni network" in the city and an excellent reputation in the region. In particular, the school is touted for its programs in finance and marketing, with a special emphasis on Chinese business. Through lecture, case studies, group work, directed research, and discussion, classes are a balance of "individual and group efforts that cultivate teamwork among students that is important for business." Group work is particularly gratifying at CUMBA, where students comprise "a very diverse group from just about every continent. Their combined work experience and life experiences has really contributed to the program."

Maintaining a working relationship with various universities in mainland China and Taiwan, the school's "administration is very dedicated and efficient." The school attracts faculty from all over the world, and the current teaching staff includes professors from Australia, Hong Kong, Europe, New Zealand, mainland China, Southeast Asia, Taiwan, and the United States. Despite their varied origins, CUMBA faculty are deeply engaged in the Hong Kong business culture. A student attests, "Teaching staff are actively involved in the business community in areas of research and consulting. So there are lots of first-hand findings and . . . information [on] local business trends." On the whole, students appreciate the school's progressive outlook, saying professors "stay abreast of the real-life market and keep up to date with their own knowledge."

While Cantonese is the dominant language spoken in Hong Kong, courses at CUMBA are taught in English, with the exception of a few elective courses whose unique nature demands instruction in Chinese. The 54-unit curriculum consists of required core course work, followed by electives. Through electives, students have the option to pursue a concentration in one of four areas: China business, finance, marketing or entrepreneurship. The full-time curriculum can be completed in 16 months of study, including internships. Without an internship, the program can be completed as quickly as 12 months. Either way, the program is intense, with a "busy workload and no breaks in between terms." In addition to the traditional MBA programs offered through the school, students may choose to pursue a joint-degree with partner universities in Mainland China or the HEC School of Management in France or the University of Texas at Austin.

Career and Placement

As part of the MBA experience, students at The Chinese University of Hong Kong are expected to develop career goals and design a plan of action to meet those goal. The Career Management Centre facilitates students looking for summer internship placements, as well as students looking for permanent positions after graduation. The center also hosts an executive development series on presentation, communication, and influencing skills project management, and a series of career talks and job search workshops.

The school has strong ties in the Hong Kong business community, as well as a large regional alumni network. In recent years, the following companies have recruited CUMBA graduates: Arthur D. Little, The Boston Consulting Group, Citigroup Inc., Goldman Sachs, IBM China/Hong Kong Ltd, JP Morgan, Louis Vuitton (China) Company Ltd, Societe Generale Corporate & Investment Banking, Walt Disney Company, UBS Investment Bank, Macquarie Securities Ltd, and Kimberly-Clark

Corporation. In 2008, 59 percent of graduates took positions in Greater China (HK, PRC & Taiwan), 50% of whom were non-local students, 41% of students were relocated to different locations outside their home countries for the post-MBA jobs. The majority of students took positions in banking, finance and investment management sectors.

Student Life and Environment

CUMBA boasts a "beautiful campus" environment, and its daytime and weekend-mode students take classes on the main campus. Beginning from the early part of 2010, the business school will move into a state-of-the-art new teaching building near its main campus, and classes from then on will be given there. For evening-mode students, they attend classes in the school's MBA Town Centre, a modern and spacious 900-square-meter facility located in downtown. In addition to the extensive computer facilities available via the larger university, MBA students have access to over 100 microcomputers in the Town Centre, connected via LAN network. MBA students have the option of living on campus in the graduate residence halls; they also have access to the school's sports facilities, including three indoor gyms and an Olympic-sized swimming pool.

One of the major attractions of CUMBA is its diverse student population, who bring experience "from a variety of professions and cultures." Totally student-run, the MBA Student's Association sponsors a broad range of social and professional events, including executive seminars, company visits, and study tours to mainland China. The school also sponsors various social and recreational events, such as charity and fund-raising activities and sports teams, although some students say "Campus life is not adapted to international students at all." Even part-timers enjoy a sense of community. One says, "I am a part-time student. Fellow students usually have dinner gatherings after school."

Admissions

To be considered for admission to CUMBA, prospective students must hold an undergraduate degree (with at least a B average), have at least 3 years of relevant work experience post-graduation, and submit current GMAT scores. The average GMAT score for accepted applicants changes every year; however, the class average usually hovers between 620–640. Interviews are required for all short-listed applicants, either in person or via telephone, as determined by the selection committee.

FINANCIAL FACTS

Annual tuition	$30,460
Cost of books	$11,500
Room & board	
(on/off-campus)	$3,000/$20,500
% of students receiving grants	69
Average grant	$6,793

ADMISSIONS

Admissions Selectivity Rating	87
# of applications received	838
% applicants accepted	56
% acceptees attending	75
Average GMAT	626
Average GPA	3.3
TOEFL required of international students	No
Application fee	$25
International application fee	$25
Regular application deadline	3/31
Regular notification	6/15
Early decision program?	Yes
ED Deadline/ Notification	12/15 / 2/28
Deferment available	Yes
Maximum length of deferment	1 year
Transfer students accepted	No
Non-fall admissions	No
Need-blind admissions	Yes

EMPLOYMENT PROFILE

		Grads Employed by Function	% Avg. Salary
Career Rating	72		
Percent employed at graduation	77	Marketing	12 NR
Percent employed 3 months after graduation	21	Consulting	7 NR
		Management	17 NR
Primary Source of Full-time Job Acceptances		Finance	48 NR
School-facilitated activities	1 (3%)	HR	2 NR
Graduate-facilitated activities	19 (45%)	Entrepreneurship	10 NR
Unknown	22 (52%)	Strategic	2 NR

Top 5 Employers Hiring Grads
Fortis Bank (2), JP Morgan (1), UBS AG (1), 3M China (1)

THE CITADEL
SCHOOL OF BUSINESS ADMINISTRATION

GENERAL INFORMATION
Type of school	Public
Academic calendar	Semester

SURVEY SAYS...
Students love Charleston, SC
Friendly students
Good peer network
Solid preparation in:
Accounting

STUDENTS
Enrollment of parent institution	3,337
Enrollment of MBA Program	266
% male/female	64/36
% out-of-state	10
% part-time	78
% minorities	19
% international	3
Average age at entry	26

ACADEMICS
Academic Experience Rating	74
Student/faculty ratio	7:1
Profs interesting rating	89
Profs accessible rating	84
% female faculty	20
% minority faculty	10

Joint Degrees
PharmD/MBA Program, 4 years; MBA with concentration in Health Care Administration, 2–6 years; MD/MBA.

Prominent Alumni
Pat Conroy, Author; Ernest Hollings, U.S. Senator, S.C.; Lt. Col Randy Bresnik, USMC, NASA Astronaut; CDR Greg McWherter, USN, Commander of the Blue Angels; Dr. Harvey W. Schiller, Former Executive Director, U.S. Olympic Committee.

Academics

The Military College of South Carolina, The Citadel operates undergraduate programs for a corps of 2,000 cadets, while simultaneously offering a range of graduate programs to 1,000 civilians in the evenings. The school's MBA program, offered through the School of Business Administration, "is accredited by the AACSB International and has an outstanding reputation for the quality of its academics." In addition to its reputation, the "low faculty to student ratio," small class sizes, and convenient evening class schedule attract a wide range of Charleston professionals to this well-recognized program. Academically, the school blends tried-and-true academic theory with practical know-how, maintaining "a good mix of some older, tenured professors, but also some new professors coming in to mix things up." Whether young or old, "the professors are all experienced professionals that are capable of lending a wide range of practical knowledge to the lessons they teach." With an excellent faculty to student ratio, "classes involve discussion and interaction," which helps to bring "theoretical and real life experiences" together in an effective manner.

By all accounts, the "School of Business office goes out of their way to answer questions, assist in admissions, class registration, and financial aid." A current student attests, "The staff is very helpful. They go out of their way to help in any way they possibly can, even if it is not their particular job." Recently, The Citadel's School of Business Administration has been busy overhauling the MBA curriculum. The recently refurbished program has a reduced number of pre-requisites and electives, and simultaneously introduces a substantial emphasis on leadership within the curriculum. Today, the MBA curriculum consists of 12 required courses and three elective courses. Students may also take additional coursework to satisfy the requirements for a certificate in health care administration, or sports management, or continue working towards one of two joint-degree programs: PharmD/MBA or MD/MBA. One unique co-curricular offering at The Citadel is the Mentor Association, which matches business students with leaders in the local business community. Students who choose to participate in this program will be matched with a powerful business leader based on common interest and career path. Current mentors include executives at companies like Corning, Xerox, Oracle Corporation, Philip Morris, Ernst & Young, Kimberly Clark Corporation, IBM, and Wachovia Bank.

Career and Placement

The Citadel's Career Services Center maintains an online job and resume database for current students and alumni. The center also has working relationships with several online job boards, which give students a wide breadth of places to begin their job hunt. In addition, the center organizes several annual career fairs, which are open to the entire school community. In recent years, the following firms have recruited students at The Citadel's career fairs: AT&T, ArborOne Financial, Computer Sciences Corporation, Elliott Davis LLC, Mass Mutual Financial Group, MetLife, and Deloitte Consulting. Students admit that "there is not as much big business in the city, therefore there is not much big-time job opportunity here." However, they are quick to point out that "the administration does the best they can at getting us totally prepared for big business."

In addition to the efforts of the Career Services team, "The Citadel's rich tradition allows its students to draw on enthusiastic alumni for guidance and support." In fact, many students feel that the school's "career network is the biggest strength" of the program, as a Citadel degree places them among the school's loyal and extensive alumni network.

ADMISSIONS CONTACT: KATHY JONES, DIRECTOR OF BUSINESS SCHOOL OPERATIONS
ADDRESS: 171 MOULTRIE STREET CHARLESTON, SC 29409
PHONE: 843-953-5056 • FAX: 843-953-6764
E-MAIL: CGC@CITADEL.EDU • WEBSITE: CITADEL.EDU/CSBA

Student Life and Environment

Given The Citadel's distinct identity as a military college, graduate students admit, "the Graduate School has a noticeable stigma of being ancillary to the corps of cadets." While they recognize the school's long-standing history and reputation, many feel the administration should "place more emphasis on graduate school (the new president has been much better about this)." While they aren't in the limelight, the business school nonetheless creates a nice, insular community, attracting "friendly and engaging" students from "a multitude of cultures and backgrounds." In the academic arena, "the student body is easy-going and willing to participate in class and group projects. Overall, the experience is one of learning and social gathering."

All students commute to campus from across Charleston and "because school is taught at night, there is little opportunity to mingle outside of the classroom." Nonetheless, students reassure us that "most people are extremely busy but they are happy to meet for a burger or beer." In addition, the school hosts an MBA Association, a social and networking group for graduate business students.

Admissions

Admission to The Citadel's MBA program is based on a student's scholastic aptitude and capacity for graduate study. To apply, students must submit official GMAT scores, undergraduate transcripts, two personal essays, a resume, two letters of recommendation, and, for international students, a TOEFL score. In addition, a personal interview with the Director of Business School Operations or the Director of External Programs may be required.

ADMISSIONS

Admissions Selectivity Rating	60*
Average GMAT	501
Range of GMAT	453–518
Average GPA	3.01
TOEFL required of international students	Yes
Minimum TOEFL (paper/computer)	550/213
Application fee	$30
Regular application deadline	7/20
Regular notification	7/20
Early decision program?	No
Deferment available	Yes
Maximum length of deferment	12 months
Transfer students accepted	Yes

Transfer application policy:
A maximum of six hours credit for graduate courses from an accredited institution (including consortia and AACSB-accredited institutions) may be approved for transfer (except BADM 740), provided: (1) that those courses are determined to be equivalent to one of the advanced or elective courses at The Citadel, (2) that grades of B or better were received in the courses being considered for transfer credit, and (3) that credit for the courses was earned within the five years prior to admission into The Citadel MBA program.

Non-fall admissions	Yes
Need-blind admissions	Yes

CITY UNIVERSITY OF NEW YORK—BARUCH COLLEGE

ZICKLIN SCHOOL OF BUSINESS

GENERAL INFORMATION

Type of school	Public
Academic calendar	Semester

SURVEY SAYS...

Students love New York, NY
Cutting-edge classes
Smart classrooms
Solid preparation in:
Accounting

STUDENTS

Enrollment of parent institution	16,734
Enrollment of MBA Program	1,662
% male/female	60/40
% part-time	91
% minorities	29
% international	38
Average age at entry	28
Average years work experience at entry	5

ACADEMICS

Academic Experience Rating	**75**
Student/faculty ratio	35:1
Profs interesting rating	76
Profs accessible rating	71
% female faculty	23
% minority faculty	5

Joint Degrees

JD/MBA, 4.5 years (full-time)

Prominent Alumni

Larry Zicklin, Former Managing Partner, Neuberger Berman; Marcel Legrand, Sr. Vice President, Monster.com; JoAnn Ryan, President, ConEdison Solutions; William Newman, Founder & Chairman New Plan Excel Realty Trust; Hugh Panero, President & CEO, XM Satellite Radio.

Academics

The Zicklin School of Business at Baruch College "gives you the biggest bang for your buck in New York City when it comes to business schools," students at this renowned public school report. If you're trying to enter the "New York network at a fraction of the price of NYU or Columbia," Baruch is a solid choice. And like other city schools in the Big Apple, Baruch attracts an "extremely culturally diverse" student body that's just right for networking around the world. "For someone like me who wants to expand his business globally, there couldn't have been a better place," one student explains.

Baruch offers a full-time honors MBA that operates as "a separate program within the business school." Honors students brag that "The school administration puts the full-time honors MBA program at the top of [its] priority list. We are able to take priority when registering for classes and our registration is taken care of by the Director of Student Affairs." Class sizes are relatively small, which "enables students to learn in a close-knit, intimate environment amid the hustle and bustle of New York City." The school offers two part-time options: the Accelerated Part-Time MBA, which is cohort-based, and the Flex-Time MBA, a more traditional part time program.

Overall, full-time students are more enthusiastic about the Baruch MBA experience than their part-time peers. All typically find the program worthwhile, but part-timers are much more likely to complain that "It is difficult to get things accomplished or figure out who is the correct person to help resolve an issue." Part-time students are also much more likely to report scheduling and enrollment difficulties. Professors throughout the program tend to be "very knowledgeable and have relevant experience in the industry because more are adjunct professors, which are better because they share their relevant work experience with us." Some instructors, however, "do not teach in a way that stimulates interest in the material," making it "difficult to do well on exams or projects." Students note that the program is strongest in accounting and finance.

Career and Placement

Zicklin's Graduate Career Management Center offers business graduate students a broad range of online career development and job search tools, including self-assessments and a variety of job boards. The office also schedules regular corporate presentation and information sessions and alumni events and holds regular career management workshops. Students tell us that there are "lots of events to attend and opportunities to network." Among graduating members of the 2009 Full-Time Honors MBA program, half found jobs in finance and accounting (mean starting salary: $64,875) and one in five found marketing positions (mean starting salary: $71,250). The financial services industry claimed two-thirds of the class. The vast majority—nearly 85 percent, more precisely—remained in the northeast after graduation.

ADMISSIONS CONTACT: FRANCES MURPHY, DIRECTOR OF ADMISSIONS
ADDRESS: ONE BERNARD BARUCH WAY, BOX H-0820 NEW YORK, NY 10010
PHONE: 646-312-1300 • FAX: 646-312-1301 • E-MAIL: ZICKLINGRADADMISSIONS@BARUCH.CUNY.EDU
WEBSITE: WWW.ZICKLIN.BARUCH.CUNY.EDU

Student Life and Environment

Baruch "is a typical urban university in the heart of New York City," meaning that "The campus is the environment that exists within the main classroom building, a massive 14-floor facility. Although the environment is unconventional, it seems to suit its students well." New York City "becomes a larger part of our campus life," as students encounter Manhattan's upscale Gramercy Park neighborhood the moment they leave the b-school building. There's no ivory tower protecting Baruch students. While "there aren't too many areas allocated to relaxation and/or personal time" in the b-school building, who needs them when are so "many restaurants and bars located in the area"?

The MBA program hosts "tons of clubs," which students say "helps us network with students from different business schools as well as professionals around the city." Part-time students may be too busy to take advantage of these, especially those in the accelerated program, who tell us that "It's like going to school full time and working full time…. A very intense program, but you form a very [close] relationship with the peers in your cohort." Full-time students' days are also "packed between classes," with "club meetings, informational seminars, and inter-university competitions." Baruch attracts an "extremely racially and ethnically diverse" student body "with a heavy emphasis on quantitative skills."

Admissions

All applicants to Zicklin MBA and MS programs must have an accredited bachelor's degree or its international equivalent (official transcripts for all postsecondary academic work is required) and must submit an official score report for the GMAT. Applications must also include a complete application form (hard copy or online), a current resume, two letters of recommendation (at least one should be from a current employer), and an essay describing career goals and explaining why a master's degree in business is important in achieving those goals. Students whose first language is not English and who have not graduated from a U.S. undergraduate or graduate school must also submit an official score report for the TOEFL/TWE. In addition to the above, international applicants must also submit translated copies of all transcripts and letters of recommendation; in some cases, applicants may be required to have transcripts evaluated by an independent evaluating agency. International applicants must also obtain a student visa and must submit a Declaration and Certification of Finances and an Affidavit of Support.

FINANCIAL FACTS

Annual tuition (in-state/ out-of-state)	$9,400/$18,240
Fees	$288
Cost of books	$1,200
Room & board	$20,000
% of students receiving aid	80
% of first-year students receiving aid	95
% of students receiving loans	19
% of students receiving grants	60
Average award package	$9,200
Average grant	$4,100
Average student loan debt	$30,000

ADMISSIONS

Admissions Selectivity Rating	80
# of applications received	1,114
% applicants accepted	60
% acceptees attending	63
Average GMAT	583
Range of GMAT	540–620
Average GPA	3.2
TOEFL required of international students	Yes
Minimum TOEFL (paper/computer)	590/243
Application fee	$125
International application fee	$125
Regular application deadline	4/30
Early decision program?	No
Deferment available	Yes
Maximum length of deferment	1 year
Transfer students accepted	Yes
Transfer application policy: Same application process as all applicants; up to 12 credits from an AACSB-accredited institution may be transferred	
Non-fall admissions	Yes
Need-blind admissions	Yes

EMPLOYMENT PROFILE

Career Rating	84	Grads Employed by Function	% Avg. Salary
Percent employed at graduation	53	Marketing	26 $63,746
Percent employed 3 months after graduation	83	Consulting	4 NR
Average base starting salary	$71,299	Finance	65 $71,907
Primary Source of Full-time Job Acceptances		**Top 5 Employers Hiring Grads**	
School-facilitated activities	15 (60%)	Ernst & Young (10), Deloitte (7), KPMG (7),	
Graduate-facilitated activities	8 (32%)	Grant Thornton (5)	
Unknown	2 (8%)		

Claremont Graduate University

The Peter F. Drucker and Masatoshi Ito Graduate School of Management

GENERAL INFORMATION

Type of school	Private
Academic calendar	Semester

SURVEY SAYS...

Students love Claremont, CA
Friendly students
Good peer network
Happy students
Solid preparation in:
General management
Teamwork

STUDENTS

Enrollment of parent institution	2,000
Enrollment of MBA Program	150
% male/female	56/44
% out-of-state	13
% part-time	31
% minorities	29
% international	36
Average age at entry	27
Average years work experience at entry	3

ACADEMICS

Academic Experience Rating	**90**
Student/faculty ratio	12:1
Profs interesting rating	89
Profs accessible rating	89
% female faculty	23
% minority faculty	8

Joint Degrees

Dual-degree programs in Human Resources, Biosciences, Economics, Arts Management, Public Health, Math, Law, and by special arrangement in other disciplines.

Prominent Alumni

Rajiv Dutta, President, Skype Technologies SA; Ming-Hsun Chen, Chairwom, China Development Financial Holding Corp; Stephen Rountree, Pres. & COO, Music & Performing Art Ctr of LA Cnty; Colin Forkner, CEO & Vice Chairman, Pacific Coast National Bank; Brad Adams, CEO & Chairman, Sunstone Systems International.

Academics

The Peter F. Drucker and Matafoshi Ito Graduate School of Management at Claremont, known as just "Drucker" for short, finds its basic philosophy in business scholar Peter Drucker's focus on the knowledge economy and in his interest in the management of people and ideas. Flowing from that is an emphasis also on values and ethics as a basis for management and economic decisions. A recently implemented and now-required seminar called the Drucker Difference introduces all beginning MBA students to how the school approaches this—not only through courses in business policy and ethics but also how it plays out in the study of topics including economics and finance.

Students at Drucker are required to complete 32 credits of core courses, comprising slightly more than half of the 60 required for the MBA. That core includes classes in marketing, finance, and operations, as well as advanced study in strategy, and a course in morality and leadership. Students may continue with a general business orientation, select a concentration from Drucker's offerings (in strategy, finance, leadership. marketing, global business, and non-profit management), or choose from topics in the university's other graduate schools and obtain dual degrees in fields such as biosciences and cultural management. Drucker also offers an executive MBA program and courses leading to the PhD in business. MBA Students can explore opportunities to study in England, Japan, the Netherlands, and other countries.

Small classes, high standards, and the focus on values are important to students in the program. "Drucker's reputation for ethical responsibility toward the notion of business" was an attraction for many in choosing the school in the first place, and "The intimate environment, which lends itself to a great deal of interaction with the faculty and other students," is another oft-cited strength. "Drucker School professors challenge you to use your whole brain and are always accessible outside of class," students agree. "I get to interact with them rather than a TA," one says. "Course work is extremely relevant and insightful." Professors with professional and academic experience "relate lessons learned into the course work."

The administration earns praise as well. When students hit a snag, "They are there to remedy the problem within the day, a couple of hours actually. Response times are amazing, compared to my undergrad state school," says one student. This supports an academic atmosphere that is "the industry leader in values-centered management training and multidimensional strategic thinking," students say. Here, there is an "emphasis on ethical management" and "on teamwork."

Career and Placement

Nearly three-quarters of Drucker's students attend full time, and opinion on how helpful the school's Career Center is to both full- and part-time students is mixed. "Career services—although improving—could be more of [a] resource, and the school should arrange for, incorporate, partner, administer, and mandate internships as part of the MBA curriculum," one student reports. "We have our own representative [at the Career Center] now, which will really change things," another counters. Assisting students with "relationships with employers and networking" is an area that could use a boost, students agree. Ernst & Young, Southern California Edison, Western Asset Management, and Northrup Grumman are among companies that often recruit Drucker graduates.

ADMISSIONS CONTACT: BRANDON TUCK, DIRECTOR, RECRUITING AND ADMISSIONS
ADDRESS: 1021 NORTH DARTMOUTH AVENUE CLAREMONT, CA 91711
PHONE: 909-607-7811 • FAX: 909-607-9104
E-MAIL: DRUCKER@CGU.EDU • WEBSITE: WWW.DRUCKER.CGU.EDU

Student Life and Environment

"We are very serious, so most of my time spent on campus is in a study room or with a study group" one student says, summing up the "intrinsically driven" but "not competitive" atmosphere that many find at Drucker. "My fellow students show a genuine interest in my success both at school and in life. We help each other through difficult times at school and in our personal lives," adds another. Many students at this school—where "Everyone knows one another by name"—come from international backgrounds, "which I think is terrific," one student notes. "The exchange and learning between people from different business and cultural background[s] has taught me quite a lot." Students agree that diversity is a benefit, but at the same time add that the school "needs more local students" and "should offer a better variety of electives during the 7:00 to10:00 P.M. time frame for students who work full-time." Those who live on campus find that "student housing is a major deficiency, especially for married students." Still, students generally agree that "Claremont is a great place to live. Weather is ideal, mountains are scenic" and the "excellent main street" is within walking distance.

Admissions

In keeping with the school's overall philosophy, the Admissions Office is committed to looking at the whole person when evaluating applicants for admission. GMAT scores are required, as are undergraduate transcripts, three letters of recommendation and a personal statement responding to questions regarding the contributions a student could make to the school's community and how the student has resolved an ethical dilemma that he or she has faced. For the executive MBA program, GMAT scores are not required; instead the school asks for at least five years of work experience at an executive level along with a personal interview. Drucker generally accepts students with an average GMAT score of 635, a GPA of 3.18, and averaged 3 years of work experience.

FINANCIAL FACTS

Annual tuition	$42,488
Fees	$250
Cost of books	$1,500
Room & board (on/off-campus)	$12,000/$13,000
% of students receiving aid	67
% of first-year students receiving aid	65
% of students receiving loans	70
% of students receiving grants	50
Average award package	$15,000
Average grant	$6,800
Average student loan debt	$42,686

ADMISSIONS

Admissions Selectivity Rating	86
# of applications received	141
% applicants accepted	70
% acceptees attending	43
Average GMAT	614
Range of GMAT	570–651
Average GPA	3.24
TOEFL required of international students	Yes
Minimum TOEFL (paper/computer)	593/243
Application fee	$60
International application fee	$60
Application Deadline/Notification	
Round 1:	11/1
Round 2:	12/1
Round 3:	2/1
Round 4:	4/1
Early decision program?	Yes
Deferment available	Yes
Maximum length of deferment	1 year
Transfer students accepted	Yes
Transfer application policy: The maximum number of transferable credits is 10 units.	
Non-fall admissions	Yes
Need-blind admissions	Yes

EMPLOYMENT PROFILE

		Grads Employed by Function	% Avg. Salary
Career Rating	85		
Percent employed at graduation	64	Marketing	28 $77,800
Percent employed 3 months after graduation	62	Operations	6 $95,000
		Consulting	17 $63,333
Average base starting salary	$70,361	Management	11 $80,500
Primary Source of Full-time Job Acceptances		Finance	22 $67,875
School-facilitated activities	7 (39%)	HR	11 $49,000
Graduate-facilitated activities	8 (44%)	MIS	5 $62,000
Unknown	3 (17%)		

CLARK UNIVERSITY
GRADUATE SCHOOL OF MANAGEMENT

GENERAL INFORMATION
Type of school   Private
Academic calendar   Semester

SURVEY SAYS...
Friendly students
Cutting-edge classes
Smart classrooms
Solid preparation in:
General management
Teamwork
Doing business in a global economy

STUDENTS
Enrollment of parent institution	3,230
Enrollment of MBA Program	263
% male/female	57/43
% out-of-state	48
% part-time	51
% minorities	2
% international	88
Average age at entry	25
Average years work experience at entry	3

ACADEMICS
Academic Experience Rating	**71**
Student/faculty ratio	23:1
Profs interesting rating	71
Profs accessible rating	77
% female faculty	40
% minority faculty	

Joint Degrees
MBA/MSF

Prominent Alumni
Isabel Hochgesand, Director Global Marketing/Proctor & Gamble; Matt Goldman, Co-founder/Blue Man Group; Lawrence Norman, Vice President Global Basketball, Adidas; Wolfgang Hammes, Managing Director/Deutsche Bank; Maria Kulsick, VP of Talent Management, Fidelity Investments.

Academics

A small graduate business program strong in finance (so strong, in fact, that it offers both an MBA with a finance concentration and a Master of Science in Finance), the Graduate School of Management at Clark University provides a "collaborative atmosphere" to a student body drawn from both the immediate region and halfway around the globe. As a result, Clark is "very diversified, which brings many different perspectives to the classroom."

Finance and accounting are standout disciplines here ("Many of the finance professors have impressive concurrent careers, running hedge funds by day and teaching courses by night; they typically have highly recognized professional certifications in addition to their PhDs," one student notes), but MBAs report other curricular strengths as well, including a "recently added concentration in social change, which allows students to take elective courses in the International Development, Community and Environment (IDCE) Department at Clark....There is also a three-year dual-degree program (MBA/MA in CD or ESP) between these two departments." Clark's forward-looking, green-leaning proclivities are further revealed in "the dual-degree program offered in environmental science and policy and the MBA."

Clark's professors are "demanding but fair." Some "are outstanding. They come from experienced fields and they help you live the experience of the new material in all its aspects. Suddenly statistics and finance become easy and enjoyable with them." Others, however, "are dull and give you tedious work that takes hours but is not interesting." Students appreciate that "The school makes sure to take the student's opinion into account when re-enlisting a professor to teach for the upcoming semesters." The program also offers "many opportunities to help real businesses in the city" in order to gain "real life experience." More of this sort of thing could be on the way; as one student observes, "I have seen a steady progression in Clark's course offerings that indicates that they understand the 'real-world' challenges facing students and are adapting appropriately. I am particularly encouraged by the apparent increase in courses addressing innovation, social sustainability, entrepreneurship, and management leadership."

Career and Placement

Many Clark students say the Stevenish Career Management Center at Clark's GSOM "does a good job of helping students prepare for their career search. They edit resumes and cover letters, provide interview coaching, and give students information on nearby career fairs."

The Center provides a range of services including individual advising, resume and cover letter assistance, workshops, career fairs, on-campus recruiting events, alumni networking events, alumni professional seminars, internship placement, and job and internship postings. Although internships are required of students with fewer than three years of professional experience, some students consider that "it shouldn't be a requirement to attain an internship as a graduate student." Others state the office does "not do a sufficient job of getting employers interested in Clark's students." Employers who have recently hired Clark GSOM graduates include Johnson & Johnson, Deloitte, Aetna Insurance, Public Consulting Group, JP Morgan, AMCOR, and Bristol-Myers Squibb.

ADMISSIONS CONTACT: LYNN DAVIS, DIRECTOR OF ENROLLMENT & MARKETING, GSOM
ADDRESS: 950 MAIN STREET, CLARK UNIVERSITY WORCESTER, MA 01610
PHONE: 508-793-7406 • FAX: 508-421-3825
E-MAIL: CLARKMBA@CLARKU.EDU • WEBSITE: WWW.CLARKU.EDU/GSOM

Student Life and Environment

Clark University's location in the urban setting of Worcester, Massachusetts, provides the same opportunities and challenges of any urban campus. Clark's University Park Partnership brings together the University and Main South communities to help create a safe and vibrant neighborhood for all. However, students must take the usual safety precautions. Some report that there are "no real student bars and the like in the Clark area and that the neighborhoods surrounding the school have been allowed to fall into poverty by the town of Worcester." Students quickly note that "Clark has a world-class police force whose mission to protect the students is paramount" and that policing on campus includes a "good and very, very helpful" escort service though "there have been cases of students being mugged from time to time."

About half of Clark's MBAs are full-time students. Many spend a lot of time on and around campus. While "undergraduate student groups are closed to graduate students," MBAs enjoy "fun social events that the business school's student council puts on, and an interesting stock market activity that happens each semester." Some report that graduate student life "feels very disconnected from the rest of the school" and that it can "get boring at times because we are a very small community." Others state that the school "provides some networking alumni activities to help us to search jobs, and for international students, they organize some specific activities, such as Asian New Year, to make students (come) together and feel (at) home."

Clark's part-time students "are mostly native(s of) Worcester or Massachusetts, with different ages and backgrounds." Full-timers typically "come from different Asian countries," with India and China especially well-represented. International students "add a richness in perspective," although some "are weak in English."

Admissions

Clark requires the following of applicants: a completed admissions application; a personal essay; a current resume; two letters of recommendation; an official score report for either the GMAT or the GRE (an uncommon option); and official transcripts from all undergraduate and graduate programs previously attended. Interviews are optional. International applicants must submit all of the above as well as an official score report for the TOEFL or IELTS (if their native language is other than English) and proof of the financial support while attending the program. The school strongly encourages, but does not require, an online application.

FINANCIAL FACTS

Annual tuition	$23,170
Fees	$1,250
Cost of books	$2,100
Room & board	$10,000
% of students receiving grants	40
Average award package	$10,000
Average grant	$9,300

ADMISSIONS

Admissions Selectivity Rating	78
# of applications received	315
% applicants accepted	72
% acceptees attending	39
Average GMAT	536
Range of GMAT	490–600
Average GPA	3.2
TOEFL required of international students	Yes
Minimum TOEFL (paper/computer)	550/213
Application fee	$50
International application fee	$50
Regular application deadline	7/1
Early decision program?	No
Deferment available	Yes
Maximum length of deferment	12 months
Transfer students accepted	Yes
Transfer application policy:	
A maximum of two graduate courses from an AACSB accredited school can be transferred into the program. Foundation courses can be waived for undergraduate business majors.	
Non-fall admissions	Yes
Need-blind admissions	Yes

CLARKSON UNIVERSITY
SCHOOL OF BUSINESS

GENERAL INFORMATION

Type of school	Private
Academic calendar	August–May

SURVEY SAYS...
Smart classrooms
Solid preparation in:
General management
Operations
Quantitative skills
Computer skills

STUDENTS

Enrollment of parent institution	2,901
Enrollment of MBA Program	67
% male/female	73/27
% out-of-state	32
% part-time	13
% minorities	3
% international	29
Average age at entry	24
Average years work experience at entry	2

ACADEMICS

Academic Experience Rating	**80**
Student/faculty ratio	3:1
Profs interesting rating	84
Profs accessible rating	79
% female faculty	29
% minority faculty	5

Joint Degrees
Master of Engineering/Master of
Business Administration (2 years)

Prominent Alumni
William, Harlow, VP Corporate
Development; Paul Hoeft, President
and CEO; Elizabeth Fessenden,
President Flexible Packaging; David
Fisher, President; Vickie Cole,
President and CEO.

Academics

Clarkson University is best known for its fine engineering programs, so it should come as no surprise that the focus at Clarkson University School of Business is on developing business acumen in engineers. Students recognize what makes their school special, telling us, "Clarkson's academic record is outstanding. It is a competitive engineering school with a growing business program." The curriculum stresses that students approach problem-solving creatively to "focus on the big picture." As one student explains, "Life at Clarkson is academically strenuous but a balance of mind, body, and spirit is encouraged by the business school." Clarkson's history as a "technical school" comes in handy for those students interested in the business side of engineering since "Many technical companies are attracted to the school" and the campus has "strong industry connections" and a "good reputation in the technology world."

Clarkson MBAs are anxious to get their degrees and move on, and the school's accelerated 1-year program suits their needs perfectly. One MBA writes, "After four years of undergrad I don't mind a little extra work load to have a master's in one year." Students agree that "the workload is intense" and places "a strong stress on the team-based experience." All this hard work pays off in the end, though, as students feel that "the group-work emphasis will help in future employment" and "The fast pace and large workload proves [their] ability to work under pressure." Despite this "challenging" atmosphere, students get a break from their studies during the *Globalization and Ethics Week* where corporate executives and alumni speak on various topics.

Clarkson MBAs note that the school's "small size does not sacrifice the quality of most professors." "They are always available and put in every effort to assist students," says one student. Another enthuses, "Professors are incredibly concerned with student progress. They are very accessible outside the classroom and more than willing to start up conversations in the middle of a hallway with any student." However, "They will not tell you the way to succeed. All they will do is guide you in your search to find success." In this way, "The faculty at Clarkson treat their students as equals," which MBAs appreciate.

Career and Placement

Clarkson MBAs receive career services from the Graduate Career Services Office and the university's Career Center, which serves all students at the university. The center schedules career fairs each semester, puts students in contact with Clarkson's alumni network, and provides students with access to the online job database MonsterTrak. MBAs give the office mixed reviews. Some wish it would "attract a more diverse pool of job recruiters in relation to the interests of the students in the program." "They could try to get more business related type firms," adds a student. However, others praise the "many helpful resources such as e-recruiting" that are provided.

Clarkson MBAs most frequently find work with IBM, Accenture, Lockheed Martin, GE, Cooper Industries, Frito-Lay, HSBC, Knowledge Systems and Research, Texas Instruments, and Whiting Turner. While the majority of graduates remain in the Northeast, students are placed throughout the country.

ADMISSIONS CONTACT: JOSHUA LaFAVE, ASSOCIATE DIRECTOR, GRADUATE BUSINESS PROGRAMS
ADDRESS: 8 CLARKSON AVE., CU BOX 5770 POTSDAM, NY 13699
PHONE: 315-268-6613 • FAX: 315-268-3810
E-MAIL: BUSGRAD@CLARKSON.EDU • WEBSITE: WWW.CLARKSON.EDU/GRADUATE

Student Life and Environment

The majority of Clarkson's student body is full-time, and they report a predictable rhythm to their school days. "You are generally on campus from 8:00 A.M. until 6:00 or 7:00 P.M. There is a lot of work and a lot of meetings to attend with group members," explains one student. As it's a business school, the prevailing mood is businesslike. Students "treat each day as if it were a work day" by dressing "business casual" and acting in "a professional manner." The business school facility follows suit with its "multiple computer labs," "student lounges," and "Learning Development Labs."

Potsdam, of course, is hardly a bustling metropolis. The closest large city is Ottawa, which lies approximately 90 miles and one international border to the north. One student simply states, "It's pretty cold, unless it's summer then it's pretty hot." With "only about three bars in town which are shared with a local SUNY school," students find "not much raucous" about the social scene, saying "It's pretty ho-hum." "Unless you skate or enjoy winter sports, there isn't much else in Potsdam to do," says one student.

Some students, however, manage to see the glass as half full instead of half empty. "A vast diversity of sports, intramurals, and clubs allow students to keep busy outside of class and to socialize with their peers," explains one student. A "majority" of Clarkson students are "involved in an activity of one sort or another." Another adds that the school provides for a "fun environment." Fortunately for all, Clarkson's accelerated one-year program keeps most students too busy to worry about what type of fun they are, or are not, missing. Students work hard all week long and through much of the weekend as well. One MBA explains, "Weekends are spent doing work all day long. You go out with friends one night a week on the weekend; that's about it."

Admissions

The admissions department at Clarkson University requires that applicants submit an undergraduate transcript, GMAT or GRE scores, TOEFL scores (if necessary), and a Test of Spoken English (TSE) (for international students whose native language is not English; the TSE can be administered via telephone), a detailed resume, two one-page personal essays, and three letters of reference. Awards of merit-based scholarships are determined during the admissions process; no separate application is required. Those requiring foundation course work prior to commencing their MBAs "may enroll in the courses at Clarkson during the summer Business Concepts Program before entering the advanced MBA program. For students doing graduate work at another university, they may be allowed to transfer in nine credit hours of graduate work."

FINANCIAL FACTS

Annual tuition	$35,385
Fees	$440
Cost of books	$2,000
Room & board (off-campus)	$7,500
% of students receiving aid	85
% of first-year students receiving aid	85
% of students receiving loans	75
% of students receiving grants	85
Average award package	$26,476
Average grant	$6,500
Average student loan debt	$34,126

ADMISSIONS

Admissions Selectivity Rating	76
# of applications received	157
% applicants accepted	57
% acceptees attending	65
Average GMAT	540
Range of GMAT	480–580
Average GPA	3.27
TOEFL required of international students	Yes
Minimum TOEFL (paper/computer)	600/250
Application fee	$25
International application fee	$35
Early decision program?	No
Deferment available	Yes
Maximum length of deferment	1 year
Transfer students accepted	Yes
Transfer application policy: Graduate students who need to complete foundation coursework may enroll in the summer business concepts program at Clarkson before entering the advanced MBA program. For students doing graduate work at another university, they are allowed to transfer in up to 9 credit hours of graduate work from another AACSB accredited institution.	
Non-fall admissions	Yes
Need-blind admissions	Yes

EMPLOYMENT PROFILE

Career Rating	87	Grads Employed by Function	%	Avg. Salary
Percent employed at graduation	36	Marketing	3	$55,000
Percent employed 3 months after graduation	75	Operations	22	$62,225
		Consulting	8	$64,333
Average base starting salary	$62,678	Management	3	$100,000
Primary Source of Full-time Job Acceptances		Finance	5	$52,523
School-facilitated activities	9 (75%)	Top 5 Employers Hiring Grads		
Graduate-facilitated activities	3 (25%)	IBM (3), Frito Lay (1), Cooper Industries (1), Bechtel (1), J&J/Duracell (1)		

CLEMSON UNIVERSITY
COLLEGE OF BUSINESS AND BEHAVIORAL SCIENCE

GENERAL INFORMATION
Type of school   Public
Academic calendar   Aug–May

SURVEY SAYS...
Students love Clemson, SC
Friendly students
Good peer network
Smart classrooms
Solid preparation in:
General management

STUDENTS
Enrollment of MBA Program   72
% male/female   71/29
% out-of-state   16
% part-time   38
% international   40
Average age at entry   29
Average years work experience
   at entry   5

ACADEMICS
Academic Experience Rating   83
Student/faculty ratio   4:1
Profs interesting rating   85
Profs accessible rating   76

Joint Degrees
Numerous dual degrees are offered with the MBA program, in which students can combine two master's and/or PhD programs. Up to 1/6 of the total hours in both programs combined may be double counted. Students must be accepted by both degree programs. Currently about 30 percent of Clemson MBA candidates are pursuing dual degrees in bioengineering, civil engineering, computer science, economics, marketing and packaging science. Clemson MBA candidates can also pursue a dual Clemson MBA and Master in International Management from ICHEC.

Academics

The College of Business & Behavioral Science at Clemson University offers a combination of daytime and evening classes to its full-time MBAs in Clemson as well as a full slate of evening classes to part-timers at the school's satellite campus in Greenville. Clemson MBAs tout the program's "rigorous curriculum" and excellent value; "The value of this degree vs. the cost of the degree appears to be very high," one student tells us.

Clemson's MBA offers concentrations in innovation and entrepreneurship; services science, supply chain management, health services (Greenville only), marketing analysis (Clemson only), and real estate (Clemson only). Full-timers are enthusiastic about "the entrepreneurial focus of the program," especially the "competitive and relevant assistantships with the Spiro Institute for Entrepreneurial Leadership." One writes, "It is rare to find relevant assistantships in an MBA program, and Clemson University provides some [of the] best opportunities for entrepreneurs to learn necessary business skills while working closely with start-up companies in South Carolina. They also do a marvelous job of bringing technologies developed by Clemson's Research Institutes to a forefront and finding their commercial value."

The program boasts "some very good professors and interesting class topics," and students praise professors for "their willingness to help outside of class" and for being "generally reasonable when it comes to grades and making changes if the general class population is not grasping the material well." Students also note that "The administration here at Clemson University is very helpful. Any time I have asked for help regarding admission, enrollment, or financial aid they have always been able to answer my questions." Finally, they report that "Clemson's study abroad programs are attractive and meaningful."

Career and Placement

Clemson University maintains an Office of MBA Career Development dedicated to its business graduates. For those who seek out the service, the Office of Career Development office offers career placement support including one-on-one professional coaching and personalized placement assistance as well as a range of self-assessment instruments, job-search counseling, interviewing and resume-writing workshops, and recruiting and networking events. Students also report that "the alumni base and networking opportunities" here are "a great strength." Companies hiring recent Clemson MBAs include Blackbaud, Bausch & Lomb, CapGemini, Colonial Life, Disney, GE, Home Depot, Lockheed Martin, Michelin, Milliken, Nestle, Northwestern Mutual, Resurgent Capital Service, Schneider, and Target. About one-third of Clemson MBAs wind up in marketing and sales; about as many find work in general management.

Student Life and Environment

The full-time and part-time degree programs are now located in downtown Greenville, South Carolina, about 45 minutes away from the main university campus. The Greenville campus, known as Clemson at the Falls, is located at Falls Park—an urban park featuring hiking and jogging paths, landscaped gardens, and an architecturally distinctive suspension bridge linking the Clemson campus building to Main Street. Students tell us that life here involves "hectic course work with case studies, quizzes, midterms, discussions, presentations and projects. Apart from the course work, we have regular MBA Student association meetings . . . to discuss and organize events related to community work, organizing events with alumni, etc. Then we have regular discussions and talks by guest speakers, which are compulsory to attend as part of our course work. We have

ADMISSIONS CONTACT: ADMISSIONS DIRECTOR, MBA PROGRAMS
ADDRESS: 55 E. CAMPERDOWN WAY, GREENVILLE, SC 29601
PHONE: 864-656-3975 • FAX: 864-656-0947
E-MAIL: MBA@CLEMSON.EDU • WEBSITE: WWW.CLEMSON.EDU/MBA

regular social gathering with MBA alumni and with faculty also." Reflecting upon all this activity, one student observes that "Clemson has a great tradition of merging academia with life. You feel like you're a part of the school and the community."

Beyond the classroom, the new location strategically places college faculty and students at the center of the Greenville business community, allowing full-time students to attend classes and simultaneously hold internships or part-time positions in local businesses.

The Clemson MBA program attracts students who "are very competitive in most facets of life: sports, academics, job-search, etc. However, this competitive spirit does not manifest itself in pettiness, but rather in a collective effort to elevate the performances of both ourselves and our peers."

Admissions

Applicants to the MBA program at Clemson must submit a current resume (two years of work experience is required for students w/undergraduate degree in business); one official transcripts representing all undergraduate work; two letters of recommendation; a one- to two-page personal statement; interview (full-time applicants only); and, an official GMAT score report (score of at least 600 preferred for applicants to the full-time program). Non-native English speakers applying to the full-time program must also submit TOEFL scores (score of 580 paper-based or 237 computer based preferred), an International Student Financial Certification Form, and translations of transcripts not in English.

Prominent Alumni

J. Strom Thurmond, U.S. Senator (died 2003); Kristie A. Kenney, U.S. Ambassador to the Phillipines; Robert H. Brooks, President, Naturally Fresh Foods.

FINANCIAL FACTS

Annual tuition (in-state/ out-of-state)	$7,338/$15,330
Fees	$736
Cost of books	$922
Room & board	$10,882

ADMISSIONS

Admissions Selectivity Rating	**79**
# of applications received	148
% applicants accepted	67
% acceptees attending	73
Average GMAT	573
Range of GMAT	510–638
Average GPA	3.28
TOEFL required of international students	Yes
Minimum TOEFL (paper/computer)	600/250
Application fee	$70
International application fee	$80
Regular application deadline	6/15
Regular notification	6/30
Early decision program?	No
Deferment available	Yes
Maximum length of deferment	1 year
Transfer students accepted	Yes
Transfer application policy: Must meet all admission requirements. Can transfer a maximum of 12 semester hours of acceptable coursework.	
Non-fall admissions	Yes
Need-blind admissions	Yes

EMPLOYMENT PROFILE

		Grads Employed by Function	% Avg. Salary
Career Rating	84		
Percent employed at graduation	27	Marketing	33 NR
Percent employed 3 months after graduation	40	Operations	17 NR
		Management	33 NR
Average base starting salary	$77,000	MIS	17 NR
Primary Source of Full-time Job Acceptances		**Top 5 Employers Hiring Grads**	
School-facilitated activities	1 (17%)	Target Corporation (1), Eaton Corporation (1),	
Graduate-facilitated activities	2 (33%)	Cintas Corporatoin (1), Trimble (1), Bluestar	
Unknown	3 (50%)	Silicones (1)	

THE COLLEGE OF WILLIAM & MARY
THE MASON SCHOOL OF BUSINESS

GENERAL INFORMATION
Type of school	Public
Academic calendar	Semester

SURVEY SAYS...
Good peer network
Smart classrooms
Solid preparation in:
Accounting

STUDENTS
Enrollment of parent institution	7,874
Enrollment of MBA Program	419
% male/female	64/36
% out-of-state	49
% part-time	47
% minorities	20
% international	39
Average age at entry	27
Average years work experience at entry	3

ACADEMICS
Academic Experience Rating	**89**
Student/faculty ratio	11:1
Profs interesting rating	95
Profs accessible rating	90
% female faculty	24
% minority faculty	14

Joint Degrees
MBA/Juris Doctor; MBA/Master of Accounting; MBA/Master of Global Management; MBA/Master of Public Policy.

Prominent Alumni
Donald Lee Lowman, MBA '82, Managing Director, Strategic Growth, Towers Perrin (consulting); Amy C. McPherson, MBA '85, President & Managing Director, European Lodging—Marriott International, Inc. (hospitality); Susan Perry O'Day, MBA '85, Sr. Vice President & Chief Information Officer, The Walt Disney Company (entertainment); James Buchanan McCabe BBA '73 & MBA '75, Sr. Vice President & Chief Financial Officer, Chick-Fil-A, Inc. (food service).

Academics

MBAs love the "personalized approach to teaching" at the Mason School of Business at the College of William & Mary. This approach results in part from the program's "smaller class sizes" and dedicated "professors who want to teach and who care about students' success." Mason's professors utilize a "holistic approach to teaching both in terms of content (challenging academics, but also specific classes on communication and leadership skills) and form (case studies, hands-on projects, traditional)." It is also the result of several value-added features of the program that many students feel are Mason's greatest assets.

Chief among these is Mason's Executive Partner Program, "a fantastic resource that pairs us up with leaders in business who live in Williamsburg (coincidently, a lot of people retire from Wall Street and move to Williamsburg)." Through the program, "Each student gets a mentor who meets with him or her on a regular basis. These executive partners are readily available to students for career advice, interview guidance, and feedback on projects and presentations." "The Executive Partner program really brought it home that [the program is] committed to teaching us the soft skills.... The aim is to teach MBAs to think and not just do," one student explains. Other unique features of the program include the "immersive Career Acceleration Modules," which "allow for you to actually work with clients and provide solutions" in such areas as "corporate finance, financial markets, entrepreneurship, B2B and B2C marketing, and consulting." Finally, there is Mason's "capstone course, a field consultancy program that allows us to consult with real companies to solve real problems."

Students report that the Mason curriculum places an "emphasis on both qualitative and quantitative skills, presentations, and teamwork to create a well-rounded education that has helped students to excel in the business world." Students also appreciate that the program "offers many opportunities to develop as a leader. There are so many options to get involved with and the cross-program bonds are stronger than any other MBA school that I have asked people about. It is commonplace to socialize with a law student just as much as a business student." Mason's administration "is open to doing things better, and if you have an idea or project, they encourage you to do it....For example, we now have green-belt six sigma certification and a project with the Department of Defense because a student took the initiative to get it started. This is just one of many examples. Students play a very active part in the school and have a large say in what happens here."

Career and Placement

Placement and recruiting services at the Mason School of Business receive mixed reviews from students. Some praise the "high quality of jobs and high job placement" and conclude that the "program is exceedingly strong," Others are less complimentary. A common complaint focuses on the fact that Mason "is a small school" in a location that isn't "ideally placed to attract MNC's and conglomerates to recruit here," putting the school "at a disadvantage when it comes to on-campus recruiting. Most companies focus on larger schools. Therefore, we need a more robust career services department to help mitigate the disadvantages that go along with that."

Top employers of Mason MBAs in recent years include: Anheuser-Busch, BearingPoint, Booz Allen Hamilton, Capital One, Deloitte, Dominion Resources, Ernst & Young, Fannie Mae, IBM, Johnson & Johnson, Lafarge, Legg Mason, Landmark Communications, National City Corporation, Rich, Seapak, Target, and Wachovia. One in four 2009 MBAs found work with the government; 15 percent took jobs in the finance sector; and 14 percent entered the consulting business.

ADMISSIONS CONTACT: JILL HUTCHKO, FULL-TIME MBA ADMISSIONS COORDINATOR
ADDRESS: ALAN B. MILLER HALL, 101 UKROP WAY, P. O. BOX 8795 WILLIAMSBURG, VA 23187
PHONE: 757-221-2900 • FAX: 757-221-2958
E-MAIL: ADMISSIONS@MASON.WM.EDU • WEBSITE: MASON.WM.EDU

Student Life and Environment

Mason recently moved into a "new 166,000 square foot facility" that students say is "fantastic." "The study rooms or the conference rooms are comparable to the offices in any high-tech company," one student writes. Within the building's confines, "students are heavily involved in projects that originate in the classroom but often move to the weekends and off time. This is balanced with social events, intramural sports, clubs, committee involvement, and community service." Clubs "ranging from community service to marketing" are "student-run and all give us experience trying out real-world situations." The student body forms a "small community...with a high level of cooperation and teamwork and very little of the competitiveness rumored at other business schools."

William and Mary is located in Williamsburg, Virginia, a "historic, safe, and picturesque" town "small enough that you go out and see your classmates and enjoy getting to know them in a non-professional setting" but with "great access to both large cities within an hour-and-a-half drive or a great oceanfront within an hour-and-a-half drive." Regardless of where they are, "students find a way to make it fun. Whether having mug night at the Greenleaf, or celebrating Diwali with the Indian students (with professors dancing!), or the Chinese New Year with the Chinese students, or random intramurals, hanging out at Miller Hall, or just having a conversation, I am thoroughly enjoying my experience here," one student writes.

Admissions

Applicants to Mason must submit: official academic transcripts for all undergraduate and graduate work; an official GMAT score report; letters of recommendation; three personal essays; and a resume. Interviews are required and are by invitation of the school only. International applicants whose first language is not English must submit official score reports for the TOEFL, the IELTS, or the PTE (applicants scoring in at least the 60th percentile on the verbal section of the GMAT and at least a 5.0 on the AWA section of the GMAT are exempted from this requirement).

FINANCIAL FACTS

Annual tuition (in-state/ out-of-state)	$19,907/$30,857
Fees (in-state/ out-of-state)	$5,093/$5,643
Cost of books	$4,500
Room & board	$8,330
% of students receiving aid	54
% of first-year students receiving aid	62
% of students receiving loans	33
% of students receiving grants	32
Average award package	$21,756
Average grant	$12,455
Average student loan debt	$46,665

ADMISSIONS

Admissions Selectivity Rating	84
# of applications received	382
% applicants accepted	56
% acceptees attending	57
Average GMAT	613
Range of GMAT	570–660
Average GPA	3.2
TOEFL required of international students	Yes
Minimum TOEFL (paper/computer)	600/250
Application fee	$100
International application fee	$100
Application Deadline/Notification	
Round 1:	11/16 / 1/8
Round 2:	1/11 / 3/12
Round 3:	3/1 / 4/23
Round 4:	4/19 / 5/14
Early decision program?	No
Deferment available	Yes
Maximum length of deferment	1 year
Transfer students accepted	No
Transfer application policy:	
Transfer credits are not accepted.	
Non-fall admissions	No
Need-blind admissions	Yes

EMPLOYMENT PROFILE

Career Rating	89	Grads Employed by Function	% Avg. Salary
Percent employed at graduation	40	Marketing	24 $62,125
Percent employed 3 months after graduation	58	Operations	6 NR
		Consulting	27 $84,444
Average base starting salary	$71,130	Management	6 NR
Primary Source of Full-time Job Acceptances		Finance	32 $6,585
School-facilitated activities	15 (41%)	MIS	3 NR
Graduate-facilitated activities	22 (59%)	**Top 5 Employers Hiring Grads**	
		Deloitte Consulting (5), Department of the Navy (2), Ernst & Young (2), IBM Global Business Services (2), Bristol-Myers Squibb (1)	

COLORADO STATE UNIVERSITY
COLLEGE OF BUSINESS

GENERAL INFORMATION
Type of school	Public
Academic calendar	August–July

SURVEY SAYS...
Good peer network
Cutting-edge classes
Solid preparation in:
Accounting
General management

ACADEMICS
Academic Experience Rating	82
Student/faculty ratio	35:1
Profs interesting rating	89
Profs accessible rating	80
% female faculty	10
% minority faculty	12

Joint Degrees
DVM/MBA: MBA is 3 years; DVM is 4 years. There is an overlap of 2 years for a total 5 year program.

Academics

Convenience and affordability define the MBA experience at Colorado State University, whether you choose to attend classes at the school's scenic Fort Collins campus, or from your home computer 1,000 miles away. Operating one of the longest-running distance MBAs in the country, CSU has online education down to a science. What makes the CSU distance MBA unique is that it runs concurrently with the Professional MBA program on the CSU campus. Together, distance and campus-based students complete the MBA simultaneously—viewing lectures, completing group projects, and turning in assignments in tandem. For distance students, "The in-class lectures are recorded and made available to distance students within 24 hours of each class ending" via the Internet, and "DVDs are mailed to you" within the week. As a result, distance students literally watch "the same lecture that is delivered to the on-campus students" and even "hear questions that the ground students have." "Technology is top-notch" and students can easily meet for group work via the school's web-based platforms. With absolutely no residency requirements or in-person orientation programs, CSU's program is "completely online and affordable," attracting professional students from every corner of the country—and the globe. While many students consider other low-residency MBAs before deciding where to apply, they say Colorado State offers the "best combination of course content, reputation, accreditation, cost, and flexibility for distance learners."

Whether taking place in the lecture hall or on the small screen, CSU classes are a "good balance of practical and theoretical ideas" and "the material is current and in-depth." Here, you'll get all the MBA essentials, with a touch of innovation; at CSU, "they continue to push the envelope academically but not at the expense of what is real and proven in the field." Professors "are knowledgeable, engaging, and bring excellent guest speakers to the lectures." Most faculty members "have real-world business experience, not just theory" to share. Classes are "demanding," yet both online and on-campus students benefit from the excellent personal relationships they build with CSU professors. As one online student explains, "The professors are responsive and really care for the success of the students." "They know my name, even though I am one of 1,200 students."

Coordinating such a large program is a feat, but the CSU administration is a well-oiled machine. Students praise the remarkable "ability of the administration and staff to assemble an impressive collection of students from around the globe, and then to effectively manage such a diverse group." A current student attests, "I cannot say enough about how much assistance I receive from professors, the distance coordinator, and administrators. I have a very unique job that requires me to be in remote areas with little or no Internet access, and my professors are more than accommodating in working with me during these times." Adds another, "Even though I am a distance student, I feel as connected as I would be if I were on campus."

Career and Placement

The Office of Career Services at the College of Business offers individual career counseling, resume critiques, and networking events for undergraduate and graduate business students. The emphasis, however, is on undergraduate students looking to start a career, rather than MBA candidates. In recent years, undergraduate and graduate students at CSU have gone on to jobs at Accenture, Oppenheimer, Target, EnCana Oil & Gas, and Ernest and Julio Gallo Winery.

For online students, career development is a different story. Most of CSU's distance students "are looking to move their careers forward, are dedicated employees, and want to gain more knowledge to make them better employees and managers." To that end, most are not seeking new career opportunities—and most, it should be added, do not live in the Colorado area. As a result, graduate student career services are not particularly robust at CSU, and "career center resources are non-existent for distance students." Fortunately, Colorado State University "has a great reputation around the country and the world," which is an asset to any career or job search.

Student Life and Environment

Drawing students from far and wide, CSU brings together a "great mix of people, from diverse work environments, from all around the world, each bringing their piece of diversity to the mix." The program is well suited to busy professionals, and distance students are "mostly mid-career with backgrounds ranging from engineering to veterinary." Needless to say, "Personal interactions are limited due to the distance format," though students are still expected to participate in group projects through the university's technology platforms. It might sound like a bit of a headache, but current students assure us that, "All the online students are courteous and willing to help."

Those who study on campus say that CSU's business school, located on "a safe and friendly campus" in the pretty town of Fort Collins, Colorado, "offers a great environment in which to learn and grow personally and professionally." With spectacular recreational opportunities in the surrounding Rocky Mountains, affordable cost-of-living, and a laid-back social scene, students ask us, "How can you complain?"

Admissions

To be eligible for admission to CSU, students must have maintained a 3.0 GPA or better from an accredited undergraduate college, or they must have completed a graduate degree and have at least four years of professional work experience. Students with a lower GPA must include a statement explaining their academic performance. Students with significant professional work experience may apply for a GMAT waiver. Applicants are advised of their admission status within three weeks of the application deadline.

FINANCIAL FACTS

Annual tuition (in-state/ out-of-state)	$12,500/$20,616
Fees (in-state/ out-of-state)	$40/$660
Cost of books	$400
% of students receiving aid	32
% of first-year students receiving aid	36
% of students receiving loans	30
% of students receiving grants	2

ADMISSIONS

Admissions Selectivity Rating	77
TOEFL required of international students	Yes
Minimum TOEFL (paper/computer)	565/227
Application fee	$50
International application fee	$50
Regular application deadline	5/1
Regular notification	6/1
Early decision program?	No
Deferment available	Yes
Maximum length of deferment	1 year
Transfer students accepted	No
Non-fall admissions	No
Need-blind admissions	Yes

COLUMBIA UNIVERSITY
COLUMBIA BUSINESS SCHOOL

GENERAL INFORMATION

Type of school	Private
Academic calendar	Semester

SURVEY SAYS...

Students love New York, NY
Good social scene
Good peer network
Solid preparation in:
Finance
Quantitative skills
Doing business in a global economy

STUDENTS

Enrollment of parent institution	26,399
Enrollment of MBA Program	1,293
% male/female	67/33
% minorities	23
% international	38
Average age at entry	28
Average years work experience at entry	5

ACADEMICS

Academic Experience Rating	**90**
Profs interesting rating	88
Profs accessible rating	88
% female faculty	16

Joint Degrees

MBA/MS: Master of Science in Urban Planning; MBA/MS: Master of Science in Nursing; MBA/MPH: Master of Public Health; MBA/MIA: Master of International Affairs; MBA/MS: Master of Science in Earth Resources Engineering, Financial Engineering, Industrial Engineering or Operations Research; MBA/MS: Master of Science in Social Work; MBA/MS: Master of Science in Journalism; MBA/JD: Doctor of Jurisprudence; MBA/MD: Doctor of Medicine; MBA/DDS: Doctor of Dental Surgery.

Academics

When it comes to business education, Columbia University has an almost unfair advantage over its competitors: its New York City address. Students here tout "the only great business school in New York City, which gives it a huge advantage over the Harvards and Stanfords of the world" because "whether or not you want to stay here, access to New York City is an unmatched experience that cannot be overstated: The connections made, the speakers we get, the opportunities to visit company offices, are incredible." As one student looking to get into the media and entertainment industry puts it, "New York city location gives access to [the] real world in whatever field one desires...there are so many alums and industry experts in my desired area that Columbia Business School connects me with."

Columbia excels in finance—a natural fit for a b-school in a world finance capital—as well as in related fields like accounting and economics. One student immersed in all three assures us that "The faculty in these departments are outstanding and widely recognized outside of the school. I've had Fed officials, C-level finance managers and well-known investment managers teaching my electives." But these disciplines are just the tip of the iceberg; Columbia also offers outstanding programs in social enterprise and development, real estate, marketing (featuring another NYC touch: a focus on luxury goods), entrepreneurship, and management. There's "a great international focus" throughout the "very analytical" curriculum, which includes "a well-rounded core curriculum and amazing electives across all disciplines."

Columbia's location means "many opportunities for part-time internships as well as networking events. These off-campus opportunities are equivalent to taking several extra classes" and "are an invaluable resource for learning about industries and a great addition to material covered in class." It also means that the school can supplement its "globally respected" full-time faculty with "many adjunct professors who are leaders in their industry and are well-positioned to incorporate real-world issues." Students warn, "The workload intensity doesn't seem to abate during the second year" as it does in other top programs; coupled with recruiting activities, this makes for "a schedule that can be overwhelming for even the most robotic among us." They also complain that CU's facilities are "old and cramped" but add that plans for a new building are in the works.

Career and Placement

The Career Management Center at Columbia benefits from a tremendous parlay: a top-flight business school located in the financial capital of the world. The office helps students coordinate internship and employment searches and also provides "a range of complementary resources...ranging from intimate workshops on interviewing and presentation skills to a five-part course on different aspects of the job," according to the school's website. The CSO also draws from the region's many business leaders for lectures, seminars, and panel discussions. The school reports: "Hundreds of employers actively recruit at Columbia Business School each year, conducting thousands of on-campus interviews and numerous corporate presentations. Columbia also receives thousands of job postings for off-campus full-time and intern positions." Students add, "Recruiting opportunities and alumni are the greatest strengths of the program. Recruiting is very intense because recruiters are all over you the minute you step in the door. This lasts until you succumb to one of them and take your resume off the market by accepting an offer."

Over forty percent of the graduating class landed in the finance sector; a third of the class found work in consulting (average starting salary $117,413). Top employers include: McKinsey & Company, Citi, Goldman Sachs & Co., Deutsche Bank, Booz & Co., JP

Morgan Chase & Co., Merrill Lynch, Morgan Stanley, Boston Consulting Group, American Express, General Electric, and IBM.

Student Life and Environment

Columbia MBAs are organized into 'clusters,' groups of "65 or so students with whom you take most of your classes." Students love the system, saying, "It's unbelievable and builds everlasting and close-knit relationships among students." One student tells us: "Most of your social life takes place with your cluster. They become your new family. However, it is completely OK to have your own life outside of school and no one judges you for not attending every event. But, if you want to do nothing but socialize with class-mates, there is something you could be doing every night of the week." And not just on campus; there's "great balance given the location" that "allows you to have your own life outside of school." Restaurants, bars, clubs, all manner of entertainment, museums, parks, and just about anything else you can imagine is a subway ride away.

Campus life is quite robust; students "have to balance the myriad activities and events taking place at and around campus. On a given day, one might have to choose between studying, listening to a Wall Street CEO speak on campus, attending one of a number of recruiting presentations, attending a club meeting, or hitting the bars with classmates. Overall, though, I'd rather have too many choices than none at all, and some of the choices are remarkable. I've crossed both Jim Cramer and John Mack (Former Morgan Stanley CEO) in the bathroom on campus." The program is home to more than "[90] student-run clubs and associations."

Admissions

The Admissions Department at Columbia notes, "Columbia Business School selects appli-cants from varied business and other backgrounds who have the potential to become suc-cessful global leaders. Their common denominators are a record of achievement, demon-strated leadership and the ability to work as members of a team." The school also reports: "By design, efforts are made to admit students who add different perspectives to the learn-ing experience. In this way, students are continually learning from the diverse profession-al experiences and cultural/geographical backgrounds of their classmates. Columbia Business School has also maintained, through a concerted strategic effort, one of the high-est enrollments of women and underrepresented minorities among top business schools. The Office of Admissions, in conjunction with the School's Black Business Students Association, Latin American and Hispanic Business Association, and African American Alumni Association, sponsors information sessions and receptions for prospective stu-dents. Fellowships are also available for minority students." Admission to the program is extremely competitive.

Prominent Alumni

Warren Buffett, Chairman, Berkshire Hathaway Inc.; Henry Kravis, Founding Partner, Kohlberg Kravis Roberts & Co.; Rochelle Lazarus, Chairman, Ogilvy & Mather Worldwide; Lew Frankfort, Chairman and CEO, Coach, Inc.

FINANCIAL FACTS

Annual tuition	$49,728
Fees	$2,212
Cost of books	$900
Room & board	$19,440
% of students receiving aid	58
% of first-year students receiving aid	54
Average award package	$56,771
Average grant	$12,915

ADMISSIONS

Admissions Selectivity Rating	99
# of applications received	6,885
% applicants accepted	15
% acceptees attending	72
Average GMAT	713
Range of GMAT	680–760
Average GPA	3.5
TOEFL required of international students	Yes
Application fee	$250
International application fee	$250
Regular application deadline	4/14
Early decision program?	Yes
ED Deadline	10/7
Deferment available	No
Transfer students accepted	No
Non-fall admissions	Yes
Need-blind admissions	Yes

EMPLOYMENT PROFILE

Career Rating	97	Grads Employed by Function% Avg. Salary	
Percent employed at graduation	61	Marketing	14 $94,300
Percent employed 3 months after graduation	77	Consulting	32 $117,413
		Management	6 $98,684
Average base starting salary	$106,246	Finance	44 $106,313
Primary Source of Full-time Job Acceptances		Top 5 Employers Hiring Grads	
School-facilitated activities	170 (41%)	McKinsey & Company (46), Boston Consulting	
Graduate-facilitated activities	69 (17%)	Group (21), Booz & Co. (20), JP Morgan	
Unknown	172 (42%)	Chase & Co. (15), Deloitte Consulting LLP (12)	

CONCORDIA UNIVERSITY
JOHN MOLSON SCHOOL OF BUSINESS

GENERAL INFORMATION
Type of school	Public
Academic calendar	Trimester

SURVEY SAYS...
Students love Montreal, QC
Friendly students
Good peer network
Solid preparation in:
Marketing
Teamwork

STUDENTS
Enrollment of parent institution	43,942
Enrollment of MBA Program	364
% male/female	63/37
% out-of-state	54
% part-time	58
% international	37
Average age at entry	29
Average years work experience at entry	6

ACADEMICS
Academic Experience Rating	**86**
Student/faculty ratio	12:1
Profs interesting rating	80
Profs accessible rating	81
% female faculty	29

Prominent Alumni
Irving Teitelbaum, Founder, Chairman and CEO, La Senza; Keith Conklin, President and CEO, Nestle Canada; Alice Keung, Senior Vice President Information Technology & C.; Lawrence Bloomberg, Former COO, National Bank; Jean-Yves Monette, Executive President & CEO Van Houtte Cafe.

Academics

The John Molson School of Business MBA program "is steeped in pragmatism," students tell us. "This isn't a theoretical program. You come out of JMSB able to apply the stuff you learned in the workplace" because "whenever possible, we learn by doing." As one student explains, "I felt at John Molson I would be able to learn more everyday tools that I can apply in the real world." In addition, "strong ties with the business community and great alumni" add further value to a JMSB MBA.

Finance and accounting are among the strongest areas here, students tell us, and John Molson professors are "leaders in their respective fields." The program is flexible and meets the needs of part-time students by providing classes on Saturdays and Sundays. To enrich the learning experience, students can take a one-credit course in New York City to learn first-hand the realities and complexities of doing business in a major international city. The John Molson MBA's core courses include "Business Ethics" and "Strategy and Social Responsibility in Action"; electives include courses on sustainability, global climate change and corporate governance. Overall the administration is "quite friendly and helpful for day-to-day questions."

One of the high points of the school's academic year is the John Molson MBA Case Competition, held on campus and billed as "the oldest global case competition in the world." JMSB students are extremely passionate about this event. The Concordia Small Business Consulting Bureau offers students another opportunity to flex their business muscles while helping local businesses fine-tune their business plans and reach new consumers. The school offers a co-op option to all full-time students; the school's big-city setting strengthens this option considerably.

Career and Placement

The Career Management Services Center rolled out many initiatives to make graduate students have a much better chance of connecting with employers and take charge of their job search. A Business Development Manager was recently hired to cultivate relationships with new prospective employers. The office has also "worked hard to foster cooperation between career placement and the co-op program," exploiting previously underutilized synergies. The center provides the standard complement of career counseling, guest lectures, mock interviews, job postings, and seminars in networking, resume writing, and salary negotiation.

Employers who most frequently hire Molson MBAs include Royal Bank, Bombardier, Deloitte Consulting, CIBC, Hasbro, Deutsche Bank, ICAO, Lafarge North America, IMS Health, and CN. Approximately one-third of Concordia MBAs take jobs in consulting; about one-quarter wind up in marketing and sales.

CYNTHIA LAW, MANAGER, GRADUATE ADMISSIONS & ENROLLMENT
ADDRESS: 1450 GUY ST., MONTREAL QUEBEC, CANADA H3H 0A1
PHONE: 514-848- 2424, EXT. 2727 • FAX: 514-848-2816
E-MAIL: GRADPROGRAMS@JMSB.CONCORDIA.CA
WEBSITE: HTTP://JOHNMOLSON.CONCORDIA.CA/MBA

Student Life and Environment

"There are many student-run clubs and thus activities abound" for Concordia MBAs, "making it extremely easy to participate beyond the regular classroom…and bond outside of school." Organizations provide "various initiatives going on throughout the year," including "a social event every Thursday, and some sort of dinner or big social networking event about twice per semester." Students engage in "some charity events as well: hockey, poker tournaments, and fundraising for Breast Cancer and Make-a-Wish Foundation." One student opines that Concordia provides "a great environment not only in which to learn but also to network."

The vibe at Concordia is "very informal and open." "Students come and go from the lounge to their classes and openly share their insights or talents to assist others," a student explains. "It's a very team-oriented atmosphere, and not as cutthroat as I thought it would be."

The new building for the John Molson School of Business opened in fall 2009 and the student social spaces are more generous. Many were "especially excited about it being a green building…whose heat and power will be generated by solar panels."

Molson students are "a diverse lot," "with a good number of international students as well as a varied range of work experience backgrounds." About half "work full time and study part time while still taking an impressive course load." "The full-time students are extremely involved in student life, even more so than the part-time students, running events and case competitions and doing extremely well at it," one student says. "The networking opportunities are amazing and you finish your business school with a large extended network of friends that have bonded with you through many shared experiences beyond the classroom." As another student puts it, "The social experience at the JMSB is phenomenal. I have made friends for life."

Admissions

Concordia admissions officers seek students with "real-world work experience, strong academic backgrounds, clear career objectives, and a commitment to excellence." Applicants must meet the following minimum requirements: undergraduate GPA of 3.0; two years of full-time work experience; a GMAT score of 580; and, for international students who have not previously completed an undergraduate degree in English or French, a TOEFL score of 600 (paper-based), 250 (computerized), or an IELTS score of at least 7.0. Career/leadership potential, level of maturity, communication skills, and how closely the student's goals match those of the program are also weighed. Complete applications include a personal essay, a resume, official undergraduate transcripts, three letters of recommendation, and test scores. Applications are processed on a rolling basis, a method that favors those applying early.

FINANCIAL FACTS

Annual tuition (in-state/ out-of-state)	$2,327/$21,870
Fees (in-state/ out-of-state)	$1,488/$1,850
Cost of books	$3,500
Room & board (on/off-campus)	$4,842/$14,400
% of students receiving aid	29
% of first-year students receiving aid	24
Average award package	$6,408
Average grant	$7,663

ADMISSIONS

Admissions Selectivity Rating	87
# of applications received	599
% applicants accepted	41
% acceptees attending	59
Average GMAT	600
Range of GMAT	580–690
Average GPA	3.43
TOEFL required of international students	Yes
Minimum TOEFL (paper/computer)	600/250
Application fee	$90
International application fee	$90
Early decision program?	Yes
ED Deadline/Notification	NR / 3/5
Deferment available	Yes
Maximum length of deferment	1 year
Transfer students accepted	Yes
Transfer application policy: Applicants may be eligible for advanced standing	
Non-fall admissions	Yes
Need-blind admissions	Yes

EMPLOYMENT PROFILE

Career Rating	82	Grads Employed by Function	% Avg. Salary
Average base starting salary	$66,155	Marketing	29 NR
		Operations	24 NR
		Consulting	9 NR
		Management	5 NR
		Finance	33 NR

Top 5 Employers Hiring Grads
Bombardier, Deloitte Consulting, National Bank, Darftfcb, BMO Financial

CORNELL UNIVERSITY
JOHNSON GRADUATE SCHOOL OF MANAGEMENT

GENERAL INFORMATION
Type of school   Private
Academic calendar   Semester

SURVEY SAYS...
Cutting-edge classes
Helfpul alumni
Solid preparation in:
Marketing
Accounting
Computer skills

STUDENTS
Enrollment of parent
  institution   21,325
Enrollment of MBA Program   274
Average age at entry   27
Average years work experience
  at entry   5

ACADEMICS
Academic Experience Rating   99
Profs interesting rating   98
Profs accessible rating   99

Joint Degrees
MBA/MILR, 5 semesters;
MBA/MEng, 5 semesters; MBA/MA
Asian Studies, 6–7 semesters;
JD/MBA, 4 years; MBA/MPS-RE, 6
semesters; MD/MBA, 5 years (only
currently available to students at
Weill Medical College of Cornell
University).

Prominent Alumni
Irene Rosenfeld '75, CEO, Kraft
Foods Inc.; H. Fisk Johnson '84,
Chairman of S.C. Johnson and Son;
Dan Hesse '77, CEO, Sprint Nextel
Corp.; Nancy Schlichtina '79, CEO,
Henry Ford Health Systems; Jim
Morgan '63, Chairman of Applied
Materials.

Academics

Students praise the "variety of MBA programs and areas of study" at Cornell University's Johnson Graduate School of Management, where an Accelerated MBA and two Executive MBA programs complement the traditional 2-year MBA. They also praise the availability of "specialized courses during the first year." The first year consists of eight required courses (Microeconomics for Management, Financial Accounting, Marketing Management, Statistics for Management, Managerial Finance, and Strategy, Managing Operations, and Managing and Leading in Organizations) and a choice of electives or participation in the Immersion Learning program. Eighty percent of students choose to participate in this "well-structured" practicum, which "provides great preparation" for internship-seekers. Second year students choose an all-elective program. The school offers concentrations in selected areas including leadership, global management, sustainable global enterprise, entrepreneurship, and consulting. This system, says one student, "allowed me to become a real expert in the field I have selected." Among other strong specializations is the Asset Management track, bolstered by a student-run trading floor with a "$14-million-dollar hedge fund," and an investment studio in the Parker Center for Investment Research. Students also reserve high praise for the Center for Sustainable Global Enterprise, which gives students "amazing access to [top] companies" and schools them in "the strategic advantages a focus on sustainability can offer to innovative private enterprise." Johnson also offers 23 international business courses and study abroad opportunities in numerous countries.

Students say that Johnson's "world-class faculty" is "very accessible." ("I have gotten rides to school by my professors who see me waiting for the bus," says one student.) They also appreciate that the academics allow for more of a work-life balance than at some other schools ("There are no regular courses on Fridays...which makes it easier to take short vacations or just relax"). In addition, "The school encourages pursuits outside Johnson," "from cooking classes at the Hotel School to athletic classes (such as sailing on the lake)."

Career and Placement

Johnson alumni "pull us into the top firms," says one MBA candidate. Another affirms, "Cornellians can call any other Cornellian anywhere in the world and we help each other." Where "others care about the consequences of helping, we just do it." In addition, "Our career center is awesome. They really help students find relevant jobs." The top employers of Johnson graduates are American Express, Citigroup, General Electric Company, Deloitte Touche Tohmatsu, JP Morgan, Amgen, McKinsey & Company, Deutsche Bank, Johnson & Johnson. The average starting salary is $100,700, with international students reporting slightly lower salaries than domestic students. Ninety percent of the last graduating class received offers before commencement.

Student Life and Environment

Students say Cornell deserves its reputation as "the 'nice' business school," where "Students get ties out of their locker to help classmates make a great impression at I-banking and consulting corporate briefings." In other words, Cornell students will "gladly help a struggling classmate out anytime." "We hunt as a pack," says one MBA candidate of his "bright and collaborative" peers. As if to underscore the "collegial" climate, Johnson students don't hesitate to praise one other. "My classmates are bright, motivated, genuine people who are all about results," says one student. "People here don't talk about themselves all the time like a lot of business types—they just get the job done." Another adds that Johnson students are "some of the smartest students amongst all schools, but the difference is that Johnson students won't tell you how smart they are." "Students, especially those in the Sustainable Enterprise program, are extremely intelligent nontraditional thinkers and intent on exploring ways new ways of doing business."

Hometown Ithaca is famous for its "beautiful scenery" and "outdoor activities such as cliff climbing, yachting, and hiking." It's also isolated and cold, qualities that foster intimacy among the small student body. "At the Johnson School, it is always 70 degrees and bright...in the atrium," jokes one student, a place where "We have frequent social hours." Students are extremely active in nearly 70 organized teams and clubs ("Spouses/partners are welcome and encouraged to join these organizations"), and spend their scanty free time winding down together. "On weekends, there is usually one big social event at night where the majority of the school will gather, and the rest of the weekend is typically spent with smaller groups of friends at a variety of locales." "Whether it's the indoor soccer club playing at 11:00 P.M. on a Sunday night, or the whole lot of us crowding the Palms (a local bar) on Thursday nights, you will always find a group of us out doing something enjoyable."

Admissions

The Johnson application is online only and includes three 400-word essays (two mandatory, one optional). Mandatory topics cover professional achievement and career goals, and the optional essay may be used to detail extenuating circumstances or provide additional bolstering information. Johnson initially reviews applicants through a two-reader system; those who make the cut receive an interview, and only disputed files go to committee. As with other systems, this simply means that it pays to present an extremely strong case for admission. Last year's entering class reported an average GPA of 3.3, average GMAT score of 700, and 5 years of work experience.

FINANCIAL FACTS

Annual tuition	$47,150

ADMISSIONS

Admissions Selectivity Rating	99
# of applications received	2,276
% applicants accepted	22
% acceptees attending	54
Average GMAT	700
Range of GMAT	640–750
Average GPA	3.3
TOEFL required of international students	Yes
Minimum TOEFL (paper/computer)	600/250
Application fee	$200
International application fee	$200
Application Deadline/Notification	
Round 1:	10/6 / 12/17
Round 2:	11/12 / 2/16
Round 3:	1/12 / 3/23
Round 4:	3/30 / 5/06
Early decision program?	No
Deferment available	No
Transfer students accepted	No
Non-fall admissions	Yes
Need-blind admissions	Yes

EMPLOYMENT PROFILE

Career Rating	98	Grads Employed by Function% Avg. Salary
		Top 5 Employers Hiring Grads
		Citigroup (8), Deloitte Consulting LLC (7), Accenture (5), Deutsche Bank (5), General Electric Company (5)

DARTMOUTH COLLEGE
TUCK SCHOOL OF BUSINESS

GENERAL INFORMATION
Type of school   Private
Academic calendar   Quarter

SURVEY SAYS...
Friendly students
Good social scene
Good peer network
Helpful alumni
Solid preparation in:
General management

STUDENTS
Enrollment of parent
  institution   5,700
Enrollment of MBA Program 510
% male/female   66/34
% minorities   18
% international   35
Average age at entry   28
Average years work experience
  at entry   5

ACADEMICS
Academic Experience Rating 97
Student/faculty ratio   9:1
Profs interesting rating   86
Profs accessible rating   90
% female faculty   20
% minority faculty   15

Joint Degrees
Tuck offers joint and dual-degrees in association with Dartmouth's other graduate programs and some of the nation's best professional schools.

Prominent Alumni
Steven Roth, Chairman and CEO, Vornado Realty Trust; Elyse Allan, President & CEO, General Electric Canada; Roger McNamee, Co-Founder & Advisory Director, Elevation Partners; Thomas McInerney, COO, ING Insurance; Debi Brooks, Co-Founder, Michael J. Fox Foundation.

Academics

There is no rest for the weary at Tuck, where the "intensive academic core for first-years is accelerated and rigorous." During the elongated (32-week) school year, students take 18 courses, two of which are electives. One of these is Tuck's trademark First-Year Project, a course in which student teams develop new business ventures or act as consultants in existing ventures, and in which grades rest on the final presentation and other outcomes. This method reflects Tuck's emphasis on "academic deliverables, such as group papers, projects, and presentations." The second year consists of 12 elective courses, which may reflect well-rounded interests or a specialization. For example, Tuck recommends that a student interested in nonprofit and sustainability management take Corporate Social Responsibility, Entrepreneurship in the Social Sector I and II, Ethics in Action, the Tuck Global Consultancy international field study, and Strategic Responses to Market Failure. One student reports, "I feel completely prepared to take on my career post-Tuck. The school does a fantastic job of working students hard in the first year, teaching them the core fundamentals of business, and letting them craft their own paths during the second year." One student notes, "Tuck could update its core curriculum and case study assignments to reflect the current business environment, i.e., more standard courses to better understand the private-market investment climate, corporate ethics, digital media/entertainment, and emerging economies."

Tuck operates through "full immersion." Students "do a lot of work in study groups, which are assigned and required for first-years." Mandatory team rotation forces each student to work closely with a wide swath of his or her peers during the first year. The small class size and rural location reinforces class cohesiveness and fosters intimacy between MBA students and Tuck faculty and staff. Professors host social "gatherings at their homes and get involved with student organizations." "I have had lunches, dinners, or drinks with the majority of my professors," reports one second-year, "and I am treated with a respect that goes beyond [typical] teacher-student interactions." Administrators are "the nicest people on Earth." Some have even been known to "come in on a Sunday evening and bring food and coffee for us when we have exams." The overall "quality" of faculty and administration alike is "extraordinary."

Career and Placement

Tuck is "very focused on helping students land the jobs they came here to get." "The Career Development Office works tirelessly on behalf of students," though this benefit is most useful for students pursuing "traditional career paths (i.e., consulting, finance, general management)." However, "students interested in other opportunities (i.e., marketing, retail) may need to do more work outside the Career Development Office." Dartmouth is a magnet for recruiters, and "one of the best parts of Tuck is that visiting executives spend meaningful time with us. They don't stop by on their way to another meeting; rather, they have lunch and/or dinner with us, hold individual office hours, and make an effort to share their experiences with members of the class." Recruitment is Northeast focused, but the career office "is continually trying to reach out to West Coast firms"—the ones who often "recruit locally at Stanford and UCLA"—"and does a couple of treks for students interested in returning to the West." The tides may be turning; one student reports seeing "Google, Microsoft, and PG&E on campus this year," a possible "indication that a more diverse lineup of firms [is] coming to Tuck."

Students seeking jobs in "nontraditional" vocations and regions will have better luck with Tuck's extremely strong, supportive alumni network. One student told this story of success: "I emailed a Tuck alum who is a managing director at a bulge-bracket investment bank in London, and he called me 5 minutes later to talk. He arranged a personal office visit…and actually talked HR into sending me straight to second round interviews, because the firm's London office didn't recruit on campus…all because I put 'Tuck' in the subject line."

Tuck's most recent graduating class reports a median total annual compensation of $165,000.

Student Life and Environment

Students call posh, pretty Hanover "the quintessential small, New England, Ivy League town," "within a short drive of many great ski resorts" and far removed "from the hustle and bustle of a big city." Unlike many schools, most first-years live on campus. Couples and families live in the Dartmouth-owned Sachem Village housing complex or elsewhere off-campus. The environment is extremely "intimate" and "supportive." Tuckies consider their school very family-friendly, telling us that partners are an integral part of the social scene, and note that "classmates who have children while at Tuck" are surrounded by a "phenomenal support network." Tuck is very inclusive of gay and lesbian students and partners.

The isolated location and clustered housing contribute to "a great deal of school spirit" and "strong camaraderie" in a "work-hard, play-hard environment." "Tuck students really transplant their lives to be here…we make friends quickly here and socialize a lot with our classmates." Students belong to more than 60 clubs, teams, and publications, and attend numerous social functions every week. "The end of the week is typically characterized by social mixers (Tuck Tails), small group dinners…and the occasional full-blown party (winter and spring formals, Tuck Vegas, beach party)." Students report that "sports are very much a part of life at Tuck."

No one gripes about the intimacy, which results in great friendships and means close business ties in the future. "I have had a substantive conversation with each of my 240 classmates and will feel very comfortable calling any of them after graduation for career advice and/or business counsel," reports one Tuckie. The class of 2011 is 35 percent international and an additional 20 percent minority, however, sometimes students note they wish there was a bit more diversity.

Admissions

Like many other schools, Tuck wants to know that you love it for what it is, not only for what it can do for you; show that you have researched the school thoroughly. The class of 2011 reports an average GPA of 3.53 and GMAT score of 712.

FINANCIAL FACTS

Annual tuition	$47,835
Fees	$300
Cost of books	$3,700
Room & board	
(on/off-campus)	$11,325/$13,850
% of students receiving aid	76
% of first-year students receiving aid	75
% of students receiving loans	87
% of students receiving grants	45
Average award package	$56,973
Average grant	$20,414
Average student loan debt	$65,365

ADMISSIONS

Admissions Selectivity Rating	98
# of applications received	2,804
% applicants accepted	19
% acceptees attending	49
Average GMAT	712
Range of GMAT	660–760
Average GPA	3.53
TOEFL required of international students	Yes
Application fee	$260
International application fee	$260
Application Deadline/Notification	
Round 1:	10/14 / 12/18
Round 2:	11/11 / 2/5
Round 3:	1/29 / 3/19
Round 4:	4/2 / 5/14
Early decision program?	Yes
Deferment available	Yes
Maximum length of deferment	Case-by-case basis
Transfer students accepted	No
Non-fall admissions	No
Need-blind admissions	Yes

EMPLOYMENT PROFILE

Career Rating	97	Grads Employed by Function	%	Avg. Salary
Average base starting salary	$105,198	Marketing	13	$97,548
		Operations	2	NR
		Consulting	40	$117,173
		Management	14	$94,102
		Finance	27	$99,452

DELAWARE STATE UNIVERSITY
COLLEGE OF BUSINESS

GENERAL INFORMATION
Type of school   Public

SURVEY SAYS...
Good peer network
Solid preparation in:
Operations Teamwork
Communication/interpersonal skills
Presentation skills
Quantitative skills
Doing business in a global economy

STUDENTS
Enrollment of MBA Program	75
% male/female	54/46
% out-of-state	40
% minorities	32
% international	62
Average age at entry	32
Average years work experience at entry	3

ACADEMICS
Academic Experience Rating	**65**
Student/faculty ratio	9:1
Profs interesting rating	62
Profs accessible rating	71
% female faculty	10
% minority faculty	60

Prominent Alumni
P. Narayan, Project Manager; Elan, Business Analyst; Sree, Financial Analyst.

Academics

Most of the students enrolled in the MBA program at Delaware State University's College of Business choose the program for its "convenient location" and for its attention to the needs of the "working professionals and aspiring managers" who attend here (classes are held exclusively during evening hours and weekends). The school describes its MBA as "an accelerated program geared towards working adults" that can be completed in 18 months by those taking two courses per eight-week term and in just 12 months by those taking three courses per term. Even those shouldering a lighter workload can complete the program in two years by attending at least one summer session.

The DSU MBA program is designed to promote integrative learning in a functional context so that students can build important managerial and organizational skills. The program requires students to complete 21 credit hours of core courses, one capstone course, and nine credit hours of electives, which can be used to pursue a concentration in a single subject. Students lacking corresponding undergraduate coursework may be required to take some or all of 18 credit hours in foundation courses. Foundation courses cover the following subjects: accounting, economics, finance, management information systems, marketing, and quantitative methods. Students may attempt to place out of any of these courses by passing a comprehensive exam, developed by the College of Business faculty, in the subject.

DSU's required core courses cover advanced economics, marketing management, business law and ethics, financial management, organizational leadership and behavior, operations analysis and management, and information and technology management. The capstone course is entitled Applied Strategic Management. Electives are offered in finance, information systems, and general management; concentrations are available in finance and information systems. Students may also participate in a case project in order to fulfill one of their elective requirements. According to the school's website, the case project "tests the student's strategic thinking and analytic skills" by requiring students either to (1) assess a company's income statement, balance sheet, annual reports, and other such documentation and provide recommendations; (2) manage an investment portfolio; or, (3) analyze "a series of general management cases that cover a broad range of strategic issues facing companies."

In order to graduate, students must earn a minimum grade point average of 3.0 with no more than six credit hours with a grade of C. Students who receive a grade of D or F during a course will be dismissed from the program; the school has procedures in place for students to appeal dismissal and/or academic probation. Students are required to complete the program in no more than five years.

Career and Placement

According to the school's website, the DSU Career Services office provides "technological and practical resources to provide students with the talent to conduct job searches, to become proficient in effective interviewing and presentation, and understanding the fit between their competencies and occupational requirements. Students also gain marketable experience through on- and off-campus collegiate activities, campus and community service, research projects, cooperative education, and internships to prepare them to manage their careers pre- and post-graduation." The service is designed primarily for the benefit of undergraduates, although graduate students and recent alumni may also utilize it.

ADMISSIONS CONTACT: KISHOR SHETH, MBA DIRECTOR
ADDRESS: 1200 N. DUPONT HIGHWAY, ROOM 106C, BANK OF AMERICA BUILDING DOVER, DE 19901
PHONE: 302-857-6906 • FAX: 302-857-6945
E-MAIL: KSHETH@DESU.EDU • WEBSITE: WWW.DESU.EDU

Student Life and Environment

Students in the DSU MBA program form "a very culturally and ethnically diverse" group. Most are "hard-working students with full-time jobs" and "many have families to support," but there are also "some fresh college grads" in the mix. These "dedicated and helpful" students contribute to an intellectually challenging atmosphere."

DSU is located in Dover, the state capital. The state government and the United States Air Force are among the area's top employers; others include Playtex, Procter & Gamble, and General Mills, all of which have manufacturing facilities in or around Dover. The city is conveniently located, with fairly easy access to Philadelphia, Washington D.C., and Baltimore.

Admissions

Applicants to the Delaware State MBA program must submit the following documentation to the Admissions Committee: a completed application; official transcripts for all previous undergraduate and graduate work; an official score report for the GMAT; two letters of recommendation from individuals capable of assessing the candidate's ability to succeed in a graduate business program; a resume; and, a personal statement of career objectives and personal philosophy. In order to earn unconditional admission, applicants must have completed all foundations courses at the undergraduate level, and they must show an undergraduate GPA of at least 2.75, a minimum GMAT score of 400, and earn a score of at least 975 under the formula [(undergraduate GPA x 200) + GMAT score]. Applicants failing to meet these requirements may be admitted conditionally if they have an undergraduate GPA of at least 2.5 and a minimum GMAT score of 400; or, have an undergraduate GPA of at least 3.0 or an upper-division GPA of at least 3.25; or, meet all requirements except for the foundations requirement. Students admitted conditionally will have their status changed to 'unconditional admission' once they have completed three MBA-level courses with a grade of at least B; they must submit a satisfactory GMAT score before being allowed to register for a fourth MBA-level course. Applicants with significant work experience (at least five years) in management may apply for admission as non-traditional students; the school may waive GPA and GMAT requirements for such applicants.

FINANCIAL FACTS

Annual tuition (in-state/ out-of-state)	$11,000/$22,000
Fees	$350
Cost of books	$1,000
Room & board (on/off-campus)	$800/$1,000
% of students receiving aid	20
% of first-year students receiving aid	40
% of students receiving loans	5
% of students receiving grants	20
Average award package	$5,000
Average grant	$6,000

ADMISSIONS

Admissions Selectivity Rating	61
# of applications received	45
% applicants accepted	98
% acceptees attending	100
Average GMAT	450
TOEFL required of international students	Yes
Application fee	$40
International application fee	$40
Early decision program?	No
Deferment available	Yes
Maximum length of deferment	Unlimited
Transfer students accepted	Yes
Transfer application policy: They must complete the application process and provide the official transcripts.	
Non-fall admissions	Yes
Need-blind admissions	No

EMPLOYMENT PROFILE

Career Rating	78	Grads Employed by Function	%	Avg. Salary
Percent employed at graduation	2	Marketing	10	NR
Percent employed 3 months after graduation	3	Operations	10	NR
		Management	40	NR
Average base starting salary	$60,000	Finance	20	NR
Primary Source of Full-time Job Acceptances		Entrepreneurship	10	NR
School-facilitated activities	NR (30%)	Strategic	10	NR
Graduate-facilitated activities	NR (40%)	**Top Employers Hiring Grads**		
Unknown	NR (30%)	Bank of America (13), Chase (15), JP Morgan (25)		

DREXEL UNIVERSITY
BENNETT S. LeBOW COLLEGE OF BUSINESS

GENERAL INFORMATION

Type of school	Private
Academic calendar	Sept–June
	with exception of 1 yr

SURVEY SAYS...

Students love Philadelphia, PA
Smart classrooms
Solid preparation in:
Accounting

STUDENTS

Enrollment of parent institution	22,493
Enrollment of MBA Program	746
% male/female	58/42
% out-of-state	48
% part-time	89
% minorities	47
% international	46
Average age at entry	29
Average years work experience at entry	6

ACADEMICS

Academic Experience Rating	84
Student/faculty ratio	26:1
Profs interesting rating	63
Profs accessible rating	76
% female faculty	29
% minority faculty	30

Joint Degrees

For most MBA programs, candidates can combine their MBA degree with either an MS in Accounting or MS in Finance. Dual degrees offered are: MD/MBA 5 years; JD/MBA, 4 years; MBA MS in Television Management, 3 years.

Prominent Alumni

Nicholas DeBenedictis, Chairman, AquaAmerica; Gary Bernstein, Vice President, IBM; Dominic J. Frederico, Chairman, President and CEO, Assured Guaranty; Raj Gupta, Chairman and CEO, Rohm & Haas; Dominic J. Frederico, Chairman, President, & CEO, Assured Guaranty.

Academics

Academics at Drexel University encompass a breadth of Colleges and Schools whose programs are designed to provide the foundation of study coupled with cooperative education experiences to produce the next generation of scholars, professionals, and leaders. LeBow College fits squarely into that tradition. Noted strengths of the MBA program include "a pragmatic approach to real-world application." Offering a "strong and dynamic curriculum" that "stresses practical education," LeBow offers "a solid emphasis on business analysis processes with a strong technology background as well." Practical application is delivered through "case studies and other real-life simulations" that "help in applying concepts and attaining a better understanding of how to approach a given situation." Students in the two-year full-time MBA program also benefit from a co-op program that provides hands-on experience while "helping students learn more about the industries in which they might wish to pursue a career."

Part-time and full-time students will find numerous options at LeBow. The school offers a one-year full-time MBA as well as the aforementioned two-year program. Those unable to attend daytime classes will likely prefer the two-year evening cohort MBA (called the LEAD MBA, for LeBow Evening Accelerated Drexel MBA). LeBow also offers a more traditional part-time Professional MBA and two online part-time MBAs. The first, called MBA Anywhere, is a conventional part-time cohort MBA delivered primarily online over 24 months (three on-campus residencies are required). The other is the Corporate MBA in Pharmaceutical Management, whose curriculum was designed in collaboration with Johnson & Johnson. All programs operate on a fast-paced quarterly academic calendar that allows "more chances to take courses during a year," and all programs place "a strong emphasis on leadership."

Students praise the LeBow administration, reporting that the school "appears to be pouring a lot of money into the marketing of the LeBow brand. That will likely produce more of a return for [us] upon graduation." One MBA happily tells us that "The administration could not make the process any easier to prevent any type of potential distraction from your academics. If you wish to pursue further study in a discipline or make local contacts in a discipline they are always there to help." Likewise, professors "are really open to meeting with students and discussing classroom ideas in a different context. They enjoy getting to know their students and sharing their own experiences." Faculty members "bring real-world issues to classroom for discussions and potential problem solutions. Some even share their consultancy experiences with the students. Overall, it is highly stimulating and excellent learning experience."

Career and Placement

LeBow's Office of MBA Career Services offers "excellent career services," according to students. Through "various career service events and networking opportunities," career counselors "really make an effort to involve as many students as possible and showcase their events in a professional way. Just in the last few months I have attended several Employer of the Week sessions that have [piqued] my interest in industries I had not previously considered. Also the Mentor Match program has been pivotal in honing my networking skills and [giving me the opportunity to interact] with alumni in both formal and informal settings." Drexel's alumni network represents another "great opportunity to see how Drexel positively impacted the careers of so many professionals who were once in our position years ago." Finally, "regular job fairs...are often good opportunities for networking."

ADMISSIONS CONTACT: JOHN ADAMSKI, DIRECTOR GRADUATE ADMISSIONS
ADDRESS: 3141 CHESTNUT STREET, MATHESON HALL 207 PHILADELPHIA, PA 19104
PHONE: 215-895-6804 • FAX: 215-895-1725
E-MAIL: MBA@DREXEL.EDU • WEBSITE: WWW.LEBOW.DREXEL.EDU

Top employers of recently graduated Drexel MBAs include: Deloitte & Touche, PricewaterhouseCoopers, Prudential Bank of America, PNC Bank, Wachovia Securities, TIAA CREF, Campbell Soup Company, Siemens, Sungard, and Exelon Corporation.

Student Life and Environment

"Drexel provides plenty of professional and social networking opportunities" for its MBAs, although full-time students benefit the most (since they are on campus most frequently). Full-timers report "an overwhelming range of opportunities available," with "clubs and competitions for every interest" that include "networking events for women in business, video game clubs, consulting groups, music labels, etc. Academics are always number one priority, but there are plenty of outside opportunities for fun." Philadelphia is an asset in that regard. It's "a city that has a ton of opportunities" and provides a "great local business and government network." Overall, students enjoy a "good life/school/work balance," with "plenty of opportunities to pursue other school-related activities without having to overcommit yourself."

LeBow has a diverse population in its MBA programs with one-third of the students coming with undergraduate degrees in business, one-third in the sciences including engineering, and one-third having liberal arts degree. Students say this mix results in "a nice balance between very intelligent and a lot of fun." The different programs draw different types of students, of course. The full-time program tends to be younger and less experienced, while the Executive MBA draws students who "have extensive work experience and understand the importance of a business graduate degree."

Admissions

Applicants to the Drexel MBA program must submit all of the following: transcripts for all undergraduate work and for any graduate study; an official GMAT score report; letters of recommendation; a personal essay; and a resume. Applicants are assessed based on academic performance, professional experience, career goals, extracurricular record, and potential to contribute positively to the Drexel MBA program. International applicants must also submit an official score report for the TOEFL if English is not their first language, unless they hold an undergraduate degree from an institution at which instruction is in English.

FINANCIAL FACTS

Annual tuition	$29,000
Fees	$800
Cost of books	$1,200
Room & board	$15,000
% of students receiving aid	76
% of first-year students receiving aid	76
% of students receiving loans	64
% of students receiving grants	42
Average award package	$29,890
Average grant	$16,246
Average student loan debt	$48,981

ADMISSIONS

Admissions Selectivity Rating	89
# of applications received	1,385
% applicants accepted	37
% acceptees attending	47
Average GMAT	620
Range of GMAT	580–680
Average GPA	3.2
TOEFL required of international students	Yes
Minimum TOEFL (paper/computer)	600/250
Application fee	$50
International application fee	$50
Regular application deadline	8/1
Early decision program?	Yes
Deferment available	Yes
Maximum length of deferment	12 months
Transfer students accepted	Yes
Transfer application policy: Completed application and all supporting materials to be reviewed by Admissions Committee. Only non-cohorted programs allow for transfer credits from an AACSB accredited school.	
Non-fall admissions	Yes
Need-blind admissions	Yes

EMPLOYMENT PROFILE

Career Rating		91	Grads Employed by Function	% Avg. Salary
Percent employed at graduation		49	Marketing	20 $48,000
Percent employed 3 months after graduation		78	Operations	5 NR
			Management	13 $63,000
Average base starting salary		$61,203	Finance	58 $64,329
			MIS	5 NR

Top 5 Employers Hiring Grads
KPMG, IBM, CIGNA, Sunoco, Johnson & Johnson

DUKE UNIVERSITY
THE FUQUA SCHOOL OF BUSINESS

GENERAL INFORMATION
Type of school   Private
Academic calendar   Terms

SURVEY SAYS...
Good social scene
Good peer network
Happy students
Smart classrooms
Solid preparation in:
Teamwork
Communication/interpersonal skills

STUDENTS
Enrollment of parent
  institution   13,662
Enrollment of MBA Program   902
% male/female   61/39
% part-time   0
% minorities   14
% international   38
Average age at entry   29
Average years work experience
  at entry   6

ACADEMICS
Academic Experience Rating   **95**
Profs interesting rating   94
Profs accessible rating   86
% female faculty   20
% minority faculty   5

Joint Degrees
MBA/JD (4 years); MBA/Master of
Public Policy (3 years); MBA/Master
of Forestry (3 years); MBA/Master
of Environmental Management (3
years); MBA/MS Engineering (3
years); MBA/MD (5 years);
MBA/MSN in Nursing (3 years).

Prominent Alumni
Jack Bovender, Chairman and CEO,
HCA (retired); Timothy D. Cook,
COO, Apple Inc; Melinda French
Gates, Co-chair and Trustee, Bill &
Melinda Gates Foundation; Kevin
Kelly, CEO, Heidrick & Struggles;
Malvinder Singh, Group Chairman,
Religare Enterprises & Fortis
Healthcare Ltd.

Academics

Students come to Duke University's Fuqua School of Business for many reasons. For some, "the opportunity to be associated with one of the premier universities in the world" is an obvious advantage, while others cite the school's "strong social entrepreneurship program." The "culture of diversity," "international programs," and "focus on developing global business leaders," are other highly attractive qualities of a Fuqua education, as are the school's many institutes and abundant areas of study. Across the board, however, almost everyone agrees that the "incredible atmosphere of collaboration" and "emphasis on teamwork" make Fuqua stand out. Both inside and outside the classroom, Fuqua maintains "an environment that highly values (and teaches) principles of communication and inter-connection between people." Coursework is collaborative, teamwork is integrated throughout the curriculum, and students are encouraged to take leadership roles in the school community. In fact, "The challenge from the administration to be "leaders of consequence" is woven throughout our activities, not just a trite phrase mentioned during orientation." A student details, "The administration gives students the freedom to shape much of our experience, and has an open-door policy when we need to confront any situations that might arise, even for items as small as thermostat settings in classrooms." In fact, "Much of the day-to-day activities of the school are student-run," and even "core functions of the school, such as admissions and career management, have great leadership opportunities for current students." With such a round and robust student experience, many feel that Duke offers "the best blend of academics and atmosphere of any of the top business schools."

The Fuqua Daytime MBA begins with a four-week term called the "Global Institute," designed to develop international business and leadership skills. Thereafter, Duke's curriculum is organized into a series of six-week terms, during which students take a blend of electives and required core courses. "Taught by seasoned, senior faculty," "the core classes truly prepare you for every aspect of business." There is also a "plentiful" selection of electives (more than 100, at present), which add "a great blend of breadth and depth" to the program. As a part of an internationally renowned university, Duke's "phenomenal" faculty is "widely recognized for its prolific research output," yet "very devoted to classes they teach." Each class crams "a full semester of material into a six week term." Therefore, you'll "learn a lot in a short period of time"—and be amply challenged, at that. A dazzled student exclaims, "The academic experience is the best one can get in the world; I have learned more in these two years than in my five years of college and 10 years of experience combined."

Career and Placement

With an excellent reputation and accomplished student body, there is "a wide breadth of companies for each discipline" who recruit on the Duke campus. In recent years, top recruiters included Citi, Deloitte Consulting, Accenture, Johnson & Johnson, Goldman Sachs, McKinsey & Company, and Boston Consulting Group. While some students hail the Career Management Center's ample contacts and recruiters, other say they would like to continue to see the school work toward implementing a "better off-campus strategy for students," a goal that the Center has recently addressed with the introduction of the LAMP model, a new, proprietary model for organizing and implementing an off-campus search. Most students note that given the current trouble in the economy, the school has responded adequately; "They have added additional sessions throughout the week to make sure students have the resources they need to have a successful job search." Further, "50 to 60 students formally assist—via Career Management Center—other students to critique resume, cover letter, and interview skills." To further assist students with their off-campus search during these difficult economic conditions, the school recently launched an institution-wide

ADMISSIONS CONTACT: LIZ RILEY HARGROVE, ASSOCIATE DEAN FOR ADMISSIONS
ADDRESS: 1 TOWERVIEW DRIVE DURHAM, NC 27708-0120
PHONE: 919-660-7705 • FAX: 919-681-8026
E-MAIL: ADMISSIONS-INFO@FUQUA.DUKE.EDU • WEBSITE: WWW.FUQUA.DUKE.EDU

initiative entitled "Hire Up." In spring 2010, 11 cross-functional teams were formed to help current job seekers in the short-term, as well as to identify and implement longer term enhancements to the job search process at Fuqua. Each team is comprised of senior staff representing Fuqua's industry centers, global regions, career center, corporate relations and alumni relations groups. A student representative also serves on each team to ensure that student perspective is heard and considered. Others relay the desire for the Center to continue to "improve in building relationships with international employers." Though, as the school notes, with more than 9 out of 10 students citing the U.S. as their preferred destination post-graduation, student employment interests have traditionally been focused in the U.S. despite the fact that Fuqua's student population is very global.

Student Life and Environment

Student leadership is a key component of the Fuqua experience, and "The business school activities and clubs are solely student-run." As a result, "Day-to-day life is very busy between classes, career search, clubs, and social activity." A student shares, "The workload (class, career search, club related) is very challenging and prepares you well for the busy life of an executive." But, with 24 hours in the day, there is even time for fun. A student marvels, "I work at 100% capacity but somehow still manage to enjoy a dynamic social life." In fact, "Team Fuqua"—as the business school community is fondly called—is a "friendly" and "tight-knit" group. As "most people come to Durham just for business school," you'll find "an instant community whose members bond very quickly and socialize very often." A popular event is the weekly "Fuqua Friday," a happy hour during which "students, partners, children, professors and administrators can decompress and have some fun." In addition, students get together for "lots of parties and barbecues at apartment complexes." For married students (which comprise about a third of the population), "The school also has a great community of spouses and partners who meet regularly which makes it easier for those who are married or in relationships."

On campus, "The facilities are amazing. There is a new building with high end technology, a top library, and 58 team rooms." When it comes to surrounding Durham, most students praise the school's comfortable "suburban location" in a city that "affords a good quality of life." Among other benefits, there is "a plethora of affordable housing," and "the weather is nice for most of the year."

Admissions

Admission to Fuqua is highly competitive; you will have the best chance of acceptance if you apply as early in the admissions cycle as possible. The admissions committee does not have any minimum GMAT scores or GPA requirements. However, for the class of 2011, the GMAT range for students in the 25th to 75th percentile was 650–720, while the average GPA range was 3.14 to 3.63.

FINANCIAL FACTS

Annual tuition	$45,850
% of students receiving aid	81
% of first-year students receiving aid	79
% of students receiving loans	70
% of students receiving grants	45
Average student loan debt	$88,050

ADMISSIONS

Admissions Selectivity Rating	96
# of applications received	2,909
% applicants accepted	31
% acceptees attending	50
Average GMAT	688
Range of GMAT	650–720
Average GPA	3.4
TOEFL required of international students	Yes
Application fee	$200
International application fee	$200
Application Deadline/Notification	
Round 1:	10/6 / 11/14
Round 2:	11/12 / 1/19
Round 3:	1/7 / 3/8
Round 4:	3/9 / 4/22
Early decision program?	Yes
ED Deadline/Notification	10/6 / 11/24
Deferment available	Yes
Maximum length of deferment	Considered on a case-by-case basis after May 1
Transfer students accepted	No
Non-fall admissions	No
Need-blind admissions	Yes

EMPLOYMENT PROFILE

Career Rating	96	Grads Employed by Function	%	Avg. Salary
Percent employed at graduation	68	Marketing	21	$92,662
Percent employed 3 months after graduation	76	Operations	2	$102,933
		Consulting	35	$114,465
Average base starting salary	$101,764	Management	19	$95,047
Primary Source of Full-time Job Acceptances		Finance	21	$96,725
School-facilitated activities	208 (71%)	Top 5 Employers Hiring Grads		
Graduate-facilitated activities	80 (27%)	Deloitte Consulting (17), Johnson & Johnson		
Unknown	4 (1%)	(12), Boston Consulting (11), Dell (11),		
		PricewaterhouseCoopers (9)		

DUQUESNE UNIVERSITY
JOHN F. DONAHUE GRADUATE SCHOOL OF BUSINESS

GENERAL INFORMATION

Type of school	Private
Academic calendar	Semester

SURVEY SAYS...

Cutting-edge classes
Happy students
Solid preparation in:
Doing business in a global economy

STUDENTS

Enrollment of parent institution	10,160
Enrollment of MBA Program	307
% male/female	57/43
% part-time	68
% international	22
Average years work experience at entry	4

ACADEMICS

Academic Experience Rating	70
Student/faculty ratio	19:1
Profs interesting rating	81
Profs accessible rating	79
% female faculty	17

Joint Degrees

MBA/MS-Information Systems Management: 3 years full time; 4 years part time; MBA/JD: 4 years full time; five years part time; MBA/MS-Nursing: three years full time; 4 years part time; MBA/MS-Environmental Science and Mgmt.: 2 years full time; 4 years part time; MBA/MS-Industrial Pharmacy: varies with changes in Pharmacy program.

Prominent Alumni

James F. Will, Vice Chancellor, St. Vincent College; Gail Gerono, Vice President Investor Relations, Communications and Human Resources, Calgon Carbon Corp; William Lyons, Executive Vice President and CFO, Consol Energy.

Academics

With the introduction of a new sustainability-focused MBA program, a growing reputation, and an unwavering emphasis on ethical approaches to business principles, students at the Donahue Graduate School of Business say "it is a truly exciting time at Duquesne University." Duquesne offers an evening MBA program for working professionals, dual degree programs, and several master's programs, as well as their flagship offering: "an 11-month full-time program, focusing primarily in sustainability." While the school has maintained a solid regional reputation for many years, a student observes, "Since launching the MBA Sustainability program, I have noticed an unstoppable momentum. Students, faculty, and administration are relentlessly involved in new research, case competitions, and program development." In addition to the academic energy the new program has produced, students say adding sustainability to the MBA is "perfect for the student looking for a career edge," as very few graduate business programs offer the highly specialized training they receive at Duquesne. On a broader scale, business courses throughout the curriculum "emphasize both the subject areas and the ethical and sustainability considerations. This holistic combination produces balanced individuals who learn to solve problems while protecting the rights of others and the environment." In addition, students can add depth to their MBA through one of ten established concentrations (including business ethics, environmental management, marketing, and taxation) or top off the experience with international business skills through a semester abroad at one of the school's partner universities in France, Colombia, Mexico, Japan, China, Belgium, or Germany.

In addition to its innovative curricular offerings, Duquesne distinguishes itself through its "genuine interest in the success of their students." Duquesne professors "like to teach and are skilled instructors." A current student shares, "With rare exception, all of my professors are wonderful teachers who take the time to explain material." In particular, students appreciate the fact that "particular professors are brought in straight from the work world and know their field inside and out." What's more, at this small school, students benefit from ample interaction with faculty. For example, "students form close relationships with faculty and often begin joint research projects out of the classroom. This research is usually published where the student is recognized as primary, secondary, or joint author."

When it comes to the workload, "Tests are killer but the papers are manageable." However, students also remind us that "this is not a heavy quant school, and there is a heavy emphasis on the soft skills in the business world." To that end, teamwork is heavily emphasized and "the MBA students come from a variety of backgrounds, bringing many perspectives to classroom discussions. This enhances the learning experience by broadening our perspectives and encouraging us to contribute to the discussions." In addition to excellence, convenience is key to a Duquesne education; the program allows undergraduate business majors to waive a large percentage of required courses, and the "program that is set up to make education accessible by conducting classes in several locations around the city of Pittsburgh."

Admissions Contact: Patricia Moore, Managing Director of Graduate Programs
Address: 600 Forbes Avenue Pittsburgh, PA 15282
Phone: 412-396-6276 • Fax: 412-396-1726
E-mail: grad-bus@duq.edu • Website: www.business.duq.edu/grad

Career and Placement

The Duquesne University Career Services Center provides career services to undergraduate students, graduate students, and alumni. Through DuqConnection, students can post their resumes, register for career fairs, and view current job openings online. On campus, the center hosts two major career fairs each year. In addition, the Career Services Center maintains contact with other universities, which sponsor more career fairs or job-related forums, giving student access to a range of career opportunities in the greater region. Recently, the following employers recruited Duquesne graduates: Allegheny Energy, American Eagle Outfitters, Bayer, Deloitte, Ernst & Young, GlaxoSmithKline, Highmark, Intel, PricewaterhouseCoopers, Roadway Express, and Verizon Wireless.

With a largely regional reputation, "Duquesne University is well-known and respected in Western Pennsylvania, but loses some credibility outside of the state." As a result, some feel the school should "allocate more resources to assisting students with finding employment nationally and internationally."

Student Life and Environment

According to its students, Duquesne graduate business programs attract a group of "intelligent people who sincerely care about their academic and professional careers." The overall "atmosphere is friendly and supportive," and students "work on projects outside of school, have started clubs, and socialize regularly. I believe that some of us will stay in close contact long down the road." A current student adds, "My cohorts spend a lot of time together, eating, studying, and going out on the drink. We have our own computer lab. It is similar to an office setting where work and chatter coexist."

Duquesne's "beautiful" campus is "located in the heart of Downtown Pittsburgh," an affordable, big city that also boasts a respectable business community. In addition to overhauling the curriculum, students are proud to report that "there are long-range plans for new construction of LEED Certified buildings, not to mention the retrofitting of current buildings." Of the many facilities available to graduate students on the Duquesne campus, "the new fitness center is a definite selling point." On the downside, "parking is terrible, which is funny considering the campus is mostly commuters."

Admissions

Applicants to Duquesne are evaluated based on their undergraduate transcripts, letters of recommendation, autobiographical statement, GMAT scores, and work experience. Generally speaking, a minimum GMAT score of 550 is required for admission to the program. Students with more than ten years of high-level business experience may be able to waive the GMAT requirement.

FINANCIAL FACTS

Annual tuition	$22,113
Fees	$2,106
Cost of books	$2,500
Room & board (on-campus)	$9,000
% of students receiving aid	70
% of first-year students receiving aid	70
% of students receiving grants	13
Average grant	$15,000

ADMISSIONS

Admissions Selectivity Rating	66
# of applications received	165
% applicants accepted	96
% acceptees attending	59
Average GMAT	521
Average GPA	3.29
TOEFL required of international students	Yes
Minimum TOEFL (paper/computer)	550/213
Regular application deadline	5/1
Regular notification	6/1
Early decision program?	No
Deferment available	Yes
Maximum length of deferment	1 year
Transfer students accepted	Yes
Transfer application policy: The Donahue School will accept up to 15 transfer credits from an accredited college or university.	
Non-fall admissions	Yes
Need-blind admissions	Yes

EMPLOYMENT PROFILE

Career Rating	83	Grads Employed by Function	% Avg. Salary
Average base starting salary	$76,600	Operations	35 NR
		Consulting	6 NR
		Management	6 NR
		Finance	29 NR
		MIS	12 NR

Top 5 Employers Hiring Grads
Westinghouse (3), Heinz North America (2), Highmark (2)

EAST CAROLINA UNIVERSITY
COLLEGE OF BUSINESS

GENERAL INFORMATION
Type of school   Public
Academic calendar   Semester

SURVEY SAYS...
Friendly students
Good social scene
Cutting-edge classes
Solid preparation in:
Teamwork
Communication/interpersonal skills
Quantitative skills
Computer skills

STUDENTS
Enrollment of MBA Program 767
% part-time   69

ACADEMICS
Academic Experience Rating **71**
Profs interesting rating   85
Profs accessible rating   84

Joint Degrees
MD/MBA full-time, 42 credits; 12 months.

Academics

East Carolina University is a medium-sized public school that offers a fully accredited MBA program both online and on campus. Academically, the MBA curriculum is designed to provide a "solid foundation in business fundamentals across the board." Students are required to complete a series of breadth classes in seven business areas, and later, may tailor their education through elective coursework in areas like finance, health care, and supply chain management. A current student attests, "I am an aspiring entrepreneur and I chose this institution for its comprehensive curriculum to build a solid, broad business foundation. I feel I chose well." In addition to coursework, "there are numerous opportunities available to become involved with department-related projects and academic groups," or to augment your experience (while lowering the tuition price) through graduate assistantships. Students can also add international experience to the MBA through one of two summer exchange programs in China and Australia.

Despite the school's low in-state tuition, East Carolina University isn't besieged by the bureaucratic hassles that plague other public institutions. Led by an administrative staff that is "very accessible and willing to lend a helping hand," students assure us that "when the university becomes aware of an improvement needed, they are quick to respond." In fact, "if you are an on-campus student, you get the opportunity to know the school's administrators on a first name basis. They are very accessible and want to help." In addition to the administrative support, students are guided in their academic career through an assigned advisor, "who is always available and always has the answers you need." Experts in the business school experience, "all of the advisors and staff for the MBA program have received an MBA from ECU; therefore they know how the courses are and how the curriculum is set up first hand."

If you are planning to pursue a degree part time, be aware that "the homework and class work is very demanding and time-consuming," which can be particularly challenging for those who are balancing a full life outside of school. A first-year student writes, "So far, I have been very stressed out adapting to the MBA program, but the program has enough flexibility to allow me time to get adjusted to the course load." For extremely busy professionals, East Carolina University also gives students the "ability to complete the entire MBA online," or the opportunity to complete the degree through a combination of online and campus classes. Fortunately, "the distance education program is well run" and online students benefit from the same quality academic programs you'll find on campus. A student attests, "Every professor I have had treats online students exactly as they treat their on-campus students and holds us to the same standards."

ADMISSIONS CONTACT: TINA WILLIAMS, DIRECTOR OF GRADUATE PROGRAMS
ADDRESS: 3203 BATE BUILDING GREENVILLE, NC 27858-4353
PHONE: 252-328-6970 • FAX: 252-328-2106
E-MAIL: GRADBUS@ECU.EDU • WEBSITE: WWW.BUSINESS.ECU.EDU

Career and Placement

Through ECU's Career Services office, students can get highly individualized counseling services and participate in a range of career development activities. Students particularly appreciate the fact that the team at Career Services "know you by name and remember speaking with you. They are quick to respond to any questions or concerns you might have." A current student adds, "They go through your entire resume and help you tweak it until it is just right, and they even hold regular mock-interviews with actual company personnel."

Career Services also maintains a monthly schedule of campus recruiting events, campus interviews, and corporate speakers. Companies that visited campus in the past year include Credit-Suisse, CIA, Wachovia Bank, Sherwin Williams, FMI, Coyote Logistics, Lowes, Vanguard, Northwestern Mutual, and BB&T Bank.

Student Life and Environment

Boasting a pleasant campus environment with a touch of Southern charm, ECU "has a great atmosphere from small-town North Carolina. Everyone at the university is friendly and always willing to help." Within the business school, "the graduate student body is professional and everyone seems genuinely eager to learn." While the school draws a predominantly local crowd, you'll still feel at home, even if you aren't from the area. A current MBA attests, "My fellow students are very helpful. I am not from North Carolina and many of them are very eager to show me around and help me out." Located in the small city of Greenville, the school's "on-campus facilities such as gym, theater, auditorium are good to excellent, and offer opportunities for staying healthy and active."

The Graduate Business Association (GBA), the largest graduate student group on the ECU campus, "is well-run and is a good association for socializing." Both the business school and the GBA host various recreational and career-development events throughout the year. Even an online student shares, "I get tons of emails about everything going on all the time, so I never feel in the dark." While they are well-apprised of the many things they are missing, part-time and online students say they rarely participate in campus life. Explains one, "Keeping up with your familial obligations and job plus school leaves almost no time for anything else."

Admissions

East Carolina University admits students using an admission index number, which is calculated using a student's standardized test scores and undergraduate GPA. To be eligible for the program, students must hold an undergraduate degree in any subject. Students in the most recent graduating class had an average undergraduate GPA of 3.29 and an average GMAT score of 519.

FINANCIAL FACTS

Annual tuition (in-state/ out-of-state)	$6,620/$16,940
Cost of books	$500

ADMISSIONS

Admissions Selectivity Rating	60*
# of applications received	223
% applicants accepted	81
% acceptees attending	78
TOEFL required of international students	Yes
Minimum TOEFL (paper/computer)	550/213
Application fee	$60
International application fee	$60
Early decision program?	No
Deferment available	Yes
Maximum length of deferment	1 year
Transfer students accepted	Yes
Transfer application policy: Maximum of 9 semester credit hours from AACSB accredited institution accepted.	
Non-fall admissions	Yes
Need-blind admissions	Yes

EAST TENNESSEE STATE UNIVERSITY
COLLEGE OF BUSINESS AND TECHNOLOGY

GENERAL INFORMATION

Type of school	Public
Academic calendar	Semester

SURVEY SAYS...
Good social scene
Good peer network
Solid preparation in:
Accounting

STUDENTS

Enrollment of parent institution	13,870
Enrollment of MBA Program	80
% male/female	55/45
% out-of-state	10
% part-time	70
% minorities	10
% international	10
Average age at entry	28
Average years work experience at entry	3

ACADEMICS

Academic Experience Rating	85
Student/faculty ratio	7:1
Profs interesting rating	94
Profs accessible rating	74
% female faculty	10
% minority faculty	2

Prominent Alumni
Pal Barger, Food Services.

Academics

There aren't many choices at the College of Business and Technology at East Tennessee State University—the small program maintains only three business and four technology departments (accounting, economics/finance—urban studies, management/marketing)—but for those who are interested in a general purpose business degree, ETSU delivers.

In addition to the traditional MBA, the school also offers an MAcc (master's of accounting), an MPA (master's of public administration), and a graduate certificate in business administration for "those who seek a basic understanding of business administration but who may not be able to make the commitment of time, effort, and money required to seek a master's degree."

MBAs at ETSU feel that "The administration and faculty here are very student-oriented. Most have set times when they are available outside of class; others excel and really go the extra mile both in class presentation and in their availability to those students that require extra instruction." Overall, "The program is very well-organized and runs smoothly. The program has been staffed administratively to be a success. Everyone is focused on their customer—the student." Professors are regarded as "very knowledgeable in their fields, and many of them are widely recognized as great scholars." One student writes, "Most of them have a work background that can lead to some very good discussions in class, and [the professors present] the applications of the concepts in the real world through their stories." Faculty members are also "easy to work with and understanding about personal matters that can arise." ETSU students are "a very diverse and accepting group. All of us have different ideals and political and social backgrounds." Another student concurs: "We are like a family at ETSU. You go through the same classes with pretty much the same group of students. We are all interested in each other's success. There is low competition." Most students agree that the school does "a very good job of getting the student prepared with the knowledge that is needed in the workplace, but there is just so much that can be taught in the classroom setting." Many students have full-time jobs, and say "true learning from the classroom is applied to the jobs that are obtained after school." Across the board, students love that "The school is large enough to offer remote-learning facilities, and classes are generally available at convenient times for working adults." Most of all, however, students appreciate that professors "show a major interest in students' ability to understand the work."

Career and Placement

The Career Placement and Internship Services Office at East Tennessee University serves the school's entire undergraduate and graduate student body. The office hosts recruitment visits from various companies, sponsors and participates in career fairs, maintains online job boards and resume books, and offers counseling in interview skills, job search, career match, and resume writing. Recent on-campus recruiters included New York Life, Norfolk Southern, Wachovia, and Wells Fargo. Students are aware that "Johnson City is a small town, which limits the amount of recruiting that is done on campus." Even so, many "believe that [the] school could improve by really showing students what is available out there and helping them find jobs when they get done. It is there right now [at the Career Placement and Internship Services Office], but a student really has to push to find it."

ADMISSIONS CONTACT: DR. MARTHA POINTER, DIRECTOR OF GRADUATE STUDIES
ADDRESS: PO BOX 70699 JOHNSON CITY, TN 37614
PHONE: 423-439-5314 • FAX: 423-439-5274
E-MAIL: BUSINESS@BUSINESS.ETSU.EDU • WEBSITE: WWW.ETSU.EDU/CBAT

Student Life and Environment

East Tennessee State University is located in Johnson City, a small Appalachian city close to both the North Carolina and Virginia borders. The surrounding area, dubbed the Tri-Cities region, also includes Bristol and Kingsport; the charming town of Abingdon, Virginia, is also not too far afield. The area is an outdoor enthusiast's paradise, offering plenty of opportunities for hiking, climbing, skiing, and nature walks. The Tri-Cities area is a rising force in the health care industry, with a developing biotech industry that could bring big players to the region.

With more than 12,000 students (about 2,000 of whom are graduate students), the ETSU campus has the population to support a busy social scene. MBAs report, "There is a very good social scene, with Thursday nights being the night that most students go out to the clubs. There are not a lot of clubs in the area, but there are many places that one can go and have a beer if they so choose." Students try to find time to support their men's basketball team, the ETSU Bucs.

ETSU has expanded in recent years, adding several new buildings, including a fitness center (students love the "fully-equipped athletic facility"). Not all MBAs take the time to enjoy the ETSU campus, however; they note that "the school is a high commuter school. This leads to a low participation level in on-campus clubs" and other activities. Those who do participate recommend the school's several national honor societies. One student touts "the university organization called 'President's Pride.' Through this organization, I am able to socialize with other students, faculty, administrators, and [members of the] community by volunteering for university/community functions."

Through its Adult, Commuter, and Transfer Services (ACTS) Office, ETSU assists its many nontraditional students in adapting to student life. ACTS staff advises students on the nuts and bolts of registration, direct them to the campus's various tutoring services, and help parents find child-care services. This last one can be a problem for MBAs, who typically attend evening classes.

Admissions

Applications to the College of Business and Technology at East Tennessee State University are considered on a rolling basis. Applicants must submit the following to the

Graduate Admissions Office: official copies of transcripts for all undergraduate and graduate work; standardized test scores (GMAT for the MBA or MAcc, GRE for the

MPA); TOEFL scores (where applicable); a personal statement; letters of recommendation; and a resume. Applicants to the MPA program must have a minimum undergraduate GPA of 3.0. All applicants are presumed to be competent with computers and math literate through calculus.

FINANCIAL FACTS

Annual tuition (in-state/ out-of-state)	$6,493/$16,320
Fees	$1,100
Cost of books	$1,000
Room & board (on/off-campus)	$5,000/$6,000
% of students receiving aid	25
% of first-year students receiving aid	25
% of students receiving grants	25
Average award package	$6,000
Average grant	$6,000
Average student loan debt	$10,000

ADMISSIONS

Admissions Selectivity Rating	74
# of applications received	70
% applicants accepted	77
% acceptees attending	85
Average GMAT	535
Range of GMAT	450–700
Average GPA	3.3
TOEFL required of international students	Yes
Minimum TOEFL (paper/computer)	550/213
Application fee	$25
International application fee	$35
Regular application deadline	6/1
Deferment available	Yes
Maximum length of deferment	1 year
Transfer students accepted	Yes
Transfer application policy: Up to 9 approved hours MAY be accepted.	
Non-fall admissions	Yes
Need-blind admissions	Yes

EMPLOYMENT PROFILE

Career Rating	79	Grads Employed by Function	% Avg. Salary
Average base starting salary	$38,000	Marketing	10 $38,000
		Management	50 $30,000
		HR	10 $30,000
		Entrepreneurship	10 $35,000

Top 5 Employers Hiring Grads
Eastman Chemical (2)

EASTERN MICHIGAN UNIVERSITY
COLLEGE OF BUSINESS

GENERAL INFORMATION
Type of school   Public
Academic calendar   4 Semester

SURVEY SAYS...
Cutting-edge classes
Solid preparation in:
Teamwork
Communication/interpersonal skills
Presentation skills

STUDENTS
Enrollment of parent institution	22,173
Enrollment of MBA Program	328
% male/female	58/42
% out-of-state	30
% part-time	64
% minorities	11
% international	27
Average age at entry	28
Average years work experience at entry	4

ACADEMICS
Academic Experience Rating	**73**
Student/faculty ratio	22:1
Profs interesting rating	76
Profs accessible rating	71
% female faculty	33
% minority faculty	32

Prominent Alumni
Raymond Lombardi, Deloitte Touche, Partner; David Mazurkiewicz, McLaren, Healthcare Corp., SVP/CFO; Robert J. Skandalaris, President, Quantum Ventures; James Webb, Chairman, AON Risk Services, Inc.; Allen D. Fazio, The Walt Disney Foundation, VP/CIO; Thomas Wells, Cisco Systems, Channel Sales Operations Mgr.; Joseph Reid, Capitol Bancorp, President.

Academics

Offering an affordable, flexible, and "very student-oriented" MBA program, Eastern Michigan University is a public school with a contemporary touch. Within the two-year MBA, Eastern Michigan excels at "staying current with business trends and developing a program aimed directly at reaching higher placement in the workforce." The "innovative curriculum" integrates fundamental business areas with contemporary business topics such as global knowledge, innovation, analytical skills, ethics, and critical thinking. "Course content is extremely current" with a pointed focus on "preparing students...through exposure to business and industry." With an emphasis on discussion and critical thinking, "professors do less lecturing and [use] a lot of case studies." Through these practical examples, students have the opportunity to "exercise their real-world experience and apply [it] to solve real-world problems." In fact, students say that EMU may very well be "the most practical and project-centric program in Michigan." Outside the core, the program offers the opportunity to specialize in contemporary fields like e-business, entrepreneurship, international business, and nonprofit management, in addition to traditional fields like marketing and supply chain management.

The most popular professors at EMU are those who are very experienced and "very active in the industry" (though, thanks to their sought-after expertise, class is sometimes interrupted when professors "travel for foreign teaching stints and conferences.") Bringing examples from the workplace to the classroom, "Their stories enhance students' understanding of how the theory is applied." On the flip side, other EMU "professors have spent their entire career in academic institutions," and therefore, "The currency of their examples, data, and anecdotes demonstrate that they learn about new ideas and trends about three to five years behind those [who] are living it daily." Whether educators or executives, the good thing about EMU professors is that "A student can tell that the faculty really care about their students and their future success." What's more, "Classes are usually limited to 30 students, so teachers and students know each other." A current student enthuses, "There is an open environment in each classroom to share your work experience and how it relates to topics and ask other opinions as well."

EMU's MBA programs are appropriate to students in every stage of their career, and classes can be taken full-time, part-time, online, or through a hybrid of online and in-class coursework. For working professionals, the campus provides "ease of access from Ann Arbor, Detroit, and Toledo"—as well as "offerings online and at extended locations." A current student shares, "The business school definitely works for working, older students like myself. Classes don't start until 6:30 so I have time to drive from work in Detroit."

Career and Placement

The Career Services Center (CSC) within the College of Business helps EMU students plan and prepare for their job search and career. Among other services, the CSC offers skills workshops, operates an internship program, and coordinates on-campus recruiting events. The CSC also hosts an annual Career Day, which combines career development workshops with a company career fair. Enrolled graduate students and EMU alumni have access to all CSC services. Even though there is a large alumni network from EMU, "The business school does not have a good 'networking community' of past students like other schools such as the University of Michigan, Wayne State, even Michigan State."

ADMISSIONS CONTACT: MICHELLE HANRY, DIRECTOR, GRADUATE PROGRAMS
ADDRESS: 300 W. MICHIGAN AVENUE, STE. 404 YPSILANTI, MI 48197
PHONE: 734-487-4444 • FAX: 734-483-1316
E-MAIL: COB.GRADUATE@EMICH.EDU • WEBSITE: WWW.COB.EMICH.EDU

While EMU enjoys a great local reputation, students would like the CSC to make contact with "better companies coming to recruit at the university" as well as more graduate-appropriate contacts. Right now, "Companies that do come to recruit are looking for low-level employees," which are more appropriate to undergraduate students. On that note, working students complain, that the "placement office is not convenient for graduate students. Most students attend classes at night or weekends, but the placement office closes before 5pm."

Student Life and Environment

Eastern Michigan University draws a friendly, "motivated," and "ethnically diverse" group of students from the local region, as well as many international students. While the program attracts "mostly working professionals," there are also plenty of younger students who "continued their studies into the graduate program without a break" after undergraduate work. A current student shares, "Everyone is different and has their own story. There are international students, young professionals like me, [and] people with young or older children going back to school to better provide for their family." For graduate students, social life is somewhat limited at EMU. Most students live in one of the surrounding cities, and "commuter students don't hang around campus very long" after class. In recent years, however, "EMU has made great strides in becoming less of a 'commuter' school. There are numerous activities to participate in, [including] clubs, and organizations."

The "university main campus has many good resources and facilities." Among other amenities, "the library is excellent," and the "student center is a very nice building to work in teams." A boon to commuters, there is "easy access to parking for the Business School." In and around EMU, there's plenty to do, and "the neighboring city of Ann Arbor, MI, has outstanding social and cultural activities."

Admissions

To be considered for Eastern Michigan University's MBA programs, students must have a cumulative undergraduate GPA of at least 2.75 from a four-year accredited institution. Students must also have a minimum GMAT score of 450, including minimum sub-scores of 20 on the verbal section and 24 on the quantitative section.

FINANCIAL FACTS

Annual tuition (in-state/ out-of-state)	$7,501/$14,787
Fees	$1,867
Cost of books	$1,000
Room & board (on-campus)	$9,014
% of students receiving aid	38
% of first-year students receiving aid	35
% of students receiving loans	29
% of students receiving grants	10
Average award package	$10,943
Average grant	$4,774

ADMISSIONS

Admissions Selectivity Rating	72
# of applications received	239
% applicants accepted	49
% acceptees attending	77
Average GMAT	479
Range of GMAT	390–600
Average GPA	3.2
TOEFL required of international students	Yes
Minimum TOEFL (paper/computer)	550/213
Application fee	$35
International application fee	$35
Regular application deadline	5/15
Regular notification	6/15
Application Deadline/Notification	
Round 1:	5/15 / NR
Round 2:	10/15 / NR
Round 3:	3/15 / NR
Round 4:	4/15 / NR
Early decision program?	No
Deferment available	Yes
Maximum length of deferment	1 year
Transfer students accepted	Yes
Transfer application policy: 6 credits may be accepted for the core and 6 credits for electives upon approval.	
Non-fall admissions	Yes
Need-blind admissions	Yes

EMPLOYMENT PROFILE

Career Rating	72	Grads Employed by Function	%	Avg. Salary
		Marketing	15	$61,500
		Operations	16	$52,600
		Consulting	7	$49,600
		Management	18	$57,500
		Finance	9	$44,500
		HR	8	$40,400
		MIS	8	$44,500

Top 5 Employers Hiring Grads
Ford Motor Company (2), Pricewaterhouse-Coopers, LLP (2), Comerica (3), Creative Solutions (3), Thomson Tax and Accounting (1)

Eastern Washington University
College of Business and Public Administration

GENERAL INFORMATION
Type of school	Public
Academic calendar	Quarter

SURVEY SAYS...
Students love Cheney, WA
Good peer network
Solid preparation in:
Marketing
Communication/interpersonal skills
Computer skills

STUDENTS
Enrollment of parent institution	11,302
Enrollment of MBA Program	90
% male/female	70/30
% out-of-state	28
% part-time	42
% minorities	5
% international	23
Average age at entry	28
Average years work experience at entry	9

ACADEMICS
Academic Experience Rating	**66**
Student/faculty ratio	25:1
Profs interesting rating	61
Profs accessible rating	62
% female faculty	46
% minority faculty	2

Joint Degrees
MBA/MPA, 82 credits, 2 years.

Academics

For the "mostly working students who take night classes" pursuing MBAs at Eastern Washington University, the College of Business and Public Administration appeals on a number of levels: It's relatively inexpensive, it is close to home, and the extremely diligent can complete their graduate degrees here in one year. "Small classes" and "professors who are friendly, great communicators, and easy to reach with questions" further bolster the school's attractiveness.

Students speak highly of the program's courses in healthcare administration. Because the business facility also houses the school's public administration program, EWU students have a unique opportunity to combine an MBA with an MPA.

The EWU MBA consists of 50 credit hours. Core courses constitute 42 hours of required work; electives take up the remaining 8 hours. Foundation courses can add up to an additional 32 hours of required coursework; many or all of these courses may be waived for students with relatively recent undergraduate business degrees. Because EWU operates on a quarterly academic calendar, students who place out of foundation courses may complete the program in one year by taking 10+ credits per semester. Students love the convenience of evening scheduling and praise their professors for their flexibility. One reports that they "are willing to tailor work to what individuals need. I'm working on a tailor-made project, and I will have a business plan and start up when done." Expanded distance-learning options are on students' short wish lists.

Career and Placement

The Office of Career Services provides counseling and placement services for the entire EWU student body. The office organizes occasional career fairs and posts notices for other career fairs held in the area. In addition, the office hosts on-campus interviews and other recruitment events and maintains an online placement files service, which provides students' resumes, letters of recommendation, and other documents to prospective employers. Most of Career Services' efforts are directed at the school's substantial undergraduate population. Students tout the program's "strong alumni connections," which can be helpful to those in the program seeking post-degree employment.

Student Life and Environment

The smallish, predominantly part-time MBA program at EWU is a mix of working professionals and EWU undergraduates continuing directly through to their MBAs. Collectively, they are "very helpful and cooperative, and good at working in teams," and are typically "smart, hard-working, going places, no-silver-spoon kids" who constitute a "very diverse group ethnically, age-wise, and in terms of previous experience."

The size and part-time nature of the program is not conducive to a cohesive student community. Students don't even get to tap into the culture of EWU's main campus because the MBA program is located on a satellite campus in downtown Spokane, 20 miles from the main campus. While the location stunts extracurricular life, it does have the advantage of convenience for those students who work in the downtown area. Most students don't have much time for bonding and after-class fun anyway. A typical student explains his situation: "I work full-time at an executive level job. I am able to juggle my work and school load, but there is not a lot of time for much else."

Classes convene at the Riverpoint Higher Education Park, located on the banks of the Spokane River. The facility is home to EWU's College of Business and Public Administration, a boon to those seeking a dual degree in those two fields. Riverpoint houses a 200-seat auditorium and a number of state-of-the-art classrooms.

Admissions

Eastern Washington University requires all the following materials from applicants to its MBA program: two copies of the completed application for admission to a graduate program; two copies of official transcripts for all post-secondary academic work; and an official GMAT score report no more than five years old. The MBA program director reserves the right to require additional information, including: a resumé, an interview, and a letter of intent. International applicants whose first language is not English must provide all of the above materials as well as an official TOEFL score report (students must score 580 for admission to the MBA program. EWU requires a minimum undergraduate GPA of 3.0 during the final 90 quarter hours or 60 semester hours of undergraduate work and a minimum GMAT score of 450. The school's website notes: "All students who graduate from the MBA program should have some practical work experience. The majority of students accepted into the program are working professionals and meet this requirement. For those students who enter the program lacking professional work experience, an internship should be part of the student's MBA program. Up to four (4) four credits earned while in an internship may be used for MBA elective credit."

FINANCIAL FACTS

Annual tuition (in-state/ out-of-state)	$6,795/$11,850
Fees	$165
Cost of books	$1,500
Room & board (on/off-campus)	$6,900/$12,000
% of students receiving aid	25
% of first-year students receiving aid	25
% of students receiving loans	20
% of students receiving grants	5

ADMISSIONS

Admissions Selectivity Rating	70
# of applications received	77
% applicants accepted	88
% acceptees attending	99
Average GMAT	510
Range of GMAT	410–610
Average GPA	3.32
TOEFL required of international students	Yes
Minimum TOEFL (paper/computer)	580/237
Application fee	$100
International application fee	$100
Regular application deadline	1/1
Regular notification	1/1
Early decision program?	No
Deferment available	Yes
Maximum length of deferment	1 year
Transfer students accepted	Yes
Transfer application policy: We will accept up to 12 transfer credits.	
Non-fall admissions	Yes
Need-blind admissions	Yes

Elon University

Martha and Spencer Love School of Business

GENERAL INFORMATION

Type of school	Private
Affiliation	United Church of Christ
Academic calendar	Trimester

SURVEY SAYS...

Cutting-edge classes
Solid preparation in:
Communication/interpersonal skills
Presentation skills
Doing business in a global economy

STUDENTS

Enrollment of parent institution	5,666
Enrollment of MBA Program	141
% part-time	100
Average age at entry	31
Average years work experience at entry	9

ACADEMICS

Academic Experience Rating	87
Student/faculty ratio	22:1
Profs interesting rating	93
Profs accessible rating	85
% female faculty	30
% minority faculty	20

Prominent Alumni

Danielle Hoversten, CFO, Senn Dunn Insurance; Steven Casey, Founder & Board Secretary, Expression Analysis; Allan Davis, CEO, AllFab Solutions; Kathleen Galbraith, Chief Hospital Ops & Bus. Dev. Officer, Durham Reg. Hosp.; Bernadette Spong, Executive VP & CFO, Rex Health Care.

Academics

The MBA program at Elon University is "a program on the rise," students tell us, citing "excellent facilities and a brand-new business school building" among the factors driving its ascent. A "globally-focused curriculum, which is important in today's economy" and a relatively low cost of attending (as compared to area competitors Wake Forest, Duke, and UNC—Chapel Hill) also draw area business hopefuls to the school.

Elon works hard to optimize its MBA experience. Students tell us that "the administration of the program is as close as you can get to flawless" and that the school is "very well-run, more like a business serving it customers well as opposed to a bureaucratic organization." "There are regular opportunities to provide feedback on courses and unmet needs to the program administrator and he will listen," one student says. The school also does a great job of soliciting "a strong corporate and alumni support system that allows for the latest technology and educational methods to be utilized." As a result, the Love School has a new three-story home that includes a state-of-the-art finance center streaming real-time data from global financial markets, a 240-seat multimedia wireless theater, and plenty of study, conference, and classroom space.

The Elon MBA is a small program, making it difficult to avoid substandard teachers—fortunately, "Only about two or three of our thirteen teachers belong in the 'not so good' category...while everyone else is excellent," one student notes. However, this intimate environment can also result in a "lack of choices for electives." A student explains, "Most are management-related and it is difficult for someone to find financial- and economic-focused electives to meet a particular career focus." In the plus column, "Most all the professors have worked in the fields that they teach in, so they have real-world experiences." Students also appreciate that "the MBA program is an experiential program in that each class requires some outside activities pertaining to the course."

Career and Placement

Career placement services are provided by Elon's Career Development office, which serves all students in the university. Services offered to MBAs include a battery of self-assessment tools, faculty advising, and seminars with business leaders. Students have met with and learned from Thomas J. Murrin, former Westinghouse exec and former Deputy Secretary at the US Commerce Department; Leslie M. "Bud" Baker, Jr., former Chair/President/CEO of Wachovia; J Richard Munro, former Chair and CEO of Time, Inc., Dr. Jim Goodnight, CEO of SAS Institute; John Allison, CEO of BB&T; and John Zeglis, former CEO of AT&T Wireless. Students tell us, "The MBA faculty goes above and beyond by assisting graduate students with support in areas such as educational mapping as well as with registration and career services." Even so, most here agree that "Career Services is not the best at Elon" and that "more corporate recruiting on campus would add much to a program that is already wonderful."

Elon MBAs work for some of the area's top employers, including Banner Pharmacaps, Ciba Specialty Chemicals, Cisco Systems, Duke Health Systems, GE, GKN Automotive, IBM, LabCorp, Sony Ericsson, UNC Hospitals, Underwriters Laboratories, and Wachovia.

ADMISSIONS CONTACT: ARTHUR W. FADDE, DIRECTOR OF GRADUATE ADMISSIONS
ADDRESS: 2750 CAMPUS BOX ELON, NC 27244
PHONE: (800) 334-8448 EXT. 3 • FAX: (336) 278-7699
E-MAIL: ELONMBA@ELON.EDU • WEBSITE: WWW.ELON.EDU/MBA

Student Life and Environment

Elon is "very big about building community among the MBA students" through "activities such as midterm pizza nights, golf outings, and social events such as football games, basketball games, and local theater trips." However, "Due to the nature of a part-time graduate program, many students are not involved in the life of the school." Some do embrace extracurricular fun, telling us, "We frequently have social gatherings on weekends and before classes so that the students have opportunities to decompress." The MBA Student-Alumni Association is active, bringing in "guest lecturers who are excellent."

The "beautiful" Elon campus is "moderately-sized but has a strong community feel." "The buildings and landscaping are gorgeous and MBA students have access to all of the same gym, dining, and event resources as undergraduates," one student explains. The school's small hometown (also called Elon) "grew up around the school and blends with the campus." The larger city of Greensboro is close by, with Winston-Salem and Durham about an hour's drive away, and Raleigh and Charlotte just a little further down the line.

Elon's student body is "a mixture of people very experienced in the business world (bankers, lawyers, senior leaders in their organizations) and a lower percentage of folks who are not very experienced." They tend to be "very helpful and all with a good sense of humor." "They're never too serious but always willing to do what is necessary to complete project work or other course assignments," one student says. "Most classmates are people that I would network with and hopefully develop friendships with."

Admissions

The Elon MBA requires a minimum of two years' professional experience of all applicants. A completed application must include three letters of recommendation (two from work supervisors), official transcripts from all post-secondary schools attended, and GMAT scores. An interview is recommended but not required. Students whose native language is not English must also submit TOEFL scores (minimum 550 written, 213 computer); those who graduated from non-English programs overseas must have their transcripts translated and the grades interpreted by a professional service. Applicants must exceed a formula score of 1000 under the formula [(undergraduate GPA x 200) + GMAT score], and must also have a minimum GMAT score of 500 and a minimum GPA of 2.5. Undergraduate classes in financial accounting, finance, microeconomics, and statistics are foundation courses in the MBA program. Students may begin in September; applications are assessed on a rolling basis.

FINANCIAL FACTS

Annual tuition	$11,394
Cost of books	$570
% of students receiving aid	33
% of first-year students receiving aid	54
% of students receiving loans	25
% of students receiving grants	7
Average award package	$11,644
Average grant	$5,110
Average student loan debt	$28,360

ADMISSIONS

Admissions Selectivity Rating	79
# of applications received	132
% applicants accepted	56
% acceptees attending	78
Average GMAT	562
Range of GMAT	510–600
Average GPA	3.2
TOEFL required of international students	Yes
Minimum TOEFL (paper/computer)	550/213
Application fee	$50
International application fee	$50
Early decision program?	No
Deferment available	Yes
Maximum length of deferment	1 year
Transfer students accepted	Yes
Transfer application policy: A student may transfer up to 9 semester hours of credit from another AACSB accredited school.	
Non-fall admissions	Yes
Need-blind admissions	Yes

Emory University
Goizueta Business School

GENERAL INFORMATION
Type of school	Private
Academic calendar	Semester

SURVEY SAYS...
Friendly students
Good social scene
Good peer network
Helpful alumni
Solid preparation in:
Communication/interpersonal skills
Doing business in a global economy

STUDENTS
Enrollment of parent institution	12,930
Enrollment of MBA Program	848
% male/female	71/29
% out-of-state	43
% part-time	38
% minorities	24
% international	23
Average age at entry	31
Average years work experience at entry	8

ACADEMICS
Academic Experience Rating	**95**
Student/faculty ratio	5:1
Profs interesting rating	88
Profs accessible rating	95
% female faculty	23
% minority faculty	7

Joint Degrees
Master of Business Administration/ Doctor of jurisprudence(MBA/JD)(4 years), Master of Business Administration/Master of Public Health (MBA/MPH)(five Semesters), Master of Business Administration/Master of Divinity (MBA/MDIV)(4 years), Doctor of Physical Therapy/Master of Business Administration (DPT/MBA) (4 years).

Academics

"The community is the greatest strength" of the Goizueta Business School at Emory, where "there are 200 other [students] happy to help with any project or connect [you] to their network." And it's not just the student body that personifies the "culture of collaboration over severe competition" that presides here. "The community outside the current students is also phenomenal," we're told. "Alumni are happy to mentor, connect you to networks, and help you find directed study [opportunities], jobs, or internships."

Collaboration is encouraged in part through Goizueta's "lack of a hard-lined grading system" (grades are evaluative and do not correspond to GPA). It "definitely helps the community atmosphere," although students "still feel pressured to do well personally." The size of the program also helps; "the smaller school size makes Goizueta thrive on the ambition, creativity and curiosity of its students," one student writes.

Given the communal vibe, some might find it ironic that Goizueta's primary curricular emphasis is leadership. Regardless, the school offers "wonderful leadership courses with guest speakers and applied learning." It's all part of a "flexible" curriculum to which "new and relevant courses are frequently added (e.g., e-marketing, globalization, and illiquid assets in times of financial crisis)," and which provides ample opportunities for students to pursue their unique interests through electives. As one MBA student explains, "Emory's curriculum is very customizable, which comes from having a small class size."

Despite the laid-back atmosphere, academics are demanding at Goizueta. As one student puts it, "you genuinely need to push yourself hard and are challenged to reach the top of any class, but the focus is on really internalizing and learning the basics and foundations well. It's not an insanely competitive environment; it's one where you can truly learn and if you want to excel with grades and recognition, you can without feeling as though such things [are] easy or commonplace." Goizueta's location in Atlanta, a major metropolis home to many *Fortune* 500 companies, provides plenty of networking opportunities and a steady stream of well-connected professors and guest lecturers. Faculty members "are leaders in their fields, passionate about the material, and very accessible." "Every one of them brings great work experience as well as academic credentials to the classroom. They are willing to bring in current business-related events into the classroom and are eager for students to bring in their work experience into class discussions," students tell us.

Career and Placement

Student perspective on the Goizueta Career Management Center is mixed. "Career services could use some love," is how one student puts it. "No one seems to be able to pinpoint what exactly goes wrong there, but in general people seem less than satisfied with their help. Placement seems to be good, though, so something is working." Several voiced the feeling that the office "struggles with attracting large companies to recruit here. Despite our name, we are not a feeder school for Coke nor do we see much of the other major companies in the Atlanta area. On the other hand, we have many alumni at all those companies who through the power of networking are happy to help students find jobs and placements."

Despite the fact that many Atlanta companies have been on a hiring freeze in recent years, over 150 companies have visited Goizueta for on-campus recruitment. Employers who most frequently hire Emory MBAs include: Accenture, AT Kearney, AT&T, Bank of America, Citigroup, Chevron, Delta Air Lines, Ernst & Young, General Electric, Georgia-Pacific, Humana, IBM, JP Morgan, Kimberly-Clark Corporation, Kurt Salmon Associates, PricewaterhouseCoopers, SunTrust, The Coca-Cola Company, and Wipro.

Student Life and Environment

Because of the small size of the program, Goizueta MBAs form a "very close group" that participates in "lots of social activities, both formal and informal." Student life "is very busy, but we learn so much in such a short time. Our networking opportunities are extensive as well, with Thursday afternoon networking activities, our mentor program, and very accessible alumni. Social activities and clubs are numerous," so much so that "it is difficult to decide which clubs to become involved in and which social activities to attend." As one student puts it, "The quality of life is great." The city of Atlanta helps in that regard; not only is it "a great place to live," it also "provides a wealth of business opportunities."

Goizueta students "are very collaborative." "We all want to see each other succeed, so although we are very competitive (all business school students are), we all want to help each other out," one student explains. Another adds, "This is not a cut-throat environment, but rather one in which everyone wants everyone else to succeed." The prevailing attitude is "nice, professional, and polished (this is the South and it does show through)."

Admissions

Applicants to the Goizueta MBA program must submit the following materials: a completed online application; official transcripts for all undergraduate and graduate schools attended; an official GMAT score report; and two letters of recommendation (the first is a narrative resume; the second offers a choice of subjects that center on your sources of inspiration or your career and life aspirations). An interview, while not required, is "strongly recommended." International students whose first language is not English must also submit official score reports for the TOEFL, PTE, or IELTS. Candidates for the one-year program must have an undergraduate degree in a business-related discipline or a strong quantitative background and "solid business experience."

Prominent Alumni

Duncan Niederauer '85 MBA, Chief Executive Officer and Director, NYSE Euronext Inc.; Paul S. Amos II, President, Aflac; Chief Operating Officer, Aflac U.S.; John Chidsey '87 JD/MBA, Chief Executive Officer and Chairman of the Board, Burger King Holdings, Inc.; Brian Gallagher '92 EMBA, President and Chief Executive Officer, United Way Worldwide; Michael Golden '84 EMBA, Vice Chairman, President, Chief Operating Officer, Regional Media Group and Director, New York Times Company; Michael F. Golden '86 EMBA, President, Chief Executive Officer and Director, Smith and Wesson Holding Corporation; Charlie Jenkins '64 BBA '65MBA, Retired Chief Executive Officer and Director, Publix Super Markets.

FINANCIAL FACTS

Annual tuition	$42,400
Fees	$476
Cost of books	$2,000
Room & board (off-campus)	$16,810

ADMISSIONS

Admissions Selectivity Rating	93
# of applications received	1,241
% applicants accepted	32
% acceptees attending	42
Average GMAT	676
Range of GMAT	610–750
Average GPA	3.3
TOEFL required of international students	Yes
Minimum TOEFL (paper/computer)	600/100
Application fee	$150
International application fee	$150
Regular application deadline	3/1
Early decision program?	No
Deferment available	Yes
Maximum length of deferment	1 year
Transfer students accepted	No
Non-fall admissions	No
Need-blind admissions	Yes

EMPLOYMENT PROFILE

Career Rating	95	Grads Employed by Function	% Avg. Salary
Percent employed at graduation	51	Consulting	29 $103,527
Percent employed 3 months after graduation	72	Finance/ Accounting	34 $87,889
		General Management	10 $93,530
Average base starting salary	$91,000	Human Resources	2 $82,333
Primary Source of Full-time Job Acceptances		Marketing	19 $75,223
School-facilitated activities	123 (70%)	Other	5 $103,333
Graduate-facilitated activities	52 (30%)	Operations	1 NR

Top 5 Employers Hiring Grads
Deloitte Consulting (6), Delta Airlines (5), Accenture (4), The Coca-Cola Company (3), PricewaterhouseCoopers (3)

ESADE Business School

GENERAL INFORMATION
Type of school   Private

SURVEY SAYS...
Students love Barcelona
Good social scene
Good peer network
Happy students
Solid preparation in:
Teamwork
Entrepreneurial studies

STUDENTS
Enrollment,of	
business school	160
% male/female	75/25
% international	80
Average age at entry	29
Average years work	
experience at entry	6

ACADEMICS
Academic Experience Rating	**61**
Student/faculty ratio	2:1
Profs interesting rating	77
Profs accessible rating	81
% female faculty	21

Prominent Alumni
Enrique Rueda, Director of
Corporate Strategy, The World
Bank; Ignacio Fonts, General
Manager, Hewlett-Packard Inkjet;
Ferran Soriano, CEO/Member of the
Board, FC Barcelona; Alex Rovira &
Fernando Trias de Bes, Authors of
the best-selling book "The Good
Luck."

Academics

The ESADE MBA's new and highly flexible format enables students to customize their MBA experience in 12, 15, or 18 months according to the individual's career objectives. With 80% of ESADE's full-time MBA participant population comprised of international students, the program will appeal to students who want to develop managerial and leadership skills in the context of a highly international environment. Academically, the school "provides a combination of case analysis and theory," complimented by an overarching "emphasis on developing interpersonal skills." "Marketing and finance are two strong fields here at ESADE" and themes in corporate responsibility are woven throughout the curriculum. ESADE's full-time MBA consists of two English tracks and a bilingual track taught in Spanish and English. Many students take advantage of their ESADE education as an opportunity to improve their language skills. For those who are already fluent in Spanish and English, the school also offers German or French courses.

While the school's appealing Barcelona location is a major attraction for many students, be forewarned that ESADE's MBA program is highly demanding. While completing core coursework, you are more likely to spend your time in the library rather than taking advantage of Barcelona's wide cultural and entertainment offerings. Fortunately, the "work load dropped to more manageable levels during the second half of the program, during the electives." Despite the rigors of the program, you won't fall through the cracks. ESADE given its focus on delivering personalized attention at all levels. As a select program open to a limited number of participants, "the school pays attention to the individual." In addition, "because of the relatively small size of the school, administration is efficient and flexible."

Drawing faculty from 13 different countries, including Argentina, Chile, India, Italy, and the United States, ESADE "professors are without exception passionate and knowledgeable about their subjects. All encourage active participation by the students." A current student attests, "The academic experience has been great, as teachers are very good in general and the environment in class with my classmates is rewarding." On that note, many ESADE students say their classmates are an indispensable part of the MBA experience, which emphasizes "building up relationships and getting exposed to different cultures." Despite the school's patently international environment, some feel "ESADE should strengthen its link with emerging countries, namely, China [and] India."

Career and Placement

ESADE's Career Services staff operates the comprehensive Career Management Programme (CMP), designed to help students advance in their professional goals, both during their studies and after graduation. Through the CMP, students have access to various career development workshops and seminars, through which they learn to assess their strengths, identify markets, interview successfully, and negotiate a job offer. Career Services also hosts a number of campus recruiting events, including two MBA career weeks and various corporate presentations held throughout the academic year. The school maintains contact with hundreds of companies in numerous countries. A current student writes, "I was impressed by the portfolio of companies that come to interview on campus."

ADMISSIONS CONTACT: ROSALIA GALAN, ADMISSIONS OFFICER
ADDRESS: AV. D'ESPLUGUES, 92-96 BARCELONA, 08034 SPAIN
PHONE: 0034 934 952 088 • FAX: 0034 934 953 828
E-MAIL: MBA@ESADE.EDU • WEBSITE: WWW.ESADE.EDU/MBA

In 2008, the ESADE student body represented 40 different nationalities. Within this diverse group, 32 percent of students found jobs in Spain and 35 percent in other Western European countries (64 percent of ESADE candidates took jobs in countries of which they were not nationals, which is a good sign for students who would like to use their ESADE education as a jumping-off point for an international career.) Marketing and sales positions were the most popular, drawing almost 35 percent of graduates, followed by consulting, which drew 20 percent of the graduating class.

Student Life and Environment

International diversity is the cornerstone of the ESADE experience, as the school draws select student body from more than 40 nationalities. On the whole, ESADE's serious students are "driven to play a role as future international leaders in their respective fields." However, the environment is distinctly cooperative, not cut-throat. A student shares, "The teamwork orientation the school prides itself on can be felt anytime, right from the group work through the cafeteria."

Obviously, the school environment is enhanced by the fact that ESADE is "located in Barcelona, one of the nicest European cities." However, be forewarned that "the heavy workload gets in the way" of enjoying cultural and recreational activities, especially during the core curriculum. Even so, "Spain puts a premium on living well" and students manage to balance work and play throughout their ESADE education. A current student reassures us, "Despite the tough academic requirements of the school, most students do enjoy a very active social live outside of pure academia." Another adds, "The first year you practically live in school [and] there is great pressure, but there is always time for social activities."

Admissions

Admissions for the full-time MBA operate on a staged application deadline basis. (Deadlines are listed on the website). Given the limited number of places on the program, competition is tough. Interested candidates are encouraged to apply early in order to increase their chances of being offered a place as well as accessing financial aid programs. Non-European candidates should also consider visa application processes, which take several weeks to approve.

When reviewing applications, the admissions team looks at: performance in previous studies, potential career trajectory, a clear sense of direction, international experience, and global outlook.

FINANCIAL FACTS

Annual tuition	$72,982
Cost of books	$3,508
Room & board	$25,263
% of first-year students receiving aid	40
Average grant	$14,035

ADMISSIONS

Admissions Selectivity Rating	60*
% acceptees attending	65
Average GMAT	670
Range of GMAT	610–780
TOEFL required of international students	Yes
Minimum TOEFL (paper/computer)	600/250
Application fee	$147
International application fee	$147
Regular application deadline	6/30
Regular notification	6/30
Deferment available	Yes
Maximum length of deferment	1 year
Non-fall admissions	Yes
Need-blind admissions	Yes

EMPLOYMENT PROFILE

Career Rating	60*	Grads Employed by Function	% Avg. Salary
		Finance	17 NR
		Marketing	35 NR
		Consulting	20 NR
		General Management	17 NR
		Other	11 NR

ESSEC BUSINESS SCHOOL
THE ESSEC MBA PROGRAM

GENERAL INFORMATION

Type of school	Private
Academic calendar	Trimester

SURVEY SAYS...
Good social scene
Solid preparation in:
Finance
General management
Teamwork

STUDENTS

% male/female	51/49
% international	20
Average age at entry	24
Average years work experience at entry	1

ACADEMICS

Academic Experience Rating	63
Profs interesting rating	69
Profs accessible rating	73
% female faculty	23

Joint Degrees
China: Peking University, Germany: Mannheim University, Korea: Seoul National University (2), Singapore: Nanyang Technological University, Mexico: EGADE, Tec de Monterrey, India: IIM Ahmedabad, Japan: Keio University.

Prominent Alumni
Christian BALMES, President Director General, Shell France; Charles BOUAZIZ, General Manager, Pepsico Europe; Emmanuelle MIGNON, President Sarkozy's Chief of Staff; Dominique REINICHE, President Europe, The Coca Cola Company; Serge VILLEPELET, President, PricewaterhouseCoopers.

Academics

If you're looking for a "flexible" MBA at "a major player on the international level among European business schools" and one of "the top business schools in France," ESSEC is a school you should consider. After completing eight management fundamentals courses, ESSEC MBAs fashion their own curricula, choosing from more than "200 electives" each semester. Students love the freedom, telling us that "each quarter, we can basically choose to take classes at ESSEC Business School in Paris or Singapore, do an internship with a company in France or abroad, or go on an exchange program abroad with one of ESSEC MBA's 80 academic partners," whose ranks include many prestigious names in the United States and around the world. The school's administration "does a great job of managing this 'a la carte' system," allowing students to "choose almost any courses we want in order to create our specialization and formation."

Because ESSEC believes that students should make "a constant connection between work and the classroom," all students must have at least 18 months of validated professional experience prior to graduation. These internships are easy to find thanks to ESSEC's "great relationship with the business world." The school "has strong links with international finance and consulting companies;" and a campus in Singapore means that opportunities to intern in Southeast Asia are constantly developing. ESSEC's practical philosophy permeates the classroom as well; here "Courses are not just theory. We have a lot of business cases given by corporate partners, and we have a lot of work every week to prepare other business cases in groups (teamwork is very important here)." Throughout the program, there is a "prominent international dimension" bolstered by "the school's ever-increasing partnerships overseas."

The faculty includes "outstanding professors recognized in their fields of specialization, people who publish a lot. They help us get most prepared for our chosen profession and they are also very available and most willing to give us useful insights." Part-time faculty are drawn from "top-notch businesswomen and men and successful entrepreneurs. In any case, they always have a great experience and very useful insights to share."

Career and Placement

Students report that "ESSEC is the best passport to great job opportunities in France and worldwide. The school administration and students are really eager to keep in very close contact with firms. There is a constant exchange between the academic, student and business world. Companies are often involved in student projects too." The school's "excellent relations with European businesses" help students procure the internships required to complete their MBAs. While ESSEC's connections are strongest in France, "Many foreign companies also recruit (largely for their French subsidies), such as the consulting companies McKinsey, BCG, etc. ESSEC is part of their main target schools for recruiting."

Employers most likely to hire ESSEC MBAs include: PricewaterhouseCoopers, L'Oréal, Renault, Societe Generale, Deloitte Touche Tohmatsu, Danone, Michelin, BNP Paribas, Capgemini, Accenture, EDF-GDF, Pinault Printemps Redoute, Procter & Gamble, Deutsche Bank, 3 Suisses International, Pfizer, LVMH, Ernst & Young, Boston Consulting Group, A.T. Kearney, SC Johnson, and Bain.

ADMISSIONS CONTACT: DR. MARIE-NOELLE KOEBEL, DEAN FOR ADMISSIONS AND ACADEMIC AFFAIRS
ADDRESS: AVENUE BERNARD HIRSCH, B.P. 50105 CERGY-PONTOISE, 95021 FRANCE
PHONE: +33 1 34 43 32 59 • FAX: +33 1 34 43 32 60
E-MAIL: DEMARS@ESSEC.FR • WEBSITE: WWW.ESSEC.EDU

FINANCIAL FACTS

Annual tuition	$32,500
Cost of books	$500
Room & board (on-campus)	$10,000

ADMISSIONS

Admissions Selectivity Rating 60*

# of applications received	5,117
Average GMAT	675
Range of GMAT	600–730
TOEFL required of international students	Yes
Minimum TOEFL (paper/computer)	600/250

Application Deadline/Notification

Round 1:	10/10 / 12/5
Round 2:	1/26 / 3/23
Round 3:	4/29 / 6/9
Early decision program?	Yes
ED Deadline/Notification	NR / 6/13
Deferment available	Yes
Maximum length of deferment	1 year
Transfer students accepted	No
Non-fall admissions	No
Need-blind admissions	Yes

Student Life and Environment

ESSEC encourages students to participate in extracurricular life, and students respond, forming "about 80 different clubs" that encompass not only business activities but also "theater, a choir, painting, photography, sports, and social groups." The area surrounding ESSEC, Cergy Pontoise, is "Parisian suburb" located "about an hour from the center of the city by commuter train." Some describe it as "a modern city with very good amenities, including an artificial lake for sailing or rowing and other water sports, a nearby skating rink, and very good town libraries." Others tell us that "living in Cergy can be a little bit disappointing for those who would prefer the dense atmosphere of Paris to ESSEC school life." Local housing "is pretty easy to find" and "not too expensive."

ESSEC is "undergoing immense changes," students tell us, reporting that new professors are being recruited at an international level. The school is going global and will become internationally known very soon." Some here tell us that "you can stay all day long at ESSEC, and there's always something to do and somewhere to go." Though in the past students have noted that"facilities here could improve." Recent renovations have been completed including several new buildings."

Admissions

Students are admitted to ESSEC either as traditional MBAs (this is the way international students enter the program), French MBAs, or as "grande école" students (French students who have attended 2 years of postsecondary school and are now ready for intensive, focused study in a discipline such as business). Students applying to the traditional MBA program must provide the school with an official GMAT or TAGE-MAGE score report, official transcripts for all postsecondary academic work, an interview, and a resume. Applicants must be under the age of 32; 1 or 2 years of professional experience is highly recommended. French MBA students follow the "French MBA" admissions path. "Grande école" applicants must meet a variety of requirements, including completion of the undergraduate period and completion of at least one six-month internship.

EMPLOYMENT PROFILE

Career Rating	60*	Grads Employed by Function	% Avg. Salary
Average base starting salary	$67,000	Marketing	21 NR
Primary Source of Full-time Job Acceptances		Operations	5 NR
School-facilitated activities	NR (50%)	Consulting	36 NR
Graduate-facilitated activities	NR (4%)	Management	5 NR
Unknown	NR (46%)	Finance	20 NR
		HR	1 NR

Top 5 Employers Hiring Grads

Cap Gemini (10), BNP Paribas (6), Ernst & Young (5), KPMG (5), McKinsey & Company (5)

FAIRFIELD UNIVERSITY
CHARLES F. DOLAN SCHOOL OF BUSINESS

GENERAL INFORMATION

Type of school   Private
Affiliation   Roman Catholic/Jesuit
Academic calendar   Semester

SURVEY SAYS...

Students love Fairfield, CT
Good peer network
Solid preparation in:
Finance
Accounting

STUDENTS

Enrollment of MBA Program   134
Average age at entry   29
Average years work experience
at entry   4

ACADEMICS

Academic Experience Rating   **84**
Student/faculty ratio   23:1
Profs interesting rating   90
Profs accessible rating   79
% female faculty   36
% minority faculty   2

Prominent Alumni

Robert Murphy, Jr., Senior VP, The
Walt Disney Company Foundation;
Christopher McCormick, President
& CEO, LL Bean, Inc.; Dr. Francis
Tedesco, President, Medical College
of Georgia.

Academics

The Dolan School of Business at Fairfield University excels in finance, a strength that dovetails nicely with the school's proximity to America's financial center, New York City. Students report that "the placement of the school in relation to key industries/businesses is a particular strength" and that "the ties with well-placed alumni are invaluable." Location also allows Dolan to draw its faculty from a powerful pool. One MBA notes, "Most all professors are either published authors or business owners (e.g., fund managers and investment advisors). This is very beneficial as they teach us in the real-world scenarios."

"Jesuit traditions and philosophies" aren't just slogans here; students pick Fairfield "for its strong commitment to Jesuit ideals." Jesuit values include an emphasis on teaching, and here students "work with professors outside of class regarding personal business situations, and all are more than willing to speak and help where they can." Professors are "flexible and accommodating;" two valuable traits in serving a working professional part-time student body. One student observes that they "want to create a comfort level for their students, knowing that will make them most successful in school. Fairfield's teachers also are thick-skinned when students challenge them in class discussions. They encourage such open-minded dialogue; the instructors are not like some of the other high-and-mighty professors who insist their way of thinking is the only way."

Part-timers here enjoy "flexible night schedules and course terms," as the school offers a variety of seven- and fourteen-week terms as well as mini-term options. "This program is tailored for working students," MBAs here agree. Resources are solid; "The school is as technologically advanced as could be expected, and is more so than some of other colleges in the area and neighboring states." Students' wish list includes "more online hybrid classes. For those of us with a long commute to school after work, online hybrids are helpful because I still get classroom interaction, but without the commute every week."

Career and Placement

The Dolan MBA program is a small, predominantly part-time program in which most students already have careers. In fact, a number of students actually attend at their employers' expense. This situation creates a relatively small demand for career services within the program, so students seeking such services must use the Career Planning Center that serves the entire university. The Dolan Graduate Business Association, run by students, is probably the most aggressive advocate for career services within the program. Professors and alumni are also regarded as valuable resources for those seeking internships or careers. Most students wish that the school would "bring a greater diversity of businesses to career fairs." "Right now every business is in the financial arena, I would like to see them expand beyond those borders," one student says.

Employers most likely to hire Dolan MBAs include General Electric, People's Bank, American Skandia, United Technologies, Pitney Bowes, The Common Fund, Bayer Corporation, UBS Warburg, Gartner, Unilever, and Pfizer.

Student Life and Environment

"There is little to no interaction outside of class," Fairfield MBAs report, explaining that "Since most students are working professionals, most are preoccupied outside of the MBA program." However, "This doesn't detract from the educational experience." Students note that "there have been many attempts to create extracurricular activities, but with little response from the graduate student population.... In practice, most part-time, fully-employed students are too busy to take part in such activities." Still, some believe that "if there were more networking opportunities for students," they "would feel better situated when searching for jobs." "The only activities for graduate students occur one night, during class time, at the beginning of each semester," one student says. On the other hand, another points out, "there have been many attempts by faculty and staff to listen to students and respond to their needs, but in practice, most part-time, fully-employed students are too busy to take part in such activities."

The Fairfield campus is "dynamic in that it's like an oasis." "It has a rural, small-school feel in a major metropolitan area. Major NYC-area and Fairfield County companies such as IBM, GE, and Pepsi, as well as many media, publishing, and financial companies are all within a 60- to 90-minute drive of the campus, allowing for students to land opportunities at a major company without having to move far."

Admissions

Applications may be submitted to Dolan via mail or the internet. Applications are processed on a rolling basis, and students may commence the program in any term. The Admissions Committee considers applicants' post-secondary academic records, GMAT scores, two letters of recommendation, and resume or other self-evaluation of work experience. In general, applicants are expected to have achieved a minimum undergraduate GPA of 3.00 and a score of at least 500 on the GMAT. International students from non-English speaking countries must submit TOEFL scores (a minimum score of 550 paper and pencil, 75 to 80 computer-based, is required). Applicants to the MS program in Accounting and Taxation must meet all the above criteria and must also provide a Statement of Certification from their accounting department faculty and a letter of recommendation from either a former employer or a faculty member outside the discipline of accounting. This program is only open to students who hold, or are in the process of earning, an undergraduate degree in accounting. All entering students in all programs must demonstrate proficiency in microeconomics, macroeconomics, calculus, and statistics. Successful completion of undergraduate work in these areas is the most common way of demonstrating proficiency.

FINANCIAL FACTS

Annual tuition	$22,680
Fees	$100
Cost of books	$1,000
Average grant	$5,000

ADMISSIONS

Admissions Selectivity Rating	83
# of applications received	75
% applicants accepted	43
% acceptees attending	94
Average GMAT	523
Range of GMAT	500–650
Average GPA	3.23
TOEFL required of international students	Yes
Minimum TOEFL (paper/computer)	550/213
Application fee	$60
International application fee	$60
Early decision program?	No
Deferment available	Yes
Maximum length of deferment	1 year
Transfer students accepted	Yes
Transfer application policy: 6 credits or Jesuit University Transfer Program	
Non-fall admissions	Yes
Need-blind admissions	No

FAIRLEIGH DICKINSON UNIVERSITY
SILBERMAN COLLEGE OF BUSINESS

GENERAL INFORMATION
Type of school   Private

SURVEY SAYS...
Cutting-edge classes
Solid preparation in:
Communication/interpersonal skills
Doing business in a global economy

ACADEMICS
Academic Experience Rating	**80**
Student/faculty ratio	20:1
Profs interesting rating	87
Profs accessible rating	85
% female faculty	22
% minority faculty	41

Joint Degrees
MBA in Management/MA in Corporate and Organizational Communications, 72 credit program.

Prominent Alumni
Cheryl Beebe, VP & CFO, Corn Products International, Inc.; Dennis Strigl, President & COO, Verizon Communications; Dick Sweeney, Co-founder, VP, Keurig Coffee; Joseph Mahady, President, Wyeth Pharmaceuticals; John Legere, CEO, Global Crossing Ltd.

Academics

Fairleigh Dickinson's MBA programs are suited to students with well-defined career goals. Attracting a largely part-time student population, this private university offers nine different MBA specializations, each focused on a specific business area. Depending on their interests, students can pursue an MBA in accounting, entrepreneurship studies, finance, information systems, international business, marketing, management, pharmaceutical management, and personalized study. In addition, Fairleigh Dickinson offers a joint MBA/master's program in Management/Corporate and Organizational Communications, as well as a full-time Global MBA, with a focus on international business. Many students specifically mention that, "The Entrepreneurial Studies program is the greatest strength," of the MBA offerings, providing a "truly a different approach while keeping within a traditional MBA." In addition, the school's international focus is incorporated into the traditional MBA programs. As students explain, "FDU has a strong focus on global learning, which is very important in doing business today," and the school offers "a lot of international exchange and study-abroad programs." Despite the fact that Fairleigh Dickinson offers an impressive range of courses and specializations, classes are "small and personal." As a result, students get "very strong attention" from their professors and develop a "network of professional contacts through group work in class."

When it comes to the faculty, Fairleigh Dickinson students say their professors' "emotional investment in each class is remarkable. This generates passion for learning which inspires students who wish to succeed in business to perform well." A student details, "Professors are very knowledgeable, easy to approach, take time to answer any queries you may have, and drive you to achieve perfection." Combining classroom smarts with real-world experience, "The professors are extremely dynamic and are in most cases active in business, which seems to give an up-to-the-minute explanation of world events and changing landscapes." In fact, some feel, "The best professors are actually the adjuncts that can offer real-world scenarios and provide classes with discussion heavy topics." That said, "Professors at FDU tend to adjust their academic demands to students who are willing to learn. A keen, hardworking student will be given additional challenging assignments in order to meet the grade, while students struggling to meet the requirements of passing the grade would be given assistance by the professor up to a point. The more you challenge the professors, the more they will challenge you."

Like the school's student-friendly professors, the "administrators are always eager and willing to help," and the school runs without a hitch. There is a "seamless organization of administrative facilities," and student support services are all in place. A current student attests, "My advisor makes life bearable for me. She is always there to help when the going gets tough." Additionally, Fairleigh Dickinson is very convenient for working students. The school's two New Jersey campuses both hold classes in the evenings, as well as accelerated classes on Saturdays. As most are juggling professional and education pursuits, students say they really "appreciate the Saturday program because it allows them to balance work, school, and life."

Career and Placement

The Career Development Center at Fairleigh Dickinson University offers a variety of recruiting and career services to both undergraduate and graduate students, including online job boards, resume critiques, and career workshops. The Career Development Center also hosts school-wide career fairs on both New Jersey campuses, attracting employers such as Bloomberg, Colgate-Palmolive, IBM, ERNST & Young, and Novartis.

ADMISSIONS CONTACT: SUSAN BROOMAN, DIRECTOR OF GRADUATE RECRUITMENT & MARKETING
ADDRESS: FAIRLEIGH DICKINSON UNIVERSITY GRADUATE ADMISSIONS, METROPOLITAN CAMPUS
1000 RIVER ROAD (T-KB1-01) TEANECK, NJ 07666 • PHONE: 201-692-2554
FAX: 201-692-2560 • E-MAIL: GRAD@FDU.EDU • WEBSITE: WWW.FDU.EDU

While some recruiting services are focused specifically on graduate students, there are no dedicated career services for the MBA program. Many students plan to keep their current job after graduation, but others would like to see the program offer more professional assistance. Specifically, students feel the business school could encourage "More interaction among business school classmates and alumni to build strong business network."

Student Life and Environment

Attracting "ambitious" working professionals from across New Jersey, Fairleigh Dickinson students are "very friendly, intelligent, [and] hard-working." An asset in the classroom, "Fellow students are generally professionals in various aspects of business (from pharmacy to accounting) and have great insight and personal experiences to offer in class." A current student elaborates, "The students are very motivated to achieve within the MBA program and within the corporate world. All of my group project experiences have made this clear." Overall, "The community is very diverse," yet students manage to build relationships through academic projects, as well as through a "mix of social events and business events" on campus. In fact, the "school is small so, if you are interested, you can really get to know everyone and have lots of fun."

Fairleigh Dickinson's business school is located on two separate New Jersey campuses: the College at Florham in Madison and the Metropolitan Campus in Teaneck. At Teaneck, students mention that the "campus could use some aesthetic improvements and renovations." At Madison, however, the "campus is beautiful," and MBA students can de-stress at the school's "great gym, pool, and other facilities for physical fitness and recreation." Madison students also appreciate the school's "great location" in a "great town with lots to do."

Admissions

Students are admitted to Fairleigh Dickinson University on a rolling basis. Once they have been accepted, students may begin the program immediately, even mid-semester. To apply, prospective students must submit an official GMAT score report and transcripts from all post-secondary work. If you are concerned about the strength of your GMAT score, Fairleigh Dickinson offers a unique option: Prospective students may enroll in a GMAT prep course on the Fairleigh Dickinson campus and, if they are accepted by and choose to attend Fairleigh Dickinson, they will receive a full reimbursement for the course.

FINANCIAL FACTS

Annual tuition	$24,024
Fees	$900
Cost of books	$3,000
Room & board (on-campus)	$9,500
% of students receiving aid	75
% of students receiving loans	45
% of students receiving grants	25
Average award package	$13,500
Average grant	$5,222

ADMISSIONS

Admissions Selectivity Rating	77
TOEFL required of international students	Yes
Minimum TOEFL (paper/computer)	550/213
Application fee	$40
International application fee	$40
Early decision program?	No
Deferment available	Yes
Transfer students accepted	Yes
Transfer application policy: Core courses can be waived by meeting FDU waiver policy. 6 graduate level credits can be transferred from other AACSB schools.	
Non-fall admissions	Yes
Need-blind admissions	Yes

EMPLOYMENT PROFILE

Career Rating	87	**Top 5 Employers Hiring Grads**
Average base starting salary	$70,000	Verizon, Deloitte, Johnson & Johnson, ADP,
Primary Source of Full-time Job Acceptances		UBS
School-facilitated activities	NR (80%)	
Graduate-facilitated activities	NR (20%)	

FAYETTEVILLE STATE UNIVERSITY
SCHOOL OF BUSINESS AND ECONOMICS MBA PROGRAM

GENERAL INFORMATION
Type of school   Public

SURVEY SAYS...
Friendly students
Good peer network
Solid preparation in:
Accounting
General management
Quantitative skills

STUDENTS
Enrollment of parent
  institution   6,800
Enrollment of MBA Program   113
% part-time   100
Average age at entry   33
Average years work experience
  at entry   5

ACADEMICS
Academic Experience Rating   **75**
Student/faculty ratio   15:1
Profs interesting rating   82
Profs accessible rating   78
% female faculty   20
% minority faculty   50

Academics

The School of Business and Economics at Fayetteville State University, a campus of the University of North Carolina system, offers both on-site and online MBA courses to both full-time and part-time students. Undergraduates pursuing a three-two BA/MBA and international students fill out the full-time population; the remaining majority of students are part-timers who typically work full-time while earning a graduate degree. The latter are well-served by UNCFSU's "flexible curriculum" and by the school's partnerships with large local employers, including the US Army at Fort Bragg and the Cape Fear Valley Health System (the school offers an MBA in healthcare, with "classes right on the hospital campus," one participant reports). The school is accredited by the AACSB International.

The UNCFSU MBA is open to all students with undergraduate degrees, including those with no background in business; such students must complete up to 15 credit hours of non-degree foundation courses covering accounting, statistics, finance, microeconomics, macroeconomics, management, communication, and marketing. Students with previous coursework or extensive experience in these areas may place out of some or all foundation courses. The degree-applicable MBA curriculum consists of 27 credit hours of core curriculum and 9–12 credit hours of electives. Students may take all electives in a single area to develop a concentration in accounting, entrepreneurship, finance, healthcare, international business, management, project management, or marketing, or they may mix and match electives to earn an MBA in general business. The school offers a fairly even mix of onsite and online classes, with the former more likely to outnumber the latter slightly in any given semester.

Students praise the "high quality of instructors and the friendly atmosphere offering students opportunities to grow intellectually. Many are "very impressed with the technology used in the classrooms and available for the students, particularly the offsite access to several software programs and library resources." Convenience and a developing local reputation seem to be the chief selling points among current students; they like how they can get a relatively inexpensive MBA "with the convenience of taking some classes online, which cuts down on added expenses" and also that the school "has greatly improved the community perception that it is doing a good job with our young people."

Career and Placement

Placement and career counseling services are provided by the Office of Advisement and Career Services Center at UNCFSU. The office serves all undergraduates, graduates, and recent alumni "in their preparation for securing meaningful employment." Services include workshops, symposia, classroom presentations, career exploration seminars, and job fairs. A Career Resource Library "offers materials and information regarding careers, the job search process, and company literature as well as graduate schools and fellowship programs." Access to online job search tools allows students to utilize a broad range of local, national, and international job-search engines.

FINANCIAL FACTS

Cost of books	$300
Room & board (on-campus)	$5,820
% of students receiving grants	2
Average award package	$7,600

ADMISSIONS

Admissions Selectivity Rating	72
# of applications received	73
% applicants accepted	71
% acceptees attending	100
Average GMAT	486
Range of GMAT	410–560
Average GPA	3.2
TOEFL required of international students	Yes
Minimum TOEFL (paper/computer)	550/213
Application fee	$35
International application fee	$35
Regular application deadline	4/15
Early decision program?	No
Deferment available	Yes
Maximum length of deferment	Normally 1 year
Transfer students accepted	Yes
Transfer application policy: Up to six credit hours could be transferred from an AACSB accredited program.	
Non-fall admissions	Yes
Need-blind admissions	No

Student Life and Environment

UNCFSU serves a student body that consists mostly of "focused, working professionals" (their rank include "doctors, accountants, bankers, and soldiers") with some undergraduates (in the three-two program) and international students in the mix. "Students in the program are extremely friendly and willing to share their experiences and collaborate with studies," one student here informs us. "Most have families, though some don't."

As at most part-time programs serving working students, extracurricular life here is minimal. Some bemoan the dearth of activities, student associations and groups, and "speakers from large businesses and corporations visiting the campus," but many wouldn't notice the difference even if all these activities arrived tomorrow. They're simply too busy with work, school, and life to make time for extracurricular activities. An international student from Romania tells us that the environment is hospitable to foreign students, saying: "It felt like home from the first day of school. Everybody is friendly and helpful and the instructors are always trying to push the students' limits towards higher achievements that will prepare them better for the job market."

Admissions

Degree-seeking applicants to UNCFSU must provide the Admissions Committee with the following materials: a completed application form; official transcripts for all undergraduate and graduate institutions attended (international students must have their transcripts evaluated by an approved agency such as the World Education Service); an official score report for the GMAT; and two letters of recommendation. Students whose native language is not English must submit an official score report for the Test of English as a Foreign Language (TOEFL). International applicants must complete a different application form and must provide proof of their ability to support themselves financially while attending the institution. Degree-seeking applicants must earn a formula score of at least 950 under the formula [(undergraduate GPA 200) + GMAT score], with a minimum GMAT score of 375. Those failing to meet the above requirements but who have a minimum GPA of 2.5 or a GMAT score of at least 450 may be admitted under the Professional Development status, and may later be reclassified as degree-seeking students. Current undergraduates who have carried a GPA of at least 3.0 for the trailing 60 credit hours and earn a formula score of at least 1,000 are eligible for the three-two BA/MBA degree program.

FLORIDA ATLANTIC UNIVERSITY
COLLEGE OF BUSINESS

GENERAL INFORMATION

Type of school	Public
Academic calendar	Semester

SURVEY SAYS...
Solid preparation in:
Communication/interpersonal skills
Presentation skills

STUDENTS

Enrollment of parent institution	27,021
Enrollment of MBA Program	599
% male/female	57/43
% out-of-state	11
% part-time	63
% minorities	27
% international	6
Average age at entry	32
Average years work experience at entry	7

ACADEMICS

Academic Experience Rating	80
Student/faculty ratio	12:1
Profs interesting rating	78
Profs accessible rating	69
% female faculty	36
% minority faculty	20

Prominent Alumni

George C. Zoley, Security Services; Robert L. Forde, Jr., Furniture Retail; Lisbeth R. Barron, Finance; Maynard G. Webb, E-Commerce; Michael Daskal, Accounting.

Academics

The Barry Kaye School of Business at Florida Atlantic University "offers some interesting and unique programs," including a well-regarded MBA in sports management, an environmental MBA, a master's in forensic accounting, and distance learning options "with no obligation to physically attend classes," which makes for an especially appealing feature to the many busy professionals earning degrees here. Students especially appreciate how online courses counter "FAU's habit of scheduling all courses at the same time" by making it possible to "take a mix of online and onsite courses to get through the program much faster."

FAU's sport management program "has a great reputation" and capitalizes on a strong local industry in order to allow students "to learn from industry professionals" and serve career-boosting internships. Likewise, FAU's graduate communications program is "intense and extensive. You must be certified in speaking and writing to graduate from this program. They give you all the tools you need to be a success and require you to do the work you need to get yourself to the level expected." Students also praise the accounting program, saying it's "just excellent—the courses offered, course content, instructors. It is a very demanding program (much more demanding than the MBA)." Students in the MBA program concur, telling us, "The academics aren't overly demanding, since the university recognizes that many of its master's students also are employed full-time, but it is important to be able to balance everything."

The FAU curriculum features "a strong focus on presentations and group work." Some approve, while others believe "there's too much focus on this. Most of the people here are career professionals and work on teams daily. Sometimes, the stress of meeting with members for assignments can be a bit overwhelming," especially when team members live in different cities. Classes include "free-flowing and wide-ranging discussions. Professors consider alternative points of view and create an environment to foster open and honest discussion." As at many large schools, "Going through the administration can be complicated. Persistence is key."

Career and Placement

FAU's College of Business houses the Career Resources and Alumni Relations Center to provide undergraduates and graduate business students with "invaluable guidance with interviewing skills, resume preparation, locating employment opportunities and locating internships." The office also compiles student resumes to be distributed to South Florida businesses. Graduate students have exclusive access to the Job Connection, an internet-based notification system that alerts them to job postings that match their qualifications. FAU participates in a statewide job fair held in the autumn, and "the school offers an online job board and hosts two large job fairs during the school year," but some complain that "there is a noticeable absence of top-tier companies recruiting graduates" at these events.

ADMISSIONS CONTACT: TIFFANY NICHOLSON, ASSOCIATE DIRECTOR OF ACADEMIC SUPPORT SERVICES
ADDRESS: 132 FLEMING WEST, 777 GLADES ROAD BOCA RATON, FL 33431
PHONE: 561-297-2786 • FAX: 561-297-1315
E-MAIL: MBA@FAU.EDU • WEBSITE: WWW.BUSINESS.FAU.EDU

Student Life and Environment

FAU MBAs are typically "employed full-time during the day so the involvement in campus activities is low; however, everyone is very friendly, and once we get to know each other we do mingle outside of the classroom (at least the students in our twenties). There are lots of activities available if you choose to take part, especially athletic events."

The FAU campus provides "a supportive environment" with "state-of-the-art technology" and plenty of "sun and palm trees." The campus is "growing as FAU is becoming a top-tier school in Florida. More buildings are being built, and they make the campus a beautiful place to be." Hometown Boca is "a fantastic location. It's close to the beach and close to Miami and Fort Lauderdale," providing plenty of opportunities for internships and career networking.

Students here "come from many walks of life" and "are all employed in various fields." "We have doctors, lawyers, entrepreneurs, professors, CPAs, etc.," one student explains. "You name it, we have it! Each of them is a professional in their own right and is seeking to enhance their knowledge base." All these commitments mean that students are "always on the run" and that "not too many have spare time to get together and study." However, when time allows, the program attendees' "diverse nationalities and backgrounds lead to great discussions." "About 90 percent of my classmates in my global culture class were not born in the United States. It's a great multicultural mix."

Admissions

Admission to a FAU MBA program requires the following: an undergraduate degree with a GPA of at least 3.0 (on a four-point scale) for the final 60 semester hours of undergraduate course work from an accredited institution; and, a score of at least 500 on the GMAT, earned within the previous five years. In addition to the above qualifications, international students whose first language is not English must also submit official score reports indicating a score of at least 600 on the TOEFL and at least 250 on the Test of Spoken English (TSE). All international applicants must submit Certification of Financial Responsibility and must provide translation and accredited evaluation of their undergraduate transcripts (the latter is necessary only if a grading system other than the American system was used at the degree-granting institution). Letters of recommendation, a resume, an interview, and a personal statement are optional for all applicants. After undergraduate record and standardized test scores, work history is the most important factor in admissions decisions.

FINANCIAL FACTS

Annual tuition (in-state/ out-of-state)	$4,867/$16,486
Fees (in-state/ out-of-state)	$849/$12,467
Cost of books	$1,100
Room & board (on/off-campus)	$9,000/$12,000

ADMISSIONS

Admissions Selectivity Rating	82
# of applications received	486
% applicants accepted	49
% acceptees attending	73
Average GMAT	550
Range of GMAT	510–605
Average GPA	3.2
TOEFL required of international students	Yes
Minimum TOEFL (paper/computer)	600/250
Application fee	$30
International application fee	$30
Regular application deadline	7/1
Early decision program?	No
Deferment available	Yes
Maximum length of deferment	Up to 1 year
Transfer students accepted	Yes
Transfer application policy: We allow the transfer of up to 6 Semester credit hours from an AACSB accredited graduate program. Credits must be no more than 7 years old.	
Non-fall admissions	Yes
Need-blind admissions	Yes

EMPLOYMENT PROFILE

Career Rating	81	Grads Employed by Function	% Avg. Salary
Percent employed at graduation	40	Marketing	14 $80,000
Percent employed 3 months after graduation	32	Operations	9 $100,000
		Management	36 $70,500
Average base starting salary	$77,380	Finance	27 $72,500
		MIS	9 $65,000

Top 5 Employers Hiring Grads
IBM (1), LexisNexis (1), Lilly (1), Ryder Systems (1), FBI (1)

FLORIDA GULF COAST UNIVERSITY
LUTGERT COLLEGE OF BUSINESS

GENERAL INFORMATION
Type of school   Public

SURVEY SAYS...
Solid preparation in:
General management
Operations
Doing business in a global economy

STUDENTS
Enrollment of parent institution	11,104
Enrollment of MBA Program	186
% male/female	53/47
% out-of-state	2
% part-time	68
% minorities	13
Average age at entry	27

ACADEMICS
Academic Experience Rating	**71**
Profs interesting rating	89
Profs accessible rating	83

Academics

The Lutgert College of Business at Florida Gulf Coast University offers both a full-time and a part-time MBA program as well as an Executive MBA, an MS in accounting and taxation, and an MS in computer information systems. The school offers a broad range of MBA courses online to facilitate distance learning. Location and cost are among the top reasons cited for attending; students also appreciate that "the College of Business, both undergrad and graduate, is very well-established in the local community."

The FGCU MBA "emphasizes the application of analytical, technical, and behavioral tools to solve organizational problems" with "a focus on teamwork and team-building so that students frequently work closely together." The program consists of 24 hours of foundation courses, 21 hours of core courses, and nine hours of concentration courses; students with solid business backgrounds or college transcripts deep in business courses may have some or all of the foundation courses waived. Concentrations are offered in general management, interdisciplinary studies, finance, information systems, or marketing. Students approve, telling us that the school has "a tremendous faculty and staff backed with a tremendous amount of intelligence." "A majority of the faculty holds PhDs and frequently publish articles and books as well," a student explains. Finance is particularly strong, as "a majority of the professors come from companies and institutions such as Gillette and the Federal Reserve. These professors hold advanced degrees from schools like Wharton and Harvard." The program itself, says one MBA, "offers a globally aligned business education through a quality Master's program. FGCU is integrated with schools in Germany and elsewhere abroad." A student population in which "multiple nationalities, ethnic groups, and minorities are represented" amplifies this international focus.

Lutgert opened in 1997, and students see its newcomer status as a plus. One explains: "Being a newer school, it has jumped headfirst into solving the...web-based education and capitaliz[es] on using the Internet to advance the teachers' ability to manage classroom assignments, work, and lessons. They are light-years ahead of most schools that may appear larger and more experienced but have failed to grasp the integration of solid web-based education." The school's novelty also pays dividends in "the modernity of its infrastructure," which includes "a great, clean, small campus" with a "great library with plenty of quiet areas and an abundance of resources and references."

Career and Placement

All career services at Florida Gulf Coast University are provided by the school's Career Development Services office, which assists undergraduates and graduate students in all areas. The office sponsors a variety of events throughout the year, including workshops, seminars, on-campus recruiting visits, and a career fair. Participants in the school's Spring 2008 Career Expo included Alliance Financial, Ameriprise, Colonial Life, Gartner, Northwestern Mutual, Orion Bank, Primerica Financial Services, and Wells Fargo. Students would like to see "a stronger showing of large international companies in recruiting season." Because the school is relatively new—FGCU welcomed its first students in 1997—its alumni network is small, but growing.

ADMISSIONS CONTACT: ANA HILL, ADMISSIONS-REGISTRAR OFFICER-GRADUATE ADMISSIONS
ADDRESS: 10501 FGCU BOULEVARD SOUTH FORT MYERS, FL 33965
PHONE: 239-590-7908 • FAX: 239-590-7894
E-MAIL: GRADUATE@FGCU.EDU • WEBSITE: WWW.FGCU.EDU

Student Life and Environment

Most FGCU MBAs have little time for campus life. Quite a few, in fact, rarely visit campus at all since the school also serves a sizeable distance-learning population. Even those who attend classes in person typically work full time. Many have family obligations too, leaving little (make that "no") time for extracurriculars. International students, who attend full time, are one exception to the rule. The other exception includes some students who have proceeded directly from undergraduate study to the MBA program. (While a number of these attend part time while working, others attend on a full-time basis.) Students tend to be "resourceful, smart, and innovative." One informs us that "this region of Florida breeds entrepreneurs, and the Florida Gulf Coast University MBA program caters to that audience. We receive a quality education for learning how to start, maintain and operate, and capitalize on all our resources to make a business successful."

The FGCU campus is located 15 minutes from the Gulf of Mexico, in a small city with great weather and a laid-back vibe. Students agree that the quality of life in the area is high. As one student puts it, "It's 76 degrees on March 11. Any other questions?" Top-area employers include Lee Memorial Hospital, SWFL Regional Medical Center, the government, local colleges and universities, and real estate and resort developers. The area is growing quickly, creating opportunities for both managers and entrepreneurs. The university is growing as well, with lots of new facilities developing all the time.

Admissions

Admission to the MBA program at FGCU is based on a combination of undergraduate GPA and GMAT scores. To be considered, applicants much have either a minimum GPA of 3.0 for their final 60 credit hours of undergraduate work or a minimum GMAT score of 500; and a formula score of at least 1050 under the formula [(undergraduate GPA × 200) + GMAT score], with a minimum GMAT score of at least 400. International students whose first language is not English must also submit TOEFL scores (minimum 550 written, 213 computerized, 79 internet-based). Students may apply for admission to either the fall or spring semester. Students may complete a maximum of nine credit hours of graduate level courses before gaining official admission to the program.

ADMISSIONS	
Admissions Selectivity Rating	**60***
Average GMAT	499
Average GPA	3.1
TOEFL required of international students	Yes
Minimum TOEFL (paper/computer)	550/213
Application fee	$30
International application fee	$30
Regular application deadline	5/1
Regular notification	7/1
Early decision program?	No
Deferment available	Yes
Maximum length of deferment	1 semester
Transfer students accepted	Yes
Transfer application policy: 6 credits of approved graduate-level coursework may be transferred from a regionally accredited institution.	
Non-fall admissions	Yes
Need-blind admissions	Yes

FLORIDA INTERNATIONAL UNIVERSITY
ALVIN H. CHAPMAN GRADUATE SCHOOL OF BUSINESS

Academics

As its moniker suggests, Florida International University offers MBAs that are "more internationally-oriented" than your standard graduate business program. This emphasis is especially pronounced in the school's one-year International Business program, but it applies to all the graduate degrees offered here. The school parlays its location in Miami, "the gateway to the Americas," to focus particular attention on Latin America and the Caribbean, regions well-represented on the faculty and among the student body.

No matter your academic interests and scheduling needs, FIU probably has an MBA program to suit you. Its 20-month Executive MBA "is an excellent program for managers with over 12 years of work experience." For less experienced professionals, the 18-month Downtown MBA or the Evening MBA on FIU's campus may be good fits. For those unable to get away from the office, the Corporate MBA delivers the program to the workplace. And if you're looking for a specialized MBA in healthcare, FIU offers that as well.

Students praise FIU's "excellent reputation in the south Florida business community," its affordability, and the "top-notch" professors and administration. Students report approvingly that "The school has a team of administrators assigned to the MBA program. They handle everything for us, and I mean everything: enrollment, books, materials, copies, meals, etc." One MBA notes, "It is especially appealing that the business program is run somewhat independently from the rest of the university to ensure higher quality services and resources." Overall students find the program "very well-organized," led by "extremely competitive and prepared" professors who "are all known leaders in their field and have great experiences to share with us." "The faculty have provided real insight into their industry[ies] and created stimulating learning environments for the most part," one student explains. Classroom discussion is enhanced by a "very international" and diverse student body. "You get investment bankers [and people in] rank and file jobs trying to get ahead, all working together" here. With all these assets, no wonder students call an FIU MBA "a superb investment at a very low price."

Career and Placement

Chapman's Career Management Services office provides graduate students and alumni with counseling and placement assistance. The office works closely with the university's general Career Services Office to coordinate career fairs, on-campus interviews, and other career-related events. Students tell us that FIU's alumni network is large and very helpful.

Top employers of FIU MBAs (including currently employed students attending one of the part-time programs) include: PricewaterhouseCoopers, B/E Aerospace, Commerce Bank, P&G, FPL, Fitch Ratings, Brightstar Corporation, Bank of America, Caterpillar, GE, and Choice Hotels International.

ADMISSIONS CONTACT: PRISCILIANA BERRIOS, GRADUATE RECRUITING
ADDRESS: 11200 S. W. 8TH STREET - CBC 200 MIAMI, FL 33199
PHONE: 305-348-7398 • FAX:
E-MAIL: CHAPMAN@FIU.EDU • WEBSITE: BUSINESS.FIU.EDU

Student Life and Environment

FIU's MBA program is housed "in a brand-new building with extremely comfortable and high-technology resources," with "many locations for classmates to gather and work in a comfortable environment." "The resources you need for research and completing assignments are readily available" here, and the school even "makes ample provision for students who are without computers; for example, access to computers whether in the computer room or the library." Full-time students report that they experience "a fast-paced environment" driven by classes, extracurriculars, and an active Student Government Association. They also tell us that "The sports program is up and coming, so the students are very excited and try hard to get the rest of us motivated to cheer for the Golden Panthers!" Part-timers tend to visit campus only for classes and schoolwork, and as a result are less engaged in campus life.

The FIU MBA program is "like the United Nations. We come from many nations: Germany, France, [United States], Central America, and South America. When they say 'Florida International University'—they mean it." Students are drawn from an equally impressive array of industries "including banking, healthcare, pharmaceutical, automotive, logistics, insurance, etc." There are a lot of "strong A-type personalities, which in my book means we 'Ace' in everything we do, be it group assignments, weekly tests, heated arguments over project submissions, or a chilled beer to commemorate the end of a quarter."

Admissions

Admissions requirements to FIU's MBA programs vary somewhat from program to program. As a general rule, students with the best combination of grade point average, applicable test scores, and pertinent work experience who also meet specific program requirements will have the first opportunity to enter the programs, according to the school's website. Applicants to the school's popular International MBA program must submit the following materials: an official copy of an undergraduate transcript, with a GPA of at least 3.0 in upper-division course work strongly preferred; official proof of undergraduate degree; a current resume; a personal statement; and an official GMAT or GRE score report. In addition to the above documents, international students whose primary language is not English must also provide an official score report for the TOEFL or the IELTS. They must also submit their transcripts to a translation agency to be forwarded to FIU, and they must provide the following documents: Declaration of Certification of Finances (DCF); a bank letter; a sponsor letter if applicable; and an F-1 transfer if they already have an F-1 Visa.

FINANCIAL FACTS

Annual tuition (in-state/ out-of-state)	$30,490/$35,490
Cost of books	$2,000
Room & board (on/off-campus)	$12,000/$18,000
% of students receiving aid	79
% of students receiving loans	75
% of students receiving grants	4
Average award package	$21,080
Average grant	$5,000
Average student loan debt	$40,000

ADMISSIONS

Admissions Selectivity Rating	60*
Average GMAT	550
Range of GMAT	450–700
Average GPA	3.29
TOEFL required of international students	Yes
Minimum TOEFL (paper/computer)	550/213
Application fee	$30
International application fee	$30
Early decision program?	No
Deferment available	Yes
Maximum length of deferment	1 year
Transfer students accepted	Yes
Non-fall admissions	Yes
Need-blind admissions	Yes

EMPLOYMENT PROFILE

Career Rating	78	Grads Employed by Function	% Avg. Salary
Percent employed at graduation	72	Marketing	30 $62,667
Average base starting salary	$59,308	Finance	10 $60,000
Primary Source of Full-time Job Acceptances		HR	10 $70,000
School-facilitated activities	NR (57%)		
Graduate-facilitated activities	NR (43%)		

FLORIDA STATE UNIVERSITY
COLLEGE OF BUSINESS

GENERAL INFORMATION
Type of school   Public
Academic calendar   Semester

SURVEY SAYS...
Good peer network
Solid preparation in:
Communication/interpersonal skills
Presentation skills

STUDENTS
Enrollment of parent institution	38,000
Enrollment of MBA Program	215
% male/female	61/39
% out-of-state	10
% part-time	76
% minorities	18
% international	4
Average age at entry	26
Average years work experience at entry	4

ACADEMICS
Academic Experience Rating	**81**
Student/faculty ratio	30:1
Profs interesting rating	85
Profs accessible rating	82
% female faculty	13
% minority faculty	3

Joint Degrees
JD/MBA Juris Doctor/Master of Business Administration, 113 credit hours completed over approximately 4 years.

Prominent Alumni
Gary Rogers, President & CEO, GE Plastics; Craig Wardlaw, Executive VP & CIO, Bank of America; Craig Ramsey, Partner, Accenture; Chuck Hardwick, Senior Vice President, Pfizer.

Academics

The College of Business at Florida State University offers a variety of options to suit the diverse needs of its MBA student body. Students straight out of college and anxious to earn a graduate degree typically find their way to the school's one-year full-time MBA program. Busy professionals can choose between an on-campus part-time program and an online program with "an asynchronous, totally web-based curriculum." The super-ambitious can pursue joint degrees in business and law or business and social work. In all programs, the reasonable tuition ("It's a prestigious school at a great value," writes one student) and "the growing reputation of the business school" are compelling factors in bringing students aboard.

Florida's full-time MBA is a cohort-based lockstep curriculum, with students remaining in the same work group throughout the twelve-month program. Students in the program may concentrate in finance or marketing and supply chain management, or they may earn a general MBA. Part-time students complete the same core courses and study with the same professors as do their full-time counterparts; however, they are not divided into cohorts and they cannot pursue a concentration. The online MBA can be completed in its entirety remotely. Again, students complete the same core courses with the same professors as do other FSU MBAs. The online MBA allows for concentrations in real estate and analysis or hospital administration. Students may also complete a general MBA.

FSU faculty members receive strong grades overall. Students tell us, "The professors in the business department are amazing. They are very congenial and well-spoken. They are helpful at all times. Most teachers are older and contain a strong sense of experience. They know how to teach a class that is entertaining, interactive, and fun." Some warn that "There are quite a few professors here with heavy accents that may take a little concentration to understand," but even they concede that "their willingness to help you outside the classroom and brilliance far outweigh this drawback." Teachers also "do a very good job of keeping class interesting by incorporating technology, group assignments, etc."

Career and Placement

Because FSU's MBA program is small and largely part time, the school does not maintain a separate career services office for graduate students in business. It does, however, sponsor an MBA Internship Program in which "carefully structured project work" allows both students and employers to "realize the benefits of this program." The school also offers coaching and career-related resources in order to help students plan their job search and marketing of their skills. The school hosts semi-annual MBA Networking Night events and on-campus and videoconference interviews. It also provides students access to a host of job-posting resources. Students report, "Our career center is great about creating internship opportunities. However, as far as full-time positions after graduation, the focus is more on undergrads. There are few recruiters that come specifically for MBAs." In the plus column, "Networking seems to be one of the biggest strengths of Florida State. Through the College of Business, my sorority, and all the amazing staff, the opportunities are endless."

Employers most likely to hire FSU MBAs include BB&T, CSX, Harris, JP Morgan, Protiviti, and Wachovia Bank.

ADMISSIONS CONTACT: LISA BEVERLY, ADMISSIONS DIRECTOR
ADDRESS: GRADUATE PROGRAMS, COLLEGE OF BUSINESS, FSU TALLAHASSEE, FL 32306-1110
PHONE: 850-644-6458 • FAX: 850-644-0588
E-MAIL: GRADPROG@COB.FSU.EDU • WEBSITE: WWW.COB.FSU.EDU/GRAD

Student Life and Environment

Full-timers at FSU basically get to extend their college years by one, albeit with a heavier workload. Students tell us: "Life is relaxed and challenging. We have a lot of work but ample time to complete it. Everyone wants to have a good time, but it's about priorities. If you go to class, you will succeed." Campus life offers "the perfect balance of challenging schoolwork, amazing social groups, and fun nightlife," and "the School of Dance and Music puts on (sometimes free) performances for the community. FSU energizes Tallahassee," a city that is "a great place to be" although "it is a small town and can get boring quick." One student suggests "picking up a hobby that you can do around town in all the parks and woods—Frisbee, mountain biking, kayaking, football, whatever—just stay involved in a physical activity."

Part-time students engage mostly in class and study groups. One observes: "It's nice being able to see the same people semester after semester. That gives us all a sense of warmth when we get into new classes. Life here is pretty busy, people running around trying to get things done on time...not much different from in the real world." Part-timers regard themselves as "more adaptable and friendly" than their full-time peers, whom they regard as "still a bit immature."

Admissions

The Admissions Office at Florida State University requires all of the following from applicants to its MBA program: two official copies of transcripts for all post-secondary academic work; an official GMAT score report; three letters of recommendation from former professors and/or employers; a current resume; a personal statement; and a Florida Residency affidavit, if appropriate. Students must have proficiency working with PCs. International students whose first language is not English must also submit an official score report for the TOEFL (minimum score: 600 paper-based test, 250 computer-based test, or 100 Internet-based test). All test scores must be no more than five years old. The school lists the following programs designed to increase recruitment of underrepresented and disadvantaged students: the FAMU Feeder Program, FAMU Graduate & Professional Days, GradQuest, MBA Advantage, Minority Student Orientation Program, Leslie Wilson Assistantships, the Delores Auzenne Minority Fellowship, and the University Fellowship.

FINANCIAL FACTS

Annual tuition (in-state/ out-of-state)	$9,600/$36,153
Cost of books	$5,750
Room & board (on/off-campus)	$13,000/$15,000
% of students receiving aid	29
% of first-year students receiving aid	29
% of students receiving grants	29
Average award package	$10,000
Average grant	$2,500

ADMISSIONS

Admissions Selectivity Rating	82
# of applications received	546
% applicants accepted	55
% acceptees attending	72
Average GMAT	558
Range of GMAT	500–610
Average GPA	3.35
TOEFL required of international students	Yes
Minimum TOEFL (paper/computer)	600/250
Application fee	$30
International application fee	$30
Early decision program?	No
Deferment available	Yes
Maximum length of deferment	12 months
Transfer students accepted	Yes
Transfer application policy: Transfer applicants must complete the same application process as all other applicants.	
Non-fall admissions	Yes
Need-blind admissions	Yes

EMPLOYMENT PROFILE

Career Rating	77	Top 5 Employers Hiring Grads
		Wachovia Bank, U.S. Staffing, CSX Corporation, Harris, Avaya

FORDHAM UNIVERSITY
GRADUATE SCHOOL OF BUSINESS ADMINISTRATION

GENERAL INFORMATION
Type of school	Private
Affiliation	Roman Catholic/Jesuit
Academic calendar	Trimester

SURVEY SAYS...
Students love New York, NY
Solid preparation in:
Finance
Accounting

STUDENTS
Enrollment of parent	
institution	14,544
Enrollment of MBA Program	1,131
% male/female	61/39
% part-time	42
% minorities	36
% international	23
Average age at entry	28
Average years work experience	
at entry	5

ACADEMICS
Academic Experience Rating	**81**
Student/faculty ratio	7:1
Profs interesting rating	86
Profs accessible rating	81
% female faculty	25
% minority faculty	27

Joint Degrees
Joint JD/MBA Program, 3.5 years full-time, 6.5 years part-time; MTA Program (MBA in Public Accounting and MS in Taxation, 99 credits; BS/MS Programs, 5 years; BS/MBA Program, 150 credits, 5 years.

Prominent Alumni
Nemir Kidar, Founder/President, Investcorp Bank; James N. Fernandez, EVP/CFO, Tiffany & Co.; Patricia Fili-Krushel, EVP, Time Warner; Frank Petrilli, Presient/CEO, TDWaterhouse; Robert Dafeo, Executive VP/CFO, Thomson Reuters.

Academics

For New York City professionals—or those who aspire to be—the Graduate School of Business at Fordham University offers a perfect blend of convenience and quality. Located in the midst of New York's thriving business world, the school's Lincoln Center campus "is accessible and beautiful," giving students the opportunity to keep their job (or start a new one) while they complete their MBA. What's more, "All classes are offered at night or during the day to fit your schedule," and the program is "very flexible," allowing students to tailor their course load each semester. In fact, "You can switch from part time to full time at your wish." Juggling work and school can be a challenge; fortunately, "Coursework is demanding but reasonable," and "If you are working, this school is very much geared for you." A typical part-time student shares, "I study 20–30 hours a week while working a full time job."

Fordham's required core curriculum provides a complete introduction to business principals through eight courses in subjects including accounting, finance, and marketing. Students admit that some professors are more engaging than others, but, on the whole, classes deliver "extremely valuable and practical knowledge." Working professionals appreciate the fact that "Professors constantly bring real-world applications into the classroom that I can apply to work the very next day." In addition to the core, "Fordham MBA offers quite a wide breadth of course topics and majors," including well-regarded finance and marketing departments and "a strong media and entertainment program." Whether concentrating on finance, media, accounting and taxation, management systems, or marketing, "The degrees and specializations can significantly assist students in focusing on a career path few other schools in the city can offer."

In line with the school's Jesuit tradition, education at Fordham extends beyond the classroom, and students are pleased to report that, "Professors have been very helpful with outside interests, discussing current events, and career advising." The academic environment is interactive, and students are encouraged to share insights from their "diverse work experience," and to "learn from other's experiences." With uniformly small class sizes, "students and professors engage in dialogs and everyone is open to one another; it is a friendly, yet serious business environment filled with people from all walks of life."

While upholding a strong reputation in New York City, Fordham doesn't rest on its laurels. In recent years, Fordham's top administrators "have worked hard to make positive improvements to the program, so that it remains competitive." In recent years, the school has kept up with recent business trends by "implementing a global sustainability designation [as well as an entrepreneurship designation] and creating international business-culture study tours for students to countries, such as China, Mexico, and Turkey." Moreover, the administrators are "receptive to student feedback and take action when students show an interest in a new subject. Overall the university has improved the curriculum every year, continuing to focus on the most important global issues."

Career and Placement

Fordham maintains a "great reputation in the New York City metropolitan region," which bodes well for students hoping to make a career change after completing their MBA. With more than 15,000 working graduates (most in the New York City region), Fordham's "alumni network is very helpful and well-placed." In particular, Fordham is "a very well-recognized school in the financial as well media sector." Despite these strengths, students feel "Career services could be more aggressive building relationships with top companies for recruiting purposes." New leadership in the Office of Career

ADMISSIONS CONTACT: CYNTHIA PEREZ, DIRECTOR OF ADMISSIONS AND FINANCIAL AID
ADDRESS: 33 WEST 60TH STREET, 4TH FLOOR NEW YORK, NY 10023
PHONE: 212-636-6200 • FAX: 212-636-7076
E-MAIL: ADMISSIONSGB@FORDHAM.EDU • WEBSITE: WWW.BNET.FORDHAM.EDU

FINANCIAL FACTS

Annual tuition	$36,605
Fees	$403
Cost of books	$1,500
Average grant	$10,443

ADMISSIONS

Admissions Selectivity Rating	**78**
# of applications received	729
% applicants accepted	74
% acceptees attending	49
Average GMAT	590
Range of GMAT	550–630
Average GPA	3.2
TOEFL required of international students	Yes
Minimum TOEFL (paper/computer)	600/250
Application fee	$130
International application fee	$130
Regular application deadline	6/1
Early decision program?	No
Deferment available	Yes
Maximum length of deferment	1 year
Transfer students accepted	Yes
Transfer application policy: ACCSB Accredited school; Prerequisite and core courses can be waived based on course work taken at other institution.	
Non-fall admissions	Yes
Need-blind admissions	Yes

Applicants Also Look At

Baruch College, Columbia University, Fairfield Univeristy, Hofstra University, New York University, Pace University, Rutgers University, St. John's University

Management has taken steps to expand the on-campus recruiting program, including full-time jobs and internships.

Through the Office of Career Management, Fordham offers resume critiques, career workshops, and on-campus recruiting. In recent years, Fordham graduates have received offers from ABN AMRO, American Express, Bank of America, Barclays Capital, Citigroup Inc., Deloitte, Duff & Phelps, Ernst & Young, General Electric, JPMorgan Chase, KPMG, MTV, NBC Universal, Nestle, Novartis, Pepsico, Pricewaterhouse, Societe Generale, Thomson Reuters, Time Inc., and Unilever. For students who want to work anywhere but New York City, be forewarned that the focus at Fordham is on the Big Apple, and Career Management places graduates primarily in the New York City/Tri-state area.

Student Life and Environment

Although Fordham has a large part-time program, the full-time student body has been growing over the past few years and leads an active coterie of student clubs. The majority of students are "hard-working professionals balancing multiple priorities in order to get ahead." In other words, Fordham students are very busy. Even so, the school's atmosphere is laid-back and convivial, lending itself to friendship and networking. "There are generally no competitive pressures" between classmates, and many students make time to "socialize on school days after class."

While many Fordham students don't have time for campus activities, there is still plenty going on around Lincoln Center. If you're so inclined, Fordham hosts "many networking events and school sponsored happy hours to meet other students." More informally, "Students typically do their studying at school rather than home and pack the study lounges and library." Drawing a large population from surrounding New York, as well as internationally, Fordham attracts students who are "passionate, fun, very diverse in their attitudes and view points, yet somewhat similar in their quest for new and challenging opportunities."

Admissions

To apply to Fordham, prospective students must submit a completed application, college transcripts, a resume, three essays, and two letters of recommendation. In recent years, successful admits have five years of professional work experience, and an average GMAT score of 577 (for part-time students) to 609 (for full-time students). Fordham students join the community from varied industries, including radio and television, public relations, real estate, financial services, publishing, and accounting, and they hail from countries as diverse as China, India, Taiwan, Italy, Brazil, Russia, Turkey, Nigeria, Mexico, and South Korea.

EMPLOYMENT PROFILE

Career Rating	**87**	**Grads Employed by Function**	**% Avg. Salary**
Average base starting salary	$76,396	Marketing	18 $79,200
Primary Source of Full-time Job Acceptances		Consulting	3 $95,000
School-facilitated activities	19 (41%)	General Management	3 $80,000
Graduate-facilitated activities	27 (59%)	Finance	69 $72,720
		MIS	7 $110,000

Top 5 Employers Hiring Grads
Ernst & Young (3), KPMG (3), Credit Suisse (2), Barclays Capital (2), Thomson Reuters (1)

FRANCIS MARION UNIVERSITY
SCHOOL OF BUSINESS

GENERAL INFORMATION
Type of school	Public
Academic calendar	Semester

SURVEY SAYS...
Friendly students
Solid preparation in:
Presentation skills
Quantitative skills
Computer skills

STUDENTS
Enrollment of parent institution	3,947
Enrollment of MBA Program	61
% male/female	49/51
% part-time	95
% minorities	20
% international	7
Average age at entry	29

ACADEMICS
Academic Experience Rating	70
Student/faculty ratio	3:1
Profs interesting rating	82
Profs accessible rating	63

Academics

The School of Business at South Carolina's Francis Marion University offers "excellent preparation for real-world business decision-making" in a "convenient" MBA program "scheduled in the evening to accommodate working students." Since FMU is a state school, it does so at a price that doesn't break the bank.

This small school—one of the smallest state universities to earn AACSB accreditation, according to the university's public relations materials—offers a "challenging learning environment" in which "professors are easy to approach" and, consequently, the almost exclusively part-time student body "gets to know professors one on one." FMU offers both a general MBA and an MBA with a concentration in Health Management. The former is designed to serve the general business population of the Pee Dee region and beyond; the latter is directed toward individuals currently employed in the health care field and/or those with backgrounds in health care. The Health Management Degree is delivered to FMU students through online classes and resources.

All FMU MBAs must complete courses in accounting for management control, managerial economics, financial theory and applications, strategic management, management science and statistics, and marketing theory and application. Students in the general MBA program must also complete classes in financial accounting, information systems, international business, management theory and applications, production management, and entrepreneurship. Students pursuing a health concentration must also complete classes in health policy, health economics, health care delivery systems, financial management for health care organizations, and health law and risk management. Students in health management may also take three hours of elective course work.

MBAs praise the program's faculty, noting that "professors with real-world experience are integrated into active businesses and graduate programs." Primarily, they appreciate the convenience afforded by the school's location and scheduling, as well as the low cost of attending to Palmetto State natives.

Career and Placement

FMU's MBA program is too small to support career services dedicated exclusively to its students. MBAs receive career assistance from the university's Office of Career Development, which serves undergraduates and graduates in all divisions. Students here also benefit from an active Alumni Association, whose newest chapter is the MBA Alumni Chapter.

ADMISSIONS CONTACT: BEN KYER, DIRECTOR
ADDRESS: BOX 100547 FLORENCE, SC 29501-0547
PHONE: 843-661-1436 • FAX: 843-661-1432
E-MAIL: ALPHA1@FMARION.EDU • WEBSITE: ALPHA1.FMARION.EDU/~MBA

FINANCIAL FACTS

Annual tuition (in-state/ out-of-state)	$3,500/$7,000
Fees	$60
Cost of books	$750
% of students receiving aid	8
Average grant	$1,000

ADMISSIONS

Admissions Selectivity Rating	**62**
# of applications received	33
% applicants accepted	85
% acceptees attending	93
Average GMAT	400
Average GPA	3
TOEFL required of international students	Yes
Minimum TOEFL (paper/computer)	550/213
Application fee	$30
Early decision program?	No
Deferment available	Yes
Transfer students accepted	No
Non-fall admissions	No
Need-blind admissions	No

Student Life and Environment

FMU draws a "driven and goal-oriented" student body that is "culturally diverse and career diverse." Life here is hectic, with most students juggling career and family obligations in addition to school responsibilities. Because of the many demands on their time, most students have little inclination to join in extracurricular activities. The program offers "many organizations" to those interested, but students warn that "they aren't as organized or publicized as well as they should be."

The school does a better job with its cultural and entertainment offerings to the general student population, hosting a wide range of performances, exhibits, and lecture series. The school houses an art gallery that displays student and faculty work as well as traveling exhibitions, film series, a planetarium and observatory, concerts, and festivals. FMU's Patriots are successful enough that the school plans to move its entire athletic program to Division I in the coming years; two teams already compete at that level, with the other ten currently competing in Division II.

FMU is located just outside of Florence, SC, a city with nearly 70,000 residents within its borders and its suburbs. Florence offers a number of movie theaters, malls, restaurants, a symphony orchestra, and professional hockey (the Pee Dee Pride skate in the East Coast Hockey League). The city is located at the intersections of I-95 and I-20, making travel in all four cardinal directions a snap. Columbia, Charleston, Myrtle Beach, and Fayetteville, NC, are all within 100 miles.

Admissions

Applicants to the FMU MBA program must submit a completed application; official transcripts for all postsecondary academic work, in a sealed envelope addressed to the applicant from the awarding school; official GMAT scores; two letters of recommendation; and a personal statement of purpose. All materials must be delivered to the school in a single envelope or package. In addition, international applicants must submit official TOEFL scores and a Confidential Financial Statement form demonstrating their ability to pay all expenses related to an FMU MBA. All successful applicants meet the following minimum guidelines: a score greater than 950 under the formula [(undergraduate GPA x 200) + GMAT score] or a score greater than 1000 under the formula [(GPA for final 60 hours of undergraduates work x 200) + GMAT score]. Also, they must earn at least a score of 400 on the GMAT. Applicants with non-business undergraduate degrees are generally required to complete the business foundation sequence prior to beginning work on their MBA. The sequence is a 33-hour, 11-course curriculum covering the basics of accounting, economics, statistics, business law, business computing, management, information systems, finance, and marketing. Students with undergraduate business degrees typically have this requirement waived.

THE GEORGE WASHINGTON UNIVERSITY
SCHOOL OF BUSINESS

GENERAL INFORMATION
Type of school	Private
Academic calendar	Semester

SURVEY SAYS...
Students love Washington, D.C.
Good social scene
Solid preparation in:
Accounting
Doing business in a global economy

STUDENTS
Enrollment of parent institution	26,220
Enrollment of MBA Program	973
% male/female	55/45
% part-time	79
% minorities	5
% international	27
Average age at entry	27
Average years work experience at entry	4

ACADEMICS
Academic Experience Rating	**87**
Student/faculty ratio	22:1
Profs interesting rating	77
Profs accessible rating	84
% female faculty	29
% minority faculty	23

Joint Degrees
MBA/JD degree, 4 years; MBA/MA in International Affairs, 30 months; MBA/MS Finance, 27 months; MBA/Project Management, 36–60 months.

Prominent Alumni
Colin Powell, MBA, Former U.S. Secretary of State; Henry Duques, BBA & MBA, Former President & CEO, First Data Corp.; Edward M. Liddy, MBA, Chairman & CEO, Allstate Insurance; Michael Enzi, BBA, US Senator; Clarence B. Rogers, Jr., MBA, Chairman, President & CEO, Equifax, Inc.

Academics

A new breed of business school, The George Washington University's Global MBA program brings ethical leadership and international savvy into the classroom. Having recently redesigned its MBA program, the school's "bold new curriculum" (combined with its historic strength in real estate, sports management, and other fields) has attracted many enthusiastic and socially-minded students to the program. At GWU's School of Business, core coursework has a heavy focus on entrepreneurship and global business, as well as an emphasis on "ethics, corporate social responsibility, and sustainability." During the first two semesters, students complete a "full-time compressed curriculum with fixed cohorts"—a series of interdisciplinary courses taught by teams of professors. A "relatively small MBA program," the GWU MBA allows more personal interaction in the classroom, and throughout the program, "Schoolwork is extremely team-based, which empowers students to develop essential teamwork skills." After completing the core, students can "tailor their second-year curriculum to their interests" through one of 17 areas of concentration.

A long-standing D.C. institution, GWU's stellar location adds incredible value to students educational experience, providing "many opportunities to supplement classroom learning with out-of-class experiences, such as seeing the treasury secretary and other politicians discuss important legislation." A student agrees, "While the academic experience is vital (and excellent), I would say it's all the opportunities outside the classroom that are most valuable to me." To supplement the academic curriculum with real-world know-how, GWU students pursue summer internships, attend lectures in the MBA speaker series, participate in school-sponsored co-curricular activities in the Washington, D.C., area, or volunteer through the "active Net Impact chapter." Of particular note, every GWU student gets hands-on experience through the "international consulting project"—a three-course sequence, which concludes with a real-world consulting experience overseas (recent destinations include Barcelona, Istanbul, and Ho Chi Minh City.)

At GWU, professors and administrators are "all very professional and very competent"—as well as student-oriented. In fact, students say, "The most impressive thing about GWU's professors is their accessibility outside of class…. Most professors display a genuine interest in the students, which is very refreshing." Even so, many think the school needs to invest more time and energy in recruiting better faculty, as "the professors are very hit or miss" in the classroom. "Some of them are very effective instructors and go out of their way to help students succeed in learning the subject matter," while others "may be better researchers than educators." Students also admit that there have been a few hiccups as the school implements its new curriculum, but "the administration is working hard to smooth out all the wrinkles." Overall, the school "functions exceptionally well" and administrators are always "very responsive to student feedback."

Career and Placement

The F. David Fowler Career Center (FDFCC) at the School of Business distinguishes itself from other MBA placement programs through its partnership with Meridian Resources, Inc, a career management consulting firm, which augments the campus program with expanded career planning and job placement resources. Students begin working with the FDFCC before they arrive on campus, and they continue to prepare for their career throughout the program through one-on-one career counseling, career development workshops, career fairs, and networking events. GWU has "a strong alumni network in the Washington, D.C., area and elsewhere," and "There are a number of programs that link students with alumni." However, given the school's global focus, many feel that "More of an effort should be made to engage international alumni."

ADMISSIONS CONTACT: JUDITH STOCKMAN, EXECUTIVE DIRECTOR, GRADUATE ADMISSIONS
ADDRESS: 2201 G ST. NW, SUITE 550 WASHINGTON, DC 20052
PHONE: 202-994-1212 • FAX: 202-994-3571
E-MAIL: GWMBA@GWU.EDU • WEBSITE: WWW.BUSINESS.GWU.EDU/GRAD

For recent MBA classes, the mean salary upon graduation was $77,600, with 16 percent of students receiving an additional signing bonus. Students took jobs at companies including AARP, AE Strategies, Booz Allen Hamilton, General Electric, Metro Associates, Samsung Securities, SAP, U.S. Department of Commerce, and U.S. Department of Health and Human Services.

Student Life and Environment

At The George Washington University, extracurricular, networking, and social activities are just as vital to the student experience as the academic program. With an emphasis on teamwork and cooperation, GWU "values the balance of networking and social relationships in conjunction with demanding academics." Taking advantage of the urban environment, the school offers "organized events around sightseeing and community service initiatives." In addition, "There are tons of ways to be involved, and nearly every student keeps exceptionally busy, through a combo of classes, internship(s), part-time work, and student clubs/activities." There really is something for everyone, and, "If you don't see a club you like, it's easy to start your own."

With its small class sizes, "The atmosphere at GWU is definitely collegial—in contrast to other schools which get fairly competitive, GWU students are happy to work together and help each other out." Socially, members of study groups often become close friends, and students say, "We go out at least once a week to socialize with each other and with other business school students as well." With its campus located in "the center of Washington D.C.," students say it is "very easy to get around in this city, and there is always a lot going on at the business school, around campus, and elsewhere." Thanks to the urban environs, "There is access to great speakers, events, and museums all the time and often for free;" however, some students complain that campus safety can be spotty, and there are "not many places to study on campus or near campus."

Admissions

To apply to The George Washington University, prospective students must submit a completed application, a resume and employment profile, two letters of recommendation, four personal essays, official transcripts from all higher education institutions attended, and official GMAT scores. In recent years, the entering class had an average 4.3 years of professional work experience, an average GMAT score of 643, and an average undergraduate GPA of 3.3.

FINANCIAL FACTS

Annual tuition	$34,428
Fees	$30
Cost of books	$3,000
Room & board (on-campus)	$18,060
% of students receiving aid	68
% of first-year students receiving aid	69
% of students receiving loans	32
% of students receiving grants	54
Average award package	$35,087
Average grant	$20,180
Average student loan debt	$66,989

ADMISSIONS

Admissions Selectivity Rating	89
# of applications received	1,087
% applicants accepted	44
% acceptees attending	61
Average GMAT	643
Range of GMAT	603–678
Average GPA	3.33
TOEFL required of international students	Yes
Minimum TOEFL (paper/computer)	600/250
Application fee	$60
International application fee	$60
Early decision program?	No
Deferment available	Yes
Maximum length of deferment	1 year
Transfer students accepted	Yes
Transfer application policy: Standard Application Procedures	
Non-fall admissions	Yes
Need-blind admissions	Yes

EMPLOYMENT PROFILE

Career Rating	91	Grads Employed by Function	%	Avg. Salary
Percent employed at graduation	46	Marketing	22	$80,500
Percent employed 3 months after graduation	75	Operations	2	NR
		Consulting	23	$84,200
Average base starting salary	$77,615	Management	12	$68,750
Primary Source of Full-time Job Acceptances		Finance	31	$67,683
School-facilitated activities	24 (NR%)	HR	6	$74,333
Graduate-facilitated activities	27 (NR%)	**Top 5 Employers Hiring Grads**		
		IBM (3), Johnson & Johnson (2), American Airlines (2), General Electric (2), Ogilvy (1)		

GEORGETOWN UNIVERSITY
McDONOUGH SCHOOL OF BUSINESS

GENERAL INFORMATION
Type of school   Private
Affiliation   Roman Catholic/Jesuit
Academic calendar   Each semester
divided into two "modules"

SURVEY SAYS...
Students love Washington, D.C.
Friendly students
Good peer network
Helpful alumni
Solid preparation in:
Doing business in a global economy

STUDENTS
Enrollment of parent institution	15,318
Enrollment of MBA Program	843
% male/female	69/31
% out-of-state	89
% part-time	40
% minorities	4
% international	24
Average age at entry	28
Average years work experience at entry	5

ACADEMICS
Academic Experience Rating	**93**
Student/faculty ratio	9:1
Profs interesting rating	74
Profs accessible rating	83
% female faculty	23
% minority faculty	21

Joint Degrees
MBA/MSFS, 3 years; MBA/JD, 4 years; MBA/MPP, 3 years; MBA/MD, 5 years.

Prominent Alumni
Michael Chasen, President and CEO, Blackboard, Inc.; Eric Bauer, Chief Financial Officer, The Gap; Brett Jenks, President and CEO, Rare; Suzanne Clark, President, National Journal Group; Christopher Gergen, Founding Partner, New Mountain Ventures.

Academics

Offering "a diverse global environment in the world's greatest capital city," the McDonough School of Business at Georgetown University offers an MBA with a strong international focus bolstered by "its international enrollment" and the second-year Global Integrative Experience, a course that culminates in a mandatory 9-day, international consulting experience. The school's location in the nation's capital—a magnet for diplomats and international business reps—further enhances the school's global scope.

McDonough's "innovative curriculum" capitalizes on the university's many strengths by "integrating other elements of the Georgetown University, such as the Public Policy Institute and the School of Foreign Service," thereby exploiting an advantage to "merge public and private interests to create well-rounded, business-minded individuals." The MBA program also benefits from "access to Georgetown University-related activities, such as speakers and workshops," and a "highly responsive alumni" who are "very receptive to networking with MBA students."

McDonough's full-time program operates on a modular calendar, a system many here wish the school would abandon. Students tell us that "five classes crammed into 6-week modules is too much," not allowing students "to delve into course material." The school has responding by moving to a 7-week module with 4 classes. The school introduced a part-time evening program during the 2006–2007 academic year. A gorgeous brand-new building in the center of campus" dedicated to the business school, opened in 2009.

MBAs at Georgetown benefit from "small class sizes" because it "encourages a great deal of interaction." Also, students appreciate "a faculty that is very dedicated to teaching, which is clearly distinct from many schools that are more research-focused." While international business is McDonough's greatest strength, it isn't its only standout discipline; students laud the "strong management" offerings and note that the school is "a hidden gem for investment banks." Students also appreciate the school's Jesuit underpinnings, which stress ethics, immersion in the liberal arts and philosophy, and the importance of community service.

Career and Placement

McDonough students have complained about career services in the past, but many now emphatically tell us that "there has been considerable improvement" in this area, and "Whereas there was a time when the Career Management Center could have stepped up its efforts, this is no longer the case." The addition of a new Dean and a new Director of Career Management sparked the transformation; today, "Career Management is very dedicated. The office is extremely helpful in providing advice and consultation. Furthermore, the quality of the companies and the job opportunities that are made available to students are outstanding."

Employers who most frequently hire McDonough graduates include: Citigroup, Booz Allen Hamilton, Credit Suisse, Merrill Lynch, AES, America Online, International Finance Corporation (IFC), 3M, American Express Company, Avaya, Bank of New York, Deloitte Touche Tohmatsu, Ford Motor Company, and JPMorgan Chase.

ADMISSIONS CONTACT: KELLY WILSON, ASST DEAN & DIRECTOR OF ADMISSIONS
ADDRESS: 37TH & O STREET, NW WASHINGTON, DC 20657
PHONE: (202) 687-4200 • FAX: (202) 687-7809
E-MAIL: MBA@GEORGETOWN.EDU • WEBSITE: MSB.GEORGETOWN.EDU

Student Life and Environment

"The workload is intense" at McDonough, with the module system rushing classes along to the point that "it can interfere with the internship/job search. Even so, students who are driven find ways to make it work." Because full-timers attend classes in four separate cohorts, "There isn't much opportunity for you to interact with the three-fourths of the class not in your own cohort," but "Significant amounts of group work help foster teamwork skills and force people to deal with uncomfortable or unfamiliar situations within their cohorts." Students do get to interact with folks outside their cohorts through "a decent number of clubs and social activities."

Georgetown University is a hub of political and intellectual activity; its many schools host "lectures and activities...that are extremely interesting. There are many opportunities to attend lectures with prominent speakers, such as Kofi Anan, [the] President of Afghanistan, etc., who are visiting town." Washington, D.C. offers even greater diversions, with "many cultural outlets that are unique to D.C. such as restaurants, nightlife, a great zoo, and museums."

McDonough MBAs enjoy a "highly cooperative environment. Classmates are not at all competitive." The student body "is extremely diverse in both background and professional experience. Even a student without a strong business/financial background would feel comfortable studying here." Part-time evening students "tend to have full-time jobs. Many are married and have kids; they have absolutely no time to socialize."

Admissions

Applicants must submit all of the following materials: an application form (online application is required); a resume; four required essays; official transcripts for all postsecondary academic work; two recommendations, from professional relationships; and an official GMAT score report. Interviews are encouraged but are conducted only at the invitation of the school after the first application deadline. International students must submit an official score report for the TOEFL, IELTS, or Pearson Test of English in addition to the above materials. McDonough requires a minimum of 2 years of post-collegiate professional experience (and prefers 3 or more) prior to admission.

FINANCIAL FACTS

Annual tuition	$41,952
Fees	$2,030
Cost of books	$2,484
Room & board (off-campus)	$14,850
% of students receiving aid	71
% of first-year students receiving aid	68
% of students receiving loans	56
% of students receiving grants	36
Average award package	$21,470
Average grant	$20,982
Average student loan debt	$78,746

ADMISSIONS

Admissions Selectivity Rating	95
# of applications received	1,760
% applicants accepted	36
% acceptees attending	38
Average GMAT	685
Range of GMAT	640–730
Average GPA	3.35
TOEFL required of international students	Yes
Minimum TOEFL (paper/computer)	600/250
Application fee	$175
International application fee	$175
Application Deadline/Notification	
Round 1:	11/1 / 1/15
Round 2:	1/2 / 3/25
Round 3:	3/20 / 5/14
Early decision program?	No
Deferment available	No
Transfer students accepted	No
Non-fall admissions	No
Need-blind admissions	Yes

EMPLOYMENT PROFILE

Career Rating	99	Grads Employed by Function	%	Avg. Salary
Percent employed at graduation	67	Marketing	33	$88,748
Percent employed 3 months after graduation	79	Operations	5	$87,400
		Consulting	40	$91,635
Average base starting salary	$89,276	Management	19	$95,000
Primary Source of Full-time Job Acceptances		Finance	52	$88,740
School-facilitated activities	86 (53%)	**Top 5 Employers Hiring Grads**		
Graduate-facilitated activities	65 (40%)	Citigroup (11), Deloitte Consulting (7),		
Unknown	12 (7%)	Johnson & Johnson (8), Booz Hamilton (9), Bank of America/Merrill Lynch (7)		

GEORGIA INSTITUTE OF TECHNOLOGY
COLLEGE OF MANAGEMENT

GENERAL INFORMATION

Type of school	Public
Academic calendar	Semester

SURVEY SAYS...

Students love Atlanta, GA
Good peer network
Happy students
Smart classrooms
Solid preparation in:
Quantitative skills

STUDENTS

Enrollment of parent institution	19,413
Enrollment of MBA Program	395
% male/female	79/21
% part-time	62
% minorities	15
% international	17
Average age at entry	28
Average years work experience at entry	6

ACADEMICS

Academic Experience Rating	97
Profs interesting rating	89
Profs accessible rating	88
% female faculty	17
% minority faculty	9

Joint Degrees

Dual degree programs with any Masters or PhD degree at Georgia Tech.

Prominent Alumni

Tom A. Fanning, Executive Vice President, The Southern Co; Michael A. Neal, Vice Chairman, GE Corporation; President and CEO, GE Commercial Finance; Stephen P. Zelnak, Jr., Chairman, CEO & President, Martin Marietta Material, Inc.

Academics

No doubt Georgia Tech boasts "a great brand name," but that's hardly all this school has to offer its MBAs. With a "curriculum designed to integrate management and technology," Georgia Tech positions its grads well in the increasingly technologically-focused world of business. Furthermore, the school's Atlanta location means access to some of the best business minds—and some of the top business employers—in the Southeast. In addition, the school "provides great value for the money."

Students find Georgia Tech's many assets in surprising places. One writes, "Before coming to school, I would have said our greatest strength was our technology focus and proximity to one of the premier engineering schools in the world. Now…I would say that our professors and career services are tied for greatest strengths. I will put either up against any top-ten business school any day." MBAs here report that Georgia Tech has "a great faculty in accounting, IT, and operations," and identify entrepreneurship, finance, and international management as other standout areas. Across disciplines, an "innovative curriculum keeps pace with the rapidly changing business and technology environment."

Georgia Tech's full-time program is limited to 75 students, which results in "strong networks and personal attention." "Small class sizes mean that students can have a high degree of impact in clubs, research assistantships, and special, self-initiated projects," one student observes (Of course, it also means that "not all electives that you may want will be offered"). The program places "an emphasis on teamwork and collaborative relationships" that students embrace, describing "a positive yet challenging work environment." The "workload can be overwhelming at times," but "the heavy emphasis on group projects means we have strong and reliable classmates to lean on if we need it."

Career and Placement

The Jones MBA Career Center provides "outstanding" support to assist students in developing a successful career strategy and plan. Each student is assigned a career advisor "who helps us find internships and jobs in our preferred fields," a service students deem "invaluable." Other resources include an in-depth career course, job search tools, and individual career coaching.

Atlanta's big-city locale is a plus for students in their job search, because the school "can get business heads and leaders from the city of Atlanta" to visit campus, meet with and mentor students, assist in networking, and provide internships and jobs. As one student sums up, "The program is very much oriented toward the job market, and the school is known to get 100 percent job placement. From the time you are accepted, you begin evaluating employers and job hunting. You are given exceptional tools and resources (however, you are also under a great deal of pressure to secure a high-paying job)."

Among the top employers of Georgia Tech MBAs are AT&T, Bank of America, Booz Allen Hamilton, Deloitte Consulting, Delta Airlines, The Home Depot, Infosys Consulting, North Highland Consulting, and Raytheon.

Student Life and Environment

There's a "friendly atmosphere" in the Georgia Tech MBA program, where "social networking events and clubs are an integral part of [the] business school experience." The b-school facility "has several common areas, comfortable lobbies, and group work areas," so "no one is ever by himself. Even if working diligently on different homework assignments, we tend to cluster together and have a social environment." Classrooms "are all equipped with a computer-managed multimedia system, which includes double projectors and screens, document camera, laptop hookups and DVD/VHS," and "Faculty offices are easily accessible in the building. The facilities are very clean and updated."

Because the program holds "no classes on Fridays," Thursday night is a time for socializing. "Every Thursday there is a social event either at a restaurant, atrium in the academic building, or elsewhere where current students, alumni, and professors interact in a relaxed environment," students tell us. Fridays aren't for hangovers, though; students "have two or three group meetings every Friday." The "Fridays off" policy, students explain, "is the only thing that makes group work possible" in this busy program.

Georgia Tech's "midtown Atlanta location" "offers numerous educational, professional, and social opportunities," although some warn that the surrounding neighborhood "has some safety issues." Most everyone agrees that the Atlanta location is a huge advantage overall, both in terms of "keeping outside 'real world' connections with professionals in our industry of choice" and culturally. "It is an exciting and vibrant life at Georgia Tech," one student reports.

Georgia Tech "attracts many people from the engineering fields, but also from financial services as well. This makes for a strong competition between teams in case reports and presentations." The program is home to lots of "Type-A driven people who are very engaging in class discussion and projects." Even so, "The culture is not over-competitive or cut-throat. We are like a family pushing each other to learn and to accomplish great things."

Admissions

GMAT scores, undergraduate GPA, work experience, and the results of a personal interview (scheduled by invitation only) are the factors that weigh most heavily with those who evaluate applicants for Georgia Tech's MBA program. Personal essays and recommendations are also important. A satisfactory grade in a college-level calculus course is a required prerequisite for enrollment. TOEFL scores are required of applicants whose first language is not English or who have not successfully completed a year of college/university level study in the United States or another English-speaking country. Applications are processed on a rolling basis, a system that typically favors those who apply early.

FINANCIAL FACTS
Annual tuition (in-state/ out-of-state)	$22,000/$33,712
Fees	$1,646
Cost of books	$1,000
Room & board	$7,294
% of students receiving aid	67
Average award package	$16,256
Average grant	$6,000
Average student loan debt	$29,312

ADMISSIONS
Admissions Selectivity Rating	98
# of applications received	443
% applicants accepted	23
% acceptees attending	74
Average GMAT	684
Range of GMAT	630–720
Average GPA	3.32
TOEFL required of international students	Yes
Minimum TOEFL (paper/ computer/web)	600/250/100
Application fee	$50
International application fee	$50
Regular application deadline	3/15
Early decision program?	No
Deferment available	Yes
Maximum length of deferment	1 year
Transfer students accepted	No
Non-fall admissions	No
Need-blind admissions	Yes

EMPLOYMENT PROFILE
Career Rating	95	Grads Employed by Function	%	Avg. Salary
Percent employed 3 months after graduation	84	Marketing	22	$77,455
		Operations	18	$82,100
Average base starting salary	$84,779	Consulting	21	$89,792
Primary Source of Full-time Job Acceptances		Management	14	$87,813
School-facilitated activities	NR (80%)	Finance	14	$85,286
Graduate-facilitated activities	NR (20%)	HR	4	NR
		MIS	7	$90,000

Top 5 Employers Hiring Grads
AT&T, Bank of America, Infosys Consulting, Deloitte Consulting, Raytheon

GEORGIA SOUTHERN UNIVERSITY
COLLEGE OF BUSINESS ADMINISTRATION

GENERAL INFORMATION
Type of school   Public
Academic calendar   Semester

SURVEY SAYS...
Solid preparation in:
Accounting
Communication/interpersonal skills
Presentation skills

STUDENTS
Enrollment of parent institution	19,086
Enrollment of MBA Program	240
% male/female	64/36
% out-of-state	13
% part-time	61
% minorities	29
% international	14
Average age at entry	27

ACADEMICS
Academic Experience Rating	**70**
Student/faculty ratio	21:1
Profs interesting rating	81
Profs accessible rating	79
% female faculty	29
% minority faculty	1

Joint Degrees
MBA with a concentration in Health Services Administration, Information Systems, and International Business, 2 years evening/part time.

Prominent Alumni
Dan Cathy, President/CEO,Chick-fil-A; James Kennedy, Director, NASA John F. Kennedy Space Flight Center; Karl Peace, President, Biopharmaceutical Research Consultants; Steven Cowan, Novelist; Tony Arata, Singer/Songwriter.

Academics

A "hidden gem" in the peach state, Georgia Southern University's small, AACSB-accredited business school offers "affordability and amicability" to a largely local population. At Georgia Southern, students can pursue an MBA degree in general management, or customize the program through a specialization in one of three areas: health services, information systems, and international business. Georgia Southern offers their part-time, evening MBA programs at their Statesboro and Savannah campuses, as well as a part-time, distance learning MBA at the Coastal Community College campus in Brunswick, GA. The school also operates an AASCB-accredited, Web MBA program, which can be completed over the course of five semesters, and MAcc degrees, with an optional concentration in forensic accounting. The "reasonable tuition" is a feature of any graduate program so, no matter what or how you choose to study, "considering the high quality of instruction, the overall cost of attending is a steal."

In the classroom, practical applications of business principles are duly emphasized, and "professors often use current events to explain business concepts." A current student writes, "The professors are detail-oriented and the instruction that they provide can be taken away from academia and applied to the real world." With a total enrollment of fewer than 200 students in the graduate business program, Georgia Southern's "greatest strengths are smaller class sizes and the availability of faculty to students outside of class." In this friendly atmosphere, "professors gave us their cell phone numbers and home numbers to help with accessibility. They were always willing to help with questions, even at home in their personal time." In addition to the faculty, "the administration is approachable" and "very sensitive and supporting of its student body."

Georgia Southern allows senior business majors in the undergraduate school to begin their work towards an MBA before they have received their undergraduate degree. Because MBA courses are taught in the evenings, these students can take undergraduate courses during the day and attend graduate-level courses at night. As a result, there is a smattering of fifth-year seniors in the MBA program; however, most students "are employed full time with several years [of] work experience." Catering to working students, "we have a diverse population and our instructors understand that most of us work or have other situations." On the whole, the academic atmosphere is stimulating and collegial, with students who are "very competitive, sharp, and goal-oriented individuals looking to advance their careers by pursuing graduate education."

Career and Placement

The Georgia Southern University Career Services Department hosts a number of university-wide events and services, and also maintains a satellite office in the business school. The department's comprehensive student services include career assessment, mock interviews, and recruiting events and career fairs, and the department will assist business students with internship and co-op placements, as well as professional placements. However, for younger students who are getting their feet wet in the business world, many feel that "more resources should be established to link business students with job opportunities," including "stronger encouragement of internships and mentoring opportunities (maybe even build it into the curriculum)."

The Career Services Department hosts several career fairs and campus recruiting events, which are open to the entire undergraduate college and graduate students. Employers who recently visited campus include AT&T, Babies R Us/Toys R US, Bank of Eastman, Enterprise Rent-a-Car, GEICO, IBM, John Deere, Mary Kay, McKesson, MetroPower, Pet Smart, Sherwin Williams, Target Stores, Verizon Wireless, and Wells Fargo Financial.

ADMISSIONS CONTACT: MRS. MELISSA HOLLAND, MBA DIRECTOR
ADDRESS: P. O. BOX 8050 STATESBORO, GA 30460-8050
PHONE: 912-478-5767 • FAX: 912-478-7480
E-MAIL: GRADSCHOOL@GEORGIASOUTHERN.EDU • WEBSITE: COBA.GEORGIASOUTHERN.EDU/MBA

Student Life and Environment

Georgia Southern University is a vivacious and "beautiful" campus environment, which offers a full range of student clubs, activities, and resources. However, a large majority of business students take classes at satellite campuses, or only arrive at GSU in the evenings. Others don't come to campus at all, as they are enrolled in the school's online MBA program. Therefore, a large percentage of MBA students don't have much opportunity to participate in campus activities. A current student explains, "Unfortunately, because all graduate classes are only offered at night, graduate students don't have much opportunity to join and be active in student organizations that hold their meetings during the times we are in class (6:30–9:15)."

Students who join the MBA program directly after undergrad are more likely to take advantage of the campus environment. A fifth-year senior explains, "I live on campus in a suite-style residence hall that is only 5–10 minutes (walking) from the business building, which makes my life extremely convenient." For younger students (and those who wish to participate), "the school sponsors many activities and events. We have great athletic events such as football, baseball, and basketball."

Admissions

Students are admitted to Georgia Southern University based on an admissions index, calculated by combining their undergraduate GPA and standardized test scores. A minimum GMAT score of 430 is required for admission. Students who have not taken the GMAT may be provisionally admitted if their undergraduate GPA was 3.25 or higher; these students will be expected to submit acceptable GMAT scores before they finish their third course at the business school.

FINANCIAL FACTS

Annual tuition (in-state/ out-of-state)	$5,040/$20,136
Fees	$1,444
Cost of books	$4,300
Room & board	$7,900
% of students receiving aid	87
% of first-year students receiving aid	87
% of students receiving loans	49
% of students receiving grants	59
Average award package	$11,821
Average grant	$6,037

ADMISSIONS

Admissions Selectivity Rating	68
# of applications received	150
% applicants accepted	79
% acceptees attending	62
Average GMAT	491
Range of GMAT	450–530
Average GPA	3.13
TOEFL required of international students	Yes
Minimum TOEFL (computer)	530
Application fee	$50
International application fee	$50
Regular application deadline	6/1
Regular notification	7/1
Application Deadline/Notification	
Round 1:	3/1 / 4/1
Round 2:	6/1 / 7/1
Round 3:	10/1 / 11/1
Early decision program?	No
Deferment available	Yes
Maximum length of deferment	1 year
Transfer students accepted	Yes
Transfer application policy:	
No more than 6 Semester hours of graduate credit may be transferred to a graduate program at Georgia Southern. Only grades of B or higher will be accepted for transfer.	
Non-fall admissions	Yes
Need-blind admissions	Yes

GEORGIA STATE UNIVERSITY
J. MACK ROBINSON COLLEGE OF BUSINESS

GENERAL INFORMATION
Type of school	Public
Academic calendar	Semester

SURVEY SAYS...
Cutting-edge classes
Solid preparation in:
Doing business in a global economy

STUDENTS
Enrollment of parent institution	30,431
Average age at entry	28
Average years work experience at entry	5

ACADEMICS
Academic Experience Rating	**85**
Student/faculty ratio	12:1
Profs interesting rating	84
Profs accessible rating	81
% female faculty	25
% minority faculty	26

Joint Degrees
Master of Business Administration/Doctor of Jurisprudence (MBA/JD): Full-time, part-time; 63 total credits required; 24 months to 6 years to complete the JD degree and 8 years to complete the MBA degree. Master of Business Administration/Master of Health Administration (MBA/MHA): Full-time; 51–63 total credits required; 2.8 to 5 years to complete program.

Prominent Alumni
Sandra Bergeron, Chairman of the Board, TraceSecurity, Inc.; Ahmet C. Bozer, President, Eurasia and Africa Group, the CocaCola Company; Richard H. Lenny, Chairman, President, and CEO (ret.), The Hershey Company; Mackey J. McDonald, Chairman (ret.), VF Corporation; Deepak Raghavan, Co-Founder and Director, Manhattan Associates.

Academics

Georgia State offers its part-time MBA in two formats. Students in its flexible MBA program determine how many or how few courses to take per semester. Most Flex MBA students graduate in three to five years, but the program can be completed within two years with a full course load. Its Professional MBA (PMBA) is for high-performing, early-career professionals with four or more years of experience. The two-year PMBA is presented in an executive format, allowing students to continue working full-time. Georgia State also offers the Global Partners MBA, a full-time, 14-month program spanning four continents with residencies in Atlanta, Rio de Janeiro, Paris, and China, and a four-month international internship.

While you can no doubt find the occasional dissenter, many students at Georgia State are rather impressed with their b-school education. The vast majority of professors are "personable," "caring," and really "work to help you understand the material." Most bring years of business experience into the classroom and make a concerted effort to "stay up to date with the latest trends in their field." Additionally, instructors are adept at "facilitating discussions...using case studies," often illustrating concepts within a practical framework. Students also laud their "engaging" professors for fostering a classroom environment that makes one "eager to learn more about the business world."

Moreover, students appreciate that "the curriculum is really geared for working professionals so you can apply your learning [in] real time." Many extol the "flexibility of the part-time programs" noting they "really try to cater to people who work full time." Most classes are "very focused on teamwork and group projects." There is also "a primary emphasis on application of ideas and techniques and a lesser concentration on theory."

Many students applaud the administration, noting the "friendly, helpful, and polite" staff ensures everything runs "very smoothly." One first-year student does offer this final piece of advice: "The Financial Aid staff is a bit overextended, due to the size of the school, but if you start efforts early, it works fine."

Career and Placement

Though some students wish career services would "promote networking outside of the classroom that is convenient for working professionals," Robinson's Career Management Center for Graduate Students does provide a variety of services. MBA candidates have access to the Robinson Career Connection, an online database where students can upload resumes, search for jobs and internships, and register for campus events. Furthermore, Robinson offers exceptional training in interview preparation. Students can take advantage of both mock interviews as well as InterviewStream, an online video system that they can access from the comfort of their home. Additionally, resources like the Executive Coaching Program present eligible students with the chance to meet, one-on-one, with business professionals. All of these opportunities help to ensure that Georgia State students meet their career goals and aspirations.

Recent recruiters of Georgia State MBAs were Deloitte Consulting; Hewitt Associate; KPMG, LLP; UNUM Corporation; Ernst & Young, LLP; Tauber & Balser, PC; Coca-Cola Enterprises Inc.; Towers Perrin; Frazier & Deeter, LLC; and Wachovia Securities Financial Network.

ADMISSIONS CONTACT: KAREN ALLEYNE-PIERRE, DIRECTOR, GRADUATE ADMISSIONS
ADDRESS: SUITE 625, 35 BROAD STREET ATLANTA, GA 30302-3988
PHONE: 404-413-7130 • FAX: 404-413-7162
E-MAIL: MASTERSADMISSIONS@GSU.EDU • WEBSITE: WWW.ROBINSON.GSU.EDU

Student Life and Environment

The Georgia State student body is comprised of "driven, currently working professionals, with high expectations." Many are "very independent and focused on their area of interest." Since the "majority of students work full time," there's a dearth of "socializing outside of class." Despite limited fraternizing, "there is a wonderful camaraderie amongst MBA students." Indeed, a number are quick to characterize their peers as "friendly," "helpful," and "articulate" as well as "willing to [both] share their experiences and learn from the experiences of others." Additionally, the majority "reach [out] to other students [to] form networking circles." Also of importance, Georgia State manages to attract an applicant pool that offers "varied backgrounds," both in terms of industry and geography. This greatly benefits students as they are privy to "additional global perspectives from classmates."

A multi-campus school, "the environment changes with locale." While "two of the campuses are dedicated to the business school," those students who "desire the traditional collegiate atmosphere" should look into attending the main campus. Regardless of where you enroll, Georgia State students have the bustling city of Atlanta at their fingertips. Offering a variety of fine dining and entertainment, Atlanta is also home to top companies such as Turner Broadcasting, Coca Cola, Bell South, and The Home Depot—perfect for the ambitious MBA candidate.

Admissions

Applicants to GSU MBA programs must submit all of the following materials to the Office of Admissions: official copies of transcripts for all postsecondary academic work; an official GMAT score report; a resume (at least two years of full-time professional experience is preferred); and two personal essays. Letters of recommendation are not required but are considered for those candidates who submit them. International students must submit, in addition to the above materials, evidence of sufficient financial resources to fund their MBA studies; an independent evaluation of all academic transcripts for work completed abroad; and, for students whose first language is not English, an official score report for the TOEFL. International students are required to carry a full-time course load.

FINANCIAL FACTS

Annual tuition (in-state/ out-of-state)	$8,112/$28,461
Fees	$1,628
Cost of books	$2,000
Room & board	$14,976
% of students receiving aid	32
% of first-year students receiving aid	41
% of students receiving loans	31
% of students receiving grants	1
Average award package	$14,482
Average grant	$1,638
Average student loan debt	$8,149

ADMISSIONS

Admissions Selectivity Rating	84
# of applications received	424
% applicants accepted	57
% acceptees attending	64
Average GMAT	603
Range of GMAT	560–640
Average GPA	3.31
TOEFL required of international students	Yes
Minimum TOEFL (paper/computer)	610/255
Application fee	$50
International application fee	$50
Regular application deadline	4/1
Regular notification	6/15
Early decision program?	No
Deferment available	Yes
Maximum length of deferment	2 semesters
Transfer students accepted	No
Non-fall admissions	Yes
Need-blind admissions	Yes

EMPLOYMENT PROFILE

Career Rating	75	Top 5 Employers Hiring Grads
		Deloitte (10), Hewitt & Associates (5), ING (5), KPMG (4), Towers Perrin (4)

GONZAGA UNIVERSITY
GRADUATE SCHOOL OF BUSINESS

GENERAL INFORMATION
Type of school	Private
Affiliation	Catholic/Jesuit
Academic calendar	Semester

SURVEY SAYS...
Happy students
Smart classrooms

STUDENTS
Enrollment of parent	
institution	6,500
Enrollment of MBA Program	238
% male/female	63/37
% out-of-state	35
% part-time	70
% minorities	10
% international	11
Average age at entry	29
Average years work experience	
at entry	3.5

ACADEMICS
Academic Experience Rating	**80**
Student/faculty ratio	10:1
Profs interesting rating	90
Profs accessible rating	84
% female faculty	21
% minority faculty	30

Joint Degrees
MBA/MAcc approximately 1–2 years to graduate. 50% complete in 12–18 months. MBA/JD and MAcc/JD approximately 3–3.5 years to graduate.

Prominent Alumni
Michael R. Coleman, VP of IBM; Jerome Conlon, Retired VP of NBC, Current VP of Brand Alchemy; Stuart McKee, National Technology Officer-Microsoft.

Academics

Jesuit-run Gonzaga University is "ethics-based, family-oriented, and strives to produce people ready for the real world and its challenges, both professionally and socially," all of which appeal to the MBA students in its Graduate School of Business. A "great reputation in the business community," especially for its "great accounting program," and an "awesome flexible curriculum structure" that "is designed with working individuals in mind (with evening and online classes)" also draw area business grads to the program.

Gonzaga's MBA curriculum consists of 22 credits in core courses (11 two-credit classes) and 11 credits in electives, through which students may develop a concentration if they wish. Students who did not major in business as undergraduates are typically required to complete a series of foundation requirements prior to beginning work on their MBA. Students report that the curriculum is "broad and covers many aspects of the modern business environment, with opportunities to specialize in finance, economics, accounting, etc." Professors "integrate course material throughout the program" and "rarely present contradicting information" as "the material in the program is well-planned." Students also appreciate that the program "has a very good grasp on current trends in the business world and effectively integrates those trends into the class curriculum." Some, however, wish for "more updated technology and computer labs," while others believe the program would benefit from "more course-end teamwork projects." "Students need to have more opportunities to simulate complex projects and the teamwork needed to solve them," one student notes.

Gonzaga's "small size and interactive environment...offers a plethora of opportunities for students looking to expand their horizons." "For those who are entrepreneurial, the Hogan Center offers hands-on experience, as do other business classes such as business consulting, which enables students to try their hand at consulting for a real local business." Gonzaga introduced a new healthcare management concentration in 2007, of which one student says, "There are some bumps, but overall, it is excellent."

Career and Placement

The Gonzaga Career Center and the School of Business Administration staff and faculty provide career counseling and placement services to MBAs here, including: Career 301 Seminars covering self-assessment, career planning, resume writing, and conducting a successful job search; mock interviews and interview critiques; on-campus recruiting and interviewing; a career-resources library; alumni events; and internship placement assistance. Students complain, "Gonzaga's only weak point is connecting students to careers after graduation....Due to the small size of both the city of Spokane and of the university, not a lot of major companies recruit at Gonzaga, and a lot more legwork is needed on behalf of the student to find his or her post-graduation path than at some other major universities. Thus, the MBA program may best benefit those who already know where they want to go after they graduate."

Employers of Gonzaga business graduates include Avista, Bank of America, Boeing, Deloitte, Ernst & Young, Honeywell, Itron, KPMG, Microsoft, PricewaterhouseCoopers, and Starbucks. Fifty percent of Gonzaga MBAs go into finance and accounting.

Student Life and Environment

Gonzaga's MBA candidates include "everything from recent college graduates to ex-military officers to professionals who have families and full-time jobs." Many feel that the population includes too many students "who have just got their bachelor's degree with no work experience and have no valuable input to conversations or the academic environment. The school really needs experienced professionals." Students tend to be "friendly and hardworking," down-to-earth, not stuck on themselves, "real," and, according to one of those ex-military officers, "very energetic and willing to take risks, similar to those that I had taken in life. I like how open-minded they are to the ideas presented and the materials."

Students are "fairly isolated from the campus in that our classes start at the end of the traditional day and our building is on one edge of the campus. The great thing, though, is our building is amazing, has everything we need in one place, and the lounge has a fantastic view of a lake beneath and downtown in the distance." Evening classes "allow working professionals to attend classes." One student notes, "I cannot say enough about the flexibility and responsiveness of the MBA program team. From professors to the administrative staff, this experience has been outstanding."

Those who choose to engage in campus life tell us that it is "full of opportunities to get involved in fun activities and helpful charities. The basketball games are free for students and are full of excitement" and, as an added bonus, revenue "generated by the basketball team is used to improve the school and the school's reputation." Local charities "love the help from grad students and rely on them for help in creating business plans, conducting market research, and planning marketing activities." Hometown Spokane is "a small town in eastern Washington, cold during the winter, and not all that exciting compared to Seattle, which is four hours away."

Admissions

Applicants to the MBA program at Gonzaga must submit two official copies of all postsecondary academic transcripts, official GMAT scores (minimum score of 500 required), resume, two letters of recommendation, and a complete application (which includes three short essays). International students must also submit official TOEFL scores (if English is not their first language) and a financial declaration form. An interview may be required of some international applicants. Work experience is not required, "but is strongly encourages, and "the majority of students who enter the program have four or five years [of] prior work experience."

FINANCIAL FACTS

Annual tuition	$12,780
Cost of books	$600
Room & board (off-campus)	$4,500
% of students receiving aid	90
% of first-year students receiving aid	90
% of students receiving loans	50
% of students receiving grants	50
Average award package	$14,000
Average grant	$2,000
Average student loan debt	$12,000

ADMISSIONS

Admissions Selectivity Rating	79
# of applications received	158
% applicants accepted	66
% acceptees attending	80
Average GMAT	561
Range of GMAT	500–610
Average GPA	3.41
TOEFL required of international students	Yes
Minimum TOEFL (paper/computer)	570/230
Application fee	$50
International application fee	$50
Early decision program?	No
ED Deadline/Notification	
Deferment available	Yes
Maximum length of deferment	4 years
Transfer students accepted	Yes
Transfer application policy: Transcripts are evaluated to ensure that desired learning objectives have been fulfilled. Up to 6 credits can be transferred in from non-Jesuit MBA programs.	
Non-fall admissions	Yes
Need-blind admissions	Yes

EMPLOYMENT PROFILE

Career Rating	84	Grads Employed by Function	% Avg. Salary
Percent employed at graduation	60	Marketing	10 NR
Percent employed 3 months		Consulting	5 NR
after graduation	35	Management	5 NR
Average base starting salary	$72,000	Finance	50 NR
Primary Source of Full-time Job Acceptances		HR	5 NR
School-facilitated activities	NR (50%)	Entrepreneurship	5 NR
Graduate-facilitated activities	NR (50%)	Nonprofit	5 NR
		Strategic	5 NR

GRAND VALLEY STATE UNIVERSITY
SEIDMAN COLLEGE OF BUSINESS

GENERAL INFORMATION
Type of school	Public
Academic calendar	Semester

SURVEY SAYS...
Cutting-edge classes
Solid preparation in:
General management

STUDENTS
Enrollment of parent institution	23,295
Enrollment of MBA Program	266
% part-time	88
Average age at entry	31
Average years work experience at entry	9

ACADEMICS
Academic Experience Rating	**74**
Student/faculty ratio	25:1
Profs interesting rating	80
Profs accessible rating	83
% female faculty	14
% minority faculty	28

Academics

With an "excellent technology infrastructure"—the DeVos Center, which houses the business program features "beautiful grounds and buildings," and "a strong program that is well-recognized within the region," Grand Valley State University provides an affordable graduate experience to its predominantly working-professional student body. As one student puts it, "Grand Valley offers an excellent value for a very good MBA program."

GVSU's Seidman College offers an MBA as well as Master's of Science degrees in taxation and accounting. Students who pursue the 33-credit MBA program part time typically complete the program in two years. The curriculum includes three electives; students may graduate with a concentration in a specific discipline by choosing all three electives from that discipline. A degree with an emphasis on innovation and technology management is available as well; it requires the completion of a fourth elective, lengthening the program to 36 credits.

Students praise GVSU for providing "small classroom size" that "seems to be very helpful when it comes to getting the help needed." The "high caliber" faculty is "very astute, visionary, shrewd, capable, and highly qualified," ensuring that students are "both challenged and adequately supported." Administrators "put themselves in the shoes of the students and give 100 percent effort to ensure that our education experience at GVSU is fruitful and worthwhile." Overall, students perceive "excellent customer service here" and appreciate that the school is "located in an economically growing area," providing access to business connections both during and after the program.

Career and Placement

The school reports that "The Seidman MBA is a program primarily for working professionals, as opposed to a full-time MBA program. Most students are employed when they begin their MBA studies and remain employed by the same firms when they graduate." Students add, however, that "there is a trend for more and more full-time students...There are also career fairs every semester where companies from around Michigan and the nation will come to talk with graduates and upcoming graduates. As more full-timers enter the program, more of these companies will come to the fairs." A central career services office serves undergraduates and graduates; one student who attended GVSU as an undergraduate tells us that "I have not had much experience with the career placement services at the graduate level; undergraduate career services are good."

ADMISSIONS CONTACT: CLAUDIA BAJEMA, GRADUATE BUSINESS PROGRAMS DIRECTOR
ADDRESS: 401 W. FULTON GRAND RAPIDS, MI 49504
PHONE: 616-331-7400 • FAX: 616-331-7389
E-MAIL: GO2GVMBA@GVSU.EDU • WEBSITE: WWW.GVSU.EDU/BUSINESS

Student Life and Environment

The DeVos Center, home to the Seidman College of Business, offers "a variety of places to eat as well as a bookstore and tuition payment center," all of which make the hectic lives of GVSU's part-time students a little bit easier. One student happily reports: "I very rarely have to leave the campus to accomplish all of my tasks. This is extremely pleasing to a student juggling family, work, and school." The school "is making a concerted effort to create study space on campus," which students also appreciate.

The atmosphere within the Seidman MBA program is "easygoing but professional." Most students visit campus only when necessary, and the school works hard to accommodate them. As one explains, "I like that I get all the information I need for class via BlackBoard or through the Library's class reserve system. That makes it much easier for me as a part-time student."

Hometown Grand Rapids is a substantial city with a metropolitan area population of nearly three quarters of a million, making it the second-largest city in Michigan. Grand Rapids has been one of the nation's furniture capitals for more than a century. Manufacturing still provides a solid base for the local economy, although shipping and the health industry also claim substantial workforces. GVSU students tell us, "The restaurants and the cultural venues in Grand Rapids are beyond compare when you look at cities of this size."

GVSU students tend to be "very busy, task-oriented, serious with their studies, and very focused in their lives." They are "mostly professionals" although there are some students fresh out of college in the mix. They tend to be "fairly young," "most are married, and some have children." Most are "friendly with good people skills," making them excellent partners for team projects.

Admissions

The GSVU Admissions Committee applies the following formula: [(undergraduate GPA for final 60 hours of coursework + 200) + GMAT score. Applicants scoring above 1100 with a GMAT score of at least 500 are admitted to the program. Applicants scoring 1100 with a GMAT score between 450 and 490 are reviewed by the admissions committee "for predictive indicators of success with respect to quantitative and qualitative GMAT scores and grades earned in courses deemed to be relevant to graduate curriculum." Some such applicants may be admitted conditionally pending successful completion of background courses. The committee may make the same recommendation to applicants who score at least 500 on the GMAT but do not earn an 1100 formula score. Applicants whose first language is not English are required to score at least 550 on the TOEFL.

FINANCIAL FACTS

Annual tuition (in-state/ out-of-state)	$5,850/$10,800
Fees	$90
Cost of books	$1,500
Room & board (on/off-campus)	$6,500/$5,000

ADMISSIONS

Admissions Selectivity Rating	75
# of applications received	146
% applicants accepted	82
% acceptees attending	85
Average GMAT	566
Range of GMAT	520–680
Average GPA	3.3
TOEFL required of international students	Yes
Minimum TOEFL (paper/computer)	550/213
Application fee	$30
International application fee	$30
Regular application deadline	12/1
Early decision program?	No
Deferment available	Yes
Maximum length of deferment	1 year
Transfer students accepted	Yes
Transfer application policy: Students may transfer up to 9 credits with B or better at discretion of program director.	
Non-fall admissions	Yes
Need-blind admissions	Yes

HARVARD UNIVERSITY
HARVARD BUSINESS SCHOOL

GENERAL INFORMATION

Type of school	Private
Academic calendar	Sept–May

SURVEY SAYS...
Good social scene
Good peer network
Cutting-edge classes
Solid preparation in:
General management
Doing business in a global economy
Entrepreneurial studies

STUDENTS

Enrollment of MBA Program	1,837
% male/female	63/37
% part-time	0
% minorities	24
% international	35
Average age at entry	26
Average years work experience at entry	3

ACADEMICS

Academic Experience Rating	96
Profs interesting rating	94
Profs accessible rating	93
% female faculty	22

Joint Degrees
JD/MBA, 4 years MPP/MPA/MBA, 3 years MD/MBA, 5 years .

Prominent Alumni
Michael Bloomberg, Mayor of New York City, Founded Bloomberg L.P.; Jamie Dimon, Chairman & CEO, J.P. Morgan Chase & Co.; Sheryl Kara Sandberg, Chief Operating Officer, Facebook; Margaret Whitman, Former President & CEO, Ebay Inc.; Daniel Vasella, Chairman & CEO, Novartis AG.

Academics

A "tried-and-true General Management focus with no concentrations or majors and no published GPAs," a "pedagogical approach that relies strongly on the case method," and most of all "a reputation as the best business program in the country" make Harvard Business School one of the top prizes in the MBA admissions sweepstakes. Applicants lucky enough to gain admission here rarely decide to go elsewhere.

The school's full-time-only program is relatively large; approximately 900 students enter the program each year. Students tell us, "Despite its large size, the school feels surprisingly small" thanks to a combination of factors. First is an administration that "could be a role model for any enterprise. This place is very well-run." Second is the subdivision of classes into smaller sections of 90 students, who together attack approximately 500 case studies during their two years here. Finally, there's a faculty that "is obviously committed to excelling at teaching and developing relationships with the students. Each faculty member loves being here, regardless of whether they are a superstar or not, and that makes a difference. Faculty guide discussion well and enliven the classroom."

The case method predominates at Harvard; explains one student, "I sit in my section of 90 students every day and debate business topics. My section mates come from all walks of life and all of them are incredibly successful. I prepare my 13 cases per week so that I can contribute to this environment." Students love the approach, although they point out that "the case method is not as great for quantitative courses such as finance." Numerous field-study classes supplement the program, especially during the second year, which is devoted to elective study. School-wide initiatives—combinations of interdisciplinary classes, field study, contests, and club work—encourage research and provide added focus in the areas of social enterprise, entrepreneurship, global issues, and leadership.

Ultimately, though, HBS' strength resides in the quality of its instructors. One student notes, "HBS is one of the few schools where a large part of the professor's evaluation is based on classroom teaching. The professors at HBS are wonderful teachers and take great interest in their students." As one first-year puts it, "If first semester is representative of the whole experience, I'll be a happy grad. My accounting professor managed to make accounting my favorite class (seems unimaginable!), and I'll definitely take whatever he teaches during the second year of elective courses."

Career and Placement

Harvard Business School maintains a robust career services office all the same, providing a full range of counseling and internship- and career-placement services, with more than 40 career coaches seen by more than 80 percent of the class. There are more than 800 recruiting events on campus each year; of those, 400 focus on full-time employment and the other 400 focus on summer internships. Nearly half of all MBAs remain on the East Coast after graduation, about a quarter of whom take jobs in New York City. Nineteen percent find international placements; 10 percent of the class work in Europe and 6 percent work in Asia.

Student Life and Environment

Life at HBS "is as hectic as you want it to be." One student writes, "My life is pretty much moving along at breakneck speed. I wouldn't want it any other way because the school offers an incredible amount and array of activities, from volunteer consulting to running conferences." Because Harvard University is a magnet for innovative and prestigious thinkers in all disciplines, "This place is like a candy store for a five-year-old; you want to eat a lot more than what's good for you. You can spend all your time on studies, lectures from academics/politicians from all over the world, visiting business leaders, conferences, sports, or the nightlife. A 60-hour day would be appropriate."

Students generally manage to find the time to enjoy "a very social and outgoing environment" at HBS. One married student writes, "Most weekends my husband and I have a choice: the 'college scene' where we can hit up the Harvard or Central Square bars with the singles, or the 'married scene' where we have dinner, play goofy board games, and drink with our 'couple friends.' Either can be a great escape from the other, and both are always a lot of fun!" Close relationships are easy to forge here, as "the section system means you have 89 close friends in the program, which makes learning and being here fun. It also means in the business world there will always be 89 incredibly smart, connected people who will go to bat for me no matter what."

The population of this program is, unsurprisingly, exceptional. As one MBA explains, "The quality of people here is unlike anything I've experienced. For the first time in my adult life, I'm surrounded by people whose interests and abilities fascinate and inspire me. All religions, nationalities, cultures, and sexual orientations exist here, happily, and together. I think Boston cultivates this kind of 'meshing of all thoughts' in such a way that everyone is comfortable, and everyone learns. The city and the school are both comfortable in their own skins, and the students take on that characteristic here."

Admissions

Applicants to Harvard Business School must submit a "complete HBS application portfolio, including personal essays, academics transcripts, and three letters of recommendation." In addition, students must provide scores from the GMAT or GRE, and applicants from non-English-speaking countries must submit scores for either the TOEFL or the IELTS (scores must be no more than two years old). Applications must be submitted online. Academic ability, leadership experience, and unique personal characteristics all figure prominently into the admissions decision. The school notes that "because our MBA curriculum is fast-paced and rigorously analytical, we strongly encourage all applicants to complete introductory courses in quantitative subjects such as accounting, finance, and economics before coming to HBS. For some candidates, we may make admission contingent upon their completing such courses before they enroll." Good luck! HBS has opened its doors to an innovative new program for college juniors. It's called HBS 2+2: two years of work, then two years of immersion in the Harvard Business School MBA program.

FINANCIAL FACTS

Annual tuition	$48,600
Fees	$7,804
% of students receiving aid	71
% of first-year students receiving aid	74
% of students receiving loans	61
% of students receiving grants	51
Average award package	$56,135
Average grant	$22,250
Average student loan debt	$76,958

ADMISSIONS

Admissions Selectivity Rating	99
# of applications received	9,093
% applicants accepted	12
% acceptees attending	91
Average GMAT	720
TOEFL required of international students	Yes
Minimum TOEFL (paper/computer)	633/267
Application fee	$250
International application fee	$250
Application Deadline/Notification	
Round 1:	10/1 / 12/15
Round 2:	1/19 / 4/6
Round 3:	4/8 / 5/13
Early decision program?	No
Deferment available	No
Transfer students accepted	No
Non-fall admissions	No
Need-blind admissions	Yes

EMPLOYMENT PROFILE

Career Rating	99	Grads Employed by Function	% Avg. Salary
Percent employed at graduation	85	Marketing	9 NR
Percent employed 3 months		Consulting	28 NR
after graduation	91	Management	16 NR
Average base starting salary	$113,880	Finance	32 NR

HEC MONTRÉAL
MBA PROGRAM

GENERAL INFORMATION
Type of school   Public
Academic calendar Starts in August

SURVEY SAYS...
Students love Montreal, Quebec
Cutting-edge classes
Solid preparation in:
General management

STUDENTS
Enrollment of MBA Program   143
Average age at entry   31
Average years work experience
   at entry   7

ACADEMICS
Academic Experience Rating   **67**
Profs interesting rating   84
Profs accessible rating   83

Joint Degrees
PhD Program joint with McGill, Concordia, EMBA McGill HEC Montréal

Prominent Alumni
Thierry Vandal, President and Chief Executive Officer, Hydro Québec; Pierre Duhaime, President and Chief Executive Officer, SNC Lavalin; Hubert Bolduc, VP Communications & Public Affairs, Cascades; Yannis Mallat, Chief Executive Officer, Ubisoft Montréal, JianWei Zhang, President, Bombardier China; Marie-Hélène Favreau, Director Medical Services, Pratt & Whitney Canada; Dominique Anglade, Consultant, McKinsey and Company.

Academics

HEC Montréal offers "a strong MBA program based on practical issues" that emphasizes "a case-based teaching style" and has "real consulting opportunities incorporated into the curriculum." That, along with the school's "strong network in Quebec and excellent reputation," has made HEC Montréal one of the world's top MBA programs outside the United States. Students here may pursue an intensive one-year program in English or French or a three-year part-time program in French. All programs are housed in a "state-of-the-art facility" with "great libraries and study rooms."

HEC Montreal's one-year program starts with two phases of core courses, followed by a specialization period and a concluding two-course sequence in corporate responsibility. The entire program evinces "a team focus," as "every person has to work in teams that are assigned and specially designed." "The whole program is very community- and net-work-oriented" and thus "forces students to realize how important it is to rely on others and to help team members in order to increase results and efficiency." Classes are delivered in six-week increments, which students describe as "very challenging." "It forces students and teachers to prepare more, and to be ready for every class," one student explains. Students appreciate how the program provides "so many resources invested to ensure the satisfaction of the student body," including "great programs like Campus Abroad," a three-week international program that includes company tours and meetings with business leaders.

Part-timers here enjoy "a good flexible program that support full-time work and MBA courses using the same quality teachers that full-timers get." Students in all programs laud the curriculum's "strong emphasis on durable growth and business ethics. The curriculum is planted on solid foundations. We're definitely not going to be Master Bulls**t Artists." They also appreciate how "HEC Montréal is extremely well-connected and well-regarded by Quebec's business community." "Several professors act as consultants for Canadian or international companies that have operations in Quebec," a student says. "Also, there are regular meetings and presentations at school with business leaders, making the whole program very 'real world.' No stale academic courses here!"

Career and Placement

The HEC Montréal Career Management Services team provides career and placement services to MBAs here. Services include online job search, with international listings and email notification of appropriate postings; workshops and consulting services; CareerLeader, a self-assessment and career-management program; the Vault online career library; mentoring; mock interviews; recruitment events, including career days and on-campus interviewing; and information sessions. Students praise the "exceptional efforts made by career services for job placement" here.

Companies that recruit on campus include Accenture, Air Canada, Bell Canada, Bombardier, CIBC World Markets, Cirque du Soleil, Deloitte, Emirates National Oil Company, Ernst & Young, GE Commercial Finance, IBM, Johnson & Johnson, L'Oreal, Matrox, McKinsey, Merck Frosst, Pratt & Whitney, Procter and Gamble, RBC Financial Group, Scotiabank, TD Financial Group, Toyota, and UPS.

Student Life and Environment

The HEC Montréal campus is "a vibrant environment with people from all over the place" with "excellent resources at our disposal such as libraries, classrooms, and technology." As one student puts it, "Our school is just amazing: The design of it is sharp, they keep it real clean, and we have access to many facilities on campus: gym, bank

ADMISSIONS CONTACT: JULIE BENOIT, ADMINISTRATIVE DIRECTOR OF THE MBA PROGRAM, OFFICE OF THE REGISTRAR
ADDRESS: 3000, CHEMIN DE LA CÔTE STE CATHERINE, MONTRÉAL (QUÉBEC) CANADA H3T 2A7
PHONE: 514 340 6957 • FAX: 514 340 7327
EMAIL: MBA@HEC.CA • WEBSITE: WWW.HEC.CA/EN/PROGRAMS_TRAINING/MBA/INDEX.HTML

machine, lounges. The food at the cafeteria is really good. We have access to a bunch of activities from dance classes to any organized sport activities (climbing, soccer, running club, volleyball, swimming). We are located next to restaurants, coffee shop, a subway entrance, all kind of stores and a lot of them are open 24/7." "The campus and buildings are beautiful and safe." The school is "located in the center of town," which "provides help for lodging and activities that are smartly connected to the school."

HEC Montréal's one-year programs are "very intensive," so "students spend a lot of time with each other" and "life is very hectic." Classes generally run from early morning to late afternoon, after which students participate in team projects and assignment discussion, "then go home and prepare for the next class." All that cooperation promotes bonding, creating "a tight-knit community that enjoys many group activities, including weekly happy hours." Clubs and associations "encourage and generate a nice social life inside and around the school." "The MBA students' association is particularly good, even if it's difficult to connect full-time and part-time students."

Admissions

Admission to the MBA program at HEC Montréal is competitive; the school reports that it is "unable to accept all eligible candidates who apply" because class space is limited. Admissions decisions are based on academic record, professional experience (three years minimum required), standardized test scores (TAGE-MAGE or GMAT), letters of recommendation, interviews and candidates' career objectives. Applicants must provide the school with official transcripts for all post-secondary academic work, a curriculum vitae, and an official score report for standardized tests. The application includes supplementary questions, to be answered in essay form. Applicants to the English-language full-time intensive program must demonstrate English proficiency via testing (TOEFL, IELTS, or HEC Montréal's own HECTOPE) if their native language is not English. Non-native French speakers applying to the French-only program must complete the Test de français international (an ETS-administered exam). Applicants who are not citizens of Canada must obtain a certificat d'acceptation du Québec (C.A.Q.) and a document attesting to their right to reside in Canada (Student Authorization or Ministerial Permit). The school recommends that accepted students apply for these documents as soon as they receive confirmation of their admission to the program.

FINANCIAL FACTS

Annual tuition	$27,000 (Canadian)
Fees	$43 (Canadian)
Room & board (on-campus)	$1,500 (Canadian per month)

ADMISSIONS

Admissions Selectivity Rating	60*
# of applications received	384
Average GMAT	625
TOEFL required of international students	Yes
Minimum TOEFL (paper/computer)	600/250
Application Deadline/Notification	
International students	2/1
Canadian students	3/15
Early decision program?	No
Deferment available	Yes
Maximum length of deferment	case-by-case basis
Transfer students accepted	No
Non-fall admissions	Yes
Need-blind admissions	Yes

Applicants Also Look At
McGill University
University of Western Ontario
York University

EMPLOYMENT PROFILE

			Grads Employed by Function	% Avg. Salary
Career Rating		60*	Marketing	15 NR
Percent employed at graduation		54	Operations	5 NR
Percent employed 3 months after graduation		69	Consulting	34 NR
Average base starting salary	$75,500 (US)		Management	5 NR
Primary Source of Full-time Job Acceptances			Finance	1 NR
School-facilitated activities	NR (21%)		MIS	15 NR
Graduate-facilitated activities	NR (42%)		**Top 5 Employers Hiring Grads**	

KPMG, Bombardier, Deloitte &Touche, RBC Financial Group, Scotiabank, TD Meloche Monnex

HEC PARIS
HEC MBA PROGRAM

GENERAL INFORMATION
Type of school	Public
Academic calendar	Quarter

SURVEY SAYS...
Friendly students
Good peer network
Solid preparation in:
Marketing
Accounting
Presentation skills

STUDENTS
Enrollment of parent institution	3,600
Enrollment of business school	214
% male/female	73/27
% international	83
Average age at entry	30
Average years work experience at entry	6

ACADEMICS
Academic Experience Rating	68
Student/faculty ratio	4:1
Profs interesting rating	80
Profs accessible rating	83
% female faculty	15

Joint Degrees
Stern School of Business, New York University; MIT Sloan School of Management; Fletcher School of Law and Diplomacy; Tufts University; Chinese University of Hong Kong (CUHK); SEM Tsinghua University Beijing; National University of Singapore; London School of Economics, UK; ESADE, Spain; Instituto Tecnologico de Monterrey (ITESM); Fundaçao Getulio Vargas (FGV) Sao Paulo; Universidad Torcuato di Tella (UTDT) Buenos Aires; Pontificia Universidad Catollica de Chile (PUC).

Academics

Located just outside Paris, HEC attracts students for its superb setting, international focus, "reputation and for being among Europe's top 10 business schools." Offering MBA and graduate business programs in both French and English, as well as an English-only program, the HEC MBA begins with a comprehensive core curriculum, including essential business coursework in marketing, business economics, corporate finance, and statistics. There is a "strong focus on ethics/corporate governance and sustainability" within the program, as well as an incredibly international perspective. Of particular note are the "opportunities to learn French and work in France for non-native speakers." In fact, "the school offers French language courses as a part of curriculum," and requires that all students (even those who are already bilingual) take a language course while pursuing their MBA. In addition to promoting language skills, the school generally excels in the "development of managerial soft skills and of teamwork."

Balancing efficiency with rigor, HEC's MBA is "a two-year program condensed into 16 months, so there is a high workload." Drawing faculty from the European business community, "professors are generally good with a few brilliant lecturers." A student in the bilingual section shares, "I am very lucky to have French professors that are very well-known in their respective fields in France and internationally." The school's administration is often described as "bureaucratic" and not always particularly efficient. At the same time, students appreciate the fact that the school helps them "adjust into the French system, like [assisting with] residence permits." Its European location means HEC is strategically placed between numerous economic powerhouses, and just a short ride to Paris and the many important corporations there.

Your classmates are an essential part of the learning experience at HEC, which draws a truly "international student body with participants from over 45 countries." When the program begins, students are divided into "work groups," designed to maximize diversity in terms of country of origin, multicultural background, and professional experience. Fortunately, "the work groups are effective and encourage collaboration rather than elitist competition." On top of that, professors generally "promote discussion so we learn from each other" in class.

Career and Placement

The HEC Career Management Center offers a range of career development workshops, as well as conferences and seminars in both French and English. Keep in mind that the majority of opportunities for HEC graduates are in Paris, which is great for those who want to work in Europe, but also means that it can be a bit more "difficult for non-French-speaking participants to get good jobs." However, students note that the school's 40,000 "alumni are a good resource" for finding jobs in France and internationally. In fact, 85 percent of students had jobs within three months of graduation, with an average salary of $109,746 for graduates who stay in France, and $106,757 for graduates who take jobs in other countries. Twenty-nine percent of graduates take positions in France.

ADMISSIONS CONTACT: PHILIPPE OSTER, DIRECTOR OF ADMISSIONS AND DEVELOPMENT
ADDRESS: 1 RUE DE LA LIBERATION JOUY-EN-JOSAS CEDEX, 78351 FRANCE
PHONE: +33(0) 1 39 67 95 45 • FAX: +33(0) 1 39 67 74 65
E-MAIL: ADMISSIONMBA@HEC.FR • WEBSITE: WWW.MBA.HEC.EDU

Student Life and Environment

With students from 45 countries and a range of professional backgrounds, HEC is characterized by its diversity. A current student shares, "I really like my fellow students; this is a truly international school so we have a great variety of nationalities and business experiences from all over the world." Student life is rewarding and active, as "there are many clubs and most of the students live on campus, especially during the core phase." In addition to the day-to-day pleasures of student life, "Cultural Weeks (Japan Week, Latin America Week) and parties on holidays such as Diwali are a strong part of the culture of the school, and a highlight in the calendar as most of the students attend the events."

The school's pretty campus is set "up a hill in a tiny town in the Paris suburbs," from which "it takes an hour to get to Paris by public transportation." The surrounding community is fairly quiet; however, students appreciate the fact that "you do not have many distractions so you can dedicate more time to studying." Fortunately, "the outdoor sports facilities and the location of the school are lovely—huge grounds, and it's great to go for walks." With a world-class city just a stone's throw away, it's not surprising that "many people go to Paris for weekend, and enjoy the cultural and entertainment life there."

Admissions

HEC admissions process is rigorous. First, each candidate is evaluated based on their standardized test scores and undergraduate performance, as well as quantitative factors as evidenced in their personal recommendations and work experience. After candidates have passed the first stage of review, they must attend two in-person interviews with HEC alumni, HEC professors, or other HEC community members. Each of these interviews begins with a 10-minute presentation by the MBA candidate, followed by a question-and-answer session. Last year's entering class had an average GMAT score of 682, with a range between 600 and 770.

Prominent Alumni

Sidney Taurel, President & CEO, Eli Lilly & Co.; Fumiaki Maeda, Managing Director, Mitsubishi Bank; Daniel Bernard, CEO, Provestis; Pascal Cagni, VP EMEA, Apple. Francois-Henri Pinault, CEO, PPR.

FINANCIAL FACTS

Annual tuition	$55,343
Cost of books	$1,353
Room & board	$10,992
% of students receiving aid	50
Average award package	$14,758

ADMISSIONS

Admissions Selectivity Rating 60*

# of applications received	3,142
% applicants accepted	14
% acceptees attending	70
Average GMAT	682
Range of GMAT	600–770
Average GPA	3.8
TOEFL required of international students	Yes
Minimum TOEFL (paper/computer)	600/250
Application fee	$200
International application fee	$200
Regular application deadline	Rolling
Regular notification	7/4
Deferment available	Yes
Maximum length of deferment	1 year
Non-fall admissions	Yes
Need-blind admissions	Yes

Applicants Also Look At

IMD(International Institute for Management Development), INSEAD, London Business School, New York University

EMPLOYMENT PROFILE

Career Rating	89	**Top 5 Employers Hiring Grads**
Average base starting salary	$97,914	Unicef, Unido, Unesco, OECD; BNP Paribas;
Percent employed	88	Johnson & Johnson; Louis Vuitton; Lilly

HHL—Leipzig Graduate School of Management

GENERAL INFORMATION

Type of school	Private
Academic calendar	Sept–March

SURVEY SAYS...

Friendly students
Solid preparation in:
Finance
Accounting
General management

STUDENTS

Enrollment of MBA Program	98
% male/female	67/33
% part-time	64
% international	70
Average age at entry	29
Average years work experience at entry	5

ACADEMICS

Academic Experience Rating	61
Student/faculty ratio	3:1
Profs interesting rating	85
Profs accessible rating	85
% female faculty	10

Prominent Alumni

Eugen Schmalenbach, Professor. Father of German Cost Accounting; Stefan Niemeier; Partner at McKinsey & Co.; Erik Theilig, CEO PVflex Solar GmbH; Jack Artman, Director of M&A Infineon Technologies; Lukasz Gadowski, Founder & CEO Spreadshirt.

Academics

HHL—Leipzig Graduate School of Management offers German and international business students an appealing mix of a well-established name and modern innovation. Founded in 1898, HHL is the oldest business school in Germany, and its students benefit from its deserved reputation as a solid training ground for European managers. The MBA program, is relatively new, having only graduated its first class in 2001. Students tell us, "It is striving to achieve more in the global ranking, so they really make an effort, as opposed to many established schools that expect their reputation to work for them." Since the program runs its course in a scant 18 months, it also appeals to the cost-conscious and to those in a hurry to climb the corporate ladder of success.

The HHL curriculum is made up of core courses arranged into three modules and six interdisciplinary modules that include electives. The full-time program focuses on leadership and international experience, applying an integrated management approach that combines soft skills with hard knowledge and that is particularly well-suited to the students "whose prior academic training was not focused on business but rather was in the natural sciences, humanities or social sciences."

Courses are taught by resident and international faculty, and students appreciate the "very well-known professors who publish a lot in their field and are on boards of corporations." HHL professors "can be contacted almost 24 hours a day," and "those who are comfortable with English can even be fun in classes." Case studies, consulting projects, and high-profile guest speakers ensure strong input from practice and round out the whole HHL experience. Internships, study abroad, and independent study options are all available.

Career and Placement

HHL MBAs report with satisfaction that "one of the big strengths of this program is its excellent contact to companies. Almost all top companies in consulting, banking, and industry come for presentation and recruiting. Companies react surprisingly positively when saying that you are from our school." One student comments, "Concerning placement, there is a huge database of direct contact people. Rather than applying over a 'website' one can contact people or alumni. This helps to stay away from the crowd that applies over recruiting websites of companies."

HHL's entrepreneurial focus is evident in the founding of 80 companies during the last 10 years. Being actively integrated into the career service, start-up companies often offer HHL MBAs various opportunities such as internships or field projects.

According to HHL, the school "has a record of placing graduates with prominent international firms—including BASF, Bertelsmann, Booz Allen Hamilton, Daimler, Deutsche Bank, RWE AG, Ernst & Young, Henkel, Johnson & Johnson, KPMG International, Nestlé, Procter & Gamble, Siemens—as well as with many German 'Mittelstand' companies such as Bauerfeind AG, Breuninger GmbH & Co., Hexaware Technologies, Robert Bosch GmbH or European Energy Exchange AG." Other companies that recruit on campus include Roland Berger Strategy Consultants, Bertelsmann Group AG, BASF AG, JP Morgan, Deutsche Bank AG, Credit Suisse AG or IBM Consulting, Citibank, Goldman Sachs, Lufthansa Cargo, and OnVista.

ADMISSIONS CONTACT: ANJA BACKHAUSS, ADMISSIONS OFFICER
ADDRESS: JAHNALLEE 59 LEIPZIG, 04109 GERMANY
PHONE: +49 341 - 9851 734 • FAX: +49 341 - 9851 731
E-MAIL: ANJA.BACKHAUSS@HHL.DE • WEBSITE: WWW.HHL.DE

Student Life and Environment

An accelerated academic schedule at HHL means that "life is somewhat focused on the courses. There is a lot of pre-work and post-work to do for almost all courses. Most courses integrate a high amount of applied case studies and group work. In some weeks/months the balance of studying and doing other things is bad (i.e., a lot of studying)." One student notes, "Classes in finance are especially tough, but teach a lot that you need later in respective jobs." Even so, there is some time leftover to socialize. One MBA writes, "The school organizes a lot of parties and integrates in social-life staff (i.e., professors) and students. The professors and students are almost on a friendship level and they help the students where they can."

Many students were attracted to the school because it represents "a somewhat wild mixture of nations, ages, and backgrounds," with about one third from Germany and the rest "from different countries in Asia, South and North America, Europe, etc. Also, they have different working experiences; some of them are businessmen, some are engineers. Some worked for law firms, some served in the Navy as IT engineers." What they all share in common is that they "are ready to help, ready to work, and ready to party." As one student observes, "They are very interesting and challenging to work with. I can't imagine better fellow students!"

Leipzig is "a great town [with] a long academic record [and] many sports facilities," students tell us. Bach and Schumann put this ancient trade center on the musical map, and their traditions are carried on today in the city's many concert halls, theaters, cafés and cabarets, jazz clubs, and discos. The city is conveniently located for travel to and from Berlin, Dresden, and Weimar, as well as to major Czech and Polish cities.

Admissions

All applicants to HHL's MBA program must submit GMAT scores, proof of undergraduate degree and transcripts, two recommendations, a resume, and a completed application form on the online application database. Non-native English speakers must also submit proof of English proficiency. HHL accepts TOEFL scores to fulfill this requirement. The applications are reviewed once a month in admissions rounds starting in September each year. Before the admissions committee meets and decides upon a candidate, an interview with the candidate is being held. HHL accepts solely complete application forms.

FINANCIAL FACTS

Annual tuition	$34,371
Cost of books	$100
% of students receiving aid	20
% of first-year students receiving aid	15
Average grant	$17,200

ADMISSIONS

Admissions Selectivity Rating	60*
# of applications received	109
% applicants accepted	33
Average GMAT	610
TOEFL required of international students	Yes
Minimum TOEFL (paper/computer)	600/250
Regular application deadline	6/30
Application Deadline/Notification	NR
Round 1:	1/11 / Yes
Round 2:	1/2 / NR
Round 3:	1/2 / NR
Round 4:	1/3 / 1/8
Early decision program?	No
ED Deadline/Notification	NR / 12/11
Deferment available	Yes
Maximum length of deferment	1 year
Transfer students accepted	Yes
Transfer application policy: Double Degree agreements with international partners.	
Non-fall admissions	Yes
Need-blind admissions	No

EMPLOYMENT PROFILE

Career Rating	60*	Grads Employed by Function	%	Avg. Salary
Percent employed at graduation	50	Marketing	11	NR
Percent employed 3 months after graduation	90	Operations	17	NR
		Consulting	28	NR
Average base starting salary	$81,500	Management	11	NR
Primary Source of Full-time Job Acceptances		Finance	28	NR
School-facilitated activities	NR (33%)	Top 5 Employers Hiring Grads		
Graduate-facilitated activities	NR (67%)	BASF, Johnson and Johnson, Siemens, Accenture, Henkel		

HOFSTRA UNIVERSITY
FRANK G. ZARB SCHOOL OF BUSINESS

GENERAL INFORMATION

Type of school	Private
Academic calendar	4–1–4

SURVEY SAYS...
Happy students
Smart classrooms
Solid preparation in:
Teamwork

STUDENTS

Enrollment of parent institution	12,068
Enrollment of MBA Program	589
% male/female	54/46
% out-of-state	70
% part-time	85
% minorities	7
% international	65
Average age at entry	27
Average years work experience at entry	3

ACADEMICS

Academic Experience Rating	77
Student/faculty ratio	10:1
Profs interesting rating	78
Profs accessible rating	79
% female faculty	18
% minority faculty	26

Joint Degrees
JD/MBA 4 years, BBA/MBA 5 years, BBA/MS 5 years

Prominent Alumni
James Campbell, President and CEO, GE Consumer and Industrial; Ellen Deutsch, SVP&Chief Growth Officer, The Hain Celestial Group; Patrick Purcell, President and Publisher for Herald Media Inc.; Bruce Gordon, CFO and SVO for Walt Disney Interactive Media Group; Kathy Marinello, Director, GM, Ceridian Corp.

Academics

With programs for both full-time students and working professionals, Hofstra University's "up-and-coming" business programs are contemporary, well-rounded, rigorous, and "highly recognized in NYC." Recently, the school introduced a new full-time day MBA to complement its long-running evening program. In the full-time program, "Students are exposed to a wide variety of subjects and topics" through the cohort-based core curriculum; thereafter, they can tailor their education through a concentration in accounting, finance, health services management, information technology, management, sports and entertainment management, or marketing, among other business areas. Described as "entrepreneurial and innovative," Hofstra excels at "meshing technology with learning," and the business school is equipped with "Blackboard, email, library databases, great technologies in the classroom, access to appropriate and relevant computer programs for download[ing] onto personal computers, and a Wi-Fi network."

Though located on Long Island, Hofstra definitely picks up the New York City vibe, with a state-of-the-art trading room with Bloomberg terminals on campus, a "reputable finance program," and "many opportunities to go on corporate visits" in the city. A strong global influence in the program (both in the curriculum and throughout the student body) seems to echo New York City's international atmosphere, and "The diverse student body and professional staff makes for a great experience and better preparation for a global economy." Despite the program's myriad strengths, some students would like Hofstra to "add environmental sustainability, as well as green topic classes, to stay ahead of the curve," while others suggest that, "The school should further incorporate writing into the program."

A private school, Hofstra University takes teaching seriously, and this commitment extends to the graduate programs. Discussion is encouraged in the classroom, and professors "work hard to engage students in well-organized, clear lectures that provide the tools to apply class material to not just assignments and exams, but also the real world." Executives, consultants, and industry leaders, Hofstra professors are "knowledgeable and have real-world experience." On a personal level, professors "all seem to genuinely care about our wants, needs, and aspirations" and "they [are] always easily accessible and flexible in scheduling meeting times." While some students observe that Hofstra's administration suffered some growing pains as it worked to get the full-time MBA off the ground, all agree that administrators "are very nice individuals that support the growth and transition of students to the MBA program."

Career and Placement

Hofstra MBA candidates work closely with counselors at the Graduate Business Career Services office. On the whole, the Career Center gets good reviews, and "The faculty in the Career Center is very helpful and offers a great variety of information for job searches and preparation for job searches." Student advocates with deep ties in New York City, "These advisors not only provide use with workshops on how to revise a resume or how to search for internships and jobs, but they also push students to get involved in activities outside of the classroom." However, those who aren't NYC-centric would like Hofstra to "reach out to other companies outside New York state."

ADMISSIONS CONTACT: CAROL DRUMMER, DEAN FOR GRADUATE ADMISSIONS
ADDRESS: 126 HOFSTRA UNIVERSITY, 105 MEMORIAL HALL HEMPSTEAD, NY 11549
PHONE: 800-463-7672 • FAX: 516-463-4664
E-MAIL: GRADSTUDENT@HOFSTRA.EDU • WEBSITE: WWW.HOFSTRA.EDU/BUSINESS

FINANCIAL FACTS

Annual tuition	$16,650
Fees	$970
Cost of books	$1,000
Room & board	
(on/off-campus)	$15,110/$14,060
% of students receiving aid	82
% of first-year students	
receiving aid	81
% of students receiving loans	17
% of students receiving grants	80
Average award package	$14,367
Average grant	$11,447

Recent graduates of Hofstra's MBA programs reported a starting salary between $40,000 and $100,000 annually, with a mean base salary of $68,000. Almost 60 percent of graduates who were seeking employment had already received a job offer by graduation, and almost 90 percent within three months. Most students (over 95 percent) stay in the Northeast region. Recent employers include AT&T, Citigroup, Con Edison, Deutsche Bank, Ernst & Young, Nokia, Pricewaterhouse Coopers, and Thomson Financial.

Student Life and Environment

Offering an excellent atmosphere for studying and socializing, Hofstra's facilities are "modern and technologically-advanced," and include a "trading room and study room" within the business school building. There is always something going on outside the classroom, and "On any given day there could be a guest speaker, conference, social event, or just a student gathering. Students typically find themselves having to choose which event or activity they wish to attend." Additionally, a variety of student organizations provide "interesting networking opportunities and clubs that are relevant to business majors." Unfortunately, part-time students often "feel that many of the beneficial workshops and seminars that are offered are not available to [them]," as they are offered during business hours. At the same time, another evening student acknowledges, "I work full time and go to school at night and find the class setup at Hofstra extremely accommodating."

At Hofstra, the character of the evening and full-time programs is somewhat divided. In the evening program, most students "work full time in the Tri-state area and attend class at night," and represent "the diverse nature of the New York metropolitan area." For the daytime MBA, Hofstra attracts students "from all over the world, which makes group work very interesting and worthwhile." In the full-time program, "students often get together outside of class to hang out and socialize." "The off-campus pubs and bars are a great place for having a drink and socializing with students while taking a break from school work." In fact, even "the libraries are fun and social."

Admissions

Prospective students may apply to begin Hofstra's part-time MBA in the fall, spring, or summer term, or they may apply for August admission to the full-time program. Students are evaluated based on their undergraduate academic performance, professional experience, leadership potential, letters of recommendation, and GMAT scores. High-achieving students have the option of applying as an Honors Scholar, a title that will be conferred at graduation and may be linked to scholarship opportunities.

ADMISSIONS

Admissions Selectivity Rating	75
# of applications received	391
% applicants accepted	85
% acceptees attending	53
Average GMAT	561
Range of GMAT	510–610
Average GPA	3.12
TOEFL required of	
international students	Yes
Minimum TOEFL	
(paper/computer)	550/213
Application fee	$60
International application fee	$60
Early decision program?	No
Deferment available	Yes
Maximum length	
of deferment	1 year
Transfer students accepted	Yes
Transfer application policy:	
Number of transferable credits is	
limited to a maximum of 9 credits.	
Non-fall admissions	Yes
Need-blind admissions	Yes

Applicants Also Look At

Baruch College; Fordham University; New York University; Rutgers, The State University of New Jersey; St. John's University

EMPLOYMENT PROFILE

Career Rating	88	Grads Employed by Function	%	Avg. Salary
Percent employed at graduation	59	Marketing	14	$56,500
Percent employed 3 months		Operations	11	$78,330
after graduation	75	Consulting	7	$60,000
Average base starting salary	$67,178	Management	4	$113,000
Primary Source of Full-time Job Acceptances		Finance	43	$66,167
School-facilitated activities	17 (39%)	MIS	4	$110,000
Graduate-facilitated activities	19 (43%)	**Top 5 Employers Hiring Grads**		
Unknown	8 (18%)	KPMG (3), North Shore Health System (3),		
		Open Link Financial Inc (3), National Grid (2),		
		Citigroup (1)		

HONG KONG U. OF SCIENCE AND TECHNOLOGY
HKUST BUSINESS SCHOOL

GENERAL INFORMATION
Type of school   Public
Academic calendar   Semester

SURVEY SAYS...
Students love Clear Water Bay,
Kowloon, Hong Kong
Solid preparation in:
Finance
Accounting
Teamwork

STUDENTS
Enrollment of MBA Program	226
% male/female	63/37
% part-time	50
% international	92
Average age at entry	30
Average years work experience at entry	7

ACADEMICS
Academic Experience Rating	70
Profs interesting rating	87
Profs accessible rating	62

Academics

For students looking to begin a career in Hong Kong or on the Asian continent, The Hong Kong University of Science and Technology operates one of the region's most well respected MBA programs, spearheaded by the "best faculty in Asia." Located in a prominent "financial hub," HKUST students benefit from the unique "opportunity to live in Hong Kong and study Asian Business in an environment unparalleled anywhere else across the continent." In addition to the exceptional contacts and experience that the school's location inherently supplies, "the program provides well-rounded foundational coursework across a spectrum of business topics." On top of required classes, "elective offerings are diverse and interesting," comprising more than 40 percent of the MBA curriculum. Many students point out the strength of the school's "world-renowned finance department," saying the program boasts "a very competitive environment, especially in more quantitatively-oriented courses."

Despite HKUST's strength in quantitative fields, the well-balanced academic program includes "abundant soft skills training." In the classroom, professors focus on "developing critical and problem-solving skills using business cases and real-world questions, in addition to teamwork." On that note, group work and class discussions are also emphasized throughout the curriculum, with good results. With over 20 nations represented within a full-time MBA class of 110 students, "the group discussions in class are enriched by such a varied mix of cultures and experiences."

Attracting a team of business experts from across the world, "HKUST has a good mix of professors who are former industry practitioners with many years of experience, as well as brilliant researchers who are on the cutting edge of what the future is going to bring." A current student enthuses, "Hong Kong is a unique place where many academic superstars want to teach. Currently there are three visiting faculty professors who are absolute experts in their fields." In the lecture hall, these expert teachers excel at "combining theory with real-life examples and making their lectures relevant and practice-oriented." When it come to the administration, students say the program is "well organized," and headed by a friendly and helpful staff. If you have a question or concern, "the MBA office representatives are always available, even during their lunch break."

Career and Placement

The HKUST Career Services Office offers individual counseling, career coaching, group workshops, a well-stocked career library, and a packed calendar of networking events and alumni activities. A current student enthuses, "The Career Office has been exceptional in providing advisory services for existing students, and in creating opportunities for students to network with existing business entities for future career placements."

The school's stellar reputation in Asia puts HKUST graduates in the running for top jobs in the region. In 2009, about half of the graduating class took jobs in Hong Kong, while another 25 percent went to mainland China. Despite their regional renown, students worry that the school's "reputation is undervalued in comparison to its quality. It is hardly known in the USA or Europe." At the same time, students are quick to point out that many US business schools operate exchange programs with HKUST, which is helping to promote the school's name internationally.

ADMISSIONS CONTACT: (852) 2358-7539
ADDRESS: CLEARWATER BAY, HKUST KOWLOON, HONG KONG
PHONE: (852) 2358-7539 • FAX: (852) 2705-9596
E-MAIL: MBA@UST.HK • WEBSITE: WWW.MBA.UST.HK

Currently, HKUST graduates who took jobs in Hong Kong reported an average annual salary of HK$548,356 (or US$70,302), and graduates on average received salaries that were 131 percent higher than their pre-MBA wages. A partial list of employers recruiting at HKUST includes ACNielsen, AXA, LVMH, Bank of China, Morgan Stanley, Nortel, PepsiCo, Philips, Royal Bank of Scotland, Blackrock, and Volkswagon.

Student Life and Environment

HKUST's challenging curriculum demands a lot of time and energy. As a result, "a great deal of the day is taken up by team meetings, preparing for presentations, and doing homework." Fortunately, the campus atmosphere is pleasant and inclusive, and "the common rooms and the MBA lounge [are] a sort of a big living room for the MBA community." Boasting an idyllic location in one of Hong Kong's quieter neighborhoods, "HKUST has arguably the best campus views in the world. The school is built into a mountain overlooking the South China Sea providing stunning views all around. It has a National Geographic feel to it." In addition, the campus "recreational facilities are excellent," including "multiple pools, gyms, tennis courts, [and] soccer fields."

Social and academic life is vibrant at HKUST. After class, "the school organizes a wide variety of networking, alumni and business leader events for students to attend, to grow their business contacts and to broaden their outlook in business in Asia." In addition, students get together to blow off steam, planning "trips to various places in Hong Kong for fun," or "socializing and partying" with their classmates.

Admissions

To apply to the HKUST MBA program, students must possess an undergraduate degree and have at least two years of full-time professional work experience. The current HKUST business student had a GMAT score between 610–700, a TOEFL score of 600 or above, and three to five years of work experience before entering the program.

FINANCIAL FACTS

Annual tuition	$53,900
Cost of books	$1,300
Room & board (on-campus)	$5,400

ADMISSIONS

Admissions Selectivity Rating 60*

Range of GMAT	610–700
TOEFL required of international students	No
Minimum TOEFL (paper/computer)	600/250
Application fee	$129
International application fee	$129
Application Deadline/Notification	
Round 1:	12/15 / 3/15
Round 2:	3/16 / 6/15
Early decision program?	No
Deferment available	Yes
Maximum length of deferment	1 year
Transfer students accepted	No
Non-fall admissions	No
Need-blind admissions	No

EMPLOYMENT PROFILE

Career Rating	88	Grads Employed by Function	% Avg. Salary
		Marketing	13 NR
		Consulting	7 NR
		Management	30 NR
		Finance	32 NR
		Strategic	8 NR

Top 5 Employers Hiring Grads

AXA, Societe Generale, Banco Santander, Bearing Point Management & Technology Consults, Louis Vuitton China.

HOWARD UNIVERSITY
SCHOOL OF BUSINESS

GENERAL INFORMATION
Type of school	Private
Academic calendar	Semester

SURVEY SAYS...
Students love Washington, D.C.
Friendly students
Good social scene
Good peer network
Solid preparation in:
Operations
Communication/interpersonal skills
Presentation skills

STUDENTS
Enrollment of parent institution	11,227
Enrollment of MBA Program	126
% male/female	49/51
% out-of-state	90
% part-time	31
% minorities	77
% international	23
Average age at entry	26
Average years work experience at entry	4

ACADEMICS
Academic Experience Rating	**79**
Student/faculty ratio	4:1
Profs interesting rating	70
Profs accessible rating	74
% female faculty	26
% minority faculty	87

Joint Degrees
JD/MBA (4 years) MD/MBA (five-year); DDS/MBA (5 years); PharmD/MBA 6 years); BBA/MBA Accounting (5 years); BSE/MBA Engineering (5.5 years or 6 years with Business Concentration).

Prominent Alumni
Vita Harris, Chief Strategy Officer, Draftfcb New York; Kerry L. Nelson, Sr. V-P, Nonprofit Foundations, Northern Trust; Rodney E. Thomas, CEO, Thomas & Herbert Consulting, LLC.

Academics

Howard University's School of Business offers "smaller classes" and an "intimate environment" bolstered by an "ideal location" and the school's status as one of the nation's best-known Historically Black Colleges and Universities, all of which translates to "a myriad of corporate exposure opportunities" for MBAs. To top it all off, a Howard MBA is "inexpensive in comparison to other schools in D.C." And it's convenient; with a full-time day program, an accelerated part-time program, and a conventional part-time program, Howard has options to accommodate a wide range of students.

Howard's entire MBA program is relatively small, with the majority of students enrolled full-time. Students tell us that the program's strengths include "a dedicated supply chain management program" and the opportunity to undertake "unique global experiences." The program consists of 54 credits, 39 of which are dedicated to foundation and core classes and 15 of which are devoted to specialization. Students may pursue a concentration in entrepreneurship, finance, marketing, supply chain management or general management with an emphasis on HR, international business, or strategy.

Students love the "helpful and flexible" professors, all "specialists in their fields of study." They "are available to answer your questions and to engage in thought-provoking discussions." The program as a whole "provides the tools you need to succeed, but it is up to the students to guide their education," one student explains, noting that "keeping up with the latest business news is crucial to making [the] class experience engaging and meaningful." In sum, "Succeeding at Howard is a lot of work, but is well worth it." Some here feel that "the school would gain in advocating even more case studies dealing with current issues in all classes."

Career and Placement

Students tell us that "the networking aspect is the greatest strength of Howard," and that the school's connections among alumni throughout the business community can translate to "great opportunities for African-Americans." MBAs at Howard are pleased with "the number and diversity of recruiters that come to our campus." Howard's Career Services Office works hard to provide students with the necessary counseling, workshops, and recruitment opportunities, both on campus and beyond.

Employers that frequently hire Howard MBAs include American Express, Bank of America, Booz Allen Hamilton, Cisco, Citigroup, Dell, Deloitte, Eaton Corporation, Ernst & Young, FMC Technology, Inc., Hanes Brand, Inc., IBM, Intel Corporation, Johnson & Johnson, KPMG, Kraft Foods, MetLife, Merrill Lynch, PriceWaterhouseCoopers, Procter & Gamble, State Street Corporation, SPG & Consultants, Inc., Sprint, Terex, Tyco, United Technologies Corporation, Unilever and W.W. Granger.

Student Life and Environment

Life at Howard's School of Business "is intense and fun," with students "heavily involved in extracurricular activities on and off campus," including "a number of workshops and activities that offer the possibility to learn." "Various CEO days, corporate modules, and leadership development series" are supplemented by "case competitions" and "exceptional...club activities" to keep students "constantly on the go." One student sums up the experience: "In a typical week students will spend six to seven hours in the class room, 40 to 50 hours studying, 10 to 20 hours working a job either on or off campus, seven to eight hours keeping up with current events, and in the remaining hours students will be at happy hours, interviewing with companies, meeting with groups for projects, attending a club meeting or event, volunteering, working out, or networking. Sometimes we can fit in sleep."

The business school's "outdated" facilities "are good but could be better. While we have everything we need, new technology and machinery could be incorporated in our current learning [environment] to improve the program." The program attracts students who "are hardworking, innovative, and are natural go-getters. If there is something that we want to improve or accomplish at Howard, we work to make it happen." The student body is "like a small family. All students care about one another and are willing to help ensure that everyone is successful. At the same time, the students are very competitive when it comes to succeeding in the classroom."

Admissions

Applicants to the Howard MBA program must submit the following materials to the Admissions Office: a completed application form; an up-to-date resume; an official score report for the GMAT (taken no more than five years before date of application); official transcripts for all undergraduate and graduate course work; three letters of recommendation, completed by at least one academic and one professional supervisor; a personal statement describing the applicant's abilities, experiences, and goals in pursuing the MBA; and proof of at least two years of significant post-collegiate professional or managerial experience. Applicants must have completed business or applied calculus at the undergraduate college level in order to be admitted. International applicants must submit all of the above plus a Statement of Financial Resources. International students who attended a non-English speaking undergraduate institution must have their transcripts translated and interpreted by a professional service. They must also submit an official score report for the TOEFL.

FINANCIAL FACTS

Annual tuition	$22,950
Fees	$805
Cost of books	$2,400
Room & board (on/off-campus)	$17,000/$20,000
% of students receiving aid	97
% of first-year students receiving aid	98
% of students receiving loans	69
% of students receiving grants	63
Average award package	$33,003
Average grant	$20,649
Average student loan debt	$43,207

ADMISSIONS

Admissions Selectivity Rating	81
# of applications received	159
% applicants accepted	50
% acceptees attending	59
Average GMAT	527
Range of GMAT	450–620
Average GPA	3.17
TOEFL required of international students	Yes
Minimum TOEFL (paper/computer)	550/213
Application fee	$65
International application fee	$65
Regular application deadline	4/1
Regular notification	5/1
Application Deadline/Notification	
Round 1:	11/15 / 1/1
Round 2:	2/1 / 3/1
Round 3:	4/1 / 5/1
Round 4:	5/15 / 6/1
Early decision program?	Yes
ED Deadline/Notification	NR / 1/1
Deferment available	Yes
Maximum length of deferment	2 semesters
Transfer students accepted	Yes
Transfer application policy: Must meet Howard's MBA Program Admission Criteria; can only transfer a maximum of 6.0 credit hours from an AACSB-accredited Graduate Business Program.	
Non-fall admissions	Yes
Need-blind admissions	Yes

EMPLOYMENT PROFILE

Career Rating	92	Grads Employed by Function	%	Avg. Salary
Percent employed at graduation	53	Marketing	24	$90,750
Percent employed 3 months after graduation	67	Operations	35	$88,800
		Consulting	7	$76,500
Average base starting salary	$91,425	Finance	28	$88,786
Primary Source of Full-time Job Acceptances		HR	3	$87,000
School-facilitated activities	21 (72%)	Other (Law)	3	$160,000
Graduate-facilitated activities	8 (28%)	Top 5 Employers Hiring Grads		
		Unilever (2), Intel (2), Cisco (1), Dell (1), IBM (1)		

IAE UNIVERSIDAD AUSTRAL
MANAGEMENT AND BUSINESS SCHOOL

GENERAL INFORMATION
Type of school   Private

SURVEY SAYS...
Good peer network
Happy students
Solid preparation in:
Finance
General management

STUDENTS
Enrollment of MBA Program	48
% male/female	69/31
% minorities	15
% international	35
Average age at entry	28
Average years work experience at entry	5

ACADEMICS
Academic Experience Rating	87
Profs interesting rating	95
Profs accessible rating	63
% female faculty	9
% minority faculty	16

Academics

Located in Pilar, Argentina, IAE Universidad Austral's intensive MBA programs maintain an "excellent reputation in Argentina and throughout Latin America," a strong global focus throughout the curriculum, and "regionally-related" course material for those interested in Latin American business. The rigorous, efficient, bilingual program (classes are taught in Spanish and English) has been honed over time to provide a quality education to its students. As the school's website states, the one-year MBA program "is the result of the 25-year experience IAE has acquired in providing part-time Executive MBA programs and the contributions of many years of delivering full-time programs supplied by the Harvard Business School and the IESE of Barcelona." IAE's "intensive" program combines 1800 hours of campus study, with a daily schedule that "runs from 9:00 A.M. to 6:00 P.M., with only a two-hour break in the middle of the day (from 12:30 P.M. to 2.30 P.M.) for sports and eating." The program begins with a computer-based "leveling course," during which students are reacquainted with fundamental quantitative skills in statistics, mathematics, and accounting. After completing these basic proficiencies, students begin the extensive core curriculum, which focuses on three areas: "technical skills in marketing, finance, etc.; critical thinking skills that teach you new ways to approach both professional problems and personal problems; and teamwork skills." While required material is extensive, the school also offers several elective courses, as well as a Team Building and Outdoor Activities module, designed to promote problem-solving skills in a playful environment. Throughout the MBA, international business is emphasized, and the school's highly international student body adds depth and perspective to the school's global focus.

Students speak highly of the program, describing their professors as "excellent." Friendly and student-oriented, "Most of them have PhDs, and they have a lot of patience. They always are able to help you inside and outside the class." A student adds, "They are always available to answer the questions or having meetings to study some specific and interesting topics." The program runs smoothly, and this ease is especially important given the amount of work piled on students; no one here has time to wade through bureaucratic red tape. As one MBA notes, "The administration provides exceptional service. It is well prepared for the needs of its classmates: Everything we need is available for us." And perhaps most important, "IAE has very good contacts with businesses in Latin America, and a very important aspect is that it provides us with internal and external mentors."

Career and Placement

The Career Services Department at IAE works with students and companies to facilitate recruitment and placement. Among other services, they offer career-related workshops, operate mentoring programs, and publish an MBA newsletter. Despite the school's international focus, students report that "the department is underdeveloped, especially in the international job market." The alumni network, on the other hand, "is unbelievable," according to students; one reports, "I could speak to many important executives from the best companies of my country because they were alumni." Today, IAE graduates are working in diverse countries, including Germany, Malaysia, the United States, Mexico, and Puerto Rico. Employers who have worked with IAE include Alto Parana SA, Hewlett Packard Argentina, Banco Galicia, Belise & Asociados, Bodegas Lagarde, CCBASA, Citibank NA, Fiat Argentina, Ernst & Young, Google, GE Capital Cia, Global Praxis, Hart Casares, Johnson & Johnson Medical SA, KPMG Consultores, Kraft Food Argentina, McKinsey & Company, Nestlé Argentina SA, Novartis Argentina SA, and The Walt Disney Company.

ADDRESS: CASILLA DE CORREO NO. 49 - MARIANO ACOSTA S/N Y RUTA NAC. 8 PILAR—
BUENOS AIRES, 1629 ARGENTINA
PHONE: 011 54.2322.48.1000 • FAX: 011 54.2322.48.1050
E-MAIL: FFRAGUEIRO@IAE.EDU.AR • WEBSITE: WWW.IAE.EDU.AR/WEB2005_ENG/HOME/HOME.HTML

Student Life and Environment

IAE's campus "is located in Pilar, 50 kilometers from the capital" of Argentina, in a beautiful setting "with a lot of trees, grass, and greenery everywhere." The "campus building and facilities are incredible," and, in the surrounding community, "you can find everything near the campus: a mall, restaurants, supermarkets, movies, gas stations, etc." Campus facilities include areas where students "can play soccer, tennis, and rugby during the two-hour lunch break." Big-city life isn't too far off, as "the campus is one hour away from Buenos Aires." Students note, however, that "since IAE's program is a one-year MBA, the workload is so heavy that there is very little time to do activities outside the classroom." Classes convene from 9:00 A.M. to 6:00 P.M.; most students "study until 9:00 P.M., then have some dinner with friends," and then call it a day. Despite the rigors of the program, "the nice environment, people, and landscape make you enjoy every moment."

Drawing a largely international student body, only about 40 percent of IAE's MBA students are Argentine; the remaining 60 percent of students come from other parts of Latin America, Europe, and the United States. Students are drawn from all sectors, including marketing, banking, consulting, engineering, services, and even agriculture. Students are "very different but open-minded," and universally described as "very supportive" of their classmates. In addition to their professional prowess, most "have great senses of humor, don't hesitate to help one another, and enjoy hanging out, drinking beer and wine, and watching movies."

Admissions

Experience is very important to IAE Austral Universidad. Applicants to the full-time MBA program at IAE must have at least three years of post-undergraduate work experience and be at least 25 years old. The admissions department requires all of the following materials: official transcripts for all postsecondary academic work; an official GMAT score report with a minimum score of 550; a resume; personal essays; letters of recommendation; a completed application form; and, for students whose first language is not English, a minimum TOEFL score of 570 (paper-based test) or 230 (computer-based test). IAE also offers its own skills exam which can be taken in lieu of the GMAT and which can be taken by appointment in Buenos Aires.

FINANCIAL FACTS

Annual tuition	$17,000

ADMISSIONS

Admissions Selectivity Rating	83
# of applications received	111
% applicants accepted	57
% acceptees attending	76
Average GMAT	618
TOEFL required of international students	Yes
Minimum TOEFL (computer)	230
Early decision program?	No
ED Deadline/Notification	
Deferment available	No
Transfer students accepted	No
Non-fall admissions	No
Need-blind admissions	No

EMPLOYMENT PROFILE			
Career Rating	83	Grads Employed by Function	% Avg. Salary
Average base starting salary	$17,000	Marketing	13 NR
		Operations	6 NR
		Consulting	11 NR
		Finance	4 NR
		HR	4 NR
		Communications	2 NR
		Entrepreneurship	2 NR
		Nonprofit	6 NR

IDAHO STATE UNIVERSITY
COLLEGE OF BUSINESS

GENERAL INFORMATION
Type of school   Public
Academic calendar   Semester

SURVEY SAYS...
Friendly students
Happy students
Solid preparation in:
Accounting
General management

STUDENTS
Enrollment of parent institution	13,977
Enrollment of MBA Program	110
% male/female	74/26
% part-time	52
% minorities	8
% international	15
Average age at entry	30

ACADEMICS
Academic Experience Rating	**77**
Student/faculty ratio	23:1
Profs interesting rating	90
Profs accessible rating	80
% female faculty	20
% minority faculty	2

Academics

The College of Business at Idaho State University offers MBA classes in two locations: on its main campus in Pocatello and at a satellite location in Idaho Falls. Students love the convenience and the cost of the program; many laud the "great return on investment" represented by an ISU MBA. One student notes that the Idaho Falls location is "very convenient for professionals working for or with Idaho National Laboratory." Evening-only classes at the location make the program even more convenient (the school notes that some emphasis areas require students to take some daytime classes).

"Class sizes are small and the professors are always available outside of class" at ISU, where "Everyone is on a first-name basis with the professors and the atmosphere is laid back yet still professional." One student writes, "I have been pleasantly surprised with the quality of teachers and students that are a part of this program. I feel that the teachers genuinely care about the success of the students and their understanding and application of the material. The students come with years of experience and willingly and beneficially contribute to the material taught." The curriculum here, while "challenging, is backed by a supportive network of professors and students. Relying on help outside of class in the way of face-to-face meetings and study groups makes the experience much more successful."

ISU offers a general MBA as well as MBAs with emphasis areas in accounting, computer information systems, management, marketing, finance, and health care administration. Students tell us that "finance and accounting are very strong at Idaho State University." As for the future, students report that the administration is "doing a good job of moving the university towards a good goal—a medical school—which is what they were hired to do." Look for the health care administration segment of this program to grow as the school continues in this direction.

Career and Placement

MBAs at Idaho State University receive career services from the Career Development Center, which serves all undergraduates, graduates, and alumni at ISU. The office provides career counseling, career testing, internship referrals, student employment opportunities, alumni connections, workshops in job search skills, resume review, on-campus interviews, and job fairs. Students tell us that the school needs to "attract recruiters from world-class companies for all areas of emphasis. It seems like the accounting department does well but that other areas of emphasis are lacking these contacts." One MBA observes: "There are not that many recruiters from outside of southeast Idaho at job fairs. This is especially a problem for the MBA students who most likely will be looking for jobs prior to and immediately after graduation."

Student Life and Environment

Idaho State University's main campus is located in Pocatello, a city with a population of about 50,000. ON Semiconductor, Alliance Title and Escrow, and the university are among the city's largest employers. Students tout the "small-town feel of the town," noting the "low crime rate and conservative values." The location provides easy access to outdoor recreation, and "most people enjoy outdoor activities on the weekend such as skiing, snowmobiling, hiking, etc." The school also offers MBA classes in Idaho Falls, a city whose motto "Where Great Adventures Begin" highlights its proximity to such attractions as Grand Teton National Park and Yellowstone National Park. Idaho National Laboratory is by far the city's biggest employer with about 7,500 employees. Healthcare, education, government, and retail are the city's other primary employers.

ADMISSIONS CONTACT: SAM PETERSON, MBA DIRECTOR
ADDRESS: STOP 8020, 921 S 8TH AVE POCATELLO, ID 83209
PHONE: 208-282-2966 • FAX: 208-236-4367
E-MAIL: PETESAM@ISU.EDU • WEBSITE: COB.ISU.EDU

Students appreciate that "ISU is very facilitating to married families," with "an incredibly family-friendly campus. There's plenty of family housing on campus and a huge day care center." Their only complaint is that "facilities are outdated." "The building is slightly in need of renovation," one student explains. Another points out that "The university has taken steps to modernize the college's building and its miscellaneous resources such as computer labs and information networks," but even she concedes that a facilities overhaul is in order.

"Most students are non-traditional students" here. This "is true of the undergraduate classes and the graduate ones. Since most students have spouses and children, college life is not as exciting as one may expect." MBA candidates "generally have at least two or three years of work experience since receiving their undergraduate degree" and are "focused and serious about learning." They tend to be typically conservative Idahoans, but "a politically liberal transplant from a West Coast city" in their midst assures that "it was easy to form great relationships with my conservative classmates."

Admissions

Applicants to the CoB MBA program at Idaho State University must apply for admission to the university Graduate School and must also meet additional CoB admissions requirements. A completed application includes: official transcripts for all post-secondary academic work; an official GMAT score report; a current resume; and two letters of recommendation. A score of at least 1150 under the formula [(200 x GPA for final 60 semester hours of undergraduate work) + GMAT score] is required for consideration; those meeting this requirement are not guaranteed admission. Applicants holding a master's degree from an accredited institution may have the GMAT requirement waived. International applicants must also submit a statement of financial support and an official score report for either the TOEFL or the IELTS. Minimum required scores: 80, Internet-based test; 213 with a 21 on Section 1, computer-based test; 550 with a score of at least 55 on Section 1, paper-based test; or 6.5, IELTS.

FINANCIAL FACTS

Annual tuition (in-state/ out-of-state)	$5,848/$15,650
Cost of books	$1,000
Room & board	$7,500

ADMISSIONS

Admissions Selectivity Rating	77
# of applications received	73
% applicants accepted	75
% acceptees attending	60
Average GMAT	540
Range of GMAT	480–580
Average GPA	3.46
TOEFL required of international students	Yes
Minimum TOEFL (paper/computer)	550/213
Application fee	$55
International application fee	$55
Regular application deadline	7/1
Regular notification	7/7
Early decision program?	No
Deferment available	Yes
Maximum length of deferment	2 years
Transfer students accepted	Yes
Transfer application policy: 9 credits max, from an AACSB program.	
Non-fall admissions	Yes
Need-blind admissions	No

EMPLOYMENT PROFILE

Career Rating	78
Percent employed at graduation	47
Average base starting salary	$59,000

ILLINOIS INSTITUTE OF TECHNOLOGY
STUART SCHOOL OF BUSINESS

GENERAL INFORMATION
Type of school   Private
Academic calendar   Semester

SURVEY SAYS...
Students love Chicago, IL
Smart classrooms
Solid preparation in:
Finance

STUDENTS

Enrollment of parent institution	7,707
Enrollment of MBA Program	102
% male/female	61/39
% out-of-state	2
% part-time	32
% minorities	1
% international	86
Average age at entry	28

ACADEMICS

Academic Experience Rating	**74**
Student/faculty ratio	26:1
Profs interesting rating	86
Profs accessible rating	72
% female faculty	20
% minority faculty	4

Joint Degrees
MBA/JD (4–6 years); MBA/MS (2–3 years); MBA/MPA (2–3 years); MBA/MSF (2–3 years); MDes/MBA (3–4 years); JD/MS (3–5 years); JD/MPA (3–5 years)

Prominent Alumni
John Calamos, President/Chief Investment Officer/Founder, Calamos Asset Management; Ellen Jordan Reidy, President/Founder, America's Food Technologies, Inc. (AMFOTEK); Robert Growney, Former President/COO, Motorola; Frank Brod, Corporate Vice President/Chief Accounting Officer, Microsoft Corporation; Thomas R. Donovan, Chairman, Quantum Crossings, LLC; Former President/CEO, Chicago Board of Trade.

Academics

The Stuart School of Business at Chicago's Illinois Institute of Technology recognizes the diverse needs of its student body and works hard to accommodate them all. Those looking to expedite their MBAs, for example, can enroll in the school's full-time program; about one-third of the students here do just that. Those who want to pursue their degrees contemporaneously with their careers have a number of part-time options, including the "customizable world-class MBA." Classes are scheduled during weekdays, evenings, and weekends for the convenience of all of Stuart's constituencies. All MBA programs consist of a minimum of 16 classes.

IIT is a world-class research institution, and, not surprisingly, Stuart MBAs benefit from the presence of the high-powered academics here. Three research centers—the Center for Financial Markets, the Center for Strategic Competitiveness, and the Center for Sustainable Enterprise—offer unique options to adventurous MBAs. There is even an optional specialization in sustainable enterprise that trains students "to identify, develop, communicate, and help implement practical and equitable business strategies that advance the ecological sustainability of the Chicago area while fostering current and future economic viability." Stuart was recently ranked among the world's leaders in incorporating environmental management.

Many here, however, prefer more traditional fare. Stuart MBAs laud the school's entrepreneurship program as well as offerings in finance and marketing. Quite a few full-timers take advantage of dual-degree programs in law, design, or public administration. Throughout the curriculum, students praise "the use of technology and real-life examples, and the application of business problems." Stuart professors "are always willing to help and provide out-of-the-classroom tutorials and further explanations," plus "their experience and techniques are outstanding." Similarly, administrators "are extremely helpful and go out of their way to get to know each student personally and help anyone." With IIT's small cohorts, "there is no crowding in the libraries, computer labs, etc. And, we get to learn a lot from group discussions." For many, though, "the school's greatest strength is its strategic location. It is because of its location that we are able to get internships and other opportunities to work." About the only weakness here, students tell us, is that "the school's image needs to be improved. The rankings need improvement and people need to know about IIT a lot more."

Career and Placement

The Office of Career Services at the Stuart MBA program provides students with one-on-one career counseling, workshops in interviewing and resume preparation, and research on companies and opportunities appropriate to each student's goals. A self-assessment, conducted as students enter the program, helps the office tailor its services to the individual needs of each MBA. The university at large conducts career fairs through its Career Development Center.

Employers who most frequently hire Stuart MBAs include Bank One, Northern Trust, Bank of America, ABN-Amro, Lucent Technologies, JPMorgan, Navistar, Johnson & Johnson, Capitol One, Vankampen, US EPA, Reuters, Cantor Fitzgerald, McLagan Partners, Motorola, Inc., and Akamal Trading. About half of all Stuart MBAs remain in the Midwest after graduation; most of the rest head to one of the two coasts.

ADMISSIONS CONTACT: DEBORAH GIBSON, DIRECTOR OF GRADUATE AND PROFESSIONAL ADMISSION
ADDRESS: 565 W. ADAMS STREET, 6TH FLOOR CHICAGO, IL 60661
PHONE: 312-906-6511 • FAX: 312-906-6549 • E-MAIL: ADMISSION@STUART.IIT.EDU
WEBSITE: WWW.STUART.IIT.EDU

Student Life and Environment

IIT's main MBA programs are located "in a separate building in downtown Chicago. That building houses law and business school students only, so there isn't much activity there really, just serious-looking students walking to and fro. The main campus has more life, and there is a free shuttle to transport you between campuses. I appreciate the peace and quiet of our building, though. It's very easy to find a nook to study in without constant interference," remarks one student. MBAs participate in "lots of study groups. We also have socials every Wednesday, and students often go out into town in small groups." Despite these opportunities, many here feel that they "need more organizations, activities, a bigger career center, and more seminars and activities with others outside the school (i.e. businesses, other universities, etc.)."

The student body includes many who have considerable work experience, as well as "a lot of diversity in terms of nationality and occupation." One student observes, "The diverse population aids in creating a learning experience unlike any other. Students learn as much (if not more) outside the classroom than in the classroom, just by interacting with everyone around them." When they can find the time, students love to take advantage of "the world's biggest financial city," which also offers plenty in the way of culture, entertainment, fine dining, and nightlife. Again, it comes back to location. "Stuart is located near the Chicago loop in the midst of big-name business companies, allowing for excellent networking and job opportunities. It's also very close to public transportation."

Admissions

The IIT Stuart School of Business requires applicants to submit GMAT scores, official undergraduate transcripts for all schools attended, two letters of recommendation from people "who can attest to your academic or professional qualifications," two required essays (personal statement and career goals) with the option to submit additional essays (describe a difficult challenge you have faced, describe your ideal company), and a resume. International students must also submit TOEFL scores no more than two years old. Undergraduate transcripts in languages other than English must be accompanied by an English translation.

FINANCIAL FACTS

Annual tuition	$25,758
Fees	$304
Cost of books	$1,200
Room & board	$14,400
% of students receiving aid	66
% of first-year students receiving aid	67
% of students receiving loans	11
% of students receiving grants	57
Average award package	$9,825
Average grant	$6,166
Average student loan debt	$25,171

ADMISSIONS

Admissions Selectivity Rating	80
# of applications received	206
% applicants accepted	50
% acceptees attending	27
Average GMAT	582
Range of GMAT	560–610
Average GPA	3.12
TOEFL required of international students	Yes
Minimum TOEFL (paper/computer)	600/250
Application fee	$75
International application fee	$75
Regular application deadline	8/1
Early decision program?	No
Deferment available	Yes
Maximum length of deferment	1 year
Transfer students accepted	Yes
Transfer application policy	
With advisor approval, may transfer up to 6 semester credits hours or equivalent.	
Non-fall admissions	Yes
Need-blind admissions	Yes

Applicants Also Look At
American University
DePaul University
John Marshall
Loyola University
Northwestern University
The George Washington University
University of Illinois
at Urbana-Champaign
The University of Wisconsin

EMPLOYMENT PROFILE				
Career Rating	76	Grads Employed by Function	%	Avg. Salary
Percent employed at graduation	33	Marketing	17	$40,000
Percent employed 3 months		Consulting	33	$64,000
after graduation	10	Management	17	$51,667
Average base starting salary	$59,117	Finance	17	$57,500
		MIS	17	$73,333

ILLINOIS STATE UNIVERSITY
COLLEGE OF BUSINESS

Academics

The MBA program at ISU "has a great relationship with central Illinois business" manifested "in the corporate partnerships the school holds," which "bring in a lot of knowledge and experience to the school." The big players in the region include "two major insurance companies, manufacturing, and agriculture...There are a lot of fields for people to study and get strong practical experience" through locally-based jobs, internships, guest lectures, and networking opportunities. "The corporate partnerships ISU has with major corporations made ISU the choice for me," a typical student tells us.

"An excellent finance and insurance reputation" as well as strength in accounting and management lead the way academically at ISU. The MBA program also offers "great international experiences." "Either internships or study abroad programs are offered," and the school maintains "good partnerships with international educational institutions that offer opportunities for students to expand their world view and get practical experience in the field." Professors here "do an excellent job balancing research, teaching, and service and are very available to students." One student reports, "Coming from a much larger, research-oriented undergraduate university, it is refreshing to come to a school that is so devoted to teaching...Having professors who are devoted to being excellent teachers keeps me looking forward to going to each class."

ISU's MBA is geared toward part-time students. Some feel the school could tweak the program for convenience's sake. One explains, "Most students I know feel we are grouped to death. There comes a time when enough group projects are enough! Because many students live out of town (many in Peoria or Champaign, 50 to 60 miles from Normal), group projects can be nearly impossible and it seems we often do just enough to get by. We do the same group project over and over and over and over, just with a different topic." On a positive note, students report that research opportunities exist, as does the chance to incorporate community projects into one's coursework.

Career and Placement

Illinois State University's career services include resume and job posting through eRecruiting. Other services are provided by the Career Center, which serves the entire undergraduate and graduate population of the university. Students report that the university's "proximity to State Farm, Financial, Mitsubishi Motors North America, Caterpillar and Growmark" creates welcome opportunities. There is "strong cooperation between companies and the business school through internships and classroom instruction from practitioners in various fields of business," students tell us. Companies visiting campus during a Sprint 2009 job fair included Archer Daniels Midland, Country Financial, Sherwin-Williams Company, and State Farm.

Student Life and Environment

The ISU MBA facility is a five-year old "palace," according to students. Classrooms have "power and hardwired Internet along with campus-wide wireless" at every seat; the building "has numerous small meeting rooms, a massive computer lab, and a graduate lounge" as well as "an in-house coffee, sandwich, and snack shop." Students brag that "the campus is wonderfully landscaped, with a nationally registered arboretum on the quad" and are especially pleased to report that "we have access to an on-site parking garage less than 100 feet from the building." On the downside, "Recreation facilities are not included with tuition. You must voluntarily sign up for and pay for the ability to go work out...It would be much better to have gym fees included in tuition cost. It would probably benefit the health of the average student, too."

The Normal-Bloomington area where ISU is located constitutes "a rather large small town" where "diversity and culture are limited, although that is changing." Some feel "the size of the school and the local community are ideal," noting that "there are no major traffic jams and no worry about being safe from crime at night." They also point out that "The local economy is based on insurance and finance with manufacturing second, so the [poor] economy seems to have a lesser impact [than it has elsewhere]. Jobs for students are always available and traffic is never a problem."

Students report that "The university culture is predominated by the undergraduate programs," which makes sense given that most business grads are rarely on campus except to attend classes. For those seeking greater involvement, "The student life and activities office offers opportunities to improve the MBA experience with support of extracurricular programs, giving MBA students opportunities to reinforce what we learn in class and apply them in original and new creative ways outside the classroom." MBAs also observe "significant improvements to both campus and surrounding area underway, which portend some change of culture around the university." The student body here constitutes "a very diverse community." Writes one student, "In my current classes, I have classmates from nine countries in four continents. Along with that there are working professionals with families, military veterans and full-time students."

Admissions

Applicants to the ISU MBA program must submit an online application to the Graduate School. Applications are due by July 1 for the fall semester; by December 1 for the spring semester; and by April 1 for the summer semester. All applications must include two official copies of transcripts for all academic work completed beyond high school. GMAT scores, a resume, and personal essays must be attached to the online Graduate School application. The two letters of reference should be sent directly to the MBA Program office. GPA for the final 60 credit hours of undergraduate work and GMAT scores are the primary determining factors in the admissions decision. In recent years, successful applicants have posted an average GPA of 3.41 and an average GMAT score of 540. International students whose first language is not English must submit TOEFL or IELTS scores. A minimum score of 600 on the paper-and-pencil TOEFL, 250 on the computer-based TOEFL, 83 in the Internet-based TOEFL, or 6.5 on the IELTS is required. Work experience is considered "beneficial" and is "strongly encouraged," but is not required.

Applicants interested in Graduate Assistantship appointments (benefits include tuition waiver and monthly stipend) need to apply for a position prior to Marchst. The application is separate from the Program application and can be found via the "jobs" link on the university's homepage.

FINANCIAL FACTS

Annual tuition (in-state/ out-of-state)	$4,752/$9,864
Fees	$1,228
Cost of books	$1,526
Room & board (on/off-campus)	$6,148/$6,455
% of students receiving aid	88
% of first-year students receiving aid	70
% of students receiving loans	43
% of students receiving grants	85
Average award package	$7,864
Average grant	$3,512
Average student loan debt	$19,534

ADMISSIONS

Admissions Selectivity Rating	73
# of applications received	94
% applicants accepted	78
% acceptees attending	59
Average GMAT	540
Range of GMAT	520–650
Average GPA	3.41
TOEFL required of international students	Yes
Minimum TOEFL (paper/computer)	600/250
Application fee	$40
International application fee	$40
Regular application deadline	7/1
Regular notification	8/1
Early decision program?	Yes
ED Deadline/Notification	2/1 / 2/15
Deferment available	Yes
Maximum length of deferment	1 year
Transfer students accepted	Yes
Transfer application policy: Must be in good academic standing and complete all regular application requirements, maximum 9 hours transfer credit accepted.	
Non-fall admissions	Yes
Need-blind admissions	Yes

EMPLOYMENT PROFILE

Career Rating	83	**Top 5 Employers Hiring Grads**
Average base starting salary	$63,000	State Farm Insurance, Country Financial, Archer Daniels Midland, Caterpillar, Heritage Enterprises

IMD INTERNATIONAL
INTERNATIONAL INSTITUTE FOR MANAGEMENT DEVELOPMENT

GENERAL INFORMATION
Type of school	Private
Academic calendar	Jan–Nov

SURVEY SAYS...
Friendly students
Good peer network
Solid preparation in:
General management
Teamwork
Communication/interpersonal skills
Doing business in a global economy

STUDENTS
Enrollment of parent institution	8,000
Enrollment of MBA Program	90
% male/female	78/22
% part-time	0
% international	98
Average age at entry	31
Average years work experience at entry	7

ACADEMICS
Academic Experience Rating	**98**
Student/faculty ratio	2:1
Profs interesting rating	91
Profs accessible rating	64
% female faculty	9

Prominent Alumni
Kjeld Kristiansen, President, LEGO;
Jurgen Fischer, President, HILTON
INTERNATIONAL; Bo Risberg, CEO,
HILTI; Mark Cornell, President and
CEO, Moet Hennessy USA, LVMH
Moet Hennessy Louis Vuitton Inc.

Academics

Within a stone's throw of Lake Geneva's shores, IMD in Lausanne, Switzerland, specializes in "leadership development with top professors and exceptional facilities." The unique aspect of this program is its emphasis on real-world learning which is supported through its "excellent faculty" who are not tenured, but rather work on a contract basis, meaning that they are effectively coming straight to the classroom from the boardroom. The school prides itself on being "a global meeting place" and this is evidenced by mix of nationalities and ages of its students and professors. "It's probably the smallest business school in the world," one student notes, "with only 90 students a year." Thanks to this "small class," students "can always enjoy one-on-one relations" with their "professors, career officers, and other resources." "The professors are often leaders or respected academics in their fields who are open to class discussion," one student says.

Many here appreciate the "opportunity for hands-on learning, with the start-up and consulting projects, in addition to the emphasis on leadership and opportunities for personal development." In line with IMD's global outlook comes an emphasis on real-world experience. "Applied learning" and "problem-based learning" reign supreme here. Be forewarned though, the workload ain't light. "The most important skill to survive here is to prioritize the heavy workload," a student advises. Part of this time management involves working together and most students at IMD are pleased to find a "very collaborative work environment." "The workload is such that it is not possible to do everything, so students tend to divide up work." Any idea what this kind of teamwork might allow? If you were thinking something along the lines of "diversity," you're right. Most students here have already been part of the workforce, with around "seven to eight years of experience," and represent "41 nationalities from all over the world." Where else could you find out about everything from "the banana business to elevators [in places as disparate] as Zimbabwe and Mauritius"? All this makes for "an intensive but life-changing year!"

For the most part, "Everything runs like Swiss clockwork." "We get very attentive staff which sorts out everything from mobile phones to setting up bank accounts," one student explains. The "friendly and helpful" staff "cooperate positively" with students. "I'm glad the campus is good because I spent 100 hours a week there," one student explains. "Part of how we managed it is due to how helpful everyone is down there." But into every MBA, a little rain must fall. Students wouldn't mind seeing the school "market itself" and "increase brand awareness among the general public" so that it would "be better known outside of Europe." As one student explains, "It has a great reputation among those who know it, but as it's a small school, it isn't well recognized in the U.S., for instance."

Career and Placement

After an "extremely busy first six months," IMD students settle into the second half of the year, where "project work is mixed with classes and recruiting." A huge part of this time involves working with career services to find a job. Many here note that since there is such a small number of students, their "career search is very individualistic and you can go for something off the usual track." IMD's career services center takes a personal approach to finding its students jobs by having them work with career coaches who help them "to better define [their] career goals" through surveys, "individual career strategy sessions," and workshops that cover everything from "networking" to "negotiating salary." Most impressive is the school's "class marketing," wherein IMD distributes short profiles of its MBA students "available for employment to over 5,000 companies and managers worldwide." The school also sends out a "résumé portfolio" to "over 250 organizations" that includes a "one-page résumé for each participant." This, in combination with ever-present "company presentations and on-campus recruiting," makes for happily-employed students. "It allowed me to make a huge career leap to another level," one student says.

Student Life and Environment

You can thank the Romans for Lausanne. They originally founded it as a military camp but it went through many, many more incarnations and occupants until it reached its present state as one of the most beautiful locales in all of Europe. With over 15 museums, film and music festivals, several universities, nearby vineyards, and a massive focus on all things related to sports (which comes as no surprise considering the International Olympic Committee's headquarters is located here), there's no shortage of things to see or do regardless of the season. That said, for IMD students, "The heavy workload sometimes hampers social activities." A common complaint here is that the school "could improve its efforts to set aside time for more networking in a social environment." More often than not—and when time allows—students take things into their own hands and "go out of their way to organize social events or trips away." "Ninety percent of my time was spent on work, although there were different clubs or parties to attend almost every weekend," one undeterred student says. Another student sums up his experience, "IMD is a particular school and program in some senses. Since it doesn't belong to a university, its campus is smaller than the average and, therefore, it doesn't have on-campus housing….Overall, life at IMD has been spectacular both for me and my family. Lausanne is a lovely town, the campus is well-located…and people are friendly and competent and the support for families and spouses is fantastic." Others note, "The sports facilities could be improved." However, one thing that gets a unanimous vote of confidence is the "fantastic lunch buffet" and "amazing dessert table."

Admissions

In considering applicants for the MBA program, IMD requires its students to have a bachelor's degree or equivalent from an accredited institution, GMAT score, a minimum of three years full-time work experience (although they stress that the average among current students is seven years), and near-fluency in English (the TOEFL is not required, but considering your year at IMD will involve writing and speaking in English, your language skills had better be up to snuff). If you're unsure of where you stand, these good people have set up a MBA Assessment Form on their website (www.imd.ch/programs/mba/Assess-your-chances.cfm) where you can enter your stats and get a clear idea of whether you're a likely candidate for admission.

FINANCIAL FACTS

Annual tuition	$49,993
Fees	$18,532
Room & board (off-campus)	$11,205
% of first-year students receiving aid	32
Average award package	$43,635
Average grant	$25,740

ADMISSIONS

Admissions Selectivity Rating	98
# of applications received	439
% applicants accepted	27
% acceptees attending	77
Average GMAT	675
Range of GMAT	620–750
TOEFL required of international students	No
Application fee	$302
International application fee	$302
Regular application deadline	9/1
Application Deadline/Notification	
Round 1:	2/1 / NR
Round 2:	4/1 / NR
Round 3:	6/1 / NR
Round 4:	8/1 / NR
Early decision program?	No
Deferment available	No
Transfer students accepted	No
Non-fall admissions	Yes
Need-blind admissions	Yes

EMPLOYMENT PROFILE

Career Rating	98	**Grads Employed by Function% Avg. Salary**	
Percent employed at graduation	63	Marketing	31 $125,000
Percent employed 3 months after graduation	83	Operations	7 $115,200
		Consulting	20 $122,600
Average base starting salary	$124,500	Management	15 $127,600
Primary Source of Full-time Job Acceptances		Finance	25 $127,800
School-facilitated activities	36 (58%)	**Top 5 Employers Hiring Grads**	
Graduate-facilitated activities	23 (37%)	McKinsey & Company (4), Philip Morris International (3), The Boston Consulting Group (2), Medtronic (2)	

INDIANA STATE UNIVERSITY
COLLEGE OF BUSINESS

GENERAL INFORMATION

Type of school	Public
Academic calendar	Trimester

SURVEY SAYS...

Friendly students
Happy students
Solid preparation in:
General management
Teamwork
Doing business in a global economy

STUDENTS

Enrollment of parent institution	10,487
Enrollment of MBA Program	61
% male/female	60/40
% part-time	40
% minorities	1
% international	55
Average age at entry	27
Average years work experience at entry	4

ACADEMICS

Academic Experience Rating	72
Student/faculty ratio	18:1
Profs interesting rating	84
Profs accessible rating	75
% female faculty	15
% minority faculty	7

Prominent Alumni

Paul Lo, Pres./CEO, SinoPac.

Academics

Designed primarily for students early in their business careers, the MBA program at Indiana State University offers graduate-level preparation to aspiring managers and business professionals. "Small classes, great teachers, good assistantships" and an affordable tuition add up to excellent value for students here.

Size is both a major asset and an occasional drawback at ISU. With fewer than 60 students in the entire program, students enjoy "individual attention that better prepares the students in a hands-on manner." Small class sizes also mean great faculty accessibility; one student points out, "All of my classes have been taught by senior professors, department chairs, etc. The mentors and connections I'm gaining are fantastic." The size of the program also helps foster a "friendly environment inside and outside the classroom." On the downside, "Class scheduling can be difficult since limited classes are offered each semester." Also, small programs often suffer from neglect in some areas, and ISU's is no exception. For example, ISU "needs to continually update case studies," an area in which students say the program is deficient. "Especially during these economic times, we need very current cases."

The Indiana State MBA consists of 33 semester units (plus foundational course work for students who did not study business as an undergraduate; students seeking a specialized concentration must complete an additional 3 semester units), which can be completed in one year and four months of full-time study. Students wishing to continue to work while they earn their MBAs may also choose to study part-time. Through core course work and electives, the program emphasizes strategic thinking, problem-solving skills, organizational change, international business, and group dynamics. Hands-on learning occurs through opportunities to assist faculty in real-world research projects in programs such as the Small Business Development Center (SBDC), which provides business planning assistance to start-up companies, and through consulting services to existing small businesses.

Career and Placement

Since 2004 when the College of Business opened the Career Experience Center (CEC), where students have had a dedicated facility where they can research positions using the Sycamore CareerLink electronic database, attend career-building workshops, and prepare for interviews. One student writes the following: "My experience with the Career Center is that they only provide the website for assistance in job searches and two career fairs per year. The staff does not provide any other help." Employers interviewing on the ISU campus during a recent recruiting year included: AFLAC, AmSouth, Caterpillar, Dauby O'Connor & Zaleski CPA, Federated Mutual Insurance Company, Marathon Oil, Travelers, and West Point Financial/Mass Mutual.

Student Life and Environment

"There is always something to be involved in for anyone who wants to get involved" in ISU's MBA community, students tell us. "Whether they are activities organized by the MBA Association (MBAA) or seminars and conferences hosted by leaders of industries, the ISU business school contributes positively towards a student's personality and mentality," a student observes. Students are particularly impressed with MBAA, whose events "allows students from all cultures to come together." Students also appreciate "a lounge for MBA students to study, eat, socialize, and plan." While students complain that "the classrooms need to be upgraded," they also point out that "they are already working on a new business building for us."

Hometown Terre Haute "has the most amazing public parks," facilitating "all [sorts] of outdoor activities. We are also very close to Indianapolis, Chicago, Louisville, and St. Louis, so we have been to Pacers games, Rams games etc. There is so much to do in this area and the cost of living is so low that you have money to enjoy life, even while in b-school."

The ISU MBA program attracts a mix of full timers—typically "young and busy," with some continuing directly from undergraduate study—and part timers adding school to a busy calendar that also includes a full-time job and family obligations. There is a large international contingent here, which makes for a "culturally diverse" campus. Students are "friendly and helpful," even when there are language barriers, and "work together on projects to make sure everyone understands." One writes: "As an international student I have never felt like a foreigner at ISU…[My classmates] always contribute positively in the classroom environment as well as outside." Academically, students describe their peers as "moderately competitive, with the occasional outstanding scholar."

Admissions

In considering applicants for the MBA program, Indiana State University considers the following criteria: acceptance to the School of Graduate Studies; successful completion of undergraduate degree; GPA of at least 2.7, or a GPA of at least 3.0 over the final 60 semester hours of undergraduate study; basic computing skills; GMAT scores; and prerequisite competency. Prerequisite course work for the program includes micro- and macroeconomics, financial accounting, finance, and US business law; additionally, marketing and production and operation management are "strongly recommended." Potential students must earn a GMAT-GPA admissions index of 1050 or higher (the admissions index numbers are calculated by multiplying GPA by 200 and adding GMAT scores), with scores ranking in at least the 50th percentile in both the math and verbal portions of the GMAT. Students failing to meet this requirement may be granted conditional admission to the program.

FINANCIAL FACTS

Annual tuition (in-state/ out-of-state)	$4,410/$8,760
Fees	$82
Cost of books	$900
Room & board	$7,800
% of students receiving aid	30
% of first-year students receiving aid	30
% of students receiving grants	30
Average award package	$12,210
Average grant	$6,210

ADMISSIONS

Admissions Selectivity Rating	70
# of applications received	61
% applicants accepted	67
% acceptees attending	37
Average GMAT	520
Range of GMAT	430–750
Average GPA	3
TOEFL required of international students	Yes
Minimum TOEFL (paper/computer)	550/213
Application fee	$35
International application fee	$35
Early decision program?	No
Deferment available	Yes
Maximum length of deferment	2 years
Transfer students accepted	Yes
Transfer application policy: Will only accept 6 credit hours from AACSB accredited universities.	
Non-fall admissions	Yes
Need-blind admissions	No

EMPLOYMENT PROFILE

Career Rating	68	Grads Employed by Function	% Avg. Salary
		Marketing	10 NR
		Management	30 NR
		HR	10 NR
		MIS	10 NR

INDIANA UNIVERSITY—BLOOMINGTON
KELLEY SCHOOL OF BUSINESS

GENERAL INFORMATION
Type of school	Public
Academic calendar	Semester

SURVEY SAYS...
Friendly students
Good peer network
Solid preparation in:
Marketing
Accounting
Teamwork
Quantitative skills

STUDENTS
Enrollment of parent institution	40,211
Enrollment of MBA Program	868
% male/female	70/30
% out-of-state	86
% part-time	47
% minorities	8
% international	32
Average age at entry	28
Average years work experience at entry	5

ACADEMICS
Academic Experience Rating	**92**
Student/faculty ratio	30:1
Profs interesting rating	94
Profs accessible rating	97
% female faculty	32
% minority faculty	14

Joint Degrees
MBA/JD-4 years; MBA/MA 3 years (area studies); MBA/MA 3 years (Telecommunications); MBA/JD 3 years.

Prominent Alumni
John T. Chambers, MBA '76, Chairman and CEO, Cisco Systems, Inc.; Phillip Francis, MBA '71, Chairman & CEO, PETsMART, Inc; Jeff M. Fettig, MBA '81, Chairman and CEO, Whirlpool Corporation; Cheryl Bachelder, MBA '78, President & CEO, AFC Enterprises/Popeye's Chicken; Bradley Alford, MBA '80, Chairman & CEO, Nestle USA.

Academics

Students enjoy "a collaborative environment" at IU's prestigious Kelley School of Business, where "life is pretty relaxed and students are not very competitive. Pretty much any person you ask for help—student, faculty, professor—will legitimately take an interest in helping you solve your problem." Maybe it's a Midwestern thing, or maybe it's just a benefit of being located far enough away from the East Coast rat race, but for whatever reason, Kelley students seem awfully happy for people who are working so hard. As one student puts it, "In some ways the culture here is so amazing that you forget things don't always operate that way outside of Kelley."

The Kelley experience begins with a 15-week integrated core curriculum that "is exciting but also very challenging; think of it as a marathon. Courses themselves are actually easier than many of my undergrad classes were in terms of content. It's the pacing and volume combined with activities outside of class that make it so difficult." Indeed, "The first semester core can be brutal, but is a team-building exercise to prepare you for the remainder of the MBA program and for your internship and post-grad employment." It helps that "the professors through[out] the core are very engaging and accomplished."

The core, along with a leadership/professional/career development module, consumes most of the first semester. During the second semester, students begin major and elective coursework. "Most classes require a team effort" at Kelley, so "students must be able to work in teams." A top school, Kelley is strong across multiple business disciplines; marketing and entrepreneurship are the standout fields here, though, with numerous respondents identifying them as the program's greatest strengths. Specialized study is enhanced by industry-focused, week long 'academies' that provide concentrated exposure to a business sector through guest speakers, seminars, field trips, and case competitions. The academies are huge crowd pleasers. One student explains why: "The Kelley Academies by far set Kelley apart from every other top b-school. When you choose your academy, you gain exposure to industry leaders that come on campus to give you their real-world perspective on their industry. The importance of the things I have learned in my academy far outweigh the things I actually learned in class, because I was learning what was 'really important' straight from industry leaders at the Director, VP, and even C-levels."

Career and Placement

"The administrative and support staff, including the graduate career staff, are very devoted to us and there to hear our questions and concerns," one Kelley MBA brags, illustrating students' high level of satisfaction with career services. Students are especially effusive about Kelley's legendary alumni network. One writes: "The alumni network here isn't just a nice phrase; it actually works for you. For example, during my admissions interview, my interviewer learned of my post-graduate plans. After the interview, he gave me contact names and phone numbers for managers at leading companies within my field of choice, and he encouraged me to reach out to them to learn what they had to say both about their jobs and their Kelley experiences. This was before I was even admitted to the program! The alumni exposure has only grown since then. I feel like I could throw a dart at any *Fortune 500* company…and have a lunch set up there within a week; it's that good."

ADMISSIONS CONTACT: JAMES HOLMEN, DIRECTOR OF ADMISSIONS AND FINANCIAL AID
ADDRESS: 1275 EAST TENTH STREET, SUITE 2010 BLOOMINGTON, IN 47405-1703
PHONE: 812-855-8006 • FAX: 812-855-9039
E-MAIL: MBAOFFICE@INDIANA.EDU • WEBSITE: WWW.KELLEY.INDIANA.EDU/MBA

Top recruiters of Kelley MBAs include Target, Bank of America, Johnson & Johnson, General Electric, 3M, Ernst & Young, and Procter & Gamble. About one-quarter of 2009 Kelley MBAs wound up in consumer products; 16 percent found jobs in pharma/biotech; 14 percent took positions in manufacturing; 12 percent were hired in financial services; and 10 percent found consulting gigs.

Student Life and Environment

At Kelley, "school is busy and challenging, but students still get together to go out and have fun." Mornings "are filled with classes. Once classes are done, your afternoons are filled with team meetings and group projects. Evenings are your free time, which you have to balance between social events and personal study time." The calendar allows "plenty of opportunities to cut loose, but you have to balance your time because the coursework is challenging." Extracurriculars include "great opportunities for all types: designated bar for MBAs most nights of the week; academic/professional lectures and activities most nights of the week; and [there are] always outdoor or sports activities going on."

Hometown Bloomington "is great. Since it is a small town, you really get to know your classmates rather than everyone going their separate [ways] during the weekends." Students call hometown Bloomington "the ideal college town—small enough to be easy to navigate, but packed with great food, culture, and people thanks to the university."

Admissions

The Kelley MBA program is highly selective. The Admissions Office considers all the following factors: academic record, including cumulative grade point average; area of concentration; balance of electives and trend of grades; GMAT scores; work experience (two or more years strongly recommended); evidence of leadership ability; two letters of reference; and personal essays. Successful applicants need not have majored in business as undergraduates but should understand algebra and statistics and have some facility with spreadsheets. Calculus is important for some majors. Kelley has four separate application deadlines, with separate screening for each batch of applicants. In general, your chances are better if you apply early; however, it is better to wait for a later deadline if doing so will improve your application. Those seeking merit scholarships should try to apply by the January 5th deadline.

FINANCIAL FACTS

Annual tuition (in-state/ out-of-state)	$22,000/$41,000
Fees	$1,592
Cost of books	$1,900
Room & board (on/off-campus)	$8,750/$8,750
% of students receiving aid	95
% of first-year students receiving aid	95
% of students receiving loans	90
% of students receiving grants	60
Average award package	$42,400
Average grant	$20,205
Average student loan debt	$48,000

ADMISSIONS

Admissions Selectivity Rating	**93**
# of applications received	1,511
% applicants accepted	32
% acceptees attending	47
Average GMAT	664
Range of GMAT	630–710
Average GPA	3.34
TOEFL required of international students	Yes
Minimum TOEFL (paper/computer)	600/250
Application fee	$75
International application fee	$75
Application Deadline/Notification	
Round 1:	11/1 / 1/15
Round 2:	1/5 / 3/15
Round 3:	3/1 / 4/30
Round 4:	4/15 / 5/30
Early decision program?	No
Deferment available	Yes
Maximum length of deferment	1 year
Transfer students accepted	No
Non-fall admissions	No
Need-blind admissions	Yes

EMPLOYMENT PROFILE

		Grads Employed by Function	% Avg. Salary
Career Rating	93		
Percent employed at graduation	82	Marketing	36 $88,043
Percent employed 3 months after graduation	89	Operations	3 $87,000
		Consulting	15 $100,050
Average base starting salary	$91,869	Management	5 $89,572
Primary Source of Full-time Job Acceptances		Finance	32 $92,188
School-facilitated activities	115 (73%)	HR	1 NR
Graduate-facilitated activities	42 (27%)	**Top 5 Employers Hiring Grads**	
		Procter & Gamble (6), Cummins (5), Kraft Foods (5), Sears Holding Corp. (5), Ernst & Young (5)	

INDIANA UNIVERSITY—KOKOMO
SCHOOL OF BUSINESS

GENERAL INFORMATION
Type of school	Public
Academic calendar	Semester

SURVEY SAYS...
Solid preparation in:
Accounting
General management
Operations
Communication/interpersonal skills
Quantitative skills
Computer skills

STUDENTS
Enrollment of parent institution	2,690
Enrollment of MBA Program	78
% male/female	44/56
% part-time	77
% minorities	6
Average age at entry	31
Average years work experience at entry	6

ACADEMICS
Academic Experience Rating	**65**
Student/faculty ratio	6:1
Profs interesting rating	61
Profs accessible rating	61
% female faculty	36
% minority faculty	1

Academics

The School of Business at Indiana University—Kokomo capably serves area professionals seeking to advance their careers through an MBA degree. Students here praise the program's "excellent reputation" with area employers as well as its "convenient location" and small class sizes that "make for an intimate setting. Students are people, not numbers here." A public school that is one of only a dozen AACSB-accredited MBA programs in the state of Indiana, Kokomo provides a compelling option to business people seeking an affordable career advancement opportunity in and around this city of 50,000.

IU Kokomo's program is "attuned to the regional industry base" of north-central Indiana but is also flexible enough to "foster effective management of resources in diverse organizational units and settings," according to the school's promotional material. Because nearly all its students work full time, the program offers flexible scheduling. All required classes are held during the week in the evening hours; electives are offered either during the day or in the evenings. Classes are alternately offered in 8- and 16-week formats, accommodating both those in a hurry to complete course work and those who wish to learn at a (somewhat) less frantic pace. Except for a capstone course, classes may be taken in any order, another accommodation to the convenience of IU's busy students. Such convenience comes with a tradeoff, however, making it impossible for the school to fully integrate the curriculum. Some here feel that "the program should add an integrated case study that encompasses at least two courses per semester," an impossibility under the current system.

Part-time students typically complete Kokomo's 30-credit MBA program in four years. The program is small, facilitating student-teacher interaction, and fortunately professors here "are very approachable and show genuine interest in the students' academic and professional success." The downside of the school's size is that it limits options. Some students complain that some courses are not offered frequently enough.

Career and Placement

IU Kokomo does not aggressively promote its career services for MBA students. Because most students in the program "are employed full-time in positions of responsibility," few actually require placement services or career counseling, and those who do generally rely on the assistance of their professors. MBAs may take advantage of the university's Office of Career Services, which maintains job boards, a Career Library and Resource Center, and online career-related databases. The program also features an MBA Association that works to schedule networking and recruitment events for current graduate students.

Student Life and Environment

IUK attracts a student body that is "diverse in gender, race, and age," with "lots of women and minorities" filling out the ranks. MBAs here tend to be "working adults looking to improve their skill sets." They have "multiple demands on their time" in addition to school, including careers and, quite often, family obligations. Some are friendly, but others "tend to stick together with fellow students from the same employer" and are "not always welcoming to outsiders."

ADMISSIONS CONTACT: LINDA FICHT, ASSISTANT DEAN AND MBA DIRECTOR
ADDRESS: PO BOX 9003 KOKOMO, IN 46904-9003
PHONE: 765-455-9465 • FAX: 765-455-9348
E-MAIL: LFICHT@IUK.EDU • WEBSITE: WWW.IUK.EDU/MBA

IUK is "strictly a commuter campus" where students "come in, go to class, and leave." It is worth highlighting the efforts of the MBA Association (MBAA), which organizes social and intellectual events for those students who do spend time on campus. The school invites business leaders as part of its distinguished lecture series, enabling students to learn from some of the business world's top players. Some here feel that "the safety of students attending night classes is an issue. I never see security at night and the lighting could be better." Statistics indicate that the city of Kokomo has a below average rate of such common crimes as assault, robbery, and automobile theft. Top employers in Kokomo include Delphi Electronics & Safety, Howard Regional Health, Saint Joseph Hospital, Haynes International, Meijer, and the university.

Admissions

Admission to the MBA program at IU Kokomo requires a bachelor's degree from an accredited college or university (business major not required); a completed application to the program; a personal statement of career goals; and official transcripts for all post-secondary academic work. Most applicants must also submit GMAT scores; those already holding graduate degrees from accredited institutions, however, are exempted from this requirement. A formula score of at least 1,000 under the formula [(undergraduate GPA + 200) + GMAT score] is required of all applicants who submit GMAT scores. Successful completion of undergraduate-level courses in calculus, statistics, and composition and a background in microcomputer applications are prerequisites to beginning the MBA program; these courses can be completed after admission to the program, however. Some qualified applicants may be denied admission due to space and resource constraints; admissions decisions are made on a rolling basis, so it pays to apply as early as possible. International applicants must meet the aforementioned requirements and must also submit TOEFL scores (minimum score 550). The MBA program admits students for fall, spring, and summer semesters. IU Kokomo accepts students with deficiencies in their business education background; such students are required to complete up to 18 credit hours of foundation courses in business.

FINANCIAL FACTS

Annual tuition (in-state/ out-of-state)	$8,130/$18,258
Fees	$417
Cost of books	$1,000

ADMISSIONS

Admissions Selectivity Rating	**65**
# of applications received	26
% applicants accepted	96
% acceptees attending	96
Average GMAT	505
Average GPA	3.1
TOEFL required of international students	Yes
Minimum TOEFL (paper/computer)	550/213
Application fee	$40
International application fee	$60
Regular application deadline	8/1
Early decision program?	No
Deferment available	Yes
Transfer students accepted	Yes
Transfer application policy: 6 credits from AACSB accredited schools	
Non-fall admissions	Yes
Need-blind admissions	Yes

INDIANA UNIVERSITY—SOUTH BEND
SCHOOL OF BUSINESS AND ECONOMICS

GENERAL INFORMATION

Type of school	Public
Academic calendar	Semester

SURVEY SAYS...

Solid preparation in:
Computer skills

STUDENTS

Enrollment of parent institution	8,300
Enrollment of MBA Program	210
Average age at entry	27
Average years work experience at entry	2

ACADEMICS

Academic Experience Rating	71
Student/faculty ratio	17:1
Profs interesting rating	84
Profs accessible rating	83
% female faculty	29
% minority faculty	6

Academics

Not all MBAs in South Bend attend University of Notre Dame. On the contrary, Indiana University at South Bend offers an "exhaustive" MBA that provides "low cost, high accreditation," and "convenience" to its locally-based, largely professional student body. An evening-classes-only schedule accommodates these students, helping to make participation in the program "a welcome addition to the weekly routine."

Small classes also help. One student reports, "Every class has 15 to 20 students in it, so the professor can take care of everyone." The faculty here includes "some of the most committed and best professors in the state" who, students speculate, "have chosen this school because of the high level of professor-student interaction." They even go the extra mile to "help graduates find jobs and match interested students with mentors to prepare them for the future." Additionally, profs "do an excellent job of integrating the actual work environment with the classroom experience." MBAs tell us that finance, accounting, and management are among the strongest areas here; marketing and operations, on the other hand, are relatively weak.

Unlike the cross-town competition, IUSB welcomes students with nominal backgrounds in business. Such students are required to complete a battery of introductory courses, which receive mixed reviews. "I had no previous business experience, so the classes have laid a good foundation for business classes," one student tells us. Another, however, complains that "The administration forces prerequisite courses that I did not see as beneficial to learning...specifically a course in Microsoft Access and Excel when my profession requires me to be proficient in both. I felt as though it was forced to increase revenue for the school versus the need/learning of the students."

Career and Placement

The Career Services Office at IU South Bend serves the entire student and alumni population of the school. The office is primarily dedicated to undergraduates, although its services are also available to MBAs. The office provides the standard complement of job-search services, skills seminars, personal assessments, and one-on-one counseling. The following is a partial list of recent recruiters on campus; 1st Source Bank, ADEC, AFLAC, Americall Group, Inc., Bounce Logistics, Career Transitions LLC, John Hancock Financial Network/Legacy Financial Partners, New York Life Insurance Company, One Communications, Primerica-Reygaert, Primerica-Saenz, State Farm, Wells Fargo Financial, WestPoint Financial Group, and WorkOne.

ADMISSIONS CONTACT: TRACY P. WHITE, GRADUATE BUSINESS RECORDS REPRESENTATIVE
ADDRESS: 1700 MISHAWAKA AVENUE, P O BOX 7111 SOUTH BEND, IN 46634-7111
PHONE: 574-520-4138 • FAX: 574-520-4866
E-MAIL: GRADBUS@IUSB.EDU • WEBSITE: WWW.IUSB.EDU/~BUSE/GRAD

FINANCIAL FACTS

Annual tuition (in-state/ out-of-state)	$4,600/$11,290
Cost of books	$700
Room & board	$12,000

ADMISSIONS

Admissions Selectivity Rating	66
# of applications received	74
% applicants accepted	93
% acceptees attending	65
Average GMAT	542
Range of GMAT	450–700
Average GPA	3.01
TOEFL required of international students	Yes
Minimum TOEFL (paper/computer)	550/213
Application fee	$48
International application fee	$60
Regular application deadline	7/1
Early decision program?	No
Deferment available	Yes
Maximum length of deferment	1 year
Transfer students accepted	Yes
Transfer application policy: Contact the office for a determination of which classes might transfer.	
Non-fall admissions	Yes
Need-blind admissions	No

Student Life and Environment

IUSB's MBA program is predominantly a part-time program designed for the convenience of students who also work. Many of these students hold full-time jobs, leaving them little time for anything other than classes, group work, and sleep. "The only time I spend on campus is during class or if a group project requires my attendance," writes a typical student. Another observes, "IUSB campus is a commuter campus and you don't see most of the students once they are done with their classes and studies."

Extracurricular opportunities do exist for those who seek them, however. "The social comfort level at IUSB is perfect," one student explains. "For those who are joiners, there are clubs and activities. Those who choose not to join are still an important part of campus life." The "many, many clubs on campus meet a wide variety of academic and social wants and needs," including the fostering of "a small community feel with a top notch university educations." The campus is small, which students generally appreciate. One writes, "I really enjoy the small size of the campus. It's very common to see people you know from past classes walking through the halls. People are very friendly and willing to chat or say 'Hi.'" They are even happier to report that "the campus is very safe, even at night." Campus amenities include a "rather extravagant recreation building," and "excellent library," and "good, reasonably-priced food service."

IUSB's MBAs "come from diverse working backgrounds and are looking to further themselves in either their own careers or prepare for new ones." There is a "variety of age groups" represented, and this "adds opportunity and flavor to the academic experience here. For the most part students are friendly and responsive." The student body includes "a large international segment as well that provides insight to business practices abroad."

Admissions

The MBA program at Indiana University—South Bend requires applicants to submit all of the following: a completed application and data sheet, available online; official transcripts for all postsecondary academic work; two letters of recommendation (recommendation form available online); a personal statement describing one's background, outlining one's goals in the program, and recounting an experience that led to personal growth; and an official score report for the GMAT. International students whose native language is not English must submit all of the above as well as an official score report for the TOEFL; minimum required score for consideration is 550 (paper-based test) or 213 (computer-based test). Applications are accepted for admission commencing with the Fall, Spring, or Summer semesters. IU South Bend admits students at two levels: full admission and probationary admission. Full admission requires a minimum GMAT score of 450 and an undergraduate business degree from an AACSB-accredited school with a minimum GPA of 2.75. Probationary admission is granted to applicants "whose GPA does not quite meet minimum standards." All students must maintain an in-program GPA of at least 2.75 in order to remain in the program, and to graduate from the program.

INDIANA UNIVERSITY OF PENNSYLVANIA
EBERLY COLLEGE OF BUSINESS AND INFORMATION TECHNOLOGY

GENERAL INFORMATION
Type of school	Public
Academic calendar	Semester

SURVEY SAYS...
Solid preparation in:
Marketing
General management
Communication/interpersonal skills
Doing business in a global economy

STUDENTS
Enrollment of parent institution	14,638
Enrollment of MBA Program	300
% male/female	68/32
% out-of-state	78
% part-time	7
% minorities	3
% international	77
Average age at entry	24

ACADEMICS
Academic Experience Rating	84
Student/faculty ratio	9:1
Profs interesting rating	85
Profs accessible rating	86
% female faculty	26
% minority faculty	33

Prominent Alumni
Richard B. Clark, '80, President & CEO Brookfield Financial Properties LP; Terry L. Dunlap, '81, President Allegheny Ludlum; Regina Dressel Stover, '75, Senior Vice President Mellon Financial Corporation; Timothy W. Wallace, '79, CEO FullTilt Solutions; Jeffrey R. DeMarco, '81, Director of Human Resources KPMG Peat Marwick.

Academics

With a broad-based curriculum, affordable in-state tuition, and uniformly small class sizes, the MBA program at Indiana University of Pennsylvania is suitable to both recent graduates and mid-career professionals. With all courses taught in the evenings, the program can be tailored to fit your schedule, as well as your educational goals. For those who want to complete the degree quickly, the school offers "a fast-paced one-year completion opportunity" (open to students with an undergraduate degree in business). However, there are also "options for doing concentrations/ specialization for those who want a longer program," or for those who wish to concentrate their studies on a field like international business, human resources, or supply chain management. Offering a great return on investment, this public school "is not expensive compared to another MBA programs, and the quality is still very good." Despite the attractive price tag, the curriculum is well-designed, the administration is efficient, and "Everything is done to allow students to work as smoothly as possible, [and] we have easy access to all resources needed."

Eberly's MBA curriculum strives to stay current with business trends, and practical business applications are constantly incorporated into class work. Drawing on their real-world credentials, "Professors are constantly reinforcing what is being taught with real life experiences or with what is going on in the world today." In some fields, however, the program is still behind on industry trends. For example, "the current advertising course does not even discuss online advertising or social media"—a significant omission in today's business environment. Another feature that stands out about the Eberly MBA is its focus on international business. This focus is reflected in both the staff and the students, as Eberly recruits "professors and students who are from all different parts of the world, as well as who have been to all different parts of the world." Here, "It is a pleasure to work in an intercultural group and we learn more about other cultures and our globalized world economy!"

Uniting intimacy with opportunity, "The greatest strength of the school is the small campus feel mixed with a big college feeling." Thanks to the low graduate enrollment, Eberly students enjoy "small class sizes" and the opportunity to work directly with their professors, while still benefiting from the larger campus environment as well as the big, state-of-the-art Eberly College of Business complex. Within the business school, "Professors are always willing to give an extra hand, and are always available during office hours." Likewise, the "School administration is very helpful and reacts very quickly to all our inquiries and demands!"

Career and Placement

The Indiana University of Pennsylvania Career Development Center assists all undergraduates, graduate students, and alumni with career preparation, internships, and job placement. The Career Development Center offers help with resume writing, interviewing skills, and job-hunting techniques, and it offers one-on-one counseling by appointment. In addition, the Career Development Center organizes job fairs and campus recruiting programs, while also maintaining an updated list of job opportunities online. While their services are open to MBA candidates, some say the Center "could use some overhauling," with a greater focus on "attracting good companies for internships and placements."

ADMISSIONS CONTACT: KRISH KRISHNAN, DIRECTOR MBA PROGRAM
ADDRESS: 664 PRATT DRIVE, RM 301 INDIANA, PA 15705-1081
PHONE: 724-357-2522 • FAX: 724-357-6232
E-MAIL: IUP-MBA@IUP.EDU • WEBSITE: WWW.EBERLY.IUP.EDU/MBA

In recent years, the mean base salary for IUP graduates was over $50,000, and over 70 percent of students had accepted a job within three months of graduation. Companies that recruit on the IUP campus include American Express, Bristol-Myers Squibb Co., Cigna, DuPont Company, EDS, Exxon Company, Federated Investors, General Motors, Georgia Pacific, Deloitte & Touche LLP; Ernst & Young LLP; PriceWaterhouseCoopers LLP, Sun Microsystems, Inc., Wal-Mart, Walt Disney World Company, and Westinghouse.

Student Life and Environment

A "very diverse" student body, over 30 percent of Eberly students are international, with more than 20 countries represented on campus. This diversity is a blessing to the academic experience, as "everyone comes to class with a clear mind, ready to share their background [and] experiences" and most "find it very interesting to learn about their cultures and societies."

Despite their different backgrounds, students at this program get along well. In fact, "Being in the MBA school at IUP is like having a small group of friends…. It's easy to get together with fellow students to study and go over things or just hang out." A student exclaims, "I've always enjoyed IUP for the vast social networking I'm able to do. Even though the town is small, I always have something to do, whether it's participating in a club, or just relaxing on weekends." An hour northeast of Pittsburgh, IUP is near a major city, yet the small-town atmosphere makes it a "peaceful place for studying" and ensures "affordable" cost of living. On that note, hometown Indiana, Pennsylvania isn't everybody's cup of tea. In fact, Indiana "is a very tiny town, so you can either enjoy it or hate it."

Admissions

To be eligible for admission to IUP, students must have a minimum undergraduate GPA of at least 2.6 (for those who graduated from college fewer than five years ago) or 2.4 (for those who graduated from college more than five years ago.) Prospective students must also present GMAT scores of 450 or better. In addition to test scores and undergraduate transcripts, students must also submit a one-page personal statement, at least two letters of recommendation, and an updated resume. High-achieving Pennsylvania residents are eligible to apply for graduate assistantships after completing the first part of the core curriculum.

FINANCIAL FACTS

Annual tuition (in-state/ out-of-state)	$6,666/$10,666
Fees (in-state/ out-of-state)	$1,631/$1,736
Cost of books	$1,000
Room & board	$6,140
% of students receiving aid	51
% of first-year students receiving aid	31
Average award package	$8,100
Average grant	$8,100

ADMISSIONS

Admissions Selectivity Rating	78
# of applications received	305
% applicants accepted	65
% acceptees attending	80
Average GMAT	538
Range of GMAT	400–720
Average GPA	3.4
TOEFL required of international students	Yes
Minimum TOEFL (paper/computer)	550/213
Application fee	$40
International application fee	$40
Regular application deadline	7/30
Early decision program?	No
Deferment available	Yes
Maximum length of deferment	1 year
Transfer students accepted	Yes
Transfer application policy: Written request for transfer required of transfer applicants. Maximum of six credits transfer.	
Non-fall admissions	Yes
Need-blind admissions	Yes

EMPLOYMENT PROFILE

Career Rating	81	Top 5 Employers Hiring Grads
Percent employed 3 months after graduation	57	American Express, Bristol-Myers Squibb Co., Champion International, Cigna, Dupont
Average base starting salary	$52,520	Company

INDIANA UNIVERSITY—SOUTHEAST
SCHOOL OF BUSINESS

GENERAL INFORMATION

Type of school	Public
Academic calendar	Semester

SURVEY SAYS...

Cutting-edge classes
Solid preparation in:
Computer skills

STUDENTS

Enrollment of parent institution	6,840
Enrollment of MBA Program	272
% part-time	94
Average age at entry	30
Average years work experience at entry	6

ACADEMICS

Academic Experience Rating	**80**
Student/faculty ratio	20:1
Profs interesting rating	94
Profs accessible rating	89
% female faculty	21
% minority faculty	18

Joint Degrees

Both degree plans (MBA and MSSF) can be completed simultaneously by taking 51 graduate credit hours (plus any necessary foundation course work).

Academics

Area business grads choose Indiana University Southeast because "it offers the best combination of cost and quality of education while still being close to home." "IU brand recognition" sways many who recognize that the school "offers the big-name IU degree" along with "an administration that runs like a small college." Flexibility is another major factor; the school fashions its schedule to accommodate its almost entirely part-time student body and offers two convenient locations; one on the IUS main campus in New Albany, the other a Graduate Center in downtown Jeffersonville that students say "makes things easier, because we don't have to go to campus at night and walk from the back of the parking lot because all the students going to class during the day have taken all the spots."

IUS offers a general MBA and a Master's of Science in Strategic Finance (MSSF), each requiring 36 credit hours; students may earn both degrees simultaneously by completing 51 credit hours. The 36-hour programs consist of 30 hours of required classes and six hours of electives; students report that the required courses "build on and contribute to the understanding of concepts taught. I always find myself relating back to other classes I have taken." Academics are "demanding." As one student puts it, "The program takes a hard line on academics. There's no 'pay your fee, get your C' at this school."

MBAs are most impressed with the faculty at IUS, whom they describe as "knowledgeable and caring," "wonderful and very accessible outside of class." The strength of the faculty contributes substantially to the program's "quality reputation in the region with area professionals." That's an impressive accomplishment given the price of attending; as one student observes, "The cost of this program was so low that I was concerned about its quality, but after looking into their reputation with colleagues that attended this and other local schools, I feel I made the right choice." Of course, that low price tag means the school has to skimp in some areas; students complain that "the library, bookstore, and other campus services close down very early, making the campus less accessible to night MBA students."

Career and Placement

IUS' Office of Career Services and Placement receives middling marks from MBAs. Some describe the office as "extremely helpful," but many more declare the office "practically nonexistent...IU Southeast MBAs are largely left on their own. Sometimes e-mails come telling you of opportunities, but that's about it." Fortunately, "Most students are currently employed in companies with growth potential" and so are not on the job market. According to one student, "Most local opportunities are in financial services, insurance, healthcare. GE, YUM, and Papa John's, and smaller companies have opportunities available, and if someone is willing to move there is more available." Attendees at a recent business and industry job fair included AFLAC, AT&T, Cox Radio, Enterprise, FedEx, Kelly Services, Kroger, Northwestern Mutual Financial, Target, and Zappos.

Student Life and Environment

IUS is "mainly a commuter campus" for MBAs, although the school "has made strides to change the perception by working on construction of dorms. I still suspect that most MBA professionals will continue living off campus." That's because most MBAs are "balancing work with class and coursework" as well as family obligations; they're not the 'live on campus' type. The school works to accommodate their needs; writes one, "The child care center on campus is very inviting. My kids love to go there and will miss it when I graduate." On the downside, "The school shuts down at about 6 P.M., which means night students have trouble getting to necessary services before they close."

The part-time environment is not especially conducive to extracurricular activities, and indeed "many attempts have been made to generate interest in clubs for MBA students, but those events are overwhelmingly poorly attended." All the same, students tell us that "there are clubs and activities for MBAs to get involved with if they desire and opportunities to network. If someone does not get involved, it's most likely the person either does not get to know fellow class members or chooses not to get involved. As a person goes through program, he/she meets more people and networks better."

The IUS student body "ranges from recent graduates to people who have been working for 25+ years and are interested in furthering their careers by moving into managing in their field." It's a "friendly, supportive" group who make "good team members" and "bring a diverse work background to the learning experience." While "gender and age group diversity are great," the school is still "much more white" than it might be, although "the diversity of ethnic groups is improving."

Admissions

Completed applications to the IUS MBA program must include an official GMAT score report, official copies of all undergraduate transcripts, and a resume. Students with undergraduate degrees in business are likely to place out of some or all of the school's eight foundation courses in business; all other admitted students must complete these foundation courses before beginning work on the actual MBA.

ADMISSIONS	
Admissions Selectivity Rating	70
# of applications received	103
% applicants accepted	89
% acceptees attending	78
Average GMAT	544
Range of GMAT	500–590
Average GPA	3.32
TOEFL required of international students	Yes
Minimum TOEFL (paper/computer)	550/213
Application fee	$35
International application fee	$35
Early decision program?	No
Deferment available	Yes
Transfer students accepted	Yes
Transfer application policy:	

Students may transfer a maximum of 6 graduate credit hours (with no grades below B) from another AACSB-accredited MBA program to count toward the 36 credit hour MBA curriculum at IU Southeast. Students may request that graduate credit not meeting this criterion be reviewed for transfer approval. The final disposition of all transfer course work is determined by the Graduate Business Programs Committee.

Non-fall admissions	Yes
Need-blind admissions	Yes

Applicants Also Look At

Bellarmine University
University of Louisville

INSEAD

GENERAL INFORMATION

Type of school	Private

SURVEY SAYS...
Good social scene
Good peer network
Cutting-edge classes
Solid preparation in:
General management
Doing business in a global economy
Entrepreneurial studies

STUDENTS

% male/female	71/29
% international	92
Average age at entry	29
Average years work experience	
at entry	55

ACADEMICS

Academic Experience Rating	62
Profs interesting rating	91
Profs accessible rating	86

Academics

INSEAD brands itself as "the business school for the world," and it can provide hard facts to support its claim. Students tell us the program is "is incredibly international, unrivaled by any other school," with a broad international student population and campuses in both France and Singapore. One student observes: "My fellow students come from 70 countries. My study group is an epitome of globalization: a Mexican investment banker, a Taiwanese accountant, a French Navy officer, an American diplomat, and a Bulgarian marketer, all exchanging knowledge in INSEAD. How much better could it be?" Further driving the point home is the fact that INSEAD is "the only prestigious MBA program that requires three languages upon exit."

Students, grateful for a program that "is not only US-centric," love the international focus at INSEAD. They also appreciate the fact that it's a 10-month program that "gives quicker return on investment" than longer, more expensive MBA programs. INSEAD has "a strong reputation in consulting and general management" that translates into "placement success with top-tier consulting firms." The school also offers "exceptional private equity and investment courses (private equity, realizing entrepreneurial potential, leveraged buyouts, etc.)." Perhaps the school's greatest strength, though, is the quality of its student body; one MBA tells us, "The work experience of all candidates is extremely high, which creates in-depth, dynamic discussions and learning in the classroom." Another adds: "At this point, any question I have about any country or industry can be solved by simply asking the right classmate."

As in most accelerated programs, "academics are extremely challenging" at INSEAD, especially "for someone completely new to business or on topics for which you have no knowledge. " However, "At the same time there is a stress toward making sure that students understand the basics and all that is necessary for business. What's more, other students who have had experience or who studied business in undergrad are always open to help and encourage each other." The large size of the program, coupled with the speed at which it is completed, "sometimes makes it feel as though you are passing through an MBA factory, which has been doing things the same way for a long time." Even so, "The administration is generally prompt and receptive, especially with regards to clubs, network and career activities," and is also very efficient. For example, "Many people change their minds during the year about which campus they want to be in for the next period, and the school is very good at trying to understand every situation and to accommodate their desires."

Career and Placement

INSEAD maintains Career Management Services (CMS) offices on both its French and Singaporean campuses. The offices promote students to employers around the globe while providing MBAs with one-on-one counseling and coaching, job search strategies, and on-campus recruiting events. Some students complain that CMS counselors are "used to a specific way of working and don't think outside the box. The focus is all on consulting, finance, and maybe a little industry." Others say, "Career Services is doing a good job, but there is room for improvement, as the school has a lot to offer on the job market." Nearly all agree that the school's substantial alumni network is "very helpful and intent on seeing current graduates succeed."

Employers most likely to hire INSEAD MBAs include McKinsey & Company; American Express; Booz Allen Hamilton; General Electric; Eli Lilly; Barclays Capital; Citigroup; Johnson & Johnson; Bain & Company; A.T. Kearney; Honeywell; Philip Morris; and Royal Dutch Shell. Nearly 40 percent of INSEAD MBAS wind up in consulting functions; one in five goes into finance and accounting.

Student Life and Environment

"The INSEAD year is a very intense period," students tell us, noting, "As there are classes every day, we have to study just like in high school and more or less all the time. There is a lot of group work...But, we all understand the quality of the people around us and the need for social interaction," and most here find time for fun.

INSEAD's Fontainebleau campus "is extremely dynamic. There's always something going on, but at the same time depends on the intake. At the end of the day, activities are driven by students. Sometimes, the one-year nature of the program makes keeping activities and clubs continuous a bit challenging." Weekends often feature "fantastic parties at chateaus in the French countryside. The school even provides shuttle buses. Can you beat that?" The Singapore campus "is superb" and "quite relaxed because of the setting."

Admissions

INSEAD has two intake points, in September and January. Students may apply to begin the program at either time; application is online only. All applicants must provide a personal profile, resume, five personal essays (with a sixth optional essay), two recommendations attesting to leadership potential and management capacity, a photograph, a statement of integrity, an official GMAT score report (the school recommends a score in at least the 70th percentile in both the verbal and quantitative sections), and official transcripts for all post-secondary academic work. In addition, all students must enter the program with proficiency in English and a second language. Non-native English speakers may submit results from the TOEFL, TOEIC, CPE, or IELTS; English speakers must provide certification of a second language. A third commercially useful language (sorry, no Latin!) is required to graduate; while language instruction is available through INSEAD, the intensity of the MBA program is such that the school recommends students get a start on their third language before the program begins. The applicant's choice of campus is not taken into account in the admission decision; however, placement at one's campus of choice is not fully guaranteed.

FINANCIAL FACTS

Annual tuition	$64,252
Cost of books	$1,008
Room & board (off-campus)	
$25,193	
% of students receiving grants	20

ADMISSIONS

Admissions Selectivity Rating	60*
Average GMAT	704
TOEFL required of	
international students	Yes
Minimum TOEFL	
(paper/computer)	620/260
Application Deadline/Notification	
Round 1:	3/11 / 6/5
Round 2:	5/27 / 9/4
Round 3:	7/22 / 10/9
Early decision program?	No
Deferment available	No
Transfer students accepted	No
Non-fall admissions	Yes
Need-blind admissions	No

IONA COLLEGE
HAGAN SCHOOL OF BUSINESS

GENERAL INFORMATION

Type of school	Private
Affiliation	Roman Catholic
Academic calendar	Trimester

SURVEY SAYS...

Cutting-edge classes
Happy students
Solid preparation in:
Teamwork
Communication/interpersonal skills

STUDENTS

Enrollment of parent institution	4,248
Enrollment of MBA Program	410
% male/female	51/49
% out-of-state	13
% part-time	80
% minorities	28
% international	4
Average age at entry	28
Average years work experience at entry	3

ACADEMICS

Academic Experience Rating	74
Student/faculty ratio	6:1
Profs interesting rating	89
Profs accessible rating	81
% female faculty	23
% minority faculty	10

Prominent Alumni

Alfred F. Kelly, Jr., President, American Express Company; Robert Greifeld, President, NASDAQ; Ron DeFeo, Chairman, President and CEO, Terex Corp; Philip Maisano, Vice Chair & CIO, The Dreyfus Corporation; Catherine R. Kinney, President and Co-COO of NYSE Group Inc.

Academics

"Iona has a good reputation in the Tri-state area," students tell us when explaining why they chose the MBA program at Iona's Hagan School of Business. Convenience is another major factor: "The proximity to Stamford, New York City, and its location in Westchester County...makes it ideal for job searches," one student writes. Familiarity with the program is a third contributing factor; many of the students in our survey attended Iona as undergraduates and "had a great experience." For them, the only question is why they wouldn't continue at Iona for their graduate degrees.

Hagan's relatively small MBA programs offer a surprising number of options to students, most of whom attend part time while working at full-time jobs. A fast-track MBA hustles students through the program in as little as 13 months. There's also a conventional MBA and a Saturday MBA. Classes are offered in a traditional classroom setting, online, or in a hybrid format that mixes on-campus and online study. Concentrations in financial management, information systems, general management, human resources management, marketing, general accounting, public accounting, and healthcare management are all available. Students speak especially highly of the HR program; many note approvingly of the entire MBA program's international focus, and several appreciate the "Christian influence" at this Christian Brothers-affiliated school.

Most of all, students love Hagan's faculty, which they describe as "outstanding." The faculty includes "some seasoned professionals with previous illustrious business careers" and teachers who "have owned companies or currently own companies, [and] who have provided a wealth of knowledge for future perspective entrepreneurs." Professors "are always available to help the students," "genuinely care about educating their students, and go the extra mile to help. They are accommodating, fair, and highly knowledgeable in their fields." The "excellent" administration "will reach out to you" as well. Campus resources, including the library and "up-to-date" technology, also earn accolades.

Career and Placement

The Gerri Ripp Center for Career Development handles counseling and placement services for all Iona students and alumni. Online job searches are facilitated by GAELlink, Iona's proprietary job database. The school also holds a career and internship fair in the spring and welcomes on campus recruiters. Students tell us it's not enough, wishing that the school did more in the way of "helping us network and bringing more recognized companies onto campus." The situation is complicated by the fact that many students attend at the expense of their current employers, who presumably do not want the school to assist students in finding better opportunities elsewhere. Professors, who "aid in networking," are considered a more dependable source of career assistance. Students tell us that the school is also beginning to reach out to its considerable alumni network on behalf of MBAs, "which should help the graduating students entering the labor market."

FINANCIAL FACTS

Annual tuition	$20,385
Fees	$350
% of students receiving aid	83
% of first-year students receiving aid	76
% of students receiving loans	51
% of students receiving grants	53
Average award package	$18,064
Average grant	$2,559
Average student loan debt	$19,988

ADMISSIONS

Admissions Selectivity Rating	**66**
# of applications received	169
% applicants accepted	77
% acceptees attending	64
Average GMAT	465
Range of GMAT	390–540
Average GPA	3.30
TOEFL required of international students	Yes
Minimum TOEFL (paper/computer)	550/213
Application fee	$50
International application fee	$50
Early decision program?	No
Deferment available	Yes
Maximum length of deferment	1 year
Transfer students accepted	Yes
Transfer application policy: Max of 6 upper-level credits accepted. 30 credit minimum required to earn a degree at Iona.	
Non-fall admissions	Yes
Need-blind admissions	Yes

Student Life and Environment

Iona's campus "is beautifully maintained and manicured," making it a welcome respite from the hectic and cluttered New York metropolitan area beyond its walls. Undergraduates will tell you it's an "active campus" with plenty of "events, entertainment, guest speakers, and sporting events." These events "are well-planned and publicized both on campus and via the web and emails," one MBA explains. The result of all this extracurricular activity is a solid community that engenders plenty of school pride, and even the MBAs feel it, even though they are mostly too busy to participate. As one explains, "Life at school is all about the classroom. Students do not hang out around school. They show up to class, then go home."

Hagan attracts a lot of young professionals as well as a substantial number of Iona undergraduates, some of whom proceed directly from undergraduate work to the MBA program. Older students include those "returning to further develop skill sets (as a result of the economy)" who "work for a diversity of companies from small organizations to large ones like Morgan Stanley." These older students sometimes complain that their younger classmates "do not care about education but [only] the title," but even they concede that "there are a great number of smart, dedicated, and committed students [in the program] that make you want to be smarter."

Admissions

Applicants to the Hagan MBA program must submit the following materials: a completed Hagan School of Business application form, along with a $50 application fee; copies of official transcripts from each undergraduate and graduate institution attended; two letters of recommendation; and an official score report for the GMAT reflecting a score no more than five years old (the GMAT requirement may be waived for applicants with at least seven years of post-undergraduate professional experience). Interviews are optional. International applicants must submit all of the materials listed above, as well as an official score report for the TOEFL, WES, and a cash support affidavit. Transcripts in languages other than English must be translated and interpreted by an approved service. Applications are processed on a rolling basis and are valid for one full year from the day they are received by the school. Applicants may request an interview, which the school recommends but does not require.

ITHACA COLLEGE
SCHOOL OF BUSINESS

GENERAL INFORMATION
Type of school   Private

SURVEY SAYS...
Students love Ithaca, NY
Solid preparation in:
Finance
Presentation skills
Quantitative skills
Doing business in a global economy

STUDENTS
Enrollment of parent institution	6,448
Enrollment of MBA Program	29
% male/female	69/31
% out-of-state	35
% part-time	21
% minorities	14
% international	20
Average age at entry	24
Average years work experience at entry	1

ACADEMICS
Academic Experience Rating	**77**
Student/faculty ratio	1:1
Profs interesting rating	87
Profs accessible rating	89
% female faculty	26
% minority faculty	26

Academics

MBA students in Ithaca College's small graduate program may choose between two programs: an MBA in business administration and an MBA in professional accountancy. Both degrees require 35 credit hours and can be completed by full-time students in 12 months—and this is the selling point of the program. As one student explains, "A one-year program offered me a faster track to my post-MBA life."

The curriculum for Ithaca's Business Administration MBA starts with function-level analysis of firms. Once students have mastered the workings of an individual business, the focus grows wider to encompass entire industries, finally concluding with a project in which students analyze an industry of their choice and assess individual firms within that industry. Classes emphasize "a balance between building technical and interpersonal skills," and students praise professors for their "hands-on teaching philosophy." "The faculty is always willing to bend over backwards to meet students' academic and professional needs," says one student. "While the professors remain rather rigid in their expectations of students, most will work tirelessly with students to ensure they succeed." Another student notes, "The school does a good job offering elective courses that are in line with students' career aspirations. Since the program is small, faculty surveys students prior to each semester. The result is a course offering that honestly reflects the interests of students. I see this adaptability as Ithaca's greatest strength because it can help overcome the obstacles often associated with a smaller business school."

Ithaca's Professional Accountancy MBA primarily functions as the culmination of a 5-year undergraduate/graduate program for students in the college's undergraduate accounting program, although candidates from other schools can gain admission. Most here agree that although "many students that graduated from Ithaca as undergrads" are now part of the MBA program, there are also "older" or "married" students in attendance.

The curriculum includes a thorough review of principles of business administration as well as advanced instruction in financial accounting and reporting, managerial and cost accounting, auditing, taxation, and principles of business law. Students in both programs are full of praise for the school. "Overall, I think the school is really starting to take off. Ithaca worked hard to receive AACSB accreditation, [and] since that happened the school has retained high standards for both students and faculty." Another adds, "Tuition is high, but you can definitely see where the money went. Everything from the smart boards in the classrooms—which help make articulating difficult accounting concepts much easier—to the trading room is state-of-the-art."

Students note that the one-year duration of the program helps offset the relatively high cost of attending. That said, while it had been a "little pricey" in the past, "Prices have come down." They also appreciate the fact that the business school administration "welcome(s) comments and suggestions from the grad students on what could help better the program. If you have any problems, they do their best to help you solve the issues." The future's looking bright here, so bring your shades.

ADDRESS: OFFICE OF GRADUATE STUDIES, ITHACA COLLEGE, 101 TERRACE CONCOURSE ITHACA,
NY 14850-7020
PHONE: (607) 274-3527 • FAX: (607) 274-1263
E-MAIL: MBA@ITHACA.EDU • WEBSITE: WWW.ITHACA.EDU/BUSINESS/MBA

Career and Placement

The Ithaca College Career Services Office provides self-assessment inventories, e-Recruiting tools, one-on-one advising, mock interviews, workshops, a library, and on-campus recruiting. The school also hosts a graduate school job fair and other special recruiting events. Though despite all this, some students find that "Ithaca could do a better job attracting recruiters from upper-tier businesses." While they appreciate the "many local recruiters on campus" and "ample alumni network and mentoring program," some still find a dearth of businesses at which they're "trying to get [their] foot in the door."

Employers who recruit on the Ithaca campus include Lockheed-Martin, Merrill Lynch, PricewaterhouseCoopers, Ernst & Young, Deloitte & Touche Tomastu, KPMG International, and an active alumni recruiting network.

Student Life and Environment

MBA students at Ithaca College enjoy "a great community atmosphere" at a school that "is just the right size, so that you can go anywhere and know somebody, and meet somebody new." One student writes, "All students are easygoing and approachable. The small size of the program means that many people have identical course schedules. This makes for a tight-knit group of students and strong, long-lasting friendships."

The demands of the program keep MBA students "pretty detached from the rest of the campus. You never deal with grad students from any of the other programs (unless they happen to take a business elective)." However, "Students work hard and play hard" when their schedule allows. "Most weekends I find myself in one or more bars or restaurants eating and drinking with classmates," says one student. Ultimately, "Life at Ithaca is good."

Admissions

Applicants to Ithaca's MBA program must have completed either a bachelor's program in business or accounting, or a bachelor's program in any field along with having taken Ithaca's Pre-MBA Modules. Post-undergraduate work experience is not required; in fact, many students enter the program immediately after completing work on their bachelor's degree. Successful applicants typically have "an undergraduate GPA of 3.0 or higher and a minimum GMAT score of 500." All applications must include official undergraduate transcripts, official GMAT scores, and two letters of recommendation in addition to the essay. Merit-based academic scholarships are also available from the program.

FINANCIAL FACTS

Annual tuition	$24,444
Cost of books	$1,500
% of students receiving grants	21
Average grant	$5,100

ADMISSIONS

Admissions Selectivity Rating	**67**
# of applications received	47
% applicants accepted	91
% acceptees attending	56
Average GMAT	542
Range of GMAT	460–590
Average GPA	3.21
TOEFL required of international students	Yes
Minimum TOEFL (paper/computer)	550/213
Application fee	$40
International application fee	$40
Regular application deadline	6/1
Regular notification	6/20
Early decision program?	No
Deferment available	Yes
Transfer students accepted	Yes
Transfer application policy: Transfer credits from AACSB-accredited institutions accepted on case-by-case basis.	
Non-fall admissions	Yes
Need-blind admissions	Yes

JACKSONVILLE STATE UNIVERSITY
COLLEGE OF COMMERCE AND BUSINESS ADMINISTRATION

GENERAL INFORMATION
Type of school — Public

SURVEY SAYS...
Good peer network

STUDENTS
Enrollment of parent institution	9,100
Enrollment of MBA Program	70
% male/female	45/55
% out-of-state	10
% part-time	70
% minorities	10
% international	15
Average age at entry	28
Average years work experience at entry	3

ACADEMICS
Academic Experience Rating	75
Student/faculty ratio	15:1
Profs interesting rating	92
Profs accessible rating	84
% female faculty	33

Academics

The blend of "affordable tuition" and an "excellent location" makes Jacksonville State University a good pick for penny-wise professionals in Northern Alabama. Despite the low cost, this public school maintains a high academic standard. JSU professors "have a wealth of experience" and they often use "real-world examples in order to show us how to apply the concepts being taught." A current student adds, "All graduate professors I have dealt with are published authors in reveered business journals." Classes are challenging, and professors are "tough, but fair. They understand what's going and realize that every student has a tough road ahead of them." At the same time, the atmosphere is participatory and collaborative, not cut-throat. At JSU, professors "see you as a well-prepared professional" and not with just a "small number of students per class," you feel that "your opinion counts in the classroom." A student adds, "I have had a great experience as an international student at JSU. The way instructors treat us inside and outside of class is terrific."

Jacksonville State University's MBA program is designed to cover business fundamentals, while also addressing the international business environment and changing business technologies. The curriculum—which can be completed through a mix of online and campus courses—consists of 24 credit hours of foundation coursework, plus 30 credit hours of graduate business coursework. Students appreciate the ease and convenience of online courses, which allow busy professionals to complete classes as their schedule permits. A current student shares, "I have never had any technical difficulties, and if it weren't for distance learning courses, it would take me longer to graduate." On the flip side, some students feel the in-person education at JSU is superior. A student shares, "I prefer the traditional class because I get more out of the lecture and it is cheaper. There is interaction among the class and professor that cannot be imitated by online classes." For those who aren't working fulltime, JSU also offers graduate assistantship programs "to help pay for school."

Known to many as the "friendliest campus in the south," graduate students report a positive experience with the JSU administration and staff. In fact, the "Business school and all of its staff knows who you are and where you are coming from; it is like a big family where you gather knowledge and meet friends." When a problem arises, "The school's administration is always able and willing to take care of any needs you may have." A student shares, "My advisor and dean are as good as they get and are available for comment and discussion conveniently. They are very respected throughout the university and community."

ADMISSIONS CONTACT: DR. JEAN PUGLIESE, ASSOCIATE DEAN
ADDRESS: 700 PELHAM ROAD N JACKSONVILLE, AL 36265
PHONE: 256-782-5329 • FAX: 256-782-5321
E-MAIL: PUGLIESE@JSU.EDU • WEBSITE: WWW.JSU.EDU

Career and Placement

JSU Career Placement Services serves the undergraduate and graduate community at the university, offering online job boards, campus career fairs, resume critiques, mock interviews, and career workshops. Students may also sign up for email notification of new job opportunities, as well as the option of having their resume automatically forwarded to employers seeking someone with their skill set. Services are principally targeted at graduating seniors from the undergraduate college, though graduate students and alumni are also invited to use the center. The Career Placement Services center also assists with internship placements and coordinates on-campus recruiting efforts with regional employers.

Student Life and Environment

There is a diverse community at JSU. Within the MBA program, "The age of the students varies greatly from fresh undergraduates to 40+, married professionals. Also, the ethnic and gender profiles are diverse with many students from other countries along with high percentages of females and African Americans." On the whole, students are "pleasant, outgoing, and friendly," and tend to "share a largely conservative opinion." However, as JSU is predominantly a "commuter school," for the great majority of MBA candidates, "life at school is strictly business." While "there are lots of activities for students to get involved with during the week," they admit that, "Most MBA students are too busy with course work and family to get involved." Come Friday, "very few students are actually on campus during the weekend unless there is a football game of merit. Even then, most students are elsewhere and only locals and local alumni are present."

While there isn't much of a social life at JSU's business school, it is still a "great environment for students." JSU is located on a "beautiful campus that is safe, friendly, and very accessible." The business school is "clean and maintained," though "newer facilities would be very welcomed." A student explains, "The business building was built about 1969 and has had few modifications, although new technologies and computers are readily available."

Admissions

Students must apply to the MBA program through a two-step process. First, students must meet acceptance criteria to the College of Graduate Studies; then they must meet admissions requirements for the business school. The business school measures applicants based on an admissions score, calculated with a prospective student's GPA and GMAT scores. A minimum 400 is required on the GMAT. Therefore, a slightly lower undergraduate GPA may be offset by higher GMAT scores, and vice versa. All forms required for the application are available on the school's website.

FINANCIAL FACTS
Annual tuition (in-state/out-of-state)	$4,500/$9,000
Cost of books	$2,000
Room & board (on/off-campus)	$3,000/$10,000
Average award package	$18,000
Average grant	$1,000

ADMISSIONS
Admissions Selectivity Rating	63
# of applications received	37
% applicants accepted	89
% acceptees attending	33
Average GMAT	508
Range of GMAT	420–610
Average GPA	3.18
TOEFL required of international students	Yes
Minimum TOEFL (paper/computer)	500/173
Application fee	$30
International application fee	$30
Early decision program?	No
Deferment available	No
Transfer students accepted	Yes
Transfer application policy: 6 hours. of approved courses with grade of A or B.	
Non-fall admissions	Yes
Need-blind admissions	Yes

JOHN CARROLL UNIVERSITY
THE BOLER SCHOOL OF BUSINESS

GENERAL INFORMATION
Type of school | Private
Affiliation | Roman Catholic/Jesuit
Academic calendar | Semester

SURVEY SAYS...
Good peer network
Solid preparation in:
Marketing
General management

STUDENTS
Enrollment of parent
  institution | 3,714
Enrollment of MBA Program | 197
% male/female | 67/33
% out-of-state | 25
% part-time | 63
% minorities | 4
% international | 1
Average age at entry | 26
Average years work experience
  at entry | 3

ACADEMICS
Academic Experience Rating | 70
Student/faculty ratio | 15:1
Profs interesting rating | 80
Profs accessible rating | 78
% female faculty | 25
% minority faculty | 12

Joint Degrees
Communications Management, 33
credits (2–3 years); Nonprofit
Adminstration, 36 credits (2–3
years.)

Academics

The Boler School of Business at John Carroll University features programs "designed for students who want to move into positions of leadership in organizations and want an in-depth knowledge of business and leadership skills that will help them achieve their goals." Many students note, "JCU does seem to cater towards accounting students more than any other area." However, others add: "Although accountancy is an important program, it is by no means the only strong concentration in the MBA. Many classes build off of accounting, as having to deal with budgets is typically found in all types of jobs, not just accounting." All in all, praise is widespread, particularly when it comes to the "erudite" and "dedicated" professors. Strangely enough, students at Boler tend to be fonder of the adjunct faculty than the tenured professors. As one student explains, "Professors are top-notch, and many are adjunct who are currently in the business world and can bring current situations and trends to the table, whereas some tenured faculty have been out of the business world (or never in it to start with) for a while and may not be as current with today's business experience as students would like." That said, despite this "unique opportunity to learn real applications," some find that "part-time professors tend not to invest as much into the development of their students."

Another thing students appreciate at Boler is the program's willingness to work around their schedules. The school states that "Our program is flexible for students who are working full-time and may want to take one class in some semesters, two classes in some semesters or may need to take a semester off from classes based on work or family demands. At the same time, our program can be completed on a full-time basis for those students who are taking a break from work." Part of this involves allowing undergraduate students who majored in business to take three courses per term in order to graduate in one year. Many JCU accounting undergrads proceed directly to Boler's accountancy program, which in turn accounts for why so many undergrad alumni are current grad students. "I went here as an undergrad and the fifth-year program was hard to pass up," one student says. Some wouldn't mind seeing a "little more in the way of resources for women," "more selection offered for electives," and "improving" financial aid.

Career and Placement

The search for a job starts at home with Boler students—literally. "The greatest strength of John Carroll is its dedicated professors and great location within the Cleveland area," one student explains. "Many companies like to recruit at John Carroll due to the abundance of great candidates." Strong alumni ties are bolstered by a career center that schedules interviews, organizes job fairs that draw a substantial number of companies to campus, offers help with resumes, and provides "career coaches" that aid students in "making sense of their own career path." "Our graduates get jobs," one student says. "Each year over 90 percent of our Boler School of Business graduates receive job offers in their chosen field of interest or have been accepted into graduate school." 'Nuff said.

ADMISSIONS CONTACT: SUZANNE KRUPA, ASSISTANT TO THE DEAN DATA AND FINANCIAL MGMT.
ADDRESS: 20700 NORTH PARK BOULEVARD, UNIVERSITY HEIGHTS, OH 44118-4581
PHONE: 216-397-4524 • FAX: 216-397-1833
E-MAIL: SMKRUPA@JCU.EDU • WEBSITE: WWW.JCU.EDU/BOLER/GRADS

FINANCIAL FACTS

Annual tuition	$14,562
Cost of books	$1,200
% of students receiving aid	53
% of first-year students receiving aid	38
% of students receiving loans	47
% of students receiving grants	9
Average award package	$14,864
Average grant	$2,833
Average student loan debt	$9,434

ADMISSIONS

Admissions Selectivity Rating	67
# of applications received	55
% applicants accepted	91
% acceptees attending	67
Average GMAT	527
Range of GMAT	490–570
Average GPA	3.21
TOEFL required of international students	Yes
Minimum TOEFL (paper/computer)	550/215
Application fee	$25
International application fee	$35
Early decision program?	No
Deferment available	Yes
Maximum length of deferment	1 year
Transfer students accepted	Yes
Transfer application policy: Applicants from members of the Network of MBA Programs at Jesuit Universities and Colleges, will have all MBA credits transferred. Otherwise, applicantions are reviewed on a case-by-case basis.	
Non-fall admissions	Yes
Need-blind admissions	Yes

Student Life and Environment

While most might love to say "Hello, Cleveland!" every night, the truth of the matter is that "The MBA program is mostly comprised of part-time students who are not interested in joining clubs or becoming involved in on-campus activities." Or, to take the word of a more blunt student, "I want to get my studies completed and move on. No interest in reliving undergraduate." Though it could be a question of the chicken-and-the-egg in terms of whether the large percentage of commuters affects how vibrant the social life is, many here bemoan the lack of student life while acknowledging that they would be too busy to partake if there were any. That said, most happily find themselves in classes surrounded by "very articulate, intelligent, friendly, and interesting" students. "The people that I have met are very down to earth, classy individuals," one student explains. "They are very intelligent, and have a desire to be there working. There is a wide variety of races, religions, as well as married and single people. Overall, the classmates I have had are ones I can resonate with." "Most are right out of undergrad so not as experienced, but yet still are able to contribute to discussions based upon past work or internship experience." The atmosphere is "competitive without being overly intense." Ultimately, while you may only "say hi when passing each other," when the chips are down and the stress-levels high, students "support each other."

Admissions

In JCU's own words, the MBA program is "open to individuals who have earned a bachelor's degree from an accredited university and who show high promise of success in graduate business study." Applicants to the program should submit official transcripts from all or any colleges attended, GMAT scores, one letter of recommendation, a resume, and need to complete both an application form (available on the school's website) and an essay entitled "Graduate Business Education: Enabling Me to Achieve My Personal Goals and Become a Leader." International students must also provide TOEFL scores, appropriate financial documentation, and, when applicable, an English translation of all documents submitted in a language other than English. The program also has a rolling enrollment, meaning that you can enter at the beginning of the spring, summer, or fall semesters.

KENNESAW STATE UNIVERSITY
MICHAEL J. COLES COLLEGE OF BUSINESS

GENERAL INFORMATION
Type of school   Public
Academic calendar   Semester

SURVEY SAYS...
Cutting-edge classes

STUDENTS
Enrollment of parent institution	22,392
Enrollment of MBA Program	766
% part-time	100
Average age at entry	33
Average years work experience at entry	9

ACADEMICS
Academic Experience Rating	**85**
Student/faculty ratio	8:1
Profs interesting rating	89
Profs accessible rating	83
% female faculty	35
% minority faculty	20

Prominent Alumni
Gregory Simone, President and Chief Executive Officer of WellStar Health Systems,Inc.; Wiliam Hayes, Chief Executive Officer of Northside Hospital-Cherokee; Lawrence Wallace, principal accountant at PricewaterhouseCoopers; Kerstin Valdes, Vice President and Chief Internal auditor at Earthlink; Carl Johnson, Principal Accountant at Coca-Cola company.

Academics

Great teaching is a trademark of the Coles College of Business, which offers flexible degree programs for working professionals in a friendly, student-oriented atmosphere. The school's talented professors are "supportive and enthusiastic to teach, and show an amazing sense of sympathy to their students. They are also very knowledgeable in their fields and are prepared to teach above and beyond what is required." Academics have a practical focus, and professors make a point of incorporating their professional experience into classroom discussions. In fact, "most of the professors are practicing professionals or have had many years of experience in their fields. The research and articles written by these professors is impressive." A current student writes, "Many of the classes have directly overlapped with functions performed in my current role at work and have enabled me to immediately add value to my company."

Kennesaw offers an MAcc degree and several MBA options, of which the most popular is the Coles MBA. This flexible, part-time degree is offered at the school's Kennesaw campus, at Cobb Galleria, and in Dalton, as well as online. Designed for working adults, the Coles MBA offers courses once a week or on the weekends, as well as "mini-mesters" three times a year. The program can be completed in just 18 months, though this remarkably flexible school allows students up to six years to complete their degree. Students appreciate the "great class scheduling for full-time workers;" however, they also note that class availability isn't consistent. While "all classes are offered at least once a year," "some semesters the elective course offerings are a little thin."

Exhibiting a genuine interest in teaching, "professors are available and genuinely care about the success of their students." Likewise, when it comes to the school's staff and directors, "the administration is very helpful and accessible all the way up to the dean of the business school." In fact, "MBA students are treated like customers of the university" and the administrative staff "arrive[s] at work everyday with the intent to serve the students." In this and other ways, students at Coles are given the respect, support, and service a professional adult would expect from their business school. A current student explains, "The greatest strength of my school is the independent yet supportive atmosphere. Students get to make their own decisions but can receive help in any way they need it."

Career and Placement

Coles is the "largest business school in Georgia," which gives it a commanding presence in the region, as well as an extensive alumni network. In addition, the school works hard to maintain a "connection with the local business community," which helps serve students while they are pursuing their degree and afterwards.

Students in the business school are served by the "great career services team" at KSU's Career Services Center, which offers interview prep, cover letter and resume review, one-on-one counseling, and access to several online job boards. The center also organizes campus career expos and career fairs throughout the year. A current student shares, "I would like to stress how much KSU tries to get employers on campus. They have career fairs in both spring and fall. They even have a separate event just for the accounting firms."

ADMISSIONS CONTACT: DAVID BAUGHER, DIRECTOR OF ADMISSIONS
ADDRESS: 1000 CHASTAIN ROAD, #9109 KENNESAW, GA 30144
PHONE: 770-423-6087 • FAX: 770-423-6141
E-MAIL: KSUGRAD@KENNESAW.EDU • WEBSITE: WWW.COLESMBA.COM

Student Life and Environment

Kennesaw State's campus has a laid-back, collegiate feel, with great facilities and plenty of resources for both undergraduate and graduate students. At the business school and the larger university, "student life around campus during the warmer months is very upbeat and you can find students lounging outside in the warm weather all of the time." A current student adds, "There are innumerable resources for students: the library, computer labs, special tutoring labs, clubs, groups, free extracurricular classes. The campus is secure, beautiful and very student-friendly." For those who live on campus, "housing is awesome and the gym facilities make you want to work out." An added advantage is the surrounding community, which "is very nice and is one of the safest in the country." In addition, "Atlanta is close enough to take advantage of the big city activities but far enough to avoid the big city problems."

Despite the appealing atmosphere at Kennesaw, most graduate students don't get too involved in the school community. A current student explains, "The undergraduate life seems very active from what I can tell, and the graduate students interact a great deal. However, because it is a commuter school, graduate activities are not as well-attended. Additionally, many events take place during the daytime when those who work cannot attend." While it doesn't foster a strong campus atmosphere, the diverse locations and flexible schedule of the graduate business programs attract "students of all ages, with families and without. I believe the youngest I have met was 24 and the oldest around [their] 50s." In addition, "KSU seems to have a very large international student body. I have met students from all over the world, and it seems that nearly 50 percent of my classmates have foreign accents."

Admissions

Admissions to Coles is based on a student's undergraduate performance, standardized test scores, and professional experience. In addition to undergraduate transcripts, GMAT scores, and a resume, students may choose to send letters of recommendation for consideration, though they are not required.

FINANCIAL FACTS
Average student loan debt $20,500

ADMISSIONS

Admissions Selectivity Rating	80
# of applications received	705
% applicants accepted	45
% acceptees attending	86
Average GMAT	585
Range of GMAT	520–720
Average GPA	3.26
TOEFL required of international students	Yes
Minimum TOEFL (paper/computer)	550/213
Application fee	$60
International application fee	$60
Regular application deadline	8/1
Early decision program?	No
Deferment available	Yes
Maximum length of deferment	1 year
Transfer students accepted	Yes
Transfer application policy: Transfer credit from AACSB International accredited universities is possible. Limits and restrictions apply.	
Non-fall admissions	Yes
Need-blind admissions	Yes

KENT STATE UNIVERSITY
THE COLLEGE OF BUSINESS ADMINISTRATION AND GRADUATE SCHOOL OF MANAGEMENT

GENERAL INFORMATION
Type of school	Public
Academic calendar	Semester

SURVEY SAYS...
Solid preparation in:
Accounting
General management

STUDENTS
Enrollment of parent institution	25,127
Enrollment of MBA Program	270
% male/female	51/49
% out-of-state	6
% part-time	60
% minorities	10
% international	16
Average age at entry	25
Average years work experience at entry	1

ACADEMICS
Academic Experience Rating	**70**
Student/faculty ratio	22:1
Profs interesting rating	76
Profs accessible rating	82
% female faculty	23
% minority faculty	9

Joint Degrees
MBA/Master of Science in Nursing (3 years), 63 hours; MBA/Master of Library Science (3 years), 70 hours; MBA/Master of Architecture (3 years), 71 hours; MBA/Master of Arts in Translation, (3 years) 70 hours.

Prominent Alumni
Drew A. McCandless, President & General Manager, Sherwin Williams; Virginia Albanese, CEO, Fedex Custom Critical; John Kapioltas, Chairman, ITT Sheraton Corporation; Michael Capellas, CEO First Data Corporation; John S. Brinzo, Retired CEO and Chairman, Cliffs Natural Resources Inc.

Academics

An affordable and efficient place to get a graduate business degree, students choose Kent State for its flexible class schedules, respected faculty, and "excellent reputation in Northeast Ohio and beyond." Operating at Kent State's main campus, the Stark campus, and at a satellite campus in Lorain, the Graduate School of Management offers full-time and part-time MBA programs, as well as a MA degree in economics and MS degrees in accounting and financial engineering. Throughout the curriculum and through co-curricular activities, Kent State emphasizes teamwork, ethical leadership, creative problem solving, applications of technology, and global perspectives. To support these educational goals, "the professors at Kent have extensive international business experience and a good grasp on what is driving the global marketplace." They are also active professionals, who offer real-world insights in the classroom. A current MBA candidate explains, "I have always admired that my professors worked for 20-plus years in their field before teaching. I appreciate learning from experienced individuals, not just people who learned how to teach." Kent State professors are nonetheless highly dedicated instructors who "have a genuine interest in giving students the tools they need to succeed."

The MBA begins with a set of core courses, which may be waived for students who hold an undergraduate degree in business. After completing the core, students have the opportunity to tailor their education through one of six concentrations in finance, marketing, human resource management, management information systems, international business, or accounting. Some students would like to see "more flexibility in what courses are required as part of the core curriculum." However, on the whole, they say the academic program is well-balanced and effective. A student writes, "It provides a very clear picture of the business world and also challenges students to go deeper into the issues. The combination of general business and specific skills was nearly perfect in my opinion."

Full-time students can complete the MBA coursework in anywhere between 15 months and two years. Professional MBA students usually need about three years to finish their degree, though the school allows up to six. Students warn us, however, that given the school's extensive foundational requirements, "as a non-business undergraduate... there's no way to realistically graduate in two years." For students who choose to pursue an MBA on a part-time basis, students reassure us that "in general, coursework isn't especially rigorous, except for final projects." Keep in mind, however, that the "workload can vary considerably by course and professor," so you may find some semesters are a bit more challenging than other. If you need a little extra help to get by, "most professors are very good, [and] advisors are accessible and helpful."

ADMISSIONS CONTACT: LOUISE DITCHEY, DIRECTOR, MASTER'S PROGRAMS
ADDRESS: P.O. BOX 5190, 475 TERRACE DRIVE KENT, OH 44242-0001
PHONE: 330-672-2282 • FAX: 330-672-7303
E-MAIL: GRADBUS@KENT.EDU • WEBSITE: BUSINESS.KENT.EDU/GRAD

Career and Placement

The Career Services Center and Employment at Kent State offers resume writing and interview coaching, an alumni job hotline, campus interviews, and updated vacancy listings. The center also hosts a number of campus career fairs and recruiting events, which bring over 500 employers to campus annually. Many students, however, come to Kent State because it has a good reputation at their current company, and they hope to use the degree as a springboard towards a better position. These students aren't looking for a new position, per se; however, they do feel Kent State will help them advance in their professional goals. A current student enthuses, "The MBA program has made me feel like I am able to move up a couple levels and eventually take that coveted top spot at CEO."

Student Life and Environment

Through the graduate school as well as the larger university, there are "many opportunities to be involved in extracurricular activities" at Kent State. Clubs and organizations targeted at graduate business students include the Graduate Management Association, a social and career development group, as well as a number of organizations offered through the larger university, such as Graduate Student Senate. With an enrollment of just 100 students in the full-time program, students "know each other well and work together. We take part in associations and share experiences." On the flip side, many students in the Professional MBA "come for class and leave right away afterward;" not surprisingly, they feel they "don't have much time for life at school," as work, home life, and homework keep them sufficiently busy. While they may not get together outside of class, the mix of older and younger students creates an excellent academic atmosphere. A student explains, "Kent benefits greatly from the many outstanding businesses that encourage employees to pursue an MBA. This real-world experience is a nice complement to the younger students' enthusiasm and technological savvy."

Admissions

There is no stated minimum GPA or GMAT score to be accepted to Kent State's MBA program. However, in recent years, the mean undergraduate GPA for students in the full-time program was 3.2–3.4, and the mean GPA for part-time Professional MBA students was 3.0–3.1. Roughly 80 percent of applicants are accepted to the programs each year.

FINANCIAL FACTS

Annual tuition (in-state/ out-of-state)	$9,282/$16,542
Cost of books	$1,200
Room & board (on/off-campus)	$9,580/$8,750
% of students receiving aid	31
% of first-year students receiving aid	13
Average award package	$15,982

ADMISSIONS

Admissions Selectivity Rating	71
# of applications received	117
% applicants accepted	98
% acceptees attending	69
Average GMAT	551
Range of GMAT	480–610
Average GPA	3.26
TOEFL required of international students	Yes
Minimum TOEFL (paper/computer)	550/213
Application fee	$30
International application fee	$60
Regular application deadline	4/1
Regular notification	4/15
Early decision program?	No
Deferment available	Yes
Maximum length of deferment	1 year
Transfer students accepted	Yes
Transfer application policy: AASCB accredited program; less than 6 years old by the time Kent degree is conferred; 12 credit hours maximum; approved by graduate committee and dean.	
Non-fall admissions	Yes
Need-blind admissions	Yes

EMPLOYMENT PROFILE

Career Rating	70	Grads Employed by Function	%	Avg. Salary
Average base starting salary	$52,208	Marketing	33	$63,750
		Finance	33	$51,250
		HR	16	$37,500
		MIS	16	$47,500

Top 5 Employers Hiring Grads
Ernst and Young (1), Goodyear Tire and Rubber (2), JM Smucker Company (1), American Medical Response (1), Key Bank (1)

LAMAR UNIVERSITY
COLLEGE OF BUSINESS

GENERAL INFORMATION
Type of school	Public
Academic calendar	Semester

SURVEY SAYS...
Solid preparation in:
General management
Teamwork
Communication/interpersonal skills
Presentation skills

STUDENTS
Enrollment of parent institution	13,992
Enrollment of MBA Program	121
% male/female	56/44
% part-time	50
% minorities	11
% international	11
Average age at entry	29

ACADEMICS
Academic Experience Rating	**72**
Student/faculty ratio	3:1
Profs interesting rating	81
Profs accessible rating	82
% female faculty	27
% minority faculty	36

Joint Degrees
MSN in Administration, 37 hours

Academics

"They are constantly trying to improve and innovate the program" at Lamar University, where students love being part of an "an outstanding university that is growing almost exponentially." Not that it needs much in the way of improvement; even as it currently stands, Lamar is seen by its students as "a great school with well-educated professors and a good learning environment." A student body drawn largely from Beaumont and the surrounding area chooses the Lamar MBA for its convenience, its low cost, its reputation, and its unwillingness to settle for "good enough."

Lamar offers a Cohort MBA, a full-time evening program that includes several experiential learning opportunities. The program is intense: Classes meet four nights a week, and the curriculum goes pretty much nonstop for 16 months, but those who tough it out are rewarded with an MBA earned in a relatively short time for relatively little money. Cohort MBA participants must have earned an undergraduate degree in business. The school also offers a traditional MBA, which also meets in the evenings, but it allows for part-time attendance. The traditional MBA program is open to all college graduates; those who lack the requisite academic business background must complete a series of leveling courses before commencing the MBA proper.

Students report that the programs have more of a cooperative than competitive feel. They appreciate the "relaxed classroom settings" and "the ability to meet with faculty and students without pressure and [to discuss] issues related to business." "Smaller classes" make it "easy to obtain one-on-one time with a professor" and also ensure that students aren't just a number or name on a list to administrators. In fact, "every student is required to be advised, which means the people in MBA office know who you are and what you are doing when you walk into the office." "The administration for the MBA program is well-organized."

Lamar professors "keep current with the latest business developments and they constantly work on outside research projects. They often present papers at conferences and work to expand their professional knowledge base. We have several professors that work as marketers or business owners so they bring their practical experience to class." The faculty consists of a "small core group of professors," which "builds relationships [between students and teachers] throughout the years."

Career and Placement

The Career and Testing Center at Lamar provides services for all undergraduates, graduate students, and, alumni of the university. Services include counseling, workshops, online job database access, and recruitment events. The majority of Lamar MBAs work full time while attending the program. Many do not plan to leave their employers during or after the program.

Employers who most frequently hire graduates include: Ernst and Young, Melton and Melton, Merrill Lynch, Smith Barney, JP Morgan Chase, Medical Center of Southeast Texas, Wells Fargo, and Verizon.

ADMISSIONS CONTACT: DEBBY PIPER, GRADUATE ADMISSIONS OFFICE
ADDRESS: P. O. BOX L0078 BEAUMONT, TX 77710
PHONE: 409-880-8356 • FAX: 409-880-8414
E-MAIL: GRADMISSIONS@LAMAR.EDU • WEBSITE: MBA.LAMAR.EDU

FINANCIAL FACTS

Annual tuition (in-state/ out-of-state)	$5,220/$12,000
Fees	$1,500
Cost of books	$1,410
Room & board (on/off-campus)	$6,290/$7,092
% of students receiving aid	74
% of first-year students receiving aid	84
% of students receiving loans	19
% of students receiving grants	49
Average award package	$2,670
Average grant	$1,748
Average student loan debt	$876

ADMISSIONS

Admissions Selectivity Rating	63
# of applications received	70
% applicants accepted	81
% acceptees attending	56
Average GMAT	473
Range of GMAT	420–510
Average GPA	3.17
TOEFL required of international students	Yes
Minimum TOEFL (paper/computer)	525/200
Application fee	$25
International application fee	$75
Regular application deadline	7/1
Early decision program?	No
Deferment available	Yes
Maximum length of deferment	1 year
Transfer students accepted	Yes
Transfer application policy: Accept 6 hours from another AACSB MBA program	
Non-fall admissions	Yes
Need-blind admissions	Yes

Student Life and Environment

"Lamar has traditionally been a commuter [school]," and while "that is changing," for the most part it's still the case that "students come to class and go home afterwards even when activities are planned." There are some "active on-campus organizations" for MBAs, but they "tend to be geared towards those living on-campus, which mainly consist of international students and those receiving full scholarships."

Lamar's business facility is "dated, and some classrooms have equipment and maps that are falling apart," which understandably rankles some. Students also complain that "more business-specific applications could be available on our college's computers, [as well as] more labs with larger work stations to accommodate groups. Much of the MBA program is centered around group work, and it is difficult to cram into a narrow row of computers set up traditional classroom-style to spread out and collaborate."

Lamar's "friendly, yet competitive" MBAs mostly "work full time, and they bring plenty of real-world experience to the class." The program creates "quite a diverse setting with many international students as well as local commuters. Lamar is very well-rounded and diverse for its size."

Admissions

Lamar University requires all applicants to provide GMAT scores, undergraduate transcripts, essays, and TOEFL scores (for students whose native language is not English). An interview, letters of recommendation, personal statement, resume, and evidence of computer experience are all recommended but not required; all are taken into account in rendering an admissions decision. Applicants must earn a score of at least 950 under the formula (200 multiplied by GPA plus GMAT score) or a score of 1000 under the formula (200 multiplied by GPA for final 60 semester hours of undergraduate work plus GMAT score). In both cases, a minimum GMAT score of 450 is required for unconditional admission; students with scores between 400 and 450 qualify for conditional admission. International applicants must provide proof of financial support.

EMPLOYMENT PROFILE

Career Rating	71	Grads Employed by Function	%	Avg. Salary
		Finance	29	$66,000

LONG ISLAND UNIVERSITY—C.W. POST CAMPUS
COLLEGE OF MANAGEMENT

GENERAL INFORMATION
Type of school	Private
Academic calendar	Trimester

SURVEY SAYS...
Students love Brookville, NY
Cutting-edge classes
Solid preparation in:
General management
Doing business in a global economy

STUDENTS
Enrollment of parent institution	8,770
Enrollment of MBA Program	269
% male/female	59/41
% out-of-state	2
% part-time	53
% minorities	15
% international	56
Average age at entry	27
Average years work experience at entry	6

ACADEMICS
Academic Experience Rating	**71**
Student/faculty ratio	15:1
Profs interesting rating	76
Profs accessible rating	68
% female faculty	23
% minority faculty	23

Joint Degrees
Dual JD/MBA JD, 3 years; MBA, 1.5 years; BS/MBA: BS, 4 years, MBA 1 year

Academics

Long Island University's C.W. Post Campus boasts "one of the top business programs on Long Island." It offers two paths to an MBA to its mostly part-time student population. In the Campus MBA program, students take "flexible night classes" Monday through Thursday. As a general rule, 48 credit hours are required to graduate. Depending on your undergraduate coursework, though, you can complete the program in as few as 36 hours. The other option is the Saturday MBA program, which features intensive, all-day classes and takes between 15 and 23 months to complete, again depending on your undergraduate work. Students in the Campus MBA program may supplement their curricula with Saturday classes. C.W. Post's advanced certificate program is also worth noting. It requires four additional electives and allows students to acquire further expertise in six areas including accounting and taxation, finance, and international business.

One of the best things about C.W. Post is its class sizes. "Classes are not too large, which makes for a better learning environment," explains one student. For the most part, "support from the advisors and faculty is great" as well. Professors are "responsible, nice, and professional." They are "knowledgeable in their respective fields" and "willing to help students" outside of class.

One student describes the administration as "very helpful." Another calls it "terrible." Also, gripes about the narrow range of elective courses are a hardy perennial here. "We have to take many core courses to graduate," says one student.

Career and Placement

C.W. Post affords its students a variety of placement services. The Office of Professional Experience and Career Planning offers self-assessment diagnostics, career counseling, resume and job-search advisement, mock interviews, job fairs, recruiting events, and online databases. Also, a broad graduate assistantship program provides advanced research opportunities. However, some students here report that career resources are "nonexistent." "Get better companies to job fairs," demands one student. "I don't see that many events to help facilitate job placement for C.W. Post graduates," observes another.

ADMISSIONS CONTACT: CAROL ZERAH, DIRECTOR OF GRADUATE AND INTERNATIONAL ADMISSIONS
ADDRESS: 720 NORTHERN BOULEVARD BROOKVILLE, NY 11548
PHONE: (516) 299-3952 • FAX: (516) 299-2418
E-MAIL: CAROL.ZERAH@LIU.EDU • WEBSITE: WWW.LIU.EDU/BUSINESS

Student Life and Environment

The MBA students at C.W. Post describe themselves as "friendly, smart, active," and "interesting." Virtually everyone here is a part-timer, attending classes in the evenings and on Saturdays. That's the nature of the program. Many students choose C.W. Post because it's close to home. There's also a tremendous population of international students. "In recent years, C.W. Post has focused on recruiting students from overseas and it has made the learning experience more global." Students vary quite a bit in their levels of experience. There are older types with fat resumes and others who "have no business experience and cannot bring real-life examples to the class discussions."

C.W. Post is "a beautiful school" spread out across a few hundred acres. Green, rolling lawns and heavily wooded areas proliferate the area. The location of the campus on the north shore of Long Island is definitely a plus. It's not far from some fabulous beaches and, at the same time, relatively "close to New York City." Parking is about the only problem. Students gripe, "The parking situation needs to improve drastically."

Socially, this is a commuter school. Beyond the MBA association and the occasional function during business hours, there are few clubs or activities. With work and families, and with the lights of Manhattan beckoning, most students "have busy lives."

Admissions

Your grades and your GMAT scores don't have to be terrifically high to get admitted to C.W. Post. Prerequisites for admission include competence in business communications, mathematics, and computers, as demonstrated through undergraduate work, successful completion of a related workshop, or successful completion of a waiver exam. In addition to transcripts and a GMAT score, you need to submit two letters of recommendation and a resume. There's also an essay. If your first language isn't English, you need to submit official results for the TOEFL. The minimum score requirement is 550 on the paper-based test, or 215 on the computer-based test, or 79 on the Internet-based test. Students who completed undergraduate degrees from institutions that teach primarily in English don't have to submit TOEFL scores.

FINANCIAL FACTS

Annual tuition	$15,876
Fees	$1,224
Cost of books	$1,500
Room & board (on/off-campus)	$10,520/$12,000
Average grant	$3,000

ADMISSIONS

Admissions Selectivity Rating	**64**
# of applications received	162
% applicants accepted	80
% acceptees attending	46
Average GMAT	465
Range of GMAT	408–523
Average GPA	3.13
TOEFL required of international students	Yes
Minimum TOEFL (paper/computer)	550/215
Application fee	$30
International application fee	$30
Regular application deadline	8/15
Regular notification	8/15
Early decision program?	No
Deferment available	Yes
Maximum length of deferment	1 year
Transfer students accepted	Yes
Transfer application policy: Maximum of 6 credits within the last five years, grades of B or better. AACSB accredited School.	
Non-fall admissions	Yes
Need-blind admissions	Yes

LOUISIANA STATE UNIVERSITY
E. J. OURSO COLLEGE OF BUSINESS

GENERAL INFORMATION

Type of school	Public
Academic calendar	Aug–Aug

SURVEY SAYS...
Friendly students
Good social scene
Solid preparation in:
Teamwork

STUDENTS

Enrollment of parent institution	28,194
Enrollment of MBA Program	379
% male/female	65/35
% out-of-state	5
% part-time	62
% minorities	5
% international	13
Average age at entry	23
Average years work experience at entry	2

ACADEMICS

Academic Experience Rating	**80**
Student/faculty ratio	1:1
Profs interesting rating	76
Profs accessible rating	83
% female faculty	27
% minority faculty	3

Joint Degrees
Dual JD/MBA (Juris Doctorate/Master of Business Administration (also awards a Bachelor of Science in Civil Law), four years.

Prominent Alumni
Harry Hawks, Executive VP and CFO of Ki2 Inc.; D. Martin Phillips, Sr. Managing Director of EnCap Investments,LLC; Ross Centanni, Chairman, President & CEO, Gardner Denver, Inc.; John H. Boydstun, President, Capital One's Banking Segment.

Academics

Looking for an MBA that offers "the perfect combination of academics, athletics, and the south?" Well, look no further than the LSU Flores MBA, part of the E. J. Ourso College of Business at Louisiana State University, which offers a "respected academic program along with very favorable financial aid," not to mention "the camaraderie of the students," "the beautiful campus," and "excellent" football. Many here note the "reasonable tuition" and flexible programs as the driving force behind their decision to enroll. "My undergraduate degree was in engineering, and LSU had the only MBA program in the state that did not require me to take undergraduate business courses before starting the program," a student says. In fact, according to the school, "49 percent" of their students "hold non-business undergraduate degrees, including education, engineering, journalism, geography, political science, criminal justice, kinesiology, and history," to name a few. This results in a student body with an impressive—and varied—set of undergraduate backgrounds. Another boon of being in the LSU Flores MBA Program is the "real work experience" the program offers both in the classroom and around campus. "On Fridays, we have speakers come in from all over the country, which really lends a practical, applicable side to the LSU MBA," one student explains. Another adds, "The internal auditing program, without a doubt, is one of the highlights of the MBA program." When it comes to professors, however, feelings are a little mixed. "Many teachers may be well-qualified academically," one student notes, "but they are completely unable to teach, or relay information to the students effectively." Another student agrees, adding, "The level of the courses is roughly that of an undergraduate degree. The professors are hit and miss. Some teach for the love of it, and it shows. Some are there only for the paycheck." That said, others have been "very impressed with the professors" who "go out of their way to get to know each student and are always available for help when you need it." Another student admits: "The courses were challenging, but not impossible. As with most things, to succeed one must put forth effort." Students also tell us that the LSU Flores MBA Program is keen on expanding. In the past few years, the MBA office has made numerous hires and expanded its services, especially in corporate relations and recruiting. These advances are making contacting corporate recruiters and finding more specialized professions easier than ever." Additionally, the "electives offerings are improving." Good news for whichever side of the spectrum of opinion you might fall on. Less divisive are the views on the school's "wonderful" and "very accessible" administration. "They are constantly assessing the curriculum to ensure that our students have the greatest preparation upon graduation," one student says. Change is indeed on its way to the LSU Flores MBA Program. Many students point out that "the school is in the midst of a multimillion dollar building campaign that will greatly improve its facilities," which they hope will also improve "the quality of the programs overall" and "the standards of new students." ("Request work experience, higher GMAT, and more extracurricular work in general," a die-hard student suggests.) Indeed, ground was broken for the college's new home—the Business Education Complex—in spring 2010. The anticipated completion date for this 156,000 square-foot facility is spring 2012. Enthusiasm for the construction runs high. "I have seen the approved plans for the new building, and it will be an incredible boost to the reputation of the Flores MBA and the icing on the cake for our recent *Wall Street Journal* ranking!" a student enthuses. As part of its globalization efforts, the program's MBAs continue to travel to China to learn business practices in emerging markets. In spring 2010, the LSU Flores MBA Program traveled to Brazil, and a trip_ to India is being planned for 2011.

Career and Placement

Options abound for jobseekers in the Flores MBA Program thanks to a multi-faceted career services department and strong alumni connections. An abundance of events, from alum-

ADMISSIONS CONTACT: DANA C. HART, ASSISTANT DIRECTOR OF ENROLLMENT & STUDENT SERVICES
ADDRESS: E. J. OURSO COLLEGE OF BUSINESS, 3176 PATRICK F. TAYLOR HALL BATON ROUGE, LA 70803
PHONE: 225-578-8867 • FAX: 225-578-2421 • E-MAIL: BUSMBA@LSU.EDU • WEBSITE: MBA.LSU.EDU

ni receptions to career expos to speaking engagements, are available to MBA students not only through the Flores Program, but the E. J. Ourso College of Business itself. Many find that the "Distinguished Speaker Series" is particularly helpful because "we have business leaders, often LSU MBA Alumni, speak to our students about current industry trends and offer career advice as well as networking!" Others opine that the career center offers "good" recruitment and job placement for those "who want to stay in Louisiana," and some note that "though vastly improving already, it could be better." Lucky for them, help is on the way. "The MBA office here at LSU now has staff that are responsible solely for placing us in great jobs, and they are already helping many of us find the jobs that are just right," one student explains. Another adds, "My graduate assistantship is awesome and there couldn't be better or more helpful alumni as far as networking is concerned."

Student Life and Environment

The "culturally rich state" of Louisiana has plenty to offer to students, but it's "being on the campus of a major university" that "affords students the great opportunities that come with a university such as performing arts and sports." And have we mentioned LSU's "national championship football team?" (Despite being in graduate school, "students still care more about football than education," a student notes.) Students here find themselves among a "diverse group" set in a "productive atmosphere of graduate students who are willing and able to learn and at the same time bring unique and realistic views to the classroom." Many note that those with a cut-throat attitude might do well to look elsewhere. "The school day does not end at the end of class," one student explains. "Students regularly get together to work on school projects, study, or even to socialize. The atmosphere is a close community with students who are willing to help each other out." Additionally, many here appreciate what the school does to get the social ball rolling. "Our MBA Association holds monthly socials where we can all meet outside of class and just hang out. For instance, our social this month is bowling. We will all get together at the bowling alley and talk about things other than school. This friendship spills over into our academic life and our careers." All in all, students find that it's "very easy to make friends here" and "life is never dull" in Baton Rouge. That said, LSU's reputation as a party school can carry over into graduate classes. Some find Flores students to be "young" and "immature." "They just party and don't work hard," one student says. Ultimately, it seems you can find what you're looking for here, whether raucous or relaxed, there's something for everyone. "As a married student, I would say that the MBA program is very conducive to married life, and although I spend many hours studying, I still feel like I have a good school/life balance."

Admissions

In considering applicants, the LSU Flores MBA Program requires prospective students to submit two sets of undergraduate transcripts (with a minimum GPA of 3.0), GMAT scores (the most recent Class had an average GMAT score of 640), record of previous work experience (not required, but considered "desirable"), a one-page resume, one letter of recommendation (this is optional, but recommended), and, in the case of international students, a financial statement and TOEFL scores (minimum score: 550 written, 213 computer-based, or 79 Internet-based).

FINANCIAL FACTS

Annual tuition	$3,215
Fees (in-state/ out-of-state)	$4,822/$13,536
Cost of books	$1,500
Room & board (on/off-campus)	$5,166/$6,011
% of students receiving aid	60
% of students receiving loans	36
% of students receiving grants	25
Average award package	$18,336
Average grant	$16,139

ADMISSIONS

Admissions Selectivity Rating	90
# of applications received	152
% applicants accepted	68
% acceptees attending	71
Average GMAT	637
Range of GMAT	610–660
Average GPA	3.36
TOEFL required of international students	Yes
Minimum TOEFL (paper/computer)	550/213
Application fee	$25
International application fee	$25
Application Deadline/Notification	
Round 1:	12/4 / 12/18
Round 2:	2/5 / 2/19
Round 3:	4/2 / 4/16
Early decision program?	No
Deferment available	Yes
Maximum length of deferment	1 year
Transfer students accepted	Yes
Transfer application policy: Applicants must have attended an AACSB accredited school and meet the entrance requirements for the Flores MBA Program. Transfer credit may be approved on an individual basis.	
Non-fall admissions	No
Need-blind admissions	Yes

EMPLOYMENT PROFILE

Career Rating	87	Grads Employed by Function	% Avg. Salary
Percent employed at graduation	57	Consulting	16 $64,407
Percent employed 3 months after graduation	90	Management	7 $58,000
		Finance	31 $55,272
Average base starting salary	$59,120	MIS	16 $63,400
Primary Source of Full-time Job Acceptances		Top 5 Employers Hiring Grads	
School-facilitated activities	24 (38%)	Deloitte & Touche (4), Chevron (3), Exxon (3),	
Graduate-facilitated activities	15 (24%)	IBM (2), Capital One (2)	
Unknown	24 (38%)		

LOYOLA MARYMOUNT UNIVERSITY
COLLEGE OF BUSINESS ADMINISTRATION

GENERAL INFORMATION
Type of school   Private
Affiliation   Roman Catholic/Jesuit
Academic calendar   Semester

SURVEY SAYS...
Solid preparation in:
Entrepreneurial studies

STUDENTS
Enrollment of parent institution	9,010
Enrollment of MBA Program	320
% part-time	100
Average age at entry	27
Average years work experience at entry	4

ACADEMICS
Academic Experience Rating	**88**
Student/faculty ratio	3:1
Profs interesting rating	93
Profs accessible rating	88
% female faculty	22
% minority faculty	27

Joint Degrees
Doctor of Jurisprudence/Master of Business Administration (JD/MBA) 4 years; Master of Systems Engineering/Master of Business Administration (SELP/MBA), 4 years

Academics

The part-time MBA program at Loyola Marymount University "is by far the most accommodating program for working professionals in the Los Angeles area," students assert. One argues that "The evening classes, small class size, strong academics, and flexible schedules make LMU an obvious choice" for mid-career business types looking for a boost, as does "the very convenient location for residents on the westside of Los Angeles." A "widely-recognized entrepreneurship program" also draws its fair share of students.

Loyola Marymount is a Jesuit school, meaning the curriculum focuses on "educating the whole person." As one student observes, "All the other MBA schools talked about how much money their graduates made. This school talked about teaching me to live up to Jesuit ideals of philanthropy, loyalty, and justice. It suited my value system." "High ethical and moral standards" infuse all course offerings here. Students tell us that the program also excels in management, finance, and operations. Students praise "everything from the classes to the extracurricular activities to the guest speakers" within the program and tell us, "If someone comes into the program knowing they want to develop their own business, they definitely have all the tools they will need here. They will be able to graduate with a viable business plan in hand."

Students attend LMU's MBA program on a full-time or part-time basis. The former option is especially appealing to LMU business undergraduates, who place out of certain MBA prerequisites and thereby complete their graduate degrees more quickly. All students conclude their study here with a series of integrative experiences, the last of which is the year-long Corporate Management Systems, through which "students are given the opportunity to spend a few weeks abroad making presentations and learning about how business is done in other countries."

Career and Placement

LMU serves two distinct student bodies: a majority of part-timers who already have full-time jobs, and a minority who attend full-time and will be looking for job placement post-MBA. The latter benefit from resume and cover-letter seminars, interview and salary-negotiation workshops, and career counseling. The CSO also offers the CareerLeader assessment tool and access to Vault.com and InterviewStream.com. The office maintains an online bulletin board for job postings.

Students tell us that "the career services department is limited," with some going so far as to say the office "needs a huge overhaul...The career services department offers little beyond what someone in a graduate program should already know when it comes to looking for a new job. Connections with recruiters and alumni should be made more readily available." A few counter: "LMU is working on delivering more to its students. As the program is growing, so are the resources available to the students. The career center is beginning to deliver more for its students, which is where the greatest improvement opportunity existed."

Admissions Contact: Elynar Moreno, MBA Coordinator
Address: One LMU Drive, MS 8387 Los Angeles, CA 90045-2659
Phone: (310) 338-2848 • Fax: (310) 338-2899
E-mail: mbapc@lmu.edu • Website: mba.lmu.edu

Student Life and Environment

The LMU campus is "very accommodating," students report, telling us, "The facilities are top-notch, there are computer facilities and multimedia stations available in every classroom." Students appreciate that "The school is nice and quiet, and still students have a social life outside of school. The school has social events that are free of cost to students." They also note, however, that "It's [largely] a part-time program, so there isn't a whole lot of structure to it besides classes, but the students are very self-organizing, and sociable, so there is no lack of academic support or networking opportunities." The program offers "frequent speakers or events planned for students and/or alumni to attend," including "networking parties to help students get to know each other."

LMU is in "a good location, close to downtown Los Angeles and close to the beach." One student reports: "The school's beauty and location are two of the greatest strengths. It is hard to feel stressed out when you can walk around and see views of the Los Angeles Basin, Pacific Ocean, Marina Del Rey, and Century City skyline. The laid-back atmosphere…is welcoming."

LMU students "are very friendly, very willing to help, and seem to be there to learn and improve their own lives as opposed to wanting to compete and run the world. They are realistic about expectations and prefer an environment where people work together to achieve success as opposed to working against each other." Most are "working professionals with busy schedules" who have "very diverse backgrounds with regards to their careers, origins, and viewpoints."

Admissions

Applicants to the LMU MBA program must provide the admissions office with the following materials: two official copies of transcripts for all post-secondary schoolwork; an official score report for the GMAT; a resumé; two letters of recommendation; and a completed application form. International students must additionally provide an official TOEFL score report (if English is not their first language) and documentation demonstrating the financial means to support themselves while attending the program. Work experience "is not required but will enhance the application," according to the school. Applicants may be admitted for fall or spring semester. Applications are processed on a rolling basis, with admissions decisions typically made within two weeks of delivery of all application materials.

ADMISSIONS	
Admissions Selectivity Rating	**84**
# of applications received	347
% applicants accepted	57
% acceptees attending	54
Average GMAT	607
Range of GMAT	570–640
Average GPA	3.31
TOEFL required of international students	Yes
Minimum TOEFL (paper/computer)	600/250
Application fee	$50
International application fee	$50
Early decision program?	No
Deferment available	Yes
Maximum length of deferment	1 year
Transfer students accepted	Yes
Transfer application policy: Students from other Jesuit MBA Programs may transfer core and electives through the Jesuit Transfer Network. Students who attend an AACSB accredited MBA Program (non-Jesuit) with equivalent course work of B or better may ONLY transfer in 6 units of upper division course credit but may be elgibile for core course waivers.	
Non-fall admissions	Yes
Need-blind admissions	Yes

LOYOLA UNIVERSITY—CHICAGO
GRADUATE SCHOOL OF BUSINESS

GENERAL INFORMATION

Type of school	Private
Affiliation	Roman Catholic/Jesuit
Academic calendar	Quarter

SURVEY SAYS...

Students love Chicago, IL
Cutting-edge classes
Solid preparation in:
Doing business in a global economy

STUDENTS

Average age at entry	27

ACADEMICS

Academic Experience Rating	77
Student/faculty ratio	26:1
Profs interesting rating	84
Profs accessible rating	84
% female faculty	22
% minority faculty	5

Joint Degrees

MBA/JD; 4 years full time; 6 years part time. MBA/MSISM; 2 years full time; 3.5 years part time. MBA/MSIMC; 2 years full time; 3.5 years part time. MBA/MS Nursing; 3 years full time; 5 years part time. MBA/MSHR; 2 years full time; 3.5 years part time. MBA/MSA; 2 years full time; 3.5 years part time. MBA/MSF; 2 years full time; 3.5 years part time.

Prominent Alumni

Robert L. Parkinson, Jr., President and CEO, Baxter International Inc.; Brenda Barnes, President and CEO, Sara Lee Corporation; Michael R. Quinlan, Retired Chairman & CEO, McDonald's Corporation; John B. Menzer, President & CEO, Wal-Mart International; John Rooney, President and CEO, U.S. Cellular.

Academics

A university founded in the Jesuit tradition, "Loyola is a school that is focused on developing the entire individual," and business ethics is a mainstay of the MBA program. While MBA course content resembles other graduate business programs, Loyola distinguishes itself in a number of ways. In particular, "Success is not measured in dollars, but rather [in] how one can contribute to society in a meaningful and productive way." To that end, "Every class incorporates ethics and ethical situations and relates them to real-world business issues." At the same time, the curriculum focuses on practical business, and "is very relevant and applicable." Through coursework, students work in teams, analyze case studies, or work on live projects in cooperation with a partner business or organization. A current student enthuses, "I take advantage of student organizations and outside consulting projects, and often feel that these have more value than my classes." To add an international perspective to the MBA, "The study abroad program is fantastic," offering numerous two-week summer courses overseas. A current student enthuses, "I will be afforded wonderful study abroad opportunities through this program and will be traveling to China, India, and Rome."

Combining expertise with excellence, the majority of Loyola professors are "highly experienced and make the learning experience worthwhile." While there are some "pure academics" on staff, they are outnumbered by current and former business leaders, who bring real-world content to the coursework. In fact, Loyola's adjunct professors "are among the best at bringing a 'real-world' perspective into the classroom." Most importantly, professors are "very enthusiastic about their subject and classes, and they all very much love teaching." As a result, "The classroom experience is dynamic and engaging," and the "thought-provoking course content" inspires discussion and critical thinking. A student enthuses, "I have enjoyed many of my classes so much, I am actually somewhat disappointed when the quarter comes to an end!" At the same time, Loyola is a large school, so it's easier to get lost in the crowds. A current student admits, "It's difficult to have good, thoughtful discussions in classes with 50 people in attendance."

Loyola's "flexible class schedule" is great for part-time students, and "the course load is perfect for a professional who has a full-time job." In addition, the "ability to switch between full-time and part-time status" gives students the opportunity to complete their degree at their own pace. Full-timers, on the other hand, sometimes feel "the course work doesn't seem as challenging as it could be." A school on the move, "The GSB has grown considerably just within the last year," and students admit, "The administration seems a little overwhelmed by the number of students currently enrolled." Fortunately, a student writes, "The school is committed to providing students with an exceptional experience. When there are hurdles to overcome, the administration is quick to identify how things might improve." .

Career and Placement

Loyola's downtown "location in a world class city" brings students within a stone's throw of many reputable employers. This private university maintains a great local reputation, and the focus on practical skills throughout the MBA curriculum helps to prepare students for the workplace. A current student agrees, "In this time of economic crisis, I feel incredibly prepared and optimistic that my MBA degree will make me stand out from the competition."

Loyola University's Career Management Services assists job seekers through resume critiques, career workshops, and advising. They also operate an online recruiting program, which allows students to research employers, post their resumes, and sign up for campus interviews via the web. Despite these services, "The school could do a much better job attracting more quality employers to recruit at Loyola." A current MBA candidate laments, "The school is in a sweet spot for business in the country but doesn't take full advantage of the networking possibilities." On the other hand, "There are students who have found great jobs through Career Management and have received excellent coaching from the staff....It all depends on what a person expects."

Student Life and Environment

Loyola is a large, urban university, which attracts "all different backgrounds, ages, interests, career paths (if working), intelligence levels, and points of life." While some students are too busy to participate in extracurricular activities, others find time to "belong to a number of clubs that meet before class once or twice a month." More informally, there are "plenty of opportunities to mingle after class and on weekends," and students attend "social events at bars or restaurants after class every month." Still, you won't get the social atmosphere you'd find on a residential campus: "Although the social life is improving, the school definitely feels like a commuter school."

"Located in the heart of downtown Chicago," Loyola's well-placed campus is a major benefit of the program. Academic resources are good, and "The library is excellent." "Getting information from any source at the school has been easy." Unfortunately, many business school classrooms lack modern technology and suffer from "a poor layout, not conducive to class discussion." A student adds, "More than 30 percent of assignments are group related, yet less than 5 percent of computers in the library cater toward group work. Options like LCD projectors (or mounted televisions with a monitor input) in group rooms would be greatly appreciated."

Admissions

At Loyola, the academic calendar is divided into quarters. Accordingly, there are four start dates each year, so the school is continuously accepting and enrolling new students. To apply, prospective students must submit an application form, two letters of recommendation, a statement of purpose, a current resume, undergraduate transcripts, and official GMAT test scores.

FINANCIAL FACTS

Fees	$320
Cost of books	$1,200
Room & board (on/off-campus)	$14,000/$15,026
% of students receiving aid	58
% of first-year students receiving aid	63
% of students receiving loans	51
% of students receiving grants	6
Average award package	$22,933
Average grant	$6,642
Average student loan debt	$62,826

ADMISSIONS

Admissions Selectivity Rating	72
# of applications received	387
% applicants accepted	82
% acceptees attending	53
Average GMAT	540
Range of GMAT	490–580
Average GPA	3.2
TOEFL required of international students	Yes
Minimum TOEFL (paper/computer)	550/213
Application fee	$50
International application fee	$50
Regular application deadline	7/15
Early decision program?	No
Deferment available	Yes
Maximum length of deferment	1 year
Transfer students accepted	Yes

Transfer application policy:
Up to 9 hours of B or better coursework can transfer from AACSB-accredited institutions. To assist students who are transferred to other cities before graduation, the MBA program at Loyola University Chicago participates in the Multilateral MBA Agreement with a number of other MBA programs at Jesuit universities. The Jesuit Business School Network (JEBNET) transfer program allows special accommodations for students transferring from most Jesuit schools of business.

Non-fall admissions	Yes
Need-blind admissions	Yes

EMPLOYMENT PROFILE

Career Rating	75	**Grads Employed by Function% Avg. Salary**	
Percent employed at graduation	20	Marketing	2 $46,000
Percent employed 3 months after graduation	10	Consulting	3 $50,000
		Management	2 $88,500
Average base starting salary	$67,513	Finance	5 $70,560
Primary Source of Full-time Job Acceptances		HR	2 $62,500
School-facilitated activities	6 (6%)	**Top 5 Employers Hiring Grads**	
Graduate-facilitated activities	48 (46%)	Loyola (4), True Partners Consulting (2),	
Unknown	50 (48%)	Northwestern Memorial (2), Accenture (2), Abbott (2)	

LOYOLA UNIVERSITY MARYLAND
SELLINGER SCHOOL OF BUSINESS AND MANAGEMENT

GENERAL INFORMATION

Type of school	Private
Affiliation	Roman Catholic/Jesuit
Academic calendar	Semester

SURVEY SAYS...
Solid preparation in:
Doing business in a global economy

STUDENTS

Enrollment of parent institution	6,067
Enrollment of MBA Program	861
% part-time	100
Average age at entry	28

ACADEMICS

Academic Experience Rating	**77**
Student/faculty ratio	10:1
Profs interesting rating	83
Profs accessible rating	76
% female faculty	26
% minority faculty	17

Academics

Loyola's Sellinger School of Business and Management offers the aspiring MBA a distinct, challenging, and flexible program. With evening classes held on both the Timonium and Columbia campuses, full-time working professionals can really take advantage of the self-paced curriculum. The average time to degree completion is less than three years, with some qualified and dedicated students finishing within twelve to fifteen months. Candidates whose undergraduate coursework involved business may be eligible for course waivers. Available concentrations include accounting, finance, information systems, international business, management and marketing.

Loyola manages to attract "extremely accessible" professors who know how to provide "practical knowledge to complement the academic theories of business." They cultivate a "very supportive environment" and "continuously seek student and outside feedback to [ensure] courses are relevant to today's business environment." Importantly, the "majority of professors are at the top of their fields" and have "an extensive background in real-world business." Many employ teaching methods that encourage students to "think in a different way rather than regurgitate information." Though students are quick to heap praise on their instructors, their enthusiasm is tempered by one qualifier. While the tenured faculty is continually described as "top-notch," some do warn that the adjunct faculty is "barely prepared."

Student opinion is decidedly mixed when it comes to Loyola's administration. As one disgruntled respondent shared, "The financial offices make more mistakes than a fourth grader with a calculator." Conversely, others assert that they are "very concerned about the well-being of their students" noting that "[administrators] make themselves readily available to students by having extended office hours and [by] being located at all satellite campuses." And an impressed second-year candidate shared, "The dean even called to inform that I will need to take two specific courses in order to graduate."

Career and Placement

Loyola's Career Center provides comprehensive services, equipping graduates with the necessary tools to succeed in the job market. Experienced officers help students identify and explore possible career paths. They also offer resume critiques and practice interviews, allowing students to sharpen their skills and apply for a job with supreme confidence. The Career Center grants access to a number of online resources and connects students with a handful of job fairs throughout the Baltimore area. Impressively, MBA candidates are privy to a network of approximately 1000 Loyola alumni. These alums become invaluable mentors, providing industry knowledge and acumen along with indispensable career advice. Lastly, there is an on-campus recruitment program, attracting roughly 150 local, regional, national, and international corporations.

Recent recruiters at Loyola University Maryland were T. Rowe Price; Northrop-Grumman; Legg Mason-Wood Walker; the U.S. government; and Verizon.

ADMISSIONS CONTACT: MAUREEN FAUX, DIRECTOR FOR GRADUATE ADMISSIONS
ADDRESS: 4501 NORTH CHARLES STREET BALTIMORE, MD 21210
PHONE: 410-617-5012 • FAX:
E-MAIL: ADMISSIONS@LOYOLA.EDU • WEBSITE: WWW.LOYOLA.EDU/SELLINGER

Student Life and Environment

Loyola's MBA program is offered on a part-time basis only, a factor that does impact student life. Indeed, the population is comprised primarily of "professionals" who maintain "busy personal and work schedules." Due to time constraints "there is limited interaction with other students outside of the classroom and study groups." However, one eager respondent did note that students do sometimes "go out for drinks after class."

Despite a scarcity of social opportunities, Loyola's MBA candidates speak highly of one another. They are quick to define their peers as "highly-motivated," "friendly" and "career-driven." And while "fellow students are competitive," they also prove themselves to be "amazing team players" who are "very supportive of each other and...create an atmosphere where everyone is committed to coming to class each week with a desire to learn as much as we can from each other." As one respondent sums up, "Doing well and receiving good grades are important to Loyola students."

Importantly, the school attracts a healthy "mix of new graduates and working adults with broad backgrounds and an extremely diverse experience base—from government [and] non-profit to commercial and private sector." Certainly this diversity within the student body enhances the learning experience by allowing "for different perspectives to be heard." And ultimately, all of this works to create an "environment very conducive not only to learning but making friends and connections too."

Admissions

A complete application to the Loyola University Maryland MBA program includes: a completed application form; a personal statement; a resume; an official GMAT score report; official transcripts for all undergraduate and graduate institutions attended; as well as international documents, where appropriate. Applicants with a 3.25 undergraduate GPA and five years of work experience may request waiver from the GMAT requirement, as may students with an advanced degree in any other discipline (e.g., an MA, a PhD, a JD, etc.). Interviews and letters of recommendations are optional, and letters of recommendations are required.

FINANCIAL FACTS

Annual tuition	$11,700
Fees	$50
Cost of books	$810
Room & board (off-campus)	$16,650
% of students receiving aid	21
% of first-year students receiving aid	26
% of students receiving loans	14
% of students receiving grants	5
Average award package	$17,630
Average grant	$8,340
Average student loan debt	$27,000

ADMISSIONS

Admissions Selectivity Rating	**74**
# of applications received	305
% applicants accepted	79
% acceptees attending	79
Average GMAT	560
Range of GMAT	530–780
Average GPA	3.14
TOEFL required of international students	Yes
Minimum TOEFL (paper/computer)	550/213
Application fee	$50
International application fee	$50
Early decision program?	No
Deferment available	Yes
Maximum length of deferment	1 year
Transfer students accepted	Yes
Transfer application policy: Only classes from another AACSB accredited school will be counted, total 6 credits.	
Non-fall admissions	Yes
Need-blind admissions	Yes

LOYOLA UNIVERSITY—NEW ORLEANS
JOSEPH A. BUTT, S.J. COLLEGE OF BUSINESS

GENERAL INFORMATION
Type of school	Private
Affiliation	Roman Catholic/Jesuit
Academic calendar	Semester

SURVEY SAYS...
Students love New Orleans, LA

STUDENTS
Enrollment of parent institution	4,676
Enrollment of MBA Program	95
% male/female	54/46
% out-of-state	60
% part-time	55
% minorities	21
% international	2
Average age at entry	25
Average years work experience at entry	2

ACADEMICS
Academic Experience Rating	77
Student/faculty ratio	18:1
Profs interesting rating	80
Profs accessible rating	86
% female faculty	26
% minority faculty	19

Joint Degrees
Master of business adminstration/Juris Doctor, 4 to 5 years; Master of Business Administration/Master of Pastoral Studies.

Academics

Loyola's "small, flexible MBA program" "really caters to each and every student," a fact appreciated by the predominantly part-time student body in the College of Business' graduate programs. MBAs here also love the "Jesuit tradition," which encourages "involvement in the New Orleans community." "I appreciate being at a place that not only educates my mind, but gives me social awareness as well," one student writes.

Loyola offers a general MBA as well as a combined MBA/JD and a combined MBA/MPS. The school does not offer concentrations, but it does offer "strands," sets of pre-selected electives in a particular discipline that function a lot like concentrations. Students may pursue a strand in finance, leadership, marketing, or supply chains, or they may use their electives to pursue other interests, including forensic accounting, international business, entrepreneurship, negotiations, or sustainability. The MBA culminates in a capstone course called Total Global Strategy, which emphasizes case study and integrative analysis.

Loyola professors "are very involved with the students. The classes are small and the faculty care about the students' well being and learning." One student writes, "I was shocked to learn how easily accessible my professors were. They really are interested in your education and your life and they want you to succeed! In fact, they will put in extra hours to make sure you do just that. The business school here is more like a family, which makes it that much easier to learn." Administrators are "excellent." One student reports, "There are a few classes the administration is trying to reorganize because of complaints from last semester. I think this is a good thing that the administration is listening to the students." Indeed, the administration seems intent on exploring all opportunities to improve the program. "The quality and experience of the new students has improved each year as admission standards have become tougher," MBAs here report approvingly.

Career and Placement

Loyola maintains a Career Development Center to serve all undergraduate and graduate students of the university. Services include self-assessment instruments, career counseling, internship and job placement services, and guidance in resume writing, interviewing, job search, and salary negotiation skills. The office organizes on-campus recruiting events. One student "is not sure how much other students utilize" the CDC, but she does use the office's service and finds it "extremely helpful, especially because I recently moved to the area." The MBA Association also contributes by organizing networking events.

In recent years, Loyola MBAs have been placed with Chevron, Cox Communications, Deloitte & Touche, Entergy, Ernst & Young, Harrah's Entertainment, JPMorgan, Northwestern Mutual, the Ochsner Health System, Shell, Prudential Financial, and the Target Corporation.

ADMISSIONS CONTACT: STEPHANIE MANSFIELD, MBA DIRECTOR
ADDRESS: 6363 ST. CHARLES AVENUE, CAMPUS BOX 15 NEW ORLEANS, LA 70118
PHONE: (504) 864-7965 • FAX: (504) 864-7970
E-MAIL: SMANS@LOYNO.EDU • WEBSITE: BUSINESS.LOYNO.EDU/MBA

Student Life and Environment

Designed to "keep your attention," "classes are interactive and fun" at Loyola, where "professors expect your best and highest quality work, but go above and beyond to provide the support you need in order to succeed. Coming to class is like meeting with friends and family every night." Students tell us that "life at school is stressful" but worth the hard work. "I do feel like I am learning more then I ever have," one writes.

Loyola classes meet once a week on weekday evenings. While most students are part-timers with full-time jobs, "there are [also] many full-time students that have part-time jobs. Everybody knows everyone. You have many of the same classes with the same people." "Significant effort has been made recently to improve the cohesiveness among students" at Loyola, with "MBA functions almost every week to bring the students closer together." One student reports, "The MBA program does a good job of organizing social events within as well as outside of the school."

Loyola is located in the fashionable uptown section of New Orleans, just down the road from Tulane University. The area is known for its fine restaurants and upscale shopping. The city's Central Business District, Garden District, and French Quarter are all easily accessible from campus via the city's picturesque streetcar line.

Most MBAs at Loyola "are just out of [their] four-year degree [programs], but there are some that have been in the workforce for a while." It's not just locals in attendance here. One student told us he was "very surprised to discover how many students are from every part of the country and so many different backgrounds." Across the board, students tend to be "very friendly and willing to help each other out. The MBA association facilitates this atmosphere by scheduling meet and greets and other social events throughout the semester."

Admissions

Loyola requires the following of applicants to its MBA program: official transcripts for all past postsecondary academic work; an official score report for the GMAT; two letters of recommendation; a 400-word personal statement of purpose; and a resume. International students whose first language is not English must also submit TOEFL scores; all international students must provide an affidavit demonstrating sufficient financial resources to support themselves during their tenure at the university. Interviews and letters of recommendations are optional, and letters of recommendations are required. Work experience, though not required, is strongly recommended.

FINANCIAL FACTS

Annual tuition	$20,520
Fees	$936
Cost of books	$1,500
Room & board (on-campus)	$11,508
Average grant	$5,000

ADMISSIONS

Admissions Selectivity Rating	**71**
# of applications received	57
% applicants accepted	85
% acceptees attending	56
Average GMAT	558
Range of GMAT	520–610
Average GPA	3.19
TOEFL required of international students	Yes
Minimum TOEFL (paper/computer)	580/237
Application fee	$50
International application fee	$50
Regular application deadline	6/15
Early decision program?	No
Deferment available	Yes
Maximum length of deferment	1 academic year
Transfer students accepted	Yes

Transfer application policy: In applicant comes from an AACSB-accredited program, the foundation work may apply to our program. Also, a maximum of 6 credit hours may be applied to the advanced level. Only B's or better are accepted.

Non-fall admissions	Yes
Need-blind admissions	Yes

MARIST COLLEGE
SCHOOL OF MANAGEMENT

GENERAL INFORMATION
Type of school   Private
Academic calendar   Semester

SURVEY SAYS...
Solid preparation in:
General management
Operations
Computer skills
Doing business in a global economy

STUDENTS
Enrollment of parent institution	6,179
Enrollment of MBA Program	192
Average age at entry	30
Average years work experience at entry	5

ACADEMICS
Academic Experience Rating	**82**
Student/faculty ratio	15:1
Profs interesting rating	70
Profs accessible rating	80
% female faculty	46
% minority faculty	17

Prominent Alumni
Marsha Gordon, Pres./CEO Business Council of Westchester Chamber; Karen Sieverding, Healthcare; Jeff Clark, Telecommunications.

Academics

For more than 30 years, Marist College has offered working professionals the opportunity to pursue an MBA degree on a part-time basis. Today, the school continues to operate a part-time, campus-based program, while also distinguishing itself as "one of the few AACSB-accredited graduate schools that offered an MBA program fully online, while being affordable." While part-time students in other MBA programs complain about the difficulties of balancing home life, work, and school, the Marist "program [is] tailored to those working long hours and still offer[s] a strong reputation with a decent curriculum." The flexibility of the program is perhaps its most attractive feature, allowing students to take traditional or online courses, or a blend of the two. Indeed, students tell us that "being able to mix online courses as well as traditional in-class courses is very beneficial for students who also work full time."

The curriculum at Marist is divided into foundation courses, core courses, and electives; however, foundation courses may be waived for students who have an undergraduate degree in business. Taking two courses per semester and one course in the summer, many students are able to earn their MBA in just 2 years. To accommodate the schedule of working professionals, traditional classroom courses are scheduled one evening per week, Monday through Thursday, on the Marist College campus, as well as in off-site classrooms. Online classes are available 24 hours a day, 7 days a week, and have no on-campus requirement whatsoever. "The high quality of the program and professors" draws many students to the school, and online students are welcome to meet with faculty in person while taking the course. Students say Marist professors are, on the whole, "accessible and very helpful."

The school is technologically and organizationally equipped to help online students plan and execute a quality educational program. A student shares, "Enrollment is a breeze, and the Assistant Dean who works with online students is very helpful." Another adds, "The administration was very helpful in getting [me] access to courses to meet my academic plan." Online classes are very similar to classroom courses in that students must be prepared to turn in assignments, take exams, participate in class, and meet deadlines. Course work is fully multimedia and includes group projects, case studies, computer simulations, and presentations. Students insist that they build a sense of community via the Internet, and "Group projects illuminate personalities pretty well even over the web." A current student enthuses, "I completed my program completely online. I have found many students to be actively engaged and willing to collaborate via online chat, e-mail, and over the phone."

Whether online or in the classroom, students say the program is high quality and challenging. One shares, "I started here after moving away from Chicago, where I attended a top-10 MBA program (Kellogg). I find the classes to be rigorous and academically competitive. I was worried that the courses would seem much easier than Kellogg['s], but my fears were misplaced." Even so, the program is fairly structured, and some students say they'd like to have the option of "more concentrations within the program" that are "structured to specific disciplines" while "removing some courses that aren't as beneficial to one's future goals."

ADMISSIONS CONTACT: KELLY HOLMES, DIRECTOR OF ADMISSION
ADDRESS: 3399 NORTH ROAD POUGHKEEPSIE, NY 12601
PHONE: 845-575-3800 • FAX: 845-575-3166
E-MAIL: GRADUATE@MARIST.EDU • WEBSITE: WWW.MARIST.EDU/MANAGEMENT/MBA

Career and Placement

Ninety-five percent of Marist students work full-time while completing their MBA. Ranging from relatively young professionals to senior managers, most students plan to stay with their current company upon termination of the program. For those who are looking for a new position, MBA students have access to the Marist College Career Services Office, which hosts career-building workshops, career conferences, career fairs, and a host of online resources. The Spring Career Conference at Marist included a number of regional employers, including: Affinity Group/Mass Mutual, Aldi, CVS Pharmacy, First Investors Corporation, Gap, Gunn Allen Financial Corporation, Household Finance, IBM, MetLife, Morgan Stanley, Northwestern Mutual Financial Network, Ryder Transportation, Target, United Parcel Service, Wells Fargo, and Worldwide Express.

Student Life and Environment

Because a large percentage of Marist courses are taught via the Internet, the student community is largely virtual. Even so, Marist students have the opportunity to get to know their classmates through the phone and Internet, describing them as "hardworking, intelligent [people], with work and family obligations." Those who attend classes on campus tell us the school promotes a "good sense of community" and "attracts people who are just plain nice and helpful both to work and teach and as students." While the business school is located on Marist's lively undergraduate campus, there aren't many social or recreational activities targeted at business students. Indeed, some would like to see "more opportunities for socializing, networking, out-of-classroom learning (speakers, etc.)."

Marist is located in Poughkeepsie, New York, a small city about 90 minutes from both New York City and Albany. A picturesque campus environment, the school is located near the Catskill Mountains, and the surrounding area is a paradise for hiking, cross-country skiing, mountain biking, and other outdoor activities. There are also a number of attractions in the town of Poughkeepsie, including the historic Barbadon Theater and Mid-Hudson Civic Center, which show opera, ballet, Broadway shows, and popular performers.

Admission

To apply to the graduate program at the Marist School of Management, students must possess an undergraduate degree in any discipline. Whether applying to the online or on-campus program, all applicants must submit a completed graduate school application, an application fee, two letters of recommendation, responses to the essay questions, official GMAT scores, and official transcripts from undergraduate study.

FINANCIAL FACTS

Annual tuition	$12,510
Cost of books	$1,350
Room & board	
% of students receiving aid	46
% of first-year students receiving aid	80
% of students receiving loans	23
% of students receiving grants	41
Average award package	$6,620
Average grant	$1,266

ADMISSIONS

Admissions Selectivity Rating	82
# of applications received	109
% applicants accepted	47
% acceptees attending	65
Average GMAT	542
Range of GMAT	475–575
Average GPA	3.4
TOEFL required of international students	Yes
Minimum TOEFL (paper/computer)	550/213
Application fee	$50
Regular application deadline	8/1
Regular notification	8/15
Early decision program?	No
Deferment available	Yes
Maximum length of deferment	1 year
Transfer students accepted	Yes
Transfer application policy: No more than six credit hours of core courses accepted from AACSB accredited programs.	
Non-fall admissions	Yes
Need-blind admissions	Yes

EMPLOYMENT PROFILE

Career Rating	83	Top 5 Employers Hiring Grads
Percent employed at graduation	73	IBM, Madison Square Garden, JP Morgan
Percent employed 3 months after graduation	92	Chase, Merrill Lynch, Hudson Valley Credit Union
Average base starting salary	$65,000	

MARQUETTE UNIVERSITY
COLLEGE OF BUSINESS ADMINISTRATION

GENERAL INFORMATION

Type of school	Private
Affiliation	Jesuit
Academic calendar	Semester

SURVEY SAYS...

Cutting-edge classes
Happy students
Solid preparation in:
Teamwork
Quantitative skills

STUDENTS

Enrollment of parent institution	11,633
Enrollment of MBA Program	532
% part-time	82
Average age at entry	29
Average years work experience at entry	6

ACADEMICS

Academic Experience Rating	**77**
Student/faculty ratio	7:1
Profs interesting rating	83
Profs accessible rating	75
% female faculty	26
% minority faculty	11

Joint Degrees

MBA/JD, 4 years; MBA/JD in sport business, 4 years; MBA/MSN, 4–6 years; MBA/MS Political Science, 3–6 years

Academics

The MBA program at Marquette University pursues "transformative education," and students tell us that it succeeds on this front. One tells us, "The Global Environment of Business Class that I took exemplified the school's mission. I definitely look at international business in a new light after taking that class. It's not too often that a business class can shape perspectives like that." This ability, along with Marquette's "strong academic reputation," its "proximity to *Fortune* 500 companies," and the "Christian ethics" infused through the school's Jesuit traditions are all reasons students come to this school.

Marquette's busy MBAs appreciate "the flexibility afforded by the part-time MBA program. It is invaluable," allowing students "to take classes at night and on the weekends, allowing us to work full time while attending school." An efficient faculty and administration also help; according to one student, "The accessibility and assistance from professors and the staff in the Graduate School of Management are among the program's great strengths. They help and guide us to make the best choices for our individual situations." Professors "recognize that the students are working and will always make time to meet [with] them." On the downside, "Electives for grad students are very limited and therefore getting a specialization on your MBA is very difficult without going past your graduation date." Students also wish that the school would "offer more online or blended courses," noting optimistically that "the program has started to experiment with this approach."

MU teaches a broad curriculum that "exposes students to a number of different types of problems, whether they are strategic or pragmatic." In addition, students tell us, "Each course blends different facets of real problems faced in industry with theoretical knowledge to fully dissect the issues and understand them." Marquette offers a number of unique joint degrees, including an MBA/JD in sports business, an MBA/MS in political science, and a Healthcare Technology Management Program offered in collaboration with the Medical College of Wisconsin.

Career and Placement

The Career Services Center at Marquette provides counseling and placement services to all undergraduates and graduate students at the university. The office organizes workshops, one-on-one counseling sessions, on-site recruiting events, and job databases. In addition, the College of Business offers career management services through its Hire Learning Program. A few students here describe the office as "second to none," but that's definitely the minority opinion; most tell us that Marquette's MBA program "could improve on providing job opportunities. Because most people in the program are employed, it does not have any on-campus interviewing. However, there are some full-time students and students looking to change careers and opportunities to interview with companies." A recent career fair promoted by exclusively for MBAs drew "primarily local firms, of various sizes. Almost all participating companies were looking for recent undergraduates for entry-level positions, rather than experienced business graduate students."

ADMISSIONS CONTACT: DR. JEANNE SIMMONS, ASSOCIATE DEAN
ADDRESS: PO BOX 1881, STRAZ HALL SUITE 275 MILWAUKEE, WI 53201-1881
PHONE: 414-288-7145 • FAX: 414-288-8078
E-MAIL: MBA@MARQUETTE.EDU • WEBSITE: WWW.MARQUETTE.EDU/GSM

Student Life and Environment

Marquette offers MBA classes in three locations: downtown Milwaukee, Waukesha, and Kohler. In all locations, "many students work full time and do not have the time to enjoy the [available] opportunities" to get involved in campus life. As one student explains, "The workload is substantial; it's like taking on a part-time job for 20 to 30 hours a week." On a positive note, the fact that nearly 90 percent of all students work full time presents excellent networking opportunities.

For those who can make the time, opportunities to get involved "are abundant for students who want to be involved," particularly at the Milwaukee campus. MBAs report that "Basketball is the major sport on campus, and I like the fact that tickets for the Marquette Fanatic Student Section are offered to graduate students. In my opinion, this helps MBAs to feel more included in the campus community." Some MBAs even find time to attend the many on-campus theater and musical productions.

Marquette MBAs "are hard-working and personable" and are also "very helpful to other students. It's a great group to learn with." The typical student is "in his mid to late twenties and is in a serious relationship. Some have just started having families. All are career-oriented and take the MBA program very seriously. Most are already in management positions." There "is some ethnic and racial diversity," and "everyone seems to get along."

Admissions

Applicants to the Marquette MBA program must provide the admissions office official transcripts for all previous post-secondary academic work, an official GMAT score report, a personal essay, and a resume. International students are additionally required to submit three letters of recommendation and an official score report for the TOEFL or another acceptable English proficiency exam. Two letters of recommendation are required for the Executive MBA program and for the MS programs in applied economics and engineering management; letters of recommendation are optional for the MBA and MS in accounting and human resource programs. Marquette encourages applicants to apply for full admission but also offers a temporary-admission option, good for one semester only. Students applying to campuses other than the downtown campus must remember to specify their campus of choice on their application.

FINANCIAL FACTS

Annual tuition	$15,300
Cost of books	$1,100

ADMISSIONS

Admissions Selectivity Rating	72
# of applications received	270
% applicants accepted	90
% acceptees attending	64
Average GMAT	578
Average GPA	3.24
TOEFL required of international students	Yes
Minimum TOEFL (paper/computer)	550/213
Application fee	$50
International application fee	$50
Early decision program?	No
Deferment available	Yes
Maximum length of deferment	Usually 1 year
Transfer students accepted	Yes
Transfer application policy: Transfers accepted from other Jesuit Schools (JEBNET agreemen) up to 6 approved credits from AACSB schools.	
Non-fall admissions	Yes
Need-blind admissions	No

MASSACHUSETTS INSTITUTE OF TECHNOLOGY
SLOAN SCHOOL OF MANAGEMENT

GENERAL INFORMATION

Type of school	Private
Academic calendar	Semester

SURVEY SAYS...
Good peer network
Cutting-edge classes
Solid preparation in:
Teamwork
Quantitative skills
Entrepreneurial studies

STUDENTS

Enrollment of parent institution	10,384
Enrollment of MBA Program	792
% male/female	62/38
% out-of-state	NR
% part-time	0
% minorities	13
% international	39
Average age at entry	28
Average years work experience at entry	5

ACADEMICS

Academic Experience Rating	97
Student/faculty ratio	7:1
Profs interesting rating	86
Profs accessible rating	79
% female faculty	22
% minority faculty	24

Joint Degrees

Leaders for Global Operations (LGO), SM or MBA in Management and SM in Engineering (one of six departments), 2 years; Biomedical Enterprise Program (BEP), 3 year dual MBA and S.M. in Health Sciences Technology; MBA and Harvard Kennedy School, 3 year dual MBA and MPA.

Academics

The MIT Sloan MBA Program has "both the best entrepreneurial program of any business school in the world and the most fantastic technology available," students insist. And that's hardly all the school offers; on the contrary, students tell us that MIT Sloan is "the best all-around program in allowing students to learn about innovative endeavors while still teaching and offering the most academically challenging traditional MBA curriculum of all schools."

MIT expertly exploits the synergies of its location in a great city and its affiliation with a great university. Students brag about "Sloan's ties to the real business world. In the last week alone, I listened to three *Fortune* 500 CEOs speak on campus and had dinner with a partner from a local VC firm and a partner from a local law firm. Many of the professors have incredibly deep experience and connections to industry and bring great insight along those dimensions." They are especially impressed with "how connected MIT Sloan is with companies in a non-recruiting season," which they justly see as "a real point of differentiation" for the program. MIT's Herculean status in the worlds of math, engineering, and science contribute substantially to the MBA program. "There are very low barriers between schools; interdisciplinary work and entrepreneurship are actively encouraged between business and engineering," one student writes. MIT's many strengths make possible such programs as the Leaders for Global Operations Program—"an operations and logistics-focused program" that students call "the best dual-degree program in business and engineering in the country"—and the Biomedical Enterprise Program, to which "Anyone who is interested in business within the life sciences should apply. This is a top-notch program that allows students to study business and science while providing the opportunity to interact in a close setting with industry leaders." (Applications will not be accepted for enrollment in the BEP program for the 2010–11 academic year.)

Throughout the program, MIT Sloan emphasizes "a strong hands-on approach to learning" and cooperative work. "At MIT Sloan, practically everything is done in teams," students tell us. The workload "is what you expect of MIT: rigorous and quantitative." Most don't mind the challenge; as one explains, "Although the workload is heavy, people actually want to prepare just for the opportunity to participate in discussions in where faculty are posing questions to the most pressing business issues. A place like MIT Sloan is a reason why people want to continue their education." The cherry on the sundae is global travel; "Everyone travels on trips or treks, both foreign and domestic. I am headed to Japan for 10 days with 200 of my classmates. These are student-planned trips that are excellent ways to get to see other cultures and get business exposure around the world."

Career and Placement

MIT Sloan's Career Development Office provides MBAs with a range of career management resources, including seminars, self-assessment tools, library materials, and online databases and services. Students tell us that "the CDO is great for traditional MBA jobs such as banking, [and] consulting and the major corporations and tech companies." Some report the office is "not as good with smaller and tougher markets such as private equity and venture capital," although students interested in those fields can make use of the "career trek" program, which offers trips around the globe to job-hunt and learn about a variety of industries. "The focus on entrepreneurship means that a lot of MIT Sloan students are starting companies or working at early-stage startups right after school," and are thus less inclined to make use of the CDO. Supplementing the CDO, "Clubs have a huge impact on career choices, setting up relationships, bringing in speakers, etc. Alumni are also a great resource, and a fantastic channel for connecting. Many Sloanies are looking to work for startups, tech, or smaller firms without traditional recruiting seasons, and alumni are very helpful in this regard."

Employers most likely to hire MIT Sloan MBAs include Bain & Company, Booz & Co., The Boston Consulting Group, Citi, Amazon.com, Fidelity, Goldman Sachs, Google, IBM, and McKinsey & Company.

Student Life and Environment

MIT Sloan keeps students plenty busy with work, but they still somehow find time to "participate in clubs and set up the many conferences we host. For example, the Sports Conference this spring had general managers from each of the top four professional sports (basketball, hockey, baseball, and football) sit on a panel. How cool is that?" Students tell us that MIT Sloan "provides more opportunities than anyone could expect. I find that I spend about 50 percent of my time on academics and the other 50 percent working with clubs and local companies, a perfect balance that allows me to take what I've learned in the classroom and apply it in a real-world setting." It's easy to get overwhelmed; according to one student, "School is a blur with so many classes, activities, guest speakers, etc. In terms of social activities, I think you have to pick your spots. Otherwise you will fall behind in your coursework and job search, but the options are pretty limitless here."

About the only area of dissatisfaction here concerns the school's facilities, and that problem will soon be addressed; the school is currently constructing a new business school building scheduled to open in fall 2010.

Admissions

Completed applications to the MIT Sloan MBA program include a cover letter, two letters of recommendation, post-secondary transcripts (self-reported prior to interview; if called for an interview, applicants must provide official transcripts), a current resumé, three personal essays, supplemental information, and GMAT or GRE scores. The school requires additional materials from applicants to the Leaders for Global Operations Program (LGO), and the Biomedical Enterprise Program. The nature of the program favors candidates with strong quantitative and analytical skills, as well as those with strong personal attributes including leadership, teamwork, and ability to make decisions and pursue goals.

Prominent Alumni

Rafael del Pino, Chairman, Groupo Ferrovial SA; Jeff Wilke, Sr VP North American Retail, Amazon.com; Robin Chase, Founder and CEO, Meadow Networks; Ron (Ronald) A. Williams, Chairman and CEO, Aetna, Inc.; Michael Kaiser, President, Kennedy Center.

FINANCIAL FACTS

Annual tuition	$48,922
Fees	$272
Cost of books	$1,800
Room & board	$27,690
% of students receiving aid	82
% of first-year students receiving aid	82
% of students receiving loans	72
% of students receiving grants	4
Average award package	$66,355
Average grant	$25,502
Average student loan debt	$92,937

ADMISSIONS

Admissions Selectivity Rating	98
# of applications received	4,125
Average GMAT	710
Range of GMAT	660–760
Average GPA	3.6
TOEFL required of international students	No
Application fee	$250
International application fee	$250
Regular application deadline	1/12
Regular notification	4/5
Application Deadline/Notification	
Round 1:	10/27 / 2/1
Round 2:	1/12 / 4/5
Early decision program?	No
Deferment available	No
Transfer students accepted	No
Non-fall admissions	No
Need-blind admissions	Yes

EMPLOYMENT PROFILE

Career Rating	98	**Grads Employed by Function% Avg. Salary**	
Percent employed at graduation	70	Marketing	7 $100,344
Percent employed 3 months after graduation	83	Operations	10 $105,478
		Consulting	39 $116,378
Average base starting salary	$106,536	Management	10 $102,024
Primary Source of Full-time Job Acceptances		Finance	20 $97,340
School-facilitated activities	236 (80%)	**Top 5 Employers Hiring Grads**	
Graduate-facilitated activities	51 (17%)	McKinsey & Company (23), Bain & Company	
Unknown	8 (3%)	(10), Boston Consulting Group (8), Deloitte Consulting (7), Amazon.com (7)	

McMASTER UNIVERSITY
DeGroote School of Business

GENERAL INFORMATION
Type of school   Public
Academic calendar   Sept–May

SURVEY SAYS...
Friendly students
Good social scene
Good peer network
Solid preparation in:
Teamwork
Communication/interpersonal skills
Presentation skills

STUDENTS
Enrollment of MBA Program   439
% male/female   54/46
% part-time   32
% international   10
Average age at entry   27
Average years work experience
    at entry   3

ACADEMICS
Academic Experience Rating   83
Profs interesting rating   66
Profs accessible rating   67

Prominent Alumni
Karen Maidment, Chief Financial & Administrative Officer, BMO; David Feather, President, Mackenzie Financial Services Inc.; Stephen Smith, Past President/CEO, Westjet Airlines; Rob Burgess, Former Chairman and CEO, Macromedia; Marco Marrone, CFO and Executive Vice President Finance, Canadian Tire Corporation.

Academics

The DeGroote School of Business at McMaster University offers conventional full-time and part-time MBAs, but its co-op program (with paid work terms) truly distinguishes it from the competition. It is a program that, in the words of one student, is "vital to the school's differentiation factor." Through co-op, students with no business experience can enter DeGroote and 2 years later emerge with an MBA and significant professional experience.

DeGroote's co-op program is especially "friendly to young grads," as it carries no prerequisite of professional experience though 46 percent have some work experience. Students appreciate that the program "offers a great way for fresh graduates to gain specialized work experience while concurrently completing their degree. The ability to simultaneously learn theory and apply it in the business world is priceless." The program also suits some already in the midst of their careers. One student revels in the fact that co-op offers "the best way to get a job in a different field" than his experience was in.

DeGroote also offers an accelerated MBA program for individuals with an undergraduate business degree. Students enter at what is traditionally the program's second year and have eight months of intensive study. Students tell us that DeGroote offers "good networking" with the biotech and pharmaceutical industries, and they praise the "innovative" curriculum for its emphasis on "leadership and ethical culture." The program also stresses "team building and cross-functional teamwork," thereby building necessary business communication skills. Some here lament that "quantitative material is afforded seemingly little attention...the material covered is cursory," while others observe that "first-year courses are too much like undergraduate [business] courses." Qualified students can enter the MBA program from any undergraduate discipline.

Even those who see problems, however, agree that the school is headed in the right direction. One student commends, "I have been tremendously impressed with the direction [the Dean] has taken the school in recent years." Another agrees, "No question about it, the leaders of our program are putting it on the map." Students like that the current Dean "is not from the academic world and has brought a practical perspective to the school and courses....He knows what he is talking about." They also love that "the price of the program (compared to other programs in the Ontario area) is low." Sums up one MBA, "Given...the cost of the program, I felt that McMaster offered a far superior return on investment than most business schools."

Career and Placement

DeGroote's Centre for Business Career Development "is an excellent resource for students." The center shows an "aggressive ambition" that "is necessary in this job market, and is beginning to pay dividends" for students. The office provides coaching and recruitment services throughout the MBA program and partners with many high end and notable Canadian employers to "deliver seamless, on-campus company information sessions and career recruiting," according to the school's website. Some here feel that "more diverse career opportunities would be nice. Currently, our on-campus recruitment is very focused on accounting and finance jobs, and they do this very well. However, opportunities in other areas such as consulting and marketing leave something to be desired."

Employers most likely to hire DeGroote MBAs include: Accenture, Bell Canada, BMO, CIBC World Markets, Gennum Corporation, Hydro One, PricewaterhouseCoopers, Scotiabank, Canadian Tire Financial Services, Eli Lilly, Scotia Capital, ArcelorMittal Dofasco, The Ministry of Health, TD Securities, and Telus.

ADMISSIONS CONTACT: STEVEN WALKER/DENISE ANDERSON, RECRUITING ADMINISTRATOR
ADDRESS: 1280 MAIN STREET WEST, DSB 104 HAMILTON, ON L8S 4M4 CANADA
PHONE: (905) 525-9140 EXT. 27024 • FAX: (905) 521-8995
E-MAIL: MBAINFO@MCMASTER.CA • WEBSITE: WWW.DEGROOTE.MCMASTER.CA

Student Life and Environment

Students enjoy a "very social atmosphere" at DeGroote. One reports, "We all spend a lot of time with each other, whether it's outside of school or just grabbing coffee. You can always find someone to get coffee within Innis (our business library) at any time of day or night." They also tell us that "life on campus is excellent. It is a home away from home for anyone who wants to make it so. Facilities are open at all hours, the environment is comfortable, and the school has gone out of its way to make MBAs a priority (e.g., the entire top floor of the building is now an MBA study space)."

Academics here "are challenging but still provide us with free time to pursue other interests as well." A new recreation center that opened recently "is state-of-the-art" while classrooms are "modern and well-equipped." The DeGroote MBA Association "plans frequent events and activities"; "There are several MBA intramural sports teams" and "opportunities to participate in case competitions." No wonder students tell us that life here is "quite busy" and things move at a "fast pace. Fortunately, there is always help when you need it."

Hometown Hamilton "is not the most attractive place to live in general, but the location of the school in the west end of the city is quite safe and attractive. The mid-range size of the school in comparison to other Canadian universities gives it the best of both worlds: small-school networking with larger-school sports and community involvement." McMaster University is located within close proximity to the vibrant and diverse city of Toronto.

Admissions

The Admissions Staff at DeGroote focuses primarily on applicants' final 2 years of undergraduate work (minimum 3.0 GPA strongly preferred) and their GMAT scores in assessing candidates. The process is highly holistic in nature. Work experience and demonstrated community leadership skills are also considered, as are evidence of ethical maturity and business aptitude. Applicants to the co-op program are assessed by interview for communication skills, initiative, leadership potential, and general experience. Applicants must submit official transcripts for all previous undergraduate and graduate work, an official score report for the GMAT, two letters of recommendation, and a current resume. One year of post-collegiate work experience is required of applicants to the full-time and part-time programs; applicants to the co-op program need not have prior professional experience. International students whose first language is not English must submit an official score report for the TOEFL (minimum score: 100, internet-based test; 250, computer-based test; or 600, paper-based test strongly preferred).

FINANCIAL FACTS

Annual tuition	$11,927
Fees (in-state/out-of-state)	$1,115
Cost of books	$967

ADMISSIONS

Admissions Selectivity Rating	**87**
# of applications received	515
% applicants accepted	56
% acceptees attending	71
Average GMAT	620
Average GPA	3.48
TOEFL required of international students	Yes
Minimum TOEFL (web based)	100
Application fee	$150
International application fee	$150
Regular application deadline	6/15
Early decision program?	No
Deferment available	No
Transfer students accepted	Yes
Non-fall admissions	Yes
Need-blind admissions	Yes

EMPLOYMENT PROFILE

Career Rating	88	Grads Employed by Function	%	Avg. Salary
Average base starting salary	$68,024	Consulting	7	$78,000
		Management	7	$49,500
		Finance	64	$70,333
		Other	22	$66,620

Top 5 Employers Hiring Grads
PricewaterhouseCoopers, Scotiabank, KPMG, St. Joseph's Hospital, Cancer Care

MERCER UNIVERSITY—ATLANTA

EUGENE W. STETSON SCHOOL OF BUSINESS AND ECONOMICS

GENERAL INFORMATION
Type of school   Private
Affiliation   Baptist
Academic calendar   Semester

SURVEY SAYS...
Solid preparation in:
Marketing
General management

ACADEMICS
Academic Experience Rating	**80**
Student/faculty ratio	20:1
Profs interesting rating	86
Profs accessible rating	79
% female faculty	38
% minority faculty	19

Joint Degrees
Joint MBA and Doctor of Pharmacy, 4 years; Joint MBA and Master of Divinity, 3 years; Joint MBA and Master of Accounting.

Prominent Alumni
Karen Romaine Thomas, Vice President, CFO, Schwan's Bakery, Inc.; John F. Hough, Dr.P.H., MPH, MBA, Health Scientist Administrator, NIH; William Astary, Sr. Vice Pres. of Sales, Acuity Brand Lighting; Paul Gianneschi, Mananging Prin. & Founder, Hatch Medical, LLC.

Academics

Atlanta is a city with many high-quality universities, making it difficult for an MBA program to stand out in the crowd. The Eugene W. Stetson School of Business and Economics at Mercer University in Atlanta seems to have found its competitive edge; it's the Flexible MBA program's unique eight-week sessions, which the school's predominantly professional student body loves. The schedule of evenings-only classes caters to the needs of students with full-time jobs; as one student explains, the calendar "allows us to focus our efforts on one class at a time while continuing to work full time." It also allows for flexibility, so that "you can miss a session if work gets too busy or for other personal matters. Other schools expect you to begin and move through at their pace, instead of your pace." The fact that the calendar "runs throughout the year, including two summer sessions," is also "great," because it "enable students to get through the program quickly."

Students tell us that finance and marketing are among Stetson's strongest disciplines. Throughout the program, "Small class sizes allow for close relationship with professors" who, students happily report, "are always available. They provide multiple email addresses as well as phone numbers that they can be reached at. The professors bring a great mix of academic and real-world experience to the classroom." "Class interaction and student discussion is encouraged" here. The Stetson curriculum includes a 27-credit Core Course sequence, 12 credits of electives (at least one of which must be an international elective), and a capstone case study seminar. The school encourages all students to study abroad; students approve, telling us that "The study abroad trip is a nice concept where students can learn as well as experience a new country."

Stetson had recently launched a one-year, daytime Master of Business Administration (MBA) degree tailored for those individuals who desire to attend an accelerated full-time MBA program to retool their career, make a career change, or re-enter the workforce. This daytime cohort program begins in the summer semester with students enrolling in 3–12 credit hours (depending on previous academic preparation), and delivers the remaining 36 credit hours over the subsequent fall and spring semesters via a 4-day a week daytime class schedule. Students enroll in 3 courses (3 credit hours each) every eight-week session, for a total of 4 eight-week sessions or 12 courses taken over the fall and spring semesters. Thus, the Day MBA can be completed in 10-12 months, depending on previous academic preparation. Admission requirements for the Day MBA are identical to those of the evening Flexible MBA. Stetson also offers an Executive MBA program on the Atlanta Campus, as well as a Professional MBA in metro Atlanta. These programs are 16-month cohort programs that meet approximately every other weekend.

Career and Placement

The Office of Career Services at Mercer provides a broad range of counseling and placement services to undergraduates and graduate students at Mercer University in Atlanta. Seminars and workshops cover job search strategies, resume preparation, networking, interviewing techniques, and compensation negotiation. The office hosts career fairs and coordinates participation in career fairs on other Atlanta area campuses. The online service BEARlink connects students, alumni, and employers to the school's career services staff and job postings. Students praise the "active and strong alumni association" here and report that "Opportunities are there for those that would like to network or participate in activities outside of work and/or school." About one in five Stetson MBAs goes into marketing and sales (average starting salary $79K). One in ten winds up in finance and accounting (average starting salary $69K).

Student Life and Environment

The Stetson Flexible MBA program convenes during weekday evenings for the convenience of the many working professionals in the student body. One student observes that "Being in the MBA program, the campus is usually pretty quiet in the evening. Upon arriving for class you will see people playing tennis, soccer, jogging, studying, or chatting with friends in the quad. It is a typical campus." Students unencumbered with a full-time job tell us that "There are numerous programs and activities that happen on campus" during the daytime, but most in the program are left "wishing that there were more events for MBA students...It would be nice to have a few activities or weekend events throughout the year, such as an MBA student holiday party, MBA student Brunch, MBA student networking event, etc." Students happily report that "The Mercer campus is beautiful and just the right size. And, they have plenty of parking spaces and they are free."

The Stetson student body "is made up of professionals and managers from many different industries, from utility companies to airlines." One student sums it up this way: "You can't describe the diversity of our students in just a couple of sentences. We have people from technical, accounting, marketing, medical, investment, customer service, and governmental backgrounds. There's always another angle on a discussion in class and it is not uncommon to have some heated debates." The professional ranks are supplemented by "a number of international students...from all over the globe. We have a very diverse class." One writes, "I have met and become good friends with several classmates and we each are originally from a different country." Because "much of the work is centered on class teamwork," students must "learn to be team focused and goal oriented." In the process, many here "make a few solid friends" who "network to help each other out in classes."

Admissions

Applicants to the Stetson MBA program at Mercer must provide the school with a completed application form, two sets of official transcripts from each postsecondary academic institution attended, a resume, and an official GMAT score report showing test results no more than five years old. In addition, international applicants whose first language is not English must demonstrate English proficiency through TOEFL scores. All students who received undergraduate degrees abroad must, at their own expense, provide an independent evaluation (and, where appropriate, a translation) of their undergraduate records. International students must additionally demonstrate the ability to finance their education at Mercer.

FINANCIAL FACTS

Annual tuition	$13,776
Fees	$160
Cost of books	$1,000
Room & board (off-campus)	$9,450
% of students receiving aid	60
% of first-year students receiving aid	60
% of students receiving loans	60
% of students receiving grants	1
Average award package	$12,666
Average grant	$1,140
Average student loan debt	$20,000

ADMISSIONS

Admissions Selectivity Rating	80
TOEFL required of international students	Yes
Application fee	$50
International application fee	$100
Regular application deadline	Rolling
Early decision program?	No
Deferment available	Yes
Maximum length of deferment	Five years past GMAT
Transfer students accepted	Yes
Transfer application policy: Will consider up to two courses (6 sem. hrs.) in transfer within past five years.	
Non-fall admissions	Yes
Need-blind admissions	Yes

EMPLOYMENT PROFILE

Career Rating	85	Grads Employed by Function	%	Avg. Salary
Percent employed at graduation	83	Marketing	21	$79,781
Percent employed 3 months after graduation	86	Operations	12	$80,281
		Consulting	2	$112,000
Average base starting salary	$73,100	Management	10	$69,528
		Finance	11	$69,000
		HR	2	$83,000
		MIS	5	$76,833

MERCER UNIVERSITY—MACON
EUGENE W. STETSON SCHOOL OF BUSINESS AND ECONOMICS

GENERAL INFORMATION
Type of school	Private
Affiliation	Baptist

SURVEY SAYS...
Good peer network
Solid preparation in:
Marketing
Accounting
Communication/interpersonal skills

STUDENTS
Enrollment of parent institution	40
Enrollment of MBA Program	40
% male/female	45/55
% part-time	99
Average age at entry	530
Average years work experience at entry	4

ACADEMICS
Academic Experience Rating	**73**
Student/faculty ratio	20:1
Profs interesting rating	92
Profs accessible rating	86
% female faculty	55

Joint Degrees
JD/MBA, 3 years

Academics

A long-standing Georgia institution with a "great reputation" and a strong "community feeling," Mercer University offers a friendly and convenient evening MBA program, specially designed for working professionals. Based at the school's main campus in Macon (though the university also operates several MBA programs in other Georgia cities, including Atlanta), this program is divided into two parts: foundational courses and core courses. For those with previous academic experience in business, the foundation courses may be waived. All students, however, must complete the core, a series of advanced courses in business fundamentals, including applied microeconomic analysis, management and leadership, and business ethics. With a focus on the relationship between business and society, the Mercer curriculum is current and contemporary. According to current students, "The administration goes to great lengths to offer courses relevant to our career goals and interests." An "outstanding offering of seminars and lecture series" augment the core, and students can take advantage of "faculty-led study abroad opportunities each year." While students generally praise the academic program, some say the school should offer a greater variety of electives, as well as coursework that is "more applicable to small business and entrepreneurs."

Mercer maintains a "low student-to-faculty ratio" and "optimal" class sizes, encouraging interaction and discussion between students and teachers. In the classroom, "Lectures are loosely structured to provide ample opportunities to contribute and share real-world perspectives." A student details, "Everyone has different educational, ethnic, and social backgrounds. Everyone likes to add to classroom discussion where they can." Fortunately, collaboration is more common than competition, and "most people work toward each person succeeding as oppose to the "cut-throat" environment some business students experience." Since most Mercer students are balancing their education with a career (and personal lives), it can definitely be challenging to keep pace with the program. Fortunately, the school is known for its decidedly "friendly atmosphere." If schoolwork proves challenging, "professors are willing to take extra time for those who need it and to lend advice in projects inside the classroom or in work life outside the classroom." Like the faculty, "The administration generally cares about students, and there is an overall open-door policy for students." Exclaims a student, "My academic experience has been hard work and time consuming, but it is worth every moment!" Another agrees, "There is a lot of work involved, but it's not impossible to get everything done. The administration is very helpful. The majority of the professors are easily accessible."

Career and Placement

The Office of Career Services at Macon serves the undergraduate and graduate communities of the main Macon campus, as well as the Eastman Center. Among other student services, the Office of Career Services hosts career fairs and campus recruiting events. At a recent career fair, Frito Lay, GEICO, Geotechnical & Environmental Consultants, Honeywell Technology Solutions, Inc, Support Systems Associates, Inc., and Universal Avionics Systems Corp. were among the employers that came to interview MBA candidates. However, for those hoping to change careers, Mercer students admit that, "Because most students are employed, emphasis on career services is not present. More energy towards helping students with career decisions would be appreciated." A current student adds, "As an MBA student, I would definitely like to see the Career Placement services improve for MBA students. The school currently tailors this program to mainly

ADMISSIONS CONTACT: ROBERT HOLLAND JR, DIRECTOR OF ACADEMIC ADMINISTRATION
ADDRESS: 1400 COLEMAN AVENUE, SSBE MACON, GA 31207
PHONE: 478-301-2835 • FAX: 478-301-2635
E-MAIL: HOLLAND_R@MERCER.EDU • WEBSITE: WWW.MERCER.EDU

undergraduate students." Nonetheless, students know that they will be able to cash in on the Mercer name during their career, as well as benefit from the school's "established network with leaders in many fields of business and economics." A student agrees, "I chose Mercer because it has a great reputation."

Student Life and Environment

According to most MBA students, it's strictly business at Mercer University. While Mercer's undergraduate college is lively and social, most MBA students "work and live off campus" and "don't seem to be involved in other organizations on campus." A current MBA candidate (and undergraduate alumni) laments, "There was a lot more to do while I was getting my undergraduate degree." At the same time, some note that the MBA student population is beginning to change as the school admits younger students, especially through the school's joint degree and work-study programs. A student explains, "There is a good mix of full-time working adults from the community, and young adult graduate assistants and law students." No matter what their age, experience, or career goals, most Mercer MBAs are "Driven individuals pursuing skills that will increase their performance in their current career or make them more marketable for a future career."

Located in downtown Macon, "The campus is quiet and safe-feeling and fosters an environment for learning." However, some say they'd like to see "More parking and more convenient food options for night class students." Others mention that, "Campus security could be better." A current student elaborates, "Students live in what they call the Mercer Bubble, protected by patrolling campus police, who do a very good job, but can't stop everything."

Admissions

Students are accepted to Mercer University based on a combination of their GMAT scores, prior academic performance, and, in some cases, previous professional experience in a management position. Mercer admits students three times a year for the fall, spring, and summer terms. In recent years, the average student was 29 years old, with 15 percent international.

ADMISSIONS	
Admissions Selectivity Rating	61
# of applications received	12
% applicants accepted	100
% acceptees attending	100
Average GMAT	530
TOEFL required of international students	Yes
Minimum TOEFL (paper/computer)	550/213
Application fee	$50
International application fee	$100
Early decision program?	No
Deferment available	Yes
Maximum length of deferment	1 year
Transfer students accepted	Yes
Transfer application policy: Can't transfer more than 6 hours from AACES accredited program.	
Non-fall admissions	Yes
Need-blind admissions	No

MIAMI UNIVERSITY (OH)
RICHARD T. FARMER SCHOOL OF BUSINESS

GENERAL INFORMATION
Type of school   Public
Academic calendar   Semester

SURVEY SAYS...
Solid preparation in:
Marketing
General management
Teamwork
Presentation skills
Doing business in a global economy

STUDENTS
Enrollment of parent institution	17,191
Enrollment of MBA Program	59
% male/female	85/15
% out-of-state	27
% part-time	56
% minorities	4
% international	12
Average age at entry	30
Average years work experience at entry	7

ACADEMICS
Academic Experience Rating	**88**
Student/faculty ratio	2:1
Profs interesting rating	91
Profs accessible rating	96
% female faculty	16

Prominent Alumni
John Smale, CEO of Procter & Gamble (retired); Richard Farmer, CEO & Chairman of Board, Cintas, retired; Michael Armstrong, Chairman, AT&T (former); Tom Stallkamp, President, Daimler/Chrysler (former).

Academics

Miami University of Ohio offers an innovative, fast-paced, and rigorous MBA program, well-suited to young professionals who want to jumpstart their careers. The school's accelerated, 14-month program is taught in a multidisciplinary, case-based format, "covering all aspects of business from finance to marketing and global strategy to IT management." The lockstep program begins with a summer-long "boot camp," a crash course in advanced business concepts and theory, including marketing, operations management, finance, economics, and statistics. After that, students begin a series of intense, integrated courses in every aspect of business. In addition to the classroom, experiential learning is essential to the MBA, and for two semesters, "academic studies are balanced with a 15-hour internship commitment to a company in the local area (Dayton/Cincinnati)." Finally, the program "concludes with a two-month global consultancy in which students consult for a company in either Europe or China." Intense and fast-paced, "The program is short, yet encompasses an amazing amount of material." As a result, "Life at Miami University as an MBA student is very busy." A current student explains, "The program requires a lot of effort and time management to accomplish the work given; however the return on our personal investment is proving rewarding for both personal and professional development."

Many students choose the Farmer School of Business for the "opportunity to capitalize on Miami's excellent professors and reputation." Fortunately, the school lives up to its name: "The professors at Miami University have great backgrounds academically and professionally." Another advantage to the Miami MBA program is its small size. With only 25 incoming students each year, "our small class ensures 100% participation and preparation along with direct interaction with all the professors." Students say, "The faculty and staff seem to genuinely care about the future of our class. The program is small, so we all have the opportunity to get to know our directors and professors." After class, professors are always available for additional help, and they are even "willing to meet outside of office hours and in some cases on weekends."

Having recently rolled out their new full-time MBA, Miami University is a "young" and up-and-coming program, with many plans for the future. The business school continues to grow with the introduction of a professional, part-time MBA program. What's more, the school is currently building a "new state-of-the-art business school," slated to open in 2010. With the school's strong reputation and big plans for the future, students are confident they'll continue to see an increase in the school's caliber and prestige. A current student enthuses, "My academic experience has been amazing, and I am confident that with a better economy my MBA ROI will continue to increase substantially."

Career and Placement

While pursuing their MBA, Miami University students have one foot in the classroom and another in the workplace. Through the school's excellent extended-internship program, students get important practical experience while completing their degrees, and they have the opportunity to make contacts at prominent local companies. During a recent academic school year, students were placed in internships at companies such as Cincy Tech, Fidelity Investments, GE Aircraft Engines, Johnson & Johnson, Kodak, Mead Westvaco, and Procter & Gamble. In addition, career planning is incorporated into the MBA curriculum. Within the first month of classes, students are expected to begin work on their personal career strategies.

At the same time, "Oxford is a small town and somewhat secluded from the city life," which means there are more limited professional opportunities in the area. Some students feel, "the Career Development Center should focus on bringing in more employers outside of the Mid-Atlantic area."

Student Life and Environment

Miami University enrolls just 25 MBA candidates each year. Even so, "Diversity is a great characteristic of our MBA class. Our work experiences have varied to a degree and our ages range from 24 to 40s, with the majority being in the 20s and young 30s." Within the small community, "There seems to be a good contrast of liberal and conservative students," and "the uniqueness of each individual is what makes the contributions of classmates so valuable." A student agrees, "My fellow students have diverse backgrounds, and each has a unique value-added contribution. Group projects, class competition, and opportunities are executed with professionalism, but the social relationships we've built complete the package."

Located on a "beautiful campus" in the small town of Oxford, Ohio, the campus boasts every amenity. "Libraries, computers, and resources are readily available" when you need to study and, when you want to burn off some stress, "the gym is two floors and includes an indoor track, rock-climbing wall, and a top-notch swimming facility." the surrounding community of Oxford is small and student-oriented, and "There are many great places to eat both on campus and uptown." Along with Miami undergrads, business students "are able to hit 'uptown' each weekend and have a good time."

Admissions

Seventy-three percent of entering students majored in business as an undergraduate, with the remaining students coming from arts, science, or engineering backgrounds. Students are required to have at least two years of professional work experience before entering the program; however, the school occasionally makes exceptions to this prerequisite.

FINANCIAL FACTS

Annual tuition (in-state/ out-of-state)	$9,000/$21,860
Fees	$2,714
Cost of books	$600
Room & board (on/off-campus)	$8,998/$10,498
% of students receiving aid	63
% of first-year students receiving aid	63
% of students receiving loans	63
% of students receiving grants	5
Average award package	$14,133
Average grant	$2,125

ADMISSIONS

Admissions Selectivity Rating	79
# of applications received	141
% applicants accepted	58
% acceptees attending	72
Average GMAT	550
Range of GMAT	440–689
Average GPA	3.16
TOEFL required of international students	Yes
Minimum TOEFL (paper/computer)	550/213
Application fee	$35
International application fee	$35
Regular application deadline	4/1
Regular notification	4/15
Early decision program?	No
Deferment available	Yes
Maximum length of deferment	2 years
Transfer students accepted	No
Non-fall admissions	Yes
Need-blind admissions	Yes

EMPLOYMENT PROFILE

Career Rating	87	**Grads Employed by Function% Avg. Salary**	
Percent employed at graduation	59	Marketing	33 $57,400
Percent employed 3 months after graduation	68	Operations	27 $62,300
		Management	20 $61,700
Average base starting salary	$63,000	Finance	13 $67,100
Primary Source of Full-time Job Acceptances		MIS	7 $90,000
School-facilitated activities	9 (60%)	**Top 5 Employers Hiring Grads**	
Graduate-facilitated activities	6 (40%)	A.C. Nielsen (2), Hewlett Packard (1), Chrysler (1), Sears (1), Eaton (1)	

MILLSAPS COLLEGE
ELSE SCHOOL OF MANAGEMENT

GENERAL INFORMATION
Type of school	Private
Affiliation	Methodist
Academic calendar	Semester

SURVEY SAYS...
Solid preparation in:
Communication/interpersonal skills

STUDENTS
Enrollment of parent institution	1,146
Enrollment of MBA Program	118
% male/female	63/37
% part-time	64
Average age at entry	28
Average years work experience at entry	4

ACADEMICS
Academic Experience Rating	84
Student/faculty ratio	12:1
Profs interesting rating	94
Profs accessible rating	92
% female faculty	39
% minority faculty	5

Prominent Alumni
Bo Chastain, CEO, MS State Hospital; John Stupka, former CEO Skytel; Richard H. Mills, Jr., CEO, Tellus Operating Group; Will Flatt, CFO Parkway Properties; Sharon O'Shea, president and CEO, e-Triage.

Academics

The Else School of Management at Millsaps College offers the academic strength of a graduate business program while maintaining the "intimate learning environment" typical of a small liberal arts school. With the ideal mix of "small class sizes and excellent professors," the academic experience is personalized and rewarding. Classes are all small and discussion-based, and professors "instruct students as individuals rather than as merely a class." Emphasizing real-world applications of academic principles, Millsaps professors "constantly bring new ideas and concepts to the table as the business world changes." In fact, most instructors "have worked in the private sector before joining Millsaps," and therefore, they "can steer the lecture to other topics outside of a textbook and focus on real-life scenarios they have encountered."

Offering MBA and MAcc degrees, the Else School confers the only graduate degrees at Millsaps College. As such, it is not surprising that the business school feels a bit more like a small college than a typical graduate program. A "casual atmosphere" pervades the academic environment, and "Everyone is on a first-name basis for the most part." Within this close-knit community, "almost all of the teachers have been at Millsaps for many years. They are easily accessible—especially by e-mail—and know everyone's name." Even more impressive, professors "really get to know the students as a person. They know their interests and value their opinions and questions in class." Like the teaching staff, "The administration is always there to help and they solve any problems quickly and efficiently." Overall, students note just one anomalous deficiency: There is only "one Academic Advisor for almost 200 students."

Many of Millsap's MBA candidates are working professionals, and the teachers and administrators are highly sympathetic to the unique needs of students who are balancing work, home life, and school. A case in point, one part-time student tells us that, after missing a few classes towards the end of the semester, "my professor met with me during my lunch hour for two days to make sure that I mastered the skills. This was so unexpected from a graduate professor, especially since she did not have to be at the school during those times." On the other end of the spectrum, professional work experience is not a prerequisite of the program, and therefore, many Millsaps undergraduates begin their MBA directly after college. Students who make this choice say "it was an easy transition from undergrad at Millsaps to post-graduate study." At many business schools, there is an obvious divide between younger full-time students and older, part-time students. At Millsaps, however, students mix comfortably. In class, professors "strive to meet the needs of a diversified business skill set for graduate students." In fact, students feel, "The collaboration of both types in group-oriented activities, as well as the classroom, is a definite benefit to the program. The younger students add a more laid back attitude while the older students inspire a deeper sense of ambition."

Career and Placement

Throughout the South, Millsaps maintains an "impeccable reputation" for academic excellence, and many say the Else School operates "the best MBA program in Mississippi." In hometown Jackson, "Millsaps graduates are highly recruited" and highly respected—a major reason that many MBA candidates chose the program. Outside the South, however, options are a bit more limited. A student explains, "It is true that Millsaps will help you get a great job in Jackson, but it won't really help if you want to get a job in another part of the country as it is not that well-known."

ADMISSIONS CONTACT: MELISSA MEACHAM, DIRECTOR OF GRADUATE BUSINESS ADMISSIONS
ADDRESS: 1701 NORTH STATE STREET JACKSON, MS 39210
PHONE: 601-974-1253 • FAX: 601-974-1260
E-MAIL: MBAMACC@MILLSAPS.EDU • WEBSITE: WWW.MBA.MILLSAPS.EDU

"There isn't a great career center" at Millsaps, and you won't find dedicated business school career counselors, as you might at larger programs. Yet students don't regret their decision to attend Millsaps, saying their education is "not just a job fair—actual learning and teaching takes place." In addition, "the relationships you form with professors are extremely helpful as you move through the program and act as a confidence booster when you pursue opportunities outside the classroom." On that note, within the business school the "administration closely focused on the needs of professionals after graduation and on networking with alumni in fields of work."

Student Life and Environment

As a part of a vibrant undergraduate campus, Millsaps "offers more than just the classroom experience, even for graduate students." In addition to intramural sports, lecture series, and other campus events, the business school hosts "a few parties to get everyone together, such as a Christmas party, a baseball game, a football game or a happy hour. These are fun and a lot of the students participate." Aside from official gatherings, most working students say, "the course load is more than enough to keep us busy." However, they do find time to "meet for study groups" or "get together off-campus for dinner or drinks."

On the "pretty" Millsaps campus, "There are a number of available resources to help students...[including] free printing, access to computers, [and] study rooms for group projects and meetings." Located in the Fondren District of Jackson, Mississippi, Millsaps is situated in the middle of "an Art District that has the right combination of activity and calmness." Students "love" the Jackson area, saying "the people in Jackson are wonderful" and the community is defined by southern hospitality.

Admissions

To be considered for admission to Millsaps MBA program, students must submit official GMAT scores, undergraduate transcripts, two letters of recommendation, and a two-page essay. The graduate admissions committee may also request an interview. Students can apply for admissions for the fall, spring, or summer semester, and they may apply for entrance directly after finishing their undergraduate studies.

FINANCIAL FACTS

Annual tuition	$26,400
Cost of books	$550
% of students receiving aid	85
% of first-year students receiving aid	100
% of students receiving grants	90

ADMISSIONS

Admissions Selectivity Rating	73
# of applications received	110
% applicants accepted	91
% acceptees attending	96
Average GMAT	560
Range of GMAT	500–730
Average GPA	3.4
TOEFL required of international students	Yes
Minimum TOEFL (paper/computer)	550/230
Application fee	$25
International application fee	$25
Early decision program?	No
Deferment available	Yes
Maximum length of deferment	1 year
Transfer students accepted	Yes
Transfer application policy: Student in Good Standing. 6 hours from a non-AACSB program; 12 hours from a AACSB accredited program.	
Non-fall admissions	Yes
Need-blind admissions	Yes

EMPLOYMENT PROFILE

Career Rating	70	Grads Employed by Function	% Avg. Salary
Percent employed at graduation	5	Marketing	2 NR
Percent employed 3 months after graduation	8	Finance	2 NR
		MIS	2 NR
		Entrepreneurship	1 NR
		Nonprofit	1 NR

MINNESOTA STATE UNIVERSITY—MANKATO
COLLEGE OF BUSINESS

GENERAL INFORMATION
Type of school   Public
Academic calendar   Semester

SURVEY SAYS...
Friendly students
Good peer network
Cutting-edge classes
Happy students
Smart classrooms

STUDENTS
Enrollment of parent institution	14,000
Enrollment of MBA Program	100
% male/female	65/35
% out-of-state	22
% part-time	33
% minorities	10
% international	15
Average age at entry	28
Average years work experience at entry	5

ACADEMICS
Academic Experience Rating	78
Student/faculty ratio	16:1
Profs interesting rating	86
Profs accessible rating	84
% female faculty	40

Academics

The MBA program at Minnesota State University Mankato's College of Business "is unique in that classes are only offered at night and in eight-week modules," an arrangement that "works out very nicely for those working full time and trying to go to school along with it." The eight-week modules create "program flexibility" that students love. MBAs here can take one or two classes per module, and they can skip a module entirely when necessary without losing too much ground. A student who takes the maximum number of classes per module can complete the program in about two years.

Convenience isn't the only attraction at the CoB. "MSU Mankato is known to have a great business program," local students report, also noting that "the program is selective" and "the cost of tuition is reasonable." Other assets include "a great atmosphere and small classes, along with a wealth of resources and technology" and an "outstanding faculty." The curriculum consists of Tool Courses (business writing, data analysis and statistics, economics), Core Courses (business law, accounting, finance, human resources, IT, and management), Strategy Courses (international business, marketing, business policy, and an executive seminar), and Concentration Courses; students may concentrate in international business (international study opportunities are available) or leadership and organizational change. Students may also fashion their own concentrations in consultation with a faculty advisor. Students report approvingly that "teamwork and ethics values are clearly interwoven into the curriculum."

Mankato professors typically "know the material they teach very well and they work well with students." One student elaborates: "The professors are aware of the present business environment and their research provides them with a keen sense of future environment. The coursework and experience have added significantly to my professional skill set." They also appreciate that Mankato "is a wired campus" and note that "all business students are required to have laptops." The university store stocks laptops that meet the campuses software, connectivity, and security software requirements, although students are free to use their own laptops so long as they meet the school's standards.

Career and Placement

MSU Mankato's Career Development Center serves all undergraduate students, graduate students, and alumni of the school. The MBA program is relatively new, with its first graduating class being spring 2006, so there is still plenty of room for growth. The College of Business has recently partnered with CareerBeam, which allows MBA students to access more than 20,000 business sources across 150 job categories. Students here should consider mining another valuable resource: the faculty. One student explains, "I think the faculty would be a very valuable resource to consult regarding future jobs and placement. Most of the faculty is very friendly and willing to help."

ADMISSIONS CONTACT: LINDA MEIDL, STUDENT RELATIONS COORDINATOR
ADDRESS: MORRIS HALL 151, MINNESOTA STATE UNIVERSITY, MANKATO MANKATO, MN 56001
PHONE: 507-389-5425 • FAX: 507-389-1318
E-MAIL: LINDA.MEIDL@MNSU.EDU • WEBSITE: COB.MNSU.EDU

Student Life and Environment

Mankato MBAs "seem to be very responsible and hard-working people" whom their classmates describe as "friendly and social," "polite and easy to get along with." They are "of various ages and backgrounds," representing a mix of recent or continuing undergraduates and professionals returning to the classroom after at least a few years of professional experience. Students here "do very well in groups and teams."

Mankato, students tell us, is "a great college town with a warm and friendly community, and a growing university with a vast support system from local businesses and leaders." The town of 36,000 is located about 65 miles southwest of Minneapolis. The surrounding region is "the health care, commercial, and cultural center of south-central Minnesota," according to the school's website. Residents have easy access to parks and ski facilities; outdoor activities are very popular here. MSU's athletic teams, which compete "in the Northern Sun Intercollegiate Conference, with the men's and women's hockey teams competing in the Division I Western Collegiate Hockey Association (WCHA) conference," and the teams enjoy strong support from area residents. The school has begun offering an off-campus MBA in Edina, a southwestern suburb of the Twin Cities, for students in the area.

Admissions

Applicants to the MBA program at MSU Mankato's College of Business must submit all of the following materials to the College of Graduate Studies: a completed application form; two official transcripts from one's degree-granting institution(s); a completed immunization form; and official score reports for the GMAT and, if applicable, the TOEFL. International applicants must also complete a Financial Statement Form demonstrating that they have sufficient funds to pay for the program. Most international applicants are required to have their undergraduate transcripts evaluated by a well-regarded credential evaluation service. All applicants must also submit a separate MBA program application form, a resume, and two letters of reference to the College of Business. Admission to the MBA program is competitive. Students earning a score of 1000 or higher under the formula $[(200 \times \text{undergraduate GPA}) + \text{GMAT score}]$ and scoring at least 500 on the GMAT will be admitted unconditionally to the program; students earning a score of at least 1000 but with a GMAT score slightly below 500 may be admitted on a conditional basis.

FINANCIAL FACTS

Annual tuition	$8,500
Fees	$523
Cost of books	$900
% of first-year students receiving aid	20

ADMISSIONS

Admissions Selectivity Rating	68
# of applications received	19
% applicants accepted	84
% acceptees attending	75
Average GMAT	500
Range of GMAT	450–680
Average GPA	3.25
TOEFL required of international students	Yes
Minimum TOEFL (paper/computer)	500/173
Application fee	$40
International application fee	$40
Application Deadline/Notification	
Round 1:	7/1 / 7/8
Round 2:	11/1 / 11/8
Early decision program?	No
Deferment available	Yes
Maximum length of deferment	1 year
Transfer students accepted	Yes
Transfer application policy: Upon evaluation, would accept a maximum of 6 credits from another MBA or graduate program.	
Non-fall admissions	Yes
Need-blind admissions	Yes

MISSOURI STATE UNIVERSITY
COLLEGE OF BUSINESS ADMINISTRATION

GENERAL INFORMATION
Type of school   Public

SURVEY SAYS...
Students love Springfield, MO
Solid preparation in:
Marketing
General management
Computer skills

STUDENTS
Enrollment of parent
institution   21,000
Enrollment of MBA Program   343
% male/female   39/61
% out-of-state   5
% part-time   53
% minorities   4
% international   29
Average age at entry   28
Average years work experience
at entry   2

ACADEMICS
Academic Experience Rating   70
Student/faculty ratio   20:1
Profs interesting rating   77
Profs accessible rating   68
% female faculty   32
% minority faculty   4

Prominent Alumni
David Glass, former CEO of Wal-
Mart and CEO of KC Royals; Todd
Tiahrt, 4-term Congressman;
Richard McClure, President of Uni
Group, Inc.; Jim Smith, President
American Banking Association,
2001–02; Terry Thompson, Former
President, Jack Henry.

Academics

Why choose Missouri State University's College of Business Administration (COBA) for your MBA? Well, how about the "accessibility, flexibility, reputation, and affordability" of the program for starters? Many students here also point out that this "well-managed" program has the "highest accreditation of all the business schools in the area," which goes a long way come job-hunting time. Along with having "the best price in the region," COBA also offers a "very flexible program." "It allowed me the freedom to tailor my MBA exactly to my needs," one student says. Part of this flexibility is evidenced by its "excellent" Accelerated Master's degree option that, according to the school, "enables outstanding Missouri State University undergraduate students to begin taking graduate course work in their junior or senior year and thus combine components of the undergraduate and graduate curriculum." Not too bad a deal, if you ask us, and it certainly accounts for the substantial number of MSU undergrads becoming COBA grads. "It provided an easy transition from my undergraduate to graduate work," one such student explains.

Another enticing component of COBA is its partnership with the International School of Management Studies in Chennai, India, that allows Indian students to "complete their foundation courses in India" and then "complete the remaining credits at MSU." "That way, I get an international MBA," one student explains. Others appreciate the "challenging courses" and the "outstanding" professors who "have an interest in teaching." "MSU employs intelligent professors that make an effort to be readily available outside the class for questions and/or comments," a student adds. Most describe the administration as "excellent" and find that the school "runs rather smoothly."

Thanks to MSU's "convenient rural location" and its rising academic reputation, it's a "large school with a small-school feel." However, despite this some students find themselves left out of the mix. "I do feel disconnected from it," one student says, "because I have never had the same teacher twice or established any consistent 'class' or group to associate with." Others are more concerned with course offerings. "I would have preferred a more developed entrepreneurial department with more small business-oriented courses to choose from." That said, for the courses that are available students appreciate the "ease of registering" and the "very positive and helpful staff." Some wouldn't mind seeing the school take a more proactive role in enhancing its visibility through "more advertising and marketing." But many here find that things are well on their way. One student sums it up, saying, "I think the school is in a transition period right now. However, I believe they are making progress."

Career and Placement

MSU is quick to point out that "The Career Center doesn't work like an employment agency." "Instead," they say, "our mission focuses upon education: We attempt to teach people job-searching skills that they can use throughout their lives." In line with this, career advisors are available to students by appointment and work to both "link" them with employers and educate them in "researching companies, occupations, or geographic locations...[so that they] won't be dependent upon someone else doing it for them." Students here can also opt to register their resumes with the Career Center so that when employers do come calling for MBAs, the office can send them info on a number of qualified individuals. Additionally, the Career Center holds career fairs where "about 90 recruiters come on campus each year to interview students." According to the school, approximately three-fourths of graduates work in Missouri after graduation, which accounts for the strong local ties MSU possesses.

Student Life and Environment

COBA students are an "intelligent" and "mostly friendly" bunch who appreciate the "culturally diverse learning experience" the MBA program offers. Despite the prevalence of "business guys" roaming the halls, most find that students here, while being competitive, are only so "against themselves" and "not really against other students." "They try very hard for the 'A,' but are very open to helping classmates succeed as well," one student states. Others opine that "Overall they lack the drive to do well. When it is possible to do just the minimum that road is taken." The student body is "primarily recent graduates or people in their early 30s," who "come from a variety of cultural backgrounds" thanks to "a large international population," all of who appreciate the "low cost of living" in Springfield.

Outside of class, the "compact campus" facilitates getting to know your fellow student. "Our campus community is safe and inviting, and allows for exploration into various activities and academic endeavors," one student says. Another adds that "Activities are planned [at] the university almost every night of the week, including lectures, panel discussions, public affairs conferences, free movie nights, Broadway shows, and athletic events (all sports Division I)." However, some believe that student involvement would take an upswing if "faculty members sponsored and recommended activities." "Life at school is very segmented from the rest of my life," one student explains. "Coming from a non-business background put me on the outside of events and other clubs." Others would like to see the improved "gym facilities" and "public transportation," but all in all, students seem more than content in "The Queen City of the Ozarks."

Admissions

Admissions officers for COBA look for applicants with a Bachelor's or Master's degree from an accredited school with a GPA of at least 2.75 for the last two years (or 60 semester hours) of academic work, a GMAT score of at least 400 (or GRE equivalent) with a minimum score in the 20th percentile for both the verbal and written portions of the test, and a minimum value of 1,000 based on this formula (200 times your GPA for the last 60 semester hours of your degree plus your GMAT score). That said, the school will consider applicants "who do not meet the normal admission requirements, but who possess high promise (usually based upon a successful record of managerial performance at increasing levels of responsibility)" for probationary admission. Additionally, international students who are not native speakers of English must submit TOEFL scores of 550 or higher.

FINANCIAL FACTS

Annual tuition (in-state/ out-of-state)	$4,536/$9,072
Fees	$508
Cost of books	$875
Room & board (on/off-campus)	$4,806/$5,200
% of students receiving aid	55
% of students receiving loans	53
% of students receiving grants	34
Average award package	$8,909
Average grant	$3,112
Average student loan debt	$16,500

ADMISSIONS

Admissions Selectivity Rating	66
# of applications received	160
% applicants accepted	98
% acceptees attending	98
Average GMAT	510
Range of GMAT	440–570
Average GPA	3.4
TOEFL required of international students	Yes
Minimum TOEFL (paper/computer)	550/213
Application fee	$30
International application fee	$30
Early decision program?	No
Deferment available	Yes
Maximum length of deferment	1 semester
Transfer students accepted	Yes
Transfer application policy: With advisor permission	
Non-fall admissions	Yes
Need-blind admissions	No

EMPLOYMENT PROFILE

Career Rating	79	Grads Employed by Function	% Avg. Salary
Average base starting salary	$56,000	Marketing	12 $43,667
Primary Source of Full-time Job Acceptances		Operations	10 $41,000
School-facilitated activities	NR (30%)	Consulting	12 $39,810
Graduate-facilitated activities	NR (20%)	Management	20 $40,988
Unknown	NR (50%)	Finance	9 $41,875
		HR	3 $33,456
		MIS	12 $48,920

Top 5 Employers Hiring Grads
BKD (10), State of Missouri (9), Missouri State University (9), Boeing (5), Wal-Mart (5)

MONMOUTH UNIVERSITY
LEON HESS BUSINESS SCHOOL

GENERAL INFORMATION
Type of school   Private
Academic calendar   Semester

SURVEY SAYS...
Students love West Long Branch, NJ
Solid preperation in:
Finance

STUDENTS
Enrollment of parent institution	6,442
Enrollment of MBA Program	222
% male/female	66/34
% out-of-state	1
% part-time	68
% minorities	11
% international	13
Average age at entry	27
Average years work experience at entry	5

ACADEMICS
Academic Experience Rating	**75**
Student/faculty ratio	7:1
Profs interesting rating	84
Profs accessible rating	79
% female faculty	24
% minority faculty	21

Prominent Alumni
Linda C Deutsch, Legal Affairs Correspondent; Noel L Hillman, Federal Judge; Christie Pearce Rampone, Olympic Gold Medalist; Herbert Butler, R & D first televised weather satellite; Robert Santelli, Executive Director GRAMMY Museum.

Academics

Leon Hess Business School at Monmouth University has long been a boon to area professionals looking to fast-track their careers. Now, thanks to "a lot of initiatives occurring to improve Monmouth's standing as a leading educational institution," the school is beginning to expand its appeal.

Among these innovations is the addition of a full-time accelerated MBA program that can be completed in one year. The school has also broadened its concentration offerings to include not only real estate and health care management (as it has in the past) but also accounting and finance. Finally, the school is expanding its selection of course formats, adding hybrid courses with an online component to its roster of traditional classroom courses.

Students here appreciate "the small-school atmosphere in getting to know and interact with your classmates," noting in contrast that "Larger universities...are very impersonal, where students are treated as numbers and figures, not as living people." Cost, convenience, and reputation with local employers all figure into students' choice of MU, as does location; as one student explains, "Being close to New York and Philadelphia helps the school develop the students to what the major employers need." MU professors "bring substantial prior work experience" to the classroom and "are very supportive. They have an interest in seeing their students learn." Students warn that the faculty can be hit-or-miss, though; one MBA informs us, "There are some very good professors and a few professors that are so awful they give poor professors a bad name."

Mostly, though, students appreciate how this program "recognizes that students have busy lives outside of school, as many work. Every effort is made to use the e-campus electronic classroom meeting-place for supplemental class work like group discussions. This allows students to log in as their time permits to contribute to discussions with classmates; the discussions are moderated by knowledgeable professors. This use of electronic tools allows for group work that allows for care of your own harried life schedules."

Career and Placement

Career services are provided to Monmouth MBAs by the Center for Student Success, which serves the entire university. The office administers aptitude tests and career inventories and provides a contact point between students and alumni and businesses. One-on-one counseling services are also available. According to one student, the Assistant Dean for Career Services at the university is energetic and caring, "but I do not get the impression that there is a full-scale service for placement at the graduate level. This is important to me as a 'career changer,' but my understanding is that I am in the minority."

Companies recruiting business grads at MU include AXA Advisors, Empire Technologies, Meridian Health, Northwest Mutual Financial, PricewaterhouseCoopers, and UPS.

Student Life and Environment

For the many part-time MBA students here with major commitments outside of school, participation in extracurriculars is a rarity. As one student aptly puts it, "I am attending night school, so all I ever see is the parking lot and the classroom." Even those who spend more time on campus say that "The school lacks any central graduate business student grouping. Perhaps an orientation each semester and a graduate business school lounge might lend some cohesiveness. Also, I'd like to see some emphasis on job placement for the graduate business school students." Most here, though tell us that they are "not looking for a full college experience again, so what I am getting now is making me happy."

Monmouth's student body is "very diverse"; most here "seem to be in their late 20s to early 30s and up." Quite a few told us that they attended MU as undergraduates and that this experience figured heavily in their decisions to return for an MBA. Some of these are "younger recent graduates" who "seem less focused, as if they are entering undergrad all over."

Admissions

Minimum requirements for conditional admission to the Monmouth MBA program include either a GMAT score of at least 500, or a formula score of at least 1000 under the formula [(undergraduate GPA x 200) + GMAT score] with a minimum GMAT score of 450. Students who hold graduate degrees in other areas (MS, MD, JD, PhD, EdD, etc.) may be exempted from the above admissions requirements. Exceptional or conditional acceptance may be granted to a small number of qualified applicants at the discretion of the MBA program director. International students whose native language is not English must submit official TOEFL score reports in addition to all required documents listed above (minimum score 550 paper, 213 computer, 79 Internet). The school will also consider results in the IELTS (minimum score 6), CAE [Certificate of Advanced English] (minimum score B2), or MELAB (minimum score 77).

FINANCIAL FACTS

Annual tuition	$13,914
Fees	$628
Cost of books	$1,000
Room & board	
(off-campus)	$14,301
% of students receiving aid	88
% of first-year students	
receiving aid	68
% of students receiving loans	31
% of students receiving grants	51
Average award package	$6,903
Average grant	$1,635
Average student loan debt	$32,198

ADMISSIONS

Admissions Selectivity Rating	68
# of applications received	151
% applicants accepted	79
% acceptees attending	55
Average GMAT	513
Range of GMAT	460–560
Average GPA	3.24
TOEFL required of	
international students	Yes
Minimum TOEFL	
(paper/computer)	550/213
Application fee	$50
International application fee	$50
Regular application deadline	7/15
Early decision program?	No
Deferment available	Yes
Maximum length	
of deferment	1 year
Transfer students accepted	Yes
Transfer application policy:	
must complete at least 30 credits at Monmouth. Transfer crds must be within 7 years and with acceptable grade.	
Non-fall admissions	Yes
Need-blind admissions	Yes

MONTCLAIR STATE UNIVERSITY
SCHOOL OF BUSINESS

GENERAL INFORMATION
Type of school   Public
Academic calendar   Year-round

SURVEY SAYS...
Students love Upper Montclair, NJ
Friendly students
Good social scene
Happy students
Smart classrooms

STUDENTS
Enrollment of parent
  institution   17,475
Enrollment of MBA Program   360
% male/female   59/41
% out-of-state   78
% part-time   77
% minorities   20
% international   10
Average age at entry   24
Average years work experience
  at entry   4

ACADEMICS
Academic Experience Rating   72
Student/faculty ratio   25:1
Profs interesting rating   75
Profs accessible rating   70
% female faculty   22
% minority faculty   34

Joint Degrees
MS in Chemistry / MBA in Business, minimum of 62 semester hours; MS in Accounting (MSU School of Business), minimum of 33 semester hours.

Prominent Alumni
Dr. Steve Adubato, Anchor, WNET NY, PBS; Dr. Paul Weber, Director Global Medical Affairs, Schering-Plough; Annette Catino, President & CEO, QualCare, Inc.; Thomas P. Zucosky, CIO, Discovery Capital Management; A. J. Khubani, President & CEO, Telebrands.

Academics

Affordability, "proximity to New York City," and "a program that caters to part-time students" are the main attractions at the MBA program at Montclair State University. The school offers a full-time program, with classes in the evenings and Saturdays; a part-time evening program; and an accelerated Saturday program. Approximately one-quarter of the student body attends full-time.

The Montclair MBA is a 48-credit sequence including nine credits of introductory management classes, a 15-credit functional core (covering accounting, finance, marketing, and information management), nine credits of advanced business courses, 12–18 credits of electives (some of which may be used to create an area of concentration), and a three-credit capstone course in advanced strategic management. Up to 15 hours of these classes can be waived based on prior academic work or through challenge examinations. Concentrations are available in accounting, economics, finance, international business, management, marketing, and MIS.

Montclair professors "have a good amount of practical knowledge and integrate current topics well, without going into overkill mode. The program design offers a good balance of individual and group assignments, papers, exams, and presentations." Instructors earn praise for being "understanding of students' other obligations, but without being pushovers," and for "bringing great real-world experience to [the] classroom." Administrators earn praise for soliciting student evaluations of their professors, and for actually listening to these comments: students claim that "some professors have actually been removed from the program upon student request." Administrators are also very approachable; one student states, they "hold lunches that are a great environment for conversation. They're really good at listening to students."

Career and Placement

The MSU Career Development Center serves all undergraduates and graduates at the school. MBAs are not impressed; one writes, "We need to establish an alumni club or organization and a career/campus recruiting office." Another agrees, "It would be nice to have a career services center active for MBAs. In all my years attending I have yet to have anyone from the MBA office or career office offer a meeting, discussion, or follow-up on my studies." Living near New York City, "the greatest free market in the world," makes it a little easier for students to find internships and jobs on their own. Most MSU MBAs attend while pursuing full-time careers; their employers include Abbott Laboratories, ADP, AT&T Wireless Services, Bank of New York, Con Edison, Deloitte Consulting, Goldman Sachs, Gucci, Kodak, the *New York Times*, the Office of the New Jersey Attorney General, PricewaterhouseCoopers, Prudential Financial, Sodexho USA, Thomson Financial, United Parcel Service, and Wyeth-Ayerst Research.

Student Life and Environment

Montclair is "mostly a commuter campus," with "about 75 percent of the students attending part-time and working full-time." As a result, "Most people don't get involved in activities because there are higher priorities (work, family, the rest of life)." The part-time student body arrives with "an interesting array of backgrounds and work experiences," we're told. The large number of part-time commuters means "group work can be difficult because we all have different schedules, but we figure out how to work together."

The town of Montclair has several major parks and lots of quiet streets. It boasts four movie theaters, an art museum and several art galleries, lots of artisan shops, two off-Broadway theater companies, a host of funky restaurants, and an abundance of coffee shops. Students remark that they often see no need to venture into New York City proper, as they are able to partake in a range of cultural activities without ever leaving the Montclair vicinity. Cross-town public transportation is also pretty good, and access to and from NYC is frequent, easy, and cheap.

Those MBAs who live on campus and attend full-time "tend to be the international students." They tell us that "overall, campus life is good. We have many graduate- and undergraduate-level clubs and organizations to choose from. There is something for everyone at MSU." Full-timers and commuters alike appreciate the fact that "there is a diner on campus, proof that this is a Jersey school."

Admissions

Applicants to the MSU/MBA program "must have at least earned a bachelor's degree from a regionally-accredited college or university (or the foreign equivalent)" and must submit two official copies of transcripts for all academic work completed after high school; an official score report for the GMAT (applicants holding a terminal degree—a PhD, MD, or JD, for example—are exempt from the GMAT requirement); a personal statement of professional goals; two letters of recommendation from "persons qualified to evaluate the applicant's promise of academic achievement and potential for professional growth;" and a completed application form. International students whose first language is not English must submit an official score report for the TOEFL. Of these elements, the undergraduate GPA and the GMAT score are among the most important factors that the Admissions Department considers. The average GMAT score was 476, and the average GPA was 3.3. Prior work experience is "strongly recommended" but is not required.

FINANCIAL FACTS

Annual tuition (in-state/ out-of-state)	$10,536/$14,490
Fees	$1,296
Cost of books	$1,200
Room & board (on/off-campus)	$8,250/$12,500
% of students receiving aid	31
% of first-year students receiving aid	40
% of students receiving loans	26
% of students receiving grants	8
Average award package	$14,446
Average grant	$10,454
Average student loan debt	$32,903

ADMISSIONS

Admissions Selectivity Rating	82
# of applications received	330
% applicants accepted	34
% acceptees attending	76
Average GMAT	476
Range of GMAT	398–550
Average GPA	3.3
TOEFL required of international students	Yes
Minimum TOEFL (paper/computer)	380/207
Application fee	$60
International application fee	$60
Early decision program?	No
Deferment available	Yes
Maximum length of deferment	1 year
Transfer students accepted	Yes
Transfer application policy: Through prior academic experience, graduate transfer credits, and/or challenge examinations, the MBA degree requirements may be reduced by up to 15 credits (SH) of Core courses. Waiver assessments are made after candidates are accepted to the MBA Program, at an initial advising appointment with the Assistant Dean for Graduate Programs in the School of Business.	
Non-fall admissions	Yes
Need-blind admissions	Yes

EMPLOYMENT PROFILE

		Grads Employed by Function	%	Avg. Salary
Career Rating	69			
Percent employed at graduation	80	Marketing	16	$75,000
Percent employed 3 months after graduation	15	Operations	4	$65,000
		Consulting	4	$50,000
Average base starting salary	$63,125	Management	40	$80,000
Primary Source of Full-time Job Acceptances		Finance	28	$60,000
School-facilitated activities	10 (NR%)	MIS	8	$60,000
Graduate-facilitated activities	90 (NR%)	**Top 5 Employers Hiring Grads**		
		Roche Laboratories, Schering Plough, Morgan Stanley, Johnson & Johnson, Prudential		

MONTEREY INSTITUTE OF INTERNATIONAL STUDIES
FISHER GRADUATE SCHOOL OF INTERNATIONAL BUSINESS

GENERAL INFORMATION

Type of school	Private
Academic calendar	Semester

SURVEY SAYS...
Solid preparation in:
Teamwork
Doing business in a global economy

STUDENTS

Enrollment of parent institution	860
Enrollment of MBA Program	124
% male/female	58/42
% part-time	5
% minorities	12
% international	38
Average age at entry	26
Average years work experience at entry	4

ACADEMICS

Academic Experience Rating	77
Student/faculty ratio	7:1
Profs interesting rating	79
Profs accessible rating	95
% female faculty	16
% minority faculty	32

Joint Degrees
MBA/MA International Policy Studies, 3 years; MBA/MA International Environmental Policy Studies, 3 years; MBA/MA International Trade Policy Studies, 3 years; MBA/MPA Non-Profit Management, 3 years; MBA/MA Translation, 3 years; MBA/MA Translation & Localization Management, 3 years.

Prominent Alumni
Fumio Matsushima, Head of Private Banking, HSBC Japan; Laurent-Gabriel Vinay, CEO/President, Hugo Boss Japan; Elizabeth Powell, Vice President of Customer Service at Motorola; Naoko Yanaghara, Vice President of AT&T Japan; Andrew Elliott, North Americas Director of Software & Services, Nokia.

Academics

As its name indicates, the graduate business program at the Monterey Institute "focuses on international business" from its curriculum (which includes "a three-semester advanced language component") to the composition of its student body (one American student calls it "the most international environment I have ever been in, and I have been living abroad since the end of high school. Half the students in every class are international students."). Part of the Graduate School of International Policy and Management, The Fisher School excels in entrepreneurship studies. Students praise its offerings in language, country and political risk assessment, cross-cultural negotiation, and corporate responsibility.

MIIS offers a "small and personal" program that is nonetheless large enough to accommodate "the ability to customize degrees, classes, specializations, and extracurricular activities." A number of our respondents noted the dual-degree programs available here, which include an MBA/MA in international environmental policy, several MBA/MA options in international policymaking, and an MBA/MA in translation. The program's size is not without its drawbacks, however. One student explains: "Being a small school with limited resources strains the ability of the faculty to offer core courses every semester. Overall, the academic experience is great, but somewhat different than most other business schools. The focus is more on language studies, negotiation and cross-cultural issues."

In addition to the above-mentioned areas, the MIIS curriculum also focuses "on ethics, corporate social responsibility, and environmental issues," an aspect of the program students find appealing. They also love how "This place is pretty laid-back, and everyone from the security folks to the Dean wants to see you succeed. Ain't no sabotaging here in Monterey!" Finally, MBAs appreciate "the strong alumni network and mentor program."

Career and Placement

The Career Management Center (CMC) for the Fisher MBA program offers "a customized approach to each individual's goals, skill set, [and] educational and personal background," according to the school. The office "acts as an 'executive search firm'" to help students "target potential employers and enhance their added-value" through online career assessments; one-on-one consultations; and workshops in interviewing skills, salary negotiation, internship, and networking. Students report that the office "is slowly pulling things together, but our size and location, definitely limits the number of recruiters coming to campus."

Employers who most frequently hire MIIS graduates include: Accenture, Bank of America, Cargill, Central Intelligence Agency, Cisco Systems, CTB McGraw Hill, Daimler Chrysler, Deutsche Bank, Deloitte & Touche Consulting, EMDAP (Emerging Markets Development Advisors Program), Ernst & Young, Frost & Sullivan, Hewlett Packard, HSBC (Hong Kong Shanghai Bank Company), Intel, JP Morgan, LanguageLine Services, Paul Kagan & Associates, PricewaterhouseCoopers, Seagate Technology, Silicon Graphics, Inc., Sun Microsystems, Target, Ubisoft, U.S. Dept of Commerce, U.S. Dept of Labor, U.S. Dept of State, US Peace Corps, Wells Fargo, and West Marine.

ADMISSIONS CONTACT: CAROLINE MANSI, ENROLLMENT MANAGER
ADDRESS: 460 PIERCE STREET MONTEREY, CA 93940
PHONE: 831-647-4123 • FAX: 831-647-6405
E-MAIL: ADMIT@MIIS.EDU • WEBSITE: FISHER.MIIS.EDU

Student Life and Environment

The MIIS MBA program is a small one; "The entering business class is about 50 students. We all know each other well and freely mingle inside and outside of class well. For the size of the school, it does very well to give each student as many opportunities to gain both intellectually and professionally as possible." MBAs report: "There is a lot of inter-action between business school students and the students of other schools. The student council organizes happy hours every month to encourage the interaction between stu-dents of all schools as well as professors." They also tell us, "There are many clubs on campus, including a golf club, scuba club, international trade and development club, women in business club, language clubs, and many others." Languages are very impor-tant, and thanks to the translation and interpretation school, one gets many opportuni-ties to practice his second language throughout the day.

The campus here "is well-equipped. All classrooms have brand-new furniture, and most have multimedia equipment. The library is top-notch; I rely on its internal collection, on the collection of the consortium to which it belongs, and on its interlibrary loan services. However, the campus has no gym and no discount arrangements, which is a shortcom-ing." Quality of life in the Monterey region "is excellent," although "because of Monterey's large student population, rents are high and housing quality is low." Monterey "is a beautiful and quiet place" that "has rich nature," but "it is isolated from centers of business activity." San Jose is about an hour's drive to the north; San Francisco is two hours off.

Admissions

Proficiency in a second language is required by the MIIS graduate business program; stu-dents are required to demonstrate reading and listening proficiency in their second lan-guage during New Student Orientation. The MBA Plus program, which is designed for students with limited proficiency in a second language, provides an intensive language immersion program in the summer prior to enrollment in the MBA program, allowing students to gain the needed language skills. Applicants whose native language is not English must demonstrate proficiency through TOEFL or IELTS testing. Applicants must have achieved a minimum 3.0 undergraduate GPA and must submit an official score report for the GMAT. Letters of recommendation, a resume, and a personal statement are also required. An interview, while not required, are strongly recommended.

FINANCIAL FACTS

Annual tuition	$29,300
Fees	$56
Cost of books	$900
Room & board (off-campus)	$13,570
% of students receiving aid	93
% of first-year students receiving aid	93
% of students receiving loans	54
% of students receiving grants	87
Average award package	$24,804
Average grant	$9,163
Average student loan debt	$25,026

ADMISSIONS

Admissions Selectivity Rating	73
# of applications received	163
% applicants accepted	77
% acceptees attending	58
Average GMAT	563
Range of GMAT	490–620
Average GPA	3.44
TOEFL required of international students	Yes
Minimum TOEFL (paper/computer)	550/213
Application fee	$50
International application fee	$50
Regular application deadline	3/15
Regular notification	5/1
Early decision program?	No
Deferment available	No
Transfer students accepted	Yes
Transfer application policy: Credits must be from an AACSB accredited college or university, must be with a B or better. Possible to transfer up to 25% of total program. Dean makes final determination.	
Non-fall admissions	Yes
Need-blind admissions	Yes

EMPLOYMENT PROFILE

Career Rating	77	**Grads Employed by Function**	**% Avg. Salary**
Percent employed at graduation	29	Marketing	70 $56,000
Percent employed 3 months after graduation	52	Consulting	10 $58,500
		Management	10 $52,000
Average base starting salary	$58,900	HR	10 $70,000
Primary Source of Full-time Job Acceptances		**Top 5 Employers Hiring Grads**	
School-facilitated activities	4 (25%)	Deloitte & Touche (1), Sun Microsystems (1),	
Graduate-facilitated activities	7 (44%)	FIJI Water (1), US Department of Commerce	
Unknown	5 (31%)	(2), Versatel AG (1)	

NATIONAL UNIVERSITY OF SINGAPORE
BUSINESS SCHOOL

GENERAL INFORMATION
Type of school   Public
Academic calendar   August

SURVEY SAYS...
Students love Singapore
Smart classrooms
Solid preparation in:
Accounting
General management
Quantitative skills

STUDENTS
Enrollment of parent institution	3,272
Enrollment of MBA Program	173
% male/female	63/37
% out-of-state	91
% part-time	30
% international	91
Average age at entry	28
Average years work experience at entry	6

ACADEMICS
Academic Experience Rating	**89**
Student/faculty ratio	21:1
Profs interesting rating	73
Profs accessible rating	76
% female faculty	29
% minority faculty	63

Joint Degrees
NUS-Peking University IMBA (24 months); UCLA-NUS Executive MBA (15 months); The NUS MBA Double Degree Masters in Public Policy with Lee Kuan Yew School of Public Policy (24–36 months full-time); The NUS MBA Double Degree Masters in Public Administration with Lee Kuan Yew School of Public Policy (24–36 months full-time); S3 Asia MBA (18 months); NUS-HEC MBA (23 months).

Academics

"Asia is fast becoming the center of global business activity," students at the National University of Singapore Business School remind us, and "NUS is one of the best schools, both to learn about how business is conducted in Asia and to network with corporations established in the region." The school is "considered one of the best universities in the world and the topmost business school in Asia." The school's location "offers a strategic advantage," because Singapore "is the financial hub of Asia and the hub of all Asian business. "NUS Business School gives the best possible value" and prepares students for a solid business career overall, "where the regional job market, especially for a career in finance, is quite good."

NUS' graduate business programs offer "a global perspective with an Asian outlook" augmented by "the ability to be part of a multicultural society in Singapore. You can enhance your understandings of, and contacts within, the Chinese, Indian, and Southeast Asian business cultures here." Students also extol "the excellent facilities, especially the libraries and auditoriums," the "very strong faculty," and the excellent "value."

NUS has long offered a part-time program. It recently added a full-time program that "has increased class sizes; the school administration has been able to handle it very well and there have been no logistical or administrative issues." Students have the option to pursue a general MBA or one with a specialization in either real estate management or health care management. Either way, they must complete a 10-course core module that "provides a holistic view of the entire business world" while giving us "exposure to all different fields of management." All of the modules "are very important, the type of courses you'd take even if they were electives."

Students also tell us that the program and the entire environment are very flexible. "We are free to do what we want (obviously within the parameter of rules), which helps us in being as creative as we want. Professors are eager to help us in various international events and competitions. This is a great impetus for students that brings out the best in them." Students tell us that "administrators are open to discussion on improving the course and integrates new business concepts in the curriculum," which they appreciate.

Career and Placement

The Career Services Office (CSO) "is a strong point of the NUS Business School," students report. One writes, "I was surprised to see so many companies coming over for on-campus recruitment." Another adds, "The CSO is changing so fast and for the better. Many job postings" are available to choose from. Some here feel that the office could do a better job bringing recruiters to campus; others counter that those who complain mostly "come from places where the placement cells actually ensure that companies come and recruit on the same day. That is not the way it works in Singapore and most of rest of the world."

Companies most likely to hire NUS MBAs include: ExxonMobil Asia Pacific, Hewlett-Packard Singapore, International Enterprise Singapore, KPMG International, Ministry of Trade and Industry, National Computer Board, NEC Singapore PTE LTD, Proctor & Gamble, Philips Electronics, Shell Eastern Petroleum, Singapore Police Force, Sony Systems Design International, and Swiss Bank Corporation.

Student Life and Environment

The NUS program carries a moderate workload, allowing for a "fantastic balance between studies and fun." The workload also means that "students have time to think about career moves, take part in business plan competitions and do some job searching." Extracurricular events include "lots of competitions, amazing speakers from the industry, lots of different activities with student clubs," and "wonderful parties like International Day and the Deepawali celebration." An annual Graduate Business Conference "brings us all together." In the past, the conference has featured such noteworthy keynote speakers as Jimmy Carter and former GM Chairperson John Smale.

On campus, "The MBA lounge is the place to be if you [want to] be a part of the 'in' group. Discussions ...range from politics, business ethics, case studies, and the venue for the next 'jam' session (basically music, booze, and fun)." Some students complain that "the layout of the school is not ideal, because it is spread out over too many buildings."

NUS draws a "mature and serious" student body of professionals "who are obviously occupied with how their careers are going and who are earnest in wanting to learn." These "well-traveled" MBA candidates are highly international; India and China are heavily represented, while students from the United States, Switzerland, Norway, Korea, and other far-flung locations fill out the student body. In terms of background, students "come from engineering, commerce, medicine, architecture, and many more fields. As the median work experience is about six years, there is a good quality of contribution that people make in the class."

Admissions

NUS seeks applicants who "have leadership capabilities and the strong desire and drive for academic and management excellence" and who are "motivated, mature, focused and have a desire to make a positive impact on business and society," according to the school's website. Applicants to the NUS School of Business must provide the Admissions Office with transcripts for all undergraduate and graduate work, GMAT scores, TOEFL or IELTS scores (for non-native English speakers), two letters of recommendation, and a resume demonstrating at least 2 years of professional experience after obtaining their first degree or equivalent. Shortlisted applicants will be interviewed and may be required to take further evaluation tests. Interviews are conducted face-to-face or via phone for candidates located overseas.

Prominent Alumni

Ms. Janet Ang, Vice President, Lenovo; Mr Wong Ah Long, CEO,Pacific Star Investments & Development Pte Ltd; Mr Hsieh Fu Hua, CEO, Singapore Exchange Ltd; Mr Peter Seah, Chairman, Singapore Technologies Engineering Ltd; Mr Pratap Nambiar, Regional Partner, KPMG Asia Pacific.

FINANCIAL FACTS

Annual tuition	$33,333
Cost of books	$800
Room & board	
(on/off-campus)	$9,171/$9,000
% of students receiving aid	46
% of first-year students	
receiving aid	46
% of students receiving grants	10
Average award package	$30,400
Average grant	$19,539

ADMISSIONS

Admissions Selectivity Rating	95
# of applications received	1,672
% applicants accepted	24
% acceptees attending	44
Average GMAT	680
Range of GMAT	620–730
TOEFL required of	
international students	Yes
Minimum TOEFL	
(paper/computer)	620/260
Regular application deadline	3/31
Regular notification	5/31
Application Deadline/Notification	
Round 1:	1/31 / 3/1
Round 2:	3/31 / 5/31
Early decision program?	No
Deferment available	Yes
Maximum length	
of deferment	1 year
Transfer students accepted	Yes
Transfer application policy:	
Admission and credit transfer applications are evaluated on a case-by-case basis, and depend on the student's record and performance within the MBA program, and the quality of the program and School.	
Non-fall admissions	No
Need-blind admissions	Yes

EMPLOYMENT PROFILE

Career Rating	93	Grads Employed by Function	%	Avg. Salary
Percent employed at graduation	83	Marketing	26	$54,229
Percent employed 3 months		Consulting	24	$68,640
after graduation	93	Management	12	$81,340
Average base starting salary	$63,709	Finance	26	$72,685
Primary Source of Full-time Job Acceptances		Top 5 Employers Hiring Grads		
School-facilitated activities	NR (55%)	LVMH (5), Procter and Gamble (5), Cognizant		
Graduate-facilitated activities	NR (45%)	Technology Solutions (4), KPMG (3), Unilever (3)		

NEW JERSEY INSTITUTE OF TECHNOLOGY
SCHOOL OF MANAGEMENT

GENERAL INFORMATION
Type of school   Public
Academic calendar   Semester

SURVEY SAYS...
Friendly students
Good peer network
Cutting-edge classes
Solid preparation in:
Accounting
General management
Teamwork
Communication/interpersonal skills
Presentation skills

STUDENTS
Enrollment of parent institution	8,828
Enrollment of MBA Program	205
% male/female	80/20
% out-of-state	25
% part-time	35
% minorities	19
% international	25
Average age at entry	33
Average years work experience at entry	5

ACADEMICS
Academic Experience Rating	79
Student/faculty ratio	13:1
Profs interesting rating	89
Profs accessible rating	80
% female faculty	5

Academics

The School of Management at the New Jersey Institute of Technology, "a solid engineering school," has "the edge in technology and related fields." This, convenience, and cost are students' main considerations when selecting the school, which offers full-time and part-time conventional MBAs as well as an Executive MBA.

NJIT's standard MBA follows a 48-credit curriculum divided into three modules: Business Fundamentals (the 27-credit core curriculum): Managing Technology Knowledge and Innovation (12 credits); and a Concentration area (9 credits; concentrations are available in finance, marketing, and MIS. Students report, "The course work is very current and discussions are lively" and "fast-paced." One writes, "My academic experience has been great. My professors are great at challenging the students. They encourage continuous dialogue and will engage students in debate quite frequently. Case studies are very relevant, as are course books and other materials."

Students are also bullish on the school's future. They admire the way this tech school is "venturing out. It will eventually establish a good management school." Some say it's already there, others that it's only a few improvements away. As one student puts it, "It's an underdog relative to other MBA programs. They are going though a lot of growing pains. However, key administration and faculty always go the extra mile to help out students. They are always willing to take student feedback and, more importantly, to implement it. Once the growth is managed it should be a solid program." Another adds, "The director is passionate about making it a great school for working people, and is an advocate." The school already has one great advantage: its proximity to major business and financial centers allows it to draw a stellar faculty. "If you're looking for an experienced economist, hedge-fund manager, corporate attorney, corporate accountant, well, name it, and NJIT has someone that has been there, done that, and will be more than willing to share their experience," students tell us.

Career and Placement

NNJIT maintains a Career Resources Center to serve all undergraduates and graduates at the university. The center includes a library, self-assessment exams, and online job postings. Counseling services are also available. Students tell us that the NJIT alumni network is "a great resource for job referrals." Employers seeking MBAs during a recent NJIT Career Fair included the Air Force, Alcatel-Lucent, Apex Technology, Associated Press, AT&T, Broadridge Financial Solutions, Census 2010, CIGNA, Makro Technologies, Maquet Cardiovascular, McKesson, MMC Systems, New York State Department of Transportation, Public Service Enterprise Group, QPharma, Schindler Elevator Corporation, Softnice, Verizon, and Vonage.

Student Life and Environment

NJIT "is a commuter school, so education is emphasized more than activities," but "there are activities going on all the time" for those who seek them out. "You could walk into the student center or any other building and find students hanging out and networking," one student informs us, adding "There are activities every day on campus to keep students entertained, as well as special guest speakers and forums for students to gain a better perspective on select issues." Furthermore, "NJIT is in the middle of other universities, so life on campus is not limited to just this college."

Full-time students occasionally have time for such activities, but part-timers generally do not; "Life is very hectic, especially if you are working and going to school at the same time," one explains. EMBA candidates appreciate how "breakfast and lunch are provided" by the school for their weekend sessions. "This may seem small, but it is a huge help," one notes. "Other than that, we come in and we leave." Campus facilities include "a well-equipped library with a good number of computers" and "a computer mall with internet and intranet access for all students." Students tell us that "One major area [for potential improvement] would be to upgrade the building, which is supposedly in the works to be completed within the next few years."

NJIT's MBA programs draw a "very diverse" student body "from both public and private sectors. Some are married, some are married with children, some are single. Students have a good mix of ethnicity." One observes, "Everyone is independent and brings something new to the table for others to learn. You can talk about one topic and have two viewpoints presented, instead of a single narrow-minded thought." The EMBAs are "experienced professionals" whose ranks include, by one student's estimate, "43 percent manager level, 21.5 percent team lead, 21.5 percent contributor, and 14 percent vice-president level."

Admissions

All applications to the NJIT MBA program must, at minimum, include complete transcripts for all work done at the undergraduate level and an official score report for the GMAT (although applicants who already hold a master's or doctoral degree from an accredited university are exempt from the GMAT requirement). Students entering the program must also demonstrate competency in economics, finance, information systems, and quantitative methods; these requirements may be met with undergraduate work or through completion of pre-degree foundation courses. International students must also provide proof of adequate funds; those whose first language is not English are required to submit scores for the TOEFL exam. All students may provide supplemental application materials, including up to three letters of recommendation, a personal statement, and a description of work experience or a resume, if they wish. The school "is proud to affirm its commitment to attracting a diverse student body," observing "NJIT has one of the most diverse campuses in the United States."

FINANCIAL FACTS

Annual tuition	$12,730
Fees	$1,624
Cost of books	$1,400
Room & board	$9,264
% of students receiving aid	64
% of first-year students receiving aid	71
% of students receiving loans	26
% of students receiving grants	34
Average grant	$10,000
Average student loan debt	$10,000

ADMISSIONS

Admissions Selectivity Rating	78
# of applications received	249
% applicants accepted	51
% acceptees attending	54
Average GMAT	522
Range of GMAT	480–550
Average GPA	3.5
TOEFL required of international students	Yes
Minimum TOEFL (paper/computer)	525/213
Application fee	$60
International application fee	$60
Early decision program?	No
Deferment available	No
Transfer students accepted	No
Non-fall admissions	Yes
Need-blind admissions	No

NEW MEXICO STATE UNIVERSITY
COLLEGE OF BUSINESS

GENERAL INFORMATION

Type of school	Public
Academic calendar	Semester

SURVEY SAYS...

Cutting-edge classes
Happy students
Solid preparation in:
Accounting
General management

STUDENTS

Enrollment of parent institution	17,000
Enrollment of MBA Program	1,900
% male/female	51/49
% out-of-state	10
% part-time	80
% minorities	60
% international	20
Average age at entry	28
Average years work experience at entry	4

ACADEMICS

Academic Experience Rating	78
Profs interesting rating	67
Profs accessible rating	77
% female faculty	17
% minority faculty	10

Prominent Alumni

John J. Chavez, Former Cabinet Secty, Dept of Tax & Revenue; Robert D. Chelberg, Retired, U.S. Army Lt. General; John M. Cordova, Former Dir. of Mktg-Milwaukee Brewers Baseball; Andres Gutierrez, Founder/Mgr Dir of New Co Production; James Hawkins, Exec. Vice President/Ranchers Bank.

Academics

The College of Business at New Mexico State University is "extremely technologically savvy," a quality that serves it well in a state that is home to several air force bases, major NASA operations, two national laboratories, Spaceport America, and several big tech players (Intel, for one, has a large manufacturing plant in Albuquerque). The tech sector is, in fact, the fastest-growing employer in the Las Cruces area.

NMSU incorporates technology in all disciplines, and has developed several specialized degrees. The school also "concentrates on entrepreneurs because of its abundant resources. It's planning new ways to convert these resources into products." NMSU is a participant in the Space Alliance Technology Outreach Program (SATOP), "which creates interactions between students and the corporate people and gives a very good exposure to the aerospace industry."

Many students simply appreciate the convenience of the program, praising its "wonderfully-located campus with a very unique and culturally-diverse academic program." The school serves both full-time and part-time MBAs, and fully understands and meets the needs of traditional and nontraditional students when it comes to education. NMSU has even "created an MBA cohort program for the Los Alamos National Laboratory. Every other weekend a NMSU professor comes to Los Alamos. We are enrolled in two classes per semester and each class meets once a month for two 5-hour sessions. This schedule is wonderfully convenient, and communication is ongoing throughout the months." A school that comes to you—you can't beat that for convenience.

Instructors at NMSU "are well-respected in their fields and apply real-world applications to their lectures and assignments," while "The administration is always very responsive whenever a conflict arises." A "socially and ethnically diverse student population" informs class discussion. One student sums up, "I have had a very positive overall academic experience. Every single administrator and faculty member has treated me with the utmost respect and professional courtesy."

Career and Placement

NMSU's Placement and Career Services Office provides university students with on-campus employment, internship listings, career listings, workshops, advising, job fairs, and online research tools. The school holds a number of job fairs and other recruiting events throughout the year, but all are primarily targeted toward undergraduates. As a result, relatively few of the many companies that visit campus seek MBAs.

Recent employers of NMSU MBAs include: Accenture, ElPaso Electric, Ernst & Young, Agilent Technologies, ConocoPhilips Company, General Motors, Hewlett-Packard, IBM, Intel, KPMG International, NASA, Los Alamos National Laboratories, Qwest, Sandia National Laboratory, TXU Energy, and Wells Fargo.

ADMISSIONS CONTACT: DR. BOBBIE GREEN, DIRECTOR, MBA PROGRAM
ADDRESS: 114 GUTHRIE HALL, MSC 3GSP LAS CRUCES, NM 88003-8001
PHONE: 505-646-8003 • FAX: 505-646-7977
E-MAIL: GRADINFO@NMSU.EDU • WEBSITE: BUSINESS.NMSU.EDU/MBA

Student Life and Environment

NMSU "is a great place to continue your education and the Las Cruces area is second to none," students report, adding that "Las Cruces is a very slow-paced, small-town type environment. It is, however, slowly changing due to this area being designated as one of the top-10 places to retire in the nation." The school is located "in its own private corner of the city, and it is very safe, clean, and spirit-oriented."

Many who attend the MBA program work part time as well; one such student writes, "This is a focused and relevant MBA that meets my needs as a nontraditional student who holds down a full-time civil engineering job." When they can manage to take a break from their responsibilities, they "enjoy attending college sporting events and special events at the Pan American Center on campus. The campus is also a nice place to take a long walk for exercise or leisure, strolling from pond to pond." The campus includes excellent facilities for workouts and for study. Some here point out that "NMSU could definitely improve in how it caters to students with families. Child care is only available to students with very low incomes, or at the standard child care rates in this city. There also don't seem to be any family-oriented extracurricular activities."

The NMSU MBA population includes "a large portion of international students, who come because of the affordability and friendly environment. Classes with widely diversified cultures and nations contribute to the discussions related to international trade and global business management." Students "have diverse work experience, which makes interaction between students interesting and useful" and results in "a very professional approach to problem-solving case studies or application of curriculum covered in course material."

Admissions

Applicants to the NMSU MBA program must apply for admission to the university's graduate school before they can be admitted to the MBA program. Admission to the graduate school requires that the applicant hold a 4-year undergraduate degree from an accredited institution with a GPA of at least 3.0 (some exceptions to the GPA requirement are possible; contact school for details). International applicants must earn at least a 530 on the paper-based TOEFL or a 197 on the computer-based TOEFL. Applicants to the MBA program must meet one of the following criteria: a minimum GMAT score of 400 and a minimum score of 1400 under the formula (GPA multiplied by GMAT); possession of a graduate degree from an accredited institution; or completion of at least 4 years of full-time professional work and an undergraduate GPA of at least 3.25.

FINANCIAL FACTS

Annual tuition (in-state/ out-of-state)	$4,543/$14,172
Cost of books	$1,000
Room & board (on/off-campus)	$5,200/$7,000
% of students receiving aid	22
% of first-year students receiving aid	10
% of students receiving loans	30
% of students receiving grants	8
Average grant	$30,000

ADMISSIONS

Admissions Selectivity Rating	74
# of applications received	102
% applicants accepted	69
% acceptees attending	100
Average GMAT	500
Range of GMAT	480–760
Average GPA	3.25
TOEFL required of international students	Yes
Minimum TOEFL (paper/computer)	530/197
Application fee	$30
International application fee	$30
Regular application deadline	7/1
Regular notification	8/4
Application Deadline/Notification	
Round 1:	11/30 / 2/15
Round 2:	2/1 / 3/30
Round 3:	3/15 / 4/15
Round 4:	4/15 / 5/15
Early decision program?	No
Deferment available	Yes
Maximum length of deferment	1 year
Transfer students accepted	Yes
Transfer application policy: A maximum of 12 semester credits from AACSB schools.	
Non-fall admissions	Yes
Need-blind admissions	Yes

EMPLOYMENT PROFILE

Career Rating	85	Grads Employed by Function	% Avg. Salary
Average base starting salary	$40,000	Marketing	5 NR
		Operations	2 NR
		Consulting	2 NR
		Management	7 NR
		Finance	2 NR
		Quantitative	2 NR

New York University

Leonard N. Stern School of Business

GENERAL INFORMATION

Type of school	Private
Academic calendar	Semester

SURVEY SAYS...

Students love New York, NY
Good social scene
Good peer network
Cutting-edge classes
Happy students
Solid preparation in:
Finance

ACADEMICS

Academic Experience Rating	91
Student/faculty ratio	12:1
Profs interesting rating	87
Profs accessible rating	83
% female faculty	19
% minority faculty	14

Joint Degrees

JD/MBA, with the School of Law, 4 years; MA/MBA, with the Institute of French Studies (GSAS), 2.5 years; MA/MBA, with the Department of Politics (GSAS), 2.5 years; MPA/MBA, with the Wagner School of Public Service, 3 years; MBA/MFA, with the Tisch School, 3 years; MBA/MS in Mathematics in Finance, 3 years; MS in Biology/MBA, 3 years; dual MBA with HEC School of Management, 2 years.

Prominent Alumni

Alan Greenspan, Former Chairman, Federal Reserve; John Paulson, Chairman, Paulson Partners; William L. Mack, Founder/Managing Partner, Apollo Real Estate; Jack Abernethy, CEO, Fox Television Stations; Robert Greifeld, President/CEO, NASDAQ.

Academics

You don't become a top-tier business school without developing strengths in a broad cross-section of fields, and the NYU Stern School of Business exemplifies that principle. With a "great finance program," a location "near all the investment banks," a "well-regarded specialization in entertainment, media, and technology," a "strong marketing program" bolstered by "recruiting opportunities with top consumer packaged-goods companies," a "great entrepreneurship program," and an "excellent reputation for strategy...and economics," to say Stern is "strong in many different business disciplines" is an understatement.

NYU's primo address is a huge asset. Access to the world's top financial institutions means "resources that no other school could offer." "Almost daily the school is able to leverage its location and prominence to bring in prominent speakers." New York is also a huge allure to the superstar professors who pepper the faculty at NYU. "Seeing your professors being quoted in The New York Times or the Wall Street Journal is [a] nice bonus," one student writes. Given their renown, it's surprising that NYU professors "make themselves extremely accessible outside of class," in part because "part of student activities funds are allocated for each professor to spend time outside the classroom with the students; last semester, I got to get to know my professors at a Knicks game, a karaoke bar, and other venues. Students also have [the] ability to 'take a professor to coffee,' where the school will pay for a once-per-semester coffee break with the professor of the specific student's choice."

NYU offers both a full-time program and a sometimes overlooked but also popular and excellent part-time program (its enrollment is actually substantially greater than full-time enrollment). One part-timer reports that "We have the same professors, same curriculum, and same degree options as full-time students—very unlike any other school I have seen." Adds another, "The greatest strength [of the part-time program] is the credentialing of the students and prospective students. There's a tremendous advantage to being able to cater to working professionals in the most powerful city in the U.S. I have no doubt that I'm surrounded by some of the most talented and driven classmates anywhere in the world!" The full-timers—who must survive one of the most demanding admissions processes in the United States—aren't too shabby either.

Career and Placement

Stern's "location in downtown New York is a huge competitive advantage when networking with recruiters," students tell us. This is especially true in finance; as one student reports, "investment banking recruiting is among the best at Stern, we have every major bank on campus." While the majority of students pursue careers in finance, the school has dramatically broadened its range of employment opportunities as student interests have diversified. However, one student writes, "I'd like to see continued diversification of on-campus recruiters. Our student body ends up working across many industries and disciplines and our recruitment opportunities need to continue to evolve to reflect that." The school has bolstered its efforts to help part-time students looking to change careers through the Langone Professional Development Program (LPDP), which "prepares students trying to shift careers by teaching them job searching techniques" and the Management Consulting Association (MCA)'s Bootcamp, which "offers training in casing and interviewing skills for students trying to get a consulting job."

ADMISSIONS CONTACT: ANIKA DAVIS PRATT, ASSISTANT DEAN, MBA ADMISSIONS
ADDRESS: 44 WEST 4TH STREET, SUITE 6-70 NEW YORK, NY 10012
PHONE: 212-998-0600 • FAX: 212-995-4231
E-MAIL: STERNMBA@STERN.NYU.EDU • WEBSITE: WWW.STERN.NYU.EDU

Hundreds of companies recruit at Stern. Some of the top employers of Stern MBAs include: American Express; Avon Products, Inc.; Bank of America Merrill Lynch; Barclays Capital; BNP Paribas; Boston Consulting Group; Booz & Company; Citi; Credit Suisse; Deloitte; Deutsche Bank; JP Morgan Chase; IBM; Johnson & Johnson; Kraft Foods; McKinsey & Company; Morgan Stanley; Pfizer; Standard & Poor's; UBS; and Unilever.

Student Life and Environment

"There is a definite split between full-time and part-time students" at NYU, where "part-timers [generally] do not interact with full-time students and are not part of the community (they are too tired after work and class to take part in extracurricular events)." The part-timers "mostly like to come in, take courses, and get the job done." Many of them prefer it that way, telling us that "The full-timers take things too seriously and I am glad we are mostly segregated. I can't deal with their competitiveness…. The part-timers are much friendlier and are open-minded and more willing to learn and share." For part-time students looking for more socialization, there are multiple happy hours each evening and other extracurricular activities. At the beginning of their first year, students are divided into smaller communities of "core groups," which plan group activities and help students form closer bonds.

While some full-timers would concede that they can be "competitive," they also say that theirs is "a strong, vibrant community" where "there are so many activities going on every night that it's like trying to drink from a fire hydrant." "There's always multiple club-sponsored happy hours and parties every weekend." Many here cite Thursday Beer Blasts as a program highlight. "No classes on Fridays allows us to have 'Beer Blast' on Thursday evenings, where we can hang out with other students on campus in an informal setting," one student explains. MBAs here are also "heavily involved and dedicated to their personal causes/interests. There is a work hard, play hard mentality at Stern, which facilitates networking and the community atmosphere."

Admissions

Admission to Stern is extremely competitive. The school reports that "admissions decisions are influenced by academic achievements and potential, professional/career progression, demonstrated potential for leadership, clearly articulated goals for pursuing an MBA, community involvement and engagement, strong communication and interpersonal skills, letters of recommendation and the admissions interview."

In its efforts to increase enrollment of underrepresented students, "NYU Stern strategically partners with a number of organizations that are committed to diversity…In partnership with these organizations, NYU Stern hosts workshops and recruiting events that educate prospective students about MBA programs and provide assistance navigating the admissions process. Additionally, NYU Stern participates in a number of diversity fellowship programs and summer "boot camps" offered by leading firms in financial services, consulting and marketing."

ADMISSIONS

Admissions Selectivity Rating	99
TOEFL required of international students	Yes
Application fee	$215
International application fee	$215
Application Deadline/Notification	
Round 1:	11/15 / 2/15
Round 2:	1/15 / 4/1
Round 3:	3/15 / 6/1
Early decision program?	No
Deferment available	No
Maximum length of deferment	Decided on case-by-case basis but rarely granted.
Transfer students accepted	No
Non-fall admissions	Yes
(for part-time only)	
Need-blind admissions	Yes

NORTH CAROLINA STATE UNIVERSITY
COLLEGE OF MANAGEMENT

GENERAL INFORMATION
Type of school   Public
Academic calendar   Semester

SURVEY SAYS...
Students love Raleigh, NC
Friendly students
Solid preparation in:
Teamwork

STUDENTS
Enrollment of parent institution	33,819
Enrollment of MBA Program	425
% male/female	72/28
% out-of-state	13
% part-time	77
% minorities	5
% international	36
Average age at entry	30
Average years work experience at entry	7

ACADEMICS
Academic Experience Rating	**84**
Student/faculty ratio	10:1
Profs interesting rating	84
Profs accessible rating	82
% female faculty	23
% minority faculty	6

Joint Degrees
Joint Masters of Microbial Biotechnology and MBA (3-year program); joint Degree in Doctor of Veterinary Medicine (DVM) and MBA (5-year program); joint Master of Accounting (MAC) and MBA (2-year program); joint Master of Global Innovation Management (MGIM) and MBA (2-year program).

Prominent Alumni
Tony O'Driscoll, Professor of the Practice, Fuqua School of Business, Duke University; John McCarley, Bowe/Bell & Howell, CIO, VP for IT; Eric Gregg, Triangle Tech Journal, Publisher; John Silvestri, Cantor Fitzgerald, VP Operations; Sam Matheny, Capital Broadcasting Group, DTV-VP & General Manag.

Academics

The Jenkins Graduate School of Management at North Carolina State University tailors its MBA program to the strengths of the surrounding area and to those of the university at large. Located in the state capital of Raleigh (with a satellite program in nearby Durham's Research Triangle Park), NCSU serves a variety of governmental and commercial interests well. For example, the school "offers strong programs that are relevant for technology companies in the area," including concentrations in Innovation Management and Entrepreneurship & Technology Innovation. These programs are "offered to people with a technical background looking to make the transition into management" and excel at "relating business skills to those with a technical background." The school's Biosciences Management program dovetails neatly with Durham's self-proclaimed distinction as 'The City of Medicine' and with the presence of several pharmaceutical and bioengineering giants in RTP. The MBA program exploits NCSU's strengths in engineering, textiles, and natural resources to provide unique business-related study opportunities in these areas. And to top it all off, the school also serves up an "excellent Supply Chain program" featuring a faculty that is "among the best in the country."

Across disciplines, NCSU professors "have a good balance of work experience and academic experience" and are "very open to discussion and welcoming of students outside the classroom." The administration here "is very responsive to the student's needs" and "encourages students to get a broad taste of many different concentrations," although it also "pushes some concentrations more than others." One student told us how much he appreciates the way the school "has increased global programs, allowed me to do independent studies so I can really focus on my marketing concentration, and encouraged networking. I also really enjoyed the public speaking class all students are required to take. That has helped me immensely in my career."

Full-time students attend NCSU's main campus in Raleigh; part-timers may choose between the main campus and the "great satellite program in Research Triangle Park," a 7,000-acre research park where nearly 40,000 people work for more than 130 companies. Part-timers tell us that they enjoy "a great program that is not too intensely scheduled." Many students in both programs would agree that NCSU offers "the best value for the money in the Raleigh-Durham area."

Career and Placement

MBAs at NC State enjoy the services of an MBA-dedicated Career Resources Center that, according to the school, is "continually building relationships with companies seeking graduates in the areas of expertise that correspond to your education...recruiting top employers to provide our students with limitless opportunities to meet their career goals...[and working] with the NC State University Career Center to stay abreast of events and networking opportunities." The MBA program also provides workshops on resume writing and cover letters, interviewing skills, and job search strategies. Companies that have paid recruiting visits to the NC State campus in the past three years include American Airlines, BB&T, Chevron, Cisco Systems, Deloitte, Eaton Corporation, Ericcson, Glaxo Smith Kline, Lab Corp, Net App, Novartis Animal Health, Novozymes, Progress Energy, Red Hat, Research Triangle Institute, SAS, Siemens Medical, and Yang Consulting.

ADMISSIONS CONTACT: PAM BOSTIC, MBA PROGRAM DIRECTOR
ADDRESS: MBA PROGRAM OFFICE / CAMPUS BOX 8114 RALEIGH, NC 27695-8114
PHONE: 919-515-5584 • FAX: 919-515-5073
E-MAIL: MBA@NCSU.EDU • WEBSITE: WWW.MBA.NCSU.EDU

Student Life and Environment

Founded as a land-grant institution in 1887, NCSU today is home to 11 schools and nearly 30,000 undergraduate and graduate students. MBA classes on NCSU's main campus are held in a remodeled facility featuring computer labs, multimedia facilities, widely available wireless service, laptop connections, and tiered-seating classrooms. The large campus is located just west of central Raleigh and is surrounded by shops that cater to the student population. Students report that the RTP facility "is very convenient" but that "the building is old" and the facilities "are only fair. However, the education is comparable to any of the better-known schools in the area." Beginning fall 2010, the RTP program was relocated to a new facility with state-of-the-art technology and equipment that is available solely for the use of NC State University's College of Management, scheduled to open in 2010. This will be a major improvement and will reflect the professional image of the working part-time student.

The majority of MBAs at NCSU have considerable professional experience. In fact, many work full time in addition to attending the MBA program. "Most of the students are from a scientific or engineering background" and "Everyone is genuinely interested in building a new business mindset and actively challenging themselves to try classes that may be outside their concentration." Other backgrounds are also represented, however; "I had someone in my study group with a PhD in Russian literature, one with a masters in engineering, and one with a masters in life sciences," one MBA reports.

Admissions

Admission to the NC State MBA program is based on academic record, GMAT scores, essays, letters of reference, and work and volunteer experience. Admission is highly competitive, with an emphasis on academic achievement and evidence of management potential and leadership skills through prior employment, volunteer, and/or military experience. Two years of full-time employment is "strongly recommended" for full-time applicants and is required of applicants to the part-time program. A background that includes coursework in calculus, statistics, and economics is "strongly encouraged." Applicants whose primary language is not English must submit TOEFL or IELTS scores; a minimum TOEFL score of 250 on the computer-based test or 100 on the Internet-based test or a minimum IELTS score of 7.5 is required. Interviews are required prior to admission; the school contacts applicants who are deemed potential candidates for the program.

FINANCIAL FACTS

Annual tuition (in-state/ out-of-state)	$12,533/$25,066
Fees	$1,585
Cost of books	$1,000
Room & board (on/off-campus)	$6,000/$11,000
% of students receiving grants	57
Average award package	$21,683
Average grant	$7,559
Average student loan debt	$31,907

ADMISSIONS

Admissions Selectivity Rating	85
# of applications received	207
% applicants accepted	56
% acceptees attending	57
Average GMAT	616
Range of GMAT	580–660
Average GPA	3.23
TOEFL required of international students	Yes
Minimum TOEFL (paper/computer)	600/250
Application fee	$65
International application fee	$75
Regular application deadline	3/1
Regular notification	4/1
Application Deadline/Notification	
Round 1:	10/5 / 11/5
Round 2:	1/11 / 2/11
Round 3:	3/1 / 4/1
Early decision program?	Yes
ED Deadline/ Notification	10/5 / 11/15
Deferment available	Yes
Maximum length of deferment	1 year
Transfer students accepted	Yes
Transfer application policy:	

The NC State MBA Program can accept up to 12 hours of transfer credit from another AACSB-accredited MBA program The grade received for a transfer class must be a B or better, and the class must have been taken no more than 6 years prior to the applicants projected graduation date from the MBA program at NC State's College of Management.

Non-fall admissions	No
Need-blind admissions	Yes

EMPLOYMENT PROFILE

Career Rating	77	Grads Employed by Function	% Avg. Salary
Percent employed at graduation	74	Operations	22 $64,977
Percent employed 3 months after graduation	78	Consulting	35 $72,325
		Management	4 $76,000
Average base starting salary	$72,730	Finance	9 $48,500
Primary Source of Full-time Job Acceptances		MIS	4 $52,000
Graduate-facilitated activities	24 (100%)	HR	4 $48,000
		Other	22 $66,984

Top 5 Employers Hiring Grads
Deloitte (3), Bank of America (2), Carquest (2), Chevron (2), Accenture (1)

NORTHEASTERN UNIVERSITY
COLLEGE OF BUSINESS ADMINISTRATION

GENERAL INFORMATION

Type of school	Private
Academic calendar	Semester

SURVEY SAYS...

Students love Boston, MA
Cutting-edge classes
Solid preparation in:
Accounting

STUDENTS

Enrollment of parent institution	26,322
Enrollment of MBA Program	638
% male/female	57/43
% out-of-state	64
% part-time	67
% minorities	10
% international	32
Average age at entry	27
Average years work experience at entry	3

ACADEMICS

Academic Experience Rating	**86**
Student/faculty ratio	7:1
Profs interesting rating	82
Profs accessible rating	78
% female faculty	22
% minority faculty	3

Joint Degrees

MSA/MBA Master of Science in Accounting/Master of Business Administration (15 months), MSF/MBA Master of Science in Finance/Master of Business Administration (2.5 years), MSN/MBA Master of Science in Nursing/Master of Business Administration (3 years), and JD/MBA Doctor of Law/Master of Business Administration (45 months).

Prominent Alumni

Richard Egan, Co-founder, EMC Corporation; Roger Marino, Co-founder, EMC Corporation; Sy Sternberg, Chairman, New York Life Insurance Company; Margot Botsford, Associate Justice, MA Supreme Judicial Court.

Academics

Northeastern University offers a broad range of full-time and part-time MBA options. The full-time program follows a 24-month curriculum that includes a cooperative work experience; specializations are available in finance, marketing, and operations and supply chain management. Part-time programs include a conventional Evening MBA, an Executive MBA, and a High Tech MBA.

For full-timers, the highlight of the program is the six-month Corporate Residency (often referred to simply as 'co-op'), during which students undertake a residency with a Boston-area business. One student puts it simply: "The six month co-op program is the best asset of the university. Through co-op I was able to affect changes at an international company and use that experience to earn a great job placement for after graduation. I wouldn't have landed my new job without the co-op experience." While "issues can arise due to the six month co-op, because you are still working in the fall when every other MBA in the nation is interviewing at large companies, banks, and consulting firms for top jobs"—making it "difficult to work out a schedule to interview for the job of your future while committing to the internship of the present"—most students cite co-op as their primary reason for choosing Northeastern.

Part-time programs do not include a co-op component at Northeastern but have much to recommend them all the same. The High Tech MBA "provides a relevant and credible education" with a schedule that "allows the flexibility to keep a full-time job that requires significant travel." One participant explains that the program "has a full-time class load (three to four classes per semester: fall, spring, and summer) with part-time flexibility (classes meet every other week Tuesday night and all day Saturday), and students complete the program in 21 months. The curriculum is preset, covering the broad spectrum of business functions and no specific specialty." Likewise, students in the EMBA program say it "has the right combination of content and environment" with "a significant level of engagement and interaction among the cohort each year."

Students in all programs tell us, "The faculty, the network, and the location are the school's greatest strengths. Our professors have been world-class and well-connected. NU is located in the heart of Boston. That is tough to beat." Dual campuses mean "easy access for many students. Classes in the satellite campus in downtown Boston are always filled with people who work in the financial district. Also, because NU has two campuses, it is more convenient for most people than going to Suffolk (only in downtown Boston) and Boston College (about an hour's commute on the subway from downtown Boston and most other points in Boston)." The school offers a variety of online MBA options.

Career and Placement

Northeastern's six-month co-op program means that the school has "good relationships ...with a wide variety of employers" in the Boston area, and these relationships pay dividends for the efforts of the school's Career Center. Recent co-op employers included Carrier, Cyprus Tree Investment, GE Supply, Gilette, Harvard Pilgrim Health Care, Hasbro, Kidde Fenwal, MasterFoods USA, Sovereign Bank, TD Securities, Thermo Fisher Scientific, UV Partners, and Wolfe Laboratories. Co-op definitely provides students with a leg up when it comes time for their co-op companies to hire new full-timers, students here agree.

Employers most likely to hire Northeastern MBAs after graduation include AC Nielsen, Amazon, Bayer Consumer Care, Citigroup, Dunkin' Brands, Fidelity, Kaiser Permanente, Liberty Mutual, Lindt & Sprungli, Mellon Financial Corporation, Proctor & Gamble/Gillette, Raytheon Corporation, and Washington Mutual.

ADMISSIONS CONTACT: EVELYN TATE, DIRECTOR, RECRUITMENT AND ADMISSIONS
ADDRESS: 350 DODGE HALL, 360 HUNTINGTON AVENUE BOSTON, MA 02115
PHONE: 617-373-5992 • FAX: 617-373-8564
E-MAIL: GSBA@NEU.EDU • WEBSITE: WWW.MBA.NEU.EDU

Student Life and Environment

The Northeastern campus "is a great place to be even when you're not in class." The Marino Center "is a superb gym and is one of the centers of campus life," and "Students participate in any number of activities and are encouraged to form their own groups" elsewhere on campus, creating "an environment that fosters learning, but it also fosters socializing and fun." Also, "Because of the sheer number of employers and outside experts visiting NU, there is always a worthwhile event going on." Students in part-time programs rarely have time for such diversions, however; they "come right from work and all are tired but power through the class." EMBA participants "attend classes all day on one day per week, on alternating Fridays and Saturdays. The support staff takes care of all of your needs: food, books, and travel are all arranged for you, so you just show-up and never have to focus on anything trivial."

The wide variety of programs available at NU draws a diverse student body that includes plenty of techies, mid-career professionals, business neophytes looking to fast track their careers, and internationals.

Admissions

All applicants to the Northeastern MBA program must provide the Admissions Office with the following: a completed online application; sealed copies of official transcripts for all post-secondary schools attended; a current resume; three essays; two professional letters of recommendation; and an official GMAT score report. In addition, international students whose first language is not English must submit TOEFL results. All international students must submit transcripts that have been translated with U.S. grade equivalents assigned for work completed, as well as a certified Declaration and Certification of Finances Statement. Neither an undergraduate degree in business nor previous work experience are required for admission to the program, although those lacking both are unlikely candidates for admission; the school advises such students to take college-level introductory business courses prior to or while applying to the school. The school prefers candidates with a minimum of two years' professional experience.

FINANCIAL FACTS

Annual tuition	$35,250
Fees	$560
Cost of books	$1,700
Room & board (off-campus)	$15,000
% of students receiving aid	79
% of first-year students receiving aid	97
% of students receiving loans	34
% of students receiving grants	75
Average award package	$26,608
Average grant	$17,539
Average student loan debt	$50,854

ADMISSIONS

Admissions Selectivity Rating	89
# of applications received	262
% applicants accepted	47
% acceptees attending	54
Average GMAT	609
Range of GMAT	560–650
Average GPA	3.3
TOEFL required of international students	Yes
Minimum TOEFL (paper/computer)	600/250
Application fee	$100
International application fee	$100
Regular application deadline	4/15
Regular notification	5/15
Application Deadline/Notification	
Round 1:	11/30 / 2/15
Round 2:	2/1 / 3/30
Round 3:	3/15 / 4/15
Round 4:	4/15 / 5/15
Early decision program?	No
Deferment available	No
Transfer students accepted	Yes
Transfer application policy:	
We may award a limited number of transfer credits for MBA courses taken at AACSB-accredited institutions.	
Non-fall admissions	No
Need-blind admissions	Yes

EMPLOYMENT PROFILE

Career Rating	93	Grads Employed by Function	% Avg. Salary
Percent employed at graduation	69	Marketing	21 $72,416
Percent employed 3 months after graduation	89	Operations	21 $65,400
		Management	8 $68,750
Average base starting salary	$74,310	Finance	38 $77,111
Primary Source of Full-time Job Acceptances		HR	4 $50,000
School-facilitated activities	23 (74%)	MIS	4 $72,800
Graduate-facilitated activities	7 (23%)	**Top 5 Employers Hiring Grads**	
Unknown	1 (3%)	IBM (3), UTC (3), State Street Global Advisors (2), Procter & Gamble (1), Hasbro (1)	

NORTHERN ARIZONA UNIVERSITY
THE W.A. FRANKE COLLEGE OF BUSINESS

GENERAL INFORMATION
Type of school   Public
Academic calendar   August–May

SURVEY SAYS...
Friendly students
Smart classrooms
Solid preparation in:
Accounting
Teamwork
Communication/interpersonal skills
Presentation skills

STUDENTS
Enrollment of MBA Program	32
% male/female	67/33
% out-of-state	38
% part-time	0
% minorities	24
% international	15
Average age at entry	26
Average work experience at entry	19 months

ACADEMICS
Academic Experience Rating	78
Student/faculty ratio	12:1
Profs interesting rating	73
Profs accessible rating	92
% female faculty	20
% minority faculty	10

Joint Degrees
Master of Business Administration-Accounting (MBA/ACC): for graduates with a bachelor's in accounting; Full-time, 31 total credits required; 10 months to complete program.

Academics

Efficiency is the name of the game at the Franke College of Business at Northern Arizona University. This school's accelerated MBA program is just "10 months from start to finish," cramming a full MBA curriculum into less than a year of coursework. Not surprisingly, the result is an "intense course load," tons of homework, and a "fast-paced, invigorating environment." A current student admits, "I'm lucky if I get more than a couple of hours on the weekends to go grocery shopping. This place will get you in and out in a hurry, but you certainly won't have time for anything else while you're doing it." At the same time, the breakneck format affords students a number of important benefits. In particular, it's a great deal: Here, students only leave the workforce for a year and tuition is "significantly lower" than at a traditional two-year program. In addition, for students who plan to take the CPA exam, NAU offers the opportunity to complete their accounting courses and earn an MBA in just two years. A popular choice, "Over half the program is enrolled in the MBA-ACC offering, while the other half navigates the traditional MBA." On that note, accounting classes get top marks, while students say "the management and finance courses add value and the principles learned will be handy going forward."

Despite the program's rigor, the Franke College of Business is a surprisingly cooperative and down-to-earth place. Throughout the business school, "The environment is one of learning and collaboration where the majority of teachers are interested in helping students achieve success." With few exceptions, "the teachers are extremely approachable," and, due to the limited graduate enrollment, "The small class sizes means we receive more individual attention from professors." Teamwork is encouraged across the curriculum, which builds soft skills while also helping to ease the stress of coursework. A student agrees, "The academic experience at NAU is demanding and high-pressured, although the group nature of a lot of our work allows students to use their best skills when contributing within this environment." Like the faculty, "the school's administration goes that extra mile" to assist students, and it truly works "to make the MBA program as stress-free as possible." The school generally runs smoothly and the curriculum is well-designed; however, some students tell us, "There does not appear to be a lot of communication between the professors" when it comes to planning and evaluating courses.

Career and Placement

By minimizing their time in the classroom, Northern Arizona University keeps students relevant to the workplace. In some cases, students don't even need to look for a new job after graduation. A current student explains, "I left my job to be in this program, but given that I will be applying back with them within a year, I don't need to go through the same hiring process." For those students looking for a new position, the Career Development Office provides undergraduate and graduate students with various career and professional development programs. Through the Career Development Center, employers recruit students for entry-level and full-time positions, as well as for internships. Companies that recently participated in one of the Career Development Office's recruiting events include Vanguard, Geico, Ecolab, Becker CPA Review, Target, Enterprise Rent-a-Car, Lohman Company, Deloitte & Touche, KPMG, Eide Bailly, and Ernst & Young. Still, students feel the MBA would improve with the addition of "more job placement opportunities." In particular, students would like to see more recruiting companies from Phoenix and other big cities.

ADMISSIONS CONTACT: JERI DENNIS, PROGRAM COORDINATOR
ADDRESS: MBA PROGRAM OFFICE, P.O. BOX 15066 FLAGSTAFF, AZ 86011-5066
PHONE: 928-523-7342 • FAX: 928-523-7996
E-MAIL: MBA@NAU.EDU • WEBSITE: WWW.FRANKE.NAU.EDU/MBA/

Student Life and Environment

Located in the beautiful mountain town of Flagstaff, NAU offers "outstanding" facilities, a professional atmosphere, and a scenic backdrop. Recently constructed, "The W.A. Franke College of Business is one of the newest buildings on campus and is LEED-certified." All classrooms "overlook a green retention area" where students can be seen "playing Frisbee, sitting and reading under the perimeter trees, or just relaxing." In addition, students have access to a "great MBA lounge that offers students a place to complete course work as well as eat lunch and socialize." "Most students are laid-back and easy-going" with their classmates, though "hardworking" and competitive in the classroom. A younger crowd, many MBA candidates are "recent graduates with no actual work experience," though you'll also meet some mid-career professionals in class.

While the atmosphere is laid-back, MBA students are definitely busy. One admits, "Honestly, in a 10-month accelerated program, I haven't much of an opportunity to have much of a life outside of school." When they want to relax, there are plenty of "outdoor activities" in the surrounding area, from local hikes and skiing, to the nearby Grand Canyon. On campus, the larger university also offers social, recreational, and cultural events. MBA students can be as involved in the school as they'd like; "Some students take full advantage of everything NAU has to offer, while others do not."

Admissions

To apply for NAU's accelerated ten-month program, students must have an undergraduate degree in business. Those without a business degree can also apply for the MBA program on a conditional basis, but they must complete a series of foundational courses before beginning the MBA core (thereby adding a year to the program.) To apply, prospective students must submit their undergraduate transcripts, official GMAT scores, a current resume, two letters of recommendation, and a set of personal essays. After submitting their application materials, prospective students are invited to interview on campus. To be eligible for the MBA, students must have an undergraduate GPA of 3.0 or better.

FINANCIAL FACTS

Annual tuition (in-state/ out-of-state)	$7,469/$17,983
Fees	$3,500
Cost of books	$2,000
Room & board	$12,181

ADMISSIONS

Admissions Selectivity Rating	75
# of applications received	35
% applicants accepted	58
% acceptees attending	58
Average GMAT	540
Range of GMAT	460–640
Average GPA	3.52
TOEFL required of international students	Yes
Minimum TOEFL (paper/computer)	550/213
Application fee	$50
International application fee	$50
Regular application deadline	6/1
Regular notification	5/15
Early decision program?	No
Deferment available	Yes
Maximum length of deferment	1 year
Transfer students accepted	Yes
Transfer application policy: 6 hours toward electives only	
Non-fall admissions	Yes
Need-blind admissions	Yes

EMPLOYMENT PROFILE

Career Rating	77
Average base starting salary	$46,375

NORTHERN KENTUCKY UNIVERSITY
COLLEGE OF BUSINESS

GENERAL INFORMATION
Type of school	Public
Academic calendar	Semester

SURVEY SAYS...
Good peer network
Solid preparation in:
Finance

STUDENTS
Enrollment of parent institution	15,000
Enrollment of MBA Program	236
% part-time	90
Average age at entry	28
Average years work experience at entry	5

ACADEMICS
Academic Experience Rating	**73**
Student/faculty ratio	22:1
Profs interesting rating	75
Profs accessible rating	78
% female faculty	27
% minority faculty	13

Joint Degrees
Juris Doctor/Master of Business Administration, minimum 5 years.

Academics

Its location "10 minutes from downtown Cincinnati, Ohio" and "affordable [overall cost] relative to other AACSB-accredited schools in the area" draws enthusiastic students to Northern Kentucky University's College of Business. About 85 percent of the students here attend part-time, and those who do appreciate that "classes are offered in the evenings"—most courses meet from 6:00 to 9:00 P.M. once a week—"so that [students] can attend all required classes without cutting into [their] work schedules." NKU also offers two 7-week summer sessions that run on accelerated evening schedules. While class times are convenient, students say that NKU's "greatest strength" is "the course work itself. NKU is very challenging and very strict with academics. Although it is not so easy to prepare for class at times, this has helped prepare me well for my professional career by pushing me to the limit." Class sizes are "small," and professors are "passionate about their subject areas" and "always willing to stay [after class] with you and meet whenever you need to." They're also, for the most part, "flexible and understand that most graduate students also work full time and have a family." Many have "very relevant real-life experience to impart," and their ranks "include the former director of human resources of a major public utility, a consultant who specializes in turning businesses around, and a finance professor who works as a Certified Financial Planner on the side. No, Jack Welch does not teach here, but those [who] do are knowledgeable and do a good job." Students love that NKU "allows specialization of the MBA" and cite its Entrepreneurship Institute, International Business Center, and finance programs as major strengths.

Overall, students find NKU to be a place where "The student is the top priority." "The staff has always been quick [when] answering my questions and available when I need them," a student writes.

Career and Placement

"There is a wonderful Career Center on campus, but it is primarily focused on meeting the needs of undergraduates," NKU business students tell us. That being said, students admit that, for the most part, they "already have jobs, so career placement is not a large need." Most are looking to move up the ranks with their current employer; those looking to jump ship turn to their fellow students for job leads. Which isn't to say there aren't those who'd like a little more help in the area of job placement: "I think we need more career counselors within the MBA program for those of us who do not come from a traditional business background," one student tells us. Another would like NKU to "improve job [placement] opportunities through alumni relations."

Student Life and Environment

Many at NKU are "on the 'slow' track to finish because of the demands of family and jobs." As such, the school differs from institutions that "have the same students begin and end the program together"; most here "meet different students each semester." Despite this, students report that their "classmates are great people who, through this MBA program, have become real friends." Such friendships are forged largely without the assistance of clubs or activities geared toward graduate students: "I'm a commuter, so most of my time at school is in class, in the library, or meeting to do group work," a typical student writes. While NKU's campus "has food/coffee stands in almost every building" and "computers everywhere with free printing," drawbacks include a "mostly concrete" aesthetic and difficult parking "at certain times of the day."

ADMISSIONS CONTACT: JIM BAST, DIRECTOR, MBA PROGRAM
ADDRESS: 209 BEP, NUNN DRIVE HIGHLAND HEIGHTS, KY 41099
PHONE: 859-572-6357 • FAX: 859-572-7694
E-MAIL: BASTJ1@NKU.EDU • WEBSITE: WWW.NKU.EDU/~COB/GRADUATE/MBA/INDEX.PHP

Students describe their "hardworking" peers as "friendly" but "competitive." NKU strongly recommends that potential applicants obtain two years of work experience before applying, and, by all accounts, its student body is "very diverse" in employment backgrounds. "Most [students here] are mid-20s to mid-30s," but "age ranges from 20 to 50." "Quite a few are married with children" and "Most have significant work experience." When students seek common ground, they need look no further than their objective: "We are all here for the same reason: to get an MBA," one student writes. That being said, most students are "eager to learn and get the most from their MBA experience, not just a credential."

Admissions

To gain admission to NKU, applicants must obtain a bachelor's degree from a regionally accredited institution and possess a cumulative undergraduate GPA of at least 2.50 on a 4.00 scale; he or she must also obtain a score of at least 450 on a GMAT taken within the last 5 years and, if applicable, obtain a score of at least 550 on the paper version of the TOEFL (or at least 213 on the computer version of the test). Applicants will be admitted if he or she obtains at least 1,000 points via the formula 200 multiplied by GPA plus GMAT score. In lieu of admission via the formula above, a student will be admitted if he or she obtains at least 1,050 points via the formula 200 multiplied by GPA for student's last 60 semester hours plus GMAT score. Exceptions to the GMAT include: GRE score within the last 5 years, possession of a Master degree, MD, or PhD, or similar advanced degree.

ADMISSIONS

Admissions Selectivity Rating	**77**
# of applications received	141
% applicants accepted	52
% acceptees attending	62
Average GMAT	513
Range of GMAT	440–630
Average GPA	3.23
TOEFL required of international students	Yes
Minimum TOEFL (paper/computer)	550/213
Regular application deadline	8/1
Application Deadline/Notification	
Round 1:	8/1 / NR
Round 2:	12/1 / NR
Round 3:	5/1 / NR
Early decision program?	No
Deferment available	Yes
Maximum length of deferment	1 year
Transfer students accepted	Yes
Transfer application policy: A maximum of 9 hours from regionally accredited institutions. To be approved by the MBA Director.	
Non-fall admissions	Yes
Need-blind admissions	Yes

NORTHWESTERN UNIVERSITY
KELLOGG SCHOOL OF MANAGEMENT

GENERAL INFORMATION
Type of school	Private
Academic calendar	Quarter

SURVEY SAYS...
Friendly students
Good social scene
Good peer network
Cutting-edge classes
Solid preparation in:
Teamwork

STUDENTS
Enrollment of parent institution	16,000
Enrollment of MBA Program	2,350
% male/female	67/33
% part-time	49
% international	27
Average age at entry	28
Average years work experience at entry	5

ACADEMICS
Academic Experience Rating	76
Student/faculty ratio	10:1
Profs interesting rating	93
Profs accessible rating	89
% female faculty	19
% minority faculty	19

Joint Degrees
JD/MBA (law school, 3 years); and
MMM (MEM/MBA) (engineering
school, 2 years)

Prominent Alumni
Peter Tan, Executive Vice President
and President, Burger King Asia
Pacific Pte Ltd; Gregg Steinhafel,
President and CEO, Target Corp.;
Colleen Goggins, Worldwide
Chairman of Consumer Products,
Johnson & Johnson; Joe De Pinto,
CEO, 7 Eleven; Axel Wieandt, CEO
and Chairman of the Management
Board, Hypo Real Estate Holding AG.

Academics

At the Kellogg School of Management at Northwestern University, you can almost feel the cooperation in the air. "It's the kind of atmosphere that even if you don't know people, you will say 'hi' in the halls," reports one student. This "collaborative," "collegial," and "student-led environment" at Kellogg means that students' input is always sought, and their voices and desires have a huge impact on the course the school takes both academically and socially. Students agree that this crash-course in democracy is "the best way to train tomorrow's business leaders" and note that it also lends the school "a certain energy around the campus that brings excitement to each and every day."

One facet of the cooperative spirit is that professors receive regular performance evaluations. However, it seems the results are rarely negative as the majority of students here praise them as "bright, accomplished, fair, and engaging." Students aren't exempt from the scrutiny of their peers, either. Through a web-based program called LeadNet, Kellogg students are able to receive "confidential, detailed, and honest feedback on how they work in teams" from fellow students, faculty, and staff. According to the school, this produces an unparalleled ability to "respond to and give confidential peer feedback, something excellent managers do well."

Another major draw to the program is the school's one-year MBA program that allows students to earn their MBAs in just 12 months. "Kellogg's one-year program is one-of-a-kind," one student says. "It's the best return on investment and offers great flexibility combined with small classes and highest quality students." There is, of course, the traditional two-year program available as well. In addition to the one-year MBA program, another unique facet at Kellogg is the MMM program, a dual-degree in conjunction with the McCormick School of Engineering at Northwestern University and designed to aid students who wish to pursue "management roles in product and/or service driven companies." In addition, the MMM program integrates management, operations, and design.

Kellogg offers a lengthy list of majors in which students can specialize, from biotechnology management to technology industry management, though some students feel that "application of technology is a little slow compared to other schools." Conversely, students single out the "breadth of the marketing, strategy, and finance departments."

Overridingly, students feel confident in regards to their prospective futures thanks to the Kellogg school's "overall atmosphere, solid reputation and ranking, [and] strength across academic disciplines."

Career and Placement

Recent recruiters with a presence at Kellogg include Merrill Lynch, Microsoft, UBS, JPMorgan Chase, and Johnson & Johnson, and Booz & Company; most students are confident that their school has a "sterling reputation among corporate recruiters." It helps, too, that professors are "student-focused" and fellow students are "willing to go out on a limb to help . . . with recruiting, career advice, and schoolwork." Students agree that the team-focused environment ensures that "networking at Kellogg is tremendous."

ADMISSIONS CONTACT: BETH FLYE, ASSISTANT DEAN, ADMISSIONS AND FINANCIAL AID
ADDRESS: DONALD P. JACOBS CENTER, 2001 SHERIDAN ROAD EVANSTON, IL 60208
PHONE: 847-491-3308 • FAX: 847-491-4960
E-MAIL: MBAADMISSIONS@KELLOGG.NORTHWESTERN.EDU
WEBSITE: WWW.KELLOGG.NORTHWESTERN.EDU

Student Life and Environment

Kellogg is situated in Evanston, Illinois, along the shores of Lake Michigan, with only a short commute on the El (elevated train) to downtown Chicago. Most here appreciate this proximity or campus "There is a lot going on [at] school." One student explains, "There are dozens, maybe hundreds of clubs at school—special interest, sports, academic, career, spouse/children, politics and government, nonprofit, gay and lesbian, etc." The student body on the whole is "alive and energetic."

The school has been steadily undergoing multiple renovations to its facilities over the years, including "new classrooms wired for network access," "group study rooms," "quiet study rooms," a "computer training facility" and "expanded computer lab," "free-standing computer terminals," a "student lounge," "lockers," and a "sky-lit atrium." Others note that "off-campus living facilities are outdated, but they're working on it!"

Admissions

Admissions Officers at Kellogg have the unenviable job of whittling a pile of approximately 5,000 applications down to an admitted class of about 600. During this process, they look for work experience, academic excellence, and personality. The school's Admissions Board conducts thousands of interviews each fall. For the entering class of 2009, the average GMAT score was 707. In addition, 34 percent of Kellogg students hail from outside of the United States, and for those applicants, TOEFL scores are required. The average TOEFL score for enrolled students is 110 on the internet-based exam.

FINANCIAL FACTS

Annual tuition	$49,074
Room & board	$14,910
% of students receiving aid	74
% of first-year students receiving aid	77
Average award package	$55,745
Average grant	$15,539
Average student loan debt	$86,336

ADMISSIONS

Admissions Selectivity Rating	60*
# of applications received	5,251
Average GMAT	707
Average GPA	3.53
TOEFL required of international students	Yes
Application fee	$250
International application fee	$250
Regular application deadline	1/14
Regular notification	3/29
Application Deadline/Notification	
Round 1:	10/15 / 1/11
Round 2:	1/14 / 3/29
Round 3:	3/4 / 5/17
Early decision program?	No
Deferment available	Yes
Maximum length of deferment	case by case
Transfer students accepted	No
Non-fall admissions	Yes
Need-blind admissions	Yes

EMPLOYMENT PROFILE

Career Rating	99	Grads Employed by Function	% Avg. Salary
Percent employed at graduation	71	Marketing	24 NR
Percent employed 3 months after graduation	81	Operations	1 NR
		Consulting	38 NR
Average base starting salary	$106,804	Management	7 NR
Primary Source of Full-time Job Acceptances		Finance	17 NR
School-facilitated activities	260 (67%)	Strategic	7 NR
Graduate-facilitated activities	116 (30%)	**Top 5 Employers Hiring Grads**	
Unknown	10 (3%)	McKinsey & Co (26), Bain & Company (13), The Boston Consulting Group (23), Deloitte Consulting (11), Johnson & Johnson (10)	

THE OHIO STATE UNIVERSITY
MAX M. FISHER COLLEGE OF BUSINESS

GENERAL INFORMATION

Type of school	Public
Academic calendar	Quarter

SURVEY SAYS...

Good peer network
Solid preparation in:
Finance
Teamwork

STUDENTS

Enrollment of MBA Program	604
% male/female	68/32
% part-time	49
% minorities	14
% international	38
Average age at entry	27
Average years work experience at entry	4

ACADEMICS

Academic Experience Rating	92
Student/faculty ratio	5:1
Profs interesting rating	86
Profs accessible rating	87
% female faculty	24
% minority faculty	18

Joint Degrees

MBA/JD (4 years); MBA/MHA (3 years); MBA/MD (5 years); MBA/PharmD (5 years); MLHR/MA in Education (3 years); MBA/MPA (3 years); MBA/MS Ag Econ Dev (3 years); MACC/BSBA (4 years).

Prominent Alumni

Mr. Leslie Wexner, Chair, CEO and Founder of Limited, Inc.; Mr. Jesse J. Tyson, President, ExxonMobil Inter-America Inc.; Mr. Lionel Nowell, Executive Vice President and CFO Pepsi Bottling Gr; Ms. Tami Longaberger, CEO, The Longaberger Company; Mr. Russell Klein, Chief Marketing Officer, Burger King Corp.

Academics

Ohio State "has a strong business school—the best in Ohio—and has a very large and dynamic reach, both in terms of academic resources [and] opportunities and in terms of alumni," students at this top-25 institution tell us. Opportunities to receive an education of this quality at a public school price are rare, and MBAs at the Fisher College of Business appreciate how good they have it. Perhaps that's the reason for the unusually "collaborative climate among the students" here. As one student observes, "Everyone is very outgoing and helpful. Your classmates want to see you do well and we celebrate each other's victories. Everyone is extremely smart and wants to succeed by doing their best, not by trying to sink others to get ahead."

Fisher is "renowned for operations management" and is also very strong in finance and accounting, but as a top school it excels in nearly every field and so "offers a great opportunity to explore different disciplines and gain hands-on experience to prepare for placement." The program's designers exploit this depth of expertise in "the interdisciplinary nature of the program," which students identify as a great strength. "Students are challenged to stretch themselves outside of their comfort zone to try new, exciting opportunities" at Fisher, where a "strong and flexible academic curriculum" gives them the freedom to explore different disciplines. Students also benefit in this regard, and have access to the "resources of the largest undergraduate university in the country." Being in a small program at a large university allows students the best of both worlds: a "small batch size that ensures personal attention" with access to near-limitless resources.

The OSU faculty "strikes a strong balance between academia and professional expertise." It's the "perfect mix between professional leaders (i.e., Jeff Rodek, CEO/Chairman Hyperion; Tony Rucci, CEO Sears S. America), and academic faculty (i.e., strategy guru Jay Barney; ex-Harvard professor and devoted student advocate Karen Wruck; etc.)," according to one student. Despite all the star power, "The professors here are very approachable and go out of their way to be accessible to students all the time, and that includes coming in on weekends for review sessions, which shows their high level of commitment to help[ing] their students."

Career and Placement

Fisher's reputation is strongest in the Midwest, the region in which two-thirds of its MBAs find employment after graduation. More than one in four finds a job overseas, primarily in Asia. OSU MBAs are most often hired by financial services companies (20 percent of graduates, $85,390 average starting salary), consulting firms (16 percent, $103,571), technology firms (15 percent, $80,000), and retailers (14 percent, $91,250). By function, graduates end up in marketing and sales (27 percent, $86,000), finance (21 percent, $90,166), and operations and logistics (17 percent, $80,285).

Companies most likely to extend offers to OSU MBAs recently included: American Greetings, Capital One, Deloitte Consulting, Emerson, General Electric, Johnson & Johnson, Kimbery-Clark, Limited Brands, Motorola, Nationwide, Nestle, Oracle Consulting, PricewaterhouseCoopers, Procter & Gamble, and United Stationers.

ADMISSIONS CONTACT: DAVID SMITH, EXECUTIVE DIRECTOR, GRADUATE PROGRAMS OFFICE
ADDRESS: 100 GERLACH HALL, 2108 NEIL AVENUE COLUMBUS, OH 43210-1144
PHONE: 614-292-8511 • FAX: 614-292-9006
E-MAIL: MBA@FISHER.OSU.EDU • WEBSITE: FISHER.OSU.EDU/FTMBA/

Student Life and Environment

Fisher "benefits from strong student organizations that provide opportunities to work on experiential learning projects outside of the classroom," such as "Fisher Professional Services (a paid MBA consulting firm working with companies like Google, Nationwide, Cardinal Health, and Microsoft)" and "Fisher Board Fellows (MBAs participate on local boards as non-voting members)." These opportunities, in addition to in-class responsibilities, make for a busy schedule. "Most regular business hours in a day are taken up with projects being done in the community and class time" while "evenings are spent doing reading and assignments. You have to be able to multitask and prioritize effectively" to survive at Fisher. As hard as they work, most students still find time for "regular[ly] scheduled social events for classmates and significant others."

OSU's hometown of Columbus "brings a lot to the table, not only in [terms of] culture (restaurants, sports, and museums), but also in [terms of the] strong companies headquartered here (Nationwide, Huntington Bank, Scotts Miracle Gro, AEP, and Limited Brands) that consistently consult with our students." On campus, "Facilities, clubs, and team sports at Ohio State are excellent and there is truly a group for every taste. The large campus includes amazing history, tradition, and great green spaces. Buckeye athletics are great for evenings and weekends."

Fisher attracts a "diverse group of people from all over the U.S. and world." Students tend to be "very bright and well spoken but still down to earth," and are "driven" and "entrepreneurial" but also "very collaborative" and "genuinely willing to help." A "strong international mix" supplements the American majority.

Admissions

The Admissions Office at Fisher requires applicants to provide two official copies of transcripts for all undergraduate and graduate institutions attended, GMAT scores, two letters of recommendation, essays, and a resume of work experience (work experience is preferred but not required). In addition to the above, international applicants whose first language is not English must provide proof of English proficiency (the school accepts several standardized tests, including the TOEFL, MELAB, and IELTS) and an affidavit of financial support. Admissions interviews are conducted only at the request of the Admissions Department.

FINANCIAL FACTS

Annual tuition (in-state/ out-of-state)	$24,003/$39,771
Fees	$1,401
Room & board	$4,643
% of students receiving aid	86
% of first-year students receiving aid	84
% of students receiving loans	44
% of students receiving grants	73
Average award package	$29,642
Average grant	$6,896
Average student loan debt	$39,364

ADMISSIONS

Admissions Selectivity Rating	96
# of applications received	727
Average GMAT	677
Range of GMAT	640–710
Average GPA	3.41
TOEFL required of international students	Yes
Minimum TOEFL (paper/computer)	600/250
Application fee	$60
International application fee	$70
Application Deadline/Notification	
Round 1:	11/15 / NR
Round 2:	12/31 / NR
Round 3:	3/15 / NR
Round 4:	5/30 / NR
Early decision program?	No
Deferment available	Yes
Maximum length of deferment	1 year
Transfer students accepted	No
Non-fall admissions	No
Need-blind admissions	Yes

EMPLOYMENT PROFILE

Career Rating	95	**Grads Employed by Function%**	**Avg. Salary**
Percent employed at graduation	59	Marketing	23 $87,928
Percent employed 3 months after graduation	31	Operations	14 $85,077
		Consulting	11 $103,000
Average base starting salary	$90,051	Management	5 $90,600
Primary Source of Full-time Job Acceptances		Finance	22 $92,415
School-facilitated activities	76 (82%)	**Top 5 Employers Hiring Grads**	
Graduate-facilitated activities	17 (18%)	Nationwide (7), Deloitte Consulting (6), Johnson & Johnson (4), Procter & Gamble (4), Sears Holding (3)	

OLD DOMINION UNIVERSITY
COLLEGE OF BUSINESS AND PUBLIC ADMINISTRATION

GENERAL INFORMATION
Type of school   Public
Academic calendar   Rolling

SURVEY SAYS...
Friendly students
Cutting-edge classes
Smart classrooms
Solid preparation in:
Accounting
General management
Doing business in a global economy

STUDENTS
Enrollment of parent
  institution   23,806
Enrollment of MBA Program   369
% male/female   60/40
% part-time   65
% minorities   15
% international   22
Average age at entry   28
Average years work experience
  at entry   6

ACADEMICS
Academic Experience Rating   77
Student/faculty ratio   17:1
Profs interesting rating   83
Profs accessible rating   78
% female faculty   22
% minority faculty   33

Joint Degrees
Students may pursure dual degrees
with nearly any degree offered at
Old Dominion University with varying degrees of course overlap.

Prominent Alumni
Elizabeth Duke, Federal Reserve
Board Member; Linda Middleton,
Senior VP; John Sanderson,
President; Larry Kittelberger, Senior
VP & CIO; Bruce Bradley, President.

Academics

Business students in the Virginia Beach-Norfolk area tell us that the MBA program at Old Dominion is a good fit for them. Not only does the program have "a good reputation in the area," but its academics are "superbly integrated into the local business community. ODU's business department is the de facto authority on economic and business [issues] in this region." Of course, you don't need to be from the immediate area to enjoy the benefits of ODU's MBA program. Folks from all over can appreciate the program's "reputation for its quantitative research orientation" and its "small class sizes."

Choices are myriad in the ODU College of Business and Public Administration. Students may pursue a traditional MBA or an MS in accounting, an MA in economics, an MPA, a Master of Urban Studies, or an MS in computer science, along with two PhD options. Furthermore, they may take classes part time or full time; in the daytime, evenings, or on weekends; and at the main campus in Norfolk or at any of several satellite campuses. Students may choose a concentration in financial analysis and valuation; international business; public administration; information technology; business and economic forecasting; or maritime and port management; or they may opt for a general MBA without a concentration. A variety of study abroad options and independent research projects round out the choices here.

Size matters at ODU. As one student who arrived from a large undergraduate program explains, "I have really enjoyed the smaller setting of this school. Every professor I've had has been readily available to meet with students when needed. Every email I've ever sent a professor has been responded to within the same day or by the next morning, even on weekends. It's been a major asset in my education here to have such accessible teachers who really care about their students more so than their research. To have professors remember my name after the semester is over when I see them in the halls is something I never experienced at the school I went to for undergrad." Of course, there are downsides to attending a school this small, and at ODU, the size of the program leaves some students complaining that "some courses are offered [only] once a year" and yearning for a "more flexible course schedule." "Specifically for the MBA curriculum, there is a serious lack of electives offered," one student observes. "I found myself taking two public administration courses that I was not very interested in because there are only one or two finance electives offered in any given semester."

Career and Placement

Old Dominion offers career services to its MBA students through the university's Career Development Center. The university dedicates one counselor in the CDC Office to serve MBAs; she assists students in finding both internship and full-time positions, helps with resume and cover letter preparation, and provides individual career consultation. MBA students also benefit from an MBA Association comprised of both current students and alumni. The association organizes numerous career-promoting events over the course of the school year, including seminars, forums, social events, community service activities, and an annual dinner. Despite all this, students say they would love to see an upgrade to career services. "ODU needs to improve [its] MBA-specific career connections," one writes.

ADMISSIONS CONTACT: Ms. SHANNA WOOD, MBA ASSOCIATE DIRECTOR
ADDRESS: CONSTANT HALL 1026 NORFOLK, VA 23529
PHONE: 757-683-3585 • FAX: 757-683-5750
E-MAIL: MBAINFO@ODU.EDU • WEBSITE: WWW.ODU-MBA.ORG

Student Life and Environment

"Most students are working professionals" at ODU; the "others are international students." There's "a very strong military background here, which tends to lead to very conservative views." During the daytime, ODU has an active campus, but during the evenings—when most MBAs attend classes—it's a different story. Students wish the school would "keep areas open longer to accommodate students will full-time jobs. The MBA lounge and computer labs close too early." Another opines, "There are many lunches and activities during the day, [but] I work about 45 minutes from campus and can not take off work to attend these activities. More activities need to be offered on the weekends. Also most night activities are offered on Friday nights, and that is not a good night for full-time workers who are part-time students, as that is normally a night of relaxation as the work week has finally ended." Further complicating matters is the fact that campus security "is tough because the school is deep in the center of the city…. There are a lot of criminal alerts when the weather is good."

Admissions

All applicants to the MBA program at ODU must submit the following materials: a completed application (paper or online) including a statement of personal objectives and resume; an official GMAT score report; official transcripts for all undergraduate and graduate work; a letter of recommendation (from a professor if you are currently a student; from a supervisor if you are currently employed); and a tuition-rate-determination form (to determine eligibility for in-state tuition). International students whose first language is not English must also submit an official score report for the TOEFL. Applications generally take four to six weeks to process once all materials have arrived at the Admissions Office. Incoming students who have not completed college-level calculus are required to complete an equivalent undergraduate course during their first semester of MBA work. ODU considers the trend of undergraduate grades as well as overall cumulative GPA; those who showed marked improvement in junior and senior years can overcome poor performance as underclassmen. Returning adults with considerable work experience may earn up to six credits toward the MBA for skills and knowledge accrued through work; credits are awarded on the basis of evaluation, examination, certifications, or portfolio.

FINANCIAL FACTS

Annual tuition (in-state/ out-of-state)	$8,592/$21,672
Fees	$207
Cost of books	$1,200
Room & board (on/off-campus)	$7,500/$8,500
% of students receiving aid	10
% of students receiving grants	1
Average award package	$40,000
Average grant	$20,000

ADMISSIONS

Admissions Selectivity Rating	75
# of applications received	261
% applicants accepted	73
% acceptees attending	75
Average GMAT	550
Range of GMAT	540–580
Average GPA	3.25
TOEFL required of international students	Yes
Minimum TOEFL (paper/computer)	550/213
Application fee	$75
International application fee	$75
Early decision program?	No
Deferment available	Yes
Maximum length of deferment	1 year
Transfer students accepted	Yes
Transfer application policy: We accept up to 12 credit hours from AACSB accredited MBA programs only.	
Non-fall admissions	Yes
Need-blind admissions	Yes

PACIFIC LUTHERAN UNIVERSITY
SCHOOL OF BUSINESS

GENERAL INFORMATION
Type of school	Private
Affiliation	Lutheran
Academic calendar	4–1–4–3

SURVEY SAYS...
Solid preparation in:
General management
Operations
Communication/interpersonal skills
Presentation skills
Doing business in a global economy

STUDENTS
Enrollment of parent institution	3,661
Enrollment of MBA Program	70
% male/female	65/35
% out-of-state	4
% part-time	34
% minorities	14
% international	20
Average age at entry	31
Average years work experience at entry	6

ACADEMICS
Academic Experience Rating	**76**
Student/faculty ratio	15:1
Profs interesting rating	81
Profs accessible rating	87
% female faculty	36
% minority faculty	7

Joint Degrees
Master of Science in Nursing and Master of Business Administration (MSN/MBA) Dual-Degree Program, 30 months.

Prominent Alumni
Brad Tilden, CEO Alaskan Air Group; Joyce Barr, Former U.S. ambassador to Namibia; Dr. William Foege, former Director, Center for Disease Control; Lois Capps, U.S. Representative; Marv Harschman, Retired UW basketball coach.

Academics

Offering a "globally-focused program" that's "well-known in the area," the School of Business at Pacific Lutheran University satisfies Tacoma area locals, who appreciate "the convenience offered to working professionals" here. With "small class sizes" facilitating plenty of "one-on-one interactions," the PLU MBA program employs a "customer service approach" that keeps students happy. This part-time program, "designed for working professionals," can be completed in less than two years.

Standout features of the PLU MBA include an emphasis in technology and innovation management, mentioned by several students as the thing that brought them to the school; PLU also offers areas of emphasis in entrepreneurship and closely-held enterprises, as well as in health care management. A general MBA without concentration is also available. All students must complete a "ten-day international trip requirement," which grateful MBAs note is "included in the cost of tuition." In past years the program has sent some students on a trade mission trip organized by the Tacoma World Trade Center, and sent others to an international destination to meet with foreign business leaders to study global business best practices. Students describe the experience as "amazing" and cite it as a major asset to the program.

Most agree, however, that the faculty and program administrators are PLU's primary selling points. The "excellent professors" at the School of Business are "experienced, flexible, always available, and professional." They go out of their way to utilize their students' professional experiences in class. As one student explains, "Professors try very hard to learn about each student and cater lessons/lectures to our professional backgrounds." Small classes mean lots of student participation. "As a student you are challenged to learn, and you are a part of the class. It's expected that the students are active in the classes," one MBA warns. The administration of PLU's MBA program "is handled almost exclusively by the program administrator/director," a great arrangement for students, who report that administrative services in their program are among the best on campus.

Career and Placement

The Career Development Office at PLU provides placement and counseling services for all undergraduates, graduate students and alumni. The office assists students with internship and career placement. The PLU Business Network is an alumni group who schedules networking events to help alumni and current BBA and MBA students connect. The School of Business' career mentoring program matches students with alumni in different industries. A significant networking opportunity open to PLU MBAs is the State Farm MBA Executive Leadership Series, a series of addresses delivered by area executives. Recent speakers have included the co-founder of Meteor Solutions, the head of the CEO's office at Russell Investments, and a Senior Director of Sales at Microsoft. But a "strong alumni network" is probably PLU's greatest placement service. Students note the "sustained good reputation of [PLU] graduates," and benefit from "having a larger number of them in key companies and industries, serving in positions of great importance and responsibility."

Employers who most frequently hire Pacific Lutheran MBAs include Boeing, Microsoft, Weyerhaeuser, State Farm Insurance, Intel, and Starbucks.

ADMISSIONS CONTACT: THERESA RAMOS, DIRECTOR OF GRAD. PROGRAMS
ADDRESS: OFFICE OF ADMISSIONS, PACIFIC LUTHERAN UNIVERSITY TACOMA, WA 98447
PHONE: 253-535-7330 • FAX: 253-535-8723
E-MAIL: PLUMBA@PLU.EDU • WEBSITE: WWW.PLU.EDU/MBA

FINANCIAL FACTS

Annual tuition	$21,802
Cost of books	$1,800
Room & board	$6,765
% of students receiving aid	64
% of first-year students receiving aid	80
% of students receiving loans	30
% of students receiving grants	35
Average award package	$12,556
Average grant	$5,352
Average student loan debt	$15,563

ADMISSIONS

Admissions Selectivity Rating	**70**
# of applications received	77
% applicants accepted	74
% acceptees attending	81
Average GMAT	540
Range of GMAT	450–670
Average GPA	3.23
TOEFL required of international students	Yes
Minimum TOEFL (paper/computer)	573/88
Application fee	$40
International application fee	$40
Early decision program?	No
Deferment available	Yes
Maximum length of deferment	1 year
Transfer students accepted	Yes
Transfer application policy: In order to graduate, a student must complete a minimum of 24 Semester hours in residence at PLU.	
Non-fall admissions	Yes
Need-blind admissions	Yes

Student Life and Environment

A "new business building" and a "beautiful campus" are among the top amenities of the PLU MBA experience. The building boasts "state-of-the-art facilities [that] cater to the unique [challenges] of working students," including "Wi-Fi available throughout the entire building." Opportunities to connect with classmates are limited as a result of the part-time nature of the program and the busy schedules most students maintain. Students do frequently interact though, through "classroom-related team project activities" that one student describes as "exciting and promising, as well as offering distinct challenges." Despite the fact that many students' schedules prevent them from spending a lot of time on campus, a "very collegial atmosphere" still manages to pervade the program.

Students in the PLU MBA program bring "very diverse backgrounds and professional experiences" to the classroom. A great many are "hardworking, family-oriented professionals with a lot going on in their lives," ranging "from stay-at-home moms and dads to army surgeons and city managers." One student reports that "when working together, I felt in all cases that we were peers, that never did one person's experience make them better than another, that everyone was able to contribute."

Admissions

At PLU, applicants are "evaluated individually based on a presentation of factors indicating equivalence to admission standards, a promise of success in graduate school, qualities of good character, and potential contributions to the educational mission of the graduate program and university." Applicants must provide the school with the following materials: official transcripts covering all undergraduate and graduate work; an official GMAT or GRE score report; a current resume; a completed application form; two letters of recommendation; and a 300-word statement of personal goals. Candidates whose native language is other than English must also submit an official TOEFL or IELTS score report. International transcripts must be submitted to the Educational Perspectives transcript translation agency for evaluation. All international applicants are required to submit an I-20 as well as a Declaration of Finances.

EMPLOYMENT PROFILE		
Career Rating	88	**Top 5 Employers Hiring Grads**
Average base starting salary	$75,000	Boeing, Intel, Russell Investments, Weyerhaeuser, Microsoft

PENNSYLVANIA STATE UNIVERSITY
SMEAL COLLEGE OF BUSINESS

GENERAL INFORMATION
Type of school   Public
Academic calendar   Semester

SURVEY SAYS...
Smart classrooms
Solid preparation in:
Teamwork
Communication/interpersonal skills
Presentation skills

STUDENTS
Enrollment of parent
  institution   44,406
Enrollment of MBA Program   187
% male/female   62/38
% out-of-state   72
% part-time   0
% minorities   14
% international   33
Average age at entry   28
Average years work experience
  at entry   5

ACADEMICS
Academic Experience Rating   94
Student/faculty ratio   2:1
Profs interesting rating   88
Profs accessible rating   89
% female faculty   20
% minority faculty   34

Joint Degrees
JD/MBA, 4 years; BS/MBA, 5–6
years

Prominent Alumni
John Surma, Chairman and CEO,
U.S. Steel; J. David Rogers, CEO,
JD Capital Management; James
Stengel, President & CEO, The Jim
Stengel Company, LLC; Karen
Quintos, VP/General Manager, Dell,
Inc.; Joan Amble, EVP and
Corporate Comptroller, American
Express Company.

Academics

Many factors combine to convince MBAs at Penn State's Smeal College of Business that their program offers "one of the best returns on investment in the world." The "reasonable tuition and amazing financial assistance from the program" certainly play a large part, not to mention the school's small-town location, which provides "a cheap place to live and study, so costs are minimal." There's also "the world-class education provided by professors who are extremely respected in their industry," and, last but not least, "the benefit of the Penn State network with the largest active alumni base in the country." One student describes the alumni as "rabidly loyal to the school and very willing to help current students.... They also come back for football tailgates, so students have a great opportunity to connect with many alumni in person."

The Smeal MBA is "a very small program" (between 75 and 110 students in each incoming class) that "facilitates a more personalized education" through "great access to professors and professional development opportunities." Students love the "many opportunities to build close relationships with a world-class faculty." One student explains, "MBAs are on a first-name basis with all faculty and staff. Everyone really goes out of their way to make sure you are on the right path in virtually everything." Administrators "join the students daily for coffee and are tremendously responsive to our needs. They also join us for social events and attend outside events." Students are especially pleased that the Dean "is committed to transforming this program into a national powerhouse."

Smeal excels in supply chain management; students tell us that finance is another strength of the program, as is business-to-business marketing (a product of Smeal's Institute for the Study of Business Markets, which "brings the thought leaders from around the world together to face the challenges in today's B2B markets"). They warn that "the first year at Smeal is packed. Students coming into the program should expect to be in class 16 hours a week and working outside the classroom around 20 hours." Things don't let up that much during the second year, but students don't mind; they tell us that the program "prepares students for the challenges they will face once they re-enter the workforce in a management capacity. Students develop both technical and leadership skills and are well-positioned to lead business in the future. In addition, the collaborative culture of the program translates well into successful behaviors in the business world."

Career and Placement

Career Services is a mixed bag at Penn State. Students grumble that "due to the small size of our MBA program, the school struggles to bring in a large number of recruiters in various disciplines." However, they also point out that "career services have been upgraded recently." The school facilitates recruitment and job searches nationally and on-campus. Students note, "contacts at every major company in the world." Overall, most agree the placement picture here is pretty good.

Companies most likely to employ Smeal MBAs include: Air Products & Chemicals, Amazon.com, Avaya, Bank of America Corporation, Bear Stearns, CIGNA, Citigroup, Dell, DuPont, ExxonMobil, Ford Motor Company, Hewlett-Packard, Honeywell International, IBM, Intel, Johnson & Johnson, Kennametal, KPMG International, Pfizer, Praxair, PricewaterhouseCoopers, Solectron, and Time Inc.

Student Life and Environment

State College, Pennsylvania, may not have Manhattan's glitz and glamour, but it is "a beautiful town and a fantastic place to spend two challenging years of your life." The town provides "great nightlife and a downtown bar scene," while the school provides the football beloved by so many here. Major events such as THON and Arts Fest pepper the academic calendar, and students report that "outside of the classroom, opportunities abound for cross-cultural learning (student organizations host numerous events), philanthropic involvement (Habitat for Humanity, etc.), and social events (we went skydiving at the beginning of the semester!)." In 2005, the business school moved into a "state-of-the-art $68 million building that takes advantage of cutting-edge technology available today. The building helps strengthen a sense of community that is already very evident at Penn State." On the downside, students tell us that "activities can be limited due to the small size of the school. There are always demands for more clubs, but not always enough students available. Several students and spouses started a partners club, Lion Partners, this year, which helps new students with domestic partners."

Admissions

The Smeal admission's website notes that Admissions Officers work hard to optimize class composition for each entering class. Diverse backgrounds in terms of both professional and life experience are sought so that a wide range of perspectives inform group work and class discussion. Applicants to the program must submit the following materials: a completed online application form; official copies of all transcripts for all postsecondary academic work; an official GMAT score report; two letters of recommendation from individuals who can assess your past professional performance; personal essays; a resume; and an interview. In addition to all of the above, international applicants must also submit an official score report for the TOEFL or IELTS; and evidence of sufficient funds to cover at least one year's expenses while in the program (approximately $50,000). The school admits some students directly from undergraduate programs, but most students enter with at least four years of professional experience.

FINANCIAL FACTS

Annual tuition (in-state/ out-of-state)	$18,948/$31,470
Fees	$1,012
Cost of books	$3,500
Room & board	$17,400
% of students receiving aid	90
% of first-year students receiving aid	88
% of students receiving loans	43
% of students receiving grants	80
Average award package	$27,828
Average grant	$24,400
Average student loan debt	$33,642

ADMISSIONS

Admissions Selectivity Rating	91
# of applications received	663
% applicants accepted	33
% acceptees attending	38
Average GMAT	652
Range of GMAT	610–690
Average GPA	3.3
TOEFL required of international students	Yes
Minimum TOEFL (paper/computer)	600/250
Application fee	$65
International application fee	$65
Regular application deadline	4/15
Regular notification	5/31
Application Deadline/Notification	
Round 1:	12/1 / 1/31
Round 2:	2/1 / 3/31
Round 3:	4/15 / 5/31
Early decision program?	Yes
ED Deadline/Notification	12/1 / 1/31
Deferment available	Yes
Maximum length of deferment	1 year
Transfer students accepted	Yes
Transfer application policy:	
A maximum of six elective credits can be transferred. All core courses must be taken.	
Non-fall admissions	No
Need-blind admissions	Yes

EMPLOYMENT PROFILE

Career Rating	93	Grads Employed by Function	% Avg. Salary
Percent employed at graduation	69	Marketing	14 $74,400
Percent employed 3 months after graduation	75	Operations	48 $93,200
		Consulting	8 $81,500
Average base starting salary	$87,940	Finance	21 $87,667
Primary Source of Full-time Job Acceptances		MIS	2 NR
School-facilitated activities	38 (46%)	**Top 5 Employers Hiring Grads**	
Graduate-facilitated activities	7 (8%)	Dell (7), Sears Holdings (3), Bristol-Myers Squibb (3), Johnson and Johnson (2), Mars (2)	

PENNSYLVANIA STATE UNIVERSITY—ERIE, THE BEHREND COLLEGE
SAM AND IRENE BLACK SCHOOL OF BUSINESS

GENERAL INFORMATION
Type of school	Public
Academic calendar	Semester

SURVEY SAYS...
Smart classrooms
Solid preparation in:
General management

STUDENTS
Enrollment of parent institution	4,633
Enrollment of MBA Program	118
% male/female	68/32
% out-of-state	14
% part-time	63
% minorities	11
% international	5
Average age at entry	25
Average years work experience at entry	4

ACADEMICS
Academic Experience Rating	78
Student/faculty ratio	5:1
Profs interesting rating	80
Profs accessible rating	84
% female faculty	27
% minority faculty	20

Academics

The Black School of Business at Penn State Behrend College "provides the best value for a working student in the local area," one MBA here explains, adding, "You get the Penn State name, an outstanding general MBA education, and student-work flexibility." Behrend enjoys "an outstanding reputation" in the region, making it an excellent choice for students looking to build their careers in and around Erie.

A general degree that aims to develop the critical-thinking skills necessary for a career in mid- and upper-level management, the Behrend MBA curriculum consists of 48 units, or 14 courses. Of these, 18 units form the foundational core courses, which are comprised of four introductory classes: Business, Government, and Society; Costs, Competition, and Market Performance; Demand, Operations, and Firm Performance; and Integrated Business Analysis. After completing these courses, students must complete 18 credits of required advanced courses and 12 credits of elective course work. For those who have already taken business courses, the program can be streamlined through the omission of certain foundation courses. Depending on their previous academic preparation, full-time students can usually complete the MBA curriculum in three semesters; part-time students usually require two to four years to complete the program.

Behrend works hard to keep its MBA program student-friendly with an "attractive and clean" campus (that includes "a new facility for the business school"), "small classes" and "accessible professors." Most faculty members "have extensive real-world experience that greatly adds to their lessons. Additionally, many are locals and have experience at the major companies in the area and understand the general job situation of the area." Students describe the curriculum as challenging, citing "tough courses" that "equate to well-educated students." Another reports, "The professors expect a lot. No class was easy. I consider myself to be an intelligent person, but have felt less so at times because of the difficulty of the work." Among the drawbacks of a Behrend MBA, "some courses are only offered one semester each year," making it "very difficult to have a consistent workload. Some semesters are much heavier than others due to course offerings." Even so, students here agree that Behrend is "the best school, academically, for the region."

Career and Placement

A high percentage of Penn State Behrend students are currently employed in professional positions and are pursuing an MBA with the intention of improving their career opportunities at their current companies. In fact, a considerable number of Penn State Behrend students receive tuition assistance from their employers. Some, however, see their MBAs as a stepping stone to a new career (or, for students pursuing MBAs straight out of college, simply a career). For those, the Penn State Behrend Academic Advising and Career Development Center serves both the undergraduate and graduate population at the college, including students in the MBA program. The CDC hosts career fairs, on-campus recruiting and interview events, seminars, and workshops. A growing number of organizations participate in Penn State Behrend career fairs each year. Employers who frequently hire Behrend MBAs include: Deloitte Consulting, Paradigm Wave, Ingentor, GE Infrastructure-Transportation Systems, IBM, Erie Insurance Group, National City Corporation, Graham Packaging, HealthAmerica, and the Pennsylvania State University.

ADMISSIONS CONTACT: ANN M. BURBULES, GRADUATE ADMISSIONS COUNSELOR
ADDRESS: 4851 COLLEGE DRIVE ERIE, PA 16563
PHONE: 814-898-7255 • FAX: 814-898-6044
E-MAIL: PSBEHRENDMBA@PSU.EDU • WEBSITE: WWW.BEHREND.PSU.EDU/MYMBA

Student Life and Environment

Behrend MBAs enjoy "state-of-the-art" classrooms that "allow us to utilize multimedia learning," which they very much appreciate. The campus itself is "very clean, safe, and attractive," "not so large that it is overwhelming but still offering most [of the] opportunities of a large school." And here's something you rarely hear at any school, much less a state institution: there's "plenty of parking" here.

Campus life offers "a number of clubs and organizations for students," and "the school also hosts a very wide array of speakers, and events," but most of these events seem planned primarily for undergraduates. "There are no solely business school programs of any kind. The most activity available is an unofficial happy hour at the end of the semester," one student writes.

There's a clear divide among the Behrend MBA population. "The morning sessions of class are more geared toward the younger generation," while "the evening sessions [consist] more of your business professionals who take things more seriously." The student body includes "a large number of engineers due to the engineering school at the Behrend School." Several full-time students reported that they were only attending full time as a result of the down economy; otherwise, they'd be working and attending part time.

Admissions

Students may apply to begin study at Penn State Behrend's Black College of Business in the fall, spring, or summer semester. Admissions decisions are made on a rolling basis. To apply, students must submit two official transcripts, official GMAT scores, a statement of purpose, an application fee, and three recommendation forms. Candidates with the highest GMAT scores and GPA are given priority in admissions. Candidates are evaluated based on the strength of their combined GMAT score and GPA; therefore, a lower GMAT score can be compensated for by a higher GPA, or vice versa. International applicants whose first language is not English must meet all of the above requirements and must also submit an official score report for the TOEFL or IELTS.

FINANCIAL FACTS

Annual tuition (in-state/ out-of-state)	$12,276/$19,026
Fees	$792
Cost of books	$1,248
Room & board (off-campus)	$10,062
% of students receiving aid	87
% of first-year students receiving aid	83
% of students receiving loans	76
% of students receiving grants	29
Average award package	$17,391
Average grant	$8,333
Average student loan debt	$17,725

ADMISSIONS

Admissions Selectivity Rating	**79**
# of applications received	47
% applicants accepted	72
% acceptees attending	94
Average GMAT	525
Range of GMAT	460–590
Average GPA	3.36
TOEFL required of international students	Yes
Minimum TOEFL (paper/computer)	550/213
Application fee	$65
International application fee	$65
Regular application deadline	7/10
Early decision program?	No
Deferment available	Yes
Maximum length of deferment	2 years
Transfer students accepted	Yes
Transfer application policy:	

Up to 10 credits of relevant graduate work completed at an accredited institution. Credits earned to complete a previous graduate degree may not be used to fulfill MBA degree requirements. Transferred graduate work must have been completed no more than five years before the student is fully admitted as a degree candidate at Penn State Behrend. Course work must be of at least a B quality and appear on the graduate transcript of a regionally-accredited institution.

Non-fall admissions	Yes
Need-blind admissions	Yes

EMPLOYMENT PROFILE

Career Rating	**80**	**Grads Employed by Function**	**% Avg. Salary**
Percent employed at graduation	23	Consulting	43 $55,500
Percent employed 3 months after graduation	9	Finance	29 $40,500
Average base starting salary	$45,000	Nonprofit	14 $12,000
Primary Source of Full-time Job Acceptances		**Top 5 Employers Hiring Grads**	
Unknown	7 (NR%)	Ernst & Young (1), Husky Energy (1), IBM (1), Bank of New York Mellon (1), Medrad (1)	

PEPPERDINE UNIVERSITY
GRAZIADIO SCHOOL OF BUSINESS AND MANAGEMENT

GENERAL INFORMATION

Type of school — Private
Affiliation — Church of Christ

SURVEY SAYS...
Students love Malibu, CA
Friendly students
Solid preparation in:
Teamwork

STUDENTS
Enrollment of parent institution	7,733
Enrollment of MBA Program	291
% male/female	52/48
% minorities	66
% international	42
Average age at entry	26
Average years work experience at entry	4

ACADEMICS
Academic Experience Rating	86
Profs interesting rating	86
Profs accessible rating	89
% female faculty	20
% minority faculty	9

Prominent Alumni
Victor Tsao, Founder, Vice President and General Manager, Linksys; John Figueroa, President, McKesson U.S. Pharmaceutical; Christos M. Cotsakos, CEO and President, Mainstream Holdings; Jose A. Collazo, Vice Chairman and Presidnet, Form I-9 Compliance, LLC; Jason Nazar, Founder and CEO, Docstoc.com.

Academics

An eminent Southern California institution, Pepperdine University offers more than just sunshine. At this small but progressive school, the MBA curriculum distinguishes itself through a "strong international outlook," as well as a pointed "emphasis on values, entrepreneurship, and environmental stewardship." Throughout the curriculum, experiential learning and teamwork are stressed, and "group study sessions and projects help simulate real team dynamics." In addition, students benefit from various co-curricular activities and "international experiences," plus "all the leadership positions and extracurricular activities available on campus." A student tells us, "I have worked on research projects with faculty and business plan projects with fellow students." Of particular note, "The education-to-business program, in which students consult for a major local company, is also excellent."

Pepperdine "Professors are excellent, especially the finance staff." The best of the best are those who "come from respected industry positions"; however, students admit that, "There are also a number of tenured professors who are disorganized [and] out of touch with current business practices." "Class sizes are small, so you have more of a chance to speak up" and "The faculty-student ratio allows for a more intimate learning environment where the professors can best manage the pace of the class and the students do not get lost in the shuffle." A current student adds, "In the five classes that I am currently taking, all professors know me by name and have made an effort to make sure that all students are on track." On this friendly campus, "Everyone from professors to senior administration is not only accessible but actively interested in helping students get the most out of the program."

Depending on your background, experience, and career goals, Pepperdine has a range of MBA options. Full-time students can complete the MBA through a 12-month, 15-month, or 24-month option, while the Fully-Employed MBA is completed in the evenings in as little as two (or as many as seven) years. The school also offers a fast-paced executive MBA, as well as "a five-year BS/MBA program in conjunction with Seaver College, Pepperdine's undergraduate school." While students in the full-time program say, "the workload is heavy but not unmanageable," evening students have the additional challenge of balancing work with academics. In fact, "As a FEMBA [fully-employed MBA student] student, time is precious. Every waking hour is spent in preparation for the next class or group project."

Career and Placement

Ever-loyal to their alma mater, the Pepperdine "alumni network is incredible, and they all go out of their way to help in any way possible." A current student enthuses, "I have reached out to no less than 25 alums and every single one of them has taken my calls, answered my questions and offered to connect me with others in their company to position myself for a job!" Professors also lend a hand with the job hunt, and many "sponsor and host alumni mixers and often try to help you [find] opportunities for post-graduation." Additionally, job seekers can get help from the Career Center, which offers one-on-one counseling to MBA candidates, as well as professional development and networking events. Unfortunately, "It is a small program and big companies do not justify the effort to come on campus to recruit." To add to students' woes, "There are several other good schools in the Los Angeles area, which means competition for jobs is intense."

In the full-time program, 57 percent of students had accepted a job within three months of graduation. The top 15 recruiting companies were AT&T, PIMCO, Bank of America,

ADMISSIONS CONTACT: DARRELL ERIKSEN, PREADMISSION ADVISOR
ADDRESS: 6100 CENTER DRIVE, STE. 400 LOS ANGELES, CA 90045
PHONE: 310-568-5555 • FAX: 310-568-5727
E-MAIL: MBABSM@PEPPERDINE.EDU • WEBSITE: BSCHOOL.PEPPERDINE.EDU

Raytheon Company, PricewaterhouseCoopers, Activision Blizzard, 20th Century Fox Film Corporation, Samsung Electronics, Morgan Stanley, Skechers USA, Wedbush Morgan, Coldwell Banker, Crystal Cruises, Neiman Marcus, and Sharp Industries. In recent years, the mean base salary was roughly $76,000.

Student Life and Environment

Pepperdine's coastal campus is the perfect place for work or play. Perched above the Pacific Ocean, "The beauty and tranquility of the environment is infectious, and everyone is in a better mood because of where we go to school." The campus also creates an ideal backdrop for student life. Here, "the students are very social and they are very active within campus clubs," providing continuous "opportunities for social and academic growth." The finance club, for example, regularly hosts "guest speakers, hands-on training from alumni and professional training firms, interview workshops, and alumni mixers."

Pepperdine attracts a fairly diverse student group, including a "good mix of international and domestic students." Within the business school, there are "some very liberal students (attracted to the school's focus on corporate responsibility) yet also some very conservative students (attracted to the school's Christian values), so no dominant political view among the class." Despite differences, "There is a great social, familial atmosphere among student body." In addition, "The mentorship program, led by second years, provides guidance and support for incoming students, strengthening the bond between the first- and second-year students." While full-time students gush over the Malibu campus, many part-time students go to school on "a satellite campus, so many of the facilities available to students at the main campus are not available to us."

Admissions

Prospective Pepperdine students are evaluated on the strength of their undergraduate record, standardized test scores, letters of recommendation, and work experience. However, there are different admissions requirements for each graduate business program. For example, students applying to the one-year MBA must have a minimum of three years professional experience before entering the program. For the two-year program, only a year of work experience is required. To determine which program is right for you, Pepperdine recommends attending a pre-admission information session.

FINANCIAL FACTS

Annual tuition	$37,516
Fees	$690

ADMISSIONS

Admissions Selectivity Rating	87
# of applications received	500
% applicants accepted	50
% acceptees attending	117
Average GMAT	640
TOEFL required of international students	Yes
Minimum TOEFL (paper/computer)	600/250
Application fee	$75
International application fee	$75
Regular application deadline	5/1
Early decision program?	Yes
ED Deadline/ Notification	12/15 / 1/15
Deferment available	Yes
Maximum length of deferment	1 year
Transfer students accepted	Yes
Transfer application policy: No more than 2 courses may be transferred, contingent upon policy committee approval.	
Non-fall admissions	No
Need-blind admissions	Yes

EMPLOYMENT PROFILE

Career Rating	82	**Grads Employed by Function**	**%**	**Avg. Salary**
Percent employed at graduation	31	Marketing	16	$73,000
Percent employed 3 months after graduation	25	Operations	4	$58,902
		Consulting	1	$75,000
Average base starting salary	$75,615	Management	9	$84,222
Primary Source of Full-time Job Acceptances		Finance	13	$77,531
School-facilitated activities	NR (37%)	HR	2	$69,000
Graduate-facilitated activities	NR (56%)	MIS	1	$72,000
Unknown	NR (7%)	**Top 5 Employers Hiring Grads**		
		AT&T (7), PIMCO (2), Bank of America (1), Raytheon Company (1), PricewaterhouseCoopers (1)		

PITTSBURG STATE UNIVERSITY
GLADYS A. KELCE COLLEGE OF BUSINESS

GENERAL INFORMATION
Type of school   Public
Academic calendar   Semester

SURVEY SAYS...
Solid preparation in:
Accounting
General management

STUDENTS
Enrollment of parent institution	7,100
Enrollment of MBA Program	136
% male/female	55/45
% out-of-state	53
% part-time	27
% international	43
Average age at entry	25
Average years work experience at entry	1

ACADEMICS
Academic Experience Rating	77
Student/faculty ratio	25:1
Profs interesting rating	90
Profs accessible rating	82
% female faculty	15
% minority faculty	10

Prominent Alumni
Lee Scott, EX-President & CEO Walmart; John Lampe, President & CEO Firestone/Bridgestone; John Lowe, Executive VP ConocoPhillips; Orvil Gene Bicknell, CEO NPC International; Richard Colliver, Executive VP American Honda.

Academics

For many an MBA student in Kansas, there's no place like home at the Kelce College of Business, which "provides a great atmosphere to receive an education." You'll find many a native Kansan here thanks to the school's "close to home" location; however its real draw is its "excellent reputation" as one of the best business schools in the area. Students here appreciate the "small class sizes" and "enlightening" curriculum, along with the "flexible study options" that allow students to earn their degrees on either a full-time (12 months of study) or part-time (two and a half years of study) basis.

The "high quality of the courses" offered are bolstered by "great" professors who "take time to get to know you as a student, and come off as real people that are there to facilitate your learning." "I have been really impressed by my professors," one student explains. "They usually have extensive real-world experience, and they are able to bring their insights into the classroom. I have found most of my professors have a good sense of humor which is often the best way to keep students' attention." Another adds, "The professors [each] have different strengths, but [many] have a business leaning rather than a purely academic one." Some here would like to see professors with "more real-world experience," and note that despite the faculty being "very well-seasoned," they might almost be too much so when it comes to "age."

PSU's administration also gets glowing reviews. "The school administrators...take an active role in your learning experience," one student says. The school is "well-organized" and many note that "difficult situations" are handled with ease by an "understanding and helpful" staff. The main issue that students report is the need for "a new building" and "more access to study or work areas." But in line with the hands-on nature of a school that students describe as "already looking ahead toward the future," "a brand-new business school...is already in the plans."

Career and Placement

The Career Services office at PSU states that their mission is "to proactively educate students and alumni to make informed career decisions and provide them with counseling, teaching, training, resources, plus consultation and employment-related services necessary to optimize their life span career development; and to support institutional outcomes through employment data collection." This attitude, combined with a "career-oriented" MBA program, accounts for a high degree of success when it comes to graduates looking for work. "Pitt State concentrates on making its education both useful to the students and to local businesses," one student explains. "Finding a job does not usually seem to be a problem for Pitt State graduates." This is further bolstered by PSU's "many high-profile alumni" and the "good working relationship" the school has with the local community. That said, when looking beyond the local community, some students find their career options limited. "The majority of companies at the university's career fair are ones I have never even heard of," a student laments.

Student Life and Environment

Students say that Pittsburg State "offers a traditional MBA with great on-campus clubs, sports, and other educational and extracurricular activities." School spirit runs high, particularly during football season, and the MBA Program Director "does a good job encouraging students to be involved." "Pitt State is truly a community," one student explains, "almost a town within a town. Everyone knows each other here!" This is helped in a large way by the school's popular standing in Pittsburg, Kansas. "The town is such a strong supporter of the college," one student notes. "The people are friendly and helpful."

By and large, students here are "amazed" at the number of school-run clubs, activities, and volunteering opportunities. As one student attests, "There is always something going on." That said, finding time for activities can sometimes prove challenging for MBA candidates. Many find that the assortment of "assignments, submissions, exams, and quizzes" keeps them "pretty busy."

The student body is comprised of a "culturally diverse" "variety of foreign and domestic students," all of whom are "extremely well-qualified" due to their "educational backgrounds and work experience." There is also a "blend of younger students and those who have come back to school [from the working world]." All in all, "most students are intent on making the most out of their education." "I feel that students in the business school are extremely focused," one student states. Students describe themselves as "friendly" and "willing to lend a helping hand." "We all seem to have the attitude that we are in this together," one student says. "Fellow students are always a pleasure to work with in groups and tend to be supportive during heavy workload periods," another adds. No surprise that many here tell us that they have "built some great relationships" during their time at Pittsburg State University. However, some international students complain that when they step off campus, they find themselves surrounded by "rednecks, racists, and rustic rascals." Additionally, they also find that they are "handicapped" if they don't have a car. Students with families would like to see the school "offer more childcare facilities to enable the attraction of more students from the working environment."

Admissions

Students looking to apply to Kelce must present official copies of undergraduate transcripts (those who didn't major in business will be required to take foundation courses to bring them up to speed), a completed application for admission to the Graduate School of Pittsburg State University, GMAT scores (a minimum of 400 is required), and, if the applicant's native language isn't English, a TOEFL score of at least 550 (or 213 on the computer-based exam). The school states that for unconditional admission, students "must submit a minimum of 1,050 points based on the following formula: 200 times the overall undergraduate grade point average plus the GMAT score."

FINANCIAL FACTS

Annual tuition (in-state/ out-of-state)	$5,152/$12,470
Cost of books	$1,200
Room & board	$5,744
% of students receiving aid	50
% of first-year students receiving aid	25
% of students receiving loans	25
% of students receiving grants	15
Average award package	$8,500
Average grant	$3,500

ADMISSIONS

Admissions Selectivity Rating	71
# of applications received	270
% applicants accepted	76
% acceptees attending	67
Average GMAT	510
Range of GMAT	400–710
Average GPA	3.5
TOEFL required of international students	Yes
Minimum TOEFL (paper/computer)	550/213
Application fee	$35
International application fee	$60
Regular application deadline	7/15
Regular notification	8/1
Application Deadline/Notification	
Round 1:	6/1 / 6/15
Round 2:	10/15 / 10/30
Round 3:	4/1 / 4/15
Round 4:	5/1 / 5/15
Early decision program?	No
Deferment available	Yes
Maximum length of deferment	1 year
Transfer students accepted	Yes
Transfer application policy:	
Up to 9 semester hours may be transferred from another MBA accredited program.	
Non-fall admissions	Yes
Need-blind admissions	Yes

EMPLOYMENT PROFILE

		Grads Employed by Function	% Avg. Salary
Career Rating	76		
Percent employed at graduation	60	Marketing	24 $44,000
Percent employed 3 months after graduation	25	Management	54 $45,000
		MIS	22 $45,000
Average base starting salary	$46,000	**Top 5 Employers Hiring Grads**	
Primary Source of Full-time Job Acceptances		Deloitte & Touche (2), Sprint (4), Kock\h (2),	
School-facilitated activities	43 (72%)	Walmart (2), AllState (2)	
Unknown	17 (28%)		

PORTLAND STATE UNIVERSITY
SCHOOL OF BUSINESS ADMINISTRATION

GENERAL INFORMATION
Type of school   Public

SURVEY SAYS...
Students love Portland, OR
Friendly students
Good peer network
Solid preparation in:
Marketing
Accounting
General management
Teamwork

STUDENTS
Enrollment of parent institution	27,972
Enrollment of MBA Program	342
% male/female	57/43
% out-of-state	20
% part-time	76
% minorities	11
% international	20
Average age at entry	28
Average years work experience at entry	6

ACADEMICS
Academic Experience Rating	**78**
Student/faculty ratio	35:1
Profs interesting rating	73
Profs accessible rating	77
% female faculty	32

Prominent Alumni
Gary Ames, former President/CEO, U.S. West; Gerry Cameron, retired Chairman of the Board, U.S. Bancorp; Scott Davis, Chief Executive Officer, UPS; Larry Huget, President/COO, ESCO Corp; J. Greg Ness, President/COO, StanCorp Financial Group.

Academics

Taking a cue from its progressive environs in Portland, Oregon, Portland State University offers an MBA+ program with a "focus on sustainability" and an emphasis on "personal development as a leader." Offering more than your standard MBA, "This school is committed to the whole student," and "creativity, along with sustainable, equitable solutions, are promoted, even prized." Throughout the hefty 72-credit curriculum, you'll never lose sight of the school's core values: "PSU also works hard to integrate sustainability into most aspects of the curriculum, from core classes to elective offerings." The MBA+ includes plenty of required coursework (as well as required hands-on projects), yet electives give students the opportunity to tailor their education. In fact, "the wide latitude given to students to pursue their studies in a multi-disciplinary manner" is a trademark of PSU's graduate program. One student, for example, chose to take "public policy classes through the school of Public Administration, an environmental economics course through the School of Liberal Arts and Sciences (Economics), and a two-term seminar on the Smart Grid, also through the school of Public Administration."

Thanks to its strong reputation and enviable Portland location, PSU can "attract and retain an extremely high-quality faculty roster." On the whole, "Professors are informed, enlightened educators as well as experts in their respective fields." Despite overall excellence, students say there are a few instructors who "seem unprepared, disorganized, and unclear on what they're supposed to be teaching us." The local community also plays an important role in the PSU experience. "Portland is truly at the center of this nation's move toward sustainability," and therefore, "Being in Portland is a huge plus—there's so much sustainable business thinking and practice here that it's easy to see in the field what I learn in school." A student adds, "I have been introduced to and met with many people that are driving regional and national movements on the cutting edge of sustainability."

PSU is a large school, but you won't get lost in the crowd. Despite its 600-plus enrollment, "The SBA manages by breaking up [its] graduate studies into discrete cohorts and providing a concrete plan of study for each. There's never much doubt what you should be doing, yet there is flexibility should you need it." Depending on your schedule, the school offers several program options. For full-time students, "MBA cohort classes are four hours long one day a week from about [noon] until four," while part-time students "typically go to class two to three evenings a week." The school also operates a "well-regarded online program," which participants describe as "very smooth and very accessible." Though students say the business school's classrooms could use a refresh, "The academic resources are great." For example, "The library has done a lot of work to make research as easy as possible, even for those of us who are only on campus a couple times a week."

Career and Placement

The largest school in the state, PSU maintains "powerful connections to the Portland-area business community." Within the business school itself, faculty and administrators are "are ultra-accessible and always willing to provide career advice or introduce you to people they know in the business community." In addition, PSU has "a good alumni network" throughout the state of Oregon. Drawing on its deep ties in the Portland community, the academic experience at PSU is augmented by various professional development activities, like expert panel discussions, alumni networking events, and a mentorship

ADMISSIONS CONTACT: JOHN STOECKMANN, GRADUATE BUSINESS PROGRAMS
ADMISSIONS COORDINATOR • ADDRESS: 631 SW HARRISON ST, SBA 540 PORTLAND, OR 97201
PHONE: 503-725-8001 • FAX: 503-725-2290
E-MAIL: GRADADMISSIONS@SBA.PDX.EDU • WEBSITE: WWW.MBA.PDX.EDU

program. At the same time, students note that career services are not as robust as they'd like. While the school affords them many opportunities, "Students are expected to leverage other offerings, such as mentoring programs, informational interviews, etc." Companies that have partnered with PSU through the mentor program, as student project partners, or as employers include Columbia Forest Products, Columbia Sportswear, Costco, Ernst & Young, Intel, Nestle, Nike, PepsiCo, and WebTrends. The average starting salary for full-time PSU students is about $70,000.

Student Life and Environment

Friendly and down-to-earth, PSU students "defy the typical business school stereotype of sharkish students dying to get ahead." A current student observes, "While I expected to enter B-school with a bunch of traders and bankers, I was surprised to find a group of students that shared my, and Portland's, sensibilities regarding the world, and who are looking forward to showing the world that businesspeople are not only out to bring down the financial system en route to earning billions." Although there is a general interest in sustainability and ethics, at PSU you'll meet students from a "wide range" of backgrounds. As such, there are "a variety of activities to participate in regardless of your industry," and, on campus, there are lots of resources for a diverse student body—including "several childcare centers."

In both the full-time and part-time MBA+ program, many "people come to class and then go home," without making time for clubs or student groups. However, most students are involved in school-related activities outside of class, such as "internships, networking opportunities, and even...regular community service." In addition, many students are "open to meet after class or on weekends to socialize." Thanks to PSU's "vibrant urban location" in downtown Portland, students enjoy everything the Pacific Northwest has to offer, including plenty of "good food and coffee locations close by."

Admissions

To be considered for the full-time MBA+ program, students must have a minimum undergraduate GPA of 2.75, or, alternately, 3.0 in nine units of graduate-level coursework. Prospective students must also have at least two years of professional work experience before entering the program. In the class of 2009, the average GMAT score was 628 and the mean undergraduate GPA was 3.26.

FINANCIAL FACTS

Annual tuition (in-state/ out-of-state)	$16,200/$18,792
Fees	$1,200
Cost of books	$2,000
Room & board (on/off-campus)	$9,600/$13,100

ADMISSIONS

Admissions Selectivity Rating	86
# of applications received	276
% applicants accepted	62
% acceptees attending	73
Average GMAT	628
Range of GMAT	580–660
Average GPA	3.26
TOEFL required of international students	Yes
Minimum TOEFL (paper/computer)	550/213
Application fee	$50
International application fee	$50
Regular application deadline	5/1
Regular notification	
Round 1	11/1 / 12/15
Round 2	2/1 / 4/30
Early decision program?	Yes
ED Deadline/Notification	1/1 / 4/1
Deferment available	No
Transfer students accepted	Yes
Transfer application policy: Maximum of 1/3 of the total number of PSU credits may transfer from a US accredited university.	
Non-fall admissions	No
Need-blind admissions	Yes

Applicants Also Look At

Oregon State University
University of Oregon
University of portland
University of Washington
Willamette university

EMPLOYMENT PROFILE

Career Rating	85	Grads Employed by Function% Avg. Salary	
Percent employed at graduation	44	Marketing	12 $58,300
Percent employed 3 months after graduation	50	Operations	12 $77,700
		Consulting	4 $85,000
Average base starting salary	$70,170	Management	23 $74,800
Primary Source of Full-time Job Acceptances		Finance	27 $60,200
School-facilitated activities	3 (12%)	MIS	4 $96,000
Graduate-facilitated activities	1 (4%)		
Unknown	22 (84%)		

PURDUE UNIVERSITY
KRANNERT SCHOOL OF MANAGEMENT

GENERAL INFORMATION

Type of school	Public
Academic calendar	Semester

SURVEY SAYS...

Smart classrooms
Solid preparation in:
Finance
Operations
Quantitative skills

STUDENTS

Enrollment of parent institution	71,988
Enrollment of MBA Program	114
% male/female	76/24
% out-of-state	68
% part-time	0
% minorities	15
% international	39
Average age at entry	27
Average years work experience at entry	4

ACADEMICS

Academic Experience Rating	93
Student/faculty ratio	2:1
Profs interesting rating	89
Profs accessible rating	88
% female faculty	25
% minority faculty	2

Joint Degrees

BS Management/MBA (5 years); BS Industrial Engineering/MBA (5 years); BS Mechanical Engineering/MBA (5 years)

Prominent Alumni

Joseph Forehand, Retired Chairman, Accenture; Marshall Larsen, Chairman, President, CEO, Goodrich Corp.; Marjorie Magner, Managing Partner, Brysam Global Partners, listed among Most Powerful Women in Business (Forbes); Venu Srinivasan, Chairman and Managing Director, TVS Motor Co.; Jerry Rawls, President and CEO, Finisar.

Academics

Purdue University's Krannert School of Management is a heavyweight in the MBA universe, especially when it comes to its "areas of strength: quantitative methods, operations, finance, and economics." Those looking to develop a "strong analytical and quantitative background" can hardly go wrong with a Krannert MBA. Best of all, at state school prices, Krannert "provides a great return on investment." But it's not just the school's low tuition that lends Krannert a kinder bottom line. As one student explains, "Many of us are actually doing this program at almost no cost thanks to the number of scholarships and assistantships [on offer]. This is very unique for a top MBA program. My friends at Wharton, MIT, Tepper, etc. are paying way more!"

Krannert excels even outside its quantitatively-focused standout disciplines. Students encounter a faculty experienced "in every aspect of management, from operations and finance to marketing and HR" here. But Krannert's academic excellence comes with high expectations. Academics are tough; there's a "'no BS' atmosphere here. Here you are expected to 'work hard, work right, and work together.'" MBAs assure us that Krannert "will push everyone to the limits, truly creating upending experiences that develop the individual along several dimensions." This is true not merely in terms of in-class work; the program "also provides several experiential learning opportunities through [its] consulting projects and study abroad programs." "The experiential learning projects give us good exposure to real-world work before we actually take the plunge," students tell us.

In terms of size, Krannert is just right. The program "is small enough for each student to stand out and become a leader if they would like to," yet "large enough and diverse enough to really learn a lot from your classmates." Krannert keeps class sizes small, which "means that students have greater one-on-one time with professors and they remain closely knit even years after graduation." Krannert professors "work to continue to contribute to research and stay involved in their respective fields," yet remain "genuinely interested in helping their students and are open and available to them any time we need."

Career and Placement

Students can prepare for interviews, contact employers, research companies, and complete career counseling through the Krannert Graduate Career Services office. The office receives mixed reviews. Some praise career services staff as attentive and "very committed to the students." Others demur, complaining that "The school should do a better job at alumni networking and improve its career services." This problem is particularly acute, we're told, when it comes to career services for international students, no small issue at a school with a 43 percent international student enrollment.

Recent employers of Krannert MBAs include: Bank of America, Citibank, Cummins, Discover Financial, General Electric, Guidant, IBM, Intel, Pratt & Whitney, Procter & Gamble, Raytheon, Samsung, United Technologies, and Wyeth. Manufacturers claimed 19 percent of Krannert's MBAs from 2007 to 2009; in that same period, 18 percent found work in consumer products, 16 percent in pharma/biotech, and 15 percent in each of technology and financial services.

Student Life and Environment

Krannert "had the best building of any school I visited," one student notes, referring to the "well-equipped facilities in the recently completed Rawls Hall," which "is consistently rated the best building on campus (inaugurated in 2003). It is in the best location on campus, next to the student union building, and the main hill where all the shops and stores are, and only literally ten steps from the most popular bar in town." The building is a nexus of activity, hosting "classes, student club activities, social gatherings, coffee [houses], call outs, company presentations, guest speakers, team assignments, study groups, etc."

The school "really tries to make a community for all of its students," through campus "organizations that help new students, international students, and families become accustomed to life in West Lafayette. They host many cultural events to show the diversity of its student body and educate everyone [on the different] cultural background[s]." Campus life offers "a huge number of activities that one can take part in or lead. Be it clubs, the entrepreneurship center (Burton D. Morgan), international trips, club trips, case competitions, taskforces, GCSMI (Supply Chain Initiative), social activities, etc." Hometown West Lafayette has "plenty of restaurants to choose from and cost of living is very affordable." Purdue athletics is another big attraction, of course.

The student body includes "a truly international population that provides for diversity in culture, thoughts, and work styles." "It has truly been a melting pot experience," one student writes. Students are also diverse in age: "There are a number of students who are married with some of them having kids," while "at the same time, there are quite a few students that graduated from undergrad within a year of starting the MBA program."

Admissions

To apply to the Krannert School of Management, all candidates must submit an official undergraduate transcript, GMAT scores, a resume, letters of recommendation, and several admissions essays. The most recent entering class had a mean GPA of about 3.3 on a 4.0 scale, and an average GMAT score in the 640s. Women comprised 34 percent of the entering class. Approximately one-third of the entering class arrived with undergraduate degrees in business; almost as many majored in engineering at the undergraduate level.

FINANCIAL FACTS

Annual tuition (in-state/ out-of-state)	$19,209/$36,445
Fees	$455
Cost of books	$3,460
Room & board	$8,710
% of first-year students receiving aid	100
Average award package	$20,320
Average grant	$7,007
Average student loan debt	$46,756

ADMISSIONS

Admissions Selectivity Rating	94
# of applications received	807
% applicants accepted	37
% acceptees attending	39
Average GMAT	643
Range of GMAT	560–690
Average GPA	3.32
TOEFL required of international students	Yes
Minimum TOEFL (paper/computer)	550/213
Application fee	$55
International application fee	$55
Regular application deadline	1/10
Regular notification	2/20
Application Deadline/Notification	
Round 1:	11/1 / 12/15
Round 2:	1/10 / 2/20
Round 3:	2/1 / 3/20
Round 4:	3/1 / 4/1
Early decision program?	No
Deferment available	Yes
Maximum length of deferment	1 year
Transfer students accepted	No
Non-fall admissions	No
Need-blind admissions	Yes

EMPLOYMENT PROFILE

Career Rating	91	Grads Employed by Function	%	Avg. Salary
Percent employed at graduation	65	Marketing	14	$92,170
Percent employed 3 months after graduation	76	Operations	23	$81,641
		Consulting	8	$89,833
Average base starting salary	$85,194	Management	8	$84,250
Primary Source of Full-time Job Acceptances		Finance	34	$86,668
School-facilitated activities	43 (52%)	HR	8	$75,467
Graduate-facilitated activities	40 (48%)	Top 5 Employers Hiring Grads		

Top 5 Employers Hiring Grads
The Procter & Gamble Co. (4), U.S. Airways (4), Amazon.com (3), Bank of America (3), Eli Lilly (3)

QUEEN'S UNIVERSITY
QUEEN'S SCHOOL OF BUSINESS

GENERAL INFORMATION

Type of school	Public
Academic calendar	12 month

SURVEY SAYS...

Cutting-edge classes
Smart classrooms
Solid preparation in:
Teamwork
Communication/interpersonal skills
Quantitative skills
Entrepreneurial studies

STUDENTS

Enrollment of MBA Program	111
% male/female	68/32
% international	45
Average age at entry	29
Average years work experience at entry	5

ACADEMICS

Academic Experience Rating	76
Profs interesting rating	96
Profs accessible rating	67

Joint Degrees

Cornell-Queen's Executive MBA
(dual degree), 18 months evenings
& weekends while working.

Academics

Queen's University quickly burst onto many prospective MBAs' radars in 2004, when *BusinessWeek* magazine named it the number one international MBA program. The school was no secret to Canadian and international employers, though; in fact, their high regard for Queen's MBAs contributed substantially to the lofty biennial BW ranking which was awarded again in 2006 and 2008.

Queen's full-time MBA uses a team-based approach to learning that mirrors today's progressive workplace. Participants work one-on-one with Personal Development Coaches throughout the program. This innovative approach to personal development enables participants to identify, enhance, and fully leverage their personal strengths.

Queen's offers a great return on investment, thanks to a 12-month calendar that allows students "to return to the work force faster." Like most one-year MBAs, the Queen's MBA "is very intense and the course load is pretty heavy." A "very strong team-based learning" approach permeates all classes. All students here are assigned to a single team for the duration of the program, and "a significant portion of a student's overall marks is derived from group work." The idea is to model the team atmosphere in which students will work throughout their careers.

With 110 students each year, Queen's runs a program that "allows the administration and students to get to know each other very well." The result is a happy student body: MBAs tell us that the "amazing administration couldn't be more helpful. It is amazingly receptive to any requests." Likewise, professors are regarded as "warm-hearted, committed, responsible, open-minded, and talented." Most of all, students appreciate the school's "excellent reputation, which is on the upswing across the world."

Career and Placement

Career and placement services to MBA students at Queen's School of Business are provided by personal career managers, who offer "one-on-one coaching to help you explore your career options and chart your career path." Career managers assist students with practice interviews, resume counseling, and self-assessment instruments. Numerous online job postings are available through the Business Career Centre, which also coordinates student-alumni contacts.

Typically, about 35 percent of Queen's MBAs find their first post-degree jobs in finance. High tech and telecommunications positions account for 25 percent and management consulting 20 percent. Placement statistics show that 93 percent of the graduating class had positions six months out.

ADMISSIONS CONTACT: 613-533-2302, PROGRAM MANAGER
ADDRESS: GOODES HALL, QUEEN'S UNIVERSITY, SUITE 414 KINGSTON, ON K7L 3N6 CANADA
PHONE: 613-533-2302 • FAX: 613-533-6281
E-MAIL: QUEENSMBA@BUSINESS.QUEENSU.CA • WEBSITE: WWW.QUEENSMBA.COM

Student Life and Environment

Queen's one-year curriculum means "a hectic academic schedule" that leaves little free time. As one student notes, "Despite efforts to balance our lifestyles as students, our lives are school. Since the program is only one year long, our friends and families are very accepting of this fact." Life here generally consists of "classes followed by preparation assignments, exams, projects, and presentations."

There are opportunities to blow off steam, however "the school organizes numerous social events such as a cruise and hockey games," for example. Most popular of all is the "Point Four" club, a "tradition that has the whole class going out for drinks every Thursday night. This tradition is continued in numerous cities in Canada after graduation." The origin of the club's name, incidentally, is the notion that "going out one day a week will only reduce your grade by 0.4 percent."

MBAs in this high-caliber program are "very bright and intelligent" and the community "friendly and close-knit," qualities that are assets to the team-oriented approach to learning. The international nature of the student body means that "people can talk about issues in North America as easily as issues in Africa or Asia."

Admissions

Minimum requirements for admission to the Queen's MBA program include: a four-year undergraduate degree from a recognized university and two years work experience. Most admitted students have an undergraduate grade point average (GPA) of at least 3.3 and a GMAT score of at least 600. Students whose first language is not English must submit a score for the TOEFL, IELTS, or MELAB. A cover letter and resume, three letters of reference, and three short-answer essays—all of which can be completed online—are also required. If you are neither a Canadian citizen nor a permanent resident of Canada you must apply for a Study Permit from the Canadian government in order to enter Canada to enroll in this program. Depending on your country of citizenship you may also be required to have a Temporary Resident Visa to enter Canada. You should begin the application process as soon as you receive your offer of admission from Queen's.

FINANCIAL FACTS

Annual tuition (in-state/ out-of-state)	$59,730/$64,520
Room & board	$25,809

ADMISSIONS

Admissions Selectivity Rating	60*
Average GMAT	675
Range of GMAT	580–780
TOEFL required of international students	Yes
Minimum TOEFL (paper/computer)	600/250
Application Deadline/Notification	
Round 1:	11/28 / NR
Round 2:	2/2 / NR
Round 3:	3/13 / NR
Early decision program?	No
Deferment available	Yes
Maximum length of deferment	1 year
Transfer students accepted	No
Non-fall admissions	Yes
Need-blind admissions	Yes

EMPLOYMENT PROFILE

Career Rating	85	Grads Employed by Function	%	Avg. Salary
Average base starting salary	$80,000	Consulting	20	$94,500
		Finance	35	$78,000
		MIS	25	$74,500

QUINNIPIAC UNIVERSITY
SCHOOL OF BUSINESS

GENERAL INFORMATION
Type of school   Private

SURVEY SAYS...
Cutting-edge classes
Solid preparation in:
Teamwork

STUDENTS
Enrollment of parent institution	7,758
Enrollment of MBA Program	208
% male/female	64/36
% out-of-state	35
% part-time	58
% minorities	10
% international	7
Average age at entry	27
Average years work experience at entry	5

ACADEMICS
Academic Experience Rating	**77**
Student/faculty ratio	16:1
Profs interesting rating	86
Profs accessible rating	84
% female faculty	25
% minority faculty	30

Joint Degrees
JD/MBA, 4 years; JD/MBA in Health Care Mgt., 4 years.

Prominent Alumni
William Weldon '71, Chairman/CEO Johnson & Johnson; Murray Lender '50, Co-Founder Lender's Bagels; Bruce Dumelin '71, CFO (retired) Bank of America; Joseph Onorato '71, CFO (retired) Echlin, Inc.

Academics

Quinnipiac University is devoting considerable effort to developing its MBA program—students brag about its "exceptional resources," professors who "go above and beyond their duties," and "a new director of the business school who has worked very hard to make QU more competitive and to bring new employers to recruit"—and students respond with enthusiastic praise. The program is made up of area professionals studying on a part-time basis, and full-time undergraduates pursuing a BA/MBA or a BS/MBA. Quinnipiac offers a conventional MBA as well as tracks in Healthcare Management and Supply Chain Management, and a track leading to CFA (Chartered Financial Analyst) certification.

The QU MBA program benefits from "high-tech equipment for presentations, a Financial Technology Center for real-time trading, HD video monitors that constantly keep us up-to-date on current news," and "classroom facilities are one of the best I've seen; they played a large part in my selection of the school." Students tell us that professors "are also a strong resource; they like to question students and speak with them about their particular field." Proximity to New York City drives the school's focus toward finance, and indeed QU has "great resources for the financial industry" and "has been great at providing work opportunities for all of the students in many diverse fields in the business world."

The program's design encourages frequent collaborative work; as one MBA explains, "You constantly have a group project that ends with a presentation. This prepares you for presentation in the real world, as well as building your skills to work with others." The Quinnipiac MBA program offers full- and part-time students flexibility in delivery methods. Part-time working professionals can take classes in the evenings or take advantage of online classes offered in accelerated seven week terms. The full-time program offers classes in the afternoons and evenings, which are available to five-year students, international full-time students and other full-time MBA students.

Career and Placement

Quinnipiac MBAs tell us that the university "has decentralized its career services" so that "each college has its own career service team. For the School of Business, the career service team actively works on developing employer relationships while assisting students on campus in their job/internship search. Students have access to powerful job databases and search engines." Observes one student, the School of Business "has an extremely devoted team that works diligently to host network receptions, maintain a career website, assist with resumes, and regularly communicate with students." Many of Quinnipiac's part-time students are concurrently employed by such prominent area concerns as SBC-SNET, Anthem Blue Cross/Blue Shield, Yale New Haven Hospital, the Hospital of St. Raphael, Bayer, and United Technologies.

ADMISSIONS CONTACT: KRISTIN PARENT, ASSISTANT DIRECTOR OF GRADUATE ADMISSIONS
ADDRESS: 275 MOUNT CARMEL AVE, AB-GRD HAMDEN, CT 06518-1940
PHONE: 203-582-8672 • FAX: 203-582-3443
E-MAIL: GRADUATE@QUINNIPIAC.EDU • WEBSITE: WWW.QUINNIPIAC.EDU

Student Life and Environment

Quinnipiac "has a beautiful campus located right outside of Sleeping Giant State Park" that "is safe and offers a great environment for learning and social life." As one student explains, "When you step foot on QU grounds, you just want to grab a book and start studying. The beauty of the school is like being in a movie where all you do is study and hang out with friends in a really nice college." Though in the past students have noted, "parking is always a problem," and "the common library is beautiful, but there is not enough space for students, especially during midterms and finals," the new graduate campus in North Haven has helped provide additional classroom and study space. While parking in Hamden remains crowded in the evenings, North Haven's campus is where most evening classes are offered and parking is readily available. Also, the study spaces on the Hamden campus are being greatly expanded in 2011.

Graduate life here "is heavily focused around academics and education," although opportunities for extracurricular engagement are available. The director of the program "aims to get everyone connected and does so through a variety of ways. He hosts meet and greets and other programs throughout the semester for everyone to get involved in. All the students are connected and stay so through a variety of ways, like going out for dinners, meeting for classes etc." In addition, the Associate Dean of Graduate Programs and MBA Director work with students to provide international experiences and career enhancements, including internships. There are "a limited number of graduate clubs," but most here feel that "the graduate population is not very interested in participating in additional activities or socials."

QU MBAs are "bright, creative, and energetic," with lots of "late 20-somethings" in this "good mix of people with families, working professionals, joint undergraduate students, full-time students, and middle-aged people." Most are "extremely friendly and helpful, and many would be good contacts to have for the future."

Admissions

Quinnipiac processes MBA applications on a rolling basis. A complete application includes official transcripts for all post-secondary academic work, a current résumé, an official GMAT score report, two letters of recommendation, and a completed application form. The school's website states that desired candidates have achieved at least a 3.0 undergraduate GPA and earned at least a 500 on the GMAT; it also notes that full-time professional work experience is preferred. International applicants must provide an official statement of sufficient financial support and, if their native language is not English, TOEFL scores. Many Quinnipiac MBAs enter through the five-year program, which is open to Quinnipiac undergraduates only.

FINANCIAL FACTS

Annual tuition	$16,030
Fees	$630
Cost of books	$3,100
Room & board (off-campus)	$14,220
% of students receiving aid	77
% of first-year students receiving aid	79
% of students receiving loans	59
% of students receiving grants	59
Average award package	$22,339
Average grant	$5,734
Average student loan debt	$25,990

ADMISSIONS

Admissions Selectivity Rating	**74**
# of applications received	138
% applicants accepted	74
% acceptees attending	80
Average GMAT	540
Range of GMAT	500–690
Average GPA	3.2
TOEFL required of international students	Yes
Minimum TOEFL (paper/computer)	575/233
Application fee	$45
International application fee	$45
Early decision program?	No
Deferment available	Yes
Maximum length of deferment	1 year
Transfer students accepted	Yes
Transfer application policy: 9 graduate transfer credits allowed from regionally accredited schools.	
Non-fall admissions	Yes
Need-blind admissions	Yes

RADFORD UNIVERSITY
COLLEGE OF BUSINESS AND ECONOMICS

GENERAL INFORMATION
Type of school   Public

SURVEY SAYS...
Friendly students
Good peer network
Solid preparation in:
General management

STUDENTS
Enrollment of parent institution	8,878
Enrollment of MBA Program	82
% male/female	56/44
% out-of-state	5
% part-time	60
% minorities	15
% international	7
Average age at entry	29
Average years work experience at entry	6

ACADEMICS
Academic Experience Rating	**72**
Student/faculty ratio	2:1
Profs interesting rating	83
Profs accessible rating	81
% female faculty	20
% minority faculty	22

Academics

Repeat business is one of the telltale signs of success in retail, and by that standard Radford University must be doing a pretty good job; a considerable number of students in our survey self-identified as former Radford undergrads, and nearly all cited their satisfaction during their first go-around as the reason for pursuing an MBA here. With an undergraduate population consisting of approximately 25 percent business majors, Radford has a large customer base from which to draw graduate students. You could say that business is booming at Radford's College of Business and Economics.

Radford now offers two MBA programs: a full-time program on the Radford campus and the Professional Part-time program on the Roanoke and Radford campuses. Radford MBAs tell us that their program "is general in nature" and that "students wanting to specialize in a specific segment of business, e.g., marketing, may be well-served to look elsewhere." They are quick to add, however, that the program "does prepare you for work in many areas of business and does not skimp on content or focus in doing so" and that "Those who want the knowledge and skills to run an organization, even a global one, will be hard-pressed to find a better school, especially for the price." Part-time students also appreciate the way the program is "geared toward people who work full-time jobs." While describing the Radford MBA as "a challenging part-time program," they note that convenient scheduling and professors who will "work with your work schedule to [help you] get through the MBA program" make it "easy for a working professional to get an MBA" here.

Radford's 24 credit hour curriculum is divided in a two-thirds, one-third spilt between required courses and electives (which constitute 12 hours). The program utilizes "a face-to-face presentation format" and includes a substantial writing component. "Small class sizes" and a faculty that "is very student-oriented (rather than concentrating on writing professional papers and books, they concentrate on teaching, which is a good thing)" makes this a very student-friendly program. Professors "do an excellent job of tying in current events and international matters of interest," although some "don't seem to have much experience in the professional corporate world. Many seem to have spent most of their time in academia." MBA courses are offered in two locations: the main campus in Radford, Virginia, and the Roanoke Higher Education Center in Roanoke, Virginia. A distance learning option is also available. The RU MBA Program is moving towards differentiating its full-time and professional part-time programs. Full-time students have classes during the day and professional part-time classes will be held in the evenings in both Roanoke and Radford. Additional program support services will be provided for each of these groups.

Career and Placement

The Career Services Office at Radford University offers a variety of resources to undergraduates, graduates, and alumni. These include a virtual resume, internship, and a jobs database "where students and employers come together to post and view resumes and position openings," as well as workshops in resume and portfolio development, career fairs, and career-assessment tools. On-campus recruiters include Ameriprise Financial, DMG Securities, Ferguson Enterprises, Northwestern Mutual, State Farm, Wachovia, and the federal government.

ADMISSIONS CONTACT: MS. ELIZABETH C. S. JAMISON, DIRECTOR, MBA PROGRAM
ADDRESS: MBA OFFFICE, P.O. BOX 6956 RADFORD, VA 24142
PHONE: 540-831-6905 • FAX: 540-831-6655
E-MAIL: RUMBA@RADFORD.EDU. • WEBSITE: HTTP://RUMBA.ASP.RADFORD.EDU

Student Life and Environment

The RU MBA program is "a mix of adult and young adult students." The latter group includes nearly all of the full-time students, a combination of recently minted American undergraduates and international students. The student body tends to be "young, eager to get into a professional setting, worried about the job market," "friendly, hard-working, and intelligent." Working professionals constitute a substantial minority whose experience and insights are welcomed by their younger peers.

Full-timers describe campus life as being "like any typical college student's life," with the "majority of time spent studying and preparing for class." Part-time students typically don't have time for the "many activities, clubs, and organizations that are at this school." Those who attend classes at the Roanoke Higher Education Center tell us that "the RHEC is a newly remodeled, high tech, and comfortable facility more suited to providing an appropriate atmosphere for educating older MBA students."

Hometown Radford is a small town in the Blue Ridge Mountains; Roanoke is about 45 miles away. The area is most amenable to outdoor enthusiasts, as it provides easy access to the Appalachian Trail, the New River, and Claytor Lake. Shopping, restaurants, nightlife, and such are not in great supply, students warn, although the proximity of Roanoke helps to make up for this deficiency. Charleston, West Virginia, and Greensboro, North Carolina, are also within a reasonable driving distance.

Admissions

Admission to Radford's MBA program is considered via a full portfolio review. Application requires successful completion of an undergraduate degree with a preferred minimum GPA of 2.75. Applicants must also submit an official report of GMAT scores (applicants with five or more years of work experience can apply for a waiver of the GMAT requirement); two letters of recommendation; a resume of work experience; and statement of intent. Also, applicants must demonstrate business proficiency through accredited collegiate preparation in the following foundation areas or equivalents: economics, accounting, finance, and statistics. Students can earn credit for some of these foundation areas through CLEP testing. In addition to meeting the above requirements, international students must also provide a certified letter of sponsorship and a bank statement proving sufficient finances to cover their first year of study. Those whose first language is not English must submit TOEFL scores.

FINANCIAL FACTS

Annual tuition (in-state/ out-of-state)	$5,688/$11,340
Cost of books	$1,100
Room & board	$6,872

ADMISSIONS

Admissions Selectivity Rating	67
# of applications received	65
% applicants accepted	69
% acceptees attending	45
Average GMAT	432
Range of GMAT	360–700
Average GPA	3.19
TOEFL required of international students	Yes
Minimum TOEFL (paper/computer)	550/78
Application fee	$50
International application fee	$50
Early decision program?	No
Deferment available	Yes
Maximum length of deferment	1 year
Transfer students accepted	Yes
Transfer application policy: Maximum of 12 credit hours	
Non-fall admissions	Yes
Need-blind admissions	Yes

RENSSELAER POLYTECHNIC INSTITUTE
LALLY SCHOOL OF MANAGEMENT AND TECHNOLOGY

GENERAL INFORMATION
Type of school	Private
Academic calendar	Semester

SURVEY SAYS...
Cutting-edge classes
Smart classrooms
Solid preparation in:
Operations
Quantitative skills
Doing business in a global economy
Entrepreneurial studies

STUDENTS
Enrollment of parent institution	7,521
Enrollment of MBA Program	79
% male/female	72/28
% part-time	23
% minorities	7
% international	40
Average age at entry	28
Average years work experience at entry	3

ACADEMICS
Academic Experience Rating	**81**
Student/faculty ratio	15:1
Profs interesting rating	86
Profs accessible rating	85
% female faculty	21
% minority faculty	5

Joint Degrees
MBA/JD, 4–5 years

Prominent Alumni
George M. Low '48, NASA administrator who headed the Apollo program; James Q. Crowe '72, Founder and Builder of telecom industry compaines; Denis Tito '64, Founder of Wilshire Associates; Ray Tomlinson '63, Inventor of email in 1971; Marcian E. "Ted" Hoff, Inventor of microprocessor.

Academics

Rensselaer Polytechnic Institute's Lally School of Management and Technology offers numerous graduate business programs with a strong focus on technology and close ties to the Northeast business community. For hard-working students, Lally's MBA is fast-paced and efficient: taking a full course load, required credit hours can be completed in a mere 12 months. Those who want to tailor their degree or make a career change can pursue a specialization module in addition to core courses, but they'll still have a diploma within 17 to 24 months. (Currently, the school offers optional specializations in technological entrepreneurship, finance, information systems, operations management, marketing, new product development, and global enterprise management.) Specially designed for the younger set, the school's unique Pathfinder program "offers entrance to an MBA program to recent undergraduates with little or no work experience." Through Pathfinder, students are allowed "to jump straight into an MBA" after college, then "gain a full year of work experience between the first and second year of the MBA degree." For local professionals, Lally also offers an accelerated executive program. In addition, the school operates numerous master's programs in related business fields, such as a MS in financial engineering and risk management. These specialized programs "raise the level of the MBA program by exposing MBA students to other advanced disciplines and specializations so that MBA students, upon graduation, are already familiar with working with field specialists such as financial engineers."

While the delivery format differs, MBA programs at Lally comprise 51 credit hours of coursework. The core curriculum takes a cross-disciplinary approach to business, and courses are taught by teams of professors from different disciplines. As students point out, Rensselaer is a "world-class research institution," and the MBA program draws on the school's historic strength in technology and applied science. Here, students benefit from a "very good mix of technology management classes with traditional finance, marketing, and operations management classes." Business issues in fields like information technology or nanotechnology are often discussed in the classroom, and "many of the MBA students are working on commercializing technologies." A student elaborates, "The greatest strength of RPI is the interdisciplinary nature of all of the degree programs. For the Lally School specifically, its strength is the integration of technology into the classroom, preparing students to work in the high-tech 21st century workplace."

"The faculty is fantastic" at Rensselaer, and "small class sizes help [students] take advantage of their experience and research." While "Professors and classes get an A-plus," students say Rensselaer's "administration gets a C-plus." Overseen by "a multi-layer bureaucracy," there can be plenty of red tape at the business school. Fortunately, the personnel are approachable and friendly. Despite hassles, "The administrators understand the issues that students have and are very patient and understanding, and go above and beyond to help students."

Career and Placement

Lally's Career Resource Center manages a comprehensive online job board, where students and alumni can view current job openings, post their resumes for employers to review, and set up on-campus interviews. The Career Resource Center also oversees employer information sessions, MBA career panels, and company site tours. Despite these services, some students feel that, "career services could use an overhaul," saying, "alumni and career placement is severely lacking." On the flip side, Lally has a strong reputation in the local region, and at least one student found that the "alumni [were] extremely helpful during my career search!"

ADMISSIONS CONTACT: DR. JEFFREY F. DURGEE, ASSOCIATE DEAN FOR ACADEMIC AFFAIRS
ADDRESS: 110 EIGHTH STREET- PITTSBURGH BUILDING 3216 TROY, NY 12180-3590
PHONE: 518-276-6565 • FAX: 518-276-2665
E-MAIL: LALLYMBA@RPI.EDU • WEBSITE: LALLYSCHOOL.RPI.EDU

FINANCIAL FACTS

Annual tuition	$38,100
Fees	$1,938
Cost of books	$1,850
Room & board	
(on/off-campus)	$10,400/$10,000

ADMISSIONS

Admissions Selectivity Rating	86
# of applications received	84
% applicants accepted	79
% acceptees attending	68
Average GMAT	628
Average GPA	3.2
TOEFL required of	
international students	Yes
Minimum TOEFL	
(paper/computer)	600/250
Application fee	$75
International application fee	$75
Regular application deadline	7/1
Early decision program?	Yes
ED Deadline/Notification	NR / 2/15
Deferment available	Yes
Maximum length	
of deferment	1 year
Transfer students accepted	No
Non-fall admissions	No
Need-blind admissions	Yes

Companies that have recently recruited at Lally include Accenture, American Express, Albany Molecular Research Corporation, Blue Slate Solutions, Citigroup, Clorox, ECG Consulting Group, Foster Miller, Honeywell, IBM, Microsoft, Mimeo.com, Phillips, Proctor & Gamble, United Technologies, and Xerox. More than 40 percent of graduates stay in the Northeast region.

Student Life and Environment

The full-time MBA program at Lally comprises "roughly 15 hours per week in class," plus "another 10-15 hours per week doing homework, projects, and readings." Stimulated by the team-oriented curriculum, "Study groups emerge between students, and project teams learn to work with each other and spend time together outside of the classroom." Beyond academics, students also might get together for mingling and career development opportunities. In particular, "The graduate management student association does a great job organizing social and networking events."

With an excellent early career MBA program, the students at Rensselaer are "a relatively young group." In fact, many join the MBA directly from RPI's undergraduate college. For those students, it is easy to participate in the multitude of activities on the larger Rensselaer campus. For example, a current MBA candidate tells us, "I am involved in multiple performing arts groups, including Sheer Idiocy, the improvisational comedy troupe; WRPI, the college radio station; and The Players, the traditional theater organization. I am also the Student Outreach Coordinator for the Admissions Office." Not everyone, however, gets so involved in campus life. At Lally, "Some students are detached from the program, but others are very engaged and make the experience very good."

Admissions

To apply to Lally's graduate business programs, students must submit a completed application form, two personal essays, standardized scores, undergraduate transcripts, two letters of recommendation, and, if applicable, TOEFL scores. Candidates are also required to schedule an interview with the admissions department. The school accepts both the GMAT and the GRE. A recent incoming class had a mean GMAT score of 628 and an average undergraduate GPA of 3.2, and more than 70 percent majored in a technical field as an undergraduate.

EMPLOYMENT PROFILE

Career Rating	88	Grads Employed by Function% Avg. Salary	
Percent employed at graduation	90	Operations	10 $85,000
Percent employed 3 months		Consulting	10 $85,000
after graduation	100	Management	40 $86,500
Average base starting salary	$86,143	**Top 5 Employers Hiring Grads**	
Primary Source of Full-time Job Acceptances		American Express (1), AT&T (1), Deloitte (1),	
School-facilitated activities	2 (20%)	EMC (1), Samsung (1)	
Graduate-facilitated activities	7 (70%)		
Unknown	1 (10%)		

RICE UNIVERSITY
JESSE H. JONES GRADUATE SCHOOL OF BUSINESS

GENERAL INFORMATION

Type of school	Private
Academic calendar	Semester

SURVEY SAYS...
Good peer network
Solid preparation in:
Finance
Accounting
Presentation skills
Quantitative skills

STUDENTS

Enrollment of parent institution	5,556
Enrollment of MBA Program	605
% male/female	65/35
% out-of-state	17
% part-time	59
% minorities	12
% international	35
Average age at entry	28
Average years work experience at entry	4

ACADEMICS

Academic Experience Rating	**91**
Student/faculty ratio	9:1
Profs interesting rating	88
Profs accessible rating	94
% female faculty	22
% minority faculty	16

Joint Degrees
MBA/MD (with Baylor College of Medicine; MBA/Master of Bioengineering; MBA/Master of Chemical Engineering; MBA/Master of Civil Engineering; MBA/Master of Computational and Applied Mathematics; MBA/Master of Computer Science; MBA/Master of Electrical Engineering; MBA/Master of Environmental Engineering; MBA/Master of Materials Science; MBA/Master of Mechanical Engineering; MBA/Master of Statistics.

Academics

Prestigious, rigorous, and well-rounded, Rice University's MBA program combines a challenging core curriculum with "cutting edge" elective coursework and practical projects. You'll hit the ground running at Rice, where the comprehensive core provides a "balance of qualitative and quantitative" material, designed to "expose you to a little bit of everything." Well-planned and executed, "the coordination between classes is incredible; the same day you review a new concept in one class you link it and review it in another one." After completing the core, students can tailor their education through academic concentrations and fieldwork. Of particular note, Rice has a "strong focus on [the] energy industry," and "close ties to energy firms in Houston." In addition, the school's finance program is "known throughout the south."

At Rice, the workload is demanding, especially in the first semester. You can expect to spend some quality time in the library; students warn us that "no one can even come close to coasting" through their classes. In particular, the program "moves very fast for someone with no business undergraduate degree." While challenges are manifold, "The faculty is dynamic, and very willing to help students fully grasp class concepts." In fact, on the whole, "Professors are warm, approachable, and foster an atmosphere for learning." With an excellent faculty to student ratio, "Every professor knows every student by name," professors integrate "teamwork into each class." A current student concurs, "I chose Rice because I wanted a smaller program where I would be able to get face time with my professors and establish a strong network with my classmates." In fact, many students describe the school community as a "big family."

Rice augments traditional classroom instruction with hands-on learning experiences, including the required Action Learning Project in the first year. A student details, "The Action Learning Project is a unique consulting experience that allows us to work with a local company on a project they select. It is a welcome addition to classroom learning, and they often implement our recommendations into their business." Students can further hone their business education through one of three functional concentrations in accounting, finance, or marketing, or one of five cross-functional industry concentrations in energy, entrepreneurship, global business, management consulting, or mastering creativity and innovation.

If Rice students have one consistent gripe, it is that the school's national rankings do not accurately convey the caliber of the MBA program. However, they also say the school distinguishes itself through a continuous commitment to improvement. In order to solicit student feedback, the administrators "run surveys and focus groups regularly, ask for feedback and apply suggestions from students." Overall, faculty, students, and staff are "truly one team working together to constantly improve ourselves and our program."

Career and Placement

Rice helps students prepare for a career through a range of curricular and extracurricular career development programs. The Career Management Center offers personal counseling, mock interviews, expert speakers, and industry panels. In addition, the Action Learning Project at the end of the first year helps students explore industries and, potentially, secure a job or internship. Strategically located, Rice is "the strongest school in Texas and the Southwest, therefore you have unparalleled access to the energy companies in Houston, the entrepreneurial companies in Austin, and all the other opportunities in this region." In recent years, more than 80 percent of Rice graduates have taken jobs in the Southwest.

While the business school is small, Rice has a "strong and supportive alumni network," and "there are a lot of companies in this area that recruit" on campus. Thirty percent of graduates took jobs in the Petroleum/energy industry; however, students take jobs in a range of fields and, in recent years, Rice students were recruited and interviewed by such diverse organizations as Amazon.com, Baylor College of Medicine, Citigroup, Deloitte & Touche, ExxonMobil, Lehman Brothers, Northwest Airlines, Toyota, and the Houston Zoo.

Student Life and Environment

Drawing students from a range of industries and backgrounds, Rice excels at "fostering class unity while maintaining class diversity." To bring students together, the school offers "dinner and beer on our school patio ("the partio") every Thursday evening, which is a great way to connect with other students." At these weekly events, "recruiters and alumni speak with students in an informal fashion," while students mingle with their classmates.

With a highly demanding curriculum, Rice students definitely keep busy; "Monday through Thursday is around-the-clock academics, networking, company presentations, student activities, and job search." Fortunately, students enjoy the comfort and amenities of the business school building, which offers, "parking underground, wireless everywhere, nice library, [and] plenty of study rooms."

Students warn us that there is a "tremendous amount of academic pressure and students do tend to worry a bit too much about grades." However, most are able to maintain a "solid balance between social and academic." If you can make the time, there are plenty of "academic lectures, competitions, social activities, or intramural games" to take your mind off classes. Of the many student clubs, "The National Association of Women MBAs chapter is particularly strong and holds many activities for the women at the school."

Admissions

To apply for admission to Rice University, applicants must submit official transcripts of all college-level work, GMAT scores, two letters of recommendation, a current resume, and three personal essays. When evaluating applicants, Rice looks for both qualitative and quantitative skills; however, a strong academic track record is paramount in an admissions decision. There are no minimum GMAT or GPA scores required for admission. The mid-50% GMAT range is 640 to 710, though a high score does not guarantee admission, just as a low score does not prohibit it.

Prominent Alumni

James S. Turley, Chairman and CEO, Ernst & Young LLP; Keith Anderson, CIO, Soros Fund Management.

FINANCIAL FACTS

Annual tuition	$40,000
Fees	$2,553
Cost of books	$1,500
Room & board (on/off-campus)	$12,000/$15,500
% of students receiving aid	94
% of first-year students receiving aid	95
% of students receiving loans	49
% of students receiving grants	84
Average award package	$34,697
Average grant	$20,243
Average student loan debt	$70,496

ADMISSIONS

Admissions Selectivity Rating	94
# of applications received	627
% applicants accepted	34
% acceptees attending	55
Average GMAT	668
Range of GMAT	640–710
Average GPA	3.27
TOEFL required of international students	Yes
Minimum TOEFL (paper/computer)	600/250
Application fee	$125
International application fee	$125

Application Deadline/Notification

Round 1:	11/9 / 12/18
Round 2:	1/11 / 2/19
Round 3:	2/22 / 4/2
Round 4:	4/5 / 5/14
Early decision program?	No
Deferment available	Yes
Maximum length of deferment	Varies depending on student's situation.
Transfer students accepted	No
Non-fall admissions	No
Need-blind admissions	Yes

EMPLOYMENT PROFILE

Career Rating	94	**Grads Employed by Function**	**% Avg. Salary**
Percent employed at graduation	55	Marketing	12 $88,875
Percent employed 3 months after graduation	83	Operations	7 $67,500
		Consulting	13 $98,650
Average base starting salary	$89,068	Management	8 $104,900
Primary Source of Full-time Job Acceptances		Finance	54 $86,340
School-facilitated activities	60 (71%)	**Top 5 Employers Hiring Grads**	
Graduate-facilitated activities	24 (29%)	ExxonMobil (5), Kalypso (4), Entessa (3), Conoco Phillips (2), Hewlett Packard (2)	

ROCHESTER INSTITUTE OF TECHNOLOGY
E. PHILIP SAUNDERS COLLEGE OF BUSINESS

GENERAL INFORMATION

Type of school	Private
Academic calendar	Quarter

SURVEY SAYS...
Cutting-edge classes
Solid preparation in:
General management
Teamwork
Communication/interpersonal skills
Doing business in a global economy

STUDENTS

Enrollment of parent institution	16,773
Enrollment of MBA Program	349
% male/female	66/34
% out-of-state	30
% part-time	40
% minorities	8
% international	30
Average age at entry	28
Average years work experience at entry	4

ACADEMICS

Academic Experience Rating	**76**
Profs interesting rating	84
Profs accessible rating	78
% female faculty	19
% minority faculty	5

Academics

Located in upstate New York, Rochester Institute of Technology is known for its academic excellence in technology and applied science. Accordingly, RIT's MBA programs provide a "great blend of management and technical education," preparing students for the realities of the workplace through practical instruction, teamwork, and applied learning. Within the MBA curriculum, "Courses are updated frequently to allow for new events, technologies, and information." (In recent years, "green sustainability is growing in importance," as is entrepreneurship.) A major benefit of the program is the "the wide array of concentrations offered," including such unique offerings as digital marketing, quality and applied statistics, and environmentally sustainable management—as well as more traditional business fields like accounting and supply chain management. In addition to established concentrations, students can tailor their education through elective courses in other RIT departments, like public policy or web programming.

The MBA can be completed on a full-time or part-time basis, with classes offered in the daytime and the evening, as well as online. Course work is "fast-paced" and challenging, yet students like the school's academic calendar, saying the "quarter system is great because it keeps things moving at a fast pace." Despite the "vigorous schedule," "Professors are extremely flexible if students need to miss class for work." On that note, most RIT instructors "know students' names and take interest in the students' personal lives." With an average class size of just 25 students, "Professors go out of their way to be sure concepts are well understood and topics are relevant and beneficial to us." Even in the classroom, RIT emphasizes practical skills, and most professors "have significant corporate experience and tie it well with the academics to offer an enriched experience." In fact, many RIT instructors "still work as consultants for major companies."

Students who received an undergraduate business degree from RIT can "waive some classes" in the MBA program, or, if they are currently enrolled, complete a BS and MBA through on accelerated five-year schedule. Taking advantage of this attractive opportunity, many "students seem to come directly from undergrad," though "Each class tends to have at least some students who have been in the workplace." Furthermore, RIT undergraduates "are required to have a good deal of co-op (internship) experience before they graduate (usually between six months to one year or more.)" For those who want to build on their real-world credentials, RIT offers plenty of "hands-on, experiential, practical learning" experiences. Here, students can participate in optional internships or co-op work experiences, business plan and case competitions, and team-based projects both on and off campus. Among other offerings, the school's "Innovation Center is a new-business incubator, and they are always asking for the business students to come and consult for them."

Career and Placement

Serving the undergraduate and graduate community, RIT's Cooperative Education and Career Services offers robust career preparation services, including an executive-in-residence program, mentorship program, online job resources, career fairs, and networking events. While the campus maintains a robust recruiting program, "the greatest weakness is the lack of opportunities for business majors at the career fairs." Based on the school's strength in engineering, technology, and science, "Most of the companies at the career fair are looking to hire tech students with very few hiring management students." As such, "The campus is still trying to get more interest from the business community to send companies here for new talent."

ADMISSIONS CONTACT: DIANE ELLISON, ASST. VICE PRESIDENT, GRADUATE AND PART-TIME ENROLLMENT SERVICES • ADDRESS: 105 LOMB MEMORIAL DRIVE ROCHESTER, NY 14623
PHONE: 585-475-7284 • FAX: 585-475-5476
E-MAIL: GRADINFO@RIT.EDU • WEBSITE: WWW.RITMBA.COM

In recent years, full-time MBA candidates reported a median starting salary of more than $52,000, with a range between $30,000 and $90,000. They took jobs at Alstom Signaling, Bausch & Lomb, Carrier Corporation, Citibank, Coopers & Lybrand, Deloitte & Touche, Eastman Kodak, Global Crossing, Harris Corporation, IBM, JP Morgan Chase, Johnson & Johnson, M&T Bank, Merck & Company Inc., Paychex, Toyota, Unisys Corp., Wegmans, and Xerox.

Student Life and Environment

Part of a large, private, comprehensive university, Saunders College of Business offers a well-rounded student experience, which appeals to both part-time and full-time students. Here, "the facilities are good and campus activities are diversified," and there are plenty of "great resources available"—including an "outstanding" gym. As you'd expect from a technical school, business students enjoy contemporary technology in the classroom and "have access to amazing equipment" to prepare their "group presentations." In fact, "The whole campus has Wi-Fi, and you can even find plugs near picnic tables and other outdoor locations for your laptop!"

On this large campus, students "come from about 20 different countries," creating a "very diverse and global environment." All totaled, you'll probably meet "more part-time, employed MBA students" than full-time students at RIT, though there are also plenty of recent graduates who are completing the MBA full-time. While they enthusiastically participate in class, "It is hard for graduate students to be more involved due to the late night classes and other obligations." Still, even these students acknowledge that "There are lots of opportunities on campus for fun and Rochester is a great place to live." Among full-timers, "The students are friendly and very focused when it comes to school, but don't shy away from playing the occasional poker game now and then."

Admissions

To be considered for admission to RIT's graduate business programs, students must have a minimum undergraduate GPA of 3.0 and a GMAT score of 520 or higher. In addition to a student's academic record and test scores, RIT evaluates a student based on his or her letters of recommendation, resume, and personal statement. While many full-time students join the program directly after undergraduate work, most part-time students have three to five years of professional experience before starting the program.

FINANCIAL FACTS

Annual tuition	$33,234
Fees	$219
Cost of books	$1,500
Room & board (on-campus)	$10,044
% of students receiving aid	24
% of first-year students receiving aid	32
% of students receiving grants	24
Average grant	$10,644

ADMISSIONS

Admissions Selectivity Rating	75
# of applications received	861
% applicants accepted	44
% acceptees attending	48
Average GMAT	585
Range of GMAT	540–650
Average GPA	3.3
TOEFL required of international students	Yes
Minimum TOEFL (paper/computer)	580/237
Application fee	$50
International application fee	$50
Regular application deadline	8/1
Early decision program?	No
Deferment available	Yes
Maximum length of deferment	1 year
Transfer students accepted	Yes
Transfer application policy: Transfer up to 3 courses if relevant to program. Grade of B or better.	
Non-fall admissions	Yes
Need-blind admissions	Yes

ROLLINS COLLEGE
CRUMMER GRADUATE SCHOOL OF BUSINESS

GENERAL INFORMATION

Type of school	Private
Academic calendar	Semester

SURVEY SAYS...

Students love Winter Park, FL
Solid preparation in:
Communication/interpersonal skills
Presentation skills

STUDENTS

Enrollment of parent institution	3,478
Enrollment of MBA Program	547
% male/female	62/38
% out-of-state	34
% part-time	63
% minorities	8
% international	18
Average age at entry	26
Average years work experience at entry	3

ACADEMICS

Academic Experience Rating	**89**
Student/faculty ratio	20:1
Profs interesting rating	88
Profs accessible rating	91
% female faculty	13
% minority faculty	13

Prominent Alumni

Al Weiss, President; Thomas Jones, Senior Vice President Operations; Steve Grune, Publisher; Charles Rice, President; F. Duane Ackerman, President & CEO.

Academics

"Set in a picturesque landscape," Rollins not only enjoys "a fantastic reputation" as the number one business school in the state of Florida, but it also "offers its students exceptional international business opportunities and experiences, in addition to a world-class faculty." With a "high level of post-graduate job placement and [a] great reputation," students say "The education and networking opportunities [at Rollins] cannot be matched for a young, ambitious future business leader."

One of Rollins greatest strengths is its diversity. The business school offers four separate programs—Early Advantage, Professional, Saturday, and Key Executive—catering to the needs of everyone from eager students fresh out of their undergraduate experiences, to working professionals looking to pursue an advanced degree in their field. Many of the younger students laud the "specially-designed" Early Advantage (EMBA) program, which "caters to those who have not had work experience prior to entering business school. It provides them opportunities to build up their experience through study trips, consultation projects, and internships." Says one, it's "a great fit for someone on the younger side. It's almost like an extension of undergrad. All the kids are about your age."

In addition to its EAMBA program, the school offers three part-time programs: the Professional MBA, open to anyone currently employed full-time; the Saturday MBA, designed for mid-to-senior-level professionals (minimum five years work experience required); and the Key Executive MBA. As one Saturday MBA students attests, " I wanted a 'traditional' classroom and learning experience but with the flexibility to meet my full-time work needs. I'm going to classes all day every Saturday and will graduate in only 19 months!"

Students are drawn to Rollins for its "prestige, quality of education, smaller class size, [and] experience of faculty." Many say the "small classroom settings create an intimate learning environment that promotes participation from all students, as well as interaction from each professor." The faculty at Rollins is "top notch." Professors "all hold the highest degree in their respective fields and all were successful in the world of business prior to entering the teaching ranks."

Overall, the academic experience is "top-flight as long as you are willing to sit through some classes in the first term that will feel remedial to some business majors." Course work is "very challenging, but manageable," and the school's administration and faculty "does everything possible to prepare students for their future. Whether it is providing mentors, leadership coaching, or career development, students are given the personal attention and support they need to be successful."

Career and Placement

Rollins boasts an "active and engaged alumni base," and connections to "some of the biggest companies in the country (Disney, Lockheed, Darden)" that all add up to a "high level of post-graduate job placement." In 2009, more than 88 percent of full-time MBA students seeking employment secured positions within three months of graduation with a mean base salary of $60,000.

Top employers of Crummer MBAs include: The Walt Disney Company, Radiant, CNL Group, FedEx, Harris Corporation, Johnson & Johnson, Marriot International, Darden restaurant Group, AT&T, Siemens Westing House, CIA, Dynetech, Citigroup, Universal Studios, General Mills,. Tupperware, and SunTrust Bank. Though 86 percent of students who procured employment within three months of graduation landed jobs in the South,

ADMISSIONS CONTACT: JACQUELINE BRITO, ASSISTANT DEAN
ADDRESS: 1000 HOLT AVE. - 2722 WINTER PARK, FL 32789-4499
PHONE: 407-646-2405 • FAX: 407-646-2522
E-MAIL: MBAADMISSIONS@ROLLINS.EDU • WEBSITE: WWW.ROLLINS.EDU/CRUMMER

students say Rollins enjoys a strong alumni network and a cache of prestige both regionally and nationally.

Student Life and Environment

Students at Rollins aren't shy about singing the praises of their gorgeous environment: "Campus is beautiful and Rollins' reputation lives up to its name." The campus boasts "a large amount of resources available for all students. Graduate students have full access to plays, music performances, athletic facilities, volunteer opportunities, etc." Facilities are nothing to shake a stick at either. Students "attend class in one centralized building where there are plenty of study rooms….Each study room is equipped with a flat-screen TV to hook up to a computer that assists groups in facilitating discussion."

Overall students describe themselves as "ambitious, energetic, supportive, and intellectual." Most are "well-informed in respect to current events and openly share their views and opinions, which adds to the in-class conversations." The atmosphere at school "isn't too competitive; instead, everyone is open to helping out others if they need it." Given the program's focus on early learning and continuing education, across the board students are "active learners" who are "very professional and driven towards having a balance in their personal life and work." With only "forty people in the class" students "become very close within the first semester. We socialize a lot and meet every Wednesday after class. We also do outside classroom activities [on] the weekends." Because of the program's nature, "Students come from diverse backgrounds. It's not unusual to be paired in a group with an engineer, an accountant, a marketing professional, an entrepreneur, and a liberal arts major. The diversity creates valuable classroom discussions and inspires students to see things from many different points of view."

Life in hometown Winter Park "is phenomenal. There is a small-town atmosphere, but you never forget that you are surrounded by some of the biggest business names in the state." Winter Park "is close enough to Orlando for all of the excitement but far enough away to avoid the traffic and population density."

Admissions

Applicants to Crummer's EMBA program must provide the school with the following: official transcripts for all undergraduate, graduate, and professional schoolwork; an official GMAT score report; statement of purpose; two confidential evaluations; and a resume. Interviews are conducted at the school's invitation. Applicants to the executive MBA program must meet all of the above requirements in addition to a required interview and proof of support from their employer. PMBA and SMBA applicants must interview as part of the application process as well.

FINANCIAL FACTS

Annual tuition	$31,200
Fees	$200
Cost of books	$2,400
Room & board (off-campus)	$15,000
% of students receiving aid	54
% of first-year students receiving aid	53
% of students receiving grants	54
Average award package	$32,274
Average grant	$32,274
Average student loan debt	$26,263

ADMISSIONS

Admissions Selectivity Rating	86
# of applications received	236
% applicants accepted	51
% acceptees attending	62
Average GMAT	598
Range of GMAT	510–693
Average GPA	3.4
TOEFL required of international students	Yes
Application fee	$50
International application fee	$50
Early decision program?	No
Deferment available	Yes
Maximum length of deferment	1 year
Transfer students accepted	Yes
Transfer application policy: The school accepts up to 6 credits transferred from an MBA program that is accredited by the AACSB.	
Non-fall admissions	Yes
Need-blind admissions	Yes

EMPLOYMENT PROFILE

Career Rating	84	Grads Employed by Function	%	Avg. Salary
Average base starting salary	$60,000	Marketing	25	$50,000
Primary Source of Full-time Job Acceptances		Operations	2	$60,000
School-facilitated activities	NR (68%)	Consulting	7	NR
Graduate-facilitated activities	NR (32%)	Management	5	$300,000
		Finance	52	$53,800
		MIS	5	NR

ROTTERDAM SCHOOL OF MANAGEMENT
ERASMUS UNIVERSITY

GENERAL INFORMATION
Type of school   Public

SURVEY SAYS...
Friendly students
Good social scene
Good peer network
Solid preparation in:
Accounting
Teamwork
Doing business in a global economy

ACADEMICS
Academic Experience Rating	**73**
Profs interesting rating	74
Profs accessible rating	77

Academics

Future international business moguls choose Rotterdam School of Mangement, Erasmus for two simple reasons: The school provides "the most international MBA" experience in the world, and Rotterdam is in the heart of the EEC, with "easy access" to Germany and the "EU labor market." RSM provides a "very challenging, positive learning environment," but its intensive 12-month MBA program is not for the faint of heart. The "workload is heavy," and the curriculum is front-loaded (students take 11 general management courses in the first two semesters). During this period, the day "starts at 9:30 A.M. with classes and ends at 7:00 P.M. with some group work or . . . [an] assignment." Overworked students take comfort in the fact that their professors are "excellent! They clearly enjoy teaching their subject matters, and because they are from all over the world, we get different perspectives in class." Students also point out that "the small class size means we have more opportunities to form close relationships with the program staff." During the third semester, students choose an advanced course from one of four areas of specialization (finance, marketing, or strategy). The final semester is an elective curriculum; about a third of students fulfill these credits in one of 30 international exchange programs. All academic work in residency at RSM is conducted in English.

With one eye trained on the executive job market and the other on skill development and business knowledge, Rotterdam is what "b-school should be"; that is, "practical and academic at the same time." The Personal Leadership Development program, a mandatory 12-month experiential course, adds additional value. One student sums it up: "In hindsight I would not have gone to any other business school. RSM offers the right balance of soft and hard skills." "The school [also] has a strong sense of social responsibility." "I am now equipped to be a stronger and more sensitive businessperson," writes one satisfied student.

Career and Placement

Students say RSM's "Career Services Department is currently understaffed. They are encouraging, but they lack manpower." For less-motivated students, this might "be an issue." Regardless, RSM Erasmus MBAs can look forward to bright and lucrative careers. While the school is responsible for connecting students with about three-quarters of internships and half of post-MBA jobs, students also find significant career opportunities within the alumni network and elsewhere. Top employers of RSM grads are ABN Amro, Barclays Capital, Campina, Coca-Cola, Eli Lilly and Company, General Electric Company, Hewlett-Packard, ING, Interbrand, Johnson & Johnson, KPN, L'Oréal, McKinsey & Company, Novartis, Orange, Philips, Reckitt Benckiser, Roland Berger, Strategy Consultants, Shell Oil Company, and Siemens Business Services.

Student Life and Environment

RSM "Students form a strong and very connected group," students say. "Everyone is automatically a member of every club. It's your responsibility to contribute as much or as little to the events. For example, though you may not be in any entrepreneurial courses, you are automatically invited to [hear] every entrepreneurial speaker on campus. And once you arrive, you are welcome in the room." The collegial atmosphere is "perfect and wonderful," says one MBA candidate. "I'd like to go back to the first semester and to start again." Even so, students are "extremely driven." "Almost half want to be entrepreneurs or have owned businesses." RSM's "inspiring and challenging" students don't shrink from competition or from giving "positive and constructive criticism."

ADMISSIONS CONTACT: MARYKE STEENKAMP, SENIOR MARKETING & ADMISSIONS MANAGER,
M STEENKAMP@RSM.NL
ADDRESS: BURGEMEESTER OUDLAAN 50, 3062 PA ROTTERDAM, NETHERLANDS
PHONE: +31104082222 • FAX: +31104529509
E-MAIL: MBA.INFO@RSM.NL • WEBSITE: WWW.RSM.NL/MBA

FINANCIAL FACTS

Annual tuition	$26,292
Cost of books	$875
Room & board (off-campus)	$9,650
% of first-year students receiving aid	27

ADMISSIONS

Admissions Selectivity Rating	60*
TOEFL required of international students	No
Early decision program?	No
Deferment available	No
Transfer students accepted	No
Non-fall admissions	Yes
Need-blind admissions	Yes

Diversity is no afterthought here—it's the reason MBA candidates choose RSM. Students say that the "international perspective was a big draw. Several other [schools] claimed to be international, but mostly had over 50 percent from one or two backgrounds." RSM, on the other hand, "has 50 nationalities and only small clusters from the same backgrounds." This means that students learn "a lot from classmates," and "There is no ruling racial group in our class." "It is just great!" enthuses one student. "A mix of cultures brings so many good things out of each student that it is almost like magic. The amount of kindness that I've experienced is just overwhelming." Demographically speaking, students are overwhelmingly European and Asian, with large Indian and Taiwanese communities; the average student is in his or her late 20s, with an undergraduate background in business or economics and more than five years of pre-MBA work experience. A quarter of MBA candidates are women. Partners and spouses "have banded together" to form "a supportive network," "and routinely have nights out on the town."

Admissions

RSM Erasmus admits more than half of all its applicants—good news to the self-selected pool of MBA candidates whose passion for international business and culture brings them to RSM. Admission is no cakewalk—successful applicants report an average GMAT score of 640 and a minimum of two years' work experience—but the numbers give good reason for optimism. The most recent application requires essays on career goals, hobbies and interests, and difficult decisions—slightly more personal topics than appear on American applications. Submit translations of your academic transcripts if they are written in languages other than English, and prepare for an interview if you make the first cut. Admission is rolling.

ROWAN UNIVERSITY
THE ROHRER COLLEGE OF BUSINESS

GENERAL INFORMATION
Type of school   Public

SURVEY SAYS...
Cutting-edge classes
Solid preparation in:
Communication/interpersonal skills
Presentation skills

STUDENTS
Enrollment of parent institution	10,271
Enrollment of MBA Program	103
% male/female	45/55
% part-time	79
% minorities	5
% international	55
Average age at entry	27

ACADEMICS
Academic Experience Rating	74
Student/faculty ratio	19:1
Profs interesting rating	62
Profs accessible rating	70
% female faculty	40
% minority faculty	32

Academics

Offering "a good location, good tuition, and good environment" in the Philadelphia area (and, thanks to the recent addition of online classes, beyond), Rowan University's Rohrer College of Business MBA program delivers what local students want. As one such student explains, "The school has a good ranking within schools in the Northeast and has a tuition rate that could not be matched by comparably ranked schools. Short of someone else paying for my education, it was the best value, period."

Part-time students love the flexible scheduling at Rowan. Classes meet for three hours once a week (typically on a weeknight, although some courses meet on Saturday mornings). Some courses are also available online, further enhancing the convenience of the program. The curriculum commences with 27 hours of required core courses covering fundamental general management skills. The curriculum also leaves room for nine hours of electives; students may choose to take a variety of courses that match their career needs or may use these courses to specialize in finance, accounting, management, marketing, or management information systems. Part-time students typically take between three to six years to complete their MBAs here. Those enrolled full-time have the option of completing the program in a single year.

Students love "the small size" of Rowan's MBA program, reporting that it increases "the accessibility of the professors." As one student tells us, "Every professor I have had you could email them a question about the course, and get a solid answer within a day usually." Administrators earn similarly high marks. One student notes, "I have had nothing but a pleasant experience at Rowan, even when I had a family emergency. The faculty and staff were very understanding and accommodating and allowed me to work around the days I needed to provide care for a relative."

Career and Placement

Rowan maintains a Career and Academic Planning Center "to provide developmental advising" to all students in their pursuit of academic and professional goals. The CAPC serves the entire school; there is no office dedicated specifically to MBAs or to business students on the undergraduate and graduate levels. CAPC Services include one-on-one counseling, workshops, online self-assessment and job databases (like Experience), career publications, and employer directories. Services are available to alumni as well as to current students. It should be noted that most current students are full-time workers looking to advance within their current places of work; relatively few students seeking MBAs at Rowan are actively searching for new jobs. Those in the job market tell us that Rowan's small size "is a strength" when it comes to academics, "while at the same time it is a weakness when it comes to companies that recruit at the school."

ADMISSIONS CONTACT: DR. HORATIO SESA, FOUNDING DEAN, COLLEGE OF PROFESSIONAL AND CONTINUING EDUCATION • ADDRESS: EDUCATION HALL, 201 MULLICA HILL ROAD GLASSBORO, NJ 08028 • PHONE: 856-256-4050 • FAX: 856-256-4436
E-MAIL: GRADOFFICE@ROWAN.EDU • WEBSITE: WWW.ROWAN.EDU/COLLEGES/GRADUATE

Student Life and Environment

Rowan's MBA program "is meant for both part-time and full-time students," with the majority attending part time, usually while also managing full-time jobs. On-campus activities "are meant for people who live on campus," which means that they are directed at undergraduates. "On-campus stuff [does not apply] to most MBAs at Rowan, since they are for the most part commuters or from the South Jersey area." Residents and non-residents alike warn that parking on or near campus can be a challenge.

Rowan's suburban New Jersey hometown of Glassboro is a mere half-hour's drive from Philadelphia; the Jersey shore is less than an hour to the east, and Atlantic City is only 50 miles away. New York, Washington, D.C., and the Chesapeake are all within easy commuting distances. All of this adds up to opportunity. To prove it, the Rowan campus is in the midst of an ambitious expansion program, with makeovers planned for most facilities and several new buildings going up. Students praise the new athletic center and enjoy watching Rowan's excellent Division III men's and women's basketball teams.

Most Rowan MBAs "are in their upper 20s to upper 30s with very diverse backgrounds and experience[s]." Rowan's considerable international population includes a large group from China. American students enjoy the international student body, whom they describe as "a pleasure to work with."

Admissions

Rowan's graduate business school students are required to complete seven foundation courses in accounting, statistics, principles of finance, principles of marketing, calculus, operations management, and economics. Students who have successfully completed equivalent courses at the undergraduate level may place out of these foundation classes. Applicants to the MBA program must submit official transcripts for all undergraduate work (with a minimum GPA of 2.5 overall), GMAT or GRE scores, two letters of recommendation, a personal statement of career objectives, and a resume. International students whose first language is not English must also provide TOEFL scores (minimum required score: 79 iBT, 550 written exam, 213 computer-based exam).

FINANCIAL FACTS

Annual tuition	$10,624
Fees	$2,258
Cost of books	$2,000
Room & board (on-campus)	$9,616
% of students receiving aid	25
% of students receiving loans	25
Average award package	$15,291

ADMISSIONS

Admissions Selectivity Rating	73
# of applications received	132
% applicants accepted	46
% acceptees attending	75
Average GMAT	509
TOEFL required of international students	Yes
Minimum TOEFL (paper/computer)	550/213
Application fee	$50
International application fee	$50
Early decision program?	No
Deferment available	Yes
Transfer students accepted	Yes
Transfer application policy: Students may transfer up to 9 credit hours.	
Non-fall admissions	Yes
Need-blind admissions	Yes

RUTGERS, THE STATE UNIVERSITY OF NEW JERSEY
RUTGERS BUSINESS SCHOOL—NEWARK AND NEW BRUNSWICK

GENERAL INFORMATION
Type of school	Public
Academic calendar	Trimester

SURVEY SAYS...
Cutting-edge classes
Solid preparation in:
Teamwork
Communication/interpersonal skills
Presentation skills

STUDENTS
Enrollment of parent institution	50,000
Enrollment of MBA Program	1,111
% male/female	62/38
% out-of-state	17
% part-time	86
% minorities	9
% international	27
Average age at entry	27
Average years work experience at entry	4

ACADEMICS
Academic Experience Rating	**84**
Student/faculty ratio	20:1
Profs interesting rating	79
Profs accessible rating	80
% female faculty	24
% minority faculty	35

Joint Degrees
BA/MBA, 5 years; BS/MBA, 5 years; MPH/MBA, 3 years; MD/MBA, 5 years; JD/MBA, 4 years; MS/MBA in Biomedical Sciences, 2.5 years; MPP/MBA, 3 years; MCRP/MBA, 3 years.

Prominent Alumni
Thomas A. Renyi (MBA '68), Chairman & CEO, The Bank of New York Mellon; Gary M. Cohen (MBA '83), President, BD Medical (Becton, Dickinson and Co.); Irwin M. Lerner, Retired Chairman of the Board, Hoffmann-La Roche; Nicholas J. Valeriani, Worldwide Chairman, Johnson & Johnson; Ralph Izzo, President & CEO, PSEG.

Academics

Just a stone's throw away from the vibrant business community in New York City, Rutgers University is a large and prestigious public school that provides a "great value" education to 1,600 graduate students. Offering a "wide variety of high-quality courses at an in-state tuition rate," Rutgers students may choose between several MBA options: a full-time MBA in Newark, New Jersey, a flexible part-time MBA and Executive MBA on multiple New Jersey campuses, and a one-year International MBA in China. With campuses across the Garden State (and two in China), "Rutgers is a large school with an overwhelming number of resources at the fingertips of students." The schools sustains "depth and variety" within the required core courses, as well as an extensive selection of advanced elective offerings. At Rutgers, MBA candidates may concentrate their studies on finance, information technology, management and global business, marketing, pharmaceutical management, and supply chain management, or they may choose a custom concentration, such as business and the arts. A current student explains, "Excellent staff and a wide variety of course offerings allow a student to challenge themselves in areas that interest them while developing broad-based business skills." Within the "multidimensional curriculum," the school prides itself on its focus on science and technology, maintaining close partnerships with many relevant businesses in the greater region, including New York City. In particular, the unique "pharmaceutical medicine concentration" draws many students to the program.

Despite the school's impressive scope, Rutgers maintains "smaller class sizes" and a friendly teaching staff. Students laud the "the real-world, relevant experience of the faculty"; in fact, most, "professors come from incredibly impressive professional backgrounds, including a portfolio manager for one of the largest funds in the world." Through the faculty, as well as through guest speakers, Rutgers "brings its corporate connections into the classroom," giving students an edge up in the business world. Fellow students are another source of business expertise, and, in the classroom, you'll rub elbows with "intellectual, well-educated, well-rounded individuals with diverse opinions. They challenge thoughts and ideas and are very receptive to critical view points of their own ideas as well." Given the school's size, you might be surprised to learn that Rutgers is well-run and managed by an "extremely friendly staff." In particular, "The Student Services, Admissions, and Office of Career Management staffs are actively involved in students' lives. They attend student organization events and meetings, and are very helpful to students organizing different initiatives." A student adds, "Dropping and adding classes was a breeze and you can even meet with the Dean of the entire program if you need to."

Career and Placement

You will receive excellent, personalized career assistance at Rutgers. "The career services department is excellent" and the accessible staff will "help you with resumes, cover letters and mock interviews. They also get feedback from companies after your interviews." A current student attests, "My relationship with the Office of Career Management (OCM) has been very rewarding as well. The administrators of OCM go to great lengths to bring top companies to recruit on campus and readily go to bat for students who seek positions at companies that would normally only recruit from ivy league schools." For a small fee, Rutgers alumni may also use the resources at the Career Services department.

ADMISSIONS CONTACT: RITA GALEN, DIRECTOR OF ADMISSIONS
ADDRESS: 1 WASHINGTON PARK SUITE 132 NEWARK, NJ 07102-1813
PHONE: 973-353-1234 • FAX: 973-353-1592
E-MAIL: ADMIT@BUSINESS.RUTGERS.EDU • WEBSITE: WWW.BUSINESS.RUTGERS.EDU

With its excellent pharmaceutical program, Rutgers maintains great "connections with pharmaceutical industry," as well as excellent "connections to New Jersey businesses" (though some students would like to see "better connection to businesses in New York.") In addition, "Rutgers Newark is home to a number of non-profit businesses including Small Business Development Center, which helps entrepreneurs prepare business plans and start their own businesses."

Student Life and Environment

A truly "diverse" community, Rutgers attracts "outstanding and friendly people from diverse social and geographical backgrounds." For students at the Newark campus, "There are many restaurant and cafeteria options within walking distance where students can gather, study, and participate in events for the community." In addition, "Public transportation is effective and easy," allowing students easily travel to school by train, or take a trip to New York City. A student agrees, "It is very nice to be able to go to school in New Jersey by train, and visit NYC at any time and with any of my peers, easily and quickly." At the same time, students complain that "The area around the campus is only moderately well-policed" and safety is a concern.

Despite the convenience of public transportation, most part-timers "live off campus and commute by car," rarely lingering on campus. A student details, "We all know each other very well, but do not spend time on campus unless we have class or meetings." While part-time students have less time for socializing, "There is plenty of social interaction among the full-time students." On campus "there are many clubs and activities," and "Many full-time students socialize every afternoon in the RBS student lounge where they eat, have group meetings, and just relax before class." A student shares, "Everyone has gotten to know one another this semester and most of us know every student's name in our class of 90 people."

Admissions

Admission to the business programs at the Newark and New Brunswick campuses is conducted at two different admissions offices, and student must apply accordingly. The full-time program is only available at the Newark campus. There are no minimum GMAT score requirements or GPA requirements (nor does the school prefer students from any particular academic background); however, at least two years of professional work experience is strongly recommended. In some cases, the admissions committee may request an interview with an MBA candidate.

FINANCIAL FACTS

Annual tuition (in-state/ out-of-state)	$20,426/$33,030
Fees	$2,082
Cost of books	$3,000
Room & board	$13,000
Average grant	$10,119
Average student loan debt	$41,000

ADMISSIONS

Admissions Selectivity Rating	89
# of applications received	250
% applicants accepted	57
% acceptees attending	61
Average GMAT	643
Range of GMAT	620–670
Average GPA	3.3
TOEFL required of international students	Yes
Minimum TOEFL (paper/computer)	600/250
Application fee	$65
International application fee	$65
Regular application deadline	5/1
Early decision program?	No
Deferment available	Yes
Maximum length of deferment	1 year
Transfer students accepted	Yes
Transfer application policy: Students may transfer a maximum of 11 applicable core credits earned at an AACSB-accredited undergraduate b-school, with a grade of B or better, taken within 5 years.	
Non-fall admissions	Yes
Need-blind admissions	Yes

EMPLOYMENT PROFILE

Career Rating	84	Grads Employed by Function	% Avg. Salary
Percent employed at graduation	68	Marketing	31 $65,378
Percent employed 3 months after graduation	18	Operations	31 $82,869
		Consulting	7 $76,000
Average base starting salary	$80,099	Management	3 $65,000
Primary Source of Full-time Job Acceptances		Finance	28 $86,158
School-facilitated activities	22 (76%)	Top 5 Employers Hiring Grads	
Graduate-facilitated activities	7 (24%)	Johnson & Johnson Companies (3), Quest Diagnostics (3), MetLife (2), Church & Dwight (2), Dow Jones (2)	

RUTGERS, THE STATE UNIVERSITY OF NEW JERSEY—CAMDEN
SCHOOL OF BUSINESS

GENERAL INFORMATION
Type of school   Public
Academic calendar   Semester

SURVEY SAYS...
Cutting-edge classes
Happy students
Solid preparation in:
Quantitative skills
Doing business in a global economy

STUDENTS
Enrollment of parent
   institution   6,000
Enrollment of MBA Program   281
% male/female   67/33
% part-time   88
% international   12
Average age at entry   26
Average years work experience
   at entry   5

ACADEMICS
Academic Experience Rating   **82**
Student/faculty ratio   9:1
Profs interesting rating   90
Profs accessible rating   83
% female faculty   26
% minority faculty   3

Joint Degrees
MBA/JD, 117 credits (4 to 7 years);
MBA/MD, 5–6 years.

Prominent Alumni
Tony D'Alessandro, Director, Global
IT, Rohm & Haas

Academics

Why attend Rutgers' MBA program? According to students, because of its "reputation," "reputation," "reputation." "The tuition is reasonable and the education is of the highest caliber for a New Jersey public university," one student explains. Add to this an MBA program that requires "only 57 total credits" for the degree, and "only three courses needed for a concentration," and the deal gets sweeter. "Convenience" is another popular factor, meaning that many students are from Camden or nearby cities and towns. "The location is perfect for where I live," one student says. "It's close to everything (Philadelphia, the New Jersey Shore, and even New York City)."

"The expectations for students are high" at Rutgers—Camden School of Business thanks to "the opportunity to learn cutting-edge, real-world applications from experienced professionals." It's these professionals who enable students here to fulfill such expectations. "The Faculty is very impressive and they bring a well of knowledge to the classroom," one student notes. Another adds, "The professors are very approachable—they understand that we are working professionals and that we all have families, jobs, and a life away from Rutgers. They are very understanding and supportive, yet still challenging." Many students with families or jobs take advantage of Rutgers' "part-time" course offerings, particularly in the "evening" and also appreciate the "great ability to accelerate [their] degrees via summer and winter sessions." Such flexibility results in "a wide variety of students from a number of different backgrounds."

The administration also gets high marks from students for "going the extra mile to make sure each student is satisfied with his or her experiences at the university." "If a problem develops, the professionals at Rutgers are eager to solve it in a timely fashion," one student notes. "You never experience the 'isolated' feeling at this school." Others praise the "great facilities," but would like to see the school "offer more classes" "online" and at its other, off-campus locations. Some would also like the "course classifications" process to run more smoothly. "Two of my arguably finance-based Special Topics courses (Raising Capital and Corporate Restructuring) were classified as Management courses, depriving me of a desired concentration in Finance," one student says. However, as one student adds, "It may not be the most attractive school, but I believe the quality of education ranks close to if not among elite MBA programs."

Career and Placement

The Career Services office at Rutgers—Camden offers a multitude of offerings to job-seeking students, including career coaching, assessment inventories, on-campus recruiting, job fairs, web-based job postings, and resume and credentials help at their career resource center. MBA graduates can join "The Graduates Club," which the school describes as a "state-of-the-art online community that [combines the features of] a traditional off-line alumni club" that "aims to become the foremost meeting place for graduates of the world's leading programs." MBA students can also join Rutgers' Alumni Career Network, "a database of over 1,200 alumni from Camden, New Brunswick, and Newark offering career information and support to current students and alumni." Another option for MBA grads is the Rutgers—Camden alliance with Drake Beam Morin ("a provider of career management and transition services) that offers "online resources such as career consultations, resume/cover letter writing, career assessments, networking, discussion boards, and more." "Many students are well known in their industries and each student wants to get as much out of class as possible," one student says.

Student Life and Environment

Many students here agree that "the business school is like a family," since despite the "many different backgrounds and experiences, [they] all have something in common: ambition!" Students note that most of their "competitive," "motivated," and "mature" peers "are established in their discipline and are looking for the opportunity to take their career to the next level." In line with this focused approach to education, these "overworked MBA students are generally only on campus for classes," meaning that a school-based social life can be "hard to find." Despite this, while they're in class together students find each other "friendly" and "helpful." "They're just swell," one student adds. After class, those who don't head home say, "The school offers a number of different clubs and activities." For those leading a double-life as student and family person, "Rutgers—Camden does a great job of allowing students to balance work life and home life with a quality MBA education."

According to some students, Camden "isn't the nicest place to be." However, "great public transportation" and "good facilities" go a long way to offset this. However, some would like to see "transport from the subway and train station to campus" improve. Others mention that the campus itself could use some "landscaping." "[The school needs to] plant some trees and acquire more of the surrounding property to better define the campus," one student says. But despite this, the school's location is its biggest asset thanks to a short distance from Philadelphia, New York, Boston, and Washington, D.C. "There is an abundance of things to do outside of class because of the proximity to Philadelphia," a student explains.

Admissions

Applicants to the Rutgers—Camden MBA program must submit the following: an online application (available via the school's website), original undergrad and—if applicable—graduate transcripts, a personal statement, two letters of recommendation, GMAT scores (the GMAT is "waived for applicants with a PhD, JD or MD degree from and accredited U.S. institution), and a current resume (optional, but recommended). Students with an LSAT score in the 80th percentile may submit that instead of the GMAT. International applicants are required to submit a minimum TOEFL score of 213 on the computer version, 550 on the paper version, or 22 (writing), 23 (speaking), 21 (reading), and 17 (listening) on the internet version. International applicants must also submit a Financial Statement Documentation (also available via the school's website).

FINANCIAL FACTS

Annual tuition (in-state/ out-of-state)	$18,622/$28,740
Fees	$1,800
Room & board	$7,494

ADMISSIONS

Admissions Selectivity Rating	78
# of applications received	206
% applicants accepted	60
% acceptees attending	61
Average GMAT	548
Average GPA	3.2
TOEFL required of international students	Yes
Minimum TOEFL (paper/computer)	550/230
Application fee	$65
Early decision program?	No
Deferment available	Yes
Maximum length of deferment	1 semester
Transfer students accepted	Yes
Transfer application policy: Students must complete at least 36 credits in our program. We will transfer courses from AACSB-accredited schools with a grade of B or better.	
Non-fall admissions	Yes
Need-blind admissions	Yes

EMPLOYMENT PROFILE

Career Rating	84	**Top 5 Employers Hiring Grads**
Average base starting salary	$58,812	Lockheed Martin (1), Campbells Soup (3),
		Deloitte & Touche (1), JP Morgan Chase (1),
		Computer Sciences Coporation (1)

SACRED HEART UNIVERSITY
JOHN F. WELCH COLLEGE OF BUSINESS

GENERAL INFORMATION

Type of school	Private
Affiliation	Roman Catholic
Academic calendar	Trimester

SURVEY SAYS...

Cutting-edge classes
Solid preparation in:
General management
Teamwork

STUDENTS

Enrollment of parent institution	6,023
Enrollment of MBA Program	200
% male/female	56/49
% out-of-state	34
% part-time	86
% minorities	27
% international	15
Average age at entry	28
Average years work experience at entry	6

ACADEMICS

Academic Experience Rating	**75**
Profs interesting rating	83
Profs accessible rating	84
% female faculty	21
% minority faculty	29

Academics

The imprimatur of Jack Welch, former CEO of General Electric, impresses many MBAs at Sacred Heart University. "I'm a big fan of Jack Welch," one current student tells us; "the name Welch being attached to the school will hopefully bring much more recognition," another adds hopefully. The GE connection isn't lost on students either; the fact that the program "is held in high regard by GE in Connecticut," where many of these graduates will eventually seek employment, is a key factor in their decision to pursue the Welch MBA.

Sacred Heart is not merely relying on a famous name to attract and satisfy students. In 2009, the school introduced a new curriculum that begins with a fixed integrated core curriculum that "is very applicable to the real world" and culminates in concentration work in accounting, finance, or management. Students note that "the new Welch MBA format has been a monumental task to get rolling" and commend "the staff and professors[, who] go above and beyond to make sure each student is heard and prepared for the tasks at hand." They call the new curriculum "an interesting and exciting new take on the traditional MBA" with a "dynamic new format [that] is very interesting and keeps us on our toes!" The program "fully embraces the fast-paced changes of the modern world" and "trains students to be more than analytical" in order to produce "effective leaders and decision makers, ready to go."

Students commend "the breadth and depth of knowledge of the faculty" at Welch, calling their teachers an "outstanding group of professors with diverse backgrounds to teach various aspects of the business world. Their skills and knowledge in their particular subject is outstanding and…[set within] today's business world." Because "the school is not too large," students benefit from "the opportunity to get to know one another" and their teachers in the classroom. Through an international MBA in Luxembourg offering concentrations in finance and general management, Welch students have the opportunity to undertake internships in finance, marketing, international business and information technology in Luxembourg.

Career and Placement

SHU's Office of Career Development offers a range of services to MBA students. Staff members provide assistance with resume creation and critique; conduct seminars on interview skills; maintain online job postings; and organize on-campus job fairs and interview sessions. The office recently hired a full-time Assistant Director whose primary focus is on MBA student internships and job placement. During a recent academic school year, 105 employers attended the school's annual career fair and 19 employers interviewed on campus, including PricewaterhouseCoopers, General Electric, Target, Ernst & Young, Sikorsky, KPMG, and Legg Mason.

ADMISSIONS CONTACT: ALEXIS HAAKONSEN, DEAN OF GRADUATE ADMISSIONS
ADDRESS: 5151 PARK AVENUE FAIRFIELD, CT 06825
PHONE: 203-365-7619 • FAX: 203-365-4732
E-MAIL: WELCHMBA@SACREDHEART.EDU • WEBSITE: WWW.SACREDHEART.EDU

Student Life and Environment

"Most students are commuters who hold jobs during the day" at Welch, although "The students who come directly from undergraduate work appear to do a lot together." MBAs agree that in its current manifestation, the school's extracurricular life "is mainly geared towards the full-time undergraduates (concerts, clubs, student activities, sports). The graduate schools tend to just focus on classes and not student life." However, they also note that "The business school is just starting to survey its students about how we want help: network with alumni and other community leaders [versus] speakers, etc." That bodes well for the future. For now, though, "If you are not already a part of the university via undergrad work or currently working at the school, there is a major gap between the university and its graduate students."

The student body is a mix of seasoned professionals and freshly minted BAs, although with the introduction of the new curriculum there seems to be "fewer and fewer adults with work experience in the program" (although students add that "that may change as the new program is rolled out"). The older students "are personable and knowledgeable without being 'know-it-alls.'" All students in the program enjoy a "strong sense of collegiality and collaboration."

Admissions

Applicants to the MBA program at SHU's Welch College of Business must submit the following materials: a completed online application; official transcripts from all undergraduate institutions attended (showing a minimum 3.0 cumulative GPA); a personal statement of career and academic goals and a summary of relevant business experience; two letters of recommendation; a current professional resume; and an official GMAT score report (applicants with at least two years professional work experience must score a minimum of 400; for all others, the minimum score is 500). International applicants, including applicants to the MBA program in Luxembourg, must submit transcripts in English; foreign language transcripts must be translated and analyzed by an approved professional service. Applicants whose first language is not English (except those with a degree from an English-language institution) must submit an official score report for the TOEFL or IELTS. Students should anticipate at least a three month wait in the issuance of student visas for the Luxembourg program. The Luxembourg program runs approximately nine six-week sessions per year; students may apply for admission and begin the program during any session. The Fairfield campus operates on a trimester calendar.

FINANCIAL FACTS

Annual tuition	$18,765
Fees	$360
Cost of books	$3,000
Room & board (off-campus)	$10,000

ADMISSIONS

Admissions Selectivity Rating	68
# of applications received	52
% applicants accepted	71
% acceptees attending	70
Average GMAT	438
Range of GMAT	400–500
Average GPA	3.35
TOEFL required of international students	Yes
Minimum TOEFL (paper/computer)	550/213
Application fee	$50
International application fee	$100
Early decision program?	No
Deferment available	Yes
Maximum length of deferment	1 year
Transfer students accepted	Yes
Transfer application policy: Transferred credits are reviewed by the Program Director.	
Non-fall admissions	Yes
Need-blind admissions	Yes

SAGINAW VALLEY STATE UNIVERSITY
COLLEGE OF BUSINESS AND MANAGEMENT

GENERAL INFORMATION

Type of school	Public
Academic calendar	Year-round

SURVEY SAYS...
Cutting-edge classes
Solid preparation in:
General management
Doing business in a global economy
Entrepreneurial studies

STUDENTS

Enrollment of parent institution	10,498
Enrollment of MBA Program	154
% male/female	68/32
% part-time	51
% minorities	1
% international	84
Average age at entry	28
Average years work experience at entry	2

ACADEMICS

Academic Experience Rating	**71**
Student/faculty ratio	10:1
Profs interesting rating	82
Profs accessible rating	68
% female faculty	13
% minority faculty	13

Academics

Saginaw Valley State University combines the personal attention and small class sizes you'd expect to get at a private college with the attractive tuition price you can only find at a public school. The result is a "great value" education that prepares students for upper-level business positions in a friendly, teamwork-oriented environment. Saginaw offers both a full-time and part-time MBA. You'll benefit from small classes and "more focus on students in terms of teacher-student relationships." In addition, cooperation is highly encouraged among the student body, as the school "integrates team work and leadership as a requirement in each class." In fact, there is a "group element in 95 percent of all the courses offered. This group element makes interacting with your classmates a necessity and allows you to get an extremely well-rounded view of the world encompassing all issues, not just business." Fortunately, "everybody is extremely friendly and works well with each other," and "the students come from diverse backgrounds and cultures," which makes group projects particularly rewarding.

In the mission statement, the Saginaw Valley College of Business and Management pledges to provide a "relevant, interactive, and quality business education" to its students. To that end, students say Saginaw Valley truly delivers. Bringing real-world relevance to the academic setting, "the professors at Saginaw Valley come from various backgrounds throughout the world and incorporate their research into the classroom." Teaching quality varies between "some very good professors and a few that could be replaced." However, the overall academic experience is excellent. A current student confirms, "I've been very happy with each professor that I have had. They all have practical experience in the field in which they are instructing." In addition, Saginaw students really appreciate the unique "ability to work on research with professors," which adds depth and personal relationships to the MBA coursework.

No matter what your personal needs or professional goals, "The administration and professors are great at custom-building the program around the student's needs." In fact, all core coursework is taught through a hybrid/online and in-person work, in order to accommodate students' varying schedules. A student says, "The education I have received to this point has been tremendously helpful in my work life and my personal life." When it comes to the inevitable round of paperwork, the "administration is very helpful and accessible. Applying and communication with the school [was] easy and smooth." A student adds, "After graduating from a large university for my undergraduate education, I was pleasantly surprised when I arrived at Saginaw Valley State University. The administrative staff has been approachable and unspeakably accommodating." The good news doesn't stop there. Students also dole out praises for "Saginaw Valley's world-class facilities. The school is widely integrated with high-tech multimedia applications to aid classroom learning." In addition, "the library is very impressive for the school's size."

Career and Placement

SVSU's Career Planning and Placement Office hosts on-campus interviews, offers resume and cover letter critiques, and organizes a range of career fairs for Saginaw students and graduates. The larger university also hosts a number of career fairs and recruiting events, which have recently drawn employers such as Abraham and Gaffney, PC; Chase; Hantz Group Financial Services; Prudential; and Wells Fargo.

In addition to these services, business students would like to see more job placement assistance for MBA graduates, including "more job fairs and developing closer ties to big corporations. These would help students better plan their careers pre-graduation." However, Saginaw students believe strongly in the value of their education, reminding us that "the program is quickly evolving and growing. Employers are starting to recognize the high value that a Saginaw Valley State University education has."

Student Life and Environment

The newest campus in Michigan's fifteen state colleges, Saginaw Valley State is located on more than 750 acres in the tri-city area. The school's large undergraduate and graduate community hosts a large range of clubs and activities, though the majority of MBA candidates say they don't have much time for extracurricular activities. In the part-time program, students are "usually working outside the home and working on their MBA at the same time." The double life doesn't leave much room for socializing, and most students come to campus for class and not much more. However, if you'd like to go out on the town, students point out that, "SVSU is central located in the middle of three vastly different cities each with its own night-life scene."

In this vibrant and academic community, "countless cultural, social, economic, and occupational segments are represented" within the business school. The school also attracts a large international population, which adds a distinctive range of opinions and cultures to the campus. A current student attests, "My fellow students could best be described as widely diverse. My undergraduate education at Michigan State University's College of Engineering had a very diverse atmosphere, but this environment is even more culturally varied."

Admissions

Saginaw Valley admits students based on an admissions index number, calculated using each applicant's GPA and GMAT scores. Therefore, a lower GMAT score can potentially be counter-balanced by a higher GPA, and vice versa. GMAT scores, however, must be above 450 to be considered for admission. In addition to official transcripts and test scores, applicants must also submit a statement of purpose, two professional letters of reference, and a current resume.

FINANCIAL FACTS

Annual tuition (in-state/ out-of-state)	$6,678/$12,571
Cost of books	$2,000
Room & board	$7,143
% of students receiving aid	38
% of students receiving loans	16
% of students receiving grants	9
Average award package	$7,787
Average grant	$2,817
Average student loan debt	$15,576

ADMISSIONS

Admissions Selectivity Rating	71
# of applications received	125
% applicants accepted	85
% acceptees attending	42
Average GMAT	575
Range of GMAT	524–620
Average GPA	3.08
TOEFL required of international students	Yes
Minimum TOEFL (paper/computer)	550/213
Application fee	$25
International application fee	$75
Early decision program?	No
Deferment available	Yes
Maximum length of deferment	7 semesters
Transfer students accepted	Yes
Transfer application policy: May transfer 6 credits	
Non-fall admissions	Yes
Need-blind admissions	Yes

EMPLOYMENT PROFILE

Career Rating	85
Average base starting salary	$75,000

SAINT JOSEPH'S UNIVERSITY
ERIVAN K. HAUB SCHOOL OF BUSINESS

GENERAL INFORMATION

Type of school	Private
Affiliation	Roman Catholic-Jesuit
Academic calendar	Semester

SURVEY SAYS...

Solid preparation in:
General management
Teamwork
Communication/interpersonal skills
Presentation skills

ACADEMICS

Academic Experience Rating	**70**
Student/faculty ratio	10:1
Profs interesting rating	84
Profs accessible rating	81

Joint Degrees

DO/MBA Program with Philadelphia College of Osteopathic Medicine (2 years for MBA component).

Academics

The "Jesuit mission and identity" of the Haub School of Business at St. Josephs University results in an "'educate the whole person approach" that appeals to many Philadelphia-area MBAs (particularly those who attended St. Joseph's as undergraduates). "The Jesuit background of the school…promotes a desire to make a difference and to care about others while furthering your career," one student explains. Others note the "focus on value and ethics…and environmental sustainability" and the "integration of worldly concepts and viewing the business field from a multidimensional point of view" as particularly Jesuitical aspects of a Haub MBA. A typical student sums up, "I strongly agree with Jesuit education principles of inclusion and diversity and think values such as these are important foundations for anyone working in a global business market."

SJU's predominantly part-time student body say that the Haub MBA is "a well-regarded program" in the Philadelphia area that "provides an ideal combination of academic quality, location, and price." Part-timers are especially enamored of the "flexibility to pick and choose your classes to better suit your schedule," the evening and Saturdays course scheduling, and the availability of the entire program at two locations, one on the school's primary campus on City Avenue in Philadelphia, the other at Ursinus College in Collegeville, PA. In addition, St. Josephs provides online course offerings.

The SJU MBA "offers a great mix of academic teachings and real-life experiences," according to students. Professors "have a lot of experience in the private industry" and "are able to apply their private industry experience to their teachings." "They are great at applying theory to practical, everyday situations and throughout the world" and are "genuinely interested and passionate about their field of study, and it shows through their teaching," MBAs here report. Teamwork is paramount in the program; it "seems like every class has a group project that incorporates your current job. It's a nice blend of theory and practical applications." Students point out that "working in teams to get projects completed is a helpful tool in learning to deal with other students and their work ethics."

Career and Placement

The Career Development Center at Saint Joseph's serves all undergraduates, graduate students, and alumni. In the past, students have told us that the office is "typical of parochial Philadelphia colleges like La Salle and Temple," with a recruiting base largely from the Philadelphia area. While some wish for a broader range of recruiters, others "think SJU caters to its students' wants, and most want to stay in the Philly area. That's why they came to school here in the first place. If you are unsure about what you want to do after [the] MBA, Career Services has a great assessment system, where they meet and counsel you on where you would be a good fit." Saint Joseph's MBAs also benefit from "tremendous alumni networking."

Admissions Contact: Janine N. Guerra, Esq., MBA, Assistant Director of Professional MBA
Address: 5600 City Avenue, Mandeville 284, Philadelphia, PA 19131
Phone: 1-888-SJU-MBA-1 • Fax: 610-660-1599
Email: sjumba@sju.edu • website: www.sju.edu/mba

Student Life and Environment

"Saint Joseph's University truly is your home away from home," students tell us, extolling the "tight-knit community of individuals seeking the same level of intellect and values" here. For those with the time to spend on campus, "there are many activities and clubs in which to participate." "There are constant opportunities for extracurricular activities, internships, meetings, etc.," as well as "opportunities for joining the gym," students report. Very little of this activity is directed specifically toward MBAs, however. While their "life is busy with assignments and presentations," they are not so busy with extracurriculars. Students say the school could "provide [more] programming for MBA students such as clubs to provide greater interaction and experiences for more students."

Haub MBAs are "hardworking, caring, and interested in making a difference in the world, not just making money." They are typically "interested in social and political issues facing the community." Their ranks include "a lot...of recent college grads who went to graduate school because of the economy and job market." Although most work in addition to attending school, "everyone is willing to work together on projects. It is hard finding a meeting time, but everyone is flexible in making it work. Other students are interested in helping you succeed in the MBA program."

Admissions

Applicants to the Haub MBA program must submit the following materials to the school: an official transcript from each undergraduate and graduate institution at which credits were earned; an official GMAT score report (not more than seven years old), GRE is also accepted; two letters of recommendation; a current resume; and a personal statement of 250 to 500 words outlining career objectives and the value of an MBA in reaching those objectives. International applicants must submit all of the following as well as a statement of financial support. International applicants who attended undergraduate institutions at which English was not the language of instruction may have their transcripts translated and interpreted by World Education Service. Students whose first language is not English must submit an official TOEFL score report. IELTS is also accepted. Saint Joseph's admits MBA students for fall, spring, and summer terms

FINANCIAL FACTS
Annual tuition	$14,688
Cost of books	$800

ADMISSIONS
Admissions Selectivity Rating	60*
# of applications received	300
Average GMAT	540
Range of GMAT	490–710
Average GPA	3.16
TOEFL required of international students	Yes
Minimum TOEFL (paper/computer)	550/213
Application fee	$35
International application fee	$35
Early decision program?	No
Deferment available	Yes
Maximum length of deferment	1 year
Transfer students accepted	Yes
Transfer application policy: They must provide a completed application including original test scores. A total of 6 credits may be transferred into the Core Course requirement provided that they receive a C or better and the school is AACSB accredited.	
Non-fall admissions	Yes
Need-blind admissions	Yes

SAINT LOUIS UNIVERSITY
JOHN COOK SCHOOL OF BUSINESS

GENERAL INFORMATION

Type of school	Private
Affiliation	Jesuit
Academic calendar	Semester

SURVEY SAYS...

Good peer network
Cutting-edge classes
Solid preparation in:
Doing business in a global economy

STUDENTS

Enrollment of parent institution	13,313
Enrollment of MBA Program	388
% male/female	54/46
% out-of-state	50
% part-time	80
% minorities	14
% international	18
Average age at entry	28
Average years work experience at entry	4

ACADEMICS

Academic Experience Rating	**78**
Student/faculty ratio	22:1
Profs interesting rating	85
Profs accessible rating	80
% female faculty	15
% minority faculty	4

Joint Degrees

Doctor of Jurisprudence/Master of Business Administration, 3.5 years; Master of Health Administration/Master of Business Administration, 2 years; Medical Doctor/Master of Business Administration, 5 years; Master of Arts (Education)/Master of Business Adminisitration, 2 years.

Academics

"The John Cook School of Business at St. Louis University gets you the most bang for the buck," students in this Jesuit-affiliated MBA program insist. Indeed, compared to some of the higher profile MBA programs in the area, SLU is "reasonably priced," and the savings are further enhanced for those who pursue the school's recently implemented full-time one-year MBA. SLU also offers a part-time MBA to serve the needs of area professionals. Students in both programs cite the "strong ethical values" of the curriculum as another major incentive to choose SLU.

Students in the new one-year MBA praise the "innovative program that really tries to integrate the whole MBA learning process," warning that it is "intense" but ultimately worth the hard work. The administration earns praise for its responsiveness to student feedback during this early stage of the program's development. As one MBA tells it, "This administration is far and away the most flexible and willing to listen of any I've ever encountered. With the one-year program in its second year, the administration is constantly encouraging students to help make the program better by providing feedback. The administration is very clearly committed to continuous improvement." Part-time students also praise the administration, reporting that it has "created a very easy environment for part-time students to get into and get going on the MBA. They make sure to resolve any problems quickly and effectively."

In past surveys, students have complained that the SLU faculty is too academically-oriented. This is changing, though, as SLU has made "a push lately to get professors with real-world experience. As a graduate student with 5+ years of work experience, I appreciate learning from the professors with real-world experience much more than from the 'typical' college professor. The main difference lies in the specific insights the teachers with real-world experience can provide. They typically have plenty of war stories to share and a lot can be learned from listening to their past experiences." While many "need to sharpen their lecturing skills," instructors are generally "easy to work with, and much is learned in most classes."

Career and Placement

The Career Resources Center at the John Cook School of Business provides career services and counseling for all MBAs here. The center offers self-assessments, personal advising, resume and cover letter assistance, mock interviews, networking workshops and counseling, and access to multiple online and hard-copy databases and reference sources. Students tell us that the school's regional reputation and alumni network are its most effective career-enhancing assets. "SLU has a good reputation in the area, which helps in getting a job," one student tells us. About one-quarter of all SLU MBAs pursue careers in finance and accounting; about as many build careers in marketing and sales. The manufacturing sector claims about one-third of each graduating class; nonprofits attract about one-fifth of each class. Recent employers of SLU MBAs include Accenture, Anheuser Busch Companies, Inc., Covidien, Ernst & Young, Edward Jones, Emerson, JC Penney Company Inc., Kaiser Permanente, Mayo Clinic, Nestle Purina PetCare Company, Northrop Grumman Corporation, and RubinBrown.

ADMISSIONS CONTACT: NANCY BISCAN, PROGRAM COORDINATOR
ADDRESS: 3674 LINDELL BLVD. SUITE 132 ST. LOUIS, MO 63108
PHONE: 314-977-6221 • FAX: 314-977-1416
E-MAIL: GRADBIZ@SLU.EDU • WEBSITE: GRADBIZ.SLU.EDU

Student Life and Environment

Saint Louis University is, of course, located in St. Louis, "a great city" with plenty of opportunities for career professionals and entrepreneurs. Full-time students exploit the city's many assets during "business school networking events such as hockey games, baseball games, etc." Because the Jesuit tradition seeks to educate the whole person, SLU brings numerous cultural events to campus. Through the campus ministry, opportunities for service and spiritual growth are readily available. SLU competes in 16 NCAA Division I sports; the men's basketball and soccer teams both draw hefty crowds. Part-timers enjoy the same extracurricular opportunities but rarely have the time to engage in clubs, daytime guest speakers and symposia, and other such events.

The SLU campus offers "excellent facilities: library, gym, buildings, etc." Classrooms "are equipped with computer/multimedia resources" and the school is conveniently "located right in downtown St. Louis, yet it is still safe, like it's in own little world" because the "beautiful campus" is self-contained. The school's midtown location provides students easy access to the Fox Theatre, the Sheldon Concert Hall, the Grandel Square Theatre, and the Powell Symphony Hall.

SLU MBAs represent "a wide range of work experiences. Some people are in their forties and have worked for Boeing or Anheuser Busch for years. Others are just out of college. Everyone is friendly and cooperative." Some feel that most full-time students "are a little younger and less experienced in the working world" than they ought to be, and that their "lack of professional experience" limits the quality of in-class discussion.

Admissions

St. Louis University accepts both online and paper-and-pencil applications; an Adobe Acrobat file of the application can be downloaded at the school's website. All applications must include a completed application form, a personal statement (500 word maximum), two letters of recommendation (at least one professional), official transcripts for all post-secondary academic work, a current resume, and an official GMAT score report. International applicants must provide all of the above plus certification of financial support and, for non-native English speakers, an official TOEFL score report representing a score no more than two years old. The part-time program admits students prior to the fall session, the spring intersession, and the two summer sessions. Full-time applicants must enter at the start of the summer session.

Prominent Alumni

August A. Busch, IV, Former President, Anheuser-Busch, Inc; Mark Lamping, CEO of New Meadowlands Stadium Company; Robert Ciapciak, General Partner, Edward Jones; Alison Talbot, VP of Operations, Miss Elaine; Patrick J. Sly, Executive Vice President, Emerson Electric Co.

FINANCIAL FACTS

Annual tuition	$49,765
Fees	$360
Cost of books	$1,250
Room & board (off-campus)	$11,000
% of students receiving aid	90
% of first-year students receiving aid	90
% of students receiving grants	90
Average award package	
Average grant	$12,597

ADMISSIONS

Admissions Selectivity Rating	74
# of applications received	76
% applicants accepted	87
% acceptees attending	70
Average GMAT	591
Range of GMAT	550–640
Average GPA	3.2
TOEFL required of international students	Yes
Minimum TOEFL (paper/computer)	570/230
Application fee	$90
International application fee	$90
Early decision program?	No
Deferment available	Yes
Maximum length of deferment	1 year
Transfer students accepted	Yes
Transfer application policy: Part-time MBA only; 6 credit hours from another AACSB accredited school. Also, member of Jesuit MBA Consortium.	
Non-fall admissions	Yes
Need-blind admissions	Yes

EMPLOYMENT PROFILE

Career Rating	86	Grads Employed by Function	%	Avg. Salary
Percent employed at graduation	39	Marketing	30	$56,943
Percent employed 3 months after graduation	69	Operations	13	$60,000
		Consulting	26	$62,567
Average base starting salary	$57,435	Finance	13	$43,667
Primary Source of Full-time Job Acceptances		Other	17	$59,000
School-facilitated activities	8 (32%)	**Top 5 Employers Hiring Grads**		
Graduate-facilitated activities	17 (68%)	Anheuser-Busch (1), The Boeing Company (1), Emerson (1), Monsanto (1), Cintas Corp. (1)		

SAN DIEGO STATE UNIVERSITY
GRADUATE SCHOOL OF BUSINESS

GENERAL INFORMATION
Type of school   Public
Academic calendar   Semester

SURVEY SAYS...
Students love San Diego, CA
Good social scene
Happy students
Solid preparation in:
Teamwork
Doing business in a global economy

STUDENTS
Enrollment of parent
  institution   29,256
Enrollment of MBA Program   571
% male/female   55/45
% out-of-state   20
% part-time   57
% minorities   29
% international   41
Average age at entry   26
Average years work experience
  at entry   4.5

ACADEMICS
Academic Experience Rating   86
Student/faculty ratio   19:1
Profs interesting rating   83
Profs accessible rating   83
% female faculty   14
% minority faculty   3

Joint Degrees
Master of Business
Administration/Master of Arts in
Latin American Studies
(MBA/MA)3–4 years. Joint MBA/JD
4 years to complete.

Academics

"The top three things about SDSU are affordability, quality of faculty, and convenience of classes," a typical student at this "excellent value" MBA program writes, adding, "My sister is paying a ton of money to attend UCLA, but I think I'm getting a much better experience." Indeed, the MBA program at SDSU's Graduate School of Business has a lot to recommend it beyond its appealing price tag. Students here laud the school's strengths in a wide array of disciplines, including entrepreneurship, international business, and sports business management.

"Programs to assist student entrepreneurs like the Entrepreneurial Management Center (EMC)" help keep SDSU's entrepreneurship program "consistently ranked in the top." One burgeoning entrepreneur understandably brags, "Our VCIC (Venture Capital Investment Competition) team got invited to the regional competition and has gained lots of exposure to VCs and start-ups. Fifty percent of people have their own business in my classes. It is so it is awesome working with people who are passionate, know what they want, and are always improving." SDSU's Sports MBA program benefits from "access to many of higher-ups in the sports industry in the San Diego and Southern California area, be they with the Padres (with whom the program has a direct affiliation), the Chargers, the San Diego Hall of Champions, AEG, Elite Racing, or…etc., etc. These are the sorts of people you need to be meeting if you want to get a job in sports."

Across disciplines, SDSU pursues "the integration of technology, networking, and sustainable business into the curriculum," which students appreciate. In fact, about the only complaint we hear from MBAs here is that the "administration is a bit understaffed, but works very hard to provide the students with the best compilation of professors, guest lecturers and volunteer opportunities." One student writes, "Sometimes it feels a bit like this program is flying by the seat of its pants. I feel like a lot of that is because it tries do so much, like packing 100 pounds of knowledge, opportunities, and events into a 50-pound bag."

Career and Placement

In the past MBA students here have seen Career Services as a weak area, commenting that "Career Services could offers more options for graduate students. Most job fairs are for undergrads." However, students point out that graduate-level management is "still a young program, so the alumni network is growing and will continue to improve every year, which will be a big plus." One student agrees, "The alumni network is improving every year and the list of companies graduates are working with is impressive."

ADMISSIONS CONTACT: DR. DAVID ELY, DIRECTOR OF GRADUATE BUSINESS PROGRAMS
ADDRESS: 5500 CAMPANILE DRIVE SAN DIEGO, CA 92182-8228
PHONE: (619) 594-8073 • FAX: (619) 594-1863
E-MAIL: SDSUMBA@MAIL.SDSU.EDU • WEBSITE: WWW.SDSU.EDU/BUSINESS

FINANCIAL FACTS

Annual tuition (in-state/ out-of-state)	$10,923/$14,850
Cost of books	$1,650
Room & board	$11,485

ADMISSIONS

Admissions Selectivity Rating	88
# of applications received	866
% applicants accepted	48
% acceptees attending	66
Average GMAT	601
Range of GMAT	570–640
Average GPA	3.3
TOEFL required of international students	Yes
Minimum TOEFL (paper/computer)	550/213
Application fee	$55
International application fee	$55
Regular application deadline	2/1
Regular notification	5/1
Early decision program?	No
Deferment available	No
Transfer students accepted	Yes
Transfer application policy: They apply through the normal admissions process and then will TR in courses according to our discretion.	
Non-fall admissions	No
Need-blind admissions	Yes

Student Life and Environment

SDSU "kind of has a reputation as a commuter school," but the MBA program's cohort system helps counteract that. As one student explains, "The program has a very intimate feel as you go through all of the classes with the same group of students. There is a lot of group work and presentations, which forces students to work on their public speaking skills. Since you are with the same people all year, the class discussions are much more beneficial than those classes where people aren't familiar with each other." A student in the Sports MBA program observes, "Even though we live all over San Diego County, it really doesn't feel that way. The 39 of us are a pretty tight knit group who both work and play together; studying, group projects, intramural sports, going out, house parties—we do all of it."

Part-time students visit the campus primarily during the evening. One part-time reports, "We have lots of restaurants on campus and within a walk distance from campus. The library is open. Parking is very available, and there's a escorting service to follow us to our car at night if we don't want to walk alone." Part-timers and full-timers agree that "SDSU is one of the most beautiful campuses in the country" and that "the area around campus is [also] beautiful and offers a lot to graduate students."

SDSU attracts a "very active student body" that is "always hanging out on campus playing sports, listening to outdoor concerts, or going to the gym or pool because its always sunny in San Diego." "There is a great diversity among students: some working full time, some going to school full time, career paths, backgrounds, undergrad education, etc." The group includes "a lot of engineers looking to enhance their skills with MBAs" and, of course, "a lot of sports fans" in the Sports MBA program (and elsewhere). The population includes "a healthy percentage are foreign students, a small percentage of whom should probably have been screened from attending here due to their severely lacking English skills, both verbal and written."

Admissions

Nearly 1,500 potential MBAs apply to SDSU's "highly competitive" program every year. The Admissions Committee considers a number of factors, including GMAT score; GPA for undergraduate academic work (minimum 2.85 for American students, 3.0 for international students; average GPA for admitted students was 3.3); letters of recommendation; resume (work experience is preferred but not required); and personal statement. None of the final three is required, but each "can enhance an application," according to the school's website. International students whose first language is not English must also submit official TOEFL scores; a minimum paper-and-pencil test score of 550, computer-based score of 213, or an Internet-based score of 80 is required. Applications are accepted for both the fall and spring terms. They are processed on a rolling basis, so it's best to apply as early as possible.

SAN FRANCISCO STATE UNIVERSITY
COLLEGE OF BUSINESS

GENERAL INFORMATION
Type of school   Public

SURVEY SAYS...
Students love San Francisco, CA
Solid preparation in:
Accounting
General management
Doing business in a global economy

STUDENTS
Enrollment of parent institution	30,000
Enrollment of MBA Program	550
% male/female	55/45
% out-of-state	5
% part-time	55
% minorities	38
% international	33
Average age at entry	28
Average years work experience at entry	3

ACADEMICS
Academic Experience Rating	**74**
Student/faculty ratio	25:1
Profs interesting rating	76
Profs accessible rating	75
% female faculty	32
% minority faculty	35

Prominent Alumni
Mohan Gyani, Director, Safeway Inc.; Gordon Hoff, VP of International Deposit Services Bank of America; Jo Malins, VP Of International Conformance, Citibank; Brian Pretti, Senior VP of Mechanics Bank; Stephen Gillette, CIO, Starbucks.

Academics

Affordable, convenient, and exceptionally well-located, San Francisco State University is a great place to get a broad-based MBA, while adding depth and distinctiveness to the program through specialized coursework in specific business disciplines. Offering the MBA on a full-time and part-time basis, working students appreciate SF State's "flexible program," which creates "no distinction between full-time and part-time students." In addition, the curriculum's flexibility gives students the opportunity to tailor the program and "focus on topics you are interested in." To that end, San Francisco State provides lots of great academic options. For example, the school boasts a strong accounting program, as well as an "excellent and growing program in sustainable business." The school's international business department also draws its share of praises, and students find the "IBUS department faculty to be extremely engaged and willing to spend time discussing a multitude of topics outside of class."

San Francisco State recently opened a new graduate business facility in downtown San Francisco (the school's main campus is located in a residential neighborhood in the city's outskirts). Thanks to this strategic move, SF State now boasts one of the best business school locations in the Bay Area, offering students unparalleled "proximity to the financial district and the access that provides to global and entrepreneurial leaders in technology, biotech, finance, sustainable business, and more." Fortunately, "the administration in the new facility has been very helpful and efficient, and have worked hard to make the transition to the new campus as smooth as possible." In this and every way, students say the program is "run very smoothly—good communication, quick responses to questions."

Academically, the SF State experience is rewarding. Uniting academic theory and practical insights, the "professors generally have a high level of working knowledge for their areas and they do indeed bring that to their lectures. Here and there you have instructors who rely too much on PowerPoint, but this honestly doesn't happen that often." Despite the program's sizable student body, students nonetheless benefit from the "availability and accessibility" of SF State professors, who "don't disappear between classes and are for the most part engaged with the success of the students... Most really want you to succeed, are patient, and very, very approachable."

Career and Placement

An up-and-coming business program, SF State has improved placement possibilities for its students in recent years, thanks to its prime location, growing reputation, and heightened focus on career development. In fact, the school recently expanded the career services programs for MBA graduates, and now provides "a high level of service to students." The career services staff offers "optional [workshops] and provides one-on-one assistance with resumes," and also coordinates career fairs and campus networking events.

A recent Graduate Business Career Fair at SF State drew a large number of prominent companies, including Bechtel, Charles Schwab, CNET Networks, Hyatt SF Hotels, Kelly Financial Resources, Media Zone, Target Corporation, Ritz-Carlton Club, and UPS. In addition, "the accounting department has two "Meet the Firms" nights where graduating students are recruited and interviewed. Most accounting students are hired through this program." Despite these noteworthy offerings, a current student laments, "My only wish is that more *Fortune* 500 firms visit the campus to recruit, because they would be pleasantly surprised how much talent is here."

ADMISSIONS CONTACT: ARMAAN MOATTARI, ASSISTANT DIRECTOR
ADDRESS: 835 MARKET STREET, SUITE 550, SAN FRANCISCO, CA 94103
PHONE: 415-817-4300 • FAX: 415-817-4340
E-MAIL: MBA@SFSU.EDU • WEBSITE: MBA.SFSU.EDU

Student Life and Environment

Drawing a mix of students from the Bay Area, as well as "a lot of international students," SF State's student community is friendly, diverse, and cooperative. Unfortunately, the student community is somewhat fragmented, as "none of the graduate students live at the downtown campus." After hours, full-time and international students are eager to hang out with their classmates, whereas "the students who work full time don't tend to socialize much, though they are friendly in class." On top of that, "due to the flexibility of the class schedule, there isn't as much opportunity to form strong networks as students have in cohort-based schools. A lack of social events and spaces further compounds this problem." On the other hand, the school's enviable urban location means there is "lots to see, lots of international students, easy to get to and from (school is on top of a subway station)." In fact, some students feel "the student life has improved since we moved downtown since all the MBA students have classes in the same building. A group of students meet up to network and socialize every Thursday night after classes."

While they can't complain about the school's stellar new campus (there is even a Starbucks in the building), students mention that "it is very difficult for students at the downtown campus to take advantage of many of the resources offered at the Main University Campus (libraries, bookstore, student organizations, and events), leaving MBA students feeling a bit cut-off from the full student experience." Of course, most quickly note that "the proximity to the financial district and the cultural offerings of downtown SF more than make up for this."

Admissions

To apply to the graduate business programs at San Francisco State, students must have an undergraduate degree with a minimum GPA of 3.0. The current incoming class had an average undergraduate GPA of 3.3, and an average GMAT score of 585. In addition to transcripts and test scores, it is required that candidates submit a statement of purpose, letters of recommendation, and a current resume for consideration.

FINANCIAL FACTS

Annual tuition (in-state/ out-of-state)	$13,116/$22,044
Cost of books	$1,500
Room & board (on/off-campus)	$1,300/$15,000

ADMISSIONS

Admissions Selectivity Rating	88
# of applications received	900
% applicants accepted	40
% acceptees attending	65
Average GMAT	585
Range of GMAT	500–730
Average GPA	3.35
TOEFL required of international students	Yes
Minimum TOEFL (paper/computer)	590/243
Application fee	$55
International application fee	$55
Regular application deadline	4/1
Regular notification	5/1
Early decision program?	Yes
Deferment available	No
Transfer students accepted	Yes
Transfer application policy: Applicants need to apply to the program and consult with our advisor on transfer units.	
Non-fall admissions	Yes
Need-blind admissions	No

EMPLOYMENT PROFILE	
Career Rating	87
Percent employed 3 months after graduation	90
Average base starting salary	$75,000

SAN JOSE STATE UNIVERSITY
LUCAS GRADUATE SCHOOL OF BUSINESS

GENERAL INFORMATION

Type of school	Public
Academic calendar	Semester

SURVEY SAYS...

Students love San Jose, CA
Good social scene
Cutting-edge classes
Happy students
Solid preparation in:
General management
Operations
Entrepreneurial studies

STUDENTS

Enrollment of parent institution	28,400
Enrollment of MBA Program	347
% male/female	45/55
% part-time	65
% minorities	3
% international	25
Average age at entry	31
Average years work experience at entry	8

ACADEMICS

Academic Experience Rating	**74**
Student/faculty ratio	28:1
Profs interesting rating	61
Profs accessible rating	72
% female faculty	29
% minority faculty	26

Joint Degrees

MBA/MSE, 32 months.

Academics

Located smack dab in the middle of the Silicon Valley, San Jose State University's business programs benefit from the energy and innovation of their famous surroundings. "No place on earth is more entrepreneurial or technology-centric" than SJSU, where the MBA programs boast an "innovative syllabus," a "global mindset," and a top-notch faculty from the region's prominent industries. For MBA candidates, SJSU offers several program options: the traditional two-year MBA program on the main SJSU campus, the MBA One (a full-time, cohort-based program that can be completed in just a year), and the Executive-Style MBA, a "flexible program for working students," offering year-round classes on the weekends and in the evenings. With accommodating teachers and a flexible schedule, the Executive-Style MBA "is an ideal program for anyone who wants an MBA, but needs to keep working full-time while getting it." A current student attests, "When I needed to be out of town for work the week of a final, the professor was very willing to reschedule the test for me so it wouldn't interfere with my business trip."

Delivered by a team of "world-class teachers" and an "accommodating" administration, the "academic experience is positive, effective, and worthwhile" at San Jose State. Academically, the program balances "a good mix of lectures, case studies, and assignment[s]." On that note, you'll get a blend of theory and practice in the classroom, as "professors are very knowledgeable and have experience in both academics and industry." "Teachers here are experienced in Silicon Valley trends and do their best to incorporate them into class work." Coursework is interactive, and "discussions in class are lively, [and] periodically include [the] latest news and trends." Friendly as well as experienced, "Professors are very easily approachable and always try to correlate classroom learning with real-world problems as closely as possible."

"Value" is another important factor in many students' decisions to attend SJSU. A state school, SJSU has a much lower price tag than other local programs, giving prospective MBA candidates an "affordable option at a respected school," without leaving the Bay Area. Unfortunately, like many public schools, budget cuts have affected San Jose State and there has been "an increase in tuition" in response. Within the business school, the "administration is struggling with budget issues beyond [its] control," and course availability isn't always what it should be. "The courses aren't offered often enough, there is usually a wait list, so it's a lottery to see if you will even get into the classes you need." Despite limitations, "the administration has been wonderful and very responsive to all concerns," and students say the program runs efficiently.

Career and Placement

The business school at San Jose State University is propitiously located "right in the middle of Silicon Valley, with access to all [the] big-shot companies, and their executives." In addition, "the majority of students in the program come from great high-tech companies," which makes networking as easy as attending class. The Career Center at SJSU helps the undergraduate and graduate student community make connections in the local job market through recruiting events and job fairs. While most SJSU grads score great post-grad positions, some full-time students would like to see Career Services provide "better help finding jobs after graduation," through the addition of new events like "job fairs specifically designed for MBA students." Many students in the part-time program

FINANCIAL FACTS

Annual tuition (in-state/ out-of-state)	$4,274/$10,376
Cost of books	$1,386
Room & board (on/off-campus)	$9,505/$9,734
% of first-year students receiving aid	10
% of students receiving loans	1
% of students receiving grants	2
Average award package	$12,226
Average grant	$2,427

ADMISSIONS

Admissions Selectivity Rating	80
# of applications received	448
% applicants accepted	55
% acceptees attending	58
Average GMAT	562
Range of GMAT	510–600
Average GPA	3.29
TOEFL required of international students	Yes
Minimum TOEFL (paper/computer)	550/213
Application fee	$55
International application fee	$55
Regular application deadline	5/1
Regular notification	7/1
Early decision program?	No
Deferment available	No
Transfer students accepted	Yes
Transfer application policy: Applicant must meet admission requirements. Up to 20% of units can be transferred from AACSB accredited institution.	
Non-fall admissions	Yes
Need-blind admissions	Yes

receive tuition assistance from their current companies and therefore aren't looking for new jobs after graduation. Currently, you'll find recent SJSU business school graduates working at diverse companies like Charles Schwab, City Bank, Apple, Applied Materials, Chevron Corporation, Cisco Systems, Ebay, E*TRADE, HSBC Group Holdings, IBM, Lockheed Martin, Intel Corporation, Hewlett-Packard, Sprint, Nortel, Genentech, Microsoft, Pepsico, Google, Starbucks Coffee, NASA, Texas Instruments, and Xerox.

Student Life and Environment

Students in SJSU's full-time MBA programs love life on their well-equipped urban campus. The school is located right in the middle of downtown San Jose, and "Food at the Student Union is great and the campus is gorgeous." Diversity is a trademark of this large public school, and within the business program, "a lot of the students speak more than one language and have lived abroad." Despite cultural, ethnic, professional, and political diversity, "Everybody makes an effort to get along, get to know each other. The teamwork required for projects is very good as it encourages intercultural interaction."

In the Executive-Style program, "Classes are taught off campus" so many part-timers "feel very disconnected from the SJSU student body." Fortunately, the auxiliary facility is "centrally-located and well-equipped," and there is plenty of parking for commuters. While full-time cohorts are tight, socializing is more limited among part-timers, who are "very busy outside of class (since we are in an evening program, almost all of my classmates also have full-time jobs)." For most, that means a "get-in and get-out" attitude about school, and "Class work outside of class is usually handled via teleconferences or face-to-face meetings when possible."

Admissions

For those considering SJSU's graduate business programs, the school offers the unique opportunity to schedule a pre-qualification interview, which allows prospective students to discuss their eligibility for the MBA program with admissions officials. In all cases, students must have an undergraduate degree with a GPA of at least 2.5 to be considered for the program. Competitive candidates will have a GPA of 3.3 or better and GMAT scores of 550 or above.

EMPLOYMENT PROFILE

Career Rating	86	Grads Employed by Function	% Avg. Salary
Percent employed at graduation	11	Marketing	14 $65,000
Percent employed 3 months after graduation	67	Operations	14 $65,000
		Management	14 $85,000
Average base starting salary	$70,000	Finance	29 $67,500
Primary Source of Full-time Job Acceptances		Communications	14 NR
School-facilitated activities	6 (86%)		
Unknown	1 (14%)		

SANTA CLARA UNIVERSITY
LEAVEY SCHOOL OF BUSINESS

GENERAL INFORMATION
Type of school   Private
Affiliation   Roman Catholic/Jesuit
Academic calendar   Quarter

SURVEY SAYS...
Cutting-edge classes
Solid preparation in:
Finance
General management
Teamwork
Doing business in a global economy
Entrepreneurial studies

STUDENTS
Enrollment of parent institution	8,758
Enrollment of MBA Program	1,098
% male/female	66/34
% part-time	82
% minorities	15
% international	22
Average age at entry	29
Average years work experience at entry	6

ACADEMICS
Academic Experience Rating	**81**
Student/faculty ratio	16:1
Profs interesting rating	92
Profs accessible rating	99
% female faculty	18
% minority faculty	10

Joint Degrees
JD/MBA, 4 years; JD/MSIS, 4 years.

Academics

The Leavey School of Business at Santa Clara University combines "Jesuit values, primarily in the quality of education and the emphasis on high integrity," with a Silicon Valley location that draws "the cream of the crop to the faculty, such as the former 3Com CEO." The result is a unique MBA program that "caters to part-time students" but also has plenty to offer full-timers.

Customer service is the name of the game at Leavey, where "the dean runs the school as if it was a company in itself. He provides quarterly reports of the progress of school and reviews student evaluations as a measure of the progress." Administrators "do everything they can to keep up with the changing trends in business and business schools. For example, recently they introduced international exposure for the student. Every summer, one or two student groups visit another country to meet with business leaders and financial institutions to understand how business is done in that country. This year, the group went to China. Next year, one group will go to China and another," to Turkey. Professors take a similar student-first approach; they are "eager to help students in the classroom and to introduce them to colleagues for future employment opportunities. They are always available for personal/professional consultation."

Leavey's curriculum employs "a great case-study approach" that "is structured to maximize teamwork abilities." Students find this pedagogical approach immediately applicable to their professional lives. MBAs also "love the 'experimental' classes that students can choose as electives, such as Spirituality and Leadership, which really gets you to focus on your inner self and become a better, less stressed person." Students tell us the school excels in accounting, general management, and marketing. Asked where the school should improve, one student comments, "For some reason, the school is not so well-recognized as other schools in the area, namely Stanford and Berkeley. But I have been quite impressed with SCU so far. The campus is good and the academic standards are excellent. I think the school will stand to gain if marketed better."

Career and Placement

Students appreciate the "great Bay Area network" connected to SCU; MBAs here benefit from "a terrific level of interaction with leaders and innovators in Silicon Valley." The Graduate Business Career Services Office capitalizes on these connections to help students procure internships ("The quarter system allows for some interesting internship opportunities in the area because local employers know some students can be available part-time or full-time for a quarter or two," explains one student) and post-graduation jobs. In the past, students have felt the service wasn't all it could be. As one observed, "Since most students are working, there are limited resources devoted to the internship/career placement program. Also, SCU also does not do enough promotion of the program out in the business community. Its reputation is only good regionally, despite its high ranking as a part-time business program." However, many changes have been implemented in career services in the past few years.

Recent employers of graduates are Applied Materials, Inc.; Cisco Systems, Inc.; eBay; Hewlett-Packard; KLA-Tencor Corporation; Silicon Valley Bank; Sun Microsystems; VERITAS Software; Wells Fargo; and Xilinx.

ADMISSIONS CONTACT: JENNIFER TAYLOR, SENIOR DIRECTOR, GRADUATE BUSINESS ADMISSIONS
ADDRESS: 116 LUCAS HALL, 500 EL CAMINO REAL SANTA CLARA, CA 95053-0001
PHONE: 408-554-4539 • FAX: 408-544-4571
E-MAIL: MBAADMISSIONS@SCU.EDU • WEBSITE: WWW.SCU.EDU/BUSINESS

FINANCIAL FACTS

Annual tuition	$28,500
Fees	$90
Cost of books	$1,000
Room & board	
(off-campus)	$14,000
Average grant	$15,000

ADMISSIONS

Admissions Selectivity Rating	**76**
# of applications received	427
% applicants accepted	85
% acceptees attending	74
Average GMAT	613
Range of GMAT	530–710
Average GPA	3.10
TOEFL required of	
international students	Yes
Minimum TOEFL	
(paper/computer)	600/250
Application fee	$75
International application fee	$100
Regular application deadline	6/1
Early decision program?	No
Deferment available	Yes
Maximum length	
of deferment	2 quarters
Transfer students accepted	Yes
Transfer application policy:	
Apply as all others.	
Non-fall admissions	Yes
Need-blind admissions	Yes

Student Life and Environment

MBAs report that SCU "provides a safe, clean, study environment coupled with a very caring and personal staff. The school really treats students as 'customers' and caters to their needs, offering extended library hours during exams. The staff wants the students to succeed." Part-timers also appreciate that "the schedule is really terrific [and] works for working folks as well as commuters." In addition, the school opened a new facility in 2008.

SCU's "gorgeous and safe campus" offers a number of top amenities, including "a state-of-the-art gym and pool, great recreation areas, and a late-night venue called The Bronco with a pool table and a large television and several couches," as well as "campus-wide wireless access, [and] a peaceful rose garden and a church for when you need serenity." Although most students are part-timers with numerous other commitments outside school, MBAs here do occasionally socialize. One writes, "There are quarter-end bar nights which are great for relaxing after your last final with current classmates, catching up with past classmates, and meeting new people." Another student points out that "life at school can be great for those who do the work to get involved. It can be a commuter school if that is all a student wants to get out of it. [But] there is always something social to do on the weekends, either sponsored by the school or just going out with other MBA students."

"Many students here have jobs," which "provides the best opportunity for networking and recruiting after graduation, as you have gained so many resources at numerous organizations," students here tell us. MBAs range from the mid 20s to the mid 40s. Their "backgrounds are extremely diverse; they come from such areas as financial services, banking, semiconductors, software, technology management, finance, and human resources, to name a few." Engineers from the Silicon Valley are the single most visible contingent.

Admissions

Applicants to Leavey MBA programs at SCU must provide the Admissions Office with all of the following: official transcripts for all postsecondary academic work; official GMAT score reports reflecting scores no more than five years old; a completed application and a copy of same; two letters of recommendation; and personal essays. A third essay is optional. Candidates whose first language is not English must also submit official score reports for the TOEFL (minimum required score: 600 paper-based test, 100 on new IBT test. Work experience is not a prerequisite to admission, although a minimum of two years of experience is recommended; on average, admitted students have between five and seven years of post-undergraduate professional experience. All applicants must demonstrate competency in four areas: college algebra, calculus, and oral communications. SCU uses targeted advertising and recruiting events to enhance its minority and disadvantaged populations.

EMPLOYMENT PROFILE

Career Rating	88	Grads Employed by Function	% Avg. Salary
Percent employed at graduation	85	Marketing	NR $111,000
Percent employed 3 months		Operations	NR $103,000
after graduation	90	Consulting	NR $92,500
Average base starting salary	$97,395	Management	NR $111,000
		Finance	NR $87,063
		MIS	NR $76,833

SEATTLE PACIFIC UNIVERSITY
SCHOOL OF BUSINESS AND ECONOMICS

GENERAL INFORMATION

Type of school	Private
Affiliation	Free Methodist
Academic calendar	Quarter

SURVEY SAYS...

Students love Seattle, WA
Solid preparation in:
General management
Operations
Communication/interpersonal skills

STUDENTS

Enrollment of parent institution	3,891
Enrollment of MBA Program	149
% male/female	56/44
% part-time	89
% international	82
Average age at entry	27
Average years work experience at entry	5

ACADEMICS

Academic Experience Rating	**78**
Student/faculty ratio	17:1
Profs interesting rating	74
Profs accessible rating	80
% female faculty	30
% minority faculty	5

Academics

A small, Christian-affiliated college in a progressive Northwest city, Seattle Pacific University offers an MBA and Masters in Information Systems Management that considers "another way of doing business." At SPU, business education "really isn't just about the bottom line, but about sustainable, ethical business practices." "Christian values" are fundamental to the school's mission, and students note a "dedication to social issues" through the curricular and extracurricular offerings. In addition, the school's Center for Integrity in Business explores the intersection of faith and business, bringing plenty of experts, new research, and special events to campus. As a result, this MBA doesn't just introduce skills; it focuses on "building character to stand in the face of obstacles." A current student enthuses, "I believe there are some great leaders that come from the school, and will go on to affect their communities and the world in a powerful way."

The MBA at Seattle Pacific is a comprehensive general management degree comprising nine core courses, 10 required advanced courses, and five elective courses. Teamwork and communication skills are emphasized throughout the curriculum, and there is a "focus on social ventures" in the coursework. To tailor the MBA, the school recently introduced two areas of concentration in technology management and international business. In addition, SPU "offers a MS-ISM degree," which "incorporates the best of the technical IT world and the business world to create leaders who can excel, and most importantly, communicate in both worlds." Despite the emphasis on technology, students feel the curriculum could include "better teaching of quantitative subjects and less reliance on qualitative." While small in size, Seattle Pacific University boasts great "connections to [the] business community" and an active "mentorship program" with local business partners through the Center for Applied Learning. In addition, the school frequently invites "community leaders into class[es]...for live demonstration."

For working professionals, "flexibility" is a major advantage of SPU's programs, which include MBA classes in the evenings. Professional students also appreciate "the willingness of the staff and faculty to work with you to accommodate a busy work life." On that note, the atmosphere at SPU is very supportive, and "most of the professors are very receptive to extending help and want feedback on their classes." The program is small, so class sizes are reduced. In the MBA program, there are rarely more than 30 students in a class (and the average class size is just 13 to 15 students.) In addition to provoking students' comments and discussion, "The small class sizes have allowed us good access to our professors." Employing both adjunct and full-time faculty, "Most of the professors are very good" and students, on the whole, are "very satisfied with the classes, professors, and classmates." Students are split on the administration, however. Some say the top brass should "be more responsive to their customers," while others assure us that "The administration is solid, wants the best for us, and works hard to get the best."

Career and Placement

At SPU, students are prepared for the workplace throughout their studies. Practical business applications are emphasized in MBA coursework, and the school's mentorship program is active and appreciated. At the same time, "There aren't very many internship opportunities for graduate business students" at Seattle Pacific University, as many students are already working when they start the program. Those who enter the MBA with more limited business experience say the program would improve if the "Internships program integrated with the grad business program, so we can get some experience before graduating with a new degree."

Open to all MBA candidates, Seattle Pacific University's serves the undergraduate, graduate, and alumni communities at the school. Through this office, graduate students can schedule one free career counseling appointment and one resume review, and also gain access to online job boards and research tools. The school also offers free career services through Drake Beam Morrin, a career management firm. Top employers of Seattle Pacific MBA candidates include Boeing, Microsoft, Starbucks, and Safeco.

Student Life and Environment

Seattle Pacific University is a small, private school, located on a 40-acre campus just 10 minutes from downtown Seattle. Within the graduate business programs, SPU attracts a small but engaging student body. For many, "What has made the classroom so interesting [is] the diverse backgrounds and experiences of...student[s]." Teamwork is a mainstay of the program, and most students are "able to work well on small group projects, have good communication skills, [and] are inclusive." Overall, students are "friendly and helpful," and "the school has a great, positive atmosphere."

Thanks to the flexible course schedule, most MBA candidates are working "professionals with full-time jobs" in Seattle. For busy evening students, life consists of "work all day, school all night, and then homework the rest of the week." If they have a little extra time after class, SPU students might attend an event hosted by the Human Resources Club, the school's most active graduate student organization.

Admissions

Prospective students with an undergraduate GPA of 3.0 and one year of full-time work experience can take up to three MBA courses or two ISM courses before officially applying to the program. SPU accepts applicants for the autumn, winter, spring, and summer terms. To be eligible for the MBA and MS-ISM programs, students must have an undergraduate degree with a 3.0 GPA and substantive work experience (at least one full year of post-undergraduate work experience.) A GMAT score over 490 is preferred.

FINANCIAL FACTS

Annual tuition	$16,416
Cost of books	$1,320
Room & board (off-campus)	$12,700

ADMISSIONS

Admissions Selectivity Rating	73
# of applications received	50
% applicants accepted	70
% acceptees attending	60
Average GMAT	529
Range of GMAT	460–580
Average GPA	3.33
TOEFL required of international students	Yes
Minimum TOEFL (paper/computer)	565/225
Application fee	$50
International application fee	$50
Regular application deadline	8/1
Regular notification	8/31
Early decision program?	No
Deferment available	Yes
Maximum length of deferment	2 quarters
Transfer students accepted	Yes
Transfer application policy: Regular Admission Process	
Non-fall admissions	Yes
Need-blind admissions	Yes

SEATTLE UNIVERSITY
ALBERS SCHOOL OF BUSINESS AND ECONOMICS

GENERAL INFORMATION
Type of school   Private
Affiliation   Roman Catholic/Jesuit
Academic calendar   Quarter

SURVEY SAYS...
Cutting-edge classes
Solid preparation in:
Teamwork

STUDENTS
Enrollment of parent institution	7,751
Enrollment of MBA Program	723
% male/female	53/47
% out-of-state	8
% part-time	78
% minorities	5
% international	22
Average age at entry	28
Average years work experience at entry	6

ACADEMICS
Academic Experience Rating	**81**
Student/faculty ratio	14:1
Profs interesting rating	81
Profs accessible rating	81
% female faculty	24
% minority faculty	22

Joint Degrees
JDMBA, 4 years; JD/MSF, 4 years; JD/MIB, 4 years; JD/MPAC, 4 years.

Prominent Alumni
Mohamed Ali Alabbar, Chairman, Emaar Properties; William Foley, Jr., Chairman and CEO, Fidelity National Financial; Paul Folino, CEO, Emulex Corporation; Soren Mills, Vice President, Operations & Services, Wal-Mart; Carol Nelson, CEO & President Cascade Financial Corporation.

Academics

The Albers School of Business and Economics at Seattle University "is focused entirely on the working professional, so the evening program receives [its] full effort and is not a watered-down version of a day program," students here happily report. The program caters almost exclusively to part-timers (a small number of students attend full time), offering "an extremely flexible part-time MBA program" that "you can complete at your own pace." "You can enroll during any term" and enjoy "the ability to take a quarter off if necessary," MBAs here point out.

Albers' location in Seattle positions it to capitalize on some major international business-es headquartered nearby, and students say the school does just that. "Albers has a great reputation with local businesses, including Microsoft, Boeing, Amazon, Costco, Starbucks, and T-Mobile," one MBA explains. Another reports, "My IT class was taught by the CTO of Alaska Air, which pioneered online ticket sales and kiosk check-in." Seattle businesses feed Albers' "excellent mentor program" and provide valuable internship opportunities for those seeking them (most here already have full-time jobs).

Seattle University is a Jesuit school, and Albers honors that tradition by "really empha-sizing personal development in addition to technical skills." The "Jesuit philosophy of social responsibility" manifests itself in a curricular "emphasis on being a good citizen and giving back to the community." As one student explains, Albers seeks to "develop ethical team players who are tuned into workplace dynamics. The basis of this program is that you can learn accounting, finance, etc., anywhere. What sets a university apart is its ability to develop students' leadership and communication skills. The school does an excellent job in this arena while never neglecting the basics."

Students praise Albers' "great resources," "diverse student body," and "wonderful" "small classroom size." Professors here "are passionate about their fields. Many have run businesses themselves and have practical, relevant knowledge. They are easy to talk to and fun to learn from." Perhaps even better, they are "great [at] recognizing that most of the students are working professionals and bringing their experiences into the educa-tional setting." Administrators "respond well to student needs and appear to be interest-ed in improving the school's reputation in the academic and professional worlds."

Career and Placement

The Albers Placement Center provides the expected complement of career counseling, internship and career placement services, job search tools, workshops, and networking events. The school's location in a major business center helps; even so, students here gen-erally yearn for "better placement opportunities and networking." "Increasing the num-ber of companies affiliated for careers and internships" would be a critical improvement, according to one MBA.

Top employers of Seattle University MBAs include: Amazon.com, The Boeing Company, CB Richard Ellis, Clark Nuber, Collier International, Deloitte & Touche, Ernst & Young, Expeditors, Foundation Bank, GMI, KPMG, Microsoft, Moss Adams, PACCAR, Russell Investment Group, Starbucks, T-Mobile, Washington Mutual, and Zymogenetics.

ADMISSIONS CONTACT: JANET SHANDLEY, DIRECTOR, GRADUATE ADMISSIONS
ADDRESS: 901 12TH AVENUE, PO BOX 222000 SEATTLE, WA 98122-1090
PHONE: (206) 296-2000 • FAX: (206) 296-5656
E-MAIL: GRAD-ADMISSIONS@SEATTLEU.EDU • WEBSITE: WWW.SEATTLEU.EDU/ALBERS/

Student Life and Environment

"The courses are all in the evening" at Albers and "most students live away from campus and commute to class," "so graduate student life is not a strong focus" here. Even so, "social/networking activities are planned at least monthly and seem fairly well-attended." Because they commute, students "are very efficient with study groups," and there is "lots of teamwork in the program." For those who can spare the time, campus life provides "lots of organizations doing all sorts of events. There is no lack of opportunity to get involved." Popular extracurricular events include "a valuable executive speaker series."

The campus, conveniently located downtown, "is full of life when the weather is nice, with people playing with their dogs on campus or having a picnic on the grass, or playing with their children." Commuters can hang in the collegium, "which is divided up by major and/or level of education, so the grad students are separate from the undergrad students. They have a kitchen, food available on an honor system, computer access, a living room-like atmosphere, music, games, activities. It really is wonderful." "A coffee stand on the main floor of the business school…stays open into the evening for the grad students." This is Seattle, after all.

Albers' student body consists primarily of "working professionals. Many are in their late 20s to early 30s and a good number are married." They "take their studies very seriously, even while juggling full-time work schedules and personal lives" and "bring a diverse range of experience to the classroom that is very helpful to furthering class discussions."

Admissions

Applicants must submit an official undergraduate transcript; transcripts reflecting any post-baccalaureate academic work (regardless of whether it led to a degree); an official GMAT score report; a current resume; and a completed application form. International students whose first language is not English must also submit an official TOEFL score report (students with low scores may be admitted but must complete the Culture Language Bridge Program). Evidence of two years continuous full-time work experience is required for the MBA, MSF, and MIB programs; work experience is not required for the MPAC program. Personal statements and letters of reference are not required but may be included, especially if there is information an applicant feels is important for the committee to take into consideration in its decision.

FINANCIAL FACTS

Annual tuition	$18,792
Cost of books	$846
Room & board (off-campus)	$8,805
% of students receiving aid	62
% of first-year students receiving aid	63
% of students receiving loans	34
% of students receiving grants	34
Average award package	$15,905
Average grant	$10,300
Average student loan debt	$41,869

ADMISSIONS

Admissions Selectivity Rating	80
# of applications received	167
% applicants accepted	80
% acceptees attending	77
Average GMAT	577
Range of GMAT	530–630
Average GPA	3.29
TOEFL required of international students	Yes
Minimum TOEFL (paper/computer)	580/237
Application fee	$55
International application fee	$55
Regular application deadline	8/20
Early decision program?	No
Deferment available	Yes
Maximum length of deferment	1 year
Transfer students accepted	Yes
Transfer application policy: Applicants must meet standard admission requirements. University will accept 9 quarter credits from AACSB accredited schools. Students transferring from an accredited Jesuit MBA program (JEBNET) may transfer up to 50% of credits.	
Non-fall admissions	Yes
Need-blind admissions	Yes

SETON HALL UNIVERSITY
STILLMAN SCHOOL OF BUSINESS

GENERAL INFORMATION
Type of school   Private
Affiliation   Roman Catholic
Academic calendar   Semester

SURVEY SAYS...
Solid preparation in:
Communication/interpersonal skills
Presentation skills
Doing business in a global economy

STUDENTS
Enrollment of parent institution	9,700
Enrollment of MBA Program	528
Average age at entry	29
Average years work experience at entry	5

ACADEMICS
Academic Experience Rating	76
Student/faculty ratio	25:1
Profs interesting rating	84
Profs accessible rating	83
% female faculty	36

Joint Degrees
MBA/JD (open to full-time students only), 115/118 credits (3.5–4 years); MBA/MSN, 54 credits (2.5–5 years); MBA/MA Diplomacy & International Relations 60 credits (2.5–5 years).

Prominent Alumni
James O'Brien, Owner, Carlton Hill Hedge Fund; Gerald P. Buccino, Chairman and CEO of Buccino & Associates; Michael Wilk, Partner, Ernst & Young; Stephen Lalor, Partner, Ernst & Young; Steve Waldis, Owner, Synchonos.

Academics

Located just outside the hustle and bustle of New York City, Seton Hall University offers a convenient, suburban alternative for city professionals looking to pursue an MBA. At Seton Hall, "the MBA program is designed for students who work full time," and features evening classes and a "convenient location" near major New Jersey roadways. (In addition to the campus-based program, the school offers "classes off campus at the Hackensack University Medical Center.") Coining its program "The Practical MBA," efficiency is a key advantage of Seton Hall, which offers "a streamlined program of 42 credits, compared to other schools with 60 credits." Even with lower credit requirements, the program can be "taxing" and students warn, "The commitment, perseverance, and dedication one has to make while working a demanding job in NYC or on the NJ business coastline across from NYC must not be underestimated." Fortunately, Seton Hall makes every effort to accommodate busy professionals. Here, professors are highly accommodating and accessible, and "Even if they can't meet for special office hours, personal cell phone calls or emails are not uncommon."

"Seton Hall University is one of the most prestigious universities in the area," and the MBA program lives up to the school's strong reputation. Throughout the MBA core curriculum, the "subject material is made very relevant to modern business," with a focus on accounting, economics, and behavioral and quantitative sciences. After the core, students can tailor their coursework through academic concentrations in fields like accounting, information technology management, and sports management. The academic experience is hands-on, so be prepared to roll up your sleeves and get busy: "Presentations, in-class discussions, and group assignments are [a] vital part of every course." In addition, every student must conceive and complete a service project before graduation. Students really appreciate the fact that Seton Hall "incorporates core values in its program: integrity, diversity, social responsibility."

In the classroom, "Professors can be hit or miss but, for the most part, they are good at what they do and teach well." A current student enthuses, "I am very impressed with how lively my professors are...even the ones teaching stats and heavy quants." In addition to tenured staff, Seton Hall can "attract excellent adjunct professors from nearby corporations in New York City and Northern New Jersey." Most are "demonstrated leaders in the field," ranging from the "CEO of a public company" to a "lawyer for the Vatican." Things run smoothly at Seton Hall and, throughout the business school, "The offices are always well-staffed with knowledgeable employees." An important compliment to the academic experience, students appreciate that "The facilities are modern and the use of technology aids with learning during a full-time work lifestyle." For example, "The trading room is equipped with a Bloomberg terminal which is also a nice touch."

Career and Placement

The Seton Hall University Career Center assists both undergraduate and graduate students with their job search through career assessment and career counseling, mock interviews, online job boards, and networking events. For MBA candidates, the Career Center maintains several counselors who are specially designated to help graduate business students find a job or internship. While many Seton Hall students are already working when they enter the program, they say, "The school has been working towards providing more support for career transition, such as networking events and career fairs."

ADMISSIONS CONTACT: CATHERINE BIANCHI, DIRECTOR OF GRADUATE ADMISSIONS
ADDRESS: GRADUATE ADMISSIONS - STILLMAN SCHOOL OF BUSINESS, 400 SOUTH ORANGE AVENUE
SOUTH ORANGE, NJ 07079-2692 • PHONE: 973-761-9262 • FAX: 973-761-9208
E-MAIL: MBA@SHU.EDU • WEBSITE: WWW.BUSINESS.SHU.EDU

FINANCIAL FACTS

Annual tuition	$24,408
Fees	$610
Cost of books	$1,700
Room & board (off-campus)	$10,200

ADMISSIONS

Admissions Selectivity Rating	**74**
# of applications received	323
% applicants accepted	59
% acceptees attending	82
Average GMAT	541
Range of GMAT	500–580
Average GPA	3.21
TOEFL required of international students	Yes
Minimum TOEFL (paper/computer)	607/254
Application fee	$75
International application fee	$75
Regular application deadline	5/31
Early decision program?	No
Deferment available	Yes
Maximum length of deferment	1 academic year
Transfer students accepted	Yes

Transfer application policy:
Students must submit a formal application and satisfy all requirements for admission. In addition to graduate transcripts, it is suggested that the student also submit a course description and syllabus for the courses he/she intends to transfer. Upon gaining admission to the MBA program, the Associate Dean for Academic Services will review the student's transcripts to determine which graduate courses may be transferred. Students are eligible to transfer up to a maximum of 12 credits.

Non-fall admissions	Yes
Need-blind admissions	Yes

Seton Hall alumni work at a wide range of companies, including Johnson & Johnson, Deloitte, Ernst & Young, Merrill Lynch, New York Life Insurance Company, Booz Allen Hamilton, New Jersey Nets, New York Mets, New York Yankees, Madison Square Garden, Masterfoods USA, Mercedes-Benz, Prudential Financial, PricewaterhouseCoopers, and Tiffany & Co.

Student Life and Environment

Located on a "very safe and clean" campus "just 10 miles from New York City," Seton Hall University offers a pleasant environment with excellent facilities. The MBA program is largely part-time, so most students "drive in for class and leave" directly afterwards. However, others tell us that they "love spending time on the green terrace anytime between or after classes," or often "grab food at the dining hall/food court, which has a diverse selection of restaurants." Housed in Jubilee Hall—"the new business building with numerous resources inside it for class"—business students enjoy a comfortable and modern facility, with "state-of-the-art" resources, wireless Internet, and web-based classroom technology.

The largely part-time student population can "create difficulties in creating and sustaining clubs on the school campus;" however, the upshot is that you get a "great mix of industry experience among students" which contributes to class discussion and "creates a stimulating learning environment." Most students have work experience before entering the program, but "The age range and experience is dramatic—from fifth years to [those seeking] career transitions, as well as dual-degree students from the Whitehead School of Diplomacy." Despite their differences, "Everyone is eager to learn and help out the others around them," and, in general, group work goes smoothly and everyone pulls their weight.

Admissions

To apply to Seton Hall's Stillman School of Business, prospective graduate students must submit transcripts from their undergraduate studies, GMAT scores, a resume of work experience and credentials, a two-paragraph personal statement, and a letter of recommendation. Every applicant is evaluated individually; however, Seton Hall generally requires admits to have a minimum undergraduate GPA of 3.0 on a 4.0 scale, and a minimum GMAT score of 500. Applications are reviewed and admissions decisions are rendered on a rolling basis.

SIMMONS COLLEGE
SCHOOL OF MANAGEMENT

GENERAL INFORMATION
Type of school   Private

SURVEY SAYS...
Good peer network
Cutting-edge classes
Solid preparation in:
General management
Teamwork
Communication/interpersonal skills
Presentation skills

STUDENTS
Enrollment of parent
  institution   5,003
Enrollment of MBA Program   183
% male/female   0/100
% part-time   60
% minorities   31
% international   17
Average age at entry   32
Average years work experience
  at entry   7

ACADEMICS
Academic Experience Rating   **81**
Student/faculty ratio   9:1
Profs interesting rating   93
Profs accessible rating   94
% female faculty   86
% minority faculty   19

Joint Degrees
Combined MBA/MSW, BA/MBA 5.5 years

Prominent Alumni
Gail Snowden, VP, The Boston Foundation, former EVP Fleet Financial; Maryann Tocio, Pres & COO, Bright Horizons; Donna Fernandes, President, Buffalo Zoo; Gail Deegan, Board Member, TJX, former CFO & EVP/Houghton Mifflin; Sue Paresky, SVP, Dana Farber Cancer Institute; Denise Coll, President W. America, Starwood Hotels.

Academics

Simmons College Graduate School of Management offers a unique, forward-thinking, rigorous, and intimate MBA program, conceived and designed especially for women. Balancing business theory and practice, the Simmons curriculum employs the case-based learning style developed at Harvard Business School. At the same time, the program is intended to provide "an alternative to the traditional B-school culture, while maintaining the academic intensity." The school distinguishes itself in many ways, such as its "unique reputation for principled leadership," which attracts a student body that is "interested in sustainability, ethics, and other social aspects of management." In addition, as an all-women's program, "Simmons gives us unique insight into gender issues and leadership." Professors are "well-versed in gender dynamics," and a majority of the case studies involve women leaders. On the whole, "The curriculum is rigorous and current," keeping up with contemporary business trends. In fact, students boast that, "The school is way ahead of a lot of the "trends"—principled leadership is part of the mission and has incorporated areas like CSR, sustainability, and ethics, long before it was trendy."

The Simmons MBA begins with a weeklong symposium entitled Foundations of Business, after which students begin core courses in decision-making, marketing, accounting, leadership, and other business fundamentals. Curriculum has a strong qualitative component, fostering leadership skills, collaboration, and innovative thinking. While some women would like "more quantitative material" and more elective offerings, they agree that the program is "rigorous" and "truly transformational." A current student attests, "my first semester in graduate school has been one of great adjustments but also one that has inspired me to think outside of the box." With a relatively small student body and an excellent teacher-student ratio, the "intimate class setting" is another major benefit of a Simmons education. The "stupendous" professors "really challenge us, but pair the challenges with support and encouragement." A current student attests, "I have had email discussions with professors at midnight and phone conversations on Sunday mornings; I've never been made to feel like I was intruding. The professors seem invested in our ability to really understand the coursework and they make it a point to leave no one behind."

Although Simmons offers a full-time MBA option, the majority of students complete their degree on a part-time basis. Most Simmons professors understand the challenges of multitasking, and "respect the fact that you work full time during the day and have family at home." In addition to the faculty, "The deans of this school are amazing and very involved in our education," and the staff is "very flexible in working with us when our work schedules wreak havoc with our course schedules." Overall, the administration runs a tight ship, and "the communications to students are always timely and informative."

Career and Placement

"The quality of the network of current and former students," is among the best aspects of a Simmons education. Currently, Simmons graduates are employed at range of companies, including American Express, Bank of America, Blue Cross Blue Shield, Deloitte, Digitas, Four Seasons Resort, The Gap, Genzyme, Harvard University, Hewlett Packard, JP Morgan, Kraft Food, Monster Worldwide, MOMA, Partners Healthcare, Pfizer, PricewaterhouseCoopers, Sun Microsystems, Time Warner, Turner Construction and Unisys.

The Career Services Office provides a variety of services including career symposiums, employer luncheons, industry panels, and company presentations. They also offer highly individualized career counseling and networking services, often employing the support of Simmons faculty, alumni, and the dean. While they appreciate these services, students would like to see Simmons "promote the school's reputation on a national level. Simmons is well-known in Boston and New England, but rarely recognized elsewhere."

Student Life and Environment

Attracting a bright, lively, and diverse group of scholars, students say they are "constantly amazed by the level of intellect in conversation inside and outside the classroom. There are amazing women at Simmons." Drawing students from diverse personal and professional backgrounds, you'll meet students who are "conservative, liberal, local, from other countries, straight, gay, in the public or not-for-profit sector, [and] in the private sector." Despite diversity, the school is small; "everyone knows each other, which fosters a very strong feeling of community and belonging."

In line with the school's forward-thinking agenda, "Simmons SOM opened a brand new "green" building on the Simmons main campus in the Fenway neighborhood. We now have a home that reflects the community-based and socially responsible concerns of the SOM community." Students absolutely love the new building, which is equipped with "excellent" technology and "great informal meeting places and areas to work that at the same time provides opportunities to connect with colleagues." Located in the Boston, the Simmons campus is "accessible via public transportation and for students on campus it is very easy to 'get around' the city."

A largely part-time program, "Fellow students are busy with the challenges of balancing home, work, and school, and yet focused and committed to completing their degree." While part-time students don't have much time for campus activities, "the administration go[es] out of [its] way to have activities both during the day and during the evening to ensure evening students who work full-time have opportunities to be involved." Among other programs, "There is a fabulous speaker series of effective women leaders and academicians."

Admissions

Candidates are evaluated individually and are selected for admission based on both their aptitude and promise. To apply, students must submit an application and essays, two letters of recommendation, official transcripts from all post-secondary education, a current resume, and official GMAT scores. International applicants must submit TEFL scores.

FINANCIAL FACTS

Fees	$230
Cost of books	$2,500

ADMISSIONS

Admissions Selectivity Rating	72
# of applications received	113
% applicants accepted	65
% acceptees attending	78
Average GMAT	548
Range of GMAT	460–610
Average GPA	3.16
TOEFL required of international students	Yes
Minimum TOEFL (paper/computer)	550/213
Application fee	$75
International application fee	$75
Early decision program?	No
Deferment available	Yes
Maximum length of deferment	1 year
Transfer students accepted	Yes
Transfer application policy: Reviewed on case-by-case basis.	
Non-fall admissions	Yes
Need-blind admissions	Yes

EMPLOYMENT PROFILE

Career Rating	89	Grads Employed by Function	%	Avg. Salary
Average base starting salary	$81,000	Marketing	9	$91,500
		Operations	7	$109,167
		Management	7	$94,167
		Finance	16	$75,833
		MIS	7	$82,500
		Nonprofit	7	$77,500

Top 5 Employers Hiring Grads
Bank of America, Blue Cross Blue Shield of New England, Harvard University, Liberty Mutual, Partners Healthcare

SOUTHEAST MISSOURI STATE UNIVERSITY
DONALD L. HARRISON COLLEGE OF BUSINESS

GENERAL INFORMATION
Type of school	Public
Academic calendar	Semester

SURVEY SAYS...
Solid preparation in:
General management
Communication/interpersonal skills
Presentation skills
Computer skills

STUDENTS
Enrollment of parent institution	10,250
Enrollment of MBA Program	118
% male/female	56/44
% out-of-state	3
% part-time	49
% minorities	2
% international	25
Average age at entry	26
Average years work experience at entry	5

ACADEMICS
Academic Experience Rating	**78**
Student/faculty ratio	19:1
Profs interesting rating	82
Profs accessible rating	79
% female faculty	40
% minority faculty	10

Joint Degrees
Joint MBA and Masters in International Business and Economics offered with University of Applied Sciences, Schmalkalden, Germany.

Academics

For a "top-notch education at an affordable price," Missouri residents recommend the business school at Southeast Missouri State University. An inexpensive public school, "The university provides an excellent bang for your buck," yet doesn't skimp on a quality education. Catering to current and soon-to-be professionals in the Cape Giradeau area, all classes are held in the evenings. However, SEMO's MBA programs can be completed either part time or full time (the former is the more popular option), and the school operates an entirely online program for students whose schedules do not accommodate classroom work. The program begins with the common core, which covers key business areas ranging from accounting and finance to quantitative and qualitative research methods. After completing the core, students can focus their studies in a single business area, such as finance, industrial management, health administration, or sports management. In addition to coursework, full-time students often augment their coursework with for-credit internships, with teaching assistant positions through the ample "graduate assistantship opportunities" (which also include tuition assistance), or through one of the school's numerous short-term overseas programs. As one appreciative student exclaims, "Their international programs were the best experience of my life!"

Appealing to mature students, "The class environment is unique, in that is very professional, as if you were going to work." Likewise, "The teachers expect all student to come prepared and [they] develop helpful but strenuous assignments." A current student adds, "They give us the responsibility to learn and take on the role as a facilitator of learning rather than keeping it very structured, letting the students do a lot on their own." The teaching staff gets strong reviews from current students, who say their instructors add "very helpful and relevant insight into what we are studying." A current student enthuses, "The professors at Southeast are wonderful. Not only are they experienced in their field, but their teaching styles are excellent."

Despite the emphasis on professionalism, the environment at SEMO is incredibly down-to-earth and friendly. Here, "class sizes are small, so professors get to know you pretty well" and in-class discussions are encouraged. For those who need extra guidance, "The teachers do a great job of making themselves available to the students outside of the classroom for one-on-one help." The small size also facilitates networking between students; "having a smaller campus helps you connect with a wide variety of people in a variety of fields," which makes "classroom discussions very interesting and relevant to the real world."

Career and Placement

As a graduate student enrolled in the MBA program, SEMO students may take advantage of the various services offered through the university's Career Services office. Career Services offers free career advising, salary projections, resume and cover letter revisions, career testing, and interview preparation by appointment. The Career Services office also organizes both job fairs and campus recruiting programs, free of charge. For a fee, students may also access a list of current job opening listings in the region. Because their efforts serve the entire school community, MBA candidates feel, "The Career Center could be greatly improved in order to better serve graduate students."

ADMISSIONS CONTACT: DR. KENNETH HEISCHMIDT, DIRECTOR, MBA PROGRAM
ADDRESS: MBA PROGRAM; SOUTHEAST MISSOURI STATE UNIVERSITY, 1 UNIVERSITY PLAZA, MS
5890 CAPE GIRARDEAU, MO 63701
PHONE: 573-651-5116 • FAX: 573-651-5032
E-MAIL: MBA@SEMO.EDU • WEBSITE: WWW.SEMO.EDU/MBA

FINANCIAL FACTS

Annual tuition (in-state/ out-of-state)	$5,688/$10,008
Cost of books	$500
Room & board	$5,200
Average award package	$11,200
Average grant	$11,200

ADMISSIONS

Admissions Selectivity Rating	77
# of applications received	137
% applicants accepted	65
% acceptees attending	90
Average GMAT	504
Range of GMAT	400–620
Average GPA	3.84
TOEFL required of international students	Yes
Minimum TOEFL (paper/computer)	550/213
Application fee	$25
International application fee	$35
Early decision program?	No
Deferment available	Yes
Maximum length of deferment	1 year
Transfer students accepted	Yes
Transfer application policy: May transfer 9 hours authorized by Director of MBA Program.	
Non-fall admissions	Yes
Need-blind admissions	Yes

While Career Service does not work exclusively with graduate business students, students say "The MBA office does a great job of making MBA students aware of job opportunities that come to its attention." In fact, many students say, "The school puts a great deal of effort [into helping] students get jobs after graduation and organizes various networking events throughout the semester." Students enrolled in the program full-time can also lay the foundation for their career through for-credit internships.

Student Life and Environment

Located in the riverside city of Cape Giradeau, the SEMO campus is a "peaceful and safe place" to work and study. Just over 100 miles from St. Louis, Cape Giradeau is a small city of 35,000, yet provides "everything that we need as students, and…is a great place to live as well." With classes held in the evenings, most SEMO students work during the day and commute to school in the evenings; therefore, they aren't actively involved in campus life. However, if you're interested in some campus camaraderie, students assure us that "There are a ton of things going on all the time, if people just look around."

On the whole, "Students at SEMO are very diverse and intelligent" joining the business program "from many different work environments." The atmosphere is more collaborative than competitive, and, for group assignments, everyone is "very helpful and work great together." Students say "The moderately-sized student body is also a strength." At this school, "It's big enough that you can meet plenty of new people, but small enough that you can walk across campus and run into several people you know on the way."

Admissions

To be eligible for admission to Southeast Missouri State University's graduate business program, students must have an undergraduate degree in business from an accredited college or university. Students who do not have an undergraduate degree in business must take a series of prerequisite coursework before they can begin the MBA. Successful applicants will generally have a minimum GMAT score of over 400 and a minimum GPA in foundational (prerequisite) coursework of a C or better. To be considered for a graduate assistantship position, applicants must have a minimum undergraduate grade point average of 2.7.

EMPLOYMENT PROFILE	
Career Rating	81
Percent employed 3 months after graduation	95

SOUTHERN ILLINOIS UNIVERSITY CARBONDALE
COLLEGE OF BUSINESS AND ADMINISTRATION

GENERAL INFORMATION

Type of school	Public
Academic calendar	Semester

SURVEY SAYS...
Good social scene
Helpful alumni
Happy students
Solid preparation in:
Teamwork
Communication/interpersonal skills
Computer skills

STUDENTS

Enrollment of parent institution	21,589
Enrollment of MBA Program	134
% male/female	61/39
% part-time	48
% minorities	10
% international	10

ACADEMICS

Academic Experience Rating	**74**
Student/faculty ratio	12:1
Profs interesting rating	83
Profs accessible rating	78

Joint Degrees
MBA/JD, 105 credits, 3 to 4 years;
MBA/Master of Science in
Agribusiness Econmics (MBA/MS),
51 credits, 12 months to 2.5 years;
MBA/Master of Arts in
Communication (MBA/MA), 51
credits, 12 months to 2.5 years.

Academics

The College of Business and Administration at Southern Illinois University Carbondale offers both a traditional MBA and off-campus EMBA options in Hong Kong, Singapore, and Taiwan. All programs are AACSB-accredited. About half the graduate students at SIUC attend full-time. While part-time students can manage the program as well, the mixed schedule of daytime and nighttime classes limits their options somewhat.

SIUC MBAs report that "the school is famous for its finance department" and that it offers "good courses in the Management of Information Systems." Classes here "are very interactive, with only 20 to 30 students in a class," and "professors work to extend the understanding of the discipline in all classes. Also, most professors seek to design classes in an unorthodox manner to develop skills needed for business." Many students cite the low cost of attending as their primary reason for choosing SIUC; relatively low tuition rates are made effectively lower by the availability of "a lot of assistantships for students." SIUC maintains a relationship with ESC Grenoble, which allows SIUC MBAs to study for a Masters of International Business (MIB) in France.

Entering students who lack the required knowledge base for an MBA program are required to complete up to 37 hours of foundation courses prior to beginning work on their MBA. It helps that students with degrees outside business may receive credit for any equivalent undergraduate business classes in which they earned a grade of C or better. Such students must present both a transcript and a course syllabus for each course in order to be considered for the exemption. Students with undergraduate degrees in business generally are exempt from all foundation course work.

Full-time students who arrive with undergraduate business degrees under their belt can finish the 33-semester hour MBA program in 12 months. The MBA curriculum includes seven core courses and four electives. Students may also pursue electives in finance, marketing, international business, management information systems, and organizational behavior. Those who wish to concentrate in a particular area can opt to take all of their electives in one discipline.

Career and Placement

Southern Illinois University maintains a separate Business Placement Center to serve the College of Business and Administration. The office serves undergraduates, graduates, and alumni of the school. The office coordinates an annual job fair, maintains e-recruiting resources, and provides career counseling to students. Some here feel that "The career center could use a more hands-on effort with graduates. The only contact I had was through e-mail notices of career center activities." On-campus recruiters include 7-Eleven, Aldi, Archer Daniels Midland (ADM), CBIZ Business Solutions, Deloitte Touche Tohmatsu, Disney, Ernst & Young, Federated Insurance, KPMG International, MB Financial, MMP&W, PricewaterhouseCoopers, Regions Financial Corporation, State Farm Insurance, Swink, Fiehler & Company, Watkins Uiberall, and Woodbury Financial.

ADMISSIONS CONTACT: DR. DON GRIBBIN, MBA PROGRAM DIRECTOR
ADDRESS: REHN HALL 133, 1025 LINCOLN DRIVE, MAIL CODE 4625 CARBONDALE, IL 62901
PHONE: 618-453-3030 • FAX: 618-453-7961
E-MAIL: MBAGP@CBA.SIU.EDU • WEBSITE: WWW.CBA.SIU.EDU

Student Life and Environment

An overall student population of more than 20,000 keeps the SIUC campus hopping. As one MBA student explains, "There are lots of things to do here, such as [hearing] guest speakers and seminars to attend. The school often has forums for students to express their opinions on politics. They also offer fun events like concerts, and many students are avid sports fans, so sporting events are social gatherings." The campus recreation center "is very good, with basketball courts, swimming pools, racquetball courts, etc. There are also weight rooms and many cardiovascular fitness machines, and the staff that works at the Rec Center is very helpful." As if all that weren't enough, "The Student Center is an excellent facility for throwing pots, woodworking, and metal smithing." Even the surrounding campus "is beautiful, with forests all around where you can go hiking if the weather allows."

The city of Carbondale has a population of about 26,000, and the surrounding county is home to nearly 60,000 Illinoisans. St. Louis is the closest big city; it's less than 100 miles to the west. Both Chicago and Kansas City are just over 300 miles away. Major employers in the area include Nascote Industries, West Teleservices, Southern Illinois Healthcare, and the Maytag Corporation.

SIUC MBAs include "many international students. There are more young students than in many MBA programs, but not at the expense of competence." To some "it seems that almost every other student in the MBA program is a recent graduate of SIUC. Although they come from varied backgrounds…they are very similar," especially in that "few seem to have undergraduate degrees in business."

Admissions

All applicants to the MBA program at SIUC must provide the admissions department with a completed application to the university's graduate school; a separate application to the College of Business; official transcripts for all postsecondary academic work; an official score report for the GMAT; and three letters of recommendation. International applicants must also provide an official score report for the TOEFL (minimum score: 550 paper, 213 computer), a financial statement for graduate international students, and a photocopy of their passport. Work experience is not required; however, students with work experience do receive special consideration. All applications are assessed individually and holistically. Admission to the program requires a minimum undergraduate GPA of 2.7 (on a four-point scale) over the applicant's most recent 60 semester hours.

FINANCIAL FACTS

Annual tuition (in-state/ out-of-state)	$5,760/$11,520
Fees	$1,414
Cost of books	$840

ADMISSIONS

Admissions Selectivity Rating	72
# of applications received	78
% applicants accepted	69
% acceptees attending	63
Average GMAT	507
Range of GMAT	440–570
Average GPA	3.4
TOEFL required of international students	Yes
Minimum TOEFL (paper/computer)	550/213
Application fee	$35
International application fee	$35
Regular application deadline	3/15
Regular notification	6/1
Early decision program?	No
Deferment available	Yes
Maximum length of deferment	1 year
Transfer students accepted	Yes
Transfer application policy: Maximum number of transfer credits accepted for core curriculum is 6.	
Non-fall admissions	Yes
Need-blind admissions	No

SOUTHERN ILLINOIS UNIVERSITY EDWARDSVILLE
SCHOOL OF BUSINESS

GENERAL INFORMATION
Type of school	Public
Academic calendar	10 weeks

SURVEY SAYS...
Good peer network
Solid preparation in:
General management
Communication/interpersonal skills
Doing business in a global economy

STUDENTS
Enrollment of parent institution	13,940
Enrollment of MBA Program	173
% part-time	100
Average age at entry	26
Average years work experience at entry	5

ACADEMICS
Academic Experience Rating	75
Student/faculty ratio	4:1
Profs interesting rating	84
Profs accessible rating	80
% female faculty	41
% minority faculty	23

Prominent Alumni
Fernando G. Aguirre, President & CEO of Chiquita Brands International; Robert Knight, Jr., CFO, Union Pacific; Michael Abbene, CIO, Arch Coal; Timothy Keenan, CEO, High Performance Technologies; Jan-Patrick Schmitz, President & CEO, Montblanc North America.

Academics

Southern Illinois University Edwardsville's School of Business offers a small, part-time MBA program that students describe as "convenient" and "more affordable than other schools." As one student observes, "SIUE is relatively inexpensive for the type of education you get. This is great for students who want a great education but cannot afford to pay inflated tuition. With the way the economy is today, everyone is looking to get the most for their dollar."

SIUE's "proximity to the city of St. Louis" provides a large base of current and aspiring professionals from which to draw its student body. These students attend part-time, sometimes during "convenient evening" hours and sometimes participating in "a weekend format that allows [them] to better manage the work-life-school balance." While some students praise the scheduling options, others suggest that the program isn't large enough to successfully sustain these options.

The SIUE curriculum includes a "very challenging" core curriculum that "requires extensive time management. The positive is excellent instruction" provided by professors who "focus on teamwork and projects as learning tools" and "take the time to really teach the material." These busy MBAs note "some professors are very understanding and respectful of working MBA students" but caution, "Others could learn from these professors and understand that just like them, we have outside responsibilities."

Career and Placement

Business students at SIUE are served by the university's Career Development Center, which provides career counseling and placement services for all students and alumni. Services include individual counseling, resume referral, mock interviews, self-assessment materials, on-campus interview sessions, workshops on various career-related skills, and a Career Resources Center with both online and hard-copy materials. SIUE holds two annual career fairs, one in the fall and one in the spring. Students observe, "The career development center focuses more on undergrads and not so much for graduate students."

Student Life and Environment

"Life at SIUE is nice," one student writes, elaborating by observing, "Everyone from the student to the professors is friendly and open. There are various activities to become active in, even more so now that the school is moving to Division I athletics." Most MBA students don't get involved in campus activities, however; "Most students are married" and "working full-time jobs" so "there is no social life outside of the classroom." Students are typically more concerned about paying fees for campus services they don't use (e.g. the gym fee) than they are about getting more involved with campus life.

SIUE's MBA facilities could stand a makeover, students tell us. One writes, "As for the classroom environment, desks and technologies need badly upgraded. For example, it would be great if each student had his own laptop plug-in, but we are restricted to using extension cords from the walls. Sometimes we are so crammed in a room with these little tiny desks that you can barely manage to fit a textbook and a notebook, let alone a laptop on one."

ADMISSIONS CONTACT: SCHOOL OF BUSINESS STUDENT SERVICES, ADMISSIONS OFFICER
ADDRESS: CAMPUS BOX 1186 EDWARDSVILLE, IL 62026
PHONE: 618-650-3840 • FAX: 618-650-3979
E-MAIL: MBA@SIUE.EDU • WEBSITE: WWW.SIUE.EDU/BUSINESS

SIUE is located near St. Louis, which "allows students to participate in professional organizations and seek practical work experience with local firms and government agencies," according to the school's website. Such opportunities are more likely to appeal to undergraduates than to graduate students, but the opportunities are available for those who can take them.

Among those who may avail themselves of the opportunity are those MBAs who "are young and have gone directly from undergrad to the MBA program." There are "many" such students, which some here see as a drawback of the program, but "there is also a good number of professionals who are returning to school while still working in their career." These "goal- and objective-oriented" students tend to be "friendly and easy to work with. Teams form up and function well," because students are "always willing to challenge you and the world around them."

Admissions

Applicants to the SIUE MBA program must apply for admission to the university Graduate School, which includes submitting official transcripts for all post-secondary academic work and an official GMAT score report (applicants holding a PhD, MD, or equivalent degree need not submit GMAT scores). Admissions decisions are based primarily on undergraduate performance and GMAT scores (recent entering class had an average GPA of 3.2 and average GMAT score of 529). The school recommends at least two years of work experience prior to entering the program. Entering students must demonstrate proficiency (typically through undergraduates coursework) in statistics and computer software; students lacking these proficiencies will be required to complete non-degree courses in the subjects in order to gain proficiency. International applicants must meet all the above criteria and submit an official TOEFL score report (minimum score of 550 paper-based test or 213 computer-based test). Rejected applicants may appeal the admissions decision to the MBA program manager. Applicants with undergraduate GPAs of at least 2.8 may be admitted conditionally, pending subsequent successful completion of six credit hours of coursework in the program.

FINANCIAL FACTS

Annual tuition (in-state/ out-of-state)	$6,011/$15,029
Fees	$2,124
Cost of books	$2,000
Room & board (on-campus)	$8,500
% of students receiving aid	42
% of first-year students receiving aid	17
% of students receiving loans	23
% of students receiving grants	7
Average award package	$9,700
Average grant	$4,505
Average student loan debt	$16,000

ADMISSIONS

Admissions Selectivity Rating	**69**
# of applications received	134
% applicants accepted	89
% acceptees attending	80
Average GMAT	529
Range of GMAT	460–620
Average GPA	3.24
TOEFL required of international students	Yes
Minimum TOEFL (paper/computer)	550/213
Application fee	$30
Early decision program?	No
Deferment available	Yes
Maximum length of deferment	1 year
Transfer students accepted	Yes
Transfer application policy: From an AACSB accredited school and up to 9 hours.	
Non-fall admissions	Yes
Need-blind admissions	Yes

SOUTHERN METHODIST UNIVERSITY
COX SCHOOL OF BUSINESS

GENERAL INFORMATION

Type of school	Private

SURVEY SAYS...
Friendly students
Smart classrooms
Solid preparation in:
Accounting

STUDENTS

Enrollment of parent institution	11,000
% male/female	72/28
% out-of-state	44
% minorities	9
% international	18
Average age at entry	27
Average years work experience at entry	4.33

ACADEMICS

Academic Experience Rating	**95**
Student/faculty ratio	12:1
Profs interesting rating	71
Profs accessible rating	82
% female faculty	25
% minority faculty	3

Joint Degrees
JD/MBA, 4 years; MA Arts
Administration/MBA, 2 years

Prominent Alumni
Ruth Ann Marshall, Former
President, Americas, MasterCard;
Thaddeus F. Arroyo, CIO, AT&T;
Martin L. Flanagan, President and
CEO, INVESCO PLC; Hugh Jones,
CEO, Travelocity; William J. O'Neil,
Chairman and CEO, Investor's
Business Daily.

Academics

A contemporary and challenging business program situated in a lively, commerce-oriented city, Southern Methodist University's Cox School of Business is touted by students as the "best program offered in Dallas/Fort Worth area" in its balance of "course offerings, rankings, network ability and recognition, and faculty quality." All MBA students are initially enrolled in the general business concentration, taking a series of courses that provide a thorough introduction to business theory, including "very deep and modernized topics in the area of finance and accounting." Once they have finished the core curriculum, students may tailor their education through one or two academic concentrations, including management, marketing, finance, information technology, and strategy and entrepreneurship. Students appreciate the fact that SMU is highly focused on the latest trends and on a practical approach to business education, saying "Teachers bring relevant material to the class and challenge students every day."

Responding to the increasingly global economy, Cox offers a "forward-thinking, cutting-edge program with a strong focus on the international marketplace." In 2000, Cox inaugurated the Global Leadership Program, a partnership with more than 90 leading businesses and government organizations throughout Asia, India, and Europe. All full-time MBA students participate in the Global Leadership Program, and take a seminar in their first semester, which provides a comprehensive study of the culture, politics, and business in Asia, India, Latin America, or Europe. At the end of the second semester, students travel to the region for a two-week, hands-on immersion into global commerce and culture. For those who wish to further enhance their international acumen, the school operates a number of international exchange programs with universities in China, Japan, Singapore, Australia, Belgium, Denmark, Spain, Argentina, Brazil, and Mexico, among others.

In addition to the traditional, two-year, full-time MBA, the school offers two part-time programs: the professional MBA for students who wish to work full-time while pursuing the MBA and the executive MBA for students who already have advanced business experience. Students in the part-time programs appreciate the camaraderie they feel among their classmates as well as the support of the faculty. One student assures, "They realize that we are all working professionals, and [they] are always there to lend a hand." Whether full-time or part-time, many say the greatest benefit of the program is "the way the b-school administration cares about the individual students." A current student shares, "Before I was even accepted, the admissions staff and administration made me feel as if I was a part of the school."

Career and Placement

For those hoping to work in Texas or the Southwest region, Southern Methodist University is an excellent choice; the school maintains a "great reputation and alumni network in the Dallas/Fort Worth area, Texas, and the Southwestern U.S. cities." In fact, 76.7 percent of graduates took jobs in the Southwest last year, many in hometown Dallas. Since Dallas itself is a "very corporate city," many stay put after graduation. However, some feel the school is too Dallas-centric and "would improve the value to its graduates by increasing the number of companies recruiting for positions in Houston, Austin, and San Antonio."

Cox graduates have a high job-placement rate, and the majority of students take finance/accounting or marketing/sales positions, comprising 45.5 percent and 11.3 percent of last year's graduates, respectively. The average salary of a Cox graduate is $83,381.

ADMISSIONS CONTACT: PATTI CUDNEY, DIRECTOR, MBA ADMISSIONS
ADDRESS: P.O. BOX 750333 DALLAS, TX 75275
PHONE: 214-768-1214 • FAX: 214-768-3956
E-MAIL: MBAINFO@MAIL.COX.SMU.EDU • WEBSITE: WWW.COXMBA.COM

Student Life and Environment

On the Cox campus, you'll find "a great group of people, most in their 20s, some in their 30s, with different backgrounds and interests, but all outgoing." Conversation and camaraderie are not limited to the classroom, and "The school makes a strong effort to have students interact outside the classroom. They host events all the time to mingle with fellow students, professors, alumni, and even guests that people bring." For those who wish to augment the academic experience through a club or recreational activity, "there are plenty of chances for anyone who wishes to get involved with extracurricular activities to do so." However, many part-time students say the demands of work and study are overwhelming. A second-year student laments, "Being in the professional MBA program I wish I had more time to take advantage of all the school offers."

Located in Dallas, Texas, the campus is within striking distance of every form of entertainment imaginable, including restaurants, museums, shopping, and seven major sports teams. On the flip side, the school's pleasant campus offers relief from the bustling city. A current student enthusiastically sums it up: "The campus is beautiful—shady, tree-lined streets with really attractive people in one of the most pro-business cities with an awesome nightlife. Seriously, who could ask for anything more!?"

Admissions

Successful applicants to SMU have leadership experience, a strong academic record, and competitive scores on the GMAT. Last year, the average GMAT score for accepted applicants was 656. Personal qualities are also heavily weighed, and Cox admits students with a history of professional and personal growth, demonstrated achievements, proven academic abilities, and leadership potential. Although an academic background in business is not a requirement for admission, SMU recommends students enter the program with a working knowledge of calculus, accounting, statistics, and microeconomics. Qualified applicants are offered the opportunity to interview with the Admissions staff.

Admissions criteria differ slightly for students seeking admission to Cox's part-time programs. In addition to the aforementioned, applicants to the PMBA program must have at least two years of professional work experience and a strong basic knowledge of accounting, statistics, and microeconomics. Applicants to the executive MBA program are expected to have a minimum of eight years of experience in mid- to upper-level management and to currently hold a senior-level title.

FINANCIAL FACTS

Annual tuition	$37,692
Fees	$3,960
Cost of books	$1,650
Room & board (off-campus)	$13,900
% of students receiving aid	78
% of first-year students receiving aid	76
% of students receiving loans	49
% of students receiving grants	58
Average award package	$45,902
Average grant	$23,231
Average student loan debt	$64,341

ADMISSIONS

Admissions Selectivity Rating	94
# of applications received	613
% applicants accepted	30
% acceptees attending	54
Average GMAT	656
Range of GMAT	610–700
Average GPA	3.24
TOEFL required of international students	Yes
Minimum TOEFL (paper/computer)	600/250
Application fee	$75
International application fee	$75
Regular application deadline	4/15
Regular notification	6/1
Application Deadline/Notification	
Round 1:	11/14 / 1/15
Round 2:	1/6 / 3/15
Round 3:	3/3 / 5/1
Round 4:	4/28 / 6/15
Early decision program?	No
Deferment available	Yes
Maximum length of deferment	1 year
Transfer students accepted	No
Non-fall admissions	No
Need-blind admissions	Yes

EMPLOYMENT PROFILE

Career Rating	96	Grads Employed by Function	% Avg. Salary
Percent employed at graduation	61	Marketing	25 $88,400
Percent employed 3 months after graduation	75	Operations	7 $75,666
		Consulting	14 $93,833
Average base starting salary	$83,381	Management	5 NR
Primary Source of Full-time Job Acceptances		Finance	46 $77,571
School-facilitated activities	22 (47%)	MIS	2 NR
Graduate-facilitated activities	21 (45%)	**Top 5 Employers Hiring Grads**	
Unknown	4 (9%)	AT&T (3), American Airlines (2), Dr. Pepper Snapple Group (2), Frito-Lay (1), ExxonMobil (1)	

ST. JOHN'S UNIVERSITY
THE PETER J. TOBIN COLLEGE OF BUSINESS

GENERAL INFORMATION

Type of school · Private
Affiliation Roman Catholic
Academic calendar Semester

SURVEY SAYS...

Students love Jamaica, NY
Happy students
Smart classrooms
Solid preparation in:
Presentation skills

STUDENTS

Enrollment of parent institution	20,348
Enrollment of MBA Program	663
% male/female	55/45
% out-of-state	40
% part-time	68
% minorities	15
% international	37
Average age at entry	26
Average years work experience at entry	3

ACADEMICS

Academic Experience Rating	72
Student/faculty ratio	12:1
Profs interesting rating	77
Profs accessible rating	67
% female faculty	18
% minority faculty	10

Joint Degrees

JD/MBA (4 years, full-time enrollment required).

Prominent Alumni

Kathryn Morrissey, President, Global Wholesale Markets, AT&T; Richard Carbone, CFO, Prudential Financial; Joseph Garcia, CFO, Spanish Broadcasting System.

Academics

A large business school in New York City, St. John's University provides a strong, general management MBA, which can be tailored to fit individual student interests through a range of concentrations and co-curricular activities. St. John's recently updated its curriculum, which now consists of eight required courses, followed by four field courses and two non-field courses in the student's chosen area of concentration. Through the school's extensive elective offerings, students may pursue a specialization in taxation, decision sciences, finance, insurance financial management, international business, marketing management, and risk management, among a number of other fields. In addition, Tobin operates several unique co-curricular activities, including a multi-million dollar student-managed investment fund, as well as an extensive service-learning and economic development program. A Catholic-affiliated school, St. John's commitment to service has been fundamental to the program since its early days, and the school distinguishes itself from other business programs through its ethical approach to academics. A student explains, "St. John's is grounded in morals and values, and the well-being of their students is always a top priority."

With a total enrollment of over 650 graduate students, you might be surprised to learn that St. John's faculty are "accessible outside of class" and are "willing to give home and cellular phone numbers so that they can be reached at any time with an questions students may have." Drawing intellectuals and business professionals from the New York community, "professors are excellent with both high academic credentials but also real-world experience." However, while students appreciate the skill demonstrated by the senior faculty, many say they'd like to see more case studies, practical instruction, and contemporary theory integrated into the curriculum. For example, a student suggests the school provide more instruction in "accounting and computer application methods, especially for finance students."

St. John's offers the MBA program on their campus in Jamaica, Queens, and on a satellite campus on Staten Island. In addition, the School of Risk Management is located in the Financial District in Manhattan. No matter where you study, the "proximity to Manhattan" is definitely among the school's major selling points, putting students in position for jobs and internships at a wide range of companies. For those who aren't entirely focused on the Big Apple, the school operates an MBA program in Rome, Italy, with an evening class schedule geared towards part-time students. Students may complete their entire MA or MBA in Rome, or simply spend a semester abroad. With the increasing need for internationally trained business professionals, "having the opportunity to study abroad while pursuing an MBA" is another attractive aspect of a St. John's education.

Career and Placement

The Career Center at St. John's University helps students and alumni define and achieve their career goals through workshops, seminars, and campus recruiting events. Serving the entire St. John's community, the Career Center hosts industry-specific and broad-based career fairs and interview days on all three New York campuses. They also host a series of Saturday speakers, who discuss careers in various professional fields.

Among the greatest advantages to St. John's is the "proximity to NYC and the career opportunities that comes with it"; however, business students must also take a proactive approach to the career search if they want to land a plum position. A current student elaborates, "On one hand, you can do the bare minimum and still come out with your

ADMISSIONS CONTACT: SHEILA RUSSELL, ASSISTANT DIRECTOR OF MBA ADMISSIONS
ADDRESS: 8000 UTOPIA PARKWAY, 111 BENT HALL QUEENS, NY 11439
PHONE: 718-990-1345 • FAX: 718-990-5242
E-MAIL: MBAADMISSIONS@STJOHNS.EDU • WEBSITE: WWW.STJOHNS.EDU/TOBIN

MBA with a mediocre job waiting for you. While on the other, you can give it all you've got and come out of SJU with that amazing six-figure-to-start career."

At the Rome campus, the "career center staff [are] able to assist students that intend to remain and work in Italy upon graduation;" however, the university points out that Italian language skills are necessary for most jobs in Italy.

Student Life and Environment

St. John's University's main campus is located on 100 acres in Jamaica, Queens. The Queens campus is home to most of the university's facilities, including the library (which includes the business school's research collection) and athletic buildings. On all three New York campuses, St. John's attracts a largely local crowd, which reflects the diversity of the greater New York metropolitan area. While many students join the program with years of professional experience, "approximately 50–65 percent seem young (early to mid-20s) with little work experience but recent academic experience. This makes class discussion an interesting mix of theory and experience." Catering to the school's majority of part-time students, most classes are taught at night.

St. John's Italian campus boasts its share of attractions, most notably, its lovely European location. Plus, the smaller student body creates a laid-back and friendly atmosphere. A student at the Rome campus says, "Since there are only about 70–100 students total we are a very tight-knit group and extremely helpful whenever one is in need."

Admissions

To apply to the Tobin School of Business, students must submit official undergraduate transcripts, a current resume, and official GMAT scores, no more than five years old. Currently, the average GMAT score for accepted applicants is 530, and the average GPA is 3.2 on a 4.0 scale. An undergraduate business degree is not a pre-requisite of the program; in fact, 37 percent of current students joined the program from other major disciplines.

FINANCIAL FACTS

Annual tuition	$23,850
Fees	$250
Cost of books	$3,000
Room & board (on/off-campus)	$12,000/$15,000
% of students receiving aid	30
% of first-year students receiving aid	14
Average award package	$14,914
Average grant	$1,812

ADMISSIONS

Admissions Selectivity Rating	76
# of applications received	644
% applicants accepted	59
% acceptees attending	62
Average GMAT	530
Range of GMAT	440–630
Average GPA	3.2
TOEFL required of international students	Yes
Minimum TOEFL (paper)	580
Application fee	$40
International application fee	$40
Regular application deadline	6/1
Early decision program?	No
Deferment available	Yes
Maximum length of deferment	1 year
Transfer students accepted	Yes
Transfer application policy: Must use regular application. Individual review of transfer credits.	
Non-fall admissions	Yes
Need-blind admissions	Yes

EMPLOYMENT PROFILE

Career Rating	80	Top 5 Employers Hiring Grads
Average base starting salary	$68,000	Merrill Lynch, PricewaterhouseCoopers, Citigroup, Deloitte and Touche

ST. MARY'S UNIVERSITY
BILL GREEHEY SCHOOL OF BUSINESS

GENERAL INFORMATION

Type of school	Private
Affiliation	Roman Catholic
Academic calendar	Semester

SURVEY SAYS...

Solid preparation in:
Marketing.
Communication/interpersonal skills
Doing business in a global economy

STUDENTS

Enrollment of parent institution	3,893
Enrollment of MBA Program	38
% male/female	53/47
% part-time	69
% minorities	34
Average age at entry	27
Average years work experience at entry	3

ACADEMICS

Academic Experience Rating	**86**
Student/faculty ratio	10:1
Profs interesting rating	96
Profs accessible rating	89
% female faculty	36
% minority faculty	4

Prominent Alumni

Bill Greehey, Chairman, Nustar Energy, LP.

Academics

The MBA program at St. Mary's University's Bill Greehey School of Business offers innovative programs designed to graduate conscientious global business leaders. Comprehensive programs include a part-time MBA for full-time business professionals, a full-time one-year MBA, a five-year combined bachelor and master's degree and a joint JD/MBA degree. The MBA program advances the university's Marianist tradition of community service through courses in ethical leadership and corporate responsibility as well as a unique host of real-world experiential learning opportunities including: a student-managed investment portfolio; a Small Business Institute for local small and non-profit businesses through which the students offer in-depth consulting services; the opportunity to study foreign business models abroad in countries like Russia, Dubai, and Mongolia; or to be a volunteer federal income tax preparer for area residents through St. Mary's Volunteer Income Tax Assistance (VITA) program.

Prerequisites to MBA study at Greehey begin with the completion of six undergraduate-level fundamentals courses. Students arriving with undergraduate degrees in business can place out of these courses, as can students who demonstrate proficiency through CLEP and DANTES examinations. After completing or placing out of these fundamentals courses, students must complete a 30 semester-hour program that includes five core courses (in human resources, accounting/finance, international business, informational technology, and marketing). Tracks are offered in financial planning, professional accountancy and general management as well as a joint JD/MBA. (Note that the financial planning track requires two additional classes, meaning that students who choose this option must complete 36 semester hours to graduate.)

MBAs here praise the faculty for "focusing on teaching and understanding" and "providing real-life experience. They bring a lot of outside experience to the classroom." St. Mary's has always been known for its personal touches, and students confirm that "classes are small and the program as a whole is small. This allows for a lot of individual attention from professors and administrators." Students here appreciate this "laid-back program with not too much pressure" but wish that the administration was sometimes a little less laid back. They tell us that administrators "are very disorganized. They lose papers way too often."

Career and Placement

The Career Services Center at St. Mary's University serves all undergraduate students, graduate students, and alumni of the school. The office provides one-on-one advisement with career counselors, a library of career-related materials including hard-copy and online job search databases, special events (Resume Drive, Business Etiquette Dinner, Mock Interview Day), a career fair, and connections to an alumni mentoring program. Students tell us that "the strong alumni network" is one of the biggest attractions of a St. Mary's degree. Employers interviewing on the St. Mary's campus USAA; HEB; the San Antonio Spurs; Union Pacific; the CIA; Fishr, Herbst & Kemble; Enterprise Rent-A-Car; the American Red Cross, Tesoro Corporation, Valero, and NuStar Engergy.

ADMISSIONS CONTACT: DR. RICHARD MENGER, MBA PROGRAM DIRECTOR
ADDRESS: ONE CAMINO SANTA MARIA SAN ANTONIO, TX 78228-8507
PHONE: 210-436-3101 • FAX: 210-431-2220
E-MAIL: LBAGLEY@STMARYTX.EDU • WEBSITE: WWW.STMARYTX.EDU/MBA

FINANCIAL FACTS

Annual tuition	$20,700
Fees	$560
Cost of books	$1,300
Room & board	$8,072
% of students receiving grants	9
Average grant	$15,000

ADMISSIONS

Admissions Selectivity Rating	78
# of applications received	109
% applicants accepted	74
% acceptees attending	90
Average GMAT	565
Range of GMAT	525–670
Average GPA	3.31
TOEFL required of international students	Yes
Minimum TOEFL (paper/computer)	570/230
Early decision program?	Yes
ED Deadline/Notification	NR / 6/30
Deferment available	Yes
Maximum length of deferment	1 year
Transfer students accepted	Yes
Transfer application policy: On recommendation of the Graduate program director may accept a maximum of 6 semester hours from AACSB-accredited programs.	
Non-fall admissions	Yes
Need-blind admissions	Yes

Student Life and Environment

St. Mary's student body includes "many Hispanic women working toward improving their careers." The school has traditionally served the Hispanic community well; over half of all undergraduates here are Hispanic. On the whole, students "are diverse in age and cultures, all striving toward a common goal." Many "have careers and a family." Their classmates describe them as "team-oriented, hard-working, and friendly."

With over one million residents within city limits and almost as many living in the metropolitan area, San Antonio is the third-largest city in Texas and one of the larger cities in the country. The military and the petroleum industry both have major presences here. With nearly 20 million visitors every year, San Antonio is also a major player in the nation's tourism trade. Students speak highly of the city, although they warn that "the school is located in a very rough part of town."

Admissions

Applicants to the MBA program at St. Mary's must apply to the graduate school for admission. Applications are reviewed by the MBA program director, who makes recommendations to the Graduate Council. The council is then responsible for the final admissions decisions. Candidates must submit all of the following materials to the graduate admissions office: a completed application form; an official score report for the GMAT (additionally, candidates can submit GRE and LSAT scores for conditional admission); two sets of official transcripts for all postsecondary academic work; two letters of recommendation "from individuals well acquainted with your academic/professional ability" (graduates of St. Mary's University are exempt from this requirement); and a completed health form (required by Texas State Law). An interview may also be required; candidates for whom an interview is required will be notified by the school. International applicants must provide all of the above materials as well as a signed financial statement; and, an official score report for the TOEFL (minimum acceptable score: 570 paper-based, 230 computer-based, 67 Internet; students with lower TOEFL scores may be allowed to attend the English Language School in order to meet minimum language proficiency requirements). Admitted students may receive regular admission, which is unconditional. Students may also receive conditional admission, which allows them to enroll in no more than nine hours of classes, after which their admission status is reappraised; or they may receive special admission as a nondegree seeking student. They may also receive auditor status, which is a noncredit option for students who are not working toward a graduate business degree.

STANFORD UNIVERSITY
STANFORD GRADUATE SCHOOL OF BUSINESS

GENERAL INFORMATION
Type of school   Private
Academic calendar   Quarter

SURVEY SAYS...
Good social scene
Good peer network
Solid preparation in:
General management
Communication/interpersonal skills
Entrepreneurial studies

STUDENTS
Enrollment of parent
  institution   15,319
Enrollment of MBA Program   765
% male/female   66/34
% minorities   21
% international   33
Average years work experience
  at entry   4

ACADEMICS
Academic Experience Rating   99
Student/faculty ratio   6:1
Profs interesting rating   74
Profs accessible rating   80
% female faculty   18
% minority faculty   9

Joint Degrees
It is possible to earn dual degrees with any other Stanford University departments. Joint degrees offered for JD/MBA, MBA/MA in Education, MBA/MS in Environment and Resources, and MBA/MPP (public policy).

Prominent Alumni
Phil Knight, Founder and Chairman, Nike Inc.; Miles White, CEO and Chairman, Abbott Laboratories; Charles Schwab, Founder and Chairman, Charles Schwab & Co.; Jeffrey Bewkes, CEO and chairman, Time Warner; Ann Livermore, Executive Vice President, Hewlett-Packard Co.

Academics

Located in the "heart of the Silicon Valley," Stanford University's top-rated business school lives up to its "amazing reputation" for innovation and excellence. It's not just the California sunshine that sets Stanford apart; at this school, there is a strong "entrepreneurial spirit" among the faculty, students, and alumni. Here, "credibility [is] given to those who follow their passions," and accordingly, the MBA curriculum can be "tailored" to a student's individual interests (an arrangement well-suited to Stanford's "very self-directed" student body.) The school's "incredible curriculum" begins with Management Perspectives, including a 16-person seminar called Critical Analytical Thinking and core courses, called Management Foundations, which are completed during the first year. In the second year, students can choose from over 100 electives within the business school alone, and they can even take classes in other graduate departments at Stanford. Recently, to increase flexibility, "There was a change allowing students to opt out of some mandatory prerequisites to enable more first-years to take electives."

Stanford redesigned its MBA curriculum in 2007, and it has continued to make "some changes over the last two years" as it perfects the program. New Dean Garth Saloner was a chief architect of the curriculum and is now readying a new $350 million complex of buildings for spring 2011 move-in. Along with other developments, students note that, "The focus on global business has improved significantly." Now, global perspectives are incorporated across the curriculum, and every Stanford student is required to complete an international experience through the Global Management Program (GMP.) Among other options, the GMP offers immersion experiences and global study trips to current students, while also overseeing a global speaker series on campus. At home, students benefit from Stanford's deep ties in the local business community. Through its active alumni network and extensive corporate contacts, "The school provides amazing opportunities for close interaction with leaders in a variety of fields." There are ample pro-bono consulting projects, board memberships, and other real-world opportunities for Stanford students to get advanced exposure to business. Students also note Stanford's historic "strength in non-profit business." The school's Public Management Program offers 20-30 electives in non-profit management, social entrepreneurship, social responsibility, and related topics.

Academically, the Stanford experience is first-rate, defined by "outstanding classes" and "distinguished professors." Various teaching methods—including group projects, role-playing, case studies, simulations, and more—are crucial to the classroom experience. For example, "The Leadership Labs program, a required class in the first year, is a great way for students to practice leadership in an experiential setting." While "academic pressure" is intense, "Professors are easily accessible and happy to help with class projects." Administrators get mixed reviews, with some describing them as "very bureaucratic," while others say they are "open to ideas and student input."

Career and Placement

Stanford GSB's robust Career Management Center offers personal career advising, resume and cover letter preparation, alumni mentoring and networking opportunities, company presentations, career workshops, and job fairs. While placement is rarely an issue for Stanford graduates, one of the greatest benefits to job seekers is the school's "amazingly helpful alums, who feel a close connection to the school and go out of their way to help current students." The excellent "proximity to high-tech firms" is a major advantage for those who want to stay in the area.

Over 2,100 organizations recruit Stanford MBA candidates through career fairs, job postings, and online resume services. Leading employers include Amazon.com, Abbott, Apple, Bain & Company, Booz & Company, Boston Consulting Group, Cisco Systems, Dell, Education Pioneers, Goldman Sachs, Johnson & Johnson, Intel, Google, Hulu, IDEO, NBC Universal, U.S. Government, Nike, VMware, Walt Disney Co., Warner Bros., and many more. More than 75 percent of Stanford business students made a change of industry or job function after the MBA. For recent graduating classes, the median base salary for graduating MBAs was $120,000, with a range between $30,000 and $250,000.

Student Life and Environment

Drawing students from a wide range of industries and backgrounds, Stanford attracts "interesting, fun, and friendly" people, who walk that fine line between over-achieving and easygoing. At Stanford, you'll sit shoulder-to-shoulder with "intensely accomplished classmates who somehow still remain down-to-earth." Despite diversity, the atmosphere is "very inclusive," and most students are "not afraid to voice their opinion even if it is likely to be different from the opinions of others." Within the graduate business program, the "close-knit atmosphere" encourages relationships both in and out of the classroom. Even the faculty and staff are accessible and friendly. At Stanford, "It is frequent to have professors and deans over to student's houses for dinner to discuss business, politics or life choices."

Set in Northern California, Stanford students bask in "mood-alteringly gorgeous weather" and spend their days on a beautiful, well-equipped campus. Current students note that the "campus buildings are outdated" within the business school—but not for long. The new campus will be a huge asset. It will include eight buildings around three quads, an auditorium, dining pavilion, study rooms, and classrooms for hands-on cross-disciplinary courses with other Stanford schools like engineering and medicine.

Admissions

Admission to Stanford is selective. Prospective students are evaluated in three areas: intellectual vitality, demonstrated leadership potential, and personal qualities and contributions. In short, Stanford is looking for outstanding candidates who will fit into the school's "innovative environment." With such subjective parameters (school officials say admissions is an art, not a science), it is not surprising that Stanford does not have any minimum GMAT score or GPA requirements. Current students have a GMAT range from 540-800, with a median score of 730.

FINANCIAL FACTS

Annual tuition	$53,118
Cost of books	$3,789
Room & board (on/off-campus)	$21,222/$25,395
% of students receiving aid	66
% of first-year students receiving aid	79
% of students receiving loans	61
% of students receiving grants	54
Average award package	$50,853
Average grant	$20,644
Average student loan debt	$75,442

ADMISSIONS

Admissions Selectivity Rating	99
# of applications received	7,536
% applicants accepted	7
Average GMAT	726
Range of GMAT	540–800
Average GPA	3.6
TOEFL required of international students	Yes
Minimum TOEFL (paper/computer)	600/250
Application fee	$265
International application fee	$265
Application Deadline/Notification	
Round 1:	10/19 / 12/16
Round 2:	1/10 / 3/31
Round 3:	4/10 / 5/19
Early decision program?	No
Deferment available	Yes
Maximum length of deferment	very limited
Transfer students accepted	No
Non-fall admissions	No
Need-blind admissions	Yes

Applicants Also Look At
Harvard University

EMPLOYMENT PROFILE

Career Rating	99	
Percent employed at graduation	69	
Percent employed 3 months after graduation	85	
Average base starting salary	$118,384	

Primary Source of Full-time Job Acceptances

School-facilitated activities	99 (42%)
Graduate-facilitated activities	112 (48%)
No response from grad	23 (10%)

Grads Employed by Function% Avg. Salary

Marketing	22 $104,660
Operations	2 $95,250
Consulting	32 $119,795
Management	4 $130,625
Finance	30 $132,171
Strategic	5 $106,500

Top 5 Employers Hiring Grads
Apple, Boston Consulting Group, Cisco, McKinsey, Morgan Stanley

STATE UNIVERSITY OF NEW YORK AT BINGHAMTON
SCHOOL OF MANAGEMENT

GENERAL INFORMATION
Type of school	Public
Academic calendar	Semester

SURVEY SAYS...
Smart classrooms
Solid preparation in:
General management
Teamwork
Presentation skills
Computer skills

STUDENTS
Enrollment of parent institution	14,711
Enrollment of MBA Program	106
% male/female	66/34
% out-of-state	3
% part-time	8
% minorities	1
% international	49
Average age at entry	23
Average years work experience at entry	1

ACADEMICS
Academic Experience Rating	**84**
Student/faculty ratio	6:1
Profs interesting rating	80
Profs accessible rating	80
% female faculty	23

Joint Degrees
Watson (School of Engineering)/MBA Fast Track 5 years (Bachelors+MBA); Harpur (College of Arts & Sciences)/MBA Fast Track 5 years (Bachelors+MBA)

Prominent Alumni
Mark Deutsch, Partner/Private Equity; Anthony Kendall, CEO/Accounting; Gary Meltzer, U.S. Advisory Leader/Investment Mgmt & Real Estate; Mark Zurack, Retired Managing Director/Finance; Allen Zwickler, Managing Director/Finance.

Academics

"Close proximity to New York City," an "excellent reputation in New York and elsewhere" (not just for the MBA program but for the entire school, as "SUNY has a worldwide reputation"), and a "small incoming class with a diverse population" that ensures students won't get lost in the crowd are among the top reasons students give for choosing the MBA program at Binghamton University. It also doesn't hurt that it "all comes with an extremely reasonable price tag."

The four-semester MBA program at Binghamton University employs "an extremely team-based approach" to education "that replicates real-world business in a way many other business programs do not," students here inform us. This is especially true in the first year, during which the program covers core essentials. One student explains, "The first year of the program requires students to stick with a set group of students to work on projects, presentations, papers, and cases. It can be difficult at times, but the lessons learned are crucial for the real world." Students also feel that "the cohort teams are really good for discussing with prospective employers, as it shows the ability to work together with many diverse people to come to one end result." The school also offers a Fast Track MBA to Binghamton undergraduates; the program allows them to earn both a BA and an MBA in five years, no small feat considering that a Binghamton MBA requires 69 credits, "more than any other university."

For a state school, BU provides excellent service. Students tell us that "The school really tries to adapt to the latest management concepts and ideals" and that administrators "continually make improvements to meet all of our needs." Professors here "want to see their students succeed and are happy to give the time to help them with any hardship they may face in the MBA program." The only knock on them is that "Many are foreign," so that "sometimes it is difficult to understand what is being said due to accents." Most often, however, instructors "can communicate easily with the students, and they do not use their native language even when conversing with students from the same country, which is very professional." Another asset to the program is that "the alumni that are in highly respected companies are great, and everyone really tries to pull for other Binghamton students."

Career and Placement

For a small program, Binghamton does a good job of bringing some major recruiters to its relatively remote location. One student informs us that "we have powerhouse recruiters from Credit Suisse, Goldman Sachs, the big four accounting, all the engineering firms, as well as many others. Without question the recruiting at this school is on an incredible climb upwards. More and more powerhouse companies are coming to Binghamton, who in the past have not." The Career Development Center here offers counseling services, career workshops, resume-development services, resume-referral services, a career-resource library, and access to the alumni network.

Top employers of Binghamton MBAs include Ernst & Young, Deloitte, KPMG, Lockheed Martin, and Target. Ninety percent of all graduates remain in the Middle Atlantic States or New England.

ADMISSIONS CONTACT: ALESIA WHEELER-WADE, ASSISTANT DIRECTOR MBA/MS PROGRAMS
ADDRESS: SCHOOL OF MANAGEMENT, P.O. BOX 6000 BINGHAMTON, NY 13902-6000
PHONE: 607-777-2317 • FAX: 607-777-4872
E-MAIL: SOMADVIS@BINGHAMTON.EDU • WEBSITE: SOM.BINGHAMTON.EDU

Student Life and Environment

"First-year classes for the fall are all held in the evenings" at Binghamton, which "leads to very long days, especially for those who also have part-time jobs" and thus hampers extracurricular involvement. As students progress through the program, however, the school offers "many opportunities for interested students to get involved, from the GSO (Graduate Student Organization) to the GMA (Graduate Management Association)." The latter "implements various activities throughout the year: coffee hours, open bars, networking events," "horseback riding, bowling, etc." The university also "has a great Division I athletic department that provides exciting competitions for the students to attend," and many do.

The city of Binghamton "has lots of things going for it besides the downtown bar scene. For one thing there is a hometown hockey team and baseball team, an opera house, numerous playhouses, and theaters, too. We are also the carousel capital of the United States. Binghamton is ethnically diverse as well, there are often ethnic festivals going on throughout the Southern Tier. Plus if you are a golf fan, we were home to a PGA tour event for 35 years, and now we are home to a Champions Tour Event." Also, "living expenses here are not much," especially when compared to the cost of living in much of the rest of the state.

Admissions

Applicants to the Binghamton MBA program must submit two copies of official undergraduate transcripts for all college work, two letters of recommendation, a personal statement, a resume, and GMAT scores. Work experience, while preferred, is not required. Additionally, international students must submit a certified statement of financial responsibility and TOEFL scores (minimum acceptable score is 580). A basic understanding of calculus is "strongly recommended" for all incoming students; strong calculus skills are necessary for those interested in studying finance or operations management.

To attract minority applicants, the School of Management offers the Clifford D. Clark Graduate Fellowship Program for Underrepresented Minority Students. According to the school, "These fellowships are granted to students entering both master's and doctoral degree programs and carry stipends of between $6,800 and $12,750 (depending on discipline) for the academic year plus a full-tuition scholarship. Renewals or graduate assistantships may be awarded in subsequent years, depending upon availability of funds."

FINANCIAL FACTS

Annual tuition (in-state/ out-of-state)	$8,610/$13,760
Fees	$1,180
Cost of books	$750
Room & board (off-campus)	$6,800

ADMISSIONS

Admissions Selectivity Rating	87
# of applications received	201
% applicants accepted	53
% acceptees attending	47
Average GMAT	626
Range of GMAT	600–650
Average GPA	3.43
TOEFL required of international students	Yes
Minimum TOEFL (paper/computer)	590/243
Application fee	$60
International application fee	$60
Regular application deadline	3/1
Early decision program?	No
Deferment available	Yes
Maximum length of deferment	1 year
Transfer students accepted	No
Non-fall admissions	No
Need-blind admissions	Yes

EMPLOYMENT PROFILE

Career Rating	89	Grads Employed by Function	%	Avg. Salary
Percent employed at graduation	41	Operations	19	$56,666
Average base starting salary	$54,818	Consulting	19	$53,333
Primary Source of Full-time Job Acceptances		Management	12	$32,950
School-facilitated activities	7 (28%)	Finance	38	$58,900
Graduate-facilitated activities	17 (68%)	**Top 5 Employers Hiring Grads**		
Unknown	1 (4%)	Ernst & Young (3),		
		PricewaterhouseCoopers (3), Lockheed		
		Martin (2), Deloitte (1), BAE Systems (1)		

STATE UNIVERSITY OF NEW YORK—OSWEGO
SCHOOL OF BUSINESS

GENERAL INFORMATION
Type of school   Public
Academic calendar   Semester

SURVEY SAYS...
Good peer network
Cutting-edge classes
Solid preparation in:
Accounting
General management

STUDENTS

Enrollment of parent institution	8,909
Enrollment of MBA Program	62
% male/female	66/34
% out-of-state	3
% part-time	29
% minorities	7
% international	13
Average age at entry	29

ACADEMICS

Academic Experience Rating	**84**
Student/faculty ratio	19:1
Profs interesting rating	85
Profs accessible rating	74
% female faculty	11
% minority faculty	22

Prominent Alumni
Al Roker, NBC Meteorologist; Alice McDermott, Award Winning Author; Ken Auleta, New Yorker Columnist & critically acclaimed author; Kendis Gibson, CNN Anchor; Heraldo Munoz, Ambassador of Chile to the United Nations.

Academics

Students who enroll in the School of Business at SUNY Oswego can expect several things: excellent value for their money, intimate classes, knowledgeable professors, state-of-the-art facilities, and an excellent hockey team. As one student puts it, "In most areas, the school of business is at the top of its class. The classes are challenging and worthwhile. Most professors are really good at their areas. They are also widely available to help students both inside and out of class," and "really want to see the students succeed." According to most of the students, the "very small classes promote learning and student-professor interaction." The program "provides a lot of hands-on work and team activities to help form a strong work ethic" among students.

Designed as a degree in general management, an MBA from SUNY Oswego provides a solid grounding in the basics of modern business organization. The school says that "this program is intended to be equally applicable to private, public, and governmental sectors of management." The foundation subjects required of students include management, accounting, marketing, organization, law, and finance. In addition, students can choose to specialize in a specific field such as international management, manufacturing management, organizational leadership, or financial services. Foundation course requirements include management information systems, managerial finance, marketing management, management science I, international business, global perspectives on organizational management, and management policy. Students have a choice of taking classes at the Oswego Campus, at the Metro Center in downtown Syracuse and online. In addition to general management electives, students can also specialize in accounting. Students in the accounting track can gain professional experience by participating in the Volunteer Income Tax Assistance (VITA) program. Students interested in finance can spend a semester at the Levin Institute's International Finance and Global Banking in New York City.

Students find their coursework both rigorous and exciting. As one puts it, "the professors are excellent and the classes are fun and challenging." Another says, "the course load is challenging, requiring solid communication and organization skills." Fortunately, the student body as a whole is "reliable and helpful." "We help each other out in our classes. I think the students in the graduate program really create a bond with one another."

ADMISSIONS CONTACT: DAVID W. KING, DEAN GRADUATE STUDIES
ADDRESS: 502 CULKIN HALL, SUNY OSWEGO OSWEGO, NY 13126
PHONE: 315-312-3692 • FAX: 315-312-3577
E-MAIL: MBA@OSWEGO.EDU • WEBSITE: WWW.OSWEGO.EDU/BUSINESS/MBA

Career and Placement

Although Oswego has a lot to offer—lovely campus, low cost, quality education, intimate program—most students wish it would go further in strengthening its Career Services department. There is little aid specifically for prospective MBAs, and the job search is often directed almost entirely by the student. As one puts it, "Connecting with employers is a difficult task. Linking up with quality employers looking for graduates with postgraduate degrees needs to be addressed." The exception is accounting, which has numerous national and regional public accounting firms actively recruiting throughout the year.

Student Life and Environment

Students say their "classmates are very intelligent. They provide a lot of feedback to one another, work well together, and create a competitive environment which prepares people for the job market." All rave about their "beautiful campus," which, they proudly point out, is also extremely "technologically-advanced and mostly wireless." The typical MBA's social life is strong, and there are "plenty of bars around for an active nightlife." As one student says, "At Oswego, I had the opportunity to make new friends from all over the world. The social life is active and I consider myself lucky." For the most part, students claim to be "very active on campus. There is a multitude of clubs and organizations to choose from." Students enjoy their "great gyms to work out in or play a game of racquetball." Plus—as is typical in upstate New York—the school's athletic life centers on their "excellent hockey team, instead of football." As one student puts it, "what's excellent about living on campus here is that there is every resource that you could possibly need available on campus. There are new buildings and renovations, from a new student center to the newly renovated freshman residence hall and new business center with technology classrooms."

Admissions

To be considered for admission to the small MBA program at the School of Business at SUNY Oswego, a candidate must have a minimum GPA of 2.6 out of 4.0. The minimum required score for the GMAT is 490. Taking the TOEFL test is also required for students whose native language is not English.

FINANCIAL FACTS

Annual tuition (in-state/ out-of-state)	$8,110/$13,760
Fees	$798
Cost of books	$800
Room & board	$12,370
% of students receiving aid	73
% of first-year students receiving aid	100
% of students receiving loans	73
% of students receiving grants	21
Average award package	$22,499
Average grant	$738
Average student loan debt	$32,560

ADMISSIONS

Admissions Selectivity Rating	81
# of applications received	62
% applicants accepted	69
% acceptees attending	67
Average GMAT	558
Range of GMAT	450–620
Average GPA	3.35
TOEFL required of international students	Yes
Minimum TOEFL (paper/computer)	560/220
Application fee	$50
Regular application deadline	4/15
Regular notification	6/1
Early decision program?	No
Deferment available	Yes
Maximum length of deferment	1 year
Transfer students accepted	Yes
Transfer application policy: Two courses may be accepted for transfer into the program.	
Non-fall admissions	Yes
Need-blind admissions	Yes

EMPLOYMENT PROFILE

Career Rating	78	Grads Employed by Function	% Avg. Salary
Average base starting salary	$38,000	Operations	10 NR
		Management	5 NR
		Finance	10 $38,000
		HR	5 NR
		MIS	5 NR
		Nonprofit	10 NR
		Quantitative	5 NR

STATE UNIVERSITY OF NEW YORK—UNIVERSITY AT ALBANY
SCHOOL OF BUSINESS

GENERAL INFORMATION
Type of school   Public
Academic calendar   Sept–May

SURVEY SAYS...
Solid preparation in:
Marketing
Accounting
Operations
Computer skills

STUDENTS
Enrollment of parent institution	17,000
Enrollment of MBA Program	286
% male/female	31/69
% out-of-state	16
% part-time	77
% minorities	31
% international	16
Average age at entry	28
Average years work experience at entry	3

ACADEMICS
Academic Experience Rating	72
Student/faculty ratio	28:1
Profs interesting rating	76
Profs accessible rating	70
% female faculty	27

Joint Degrees
Master of Science, Nanoscale Engineering and Nanotechnology/MBA (2 years), JD/MBA.

Prominent Alumni
Kimberly Welsh, Managing Director, Morgan Stanley; Dale Carleton, Vice Chairman, Retired, State Street Corporation; Steve Rotella, President and CEO, Chase Manhattan Mortgage Corp.; Harold Cramer, VP, ExxonMobil Fuels; Anthony McCarthy, Global CIO-Investment Banking, Deutsche Bank.

Academics

Students praise "the diversity of options" available at the State University of New York at Albany's School of Business. In addition to a full-time program, the school offers an evening-based part-time program, and "a special executive-weekend program is offered offsite in Clifton Park." Not surprisingly, most students list convenience high among the school's assets. Part timers note that "the program is great for someone who is working. It is challenging but realistic"; while weekend students appreciate how "the convenience of alternative weekend classes helps me to manage work and home responsibilities."

Albany's full-time program takes two years to complete. The first year is dedicated to core competencies; students undertake in-depth study in accounting, economics, finance, human resources, management, information systems, and marketing. Case studies play a central role in classroom study, as do reading assignments and classes that divide time between lectures and discussions. Group projects supplement the curriculum and offer students opportunities to develop important teamwork skills. The first year culminates in a one-week integrative course that addresses social, legal, and political issues in international business. According to students, the first-year curriculum "is heavily weighted toward global business and the changing economy."

The second year of the full-time program—which also allows students to develop an area of specialization—focuses on technology, an area in which Albany excels. Students' work in this area reaches its high point in an information systems-based field project during which students provide consulting services to such organizations as the Albany Medical Center, DuPont, GE, KeyCorp, PepsiCo, Tiffany & Co., Towers Perrin, and a variety of regional nonprofits. The field project consumes one-third of the second-year curriculum, with a hands-on approach that prepares students for full-time employment.

Career and Placement

Albany's School of Business maintains its own Career Services Office, whose work is supplemented by the school's Career Development Center, which serves the entire university. The Career Services Office provides workshops on cover letter-writing, resume writing, interviewing, developing job-search skills, and honing business-related social skills. MBAs who graduate from Albany receive job offers from many small and medium-sized businesses as well as from such business giants as Accenture, CPI, Deloitte Consulting, Deutsche Bank, Ernst & Young, Goldman Sachs, IBM, KPMG, and PricewaterhouseCoopers. Even so, some feel the school could do better; "If we could get better national recognition, we might be able to offer more employment recruiting from leading companies and firms," one student writes. The school reports that more than half of its graduates are placed in consulting positions (average starting salary: $60,0000). About 13 percent find work in finance and accounting (average starting salary: $55,000).

Student Life and Environment

Albany MBAs are a "generally diverse group" with "many engineers seeking the MBA" (and probably more to come, given the "growing technology/IT department" and the students it attracts). "It's curious that there are not as many business-based students [as engineers]," one student observes. These "friendly, goal-oriented," "highly motivated" students include "older professionals with work experience." The program also draws "many international students and a variety of ethnicities. All are social, helpful, and hard-working." One student sums up: "Our population is very diverse and really serves as a great way to learn about and interact with people of other backgrounds."

Most students attend this program part time while also attending to full-time jobs, family, etc. Accordingly, they have little time for non-academic school activities. Full-timers are also kept busy with "a big load between classes and internships," but some still manage to find time for "Division I sports, clubs, activities, and community involvement." MBA facilities include classrooms and computer labs equipped with the latest high-tech accoutrements; these serve the program's focus on technology well. the school will break ground on a new facility in 2010, but students complain that the current buildings should be spruced up a bit. The buildings are old and unattractive."

Nearly 17,000 students are enrolled in the nine degree-granting schools and colleges at the State University of New York at Albany. Like all large state universities, it pursues the mission of offering an affordable education to state residents while also providing the state and country with cutting-edge research. The university was founded in 1844; undergraduate business study was not added to the curriculum until 1970. Graduate business programs began a few years later.

Admissions

Applicants to the MBA program at the State University of New York at Albany School of Business must provide the graduate admissions department with all of the following: official copies of transcripts for all postsecondary academic work, an official score report for the GMAT, a resume, three letters of recommendation, a personal statement of purpose, and a completed application. International applicants whose undergraduate degrees were earned at non-English language institutions must provide all of the above plus an official score report for the TOEFL (minimum acceptable score: 580 paper-based; 450 computer-based); must submit a financial affidavit accompanied by appropriate supporting documentation to demonstrate the applicant's "ability to meet all educational and living expenses for the entire period of intended study"; and, must past a SPEAK test during orientation. Furthermore, international academic transcripts in languages other than English must be accompanied by a certified English translation.

FINANCIAL FACTS

Annual tuition (in-state/ out-of-state)	$8,610/$13,760
Fees (in-state/ out-of-state)	$1,173/$1,253
Cost of books	$1,000
Room & board (on/off-campus)	$9,900/$8,250
% of students receiving aid	30
% of first-year students receiving aid	30
% of students receiving grants	30
Average award package	$7,650
Average grant	$3,550

ADMISSIONS

Admissions Selectivity Rating	**75**
# of applications received	244
% applicants accepted	90
% acceptees attending	53
Average GMAT	575
Range of GMAT	550–660
Average GPA	3.24
TOEFL required of international students	Yes
Minimum TOEFL (paper/computer)	600/250
Application fee	$75
International application fee	$75
Regular application deadline	5/1
Regular notification	6/1
Early decision program?	No
Deferment available	Yes
Maximum length of deferment	1 year
Transfer students accepted	Yes
Transfer application policy: We accept up to 50% transfer credit in each program of study.	
Non-fall admissions	Yes
Need-blind admissions	Yes

EMPLOYMENT PROFILE

Career Rating	78	Grads Employed by Function	% Avg. Salary
Percent employed at graduation	63	Operations	2 $65,000
Percent employed 3 months after graduation	21	Consulting	52 $60,000
		Management	13 $55,000
Average base starting salary	$54,083	Finance	13 $55,000
Primary Source of Full-time Job Acceptances		HR	13 $50,000
School-facilitated activities	NR (43%)	MIS	7 $60,000
Graduate-facilitated activities	NR (57%)	**Top 5 Employers Hiring Grads**	
		Ernst & Young (2), KPMG (2), Deloitte & Touche (1), General Electric (1), Lockheed Martin (1)	

State University of New York—University at Buffalo
School of Management

GENERAL INFORMATION

Type of school	Public
Academic calendar	Semester

SURVEY SAYS...
Solid preparation in:
Teamwork
Communication/interpersonal skills
Presentation skills
Quantitative skills

STUDENTS

Enrollment of parent	
institution	28,192
Enrollment of MBA Program	429
% male/female	68/32
% out-of-state	4
% part-time	55
% minorities	7
% international	26
Average age at entry	24
Average years work experience	
at entry	2

ACADEMICS

Academic Experience Rating	84
Student/faculty ratio	9:1
Profs interesting rating	74
Profs accessible rating	83
% female faculty	29
% minority faculty	3

Joint Degrees
JD/MBA; MD/MBA;
Architecture/MBA; Pharmacy/MBA;
Geography/MBA; BS/MBA Business
or Engineering; MBA/MSW;
AuD/MBA; MBA/MPH.

Prominent Alumni
Robert W. Black, Group President,
Kimberly-Clark Corp.; Jeremy
Jacobs Sr., CEO, Delaware North
Cos.; Millard S. Drexler, Chairman
and CEO, J.Crew Group, Inc.; John
Q. Doyle, Pres., American Home
Assurance Co. (an AIG Co.).

Academics

Offering AASCB-accredited graduate programs since the 1930s, the University at Buffalo's School of Management has a long history of excellence, operating both a full-time and part-time MBA, as well as a 22-month executive MBA for seasoned professionals. The academic programs are "very well-organized" and "the school does a great job of emphasizing 'management' as an underlying factor in each course" in the core curriculum. While covering business fundamentals like finance and marketing, the curriculum moves ahead with the times, and "Courses are constantly updated and altered to reflect real-world experience based on current events." Unfortunately, not every course is up to speed. In the required ethics course, a student recollects, "We talked about ethics as if it was some abstract moral issue, while ignoring tough practical questions that a manager might face today." Getting a strong practical perspective isn't a problem, though: UB compliments the academic offerings with "great opportunities outside the classroom," including "professional speakers, networking events, country forums, [and] community service," as well as case competitions and special offerings, like "marketing projects with GM or Smart Car USA." To further augment the curriculum, UB operates several formal exchange programs with business schools overseas, as well as shorter "trips to China for international business classes."

Despite the affordable tuition and high enrollment, UB offers a "smaller, more intimate MBA experience" with an "emphasis on teamwork and leadership skills" throughout the curriculum. Within each incoming class, full-time students are divided into fixed cohorts then assigned to a fixed study group of five to six students. "Group meetings outside of class require a lot of time and commitment" and can be among the most challenging aspects of the program. A student elaborates, "The curriculum is difficult and pushes students to their limits in all realms, especially in regards to working in a team environment with people you may not know to start out or who have very different perspectives than you." Despite the challenges, the focus on teamwork "simulates the real world" and "provides for a great learning environment." A student admits, "I have created a great network here, both with the students, professors, alums and other community members." Adds another, "The students are all very close and the faculty and administration are extremely involved." While the environment is friendly, the teaching staff can be "hit and miss" in the classroom, and some professors are universally disliked. Fortunately, "professors are very good overall" and "many are leaders in [their] fields." Even more importantly, "The professors have been great and are always accessible if needed, whether...after class, during weekly office hours, or by setting up a special time to meet."

Career and Placement

At UB, career planning begins—quite literally—the moment you step on campus. As a requirement of graduation, all students must complete the MBA Advantage, a comprehensive professional development program in August before your first year (with additional sessions in January and September.) In addition to the MBA Advantage, the Frank L. Ciminelli Family Career Resource Center (CRC) helps students prepare for the job hunt through career development workshops, mock interviews, career advising and more. The CRC also hosts various networking and recruiting events to link current students with local employers and alumni. UB is "very well-known in Western New York," and students benefit from the school's "great reputation and strong regional recruiting" program. For those who plan to stay in the area, UB has a "strong alumni network, especially locally."

In recent years, MBA graduates report an average base salary of more than $58,000, with a range between $41,000 and $90,000. Sixty percent of students were employed within three months of graduation. More than half the class took positions in Western New York, with another 17 percent landing jobs in downstate New York. Over the past few years, the top employers of MBA graduates include M&T Bank, Citigroup, BAE Systems, Deloitte & Touche, Independent Health, Toys R Us, Amgen, IBM, Lockheed Martin, Corning, Freed Maxick & Battaglia, Capital One, PriceWaterhouseCoopers, Ernst & Young, and KPMG, among others.

Student Life and Environment

Group work is an integral part of the UB curriculum and for many, "the variety of students from varying backgrounds/majors" and "The great presence of international students from all around the world make this academic experience tremendous both in and out of class." While teamwork can be challenging, "Everybody gets along well and builds great relationships." Throughout the MBA, "classes are all in one building," a recently completed facility, complete with high-tech classrooms, conference rooms, breakout rooms, and a cafe. With everything concentrated into one space, "it has become like a family atmosphere." Unfortunately for MBA candidates, the building is "often monopolized by the very large undergraduate student population in the school of management."

Outside of course work, many full-time students are involved in extracurricular activities, like case competitions, student clubs, and special programs like "alternative spring break events." The most active campus club, the Graduate Management Association hosts happy hours and daytrips, among other activities. On campus, "Frequent student-focused events are held, including a formal dinner with students and faculty [at] the end of each semester, in addition to charity drives and social events." A great place to call home, "Buffalo is a small city, but many of the students are from the area and know where the hangouts are."

Admissions

In 2007, SUNY University at Buffalo reduced [its] MBA class size by almost a third, limiting enrollment to 100 and imposing more stringent admissions standards on the incoming class. There are no minimum GMAT score requirements for entry into UB's MBA program; a student's full background is considered when making an admission's decision.

FINANCIAL FACTS

Annual tuition (in-state/ out-of-state)	$8,110/$13,760
Fees (in-state/ out-of-state)	$2,414/$2,500
Cost of books	$1,627
Room & board	$9,300
% of students receiving aid	25
% of first-year students receiving aid	20
% of students receiving grants	25
Average award package	$14,000
Average grant	$5,000

ADMISSIONS

Admissions Selectivity Rating	88
# of applications received	405
% applicants accepted	44
% acceptees attending	49
Average GMAT	619
Range of GMAT	580–650
Average GPA	3.43
TOEFL required of international students	Yes
Minimum TOEFL (paper/computer)	573/230
Application fee	$75
International application fee	$75
Application Deadline/Notification	
Round 1:	11/20 / 12/20
Round 2:	2/1 / 2/26
Round 3:	3/12 / 4/9
Round 4:	4/9 / 4/30
Round 5:	5/21 / 6/4
Early decision program?	No
Deferment available	Yes
Maximum length of deferment	1 year
Transfer students accepted	No
Non-fall admissions	No
Need-blind admissions	Yes

EMPLOYMENT PROFILE

Career Rating	84	Grads Employed by Function	% Avg. Salary
Percent employed at graduation	49	Marketing	19 $50,367
Percent employed 3 months after graduation	60	Operations	12 $58,460
		Finance	65 $60,727
Average base starting salary	$58,132	HR	2 NR
Primary Source of Full-time Job Acceptances		MIS	2 $51,600
School-facilitated activities	23 (55%)	Top 5 Employers Hiring Grads	
Graduate-facilitated activities	19 (45%)	M&T Bank (6), Citi (4), BAE Systems (2), Delloitte (2), Toys R Us (2)	

STETSON UNIVERSITY
SCHOOL OF BUSINESS ADMINISTRATION

GENERAL INFORMATION
Type of school	Private
Academic calendar	Semester

SURVEY SAYS...
Solid preparation in:
Finance
Accounting
Doing business in a global economy

STUDENTS
Enrollment of parent institution	2,800
Enrollment of MBA Program	204
% male/female	57/43
% out-of-state	24
% part-time	31
% minorities	17
% international	5
Average age at entry	26
Average years work experience at entry	2

ACADEMICS
Academic Experience Rating	**79**
Student/faculty ratio	15:1
Profs interesting rating	81
Profs accessible rating	86
% female faculty	25
% minority faculty	4

Joint Degrees
MBA/JD 3 Years

Academics

Stetson University offers fast-paced MBA programs for working professionals on three of its four central Florida campuses. In broad strokes, the Stetson MBA is divided into the following areas: foundational course work (or prerequisite courses), advanced course work, and electives. Stetson's is a general MBA, so students do not have the option of selecting an area of concentration; however, they can tailor their education through elective courses in fields like decision science, finance, management, information technology, and marketing. In addition, the MBA International Summer Program gives students the opportunity to spend two or four weeks overseas, where they tour local companies, meet with executives, and learn about the culture (current destinations include Austria, Italy, Germany, or China). Throughout the MBA course work, professors emphasize case studies and real world applications, giving students important skills they can take back to the workplace.

Depending on your location, Stetson offers the MBA degree on their main campus in DeLand, as well as on their auxiliary campuses in Celebration (Orlando) and Gulfport. In all locations, the school offers a "great class schedule" for working professionals, with MBA courses offered once a week in the evenings. While Stetson's flexible MBA allows students to take as many courses as fit their schedule, the "accelerated program" is both fast and efficient. Students who have already fulfilled the prerequisites can complete the program in just over a year by attending full-time. Even part-time students often finish the entire MBA in just two years of study. (Stetson will review an applicant's undergraduate transcript to estimate how many prerequisite courses are required; often, students with an undergraduate degree in business are required to complete fewer courses.) In addition to the traditional MBA, Stetson offers a challenging, cohort-based, 51-credit hour MBA for executives (more than four years of work experience is required for this program) on the school's Celebration campus. The school also offers a joint MBA/JD at Gulfport, which can be completed at lightening speed: just three years for both degrees, start to finish.

A recommendation in itself, many students come to Stetson's graduate business program after completing their undergraduate degree at the college. Indeed, Stetson's graduate programs retain many of the qualities—like intimacy and friendliness—that define the undergraduate experience. A particular advantage, the Stetson MBA is a relatively small program, giving students excellent access to their professors, and an emphasis on "one-on-one discussions." Even more importantly, "the professors are excellent and outstanding mentors on campus," providing insight and support to their students. While many professors are accomplished professionals, they are "dedicated to the educational services, not busy with their own research." Course delivery is in-person (not online), but professors incorporate technology, using Blackboard software to post syllabi, assignments, grades, and, occasionally, discussion forums online.

ADMISSIONS CONTACT: DR. FRED AUGUSTINE, DIRECTOR, GRADUATE BUSINESS PROGRAMS
ADDRESS: 421 NORTH WOODLAND BOULEVARD, UNIT 8398 DELAND, FL 32723
PHONE: 386-822-7410 • FAX: 386-822-7413
E-MAIL: MBA@STETSON.EDU • WEBSITE: WWW.STETSON.EDU/BUSINESS

Career and Placement

Stetson's campuses are located throughout central Florida, keeping students close to the job markets in Orlando, Daytona Beach, and St. Petersburg. The university operates a Career Services Office on the main campus, open to current students and alumni. Students can sign up for individual counseling appointments, or they may attend career-related events, such as skills presentations, expert speakers, or on-campus interviews. Most services are directed towards the undergraduate community. All things considered, Stetson's placement programs aren't as robust as at other MBA programs; however, Stetson's MBA is designed for working professionals who are hoping to advance in their current positions, rather than those looking for a new position.

Student Life and Environment

With a convenient evening course schedule and several campus locations, Stetson attracts many "working professionals who are striving to advance their careers." On the whole, these students comprise a "very driven group," who are "goal-oriented" and "serious about academics." At the same time, the atmosphere is collaborative, as most students are also "interested in diversifying their skills in both business and networking." For professionals the atmosphere is supportive, and students find they "can relate with classmates, since many also have full-time jobs."

Located in central Florida, students at Stetson enjoy proximity to both local businesses and the beach—and everyone loves Florida's year-round sunny weather. On the main campus, the Lynn Business Center is equipped with high-speed Internet and numerous computer terminals. Despite the nice campus environment, prospective students should be aware that Stetson's MBA is principally designed for working professionals, so most students come to campus for class—and nothing more. Accordingly, some students would like to see "more of a sense of community" at Stetson, as "the campus is a ghost town on the weekends."

Admissions

Stetson accepts new students to the MBA program on a rolling basis. Generally speaking, students must apply at least 45 days before the start of the new term; once all application materials are received, students can expect a reply from the university immediately. To be considered for the joint MBA/JD on the Gulfport campus, students must first meet the requirements of the Stetson School of Law. Undergraduate GPA and GMAT scores are typically the two most important factors in an admissions decision.

FINANCIAL FACTS

Annual tuition	$21,750
Cost of books	$1,400

ADMISSIONS

Admissions Selectivity Rating	70
# of applications received	240
% applicants accepted	95
% acceptees attending	90
Average GMAT	540
Range of GMAT	440–710
Average GPA	3.3
TOEFL required of international students	Yes
Minimum TOEFL (paper/computer)	550/213
Application fee	$25
International application fee	$25
Regular application deadline	5/31
Regular notification	6/30
Early decision program?	No
Deferment available	Yes
Maximum length of deferment	1 year
Transfer students accepted	Yes
Transfer application policy: The graduate business programs require a basic foundation in business administration courses.	
Non-fall admissions	Yes
Need-blind admissions	Yes

EMPLOYMENT PROFILE	
Career Rating	79
Average base starting salary	$47,500

SUFFOLK UNIVERSITY
SAWYER BUSINESS SCHOOL

GENERAL INFORMATION
Type of school	Private
Academic calendar	Semester

SURVEY SAYS...
Students love Boston, MA
Solid preparation in:
Communication/interpersonal skills
Doing business in a global economy

STUDENTS
Enrollment of parent institution	7,911
Enrollment of MBA Program	692
% male/female	62/38
% out-of-state	9
% part-time	81
% minorities	8
% international	57
Average age at entry	27
Average years work experience at entry	4

ACADEMICS
Academic Experience Rating	72
Student/faculty ratio	15:1
Profs interesting rating	78
Profs accessible rating	75
% female faculty	30
% minority faculty	16

Joint Degrees
MBA/MS Accounting, 18–24 months full time, 20–32 months part time; MBA/MS Finance, 18–24 months full time, 20–32 months part time; MBA/MS Taxation, 18–24 months full time; 20–32 months part time; JD/MBA, 4 years full time, 5 years part time; JD/Masters in Public Administration, 4 years total full time, 5 years part time. JD/Masters in Finance, 4 years full time, 5 years part time.

Academics

Boston's Suffolk University offers a conventional MBA as well as specialized MBAs in health administration, nonprofit management, and accounting. The school also offers a Global MBA in which students combine upper-level course work focused on international finance and marketing with a required international internship. Students laud the "diversity [of] hands-on learning experiences through global travel seminars" in the Global MBA program. One reports, "I will be going to Brazil and London for week-long seminars this year." Another adds, "The company that currently employs me does business throughout the world. This program would allow me to advance within this organization."

Suffolk "caters to the working professionals" who make up the majority of its MBA student body with "great scheduling" and "program flexibility" that "allow us to balance both work and school." "Classes are offered at night, on the weekends, online, and through the summer" to maximize students' opportunities to complete needed classes. A convenient "urban setting close to work" is another boon for those who work in and around the Financial District.

To many though, "Suffolk's greatest strength is the professors' holistic approach to management." Suffolk professors are "working professionals teaching relevant courses" emphasizing "a balance of quantitative management skills while recognizing the importance of interpersonal qualitative skills." "Many professors have a 'This is your class' mentality, where they are open to student input on the structure of the class," one student writes approvingly, adding "I have learned a tremendous amount."

Career and Placement

Suffolk prides itself on preparing students for the real world, and effective, long-term career planning is a major piece of the puzzle. In fact, every student at Suffolk must take an introductory course aptly named Effective Career Planning, designed to help students evaluate their professional skills and career paths and to make a solid plan for what they wish to accomplish with an MBA. In addition, the Suffolk MBA EDGE offers professional development events throughout the academic year. These events run the gamut from seminars on power lunches and the professional image to MBA Networking Week and Technology Day. MBA EDGE also hosts a number of career services events such as workshops on resume writing and salary negotiations. Students tell us that these "programs and classes required for new students have been great. They really push us to develop career plans and help us develop many different skills that will help us in planning and pursuing our careers."

Student opinion of Suffolk's career services office is mixed, with a number of supporters observing that recruiting and placement disappointments "may be a product of the poor economy and lack of jobs due to the recession" rather than shortcomings in the placement office. Top employers of Suffolk MBAs include: Bank of America, Fidelity Investments, Investors Bank & Trust, KPMG, PricewaterhouseCoopers, and State Street Bank.

Student Life and Environment

Over 80 percent of Suffolk MBAs are part-time students, and the university designs its program to accommodate their schedules. "Classes are [almost] always offered during evenings," with "very few day classes for full-time students." The downside is that the system necessitates a very long day for some. "When you are taking two classes back to back from 4:30 P.M. to 10 P.M., it is tough," one student explains, adding "I worked full time this last semester and went to school full time. It was tough but doable." Overall,

ADMISSIONS CONTACT: JUDITH L. REYNOLDS, DIRECTOR OF GRADUATE ADMISSIONS
ADDRESS: 8 ASHBURTON PLACE BOSTON, MA 02108
PHONE: 617-573-8302 • FAX: 617-305-1733
E-MAIL: GRAD.ADMISSION@SUFFOLK.EDU • WEBSITE: WWW.SUFFOLK.EDU/BUSINESS

however, students appreciate the lengths to which Suffolk goes to serve its evening students. The school "has amazing networking events and an exceptional 'Meet the Firms Night,'" and is also "very active in promoting networking and helping to improve social interactions in preparation of interviews." As one student observes, "As a full-time professional, work, school, and life are a balancing act. I would say that Suffolk caters to my needs, extends my breadth of knowledge, and positions me well for future success."

The school is not without its shortcomings, however. "The gym is awful," says one. Worse, "The actual b-school building is old and resembles a high school in some regards. They need a dedicated facility for the business school." Students wish there were "more resources for graduate students. There is a graduate student lounge, but it only accommodates about seven people. The computer lab is always full. The dining options in the graduate school are nothing special."

Suffolk MBAs are "a very diverse group," with many part-time students who are "mid- to upper-20-somethings in their second or third jobs" and "full time students from India, the Middle East, and Eastern Europe" as well as from the United States (the majority of full-timers are international students who "add a global perspective"). Part-timers note that "Everyone is at a different point in the program, so it is hard to foster and maintain friendships since everyone has busy and changing schedules."

Admissions

To apply to the Suffolk University Sawyer School of Business, students must submit undergraduate transcripts, a resume, and a completed application, including essays. Those applying to the full-time program must have at least one year of work experience; however, the average admit has logged three years in a professional position. Part-time applicants are expected to have spent more time in the professional world and average five to seven years of work experience. Applicants must also submit GMAT scores, though exceptions may be made for practicing CPAs and attorneys. In addition to the requirements above, international applicants must submit TOEFL scores.

Prominent Alumni

Robert Mudge, New England Region President, Verizon; Tara Taylor, VP, State Street Global Advisors; Patrick Callaghan, President Pepperridge Farms; Peter Gicheru, Finance Controller, Coca-Cola South Africa.

FINANCIAL FACTS

Annual tuition	$33,000
Fees	$20
Cost of books	$1,000
Room & board (off-campus)	$13,350
% of students receiving aid	61
% of first-year students receiving aid	66
% of students receiving loans	36
% of students receiving grants	38
Average award package	$30,162
Average grant	$15,036
Average student loan debt	$47,816

ADMISSIONS

Admissions Selectivity Rating	69
# of applications received	447
% applicants accepted	71
% acceptees attending	51
Average GMAT	498
Range of GMAT	440–560
Average GPA	3.12
TOEFL required of international students	Yes
Minimum TOEFL (paper/computer)	550/213
Application fee	$50
International application fee	$50
Regular application deadline	6/15
Early decision program?	No
Deferment available	Yes
Maximum length of deferment	1 year
Transfer students accepted	Yes
Transfer application policy: Same as for regular applicants	
Non-fall admissions	Yes
Need-blind admissions	Yes

EMPLOYMENT PROFILE

Career Rating	84	Grads Employed by Function	% Avg. Salary
Percent employed at graduation	54	Marketing	8 $49,000
Percent employed 3 months after graduation	46	Consulting	8 $50,000
		Management	23 $105,000
Average base starting salary	$76,600	Finance	46 $62,800
Primary Source of Full-time Job Acceptances		**Top 5 Employers Hiring Grads**	
School-facilitated activities	4 (31%)	State Street Corporation (1), Ernst and Young	
Graduate-facilitated activities	9 (69%)	(1), Intel Corporation (1), NEPC (1), Tufts University (1)	

SYRACUSE UNIVERSITY
MARTIN J. WHITMAN SCHOOL OF MANAGEMENT

GENERAL INFORMATION

Type of school	Private
Academic calendar	Semester

SURVEY SAYS...

Smart classrooms
Solid preparation in:
Operations
Entrepreneurial studies

STUDENTS

Enrollment of parent institution	19,366
Enrollment of MBA Program	314
% male/female	75/25
% out-of-state	76
% part-time	70
% minorities	9
% international	50
Average age at entry	25
Average years work experience at entry	3

ACADEMICS

Academic Experience Rating	88
Student/faculty ratio	4:1
Profs interesting rating	68
Profs accessible rating	70
% female faculty	19
% minority faculty	7

Joint Degrees

MBA/Juris Doctorate (4 years); MBA/Master of Public Administration (3 years); with any other degree-bearing graduate program offered at Syracuse University.

Prominent Alumni

Martin J. Whitman, Founder of Third Avenue Value Fund; Dick Clark, Chairman and CEO of Dick Clark Productions; Dan D'Aniello, Founding Partner of the Carlyle Group; The Honorable Alfonse D'Amato, former U.S. Senator; Arthur Rock, venture capitalist, Arthur Rock & Company.

Academics

A tiny MBA program at a "great, nationally-recognized" university, the Whitman School of Business at Syracuse University provides a thorough business education in an intimate academic setting. With fewer than 30 students per entering class, students benefit from uniformly small class sizes, and "the opportunity to develop relationships with every classmate as well as professors." These relationships are incredibly valuable, as "Professors get to know students on a personal level and help out in every way they can." One student elaborates, "By talking with faculty and administration, I have been put in close personal contact with a number of prominent alumni and have even been offered internship positions at some of the top firms in their respective fields due to these alumni relationships."

Whitman's challenging 54-unit curriculum includes a year of core course work in essentials like economics and finance. Core courses extend into the second year; however, by the final semester, course work is comprised entirely of electives, and students may complete a concentration in accounting, entrepreneurship, finance, general management, supply chain management, or marketing management. In addition to the traditional program, the school offers an accelerated MBA for students with a business background. Students may also pursue a joint-degree with any other graduate department at the university, including "a great JD/MBA program with a lot of connections in and around New York City."

Mixing traditional lectures with hands-on projects, Whitman's curriculum introduces Syracuse students to both the practical and theoretical sides of business. A student shares, "Our leadership class was mostly lectures and reading and more of an in-class discussion that did not require intensive study. Our GEM class [involved] creating a whole new business from scratch, presenting to a venture capitalist and having a certain number of deliverables ready in three months." As a result of this variety, "The workload can be anywhere from easy to killer depending on deadlines and classes." Fortunately, students find lots of support: "Professors are regularly available, but especially on days they know students will need them—they are in their offices later than most students remain at school."

A great option for those early in their careers, Syracuse does not require previous professional experience for entry into the MBA program and "The majority of the MBA students in my class have had less than 5 years work experience, so [they] are fairly young." As one student explains, "I had internship experiences but no professional work experience. Syracuse University was one of the only universities that allowed me to get a quality MBA earlier in life when I have the time to go to school versus later in life when family and work become a higher priority than education."

Career and Placement

Career placement is taken seriously at Syracuse. During their studies, students hone their skills through internships at local companies, and "Every week there is some event for students to take part in, whether it is a guest speaker or networking reception." When it comes to permanent placements, "The school's strong accounting and supply chain [management] programs are well-recognized nationally, and students in those fields get good job offers." However, with a young and largely international student body, placements can occasionally be more difficult. A current student explains, "Part of the problem is that because they accept students with little to no work experience, it is also tougher to place those MBA students in jobs, specifically international students in finance and marketing fields."

ADMISSIONS CONTACT: SHANNON HIEMSTRA, ASSISTANT DIRECTOR OF ADMISSIONS
ADDRESS: 721 UNIVERSITY AVENUE, SUITE 315 SYRACUSE, NY 13244-2450
PHONE: 315-443-9214 • FAX: 315-443-9517
E-MAIL: MBAINFO@SYR.EDU • WEBSITE: WHITMAN.SYR.EDU

Companies that offered positions to graduates include: Bear Stearns, ChinaTrust Commercial Bank, Citigroup, Deloitte Touche Tohmatsu, Ellis Deming Development, Ernst & Young, Health Net, JPMorgan Chase, PricewaterhouseCoopers, Rockefeller & Co., Samsung SDI, and Verizon Wireless. Another nice perk is that the school "pays for CFA testing and travel expenses for job interviews."

Student Life and Environment

You might be surprised how much you'll learn from your classmates on this tiny but diverse campus. A student praises, "Many of the students have international backgrounds and offer an international/alternative perspective to traditional North American ways of thinking." Despite students' cultural differences, the environment is noncontentious and friendly, and "People here really care for others, especially new students." There are many ways to fill your free time at Syracuse, and students say the "Many academic, social, and cultural activities to choose from [make] the experience rewarding." When they aren't hitting the books, students "plan trips together (to national and international destinations), events together (i.e., bowling night, international day), and involve the faculty as well (i.e., student versus faculty softball)."

While the city of Syracuse isn't the most happening location, students reassure us that communities outside Syracuse are "clean, crime-free, and cater to professionals. We have golf courses and ski resorts around the area that cater to people with those interests. There is also plenty to do in term of hiking, camping canoeing." In addition, many Syracuse students "take part in charity work around the city, offering their business skills and acumen to small business owners who may not always have a solid business background."

Admissions

Admission to Syracuse is competitive. Last year's entering class (for the full-time program) had an average GMAT score of 635, with a range of 610–660 and an average undergraduate GPA of 3.3. To apply to the accelerated program, students must have an undergraduate degree in business, a GMAT score of 650 or better, and four or more years of professional work experience. Reviews are made on a rolling basis and students are notified of their acceptance or nonacceptance within 4 to 6 weeks.

FINANCIAL FACTS

Annual tuition	$33,510
Fees	$1,302
Cost of books	$1,325
Room & board	$12,490
% of students receiving aid	96
% of first-year students receiving aid	93
% of students receiving loans	19
% of students receiving grants	96
Average award package	$30,453
Average grant	$23,199
Average student loan debt	$48,546

ADMISSIONS

Admissions Selectivity Rating	88
# of applications received	177
% applicants accepted	63
% acceptees attending	88
Average GMAT	635
Range of GMAT	610–660
Average GPA	3.32
TOEFL required of international students	Yes
Minimum TOEFL (paper/computer)	600/250
Application fee	$75
International application fee	$75
Regular application deadline	4/19
Regular notification	5/17
Application Deadline/Notification	
Round 1:	11/30 / 12/21
Round 2:	1/1 / 2/1
Round 3:	2/15 / 3/15
Round 4:	4/19 / 5/17
Early decision program?	No
Deferment available	Yes
Maximum length of deferment	1 year
Transfer students accepted	No
Non-fall admissions	Yes
Need-blind admissions	Yes

EMPLOYMENT PROFILE

Career Rating	**92**	**Grads Employed by Function% Avg. Salary**	
Percent employed at graduation	57	Marketing	11 NR
Percent employed 3 months after graduation	79	Operations	37 $59,065
		Management	11 NR
Average base starting salary	$60,076	Finance	37 $63,500
Primary Source of Full-time Job Acceptances		**Top 5 Employers Hiring Grads**	
School-facilitated activities	14 (64%)	Win-Holt (2), Apple (1), Deloitte (1), KPMG (1)	
Graduate-facilitated activities	8 (36%)		

TEMPLE UNIVERSITY
THE FOX SCHOOL OF BUSINESS AND MANAGEMENT

GENERAL INFORMATION
Type of school   Public

SURVEY SAYS...
Smart classrooms
Solid preparation in:
Accounting
Doing business in a global economy

STUDENTS
Enrollment of parent institution	37,748
Enrollment of MBA Program	449
% male/female	64/36
% out-of-state	39
% part-time	67
% minorities	4
% international	35
Average age at entry	28
Average years work experience at entry	5

ACADEMICS
Academic Experience Rating	86
Student/faculty ratio	15:1
Profs interesting rating	82
Profs accessible rating	82
% female faculty	18
% minority faculty	27

Joint Degrees
JD/MBA, 4 years, DMD/MBA, 4 years, IMBA/MS, 1.5 years

Prominent Alumni
Larry G. Miller, President, Portland Trail Blazers, NBA Franchise; Norman Braman, President and CEO, Braman Management; Owner: Philadelphia Eagles; Sultan Ahmed Bin Sulayem, Chairman, Dubai Ports World; Nakheel Executive Chairman; Debra J. Chrapaty, Corporate Vice President, Windows Live Operations, Microsoft Corporation; Dr. Raza Bokhari, President and CEO, Lakewood Pathology Associates (LPA).

Academics

With a view of Philadelphia's skyline and deep ties in the local business community, Temple University's Fox School of Business offers big city opportunities with a surprisingly personal touch. Academically, Temple's strength lies in its small program size, contemporary curriculum, and excellent teaching staff. The core curriculum (required for both full-time and part-time students) is integrated and interdisciplinary, and "professors work together to develop case studies between classes, such as finance and accounting." On the whole, students are "extremely happy with the professors, especially those in the core classes," saying they "take pride in teaching their students the most up-to-date trends in the industry." Outside the core, students can take electives across nine departments, and "there are opportunities for students to pursue their own specific interests" through 12 areas of concentration. Thanks to a well-planned course of study, "The rigor of course work is very strong, but it is delivered in such a way that we rarely feel completely overwhelmed or helpless."

Dynamic and interactive, "Professors facilitate engaging discussions in the classes," and the academic environment "fosters creativity and individual thought." In the classroom and through co-curricular activities, real-world situations take center stage, and "the academics are heavily weighted towards case-study learning, and application of skills." "Team-building exercises, leadership courses, and consulting projects" augment classroom education with hands-on experience. Finally, to round out their experience, full-time students must complete the capstone course, Enterprise Management Consulting Practicum, a "one-year long consulting project," which gives students the "chance to apply skills and knowledge learned in a real business environment." Part-time students complete the consulting practicum over the course of one semester. With small class sizes and a great faculty-to-student ratio, Temple's MBA "allows students to learn with and from their peers in an intimate setting and class size." Here, "Professors are personable outside of the classroom and challenging inside [of it].""The school's administrative staff is incredibly friendly, easily approachable, extremely helpful, very knowledgeable, and definitely did their best to enhance the overall experience at the school."

Students with a specific focus on international business may also consider Temple's intense, one-year International MBA program, which gives students the opportunity to "live, network, and study abroad" in multiple locations worldwide (including India, China, France, and Japan.) In this unique program, the "first semester is spent at a partner school overseas," before returning to the Temple campus to take classes with a "culturally and ethnically diverse group," of students. During their time in Philadelphia, international program students "have courses almost every day of the week," saying "Our schedule is very tight as we are trying to fit two years of courses into one year." The program culminates with a six week experience in Asia.

Career and Placement

The Graduate Career Management Center offers a wide array of programs to assist MBA students entering the job market or wishing to make a career change, including individualized career counseling, career development workshops and networking events, online job boards, and an executive speaker series. In addition to current MBA candidates, Temple alumni may also take advantage of many of these services.

A long-standing Philadelphia institution renowned for academic excellence, Temple University maintains "strong alumni ties within the surrounding business community." Building on these ties, the Graduate Career Management Center maintains relationships with Philadelphia companies, and on-campus recruiting programs are robust. In recent years, Temple graduates took jobs at companies including Accenture, Bloomberg, Bristol-

FINANCIAL FACTS

Annual tuition (in-state/ out-of-state)	$20,304/$30,132
Fees	$940
Cost of books	$1,200
Room & board	$15,000
% of students receiving aid	75
% of first-year students receiving aid	•
	75
% of students receiving loans	73
% of students receiving grants	25
Average award package	$23,139
Average grant	$9,652
Average student loan debt	$13,360

ADMISSIONS

Admissions Selectivity Rating	86
# of applications received	492
% applicants accepted	54
% acceptees attending	56
Average GMAT	624
Range of GMAT	580–660
Average GPA	3.23
TOEFL required of international students	Yes
Minimum TOEFL (paper/computer)	600/250
Application fee	$60
International application fee	$60
Regular application deadline	6/1
Early decision program?	No
Deferment available	Yes
Maximum length of deferment	1 year
Transfer students accepted	Yes
Transfer application policy: Reviewed on a case-by-case basis for the Professional MBA (part-time) program.	
Non-fall admissions	Yes
Need-blind admissions	Yes

Meyers Squibb, Comcast, Ernst & Young, Pfizer, Merrill Lynch, PricewaterhouseCoopers, The Gap, and Wachovia. Overall, financial services and marketing are the popular industries for Temple graduates. In the past three years, Fox graduates' annual average compensation was $80,000.

Student Life and Environment

From day one, you'll have a lively, friendly, and team-oriented experience in Temple's MBA program. Teamwork is emphasized throughout the curriculum, and in the full-time program "each cohort has a very strong bond that is fostered during the four-week orientation leading up to the first semester of classes." Despite the small size, "Classmates have varied upbringings, educational, and professional backgrounds, so in-class discussions are spirited, engaging, and entertaining." You'll find that "about 50 percent of the class came from the business world, either IT or finance;" however, "work experience ranges from the investment banker and former business owner to the Hollywood talent scout." Emphasizing cooperation not competition, a Temple student explains, "When classes become stressful, we help each other out, and learning is very much a shared activity at Fox."

"The facilities at Fox are top-of-the-line with the new addition of Alter Hall on the main Temple University Campus," which includes "tons of breakout rooms for team meetings," changing rooms, and "outstanding" tech equipment. Students are also quick to praise "the MBA commons area, which overlooks the skyline of Philadelphia." Outside the classroom, the "School has lots of guest lectures and networking events" and "Many of the students are involved in clubs on campus, including Net Impact, AMA, entrepreneurship and finance clubs." In fact, "Between networking, speakers, happy hours, etc., there are at least 10-15 events or extras per month that are hard to pass up." In their free time, "Students are also highly social with each other outside of school. We try to mix in weekly happy hours to de-stress from the week's work."

Admissions

Admission into the Fox MBA programs is a competitive process that takes careful consideration of students' personal experience, goals, academic aptitude and professional credentials. Fox creates diverse classes each year with varied backgrounds and experiences. The suite of MBA programs include: Fox Full-time MBA, International MBA, Professional MBA, Online MBA and Executive MBA.

The full-time two-year Fox MBA brings real world perspectives to a classroom experience. The accelerated one-year Fox International MBA provides global exposure, delivered through multiple international partnerships. The Fox Professional MBA is a flexible part-time evening program for working professionals. The Fox Online MBA provides the opportunity to earn a top-ranked MBA with the convenience of online education. The Executive MBA is a twenty-two month program designed for senior level professionals.

EMPLOYMENT PROFILE

		Grads Employed by Function	% Avg. Salary
Career Rating	86		
Percent employed at graduation	56	Marketing	28 $64,875
Percent employed 3 months after graduation	75	Consulting	28 $61,250
Average base starting salary	$61,759	Finance	24 $64,285
Primary Source of Full-time Job Acceptances		Top 5 Employers Hiring Grads	
School-facilitated activities	20 (56%)	Advanta (2), SAP (1), PWC (1), TEVA (1),	
Graduate-facilitated activities	16 (44%)	Kellogg's (1)	

TENNESSEE TECHNOLOGICAL UNIVERSITY
COLLEGE OF BUSINESS

GENERAL INFORMATION
Type of school	Public
Academic calendar	Semester

SURVEY SAYS...
Cutting-edge classes
Solid preparation in:
Finance
Accounting
General management
Computer skills
Doing business in a global economy

STUDENTS
Enrollment of parent institution	10,847
Enrollment of MBA Program	227
% male/female	57/43
% out-of-state	7
% part-time	52
% minorities	8
% international	3
Average age at entry	27
Average years work experience at entry	4

ACADEMICS
Academic Experience Rating	**79**
Student/faculty ratio	25:1
Profs interesting rating	90
Profs accessible rating	81
% female faculty	6
% minority faculty	1

Prominent Alumni
Scott Cochran, The Krystal Company; Susan Williams, O'Charley's, Inc.; Allen Washburn, Dynetics; Victor Widiasana, FedEx Corporation; Cass Larson, Tennessee Valley Authority; Aaron Anderson, AT&T.

Academics

Tennessee Technological University offers a flexible, affordable, and student-oriented MBA, designed to meet the needs of working professionals. Tech's MBA is a general management program, with an emphasis on practical and interactive learning through research, case studies, computer simulation, business mentoring, workshops, consulting assignments, field trips, and more. "Professors encourage professional growth by designing classes to build teamwork among students in a global atmosphere," while simultaneously weaving appropriate co-curricular experiences into the MBA. For example, students pursuing a concentration in finance have the opportunity to manage a real investment portfolio during their studies. Students also have the opportunity to augment their education by working at the school's external-focused centers, designed to transfer technology and knowledge from the school community to the business world. These centers include the Business Media Center, the J.E. Owen Center for Information Technology Research, and the Small Business Development Center. With a name like "Tech," it's not surprising that the school is also "leading the way in combining education and technology."

At Tech, the classroom experience is top-notch and professors "go out of their way to make the material interesting." If you have questions, doubts, or just want to talk over a concept, you'll find professors are " surprisingly accessible." In fact, at this small school, "it is easy to get to know your professors and administration" as both the faculty and staff take a genuine interest in the student experience. A case in point, a current MBA candidate shares, "Tennessee Tech extended a warm welcome when I applied to the MBA program. The director . . . met personally with me and helped me develop a strategy both for classes chosen and handling homework load." On that note, busy professionals should keep in mind that, despite the prevalence of "very cool and easy-going professors," Tech is "very demanding in terms of course deadlines."

If your work schedule suddenly changes or you don't have time to visit campus for class, "TTU also runs an excellent distance program that has the feel and personal touch of a campus degree." A current online student shares, "I feel as though Tech is also spending lots of time to improve their DMBA website. They just recently released a new version for the DMBA and it is getting better and better." Another adds, "The MBA program support staff have been very help to me as a distance student. They have hand-carried paperwork that needed signatures from person to person for me so that I didn't have to take a couple of days off work in order to travel to the university." Whether online or in the classroom, one thing unites all of Tech's MBA offerings: "This school provides a very high quality education at a very reasonable price."

Career and Placement

Tennessee Tech's Career Services Center serves the entire campus community, including the business school. Throughout the year, the center hosts on-campus interviews and career fairs. A recent career fair drew large employers such as AFLAC, Axciom Digital, Honda, Federal Bureau of Investigation, 21st Mortgage Corporation, Denso, Alstom, Lennox, Greystone Healthcare Management, Regions Financial Corporation, Sonoco Products Company, Schneider Electric, Enterprise, Unifirst Corporation, Central Intelligence Agency, and State Farm Insurance. A number of these employers were specifically seeking MBA graduates. According to the business school literature, Tennessee Tech is usually successful in placing all candidates who are seriously seeking employment after graduation.

ADMISSIONS CONTACT: MBA STUDIES
ADDRESS: BOX 5023 TTU, 1105 N. PEACHTREE JH 112 COOKEVILLE, TN 38505
PHONE: 931-372-3600 • FAX: 931-372-6544
E-MAIL: MBASTUDIES@TNTECH.EDU • WEBSITE: WWW.TNTECH.EDU/MBA

Student Life and Environment

Thanks to the flexible scheduling and affordable tuition price, Tech draws a fairly diverse group of students, who "range in age from 20s to 50s. The majority are working professionals intent on getting a good education." Within the business school, there is a "very social life with frequent pizza sessions in class and [an] end-of-the-semester outing." In fact, "students at Tech tend to bond together. They study together, hang out together, and go out together." A current student writes, "One of the things I like best about Tech is that the school is just small enough to encourage a tight group of people. When you go out, everybody knows your name." To add to the appeal, "the campus is beautiful with buildings easily accessible on foot," and is located in the "darling, small town" of Cookeville, Tennessee, seventy miles from Nashville.

There are a number of extracurricular activities aimed specifically at graduate business students, including the MBA Student Association, study abroad programs, investment challenge courses, and the Rural Economic Development Conference, for which MBA students assist in planning. Needless to say, online MBA students say that the campus itself does not play a large role in their graduate school experience. However, "the MBA program does try to do one or two events a semester that involve distance students (e.g., hockey game and group tours)."

Admissions

To be admitted to Tennessee Tech's MBA programs, you need an undergraduate degree with a minimum GPA of 2.5 on a 4.0 scale. A minimum GMAT score of 450 is also required. In addition, students must meet a computer efficiency requirement, and competency requirements in accounting, business law, economics, finance, marketing, managements, and statistics. Students who did not major in business can fulfill these competency requirements through college coursework or through pre-MBA, self-study courses.

FINANCIAL FACTS

Annual tuition	$9,240
Fees	$1,575
Cost of books	$2,000
Room & board (on/off-campus)	$7,500/$9,800
% of students receiving aid	60
% of first-year students receiving aid	45
% of students receiving loans	40
% of students receiving grants	25
Average award package	$14,700
Average grant	$13,780
Average student loan debt	$10,000

ADMISSIONS

Admissions Selectivity Rating	74
# of applications received	131
% applicants accepted	100
% acceptees attending	77
Average GMAT	540
Range of GMAT	410–720
Average GPA	3.33
TOEFL required of international students	Yes
Minimum TOEFL (paper/computer)	550/213
Application fee	$25
International application fee	$30
Early decision program?	No
Deferment available	Yes
Maximum length of deferment	1 year
Transfer students accepted	Yes
Transfer application policy: TTU will transfer 9 hours or less from an AACSB accredited school.	
Non-fall admissions	Yes
Need-blind admissions	Yes

EMPLOYMENT PROFILE

Career Rating		81	Grads Employed by Function	% Avg. Salary
Percent employed at graduation		90	Marketing	5 NR
Percent employed 3 months after graduation		95	Consulting	5 NR
			Management	20 NR
			Finance & Accounting	40 NR
			HR	10 NR
			MIS	5 NR

Top 5 Employers Hiring Grads
Nissan, FedEx, Tennessee Valley Authority, HCA Corporation, Deloitt

TEXAS A&M INTERNATIONAL UNIVERSITY
COLLEGE OF BUSINESS ADMINISTRATION

GENERAL INFORMATION

Type of school	Public
Academic calendar	Semester

SURVEY SAYS...
Friendly students
Cutting-edge classes
Happy students
Solid preparation in:
Finance
General management
Teamwork

STUDENTS

Enrollment of parent institution	5,188
Enrollment of MBA Program	161
% male/female	64/36
% part-time	78
% minorities	33
% international	58
Average age at entry	29
Average years work experience at entry	6

ACADEMICS

Academic Experience Rating	**70**
Student/faculty ratio	20:1
Profs interesting rating	85
Profs accessible rating	62
% female faculty	10
% minority faculty	76

Academics

The College of Business Administration at Texas A&M International University "is dedicated to the delivery of a high quality professional and internationalized education to a graduate student population that is drawn from a wide variety of countries and cultures," according to the college's website, which also points out that "these programs [are intended to] contribute to the students' success in leadership positions in both domestic and international settings." This AACSB-accredited school offers a general MBA, an MBA in international banking (MBA-IBK), an MBA in international trade (MBA-IT), and a PhD in International Business Administration.

All MBA programs at TAMIU require mastery of eight foundation areas: accounting, information systems, quantitative methods, economics, finance, management, marketing, and operations. Students may fulfill these requirements by completing corresponding undergraduate courses at TAMIU, by showing evidence of equivalent course work at another undergraduate institution, or by having earned an undergraduate business degree from an AACSB-accredited program. Waivers are only granted for course work completed within the previous seven years.

TAMIU's general MBA is taught in both English and Spanish. The 30-hour program allows students to concentrate in one of the following areas: accounting, information systems, international business, international finance, international trade economics, logistics, and management marketing. The strong international focus of the program "gives students the opportunity to immerse themselves in an international environment in which we can analyze situations of different countries. The diversity of the student body helps." Students also praise the "extremely optimistic" professors who "honestly care about their students and are always willing to offer a helping hand." One student writes, "Teachers are very good and highly cooperative, with great academic ability. They have the knowledge to impart, help the students, and offer their valuable suggestions to guide their further course of action."

Students also point out that "the small size of the program is a great strength. The student population is not big, so there is enough opportunity to interact with your professors and get to know everyone in your college." MBAs here appreciate how "professors acknowledge that the majority of the class works full time and also goes to school, so they make the assignments challenging, but not impossible." In addition to the above-mentioned degrees, TAMIU also offers a master of professional accountancy (MPAcc), a master of science in international logistics (MS/IL), a master of science in information systems (MS/IS), and a doctorate in international business administration (PhD/BA).

Career and Placement

The Texas A&M International Career Services Office provides counseling and placement services to the entire undergraduate and graduate student body. The office organizes on-campus recruiting events, career expos, and job fairs. It also offers one-on-one counseling, workshops, library services, and resume review.

ADMISSIONS CONTACT: IMELDA LOPEZ, GRADUATE ADMISSIONS ADVISOR
ADDRESS: 5201 UNIVERSITY BLVD. LAREDO, TX 78041
PHONE: 956-326-2485 • FAX: 956-326-2479
E-MAIL: LOPEZ@TAMIU.EDU • WEBSITE: WWW.TAMIU.EDU/COBA

Student Life and Environment

Around 47 percent of TAMIU's MBA students attend full-time, providing a sizeable base for clubs, organizations, and extracurricular activity. Students tell us that "campus life offers a diverse field of organizations. New clubs and sports are always developing." They also report that "seminars provided by the school are good. Many important speakers visit the campus to deliver inspirational speeches on important current topics, including politics, finance, economics, and health." Part-timers generally "don't get to spend much time on campus, but rather just get here for class at night and leave once classes are done." They "visit the computer labs and library to do research and work," but otherwise spend little extra time socializing.

Hometown Laredo "is poised at the gateway to Mexico," placing it "at an enviable crossroads of international business and life." One hundred and fifty-six miles south of San Antonio and 153 miles north of Monterrey, Mexico, this city of over 150,000 is the fastest growing in the state of Texas. The area's growth has been spurred by Laredo's increasing role as a center for international manufacturing and trade. Top employers in the area, outside of education and government, include the Laredo Medical Center, the H-E-B Grocery Company, Doctor's Hospital, Laredo Candle, and area banks.

TAMIU's "friendly, frank, cheerful and helpful" students "enjoy the challenge of studying in a foreign country and expect the experience to give them a better professional future." More than half the MBAs here are international students; most of whom are Mexican and Latin American. Almost twenty percent of the international student body comes from Asia.

Admissions

Applying to the TAMIU MBA program is a two-step process, as applicants must be admitted to both the university at large and the College of Business in order to enroll in the MBA program. Applicants must submit the following materials to the Office of Graduate Admission: a completed application; an official copy of transcripts for all postsecondary academic work undertaken; and an official score report for the GMAT. Applicants must also provide a statement of purpose, a resume, and two letters of recommendation. The TOEFL is required of all students who completed undergraduate study in a country where English is not the language of instruction; a minimum score of 550 paper-based or 213 computer-based is required. International students must also submit documentation demonstrating the ability to support themselves financially while studying at TAMIU.

FINANCIAL FACTS

Annual tuition (in-state/ out-of-state)	$1,170/$6,174
Fees	$2,324
Cost of books	$2,825
Room & board (on/off-campus)	$6,630/$5,814
% of students receiving aid	24
% of first-year students receiving aid	23
% of students receiving loans	22
% of students receiving grants	23
Average award package	$4,400
Average grant	$1,117

ADMISSIONS

Admissions Selectivity Rating	**61**
# of applications received	61
% applicants accepted	98
% acceptees attending	70
Average GPA	3.2
TOEFL required of international students	Yes
Minimum TOEFL (paper/computer)	550/213
Application fee	$25
International application fee	$25
Regular application deadline	4/30
Early decision program?	No
ED Deadline/Notification	
Deferment available	Yes
Maximum length of deferment	1 year
Transfer students accepted	Yes
Transfer application policy: In terms of the application process, this remains the same as first-time applicants. However, for F1 applicants, it is critical these applicants be in-status at their current institutuion.	
Non-fall admissions	Yes
Need-blind admissions	Yes

TEXAS A&M UNIVERSITY—COLLEGE STATION
MAYS BUSINESS SCHOOL

GENERAL INFORMATION

Type of school	Public
Academic calendar	Semester

SURVEY SAYS...

Good peer network
Smart classrooms
Solid preparation in:
Accounting
General management
Operations

STUDENTS

Enrollment of parent institution	48,000
Enrollment of MBA Program	149
% male/female	74/26
% out-of-state	32
% part-time	0
% minorities	13
% international	27
Average age at entry	28
Average years work experience at entry	4

ACADEMICS

Academic Experience Rating	92
Student/faculty ratio	8:1
Profs interesting rating	91
Profs accessible rating	88
% female faculty	11
% minority faculty	11

Joint Degrees

MBA/MS Management Information Systems, 24 months; MBA/MS-Finance, 24 months.

Prominent Alumni

Don Davis, Chairman/CEO, Rockwell Automation; Andrew Hansen, CEO, Heart Surgery Center of the Southwest; Karl Heilscher, President and CEO, METL-Span, LTD; Rick Cashen, CEO, Cabinrock Investments, LLC; Greg Coleman, Former Solicitor General, State of Texas.

Academics

Business-minded MBA candidates say you get a "great return on investment" at Texas A&M. While tuition at this public university is "relatively inexpensive," the business school offers a "high-quality education," spearheaded by an "unmatched teaching staff." The "academically-challenging and quantitatively-focused" curriculum is incredibly intense, compressing the equivalent of a two-year fulltime MBA into just sixteen months. Students praise the efficiency of the school's accelerated schedule, which reduces costs and career interruption while nonetheless providing "well-rounded" business training. In fact, "The ability of the professors and the program to crunch so much information into that time is outstanding." On the flip side, some students feel the program's speed isn't necessarily an advantage, as "we never have to time to prepare sufficiently and then discuss it in depth." Fortunately, those who'd like to extend their education may decide to stay at Texas A&M for an extra semester, during which time they can specialize in accounting, consulting, e-commerce, finance, marketing, and real estate, among others.

Teaching is taken seriously Texas A&M, and the school's "excellent" faculty are truly involved with the educational process. In class, "The teachers are engaging and concerned about student learning," and "try hard to make sure everybody understands the course material." Outside of class, "Professors and administration are extremely helpful. They have open-door policies and are easily accessible." In addition, the school's administration is friendly and student-oriented. From top to bottom, "Everybody in the MBA office goes out of their way to make sure we have great opportunities to learn outside the classroom, hear great speakers, and succeed in the program."

Every Texas A&M business school class is small, allowing plenty of individual attention while simultaneously encouraging interaction and discussion in (and outside) the classroom. Explains a student, "The classes are a perfect size to harness great discussions—a lot of opinions and viewpoints, but not so many that it's difficult to be heard in a single class period." At the same time, the intimate classroom environment means no one can slack off or slip through the cracks; "The classes are discussion-intensive, so every day requires a good bit of preparation." On the whole, students admit that Mays is a "very, very competitive environment," and, to keep up with the program's demands, students "often spend weekends studying and preparing for the upcoming week."

If Mays students didn't already have enough on their plate, the program includes a plethora of curricular and extracurricular activities that are designed to add depth and practical experience to the program. Of particular note, the MBA includes a required consulting project, which gives students the opportunity to apply classroom principals to a real-world business environment. Students can also sharpen their investment acumen through the Reliant Energy Securities & Commodities Trading Center, where Bloomberg terminals keep finance students in touch with the market. Beyond curricular offerings, the program incorporates enrichment features like the "Technology Transfer Challenge" case competition, a "Dean's Speaker Series" and opportunities for executive coaching and leadership development and training.

Career and Placement

With an excellent 98 percent job placement rate, it's no surprise that students sing the praises of the Graduate Business Career Services Office. The Career Services staff is "professional, respectful, and wonderful to work with," and is lauded for coming up with "creative ideas in a challenging internship/job market." Another unique advantage of the school's sixteen-month format is that A&M students graduate in December, making them "available for that recruiting period when there is not a large supply of MBA students attempting to be recruited."

In addition to the business school's job placement services, the school's active alumni network is another benefit of attending Texas A&M. With graduates all over Texas and beyond, "the Aggie network is famous for how in-touch alumni are to students." In a recent academic year, the majority of Texas A&M graduates (almost 60 percent) took jobs in the southwest, and most students went on to work in consulting, finance, management, or marketing. Last year, the median starting salary was $88,000.

Student Life and Environment

Between classes, homework, lectures, and social life, there is "never a dull moment" at Texas A&M. Though most MBA candidates say their coursework keeps them supremely occupied, they also appreciate the openness and camaraderie that exists between the students at Mays Business School. While students are "determined to succeed," "everybody in the class is very social and works together." Within the Mays community, "Friendliness and professionalism abound."

The business school is located on Texas A&M's main campus, home to 48,000 students. Politically and socially, "A&M is a very conservative school and the students, for the most part, are very conservative" in the business school as well. As a part of a large, research university, "It is very easy to get involved in Texas A&M's culture. Football games and other outside activities are a "must see" and current students make it a point to take new students to these events." School spirit surges—even in the graduate programs—and students tell us, "The Aggie Spirit is something one ought to experience." Surrounding College Station is a "quiet, largely safe" town of 125,000, which grew alongside the university. If you're craving something a little more urban, the campus is just a few hours drive from Austin, Dallas/Fort Worth, Houston, and San Antonio.

Admissions

Texas A&M deliberately limits the size of each incoming class, and admissions are competitive. Prospective students must have fulltime post-baccalaureate work experience to be considered for the program; however, Peace Corps, missionary work, or military service is counted as work experience, even if it took place before the college degree. Select applicants may be invited to interview with the Admissions Committee.

FINANCIAL FACTS

Annual tuition (in-state/ out-of-state)	$8,136/$18,108
Fees	$11,442
Cost of books	$2,114
Room & board (off-campus)	$9,986
% of students receiving aid	75
% of first-year students receiving aid	75
% of students receiving loans	65
% of students receiving grants	75
Average grant	$7,724
Average student loan debt	$28,341

ADMISSIONS

Admissions Selectivity Rating	96
# of applications received	576
% applicants accepted	23
% acceptees attending	53
Average GMAT	652
Range of GMAT	610–700
Average GPA	3.38
TOEFL required of international students	Yes
Minimum TOEFL (paper/computer)	600/250
Application fee	$125
International application fee	$150
Application Deadline/Notification	
Round 1:	11/1 / NR
Round 2:	1/4 / NR
Round 3:	2/28 / NR
Round 4:	4/15 / NR
Early decision program?	No
Deferment available	Yes
Maximum length of deferment	1 year
Transfer students accepted	No
Non-fall admissions	No
Need-blind admissions	Yes

EMPLOYMENT PROFILE

Career Rating	92	**Grads Employed by Function**	**% Avg. Salary**
Percent employed at graduation	67	Marketing	6 $91,640
Percent employed 3 months after graduation	89	Operations	13 $74,000
		Consulting	30 $84,267
Average base starting salary	$85,229	Management	7 $87,333
Primary Source of Full-time Job Acceptances		Finance	30 $88,500
School-facilitated activities	21 (39%)	HR	4 $83,525
Graduate-facilitated activities	33 (61%)	MIS	11 $81,667

Top 5 Employers Hiring Grads
Hewlett-Packard (5), AT&T (3), Lockheed Martin (2), Intel (2), Cameron International (2)

TEXAS A&M UNIVERSITY—CORPUS CHRISTI
COLLEGE OF BUSINESS

GENERAL INFORMATION

Type of school	Public
Academic calendar	Semester

SURVEY SAYS...
Happy students
Smart classrooms

STUDENTS

Enrollment of parent institution	9,468
Enrollment of MBA Program	184
% male/female	54/46
% part-time	55
% minorities	6
% international	76
Average age at entry	27

ACADEMICS

Academic Experience Rating	68
Profs interesting rating	79
Profs accessible rating	79
% female faculty	30
% minority faculty	23

Academics

Students at Texas A&M University—Corpus Christi (TAMUCC) say that in order to truly appreciate their school's stellar MBA programs, you must first put them in proper geographical perspective. TAMUCC "is a regional school, so comparing it with the experience of [students] at Top-25 schools is not fair," one such student points. However, "Given its status as a regional school and the mission of the university as it relates to the regional approach, the TAMUCC MBA program is excellent." Indeed, most here want a program that is first and foremost convenient, affordable, and flexible enough to accommodate students with full-time jobs. In these areas and more, students here tell us, TAMUCC delivers.

Point in case: TAMUCC "has a great core foundation and the potential to become a great public university." MBAs here benefit from the "wide variety of students [from] different countries" which broadens their educational experience. There is a particularly strong Hispanic student presence and a concurrent focus on business matters of interest to the American-Hispanic community. And then, of course, there's the "affordable tuition," the "small size of most classes"—the program is "not...too congested while still being large enough to have good facilities"—and the "easy-to-deal-with university administration," which works hard to ease the burdens of the school's overtaxed students. One student took special note of the program's "flexibility for working parents. I'm a single parent and have felt supported and encouraged by all of my professors and my advisor."

Similarly, professors "take the students' welfare into consideration" and "will always create extra time outside the class to answer questions to help make the learning process easy." Most instructors here "are very passionate about their work and it shows in their lecturing. They have relevant experience in their disciplines that they can relate to students showing real-life applications of the material." As one student explains, "I believe that the professors are the greatest strengths [of the program]. The passion and experience that they bring to the classroom is great. There are a couple who are not so great, but the majority are fantastic. Their enthusiasm makes you want to learn, and the material is challenging." TAMUCC offers its MBAs two areas of concentration: international business, and health care management.

Career and Placement

The TAMUCC Career Services office provides counseling and placement services for all undergraduates, graduate students, and alumni of the university. Frequent seminars and presentations are offered on such topics as "How to Job Search in the 'Hidden Market,'" "The Second Interview and Salary Negotiation," and "How to Get a Federal Job." The office also provides career counseling, computer-based self-assessments, job search advisement, online and hard-copy job postings, a career resource library and computer lab, videotaped mock interviews, and job fairs and on-campus recruiting events.

Top employers in the area include the Naval Air Station Corpus Christi, Christus Spohn Health System, the Corpus Christi Army Depot, H-E-B Grocery Co., Bay Limited, SSP Partners/Circle K, Driscoll Children's Hospital, APAC, First Data, and Gulf Marine Fabricators.

ADMISSIONS CONTACT: SHARON POLANSKY, DIRECTOR OF MASTER'S PROGRAMS
ADDRESS: 6300 OCEAN DRIVE UNIT 5808 CORPUS CHRISTI, TX 78412-5808
PHONE: 361-825-2655 • FAX: 361-825-2725
E-MAIL: SHARON.POLANSKY@TAMUCC.EDU • WEBSITE: WWW.COB.TAMUCC.EDU

Student Life and Environment

"There is a very diverse population from a multitude of cultures" within the TAMUCC MBA program, and "this is very important…in South Texas, [where] the majority of the population is either Hispanic or white." Students here are "very ambitious and amiable," and while "discussions in class are heated, there is a mutual respect." The student body "is about 30 percent international," "which gives a very diverse, unique experience in the classroom." A sizeable group of military personnel further adds to the diverse backgrounds and perspectives. Except for the international students, most here are "balancing a full work load, course load, family life and other extracurricular activities."

TAMUCC's "attractive campus by the ocean" engenders a "laid-back, casual, 'feels like island time'" atmosphere. "Don't let people wearing flip flops fool you," though; these are "very hardworking/studying individuals." The program forces them to be actively involved in class, as the classroom "is very participation-oriented rather than the professor only lecturing." Fortunately TAMUCC students are up to the challenge.

Admissions

All applicants to the TAMUCC MBA program must submit the following materials: official transcripts for all undergraduate and graduate work; an official score report for the GMAT (test score can be no more than five years old); two letters or recommendation; a current resume or curriculum vitae; a personal essay stating your reasons for pursuing the MBA; and a completed application form. In addition, international students whose first language is not English must submit an official score for the TOEFL and an evaluation of non-English language transcripts executed by Education Credential Evaluators, Inc., International Education Research Foundation, Inc., or World Education Services. All international applicants must submit an I-34 form or other notarized confirmation of adequate financial support, a copy of their current visa, and proof of medical insurance.

FINANCIAL FACTS

Annual tuition (in-state/ out-of-state)	$3,114/$8,100
Fees	$1,252
Cost of books	$726
Room & board (on/off-campus)	$9,250/$8,941

ADMISSIONS

Admissions Selectivity Rating	**69**
# of applications received	47
% applicants accepted	87
% acceptees attending	80
Average GMAT	515
Range of GMAT	460–563
Average GPA	3.17
TOEFL required of international students	Yes
Minimum TOEFL (paper/computer)	550/213
Application fee	$50
International application fee	$70
Regular application deadline	7/15
Early decision program?	No
Deferment available	Yes
Maximum length of deferment	1 year
Transfer students accepted	Yes
Transfer application policy: Possibility of transferring in 6 credits from accredited school with grade of B or above.	
Non-fall admissions	Yes
Need-blind admissions	Yes

TEXAS CHRISTIAN UNIVERSITY
THE M. J. NEELEY SCHOOL OF BUSINESS

GENERAL INFORMATION
Type of school   Private
Academic calendar   Semester

SURVEY SAYS...
Good peer network
Solid preparation in:
Operations
Communication/interpersonal skills

STUDENTS
Enrollment of parent institution	8,853
Enrollment of MBA Program	224
% male/female	69/31
% part-time	55
% international	25
Average age at entry	27
Average years work experience at entry	4

ACADEMICS
Academic Experience Rating	**90**
Student/faculty ratio	7:1
Profs interesting rating	89
Profs accessible rating	91
% female faculty	25
% minority faculty	10

Joint Degrees
Educational Leadership, MBA/EdD, 3 academic years; physics PhD/MBA, 6 academic years including dissertation; Master of International Management, 2 academic years.

Prominent Alumni
Bob McCann, President, Global Private Client Gp, Merrill Lynch; Luther King, Luther King Capital Management; Gordon England, Secretary of the Navy; John Davis III, CEO and Chairman, Pegasus Systems; James I Cash Jr, Ph.D., Former James Robison Prof, Harvard Business School.

Academics

Just five miles from downtown Fort Worth, the Neeley School of Business at Texas Christian University maintains "great connections" in the area, bringing in "the best faculty, who are well-published and have been in their industries or departments for a long time." Real-world applications are definitely emphasized here, and "The professors have lot of industry experience and this makes the teaching very effective." Of particular note, the school operates the "the best supply chain program in Texas," as well as a reputable program in finance.

At TCU, the MBA workload is substantial. Students warn, "The first two semesters can be completely exhausting"—but you'll get plenty of support, too. Despite TCU's big city opportunities, intimacy is what sets this MBA program apart. At TCU, "Faculty bends over backwards to maximize our experiences" and they "genuinely care about the success of the students." A student praises, "TCU's faculty has an open-door policy that, for the first time in my educational and occupational history, actually exists. I have never had any trouble or delay in receiving an answer to a question or feedback to an idea." In addition to their relationship with the faculty, the small class sizes also allow students "to get to know each of my classmates on a personal level, providing more fulfilling networking opportunities in the future."

On that note, TCU's curriculum is specifically designed to "develop more soft skills," in addition to honing quantitative ability. "First-years complete almost all assignments in the first semester in teams," which is both a challenge and a benefit; "Learning how to work in the team environment has been a challenge in of itself but also very rewarding"—not to mention, "great practice for the workplace." Students also prepare for the workplace through TCU's myriad experiential learning programs, such as the sales and marketing case competition, business simulations, and through the unique "Neeley and Associates, a class offered where students act as consultants to help real businesses solve real problems." To encourage participation in co-curricular activities, the university even offers "scholarships for international trips and MBA conferences."

The MBA program at TCU is dynamic, committed to improvement, and responsive to student opinion. With an eye to the future, "The administration really cares about the students and makes quite an effort to hear what our concerns are and is always looking for feedback from events, speakers, and classes." Equally impressive, "The administration is very interested in obtaining and acting on feedback from employers." Recently, for example, "Employers had provided feedback that past interns did not have as much financial modeling skill as they would like, so the administration addressed this by implementing financial modeling courses."

Career and Placement

At TCU, "Career services is outstanding," providing students with individualized career coaching, a variety of interview preparation strategies, networking events like employer roundtables, numerous career development seminars, and special programs—including a trip to Wall Street in New York City. Considered a business powerhouse in the Dallas-Fort Worth area, "*Fortune* 500 companies regularly visit campus," and the list of important employers is extensive. In recent years, top employers include Accenture, American Airlines, Bank of America, Countrywide Financial, Dell Computer, DHL, Honeywell, Goldman Sachs, Lockheed Martin, Morgan Stanley, Microsoft, Nestle Purina, Nokia, Texas Instruments, Toyota, Verizon, and Wachovia Corporation. The career center also helps MBA candidates find their summer internships, with 98 percent of students receiving an internship position each year.

In recent years, TCU students were offered an average salary of over $70,000 upon graduation, with a quarter of the class also receiving signing bonuses. Almost 80 percent of students had accepted a position within 90 days of graduation. What's more, these great placements will pay off for TCU graduates in many years to come. One of the major benefits of TCU is the "active alumni who are willing to help out current students."

Student Life and Environment

Academics are challenging at TCU, and "There are always deadlines, projects, cases, homework and readings due." Therefore, "Time management is one of the most important skills to have" as a TCU student. Fortunately, the school offers the pleasant atmosphere and modern facilities that busy business students need to succeed. The recently constructed Smith Hall offers "an abundance of study rooms with white boards for MBA students," as well as "an MBA lounge with printer, couches, and lockers for each student."

TCU students are united by a "strong community and conservative values," and students say, "The Neeley School does an outstanding job of recruiting down-to-earth people that would rather help one another succeed than aggressively compete against each other."

The community is open and inclusive, and "There are weekly social events for MBA students and their significant others or friends." In fact, for students with families, "Spouses are invited to all social gatherings, and they were invited on a study abroad class over winter break." With so many activities to juggle, it's no surprise that, "by the weekend everyone is fairly exhausted from school," yet students "try to get together for the football game or a class party or something." To blow off steam, others "play intramural sports and take workout classes at the rec center."

Admissions

Students in the MBA program have an average GMAT score of 634, though students have been accepted with GMAT scores anywhere in the 500 to 700 range. Four years of professional work experience is the average among applicants. The average age is 27. Professional recommendations are preferred over academic recommendations. A small percentage (about 10 percent) is admitted to the full-time program directly out of college. Applicants with potential for admission will be invited to interview.

FINANCIAL FACTS

Annual tuition	$26,460
Fees	$4,200
Cost of books	$1,600
Room & board	
(off-campus)	$12,000
% of students receiving aid	96
% of first-year students	
receiving aid	91
% of students receiving loans	51
% of students receiving grants	96
Average award package	$33,069
Average grant	$20,042

ADMISSIONS

Admissions Selectivity Rating	86
# of applications received	178
% applicants accepted	56
% acceptees attending	58
Average GMAT	634
Range of GMAT	590–680
Average GPA	3.25
TOEFL required of	
international students	Yes
Minimum TOEFL	
(paper/computer)	600/250
Application fee	$75
International application fee	$75
Application Deadline/Notification	
Round 1:	11/15 / 12/15
Round 2:	1/15 / 2/15
Round 3:	3/1 / 4/1
Round 4:	4/15 / 5/15
Early decision program?	Yes
ED Deadline/Notification	NR / 12/15
Deferment available	Yes
Maximum length	
of deferment	1 year
Transfer students accepted	Yes
Transfer application policy:	
Maximum transferable credits are	
six semester hours from an	
AACSB accredited institution.	
Non-fall admissions	Yes
Need-blind admissions	Yes

EMPLOYMENT PROFILE

		Grads Employed by Function	% Avg. Salary
Career Rating	86		
Percent employed at graduation	40	Marketing	22 $76,640
Percent employed 3 months		Operations	19 $69,250
after graduation	56	Management	11 $61,333
Average base starting salary	$69,169	Finance	26 $71,045
Primary Source of Full-time Job Acceptances		HR	7
School-facilitated activities	NR (66%)	MIS	4
Graduate-facilitated activities	NR (34%)	**Top 5 Employers Hiring Grads**	

Top 5 Employers Hiring Grads
American Airlines (4), Sabre Holdings (4), Lockheed Martin (2), Energy Future Holings (1), Texas Health Resources (1)

TEXAS SOUTHERN UNIVERSITY
JESSE H. JONES SCHOOL OF BUSINESS

GENERAL INFORMATION

Type of school   Public
Academic calendar   Trimester

SURVEY SAYS...

Solid preparation in:
Finance
General management
Operations
Entrepreneurial studies

STUDENTS

Enrollment of parent
  institution   9,273
Enrollment of MBA Program 174
% part-time   100
Average age at entry   25
Average years work experience
  at entry   2

ACADEMICS

Academic Experience Rating 70
Student/faculty ratio   22:1
Profs interesting rating   61
Profs accessible rating   70
% female faculty   7
% minority faculty   28

Joint Degrees

JD/MBA, 5 years.

Prominent Alumni

Gerald B. Smith, Finance &
Investment; Kase Lawal, Oil & Gas.

Academics

Students at the Texas Southern University's Jesse H. Jones School of Business have a lot of great things to say about their program, not the least of which is the school's focus on "diversity and entrepreneurship." Students enrolled in the MBA program at this historically black college have four degree tracks to choose from. JHJ offers an MBA degree with a general business concentration, an MBA with a health care administration concentration, a dual MBA/JD degree, and a Master's of Science degree in Management Information Systems. Whatever degree program they ultimately choose, students across the board speak of a "very intense program with very friendly and accessible staff members" and a "challenging" curriculum. "Professors are awesome," students say, and they "love the relationship between students and professors." In fact, one of the most common reasons that students choose Texas Southern is because of the school's visionary and "awesome" professors. Of these luminaries, students say, "They are highly competitive and knowledgeable about their professions," and students appreciate the "quality of their experience and expertise." Also, as one student points out, the professors show a distinct "ability to steer students' creativity and innovation." Despite these accolades, a few students commented that there could be "more professors" and that the "administration needs major work."

Beyond the "convenience" and "academic excellence" along with "a unique perspective" that Texas Southern offers, other strengths cited by students were the school's "location, cost, [and] small classes." "My MBA class is like a small family," one student said. While the small class sizes are a boon when it comes to gaining access to faculty, students say it can also be a limitation, especially when it comes to course selection. "We need more marketing courses," one student says. One student believes the problem is that "the business school does not fully challenge the academic potential of the students." Another adds that the school needs to "broaden the curriculum and course offerings," and that the administration should "design classes around the application of curriculum." But on the whole, however, student comments lean more toward the positive. "My overall academic experience has been great," one student says. "It's a good school," another sums up.

Career and Placement

According to the school, Texas Southern is a "major historically black college and university located in a leading international business environment." Located in Houston, Texas, the school prides itself—and students enjoy the benefits of—its "location, location, location," which any business student knows is a key component to landing the right job post-graduation. Hometown Houston offers "good career and placement" according to students. The largest city in Texas and the fourth largest city in the United States, Houston and its "booming economy" attract "31,000 new jobs among the 18 *Fortune* 500 companies and thousands of energy-related firms headquartered here," according to the school's website.

The Cooperative Education and Placement Services Center at Texas Southern University works every year to capitalize on the school's great location, and bring more companies on campus to recruiting events. The center hosts information sessions throughout the year where students can meet with company representatives to learn more about opportunities with their firm. Some of the companies that have conducted sessions recently are: Black & Decker, CITGO, Continental Airlines, Shell Oil Company, Target, Pfizer, and Kraft Foods. Other companies have visited the campus as part of a career development series, and they include: Wells Fargo, JPMorgan Chase, American Express Company, Merrill Lynch, and ING.

ADMISSIONS CONTACT: BOBBIE J. RICHARDSON, COORDINATOR - GRADUATE BUSINESS PROGRAMS
ADDRESS: OFFICE OF GRAD. PROGRAMS IN BUSINESS, JHJ SCHOOL OF BUSINESS HOUSTON, TX 77004
PHONE: (713) 313-7309 • FAX: (713) 313-7722
E-MAIL: RICHARDSON_BJ@TSU.EDU • WEBSITE: WWW.TSU.EDU/ACADEMICS/BUSINESS

Student Life and Environment

When it comes to student life at Texas Southern, it's literally all about the students. Given Texas Southern's small class size and "intimate" learning environment, it's no wonder that student life at the school is characterized by a sense of "community" and a "welcoming" atmosphere. In fact, the "intimacy of the students in the program" is a common theme running throughout student comments about Texas Southern. Students say the class is like a "tight-knit family," characterized by "supportive instructors" and "diverse," "open communications." Students here appreciate the "unique perspective" their peers bring to the campus, and note that they "cut across every strata—social, economic, business experience, [and] age." Despite their differences, these "talented," and "career-oriented" students "have similar goals and objectives," commonalities that are bolstered by the school's "encouragement of teamwork" and "smart, competitive, and fun" learning environment. It helps that students in the program are "nice and professional" and "encouraging and compassionate about education." It's clear that Texas Southern's "professional, career-focused, results-driven, friendly, and down-to-earth" MBAs feel they are in good company.

Admissions

Students seeking admission to any of Texas Southern's four degree programs will need to submit, along with the application fee and completed application, official transcripts from all colleges and universities previously attended; GRE, GMAT and TOEFL scores; a personal statement; a current resume; and two letters of recommendation. There is an English Proficiency Requirement. Each graduate student who is admitted must have an analytical writing score of 3.5 or higher on the GRE or GMAT exam or enroll in a graduate-level English class. Admission is for the fall semester only. Conditional admission may be offered to students who do not meet all of the application requirements but demonstrate promise and ability.

FINANCIAL FACTS

Annual tuition (in-state/ out-of-state)	$1,800/$6,165
Fees	$3,593
Cost of books	$500
Room & board (on/off-campus)	$6,500/$8,000
% of students receiving aid	25
% of first-year students receiving aid	40

ADMISSIONS

Admissions Selectivity Rating	74
# of applications received	131
% applicants accepted	50
% acceptees attending	95
Average GMAT	435
Range of GMAT	397–588
Average GPA	3.12
TOEFL required of international students	Yes
Minimum TOEFL (paper/computer)	550/213
Application fee	$50
International application fee	$78
Regular application deadline	7/15
Regular notification	8/15
Early decision program?	Yes
ED Deadline/Notification	NR / 6/15
Deferment available	Yes
Maximum length of deferment	1 year
Transfer students accepted	Yes
Transfer application policy: Apply similar to regular applicants.	
Non-fall admissions	Yes
Need-blind admissions	Yes

EMPLOYMENT PROFILE

Career Rating		80	Grads Employed by Function	% Avg. Salary
Primary Source of Full-time Job Acceptances			Marketing	35 NR
School-facilitated activities	59 (62%)		Finance	20 NR
Unknown	22 (23%)		HR	10 NR
			MIS	20 NR

Top 5 Employers Hiring Grads
Sysco, Citgo, City of Houston, Accenture, State of Texas

TEXAS TECH UNIVERSITY
JERRY S. RAWLS COLLEGE OF BUSINESS ADMINISTRATION

GENERAL INFORMATION
Type of school   Public

SURVEY SAYS...
Good social scene
Happy students
Solid preparation in:
Finance

STUDENTS
Enrollment of parent institution	30,049
Enrollment of MBA Program	546
% male/female	75/25
% out-of-state	10
% part-time	89
% minorities	8
% international	27
Average age at entry	31
Average years work experience at entry	8

ACADEMICS
Academic Experience Rating	80
Student/faculty ratio	9:1
Profs interesting rating	87
Profs accessible rating	85
% female faculty	18
% minority faculty	3

Joint Degrees
MD/MBA, 4 years; JD/MBA, 3 years; MA foreign language/MBA, 2 years; MA Architecture/MBA; 2.5 years; dual MBA programs with: Universidad Anahuac/Mexico, 2 years; Sup de Co Montpellier, 2 years.

Prominent Alumni
Jerry V. Smith, President, J. V. Smith Professional Corporation-CPA; James C. Wetherbe, PhD, TTU-Bobby G. Stevenson Chair in Info. Tech.

Academics

Busy West Texas professionals seeking an MBA program with "affordable tuition, friendly professors, and a broad curriculum" may find a home at the Rawls College of Business at Texas Tech. Rawls' MBA program offers evening courses to part-time and full-time students. In addition, Executive-style MBA programs offer the option of a convenient block scheduling system that students like ("We meet twice a year for nine days straight, eight hours a day") or a one-weekend-a-month calendar. Rawls has custom designed a number of combined degrees and Executive-style MBA programs to fit the needs of professionals of all stripes. A combined MD/MBA "is a unique opportunity providing the experience and preparation for a future in healthcare administration or private practice." Dual business degrees are also available in architecture, foreign languages, law, personal financial planning, and environmental toxicology. An Executive-style MBA for Physicians and Dentists helps train medical professionals who are as proficient at business as they are at healing.

Students praise the Rawls MBA for "the flexibility it offers to working professionals" and for a "benefit/cost ratio much greater than similar programs" in the area. They are especially effusive about the administration, which "takes care of everything for the students. They register us for classes, feed us, and provide us with all of the materials and resources needed for our classes." As one student puts it, "The administration is a joy to work with. If you have any questions about courses, registration, etc. they respond quickly to emails and have an open-door policy." Likewise, students are "especially impressed by the willingness of the professors to accommodate students with full-time jobs and families. As a group, they have been very helpful in making sure that my workload is effective in the curriculum and works with my schedule."

Tech, one student observes, is "not so large and accomplished that everyone has a sense of entitlement and arrogance, yet it's not small and struggling to keep its head above water." It is large enough to offer a broad selection of concentrations, including agribusiness, entrepreneurship, health organization management, MIS, real estate, and international business. Instructors in these disciplines "are beyond knowledgeable in their fields and are also easy to access for questions about course work or the job market in their particular field. I have never met anyone within the program that was not willing to help the students succeed," one student writes.

Career and Placement

Texas Tech serves a full-time and part-time student body. Many of the students in the Executive-style MBA program attend at the expense of their employers and who intend to remain with those employers after graduation. Companies likely to employ Texas Tech MBAs include Accenture, Blue Linx Corp., CINTAS, Comerica, Conoco Phillips, Consolidated Graphics, Cox Communications, Deloitte & Touche, Enterprise Rent-a-Car, Ernst & Young, Exxon Mobil, Geico, Health Smart Preferred Care, JC Penney, JPMorgan Chase, KPMG, Lockheed Martin, National Instruments, Phillip Morris USA, Plains Capital, PricewaterhouseCoopers, Pulte Homes, Rolled Alloys, Ryan and Company, SBC, Sherwin-Williams, Southwest Bank of Texas, Target, Texas Bank, Texas Tech University, USAA, USG Corp., Wal Mart, Walgreens, Wells Fargo Bank, and Wells Fargo Financial.

ADMISSIONS CONTACT: CINDY BARNES, DIRECTOR, GRADUATE SERVICES CENTER
ADDRESS: RAWLS COLLEGE OF BUSINESS, GRADUATE SERVICES CENTER LUBBOCK, TX 79409-2101
PHONE: 806-742-3184 • FAX: 806-742-3958
E-MAIL: MBA@TTU.EDU • WEBSITE: MBA.BA.TTU.EDU

Student Life and Environment

The Texas Tech campus "has excellent facilities overall," and while the b-school facilities themselves "need to be improved," the school is in the process of effecting those improvements. One student explains: "They've finished the campaign for a new building, and it will be open in a few years. In fact, it's going to be the first LEED-certified 'green' building on campus, and will be a much better place to house the COB. As forward-thinking as the Rawls College of Business is, their facilities don't reflect their innovation and accolades." Not yet, but they will soon enough.

The rest of the "beautiful" Tech campus is "filled with art from around the world," and "its Spanish-style architecture is unique and beautiful." Campus amenities include "a gym [that] has outstanding equipment and a library [that] has an extensive availability of resources, including media resources and things through interlibrary loan (the staff is very helpful with this)." It's a welcoming atmosphere on campus, according to one student: "I have always felt comfortable on Tech campus, especially walking around at night." It's a busy place; "there are always sporting events to attend on the weekends and the Center for Campus Life and Student Government Association [is] always hosting free events for students. The graduate association also makes sure students are involved with monthly socials, philanthropy events (especially during the holidays), and campus-wide events, like tailgating before football games. The Rawls Graduate Association works especially hard to connect students in the program together, making classes more comfortable and provides more networking overall."

Admissions

Texas Tech requires applicants to submit undergraduate transcripts, GMAT scores, and a resume. Other optional elements of the application considered by the school include research experience, awards, leadership positions held in college and/or industry, civic and volunteer activities, motivation, evidence of past success, letters of recommendation, and the admissions office's assessment of the applicant's potential to provide a unique perspective within the program. To boost minority recruitment, the school advertises in minority magazines, recruits on minority college campuses in New Mexico and Texas, and attends and recruits at minority forums and at conferences such as the National Black Graduate Student Conference.

FINANCIAL FACTS

Annual tuition (in-state/ out-of-state)	$5,100/$11,750
Fees	$3,000
Cost of books	$1,500
Room & board	$6,000
% of students receiving aid	100
% of first-year students receiving aid	100
% of students receiving grants	100
Average grant	$2,000
Average student loan debt	$10,528

ADMISSIONS

Admissions Selectivity Rating	72
# of applications received	477
% applicants accepted	82
% acceptees attending	78
Average GMAT	547
Range of GMAT	510–590
Average GPA	3.22
TOEFL required of international students	Yes
Minimum TOEFL (paper/computer)	550/213
Application fee	$50
International application fee	$75
Early decision program?	No
Deferment available	Yes
Maximum length of deferment	1 year
Transfer students accepted	Yes
Transfer application policy: Up to six hours may transfer.	
Non-fall admissions	Yes
Need-blind admissions	Yes

EMPLOYMENT PROFILE

Career Rating	81	Grads Employed by Function% Avg. Salary	
Percent employed at graduation	40	Operations	40 $55,000
Percent employed 3 months after graduation	47	Finance	60 $54,333
Average base starting salary	$54,600	**Top 5 Employers Hiring Grads**	
Primary Source of Full-time Job Acceptances		Ryan & Co., Texas Instruments, Chevron	
School-facilitated activities	1 (20%)	Phillips, Comerica Bank,	
Graduate-facilitated activities	4 (80%)	PricewaterhouseCoopers	

THUNDERBIRD
SCHOOL OF GLOBAL MANAGEMENT

GENERAL INFORMATION

Type of school	Private
Academic calendar	Trimesters

SURVEY SAYS...
Friendly students
Good social scene
Good peer network
Solid preparation in:
General management
Teamwork
Communication/interpersonal skills
Doing business in a global economy

STUDENTS

Enrollment of parent institution	1,385
Enrollment of MBA Program	589
% male/female	68/32
% out-of-state	85
% part-time	0
% minorities	8
% international	44
Average age at entry	28
Average years work experience at entry	5

ACADEMICS

Academic Experience Rating	**88**
Student/faculty ratio	26:1
Profs interesting rating	82
Profs accessible rating	79
% female faculty	24
% minority faculty	24

Joint Degrees
MBA/Master of Global Management, full-time, 12–18 months to complete program; MBA/JD from Vermont Law School, full-time, approximately 33–36 months to complete program; MBA/Master of Environmental Law from Vermont Law School, full-time, 24–27 months to complete program; MA-GAM or MS-GM/JD from Vermont Law School, full-time, 33–36 months to complete; MA-GAM or MS-GM/Master of Environmental Law and Policy from Vermont Law School, full time, 15 months to complete.

Academics

Offering the "#1 ranked global MBA" in the United States," with 44 percent of students hailing from abroad, the Thunderbird School of Graduate Management reflects the "melting pot of the global community." Due to the school's "excellent reputation, top ranking in international specialization, good mix of corporate social responsibility, [and] distance education options," Thunderbird offers "a truly global curriculum that prepares graduates to enter a global business environment." With students matriculating from over 50 countries, Thunderbird MBAs are "very willing to help each other and create a strong learning atmosphere; are truly passionate about global business; are well-traveled and informed about social issues; [and are] committed to sustainable development, corporate social responsibility and creating good around the world." As one MBA explains, "When students are asked 'Where are you from?' the typical answer is, 'It is complicated'"

Much like their students, professors at Thunderbird are "passionate and thought-provoking; they breathe ambition into me and my cohorts by holding us to high standards." Academically, the program is "very challenging." The "global curriculum, access to quality professors with diverse backgrounds, exposure to foreign cultures, and a mandatory second language requirement," "stretches you and causes you to grow as a leader." In addition, students are "ethnically diverse" and bring "various work experiences from many countries" to the classroom.

"While the professors are incredible," some feel "the administration is not student-focused" and can be "somewhat unorganized and rigid." Says, another, "There have been several occasions where their decisions or inaction have left students high and dry." Students band together however to initiate change. As one MBA says, "this school's greatest asset, I think, is its student culture of camaraderie and solidarity."

Career and Placement

The Career Management Center actively initiates relationships with Thunderbird MBA students from Day One. Students meet with a career counselor before even beginning course work. However, students say "the Career Center has a tough challenge: Hundreds of students from over 50 countries all trying to find jobs in different industries. If you know exactly what you're looking for, they're fantastic. But they're stretched too thin to handle the workload." However, any strain on the Career Management Center is easily countered by "strong networking and alumni connections."

In 2009, 61 percent of full-time MBA students seeking employment had secured positions within three months of graduation with a mean base salary of $76,309. Top employers included: Johnson & Johnson, Depository Trust & Clearing Corporation, FDIC, American Express, and Cisco.

Student Life and Environment

Students at Thunderbird "come from every walk of life, continent, culture, [and] functional background you can imagine." An "optimistic, active, intelligent" set, the student body is "very diverse, [and] well-traveled." Most "have lived outside the U.S. for most of their lives and most speak at least two languages." As one student says, "[E]ach person is unique. Everyone has a very different story." What they have in common is that they all "want to make a difference in the world." Thunderbird MBAs are "interested in positions in NGO's, government, entrepreneurship, as well as corporat[ions], [and] want to live and work in other countries." Despite their diversity, students are united by a desire for seeking adventure; "The best thing is everyone has a great sense of humor. We're all hard working and nobody makes excuses. We help each other out a lot and push everyone to succeed."

School life "is fantastic. It's a small campus, but a welcome[ing] one." Club activities are "very active. We have Regional Night such as Asian Night, American Night, African Night, where we can experience diverse culture[s] with food and performances." In addition, there are "plenty of networking events and social/athletic activities. The campus has a pub located on campus that enables social interaction. Every time you meet with a new cohort from a different part of the world at the pub you get a feeling that you are transported to an alternate part of the globe."

Others say "life [at Thunderbird] is largely dedicated to studies." "The workload keeps you in the library or locked in team meetings. Lunch is a social experience and [then it's] off to class with time for sports later and [attending] the big thing on campus." Some say hometown Glendale can be a bit of a "dull town. . .but that keeps us from being distracted from studies." Others reflect on it differently: "[B]ecause I want to work for good grades, school is busy. I also love learning." Students say the facilities and infrastructure could some updating; "the buildings are really old, and until some time ago there was no wi-fi. Students studying remotely say the school could make efforts to "improve remote access to TA and other on-campus programs for commuters."

Admissions

To apply to Thunderbird, students must submit a completed online application, three personal essays, GMAT scores (and TOEFL scores for international students), two letters of recommendation, official transcripts, and a resume. For the accelerated program, applicants must have the above requirements and the following additional requirements: an undergraduate degree in business or completed course work in statistics, accounting, finance and management, or a minimum of five years work experience with managerial and budget responsibilities. Prior to the beginning of the traditional or accelerated MBA program, all students must have completed course work in microeconomics and macroeconomics. Thunderbird offers an online economics boot camp prior to the beginning of Foundations Week that will satisfy the micro- and macroeconomics requirement. Waivers for micro- and macroeconomics are evaluated and granted during the admission review. While there are no prerequisite requirements for statistics, accounting and finance, applicants lacking course work or expertise in these subjects can take part in a series of pre-MBA programs on campus, two weeks prior to the beginning of Foundations Week.

Prominent Alumni

Frances Sevilla-Sacasa, President, U.S. Trust Corporation; Luis Moreno, President, Inter-American Development Bank.

FINANCIAL FACTS

Cost of books	$1,435
Room & board	
(on/off-campus)	$5,640/$9,205
% of students receiving aid	92
% of first-year students	
receiving aid	75
% of students receiving loans	63
% of students receiving grants	50
Average award package	$41,444
Average grant	$12,970
Average student loan debt	$29,319

ADMISSIONS

Admissions Selectivity Rating	90
# of applications received	593
% applicants accepted	75
% acceptees attending	59
Average GMAT	610
Range of GMAT	560–650
Average GPA	3.31
TOEFL required of	
international students	Yes
Minimum TOEFL	
(paper/computer)	600/250
Application fee	$125
Regular application deadline	3/3
Application Deadline/Notification	
Round 1:	1/7 / NR
Round 2:	3/3 / NR
Round 3:	4/28 / NR
Round 4:	6/30 / NR
Early decision program?	No
Deferment available	Yes
Maximum length	
of deferment	1 year
Transfer students accepted	No
Non-fall admissions	Yes
Need-blind admissions	Yes

EMPLOYMENT PROFILE

Career Rating	86	Grads Employed by Function	% Avg. Salary
Percent employed at graduation	42	Marketing	34 $82,313
Percent employed 3 months		Operations	11 $80,363
after graduation	67	Consulting	14 $92,014
Average base starting salary	$84,295	Management	14 $80,150
Primary Source of Full-time Job Acceptances		Finance	21 $85,444
School-facilitated activities	79 (64%)	HR	3 $97,000
Graduate-facilitated activities	45 (36%)	**Top 5 Employers Hiring Grads**	
		Cisco (6), Hilti (6), General Electric (5), American Express (4), IBM (4)	

TULANE UNIVERSITY
FREEMAN SCHOOL OF BUSINESS

GENERAL INFORMATION
Type of school	Private
Academic calendar	Semester

SURVEY SAYS...
Good social scene
Smart classrooms
Solid preparation in:
Finance
Doing business in a global economy
Entrepreneurial studies

STUDENTS
Enrollment of parent institution	13,410
Enrollment of MBA Program	218
% male/female	76/24
% out-of-state	55
% part-time	15
% minorities	24
% international	38
Average age at entry	26
Average years work experience at entry	4

ACADEMICS
Academic Experience Rating	**88**
Student/faculty ratio	22:1
Profs interesting rating	82
Profs accessible rating	87
% female faculty	38
% minority faculty	5

Joint Degrees
MBA/MD, 5 years, MBA/JD, 4 years; MBA/Master of Arts in Latin American Studies, 2.5 years; MBA/Master of Health Administration, 2.5 years; MBA/Master of Political Science, 2.5 years; MACCT/JD, 4 calendar years; MACCT/MBA, 2 calendar years; MACCT/JD, 3.5 years; MBA/MEng, 2.5 years.

Academics

A number of outstanding features distinguish the Freeman School of Business at Tulane University, particularly in the area of finance, where enrolled students enjoy "one of the best finance programs in the country." The program is equipped with an "unmatched" trading floor that serves as the nexus for two key endeavors: management of the Darwin Fenner Fund, and investment analysis through the Burkenroad Reports. The former is a student-managed fund worth approximately $2.5 million; the latter allows teams of students to work with companies to analyze their industries and make recommendations.

Finance has such a "well-deserved great reputation" at Freeman that other strengths of the program are sometimes overlooked. Marketing "continues to grow here, while the energy specialization "is very smart for this area of the country." Freeman also excels in entrepreneurial studies; as one student explains, "I chose Tulane because of the ability to focus on entrepreneurship and the school's access to successful entrepreneurs, through whom I could learn to be a more effective business owner." Finally, the school recognizes the speed at which all business is becoming international through its "strong experiential Global Management program," which "sends the entire class on three trips abroad," thereby "emphasizing the global business curriculum in a truly hands-on environment."

The sum is greater than the considerable parts at Freeman, students tell us. One writes, "The greatest strengths of Tulane are its abilities to integrate the different segments of business and make them relevant, not just to corporate America, but also to small business and global business. Tulane also facilitates discussion on how your business or company can align its operations to take into consideration all stakeholders, thus becoming an organization that creates both profit and social good." An "excellent" relationship with the local community means that "business leaders around the community are accessible and supportive." Students also appreciate how the "school administration has done a great job in the recovery efforts since Katrina." Be forewarned that the program operates on seven-week terms that can fly by; "the first is by far the most intense, and they get gradually easier," one student explains.

Career and Placement

Tulane's Career Management Center earns mixed reviews from students. Several complain that "On campus recruiting is weak. We miss almost all of the big companies due to our location. We only get energy companies or a few other random companies based in Texas or the rest of the South to come to Tulane." Some simply wish the office would be "more proactive," but some go further, calling it the school's "weakest area" and asserting that "Students are practically on their own when it comes to acquiring an internship or employment." Several acknowledged that the down economy was certainly a factor in the Center's disappointing outcomes.

Companies most likely to hire Freeman MBAs include BearingPoint, Capital One, Citibank, Daymon Worldwide, Deloitte & Touche, Entergy, Federal Express, First Albany Capital, Hibernia, Johnson & Rice, JPMorgan Chase, Latitram, Piper Jaffray & Co., RBC, Simmons & Company, Teracore Consulting, Tidewater Marine, TXU, Verizon, and Wachovia.

ADMISSIONS CONTACT: BILL D. SANDEFER, DIRECTOR OF GRADUATE ADMISSIONS AND FINANCIAL AID
ADDRESS: 7 MCALISTER DRIVE, SUITE 401 NEW ORLEANS, LA 70118
PHONE: 504-865-5410 • FAX: 504-865-6770
E-MAIL: FREEMAN.ADMISSIONS@TULANE.EDU • WEBSITE: FREEMAN.TULANE.EDU

Student Life and Environment

Tulane is in New Orleans, so it should come as no surprise that life here can be "a lot of fun." "Many people socialize heavily on the weekends (we go out a lot). New Orleans literally has events every weekend. If you can't find something to do here, you're not looking at all," is how one student sums things up. The city is so focused on socializing that "school slows down during busy periods, such as Mardi Gras." Accordingly, many here enjoy a "very good mix of school and entertainment. New Orleans is the best place to go to school. Mardi Gras, Jazz Fest, and the food [all add up to] a once-in-a-lifetime experience."

Within the program, "the numerous clubs are mostly strong. The strongest is [the] entrepreneurship club, [which] is very good with matching people [with] local small business owners who can be mentors/potential employers." The local business community "truly embraces the MBA students, with leaders often speaking on campus and offering to meet with us individually on our own time. People are simply friendly here and take an interest in Tulane students. It makes networking locally incredibly easy." Freeman classes "are hard but not impossible," and for many, "juggling so many opportunities...is probably the hardest part of attending grad school [at Tulane]."

Tulane MBAs "are a diverse group from all over the world, many with different political views and worldviews." "One-third of our class is made up of international students, so it makes everything—discussion, group work, assignments—much more interesting," one student tells us.

Admissions

Freeman reviews applications to its graduate programs in three separate rounds, and the school encourages students to apply as early as possible to maximize their chances of gaining admission. The following is required to apply: an undergraduate transcript, an affidavit of support, an official GMAT score report, TOEFL scores (for international students whose first language is not English), two letters of recommendation, a current resume, personal statement, and interview. Minority recruitment efforts include Destination MBA, the National Black MBA Association Career Fair, targeted GMASS searches, and minority fellowships. For the incoming class of 2011, entering students earned a median GMAT score of 660 and boasted a median 3.3 undergraduate GPA.

Prominent Alumni

Burdon Lawrence, Chairman, Kirby Corp., Nations largest tank barge operator; Wayne Downing, General, Natl Director of Security for Combating Terrorism; Frank Stewart, Chairman, Stewart Enterprises; Larry Gordon, Film Producer, former pres. of 20th Century Fox.

FINANCIAL FACTS

Annual tuition	$40,230
Fees	$1,800
Cost of books	$1,600
Room & board	$11,000
% of students receiving aid	80
% of first-year students receiving aid	74
% of students receiving loans	42
% of students receiving grants	47
Average award package	$41,055
Average grant	$11,250

ADMISSIONS

Admissions Selectivity Rating	90
# of applications received	425
% applicants accepted	49
% acceptees attending	47
Average GMAT	660
Range of GMAT	540–710
Average GPA	3.30
TOEFL required of international students	Yes
Minimum TOEFL (paper/computer)	600/250
Application fee	$125
International application fee	$125
Regular application deadline	5/1
Regular notification	6/1
Application Deadline/Notification	
Round 1:	11/15 / 12/15
Round 2:	1/15 / 2/15
Round 3:	3/15 / 4/15
Round 4:	5/1 / 6/1
Early decision program?	No
Deferment available	No
Transfer students accepted	No
Non-fall admissions	No
Need-blind admissions	Yes

EMPLOYMENT PROFILE

Career Rating	89	Grads Employed by Function	% Avg. Salary
Percent employed at graduation	42	Marketing	21 $67,000
Percent employed 3 months after graduation	80	Operations	13 $67,800
		Consulting	7 $72,000
Average base starting salary	$72,800	Management	3 $75,000
Primary Source of Full-time Job Acceptances		Finance	52 $74,000
School-facilitated activities	NR (47%)	Top Employers Hiring Grads	
Graduate-facilitated activities	NR (33%)	Sequent Energy (2), FEDEX (2), Fluor Global Services (2)	

THE UNIVERSITY OF AKRON
COLLEGE OF BUSINESS ADMINISTRATION

GENERAL INFORMATION

Type of school	Public
Academic calendar	Fall

SURVEY SAYS...
Cutting-edge classes
Solid preparation in:
Finance
Accounting
General management
Operations
Communication/interpersonal skills
Presentation skills
Quantitative skills
Doing business in a global economy
Entrepreneurial studies

STUDENTS

Enrollment of parent institution	27,911
Enrollment of MBA Program	306
% male/female	68/32
% out-of-state	2
% part-time	58
% minorities	5
% international	36
Average age at entry	28
Average years work experience at entry	4

ACADEMICS

Academic Experience Rating	76
Student/faculty ratio	8:1
Profs interesting rating	99
Profs accessible rating	68
% female faculty	16
% minority faculty	6

Joint Degrees
MBA/Juris Doctor, 3–4 years; M. Tax/Juris Doctor, 3–4 years; MSM-H.R./Juris Doctor, 3–4 years.

Academics

MBAs at the University of Akron's College of Business Administration praise the school's "great academic environment," "outstanding faculty," "strong curriculum," and "low cost" of attending. The flexibility of its programs—a crucial element for the school's many part-time students—is another frequently cited asset at this impressive public university.

UA offers an evening MBA program, which can actually be completed in an accelerated 12-month program by those with the requisite undergraduate course work to place out of all foundation courses or in two years full-time. The school also offers a part-time MBA, a master's of science (MS) in accounting, an MS in management, and a master's of taxation degree. Because it has a large MBA program, Akron can offer a broad selection of concentrations, including direct integrated marketing, e-business, entrepreneurship, finance, healthcare management, international business, international finance, management, management of technology and innovation, strategic marketing, and supply-chain management. Students report a "substantial focus on international business environments and global operations" throughout the curriculum and also single out the "information and technology focus." A few feel this big program might be a bit too big; one writes, "Akron has too many students, so it's easy to fall into the cracks if you do not make an effort to not be ignored."

Akron business professors "are very experienced in their fields" and "balance knowledge with practical business experience." Many here "had work experience and then entered the world of academia" and "have various backgrounds in many countries. Most were top executives or had a strong influence on senior-level management at the companies they worked for." Students report that the workload is "good, not overbearing" and that "the application of theory is very emphasized in the course work." The school's strong ties to the city of Akron—which is in "a great location"—promotes "ties with many of the area companies," resulting in a "positive environment fostering practical learning experiences." One student reports: "The university is very connected within the Akron community. [It] attracts a diverse array of students and caters to working professionals, making the classroom learning experience richer and more fulfilling."

Career and Placement

The University of Akron's Center for Career Management provides career services for all undergraduates, graduate students, and alumni; the school does not maintain a separate career office for graduate students or business students. The office provides assistance in career planning, procuring a summer internship, developing job-search, interviewing, and resume-writing skills, and locating potential employers. One student praised the both the office's effectiveness in job placement and the various student groups "that allow students, professors, and professionals to get involved and network with one another." Among employers who have recently hired Akron MBAs are Goodyear Tire & Rubber Company, Delloite & Touche, Babcock & Wilcox, Dominion, FirstEnergy, Enterprise, Progressive, National City Bank, and J.M. Smuckers.

ADMISSIONS CONTACT: MYRA WEAKLAND, ASSISTANT DIRECTOR
ADDRESS: THE UNIVERSITY OF AKRON, CBA 412 AKRON, OH 44325-4805
PHONE: 330-972-7043 • FAX: 330-972-6588
E-MAIL: GRADCBA@UAKRON.EDU • WEBSITE: WWW.UAKRON.EDU/CBA/GRAD

Student Life and Environment

UA's College of Business holds classes in "a newer building that is equipped with all the modern teaching conveniences." "The facilities that the university has are endless, such as the computer labs, quiet study areas, the recreation and wellness center,' etc.," one student reports. The university's MBAs don't get to spend as much time on campus as they'd like though; since "most students are part-time commuters," they generally "don't spend time on campus except when [they're] attending class or meeting with a project group." Those who do manage to get involved in extracurricular activities tell us that the program's groups and organizations "allow students to build relationships and also are a great networking tool for professionals to help achieve a full-time job and/or co-op and internship opportunities." Classes are typically held in the evening; full-time students usually keep busy during the day "with graduate research assistant duties and class preparation." Some students cite campus safety concerns and lack of adequate parking as downsides to the UA MBA. Though hometown Akron is small, entertainment options abound outside of class, and Cleveland, an hour to the north, offers many cosmopolitan amenities.

Akron's "very diverse" MBA group comes "from many different countries and backgrounds" and includes a "good mix of U.S. and foreign students." Most here "are younger, [either] straight out of college or coming back after a couple years," and "the majority...balance a full-time work schedule, a family, and a challenging MBA curriculum. The combination of every element leads to a hard-working, determined, knowledgeable student body."

Admissions

The admissions committee at the University of Akron considers all of the following components of a student's application: undergraduate GPA (minimum GPA of 2.75 required), GMAT scores (minimum score of 500 required), TOEFL scores (international applicants), two letters of recommendation, a letter of purpose, resume, previous graduate and post-baccalaureate performance, and professional association and student organization memberships. International applicants must apply at least six months prior to their intended date of entry into the program. The Graduate School of the University of Akron sponsors a diversity program to enhance minority recruitment within the MBA program.

Prominent Alumni

Mary Taylor, Ohio State Auditor; Anthony Alexander, President and CEO, FirstEnergy Corp.; Don Misheff, Managing Partner, Ernst & Young, LLP; Ernest E. Pattou, President & CEO, Harwick Standard Distribution; John Costello III, Chief Global Customer & Marketing Officer, Dunkin Brands; Thomas W. Roy III, VP of Financial & CFO, Frank Fletcher Companies.

FINANCIAL FACTS

Annual tuition (in-state/ out-of-state)	$15,572/$24,932
Fees	$919
Cost of books	$1,400
Room & board	$11,000
% of students receiving aid	19
% of first-year students receiving aid	20
Average award package	$20,968

ADMISSIONS

Admissions Selectivity Rating	80
# of applications received	178
% applicants accepted	72
% acceptees attending	70
Average GMAT	572
Range of GMAT	530–610
Average GPA	3.23
TOEFL required of international students	Yes
Minimum TOEFL (paper/computer)	550/213
Application fee	$30
International application fee	$40
Regular application deadline	8/1
Regular notification	8/15
Early decision program?	No
Deferment available	Yes
Maximum length of deferment	2 years
Transfer students accepted	Yes
Transfer application policy: Up to 24 credits of foundation courses may be waived. Nine credits of the core may transfer from AACSB accredited schools if approved by the Director.	
Non-fall admissions	Yes
Need-blind admissions	Yes

EMPLOYMENT PROFILE

Career Rating	79	Grads Employed by Function	%	Avg. Salary
Average base starting salary	$68,300	Marketing	15	$83,168
		Management	27	$72,182
		Finance	40	$58,688
		Nonprofit	5	$56,000

Top 5 Employers Hiring Grads
J.M. Smucker Company, Cisco Systems, Goodyear Tire and Rubber Company, Wright Patterson Air Force Base Aeronautical Systems, Jo-Ann Fabric and Craft Stores

The University of Alabama at Birmingham

School of Business

GENERAL INFORMATION

Type of school	Public
Academic calendar	Semester

SURVEY SAYS...

Cutting-edge classes
Solid preparation in:
Teamwork
Presentation skills

STUDENTS

Enrollment of parent institution	16,000
Enrollment of MBA Program	398
% male/female	56/44
% out-of-state	5
% part-time	66
% minorities	5
% international	17
Average age at entry	27
Average years work experience at entry	4

ACADEMICS

Academic Experience Rating	**74**
Student/faculty ratio	30:1
Profs interesting rating	80
Profs accessible rating	80
% female faculty	18
% minority faculty	9

Joint Degrees

Master of Business Administration/Master of Public Health (MBA/MPH): full time or part time; 72 total credits required; 2–3 years to complete program. Master of Business Administration/Master of Science in Health Administration (MBA/MS): full time; 72 total credits required; 2–3 years to complete program. Master of Business Administration/Master of Science in Nursing, 2–3 years.

Prominent Alumni

John Bakane, CEO, Mills; Daryl Byrd, CEO and President, Iberia Bank; Susan Story, CEO and President, Gulf Power Company; James Woodward, Chancellor, UNC.

Academics

Offering a "strong curriculum" in an "urban location with close ties to local business," the Graduate School of Management serves a primarily part-time student body looking to advance their careers for a "reasonable" tuition. Through evening classes offered on a "flexible schedule," students at UAB can earn an MBA with a concentration in finance, information technology management, or healthcare management. Healthcare is a standout discipline at the university, and UAB exploits that by offering not only a concentration in the field but also a combined MBA/Master of Public Health, MBA/Master of Science in health administration, and MBA/Master of Science in nursing.

MBA students at UAB who lack an undergraduate business background are required to take foundational courses in subjects including organizational behavior, corporate finance, marketing concepts, and microeconomic analysis. These comprise 21 of the 51 credits required for graduation. Five advanced courses in specific areas, including a seminar in marketing policy and at least one course relating to international business, are also required, and the remaining classes focus on the student's area of specialization.

UAB professors and administration "are, for the most part, knowledgeable and willing to help." Professors "have had experience in the corporate environment (which is helpful for relating the material and applying it)." "I liked the fact that UAB professors all had much field experience and had been in the workplace several years before coming to teach at UAB," one student explains, adding "as a student, that makes a huge difference because one can see that they know what they are talking about, even [down] to the specific details." Across the board, teachers are "solid instructors, and most of them are very approachable after class. They were all very flexible and willing to work with us when a work conflict came up, even if sometimes it meant extra work."

Career and Placement

The Career Services Office is located in the School of Business building at UAB, which offers career counseling, coaching, practical workshops on areas such as resume writing and job searching, and an online database of jobs as well as a database to which students may upload their resumes. The office hosts recruiting visits from employers, coordinates career fairs, maintains job bulletin boards, and does resume referral. In addition, the School of Business works to arrange internships for MBAs who seek them; however, most MBAs at UAB are currently employed. Despite these opportunities, some here complain that "job placement/recruitment coordination is nonexistent," with "no opportunities to talk with big companies that one would expect a business school to help arrange."

Employers who frequently hire UAB graduates include AmSouth Bank, Southern Company, Southern Progress, UAB, and Wachovia.

Admissions Contact: Christy Manning, MBA Program Coordinator
Address: 1530 3rd Avenue South BEC 203 Birmingham, AL 35294-4460
Phone: 205-934-8815 • Fax: 205-934-9200
E-mail: cmanning@uab.edu • Website: www.business.uab.edu/mba

Student Life and Environment

UAB "is well-suited for both the traditional full-time student as well as students that are getting a degree around a full-time job." Most fall into the latter category; they "work full time, then attend classes at night" and consequently have "little interaction with on-campus life and activities." They barely have time "to meet outside of class multiple times a week" to complete group work. "The level of group work required does not fit the student body of the MBA school," one student tells us.

UAB is located "in an urban setting with all of the advantages and disadvantages that come with being in an urban environment: traffic, occasional crimes, easy access to cultural centers, unique restaurants, and entertainment venues." One student feels the positives outweigh the negatives, telling us that she "loves walking out the front door of the school and seeing downtown Birmingham! The campus comes alive in the evening with grad students pouring in after they get off work." Campus amenities include "a great, free student activity center" and "good computer rooms."

UAB hosts a "very diverse student body [that] provides a unique and real-life view of the conditions that are encountered in the business world," which "allows for many unique perspectives which contribute to a more practical learning environment." They "range from straight out of undergrad to retired and looking for new opportunities," and "they come from a wide variety of jobs and bring a lot of different experiences to the classroom." The banking industry is well-represented.

Admissions

Academic GPA, rank, and scores on the GMAT are considered very important by those making admissions decisions for the graduate business programs at UAB. Work experience, personal essays, and letters of recommendation also receive consideration. Applicants to the program must submit an official GMAT score report, official transcripts from all colleges and universities attended, two letters of reference, and a current resume. Students must demonstrate aptitude in calculus with a grade of C or better in a calculus course completed within the previous five years. The admissions committee may request an interview, but otherwise interviews are not required. Non-native English speakers must score at least 550 on the TOEFL and provide an ECE report to accompany their transcripts. It is recommended that international applicants apply six months in advance of the application deadline to ensure adequate time to process appropriate visas.

ADMISSIONS

Admissions Selectivity Rating	**73**
# of applications received	276
% applicants accepted	81
% acceptees attending	77
Average GMAT	553
Range of GMAT	510–600
Average GPA	3.2
TOEFL required of international students	Yes
Minimum TOEFL (paper/computer)	550/213
Application fee	$50
International application fee	$75
Regular application deadline	7/1
Regular notification	8/1
Early decision program?	No
Deferment available	Yes
Maximum length of deferment	1 year
Transfer students accepted	Yes
Transfer application policy: Must meet UAB MBA admission requirements, transfer courses must be from AACSB accredited program and equivalent to our required courses. We will accept up to 25% of the degree program in transfer work with a minimum B grade.	
Non-fall admissions	Yes
Need-blind admissions	Yes

EMPLOYMENT PROFILE

Career Rating	**81**
Average base starting salary	$59,400

THE UNIVERSITY OF ALABAMA AT TUSCALOOSA
MANDERSON GRADUATE SCHOOL OF BUSINESS

GENERAL INFORMATION
Type of school	Public
Academic calendar	Semester

SURVEY SAYS...
Solid preparation in:
Operations
Communication/interpersonal skills
Computer skills

STUDENTS
Enrollment of parent institution	27,050
Enrollment of MBA Program	140
% male/female	62/38
% out-of-state	23
% part-time	0
% minorities	20
% international	11
Average age at entry	24
Average years work experience at entry	2

ACADEMICS
Academic Experience Rating	91
Profs interesting rating	89
Profs accessible rating	89

Joint Degrees
JD/MBA Program, 3–year or 4–year options; MBA/MS-Mechnical Engineering, 2.5 years; MBA/MS-Civil Engineering, 2.5 years.

Prominent Alumni
Sam DiPiazza, Jr, CEO PricewaterhouseCoopers; Gary Fayard, Sr. VP & CFO Coca-Cola; Richard Anthony, Chairman and CEO, Synovus Financial Corp; Don James, Chairman and CEO, Vulcan Materials Company; Clyde Anderson, Executive Chairman of the Board, Books-A-Million.

Academics

Weighing cost and quality, shrewd business students say the MBA program at University of Alabama at Tuscaloosa offers a "great return on investment." A two-year, full-time lock-step program, the Alabama MBA begins with core coursework—an integrated curriculum that covers all functional areas of business through a combination of lecture and case study. Throughout the program, students review "many real-world cases for regional firms, as well as nationally," gaining "valuable insight and knowledge regarding multiple fields of business." Teamwork is also fundamental to the experience. In fact, collaboration is not just encouraged, it's required: "There is teamwork in every class for the first year." As such, "Classes have an equal emphasis on communication and analysis such that strictly quantitative or communicative classes don't really exist." Within the curriculum, Alabama students praise "the constant and comfortable use of technology" in the classroom. Here, "most classes involve use of laptops in class" (though students say "more laptop plug-ins" would be nice, a request the school is honoring with recent renovations), and all first-year students learn "advanced spreadsheet modeling, JIT inventory, process simulations, six sigma, and case-based modern operations methods" through the required operations and supply chain management courses. On the other hand, students would like to see the school keep up with current business trends by introducing "a more international focus" to the coursework (an area the school is currently expanding), as well as more emphasis on entrepreneurship and sustainability.

In their second year at Alabama, MBA candidates continue to take core coursework while tailoring their studies through elective courses in an area of concentration. For many, the school's top-ranked operations and supply chain management concentration was a major reason for choosing the program, though Manderson also offers academic concentrations in business intelligence, enterprise consulting, finance, and strategy. In most fields, the faculty receives "overwhelmingly positive" reviews. Not only are they "leaders in their fields," but most are also "devoted and patient" teachers, who "are engaged with the students and concerned about each one's success." When a student needs extra assistance, most professors are "very willing to help students outside of class." With fewer than 100 students in each incoming class, the business program is "small enough that...the staff knows everyone's name and background, and [is] completely willing to drop what they're doing to speak when a student comes in their office." Business students know a well-run institution when they see it, and many are pleased to report that Manderson's administrative team is efficient and service-oriented. Here, "The administration is very sound and always willing to listen to ideas and answer any questions."

Career and Placement

The Manderson Graduate School of Business employs a dedicated career coordinator for MBA students who arranges individual advising sessions, resume revisions, skills workshops, alumni career panels, and on-campus recruiting programs for both jobs and internships. "Required summer internships" are also fundamental to the job preparation process, and business students are offered choice placements in Tuscaloosa and other Southern cities. In recent years, students took internships at companies including Alabama Power, Compass Bank, Sterne Agee, PriceWaterhouseCoopers, Chesapeake Consulting, BMW, Red Cross, Wal-Mart, Hewlett Packard, Procter & Gamble, and St. Vincent Hospital. Importantly, students note that alumni relations are very strong at Alabama, and the school enjoys an "outstanding reputation" in the local area.

ADMISSIONS CONTACT: BLAKE BEDSOLE, MGR. OF ADMISSIONS AND STUDENT SERVICES
ADDRESS: MANDERSON GRADUATE SCHOOL OF BUSINESS, BOX 870223 TUSCALOOSA, AL 35487
PHONE: 205/348-6517 • FAX: 205/348-4504
E-MAIL: MBA@CBA.UA.EDU • WEBSITE: MANDERSON.CBA.UA.EDU

Last year, half of Manderson graduates had accepted a job offer by graduation, with close to 70 percent accepting an offer within three months of graduation. The median salary for recent graduates was about $61,000 annually, with a range between $30,000 and $97,000. Drawing about a third of graduates respectively, finance/accounting and operations are the two most popular industries for Alabama MBAs. Most placement efforts are focused on the surrounding region; however, in recent years, "there have been great strides to bring in companies outside of the Southeast." In 2010, 68 percent of graduates accepted job placements outside the state of Alabama.

Student Life and Environment

Many Alabama students say that it's the people—the students, faculty, and staff—who make their MBA program truly special. Here, you'll meet a great group of "young, type-A, curious, collaborative, friendly, and good-looking" people from "very diverse" backgrounds. Team-oriented and collaborative, "classmates are very engaged and promote a good learning atmosphere," and "students work together on every assignment or project even if they are individual assignments." Outside of academics, "almost every MBA student is a member of MBAA, NAWMBA, or some other active group." What's more, "several new clubs and organizations have been developed," including "the Society of Global MBAs, and 'Manderson Matters 1000,' a 1,000-hour, goal-based community service organization for every graduating class year."

Located on a "very beautiful campus" in Tuscaloosa, "the facilities are outstanding" at the Manderson School of Business (and UA at large). Facilities are well-equipped and "the Bruno Bashinsky Library and Computer Center are top-of-the-line and have multiple features of which students may take advantage." A medium-sized city, Tuscaloosa offers a range of recreational activities, arts festivals, and museums, and, of course, the famous Crimson Tide. Even among graduate students, "the university sport teams are very popular, particularly football."

Admissions

University of Alabama admits one class of about 90 students every year; classes begin in the fall. To apply, students must submit a current resume, GMAT or GRE scores, three letters of recommendation, and official undergraduate transcripts. Admissions decisions are made on a rolling basis; however, to ensure financial assistance, students are encouraged to apply by the priority deadlines. Students are not required to have significant professional experience before matriculation; about 40 percent of the class enters the program directly after college.

FINANCIAL FACTS

Annual tuition (in-state/ out-of-state)	$6,400/$18,000
Fees	$2,000
Cost of books	$950
Room & board (on/off-campus)	$4,100/$6,000
% of students receiving aid	70
% of first-year students receiving aid	70
% of students receiving grants	55
Average grant	$5,700

ADMISSIONS

Admissions Selectivity Rating	92
# of applications received	282
% applicants accepted	43
% acceptees attending	66
Average GMAT	628
Range of GMAT	580–660
Average GPA	3.44
TOEFL required of international students	Yes
Minimum TOEFL (paper/computer)	550/213
Application fee	$30
International application fee	$30
Regular application deadline	3/15
Regular notification	3/25
Early decision program?	Yes
Deferment available	Yes
Maximum length of deferment	1 year
Transfer students accepted	Yes
Transfer application policy: Applicants may be able to transfer up to 12 hours of elective credit from another AACSB-accredited graduate program. However, the MBA core must be taken in our program.	
Non-fall admissions	No
Need-blind admissions	Yes

EMPLOYMENT PROFILE

Career Rating	84	Grads Employed by Function	% Avg. Salary
Percent employed at graduation	82	Marketing	13 $55,400
Percent employed 3 months after graduation	91	Operations	8 $66,666
		Consulting	15 $65,367
Average base starting salary	$69,180	Management	5
Primary Source of Full-time Job Acceptances		Finance	25 $63,950
School-facilitated activities	33 (62%)	MIS	8 $79,333
Graduate-facilitated activities	20 (38%)	**Top 5 Employers Hiring Grads**	
		Fedex (4), Procter and Gamble (2), Compass Bank (2), Hess (2), Accenture (2)	

UNIVERSITY OF ALBERTA
SCHOOL OF BUSINESS

GENERAL INFORMATION
Type of school — Public
Academic calendar — September

SURVEY SAYS...
Good peer network
Smart classrooms
Solid preparation in:
Doing business in a global economy

STUDENTS
Enrollment of parent
institution — 36,836
Enrollment of MBA Program — 396
% male/female — 69/31
% part-time — 56
% international — 54
Average age at entry — 28
Average years work experience
at entry — 5

ACADEMICS
Academic Experience Rating — 86
Student/faculty ratio — 4:1
Profs interesting rating — 75
Profs accessible rating — 76
% female faculty — 26

Joint Degrees
MBA/LLB (Master of Business
Admin./Bachelor of Law), 4 years;
MBA/MEng (Master of Business
Admin./Master of Engineering), 2
years; MBA/MAg (Master of
Business Admin./Master of
Agriculture), 2 years; MBA/MF
(Master of Business Admin./Master
of Forestry), 2 years.

Prominent Alumni
Guy Kerr, President & CEO /Workers
Compensation Board; Brian Vaasjo,
CE/Capical Poer; Gary Mitchell,
Deputy Chairman/RBC Wealth
Management; Guy Turcotte,
CEO/Stone Creek Resorts; Michael
Lang, Chairman/Stonebridge
Merchant Capital.

Academics

The first business school in Canada to receive accreditation from the American Assembly of Collegiate Schools of Business, University of Alberta operates a full-time and part-time MBA on its Edmonton campus, an accelerated executive MBA, and a part-time program in Ft. McMurray. Integrating quantitative know-how with important qualitative skills, University of Alberta offers a "well-balanced education" through a mix of core course work and electives. Lectures are enhanced by "up-to-date case analyses," and throughout the curriculum there is a "focus on interpersonal skills and relationships." "There is a lot of group work in the MBA program," and therefore, "who you choose to work with, identifying your working style, and how to work with others are all vital components of a success strategy for the MBA." In complement to course work, students can participate in co-curricular opportunities, like the annual International Study Tour and MBA mentorship program. Students also note that the school's excellent lecture series is "worth attending" and "case competitions are fantastic."

"Since it's a research university, most professors have PhDs;" however, the Alberta faculty comprises a "good mix of academics and professionals." The classroom experience is generally rewarding, and "Most professors are well-prepared and appropriate for their specific classes." At the same time, some professors "deliver a better course than others and who you get is simply the luck of the draw." Fortunately, the administration is receptive to student input, and "feedback is given from students to professors at the end of each term regarding the class and their teaching." A current student assures us, "They truly care and listen to suggestions on how to make things better."

When it comes to the nuts and bolts, things run smoothly at Alberta. "The MBA Programs Office does a great job behind the scenes," and, for the most part, the "registration process for class is well-run, smooth, and easy." At the same time, there is a bit of a divide between full-time students and their part-time counterparts. In many cases, "the part-timers do not feel as connected to the administration as the full-timers as we are not at school during the day." On the flipside, part-timers praise the fact that the "part-time program is excellent—flexible around work schedules and amenable to work-life balance." When it comes to the bottom line, students agree that the University of Alberta is an "excellent value." "Highly-regarded" in the Edmonton area, tuition is inexpensive, the area offers an "affordable cost of living," and the program is efficient (the full-time program can even be completed in as little as 16 months).

Career and Placement

Through the MBA Career Services Office, students have access to professional career coaching and myriad career management resources. For first-year students, Career Services also offers the workshops, "Business 504," a crash course in career management. With 20,000 Alberta alumni, the school maintains a strong local network, and many corporate speakers, recruiters, and representatives visit campus. In fact, some students say "the network[ing] opportunities that are made available" are the program's greatest strength. Unfortunately, part-time students often feel they weren't invited to the party. A part-time student complains, "If there are company info sessions they are held during the day, so it is hard for part-time students to attend a lot of the sessions."

Over the past five years, 90 percent of Alberta graduates had accepted a position within three months of graduation. Alberta graduates have been hired by Accenture, Alberta Economic Development, ATB Financial, Bell, Bearing Point, CEMEX, China Zheshang Bank, Deloitte & Touche, Ernst & Young, Edmonton Airports, Direct Energy, HSBC Bank

ADMISSIONS CONTACT: JOAN WHITE, ASSOCIATE DEAN, MBA PROGRAMS
ADDRESS: 2-30 BUSINESS BUILDING, UNIVERSITY OF ALBERTA EDMONTON, AB T6G 2R6 CANADA
PHONE: 780-492-3946 • FAX: 780-492-7825
E-MAIL: MBA@UALBERTA.CA • WEBSITE: WWW.MBA.NET

Canada, Intuit, KPMG, Newell Rubbermaid, Parks Canada, Saudi Aramco, Sierra Systems, TD Canada Trust, and TEC Edmonton, among many others. Full-time graduates had an average starting salary of over $75,000 annually, and part-time students reported an average salary of over $95,000.

Student Life and Environment

With a broad-based core and numerous areas of specialization, Alberta attracts students from "many different business and non-business backgrounds"—as well as from many countries across the world. While students are "very diverse in every aspect," most agree that Alberta students are generally "knowledgeable, hard-working, respectful, and intelligent." In the part-time program, "most classmates are busy people, majority married and working," and they rarely have time to participate in extracurricular activities on campus. Spare time is squeezed even tighter because "all collaboration [has] to take place outside of normal business hours and outside of class time." (Fortunately, the business school is well equipped, and "there is an MBA specific lounge and study area that is very useful for group work and activities.")

Full-time students have a different take on life at Alberta. For them, "School life is filled with a multitude of opportunities, movies, social events, case competitions, [and] athletics." In the evenings, "there are numerous social events put on by the MBA association, which includes high-ranking guest speakers, free food, and great information." A second-year student tells us, "Life at school is a lot of fun. I spend more time in group meetings and extra-curricular activities (e.g., case competitions) than in class." Another student chimes in: "From the courses offered to the students in the program (55 percent international) to the social events and clubs to join, there is truly something here for everyone."

Admissions

To be considered for admission to the University of Alberta, students must have a minimum undergraduate GPA of 3.0, a minimum GMAT score of 550, and at least two years of professional work experience. Students must also submit two letters of recommendation and a personal statement. In the part-time and full-time programs, the recent incoming class had an average undergraduate GPA of 3.4 and average work experience of more than five years.

FINANCIAL FACTS

Annual tuition (in-state/ out-of-state)	$10,666/$21,333
Fees	$948
Cost of books	$1,300
Room & board (on/off-campus)	$7,000/$9,500
% of students receiving grants	100
Average grant	$4,930

ADMISSIONS

Admissions Selectivity Rating	87
# of applications received	294
% applicants accepted	47
% acceptees attending	61
Average GMAT	608
Range of GMAT	570–660
Average GPA	3.4
TOEFL required of international students	Yes
Minimum TOEFL (paper)	600
Application fee	$100
International application fee	$100
Regular application deadline	4/30
Early decision program?	No
Deferment available	Yes
Maximum length of deferment	1 year
Transfer students accepted	Yes
Transfer application policy: Transfer students are reviewed on an individual basis. Transfer credit is normally limited to 18 credits and must be from an AACSB accredited school.	
Non-fall admissions	No
Need-blind admissions	Yes

EMPLOYMENT PROFILE

Career Rating	87	
Percent employed at graduation	31	
Percent employed 3 months after graduation	72	
Average base starting salary	$71,709	
Primary Source of Full-time Job Acceptances		
School-facilitated activities	11 (41%)	
Graduate-facilitated activities	15 (55%)	
Unknown	1 (4%)	

Grads Employed by Function	%	Avg. Salary
Marketing	12	$55,000
Management	19	$63,680

Top 5 Employers Hiring Grads
Government of Alberta (3), ConocoPhillips (2), United Nations (1), ATB Financial (1), EPCOR (1)

UNIVERSITY OF ARIZONA
ELLER COLLEGE OF MANAGEMENT

GENERAL INFORMATION
Type of school	Public
Academic calendar	Semester

SURVEY SAYS...
Friendly students
Solid preparation in:
Teamwork
Communication/interpersonal skills
Presentation skills

STUDENTS
Enrollment of parent institution	37,000
Enrollment of MBA Program	393
% male/female	70/30
% out-of-state	37
% part-time	48
% minorities	10
% international	17
Average age at entry	28
Average years work experience at entry	4

ACADEMICS
Academic Experience Rating	**90**
Student/faculty ratio	5:1
Profs interesting rating	76
Profs accessible rating	85
% female faculty	31
% minority faculty	22

Joint Degrees
JD/MBA, 4 years; MD/MBA, 5 years; MBA/Master of International Management, 2–3 years; MS MIS/MBA, 3 years; MBA/PharmD, 5 years; MBA/MMF, 2–3 years; MBA/MS in Engineering and Optical Science, 2–3 years; MBA/MPH, 3 years.

Prominent Alumni
Mark Hoffman, CEO, Commerce One; President, Knowledge Universe; Chairman, LeapFrog; Jim Whims, Managing Partner, Tech Fund; Stephen Forte, Sr. VP, Flight Operations, United Airlines; Cephas Bowles, General Manager, WBGO-FM Jazz Radio.

Academics

The Eller College of Management at the University of Arizona is "recognized as one of the nation's leading business schools" in MIS and entrepreneurship, many students here report. And "the weather doesn't hurt, either" adds one happy student.

Experiential learning plays an important part in the Eller curriculum; students identify this as "one of the greatest strengths" of the program. One MBA explains how it works: "In the spring semester, MBAs work in teams with local businesses to assess real-world problems, make strategic recommendations, and ultimately assist the businesses in solving those problems." Another tells us that "The experiential learning is more than just a resume builder. It's a very real, very challenging experience, designed to prepare students for future leadership positions." The school's strong "relationship with key businesses" in the area plays a key role in making the experiential learning component a success.

Students also appreciate that class sizes at Eller "are small enough that the students have easy access to professors.... Students are able to develop relationships and personal bonds with professors." These personal touches permeate the program's administration as well. One student reports that "The administrative staff adds great value to the student experience...[and] goes out of its way to help students find whatever they need. Cross-discipline courses, job opportunities, highly tailored informational interviews— the administration works hard to provide students with any resources they need." At the other end of the size spectrum is the university-at-large. It is huge, and this too is seen as an asset; "With a large campus, the business students can take advantage of wonderful resources for the entire school," one student explains.

Eller professors "are very engaging and add significant value. The tenured staff places a strong emphasis on real-world experiences, ranging from case competitions judged by working professionals to company site visits." Instructors "are also very available for office hours and discussion outside of class. This creates an atmosphere of '24-hour learning.'"

Career and Placement

The Office of Career Management aims to provide highly personalized service to each individual student, in the process of helping them plan and achieve their career goals. The office further supports students in their job search through professional development workshops, interview preparation, resume preparation, and professional mentoring.

Companies most likely to hire Eller MBAs include: Astec Power; Deloitte; Dial; Sunquest; Roche; Emerson Network Power; E.& J. Gallo Winery; FedEx Services; Honeywell, Inc.; Intel Corporation; Los Alamos National Laboratory; PetSmart, Inc.; Raytheon Defense Systems; and U.S. Airways.

Student Life and Environment

"Great weather and a very nice campus" soften the edges of Eller's intense program in graduate business study. So too does the perception that "no one in the MBA program needs to kill themselves to pass." Those who want to do better than scrape by will need to exert themselves, however; "excelling in all classes and electives requires an intense work week," students report. Program cohesion is enhanced through group work (the program requires "continuous case competitions, group projects, and presentations") and "lots of networking activities (e.g., happy hours, philanthropy, coed intramural sports teams)." Eller hosts "numerous guest speakers and [provides] chances to learn more with outside class activities." Students "work very hard but play hard as well. Everyone knows everyone else and there is a standing invite to any social events."

ADMISSIONS CONTACT: MARISA COX, DIRECTOR OF MBA ADMISSIONS
ADDRESS: MCCLELLAND HALL, BUILDING 108, RM 210, P.O. BOX 210108 TUCSON, AZ 85721-0108
PHONE: 520-621-4008 • FAX: 520-621-2606
E-MAIL: MBA_ADMISSIONS@ELLER.ARIZONA.EDU • WEBSITE: ELLERMBA.ARIZONA.EDU

Eller's "friendly, conservative, helpful, hard-working, social, busy" students form "a small group" who as a result are "very close. Everyone works together and helps others succeed while remaining competitive with people from other schools (instead of walking over people from the same program)." It's "a very diverse [group] with backgrounds ranging from Peace Corps workers to former hedge fund traders. We have military officers and students with private consulting backgrounds."

Admissions

Eller admissions officers seek candidates with a strong academic background, professional experience that demonstrates progress and the desire for challenges, leadership potential, and integrity. All applicants must submit two copies of official transcripts for all post-secondary academic work, an official GMAT score report, a professional resume, two professional letters of recommendation, and two comprehensive personal essays (and a third for scholarship applicants). Interviews are required but are scheduled at the request of the school only; in other words, only those who make the first cut are asked to interview. International applicants must meet all the criteria above and submit TOEFL scores (if English is not their first language), official transcripts and two copies of their diploma(s) (translated by a recognized service if not granted by an English-language institution), and a statement of financial self-sufficiency.

In its efforts to maximize the presence of underrepresented groups, the Eller MBA Program attends regional and national job/recruiting fairs organized by National Society of Hispanic MBAs (NSHMBA), Society of Hispanic Professional Engineers (SHPE) and National Society of Black Engineers (NSBE). In addition, the Eller MBA program is listed in Hobsons' Black MBA and Hispanic MBA Students' Guides and maintains partnerships with the Association of Latino Professionals in Finance and Accounting (ALPFA). It also participates in on-campus recruitment fairs geared toward underrepresented minority students.

FINANCIAL FACTS

Annual tuition (in-state/ out-of-state)	$16,830/$31,742
Fees	$315
Cost of books	$800
Room & board	$8,400
% of students receiving grants	79
Average grant	$10,259
Average student loan debt	$30,902

ADMISSIONS

Admissions Selectivity Rating	94
# of applications received	263
% applicants accepted	28
% acceptees attending	65
Average GMAT	635
Range of GMAT	500–760
Average GPA	3.38
TOEFL required of international students	Yes
Minimum TOEFL (paper/computer)	600/250
Application fee	$100
International application fee	$100
Application Deadline/Notification	
Round 1:	11/15 / 12/15
Round 2:	1/15 / 2/15
Round 3:	3/15 / 4/15
Early decision program?	No
Deferment available	Yes
Maximum length of deferment	1 year
Transfer students accepted	No
Non-fall admissions	No
Need-blind admissions	Yes

EMPLOYMENT PROFILE

Career Rating	84	Grads Employed by Function	% Avg. Salary
Percent employed at graduation	40	Marketing	6 $73,000
Percent employed 3 months after graduation	65	Operations	6 NR
		Consulting	29 $103,250
Average base starting salary	$82,000	Management	12 NR
Primary Source of Full-time Job Acceptances		Finance	35 $82,500
School-facilitated activities	9 (40%)	MIS	12 NR
Graduate-facilitated activities	13 (60%)	**Top 5 Employers Hiring Grads**	
		Sunquest (2), Roche (2), US Airways (1), Deloitte (1), Intel (1)	

UNIVERSITY OF ARKANSAS—FAYETTEVILLE
SAM M. WALTON COLLEGE OF BUSINESS

GENERAL INFORMATION

Type of school	Public
Academic calendar	Semester

SURVEY SAYS...
Good peer network
Cutting-edge classes
Smart classrooms

STUDENTS

Enrollment of parent institution	19,849
Enrollment of MBA Program	183
% male/female	71/29
% out-of-state	35
% part-time	60
% minorities	7
% international	31
Average age at entry	29
Average years work experience at entry	6

ACADEMICS

Academic Experience Rating	86
Profs interesting rating	87
Profs accessible rating	86
% female faculty	26
% minority faculty	17

Academics

Named after one of America's most famous businessmen, the Sam M. Walton College of Business has many reasons to thank its namesake. With the company's corporate headquarters just 20 miles down the road, "Wal-Mart has been a wonderful resource" for this small business school, and "the proximity to the 'Wal-Mart World' opens up a lot of doors" with regards to internships, as well as job placement. What's more, "being very near to the world's largest retailer" makes certain business fields both relevant and accessible, such as the school's "spectacular" supply chain management program. Even so, Arkansas students say it isn't all Wal-Mart, all the time. On the contrary, the school has taken advantage of its propitious location and tapped into the many vendors and *Fortune* 500 companies located in the region (many of which relocated here to be closer to Wal-Mart); "The relationships they have built within that community shows through the quality of guest speakers and their post-grad placement rate." In addition, students point out the increasing prominence of "the Green Valley movement, which is bringing a lot of money to entrepreneurs and start-ups for a green economy. This is in a complementing role to Wal-Mart's network, and extremely valuable to many students."

Within the academic curriculum, there is an emphasis on "critical thinking to solve theoretical and application questions," as well as a focus on teamwork and collaboration. As one student describes the experience: "It's less of a school and more of a corporate company with 36 executives meeting to discuss some of the most important issues related to the company for four to five hours in a day. Everybody is a chief officer in the company working, studying, discussing, socializing and competing for success." Th Walton MBA is spearheaded by a talented faculty. "The professors are extremely knowledgeable in their fields" and "effectively tie theory to real case studies and actions." Equally pleasing, "The faculty is very interested in each student's lives and goals," and with only 36 students in the full-time class, "it is a very close-knit group." A "step above" the rest, Arkansas's competent and active administrative team oversees the MBA and related activities. Students praise the fact that "The communication from the administration regarding classes, special events, upcoming speakers, and job opportunities is excellent." Offering a "great education at an affordable price," students say the only disappointment is that the University of Arkansas doesn't get its fair share of praise on a national level. A student worries, "We need to be ranked nationally, that is the only distinguishing mark we lack. That would bring national and international prestige to an otherwise wonderful program."

Career and Placement

Career prospects look good for University of Arkansas graduates. Here, the abundance of large companies and Wal-Mart suppliers "make for, arguably, the most stable economic centers in America, if not the entire world," and "the networking potential at the school with local companies and corporations cannot be matched." In fact, "All the world's greatest corporations have offices here, and most of them recruit Walton College graduates." From personal career counseling, to networking events, to advice on negotiating job offers, "The people in the Career Center work hand-in-hand with the MBA candidates before they even arrive, helping them to find an internship that is right for them and eventually a rewarding career." On campus, their efforts are visible: "Every other day there is a different S&P 500 company here interviewing."

In recent years, Arkansas students have been recruited or taken jobs at Acxiom Corporation, Chesapeake Energy Corporation, CITGO Petroleum Corporation, Deloitte & Touche, Dial Coporation, Ernst & Young, General Mills, IBM, KPMG, Newell

ADMISSIONS CONTACT: MARION DUNAGAN, ASSISTANT DEAN
ADDRESS: 310 WILLARD J. WALKER HALL, UNIVERSITY OF ARKANSAS FAYETTEVILLE, AR 72701
PHONE: 479-575-2851 • FAX: 479-575-8721
E-MAIL: GSB@WALTON.UARK.EDU • WEBSITE: GSB.UARK.EDU

Rubbermaid, PepsiCo, Shell Oil, Sears Roebuck Co., Tyson Foods, and Wal-Mart Stores Inc, to name a few. For recent graduates, the average starting salary was almost $75,500, with a salary range between $62,000 and $110,000. Not only do they get great positions, there is a "proven track record of Walton graduates rising up the corporate ladder."

Student Life and Environment

A typical day in the life of a full-time MBA student includes classes in the morning and "lunch with a group of students," followed by afternoon study sessions or group work. As they go through their day, "life revolves around one building"—Willard J. Walker Hall—a new, spacious, and well-equipped facility. Among other amenities, Walker Hall offers "plenty of small case rooms for a small group or individual use. All of these rooms have flat-screen televisions and sound systems to accompany." A student enthuses, "We have everything we need at our disposal. Study rooms are available to grad students, as well as state-of-the-art classrooms and technology."

More than offering just a degree, "The University of Arkansas is a great place to attend school, and not just for the academics." "The environment is friendly and open," with "a seemingly perfect mix of Midwest values and Southern hospitality." What's more, the surrounding town of "Fayetteville is an extremely beautiful place to live," and there is "abundant hiking and world-class trout fishing" in the area. If you're looking for some good old-fashioned fun, "The atmosphere on campus is electric during football season when the best fans in the world converge upon Fayetteville to tailgate and then make the ground rumble with their cheers."

Admissions

At University of Arkansas, the most important factors in an admissions decision are a student's standardized test scores, undergraduate academic performance, and professional experience. Students are also required to submit three letters of recommendation plus two personal essays discussing their background and goals. Competitive applicants usually have a GMAT score of 600 or better and a GPA of 3.0 or better. For the full-time program, work experience is preferred, but not required.

FINANCIAL FACTS

Annual tuition (in-state/ out-of-state)	$12,942/$29,907
Fees	$1,803
Cost of books	$1,600

ADMISSIONS

Admissions Selectivity Rating	79
# of applications received	169
% applicants accepted	69
% acceptees attending	79
Average GMAT	581
Range of GMAT	470–710
Average GPA	3.3
TOEFL required of international students	Yes
Minimum TOEFL (paper/computer)	550/213
Application fee	$40
International application fee	$50
Regular application deadline	9/15
Regular notification	10/15
Early decision program?	Yes
ED Deadline/Notification	4/1 / 5/1
Deferment available	No
Transfer students accepted	Yes
Transfer application policy: 6 hours may transfer from AACSB Institutions	
Non-fall admissions	Yes
Need-blind admissions	Yes

Applicants Also Look At
Tulane University
Universityo Nevada—Las Vegas
University of Tulsa
University of Missouri
Ohio State University
Oklahoma State University

EMPLOYMENT PROFILE

Career Rating	92	Grads Employed by Function	% Avg. Salary
Percent employed at graduation	72	Marketing	59 $56,663
Percent employed 3 months after graduation	84	Operations	5 $50,000
		Consulting	5 $124,000
Average base starting salary	$60,619	Finance	9 $50,000
Primary Source of Full-time Job Acceptances		MIS	5 $57,000
School-facilitated activities	17 (81%)	Strategic	4 $45,000
Graduate-facilitated activities	3 (14%)	**Top 5 Employers Hiring Grads**	
Unknown	1 (5%)	Wal-Mart (3), Central State Manufacturing (2), Dial/Henkel (1), Hershey Co. (1), Hewlett-Packard (1)	

THE UNIVERSITY OF BRITISH COLUMBIA
SAUDER SCHOOL OF BUSINESS

GENERAL INFORMATION
Type of school   Public
Academic calendar   Unique

SURVEY SAYS...
Students love Vancouver, BC
Friendly students
Good peer network
Solid preparation in:
Accounting
Teamwork

STUDENTS
Enrollment of parent
  institution   49,000
% international   54
Average age at entry   29
Average years work experience
  at entry   6

ACADEMICS
Academic Experience Rating   86
Student/faculty ratio   20:1
Profs interesting rating   78
Profs accessible rating   86
% female faculty   17

Joint Degrees
Joint MBA/JD, 4 years; joint
MBA/MAPPS (Master of Arts, Asia
Pacific Policy Studies), 2 years;
Combined MBA/CMA, approx. 2
years.

Academics

The Sauder School of Business at the University of British Columbia offers both a 15-month full-time and 28-month part-time MBA in the Robert H. Lee Graduate School. The full-time program convenes at the school's 100-acre campus west of Vancouver's downtown core; the part-time program meets at the school's downtown campus in Robson Square.

Sauder's full-time program commences with a fully integrated core curriculum that "integrates 11 subjects to create one hectic but excellent learning environment." Students describe this intensive 13-week sequence, which imposes a heavy workload and requires a high level of complex analysis, as a boot camp-like experience. The remainder of the program is devoted primarily to specialization electives and professional development. Students tell us that finance is one of the school's strongest areas, although supply chain management, entrepreneurship, and international business also earn praise. An "option to partake in international exchange and an internship" during the final six months of the program means students can leave UBC with two unique and valuable experiences; the former reinforces the international focus of the curriculum as a whole.

Part-time students at Sauder experience the same faculty and curriculum as do full-timers, including the rigorous Integrated Core. The chief difference is scheduling; the part-time program is offered on Friday evenings and on weekends to accommodate students' work schedules. Students in both the full-time and part-time programs describe professors as "a mixed bag. Some are excellent scholars, some are accomplished business leaders, but others don't seem fit to teach master's level courses. Thankfully this last group is a minority." They also tell us that "The support the MBAs receive from the dean, the library staff, the career center, and the MBA office is unbelievable" and that "UBC also has excellent research facilities."

Career and Placement

UBC's Hari B. Varshney Business Career Centre offers "both personal consultation and a structured program" to help students identify goals and develop strategies to meet those goals. Self-assessment, coaching sessions, skills-training programs in resume-writing, interviewing, and networking, recruiting events that bring "corporate recruiters from prominent companies" to campus to interview job candidates, and job postings all figure into the mix here. Some here tell us that "The career center is also very helpful when it comes to finding internships, preparing for interviews or just researching industries," while others complain that the office still needs to improve its performance "if the school wants to be taken seriously at a global level."

Employers likely to hire UBC MBAs include Accenture, BC Hydro, Bell Mobility, Best Buy/Future Shop, BP, Business Objects, Cadbury, Elecronic Arts, Elli Lilly, Fraser Health Authority, GE, Health Canada, Hilti, Honeywell, HSBC, Intrawest, Kodak, Kraft, L'Oreal, Lululemon Athletica, Nike Inc, Nokia, Pepsi Bottling Group, Pivotal Corporation, PMC-Sierra, PricewaterhouseCoopers, Royal Bank Canada, Teekay Shipping Corporation, Telus, Terasen, Vancity, Vancouver Coastal Health, Vancouver International Airport Authority, Vancouver Port Authority, VANOC, and Weyerhauser.

Student Life and Environment

The Sauder School "treats the MBA students extremely well. We're spoiled, in fact," with loads of opportunities for career-building extracurricular clubs, recreation, and study-related travel. One student reports: "I have traveled to Nashville and Hamilton, and before this degree is completed I will have been to London (Ontario), Harvard, Philadelphia, and Porto Fino, Italy. Each of these trips is heavily subsidized by our dean. It is his mission to get as many students involved in activities that help promote the Sauder name." The full-time program also has "an excellent social rep who is constantly creating new excuses for us to take a night off from studying." Hometown Vancouver "is amazing," students tell us. "There is always a group of students going for a run, a bike, a hike or a sail," and skiing is accessible during much of the year, thanks to the proximity of Whistler Mountain.

The full-time program at Sauder draws "a very diverse group" that is "nearly 60 percent international, bringing to the classroom "diverse backgrounds of experience and culture." While "quite competitive," students here are quite willing to "help each other with course issues." The school has "a great MBA office to assist students with any problems." It also has a language center to help international students edit their papers and improve their proficiency in English."

Admissions

Admission to the Sauder MBA program is extremely competitive. All applicants must submit official transcripts for undergraduate work (students who attended schools where English was not the primary language must arrange for a certified translation of their transcripts to be delivered to UBC), official GMAT score reports, evidence of English proficiency (TOEFL scores for students whose first language is not English) essays, a resume, and three letters of reference. Interviews are by invitation only; the school interviews roughly half its applicant pool. The school's brochure notes, "Competitive applicants generally have more than two years of full-time post-baccalaureate work experience for admission to the program." On average, students enter the program with six years' full-time professional experience. Applications are processed on a rolling basis; the process favors those who apply early. Admitted students may not defer admission.

FINANCIAL FACTS

Annual tuition	$31,000
Cost of books	$2,200

ADMISSIONS

Admissions Selectivity Rating	88
# of applications received	372
% applicants accepted	61
% acceptees attending	50
Average GMAT	628
Range of GMAT	550–710
Average GPA	3.3
TOEFL required of international students	Yes
Minimum TOEFL (paper/computer)	600/250
Application fee	$125
International application fee	$125
Regular application deadline	4/30
Early decision program?	No
Deferment available	No
Transfer students accepted	No
Non-fall admissions	No
Need-blind admissions	Yes

EMPLOYMENT PROFILE

Career Rating	88	Grads Employed by Function	% Avg. Salary
Percent employed 3 months after graduation	93	Marketing	22 $77,000
Average base starting salary	$78,000	Operations	4 $65,000
		Consulting	18 $80,000
		Management	27 $79,000
		Finance	26 $90,400
		MIS	4 $68,000

UNIVERSITY OF CALGARY
HASKAYNE SCHOOL OF BUSINESS

GENERAL INFORMATION
Type of school   Public
Academic calendar   Semester

SURVEY SAYS...
Good peer network
Solid preparation in:
Accounting

STUDENTS
Enrollment of parent institution	28,200
Enrollment of MBA Program	280
% male/female	67/33
% part-time	75
% international	27
Average age at entry	30
Average years work experience at entry	6

ACADEMICS
Academic Experience Rating	81
Student/faculty ratio	3:1
Profs interesting rating	73
Profs accessible rating	72
% female faculty	25
% minority faculty	

Joint Degrees
MBA/LLB, 4 years; MBA/MSW, 2 full calendar years (year-round); MBA/MD, 5 full calendar years; MBA/MBT, 2 full calendar years.

Prominent Alumni
Al Duerr, President and CEO, Al Duerr & Associates; Charlie Fisher, President and CEO, Nexen; Hal Kvisle, President & CEO, Trans Canada; Brett Wilson, Managing Director/First Energy Capital; Byron Osing, Chairman, Launchworks Inc.

Academics

Located in Canada's "second business center (behind Toronto)," University of Calgary's Haskayne School of Business "has close connections with local business." That's a big deal when you're in "the heart of the energy sector of Canada" and those connections forge a "link to the oil and gas business environment and high-level executives." Students note that "the integration into the oil and gas community is very evident here (e.g., speaker panels with oil execs, etc)." With an eye toward the future, Haskayne's energy-related specialization is in "energy management and sustainable development."

Energy isn't the sole focus of a Haskayne MBA, though; on the contrary, "there is a good emphasis on bringing in execs from a wide range of industries," with finance and accounting among the program's other strengths. Across the curriculum, Haskayne employs "a mix of both...cases and structured lectures...and methods even beyond the two...to provide all the learning that's essential to make good leaders for tomorrow." "In some courses, the guest speakers alone provided the ROI in the course," one student exclaims. "Really, really interesting" electives include "entrepreneurship and new venture courses that are so much fun." "Leadership panel discussions and other networking and learning events for students" add further value. Speaking of value, "the cost of living as well as the tuition rates are reasonable" here, meaning that Haskayne "offers an outstanding graduate education at a fairly affordable price."

Haskayne "is still a young program and has had a fair amount of turnover within the administration leadership." Students detect "definite improvement, and there is a lot of potential to leverage the active business community in Calgary in strengthening the student experience." Students also see, and appreciate, the program's "willingness to be innovative and [administrators'] willingness to receive student input." Haskayne offers a twenty-month full-time daytime MBA, an evening MBA, an executive MBA, and a thesis-based MBA for those interested in pursuing business research.

Career and Placement

Students are very enthusiastic about the career opportunities afforded by Haskayne's "close connections with local businesses," and the Career Center earns praise for "providing access to new job opportunities." In surveys, the school's location is consistently listed as one of its major benefits. As one student explains, the program "takes advantage of being located in an energy industry hub to provide relevant courses of study and integrat[ion] with the local business community." Some feel there's too much focus on the energy sector; one student tells us that "the Career Center is great, but a lot of the companies they bring in are oil- and gas-focused. It would be nice if they also engaged other industries."

Companies that frequently hire graduates include Enmax Corporation, Nexen Inc., Enbridge Inc., Suncor Energy, Bell Canada, CIBC World Markets Inc., Scotia Bank, SMART Technologies Inc., TransCanada, TELUS Communications Ltd., Devon Canada, Shell Canada, Imperial Oil LTD, ATB Financial, Mercer Management, and Deloitte Consulting.

Student Life and Environment

Life at Haskayne "allows each student to be as involved or uninvolved as we want to be. Those who want to get involved can join the MBA Society. Those who don't have time to get involved...simply go to classes and that's it." Involvement is strongest among full-time students, one of whom reports "that following great classes and group meetings there is a large proportion of students that get together and go out for drinks. We have great networking and social events planned throughout the year such as 'Iron Chef MBA,' curling, ski trips, etc. Just a great relaxing break from the busy schoolwork." Those in the part-time program, on the other hand, usually "do not get the benefit of experiencing school life to its fullest." School, work, and family obligations typically leave them little time for networking events.

Haskayne MBAs "range in age from 22 to 42, single to married and having five kids, no experience to amazing experience. Despite my classmates coming from different regions of the planet and different regions of Canada, we have a strong sense of camaraderie and good communication." The program includes "a lot of creative people and well-rounded people...just the kind of people that you wouldn't expect to run into in an MBA program." Students represent "a broad range of industries...but many are experienced professionals from the oil and gas sector."

Admissions

Applicants to Haskayne must submit the following materials: two sets of official transcripts for all post-secondary work (minimum undergraduate GPA of 3.0 over final two years of course work required), an official GMAT score report, two letters of reference, two copies of a current resume (three years appropriate professional experience is preferred), and two copies of a personal statement explaining their purpose in pursuing a Haskayne MBA and detailing any special attributes they can contribute to the program. College transcripts in a language other than English must be translated by a recognized translation service. Applicants for whom English is a second language must submit an official score report for either the TOEFL or IELTS.

FINANCIAL FACTS

Annual tuition (in-state/ out-of-state)	$11,450/$20,350
Fees)	$843
Cost of books	$2,000
Room & board	$12,000
% of first-year students receiving aid	75
Average grant	$5,000

ADMISSIONS

Admissions Selectivity Rating	83
# of applications received	200
% applicants accepted	60
% acceptees attending	54
Average GMAT	614
Range of GMAT	550–680
Average GPA	3.3
TOEFL required of international students	Yes
Minimum TOEFL (paper/computer)	600/250
Application fee	$100
International application fee	$130
Regular application deadline	5/1
Application Deadline/Notification	
Round 1:	11/15 / 1/15
Round 2:	1/15 / 3/1
Round 3:	3/1 / 5/1
Round 4:	5/1 / 6/15
Early decision program?	No
Deferment available	Yes
Maximum length of deferment	1 year
Transfer students accepted	Yes
Transfer application policy: We can accept up to nine courses.	
Non-fall admissions	No
Need-blind admissions	Yes

EMPLOYMENT PROFILE

Career Rating	96	Grads Employed by Function	% Avg. Salary
after graduation	93	Marketing	11 NR
Average base starting salary	$95,351	Operations	36 NR
Primary Source of Full-time Job Acceptances		Consulting	14 NR
School-facilitated activities	NR (44%)	Finance	31 NR
Graduate-facilitated activities	NR (56%)	HR	3 NR
		MIS	3 NR

UNIVERSITY OF CALIFORNIA—BERKELEY
HAAS SCHOOL OF BUSINESS

GENERAL INFORMATION

Type of school   Public
Academic calendar   Semester

SURVEY SAYS...
Friendly students
Good social scene
Good peer network
Happy students
Solid preparation in:
Teamwork
Entrepreneurial studies

STUDENTS

Enrollment of parent institution	32,714
% out-of-state	70
% part-time	64
Average age at entry	29
Average years work experience at entry	5

ACADEMICS

Academic Experience Rating	97
Student/faculty ratio	12:1
Profs interesting rating	91
Profs accessible rating	92
% female faculty	25

Joint Degrees

MBA/MPH in Public Health, 5 semesters; MBA/JD, 6 semesters (3–4 academic years); MBA/MIAS, 3 years.

Prominent Alumni

Arun Sarin, Former CEO, Vodafone; Rodrigo Rato, Former Managing Director, International Monetary Fund; Barbara Desoer, Exec VP, Bank of America; Paul Otellini, CEO of Intel; Jorge Montoya, President, Procter & Gamble Latin America, Shantanu Narayen, CEO, Adobe; Joe Jiminez, CEO, Novartis.

Academics

The Haas School of Business at the University of California—Berkeley is a "top school for academics and recruitment opportunities," especially "on the West Coast." Students here note that the MBA program is "Outstanding on all levels: professionally, academically, and socially." Thanks to an environment that encourages student involvement and input, most here "feel like they have a real role in shaping their own academic experiences." As one student explains, there are "a million ways to get involved and really make a difference. Experiential learning opportunities everywhere you turn." Things "move fast here" thanks to the structure of the courses, but students find themselves supported by "fantastic" and "accessible" professors who "sincerely care" about these future entrepreneurs. "We learn from professors who not only are recognized as top academics in their respective fields, but also professionals who shape the direction of the industry," explains one student. Additionally, Haas' administration "seems to have a singular focus on improving the experience for students." According to students, "They go to great lengths to take in, process, and change the program per student recommendations."

Students praise the "small, intimate program" for being exactly that: "small" and "intimate." "We only have 240 students per class (at least officially...sometimes one or two more get added)," says one student. This "tight-knit" environment creates a distinctly "collaborative culture" that forges lasting connections (which come in handy after graduation). The "caliber of students, faculty, administration, and career services staff" are all "top-notch," which provides a solid base for development. "Haas excels at entrepreneurship (not just social entrepreneurship)," explains one student. "Its heavy involvement and leadership in the Berkeley Energy Resources Collaborative (BERC) provides great opportunities in alternative/green energy entrepreneurship." The school also offers a "health care and international business focus." Another key component of the program is its "close ties" and proximity "to Silicon Valley." Students also single out their "excellent" new dean, Richard Lyons, for praise. As one student says, "He's an energetic, reputable professor who spent time in the real world on Wall Street."

Career and Placement

After graduation, Berkeley MBAs breathe easy knowing that their program's high profile and sound reputation go a long way in providing job opportunities for them—not to mention that it also has "an alumni network that spans the globe." As is often the case at such schools, the Haas Career Center provides a broad range of excellent services. Students here benefit from one-on-one advisement, access to numerous online job databases, industry clubs, workshops, seminars, and a mentoring program in which second-year students counsel first years in their search for internships. Employers most likely to hire Berkeley MBAs include Google, Amazon, Apple, Bain & Company, Deloitte Consulting LLP, Pacific Gas and Electric, Mekinsey, Genentech.

Student Life and Environment

According to students, life at Haas is "extremely busy and involved." "Beyond school-work—which is the focus—almost every student is involved in at least one if not two or three extracurricular activities, most of which are student-run," says one student. "There are often symposiums, speakers, new clubs forming, and conferences to attend." The extracurricular activities, just like the school, are largely "student-driven," meaning that "If a student can dream of an activity, club, or academic venture...it can be done, and in fairly easy fashion." "Life at school is a whirlwind," explains one student. "There are so many clubs, speakers, and events to check out—but never enough time in the day. Last week, I was involved in organizing a panel on sustainable design with speakers from IDEO, Patagonia, and Nike, while also participating in a chili cook-off!"

Needless to say, "Life at Haas is rich and very intensive." Despite being "very active and busy between academic and social opportunities," students find time for the "important things in life." "Dodgeball on Mondays, softball on Tuesdays, and bar of the week on Thursdays—I love b-school!" says one student. Berkeley is "a great college town" with "amazing access to San Francisco, Napa Valley, and Lake Tahoe" (no surprise that the student body reports an "overall appreciation for the outdoors). In addition, the location in the Bay Area "provides a wealth of opportunity for networking."

Thanks to the school's "small class size" Haas has "a very strong sense of community." "People are trustworthy and helpful," says one student. "Friendly," "easygoing," and "international" are all words that could be used to describe the student body here. The "collaborative" environment means that there "isn't the typical cutthroat competition apparent at other business schools." The "diverse" and "welcoming" students here are "keen to support each other." As one student explains, "Life at Haas is unique to every individual, and yet there are so many opportunities for shared experiences."

Admissions

Applicants to Haas graduate programs must submit all the following materials to the admissions department: official copies of transcripts for all postsecondary academic work, an official GMAT score report, letters of recommendation, a personal statement, and a resume. Interviews are conducted on an invitation-only basis. In addition to the above materials, international applicants whose first language is not English must also submit official score reports for the TOEFL or IELTS. The school considers all of the following in determining admissions status: "demonstration of quantitative ability; quality of work experience, including depth and breadth of responsibilities; opportunities to demonstrate leadership, etc.; strength of letters of recommendation; depth and breadth of extracurricular and community involvement; and strength of short answer and essays, including articulation of clear focus and goals."

FINANCIAL FACTS

Annual tuition (in-state/ out-of-state)	$36,670/$47,637
Cost of books	$2,500
Room & board	$20,226
% of students receiving aid	100
% of first-year students receiving aid	100
% of students receiving loans	59
% of students receiving grants	27
Average award package	$38,628
Average grant	$10,851
Average student loan debt	$68,333

ADMISSIONS

Admissions Selectivity Rating	99
# of applications received	4,064
% applicants accepted	11
% acceptees attending	54
Average GMAT	718
Range of GMAT	680–760
Average GPA	3.59
TOEFL required of international students	Yes
Minimum TOEFL (paper/computer)	570/68
Application fee	$200
International application fee	$200
Application Deadline/Notification	
Round 1:	10/13 / 1/13
Round 2:	12/2 / 3/3
Round 3:	1/20 / 4/21
Round 4:	3/16 / 5/26
Early decision program?	No
Deferment available	No
Transfer students accepted	No
Non-fall admissions	No
Need-blind admissions	Yes

EMPLOYMENT PROFILE

Career Rating	98	Grads Employed by Function	% Avg. Salary
Percent employed at graduation	65	Marketing	22 $104,825
Percent employed 3 months after graduation	81	Consulting	30 $113,887
		Management	9 $111,753
Average base starting salary	$108,428	Finance	15 $103,403
Primary Source of Full-time Job Acceptances		MIS	1 NR
School-facilitated activities	116 (65%)	**Top 5 Employers Hiring Grads**	
Graduate-facilitated activities	56 (32%)	McKinsey (15), Adobe (8), Deloitte	
Unknown	6 (3%)	Consulting (8), AT Kearney (4), Boston Consulting Group (4)	

UNIVERSITY OF CALIFORNIA—DAVIS
GRADUATE SCHOOL OF MANAGEMENT

GENERAL INFORMATION
Type of school   Public
Academic calendar   Quarter

SURVEY SAYS...
Good peer network
Solid preparation in:
Teamwork
Communication/interpersonal skills

STUDENTS
Enrollment of parent
  institution   31,426
Enrollment of MBA Program   540
% male/female   70/30
% out-of-state   7
% part-time   78
% minorities   37
% international   12
Average age at entry   29
Average years work experience
  at entry   5

ACADEMICS
Academic Experience Rating   **94**
Student/faculty ratio   15:1
Profs interesting rating   88
Profs accessible rating   87
% female faculty   42
% minority faculty   16

Joint Degrees
JD/MBA, 4 years; MD/MBA, 6 years;
Engineering/MBA, 2 years; Ag
Econ/MBA, 2 years; MS/MBA, 3
years.

Prominent Alumni
David Russ, Managing Director,
Credit Suisse; May Ngai Seeman,
CEO, MEAG New York; Gordon C.
Hunt, Jr., Senior VP & Chief Medical
Officer, Sutter Health; Timothy
Freeman, Head of U.S. Derivatives
Sales, Capstone Global Markets;
John Clare, CIO International
Division, Yum! Brands Inc.; Yvette
Conner, Director, Risk Management,
Vulcan, Inc.

Academics

The Graduate School of Management at University of California—Davis "maintains the perfect balance between size and quality of institution," students here report. The smaller scale of operations here means that students enjoy "amazing professors who we are in constant contact with and have easy access to" and an administration that "is responsive to student needs. Most students are on a first-name basis with staff." In short, Davis' "small program with good course options" results in a "personal nature of education [that] is amazing compared to many similarly ranked schools."

The Davis MBA program exploits its presence within a greater university—one that excels in the sciences, among other fields—to create more opportunities than would typically be available in a program of this size. A "thriving interdisciplinary environment" encourages students to seek these opportunities. One student pursuing "degrees in economics and transportation technology while earning the MBA" notes "close collaboration in these programs with industry and government sponsors (auto and energy, state and federal agencies), [which] has positioned me well for my desired career at the intersection of energy and transportation." Other survey respondents identify business opportunities springing from the university's work in biotech, viticulture (the school has "good ties to the wine industry"), and sustainability and clean energy industries. Students note approvingly the emphasis on social responsibility throughout the Davis curriculum.

Davis attracts an "excellent faculty" whose members "are not just academics; they are board members and former CEOs, which makes class work a lot more relevant." Teaching "focuses on case curricula" and professors "integrate a lot of material that is currently happening around us whenever they can." The "very qualified, effective, and communicative" administration "bends over backwards to help the students," helping to ease the stress that invariably accompanies graduate study. On the downside, the relatively small size of the program means that "getting into popular classes can be difficult due to faculty size and course offerings."

Career and Placement

Students report that Davis' cozy size is a drawback when it comes to job-hunting season. "Even though our small size is one of our greatest strengths, it also hinders us from making an impact with recruiters," a student warns. A "tightly knit alumni network" helps ease the pain a bit. Although that alumni network is relatively small, its members are committed to helping fellow alums find their place in the business world

Employers that most frequently hire Davis MBAs include: CalPERS; Blue Shield; Wells Fargo; CalSTRS; Hewlett Packard Company; Agilent Technologies; Intel Corporation; Kaiser Permanente; AT&T; Brocade; Elite Capitol; Ernst & Young; KPMG; PricewaterhouseCoopers; Rabobank International; Deloitte & Touche, LLP; and PG&E. Approximately two in five members of the class of 2009 found work as finance/accounting professionals (median starting salary: $78,500); one in five took jobs in consulting ($64,000) and about as many entered general management ($74,500). Most graduates remain in the area; two in five find work in San Francisco or the surrounding Bay Area, one in five finds a job in the greater Sacramento region, and the rest are split between Silicon Valley and destinations farther afield.

Student Life and Environment

The Davis MBA program operates out of a "brand new state-of-the-art building" on a "new campus that is clean and high tech." "There are plenty of places to study and I can find access to any needed resource," one student reports. The school's proximity to San Francisco and Sacramento creates opportunities for connections in business and government. Hometown Davis "is a growing midsize city. It is called 'bike town U.S.A.' because there is no need to own a car (this is rare in California).... There is a diverse mix of restaurants, including Thai, Chinese, Japanese, Mexican, Czech, Bavarian, French, European, Indian, American fare, and others."

The Davis campus engenders "a good sense of community," according to students. While "full-time students have opportunities to participate in clubs," those who attend part time either "work or have classes during club meetings." Either way, their participation is limited, which suits them. As one explains, "As working professionals, we all have established lives. We have homes. Most of us are married and many of us have children. Because of this school is less central in our lives."

Davis MBAs are "great team players" and "friendly people" "with a diverse array of skill sets and career aspirations." Many "care about the environment and the impact they make on the world." "Many are very liberal," which is not that common in graduate business programs, but "then you have about half who are more stereotypical business-minded people."

Admissions

Admissions Officers for the full-time MBA program at UC Davis consider the following factors in assessing candidates: academic potential, professional potential, and personal qualities. Full-time work experience is not required for admission, but most students have at least a few years of work experience. Applicants must submit the following materials: a completed application form (online or hard copy); a current resume; a list of outside activities and honors; three short personal essays; official transcripts from each undergraduate and graduate institution attended; two letters of recommendation; and an official GMAT score report. Applicants whose native language is not English must submit an official TOEFL score report or IELTS reflecting a score no more than two years old. Applications to the full-time program are accepted for the fall semester only.

FINANCIAL FACTS

Annual tuition	$13,516
Fees	$18,484
Cost of books	$1,753
Room & board	$13,709
% of students receiving aid	88
% of first-year students receiving aid	85
% of students receiving loans	46
% of students receiving grants	77
Average award package	$23,491
Average grant	$11,273
Average student loan debt	$34,162

ADMISSIONS

Admissions Selectivity Rating	97
# of applications received	575
% applicants accepted	21
% acceptees attending	50
Average GMAT	684
Range of GMAT	640–730
Average GPA	3.4
TOEFL required of international students	Yes
Minimum TOEFL (paper/computer)	600/250
Application fee	$125
International application fee	$125
Regular application deadline	3/11
Regular notification	5/31
Application Deadline/Notification	
Round 1:	11/3 / 1/31
Round 2:	1/5 / 3/31
Round 3:	3/2 / 5/31
Round 4:	5/18 / 6/30
Early decision program?	Yes
ED Deadline/Notification	1/5 / 3/31
Deferment available	Yes
Maximum length of deferment	1 year
Transfer students accepted	Yes
Transfer application policy: A maximum of 12 quarter units from a University of California campus or 6 quarter units from another university can be applied toward the fulfillment of our elective requirement.	
Non-fall admissions	No
Need-blind admissions	Yes

EMPLOYMENT PROFILE

Career Rating	94	Grads Employed by Function	%	Avg. Salary
Percent employed at graduation	58	Marketing	11	$45,000
Percent employed 3 months after graduation	82	Operations	11	$104,333
		Consulting	19	$62,200
Average base starting salary	$74,040	Management	18	$70,625
Primary Source of Full-time Job Acceptances		Finance	41	$81,350
School-facilitated activities	16 (59%)	**Top 5 Employers Hiring Grads**		
Graduate-facilitated activities	11 (41%)	Agilent Technologies, AT&T, Gartner Consulting, Kaiser Permanente, Hewlett Packard		

UNIVERSITY OF CALIFORNIA—IRVINE
THE PAUL MERAGE SCHOOL OF BUSINESS

GENERAL INFORMATION
Type of school	Public
Academic calendar	Sept–June

SURVEY SAYS...
Friendly students
Good social scene
Good peer network
Smart classrooms
Solid preparation in:
Teamwork
Presentation skills

STUDENTS
Enrollment of parent institution	24,000
Enrollment of MBA Program	800
% male/female	68/32
% part-time	74
% international	40
Average age at entry	28
Average years work experience at entry	5

ACADEMICS
Academic Experience Rating	**89**
Student/faculty ratio	7:1
Profs interesting rating	80
Profs accessible rating	88
% female faculty	25

Joint Degrees
MD/MBA: Five or six year program
3/2 program for UC Irvine undergraduate students.

Prominent Alumni
Lisa Locklear, Vice President,
Ingram Micro; Darcy Kopcho,
Executive Vice President, Capital
Group Companies; George
Kessinger, Pres. and CEO, Goodwill
Industries International.

Academics

"Strong ties to the local business community" are among the many assets that make the Merage School of Business at University of California—Irvine a top choice among southern California business students. Consulting is a particular strength, and students here crow about "the access to great consulting firms"—"I am currently mentoring under a senior associate at Booz Allen Hamilton," one writes. Irvine's "strong ties to the local healthcare industry" are also lauded for affording "networking opportunities in the medical device industry" and elsewhere.

Merage admits only about 100 full-time students per year, resulting in "small class sizes" that "really make a difference and give more people an opportunity to participate in discussions so we can learn from one another." Students "are able to connect very closely with each other and don't have to fight for time with faculty and staff. Professors know all our names by heart and have had a genuine interest in our education and careers. Some of my professors have even become my mentors and have connected me very well with the industries and functions I am interested in."

Merage MBAs appreciate "the effort that every single department makes to create a 360-degree program. From career development to research opportunities to great professors…to the Centers of Excellence that cooperate with the community, to...you get the idea. Every facet of Merage is well-thought out, well-executed and well-maintained." Administrators are "very accessible and friendly and professional," and "they listen to and react to feedback from students." Professors, too, "are very in tune with…students' needs and wants. . .and are willing to adjust when appropriate." In short, the school "actually operates like a business and not like academia, which is really refreshing."

The curriculum here "focuses on innovation and entrepreneurship," with a strong emphasis on teamwork. Students "are placed in diverse teams of five" during their first year "and expected to work together all year. It keeps you thinking in terms of team management, motivation, etc." Aside from the full-time MBA, Merage offers a fully employed MBA, an executive MBA, and a healthcare executive MBA. Merage also offers a doctoral program.

Career and Placement

Merage has "clout" with employers in Orange County, and that's a huge plus. Still, students wish the school would "build stronger relationships with employers across a greater variety of industries," telling us that "Merage seems to have strong ties with only a few companies (Mattel, Beckman Coulter, Blizzard, Disney, Broadcom, Marriott), so if you're looking to become a financial analyst, this isn't a great place for you. However, if you want to go into healthcare and/or IT, this place is fabulous." Counselors at the Career Center earn generally high marks, and the office's Career Visioning Program "really helps you tailor your job search. They have you put together a personal marketing plan at the beginning of the program to help guide you through the two years. You can adjust that marketing plan, but it keeps you focused and helps you identify where you want to be and how you are going to get there."

Students tell us that the most prominent recruiters of Merage MBAs include Allergan, Amgen, AT&T, Beckman Coulter, Deloitte & Touche, Disneyland Resort, Edwards Lifesciences, Experian, Johnson & Johnson, Mattel, Mazda, Niagra, Taco Bell, and Verizon.

ADMISSIONS CONTACT: CHRISTINE HOYT, ASSISTANT DIRECTOR RECRUITMENT AND ADMISSIONS
ADDRESS: SB 220 IRVINE, CA 92697-3125
PHONE: 949-824-4622 • FAX: 949-824-2235
E-MAIL: MBA@MERAGE.UCI.EDU • WEBSITE: WWW.MERAGE.UCI.EDU

Student Life and Environment

"The student life balance is amazing" at Merage, where "Students visit the beach, go to Laguna art walks, and have lots of wonderful companies to visit close by." Students' schedules are "always busy between classes and other activities on campus, so you have to be organized and [have] high energy to take advantage of so many opportunities the school offers." Many here "are very active in the community through volunteering, networking, and social activities," which include "school-sponsored mixers every week to bring together students from the different classes" and "a non school-sponsored party night every Thursday." The program vibe is "very collaborative," with students "leading review sessions for finals and midterms. It's that kind of environment. No one gets left behind."

Irvine is in SoCal with "the beach and the mountains close by," so unsurprisingly "the quality of life could not be any better." The "heart of OC" is always "sunny, warm, beautiful...for undergrads it may be too quiet or residential, but for graduate students, [it] is perfect." Hometown Irvine "has for the past decade been ranked as one of the safest cities in America, so students are comfortable living here and [trust] the community." And while "Irvine is more of a suburb than a college town, the Newport Beach Peninsula and Laguna Beach Art Walks are hip, classy, close-by entertainment for the young crowd," and Los Angeles "is close," yet "just far enough to be out of the traffic and congestion."

Admissions

Merage admissions officers consider applicants' undergraduate records (an overall GPA of at least 3.0 is preferred; post-undergraduate degrees are considered as well); GMAT scores (middle 80 percent of students admitted to the full-time program score between 620 and 730); work experience (most in the full-time program arrive with at least five years professional experience); two self-evaluation essays (plus an optional third essay, if applicants choose to submit it); a mandatory interview, conducted by invitation only; and two letters of recommendation (at least one should be from a current or former supervisor). International students whose undergraduate records do not demonstrate English proficiency will likely be required to also submit an official score report for the TOEFL.

FINANCIAL FACTS

Annual tuition (in-state/ out-of-state)	$27,815/$38,949
Cost of books	$2,947
Room & board (on/off-campus)	$11,039/$14,425

ADMISSIONS

Admissions Selectivity Rating	96
# of applications received	700
% applicants accepted	31
% acceptees attending	46
Average GMAT	675
Range of GMAT	620–730
Average GPA	3.35
TOEFL required of international students	Yes
Minimum TOEFL (paper/computer)	600/250
Application fee	$150
International application fee	$150
Application Deadline/Notification	
Round 1:	11/1 / 1/15
Round 2:	12/1 / 3/1
Round 3:	2/1 / 4/1
Round 4:	4/1 / 6/15
Early decision program?	No
Deferment available	No
Transfer students accepted	No
Non-fall admissions	Yes
Need-blind admissions	Yes

EMPLOYMENT PROFILE

Career Rating	94	Grads Employed by Function	%	Avg. Salary
		Marketing	35	$78,529
		Operations	6	$84,000
		Consulting	18	$86,333
		Management	2	NR
		Finance	29	$72,583
		MIS	2	NR

Top 5 Employers Hiring Grads
Experian (4), Deloitte & Touche (5), Countrywide/Bank of America (3), Southern California Edison (2), Niagra Waters (2)

UNIVERSITY OF CALIFORNIA—LOS ANGELES
ANDERSON SCHOOL OF MANAGEMENT

GENERAL INFORMATION
Type of school   Public
Academic calendar   Quarter

SURVEY SAYS...
Students love Los Angeles, CA
Friendly students
Good social scene
Good peer network
Helpful alumni
Happy students
Solid preparation in:
Entrepreneurial studies

STUDENTS
Enrollment of parent
  institution   39,984
Enrollment of MBA Program   1,743
% male/female   65/35
% part-time   58
% international   32
Average age at entry   28
Average years work experience
  at entry   5

ACADEMICS
Academic Experience Rating   **98**
Profs interesting rating   89
Profs accessible rating   89
% female faculty   15

Joint Degrees
MBA/JD; MBA/MD; MBA/DDS;
MBA/MPH; MBA/Master of Latin
American Studies; MBA/Master of
Urban Planning; MBA/Master of
Computer Science; MBA/Master of
Public Policy; MBA/Master of
Library and Information Science;
MBA/Master of Nursing;
MBA/Master of Public Health.

Prominent Alumni
Jeff Henley, Chairman, Oracle
Corporation; William Gross,
Founder & Chief Investment Officer,
PIMCO; Hwee Hua Lim, Cabinet
Minister, Singapore; Lisa Brummel,
Vice President of Home
Products/Microsoft; Mitch Kupchak,
General Manager, Los Angeles
Lakers.

Academics

With its focus on sustainability, diversity, and global management, the University of California—Los Angeles, Anderson School of Management pairs a "collaborative environment" and "entrepreneurial spirit," with an "outstanding reputation." "UCLA Anderson students work hard, work together, and give back. The leadership that students take on with professional clubs, case competitions, and volunteerism is inspiring." Located in Los Angeles, with prime access to Hollywood and all the trappings of the entertainment industry, for those seeking a "career in sports, entertainment, [or] media," UCLA Anderson offers "[a] strong entertainment and entrepreneurial focus" in an "extremely diverse and collaborative community."

"Academics are tough," admits one student. "I've had to utilize professors' office hours, TAs and tutors but feel I'm learning what I need to prepare me for my summer internship (on Wall Street)." UCLA, Anderson's program is built around a rigorous core which culminates at the end of the MBA program with a 20-week course entitled Applied Management Research, through which students work in groups to build a business plan, conduct management field study, or collaborate on a special project. "I have been very impressed with our core classes. The professors who teach them are outstanding, and some of the most senior and well-respected faculty...teach core courses because they love the interaction with first-year students."

Beyond the strength of its concentrations and its focus on leadership, UCLA Anderson has the added benefit of an "excellent alumni network," and professors who are "top researchers in their fields." The faculty here offers a "very good mix of academics and entrepreneurs. Very well-connected, recognized leaders. You would expect leaders in their field to be at Harvard, or Stanford, etc. But in fact the best leaders are here."

In addition, students are drawn to UCLA for the "strength of [its] real estate and finance faculty and curriculum." The school also boasts a strong real estate concentration. As one MBA attests, "I couldn't say no to it. Awesome people, engaged faculty, great facilities. The in-state tuition (while being in a whole different metro area) was a nice bonus."

UCLA Anderson's spirit of collaboration "trickles down from the top." "The administration is incredibly helpful, and easily accessible especially with the small class size." Professors encourage students "to come to office hours and introduce themselves personally, and most even offer [a] lifetime guarantee that they will always be willing to answer questions related to their field." True to its global focus, UCLA Anderson provides many opportunities for students to study abroad and engage in global field studies through international exchange partnerships with over 50 leading business schools around the world. In addition to its MBA, FEMBA and EMBA travel studies, UCLA Anderson offers a Global Executive MBA program in partnership with the National University of Singapore conducts classes in Los Angeles, Singapore, Shanghai and Bangalore.

Career and Placement

With its "highly regarded entrepreneurial program," "extensive and highly involved alumni network in the media, entertainment, and high-tech industries," and "on-site recruiting events," UCLA Anderson students enjoy high returns when it comes to career placement. In 2009, 71 percent of full-time MBA graduates seeking employment had received a job within three months of graduation.

ADMISSIONS CONTACT: MAE JENNIFER SHORES, ASST. DEAN AND DIR. OF MBA ADMISSIONS & FINANCIAL AID • ADDRESS: 110 WESTWOOD PLAZA, GOLD HALL, SUITE B201 LOS ANGELES, CA 90095-1481 • PHONE: 310-825-6944 • FAX: 310-825-8582
E-MAIL: MBA.ADMISSIONS@ANDERSON.UCLA.EDU • WEBSITE: WWW.ANDERSON.UCLA.EDU

Top employers in 2009 included McKinsey & Co., Deloitte, Credit Suisse, DaVita Corporation, and Toyota with consulting, financial services, and technologies being the industries with the biggest draw for recent graduates.

Student Life and Environment

The "student body is extremely intelligent yet personable" at UCLA Anderson, and are "often of the 'collectively competitive' type." Students "work very hard at school and are serious about their careers. Most work is done in teams, a reality which students embrace;" students "take ownership in the success of their teammates." Outside of school, "students love to socialize." In addition, "the good-sized international student population contributes to diversity and intellectual challenge." As one students says, UCLA Anderson MBAs "are all incredibly intelligent and ambitious, but do not have any sense of arrogance about them. They challenge each other, but collaborate on all aspects of assignments and final projects." In a nutshell, the community here is rife with "the kind of people you can work on a challenging problem with one night and have a beer with the next."

Daily life is "much more social than I expected, which is significantly aided by the weather. Every day between classes, you can find a majority of your classmates relaxing in the sun in the courtyard buzzing about school or weekend plans. The students socialize regularly together, with frequent beach volleyball games, hiking trips, surf outings, or beach bonfires." In addition to the more relaxed gatherings, "there seems to be a student group to match all students' needs, from identity groups to professional associations." One student attests, " I am active in the Real Estate Association which plans 'day on the jobs' with industry leading companies, brings in distinguished speakers, plans a career night with more than 30 real estate companies in attendance, facilitates relationships with alumni and provides practical training."

Admissions

UCLA Anderson's admissions criteria emphasize academic ability, leadership, work experience, and breadth of life experiences. For admissions officials here it's all about building a community of future leaders with diverse backgrounds and the ability to bring unique contributions to the UCLA Anderson community. There are no minimum requirements for GMAT scores, undergraduate GPA, or prior work experience. Students must submit an online application, two letters of recommendation, and TOEFL scores (when applicable). Optional interviews are available for prospective students.

FINANCIAL FACTS

Annual tuition (in-state/ out-of-state)	$35,852/$44,093

ADMISSIONS

Admissions Selectivity Rating	98
# of applications received	3,041
% applicants accepted	25
% acceptees attending	47
Average GMAT	712
Range of GMAT	670–750
Average GPA	3.53
TOEFL required of international students	Yes
Minimum TOEFL (paper/computer)	560/220
Application fee	$200
International application fee	$200
Application Deadline/Notification	
Round 1:	10/14 / 1/13
Round 2:	1/6 / 3/31
Round 3:	3/17 / 5/19
Early decision program?	Yes
ED Deadline/Notification	10/14 / NR
Deferment available	No
Transfer students accepted	No
Non-fall admissions	No
Need-blind admissions	Yes

EMPLOYMENT PROFILE

		Grads Employed by Function	%	Avg. Salary
Career Rating	97	Marketing	18	$93,277
Percent employed at graduation	51	Operations	2	$93,750
Percent employed 3 months after graduation	71	Consulting	23	$106,484
Average base starting salary	$95,922	Management	5	$95,222
Primary Source of Full-time Job Acceptances		Finance	36	$93,364
School-facilitated activities	128 (67%)	HR	1	NR
Graduate-facilitated activities	64 (33%)	MIS	1	NR

Top 5 Employers Hiring Grads
McKinsey & Co., Deloitte, Credit Suisse, DaVita Corporation, Toyota

UNIVERSITY OF CALIFORNIA—RIVERSIDE
A. GARY ANDERSON GRADUATE SCHOOL OF MANAGEMENT

GENERAL INFORMATION

Type of school	Public
Academic calendar	Quarter

SURVEY SAYS...

Friendly students
Good social scene
Smart classrooms
Solid preparation in:
Finance
Accounting
General management

STUDENTS

Enrollment of parent institution	17,000
Enrollment of MBA Program	140
% male/female	58/42
% out-of-state	4
% part-time	2
% minorities	31
% international	55
Average age at entry	26
Average years work experience at entry	4

ACADEMICS

Academic Experience Rating	**75**
Student/faculty ratio	5:1
Profs interesting rating	78
Profs accessible rating	84
% female faculty	19
% minority faculty	43

Academics

Combine the Southern California climate with a "fantastic school" offering "generous financial aid, and it's easy to understand why the A. Gary Anderson Graduate School of Management at UC—Riverside gets such high marks from students. One raves, "I am having the time of my life [and]…feel very privileged to be here." Many MBA candidates here are taking their first steps in the business world, as applicants are not required to have work experience—which can be a good or bad thing depending on who you talk to. Some feel that the program only offers a "surface-level understanding of business." Other students laud the "challenging" classes, bolstered by the "very accessible" professors who "care very much about their students' learning and understanding of the course material." However, some gripe that a few seem "more focused on research, and not curriculum."

The six components of an MBA from AGSM are the core courses, an internship, the communication workshop, the electives, a "capstone course," and a case project or thesis.

Though the core courses take up more time than any other single component, students are most enthusiastic about the "wide diversity of electives," which are all seminar size and designed to "encourage participative learning." One student explains, "I love coming to a small school like UCR's AGSM. You get real interaction with professors, and all of the students know each other, which allows for tighter bonds and networks." There are 10 areas of electives, and students are allowed to take up to nine courses from any area, such as accounting, entrepreneurial management, finance, general management, human resources management/organizational behavior, international management, management information systems, management science, marketing, and production and operations management.

Most students agree that "discussion is greatly encouraged" in class. A fair number of courses "require presentation with business formal attire" and some "even require group debate." One student notes, "It gives you some pressure, but it's fun." Some lament the feeling that the university "does not attach [enough] importance to our business school," and hope for this to change in the near future. Others, though conscious that the school is a "research-oriented university," wouldn't mind getting more "attention from some professors" who they find to be "mostly researchers and not lecturers."

Career and Placement

Aside from recent budget cuts, the thing that has most students at AGSM up in arms is the Career Resources Center. As one student says, "The school desperately needs a stronger Career Counseling Center designed just for the MBA students." Another adds, "I really think the school should begin to target the school's alumni more. There are many UCR MBAs in the industry and they could be a real resource and asset to the school." The MBA now has its own Career Services, which should help alleviate many of the students' concerns regarding "job placement," "internships," and "professional networking."

Student Life and Environment

In recent years, Riverside, California has undergone both something of a renaissance and an influx of people. Gone are the days of quiet orange groves, and in their place resides the veritable capital of the Inland Empire. Whether your tastes run to the great outdoors or to great shopping, students find "plenty of unique hangouts, interesting shopping, and a wide variety of eats to fit anyone's desires (and budget)." Some MBA students feel that they "lack social activities" within the program, though in many instances this could be blamed on the large amount of "homework" these students undertake. That said, as the university (and those that surround it) continue to grow, students can expect more avenues to their social outlets to open.

The school itself is housed in a 30,000-square-foot building that features "state-of-the-art research and teaching facilities." MBA students agree that their "computer lab is very nice" and relish that they, as MBAs, "have priority over all computers in the lab." Other students gripe that they're stuck in "a small building that consists of one lecture room and one classroom. Our school has suffered greatly from the previous budget cuts." Still, the building must have something going for it because "MBA students rarely venture onto the main campus at [UC Riverside], unless it's to go to the library or bookstore."

Students report that "most people are very nice, and it is easy to meet new people if you try." These "very laid-back and friendly" students have formed "a tight-knit community here because our graduate program is so small." "I pretty much know and am friends with every other MBA student," says one. Due to the proximity of students, there is "a level of competition between students during academic competitions and presentations," but most happily note that "it is healthy and in good fun."

Admissions

At AGSM, students from all undergraduate majors and levels of business experience are eligible for admission. In fact, more than 30 percent of all incoming students come from a background other than business and have little—if any—experience in the business world. According to the school, "There is no minimum GPA or GMAT requirement for MBA admission consideration." However, they also say "Satisfying minimal standards does not guarantee admission, since the number of qualified applicants far exceeds the number of places available," meaning that you'd best do your best. It is worth noting that because the school doesn't require prior work experience, all prospective MBAs must complete an internship "to ensure your success upon graduation."

FINANCIAL FACTS

Annual tuition	$12,245
Fees	$29,271
Cost of books	$2,000
Room & board	$10,000
% of students receiving aid	45
% of first-year students receiving aid	46
% of students receiving grants	45
Average award package	$23,000
Average grant	$17,700

ADMISSIONS

Admissions Selectivity Rating	77
# of applications received	488
% applicants accepted	185
% acceptees attending	43
Average GMAT	574
Range of GMAT	540–710
Average GPA	3.35
TOEFL required of international students	Yes
Minimum TOEFL (paper/computer)	550/213
Application fee	$100
International application fee	$125
Regular application deadline	5/1
Regular notification	6/1
Early decision program?	No
Deferment available	No
Transfer students accepted	Yes
Transfer application policy: A maximum of 8 graduate units taken in residence may be transferred.	
Non-fall admissions	Yes
Need-blind admissions	Yes

University of Central Arkansas
College of Business

GENERAL INFORMATION
Type of school   Public
Academic calendar   Semester

SURVEY SAYS...
Students love Conway, AR
Cutting-edge classes
Helfpul alumni

STUDENTS
Enrollment of parent institution	13,000
Enrollment of MBA Program	101
% male/female	61/39
% out-of-state	28
% part-time	36
% minorities	11
% international	17
Average age at entry	27
Average years work experience at entry	4

ACADEMICS
Academic Experience Rating	63
Student/faculty ratio	28:1
Profs interesting rating	64
Profs accessible rating	61
% female faculty	19
% minority faculty	19

Academics

University of Central Arkansas operates a number of graduate business programs, including full-time and part-time MBA programs, a master of accountancy, and a master's program in community and economic development. One testament to the quality of education at University of Central Arkansas is that many undergraduate students choose to return to the university for a graduate degree, directly out of college or many years later. A current student writes, "I attended UCA for my undergrad degree and it is such a good fit for me that it was an easy decision to stay."

Before students can begin the MBA program at UCA, they must complete prerequisite coursework in accounting, economics, and finance. After they have completed the prerequisites, the MBA program consists of ten business courses. Students also have the option of pursuing an international specialization through an additional six credit hours in an approved elective or internship experiences related to international business. Focused on advanced, general management principles, the MBA coursework is quite traditional. In fact, a number of students say they'd like a more interactive business school experience, as UCA's program includes "no group work, few papers, and hardly any projects."

When it comes to the teaching staff, student opinions run the gamut; however, a current student assures us, "With the exception of a small portion of my professors, I have had great relationships with all my teachers. I feel I have been given a solid education at UCA, facilitated by small class sizes, a large college atmosphere, and attentive professors." With an entering class of just 50 students each year, class sizes are small and instructors generally encourage students to add their personal experiences to academic material. As a result, "classroom discussion is rarely dry. We all get along well and enjoy each other's thoughts and input, whether in or out of the classroom."

University of Central Arkansas is rapidly expanding its offerings and campus facilities. The College of Business is likewise on the up-and-up. A student writes, "The administration is in a transition to make the College of Business one of the best in the state. The transition is not complete, but it is well on its way." A case in point, a new business school building, including state-of-the-art case study classrooms, a student commons, a graduate student lounge with lockers, and a professional conference room opened in January 2010.

Career and Placement

Attracting a large part-time population of students who already have professional jobs, the College of Business doesn't dedicate many resources to career planning and placement. However, business students can use the University of Central Arkansas Career Services office, which offers resume writing assistance, campus interviews, current job listings, career fairs, and workshops for job seekers. Even so, those who'd like to start a new career after graduation say the business school could do more to "help with job placement and recruitment." After graduation, UCA students can keep networking with other alums through the MBA Alumni Association or at events like the MBA Scholarship Golf Classic.

ADMISSIONS CONTACT: MICHAEL RUBACH, MBA DIRECTOR
ADDRESS: COLLEGE OF BUSINESS, UNIVERSITY OF CENTRAL ARKANSAS CONWAY, AR 72035
PHONE: 501-450-5316 • FAX: 501-450-5302
E-MAIL: MRUBACH@UCA.EDU • WEBSITE: WWW.UCA.EDU/MBA

Student Life and Environment

Located "right in the middle of Arkansas," UCA boasts a "beautiful" campus with ever-improving facilities, including a "brand new medical and self-wellness center." Plans are under way to keep the positive changes going, and currently "the student center is being expanded to house more eating establishments and office/meeting space" and the student recreation center is constructing a new, Olympic-size swimming pool. On the larger campus, "there are hundreds of student organizations that any student can get involved in." However, most MBA students feel they are "left to fend for themselves," with few networking events or campus activities expressly for them.

Within the MBA program, "the students are divided between professionals and those who did their undergraduate work here"—the former group usually comprised of younger, recent graduates. Those who did their undergraduate degree at UCA tend to feel more connected to the university than those who entered the university to pursue an MBA or masters degree. Both full-time and part-time students at UCA are "all are very busy between their personal, business, and academic activities." As a result, "there is not much time for socializing." The surrounding town of Conway is a growing city of 50,000, which offers modest recreational activities for students. However, be advised that "you have to travel over 30 miles to get a drink" after class.

Admissions

To be considered for admission at University of Central Arkansas, students must submit a minimum GMAT score of 500 and a minimum undergraduate GPA of 2.7. Along with their application, students must submit a two-page statement of purpose. Last year's entering class had an average GMAT score of 552 and an average undergraduate GPA of 3.17.

FINANCIAL FACTS

Annual tuition (in-state/ out-of-state)	$5,988/$11,028
Fees	$298
Cost of books	$1,000
Room & board (on/off-campus)	$6,578/$6,300

ADMISSIONS

Admissions Selectivity Rating	75
# of applications received	28
% applicants accepted	100
% acceptees attending	71
Average GMAT	552
Range of GMAT	510–580
Average GPA	3.17
TOEFL required of international students	Yes
Minimum TOEFL (paper/computer)	550/213
Application fee	$25
International application fee	$40
Early decision program?	No
Deferment available	Yes
Maximum length of deferment	3 years
Transfer students accepted	Yes
Transfer application policy: A maximum of 6 graduate hours is transferrable from a AACSB institution.	
Non-fall admissions	Yes
Need-blind admissions	No

UNIVERSITY OF CENTRAL FLORIDA
COLLEGE OF BUSINESS ADMINISTRATION

GENERAL INFORMATION

Type of school	Public
Academic calendar	Semester

SURVEY SAYS...

Solid preparation in:
Accounting
General management
Quantitative skills
Entrepreneurial studies

STUDENTS

Enrollment of parent institution	53,644
Enrollment of MBA Program	507
% male/female	60/40
% out-of-state	3
% part-time	55
% minorities	22
% international	5
Average age at entry	31
Average years work experience at entry	7

ACADEMICS

Academic Experience Rating	**70**
Student/faculty ratio	41:1
Profs interesting rating	74
Profs accessible rating	72
% female faculty	18
% minority faculty	24

Joint Degrees

MBA/Master of Sport Business Management (21 months)

Prominent Alumni

Kenneth G. Dixon, CPA, Real Estate Developer; J. D. Atchison, Exec. VP, Sea World; Andrew J. Fore III, Exec. Director, Citigroup Business Services; Nan McCormick, Partner, Sr. VP, CB Richard Ellis.

Academics

Students pursuing an MBA at the University of Central Florida have four options: the traditional MBA, a lockstep evening program designed for working professionals; the full-time one-year MBA, a daytime program for freshly minted BAs as well as mid-career professionals looking to jumpstart their careers; an Executive MBA, designed for current executives and managers with at least five years experience; and a Professional MBA, which reduces the EMBA experience requirement from five years to three. In addition, the school offers a variety of master's degrees in business, including a well-regarded program in sport business management.

UCF draws a predominantly local student body that turns to the school because it is "affordable and convenient." Some cite the program's "emphasis on diversity and community service" as further incentives to attend. Others tout the "outstanding professors" whose "actual work experience for almost all of their classes is their greatest strength" but who are also "always willing to help students whether it be with class material or outside counsel." The one-year program appeals to "individuals who want to move right into their MBA before or while beginning their career search."

UCF is a relatively "younger school, so many of the facilities are well-equipped with up-to-date computer systems and fully functional (as opposed to antiquated buildings on older campuses)." Resources "are excellent; there are computer and study labs with peer help available 24/7, the online resources are great, teachers are always available, advisors help with planning, and courses are easy to find and register for." Like many newer schools, UCF is constantly developing, and students tell us that "The MBA program has made good [strides forward] in helping with the selection of electives by introducing various certificate programs (i.e., entrepreneurship). However, it could still offer more, especially in terms of international business considering the number of foreign students." Students see UCF's Orlando location as a big plus, "providing a variety of outside opportunities to get experience while in school."

Career and Placement

UCF's Office for Corporate Partnerships & Career Management (OCPCM) provides career management, and internship and job and placement services to MBA and other graduate business students. The office includes a Career Information Library stocked with reading materials. Workshops are offered in resume-writing, job search strategies and interviewing techniques. Advisors are also available to assist with internship and full-time job search.

Employers who most frequently hire UCF MBAs include Lockheed Martin, Darden Restaurants, Siemens, SunTrust, Adventist Health System, Walt Disney World, Bank of America, CNL and FedEx. Almost a third of UCF MBAs find work in consulting (mean starting salary: $57,333). Marketing claims just over one quarter of each graduating class.

Student Life and Environment

For full-time MBAs at UCF, "There is always something to do, something to see, something to learn. The UCF campus is always alive." Classes meet "early in the morning, and then most students have graduate assistantships where they work in the afternoon. There are group projects due nearly every week, so the ability to get to campus quickly and easily is imperative. Fortunately, although the university has more than 50,000 students, the graduate business school does not have a crowded feel. In fact, it sometimes seems like a separate bubble, but in a way that promotes intense focus and cooperation

ADMISSIONS CONTACT: JUDY RYDER, DIRECTOR OF GRADUATE ADMISSIONS
ADDRESS: P.O. BOX 161400, BA I, ROOM 240 ORLANDO, FL 32816
PHONE: 407-823-4723 • FAX: 407-823-0219
E-MAIL: CBAGRAD@BUS.UCF.EDU • WEBSITE: WWW.BUS.UCF.EDU

on common goals." The school hosts " many different types of clubs, societies, and groups to join" to keep students busy when they're not in class or studying.

Students love UCF's "blue skies with nearly constant sunshine and green grass. It is a genuine pleasure simply to walk to class" across this "beautiful campus." As one student puts it, "There are four Starbucks locations and three different places to get pizza. What else do you need to know?" For those who need to know more: UCF has "excellent resources ranging from a great library to an enormous gym to restaurants and more," "the new stadium and arena are awesome," and the campus is host to "lots of activities, concerts, comedy, etc." As an added bonus, the school's "sports teams are becoming more recognized nationally."

Not all students have time to enjoy campus amenities. UCF's part-timers typically "don't do much outside of academics at my school" because they're simply too busy. They are working professionals whose experience "helps make the part-time program what it is. The interaction of the students and the professors is at a high level that keeps you wanting to attend class." In both the part-time and full-time programs "there is a broad range of students of all races and backgrounds," infusing each cohort with "different personalities and backgrounds that provide different points of view. Our class helps each other out a lot."

Admissions

Applicants to the UCF College of Business MBA program must complete an online application to the UCF School of Graduate Studies. Additionally, applicants must submit official transcripts for each university or college attended, an official GMAT score report, a personal essay, a current resume, and three letters of recommendation. International students whose first language is not English must also submit TOEFL scores (minimum score: 577 paper-based; 233 computer-based; 90–91 Internet-based); all international students need to provide translations of non-English documents and an accredited course-by-course evaluation of transcripts from institutions that do not employ the American grading system. UCF requires a minimum GMAT score of 540 (550 for the one-year full-time program) for its MBA programs; requirements for other Master's programs are less restrictive. An undergraduate GPA of at least 3.0 over the final 60 semester hours of coursework (3.3 for the One-Year MBA) is also required.

FINANCIAL FACTS

Annual tuition (in-state/ out-of-state)	$7,450/$26,400
Cost of books	$2,000
Room & board (on/off-campus)	$8,500/$14,000
% of students receiving aid	47
% of first-year students receiving aid	59
% of students receiving loans	20
% of students receiving grants	53
Average award package	$15,625
Average grant	$6,500
Average student loan debt	$24,822

ADMISSIONS

Admissions Selectivity Rating	78
# of applications received	7,450
% applicants accepted	49
% acceptees attending	74
Average GMAT	570
Range of GMAT	470–710
Average GPA	3.3
TOEFL required of international students	Yes
Minimum TOEFL (paper/computer)	575/233
Application fee	$30
International application fee	$30
Regular application deadline	6/15
Early decision program?	Yes
ED Deadline/Notification	NR / 3/15
Deferment available	No
Transfer students accepted	Yes
Transfer application policy:	
Transfer applicants must be from a regionally or nationally accredited university. May transfer in up to 9 hours.	
Non-fall admissions	No
Need-blind admissions	Yes

EMPLOYMENT PROFILE

Career Rating	78	Grads Employed by Function	% Avg. Salary
Percent employed at graduation	48	Marketing	26 $52,333
Percent employed 3 months after graduation	17	Operations	5 NR
		Consulting	32 $57,333
Average base starting salary	$52,322	Management	16 $46,160
Primary Source of Full-time Job Acceptances		Finance	16 $45,667
School-facilitated activities	3 (16%)	HR	5 NR
Graduate-facilitated activities	16 (84%)	**Top 5 Employers Hiring Grads**	
		Protiviti (2), Lockheed Martin (1), KPMG, LLP (1), PricewaterhouseCoopers (1), Talk of the Town Restaurants, Inc. (1)	

THE UNIVERSITY OF CHICAGO
BOOTH SCHOOL OF BUSINESS

GENERAL INFORMATION
Type of school   Private
Academic calendar   Quarter

SURVEY SAYS...
Students love Chicago, IL
Good peer network
Happy students
Smart classrooms
Solid preparation in:
Finance
Accounting
Quantitative skills

STUDENTS
Enrollment of parent
  institution   15,149

ACADEMICS
Academic Experience Rating   99
Profs interesting rating   75
Profs accessible rating   89
% female faculty   16

Joint Degrees
MBA/MA Area Studies and
Business, MBA/MA International
Relations and Business, MBA/JD
Law and Business, MBA/MD
Medicine and Business, MBA/MPP
Public Policy Studies and Business,
MBA/MA Social Service
Administration and Business.

Prominent Alumni
Mary Tolan, CEO, Accretive Health;
Frederic de Bure, Managing
Director, eBay, Singapore; Robert
Lane, Chairman, Deere & Company;
Joe Mansueto, CEO/Founder,
Morningstar; Brady Dougan, CEO
Investment Banking, Credit Suisse.

Academics

"The emphasis on [students] learning the basics rather than some predigested goo" along with "an unbeatable faculty" are "what make the University of Chicago's Booth School of Business one of the best, especially in hard-core areas such as finance and accounting," students tell us. A "rigorous quantitative program that compels students to think critically and analytically" is the hallmark of a Chicago Booth MBA, although students hasten to add that Booth also "emphasizes persuasion, communication, and negotiation skills."

Chicago Booth offers a full-time, part-time evening, part-time weekend, and executive MBA program. All four tracks share "top-notch" faculty, wide-ranging academic options, and an approach that "doesn't chase new trends in business but instead relies on teaching sound fundamentals that can then be applied to any situation." The programs differ in some details; full-time students, for example, enjoy a student-enacted grade nondisclosure policy that creates a conducive environment for "teamwork and sharing of ideas." Students must also complete the Leadership Exploration and Development (LEAD) program, which "provides analytic frameworks for leadership that are very helpful in determining the best way to use [one's] strengths and where to improve." Part-timers enjoy "great flexibility," noting that "most classes have several sessions taught by the same professor during the same quarter, enabling students to make up class sessions if for some reason they cannot attend their normal session." Booth's weekend MBA and Executive MBAs have "students flying to Chicago from across the U.S. and world to attend classes on Saturdays. This connects a much broader and more diverse group of people than other MBA programs can."

Chicago Booth's faculty includes Nobel laureates and cutting-edge researchers "who also excel in the classroom." One accounting student reports, "Both my corporate tax strategy professor and my M&A accounting professor consult for corporate and government clients, so they have intimate knowledge of how to apply what they teach in the real world." Booth is best known for its faculty in finance, economics, and accounting, but students note that the school should work to "increase awareness of its excellence in marketing, entrepreneurship, and general management disciplines." Many students also "do a one-term or full-year exchange program at a foreign business school," and "These international career development opportunities are a big part of the experience for many Booth students."

Career and Placement

The Booth Career Services Office doesn't have to work hard; as one student explains, "The network and doors that open up to a graduate from Chicago Booth are outstanding. Gaining an MBA from this school carries a lot of weight and in the job market no one will question your education." That doesn't mean that Career Services slacks off, however; on the contrary, it "is an excellent resource and deserves praise," and does a good job attracting recruiters in consulting, accounting, and finance including McKinsey & Company, Citigroup, The Boston Consulting Group, UBS, A.T. Kearney, Credit Suisse, Goldman Sachs, Bank of America/Merrill Lynch, and Booz and Company.

Chicago Booth also excels at "preparing career changers. You learn from the best faculty in the world to attain the skills you need to succeed in your given career. The alumni, and especially second-year students at the school, are available to answer any questions. Career Services does an excellent job of helping you identify your transferable skills to your new targeted career.... I would highly recommend the school for people looking to change careers."

Student Life and Environment

"The social aspect of University of Chicago is often overlooked," students in the full-time program tell us, reporting that "There are all kinds of opportunities to get together with other students in social or more formal settings, including school-sponsored happy hours, etc." Although "MBAs here work as hard as students at any other b-school, we know how to have fun too." One student writes, "If anything, there are too many programs and opportunities to be involved. You need to carefully consider them all to properly juggle [your] schedule." And with "the great city of Chicago is at our doorstep," students don't have to look far to find a wide range of fun diversions.

The school is located on Chicago's South Side in the Hyde Park neighborhood, which "is too often made out to be a scary place when, in fact, it's not. There is a pretty unique mixture of socioeconomic groups here, so you can drive by a building with three poor families living in it and four blocks later be at a stop sign next to a million-dollar (or more) home. The fact is that it's on the South Side of Chicago so people automatically say, 'bad, scary neighborhood.'" Part-time students attend classes at the Gleacher Center, "a beautiful building" in downtown Chicago, just off the Magnificent Mile. For students whose activities keep them in the Hyde Park area, Booth's Charles M. Harper Center boasts a "winter garden," a "dramatic foyer in the center of the building" where "People can catch up, do work, or just relax for a moment."

Admissions

Admission to the Chicago Booth School of Business is extremely competitive. Admissions Officers scrutinize a wide array of qualifications, including academic record (quality of curriculum, scholarships, special honors, etc.), work experience (quality as well as quantity), and overall "fit"(interpersonal skills, unique experiences, philanthropic activity). Applicants must provide the Admissions Office with transcripts for all postsecondary academic work, an official GMAT score report, letters of recommendation, personal essays, and TOEFL/IELTS scores (for international students only). Interviews are required for all candidates. Applicants to the full-time program interview on a "by invitation only" basis.

FINANCIAL FACTS

Annual tuition	$50,900
Fees	$780
Cost of books	$2,100
Room & board	$18,900

ADMISSIONS

Admissions Selectivity Rating	98
TOEFL required of international students	Yes
Minimum TOEFL (paper/computer)	600/250
Application fee	$200
International application fee	$200
Application Deadline/Notification	
Round 1:	10/14 / 12/16
Round 2:	1/6 / 3/24
Round 3:	3/10 / 5/12
Early decision program?	No
Deferment available	No
Transfer students accepted	No
Non-fall admissions	No
Need-blind admissions	Yes

EMPLOYMENT PROFILE

Career Rating	92	Grads Employed by Function%	Avg. Salary
Primary Source of Full-time Job Acceptances		Marketing	NR $94,131
School-facilitated activities	338 (84%)	Operations	NR $120,200
Graduate-facilitated activities	67 (NR%)	Consulting	NR $118,211
		Management	NR $100,696
		Finance	NR $100,223

University of Cincinnati
College of Business

GENERAL INFORMATION
Type of school   Public
Academic calendar   Quarter

SURVEY SAYS...
Smart classrooms
Solid preparation in:
Teamwork

STUDENTS
Enrollment of parent institution	39,667
Enrollment of MBA Program	183
% male/female	66/34
% out-of-state	34
% part-time	53
% minorities	9
% international	31
Average age at entry	27
Average years work experience at entry	4

ACADEMICS
Academic Experience Rating	79
Student/faculty ratio	4:1
Profs interesting rating	78
Profs accessible rating	68
% female faculty	34
% minority faculty	17

Joint Degrees
MBA/JD, 4 yrs; MBA/MA in Arts Administration, 3 yrs; MBA/MD, 5 years; MBA/Nursing, 3yrs; MBA/MS in Accounting, Information Systems, Marketing or Quantitative Analysis, 2 years.

Prominent Alumni
Robert Taft, Governor of Ohio; John F. Barrett, President & CEO, Western-Southern Life; Myron E. Ullman, III, CEO, JCPenney; Dr. Candace Kendle, Chairman & CEO Kendle International; Richard E. Thornburgh, Vice-Chairman, Credit Suisse First Boston.

Academics

Offering an efficient, one-year MBA program, the University of Cincinnati is a great place to jumpstart your career with a general business degree, or pursue a specialized graduate program that will prepare you to work in a specific industry. Described as "rigorous but manageable," the school's "one-year MBA program is very attractive to those who are taking time off of their career to pursue extra education." If you don't want to drop out of the workforce, even for just a year, the school offers part-time evening and weekend programs as well. These programs are flexible and suited to a working student; if you can't make it to campus on certain evenings, "core classes are recorded and available for viewing online." Keep in mind, however, that while these programs are designed to accommodate busy schedules, they're no walk in the park. Part-timers should "plan on 24 hours of coursework and homework per week" in addition to their professional and personal commitments.

Depending on your career interests, there are lots of educational avenues at UC. Within the MBA program, students may choose to tailor their education by taking classes within nine areas of concentration, including Operations Management and International Business. In addition, "the study abroad opportunities are plentiful" and every year, the school offers seminars in important international business locations, such as France, India, China, Thailand, and Germany. UC also offers four joint degree and various master's programs. Of particular note, University of Cincinnati's joint degree in arts administration is "unique among business schools in North America" and confers a special prestige, considering the school's fine reputation in the arts and their world-famous music conservatory. At this "top research organization," students may also pursue their specific interests through the school's research centers, like the Goering Center for Family and Private Business, and the Center for Entrepreneurship Education and Research.

In the classroom, you'll be treated to "several standout professors supported by a solid core that ensures rewarding class experiences." The majority of UC faculty is "recognized as leaders in their fields" who bring real-world expertise to the learning environment—though some students feel they would benefit from a more hands-on, case-based approach across the curriculum, rather than lecture. If you are struggling, most professors are "willing to provide extra assistance when needed." Evening classes can sometimes be a bit over-stuffed, but during the daytime, "classes are often very small and the teachers really care about their students and support you whenever you have problems and need them." On the whole, "the academic experience is very intense, but the faculty and staff try to keep everyone at ease."

Career and Placement

MBA Career Services offers workshops, counseling, career panels, mock interviews, and other services for career seekers. Their efforts clearly pay off, as 80 percent of UC graduates have accepted a job within three months of graduation. Recently, students held internships or took jobs at companies including Procter & Gamble, Citi, Deloitte & Touche, Ernst & Young, Johnson & Johnson, Kendle International, Dunnhumby, Duke Energy, Rivercities Capital Fund.

ADMISSIONS CONTACT: ANDREW VOGEL, ASSOCIATE DIRECTOR, ADMISSIONS
ADDRESS: CARL H. LINDNER HALL, SUITE 606, P.O. BOX 210020 CINCINNATI, OH 45221-0020
PHONE: 513-556-7024 • FAX: 513-558-7006
E-MAIL: GRADUATE@UC.EDU • WEBSITE: WWW.BUSINESS.UC.EDU/MBA

Most students who come to University of Cincinnati plan to stay in the region, and the majority of jobs and internships placements are made within the larger metropolitan area. In fact, 100 percent of last year's internship placements were with Cincinnati companies. Unfortunately, students who'd like to consider a wider geographical region feel the school needs to "tap into other regions, especially the close ones like Chicago, Cleveland, and the northeast."

Student Life and Environment

As at many schools that have traditional and part-time programs, you'll see a bit of a split within the UC student body. Generally speaking, "the full-time MBA program is characterized by younger students, most just out of undergrad, with limited work experience. Part-time students are mostly older, more diverse, and knowledgeable about various fields." Especially among younger students, "the social setting is pretty good, and most of the students are open to out-of-class experiences."

UC is an urban campus; however, the school grounds have recently received a facelift, and now have "a lot more green space and new workout facility." In addition, the "computer lab and library are excellent." Outside of attending class, the business school and the larger university provide a range of extracurricular and recreational options to those who are interested. A current student explains, "For me it was important to have things to do in my spare time beside school. There are a lot of opportunities on and around campus to go out, relax. The new recreation center was just perfect for me." Adds another, "There are a lot of socializing options around the school and all over the city. The school has also developed a strong football culture over the last few years and that has gone on to strengthen the community."

Admissions

This year's admitted MBA class achieved an average GPA of 3.36 and an average GMAT score of 585, plus more than three years of full-time work experience. UC considers any student with an undergraduate degree for their master's and MBA programs, regardless of discipline. UC admits students whose success in their undergraduate studies, in addition to professional experience, will make them successful in the MBA program. GMAT scores, GPA, work history, communication skills (written and oral), and teamwork experience are among the most important factors in an admissions decision.

FINANCIAL FACTS

Annual tuition (in-state/ out-of-state)	$24,588/$30,264
Fees	$2,004
Cost of books	$4,000
Room & board (on/off-campus)	$14,500/$16,000
% of students receiving aid	80
% of first-year students receiving aid	80
Average award package	$18,968
Average grant	$9,110

ADMISSIONS

Admissions Selectivity Rating	83
# of applications received	247
% applicants accepted	73
% acceptees attending	57
Average GMAT	585
Range of GMAT	550–610
Average GPA	3.36
TOEFL required of international students	Yes
Minimum TOEFL (paper/computer)	600/250
Application fee	$45
International application fee	$45
Application Deadline/Notification	
Round 1:	1/15 / 3/15
Round 2:	4/1 / 6/1
Round 3:	7/15 / 8/1
Early decision program?	Yes
ED Deadline/Notification	NR / 3/15
Deferment available	Yes
Maximum length of deferment	1 year
Transfer students accepted	Yes
Transfer application policy: Transferring from an AACSB accredited institution, no more than 16 credit hours, must have 3.0 in transferred class.	
Non-fall admissions	No
Need-blind admissions	Yes

UNIVERSITY OF CONNECTICUT
SCHOOL OF BUSINESS

GENERAL INFORMATION
Type of school   Public
Academic calendar   Semester

SURVEY SAYS...
Friendly students
Smart classrooms
Solid preparation in:
Finance
Accounting
Teamwork

STUDENTS
Enrollment of parent institution	28,372
Enrollment of MBA Program	1,214
% male/female	71/29
% out-of-state	25
% part-time	91
% minorities	9
% international	29
Average age at entry	28
Average years work experience at entry	5

ACADEMICS
Academic Experience Rating	**86**
Student/faculty ratio	13:1
Profs interesting rating	77
Profs accessible rating	80
% female faculty	14
% minority faculty	28

Joint Degrees
MBA/JD; MBA/MD; MBA/MSW;
MBA/MA International Studies;
MBA/Master of International
Management; MBA/MS Nursing.

Prominent Alumni
Mr. Robert E. Diamond, CEO,
Barclays Capital; Mr. John Y. Kim,
President & CEO, New York Life
Investment Management, LLC; Mr.
Denis Nayden, Managing Partner,
OakHill Capital Management.

Academics

A great place to develop real-world credentials, the University of Connecticut's MBA program teaches business fundamentals while maximizing students' access to practical learning experiences. Comprising 57 hours of course work, the school's full-time MBA is a two-year, lock-step program located primarily on the UConn campus in Storrs, while the part-time program is completed at a slower pace on one of UConn's auxiliary campuses in Waterbury, Hartford, or Stamford. UConn is "highly-regarded in the areas of finance and risk analytics," but the first-year core covers all functional areas of business in an integrated fashion. In the second year of the MBA, "You are given a lot more freedom in choosing your classes" and the schedule is more flexible, which allows for more co-curricular activities. In addition to an active internship program, "UConn's MBA program [is] unique in that it offers numerous experiential learning accelerators," which are practice-based programs, often operated in conjunction with a corporate partner. For example, through an "exclusive partnership with GE," students work on strategic projects for the company, in collaboration with UConn faculty and GE managers." A current student elaborates, "I've been able to complete three semester-long consulting projects for real companies and non-profits, and have participated in two study abroad programs."

A relatively small program, the full-time MBA "intimate class size" makes it easier for UConn students to build relationships with both their teachers and classmates. With roughly 60–70 students in each full-time class, "Being part of this small cohort allows for personal attention and focused learning." In general, professors are "receptive to any type of question" in class, and many are "extremely motivated and genuinely interested in the academic success of their students." However, students admit that when it comes to teaching style, "professors run a wide gamut," including some highly-skilled instructors, and some professors who seem more focused on their own projects.

For Connecticut residents, "the price of attending a state school was more reasonable" than attending a similar, private institution. On the downside, "The effects of state budget cuts can be seen throughout UConn as a whole, as well as the business school." Currently, "UConn is undergoing a great deal of change under the leadership of a new Dean," and there have been some bumps in the road as the program changes course. However, optimistic students observe, "The dean and the MBA director are very responsive to students' concerns, and changes have been made and continue to be made to improve the value of the school."

Career and Placement

While UConn enjoys great "local brand recognition" and "very good connections in the state of Connecticut," many students are disappointed with their school's career center. Drawing the majority of its business contacts from the immediate region, many feel that the "career center perhaps needs to widen its focus," and try "digging deeper into Wall Street or Boston" to make contact with more recruiters. On the flipside, a current student counters, "I have had interviews with Covidien, Pitney Bowes, General Electric, and Travelers Insurance, and I know UConn has a strong presence when I see that I am competing in the second round interviews with students from Yale and Cornell."

In a recent year, 58 percent of UConn graduates were working, negotiating a job offer, or pursuing further study within three months of graduation. By six months, that number had jumped to 71 percent of students. The mean salary for recent UConn grads was

ADMISSIONS CONTACT: MICHAEL DEOTTE, DIRECTOR
ADDRESS: 2100 HILLSIDE ROAD UNIT 1041 STORRS, CT 06269-1041
PHONE: 860-486-2872 • FAX: 860-486-5222
E-MAIL: UCONNMBA@BUSINESS.UCONN.EDU • WEBSITE: WWW.MBA.UCONN.EDU

$95,120 in the previous year, with a high of $120,000. Companies hiring UConn graduates include AC Nielsen, Aetna, Atlantic Records, Barclays, CIGNA, Citigroup, CVS Caremark, Deloitte Consulting, ESPN, General Electric, Hasbro Hewitt, Hubbell, Inc, IBM, ING, Liberty Mutual, Nestle, Nasdaq, PepsiCo, Pitney Bowes, Prudential Financial, Siemens, Sun Products Corporation, Travelers, Webster Bank, and XL Global Insurance.

Student Life and Environment

On University of Connecticut's Storrs campus, "The School of Business is new and modern with all the requisite amenities," including an MBA lounge, comfortable classrooms, and lockers. While "dining hall food is unimpressive," "the Student Union is newer," boasting a larger food court with better options. Attracting a "diverse group from all over the world," almost 40 percent of University of Connecticut's full-time MBA candidates are international. A collaborative cohort environment, "team activities are an integrated part of our school culture," and students are generally "smart, cheerful, [and] enthusiastic."

For first-year students, "School days are treated similar to a nine to five job," with class in the morning and homework to complete in the evening. Within this small program, everyone knows everyone, and students "typically socialize with the entire MBA class in-between classes." On campus, "mixers with students are fairly regular" and "some people are very motivated and active in clubs and networking events." However, "the full-time MBA is comprised of mostly commuter students, so we do not generally stay on campus when we are not in class." Plus, the school's campus in Storrs is "out in the middle of nowhere"—affording a great view of the New England woods, but limiting the scope of extracurricular and recreational activities in the immediate vicinity. On that note, prospective students "should keep in mind that a car is all but required to participate in local internships over the summer."

Admissions

To be considered for UConn's MBA program, students must have at least two years of professional work experience, strong GMAT scores (usually between 580 and 660), and a solid undergraduate academic record. In recent years, the UConn incoming class had an average undergraduate GPA of 3.4 and an average GMAT score of 621. Full-time students had an average of five and a half years in the work force, while part-time students had eight years of professional experience.

FINANCIAL FACTS

Annual tuition (in-state/ out-of-state)	$9,450/$24,534
Fees	$1,776
Cost of books	$3,000
Room & board (on/off-campus)	$11,080/$12,500
% of students receiving aid	80
% of first-year students receiving aid	66
% of students receiving loans	21
% of students receiving grants	37
Average award package	$29,555
Average grant	$15,000

ADMISSIONS

Admissions Selectivity Rating	93
# of applications received	335
% applicants accepted	26
% acceptees attending	60
Average GMAT	621
Range of GMAT	580–670
Average GPA	3.4
TOEFL required of international students	Yes
Minimum TOEFL (paper/computer)	575/233
Application fee	$55
International application fee	$55
Regular application deadline	3/1
Early decision program?	No
Deferment available	Yes
Maximum length of deferment	12 months
Transfer students accepted	Yes
Transfer application policy: All students requesting to transfer are required to meet with the Director of the MBA Program.	
Non-fall admissions	No
Need-blind admissions	Yes

EMPLOYMENT PROFILE

		Grads Employed by Function	% Avg. Salary
Career Rating	82		
Percent employed at graduation	33	Marketing	18 $86,250
Percent employed 3 months after graduation	27	Operations	3 $90,000
		Consulting	12 $83,375
Average base starting salary	$95,120	Management	3 $95,000
Primary Source of Full-time Job Acceptances		Finance	55 $79,100
School-facilitated activities	22 (54%)	Top 5 Employers Hiring Grads	
Graduate-facilitated activities	14 (38%)	IBM (5), The Hartford Financial Services (4), Covidien (2), Aetna (2), Wal-mart (1)	

UNIVERSITY OF DAYTON
SCHOOL OF BUSINESS ADMINISTRATION

GENERAL INFORMATION
Type of school   Private
Affiliation   Roman Catholic
Academic calendar   Semester

SURVEY SAYS...
Cutting-edge classes
Happy students
Smart classrooms
Solid preparation in:
Teamwork

STUDENTS
Enrollment of parent
  institution   10,930
Enrollment of MBA Program   460
% male/female   60/40
% part-time   80
% minorities   10
% international   30
Average age at entry   29
Average years work experience
  at entry   5

ACADEMICS
Academic Experience Rating   83
Student/faculty ratio   7:1
Profs interesting rating   88
Profs accessible rating   84
% female faculty   20
% minority faculty   5

Joint Degrees
Joint Juris of Doctor of Law (JD)
and Master of Business
Administration (MBA) 3–4 years
(combined JD and MBA degrees).

Prominent Alumni
Keith Hawk, Vice President, Lexis-
Nexis; Phil Parker, President & CEO,
Dayton Area Cham. of Commerce;
Mike Turner, U.S. Congressman,
OH; Linda Berning, Berning
Investments.

Academics

Students tell us that UD's integrated curriculum "is one of...the program's biggest strengths. It is unlike what any school in the region is offering, and it results in a more thorough educational experience." The school "utilizes a team-taught program where two professors from separate disciplines teach a class together. This lets students see various perspectives," which typically include an emphasis on "new management techniques. The Toyota Way and Lean Manufacturing are very popular" here. Students also boast of UD's "Marianist identity and values, which leads to a great sense of family. Students, staff and faculty are really close to one another. People help each other a lot." As one MBA explains, "If I get a B, someone is asking me what they can do to help. If I get an A, someone is asking me if I can help them, and I always agree. We're a team, no doubt."

The five-year bachelor's/MBA program at the University of Dayton's School of Business Administration attracts many UD undergraduates, making for a young and ambitious but not highly experienced student body. The school compensates by providing students with numerous opportunities to broaden their business resumes. One student reports that he is "really impressed by all the opportunities UD provides its students with outside classes. Its entrepreneurship program is supported by out-of-class valuable experiences. For example, the Business Plan Competition...offers us the possibility to create a real business plan and to receive funds to implement it. I also heard finance students telling me that they can't believe that they are allowed to manage millions of dollars on behalf of UD at the Davis Center. I really like being able to turn my theoretical knowledge into practical experience at UD, because now, I feel more confident that I will be able to apply what I learned to real-life situations."

The University provides students with numerous chances to broaden their business resumes. One student reports that he is "really impressed by all the opportunities UD provides its students with outside classes.... For example, the Business Plan Competition offers...us the possibility to create a real business plan and to receive funds to implement it...I really like being able to turn my theoretical knowledge into practical experience at UD, because now, I feel more confident that I will be able to apply what I learned to real-life situation."

UD also offers a very popular five-year bachelor's/MBA program in which University of Dayton undergraduates are "able to achieve 150 hours for the CPA exam and get an MBA degree." The school's "administration is good and getting better" and "cares about what the students think," professors are "passionate and well-prepared leaders who are engaging and challenging," and students enjoy "many opportunities to gain experience in your particular field, whether with student organizations, access to alumni, or career/academic development programs and workshops." With all that going for the school, it's no wonder students tell us that "UD's MBA program is probably one of the best-kept secrets in Ohio."

Career and Placement

MBAs at the University of Dayton are served by the Career Services Office, which assists undergraduates, graduates, and alumni in their development and placement needs. The office provides graduate students with the following services: career advisement; job search and résumé critiquing workshops, career fairs, online résumé referral, on-campus recruiting events, mock-interviews, and contact with the alumni career network. Students tell us that the school "has an excellent reputation and a great relationship with local/regional employers." Top employers of U Dayton MBAs include Wright Patterson

Air Force Base, Emerson Climate Technologies, Fifth Third Bank, Reynolds & Reynolds, and LexisNexis. Other employers include AK Steel, AT&T, Greene Memorial Hospital, Honda, IBM, Kettering Medical Center, and Premier Health Partners.

Student Life and Environment

Students brag that UD is a collegial campus, the sort of place where "every time you pass someone, whether that be a student, professor, or even the custodial staff, a pleasant 'Hello, how is your day?' is exchanged. This allows for a comfort in the classroom that, in turn, allows for education beyond the text to flourish." This open dialogue is equally available to international students; writes one from France, "UD is reputed for taking care of its international students. I knew before my arrival here that faculty and staff would be very accessible and helpful, and that I would be individually recognized by them."

SBA accommodates "a lot of MBA social events and opportunities as well as seminars for career and professional skill development," while the university at large offers "plenty of activities organized by the students and university-sponsored events that give the students plenty of options to take a break and get away from school work for a while."

While "there is an overwhelming majority of Caucasian students" here, there are also "students from France, Germany, China, and various racial minorities as well. Age covers the vast spectrum from recent graduate to retired. Non-traditional students mix well with young professionals."

Admissions

All applications to the University of Dayton MBA program must include official transcripts for all postsecondary academic work, a completed application, and an official GMAT score report; the GMAT entrance requirement may be delayed for students with strong academic records, allowing them to enroll conditionally for one semester before submitting GMAT scores. A cover letter, current resume, and letters of recommendation from employers or professors are recommended but not required. International applicants must meet all of the above requirements and must also provide a translation of any non-English language transcripts and official scores for the TOEFL (minimum score of 550 paper exam, 213 computer exam, or 80 Internet-based exam required for unconditional admission. Alternatively, international students may submit an IELTS score of 6.5 or higher in lieu of the TOEFL requirement.

FINANCIAL FACTS

Annual tuition	$18,312
Fees	$75
Cost of books	$650
% of students receiving aid	30
% of students receiving loans	25
% of students receiving grants	8
Average grant	$1,000

ADMISSIONS

Admissions Selectivity Rating	75
# of applications received	334
% applicants accepted	80
% acceptees attending	80
Average GMAT	579
Range of GMAT	460–670
Average GPA	3.28
TOEFL required of international students	Yes
Minimum TOEFL (paper/ computer/web)	550/213/80
International application fee	$50
Early decision program?	No
Deferment available	Yes
Maximum length of deferment	1 year
Transfer students accepted	Yes
Transfer application policy: Students may request up to 6 Semester hours of approved graduate transfer post-foundation credit of course work of B or better graded quality completed in acceptable time frame.	
Non-fall admissions	Yes
Need-blind admissions	Yes

EMPLOYMENT PROFILE

Career Rating	77	Top 5 Employers Hiring Grads
		Wright Patterson Air Force Base, Emerson Climate Technologies, Fifth Third Bank, Reynolds & Reynolds, LexisNexis

UNIVERSITY OF DENVER
DANIELS COLLEGE OF BUSINESS

GENERAL INFORMATION
Type of school	Private
Academic calendar	Quarter

SURVEY SAYS...
Students love Denver, CO
Good social scene
Solid preparation in:
Teamwork

STUDENTS
Enrollment of parent institution	11,731
Enrollment of MBA Program	373
% male/female	82/18
% out-of-state	36
% part-time	50
% minorities	7
% international	10
Average age at entry	27
Average years work experience at entry	5

ACADEMICS
Academic Experience Rating	**77**
Student/faculty ratio	30:1
Profs interesting rating	85
Profs accessible rating	85
% female faculty	23
% minority faculty	8

Joint Degrees
JD/MBA; JD/IMBA; JD/MSRECM, approximately 3–4 years in length; IMBA/MA in Global Finance, Trade, and Economic Integration, approximately 2–3 years in length; flexible Dual Degree offered with any other approved University of Denver degree; combined degree with any other approved Daniels degrees.

Prominent Alumni
Joseph W. Saunders, Chairman and CEO of Visa; Jim Lentz, President, Toyota USA; Ted Kleisner, President and CEO of Hershey Entertainment and Resorts Company; W. Patrick McGinnis, President and CEO of Nestle-Purina; Andrew C. Taylor, Chairman and CEO of Enterprise Car Rental.

Academics

The University of Denver's Daniels College of Business fuses its focus on "values-based leadership," "sustainability," and "ethics," with its "strong reputation" and extensive "business network within the Denver community." The result is a well-balanced program which builds a community of "sharp, young professionals" who enjoy the school's status as "the best in the region."

As a private institution, students say "networking is better and class sizes are smaller." In addition to attracting a large number of students who hail from abroad, the school offers high-achieving undergraduates the opportunity to pursue their MBA in only one extra year of course work. Thus, the student body at Daniels College of Business tends to be divided between younger faces fresh out of their undergraduate studies and those working professionals looking to pursue an advanced degree in their field through the Daniels' part-time MBA program. One student characterizes the population thusly, "the [average] age range is 23–32 years old. Most have or are working for Fortune 1000 companies. The type of experience is diverse, ranging from Finance to Engineering to Medicine. All are in a similar situation of balancing work, school, and family." A part-timer adds, the "part-time program lets me work full-time while in school, so my career isn't put on pause."

Overall, the professors at the University of Denver "are very knowledgeable in their areas." Many professors and staff "are world-class, with incredible business knowledge and experience outside of academia, as well as within academia." Although "some of the lectures may not be entirely interesting and difficult to stay focused on, it is easy to see the teachers really do enjoy their profession and want to see their students excel." Others say, "some of the professors are subpar"; however, as at any MBA program, it's all about seeking out leaders in your field as "many of [the professors] are excellent" and are quick to provide "mentoring opportunities." In addition, "the tenured faculty tends to be quite good."

The administration here is generally viewed as "average." Part-timers lament, "I do not believe the administration has a firm grasp on the part-time MBA program, unfortunately. They are undercutting the students and lowering expectations." Others say the top brass sets their sights high and "tries to empower their students to achieve big goals while supporting their communities, but they do very little to support their students to achieve this success...corporation/partnership with the school is very limited."

Career and Placement

With the school's focus on "networking, business plan deliverables, and connections with [the] Denver community," students here enjoy a competitive edge within the local business sector. In addition, DU has "a fabulous executive mentor program" and "one-of-a-kind class consulting opportunities with major companies like Newmont Mining and Deutsche Bank with an international component that includes projects in sustainability and social entrepreneurship."

Some students report that the "Career Center is not very helpful." The Center could "bring in more companies for career fairs [and] improve its offerings for people interested in entrepreneurship." Says one student, "Graduate recruitment is mostly focused on finance/accounting concentrations. If you are not interested in those areas, you really have to look outside of the companies that come to recruit." In 2009, 45 percent of full-time MBA graduates seeking employment had received a job offer previous to graduation with a mean base salary of $62,000. Media and entertainment, financial services, technology, and government were industries with strong draws with approximately 12 to 15 percent of the graduating class matriculating into these fields.

Student Life and Environment

Students at University of Denver Daniels College of Business "are highly-motivated, intelligent, fun people who are very diverse." This leads to "an energized environment and creates an atmosphere that is inspiring." When it comes to their academic camaraderie, students are "competitive in that we like to challenge each other. There is a high bar set, and everyone works to help each other." However, "they are also great friends."

Set at the foot of the Rocky Mountains, hometown Denver offers ample recreation and outdoors activities. This tends to attract students who are "physically active, outdoors-oriented, laid-back, interested in social and environmental responsibility, ethical and conscientious, caring and accepting." The atmosphere "is one of fun and appreciation for a good work/life balance (outdoor activities, skiing, mountain biking, etc) with focus on new ideas, innovation, sustainability, all within the framework of values-based leadership." In addition, the school hosts bimonthly happy hours, many of which are hosted by local companies. This is a good thing as many students here might be characterized as "bright people with a passion for business and a thirst for beer."

Admissions

Daniels seeks out students who embody its mission statement of leadership potential, commitment to advanced learning, and strong ethical standards. Admission is selective and officials consider each student's whole package including the candidate's personal, professional, and intellectual background. In 2009, the matriculating class had an average high school GPA of 3.16 and an average GMAT of 584. Work experience is required for the professional MBA and executive MBA programs. However, undergraduate students who wish to pursue a business major may apply to Daniels College of Business in the fall quarter of their sophomore year and are subject to a "whole-person" assessment of their academic performance, community engagement, personal character, future potential and overall well-roundedness. The admission interview is an integral part of the Daniels selection process. Interviews are offered on an invitation only basis for the full-time program and required for the part-time and Executive MBA programs.

FINANCIAL FACTS

Annual tuition	$36,640
Fees	$785
Cost of books	$1,698
Room & board (on-campus)	$9,765
% of students receiving aid	70
% of first-year students receiving aid	72
% of students receiving loans	53
% of students receiving grants	46
Average award package	$25,362
Average grant	$5,714

ADMISSIONS

Admissions Selectivity Rating	73
# of applications received	372
% applicants accepted	72
% acceptees attending	59
Average GMAT	584
Range of GMAT	540–630
Average GPA	3.16
TOEFL required of international students	Yes
Minimum TOEFL (paper/computer)	570/230
Application fee	$100
International application fee	$100
Regular application deadline	3/15
Regular notification	5/1
Application Deadline/Notification	
Round 1:	11/15 / 12/15
Round 2:	1/15 / 2/15
Round 3:	3/15 / 5/1
Round 4:	5/15 / 6/15
Early decision program?	No
Deferment available	Yes
Maximum length of deferment	1 year
Transfer students accepted	Yes
Transfer application policy: 8 quarter hours (6 semester hours) toward electives.	
Non-fall admissions	Yes
Need-blind admissions	Yes

EMPLOYMENT PROFILE

Career Rating	78	Grads Employed by Function	% Avg. Salary
Percent employed at graduation	44	Marketing	22 $55,000
Percent employed 3 months after graduation	12	Operations	5 $55,000
		Consulting	5 $65,000
Average base starting salary	$62,000	Management	13 $61,000
Primary Source of Full-time Job Acceptances		Finance	40 $66,000
School-facilitated activities	20 (50%)	MIS	5 $55,000
Graduate-facilitated activities	20 (50%)	**Top 5 Employers Hiring Grads**	
		Dish Network (3), KPMG (2), Hitachi (1), Qwest (1), Cricket (1)	

UNIVERSITY OF FLORIDA
HOUGH GRADUATE SCHOOL OF BUSINESS

GENERAL INFORMATION

Type of school	Public
Academic calendar	Semester

SURVEY SAYS...

Good social scene
Good peer network
Solid preparation in:
Marketing
Communication/interpersonal skills

STUDENTS

Enrollment of parent	
institution	53,000
Enrollment of MBA Program	1,024
% male/female	71/29
% out-of-state	31
% part-time	86
% minorities	13
% international	25
Average age at entry	27
Average years work experience	
at entry	4

ACADEMICS

Academic Experience Rating	**96**
Student/faculty ratio	10:1
Profs interesting rating	86
Profs accessible rating	85
% female faculty	16
% minority faculty	20

Joint Degrees

MBA/JD (4 years); MBA/MS in
Medical Sciences, Biotechnology;
MBA/PhD in Medical Sciences,
Biotechnology; MBA/BS in Industrial
and Systems Engineering;
MBA/Doctor of Pharmacy;
MBA/PhD in Medical Sciences;
MBA/MD; MBA/Master of Exercise
and Sport Science (3 years).

Academics

No matter what your educational background, professional experience, or career goals, you're likely to find a fit at the University of Florida. This large university caters to a diverse student body, offering a slew of MBA and master's programs for business mavens at every stage of their professional development. Among the school's three full-time MBAs, there are two one-year programs and a traditional two-year program. The school also offers a professional MBA for working students and an executive MBA for advanced professionals. In both "convenient" part-time programs, students come to campus one weekend each month, and "Assignments are turned in electronically during the intervening month between classes." In addition to its campus-based programs, University of Florida offers one of the top-ranked distance MBAs in the country.

Across programs, the curriculum is well-balanced, designed to "teach students about fundamentals, as well as real-world applications of course materials." Emphasizing creative thinking, "The experience does not only provide students with skills; it expands their minds enormously and teaches the critical thinking and insightful and thoughtful analysis required of business leaders." Lessons are further augmented by the MBA executive speaker series, alumni mentoring programs, and ample group work outside the classroom. Within the full-time program, "Teamwork is a must, and we change up the teams so you work with different people which has been great to really meet new people."

Professors come in every flavor, from those who are "very current on events and management issues" to those who are "very quantitative and have you learn financial formulas." What they share is excellence. At this top-ranked business school, "The professors are not only accomplished, but are very good at relaying the required material in interesting and meaningful ways." At the same time, the curriculum is very challenging. Here, "academic expectations are intense" and, even for high-achieving students, "A's are definitely hard-earned." A satisfied student declares, "I have never felt so uncomfortable and out of league in my life. And, isn't that the point? An MBA should be difficult and enriching."

Despite the scope of the graduate programs, the school runs smoothly and students are amply supported. To the delight of many, administrative staffers "assist with all enrollment issues, tuition, and course arrangements for working professional students." A current student explains, "When we arrive in Gainesville for the first day of a new semester, our books and meal vouchers are waiting for us." While excellence and ease are the program's greatest strengths, the icing on the cake is the school's great value: "Scholarships combined with small class sizes and the resources of one of the nation's great research universities have combined to make the UF MBA the best value in the nation."

Career and Placement

The Graduate Business Career Services (GBCS) works exclusively with MBA candidates, helping them prepare for a career through individualized counseling, mock interviews, an active on-campus recruiting program, and corporate site visits. Career counselors also send out a bi-weekly email update with job listings, and maintain a database of alumni who are willing to serve as job contacts and advise current students. For part-time students who receive tuition assistance from their employers, Career Services are provided by an outside career consulting company; however, to avoid ethical conflicts, their participation in recruiting programs is limited (part-timers who pay their own tuition may participate in recruiting.) All MBA candidates may also use the school's university-wide Career Resource Center.

ADMISSIONS CONTACT: MICHELLE LOVELL-HELMER, DIRECTOR OF ADMISSIONS
ADDRESS: 134 BRYAN HALL, P.O. BOX 117152 GAINESVILLE, FL 32611-7152
PHONE: 877-435-2622 • FAX: 352-392-8791
E-MAIL: FLORIDAMBA@WARRINGTON.UFL.EDU • WEBSITE: WWW.FLORIDAMBA.UFL.EDU

University of Florida has a "very strong alumni network," which is an enormous asset to professional students, as well as those looking to start a new career. UF alumni are represented at a wide range of companies, including AIG, Allstate, AOL, Bank of America, Ashland Chemical, Bell South, Blue Cross Blue Shield, Citicorp, Delta Airlines, Deloitte & Touche, Ericsson, EDS, Ernst & Young, FedEx, General Electric, Morgan Stanley, Nissan, Motorola, Proctor & Gamble, Siemens, Time Warner, Wachovia, Walt Disney World, Wells Fargo, and many more.

Student Life and Environment

Gator pride is alive and well at the University of Florida. On this lively campus, the student experience is "very reminiscent of undergraduate studies many years ago, despite everyone being older, more professional, and focused on academics now." "Social life is vibrant," there are numerous clubs and activities, and Gator sports are a huge draw. In the part-time programs (which meet on campus once a month), most students don't live within driving distance. However, almost everyone "stays overnight near campus on the weekends we attend class," and, during that time, "Everyone tends to eat together, attend basketball games together, party together, study together, etc."

In and around the business school, "Facilities are convenient, with food and coffee shops everywhere." Of particular note, "The library system is ample and well-integrated, and the newer libraries are great places to study or meet for group meetings." In addition, there are "excellent gym facilities" and plenty of "opportunities for activities such as intramural sports, museum/library lectures, and the arts." A medium-sized city, Gainesville is a "cozy college town" boasting a "'low cost-of-living" and plenty of recreational activities. And, don't forget, it's Florida, so the "weather is fantastic."

Admissions

The first step in the admissions process is to decide which of the many Florida MBA programs is the right fit for you and your career goals. You can only apply to one MBA program at a time; however, after reviewing an application, the admissions staff may recommend a student for another MBA program. For traditional full-time students, the average GMAT score is about 670. In the executive, online, and professional programs, the average GMAT score for entering students is about 600. All UF MBA programs admit students on a rolling basis.

FINANCIAL FACTS

Annual tuition (in-state/ out-of-state)	$8,190/$23,315
Fees	$1,368
Cost of books	$2,880
Room & board (on/off-campus)	$9,900/$10,680
% of students receiving aid	58
% of first-year students receiving aid	61
% of students receiving loans	23
% of students receiving grants	56
Average award package	$19,596
Average grant	$9,643
Average student loan debt	$11,372

ADMISSIONS

Admissions Selectivity Rating	95
# of applications received	413
% applicants accepted	38
% acceptees attending	60
Average GMAT	687
Range of GMAT	660–720
Average GPA	3.3
TOEFL required of international students	Yes
Minimum TOEFL (paper/computer)	600/250
Application fee	$30
International application fee	$30
Regular application deadline	4/15
Early decision program?	No
Deferment available	Yes
Maximum length of deferment	1 year
Transfer students accepted	No
Non-fall admissions	Yes
Need-blind admissions	Yes

EMPLOYMENT PROFILE

Career Rating	90	**Grads Employed by Function**	**% Avg. Salary**
Percent employed at graduation	82	Marketing	20 $74,750
Percent employed 3 months after graduation	93	Consulting	15 $77,250
		Management	7 $82,833
Average base starting salary	$76,559	Finance	39 $77,063
Primary Source of Full-time Job Acceptances		HR	7 $66,667
School-facilitated activities	26 (45%)	**Top 5 Employers Hiring Grads**	
Graduate-facilitated activities	21 (36%)	Florida Power & Light (2), ExxonMobil (1),	
Unknown	11 (19%)	AT&T (1), General Electric (1), Walt Disney (1)	

UNIVERSITY OF GEORGIA
TERRY COLLEGE OF BUSINESS

GENERAL INFORMATION

Type of school	Public
Academic calendar	Semester

SURVEY SAYS...
Students love Athens, GA
Good social scene
Happy students
Smart classrooms
Solid preparation in:
Operations

STUDENTS

Enrollment of parent institution	34,180
Enrollment of MBA Program	
% male/female	75/25
% out-of-state	57
% minorities	9
% international	27
Average age at entry	28
Average years work experience at entry	5

ACADEMICS

Academic Experience Rating	**90**
Student/faculty ratio	25:1
Profs interesting rating	80
Profs accessible rating	85
% female faculty	29
% minority faculty	6

Joint Degrees
JD/MBA, 4 years; 5–year BBA/MACC.

Prominent Alumni
Daniel P. Amos, Chairman & CEO, Aflac Incorporated; Phillip E. Casey, Chariman of the Board and former CEO, Gerdau Ameristeel; M. Dougas Ivester, President, Deer Run Investments LLC, Retired Chairman of the Board and CEO, The Coca-Cola Company; James H. Blanchard, Retired Chairman of the Board and CEO, Synovus Financial Corp.; O. Mason Hawkins, Chairman & CEO, Southeastern Asset Management, Inc.

Academics

Students realize a "high ROI opportunity" at the University of Georgia's Terry College of Business, where low in-state tuition and generous scholarships add pocketbook appeal to an already compelling Top-50 program. There's even a cherry on the proverbial sundae: this university's legendary school spirit. Georgia's fiercely loyal alumni revel in "a rich history and incredibly strong solidarity" to form an "alumni base that provides access to practically all top companies in the region." In this, Terry benefits from "a great location" that is convenient "to Atlanta, Charlotte, Greenville, Savannah, Jacksonville and many other towns that have many job opportunities, learning and educational activities outside of the classroom, and social events." "I have had the opportunity to get involved with companies while working on my MBA," one student writes, which he feels was instrumental "in getting me additional experience and actually allowing me [how] to apply what I am learning."

Terry boasts "a strong finance department," "a good entrepreneurship program," a "reputable real estate program," and "a strong focus on leadership development" throughout its MBA program. That's not a bad spread for such a small program, and Terry is indeed relatively small, small enough to "have a great capacity to work one-on-one and uniquely cater to the focus" of individual students. The Terry curriculum takes a "pragmatic approach, combining theory with cases and backed by research" in order to "provide a fundamental foundation for future." Classes are structured to require "heavy student involvement," and "students are willing and ready to work hard in and out of the classroom." "Team building and working in groups" permeates the curriculum. Terry professors "are incredibly accessible and involved with student life."

University of Georgia operates a full-time two-year program. The first year consists of foundational course work, followed by a summer internship. In the second year, students tailor their studies through elective course work. Through the Terry International Business program, the school runs week-long international trips during spring break, with lectures, company visits, and cultural exposure.

Career and Placement

The Terry MBA Career Management Center has recently expanded its advisement staff. However, as with many small programs, Terry sometimes has trouble generating recruitment traffic. One student notes that "we are too small...so we don't have a big network of graduate MBA alumni out there (although we have a huge network of undergraduate alumni). We need to position ourselves uniquely to attract more recruiters from competition like Emory and Georgia Tech." One student appreciates the school's efforts on behalf of MBAs; "the school has even sponsored us for career fairs in far off cities and they do their best to help students," she writes.

Companies with which recent Terry MBAs have been placed include: Accenture, Bank of America, BB&T, Coldwell Banker, Deloitte, Eli Lilly, Gould Investments, IBM, JD Power, Johnson & Johnson, KPMG, Nissan, PriceWaterhouseCoopers, Rubbermaid, Scantech Holdings, Tyson Foods, Unisys, Wachovia Securities, Waffle House, and WestWayne. One in three students found work in finance and accounting (median salary: $75,000), about one in five found work in marketing and sales ($45,000), and one in eight hooked up a consulting gig ($85,000).

ADMISSIONS CONTACT: ANNE C. COOPER, DIRECTOR, FULL-TIME MBA ADMISSIONS
ADDRESS: 361 BROOKS HALL ATHENS, GA 30602-6264
PHONE: 706-542-5671 • FAX: 706-583-8277
E-MAIL: TERRYMBA@TERRY.UGA.EDU • WEBSITE: WWW.TERRY.UGA.EDU

Student Life and Environment

"While [the] Terry MBA [program] is relatively small with regard to class size, I am willing to bet that we have just as much (if not more) opportunities to get involved outside of class than the much larger programs," one MBA opines. "On any given week, we have multiple club events (planned company visits, alumni or company representatives brought in to share knowledge/experience on any given subject matter), social activities (mixers with students/faculty/alumni), and community events (unique fundraisers). Almost all of these are student-led initiatives." The result is a "very communal and fun" program with "activities and opportunities for a very diverse population." Hometown Athens "is awesome, one of the best town[s] in the country."

Terry "has a strong reputation in the Southeast and thus attracts a diverse group of students." "Some are conservative and some are liberal, but all respect each other" and "are open to helping each other." A sizeable international population offers "a balanced contribution in and out of class."

Admissions

Applicants to UGA are evaluated for academic and intellectual ability, personal qualities, professional experience, and management potential. The school evaluates these factors based on a student's academic transcripts, admissions essays, GMAT scores, professional resume, honors and activities, letters of recommendation, and, for international students, TOEFL scores. In addition, because personal factors are highly important to the program, personal interviews with admissions staff are highly encouraged, though not mandatory. UGA usually receives about 400 applications for the MBA program. Last year's entering class had an average GMAT score of 646 and a GPA of 3.26, with professional work experience of 4.5 years on average. Work experience is very important and heavily weighed in an application. If a student has fewer than two years of experience, chances of admission are limited. University of Georgia admits students in rounds, so students (especially those seeking scholarships and assistantships) are encouraged to apply early.

FINANCIAL FACTS

Annual tuition (in-state/ out-of-state)	$8,918/$27,840
Fees	$1,174
Cost of books	$1,000
Room & board (on/off-campus)	$12,000/$13,200
% of students receiving aid	90
% of students receiving grants	78
Average grant	$23,963
Average student loan debt	$12,554

ADMISSIONS

Admissions Selectivity Rating	95
# of applications received	243
% applicants accepted	33
% acceptees attending	54
Average GMAT	646
Range of GMAT	610–680
Average GPA	3.26
TOEFL required of international students	Yes
Minimum TOEFL (paper/computer)	577/233
Application fee	$100
International application fee	$100
Application Deadline/Notification	
Round 1:	10/15 / 12/1
Round 2:	12/1 / 1/15
Round 3:	1/15 / 3/15
Round 4:	3/1 / 5/3
Early decision program?	No
Deferment available	Yes
Maximum length of deferment	1 year
Transfer students accepted	Yes
Transfer application policy: The University of Georgia will accept up to six credit hours of transfer credit.	
Non-fall admissions	No
Need-blind admissions	Yes

EMPLOYMENT PROFILE

Career Rating	83	**Grads Employed by Function**	**% Avg. Salary**	
Percent employed at graduation	38	Marketing	21	$50,430
Percent employed 3 months after graduation	64	Operations	10	$68,750
		Consulting	13	$92,000
Average base starting salary	$66,020	Management	5	NR
Primary Source of Full-time Job Acceptances		Finance	33	$67,273
School-facilitated activities	22 (56%)	MIS	8	$52,067
Graduate-facilitated activities	16 (41%)	**Top 5 Employers Hiring Grads**		
Unknown	1 (3%)	Bank of America, Deloitte, Credit Suisse Group, Johnson & Johnson, PepsiCo		

UNIVERSITY OF HARTFORD
THE BARNEY SCHOOL OF BUSINESS

GENERAL INFORMATION
Type of school   Private

SURVEY SAYS...
Solid preparation in:
Accounting
General management
Operations
Communication/interpersonal skills
Presentation skills

STUDENTS
Enrollment of parent institution	7,366
Enrollment of MBA Program	428
% male/female	64/36
% out-of-state	2
% part-time	76
% minorities	8
% international	40
Average age at entry	32

ACADEMICS
Academic Experience Rating	77
Student/faculty ratio	9:1
Profs interesting rating	80
Profs accessible rating	76
% female faculty	36
% minority faculty	33

Joint Degrees
E2M (MBA & ME Engineering)

Prominent Alumni
Robert Saunders, CEO, Kaman Music Corp.; Roger Klene, CEO, MOTT Corp.; Thomas Barnes, Chairman of the Board, The Barnes Group.

Academics

"Class flexibility and reputation" draw area business students to the MBA program at the University of Hartford's Barney School. As one explains, "The program was created for working students. The program structure allows me to continue with my career and still attend school." The school's many full-time workers especially enjoy the convenience of the school's "No Hassle MBA program," under which "the MBA advisor takes full care to register No Hassle MBA students for all of their classes. In addition, books are waiting for graduate students in the No Hassle program on the first night of classes during each term. There is no need to wait on lines at the bookstore or other cumbersome activities typical of registration each term." Students tell us that "The No Hassle option really does work. I don't have to worry about anything but showing up for class. My ID, parking permits, registration, and books are all taken care of for me."

The Barney School benefits from a location that is both convenient to area working people and advantageous to full-time students seeking summer work and internships. Hartford is one of the nation's insurance centers and is also home to numerous financial, manufacturing, and technological concerns (it should be noted that several students feel that finance is among the weaker disciplines here). Most who teach here "have real-life experience, not just book experience, and bring this to the classroom." That expertise, combined with the professional experience of students, makes for "a high quality of class dialogue and discussion among peers from various sectors." One student reports: "In my Capstone course, I am in the company of other full-time professionals who include engineers, insurance industry professionals, an actuary, government executives, retail executives, self-employed entrepreneurs, and business analysts, to name a few."

Several students report that classroom facilities here need an upgrade. One tells us, "Classrooms have a very dated look to them," with "desks and chairs rather than tables and chairs," which would "make the classrooms more team-friendly." They would also like to see an expansion of the curriculum, with additions made in project management, "a hot topic and a necessity in industry today. Also, more courses in operations management and international studies would be pertinent." Students praise the current curriculum for its "global viewpoint" and "engaging and practical" approach to the material. They also love the recently initiated study abroad options, describing them as "great opportunities for the students who can afford to go."

Career and Placement

Placement and career-counseling services are provided to Barney MBAs by the Career Services Office (CSO), which serves the entire undergraduate and graduate student body of the university. Services include resume and cover-letter writing workshops, seminars on networking and interviewing strategies, job banks, on-campus interviewing, and job fairs. Students warn that the office "is primarily for undergraduate students. It's rare that there is an event that would be of any interest to an MBA." Independently of the CSO, the Barney School offers a series of Saturday morning "enrichment workshops" covering such subjects as business presentations, negotiations, career planning, and job search strategies. The school also sponsors a mentoring program for MBAs.

ADMISSIONS CONTACT: CLAIRE SILVERSTEIN, DIRECTOR OF MBA PROGRAM
ADDRESS: 200 BLOOMFIELD AVENUE, CENTER FOR GRADUATE & ADULT SERVICES, CC231 WEST
HARTFORD, CT 06117
PHONE: 860-768-4444 • FAX: 860-768-4821
E-MAIL: ADMISSIONS@HARTFORD.EDU • WEBSITE: BARNEY.HARTFORD.EDU

Student Life and Environment

The Barney School attracts "friendly, smart, motivated" people, "about half of whom are in their twenties and the other half are in their forties. Generally, they are working people looking to take that next step." They arrive from "various industries such as insurance, banking, and financial services." About one in five attends full time; about half of full-time students are international students who "appear to enjoy the university environment and are engaged in various programs as this institution." Students also point out that the "good mix of international and domestic students allows you to develop better understanding of international issues." Full-time students "work in a cohort environment" that allows them to "bond deeply and quickly." Part-timers tell us that there is generally "no out-of-class mingling, which is fine for most classmates because no one has time between working and family life."

The University of Hartford campus offers "many arts and music activities to attend" through the Hartt School Program, which mounts theatre productions, concerts, and similar events. Students also have access to lecture series and other campus-wide activities. Most here, however, simply "take classes after work and then go home," with "participation in the activities at this institution limited to group meetings, project analysis, and data gathering (i.e., using the school's library and computer resources)."

Admissions

The Barney admissions office requires all MBA applicants to submit: official transcripts from all previously attended post-secondary schools; two letters of recommendation; official GMAT results; a current resume; a letter of intent describing the applicant's academic and career goals; and, a completed application. Applicants with at least three years of continuous work experience may apply for a GMAT waiver, as may applicants who have already successfully completed another master's program. International students must submit TOEFL scores and a Guarantor's Statement of Financial Support in addition to the above. Applications are processed on a rolling basis; because space in each incoming class is limited, it greatly benefits applicants to apply as early as possible.

FINANCIAL FACTS

Annual tuition	$10,800
% of students receiving aid	26
% of first-year students receiving aid	38
% of students receiving loans	18
% of students receiving grants	7
Average award package	$5,813
Average grant	$114

ADMISSIONS

Admissions Selectivity Rating	75
# of applications received	240
% applicants accepted	50
% acceptees attending	79
Average GMAT	510
Range of GMAT	450–720
Average GPA	3
TOEFL required of international students	Yes
Minimum TOEFL (paper/computer)	550/213
Application fee	$45
International application fee	$45
Early decision program?	No
Deferment available	Yes
Maximum length of deferment	1 year
Transfer students accepted	Yes
Transfer application policy: Based on individual cases.	
Non-fall admissions	Yes
Need-blind admissions	No

UNIVERSITY OF HOUSTON
C.T. BAUER COLLEGE OF BUSINESS

GENERAL INFORMATION
Type of school   Public
Academic calendar   Semester

SURVEY SAYS...
Students love Houston, TX
Friendly students
Good peer network
Cutting-edge classes

STUDENTS
Enrollment of parent institution	37,000
Enrollment of MBA Program	824
% male/female	60/40
% out-of-state	3
% part-time	84
% minorities	11
% international	24
Average age at entry	27
Average years work experience at entry	4

ACADEMICS
Academic Experience Rating	84
Student/faculty ratio	5:1
Profs interesting rating	89
Profs accessible rating	82
% female faculty	24
% minority faculty	23

Joint Degrees
MBA/JD - 111 credits (4–6 years); MBA/MIE in Industrial Engineering—72 credits (2–5 years); MBA/MA in Spanish—64 credits (2–5 years); MBA/M.S. in Hospitality Management—78 credits (2–5 years); MBA/MSW—87 credits (3–5 years); MBA/Master's in International Management—66 credits (3–5 years).

Prominent Alumni
Mark Papa, Chairman and CEO, EOG Resources, Inc.; Karen Katz, President and CEO, Neiman Marcus Stores; Marvin Odum, President, Shell Oil Company; Fran Keeth, Retired CEO, Shell Chemicals, Inc.; David McClanahan, President and CEO, CenterPoint Energy.

Academics

Marshaled by a team of experienced business leaders and located in a patently commerce-friendly city, Bauer College of Business enjoys "prominence in the Houston business community" and distinguishes itself from other Texas schools through its "very strong academic focus on the energy industry." If you want to learn about business straight from the mouth of high-power executives, you'll have ample opportunity at Bauer, where "professors are knowledgeable and generally have experience from industry, not just academia." A current student enthuses, "My professors in the past year, for example, included the senior M&A executive for a global *Fortune* 500 company, and a former Treasurer of Exxon-Mobil."

Each entering student is assigned to a "cohort," which is a group of students that works through the MBA curriculum together. Providing continuity throughout the program, as well as an excellent opportunity to begin networking, "the cohorts allow you to get to know the other students and each semester's classes are tied together very well." In fact, many Bauer students say the "most valuable part of class is often the insight that your colleagues bring to the table." Drawing students from "almost every industry" you'll meet plenty of energy industry folks, with "other experiences are sprinkled throughout: high tech, real estate, non-profit, health care, government, aerospace, banking, commodities trading, all contributing to a very diverse experience."

Another benefit to the University of Houston is the ample extracurricular opportunities to enhance your education. Special programs like the Leadership and Ethics Week, "the Distinguished Lecture series, the Rockwell Career Center, and the active students organizations also enrich the academic experience." For future investors, the school also offers "excellent Financial Services Management program that involves participation in the Cougar Fund. This fund is a mutual fund that affords students enrolled in the concentration the opportunity to serve as portfolio managers and analysts for over a year." To put the icing on the cake, University of Houston's "administration is so well-run that you hardly ever have an issue or question that is not answered even before you can come up with them."

Career and Placement

After graduation, Bauer students have plenty to look forward to: "the city of Houston has lots of career opportunities and Bauer has an exceptional reputation. Our graduates are synonymous with hard work and dedication." In fact, the Houston job market is so hopping that a current student tells us, "Several of my classmates have offered me very well-paying jobs at their companies. Most of my close friends work in management positions at major *Fortune* 500 companies."

In addition to the networking that naturally takes place between students, the Rockwell Career Center is always busy helping students make connections. Their full events calendar includes "two huge and industry-diverse career fairs specifically for Business and MBAs." Among the numerous companies that bought booths at recent career fairs are A-AIG, Allied Waste, Cameron, CenterPoint Energy, Central Intelligence Agency, Chevron, Chevron Phillips, CITGO Petroleum, Commerce Bank, Compass Bank, Continental Airlines, Deloitte Consulting, EC Power, El Paso Corporation, Intel Corporation, Koch, Merrill Lynch Commodities, Million Air, Nabors Industries, Prudential Financial, Sears Holdings, Sequent Energy Management, Serenity Systems, Shell Oil, Smith Barney, Spectra Energy, Suez Energy, SunGuard Consulting, Tesoro Corporation.

ADMISSIONS CONTACT: DALIA PINEDA, DIRECTOR OF STUDENT SERVICES
ADDRESS: 334 MELCHER HALL, ROOM 330 HOUSTON, TX 77204-6021
PHONE: 713-743-0700 • FAX: 713-743-4807 • E-MAIL: HOUSTONMBA@UH.EDU
WEBSITE: WWW.BAUER.UH.EDU/MBA

Student Life and Environment

Bauer students describe their classmates as "bright, ambitious, stimulating people with diverse personal, cultural, and professional backgrounds. They range from recent undergrads to successful executives." It's fortunate that students express such respect for their cohorts, because networking, group work, and collaboration are fundamental to the Bauer experience. Happily, "students are respectful of one another, and group projects generally go well." In fact, the spirit of work and collaboration seems to permeate the entire Bauer community, and "the academic advisors, career center, Dean's office, and even Starbucks, work long late hours, just like the students."

Hailing from across the greater Houston metropolitan area, "the MBA students are virtually all commuters. There are strong student chapters [and] professional organizations, but in general, MBA students do not participate much in campus life." Even study groups tend to form away from campus, that is, if they physically form at all. A student in the evening program explains, "I do a lot of collaboration with classmates via conference call and e-mail. Since Houston is so large, commuting to campus for every group meeting would be challenging. Working in virtual teams is a huge plus for those of us with a lot going on." But don't fret if you'd like to make a friend or two in business school; social life isn't totally non-existent. As proof, a student shares this perspective: "While a lot of student gatherings on the weekend are for group work, I would venture to say that students form very strong relationships with others from our classes and some of us do meet up socially [when] we have the time." In addition, the commuter vibe may soon be a thing of the past, as "recent and ongoing campaigns have been focused on creating a family atmosphere, where more MBA students live in new on-campus housing and commuting students spend more time on campus to socialize. These efforts have largely been successful, and even professors will occasionally attend after-hours functions."

Admissions

The University of Houston prides itself on diversity, and therefore, they understand that the strengths of each student vary. However, on the whole, the school seeks to admit students with a strong academic background, quantitative aptitude, management potential, and diversity of experiences. There are no minimum test scores or GPA required for admission; however, average Bauer admits had GMAT scores of 570 and an undergraduate GPA of 3.2. Entering students have an average of five years' work experience; however, two is generally considered the minimum acceptable years of professional experience.

FINANCIAL FACTS

Annual tuition (in-state/ out-of-state)	$10,015/$16,663
Fees (in-state/ out-of-state)	$5,735/$6,837
Cost of books	$1,600
Room & board (on-campus)	$9,600
Average student loan debt	$13,210

ADMISSIONS

Admissions Selectivity Rating	78
# of applications received	490
% applicants accepted	69
% acceptees attending	73
Average GMAT	570
Range of GMAT	530–610
Average GPA	3.2
TOEFL required of international students	Yes
Minimum TOEFL (paper/computer)	603/250
Application fee	$75
International application fee	$150
Regular application deadline	5/1
Regular notification	6/1
Early decision program?	No
Deferment available	Yes
Maximum length of deferment	1 year
Transfer students accepted	No
Non-fall admissions	Yes
Need-blind admissions	Yes

EMPLOYMENT PROFILE

Career Rating	83	Grads Employed by Function	% Avg. Salary
Percent employed at graduation	31	Marketing	25 NR
Percent employed 3 months after graduation	50	Operations	25 NR
		Consulting	25 NR
Average base starting salary	$63,125	Finance	13 NR
Primary Source of Full-time Job Acceptances		HR	13 NR
School-facilitated activities	6 (75%)		
Graduate-facilitated activities	2 (25%)		

UNIVERSITY OF HOUSTON—VICTORIA
SCHOOL OF BUSINESS ADMINISTRATION

GENERAL INFORMATION

Type of school	Public
Academic calendar	Academic

SURVEY SAYS...
Cutting-edge classes
Solid preparation in:
General management
Doing business in a global economy

STUDENTS

Enrollment of parent institution	3,680
Enrollment of MBA Program	818
% male/female	61/39
% out-of-state	22
% part-time	72
% minorities	64
% international	25
Average age at entry	32

ACADEMICS

Academic Experience Rating	70
Profs interesting rating	86
Profs accessible rating	81
% female faculty	31
% minority faculty	91

Academics

Efficiency and convenience define the University of Houston—Victoria MBA. No matter what your previous preparation or current time restraints, you can get a quality education from this regional college. UHV offers two MBA program options: The Strategic MBA, which can be completed fulltime in 18 months or part-time over the course of three years, and the Global MBA, which provides a specialized curriculum for students interested in international business. UHV also offers a unique Bridge MBA, designed for international students with a three-year undergraduate degree. All of University of Houston—Victoria's MBA programs can be completed entirely online, entirely in person, or through a combination of both classroom and distance delivery. For many, the "flexibility of taking classes online or face-to-face" is one of the school's major selling points. In fact, most students cite convenience as a key factor in their decision to attend the University of Houston—Victoria, lauding the school's "ability to provide degree programs online that are appropriate for working adults."

UHV students are serious about their education, and they insist that, even online, you will get a strong business education at University of Houston—Victoria. With all the same requirements of a traditional MBA, the "Rigor of online program is excellent," and professors "maintain a focus on state-of-the-art practices." Expectations are high, and even remote students find that "Professors are accessible and demand the best from us." A current MBA candidate adds, "I don't feel I'm at a diploma mill—they have done a good job in creating the program." The UHV online program also draws praises for being "very organized with their computer based learning systems," employing easy-to-use web technology. Still, students would like to see "more multimedia in online courses such as videos of professors explaining concepts."

Designed with working professionals in mind, "Face-to-face classes are usually in the evening, [which] helps most employed students to attend classes after work." To add to the accessibility, classes are offered at "many different locations," including the Sugar Land campus and Cinco Ranch. Students who attend school at an auxiliary facility are a bit envious of the resources available at the larger university campus, saying, "Technology, such as computer lab equipment, is very old and way behind as compared to University of Houston Victoria main campus." Nonetheless, they are generally impressed by the remote student services, saying, "Administration is professional and well run" and "The student services staff is outstanding."

No matter how or where you decide to take your courses, the school's curriculum includes comprehensive coursework in economics, management, finance, marketing, and leadership, with an "excellent entrepreneurial and economic development focus." In addition to the core curriculum, the Strategic MBA offers a "good amount of concentrations to choose from," including accounting, finance, general business, management, marketing, and international business. When it comes to the practical application of business principals, students are happy to report that UHV faculty has real-world business credentials, bringing "relevant discussions into the classroom." A current student shares, "All the professors I have met so far (I am in my sixth course) are all seasoned professionals in their field."

ADMISSIONS CONTACT: TRUDY WORTHAM, WORTHAMT@UHV.EDU
ADDRESS: OFFICE OF ADMISSIONS/RECORDS, 3007 N BEN WILSON ST VICTORIA, TX 77901
PHONE: 361-570-4848 • FAX: 361-580-5500
E-MAIL: ADMISSIONSANDREGISTRATION@UHV.EDU • WEBSITE: WWW.UHV.EDU

Career and Placement

While the UHV MBA program offers almost every benefit of a traditional, fulltime, in-person program, students admit that, "Career placement/resources are almost non-existent." Many feel the school should offer, "career support and job placements for graduates," such as job fairs or recruiting programs. A current student laments, "I feel that you really have to go out of your way to find a job from UHV career services." Students would also like to see "more alumni participation" with regards to networking and placement.

While there aren't dedicated career services for the business school, students can use the campus Career Services center, where you can get job search assistance, as well as interview, resume, and cover letter help. However, the majority of students at UHV are already working and, therefore, not looking for a new job after graduation.

Student Life and Environment

Most UHV students take the majority of their classes online, and therefore, they have little interaction with the physical campus. However, most are "very happy with the service and effectiveness" of the MBA program, often saying they receive everything one would expect from a traditional graduate program. A student assures us, "I have discussed my courses with friends who are enrolled and taking MBA courses in a face-to-face setting at another university, and the courses and experiences are very similar."

Needless to say, the "Lack of face-to-face interaction limits the socializing between students." At the same time, most students live in the local region, and they occasionally make it to campus to meet with staff or administrators. An online student explains, "I don't really have much interaction on-campus. For the little I have, the campus has been really nice. Staff is really helpful and the buildings are laid out so that rooms are easy to find." Face-to-face students do make contact with the UHV campus, but echo the general sentiments of their online counterparts. An evening student shares, "Student only goes there to learn and leave after class... Our lives are too busy already to commit to socialize with others."

Admissions

Unconditional admission to any of University of Houston—Victoria's MBA programs is granted to students with a four-year undergraduate degree, an undergraduate GPA of 2.5 or higher, and GMAT scores of at least 450 or higher. Under some circumstances, a student may be admitted without taking the GMAT.

ADMISSIONS	
Admissions Selectivity Rating	**61**
# of applications received	296
% applicants accepted	95
% acceptees attending	81
Average GMAT	457
Range of GMAT	398–520
TOEFL required of international students	Yes
Minimum TOEFL (paper/computer)	550/213
Early decision program?	No
Deferment available	Yes
Maximum length of deferment	1 year
Transfer students accepted	Yes
Transfer application policy: Graduate business students may transfer up to 6 hours of graduate-level business coursework from an AACSB-accredited program with the approval of the Director of Services.	
Non-fall admissions	Yes
Need-blind admissions	Yes

UNIVERSITY OF ILLINOIS—CHICAGO
LIAUTAUD GRADUATE SCHOOL OF BUSINESS

GENERAL INFORMATION

Type of school	Public
Academic calendar	Semester

SURVEY SAYS...

Students love Chicago, IL
Happy students
Solid preparation in:
General management
Teamwork
Entrepreneurial studies

STUDENTS

Enrollment of parent institution	24,000
Enrollment of MBA Program	318
% male/female	53/47
% out-of-state	11
% part-time	67
% minorities	19
% international	20
Average age at entry	29
Average years work experience at entry	5

ACADEMICS

Academic Experience Rating	**85**
Student/faculty ratio	13:1
Profs interesting rating	86
Profs accessible rating	82
% female faculty	38
% minority faculty	42

Joint Degrees

Master of Business Administration/ Master of Science in Accounting (MBA/MSA): Full-time, part-time; a minimum of 68 semester hours required; 3 to 6 years to complete program. Master of Business Administration/Master of Public Health (MBA/MPH): Full-time, part-time; a minimum of 70 semester hours required; 3–6 years to complete program. Master of Business Administration/Master of Science Nursing (MBA/MSN).

Academics

With its "incredibly affordable tuition and access to a Tier One research university," the MBA program at the Liautaud Graduate School of Business "provides the best value for the cost. It offers a top-quality education for a fraction of the cost of Northwestern or University of Chicago." The MBA candidates at the school value "the flexibility of an evening program" since many of them are "currently employed and trying to balance it all." They also rave about the business school's "strong" entrepreneurship department which "will soon put Liautaud on the map." Many highlight the "excellent programs like Technology Ventures Program on experience." Liautaud's many academic assets also include its Professional Topics courses, which are "two-hour courses that focus on current topics." One student explains, "I took 'Social Entrepreneurship' last fall, and it has been a major springboard for me. We had real practitioners visit class and we engaged with them, solving a business 'problem' of theirs throughout the course. It changed the way I thought a business needs to run."

Students across the board are quite satisfied with their professors who "are world-class researchers in their fields" and who "stand [out] for their passion for teaching and encouraging creativity." These "professors effectively prompt feedback from students, who often engage in constructive debate." Students consider themselves "lucky to have professors of diverse backgrounds." One particularly impressed student shares, "It's exciting when you turn on the TV and see your professor being interviewed about Al Capone's finances right on the History Channel. It's even more exciting when he integrates this topic into his classroom lecture." Students generally feel that the learning experience at the school is supported and enhanced by their classmates because "many work full-time at large companies and provide great experience[s] to discuss in class." One student notes, "I also appreciate that UIC requires prior work experience, so we are surrounded by other bright peers that can offer insight from their own experiences at work." While overall satisfied with their course work, professors, and peers, the students at Liautaud are less enamored with their facilities. They lament that "some of the classrooms are inadequate and out of date technologically" and wish for "wireless system improvement and more outlets to plug in laptops."

Career and Placement

Advantageously situated next to "banker's row" in Chicago, the university's "proximity and connections to [the] Chicago Financial District" serve as a resource for Liautaud students. According to the school's website, the Liautaud Career Services Office provides a range of services for its students including "seminars, workshops, and online tools covering all aspects of the career development process." These workshops and tools focus on resume-building, career-mapping, personal branding, networking and salary negotiation. Students also have access to advising, employer contacts, online job postings and career fairs. The Career Services Office also provides special services for its international students including assistance with learning about U.S. protocol and business writing.

Some of the notable companies that have recruited and hired graduates of Liataud include Abbott Laboratories, Caterpillar, Deloitte & Touche, PriceWaterhouseCoopers, Morningstar, Navigant Consulting, TransUnion, and Wells Fargo.

Student Life and Environment

The reputation of Liautaud's MBA program along with the allure of Chicago attracts students ranging "from helicopter pilots to surgeons, and consultants to bankers." The mix also includes "mid-career types [who] are attending classes part-time" and "students raised in India and China [who] are having their first U.S. experience at UIC."

One student proclaims, "These are down-to-earth people who are future entrepreneurs and the people that keep Chicago's small- to mid-size businesses going." Described as "competitive, bright, caring, social, and heartwarmingly nerdy," these students "group within their concentrations and have many opportunities to network outside of class." "There several active student organizations, including Net Impact and the MBAA" on campus.

Despite the many opportunities to socialize and network, it can sometimes be a challenge for Liautaud sudents to meet up in person. "All classes are held in the evenings so students have to make a deliberate effort to schedule time to get involved," observes one student. In addition, "most graduate students live off campus, and many have full-time jobs. This means that group collaboration occurs mostly online." Given its high population of commuters, students are pleased that "the campus itself is in a great spot for commuters from around Chicago, just west of downtown. And there are great places to eat nearby."

Admissions

All applicants to the MBA program at the Liautaud Graduate School of Business must submit an online application, an application fee, two copies of official transcripts for all post-secondary academic work, two letters of recommendation, a personal statement, resume, and official GMAT score. Students who are non-native speakers of English must also submit a TOEFL score. A minimum of a B average is required in at least the last 60 hours of undergraduate course work (though provisional acceptance may be extended to promising applicants who fail to meet this benchmark). For the best results, applicants' GMAT scores should be at or above the average GMAT scores of the incoming class. The school also places emphasis on professional work experience. After submitting their materials for review, qualified applicants will be invited to interview with the admissions committee.

Prominent Alumni

Charles B. Edlestein, Director/CEO, Apollo Group Inc.; William L. Gaultier, Principal, E-Storm international; Dennis P. Neumann, CEO, Bank of New York Capital Funding.

FINANCIAL FACTS

Annual tuition (in-state/ out-of-state)	$16,568/$28,566
Fees	$3,586
Cost of books	$1,389
Room & board (on-campus)	$11,250

ADMISSIONS

Admissions Selectivity Rating	84
# of applications received	394
% applicants accepted	49
% acceptees attending	46
Average GMAT	600
Range of GMAT	550–640
Average GPA	3.18
TOEFL required of international students	Yes
Minimum TOEFL (paper/computer)	570/230
Application fee	$50
International application fee	$60
Regular application deadline	5/15
Early decision program?	No
Deferment available	Yes
Maximum length of deferment	1 semester
Transfer students accepted	Yes
Transfer application policy: Need to apply and be accepted to the UIC MBA Program. Can submit transcripts fror previous coursework with a grade of B or better and a course description. Must be from an AACSB accredited institution. Maximum of 12 semester hours may transfer.	
Non-fall admissions	Yes
Need-blind admissions	Yes

EMPLOYMENT PROFILE

Career Rating	83	**Grads Employed by Function**	**% Avg. Salary**
Percent employed at graduation	53	Marketing	20 $74,750
Percent employed 3 months after graduation	82	Consulting	15 $77,250
		Management	7 $82,833
Average base starting salary	$64,533	Finance	53 $52,875
Primary Source of Full-time Job Acceptances		**Top 5 Employers Hiring Grads**	
School-facilitated activities	NR (67%)	Bosch (1), Thomson/Rueters Financial (1),	
Graduate-facilitated activities	NR (33%)	Wells Fargo (1), Northern Trust (1), Mercer Consulting (1)	

UNIVERSITY OF ILLINOIS AT URBANA-CHAMPAIGN

COLLEGE OF BUSINESS

GENERAL INFORMATION

Type of school	Public
Academic calendar	Semester

SURVEY SAYS...

Smart classrooms
Solid preparation in:
Finance
Teamwork

STUDENTS

Enrollment of parent institution	43,720
Enrollment of MBA Program	307
% male/female	69/31
% part-time	34
% international	45
Average age at entry	27
Average years work experience at entry	4

ACADEMICS

Academic Experience Rating	**90**
Student/faculty ratio	14:1
Profs interesting rating	85
Profs accessible rating	86
% female faculty	21
% minority faculty	31

Joint Degrees

MBA/MA Architecture, 3 years; MBA/MS Electrical & Computer Engineering, 3 years; MBA/MS Civil and Environmental Engineering, 3 years; MBA/MS Electrical Engineering, 3 years; MBA/MS Industrial Engineering, 3 years; MBA/MS Mechanical Engineering, 3 years; MBA/MD Medicine, 5 years; MBA/MS Journalism, 3 years; MBA/JD Law, 4 years; MBA/MS Human Resource Education, 3 years; MBA/ILIR, 3 years; MBA/MS Materials Science & Engineering.

Academics

With a large university setting and a low in-state price tag, you might be surprised to learn that the University of Illinois at Urbana-Champaign brings a decidedly personal touch to the MBA experience. With only 100 students in each entering class, "the smaller class size" helps to "foster the interactions and provide a forum for students and professors to learn from each other." In the first year, full-time MBA students take a sequence of eight-week courses in business fundamentals, which comprise a "good mix of case study and theoretical knowledge." In this well-organized core curriculum, "The courses are structured, goals are communicated early, and all work done for the course is relevant and educational." In the second year, students take 16 credits of electives and 16 credits towards a concentration in fields like marketing, finance, information technology, or general management. Students are encouraged to tailor their MBA to their own career goals, and there is "a lot of flexibility with concentrations" and electives, including several opportunities to study overseas, as well as joint master's degree programs with other Illinois departments. Students may also take electives outside the College of Business.

Group work and class discussion is stressed at Illinois, allowing students to network with their classmates, as well as their professors. Due to "the cultural and functional diversity in the class," the team-based format helps students to "expand my understanding and my knowledge concerning the business world in China, India and other countries around the world." Equally attractive, "The professors have a one-to-one relationship with most students" and many are very accessible outside the classroom. In addition to their accessibility, business faculty is "very well-regarded in their field and most [take] teaching seriously." In the lecture hall, professors "continue to innovate their teaching styles and course materials to prepare students for the realities that will be faced immediately upon graduation." While not every professor is universally adored, "The school has an unbelievable roster of finance and accounting professors who are great teachers with practical experience." To augment the traditional curriculum, the administration invites "Nobel Prize winners and industry leaders as guest speakers at the university."

Many students enter the Illinois MBA with just a few years of work experience, and the program makes every effort to promote their professional development through hands-on education and training. There are many ways to get your feet wet at Illinois, including "vast amount of case competitions, clubs, and real consulting experience." Of particular note, every student must complete "practical consulting experience through Illinois Business Consulting," or IBC, through which MBA candidates do "management consulting work for small to Fortune 100 companies." In overseeing IBC and other programs, the administration "runs very smoothly"—and seems to be ever-improving. The school "hired a new dean in 2009" and students say the new leadership is "completely flexible to student needs."

Career and Placement

The Illinois MBA Career Services office provides individual counseling to MBA candidates, helping them prepare for the workforce and to secure internships during the program. Career Services also works with local employers and alumni (the school boasts a 6,000-plus alumni network) to operate its campus recruiting program. However, students admit, "Recruiting is our biggest weakness and challenge, since we are a relatively small MBA program." In particular, many students think the school should have more corporate ties in big cities, like Chicago. International students (a large percentage of the class) also say there could be more "assistance for international students in job placement." In response to these issues, the MBA Career Services Organization has been integrated into a new college wide Business Career Services Organization aimed at providing increased visibility for MBA students to companies that recruit at the college.

In recent years, graduates of the Illinois MBA program accepted a median base salary of almost $90,000 annually, with a salary range between $60,000 and $160,000. About half of the student body took jobs in the Midwest, with general management and finance fields drawing the highest number of graduates. The top hiring companies included AT&T, Cisco Systems, Ernst & Young, ExxonMobil, Hewitt Associates, LG, Peabody Energy, Procter & Gamble, Robert Bosch Corporation, and Sears Holdings Corporation.

Student Life and Environment

At Illinois, 40 percent of current MBA candidates come from overseas, and students say it's an "amazing experience getting to know people from all over the globe with [so] many backgrounds and experiences." In addition to attending class, many students "spend a lot of time in our business building talking with other students, sometimes about a class project, but sometimes just about the current business environment." In addition, "There are seven or eight student clubs run by students in the U of I MBA program," and "Each weekend, one or two clubs put on events in order for students to interact with one another outside the classroom."

Drawing praise all around, the business school's "new $50 million LEED-certified building" is "state-of-the-art, with many multimedia resources." The workload will keep you busy on campus, but "the business school itself is a place where you can spend your whole day studying," and is auspiciously located "within a block of a library and many restaurants." Surrounding Urbana-Champaign is "a nice Midwestern town" that offers "something for everyone, from Big 10 sporting events, musical and artistic performances, [to] outdoor activities." To blow off steam, "The nightlife both on and off campus is great and weekends are always filled with options."

Admissions

If you want to learn more about the Illinois MBA, you can chat online with one of the school's admission's officers, or attend an admissions event in your area. There are no minimum GMAT scores required for entry to the program; however, recent classes had median GMAT score of 650, with an 80 percent range between 540 and 710. At least two years of work experience are strongly recommended; the average student had about four years of professional experience before entering the full-time program.

Prominent Alumni

Mike Tokarz, Chairman, The Tokarz Group; Tom Siebel, Founder, Chairman & CEO, Siebel Systems, Inc.; Jan Valentic, Senior VP Marketing, Scotts Miracle-Gro Company; Alan Feldman, President & CEO, Midas, Inc.

FINANCIAL FACTS

Annual tuition (in-state/ out-of-state)	$17,500/$26,500
Fees	$3,338
Room & board	$10,764

ADMISSIONS

Admissions Selectivity Rating	91
# of applications received	707
% applicants accepted	33
% acceptees attending	44
Average GMAT	635
Range of GMAT	540–710
Average GPA	3.3
TOEFL required of international students	Yes
Application fee	$60
International application fee	$75
Regular application deadline	3/1
Early decision program?	Yes
ED Deadline/Notification	12/1 / 2/15
Deferment available	No
Transfer students accepted	No
Non-fall admissions	No
Need-blind admissions	Yes

EMPLOYMENT PROFILE

Career Rating		Grads Employed by Function	%	Avg. Salary
Percent employed at graduation	89	Marketing	17	$88,500
Percent employed 3 months after graduation	52	Operations	5	NR
Average base starting salary	81	Consulting	32	$91,490
	$87,441	Management	10	NR
Primary Source of Full-time Job Acceptances		Finance	25	$82,400
School-facilitated activities	36 (61%)	HR	2	NR
Graduate-facilitated activities	23 (39%)	MIS	1	NR

Top 5 Employers Hiring Grads

LG Corporation (3), Sears Holdings (2), Ernst & Young (2), Robert Bosch Corporation (2), Nalco Company (2)

THE UNIVERSITY OF IOWA
HENRY B. TIPPIE SCHOOL OF MANAGEMENT

GENERAL INFORMATION
Type of school   Public
Academic calendar   Semester

SURVEY SAYS...
Good social scene
Helpful alumni
Solid preparation in:
Finance
Quantitative skills

STUDENTS
% male/female	84/16
% out-of-state	71
% minorities	4
% international	26
Average age at entry	27
Average years work experience at entry	3

ACADEMICS
Academic Experience Rating	**93**
Profs interesting rating	89
Profs accessible rating	90

Joint Degrees
Joint-degree MBA programs with Law, 4 years; Hospital and Health Administration, 3 years; Medicine, 5 years.

Prominent Alumni
Chris Michel, HR Manager/Ford Motor Co.; Jim Woo So, President, SK Telecom, Seoul, Korea; Marie Ziegler, VP, Investor Relations, Deere & Company; Michael Maves, M.D., Executive VP & CEO, American Medical Assn.; Thomas Koos, President & CEO, Jacuzzi Group Worldwide.

Academics

While some students extol the "wonderful experiential learning," and the "breadth of courses unmatched by most other institutions" that are offered at the Henry B. Tippie School of Management at The University of Iowa, others praise its "small class sizes along with the unique Academy structure." The recently implemented Academy structure requires students to select "one of three academies based on their interests: Finance, Marketing, [or] Strategic Innovation," the latter which encompasses both Strategic Management of Innovation and Process Excellence tracks. The school has also revamped its curriculum from "two 16-week semesters to four eight-week modules. This allows students to take fewer classes at one time and focus all attention on the subject matter at hand." With so many structural and administrative changes occurring at the same time, students admit that there have been some "growing pains" and "some glitches."

Nevertheless, students generally laud the school's "high return on investment" and feel that "the greatest strengths of the University of Iowa are the [number] of opportunities that are available in academics, athletics, government, and volunteer work." They also highlight that "the Tippie School's Process Excellence courses and association with the John Pappajohn Entrepreneurial Center are outstanding resources whether you want to start or improve a business." The Entrepreneurial Center, in particular, is "a hidden gem" that "offers many business competition events throughout the year that provide funding for startups, access to successful entrepreneurs and business mentorship." Students also boast that "the school's Henry Fund"—a $1.3 million student managed investment fund—"has received the top honors for performance the past five years as well."

Classes at Tippie provide a "comfortable environment" where there is a "good mix of readings, lectures, simulations, and real-world applications" that helps to nurture "thought and healthy conversation." The small size of the program creates "opportunity for involvement, interviews, and faculty interactions" and "more personalized attention."

The students are also impressed by their "outstanding" and "top-notch" professors who are often "national experts [in] their subject area." These "approachable" professors "do a very good job getting to know the students and build a personal relationship with most." The school's administration also received kudos from the students who observe that "the administration and professors meet frequently to incorporate ideas that they have gained from other schools, their own insight, and feedback from students."

Career and Placement

Tippie students reveal, "We can do a little better with career services. As such, it is good but we have faced some challenges during the economic downturn." Another student says they feel "disappointed with the efforts given by the University of Iowa for career guidance." Other students offer a more positive view of the Career Services and Placement Office, saying that they "motivate you and they also are as demanding as our professors in doing things like mock interviews, networking events etc. Also there is a leadership course that offers help to prepare one to present in professional and personal setting[s]."

Although they long for "more geographically diverse recruiters" and feel that there needs to be more effort put into "attracting more companies to visit on campus," Tippie students have noticed some recent improvement in recruiting on campus. "During the past year we have begun attracting high-tech firms and investment banks due to the efforts of career services and alumni. We have recently had Amazon recruit on campus...and are seeking to expand Goldman-Sachs undergraduate recruitment to include MBAs. We are also seeing many mid-market investment banks and private equity groups recruit on campus."

Student Life and Environment

Students are enthusiastic in their praise of Iowa City's "vibrant atmosphere which helps you both learn and relax." The city's "night-life is great and there are also a lot of hole-in-the-wall restaurants that provide a lot of diversity in dining." Iowa City also "has easy access to Chicago, Minneapolis, St. Louis, and Kansas City, and is 20 minutes from the airport for longer journeys."

Students count their school's "friendly atmosphere from admissions to faculty and students" as one of its strengths. When not immersed in their studies, students can participate in "lots of social activities as well as many school-related activities" including "company presentations and speaker sessions every fortnight." One student gushes, "The guest speakers are phenomenal—John Rice [Vice Chairman of General Electric], Fred Whyte [President of Stihl] and Clay Jones [CEO of Rockwell Collins]—are just a snapshot of the leaders that spoke at our school while I was a student." For the more athletically-inclined students, "the football atmosphere is awesome and something that should be experienced."

The school's "small community of students" is self-described as "classic Midwest[ern] people—hardworking, fairly narrow life experience, super friendly, outcome-oriented, family people." "There is a strong moral compass, and you do not have to be worried about being stabbed in the back by a fellow student for an A." These "very friendly, welcoming, and supportive" students who are "top-of-the-line performers" include "motorbike racers, go-cart racers, triathlon/marathon runners, musicians, math geeks, entrepreneurs, ex-military men, etc."

Admissions

Applicants to Tippie's MBA programs must submit an online application, official transcripts of post-secondary work, essays, a professional resume, a list of three references, an official GMAT score report, an admissions interview, and a TOEFL or IELTS score for international students. The school also strongly encourages applicants "to have a minimum of two years full-time, post-baccalaureate work experience."

FINANCIAL FACTS

Annual tuition (in-state/ out-of-state)	$17,218/$31,596
Fees	$1,311
Cost of books	$1,000
Room & board	$14,430
% of students receiving aid	74
% of first-year students receiving aid	75
% of students receiving grants	74
Average award package	$16,376
Average grant	$6,819

ADMISSIONS

Admissions Selectivity Rating	94
# of applications received	334
% applicants accepted	34
% acceptees attending	60
Average GMAT	662
Range of GMAT	630–700
Average GPA	3.41
TOEFL required of international students	Yes
Minimum TOEFL (paper/computer)	600/250
Application fee	$60
International application fee	$100
Regular application deadline	4/15
Early decision program?	No
Deferment available	Yes
Maximum length of deferment	1 year
Transfer students accepted	Yes
Transfer application policy: Maximum number of transferable credits is nine (from AACSB-accredited programs only).	
Non-fall admissions	Yes
Need-blind admissions	Yes

EMPLOYMENT PROFILE

Career Rating	94	**Grads Employed by Function**	**%**	**Avg. Salary**
Percent employed at graduation	69	Marketing	26	$73,001
Percent employed 3 months after graduation	85	Operations	11	$82,167
		Management	19	$78,400
Average base starting salary	$77,019	Finance	41	$77,091
Primary Source of Full-time Job Acceptances		HR	3	NR
School-facilitated activities	19 (58%)	**Top 5 Employers Hiring Grads**		
Graduate-facilitated activities	14 (42%)	Aegon USA, Inc. (5), Sears Holding Corporation (2), State of Wisconsin Investment Board (1), United Stationers (1), Eaton Corporation (1)		

UNIVERSITY OF KANSAS
SCHOOL OF BUSINESS

GENERAL INFORMATION
Type of school   Public
Academic calendar   Semester

SURVEY SAYS...
Students love Lawrence, KS
Happy students
Solid preparation in:
Doing business in a global economy

STUDENTS
Enrollment of parent institution	29,272
Enrollment of MBA Program	331
% male/female	76/24
% part-time	72
% minorities	5
% international	16
Average age at entry	26
Average years work experience at entry	3

ACADEMICS
Academic Experience Rating	77
Student/faculty ratio	10:1
Profs interesting rating	81
Profs accessible rating	76
% female faculty	32
% minority faculty	26

Joint Degrees
MBA/MA East Asian Languages and Cultures, 2 years; MBA/MA Latin American Studies, 2 years; MBA/MA Russian, Eastern European and Eurasian Studies, 2 years; MBA/Master in Management, 2 years; MBA/JD, 4 years; MBA/PharmD, 7 years; MBA/Architecture, 3 years.

Prominent Alumni
Ketchum Kreig, Google, VP International Marketing; Ronald G. Harper, Chairman/CEO of MPSI; Robert S. Kaplan, Lecturer at Harvard; Edward A. Kangas, Former Chairman and CEO, Deloitte and Touche.

Academics

Students at the University of Kansas' School of Business describe their institution as "the best business school in the Midwest," and they have good reason to be so complimentary. "Positive, up-tempo, friendly, and lots of work," the Kansas program is "vastly underrated" and a "truly wonderful" grad school experience. The students characterize the professors as "second to none" and are impressed with their academic and professional backgrounds." KU profs, who are "active in the business world within their fields," exhibit "a great blend of teaching skills and real-world experience."

Students are held to a high standard and are "expected to be well-prepared, well-read, and well-spoken in course discussions." The "fantastic" administration receives high praise as well. One MBA candidate reported that "if you want to try something different or want to attend a conference, they support you 100 percent of the time." Students also mention the administration's constant efforts "to improve facilities, encourage student involvement and input, and expand the faculty and curriculum."

On top of the full-time MBA offered at KU, the school also offers an evening-professional MBA, a Master's in Accounting, Master's in Finance, and several dual-degree MBAs, including a JD/MBA, MBA/MIM, MBA-PharmD, MBA/PM (petroleum management), as well as three international-themed dual degrees involving Latin American, European, and Asian studies. KU also has an extensive PhD program in which students can concentrate in accounting, information systems, finance, marketing, decision sciences, and management. KU's "focus on the global business environment" is a huge draw for many applicants, who feel that the school provides "an exceptional international business program for being in the middle of the United States and far from the coasts." Reasonable fees also are a major plus, and many students feel they're receiving a great deal of value for their money.

As one might expect from a school that focuses a great deal on international business, KU has an international program that allows students to obtain real-world experience in the global marketplace. The KU School of Business partners with the Center for International Business Education and Research to facilitate study abroad with an array of businesses across the globe. In the past few years students have traveled to India, China, Germany, France, Brazil, and Mexico as part of the program. With these types of experiences available to students, it's no wonder they describe the KU program as a "good value for the money that offered many options in terms of international experience."

Career and Placement

On its website the school boasts that "KU Business alumni are chief officers and senior executives of dozens of *Fortune* 500 companies." Fortunately for KU students who aspire to such heights, Kansas City is home to many large corporations, including Sprint and Hallmark, and the metropolitan area has been named one of the "Top 20 Areas to Start and Grow a Company" by Inc.com. KU also has a second campus (Edwards Campus) located in nearby Overland Park, which was named one of the top 10 cities for doing business by Business Development Outlook.

Students give glowing reviews to the school's Career Services Department, which does a "fantastic job of preparing students for the job-search process and facilitating that process through two massive career fairs, many interview and resume workshops, one-on-one counseling, and more." One student says, "I already have a job waiting for me when I complete the master's program, thanks to the business school's Career Services, and KU's strong reputation in the region."

ADMISSIONS CONTACT: DEE STEINLE, ADMINISTRATIVE DIRECTOR OF MASTER'S PROGRAMS
ADDRESS: 206 SUMMERFIELD HALL, 1300 SUNNYSIDE AVENUE LAWRENCE, KS 66045
PHONE: 785-864-7500 • FAX: 785-864-5376
E-MAIL: BSCHOOLGRAD@KU.EDU • WEBSITE: WWW.BUSINESS.KU.EDU

Approximately 66 percent of Kansas students accepted job offers before graduating in a recent academic year, and by three months after graduation, that number had grown to 100 percent. The average salary for graduates was $67,139 (not including bonus). The majority of students accepted jobs in marketing and finance, although there were quite a few who went into operations and consulting. A range of companies recruit on campus, and the ones who hire graduates most frequently include Tradebot, MarketSphere, United Missouri Bank, EMBARQ, Sprint Nextel.

Student Life and Environment

KU students enjoy life on campus, which many describe as "great." The only complaint is that "there are really more things that I'd like to be able to participate in than I have time to do!" One student described life at KU as "filled with a variety of activities, including extracurriculars (Net Impact, MBA Ambassadors), social events put on by MBA student organizations, working for the MBA Admissions Office, and of course, course work."

Although the majority of the class is "ambitious and concentrated on their future," students are also "very fun people." There is diversity among the MBA candidates, and the students "vary from people straight out of undergrad to people 35 years old, and they all have different goals and lifestyles, but they communicate well and make the classes enjoyable by opening up discussion without judging others." Some say their classmates "are the very best part about my experience in the KU MBA program." Overall, students are more than satisfied with their experiences at KU. As one student said, "I cannot thank KU enough for preparing me to excel in my future endeavors."

Admissions

Applications are accepted at anytime, up until posted application deadlines. KU is now accepting applications for all programs for the fall 2010 semester. In a recently admitted class, students' average undergraduate GPA was around 3.2, and the average GMAT was approximately 568. Students had an average of three years of work experience.

FINANCIAL FACTS

Annual tuition (in-state/ out-of-state)	$11,925/$21,175
Cost of books	$2,000
Room & board	$9,500
% of students receiving aid	70
% of first-year students receiving aid	70
% of students receiving loans	90
% of students receiving grants	50
Average grant	$5,000

ADMISSIONS

Admissions Selectivity Rating	**76**
# of applications received	66
% applicants accepted	73
% acceptees attending	88
Average GMAT	568
Range of GMAT	500–650
Average GPA	3.2
TOEFL required of international students	Yes
Minimum TOEFL (paper/computer)	53/20
Application fee	$60
International application fee	$60
Regular application deadline	6/1
Early decision program?	No
Deferment available	Yes
Maximum length of deferment	1 year
Transfer students accepted	Yes
Transfer application policy: Maximum number of transferable credit hours is six.	
Non-fall admissions	Yes
Need-blind admissions	Yes

EMPLOYMENT PROFILE

Career Rating	80	**Top 5 Employers Hiring Grads**
Average base starting salary	$67,139	Tradebot, MarketSphere, United Missouri
Primary Source of Full-time Job Acceptances		Bank, EMBARQ, Sprint Nextel
School-facilitated activities	74	
Graduate-facilitated activities	21	

UNIVERSITY OF KENTUCKY
GATTON COLLEGE OF BUSINESS AND ECONOMICS

GENERAL INFORMATION
Type of school   Public
Academic calendar   Semester

SURVEY SAYS...
Students love Lexington, KY
Friendly students
Solid preparation in:
Teamwork

STUDENTS
Enrollment of parent institution	26,545
Enrollment of MBA Program	167
% male/female	78/22
% out-of-state	15
% part-time	55
% minorities	4
% international	5
Average age at entry	24
Average years work experience at entry	3

ACADEMICS
Academic Experience Rating	**79**
Student/faculty ratio	3:1
Profs interesting rating	78
Profs accessible rating	82
% female faculty	16
% minority faculty	7

Joint Degrees
MBA/JD (4 years); BS Engineering/MBA (5 years); MD/MBA (5 years); PharmD/MBA (4 years); MBA/MA International Relations (3 years).

Prominent Alumni
Chris Sullivan, Founder, Outback Steakhouse, Current Chairman, OSI Restaurant Partners, Inc.; W. Rodney McMullen, President, Kroger Company; Joseph W. Craft, Chairman, President, & CEO, Alliance Coal, LLC; Paul C. Varga, Chairman, President, & CEO, Brown-Forman Corporation; James E. Rogers, Jr., Chairman, President & CEO, Duke Energy Corporation.

Academics

The Gatton College of Business and Economics at the University of Kentucky offers both a part-time MBA designed for the needs of local professionals and a full-time, 11-month immersion MBA. Many students in our survey identified the accelerated pace of the full-time program as a major attraction. It's "a quick program that offers a more intense learning experience along with the opportunity to work with executives at some of the largest world corporations" through "Project Connect, a partnership between the university and industry to provide practical education via projects" with regional businesses.

Students in both programs appreciate that Gatton "is recognized [as] the best graduate business school in the state," which "is very helpful in getting a job." "Good professors" and the "relatively low" tuition is also appealing, of course. The Gatton curriculum "is broken into modules such as new product development, mergers and acquisitions, supply chain management, and financial analysis," and "all tools and skills (finance, accounting, ops) are taught around the basis of these modules." The program "stays on top of the latest trends and technologies in business," another plus. This "very structured" program requires "a lot of group work." "The whole program is team-based, which is going to be helpful in the future," one student writes.

The Gatton MBA emphasizes new product development, supply chain management, and mergers and acquisitions. Cross-functional teams of five are created and work with companies on projects in each of the three areas of emphasis. This is complemented by professors who are generally "very good and have a fairly structured teaching style" and blend "theory and real-world experience." In recent years the school "has added many faculty with real-world experience and shaped the program and skill sets you learn around executives' requests for incoming employees. It is amazing how tailored this program is to real work experience." Part-timers appreciate how "the professors understand that their students are also working professionals and have other lives besides the classroom." As a result, "The course load has not been unbearable, but it keeps you busy."

Career and Placement

The MBA Center provides MBA Career Services in conjunction with the James W. Stackert Career Center. Among other services, MBA Career Services hosts a mentoring program and offers a MBA career development course. Two large, two-day career fairs are hosted each semester as well as a MBA Networking Reception in the spring. To help students prepare for these events, MBA Career Services offers individualized coaching sessions on topics including: resume writing, job searching, networking, interviewing, salary negotiating, etiquette, and more.

Last year the average salary for a Gatton graduate was $53,385. Companies hiring Gatton MBAs include Alltech, Brown-Forman, Cummins, Deloitte, Eastman Chemical, Eli Lilly & Company, Ernst & Young, Fifth Third Bancorp, Humana, Kaba Mas, KPMG, Lexmark International, Inc., P & G, PriceWaterhouseCoopers, LLP, Ryder Integrated Logistics, Tempur-Pedic, Toyota, U.S. Department of Labor, IBM, Wright-Patterson Air Force Base, Aldi, BB&T, and Wal-Mart.

Student Life and Environment

For full-time MBAs, "Life at UK is focused on school rather than extracurricular activities, largely because of the length and intensity of the program." Cramming two years' worth of learning into eleven months doesn't leave a lot of time for extracurriculars or socializing. Full-timers generally live in "nice...well-priced" housing located "relatively close" to campus, "which is nice considering we are all working with companies [on Project Connect projects] and we have to meet daily." The MBA group forms "a very strong community." On days we have class, nearly all students arrive 45 minutes to an hour early to socialize and visit" in the "dedicated MBA lounge...Professors will stop by as well." When time permits, students enjoy getting out and about in Lexington, an "exciting" and "excellent city" with "plenty to do."

Gatton full-timers don't have "as much work experience as [students at] some schools," but they are "hard workers and add a certain competitive edge in the classroom which I feel improves the overall experience. Outside of class, many of us commonly get together to socialize and even discuss business-related topics/concerns that arise in our workplaces and in the economy." The part-time student body includes a substantial number of "engineer-schooled and extremely goal-oriented" professionals.

Admissions

Applicants to the Gatton MBA program must submit the following materials: official transcripts for all undergraduate study (minimum GPA of 2.75 on a 4.0 scale required); an official score report for either the GMAT or the GRE; three letters of recommendation from individuals who can objectively assess the applicant's character and capabilities; a current resume; and a completed application. International applicants who do not hold undergraduate degrees from a U.S. institution must also submit an official score report for the TOEFL or the TWE. Gatton admits MBAs for the fall semester only. Among those accepted to the most recent class, the average GMAT score was 603 and the average undergraduate GPA was 3.34.

FINANCIAL FACTS

Annual tuition	$9,387
Fees (in-state/ out-of-state)	$8,000/$9,000
Cost of books	$2,500
Room & board (on/off-campus)	$8,250/$9,100
% of students receiving aid	28
% of first-year students receiving aid	28
% of students receiving grants	28
Average award package	$11,195
Average grant	$11,195

ADMISSIONS

Admissions Selectivity Rating	80
# of applications received	191
% applicants accepted	70
% acceptees attending	73
Average GMAT	603
Range of GMAT	510–730
Average GPA	3.34
TOEFL required of international students	Yes
Minimum TOEFL (paper/computer)	550/213
Application fee	$50
International application fee	$65
Regular application deadline	6/1
Early decision program?	No
Deferment available	Yes
Transfer students accepted	Yes
Transfer application policy: File must be completed and applicant is considered as a regular applicant only for Evening program.	
Non-fall admissions	No
Need-blind admissions	Yes

EMPLOYMENT PROFILE

Career Rating	82	Grads Employed by Function	% Avg. Salary
Percent employed at graduation	35	Marketing	3 $59,500
Percent employed 3 months after graduation	72	Operations	16 $49,513
		Consulting	1 NR
Average base starting salary	$53,385	Management	3 $70,000
Primary Source of Full-time Job Acceptances		Finance	9 $52,333
School-facilitated activities	19 (50%)	HR	1 NR
Graduate-facilitated activities	17 (47%)	**Top 5 Employers Hiring Grads**	
		Wright Patterson Air Force Base (6), Aldi (3), GE (1), YumBrands (1), IBM (1)	

UNIVERSITY OF LOUISIANA—LAFAYETTE
B. I. MOODY III COLLEGE OF BUSINESS

GENERAL INFORMATION
Type of school   Public
Academic calendar   Semester

SURVEY SAYS...
Solid preparation in:
General management
Computer skills

STUDENTS
Enrollment of parent
  institution   16,361
Enrollment of MBA Program   200
% male/female   63/37
% out-of-state   6
% part-time   50
% minorities   28
% international   28
Average age at entry   26
Average years work experience
  at entry   5

ACADEMICS
Academic Experience Rating   80
Student/faculty ratio   10:1
Profs interesting rating   65
Profs accessible rating   74
% female faculty   40
% minority faculty   15

Prominent Alumni
Phillip Burguieres, Oil and Gas/VP
Houston Texans Professional
Football Team; Mike DeHart, Stuller
Management Services, Inc.; John
Breaux, Former U.S. Senator;
Charles DeBellevue, Colonel, U.S.
Air Force; Dr. Ross Judice, Acadian
Ambulance and Air Med, EVP and
CMO.

Academics

Convenience and local reputation are the reasons most aspiring business people choose the Moody MBA program at the University of Louisiana—Lafayette. The majority of Moody students work full time in the area and attend classes in the evenings, thus limiting their choices of programs in which to enroll. Few mind though, as Moody is "a really good school," especially "for students who work full time," and offers a "cozy college atmosphere" where "just about everyone knows everyone else," and the faculty "really cares about the students."

Students at Moody report that the school has a "great reputation in the computer sciences" and is "the best and closest" when it comes to the health care industry. In fact, ULL offers an MBA with a concentration in health care administration, an appealing option to the area's many health care professionals. Professors have a lot of experience in their fields and "can relate to what we need better than those who just teach us with no experience to back it up." Among students' few complaints was that the relatively small size of the program limits course selection. "Schedule conflicts are common, and this is causing me to graduate at a later date than I anticipated," writes one student.

The Moody MBA requires students to complete 33 semester hours consisting of 27 hours of required core courses and six semester hours of electives (the health care MBA also consists of 33 semester hours but divides those hours between business and health care administration classes). Students who did not major in business as undergraduates are typically required to complete an additional 15 semester hours in foundation courses; these courses are prerequisite to, but do not count toward, the graduate degree.

Career and Placement

The Moody MBA program coordinates with the university's Career Services Center and the Internship Office to offer MBA N-Work, a service dedicated to finding jobs for past and current students. The Career Services Center offers Moody students on-campus job fairs and other placement services, but its primary mission is to serve undergraduates. The MBA Association is probably students' most effective conduit to employment. It should be noted that many Moody MBAs are currently employed, often by companies funding their graduate education, and thus are not actively seeking jobs. Top employers of Moody MBAs include Stuller, Lafayette General Medical Center, The Schumacher Group, Schlumberger, Acadian Ambulance Service and Air Med Services, Our Lady of Lourdes Regional Medical Center, Chevron, Texaco, and Louisiana Health Care Group Lafayette.

Student Life and Environment

Most students in the Moody MBA program attend part time, with lives so full of family and work obligations that they rarely linger unnecessarily on campus. Don't expect the hustle and bustle of a Northeastern b-school here, however; even the busiest MBAs tell us that "the school has a very laid-back attitude." That's simply the way life is in this section of Louisiana, known as Acadiana; students tell us that "in this part of the state, things are very relaxed and fun, and school is no different. We work hard, of course, but the overall feeling is more relaxed than, I assume, other business schools to be." Hometown Lafayette is "a great place to live" with an "excellent culture" that is "very attractive" to students. Students who can find time for campus events tell us that the schools "provide great opportunities to network and learn more about specific fields of work and study" and that the MBA Association does an especially good job "hosting socials and banquets and helping students and faculty get to know each other."

ADMISSIONS CONTACT: DR. C. EDDIE PALMER, DEAN OF THE GRADUATE SCHOOL
ADDRESS: MARTIN HALL, ROOM #332, P. O. BOX 44610 LAFAYETTE, LA 70504-4610
PHONE: 337-482-6965 • FAX: 337-482-1333
E-MAIL: GRADSCHOOL@LOUISIANA.EDU • WEBSITE: MOODY.LOUISIANA.EDU

Moody MBAs are "are competitive and, for the most part, have a positive attitude toward learning," although "Some are happy to settle for B's and socialize too." Students note that the school draws "an ethnically diverse" population and that "the 'joie de vivre' of the Cajun students at UL promotes a friendly but competitive atmosphere that you won't find elsewhere." While most students here are "older people coming back to school," Moody also has a number of students "just out of undergraduate school." Most feel their classmates "are mature and very helpful," a good thing since "In this program there are a lot of group projects. In every group I have been in, everyone pulls their own weight."

Admissions

Applicants to the Moody MBA program must meet the following minimum requirements for admission: a bachelor's degree from an accredited U.S. college or university or an equivalent degree from a foreign school; a minimum overall undergraduate GPA of 2.75; an "acceptable" score on the GMAT (average score for the entering class was approximately 520; analytical writing scores are also considered); three letters of recommendation from people capable of assessing your academic ability and potential to succeed in a graduate program; a written personal statement (up to 750 words describing why you wish to pursue an MBA); a current resume (include degrees earned, employment history, honors and awards received, summary of computer skills, and list of overseas travel and foreign language abilities); and, for international students, TOEFL scores. The school prefers but does not require previous work experience. The school accepts electronically submitted applications.

FINANCIAL FACTS

Annual tuition (in-state/ out-of-state)	$4,598/$13,169
Cost of books	$1,200
Room & board (on/off-campus)	$4,600/$8,400
Average award package	$12,098
Average grant	$3,000

ADMISSIONS

Admissions Selectivity Rating	77
# of applications received	153
% applicants accepted	55
% acceptees attending	81
Average GMAT	510
Range of GMAT	470–560
Average GPA	3.19
TOEFL required of international students	Yes
Minimum TOEFL (paper/computer)	550/213
Application fee	$25
International application fee	$30
Regular application deadline	7/15
Regular notification	8/1
Early decision program?	No
Deferment available	Yes
Maximum length of deferment	12 months
Transfer students accepted	Yes
Transfer application policy: Can transfer a maximum of 9 credit hours. Must apply through regular process. All transfer credits must be approved by MBA Director.	
Non-fall admissions	Yes
Need-blind admissions	Yes

UNIVERSITY OF LOUISVILLE
COLLEGE OF BUSINESS

GENERAL INFORMATION

Type of school | Public
Academic calendar | Year-round program

SURVEY SAYS...
Cutting-edge classes

STUDENTS

Enrollment of parent
institution | 22,031
Enrollment of MBA Program | 215
% part-time | 100
Average age at entry | 28
Average years work experience
at entry | 6

ACADEMICS

Academic Experience Rating | **88**
Student/faculty ratio | 10:1
Profs interesting rating | 91
Profs accessible rating | 85
% female faculty | 21
% minority faculty | 24

Joint Degrees

Joint degree oppurtunities are available with all graduate and professional programs at U of L, including the Law and Medical schools.

Prominent Alumni

David Jones, Founder/Former Chairman, Humana; Terry Forcht, Owner, Forcht Group; James Patterson, Founder/Former Chairman, Long John Silver's, Rally's; David Moran, Executive Vice President, President & CEO, Heinz Europe; Robert Nardelli, CEO Cerberus Operations & Advisory Company, LLC; Former Chairman & CEO, Chrysler, LLC.

Academics

The College of Business at the University of Louisville offers three primary MBA options. The first is the Professional MBA, a two-year accelerated program offered in two formats (two nights per week and occasional Saturdays, or all-day Saturday), and taught in six-week modules across 14 terms, including a consecutive two-term capstone project, five professional development Saturdays per year, and six elective choices. The second is the IMBA, an integrated, two-year lockstep program that focuses primarily on entrepreneurship. The IMBA is scheduled for the convenience of both full-time and working students, meeting twice weekly in the evenings. A new innovative option—the UofL Full Time MBA—will be offered in the fall of 2010. The 13-month program will feature evening classes, two nights per weekend and classes on friday afternoons, and an 11-month internship with a local company. The university also offers a number of joint-degree MBA programs. Both MBA programs offer a cohort-based team learning environment in a two year, year-round format, include an international learning experience and guarantee no tuition increase for students who complete the program with their cohort.

Students tell us that "Most of the professors have an innovative approach to teaching, and they look for ways to make their classes better. If I were to restart the program three years after graduating, I am sure it would be a unique experience." Students appreciate that this approach "is essential given the ever-changing business environment," adding that "We may not be a Harvard or Wharton, but we still produce some of the world's leaders in business. In addition, the program offers a great work/life balance." Students praise their professors for "demonstrating meaningful real-world knowledge through prior experiences. The course work they present is very applicable to situations I face as a manager at a bank each day."

Louisville's IMBA is a lockstep program with an entrepreneurial focus. This approach allows for greater integration within the curriculum; classes can be team-taught to highlight the interconnectedness of two or more business disciplines, for example. It also allows the school to vary course lengths. Because all students are taking all courses together, scheduling need not be restrained by traditional semester intervals, and students love the results. One participant writes, "I feel that it's designed to give me everything I wanted in a graduate business program. Everything that I have learned thus far has been applied in my professional life."

Career and Placement

Louisville MBAs receive career counseling and placement services from the Ulmer Career Management Center, a state-of-the-art, 3,800 square foot facility that includes a career management resource library, career shift and career trak databases, conference rooms, and interview rooms. The center also offers the new JAVS high-tech communications and sales lab. The office provides resume assistance, training seminars on interviewing skills, and on-campus recruiting events supported by CareerLeader tools and Symplicity software. Students confess that "the school still needs to improve in its career management for graduate students. Although some jobs have been posted, the majority are geared towards undergraduates or students who have graduated from the MBA program and already have several years of experience." On the bright side, students find that attending Louisville creates "many networking opportunities. Most classmates have full-time jobs and experience in the 'real world.' You can make connections with students throughout Louisville that will stay with you a long time." Opportunities to network are also enhanced in the Professional and full-time MBA programs through the capstone project, which is a team-based, external consulting project.

Student Life and Environment

Most MBAs at Louisville "have little involvement with the rest of campus (library, gym, etc.) because most work full-time and attend classes in the evenings." Students spend so little time on campus that "they are secluded from other graduate students and, to a certain extent, from the other MBA students," though the recent creation of the Professional MBA program offers more opportunities to network and utilize campus facilities with other members of their cohort. Even the busiest MBAs, however, know that "our basketball team is nationally-recognized and dominates both the school and the town during the season." Those who find time to spend on campus boast that it is "very accommodating, with a recently renovated state-of-the-art library and a great athletic program (activities MBAs can attend when not studying!)." One student notes, "Although it's an urban campus, you would never know it given the quaint, friendly atmosphere." MBA 'campus life' will be enhanced in 36 months with the planned relocation of the College's graduate business programs to the heart of downtown Louisville.

The metropolitan Louisville area is home to over one million people. Students describe it as "a city full of opportunities for recent or upcoming MBA grads. Openings for MBAs are frequently e-mailed to students by school officials, which is a great service." A recent Wall Street Journal supplement ranked Louisville "the nation's fourth best city for job opportunities for recent graduates." Papa John's, YUM!, Humana Health Insurance, UPS Worldport, and GE all have a large presence in the city; some are headquartered here. Students report that the area surrounding the school "is not the best residential area, it's not good housing. There is good, safe housing about 15 minutes from campus, though, over in the Highlands."

Admissions

Admission to the University of Louisville MBA program is, without a doubt, competitive. Students in the program rank in the top third of MBA candidates nationwide. Applicants must submit all of the following to the Admissions Office: a completed application; an official copy of all undergraduate transcripts; an official GMAT score report; a one-page personal statement; two letters of recommendation from professors (or employers for applicants who have been out of school for a substantial period); and a current resume. International students must provide, in addition to the above, an official TOEFL score report (minimum score: 170 computer-based test, 550 paper-and-pencil test). All candidates must be proficient in computer and quantitative skills prior to the commencement of their MBA work.

FINANCIAL FACTS

Annual tuition	$31,000
Cost of books	$1,500
Room & board	
(on/off-campus)	$10,000/$12,000
Average award package	$16,557
Average grant	$6,771
Average student loan debt	$33,615

ADMISSIONS

Admissions Selectivity Rating	82
# of applications received	181
% applicants accepted	112
% acceptees attending	99
Average GMAT	575
Range of GMAT	540–600
Average GPA	3.3
TOEFL required of	
international students	Yes
Minimum TOEFL	
(paper/computer)	557/213
Application fee	$50
International application fee	$50
Regular application deadline	7/31
Early decision program?	No
Deferment available	Yes
Maximum length	
of deferment	Case-by-case basis, generally 1 year
Transfer students accepted	Yes
Transfer application policy:	
Up to 9 credits are accepted (grade B or better) from an AACSB accredited MBA program, reviewed on a case-by-case basis.	
Non-fall admissions	Yes
Need-blind admissions	Yes

EMPLOYMENT PROFILE

Career Rating	76	Grads Employed by Function	%	Avg. Salary
Primary Source of Full-time Job Acceptances		Marketing	5	$49,944
School-facilitated activities	2 (5%)	Operations	10	$56,333
Graduate-facilitated activities	10 (95%)	Consulting	7	$61,000
		Management	12	$87,333
		Finance	17	$43,454
		HR	5	$91,000
		MIS	9	$103,625
		Nonprofit	12	$32,500
		Quantitative	1	$26,000

Top 5 Employers Hiring Grads
University of Louisville (9), Humana (8), UPS (3), General Electric (3), Aegon (2)

UNIVERSITY OF MARYLAND—COLLEGE PARK
ROBERT H. SMITH SCHOOL OF BUSINESS

GENERAL INFORMATION
Type of school	Public
Academic calendar	Semester

SURVEY SAYS...
Friendly students
Cutting-edge classes
Solid preparation in:
General management
Teamwork
Quantitative skills
Doing business in a global economy

STUDENTS
Enrollment of parent institution	37,195
Enrollment of MBA Program	1,352
% male/female	67/33
% out-of-state	72
% part-time	81
% minorities	21
% international	31
Average age at entry	28
Average years work experience at entry	5

ACADEMICS
Academic Experience Rating	**89**
Student/faculty ratio	7:1
Profs interesting rating	88
Profs accessible rating	81
% female faculty	25
% minority faculty	24

Joint Degrees
MBA/MS, 66 credits (21 months–5 years); MBA/JD, 108 credits (3–5 years); MBA/Master of Public Management, 66 credits (2.3 year–5 years); MBA/Master of Social Work, 88 credits (2.3–5 years); MBA/MS in Nursing, 66 credits (3–5 years).

Academics

A large school with a commanding reputation in the D.C. and Baltimore metropolitan areas, the Robert H. Smith School of Business offers a wide range of MBA options to a diverse student body of more than 1,000 graduate students. Depending on their professional experience, work schedule, and academic objectives, students can apply to Smith's full-time MBA program, Executive MBA, Accelerated MBA, or the part-time Evening MBA or Weekend MBA. While each of these programs differs in terms of class schedules, enrollment, admissions requirements, overall length, and location, they share an emphasis on the global economy, the integration of technology and business, and entrepreneurship. At the same time, real-world experience is paramount to a Smith education, and the school "allows many opportunities for students to learn outside the classroom, such as case competitions, consulting projects, and international teams." In addition to the aforementioned, "the school has a special program called the Mayer Fund where 12 selected MBA students from the entire school get to manage a $1.2 million endowment fund." Adding to the school's dynamic atmosphere is its urban location (Smith maintains campuses in College Park, Washington, D.C., Baltimore, and Rockville), which helps "attract some top-notch students to join the school, and also allows the school to offer many opportunities for growth outside the classroom."

Smith attracts a team of "incredible" faculty, who "are at the top of their fields in the industry and in research." Fortunately, the classroom experience does not come second to the faculty's research interests; at Smith, professors are "not only experts in their fields, but are also superb teachers (a rare combination)." In fact, evening students tell us that Smith professors "are very good at holding the attention of the class, even late at night." Drawing talent from the local business community, most Smith "professors have been very involved in both the Baltimore and Washington business communities" throughout their career, adding an important practical dynamic to the classroom. In addition to their expertise, Smith professors "are also just great people to be around; very personable and approachable. They work as hard for us as we work for them."

Career and Placement

A large percentage of Smith's part-time students plan to stay at their current company after graduation (in fact, many are receiving tuition reimbursement for their studies.) However, for students seeking a new position or career change after graduation, the Smith School of Business boasts "excellent job placement rates" and lots of deep ties in the local community. On campus, Smith's Office of Career Services offers a full range of professional development resources, including career and communication coaching, an online job database, an active alumni network, research materials, and more. Students can get highly individualized assistance from one of the office's professional staff. Recent companies that have recruited Smith grads include American Express Financial Advisors, Bank of America, Barclays Capital, Capital One, Chase Card Services, Citigroup, Deloitte Services, DuPont, Fannie Mae, FedEx, IBM, Intel Corporation, Lockheed Martin, Morgan Stanley, Motorola, The Washington Post, and The World Bank.

ADMISSIONS CONTACT: LeAnne Dagnall, Associate Director, MBA/MS Admissions
Address: 2308 Van Munching Hall, University of Maryland College Park, MD 20742-1871
Phone: 301-405-2559 • Fax: 301-314-9862
E-mail: mba_info@rhsmith.umd.edu • Website: www.rhsmith.umd.edu

Student Life and Environment

Smith has MBA programs on four campuses in College Park, Rockville, Washington, D.C., and Baltimore. At each campus, you'll find a different range of resources and opportunities; however, in general, Smith facilities are excellent. For example, students who attend class at the Ronald Reagan Building in Washington, D.C., describe it as a "top-notch business atmosphere" with "recently renovated rooms with electronic everything." The school's reputation and selective admissions draws a group of students who are "intelligent, well-informed, confident, hardworking, kind, and dependable." You'll also find a range of professional experience amongst the student body, with some students who are "young and fresh without much work experience, while others are seasoned and settled in their careers."

In College Park, there is a wide range of student organizations for full-time MBA students, including the Entrepreneurship Club and the International MBA Association. In addition, students and administrators are "working to ensure more community service is woven into student life." When it comes to having fun, students report a lively and social atmosphere among MBAs, including "great happy hours and frequent memorable cultural and variety nights." Luckily, part-time students don't miss out on the fun; while their schedules leave little downtime, part-timers still find time for "happy hours after class, if we are still awake.... We also have parties on weekends."

Admissions

To apply to Smith, students must submit an official copy of their undergraduate transcripts, official GMAT scores, two letters of recommendation, and a set of personal essays. In the full-time program, the entering class had GMAT scores ranging from 580–730, and an average undergraduate GPA of 3.3. The part-time class submitted GMAT scores between 550–670, and an average undergraduate GPA of 3.26. Students have an average of five years' professional work experience before beginning the part-time program.

Prominent Alumni

Kevin Plank, CEO and Founder, Under Armour; Carly Fiorina, Head of Carly Fiorina Enterprises; Richard Shaeffer, Chairman, NYMEX Holdings; Donta' Wilson, Regional President, BB&T; Robert H. Smith, Chairman, Charles E. Smith Commercial Realty.

FINANCIAL FACTS

Annual tuition (in-state/ out-of-state)	$15,642/$28,818
Fees	$17,777
Cost of books	$1,500
Room & board	15,000
% of students receiving grants	36
Average grant	$21,451

ADMISSIONS

Admissions Selectivity Rating	91
# of applications received	987
% applicants accepted	34
% acceptees attending	37
Average GMAT	658
Range of GMAT	620–690
Average GPA	3.31
TOEFL required of international students	Yes
Minimum TOEFL (paper/computer)	600/250
Application fee	$60
International application fee	$60
Regular application deadline	3/1
Regular notification	5/1
Application Deadline/Notification	
Round 1:	11/1 / 1/15
Round 2:	12/15 / 2/15
Round 3:	1/15 / 4/1
Round 4:	3/1 / 5/1
Early decision program?	Yes
ED Deadline/Notification	11/1 / 1/15
Deferment available	Yes
Maximum length of deferment	1 year
Transfer students accepted	No
Non-fall admissions	No
Need-blind admissions	Yes

Applicants Also Look At

Carnegie Mellon University, Georgetown University, Indiana University, University of North Carolina at Chapel Hill, University of Virginia

EMPLOYMENT PROFILE

Career Rating	93	**Grads Employed by Function% Avg. Salary**	
Percent employed at graduation	56	Marketing	22 $74,898
Percent employed 3 months after graduation	85	Operations	4 $68,833
		Consulting	29 $86,708
Average base starting salary	$78,462	Management	5 $55,164
Primary Source of Full-time Job Acceptances		Finance	29 $80,394
School-facilitated activities	55 (66%)	MIS	4 $75,533
Graduate-facilitated activities	27 (34%)	**Top 5 Employers Hiring Grads**	
		Booz Allen Hamilton (9), IBM (4), University of Maryland (4), Bank of America (3), Proctor & Gamble (3)	

UNIVERSITY OF MASSACHUSETTS—AMHERST
ISENBERG SCHOOL OF MANAGEMENT

GENERAL INFORMATION
Type of school	Public
Academic calendar	Semester

SURVEY SAYS...
Friendly students
Good social scene
Good peer network
Cutting-edge classes
Smart classrooms
Solid preparation in:
Accounting
General management

STUDENTS
Enrollment of parent institution	26,359
Enrollment of MBA Program	1,036
% male/female	54/46
% out-of-state	70
% part-time	93
% minorities	3
% international	26
Average age at entry	26
Average years work experience at entry	3

ACADEMICS
Academic Experience Rating	**90**
Student/faculty ratio	13:1
Profs interesting rating	86
Profs accessible rating	89
% female faculty	28
% minority faculty	23

Joint Degrees
MBA/MS in Sport Management, 2 years; MBA/MS in Hospitality & Tourism Management, 2 years; MBA/Master of Public Policy, 2.5 years MBA/MS in Industrial Engineering, 3 years; MBA/MS in Civil Engineering, 3 years; MBA/MS in Environmental Engineering, 3 years; MBA/MS in Mechanical Engineering, 3 years.

Academics

For savvy business students, University of Massachusetts—Amherst unites convenience, quality, and cost. Any way you slice it, University of Massachusetts—Amherst is an "exceptional value," boasting a low in-state tuition, yet all the prestige and resources you'd expect from the UMass name. For students who participate in the school's full-time graduate assistantship program, the deal is even sweeter. A student enthuses, "The best business decision I've made so far is to get my MBA in the full-time program where all of my tuition and fees are waived and I get paid to be a research assistant!" A comprehensive 55-unit program, the full-time MBA at UMass is completed on the school's main campus over the course of two years. For those already in the workforce, Isenberg "caters to part-time students who have to work full time" by offering a convenient part-time MBA, which can be completed "in class at Pittsfield, Holyoke, Amherst, or online." In addition, UMass offers dual degree programs in many fields, including sports management, public policy and industrial engineering.

Although the full-time MBA enrolls only 35 students each year, UMass is a large, public university. Therefore, it can be "hard to get a hold of the administrators because they're very busy." A student continues, "The administration has been nearly invisible, which is exactly how it should be—there have been no hassles over courses or deadlines." One exception: scheduling is often disorganized, and many students receive their "course schedule and textbook requirements sometimes just a week or two before classes begin"—creating lots of headaches at the beginning of the term. In contrast, the academic experience is surprisingly intimate, boasting small class sizes and "very supportive" professors. In the classroom, "Discussions are interesting and it's easy to participate," and professors "welcome discussion and feedback and are willing to let students run with ideas while still...keep[ing] us on track."

Uniting practical knowledge with academic savvy, "professors are very knowledgeable within their respective fields" and "very current" on industry trends. Students also get a taste of the real world through various experiential learning opportunities. After completing the core curriculum, students have "freedom to choose courses, practicum, and search for jobs." Among other offerings, the "Practicum" is a semester-long consulting project, which lets second-year students test their business acumen while working directly with for-profit and not-for-profit local businesses. A current student enthuses, "The end-of-program practicum project is extremely well put together, and is valuable for both real-world experience and resume-building."

Career Placement

Isenberg's MBA Career Management Office helps MBA candidates prepare for their career through a variety of services and networking programs. Among other offerings, the office operates a mandatory first-year Professional Seminar, which teaches full-time students how to research companies, market themselves, and align their career goals with the marketplace. While "the career center is good if you have specific questions," students admit that, "you really need to go out there and work for yourself to get anywhere" with the job search. Among students, "We rely on each other to bring our personal networks into the program." Here, "people know what you are looking to do and keep their ears open for opportunities to pass along."

On campus, students have access to career fairs and networking events; however, MBA candidates would also like to see more upper-level recruiting at UMass. In fact, companies "often come to campus to recruit undergrads but have no interest in the MBAs." A student adds, "Since the program is so small there are no visits from recruiters. While the

ADMISSIONS CONTACT: ERIC N. BERKOWITZ, ASSOCIATE DEAN, PROFESSIONAL PROGRAMS
ADDRESS: 305 ISENBERG SCHOOL OF MANAGEMENT, UMASS—AMHERST, MA 01003
PHONE: 413-545-5608 • FAX: 413-577-2234
E-MAIL: GRADPROG@SOM.UMASS.EDU • WEBSITE: WWW.ISENBERG.UMASS.EDU/MBA

career center has been infinitely useful for me, it would be more beneficial if they could interest recruiters in the MBA class." In recent years, Isenberg graduates have taken jobs at Bose, Canon, EMC, General Electric, Hearts of Fire, Kaufman Bros., KPMG, MassMutual, PriceWaterhouseCoopers, and United Technologies Corp.

Student Life and Environment

Amherst, Massachusetts, is the quintessential college town, and students in the business program aren't immune to their lively surroundings. Here, the atmosphere is collegial and friendly, and "students are active in clubs, sports/healthy living, arts activities, and more." Moreover, "Being a small program affords the majority of us to continue to practice our leadership skills in clubs, which provides a semblance of running a business and gives us high visibility in the university, with alumni, and in the broader community."

With only 70 students in the full-time program, UMass is "truly a community." During the challenging first-year curriculum, "the class gets very close, works hard together, and works to help each other." In addition, "Second-years are very active in helping the first-years adjust to the work load." In their free time, MBA candidates get together for "hikes, pot-luck dinners, [or] ice skating," and many attend the "weekly Thursday Night Out event sponsored by the Graduate Business Association." On the school's satellite campuses, students rarely get involved in any activities beyond classes. Nonetheless, they "enjoy interacting with the other students," and tell us that, "the facilities function well for what we need to accomplish."

Admissions

Isenberg accepts students based on their demonstrated record of academic achievement, promise for success in graduate school, personal motivation, and managerial experience. To be eligible for Isenberg's full-time or part-time programs, students must have at least three years of professional, post-undergraduate work experience. The school accepts either GMAT or GRE scores. The part-time program enrolls students three times a year; the full-time program begins once a year, in the fall.

Prominent Alumni

Eugene M. Isenberg, Chairman and CEO, Nabors Industries, Ltd.; Michael G. Philipp, Chairman, Credit Suisse Inc.; Nancy S. Loewe, CFO, GE Industrial Consumer & Industrial Division; Jeffrey C. Taylor, Founder, monster.com, Founder & CEO, aeons.com; Vivek Paul, Partner, Texas Pacific Group Ventures.

FINANCIAL FACTS

Annual tuition (in-state/ out-of-state)	$3,025/$11,385
Fees (in-state/ out-of-state)	$7,766/$10,471
Cost of books	$2,500
Room & board (on/off-campus)	$8,500/$9,500
% of students receiving aid	95
% of first-year students receiving aid	88
% of students receiving grants	5
Average award package	$24,000

ADMISSIONS

Admissions Selectivity Rating	96
# of applications received	248
% applicants accepted	25
% acceptees attending	56
Average GMAT	660
Range of GMAT	620–698
Average GPA	3.4
TOEFL required of international students	Yes
Minimum TOEFL (paper/computer)	600/250
Application fee	$40
International application fee	$65
Regular application deadline	2/1
Early decision program?	No
Deferment available	Yes
Maximum length of deferment	1 year
Transfer students accepted	No
Non-fall admissions	No
Need-blind admissions	Yes

EMPLOYMENT PROFILE

Career Rating	89	Grads Employed by Function	% Avg. Salary
Percent employed at graduation	58	Marketing	25 $72,500
Percent employed 3 months after graduation	100	Operations	8 $88,000
		Consulting	8 $95,000
Average base starting salary	$81,700	Finance	25 $95,000
		HR	8 $58,000
		Nonprofit	17 NR

Top 5 Employers Hiring Grads
Johnson & Johnson, GE, Wind Division, Staples, Inc., Lowe's, Inc., Canon, Inc.

University of Massachusetts—Boston

Graduate College of Management

GENERAL INFORMATION

Type of school	Public
Academic calendar	Semester

SURVEY SAYS...

Solid preparation in:
Teamwork
Communication/interpersonal skills

STUDENTS

Enrollment of parent institution	14,912
Enrollment of MBA Program	439
% male/female	52/48
% out-of-state	47
% part-time	67
% minorities	22
% international	39
Average age at entry	30
Average years work experience at entry	6

ACADEMICS

Academic Experience Rating	87
Student/faculty ratio	9:1
Profs interesting rating	81
Profs accessible rating	81
% female faculty	35
% minority faculty	38

Joint Degrees

MBA/MS in Accounting, 3 years; MBA/MS in Finance, 3 years; MBA/MS in International Management, 3 years; MBA/MS in Information Technology, 3 years.

Prominent Alumni

Thomas M. Menino, Mayor, City of Boston; Joseph Abboud, Fashion Designer; George Kassas, Founder, Cedar Point Communications; Mark Atkins, CEO, Invention Machine; Joseph Kennedy, U.S. Congressman.

Academics

"If you're looking for a quality education at a good price," University of Massachusetts—Boston is a solid choice for current and future East Coast professionals. At this large and prestigious public university, you'll get a strong, practical, "no-frills education," which costs "considerably less than other graduate schools in the greater Boston area." Convenience is another major selling point at this urban school. A majority of students in the UMass MBA program are already working full-time, and the school is very "accommodating to working professionals." "Full-time and part-time students take classes together" in the evening, and the academic experience is "challenging but manageable while balancing a career and home life."

At UMass Boston, the MBA begins with 10 core courses in major business areas, followed by eight electives—four of which must be distributed across functional areas. Depending on their career goals, students have the option of pursuing a general management MBA, or they may choose to specialize their education through one of 10 concentrations. Students appreciate the "highly diverse course work" offered at UMass Boston, including electives in non-profit management, environmental management, information systems, and healthcare management. The school also offers international programs during the summer and the winter intersession recently, courses were held in India and China. At the same time, students feel that "a focus on international exchange and technology learning could be better integrated" into the general curriculum.

You'll find "great people working in the administration" at UMass Boston, and the program generally runs smoothly. Attracting a talented faculty from local colleges and corporations, the university's accomplished teaching staff is comprised of "experienced professors who are graduates from the best academic institutions." Most blend an appealing classroom demeanor with "a lot of knowledge and experience to share." Despite the program's large size, the faculty is surprisingly accessible and student-friendly. A current student shares, "[A] professor accompanied me to [an] internship appointment as [a] contributor for [a] Google Ad Word Statistics study in Cambridge. Another Professor invited me into his famous Boston film study, as he recognized my experience from work in California. Amazing professors!"

Career and Placement

The majority of MBA candidates at UMass Boston's College of Management are already in the workforce, balancing their studies with a full-time career. However, for those who'd like to explore new career opportunities, UMass students don't have to look any further than the classroom: "Since so many of my classmates are also working full-time there are tremendous networking opportunities within the local business community." While many UMB students hope to move ahead in their careers, they are also realistic about their expectations after graduation. A current student says, "I haven't met anyone who thinks that an MBA alone will catapult them to a CEO position or make them an instant millionaire right after graduation. My classmates understand that the value of an education comes from what it allows you to bring to the table at work."

The College of Management Career Services helps place students in part-time, full-time, and internship positions. It offers professional career counseling and resume revisions, hosts on-campus interviews, and maintains an updated list of open positions for undergraduates and graduate business students, as well as alumni. They also offer one-on-one career counseling by appointment. In addition, the center operates a career development series known as the Management Achievement Program, or MAP—a series of "business

ADMISSIONS CONTACT: OSCAR GUITERREZ, ASSOCIATE DEAN
ADDRESS: 100 MORRISSEY BOULEVARD, MBA OFFICE BOSTON, MA 02125-3393
PHONE: 617-287-7720 • FAX: 617-287-7725
E-MAIL: MBA@UMB.EDU • WEBSITE: WWW.MANAGEMENT.UMB.EDU

events that help students in many aspect of life." Among other offerings, MAP events include a campus speaker series, company visits, and networking events. Students may also take advantage of the services provided by the UMB Career Services office for the larger university, which include numerous recruiting events on campus.

Student Life and Environment

On the UMB campus, you'll meet a "good mix of professional international students and Massachusetts natives." For the most part, students are "in their late 20s [or] early 30s, with families, and are full-time professional employees pursing an MBA in the evenings." Because students are balancing busy schedules, "there really isn't very much opportunity for students to attend campus events other than class." At the same time, students say they "get together informally off campus to network and develop ties." You'll also find a smattering of "student-organized social events and business lectures" on campus.

Urban and accessible, the UMass campus boasts "the best possible location" on the Columbia Point peninsula, with views of Boston's downtown skyline. The business school is located on the fifth floor of McCormack Hall, "a very modern building with lots of places to study and hang out." Unfortunately, students admit that, "Many of the classrooms are outdated," though serviceable. On the whole, UMB is a "good school for working professionals," but the "lack of student housing and area resources would make it a tough sell for me to attend as a full-time student." But, prospective students should stay posted: "They are planning to build dorms in the future," so UMB's reputation as a "commuter school" may someday be history.

Admission

To be eligible for the MBA program at UMass Boston's College of Management, prospective students must have an undergraduate degree from an accredited college or university and a GMAT score of 450 or higher. In addition to test scores and undergraduate record, the admissions department evaluates students based on their recommendations, personal essays, and interview with the admissions department.

FINANCIAL FACTS

Annual tuition (in-state/ out-of-state)	$2,590/$9,758
Fees (in-state/ out-of-state)	$6,896/$10,235
Cost of books	$1,000
Room & board (off-campus)	$10,000
% of students receiving aid	65
% of first-year students receiving aid	55
% of students receiving loans	62
% of students receiving grants	21
Average grant	$17,000
Average student loan debt	$13,000

ADMISSIONS

Admissions Selectivity Rating	88
# of applications received	418
% applicants accepted	38
% acceptees attending	62
Average GMAT	585
Range of GMAT	530–650
Average GPA	3.34
TOEFL required of international students	Yes
Minimum TOEFL (paper/computer)	600/240
Application fee	$40
International application fee	$60
Regular application deadline	6/1
Regular notification	7/1
Application Deadline/Notification	
Round 1:	3/1 / 4/1
Round 2:	6/1 / 7/1
Early decision program?	No
Deferment available	Yes
Maximum length of deferment	1 semester
Transfer students accepted	Yes
Transfer application policy: Same applicant procedure. Transfer credits and waivers will be considered.	
Non-fall admissions	Yes
Need-blind admissions	Yes

EMPLOYMENT PROFILE

Career Rating	93	Grads Employed by Function% Avg. Salary	
Percent employed at graduation	50	Marketing	8 NR
Percent employed 3 months after graduation	89	Operations	12 NR
		Management	2 NR
Average base starting salary	$78,500	Finance	38 NR
Primary Source of Full-time Job Acceptances		HR	8 NR
School-facilitated activities	12 (25%)	MIS	22 NR
Graduate-facilitated activities	26 (54%)	Top 5 Employers Hiring Grads	
Unknown	6 (13%)	State Street Corporation (4), Bank of America (4), Ernst & Young (6), Fidelity Investments (2), PricewaterhouseCoopers (2)	

UNIVERSITY OF MASSACHUSETTS—DARTMOUTH
CHARLTON COLLEGE OF BUSINESS

GENERAL INFORMATION
Type of school   Public
Academic calendar   Sept–May

SURVEY SAYS...
Solid preparation in:
Marketing
General management
Communication/interpersonal skills
Doing business in a global economy

STUDENTS
Enrollment of MBA Program   250
% male/female   50/50
Average age at entry   26
Average years work experience
   at entry   6

ACADEMICS
Academic Experience Rating   **64**
Profs interesting rating   79
Profs accessible rating   68
% female faculty   10
% minority faculty   16

Joint Degrees
JD/MBA in conjunction with
Southern New England School of
Law.

Academics

The University of Massachusetts Dartmouth's Charlton College of Business goes the extra mile to make its MBA program as convenient as possible. The student body, largely made up of busy young professionals, appreciates the effort. Three locations (the main campus in North Dartmouth, Fall River, and Cape Cod Community College) make it easier for students to attend classes; "the ability to take online/blended courses" means they can sometimes skip the classroom entirely. An accommodating curriculum also helps; as one student explains, "I love the flexibility in the program. I can choose my classes in any order. Although it will be a four-year period before I finish in total, the slower pace is flexible and the option to take one course at a time is the only way I could have done it."

Cost is also a factor; students declare the UMD MBA "the least expensive AACSB-accredited business program in the area." Students also praise "a stellar international core of professors with a wide range of professional and academic experience," noting their instructors' "focus on group work and presentations," which they regard as "very realistic in the business world." They're less bullish on the administration, describing it as "disjointed." "The administration needs to work more diligently at ironing out some of the bureaucracy in the system," one student explains. "On more than one occasion, I have received multiple answers to the same question, depending on who I speak with."

Students also note "there is sometimes trouble with the offerings in certain concentrations." Class availability sometimes diminishes the convenience of the program; students wish the school would "rotate the elective course offerings and have courses available for all concentrations that are offered" in order to mitigate the problem. Even so, students' opinion of the program as a whole is favorable; one writes, "The overall academic experience is challenging and engaging, [leaving me] very optimistic about potential for more success after graduation."

Career and Placement

The MBA program at UMD utilizes the university's Career Resource Center, which serves all undergraduates, graduate students, and alumni. The office provides a battery of career services, including workshops in resume-writing, interviewing, and salary negotiation; online job and resume listings; and on-campus recruiting events, including job fairs. Efforts here are primarily directed toward the undergraduate population. One MBA explains, "The majority of MBA students are usually using the MBA program to advance in their current occupation, with many large local corporations paying their tuition. The CRC is available and encouraged to be utilized for students seeking employment after graduation." Some students are less than satisfied with the situation; "They need to build their network of companies up badly. In so doing, they need to get more companies to come on campus and recruit," one such student writes.

ADMISSIONS CONTACT: NANCY LUDWIN, MBA COORDINATOR
ADDRESS: 285 OLD WESTPORT ROAD NORTH DARTMOUTH, MA 02747-2300
PHONE: 508-999-8543 • FAX: 508-999-8776
E-MAIL: GRADUATE@UMASSD.EDU • WEBSITE: WWW.UMASSD.EDU/CHARLTON/

FINANCIAL FACTS

Annual tuition (in-state/ out-of-state)	$12,150/$22,680

ADMISSIONS

Admissions Selectivity Rating	**60***
Average GMAT	500
Average GPA	3.4
TOEFL required of international students	Yes
Application fee	$40
Early decision program?	No
Deferment available	Yes
Maximum length of deferment	1 semester
Transfer students accepted	No
Non-fall admissions	No
Need-blind admissions	Yes

Student Life and Environment

The business school facility on UMD's main campus is of recent vintage; the ultramodern building, funded by a three million dollar grant from the Earle P. Charlton Family Trust, opened in 2004. Students speak highly of the main campus. They are less enthusiastic about the Fall River site, which one MBA complains "has broken windows" and "is in a scary area."

Students describe the UMD MBA program as "commuter-based," with students' involvement "mostly limited to evening courses, with little interaction on campus during the day unless attending a special lecture." "There's no mandatory participation" in extracurricular activities, "which is good for me," a typical student offers. That's because most here "are working full time and do not have time to get involved in other things outside of class."

The student body here "is a mixture of students that have just graduated from college and others who are working and raising a family." One reports, "Some are young—in their twenties—but there is a good mix of twenties, thirties, and forties. I'm 52 but feel comfortable in the environment." The program is "internationally diverse," with "people from all around the world. It is much more diverse than I would have expected," a locally based student observes. "The international students are extremely friendly and bright. I enjoy working with them on projects," one student notes.

Admissions

Applicants to the UMD MBA program must submit the following materials to the Admissions Committee: official transcripts from all post-secondary academic institutions attended (transcripts from institutions outside the US must be translated when not in English and evaluated by a Credit Evaluation service where the grading system deviates from the standard American four-point system); an official GMAT score report; two letters of recommendation, preferably one reflecting academic ability and one reflecting professional experience; a personal essay; and a current resume. International applicants must submit all the above plus an official score report for the TOEFL (minimum score 533 paper-based test, 200 computer-based test) and visa-related paperwork. Admissions are processed on a rolling basis, with decisions typically coming with a month after the completed application is received. International applicants must apply by March 1 for fall entry and by October 1 for spring entry.

UNIVERSITY OF MASSACHUSETTS—LOWELL
COLLEGE OF MANAGEMENT

GENERAL INFORMATION

Type of school	Public
Academic calendar	Sept–May

SURVEY SAYS...

Cutting-edge classes
Solid preparation in:
Accounting
General management
Operations

STUDENTS

Enrollment of parent institution	13,000
Enrollment of MBA Program	353
% male/female	57/43
% out-of-state	57
% part-time	93
% minorities	14
% international	7
Average age at entry	31
Average years work experience at entry	8

ACADEMICS

Academic Experience Rating	82
Student/faculty ratio	12:1
Profs interesting rating	82
Profs accessible rating	78
% female faculty	27
% minority faculty	27

Academics

Providing a "good balance between reputation and affordability" to business grads in and around the northeast corner of Massachusetts, the University of Massachusetts—Lowell's College of Management offers an MBA "tailored to meet the busy working person's schedules." With "evening classes," a "practical approach to tests and assignments," and, most conveniently of all, an "excellent online program" that "allows you to blend online with on-campus courses" (or even take all classes online, if you prefer), a Lowell MBA offers enough "freedom and flexibility" to suit its student body, which largely consists of professionals looking for a leg up to management positions.

The UML MBA commences with 12 hours of foundation courses in subjects traditionally covered in undergraduate business programs. Students who have completed equivalent undergraduate classes within the last five years and have earned at least a B may receive a waiver for some or all of these courses; alternately, students may attempt to place out of these classes through written exams. The curriculum also includes seven core courses in accounting, finance, analysis of customers and markets, MIS, operations, managing organization design and change, and strategy. The program concludes with three electives, which students may use to develop a concentration in accounting, finance, or information technology. They may also take an MBA in general business.

UML professors "are excellent and helpful," "not pretentious," and "demanding, which helps students do a better job." The school works hard on the service end; professors and administrators "are hands on, always follow up, and contact you regarding any questions." That said, UML is a state school, so naturally "sometimes there is non-applicable red tape, like when I was asked for proof of immunizations even though I take all my classes online." All in all, students appreciate what they have here, reporting that "Administrators do the best they can on limited staff and resources." As one student sums up, "the campus lacks the glossy touch, but I guess most here would agree that it gives the best value for your money. You have to remember that you are paying less than a third of what you would have paid at any private college [and] you still get a highly accomplished and dedicated faculty [that] works hard to embed the right kind of morals and values into your brain. The course textbooks, HBR case studies, and other miscellaneous materials are mostly the same as the ones used by the Ivy Leagues. The discussions are intense, and many ideas are innovative. I really don't think therefore that there is anything lacking academically."

Career and Placement

The UML Career Services Office provides counseling and placement services to all undergraduates, graduates, and alumni of the university. The office organizes a variety of job fairs throughout the school year. It also provides mock interviews, counsels students on resume writing and job-search skills, schedules corporate information sessions on campus, and offers access to online job search engines such as MonsterTRAK. The office coordinates the efforts of the University Career Advisory Network, which is essentially an online community of alumni and current students. Employers who most frequently hire UMass Lowell MBAs include: Bank of America, TD Bank, Fidelity, Putnam Investments, Raytheon, Pfizer, Procter & Gamble, EMC, Cisco, US Air Force and U.S. Government.

ADMISSIONS CONTACT: GARY M. MUCICA, DIRECTOR, GRADUATE MANAGEMENT PROGRAMS
ADDRESS: ONE UNIVERSITY AVENUE, PA 303 LOWELL, MA 01854-2881
PHONE: 978-934-2848 • FAX: 978-934-4017
E-MAIL: KATHLEEN_ROURKE@UML.EDU • WEBSITE: WWW.UML.EDU/MBA

Student Life and Environment

Over the years, online course offerings at Lowell have steadily grown in popularity. Today, one MBA explains, "Students are commuters or online, so the experience is not intimate. You don't form personal relationships with mentors/instructors" to the extent that students do elsewhere. Connections can be made with effort, however. Some students report "great opportunities for building relationships with professional networks," and others note that "there are many clubs and organizations for students to join. The office of student activities does a great job in matching students with their activities." These options are only really pursued by the program's few full-time students or by part-timers who don't also hold demanding full-time jobs.

Most here don't fit those descriptions. They're "working professionals" who "have at least a few years of professional experience and are part-time students who work full-time jobs." Their experiences "help in discussions in the class, as most of the arguments given are very practical and time-tested, and there is a lot to learn from everyone's experiences."

Admissions

The MBA program at the University of Massachusetts Lowell admits new students for both the fall and spring terms and requires applicants to submit the following materials: an official transcript of undergraduate grades; an official GMAT score report; three letters of recommendation from "employment-related sources" demonstrating a minimum of two years of relevant work experience; a current resume; and a one-page essay describing academic and career objectives. Applicants must complete prerequisite courses in microeconomics and statistics prior to entering the program. According to the school's website, "An aptitude for management decision-making and demonstrated academic ability are the most important qualifications for admission." International students whose first language is not English must submit an official score report for the TOEFL.

FINANCIAL FACTS

Annual tuition (in-state/ out-of-state)	$1,637/$6,425
Fees (in-state/ out-of-state)	$6,603/$10,037
Cost of books	$1,000
Room & board	$7,519
% of students receiving aid	10
% of first-year students receiving aid	10
% of students receiving loans	10

ADMISSIONS

Admissions Selectivity Rating	77
# of applications received	105
% applicants accepted	72
% acceptees attending	86
Average GMAT	550
Range of GMAT	505–610
Average GPA	3.26
TOEFL required of international students	Yes
Minimum TOEFL (paper/computer)	600/250
Application fee	$20
International application fee	$35
Early decision program?	No
Deferment available	Yes
Maximum length of deferment	1 year
Transfer students accepted	Yes
Transfer application policy: Must be fron an AACSB accredited program. Maximum of 12 tranfer credits.	
Non-fall admissions	Yes
Need-blind admissions	Yes

Applicants Also Look At

Bentley University, Boston University, Northeastern University, Suffolk University, University of Massachusetts—Amherst, University of Massachusetts—Boston

EMPLOYMENT PROFILE

Career Rating	76	Grads Employed by Function	% Avg. Salary
Percent employed at graduation	98	Marketing	8 NR
Percent employed 3 months after graduation	99	Operations	28 NR
		Management	10 NR
Average base starting salary	$71,247	Finance	21 NR
		MIS	13 NR
		Nonprofit	8 NR

UNIVERSITY OF MEMPHIS
FOGELMAN COLLEGE OF BUSINESS AND ECONOMICS

GENERAL INFORMATION

Type of school	Public
Academic calendar	Semester

SURVEY SAYS...
Cutting-edge classes
Solid preparation in:
General management
Computer skills
Doing business in a global economy

STUDENTS

Enrollment of parent institution	21,424
Enrollment of MBA Program	253
% male/female	59/41
% out-of-state	23
% part-time	47
Average age at entry	30
Average years work experience at entry	5

ACADEMICS

Academic Experience Rating	78
Profs interesting rating	65
Profs accessible rating	79
% female faculty	27
% minority faculty	

Joint Degrees
MBA/JD, 54 credits (4 years)

Academics

Fogelman College of Business and Economics at the University of Memphis is a no-non-sense professional MBA program designed for working people "from all walks of business life" who are looking to further their careers but who don't have a lot of time or energy to waste. The school has a solid reputation among locally-based businesses like FedEx. One student holds Memphis in such high regard that she has two degrees from there: "The University of Memphis is where I received my BBA in accounting. I liked my experience there, and I knew that an MBA from there would open many doors in the company that I work for."

Students say their "very knowledgeable" professors "present concepts completely" and help them relate the course material to practice. "Each of them has done extensive research in their field and [is] noted to be among the best in the country for their area of expertise." Another student says: "Every professor is interested in the development of each student into future managers and business leaders." The administration does not receive the same ringing endorsement, however. Some take issue with the allocation of funds in certain areas. One student was succinct and blunt: "Solid professors, good academic experience, but really bad administration that spends money" excessively.

Some students also have difficulty with course selection and enrollment; many required or desired classes are offered only once per semester under limited enrollment, and these courses "often conflict with each other." Since pretty much all of the courses take place in the evenings to accommodate the vast majority of students who have day jobs, there's very little leeway in terms of scheduling. But these night classes also give part-time and full-time students the opportunity to interact with each other through "small classes and heavy teamwork," something not found in a lot of MBA programs. "A lot of projects are team-based, so you get to know classmates very well." One student takes away warm feelings about the camaraderie he felt at the school: "I have a new set of best friends. I never thought it was possible after reaching age 40."

In keeping with the no-frills approach to the program, however, the facilities tend toward the sparse side. Several students expressed disdain for the academic buildings and equipment and spoke of the need for "more technology in the classroom." One student said the classrooms "need better seating. The desks were made for 4th graders."

Career and Placement

Some students say the program needs better ties to "big industries" to provide those students seeking out new or nonlocal careers with better job prospects. Fortunately for the students looking to stay in the area (and there are many), "There are several excellent companies in the area, also, that recruit heavily," and since the student body is, as one student puts it, "not nearly as competitive as I expected," everyone is "very supportive" and happy to help each other land available positions. Another boon to the school's local reputation is the recently formed partnership with the Leadership Academy. The partnership, known as the Community Internship, gives MBA students the chance to team with Leadership Academy fellows on projects designed to benefit the community.

ADMISSIONS CONTACT: MARK GILLENSON, DIRECTOR OF MASTER'S PROGRAMS
ADDRESS: GRADUATE SCHOOL ADMINISTRATION BUILDING RM. 216 MEMPHIS, TN 38152-3370
PHONE: 901-678-2911 • FAX: 901-678-5023
E-MAIL: GRADSCH@MEMPHIS.EDU • WEBSITE: FCBE.MEMPHIS.EDU

Student Life and Environment

The school is located in the midtown area of Memphis, which "is great for students because there are a lot of social establishments nearby" offering "a lot of things for students to do recreationally." Of course, there are the well-traveled destinations like Graceland (check out Elvis' gaudy yellow and black rec room), Sun Studios, and the famous Beale Street, with its string of live-music joints and soul food. And the National Civil Rights Museum, located at the old Lorraine Motel where Martin Luther King, Jr., assassinated in 1968, is a haunting must-see for tourists and locals alike. Overall, "The University of Memphis, like the city of Memphis, is greatly underrated," one student says.

Since "Most graduate students work and commute," little time is left for a social life outside of the classroom, but there's a foundation for friendship and networking among the "outgoing" and "friendly" individuals that attend Fogelman. Though some think "The school could put more effort into organized activities for students outside of class," the "busy" nature of the student body doesn't lend itself to much free time anyway, so complaints are few. Everyone is in agreement over the variety of backgrounds provided by their classmates: "The graduate population is very diverse, which makes things more interesting." "You have a great opportunity to meet people from various backgrounds (educational and ethnic)," another student says.

Admissions

Admittance to the professional MBA program at the Fogelman College of Business and Economics is not terribly selective, and the admissions requirements are fairly standard. Applicants to the school's professional MBA program must submit the following materials: a completed application (either online or via mail); an official copy of undergraduate transcripts from all colleges and universities attended (even if you did not graduate); a copy of your current resume; a statement of personal interest; a 1,000-word essay answering one of the acceptable questions provided on the school's admissions website; two letters of recommendation; and an official GMAT or GRE score report. Interviews and previous work experience are optional. In addition to the above documents, international students whose primary language is not English must also provide an official score report for the TOEFL (minimum score: 550, paper-based test; 213, computer-based test).

FINANCIAL FACTS

Annual tuition (in-state/	
out-of-state)	$7,470/$17,118
Fees	$420
Cost of books	$2,000
Room & board	
(on/off-campus)	$8,000/$12,000

ADMISSIONS

Admissions Selectivity Rating	**73**
# of applications received	240
% applicants accepted	75
Average GMAT	558
Range of GMAT	500–610
Average GPA	3.27
TOEFL required of	
international students	Yes
Minimum TOEFL	
(paper/computer)	550/213
Application fee	$35
International application fee	$60
Regular application deadline	7/1
Early decision program?	No
Deferment available	Yes
Maximum length	
of deferment	1 year
Transfer students accepted	Yes
Transfer application policy:	

Approved transfer credit may be accepted in the fogelman Colletge for not more than 9 semester hours of course credit toward a master's degree. Grades earned at another institution will not be computed in the University cumulative grand point average, nor will they be accepted for transfer, unless they are B (3.0) or better. No credit will be transferred unless it meets with the approval of the major advisor or program graduate coordinator.

Non-fall admissions	Yes
Need-blind admissions	No

EMPLOYMENT PROFILE	
Career Rating	87
Average base starting salary	$63,800

UNIVERSITY OF MIAMI
SCHOOL OF BUSINESS ADMINISTRATION

GENERAL INFORMATION

Type of school	Private
Academic calendar	August–May

SURVEY SAYS...
Good peer network
Cutting-edge classes
Happy students

STUDENTS

Enrollment of parent institution	15,323
Enrollment of MBA Program	172
% male/female	69/31
% out-of-state	47
% part-time	0
% minorities	22
% international	26
Average age at entry	26
Average years work experience at entry	3

ACADEMICS

Academic Experience Rating	91
Profs interesting rating	93
Profs accessible rating	89
% female faculty	30
% minority faculty	18

Joint Degrees
JD/MBA, can be completed within a period of 3.5–4 years; MD/MBA, can be completed in 5 years; BArch/MBA, can be completed in 5 years.

Prominent Alumni
Raul Alvarez, Former President and COO, McDonald's Corporation; Gerald Cahill, Chairman and CEO, Carnival Corporation; Matthew Rubel, Chairman, CEO and President, Collective Brands Inc.; Lyor Cohen, Vice Chairman, Warner Music Group and Chairman and CEO, Recorded Music Americas and the U.K.; Ray Rodriguez, President and COO, Univision Network.

Academics

Miami is a "fast growing...multicultural" city "full of opportunities for development," a fact the School of Business Administration at University of Miami appears to have considered strongly in developing its graduate business programs. Not only does UM offer the expected full-time, and executive MBA options, it also offers an Executive MBA in health sector management and policy, an MD/MBA, and even a unique Spanish-language-only MS is professional management. Students who arrive here uncertain of their career objectives can take comfort in the unusually broad range of options open to them. By the time they leave, they'll have had ample opportunity to find their niche.

UM excels in numerous disciplines. Students laud the "strong finance department," the "great MBA in international business," the "strong marketing curriculum," and UM's "good slant towards the health fields, with a strong emphasis on problems we are facing today, including Obama's health plan, universal health care, and global health care, including tourist medicine." Across disciplines, UM "is a leader in designing programs that are innovative" and "is driven to be an academic leader. They are putting the resources toward making the overall school better, but the business school in particular is gaining forward momentum." Wherever possible, the program exploits hometown Miami's identity as "the Capital of Latin America" to "bring many globally active companies to the business school."

UM faculty is "renowned for its research and corporate experience and are able to speak to us using its experiences." Students appreciate that their professors "are very accessible. They even provide you their home phone if you need to address any questions." They expect a lot from MBAs here; tests "are very challenging but very fairly graded if you do your part in terms of reading, asking questions, and knowing the course material. There are no 'multiple choice/guess' tests. All the tests are very much 'apply the concepts to modern day business problems.'" Students sum up the program's strengths this way: "Solid rigorous education, lots of teamwork. The school is under-recognized for the benefit is offers its students."

Career and Placement

The Ziff Graduate Career Services Center at the University of Miami is available to graduate business students only and offers career advising, online and on-campus recruiting, a career library, and periodic workshops on resume-writing and job search strategy. Students have mixed opinions on the service. Some complain that "An adequate stream of companies are brought in to speak, but there is no real urgency to hire. Several students pointed out that some of the problems may be more related to the economic downturn than to the Career Services Center. With the one of the largest alumni network in the world, the University of Miami provides students access to a large, international employment base. Companies recruiting UM MBAs in recent years include: American Express, Banco Pichincha, Disney, General Mills, Hewlett Packard, Ocasa, Royal Caribbean Cruises, UBS, and Wyeth Consumer Healthcare.

Student Life and Environment

UM's main campus, where full-time and some part-time students convene, is "beautiful," with "facilities that are very modern" (they include "an up-to-date library") and "a campus that is very well-kept, with all of the comforts even on the weekends." The b-school "is centered in the middle of the campus, with the large library and gym located nearby. Places such as the graduate lounge and tables downstairs encourage students to gather even when classes are not in session." Full-timers keep busy, as "there is never a lack of opportunity to involve oneself in various activities, groups, functions or social events. Dean's Happy Hours (every six weeks) allow students, faculty and administrators to interact in a casual environment. Various social activities sponsored by area restaurants, bars, clubs enable students to interact outside of class." When they can shake free of their school responsibilities, MBAs enjoy "plenty of opportunities to mingle with students or enjoy a good football, basketball or baseball game." UM also offers an Executive MBA program in Palm Beach and in Puerto Rico.

UM "has a heavily international student body." "About 20 percent are straight from college." Others are working professionals "with 12 to 15 years of previous work experience." One observes, "Students are very diverse in terms of nationality, work experience and skill sets. For example in the current class, there are people with CFA, PhD, CPA, published writers, medical students etc." Most here "have a good team spirit and a sense of healthy competition."

Admissions

To apply to the MBA program, students must submit a completed application, official transcripts from any undergraduate and postgraduate course work, a current resume, one letter of recommendation (preferably from a employer, or immediate supervisor at work), official GMAT score reports, and TOEFL test scores for non-native speakers of English (minimum required score 550 paper-and-pencil test, 80 Internet-based test, 213 computer-based test). Students are evaluated on the strength of all application materials. Admissions decisions are made on a rolling basis until the class is full; students are encouraged to apply at least three months before the beginning of the term. Students who wish to be considered for merit-based scholarships, fellowships, or graduate assistantship are advised to apply early, as they are limited and available for fall applicants only.

FINANCIAL FACTS

Annual tuition	$35,520
Fees	$280
Cost of books	$1,250
Room & board	
(off-campus)	$12,395
% of students receiving aid	77
% of first-year students	
receiving aid	77
% of students receiving loans	51
% of students receiving grants	51
Average award package	$35,626
Average grant	$20,455
Average student loan debt	$40,590

ADMISSIONS

Admissions Selectivity Rating	88
# of applications received	418
% applicants accepted	45
% acceptees attending	47
Average GMAT	636
Range of GMAT	600–670
Average GPA	3.2
TOEFL required of	
international students	Yes
Minimum TOEFL	
(paper/computer)	600/235
Application fee	$100
International application fee	$100
Application Deadline/Notification	
Round 1:	12/1 / NR
Round 2:	2/2 / NR
Round 3:	4/1 / NR
Round 4:	6/1 / NR
Early decision program?	Yes
ED Deadline/Notification	10/1 / 12/1
Deferment available	Yes
Maximum length	
of deferment	1 year
Transfer students accepted	No
Non-fall admissions	No
Need-blind admissions	Yes

EMPLOYMENT PROFILE

Career Rating	84	Grads Employed by Function	%	Avg. Salary
Percent employed at graduation	45	Marketing	14	$63,250
Percent employed 3 months		Consulting	11	$95,000
after graduation	65	Management	7	$59,000
Primary Source of Full-time Job Acceptances		Finance	57	$58,234
School-facilitated activities	20 (57%)	**Top 5 Employers Hiring Grads**		
Graduate-facilitated activities	19 (53%)	Kaplan University (3), Systemex Technology Worldwide (2), Visa International (2), Deloitte (1), Unilever (1)		

UNIVERSITY OF MICHIGAN—ANN ARBOR
STEPHEN M. ROSS SCHOOL OF BUSINESS

GENERAL INFORMATION

Type of school	Public
Academic calendar	Semester

SURVEY SAYS...
Good social scene
Good peer network
Cutting-edge classes
Happy students
Solid preparation in:
Teamwork

STUDENTS

Enrollment of parent institution	41,042
Enrollment of MBA Program	1,600
% male/female	66/34
% out-of-state	92
% part-time	48
% minorities	25
% international	33
Average age at entry	28
Average years work experience at entry	5

ACADEMICS

Academic Experience Rating	**96**
Student/faculty ratio	12:1
Profs interesting rating	92
Profs accessible rating	94
% female faculty	27
% minority faculty	25

Joint Degrees

MBA/JD and MBA/MD: Architecture Asian Studies; Chinese Asian Studies; Japanese Asian Studies; South Asia Asian Studies; Southeast Asia Education; Construction Engineering; Management Health Services Admin (Public Health); Industrial and Operations Engineering; Information Law; Management of Patient Care Services (Nursing); Manufacturing Engineering; Medicine (MD) Modern Middle Eastern and North African Studies; Music.

Academics

After the $100 million donation in 2004 from Stephen M. Ross—the largest gift ever bestowed upon any U.S. business school—the school has benefited from an exponential increase in both construction and curriculum, including a new $145 million facility and a revised MBA curriculum whose benefits include carefully sequenced core courses, more electives, and the opportunity to focus on specific areas of interest prior to internship interviews. Most students agree that the program "ranks high in everything," but note that it is "extremely strong in corporate strategy, entrepreneurial studies, management accounting, marketing, organizational behavior, nonprofit organizations, social venturing, and venture capital/private equity/entrepreneurial finance."

Much of the program's strength comes from the "great professors who respond to the individual classes' needs and interests." Students appreciate that the "helpful and challenging" faculty "push you to think," adding that "classes are a great mix of lecture and performance." Because the business school does not require students to specialize, MBAs "have a lot of flexibility in the second-year schedule to focus on the classes [they] want." Just keep in mind the rigorous core curriculum must be completed before students can take on the multitude of electives the school has on offer. (Some of these courses are so "popular" that the administration works "with the professor to expand the number of sections they teach in order to give the most opportunity to people to take the class.)

MBAs add that the workload is fairly heavy, but "That's what we're paying for." One student explains, "We take five classes per semester, and each class usually meets twice a week for one and a half hours at a time. For every one-and-a-half-hour class, there's probably about that much preparation time that is put in outside of class." As a major research institution, Michigan gives its MBAs access to world-class research facilities. And don't forget about the "breadth and depth" of the "second-to-none" opportunities offered, such as "dual degrees, academic programs, International Multidisciplinary Action Projects, and [access to] institutes such as The William Davidson Institute for International Studies and the Zell Lurie Institute for Entrepreneurial Studies."

On the aesthetic front, many note that "classrooms need to be upgraded" and that "facilities could be improved." The good news in this is that the school's administration "is driven to improve the school" and has "a strategic plan for the school." And that $100 million mentioned earlier has come a long way to make these students' hopes for the campus become a foreseeable reality.

Career and Placement

The university is home to a "powerful and active alumni movement," meaning that MBA graduates have exceptional access to career opportunities; "Alums seem to go out of their way to help you." U of M's Student Career Services Office at the Ross School of Business, serves both undergraduates and graduate students, and reports that an impressive 90.6 percent of recent MBA graduates received their first job offer within three months of graduating.

Top employers of Michigan MBAs include Citigroup, Booz Allen Hamilton, Dell, McKinsey & Company, American Express Company, JPMorgan Chase, A.T. Kearney, Eli Lilly and Company, Bain & Company, Ford Motor Company, Medtronic, 3M, Cummins, General Mills, Guidant Corporation, Intel, Kraft Foods, Microsoft, National City Corporation, and SC Johnson.

ADMISSIONS CONTACT: SOOJIN KWON KOH, DIRECTOR OF ADMISSIONS
ADDRESS: 701 TAPPAN STREET ANN ARBOR, MI 48109-1234
PHONE: 734-763-5796 • FAX: 734-763-7804
E-MAIL: ROSSMBA@UMICH.EDU • WEBSITE: WWW.BUS.UMICH.EDU

Student Life and Environment

"If you like college towns, you will love Ann Arbor," students at U of M agree. In addition, on campus you'll find the "friendliest group of people I've ever met," says one student. "This is my new extended family." And this family has no shortage of social opportunities. "There's happy hour every Thursday, tailgates every Football Saturday, and numerous club parties in between," explains one student. "You can't beat Michigan football, hockey, and basketball." With "jazz [clubs], dance clubs, and restaurants" in the city, students find a "heck of a lot of fun" everywhere they go. Some even venture to Detroit. But beware the winter months, warn students: "The weather is cold...and students do spend too much time studying because there's not much else to do when it's 15 degrees out."

The MBA program offers "abundant opportunities to get involved, from professional to social clubs, newspaper, admissions, and career counseling. There's even a wine-tasting club." One student mentions that "without the energy the other students provide, many of the clubs/activities would not happen and our experience here would not be as rich." And students work together here to find a "good work-life balance." "We work quite hard, but on Thursday evenings, practically all MBAs flock to the b-school happy-hour bar, Mitch's," says one. "No weekend goes by without lots of prep for class, several group meetings, and at least one party or social/fun activity." The program also "provides lots of opportunities for spouses to get together. It also has joint programs with other schools in the university, which provide meaningful activities."

Admissions

Applications to the University of Michigan MBA program must include undergraduate transcripts, GMAT test scores (on average, successful applicants score 700), TOEFL test scores (for international students), letters of recommendation, a personal statement, and a resume. The school also looks at an applicant's record of success, clarity of goals, and management and leadership potential. The program does require previous work experience and, though not required, interviews are "highly recommended." There are many minority recruitment efforts, such as the Consortium for Graduate Study in Management, Robert F. Toigo Fellowships in Finance, National Society of Hispanic MBA Conference, National Black MBA Conference, and many more.

Prominent Alumni

John M. Fahey, President & CEO, National Geographic Society; Mary Kay Haben, Group VP, Kraft North America; Pres, Kraft Cheese.

FINANCIAL FACTS

Annual tuition (in-state/ out-of-state)	$38,100/$43,100
Fees	$189
Cost of books	$8,170
Room & board	$10,884
% of students receiving aid	75
% of first-year students receiving aid	75
% of students receiving loans	64
% of students receiving grants	56
Average award package	$62,343
Average grant	$17,224
Average student loan debt	$67,576

ADMISSIONS

Admissions Selectivity Rating	99
# of applications received	2,983
% applicants accepted	20
% acceptees attending	70
Average GMAT	700
Range of GMAT	640–760
Average GPA	3.3
TOEFL required of international students	Yes
Minimum TOEFL (paper/computer)	600/250
Application fee	$180
International application fee	$180
Regular application deadline	3/1
Regular notification	3/2
Application Deadline/Notification	
Round 1:	11/1 / 1/15
Round 2:	1/3 / 3/15
Round 3:	3/1 / 5/15
Early decision program?	No
Deferment available	Yes
Maximum length of deferment	1 year
Transfer students accepted	Yes
Transfer application policy: Transfer applicants are welcome to apply, but no credits will transfer into our program.	
Non-fall admissions	No
Need-blind admissions	Yes

EMPLOYMENT PROFILE

Career Rating	98	Grads Employed by Function	%	Avg. Salary
Average base starting salary	$99,265	Marketing	28	$93,779
Primary Source of Full-time Job Acceptances		Operations	2	$99,143
School-facilitated activities	265 (73%)	Consulting	31	$111,044
Graduate-facilitated activities	96 (27%)	Management	6	$99,947
		Finance	25	$93,317
		Strategic	4	$3,287

Top 5 Employers Hiring Grads

Citigroup (11), Deloitte Consulting (10), A.T. Kearney (9), Kraft Foods (8)

UNIVERSITY OF MICHIGAN—DEARBORN
SCHOOL OF MANAGEMENT

GENERAL INFORMATION
Type of school   Public
Academic calendar   Semester

SURVEY SAYS...
Solid preparation in:
General management
Operations

STUDENTS
Enrollment of parent
  institution   8,569
Enrollment of MBA Program   328
% male/female   85/15
% part-time   89
Average age at entry   31
Average years work experience
  at entry   5

ACADEMICS
Academic Experience Rating   82
Student/faculty ratio   18:1
Profs interesting rating   82
Profs accessible rating   80
% female faculty   32

Joint Degrees
Dual MBA & Master of Science in
Finance, 2–5 years, part time; dual
MBA & MSEngineering in Industrual
Engineering, 4–5, years part time;
dual MBA & Master of Health
Services Administration.

Academics

After comparing MBA programs, many students choose University of Michigan—Dearborn for the unbeatable triumvirate of "value, location, and name brand" its College of Business offers. The program is geared toward part-time students, and the combination of "evening and online MBA classes are perfect for professionals already in the workforce." Courses begin three times a year (in September, January, and May), and through the "flexible online program," students can take as many (or as few) classes as fit their schedule. Core courses cover all functional business areas and comprise more than half the 60 units of required course work; however, students with undergraduate business degrees may be eligible to waive core course work, thereby completing the program in less time. After the core, students can choose to take various electives, or complete a concentration in finance, international business, marketing, supply chain management, human resource management, or accounting. The school has long maintained a strong local reputation (not to mention, it boasts the excellent University of Michigan name). Even so, students say things are always improving: "In the last few years, the program has become increasingly relevant and well-suited for graduate studies." In particular, students note that, "Under the administration of Dean Schatzel, the transformation from the School of Management to the College of Business has improved the academic experience significantly."

Just as they praise the school's dean, UMD students are pleased to report that the administration is "very accommodating and helpful," assisting students with everything from scheduling to academic advising. With a fairly large student body, it "can be difficult to get into popular classes, but the school has offered several options to help students get the classes they need." For students who take their classes on campus, the facilities are modern, and the school "provides the variety and excellence expected of a satellite campus of a world-class university." And, like the academic offerings, facilities are consistently improving. For example, "They are adding a finance lab this year for investments class," which will help bring real-world capacities to the classroom.

In terms of faculty, "There is a wide range of professor capability at this school." Many "are clearly experts in their fields," while others are less prepared for their important posts. On the whole, however, professors are "friendly and easily approachable" and "Lectures are well-organized, and there is plenty of opportunity provided for discussion on topics of current interest." With an average of 35 students in each classroom, "Small class sizes help the interaction between students and professors, as well as among our peers." If you'd like assistance outside of class, "Most of the professors will give you their home telephone number to reach them if you can't make office hours. They are as committed to us as we are to learning."

Career and Placement

A large percentage of UMD students are already working full-time, and many receive tuition assistance from their employers. For those who are looking for a new job (or to make a career change), the College of Business's Career Planning and Placement Office assists graduate students with their job and internship search through resume critiques, online job and internship boards, and career fairs. On the Career Planning and Placement Office's website, students can get information about upcoming events and workshops, or peruse current job listings and links to local employment assistance. Students are often surprised to find that their professors can be a great way to get a foot in the door of the local job market. A current student attests, "They are quite supportive even when you're finished with their class—it is not uncommon for professors to help with networking or career searches."

Student Life and Environment

On this urban campus, most students are "working professionals" with a "few full-time students" added to the mix. While many are busy with work and family, this professional group takes their studies seriously, and most students are "eager to participate in class and highly focused on their academics." "Being a commuter university, there is not much networking outside of class," and clubs and extracurricular activities are limited. Still, some part-time students say they use "the library, health club, and all of the business offices" while others get together for "study groups outside of class time to prepare for exams or group projects."

For those who'd like a bit more camaraderie, the "COB has worked hard to improve student life," and many full-time MBA candidates say, "I have made friends that I expect to have the rest of my life." In addition, the larger university is home to over 8,500 students. There, "You will always find clubs sponsoring and advertising activities to try and get other students engaged." Campus facilities get good reviews, and recently, "A new food court and study lounge was added" to the business school area. "Research and technologies are top notch and on par with other major business schools," and "The College of Business has its own computer lab" with Internet access and printers.

Admissions

Applications to University of Michigan—Dearborn are accepted on a rolling basis; however, students are encouraged to apply by the priority deadline. Usually, once the university has received all of a student's application materials, an admissions decision will be made in just a few days. Most accepted applicants have a GMAT score in the mid-500s and an undergraduate GPA of 3.2 on a 4.0 scale. At least two years of full-time work experience is required before entering the program.

FINANCIAL FACTS
Cost of books	$1,200
Average grant	$1,500

ADMISSIONS
Admissions Selectivity Rating	82
# of applications received	100
% applicants accepted	58
% acceptees attending	60
Average GMAT	557
Average GPA	3.35
TOEFL required of international students	Yes
Minimum TOEFL (paper/computer)	560/220
Application fee	$60
International application fee	$60
Regular application deadline	8/1
Early decision program?	No
Deferment available	Yes
Maximum length of deferment	1 year
Transfer students accepted	Yes
Transfer application policy: For courses equivalent to our MBA core courses, waivers will be given. Up to six credits of transfer may also be given for other MBA courses.	
Non-fall admissions	Yes
Need-blind admissions	Yes

UNIVERSITY OF MICHIGAN—FLINT
SCHOOL OF MANAGEMENT

GENERAL INFORMATION

Type of school	Public
Academic calendar	Semester

SURVEY SAYS...

Cutting-edge classes
Solid preparation in:
Operations

STUDENTS

Enrollment of parent institution	7,260
Enrollment of MBA Program	187
% male/female	61/39
% out-of-state	7
% part-time	90
% international	11
Average age at entry	32

ACADEMICS

Academic Experience Rating	85
Student/faculty ratio	13:1
Profs interesting rating	87
Profs accessible rating	80
% female faculty	7
% minority faculty	14

Joint Degrees

MSMO/MBA

Prominent Alumni

J. Donald Sheets II, VP and CFO, President America Area, Dow Corning Corp., MBA SOM; Robert J. Joubran, COO & Treasurer, Plantinum Equity LLC, BBA SOM; Michelle Goff, Senior VP & CFO, R. L. Polk & Co., BBA SOM; Cristin Reid English, President, Corp. Operations, Capital Bank Limited, MBA SOM; Kimberly K. Horn, President 7 CEO, Priority Health, BBA SOM.

Academics

With a friendly faculty and staff, "small class sizes," and a pretty riverfront campus, the University of Michigan—Flint offers a "small town feel in a large university." For Flint area residents, this friendly, convenient, and "flexible" MBA program offers a "great schedule to accommodate working people." All classes in the Traditional MBA program are held in the evenings and the school's administration makes it "very easy for working students to register and get things done." In addition to the traditional program, the school offers the innovative *NetPlus!* MBA, which combines both online and in-class content. The major advantage to *NetPlus!* is that, because classes only meet once every six weeks, it is possible to attend the program even if you don't live in Flint. Therefore, *Netplus!* "Students are from the top companies from across the nation. Some of the students come from as far as California on residency days." With intensive, 12-week terms, the *NetPlus!* program maintains a "fast pace," and students must be self-disciplined to keep up with coursework. In most cases, however, students like the independent nature of the program, saying, "Professors give us what is important and let us learn on our own." A "very progressive school," technology is well-employed and remote course delivery is smooth. However, some students dream of even more efficient technological systems; says one, "I'd like them to switch to electronic text books when they can. I'd also like to have lectures in podcasts."

No matter which program format you choose, the teaching staff is "very accomplished, published, respected. They are young and understand students, current events and make the classes interesting." Be aware, however, that, "MBA classes are tough." Depending on the professor, University of Michigan—Flint's grading policies can be intimidating, and "there is a lot of work to be completed for each class." A current student details, "The work is hard, but you do learn. To get the good grade (A), you have to earn it and not just show up for class." Fortunately, you are likely to be surprised by the friendliness and responsiveness of the University of Michigan—Flint faculty and staff. Online or in-person, "The professors are all very responsive and knowledgeable." A student adds, "The professors are well-educated, and willing to work with students on a more personal level to ensure the highest degree of learning." A *Netplus!* student adds, "I'm always surprised at how quickly professors respond to emails and queries." On top of that, "The administration is very accommodating and attentive—they are very proactive. They make it very easy for working students to register and get things done." Whenever a doubt arises, administration and staff are "Very quick returning questions, and they give a very good outline of your expected program."

ADMISSIONS CONTACT: D. NICOL TAYLOR-VARGO, MBA, MBA PROGRAM DIRECTOR
ADDRESS: SCHOOL OF MANAGEMENT, UM-FLINT, 3139 WILLIAM S. WHITE BLDG, 303 EAST
KEARSLEY STREET FLINT, MI 48502-1950 • PHONE: 810-762-3163 • FAX: 810-237-6685
E-MAIL: UMFlintMBA1@UMICH.EDU • WEBSITE: MBA.UMFLINT.EDU

FINANCIAL FACTS

Annual tuition	$12,650
Fees	$368
Cost of books	$1,000
Room & board (on-campus)	$7,900
Average award package	$14,572
Average grant	$1,777

ADMISSIONS

Admissions Selectivity Rating	83
# of applications received	155
% applicants accepted	26
% acceptees attending	154
Average GMAT	527
Range of GMAT	470–593
Average GPA	3.24
TOEFL required of international students	Yes
Minimum TOEFL (paper/computer)	550/213
Application fee	$55
International application fee	$55
Early decision program?	No
Deferment available	Yes
Maximum length of deferment	1 year
Transfer students accepted	Yes
Transfer application policy: AACSB accredited, B or better, grad level, 9 credit hours only, not part of any other degree program	
Non-fall admissions	Yes
Need-blind admissions	Yes

Career and Placement

Many students choose Flint because of the "reputable U of M name," which carries a great deal of weight with employers in Michigan and beyond. The Academic Advising & Career Center (AACC) at University of Michigan—Flint offers career guidance and counseling to undergraduates, alumni, and graduate students. The center hosts career fairs and offers advising services—though these services cater principally to undergraduates. Not surprisingly, MBA students say "the biggest area my school needs to improve in is on-campus recruiting by employers." Others suggest that, "UM—Flint MBA students should be allowed to attend UM—Ann Arbor recruitment events." However, the MBA program is geared towards working professionals, and therefore, many students aren't actively looking for a new job after graduation. In fact, most UM—Flint MBA candidates say their "employers are paying tuition" to the program. Almost seventy percent of recent Flint graduates work in general management fields.

Student Life and Environment

At UM–Flint, "The typical student is a tested and tried worker who is looking to further their career or secure their position." Many join the MBA program from business, engineering, and health care fields, though students have "diverse backgrounds" and are constantly "learning from each other's experiences." While students don't necessarily see each other on a regular basis, the curriculum encourages collaboration and exchange. A *Netplus!* student shares, "Most of my group project experiences have been great. Since we only see each other once every six weeks, I always look forward to seeing everyone."

Social activities at University of Michigan—Flint are focused on undergraduate students, but the campus is still welcoming to graduate students. A current student agrees, "My school life is mostly online interaction with students; however, I regularly work out in the recreation center which is provided free to students and helps to manage stress of the work/school load. Additionally, I enjoy free activities hosted by the school, such as movie night at the local theatre." On campus, "The facilities are well cared for and the riverfront location is gorgeous. The building which houses the business school is the newest academic building." A boon to commuters, there is also "lots of parking." In the surrounding area, hometown Flint offers "a wonderful art community, top flight cultural activities with The Whiting and the Flint Institute of Art, and the downtown area is very safe."

Admissions

Prospective students are considered for admission to University of Michigan—Flint based on their undergraduate GPA, GMAT scores, and work experience. Students must also submit three recommendations and a personal statement along with the application materials. The Traditional MBA program starts classes twice a year, whereas the *NetPlus!* MBA enrolls students four times a year.

EMPLOYMENT PROFILE			
Career Rating	70	Grads Employed by Function% Avg. Salary	
		Management	68 NR

UNIVERSITY OF MISSISSIPPI
SCHOOL OF BUSINESS ADMINISTRATION

GENERAL INFORMATION
Type of school   Public
Academic calendar   Semester

SURVEY SAYS...
Good social scene
Cutting-edge classes
Solid preparation in:
Finance
Accounting
Teamwork
Doing business in a global economy

STUDENTS
Enrollment of parent institution	14,000
Enrollment of MBA Program	59
% male/female	72/28
% out-of-state	37
% part-time	22
% international	6
Average age at entry	26
Average years work experience at entry	2

ACADEMICS
Academic Experience Rating	**68**
Student/faculty ratio	30:1
Profs interesting rating	82
Profs accessible rating	70
% female faculty	18

Academics

The University of Mississippi—known affectionately as "Ole Miss" to its many students and supporters—offers students two MBA options. The first is an intensive, one-year full-time MBA, which does not require post-undergraduate professional experience for admission; the other is the two-year professional MBA for working adults, which gives strong preference to students with at least two years of post-undergraduate business-related employment.

Ole Miss' one-year program runs 11 months, commencing in July and ending in May. The curriculum consists of 13 prescribed courses, taught cohort-style with an emphasis on "the integration of subjects into real business applications." Students warn that the program is intense. As one explains, "Overall, you have to be very serious if you want to be in a one-year program. Don't let the kind recruiters fool you: You are in for hell if you are not 100 percent committed...There is hardly any time to breathe. This is only for the extremely serious." Instructors "expect a lot out of us," and even "The administration is concerned with our performance and takes measures to continually monitor our progression through the classes. Overall, the academic experience is rigorous." One student concurs, "The program could use more breaks. Or, they could lengthen it to ease the stress."

The part-time MBA at Ole Miss is more flexible, using "alternate methods of delivering course content" that include interactive CD-ROMs, DVDs, videoconferencing, conference calls, and Internet learning. Some on-campus sessions are required, but most of the program can be completed remotely. In both the part-time and full-time program, "Professors all have business backgrounds and have been tenured for a long time, or they have short academic careers and long, successful business careers in the fields they teach." Instructors typically employ "real-world examples and tie your education from them into your own work experiences. Dictation seldom happens. Discussion of the assigned readings is the primary classroom focus."

Career and Placement

Ole Miss MBAs receive career support from the university's Career Center. Students report that many of the best career opportunities come via the alumni network, which is "very supportive. The Ole Miss 'brand' is well-respected in the Southeast." Employers that recruit on the Ole Miss campus include Axciom, Allstate, Bancorp South, FedEx, Harrah's, IBM, International Paper, Regions Bank, and the Tennessee Valley Authority.

Student Life and Environment

The swift pace of the full-time MBA program means that many students "study so much that it is hard to have a life. But when there are small breaks, the potential to have a great time is definitely there." First and foremost, is Ole Miss football and the requisite tailgate parties beforehand, but there's much more to the social scene than sports. The school "offers a wide variety of activities socially and academically that you can become involved in. This place has a lot of great traditions." Students appreciate the Ole Miss grounds, which one describes as "a walking campus that promotes and produces beautiful people!"

ADMISSIONS CONTACT: DR. JOHN HOLLEMAN, DIRECTOR OF MBA ADMINSTRATRION
ADDRESS: 319 CONNER HALL UNIVERSITY, MS 38677
PHONE: 662-915-5483 • FAX: 662-915-7968
E-MAIL: JHOLLEMAN@BUS.OLEMISS.EDU • WEBSITE: WWW.OLEMISSBUSINESS.COM

FINANCIAL FACTS

Annual tuition (in-state/ out-of-state)	$7,000/$13,000
Cost of books	$5,000
Room & board (on/off-campus)	$8,800/$10,000
Average grant	$1,469

ADMISSIONS

Admissions Selectivity Rating	**81**
# of applications received	189
% applicants accepted	54
% acceptees attending	45
Average GMAT	562
Range of GMAT	500–610
Average GPA	3.65
TOEFL required of international students	Yes
Minimum TOEFL (computer)	600
Application fee	$25
Regular application deadline	3/1
Regular notification	4/1
Early decision program?	No
Deferment available	No
Transfer students accepted	No
Non-fall admissions	Yes
Need-blind admissions	Yes

Hometown Oxford is a small, Southern college town distinguished by the university and the residences of several famous writers, including John Grisham. The town has become a travel destination for many, not only for Ole Miss sporting events but also for festivals such as the Double Decker Arts Festival and conferences as the Faulkner & Yoknapatawpha Conference (named after the author William Faulkner, who made his home in Oxford, and the fictional county in which much of his work is set). The city of Memphis is just 70 miles to the north.

Full-timers at Ole Miss tend to be "very young. The majority are 22 years old. Some have had internships, but none have actually worked. It's very difficult to have a discussion about business if you've never been involved in one. The few students with work experience talk 95 percent of the time." The student community is close. As one student explains, "One thing about going through an MBA 'boot camp' like this is that you come together very quickly. Because you're all suffering together, people are very friendly and quick to help you out."

Admissions

All applicants to the full-time MBA program at Ole Miss must provide an official transcript of undergraduate work showing a minimum 3.0 GPA for the final 60 semesters hours of academic work; an official GMAT score report (the school lists 550 as the cut-off for "acceptable" scores); two letters of recommendation; and a 400-word personal statement of purpose. Students who have not completed prerequisite course work in undergraduate business disciplines will be required to complete such courses successfully before commencing work on their graduate degrees. International students must meet all of the above requirements and submit TOEFL scores (minimum acceptable score is 600). Applicants to the professional MBA program "with two or more years of post-baccalaureate degree professional work experience" receive "particular consideration" from the Admissions Committee. The professional MBA program is "very competitive."

EMPLOYMENT PROFILE				
Career Rating	**79**	**Grads Employed by Function**	**%**	**Avg. Salary**
Average base starting salary	$51,500	Marketing	15	NR
		Consulting	10	NR
		Management	5	NR
		Finance	15	NR
		MIS	20	NR
		Entrepreneurship	5	NR
		Internet	25	NR

University of Missouri—Columbia
Robert J. Trulaske, Sr. College of Business

GENERAL INFORMATION
Type of school	Public
Academic calendar	Semester

SURVEY SAYS...
Students love Columbia, MO
Good social scene
Happy students
Solid preparation in:
Teamwork
Communication/interpersonal skills

STUDENTS
Enrollment of parent institution	30,200
Enrollment of MBA Program	214
% male/female	65/35
% out-of-state	36
% part-time	5
% minorities	5
% international	24
Average age at entry	25
Average years work experience at entry	2

ACADEMICS
Academic Experience Rating	**89**
Student/faculty ratio	9:1
Profs interesting rating	87
Profs accessible rating	81
% female faculty	22
% minority faculty	22

Joint Degrees
MBA/Bachelors in Industrial Engineering (1 year); MBA/MS in Industrial Engineering (3 years); MBA/JD (4 years); MBA/Master of Health Administration (3 years)

Academics

"Low tuition costs" and "a good ranking and reputation in the region" attract future MBAs to the Trulaske College of Business at the University of Missouri (MU) in Columbia. The Crosby MBA program—named after Gordon E. Crosby, Jr., the former USLIFE CEO who made a $10 million donation to the program in 2002—features "a capable faculty, good program design, and excellent value" for a student body that includes a substantial number of "straight-through undergraduates." It's "the best in the area," students assure us.

The recently redesigned curriculum at MU is streamlined to allow students with solid academic backgrounds in business to graduate in as little as 12 months. All students begin the program by formulating an Individual Program of Study in consultation with their advisor. A modular calendar format allows "for intense study and more choices," according to the school; two team-based consulting projects (students describe them as "good research projects") are part of every student's experience here. Students may pursue concentrations in marketing analytics, finance, marketing, or management, or they may take a general degree in business. "Management and marketing are quite good," a student advises. The school offers dual degree options in law, health services, and industrial engineering, as well as certificate programs in nonprofit management and European Union studies. Students may fashion certificate programs of their own in consultation with the faculty.

Students see much to appreciate here. Professors have "extensive knowledge" and offer "one-to-one interaction. They can be contacted any time by email or appointments." "They continually challenge us with relevant case material and, thanks to the economic environment, have given us a lot of insight into problem identification and solutions," one student reports. The administration provides "a high level of support" that demonstrates "good practices" and "great service." And, students here love the direction in which the program is headed: "The Crosby MBA program has been improving for years, and its future looks bright," one MBA observes.

Career and Placement

The Crosby MBA Program Career Services dedicates two staff members exclusively to MBAs. The office provides a broad range of services, including counseling, a mentoring program, on-campus interviews and company presentations, workshops in job search skills, e-recruiting, and career fairs. Students give the office mixed reviews. One reports, "The Career Services Department is well-organized and very visible." Others, however, complain, "Not very many companies from outside the Midwest visit us during recruiting fairs." In 2008, one-third of graduating MBAs found jobs in finance and accounting (average starting salary $56,600). Nearly as many were placed in consulting positions ($56,500). Top employers of Crosby MBAs include Marketsphere, Sprint, Hallmark Cards, Inc., Protiviti, Boeing, Burlington Northern Santa Fe Railway (BNSF), Chevron Corporation, Deloitte, Edward Jones, Cerner, Express Scripts, Junction Solutions, Lord, AT&T, Abbett & Co., Monsanto, PricewaterhouseCoopers, and the U.S. Patent Office.

ADMISSIONS CONTACT: BARBARA SCHNEIDER, DIRECTOR OF RECRUITING AND ADMISSIONS
ADDRESS: 213 CORNELL HALL COLUMBIA, MO 65211
PHONE: 573-882-2750 • FAX: 573-882-6838
E-MAIL: MBA@MISSOURI.EDU • WEBSITE: MBA.MISSOURI.EDU

Student Life and Environment

Roughly half the Crosby MBA program is populated "by "straight-through undergraduates with little or no real-world experience." They "tend to have stronger verbal than analytical skills" and are "competitive in the classroom but not very ambitious to go to business competitions etc. outside the university if not sponsored." There is some variation within the student body, of course; "50 percent have one or more years work experience. "Those with experience are much nicer and more humble," one student opines. About 30 percent of the student body is made up of international students.

The Crosby MBA program is housed in a "fantastic" new building with "excellent facilities." Full-time students report numerous "cultural activities, Happy Hours, social gatherings, sporting events, and social activities" to keep them busy when they aren't preoccupied with their studies or internships. The campus also features an "amazing" recreation center. The campus itself "is beautiful and friendly." Part-time students are generally too busy with work and family obligations to get deeply involved in campus life.

Hometown Columbia is "a small, friendly town" where "living expenses are affordable." With "great restaurants," "a lot to do" in town, and a location "close to big cities," Columbia is "really cool," a "great place to live and go to school." The university is the city's biggest employer. The insurance and health care industries also have a significant presence here.

Admissions

Crosby admissions officers consider the quality of applicants' undergraduate work, as reflected in the official transcripts they submit; GMAT scores; prior work experience, if any; and evidence of leadership skills. International students whose primary language is not English must submit an official TOEFL or IELTS score report. Minimum score requirements: 550, paper-based TOEFL; 213, computer-based TOEFL; 79–80, Internet-based TOEFL; or 5.5, IELTS. All applicants must submit two applications, one to the MBA program and another to the Graduate School of the University of Missouri Columbia. Applicants to the Crosby MBA program may apply for admission for fall, spring, or summer entry. The school encourages all students—and especially international students—to apply early in the semester preceding their desired entry date.

FINANCIAL FACTS

Annual tuition (in-state/ out-of-state)	$10,000/$24,174
Fees	$1,092
Cost of books	$1,000
Room & board (off-campus)	$8,590
% of students receiving aid	58
% of first-year students receiving aid	75
% of students receiving grants	58
Average award package	$17,658
Average grant	$5,327
Average student loan debt	$7,815

ADMISSIONS

Admissions Selectivity Rating	95
# of applications received	521
% applicants accepted	32
% acceptees attending	64
Average GMAT	648
Range of GMAT	620–670
Average GPA	3.53
TOEFL required of international students	Yes
Minimum TOEFL (paper/computer)	550/213
Application fee.	$45
International application fee	$60
Regular notification	
Round 2:	1/1 / 3/1
Round 3:	2/15 / 4/15
Round 4:	4/1 / 5/15
Early decision program?	Yes
ED Deadline/Notification	
Deferment available	Yes
Maximum length of deferment	2 semesters
Transfer students accepted	Yes
Transfer application policy: Students may waive up to 27 credit hours and may transfer 6 credit hours from an AACSB MBA program.	
Non-fall admissions	Yes
Need-blind admissions	Yes

EMPLOYMENT PROFILE

Career Rating	**88**	**Grads Employed by Function% Avg. Salary**	
Percent employed at graduation	45	Marketing	12 $47,000
Percent employed 3 months after graduation	78	Operations	10 $61,580
		Consulting	24 $49,618
Average base starting salary	$52,463	Management	8 $63,500
Primary Source of Full-time Job Acceptances		Finance	32 $51,583
School-facilitated activities	39 (78%)	HR	2 $40,000
Graduate-facilitated activities	11 (22%)	**Top 5 Employers Hiring Grads**	
		Cerner (7), Boeing (3), AT&T (2), Edward Jones (2), Federal Reserve—Kansas City (2)	

UNIVERSITY OF MISSOURI—KANSAS CITY

HENRY W. BLOCH SCHOOL OF BUSINESS AND PUBLIC ADMINISTRATION

GENERAL INFORMATION

Type of school	Public
Academic calendar	Semester

SURVEY SAYS...

Solid preparation in:
Teamwork
Communication/interpersonal skills
Presentation skills

STUDENTS

Enrollment of parent institution	14,818
Enrollment of MBA Program	349
% part-time	100
Average age at entry	29
Average years work experience at entry	3

ACADEMICS

Academic Experience Rating	**77**
Student/faculty ratio	14:1
Profs interesting rating	83
Profs accessible rating	69
% female faculty	31
% minority faculty	9

Joint Degrees

JD/MBA (81 law school credit hours + 30–48 MBA credit hours); JD/MPA (81 law school credit hours + 36–39 MPA credit hours).

Prominent Alumni

Mark Funkhouser, Mayor, Kansas City, Missouri; Terry Dunn, President and CEO, Dunn Industries, Inc.; Bob Regnier, President, Bank of Blue Valley; Tom Holcom, President, Pioneer Financial Services, Inc.; Steven A. Bernstein, President & COO, Bernstein Rein Advertising.

Academics

The combination of academic excellence and low in-state tuition make University of Missouri—Kansas City an unbeatable deal for Missouri residents. One of the "best business schools in the area, as well as one of the most affordable," UMKC operates an EMBA and a part-time MBA program for early-career and mid-level professionals. The curriculum begins with a series of core courses in marketing, management, finance, and supply chain and operations management (which can be waived based on a student's previous academic preparation), after which students complete their credit requirements through a concentration in entrepreneurship, finance, general management, international business, leadership, management information systems, marketing, or supply chain and operations management. Of particular note, the school's "Entrepreneurial program is one of the best in the country," managed by "well-respected" and "outstanding" professors. While the MBA program "prepares students for their future careers thoroughly," many say that, "UMKC could also add a little more structure to their program. Students can take any courses they want and only choose an emphasis area where they have to take 12 hours."

In addition to the traditional part-time program, UMKC offers an Executive MBA for experienced business leaders, defined by a "curriculum with [a] combined focus on business, leadership, policy and innovation designed for executive professionals." In the EMBA program, "classes meet three full days during each month, 8 to 5"—a convenient arrangement for students with demanding professional schedules. No matter which program you choose, UMKC professors are competent and caring. A student shares, "The professors I have had last fall and this semester at UMKC have all been great. They have a lot of real-world career experience and make themselves available for questions or concerns outside of class." In addition to the full-time faculty, "Another value-add is the community business leaders that are brought in as guest speakers who relate relevant and current real-world business leadership experiences." At the same time, there is no uniform pedagogic approach, and "The professors range from easy to challenging." A current student reports, "I have had professors that use a lot of real world examples, which is helpful, but do not focus on theory at all. Conversely, I have had professors teach all theory and not apply it to the real world much at all." By extension, students admit that classes can be hit-or-miss, and, as such, the UMKC education is really what you make it. However, for those willing to put in the effort, you will find that "tenured faculty is interested in you if you are interested in your education."

When it comes to the practical details, students remind us that UMKC is "a large university," which can lead to administrative headaches. For example, "the offices are hard to reach by phone, so you have to go in and sit and wait, sometimes for more than an hour." A current student admits, "I found enrolling at UMKC to be very frustrating." At the same time, the administrators maintain a high "level of professionalism," and most day-to-day functions are "very smooth."

Career and Placement

The Career Services Center serves at UMKC serves the entire school community. Among other services, they offer resume help, internship placements, career fairs, and campus recruiting to both undergraduate and graduate students. Many MBA candidates complain that "UMKC's Career Services Center is out of date and not in touch with job trends or needs." Fortunately, the business school recently introduced a dedicated career counselor, who has "created the Career Connection (a totally separate entity of UMKC Career Services) which focuses on companies looking to recruit from the Bloch School of

ADMISSIONS CONTACT: JENNIFER DEHAEMERS, DIRECTOR OF ADMISSIONS
ADDRESS: 5100 ROCKHILL ROAD KANSAS CITY, MO 64110
PHONE: 816-235-1111 • FAX: 816-235-5544
E-MAIL: ADMIT@UMKC.EDU • WEBSITE: WWW.BLOCH.UMKC.EDU

Business and Public Administration. Although the program is only in it's infant stages, once the economy picks back up the program will be able to execute many placements with already established relationships with local and national companies." Students in the executive MBA aren't generally looking for new positions after graduation; however, they report that their education offers a high return-on-investment at their current job.

Student Life and Environment

Many students choose UMKC for its excellent "location within Kansas City," the second-largest metropolitan area in the state of Missouri. Home to almost 15,000 students, UMKC's vibrant campus is located in the central Rockhill area. In addition to events on campus, there are plenty of cultural and recreational opportunities in the neighborhood, including several art museums and the Country Club Plaza mall.

Within the "comfortable and convenient" business school facilities, students appreciate perks like "free newspaper, TV, and accessible PCs." In addition, "Parking is accessible"—a great boon to students who commute to school every day (the great majority.) Most students are happy to visit campus for class and nothing more, saying "the part time MBA program works very well for me." Others feel "it would be nice to have more networking and social organizations within the MBA program."

Admissions

Students may begin the MBA program any semester. For students admitted to the part-time or fulltime programs, the average GMAT score is 560, and the average undergraduate GPA is 3.2. Letters of recommendation are not required; however, students must submit a one-page statement of purpose, along with their resume. For the executive MBA, students are highly experienced, with an average of 15 years professional work experience before entering the programs. EMBA students join the program from prestigious companies including Accenture, H&R Block, Great Plains Energy, JP Morgan, and the United States Army.

FINANCIAL FACTS

Annual tuition (in-state/ out-of-state)	$5,377/$13,882
Fees	$640
Cost of books	$1,180
Room & board (on/off-campus)	$9,560/$8,320
% of students receiving aid	38
% of first-year students receiving aid	80
% of students receiving loans	9
% of students receiving grants	7
Average award package	$11,595
Average grant	$6,865
Average student loan debt	$31,974

ADMISSIONS

Admissions Selectivity Rating	80
# of applications received	204
% applicants accepted	59
% acceptees attending	75
Average GMAT	560
Range of GMAT	500–620
Average GPA	3.21
TOEFL required of international students	Yes
Minimum TOEFL (paper/computer)	550/213
Application fee	$35
International application fee	$50
Regular application deadline	5/1
Early decision program?	No
Deferment available	Yes
Maximum length of deferment	1 year
Transfer students accepted	Yes
Transfer application policy: We will accept up to 6 hours of grad credit from an AACSB accredited institution.	
Non-fall admissions	Yes
Need-blind admissions	Yes

UNIVERSITY OF MISSOURI—ST. LOUIS
COLLEGE OF BUSINESS ADMINISTRATION

Academics

The University of Missouri—St. Louis is a smart choice for local professionals who want to complete an MBA without interrupting their career. "One of three AASCB-accredited schools in the St. Louis area," UMSL offers several MBA options: the traditional evening MBA, the professional MBA, and the international MBA, offered in conjunction with partner universities overseas. For students in the evening program, "convenient class schedules" make UMSL a great choice (though evening students also say, "there is a great need for online course options" to provide greater flexibility.) While classes in the evening program meet once a week, the professional MBA is a hybrid program, which combines weekend course work with web-based classes and online communication. As these options illustrate, the school's programs are principally geared toward "working professionals that attend UMSL and come to class and go home." However, the student body seems to be "shifting to younger students as they recognize the education level being received...surpasses the minimal cost to attend." On that note, USML is an excellent value. This school maintains a "good reputation in the St. Louis area for providing a good, quality business education," while also maintaining a "very affordable" tuition price.

In both the evening and professional format, the MBA at UMSL is a general program, with a core curriculum built around functional areas of business, including accounting, finance, information systems, supply chain management, and marketing (though students may also pursue an area of emphasis through elective course work.) By all accounts, the administration is very "well-organized" and the curriculum is "up-to-date on trends and technology." At the same time, some students would like to see the core courses more ably synched. In some cases, "courses are repetitive," and students feel the MBA "should encompass a more general/integrated look at business and manage[ment]." Throughout the MBA, there is an emphasis on "combining the practical knowledge with the theoretical knowledge" in the classroom. At UMSL, "The professors are almost all professionals in their field," who "teach about real-world work experience and tie current events into the curriculum." Here, talented professors "make the course work interesting by providing practical knowledge in addition to theoretical knowledge, and truly being engaged in the industry." In fact, in the rare case that a teacher doesn't excel in the classroom, they nonetheless are experts in their fields. A student remembers, "There have been a few that were poor teachers but were good technically on the subject matter." Despite their real-world credentials, faculty "all seem to teach for the love of teaching versus for the pay," and they are "readily available outside of class and are always willing to help."

Career and Placement

Most USML programs are designed for working professionals who are looking to advance in their current position, rather than find a new job. However, for those seeking a career change, the USML Office of Career Services helps undergraduate and graduate students prepare for the job search through career counseling and job preparation workshops. The Office of Career Services also connects the university with local employers through networking events and job fairs. (At recent USML job fairs, numerous prominent companies attended, including Aflac Insurance, AT&T, Bank of America, Boeing, Commerce Bank, FedEx, Maxim Healthcare Services, Mutual of Omaha, Northwestern Mutual, Sherwin-Williams, St. Luke's Hospital, Target, Walgreens, and many more.) Through Career Services, students can also post their resume online, where it can be electronically matched with recruiting companies.

ADMISSIONS CONTACT: THOMAS EYSSELL, ASSOCIATE DEAN AND DIRECTOR OF GRADUATE STUDIES
ADDRESS: ONE UNIVERSITY BOULEVARD, 250 UNIVERSITY CENTER ST. LOUIS, MO 63121-4499
PHONE: 314-516-5885 • FAX: 314-516-7202
E-MAIL: MBA@UMSL.EDU • WEBSITE: MBA.UMSL.EDU

Student Life and Environment

With a convenient evening or weekend schedule, UMSL attracts a lot of working professionals, who are "busy juggling work, school, and home responsibilities." While they have worries outside the classroom, this is a "hardworking" bunch, and "students are focused on doing well in their classes while also working a full-time job." When course work requires collaboration between classmates, students are "friendly and professional," and they "work well together in groups." By and large, "UMSL is a commuter school" and most people "are there to learn and leave."

As a part of the largest research university in the St. Louis area, UMSL has an "ethnically diverse" and active student body. As graduate business students, MBA candidates have access to numerous facilities on this 350-acre campus. For example, "The campus houses the largest Performing Arts Center in the Saint Louis Area. There are weekly and something nightly events on campus, available for free or at a discount to UMSL students." Within the business school, however, students would like the administration to "upgrade our facilities and buildings." Located in urban St. Louis, this school offers excellent access to the largest metropolitan center in Missouri. However, the campus is "set in a rough part of St. Louis," so there aren't many options for recreation or nightlife in the local area.

Admissions

The traditional (evening) MBA enrolls students three times a year, in the fall, spring, and summer terms. For the professional MBA and the international MBA, classes only start once a year, in the fall term. To apply, all programs require undergraduate transcripts, two letters of recommendation, and GMAT scores. Admission is selective, with only about 60 percent of applicants receiving an offer of admission. To be competitive, students should have a GMAT score of 500 or better, and an undergraduate GPA of at least 3.0. Promising students who fall short of these minimum standards may be considered for provisional admission.

FINANCIAL FACTS

Annual tuition (in-state/ out-of-state)	$6,316/$16,313
Fees	$1,287
Cost of books	$3,000
Room & board (on/off-campus)	$5,600/$6,180
% of students receiving aid	53
% of first-year students receiving aid	48
% of students receiving loans	32
% of students receiving grants	24
Average award package	$10,139
Average grant	$6,159
Average student loan debt	$5,933

ADMISSIONS

Admissions Selectivity Rating	72
# of applications received	106
% applicants accepted	80
% acceptees attending	71
Average GMAT	550
Range of GMAT	470–590
Average GPA	3.2
TOEFL required of international students	Yes
Minimum TOEFL (paper/computer)	550/213
Application fee	$35
International application fee	$40
Regular application deadline	7/1
Early decision program?	No
Deferment available	Yes
Maximum length of deferment	1 year
Transfer students accepted	Yes
Transfer application policy: Transcripts are evaluated for relevant course work. Maximum of nine hours of acceptable graduate credit allowed to transfer in.	
Non-fall admissions	Yes
Need-blind admissions	Yes

EMPLOYMENT PROFILE

Career Rating	79	Grads Employed by Function	%	Avg. Salary
Average base starting salary	$48,067	Consulting	17	$42,500
		Finance	50	$51,600
		Communications	16	$43,000

UNIVERSITY OF NEVADA—LAS VEGAS
COLLEGE OF BUSINESS

GENERAL INFORMATION
Type of school	Public
Academic calendar	Semesters

SURVEY SAYS...
Students love Las Vegas, NV
Good social scene
Smart classrooms

STUDENTS
Enrollment of parent institution	29,086
Enrollment of MBA Program	289
% male/female	66/33
% out-of-state	34
% part-time	30
% minorities	6
% international	11
Average age at entry	29
Average years work experience at entry	4

ACADEMICS
Academic Experience Rating	70
Student/faculty ratio	30:1
Profs interesting rating	75
Profs accessible rating	70
% female faculty	18
% minority faculty	6

Joint Degrees
MS Hotel Administration/MBA, 2.5 years; MS Management Information Systems/MBA, 2.5 years; JD/MBA 4 years full time, 5 years part time; MBA/DDM Dental Medicine.

Academics

The College of Business at the University of Nevada—Las Vegas offers both a full-time and part-time evening MBA as well as a cohort-based weekend Executive MBA program for more experienced professionals. Roughly half the students in these programs attend the college full time.

UNLV's evening MBA consists of 48 credit hours, 33 of which are devoted to core courses. Students must devote five electives to a single area in order to achieve a concentration; the college offers concentrations in finance, management information systems, service marketing, and venture management. An accelerated program is open only to evening students who score at least a 600 on the GMAT (with a score exceeding the 50th percentile in both verbal and quantitative skills) and an undergraduate business degree awarded in past years from an AACSB-accredited university. Students who meet these conditions may be allowed to waive up to six of the ten required core courses.

The 18-month Executive MBA program offers a general course of study; in order to preserve the program's cohort-based approach to learning, all students follow the same curriculum. The program begins with a week of intensive work; afterwards, students meet every Friday and Saturday from 8:30 A.M. to 5:30 P.M. Applicants to the program must have at least seven years of professional experience, at least three of which have been spent in "a key decision-making role."

UNLV also offers combined-degree programs in hotel administration, dental medicine, management information system and a JD/MBA. Students point out that the "hotel concentration feeds off the Las Vegas resort market."

Career and Placement

The UNLV College of Business Career Services Center serves only graduate students in business. According to the College's website, the office seeks to help students define career goals, develop a career plan, market themselves, develop job-search skills, sharpen interviewing skills, and contact alumni. The office serves as a liaison to the local business community, maintains a number of hard-copy and online job databases, and organizes lectures and on-campus recruiting events.

Industries most likely to hire UNLV MBAs include gaming, engineering, state and federal government. A plurality of students in a recent graduating class wound up in the gaming industry, and almost everyone had found employment by graduation.

ADMISSIONS CONTACT: LISA DAVIS, MBA PROGRAMS RECRUITMENT DIRECTOR
ADDRESS: 4505 MARYLAND PARKWAY BOX 456031 LAS VEGAS, NV 89154-6031
PHONE: 702-895-3655 • FAX: 702-895-3632 • E-MAIL: COBMBA@UNLV.EDU
WEBSITE: BUSINESS.UNLV.EDU

Student Life and Environment

Las Vegas is one of America's top tourist destinations, primarily because "it's fun every single night." Those who live here know that Vegas has a lot more to offer than just gambling, over-the-top floor shows, and cheap buffets. The Las Vegas metropolitan region is home to 1.8 million residents, many of whom never set foot inside a casino. The city boasts all the amenities of a midsize metropolis and adds to the mix a perennially sunny climate and proximity to plenty of outdoor fun; Lake Mead, the Colorado River, and the Hoover Dam are all within a half-hour's drive of the city. Some fabulous skiing and hiking awaits residents on Mount Charleston, less than an hour northwest of Sin City.

UNLV does its part to keep things interesting, providing "new cultural and entertainment attractions to the community every day," according to the college's website. Prominent lecturers and touring performing artists regularly stop by this desert campus.

Admissions

Applicants to the MBA program at UNLV must submit the following to the Admissions Committee: official transcripts for all postsecondary academic work undertaken; an official score report for the GMAT; two letters of recommendation; a personal essay; and a resume. An interview is required for admission to the Executive MBA but not for MBA graduate programs. The TOEFL is not required of students who completed degree programs conducted in English or the U.S., U.K., Australia, Canada, or New Zealand. All international applicants must provide financial certification documents.

FINANCIAL FACTS

Annual tuition	$5,748
Fees (in-state/ out-of-state)	$1,000/$15,474
Cost of books	$1,600
Room & board (on/ off-campus)	$11,000/$13,500
% of students receiving aid	30
% of students receiving loans	21
Average student loan debt	$18,178

ADMISSIONS

Admissions Selectivity Rating	**81**
# of applications received	203
% applicants accepted	55
% acceptees attending	69
Average GMAT	592
Range of GMAT	560–740
Average GPA	3.28
TOEFL required of international students	Yes
Minimum TOEFL (paper/computer)	550/213
Application fee	$60
International application fee	$75
Regular application deadline	6/1
Regular notification	7/1
Early decision program?	No
Deferment available	Yes
Maximum length of deferment	1 semester
Transfer students accepted	Yes
Transfer application policy Total of 15 credits from an AACSB accredited school.	
Non-fall admissions	Yes
Need-blind admissions	Yes

EMPLOYMENT PROFILE

Career Rating	81	Grads Employed by Function	%	Avg. Salary
Average base starting salary	$72,000	Marketing	20	$45,000
		Operations	2	$65,000
		Consulting	3	$60,000
		Management	10	$70,000
		Finance	40	$52,000
		HR	2	$50,000
		MIS	3	$50,000

UNIVERSITY OF NEVADA—RENO
COLLEGE OF BUSINESS ADMINSTRATION

GENERAL INFORMATION
Type of school   Public
Academic calendar   Semester

SURVEY SAYS...
Solid preparation in:
General management
Doing business in a global economy

STUDENTS
Enrollment of parent
     institution   16,862
Enrollment of MBA Program   195
% part-time   100
Average age at entry   30
Average years work experience
     at entry   5

ACADEMICS
Academic Experience Rating   81
Student/faculty ratio   28:1
Profs interesting rating   88
Profs accessible rating   84
% female faculty   24
% minority faculty   20

Academics

The University of Nevada—Reno's College of Business offers "a challenging and well-rounded" MBA program that "prepares business students to take on a myriad of business functions," MBAs at this predominantly part-time program tell us. UNR gears its program toward part timers through "class times convenient for those of us working full time" and a curriculum "focused on working professionals making the move to the next level." High tech, distribution, hospitality, tourism, and gambling industries dominate western Nevada's business landscape, and UNR's business school curriculum takes note, offering specializations in accounting, finance, gaming management, information technology, and supply chain management.

All MBA students at UNR are required to follow a core curriculum intended to provide them with a foundation in statistics, operations, marketing, economics, management, and finance; the core curriculum takes up roughly half the credits required for the degree. Students must also take classes in managing computer-based systems and understanding changing business environments, and must choose courses from several other areas of business before moving into their area of specialization. Specialized classes make up about one quarter of the credits required for the degree.

Students praise the program's approach, which "groups students with real-word people (not academics) who can give us experiences, ideas etc." "A lot of the work" here "is case study and team-oriented," helping students build important soft skills and analytical acuity. The presence of "high-end technology" is another boon to the program. Best of all, however, is a faculty that is "extremely knowledgeable in their fields and also understand[s] that most of us work full-time jobs while going to school." Instruction is supplemented by "retired executives who drive down from Lake Tahoe to guest lecture," a fringe benefit of the school's location "in an area that is world-renowned for its ski resorts and beauty." The "condensed and accelerated" academic calendar here "helps us make the most of our time. It is a quite rigorous but worthwhile program."

Career and Placement

While some students comment that "the Career Center needs to be more visible and active," others take advantage of career fairs, recruiting appointments, and networking among fellow students to find jobs. "It is certainly [a] very...helpful source of finding challenging opportunities, even in this period of recession" one student reports, adding "I am also confident that new initiatives...in improving professional connections will give the Career Center a competitive edge." The Career Connections Center does offer a variety of workshops targeted to the general university population on topics such as resume writing, effective networking, and developing interviewing skills in which MBA student may participate.

Reno MBAs have been recruited by the following companies: Genentech, The Peppermill Casinos, Wells Fargo, the Bureau of Land Management, Coventry Health Care, and International Game Technology.

ADMISSIONS CONTACT: VICKI KRENTZ, COORDINATOR OF GRADUATE PROGRAMS
ADDRESS: MAILSTOP 0024 RENO, NV 89557
PHONE: 775-682-9140 • FAX: 775-784-1773
E-MAIL: VKRENTZ@UNR.EDU • WEBSITE: WWW.COBA.UNR.EDU/MBA

Student Life and Environment

UNR's "beautiful campus" sits on a hill north of downtown, and the original campus design (it's the oldest university in Nevada) was modeled on Thomas Jefferson's ideal of an academic village. Standout features of the campus include a state-of-the-art Knowledge Center that has students crowing. "It's one of the best libraries in the country," one student writes. Another says, "with [the] latest cool gadgets and [an] automated library system, it goes without saying that UNR has one of the best library systems in the USA." B-school facilities include a student lounge and "multiple computing centers." Some MBAs participate in "a graduate student club for business majors that meets off campus usually every other week. It is a great way to make friends, network, and socialize in general." Most, however, have little time for extracurriculars, as they are juggling full-time careers along with their academic responsibilities. Students describe their campus as "a welcoming environment that is determined to have you succeed in academia as well as life!"

UNR's MBA program "has a diverse student body in background, interests, and ambitions." One student writes, "I think the diversity of the class is the key component in UNR's graduate program. I got to know a lot about construction, accounting and gaming through my peers. Most of my peers have five to 10 years of experience and I am learning something new from them every day." About one in twelve students is international; the program's student body includes representatives from Brazil, China, India, Iran, Kenya, Poland, Russia, and Turkey.

Admissions

Two or more years of work experience, a minimum GPA of 2.75 on a 4.0 scale, and a GMAT score of at least 500 are required for admission to the College of Business at UNR. A resume, two letters of reference, and a two- to three-page personal statement concerning background and goals are also needed. A minimum TOEFL score of 550 paper-based, 213 computer-based, or 79 iBT (or an IELTS score of at least 7.0) is required from nonnative English speakers. The average GMAT score for those admitted in 2009 was 542, the average GPA was 3.29, and the average length of work experience was five years. Slightly less than half the students admitted in 2009 majored in business at college. About one-fourth majored in engineering; another 13 percent were mathematics majors.

FINANCIAL FACTS

Room & board	
(off-campus)	$12,000
% of students receiving aid	10
% of first-year students	
receiving aid	10
% of students receiving grants	8
Average grant	$7,000

ADMISSIONS

Admissions Selectivity Rating	73
# of applications received	110
% applicants accepted	89
% acceptees attending	84
Average GMAT	542
Average GPA	3.2
TOEFL required of	
international students	Yes
Minimum TOEFL (paper)	550
Application fee	$60
International application fee	$100
Regular application deadline	3/15
Early decision program?	No
Deferment available	Yes
Maximum length	
of deferment	1 year
Transfer students accepted	Yes
Transfer application policy:	
The university's graduate school will only accept 9 transfer credits from another program.	
Non-fall admissions	Yes
Need-blind admissions	No

EMPLOYMENT PROFILE

Career Rating	85
Average base starting salary	$50,000

UNIVERSITY OF NEW HAMPSHIRE
WHITTEMORE SCHOOL OF BUSINESS AND ECONOMICS

GENERAL INFORMATION

Type of school	Public
Academic calendar	Five terms

SURVEY SAYS...
Students love Durham, NH
Solid preparation in:
General management
Teamwork
Communication/interpersonal skills
Presentation skills
Computer skills

STUDENTS

Enrollment of parent institution	14,964
Enrollment of MBA Program	206
% male/female	62/38
% out-of-state	43
% part-time	82
% minorities	10
% international	22
Average age at entry	28
Average years work experience at entry	5

ACADEMICS

Academic Experience Rating	**69**
Student/faculty ratio	5:1
Profs interesting rating	75
Profs accessible rating	78
% female faculty	5
% minority faculty	15

Joint Degrees
Current UNH seniors can apply early admission to MS Accounting program and count one graduate course towards both degree requirements.

Prominent Alumni
Dan Burnham, retired President of Raytheon, Defense; Terry Tracy, Managing Director, Citigroup; Garrett Ilg, President, Adobe Japan; David Cote, Chairman/President/CEO of Honeywell; Arthur B. Learmonth, President, Magtag Service Business Unit.

Academics

The Whittemore School of Business and Economics at the University of New Hampshire has all the bases covered. For those in a hurry to get an MBA, the school offers an intensive one-year full-time program. For young professionals looking for a leg up the corporate ladder, the school has a part-time evening program (offered on both the main campus and in Manchester) that can be completed in two to six years. And for established managers lacking that all-important sheepskin, UNH has a nineteen-month Executive MBA program that meets on alternating Fridays and Saturdays on the school's Durham campus.

Students praise Whittemore's entrepreneurial track as "one of the best in the nation," touting the school's "reputation for developing business leaders in the field of entrepreneurship and venture capital." Professors earn high marks for "their 'real world' experience" and for being "very available and friendly." Students also see the school's "desirable location (proximity to Boston)" and affordability as great assets.

Full-time students warn that the workload can be overwhelming. "The schedule is so compressed that most time is spent on completing coursework and not on understanding," one writes. Another sees an upside; "You learn about yourself through group work and intense deadlines," he explains.

Career and Placement

MBA students at UNH have their own placement service, which works in partnership with the university-at-large placement office, the University Advising and Career Center. Placement staff work with business undergraduates, graduates, and alumni to forge career strategies, identify potential employers, and navigate the recruitment process. Students tell us that the school "could definitely improve in the area of career placement." One writes, "Career placement is not a priority for the school because we already have jobs for the most part. However, "it still should be offered to us because [some of us] are looking to leave our present situations. That is why we enrolled."

Recent employers of Whittemore School graduates include BAE Systems, Coastal Forest Products, Dartmouth Hitchcock, Newmarket International, Sikorsky, Sprague Energy, State Street, ThermoFisher, Wackenhut, and Windward Petroleum. About half of UNH MBAs enter the field of marketing (avg. mean base salary, of that group $48,750).

Student Life and Environment

Whittemore's MBAs proclaim that their peers are one of the school's greatest assets. Indeed, "the students bring a diversity of work experience and perspective to class." As one student shares, "Currently, I am in classes with military budget officer, a bank CFO, a manager of a vineyard, and many other interesting individuals."Importantly, there's also a sense of camaraderie and though, "homework can be demanding, the students band together and help each other out as much as possible."

Full-timers says that, despite the "heavy workload...we still find time to be social. Half the class attends. There is strong support for UNH hockey team." For eMBAs, however, "life is not as rosy. I haven't skied once in the two years I have been enrolled because there is already not enough time to get the homework done as it is.... It would be great to partake in some of the entrepreneurial extracurriculars but there is just not enough bandwidth with the workload." Students attending the Manchester satellite campus report that "life at school is solely in the classroom."

ADMISSIONS CONTACT: CHRISTINE SHEA, ASSOCIATE DEAN, GRADUATE AND EXECUTIVE PROGRAMS
ADDRESS: 116 McCONNELL HALL, 15 ACADEMIC WAY DURHAM, NH 03824
PHONE: 603-862-1367 • FAX: 603-862-4468
E-MAIL: WSBE.GRAD@UNH.EDU • WEBSITE: WWW.MBA.UNH.EDU

Admissions

Applicants to the MBA program at UNH's Whittemore School must provide the Admissions Department with all of the following: official copies of transcripts for all post-secondary academic work; an official score report for the GMAT; three letters of reference focusing on the candidate's "strengths, weaknesses, and potential for academic and managerial success"; responses to essay questions, which the school deems a "crucial" aspect of the application; a current resume; and any evidence of leadership skills that the applicant wishes to provide. Applicants to the Executive MBA program must undergo an admissions interview. Applicants to other MBA programs may request an interview but are not required to do so. (It is, however, "strongly recommended" that applicants who have "one or more weak components in their profile" schedule an appointment.) Two years of work experience is "recommended but not required" for the full-time and part-time MBA programs; a minimum of five years of professional experience is required for the Executive MBA program. International applicants must meet all of the above requirements and must submit an official score report for the TOEFL (minimum required score: 550 paper-based test, 213 computer-based test).

Annual tuiti_ (out-of-state)	
Fees	
Cost of books	
Room & board (on/off-campus)	$9,702/$9,9_
% of students receiving aid	80
% of first-year students receiving aid	80
% of students receiving loans	47
% of students receiving grants	63
Average award package	$18,921
Average grant	$6,868
Average student loan debt	$27,664

ADMISSIONS

Admissions Selectivity Rating	**69**
# of applications received	174
% applicants accepted	87
% acceptees attending	79
Average GMAT	550
Range of GMAT	500–600
Average GPA	3.19
TOEFL required of international students	Yes
Minimum TOEFL (paper/computer)	550/213
Application fee	$60
International application fee	$60
Regular application deadline	7/1
Application Deadline/Notification	
Round 1:	1/31 / 3/15
Round 2:	4/1 / 5/15
Round 3:	6/1 / 7/15
Early decision program?	Yes
ED Deadline/Notification	4/1 / 5/15
Deferment available	Yes
Maximum length of deferment	1 year
Transfer students accepted	Yes
Transfer application policy: A maximum of 8 credits may be considered for transfer credit.	
Non-fall admissions	Yes
Need-blind admissions	Yes

FINANCIAL FACTS

(in-state)
$18,170/$29,450
$1,550
$2,500

Friendly stud...
Good social scene
Good peer network
Helpful alumni
Solid preparation in:
Teamwork

STUDENTS

Enrollment of parent institution	23,000
Enrollment of MBA Program	298
% male/female	72/28
% out-of-state	77
% part-time	0
% minorities	16
% international	22
Average age at entry	28
Average years work experience at entry	5

ACADEMICS

Academic Experience Rating	**94**
Student/faculty ratio	5:1
Profs interesting rating	88
Profs accessible rating	95
% female faculty	26
% minority faculty	1

Joint Degrees

MBA/JD, 4 years; MBA/Master of Regional Planning, 3 years; MBA/Master of Health Care Administration, 3 years; MBA/Master of Public Health, 3 years; MBA/Master of Science in Information Sciences, 3 years; MBA/Master of Public Policy, 3 years.

Academics

With its "solid academic reputation, strong leadership and teamwork focus, and case-based methodology," The University at Chapel Hill's Kenan-Flagler Business School offers the perfect balance of "sustainability, entrepreneurship and traditional business disciplines." Students across the board laud the school's "collaborative culture" which applies to everything from academics to campus life; "The students at Kenan-Flagler are focused upon the betterment of their own careers—but not at the expense of the greater good. They seem to effectively balance larger perspectives with individual needs." In addition to their Full-time MBA program, the school offers a OneMBA for Executives (catering to executives with 14-plus years of experience), as well as an MBA for Executives Weekend and Evenings programs (for business professionals with an average of 10 years experience).

The Kenan-Flager MBA begins with a rigorous core curriculum which exposes all students to the full cycle of running a business. With a "focus on teamwork, leadership, and the 'soft skills,'" and an emphasis on case studies, "core courses are taught by senior faculty" and "class sizes are appropriate for materials." The school is noted for its "strong sustainable enterprise, entrepreneurship, [and] real estate programs among other top-ranked b-schools." Those searching to stay ahead of the trend in terms of becoming the next leaders of sustainable business practices are drawn to the unique sustainable energy concentration. Other strengths include consulting, marketing, and finance. As forward-thinking as their students, the Kenan-Flagler program remains committed to innovation; twenty percent of the school's elective offerings change annually in response to new business trends. In addition, students applaud the school's "proximity to the Research Triangle Park, top-20 national ranking, [and] attractive financial package."

With its collaborative atmosphere and forward-thinking inclinations, it's no surprise that the alumni network at UNC—Chapel Hill is a huge asset to recent graduates. Says one, "I've never met any other alumni who spoke so well of their school; they all seemed to love their Chapel Hill experience in a unique way." The faculty is "first class." Professors are "extremely available. Many professors give up their weekends to meet with students to discuss cases and review the prior week's material." However, others caution that while "the core course professors are extremely good and well-respected within their fields of study," non-core professors "can be hit or miss. I have had some great non-core professors and some new professors [with whom] I feel I did not get the full benefit of the courses." The administration "does a good job incorporating overall initiatives and adapting to changing environments in business education." Furthermore, "the weather is great"—"there are beaches and mountains just a couple of hours away"—and you can't beat the school's "outstanding reputation."

Career and Placement

A "top-20 school," with a strong alumni network, "prestigious reputation," and a long arm into "recruiting firms," students at UNC Kenan-Flagler enjoy great job placement opportunities. In 2009, 71 percent of job-seeking, full-time MBA graduates had secured employment three months after graduation with a mean base salary of $93,966. Despite its impressive numbers, the career management center is "loved by some and dismissed as useless by others." Students say the CMC "could be more effective getting in touch with a diverse set of companies."

The top five employers of UNC Kenan-Flagler grads in 2009 included: Bank of America, Deloitte Consulting, Johnson & Johnson, Morgan Stanley, and Barclays. Financial Services, Pharmaceutical/Biotech/Healthcare, Consumer Products, and Consulting were the leading career sectors.

Student Life and Environment

True to their "collaborative nature," students at UNC Kenan-Flagler are "incredibly smart individuals with an amazing sense of humility and sense of awareness to the others in our class." Driven to seek out new paths in their respective fields, here is a "smart and dynamic" group of "joiners and doers" who are "unafraid to say what they think." As one MBA notes, students "are as competitive yet collaborative as any group of people that I have come across. They push me to be the best that I can be."

Beyond their drive and intelligence, students are "friendly, family-oriented, [and] people with lives outside of school work." Diversity is abundant. One student reflects, "It's a hysterical mix—in one class I've got an actress, an NFL player, two ex-military guys, two non-profiteers, and a guy with a Ph D."

The campus that UNC—Chapel Hill offers is "unbeatable," offering a "college town atmosphere" at a "top school." UNC—Chapel Hill boasts "a very social crowd that hangs out often. The small overall class size[s] allow you to know the majority of your class[mates] within the first semester and a half. Due to the close relationships of the class, everyone is willing to help out with other students' career searches and learning." In addition, "students here get heavily involved in both clubs and social activities." "The basketball team (despite having a rough year) is a highlight always."

Admissions

UNC Kenan-Flagler admits students who demonstrate leadership and organizational skills, communication ability, interpersonal skills, teamwork ability, analytic and problem-solving skills, drive and motivation, prior record of academic excellence, and strong career progression and commitment to career goals. Though no specific coursework is necessary, students must have knowledge of financial accounting, statistics, macroeconomics, and calculus.

Prominent Alumni

Hugh McColl, Former Chairman & CEO, Bank of America; Brent Callinicos, VP & Treasurer, Google, Inc.; Gary Parr, Deputy Chairman, Lazard Freres and Co.; Michele Buck, Global Chief Marketing Officer, Hershey; Donna Dean, Chief Investment Officer, Rockefeller Foundation.

FINANCIAL FACTS

Annual tuition (in-state/ out-of-state)	$20,525/$41,050
Fees	$2,899
Cost of books	$4,540
Room & board	$17,932
% of students receiving aid	70
% of first-year students receiving aid	80
% of students receiving loans	70
% of students receiving grants	65
Average award package	$45,660
Average grant	$8,975
Average student loan debt	$77,124

ADMISSIONS

Admissions Selectivity Rating	93
# of applications received	1,873
% applicants accepted	35
% acceptees attending	45
Average GMAT	677
Range of GMAT	640–710
Average GPA	3.3
TOEFL required of international students	Yes
Minimum TOEFL (paper/computer)	600/250
Application fee	$140
International application fee	$140
Regular application deadline	3/19
Regular notification	5/3
Application Deadline/Notification	
Round 1:	10/23 / 12/14
Round 2:	12/4 / 2/8
Round 3:	1/8 / 3/22
Round 4:	3/19 / 5/3
Early decision program?	Yes
ED Deadline/Notification	NR / 12/14
Deferment available	Yes
Maximum length of deferment	1 yr emergency only
Transfer students accepted	No
Non-fall admissions	No
Need-blind admissions	Yes

EMPLOYMENT PROFILE

Career Rating	95	Grads Employed by Function	% Avg. Salary
Percent employed at graduation	78	Marketing	19 $93,136
Percent employed 3 months after graduation	86	Operations	2 $86,500
		Consulting	19 $113,739
Average base starting salary	$95,647	Management	4 $88,750
Primary Source of Full-time Job Acceptances		Finance	45 $92,584
School-facilitated activities	185 (85%)	HR	3 $83,333
Graduate-facilitated activities	32 (15%)	**Top 5 Employers Hiring Grads**	

Bank of America (18), Deloitte Consulting (11), Johnson & Johnson (3), American Express (3), IBM (2)

The University of North Carolina at Charlotte
Belk College of Business

GENERAL INFORMATION
Type of school	Public
Academic calendar	Semester

SURVEY SAYS...
Students love Charlottesville, NC
Happy students
Solid preparation in:
Quantitative skills

STUDENTS
Enrollment of parent institution	23,300
% part-time	70
Average age at entry	30
Average years work experience at entry	9

ACADEMICS
Academic Experience Rating	83
Student/faculty ratio	25:1
Profs interesting rating	82
Profs accessible rating	83
% female faculty	13
% minority faculty	15

Prominent Alumni
Gene Johnson, Chairman & CEO, Fairpoint Communications; Robert Niblock, Chairman & CEO, Lowe's Home Improvement; David Hauser, CFO, Duke Energy; Robert Hall, CFO, Lowe's Home Improvement; Joe Price, CFO, Bank of America.

Academics

A "wise investment" for future business leaders, UNC Charlotte offers a selection of high-quality, affordable, flexible, and student-oriented graduate programs through the Belk College of Business. UNC Charlotte offers MBA candidates the flexibility to complete the program at their own pace. Full-time students may opt to complete the program in as little as 17 months, while working professionals may take 18 to 36 months. A student shares, "I'm even taking one course in the evenings live over the Internet this term, and I love it. The flexibility and choices for constructing your own educational experience are wonderful." Even paying for your education is super student-friendly and flexible at Belk College; students are able to "split tuition payments up throughout the semester."

While all MBA students get a thorough introduction to essential business principles, the UNC Charlotte education is greatly enriched by "the diversity of concentrations within the MBA program and its relationships within the local business community." Students praise the school's programs in supply chain management and real estate (for which the school offers a specific certificate program), as well as the strength of the finance and communications faculty. Belk also offers an MBA in Sports Marketing and Management, a unique graduate program that incorporates a full-time internship in the sports industry, as well as special electives in various sports fields.

Academic and administrative departments work hard to "accommodate business students at an individual level," and "the faculty and administrators are very accessible and show obvious concern" for each student's success. A current student writes, "I love that if I have a question about anything, from a homework problem to internship opportunities, the Belk College faculty and support staff are always available and willing to help." Academics focus on practical as well as theoretical business principles, and "most professors are or have held high-level positions in their respective fields." In the words of a student: "I haven't had a bad professor yet; although some are more eccentric than others. My overall experience has been excellent."

The curriculum is challenging and "it's generally pretty hard to get A's" at the Belk College. A current student shares, "I appreciate the fact that my classes and professors push me to think on my own instead of spoon-feeding me information that they expect to be regurgitated on quizzes or exams." Still, the MBA is manageable and "life is, for the most part, laid-back. You have to get your work done, but professors understand when work occasionally takes time away from studying."

Career and Development

Many part-time MBA candidates hope their new degree will help them move up the ladder with their current employer. To that end, Belk College is highly successful, arming graduates with a slew of new skills and professional contacts in Charlotte. Since joining the program last year, a student says, "My supervisor at my current job has commented numerous times on my development."

In addition, the Belk College offers a variety of career development services, including career counseling and career fairs, and workshops on topics like interviewing and business etiquette. The school also works its "ties to the local business community" to schedule an interesting campus speaker's series. For those looking for contacts within the local community, UNC Charlotte offers superb "networking opportunities with classmates and Charlotte professionals."

ADMISSIONS CONTACT: JEREMIAH NELSON, INTERIM DIRECTOR OF THE MBA PROGRAM
ADDRESS: 9201 UNIVERSITY CITY BOULEVARD CHARLOTTE, NC 28223-0001
PHONE: 704-687-7566 • FAX: 704-687-2809
E-MAIL: MBA@UNCC.EDU • WEBSITE: WWW.MBA.UNCC.EDU

Student Life and Environment

Three-quarters of Belk students are working professionals, who "range in age from fresh out of undergrad, to early-to-mid 40s." In particular, many Belk College students come from the banking industry; though there are "many who are from other interesting companies in the area (NASCAR, Real Estate companies, health care)." On the whole, students "bring a lot of different views and experiences into discussions" and "the diversity and quality of the student body gets better every year" at Belk College.

As you'll find at many graduate and professional programs, UNC Charlotte is "very decentralized; and most people's lives take place separately." Older students admit that, "in the evenings and weekends program, most of us with families have little time for socializing." While the hands-off attitude works for some students, many say they "would like to see more social events/functions for the younger crowd." A student writes, "Charlotte is a fun city; I'd like to share some of that fun with my classmates." In the meantime, those who'd like a little extracurricular stimulation can participate in the MBA Association, which hosts speaker series and social events.

Admissions

For admission to Belk College, students are evaluated based on their undergraduate record, GMAT scores, resume, personal essays, and three letters of recommendation. The average GMAT score for entering students currently hovers around 600. Work experience is strongly recommended, but not required.

FINANCIAL FACTS

Annual tuition (in-state/ out-of-state)	$10,000/$20,000

ADMISSIONS

Admissions Selectivity Rating	**84**
# of applications received	252
% applicants accepted	57
% acceptees attending	73
Average GMAT	597
Range of GMAT	560–620
Average GPA	3.2
TOEFL required of international students	Yes
Minimum TOEFL (paper/computer)	557/220
Application fee	$55
International application fee	$55
Application Deadline/Notification	
Round 1:	1/15 / 3/15
Round 2:	3/1 / 5/1
Early decision program?	Yes
ED Deadline/Notification	NR / 3/15
Deferment available	Yes
Maximum length of deferment	1 year
Transfer students accepted	Yes

Transfer application policy:
All students have to complete the graduate application materials and submit official test scores. With permission, it may be possible to transfer graduate level work from an AACSB-accredited university. This will be considered when the application materials are officially reviewed. At least 30 hours of graduate level coursework must be completed in residence at UNC Charlotte.

Non-fall admissions	Yes
Need-blind admissions	Yes

EMPLOYMENT PROFILE

Career Rating	**86**
Average base starting salary	$83,000

THE UNIVERSITY OF NORTH CAROLINA AT GREENSBORO
JOSEPH M. BRYAN SCHOOL OF BUSINESS AND ECONOMICS

GENERAL INFORMATION
Type of school	Public
Academic calendar	Semester

SURVEY SAYS...
Solid preparation in:
General management
Operations
Quantitative skills
Computer skills
Doing business in a global economy

STUDENTS
Enrollment of parent institution	18,433
Enrollment of MBA Program	182
% out-of-state	47
% part-time	64
% minorities	5
% international	42
Average age at entry	27
Average years work experience at entry	5

ACADEMICS
Academic Experience Rating	**78**
Student/faculty ratio	21:1
Profs interesting rating	87
Profs accessible rating	81
% female faculty	11
% minority faculty	5

Joint Degrees
MSN/MBA, 42–54 credits, 2–5 years; MS Gerontology/MBA, 57 credits, 2–5 years.

Prominent Alumni
James Kahan, Senior Executive VP, Corporate Development, AT&T; Dianne Neal, Executive VP & CFO, RJ Reynolds Tobacco Company; Steve Strader, President, Midwest District, AutoNation, Inc.; Boyd Rogers, VP & President (Supply Chain), VF Corporation; Dean Priddy, CFO and VP of Administration, RF Micro Devices.

Academics

The Bryan MBA program at The University of North Carolina—Greensboro offers a very affordable price, a great location, and a tremendous faculty. The full-time MBA program requires 48 credit hours of required coursework. "UNCG has a very flexible evening program which allows students to work during the day and attend classes at night." There's also a day program for students with a limited amount of professional experience that emphasizes practical learning experiences and includes a capstone consulting course.

Courses are taught in full, 16-week semester formats, and in addition to lectures, group projects, and case studies, students at UNCG frequently work on projects with local firms and interact with bigwigs from area industries. "The flexibility of the program structure" is outstanding and electives are very abundant. Students can specialize by pursuing a concentration in a host of areas including finance, marketing, IT, and supply chain management. Bryan's weeklong study-abroad programs in Brazil and Germany are another great perk. They allow students to tour cultural and business centers and attend roundtable discussions with business leaders and professors. If you want more substantial experience overseas, semester-long exchange programs with over 40 institutions around the world are also available.

UNCG's "efficient and accommodating" administration reportedly runs the school "very well." The MBAs here also think quite highly of their professors and the "non-tenured professionals" who teach many elective courses. "The fact that I have access to this quality of faculty at a reasonably priced school is fantastic," beams one impressed student. Outside of class, professors are "willing to help either through phone calls or through scheduled meetings."

Facilities are hit or miss. The wireless network is very good and the school's cafe "provides an excellent area to study and meet with other students." The library is certainly adequate. "The main business building is a little dated," though."

Career and Placement

UNCG has a "good reputation" in the region and career prospects are reportedly pretty bright. "The setting in Greensboro has been changing over the past few years," explains one student. "More people are moving in and more jobs are available." Career Services is "excellent" and "very proactive in providing opportunities to network with local employers." "Evaluation, coaching, and mentoring programs" are readily available. A summer internship program allows day students to gain practical experience and, perhaps more importantly, get paid. There are several on-campus recruiting events and a lot of the MBA social events include alumni, who help tremendously with networking. Also, Bryan's unique targeted recruiting service works to actively partner with local employers and promote current students for their specific needs. Companies that employ Bryan MBAs include Volvo, Lincoln Financial Group, Wachovia, BB&T, Hanes, Tyco Electronics, American Express, Deloitte, AT&T, IBM, and Moses Cone Health System.

Student Life and Environment

In the smaller day program at UNCG, students are usually "only a few years out of undergrad" and they average one or two years of work experience. Evening students are an older crowd. Their average age is 31 and they have around eight years of career experience. Students here describe themselves as "smart, driven," and "extremely motivated" "business folks who want to climb the corporate ladder." There is a large group of international students and the population as a whole comes "from various lifestyles" and "a wide array of backgrounds and disciplines." The variety of educational and working backgrounds "leads to very interesting and stimulating classroom discussions."

The first week for day students is a thorough four-day orientation. UNCG even calls it "Base Camp." Day students are "energetic" and often more "idealistic" than their peers in the evening program. They also tend to have stronger bonds with each other. "There is essentially no campus life among the students" in the evening program. For them, "life outside of school is totally separate." "Everyone just wants to go to class, get done, and go home. After already working eight hours then taking a three-hour class everyone is tired."

The surrounding midsize city of Greensboro is very affordable and it's calm enough to be "a good place for studying." If you prefer to socialize, though, Greensboro is also full of entertainment options. The downtown area boasts a good number of lively bars and restaurants and the city is part of North Carolina's Triad metropolitan region (which also includes High Point and Winston-Salem), home to 11 colleges and universities. The location provides easy access to mountain getaways, golf, and North Carolina's two largest cities, Charlotte (a major banking center) and Raleigh (the state capital).

Admissions

You have to submit transcripts, a GMAT score, three letters of recommendation, and an essay. Previous work experience is preferred but not required. International students must also submit TOEFL scores and an affidavit of financial support. UNCG states on its website that the lowest GMAT score it will accept is a 550 and the lowest grade-point average it will accept is a 3.0. Don't take that as gospel, though. At least some successful applicants fail to meet those benchmarks. It's also worth noting that fellowships, scholarships, and graduate assistantships are available to defray the already low tuition.

FINANCIAL FACTS

Annual tuition (in-state/ out-of-state)	$4,724/$16,204
Fees	$1,644
Cost of books	$1,282
Room & board (on/off-campus)	$6,836/$9,534
% of students receiving aid	32
% of first-year students receiving aid	35
% of students receiving grants	19
Average grant	$3,866

ADMISSIONS

Admissions Selectivity Rating	84
# of applications received	205
% applicants accepted	47
% acceptees attending	66
Average GMAT	572
Range of GMAT	530–620
Average GPA	3.14
TOEFL required of international students	Yes
Minimum TOEFL (paper/computer)	550/213
Application fee	$55
International application fee	$55
Regular application deadline	7/1
Early decision program?	No
Deferment available	Yes
Maximum length of deferment	1 year
Transfer students accepted	Yes
Transfer application policy: They must be in good standing at a fellow AACSB Accredited MBA Program and may transfer no more than 12 semester credit hours of approved coursework.	
Non-fall admissions	Yes
Need-blind admissions	Yes

THE UNIVERSITY OF NORTH CAROLINA AT WILMINGTON
CAMERON SCHOOL OF BUSINESS

GENERAL INFORMATION
Type of school   Public

SURVEY SAYS...
Students love Wilmington, NC
Cutting-edge classes

STUDENTS
Enrollment of parent institution	10,300
Enrollment of MBA Program	120
% male/female	61/39
% part-time	100
% minorities	3
Average age at entry	31
Average years work experience at entry	8

ACADEMICS
Academic Experience Rating	83
Profs interesting rating	82
Profs accessible rating	76

Academics

Uniting a top-notch business faculty with an intimate campus atmosphere, getting an MBA at the University of North Carolina at Wilmington's Cameron School of Business is a "warm, rewarding experience." This small public school offers several graduate business programs, including the popular Professional MBA, as well as a full-time International MBA (conferred in conjunction with partner universities overseas.) For working professionals in the PMBA program, convenience is a key factor in their decision to attend UNCW. "The campus is conveniently located in the center of Wilmington" and all classes are held in the evenings or on the weekends. The school offers a "lock-step program where all students take the same classes together," and the curriculum spans two years, with eight courses per semester. While the course load is demanding (especially for those holding down a full-time job), "classes are...manageable" and professors are friendly, accessible, and "reasonable regarding student expectations."

With a competent administrative team at the helm, "The MBA program is well-designed and run," and many students say the "caliber of professors and course material has exceeded my expectations." Group work is encouraged, and through assignments, "You to learn to work with all different types of people—just like the real work force." Among many of the school's special programs, the Learning Alliance is a 15-month course through which "students are put into groups and assigned a local company" where they study and consult on business procedures. A student elaborates on the Learning Alliance: "Rather than just writing a marketing report based on a case study, an actual marketing project will be performed where students work with local businesses on their particular marketing needs." On the flipside, students would like the curriculum to include a broader international perspective, while others would like to see more specialized course offerings, as well as "more freedom to choose classes within the program."

UNCW students are impressed with the teaching staff, describing them as "highly educated with a lot of "hands-on" work experience." Drawing from a wide range of industries, Wilmington professors range "from economics teachers who have worked at the Fed for 30 years, to management teachers who have worked for large corporations in high positions globally, to significantly published authors and highly sought-after consultants." In the classroom, they are on top of their game; "Professors of UNCW exhibit strong, experienced leadership in preparing, teaching, and guiding students through the business program." Likewise, "The administration is very service-oriented and goes out of [its] way to make student administrative obstacles easy [to overcome]." "Affordability" is the cherry on top of the cake—here, in-state tuition runs less than 50 percent the price at comparable private schools.

ADMISSIONS CONTACT: KATHY ERICKSON, GRADUATE PROGRAMS ADMINISTRATOR
ADDRESS: 601 SOUTH COLLEGE ROAD WILMINGTON, NC 28403-5920
PHONE: 910-962-3903 • FAX: 910-962-3815
E-MAIL: GRADSTUDIES@UNCW.EDU • WEBSITE: WWW.CSB.UNCW.EDU/MBA/INDEX.STM

Career and Placement

The UNCW Career Center serves both the undergraduate and graduate student community, assisting with internships, as well as full-time and part-time job placements. The Career Center organizes annual career fairs and networking events on campus, and offers an online job board and resume posting service for UNCW students. However, the business school does not have graduate-specific resources for career planning, and students say, "There is very little discussion about various fields and ways in which to apply an MBA degree." At the same time, the school does provide opportunities for networking through speaker panels, alumni events, and special events for local executives.

For students who would like to make a career change after completing their MBA, career services at UNCW can be a disappointment. A current student admits, "UNCW needs to do a better job with attracting recruiters to hire their MBA students. With top-level faculty and a top-level business education, our MBA students should be given networking and interviewing opportunities with various businesses in different fields on a regular basis." On the other hand, students point out that, "So many people's employers are paying for their MBA education, they feel it is a violation of ethics to strongly encourage us to find new jobs."

Student Life and Environment

While they come from diverse professional and educational backgrounds ("from engineers to business students"), MBA candidates at UNCW are generally "Hard-working, funny, and willing to support and help others." Competitiveness is kept to a minimum, and within cohorts, "a tight-knit bond forms between classmates." On campus, business students have access to "quiet study lounges in each building" and a "well-equipped library;" however, the classroom experience could improve with the introduction of "more technology tools." In fact, some students think, "CSB could really use a new building" altogether.

In the professional MBA program, "Most all of the students are working professionals, so they are not involved in the day-to-day campus activities." However, graduate students do have access to the facilities and resources on the greater campus, and "about 10 percent use the gym facilities and library during non-class hours." Nonetheless, the atmosphere is friendly and social, boasting "that homey feeling of a small town where everyone knows and cares about everyone else." While they may not go out every weekend, "Most of the students belong to the MBA Association, and participate in social events with each other outside of class." Even in the classroom, the feeling is laid-back; "Because of the warm climate and laid back atmosphere, I believe some students have never worn footwear besides flip flops ever."

Admissions

At UNCW, the MBA Program Committee—a group of 10 faculty members—reviews applications and makes all admissions decisions. In recent years, the average incoming student had an undergraduate GPA of 3.05 and a GMAT score of about 555 (in most cases, the school only considers applicants with a GMAT of 520 or better.) Most years, the school accepts about 75 percent of applicants annually.

FINANCIAL FACTS

Annual tuition (in-state/ out-of-state)	$4,696/$9,267

ADMISSIONS

Admissions Selectivity Rating	87
# of applications received	147
% applicants accepted	44
% acceptees attending	92
Average GMAT	555
Average GPA	3.5
TOEFL required of international students	Yes
Minimum TOEFL (paper/computer)	550/213
Application fee	$45
International application fee	$45
Regular application deadline	2/1
Early decision program?	No
Deferment available	Yes
Maximum length of deferment	1 year
Transfer students accepted	No
Non-fall admissions	Yes
Need-blind admissions	No

THE UNIVERSITY OF NORTH DAKOTA
COLLEGE OF BUSINESS AND PUBLIC ADMINISTRATION

GENERAL INFORMATION
Type of school	Public
Academic calendar	Academic

SURVEY SAYS...
Solid preparation in:
General management
Computer skills

STUDENTS
Enrollment of parent institution	12,748
Enrollment of MBA Program	88
% male/female	73/27
% out-of-state	45
% part-time	50
% minorities	18
% international	22
Average age at entry	27
Average years work experience at entry	5

ACADEMICS
Academic Experience Rating	75
Student/faculty ratio	2:1
Profs interesting rating	82
Profs accessible rating	83
% female faculty	20
% minority faculty	18

Joint Degrees
JD/MBA, 81 JD credit hours and 26 MBA credit hours, 4–8 years.
BBA/MBA, 122–123 BBA credits and 32 MBA credits, 5–7 years.

Prominent Alumni
Jason Coffel, Finance Manager; Dave Goodin, Vice Pres of Operations; Odella M. Fuqua, Assistant Dean of Finance & Information Technology; Rick Pauls, Managing Director.

Academics

With just 100 students in the graduate program, University of North Dakota is a convenient and affordable place to get an MBA, while also benefiting from an intimate, student-friendly atmosphere. Incorporating a practical perspective into classroom material, "UND is very focused on offering students the resources they need for a flourishing future." Most professors "have great experiences prior to their professorships and do an excellent job of sharing these experiences" within their students. Thanks to the low enrollment, it's easy to make contact with the school's faculty and staff, and "class sizes are small enough, allowing students to interact more openly." What's more, "the professors are always accessible and all have an open-door policy with a positive attitude when someone interrupts their research." A satisfied student shares, "I feel that a number of my professors are great mentors and will be lifelong connections." In the same vein, students say administrators are friendly, accessible, and efficient, and "academic advisors are more than happy to assist you" with questions about coursework and schedules.

Located in the middle of a large agricultural zone, the professors at UND have an understanding of both rural business and big-city business, which makes UND somewhat unique among business schools. The curriculum also focuses on business technology—a focus that is supported by the school's state-of-the-art classroom facilities, a marketing research center, and modern computer labs. The North Dakota MBA program consists of 32 credit hours, with the opportunity to focus your studies through a concentration in accounting or international business. For students enrolled in the undergraduate business program, UND allows them to begin coursework toward an MBA during their last two years of undergraduate studies. Therefore, these students have the opportunity to earn a bachelor's degree and an MBA in just five years. However, the school also goes out of its way to cater to working professionals, who have quite different scheduling, personal, and academic needs than recent graduates. In fact, convenience is central to the University of North Dakota experience, and because classes are offered during the day, in the evening, or via the distance education, they "can easily be fit into your busy schedule," no matter what you do.

Career and Placement

Career Services at University of North Dakota helps coordinate job and internship placements for the UND undergraduate and graduate community. Among other functions, the office offers career counseling and professional development workshops, an annual career fair each fall, and on-campus interview sessions throughout the spring. Some MBA students feel that the College of Business and Public Administration might improve its services by hosting "its own career fair, separate from the campus career fair," which would help MBA candidates link up with corporations specifically seeking their skill set.

After graduation, about 20 percent of MBA students take jobs in manufacturing and another 20 percent take military jobs. The third most popular career field is financial services, which attracts roughly 12 percent of graduates. The placement percentage for the entire business school (undergraduate and graduate combined) is 97.2 percent. Current UND alumni hold top positions at Coca-Cola, Bank of America, General Motors Defense, Modern Information Systems, Nodak Electric Cooperative, Legacy Consulting, and Alerus Financial ND.

ADMISSIONS CONTACT: MICHELLE GARSKE, GRADUATE ADVISOR/ACCREDITATION COORDINATOR
ADDRESS: 293 CENTENNIAL DRIVE, STOP 8098 GRAND FORKS, ND 58202
PHONE: 701-777-2397 • FAX: 701-777-2019
E-MAIL: MBA@MAIL.BUSINESS.UND.EDU • WEBSITE: BUSINESS.UND.EDU/MBA

Student Life and Environment

The largest university in the region, University of North Dakota offers a pleasant, collegiate atmosphere to a student population of 13,000 undergraduate and graduate students. While many commute, graduate business students have the option of living in the school's nice apartments or dormitories, and all graduate students enjoy access to the university's myriad facilities; in particular, the "wellness center gym facility is outstanding." Students are friendly with one another, and the "social atmosphere contributes to the great learning environment at UND." For those who'd like to participate, the MBA Student Association hosts weekly roundtable discussions and social activities. In addition, if you want to blow off steam, UND students "take pride in our hockey team" and games are well attended.

The population of Grand Forks numbers just under 700,000, which is large enough to create a substantial business and cultural community, while at the same time maintaining a more laid-back, small-town feeling. A student explains: "The life in Grand Forks is not as diversified as that in the big cities. However, we have good social events and networks with the companies around Midwest." An international student adds that North Dakota is "a safe and easygoing place where foreign students can easily concentrate on their studies and be familiar with American culture."

Admissions

For admission to the graduate business program, University of North Dakota requires a minimum undergraduate GPA of 3.0 and a minimum GMAT score of 500. Students who fail to meet the minimum admissions standards but show potential for success may be admitted on a provisional basis if their GMAT score is high enough to balance out a lower GPA, or vice versa. However, under no circumstance will a student with a GMAT score below 450 be admitted to the program. In recent years, the average GMAT score was 560.

FINANCIAL FACTS

Annual tuition (in-state/ out-of-state)	$6,912/$16,390
Fees	$553
Cost of books	$3,600
Room & board (on-campus)	$3,980
% of students receiving aid	67
% of first-year students receiving aid	24
% of students receiving loans	37
% of students receiving grants	17
Average award package	$11,149
Average grant	$4,600

ADMISSIONS

Admissions Selectivity Rating	71
# of applications received	34
% applicants accepted	88
% acceptees attending	80
Average GMAT	560
Range of GMAT	450–700
Average GPA	3.4
TOEFL required of international students	Yes
Minimum TOEFL (paper/computer)	550/213
Application fee	$35
International application fee	$35
Early decision program?	No
Deferment available	Yes
Maximum length of deferment	Up to 1 year
Transfer students accepted	Yes
Transfer application policy: Up to 9 credits of approved coursework can be transferred.	
Non-fall admissions	Yes
Need-blind admissions	Yes

UNIVERSITY OF NORTH FLORIDA
COGGIN COLLEGE OF BUSINESS

GENERAL INFORMATION
Type of school   Public

SURVEY SAYS...
Good peer network
Cutting-edge classes
Solid preparation in:
Computer skills

STUDENTS
Enrollment of parent institution	16,719
Enrollment of MBA Program	403
% male/female	61/39
% out-of-state	5
% part-time	68
% minorities	15
% international	6
Average age at entry	27

ACADEMICS
Academic Experience Rating	**83**
Student/faculty ratio	9:1
Profs interesting rating	84
Profs accessible rating	82
% female faculty	17
% minority faculty	6

Joint Degrees
Global MBA, 63 hours; Ibero-American MBA, 63 hours.

Prominent Alumni
Nathaniel R. Herring, City President of Fifth Third Bank; Anna L. Brosche, Chier Operating Officer for Ennis, Pellum & Associates; Mark Vitner, Chief Economist, Wachovia; Steve Perez, CFO, Nextran, Inc.; Donna Harper, Founder, SystemLogics.

Academics

Serving a diverse group of working professionals from the Jacksonville and North Florida region, students come to Coggin College of Business for its "excellent in-state tuition, convenience, and location." However, a Coggin education is more than just an efficient way to get a diploma in your hand. At this large college, class sizes are small and the teaching staff is knowledgeable and student-oriented. A current student says, "Professors are very committed to meeting students' needs. Overall [this] has been a very positive academic experience and [I] would enroll here again." In addition to the faculty, the "administration office is very committed to helping with school or personal issues." In particular, students point out the efforts of the school's "great president, who is looking to make the university grow."

For MBA students, UNF offers a general business degree, which can be tailored to a student's educational interests in a number of contemporary and traditional areas of concentration, including accounting, e-commerce, human resource management, finance, international business, construction management, and logistics. The school also operates a number of centers and institutes, as well as some unique curricular and extracurricular options. For example, the Osprey Financial Group is a student-managed investment fund, through which students can earn elective credits for their work researching and reporting on financial markets in support of the fund.

Coggin enrolls about 450 students in its MBA program, and 80 percent of the student body works full time while attending school. In fact, the program is specifically designed for working professionals and, to accommodate their needs, all MBA classes are taught one day a week, in the afternoon or evening. While the school caters to the working student, keep in mind that "the projects are quite time-consuming" and often require group work, so the decision to enroll should not be taken lightly. For those who can take time off from work (or are studying full time), the school also offers an excellent range of abroad programs through their partnerships with numerous universities in France, Germany, Belgium, China, Poland, and Sweden. Students may choose to participate in semester-long programs, or participate in a short-term study program at select universities.

In addition to the traditional MBA program, University of North Florida offers a unique Global MBA, in conjunction with four other international universities. This program allows students to mix traditional academics with residential experiences in the United States, China, Germany, and Poland. Global MBA participants join a cohort of about forty students, which spends a semester at a university in each of these four countries. Global MBA students add a unique dimension to the North Florida campus during their semester in Jacksonville. A new cohort starts every fall.

Career and Placement

The Career Management Center serves Coggin students and alumni, offering services like career counseling, recruiting and networking events, resume assistance, and internship programs. The center also prints individual business cards for Coggin students.

While it serves the whole university, the Career Management Center hosts a number of networking events just for Coggin students. Companies who have attended previous events include: Adams & Harper P.A., Alluvion Staffing, ATS Executive Search, Bank of North Florida, CitiGroup, Client Focused Media, COACH, CSX, Crowley, Educational Tools, Inc., EverBank, Fidelity Investments, Fidelity National Information Services, GEICO, Henry Schein, IDEAL, LBA, Liberty Mutual, Merrill Lynch, Morgan Stanley,

ADMISSIONS CONTACT: KIERSTEN JARVIS, THE GRADUATE SCHOOL COORDINATOR
ADDRESS: 1 UNF DRIVE JACKSONVILLE, FL 32224-7699
PHONE: 904-620-1360 • FAX: 904-620-1362
E-MAIL: KIERSTEN.JARVIS@UNF.EDU • WEBSITE: WWW.UNF.EDU/COGGIN

MPS/Parker&Lynch, Northwestern Mutual Financial Network, PSS World Medical, Staples, State Farm, Tensolite Company, The Suddath Companies, Total Military Management, Trailer Bridge, VyStar Credit Union, Website Pros. Inc.

Student Life and Environment

University of North Florida's flexible scheduling and contemporary programs draw "people from a variety of backgrounds and with diverse experiences." There are "not many 'traditional' full-time MBA students and those who have limited work experience." Instead, most students are "focused professionals seeking an advanced degree sprinkled with some students coming directly from the undergraduate programs." In this serious environment, group work is a pleasure, since most students "are friendly and helpful and all will do their best to pull their own weight."

Coggin is "really a commuter school," where students arrive for classes in the evening then head home in the greater North Florida region. While they don't spend much time on campus, students nonetheless note that the "university has nice facilities" and a "comely" environment. Plus, the business school maintains an appealing "small-town atmosphere," where "you tend see students and professors you know a lot around campus." In addition to curricular activities, the business school brings students together for speakers, as well as academic and social clubs such as the Student Business Advisory Council, Toastmasters, Finance and Investment Society, Economics Society, and International Business Society.

Admissions

Admission to all programs, with the exception of the GlobalMBA, is based upon a candidate's undergraduate grade point average (GPA) and GMAT score. Currently, the average GMAT score for entering students is 568. The average age of an entering MBA candidate is 27 years old, with an average of three years of work experience. Admission for the Global MBA varies slightly, and includes a full set of prerequisites in each of the following seven areas: business law, financial accounting, corporate finance, macroeconomics, microeconomics, management, and marketing.

FINANCIAL FACTS

Annual tuition (in-state/ out-of-state)	$7,634/$23,955
Cost of books	$900
Room & board (on/off-campus)	$9,982/$11,232
% of students receiving aid	58
% of first-year students receiving aid	54
% of students receiving loans	47
% of students receiving grants	28
Average award package	$14,020
Average grant	$2,203
Average student loan debt	$15,937

ADMISSIONS

Admissions Selectivity Rating	86
# of applications received	188
% applicants accepted	37
% acceptees attending	51
Average GMAT	568
Range of GMAT	530–590
Average GPA	3.19
TOEFL required of international students	Yes
Minimum TOEFL (paper/computer)	550/213
Application fee	$30
International application fee	$30
Regular application deadline	7/1
Early decision program?	No
Deferment available	Yes
Maximum length of deferment	1 semester
Transfer students accepted	Yes
Transfer application policy: On a case-by-case basis	
Non-fall admissions	Yes
Need-blind admissions	Yes

EMPLOYMENT PROFILE

Career Rating	73		
Primary Source of Full-time Job Acceptances		**Grads Employed by Function**	**% Avg. Salary**
School-facilitated activities	5 (25%)	Marketing	15 $35,100
Graduate-facilitated activities	16 (89%)	Operations	21 $49,800
		Consulting	1 $52,000
		Management	16 $40,000
		Finance	33 $44,000
		HR	2 $42,000

Top 5 Employers Hiring Grads
Deutsche Bank (7), CSX Transportation (5), KPMG (3), Deloitte (2), Ceva Logistics (3)

UNIVERSITY OF NORTHERN IOWA
COLLEGE OF BUSINESS ADMINISTRATION

GENERAL INFORMATION
Type of school	Public
Academic calendar	Trimester

SURVEY SAYS...
Solid preparation in:
Marketing
Accounting
General management
Operations

STUDENTS
Enrollment of parent institution	12,908
Enrollment of MBA Program	64
% male/female	36/64
% out-of-state	72
% part-time	84
% international	72
Average age at entry	31
Average years work experience at entry	8

ACADEMICS
Academic Experience Rating	**85**
Student/faculty ratio	25:1
Profs interesting rating	87
Profs accessible rating	82
% female faculty	17
% minority faculty	19

Prominent Alumni
Nancy Aossey, CEO, International Medical Corporation; Mark Baldwin, CEO, Iowa Laser Technology (retired); Kevin Lentz, Sr. VP, Cuna Mutual Insurance; Gary Rolling, President and CEO J-Tec Associates, Inc.; Kyle Selberg, VP Marketing, Principal Financial Group.

Academics

"Quality, speed, and cost" are among the top reasons students cite for choosing the MBA program at University of Northern Iowa's College of Business Administration. "The University of Northern Iowa offers a superior program to others in my area," one student explains. "It allows for a quick completion time while providing the business instruction I need."

The UNI MBA requires 30 hours of course work culminating in an integrative one-hour client project, which students say is "a great way to link class work and real-world business experience." A required course in cross-functional operations demonstrates the program's focus on interdisciplinary approaches; a number of one-hour electives covering international business matters evince a global approach, as do the opportunities to study in Paris, Hong Kong, and Duisburg, Germany. The curriculum also includes classes in finance, MIS, accounting, economics, marketing, statistics, and strategic planning and organizational analysis. "Accounting, finance, and strategic management are strong," one student tells us. Overall, students here see "a cutting-edge program for the changing business world" and praise the school for "adjusting to the financial changes and how that affects the business world."

Students also appreciate the school's efforts on their behalf. One writes, "UNI's motto is Students First, and the MBA program lives up to it. Most professors are truly outstanding, student-oriented, helpful and resourceful" and "have actual work experience in their fields, so they can relate to the difference of the classroom to the office." Administrators "interfere only if there is a potential conflict situation, and they are most supportive of students. They seek solutions that are both efficient and psychologically comfortable for students." Part-timers note with satisfaction that "the program caters to full-time employees by offering only night classes." As one student puts it, "From the Dean to the newest professor, everyone at the University of Northern Iowa is available and willing to help you be successful."

Career and Placement

In the Cedar Falls area, UNI is "well known for its finance and business degrees," giving graduates a step up in the local market. For extra support, the Academic Advising and Career Services Center at UNI offers workshops, resume reviews, cover letter advice, mock interviews, and Internet resources for job seekers. Recruiters visit the campus throughout the year, and the school also hosts the Fall Career Fair Day and the Spring Job and Internship Fair for job seekers. Top employers of UNI graduates include Klaussner, Loparex, Progressive, Target Distribution, US Bank, and Venture Computer Systems.

ADMISSIONS CONTACT: NANCY L. HOFFMAN, MBA PROGRAM ASSISTANT
ADDRESS: COLLEGE OF BUSINESS ADMINISTRATION, CURRIS BUSINESS BUILDING 325 CEDAR FALLS,
IA 50614-0123 • PHONE: 319-273-6243 • FAX: 319-273-6230 • E-MAIL: MBA@UNI.EDU
WEBSITE: WWW.CBA.UNI.EDU/DBWEB/PAGES/PROGRAMS/GRADUATE-BUS-ADMIN.CFM

Student Life and Environment

The UNI MBA program "is designed for working professionals, with all classes offered at night." Students here "have the chance to go to events, clubs, and the recreation center on campus," and the school even "organizes trips and entertainment activities for all students," but "most of the students here work full-time, have families and do not care much about campus activities." Undergraduates, international students, and a few domestic full-time MBAs are the primary beneficiaries of these extracurricular opportunities.

The MBA program is housed in the Curris Business Building, a $10.8 million facility that opened in 1990. Facilities include a large lecture auditorium, three computer laboratory/classrooms, and 15 seminar or lecture classrooms. Wireless Internet service is available throughout the building. The university is located in Cedar Falls, "a really cheap town and small city. Everything is close and cheap," which busy students appreciate. Top area employers include John Deere, Wheaton Franciscan Healthcare, Tyson Fresh Meats, the university, Omega Cabinet, Bertch Cabinet, GMAC Mortgage, The CBE Group, and Target Regional Distribution.

UNI's MBA program attracts "a large group of international students," the result of the school's aggressive international study and exchange programs. Students from overseas "bring some diversity and other perspective to the class," their peers tell us. The "friendly and helpful American students" (according to their international peers) are "quite diversified, from different fields and industries," except for those who "are just out of their undergraduate programs."

Admissions

Applicants to the University of Northern Iowa must submit official GMAT scores, transcripts from all colleges and universities attended, and three essays that address the applicant's professional and personal background. The Admissions Committee selects applicants based on their communication skills, demonstrated leadership potential, intellectual capability, and academic success during undergraduate and graduate work. The Admissions Committee considers each applicant's particular accomplishments individually, and admissions essays are strongly weighted in a decision. Applicants must have a bachelor's degree from an accredited university or college. In the past three years, successful applicants have submitted GMAT scores averaging 530 to 630. International applicants must demonstrate the financial means to support themselves while in the program; those whose first language is not English must submit an official TOEFL score report (minimum score 600 paper-based test, 250 computer-based test).

FINANCIAL FACTS

Annual tuition (in-state/ out-of-state)	$6,446/$14,874
Fees	$852
Cost of books	$2,000
Room & board	$6,800
% of students receiving aid	31
% of students receiving loans	62
% of students receiving grants	18

ADMISSIONS

Admissions Selectivity Rating	**86**
# of applications received	65
% applicants accepted	43
% acceptees attending	75
Average GMAT	580
Range of GMAT	530–630
Average GPA	3.1
TOEFL required of international students	Yes
Minimum TOEFL (paper/computer)	600/250
Application fee	$30
International application fee	$50
Regular application deadline	7/20
Early decision program?	No
Deferment available	Yes
Maximum length of deferment	1 year
Transfer students accepted	Yes
Transfer application policy: Students may transfer up to 10 hours of AACSB-accredited, graduate credit	
Non-fall admissions	Yes
Need-blind admissions	Yes

EMPLOYMENT PROFILE	
Career Rating	**80**
Percent employed 3 months after graduation	100

UNIVERSITY OF NOTRE DAME
MENDOZA COLLEGE OF BUSINESS

GENERAL INFORMATION

Type of school	Private
Affiliation	Roman Catholic
Academic calendar	7–week module

SURVEY SAYS...
Good social scene
Good peer network
Helpful alumni
Solid preparation in:
Communication/interpersonal skills

STUDENTS

Enrollment of parent institution	11,731
Enrollment of MBA Program	344
% male/female	76/24
% out-of-state	74
% part-time	0
% minorities	15
% international	13
Average age at entry	27
Average years work experience at entry	5

ACADEMICS

Academic Experience Rating	**97**
Student/faculty ratio	4:1
Profs interesting rating	89
Profs accessible rating	96
% female faculty	16
% minority faculty	4

Joint Degrees
JD/MBA, 4 years; Science/MBA, 5 years; Engineering/MBA, 5 years.

Prominent Alumni
James Corgel, General Mgr., ISV and Developer Relations, Software Group, IBM; Paul J. Stich, Director, Procera Networks, Inc.; Paul Reilly, President, Raymond James Financial; Scott Malpass, Vice President and CIO, University of Notre Dame; William M. Sheedy, Group President, The Americas, Visa Inc.

Academics

Students come the University of Notre Dame to become part of the "Notre Dame family," and few leave disappointed; the MBA program at the Mendoza College of Business fosters a strong sense of community that, coupled with the campus-wide school spirit, quickly makes Notre Dame feel like home. Add "outstanding professor-student interaction" and "great potential for alumni networking" and you understand why student satisfaction levels are so high here.

The Mendoza MBA program "excels at providing an overall business understanding," students tell us. The school offers a two-year full-time program that "is perfect for non-business undergraduate majors to gain a well-rounded understanding of business fundamentals," as well as a one-year program for those with exceptionally strong business backgrounds. Students say, "Ethics is a hallmark of the school and it can be seen in every course," and "The school's reputation for producing ethical graduates is more important in recent years than ever before."

Mendoza implemented a modular curriculum a few years back, and "The 2007 class was the first to complete our entire course work under the current 'module' system. The module system will allow Notre Dame MBAs to be better prepared than were previous classes. Although "There was some negative press after the transition," "now that the transition is completed, Notre Dame will move quickly [back] up the rankings." The faculty here "is top-notch." Their research, publications, work experience, and generally great personalities inspire confidence in their ability to prepare [students] for the business world."

Career and Placement

"The majority of recruiting is Midwest-based" at Notre Dame, and while some complain about the dearth of New York finance-sector recruiters, most students feel that "the Career Office does a good job of locating companies from various regions." Mendoza MBAs recognize that "our small class size hinders our ability to get a large selection of companies from each region, but they are represented." However, "The situation is greatly improving, with some bulge-bracket and many middle-market banks already recruiting on campus. This will improve over time as the school moves toward its long-term mission of improving rank."

Of course, Notre Dame's storied alumni network helps with placement. Students tell us that "the Career Development Office recently made it easier for current MBA students to get in contact with alumni. Prior to this, it was a very prolonged process that involved Career Development responding to individual student's requests for alumni contact information in their respective field." These contacts can be invaluable. As one student reports, "I went to a conference with several classmates for the weekend where we met a ND alum recruiter for a major corporation. We were invited over his house to talk and have a couple of drinks. This is what you get at Notre Dame: family. And our family is everywhere in every kind of position." No wonder students brag that "becoming a member of the alumni network is worth more than the cost of tuition."

Companies recruiting Mendoza MBAs include: Avaya Systems, DaimlerChrysler, Deloitte Touche Tohmatsu, Ernst & Young, Ford Motor Company, GE, Hewlett-Packard, Honeywell, IBM, Intel, Johnson & Johnson, Kraft Foods, PricewaterhouseCoopers, SAP, Sandler O'Neill, Sprint, Textron Financial, The Gallup Organization, Western & Southern Life, and Whirlpool.

Student Life and Environment

There's no doubt that Notre Dame is a very social campus, but the extent to which MBAs can partake in that social life depends on whether they're in their first or second year of the program. First year is "very difficult" with a massive workload. Many students "spend twice as much time on schoolwork" during their first year, and find it difficult to "juggle [classes] with career pursuits." Those who can carve out some leisure time agree that "Notre Dame has a culture that is contagious! It's not hard to keep yourself busy with a broad range of activities, whether it's class, a group meeting, intramural game, community-service event, or a football tailgate. There's never a dull moment." Football unites the campus and provides more than mere entertainment; it also "lures large corporations for networking events." Also, alumni return to campus for football games "for years after graduation and usually for life." Hometown South Bend is a small town, with only a "few good places to go out." The "students make up for it, though. We host a lot of social gatherings."

Mendoza MBA's benefit from "a strong esprit de corps" built on team projects and "an ethical foundation that is reinforced constantly so that it actually has an effect." Most are "married, with families and children." They represent "more diverse backgrounds than some of the 'big' schools back East, meaning we have folks from engineering, the public sector, and other nontraditional or non-business backgrounds. These are very sharp people who may have had the 'wrong' undergrad pedigree but are every bit as bright as those at any b-school anywhere."

Admissions

Applicants to Mendoza's two-year MBA program must provide the Admissions Department with all of the following: proof of an undergraduate degree from an accredited college or university; official transcript(s); GMAT scores; a current resume; three essays (topics provided by school); and two letters of recommendation. Transcripts and/or resume must demonstrate familiarity with basic quantitative processes and accounting methods. A background in statistics is strongly recommended. International students must also provide TOEFL scores and visa documentation. Applicants to the one-year program must present academic transcripts showing successful completion of six credit hours each of mathematics, accounting, and economics and three credit hours each of marketing and MIS. All applicants must have at least two years of meaningful work experience.

FINANCIAL FACTS

Annual tuition	$40,803
Fees	$1,775
Cost of books	$1,400
Room & board	$8,925
% of students receiving aid	86
% of first-year students receiving aid	84
% of students receiving loans	61
% of students receiving grants	70
Average award package	$40,466
Average grant	$18,550
Average student loan debt	$72,519

ADMISSIONS

Admissions Selectivity Rating	92
# of applications received	894
% applicants accepted	36
% acceptees attending	43
Average GMAT	683
Range of GMAT	650–720
Average GPA	3.3
TOEFL required of international students	Yes
Minimum TOEFL (paper/computer)	600/250
Application fee	$100
International application fee	$100
Regular application deadline	1/18
Regular notification	2/18
Application Deadline/Notification	
Round 1:	11/16 / 12/18
Round 2:	1/18 / 2/18
Round 3:	3/15 / 4/16
Round 4:	5/17 / 6/7
Early decision program?	Yes
ED Deadline/Notification	NR / 12/18
Deferment available	Yes
Maximum length of deferment	1 year
Transfer students accepted	No
Non-fall admissions	Yes
Need-blind admissions	Yes

EMPLOYMENT PROFILE

Career Rating	93	Grads Employed by Function	%	Avg. Salary
Percent employed at graduation	61	Marketing	21	$84,553
Percent employed 3 months after graduation	80	Operations	3	$76,667
		Consulting	19	$88,706
Average base starting salary	$87,849	Management	11	$91,400
Primary Source of Full-time Job Acceptances		Finance	39	$90,765
School-facilitated activities	71 (63%)	HR	2	NR
Graduate-facilitated activities	26 (23%)	MIS	2	NR
Unknown	16 (14%)	Top 5 Employers Hiring Grads		

Top 5 Employers Hiring Grads
IBM (7), General Electric (6), Whirlpool Corp. (5), Ernst & Young (4), Intel Corp. (4)

UNIVERSITY OF OKLAHOMA
MICHAEL F. PRICE COLLEGE OF BUSINESS

GENERAL INFORMATION
Type of school   Public
Academic calendar   Semester

SURVEY SAYS...
Students love Norman, OK
Smart classrooms
Solid preparation in:
Teamwork
Communication/interpersonal skills
Computer skills

STUDENTS
Enrollment of parent institution	30,591
Enrollment of MBA Program	117
% male/female	73/29
% out-of-state	22
% part-time	0
% minorities	10
% international	16
Average age at entry	24
Average years work experience at entry	2

ACADEMICS
Academic Experience Rating	82
Student/faculty ratio	9:1
Profs interesting rating	73
Profs accessible rating	71
% female faculty	13
% minority faculty	2

Joint Degrees
MBA/JD, 4–5 years; MBA/MS in MIS, 2–3 years; MBA/MAcc, 3 years; BS in IE/MBA, 5 years; BBA/MAcc, 5 years; Generic Dual (MBA and any other Masters program); length varies.

Prominent Alumni
Michael F. Price, Mutual Fund Investor; Richard Moore, President/Lazard Freres and Co.; Steve Moore, CEO/OG&E; Archie Dunham, CEO Retired/Conoco-Phillips.

Academics

The Price College of Business at the University of Oklahoma is "fittingly identified with a legendary value investor," students tell us, justifying the claim by pointing out that the program "offers small class sizes and destination internship opportunities at a low cost with numerous financial aid opportunities." That sounds like value to us, too. A Price MBA "is very affordable for students in comparison to other graduate programs" and is an especially good value for those interested in careers in the energy and banking sectors. Students describe Price's concentrations in risk management and energy management as "most sought after," with finance also drawing plenty of interest.

Price boasts "beautiful facilities," "professors who work their hardest for the students," and a "high diversity of concentration options" for a school of its size. Students may pursue the MBA either full-time (in a 16-month program) or part-time (in an evening program). Full-time students report that "a majority of our [first-year] courses take place in two-hour blocs between the hours of 9 A.M. and 1:30 P.M." while all classes after your first year are at night. "Full-time MBA students are essentially moved to part-time MBA students taking classes at night after your first three-quarters of a year. This is one huge disadvantage of such a small program."

Despite their dedication, Price professors earn mixed reviews. Some observe that the College of Business is located in "a research-based university," saying this explains why "many of the professors are not real effective teachers." One feels instruction would benefit from "a greater balance between real-world applications and textbook learning for some classes. Many of the professors seem to be fixated on tests as a method of learning and not enough on applications like cases, projects, etc." Students tell us that the problems are primarily isolated to the front end of the program. "[Intro] courses lack substance," they say, but fortunately, the teaching "gets much better as the program progresses." Students also approve of the "guest faculty and the seminars on current economic and financial challenges."

Career and Placement

At Price, the primary responsibility for career counseling and placement services falls to the MBA Student Support Center. The Center provides one-on-one mentoring, assistance with resume preparation and interviewing skills, and contacts with corporate recruiters. Students see the school's "ties to the energy industry" as a big asset and note that alumni connections in these industries are especially helpful. Finance is another strong suit. However, students warn that placement opportunities are minimal outside these areas. "The Student Support Center does very little to help students interested in marketing obtain an internship or a job, while working very hard for those with a concentration in finance," writes one marketing student. Some critics concede that "job placements were good here until the recession hit the economy." On the bright side, "there is a strong focus on finding internships for first-year students," although "the school expects students to do their fair share of the internship search as well."

Employers who hire Price MBAs include: ExxonMobil, Bank of Oklahoma, OGE, RiskMetrics, ConocoPhillips Company, Fujitsu, SBC, American Airlines, Devon Energy, Schlumberger, Shell, KPMG International, Halliburton, Raytheon, Mary Kay, BancFirst, Michelin, Ernst & Young, and Liquidnet.

ADMISSIONS CONTACT: GINA AMUNDSON, DIRECTOR OF GRADUATE PROGRAMS
ADDRESS: 1003 ASP AVENUE, PRICE HALL, SUITE 1040 NORMAN, OK 73019-4302
PHONE: 405-325-4107 • FAX: 405-325-7753
E-MAIL: GAMUNDSON@OU.EDU • WEBSITE: PRICE.OU.EDU/MBA

Student Life and Environment

Price's "recently built" building "is one of the greatest strengths of the school," providing "exceptional classrooms equipped with all of the technological benefits to teach today's students." Grad students especially appreciate their dedicated lounge, where they have "lockers, a fridge, a microwave, coffee, tables for working on projects or homework, and couches for hanging out...or the occasional between-class nap."

Life on the OU campus offers "a good mix of study, extracurricular activities, and social events." MBAs have "a very active Graduate Business Association that sets up events ranging from networking, cultural diversity (the International Food Night is always popular), and community service (Relay for Life), to general social or special interest events (such as a Wine 101 night)." Norman "is a great college town," and "OU has so many great traditions that it's nearly impossible not to feel like you are a part of something bigger, something really special. Football season is always a hit, and game days are indescribably fun and special. Many MBA students choose to participate in tailgating and other various pre-game activities." The school "has a really rich fine-arts community as well, with a wonderful art museum right on campus and a performance center and music hall that boast numerous productions and performances throughout the year."

Admissions

Applicants to the Price MBA program must submit the following materials to the Office of Admissions and Records: an application for admission to the university; an official transcript from every undergraduate and graduate institution attended; and, for international applicants, a financial statement as well as an official TOEFL score report if English is not their first language. In addition, all applicants must also submit the following materials to the MBA Admissions Office: a completed supplemental application for graduate study in business; an official score report for the GMAT; a current resume; and a personal statement of career and educational goals. Two years of work experience is preferred but not required.

FINANCIAL FACTS

Annual tuition (in-state/ out-of-state)	$5,148/$18,645
Fees	$5,493
Cost of books	$1,221
Room & board	$9,202

ADMISSIONS

Admissions Selectivity Rating	88
# of applications received	153
% applicants accepted	57
% acceptees attending	74
Average GMAT	619
Range of GMAT	530–740
Average GPA	3.43
TOEFL required of international students	Yes
Minimum TOEFL (paper/computer)	600/250
Application fee	$40
International application fee	$90
Regular application deadline	6/1
Early decision program?	No
Deferment available	Yes
Maximum length of deferment	1 year
Transfer students accepted	Yes
Transfer application policy: Students may transfer into our PT MBA program from other AACSB accredited institutions.	
Non-fall admissions	No
Need-blind admissions	Yes

EMPLOYMENT PROFILE

Career Rating	82	Grads Employed by Function	% Avg. Salary
Percent employed at graduation	37	Marketing	NR $80,000
Percent employed 3 months after graduation	67	Operations	NR $62,333
		Consulting	NR $67,417
Average base starting salary	$71,226	Management	NR $84,000
Primary Source of Full-time Job Acceptances		Finance	NR $84,333
School-facilitated activities	(63%)	MIS	NR $52,500
Graduate-facilitated activities	(37%)	**Top 5 Employers Hiring Grads**	
		KPMG (3), RiskMetrics (2), ExxonMobil (1), AT&T (2), Conoco Phillips (1)	

UNIVERSITY OF OREGON
CHARLES H. LUNDQUIST COLLEGE OF BUSINESS

GENERAL INFORMATION

Type of school	Public
Academic calendar	Quarter

SURVEY SAYS...

Good social scene
Smart classrooms
Solid preparation in:
Marketing
Entrepreneurial studies

STUDENTS

Enrollment of parent institution	21,507
Enrollment of MBA Program	94
% male/female	69/31
% out-of-state	40
% part-time	0
% minorities	6
% international	26
Average age at entry	28
Average years work experience at entry	4

ACADEMICS

Academic Experience Rating	**79**
Student/faculty ratio	3:1
Profs interesting rating	77
Profs accessible rating	78
% female faculty	19
% minority faculty	8

Joint Degrees

JD/MBA (4 academic years)
JD/MBA in Sustainability (4 academic years) MA/MBA in International Studies or Asian Studies (3 academic years)
MBA/M.Actg (3 academic years)
MBA/MPA (3 academic years)
MBA/MS (customized program, generally about 3 academic years)

Academics

A green-oriented, left-coast business program in the pretty city of Eugene, University of Oregon offers a small but diverse MBA program at a low, public school price. The location and regional reputation are among the school's most attractive features, although many students say they chose Oregon because they wanted to study sustainable business or participate in "one of the best sports business programs nationally."

No matter what your field of interest, Oregon's extensive core curriculum ensures that every student receives a strong foundation in the quantitative principles of business. During the second year, full-time MBA students also participate in the Strategic Planning Project over the course of two terms. Through this experiential learning program, small groups of Oregon students work as consultants to major Northwest businesses, including such big names as Adidas, Amazon.com, Hewlett Packard, and Intel.

After finishing the core curriculum, students take elective coursework, with the option of focusing their studies in innovation/entrepreneurship, finance/securities analysis, sports business, or sustainable business practises. Your academic experience will depend on your field of study; however, the "bright and accessible" teaching staff gets high marks in almost every area. However, with small, intensive classes, professors "don't let you just sit back and take in the class to float through. They expect you to participate, make presentations, and contribute." Despite the challenges of the curriculum, "a collaborative environment is fostered to breed the entrepreneurial spirit." A second-year student explains, "We encourage competition in the classroom and on the field but collaborative learning continues right up until exam time."

An extraordinarily pleasant campus atmosphere, "each classroom is high-tech" and "the facilities are fantastic and enhance the learning in countless ways." With four centers for experimental learning, plus a leadership of communication center, students assure us, "if you want to learn about something, you can find a resource to learn it." To give one example, "the entrepreneurship center gives students access to a breadth of resources and contacts as well as numerous opportunities for additional external education experiences."

Career and Placement

When it's time to begin the job hunt, University of Oregon students benefit from the efforts of the school's active career service center and "strong reputation in Seattle, Portland and San Francisco." On campus recruiting is affected by school's small-town "location and the program's small size." However, "the career services office is fantastic about organizing company visits in Portland, Seattle, and San Francisco, as well as providing shuttle service to MBA career fairs held in Portland for programs throughout the Pacific Northwest." In addition, the Ducks have a great many loyal graduates, and "the alumni are always willing to help current students." Beyond the local offerings, the school hosts "a networking trip to New York City for students in the sports marketing program."

The average salary for a recent graduating class was $55,819, with a range from $30,000 to $120,000. However, U of O students point out that many students prefer to take their "dream job" in sports for a lower income, or plan to work in nonprofit areas, which can make entering salaries look lower for Oregon graduates than for graduates of other schools. In fact, they assure us that Oregon graduates are highly competitive and that "there are more jobs available than there are MBA candidates." A second-year student confides, "Specifically for accounting, recruiting is amazing! All Big 4 visit almost monthly, many regional and local firms are just as competitive in recruiting."

ADMISSIONS CONTACT: HOLLY PHILLIPS, ADMISSIONS COORDINATOR
ADDRESS: 1208 UNIVERSITY OF OREGON, 302 PETERSON HALL EUGENE, OR 97403-1208
PHONE: 541-346-2151 • FAX: 541-346-0073
E-MAIL: INFO@OREGONMBA.COM • WEBSITE: WWW.OREGONMBA.COM

Student Life and Environment

With an average age of 28 at entry at University of Oregon, you'll find a mixture of some young recent graduates, as well as a "slightly older, 30-plus crowd, who have more experience" in the workplace. Old or young, married or single, everyone remarks on the business school's incredibly collegial atmosphere. With fewer than 200 students in the graduate business programs (and just over 100 pursuing an MBA), "the small class sizes allow the student to develop long-lasting friendships and future networking opportunities."

When it comes to social life, you can choose your own adventure at the University of Oregon. Depending on your lifestyle, "you can strictly stay to school work and use your free time to yourself, or you can enter many clubs and groups and consume your time within those." To connect with classmates, "the program offers weekly social activities for its students and the B-school and law school often have social activities together." In addition, the Ducks have "a strong athletics program so football and basketball seasons are fun." Older students note that the "school is very supportive of married students and family life," and spouses are welcome to join in campus activities, such as intramural sports.

Around Eugene, "housing is convenient and affordable," and "public transportation is everywhere (lots of free buses for students)." Of particular note, outdoor activities are plentiful, as "skiing is only a short drive away, the coast is within two hours, running trails can be found all over town and there are great places to go hiking."

Admissions

To be accepted to the MBA program at the University of Oregon, students must have a minimum GMAT score of 600 and a minimum 3.0 GPA on a 4.0 scale. However, when making an admissions decision, this small school considers factors beyond the numbers, examining the quality of an applicant's leadership and professional experiences, the rigorousness of their undergraduate curriculum, letters of recommendation, and interview feedback.

FINANCIAL FACTS

Annual tuition (in-state/ out-of-state)	$12,144/$17,166
Fees	$3,414
Cost of books	$1,500
Room & board (on/off-campus)	$11,210/$12,820
% of students receiving aid	70
% of first-year students receiving aid	73
% of students receiving loans	54
% of students receiving grants	41
Average award package	$25,740
Average grant	$12,350
Average student loan debt	$23,620

ADMISSIONS

Admissions Selectivity Rating	87
# of applications received	131
% applicants accepted	56
% acceptees attending	63
Average GMAT	626
Range of GMAT	560–700
Average GPA	3.25
TOEFL required of international students	Yes
Minimum TOEFL (paper)	600
Application fee	$50
International application fee	$50
Regular application deadline	3/15
Regular notification	4/15
Application Deadline/Notification	
Round 1:	11/15 / 12/15
Round 2:	2/15 / 3/15
Round 3:	3/15 / 4/15
Early decision program?	Yes
ED Deadline/ Notification	11/15 / 12/15
Deferment available	Yes
Maximum length of deferment	1 year
Transfer students accepted	No
Non-fall admissions	No
Need-blind admissions	Yes

EMPLOYMENT PROFILE

		Grads Employed by Function	%	Avg. Salary
Career Rating	77	Marketing	31	$51,920
Percent employed at graduation	26	Operations	6	$57,000
Percent employed 3 months after graduation	59	Consulting	6	$41,500
Average base starting salary	$55,819	Management	6	$73,500
Primary Source of Full-time Job Acceptances		Finance	13	$67,250
School-facilitated activities	7 (44%)	HR	6	$80,000
Graduate-facilitated activities	9 (56%)	MIS	6	$52,000

Top 5 Employers Hiring Grads
NIKE (2), Adidas (1), Hewlett Packard (1), Intel (1), Premier Sports Management (1)

UNIVERSITY OF OTTAWA
TELFER SCHOOL OF MANAGEMENT

GENERAL INFORMATION
Type of school	Public
Academic calendar	Aug–Aug

SURVEY SAYS...
Smart classrooms
Solid preparation in:
Teamwork

STUDENTS
Enrollment of parent institution	36,244
Enrollment of MBA Program	244
% male/female	55/45
% part-time	59
% international	18
Average age at entry	31
Average years work experience at entry	8

ACADEMICS
Academic Experience Rating	**83**
Profs interesting rating	79
Profs accessible rating	81
% female faculty	25
% minority faculty	59

Joint Degrees
MBA/LLB (MBA and Law), 40 months).

Prominent Alumni
Ian Telfer, Chairman of Goldcorp Inc.; Paul Desmarais, Chairman of the Executive Committee, Power Corp.; Robert Ashes, General Manager, Business Intelligence & Performance Management at IBM; Guy Laflamme, VP Mkg & Comm., National Comission; Dominique DeCelles, VP & General Manager, L'Oreal Montreal.

Academics

With "government ties and roots in the high-tech industry," the Tefler School of Management at the University of Ottawa offers important connections to go with its top-flight academics. As a result, whether they enroll in the "short, intensive" one-year full-time program or the "convenient" part-time evening program, Telfer students benefit from "professors who have impressive industry connections" in a city where they are "surrounded by great high-tech companies."

Telfer offers a broad, cross-functional curriculum with a "focus on leadership" and "integration of the newest technology and learning principles." "Opportunities for global projects" and "exposure to leaders in business" are interspersed through a curriculum that builds core skills, integrates them into complex applications, and then sends students on to electives in marketing, finance, entrepreneurship, public policy, and international management. All students participate in a consulting project in which they "deal with a real project provided and coordinated by a real company, along with [a] senior professor and a mentor who is a certified consultant." Full-time students also participate in a one-week international trip.

Ottawa professors "are very accessible and care about the students. They are available outside of class, in person or by email, to answer any questions." Part-time students appreciatively report that "there is clear recognition of the needs of the part-time students with current careers who are obtaining this graduate degree on top of everything else," both from professors and administrators. Ottawa is a bilingual school, with instruction available in English and French. The Telfer School of Management offers a general management MBA. Some here wish the school would "allow subject-area concentrations and a thesis option to avoid losing academically-oriented students to other schools."

Career and Placement

Ottawa's Telfer School of Management Career Centre offers "one-on-one counseling, mock interviews, resumé critique, and trips to different employers in neighboring cities." The office has access to online job search tools and exclusive job postings.

Employers who most frequently hire Ottawa MBAs include Accenture, Adobe Systems, Alcatel, Bank of Nova Scotia, Bell Canada, BMO Nesbitt Burns, Business Development Bank of Canada, Canada Mortgage and Housing Corporation (CMHC), Canadian Commercial Corporation (CCC), CIBC, Clarica, Cognos, Costco, Deloitte, Ernst & Young, IBM Canada, KPMG International, Laurentian Bank of Canada, L'Oréal, National Bank of Canada, Natural Research Council of Canada (NRC), Nortel, PriceWaterhouseCoopers, Primerica Financial Services, Public Service Alliance of Canada, QMR Staffing Solutions, RBC Royal Bank, SwiftTrade Securities, TD Waterhouse Investment, Toyota Canada, Veritaaq Technology House, and Xerox Canada.

Student Life and Environment

Socially, "many, many opportunities are available" for Tefler students, including "pubs, dinners, business games, sugar bush, meet and greet, [and] ski trips." While "there is always an effort to include the part-time cohort, uptake is minor from this cohort given family and work-life commitments." Full-timers, on the other hand, enjoy a full extracurricular calendar, as "the MBA Student Association runs many different events" and "the Graduate Student Association is also very active. Life at our school is active for those that want to be active." Events include "many opportunities to meet recruiters...and invited guests in the specific fields (economics, marketing, management principles) as well as many breakfast, luncheon, and seminar opportunities. There is a luncheon series specifically directed to women in leadership, with excellent speakers and opportunities for translational learning."

Telfer is housed "in a very modern building" where "the MBA program has its own floor. There are many study rooms complete with everything needed for conference calls and also [a] white board." One student calls the facilities "the best and cleanest I've seen. The school is equipped with all the necessary technology to accommodate students' needs." The area surrounding campus is "safe and attractive. There are many restaurants and annual events that occur very near the School of Business."

The full-time student body creates "a very multicultural environment," writes one student. "I am myself from Europe and have the chance to be with Indians, Brazilians, Chinese, etc. It is a tremendous opportunity and we come from such diverse background that we offer personal growth to each other at every conversation." Part-timers tend to be local professionals, which makes for "an impressive student body...due to the captive market in Ottawa (i.e., federal government and high tech)."

Admissions

All applicants to the Telfer MBA program must submit the following materials to admissions: a completed online application form, printed out; official academic transcripts from all post-secondary institutions attended; a current resume reflecting at least two years of professional or managerial experience; two letters of recommendation (at least one from a recent employer); a 500-word personal statement describing goals in pursuing the MBA; an official GMAT score report demonstrating at least 50th percentile performance with a strong showing in each subsection and a minimum score of 4.5 on the analytical writing section; proof of language proficiency for the applicant's desired program (English or French). English proficiency may be demonstrated through the TOEFL, IELTS, or CAN-TEST. The school reserves the right to request an interview of applicants. International students seeking full-time study must obtain a study permit from the Canadian government.

FINANCIAL FACTS

Annual tuition (in-state/ out-of-state)	$14,998/$24,720
Fees	$1,169
Cost of books	$1,209
Room & board (on/off-campus)	$8,668/$5,796
Average grant	$7,784

ADMISSIONS

Admissions Selectivity Rating	85
# of applications received	242
% applicants accepted	44
Average GMAT	607
Range of GMAT	570–640
Average GPA	3.1
TOEFL required of international students	Yes
Minimum TOEFL (paper/computer)	600/250
Application fee	$60
Regular application deadline	4/1
Early decision program?	No
Deferment available	No
Transfer students accepted	Yes
Transfer application policy: A maximum of 24 credits could be retained for graduate courses in management completed in a Canadian MBA program or AACSB accredited program.	
Non-fall admissions	No
Need-blind admissions	Yes

EMPLOYMENT PROFILE

Career Rating	89	Grads Employed by Function	% Avg. Salary
Percent employed at graduation	71	Marketing	8 NR
Percent employed 3 months after graduation	85	Operations	2 NR
		Consulting	8 NR
Average base starting salary	$66,000	Management	22 NR
		Finance	13 NR
		HR	5 NR
		MIS	5 NR

Top 5 Employers Hiring Grads
Government (13), IBM (7), Export Development Canada (4), Alcatel-Lucent (3), Accenture (1)

UNIVERSITY OF THE PACIFIC

EBERHARDT SCHOOL OF BUSINESS

GENERAL INFORMATION

Type of school   Private
Affiliation   Non-denominational,
                Methodist founded
Academic calendar   Semester

SURVEY SAYS...

Friendly students
Good social scene
Smart classrooms
Solid preparation in:
Presentation skills
Entrepreneurial studies

STUDENTS

Enrollment of parent institution	6,251
Enrollment of MBA Program	58
% male/female	65/35
% out-of-state	29
% part-time	7
% minorities	38
% international	19
Average age at entry	24
Average years work experience at entry	1

ACADEMICS

Academic Experience Rating	**82**
Student/faculty ratio	3:1
Profs interesting rating	82
Profs accessible rating	82
% female faculty	32
% minority faculty	7

Joint Degrees

MBA/JD, 4 years; MBA/Peace Corps, 3.5 years; MBA/PharmD, 4 years

Prominent Alumni

A.G. Spanos, Real Estate Development; David Gerber, MGM/UA—Film & TV Production; Dave Brubeck, Jazz Composer/Musician; Jaime Lee Curtis, Actress; Chris Isaak, Rock Musician/Actor.

Academics

Located in Stockton, California, University of the Pacific is a small college that boasts a "very high standing both academically and professionally throughout our local community and state." Ideal for early career professionals, the school's full-time "16-month program allows students without a business undergraduate degree to obtain an MBA in a highly intensive and challenging program." Fast-paced and efficient, the first term is "an intensive phase 18-unit semester broken down into nine modules of 4 to 6 classes each. This intensive phase allows students to learn the fundamentals necessary for a business degree and requires spending most of the students' time at school." During this time, students are placed "in a cohort of between 20 to 35 students and share all required classes." Therefore, each entering class is incredibly tight-knit, creating a unique learning environment. A current student explains, "This cohort of students is a wide array of culturally- and educationally-diverse students coming from various countries and experience levels. These factors contribute to an intellectually challenging classroom experience [that] goes beyond traditional book- or case-based classes." In addition to traditional business students, the "MBA program offers joint programs with Pacific's PharmD and JD programs...having the interaction from the other schools is a great resource."

After the first term, Pacific's MBA program follows a typical semester model, with a more "moderate workload." At that point, students can tailor their educational experiences by choosing to specialize in entrepreneurship, finance, healthcare management, sports management, or marketing. They also take advantage of "the unique opportunity to study abroad in another country," through the school's overseas program, or specialize in international issues through the school's Cooperative Peace Corps/MBA. Future finance mavens can also hone their skills through the school's $1.5 million Eberhardt Student Investment Fund. While University of the Pacific boasts many world-class opportunities, students are most impressed by the small and intimate feeling that pervades this small Northern California school. With a faculty-student ratio of 13 to 1, "The greatest strengths of this school are the small classroom sizes [and] the professors' willingness to help students and get to know them on a one-on-one basis." A current student agrees, "I have been pleased with the teacher's performance and one-on-one help outside of classrooms. Teachers really take the time make sure students understand the material and frequently check to make sure everyone is on the same page." Another adds, "Students are always welcome to question or seek help from professors and the professors offer a more peer-to-peer interaction, rather than the typical student-teacher relationship, which further encourages a beneficial educational experience." In addition to their friendliness and accessibility, Pacific professors are strong class leaders. On the whole, students are "very impressed with the quality of the teaching," saying their professors are "professional and can apply the material to real-life situations."

Career and Placement

Career development is directly incorporated into the University of the Pacific curriculum. Throughout the first term, students are required to take a weekly Career Development course to help them build a job search strategy and prepare for the professional world. Students are also required to complete a summer business internship, which offers the opportunity to build real-world skills and contacts. In addition, the MBA Career Services Center hosts various on-campus recruiting events and interviews. Located a stone's throw away from the San Francisco Bay Area and the Silicon Valley, "the network of contacts built from attending UOP is excellent." The average student interviews with about five different companies and receives three job offers by graduation. With a salary range between $42,000 and $62,000, recent graduates have taken jobs at Accenture, E. & J. Gallo, Ernst & Young, and Foster Farms, among others.

Student Life and Environment

Pacific's enthusiastic students dole out praises for their diligent classmates, saying, "Fellow students are both driven and work as a team. Together, we hope to succeed and push past boundaries." Due to the intense cohort format, "each class that comes through is extremely close-knit and shares their experiences like a single unit." A current MBA candidate elaborates, "Students are very genuine and really look out for one another. Because we spend all week together, many students have found strong friendships and even business partners for future ventures." While the school draws a few students from further a field, "the MBA student population is predominantly local—though they may have originated from somewhere else."

Based in the small city of Stockton, California, "The campus is like a world of its own within the community"—a place where students feel comfortable studying and relaxing. To burn off steam, MBA students can participate in "intramural sports like evening basketball and flag football that are played against other schools on campus." Thursdays are a popular night for gatherings, and "the MBAs also spend a lot of time together outside of campus at dinner and studying." Attracting a younger crowd, some say the school could "try to make more programs available for full-time working students and their families." One explains, "Being a father and husband, my time is very limited. There are several times that I would've liked to involve my wife and children in my school activities, but that seemed out of place."

Admissions

To be considered for admission to University of the Pacific's graduate programs, students must have a minimum GMAT score of 500. Prospective students are evaluated based on their performance in prior coursework, recommendation letters, GMAT scores, and an admissions interview. Admissions decisions are made on a rolling basis, and a new cohort of 35 students is admitted each fall.

FINANCIAL FACTS

Annual tuition	$31,350
Fees	$500
Cost of books	$1,600
Room & board (on/off-campus)	$12,000/$14,000
% of students receiving aid	85
% of first-year students receiving aid	82
% of students receiving loans	60
% of students receiving grants	55
Average award package	$22,500
Average grant	$4,156

ADMISSIONS

Admissions Selectivity Rating	81
# of applications received	68
% applicants accepted	50
% acceptees attending	71
Average GMAT	587
Range of GMAT	540–670
Average GPA	3.36
TOEFL required of international students	Yes
Minimum TOEFL (paper/computer)	550/213
Application fee	$75
International application fee	$75
Regular application deadline	3/1
Early decision program?	No
Deferment available	Yes
Maximum length of deferment	1 year
Transfer students accepted	Yes
Transfer application policy: Students may transfer up to 2 Advanced courses from another AACSB accredited MBA Program.	
Non-fall admissions	No
Need-blind admissions	Yes

EMPLOYMENT PROFILE

Career Rating	78	Grads Employed by Function	% Avg. Salary
Percent employed at graduation	58	Marketing	17 NR
Average base starting salary	$54,583	Consulting	33 NR
		Finance	33 NR
		HR	17 NR

Top Employers Hiring Grads
PricewaterhouseCoopers (1), Clorox (1), FactSet Research (1), E&J Gallo (1)

UNIVERSITY OF PENNSYLVANIA
WHARTON SCHOOL GRADUATE DIVISION

GENERAL INFORMATION
Type of school	Private
Academic calendar	Semester

SURVEY SAYS...
Good social scene
Good peer network
Smart classrooms
Solid preparation in:
Finance
Accounting
Quantitative skills

STUDENTS
Enrollment of parent institution	24,107
Enrollment of MBA Program	1,619
% male/female	64/36
% part-time	0
% minorities	13
% international	45
Average age at entry	28
Average years work experience at entry	6

ACADEMICS
Academic Experience Rating	98
Profs interesting rating	93
Profs accessible rating	67
% female faculty	24

Joint Degrees
MBA/JD (3 yr and 4 yr options);
MBA/MD; MBA/DMD; MBA/MSE;
MBA/MArch; MBA/MA-Lauder;
MBA/MA-SAIS at Johns Hopkins;
MBA/MPA-Harvard's Kennedy
School of Government; MBA/MSW;
MBA/PhD; MBA/VMD; MBA/MSN;
MBA/MA in Environmental Studies.

Prominent Alumni
J.D. Power III, Founder & Chairman,
JD Power & Assoc.; Jacob
Wallenberg, Chairman, Investor AB;
Harold McGraw III, CEO, McGraw-
Hill International; Anil D. Ambani,
Chairman, Reliance ADA
Enterprises; Risa Lavizzo-Mourey,
President and CEO, Robert Wood
Johnson Foundation.

Academics

The University of Pennsylvania's Wharton School, one of the premier MBA programs in the world, is best known for its "strong finance reputation," but the curriculum's "strong emphasis on quantitative analysis" extends "across many disciplines, not just finance but marketing, entrepreneurship, operations, international business, real estate, etc." as well. All areas present a "holistic program with a mix of case studies, traditional lecture formats, experiential learning opportunities, and strong co-curricular programs."

Students brag that Wharton "provides all the resources necessary for us to succeed, and then some," reporting that "the difficult part here is deciding between which resources—lectures, seminars, simulations, clubs, special events—one can fit into one's schedule." Writes one student, "The breadth and depth of the academic curriculum and the extracurricular activities is so huge that I would need at least six MBA years to experience 20 percent of it all." A heavy workload, described as "difficult for everyone but the most brilliant to manage," makes those choices even tougher. But what impresses students most here is the degree to which students themselves contribute to the learning experience. Wharton uses a "co-production model of learning" that "requires engagement from all participants in the Wharton community." One MBA observes, "Students sometimes add more value than assigned readings. Students make Wharton. 'Student-run' is an understatement." Another agrees, "The 'co-production model' is not just a buzz word; it really exists here."

Under the Wharton pedagogic system, "Classes build on each other. Professors are known to coordinate timing of discussing certain topics to ensure that the student has mastered the concept in another class." Much work here is done in teams. To promote cooperation and reduce competitiveness, Wharton policy currently forbids grade disclosure to recruiters. Students report that the policy "fosters an environment of helping at the school." Nondisclosure apparently has little impact on students' motivation to work. One notes, "The school has high expectations for each admit, and the overall performance of the students rises to that expectation."

Career and Placement

Wharton is a brand that pretty much sells itself, so it's no surprise that the school's career services are highly regarded and widely appreciated by students. Each year brings the following career placement services to the campus: over 200 employer information sessions; almost 300 recruiting companies; and, more than 5,000 job-board postings. Wharton's Career Management Services Office also offers resume review and distribution, mock interviews, internship placement, one-on-one counseling, and over 25 career treks both in and outside the U.S. No wonder students praise the "fantastic career opportunities and resources." About 55 percent of Wharton MBAs take jobs in the finance sector; 28 percent wind up in consulting; and seven percent find jobs in the marketing arena.

ADMISSIONS CONTACT: ANKUR KUMAR, SENIOR ASSOCIATE DIRECTOR OF ADMISSIONS
ADDRESS: 420 JON M. HUNTSMAN HALL, 3730 WALNUT STREET PHILADELPHIA, PA 19104-6340
PHONE: 215-898-6183 • FAX: 215-898-0120
E-MAIL: MBA.ADMISSIONS@WHARTON.UPENN.EDU • WEBSITE: WWW.WHARTON.UPENN.EDU/MBA

Student Life and Environment

Life at Wharton offers "an amazing number of choices in terms of classes, activities, clubs, etc." It's an atmosphere students tell us is filled with a constant stream of unique opportunities they wouldn't otherwise have. One student cites these personal examples: "At Wharton I have done a four-week study trip to greater China; a consulting project to an Israeli company that wanted to enter the U.S. market; a marketing consulting project for AOL for the mobile location-based services product; a leadership venture to Ecuador next spring to learn about teamwork through a mountain climbing expedition; dozens of fantastic speakers; and finally, some great parties." MBAs appreciate that their "partners are involved in almost all campus-related activities here." One reports, "My wife and one-year-old daughter enjoy going to activities every Wednesday and Friday with the Wharton Kids Club. This has proved to be very helpful in providing an environment where my wife can make lots of friends in a new city, and my daughter can play with other kids her own age."

Hometown Philadelphia "is underrated but still needs work." One Bay Area native notes, "I was worried about Philadelphia after living in San Francisco, but I have been pleasantly surprised by the depth of culture, fun, and good food." Wharton's new facility, Huntsman Hall, is "top-of-the-line" but MBAs gripe that "sharing the building with undergraduates leads to scarce group study rooms. Most students do not use the library because it is overrun with undergrads." Still, Wharton does most things right. You realize this when you ask students what most needs improving here and all they can think to mention is "full-size lockers for each student."

Admissions

Wharton is among the most selective MBA programs in the country. On average, the school receives between seven and 10 applications for each available slot. The school's website notes that "approximately 75 to 80 percent of all applicants are qualified for admission." Applicants are evaluated holistically by at least three members of the Admissions Committee. All prior academic experience, including graduate work and certifications, is considered. GMAT scores also figure into the decision. Quality of professional experiences, career choices, and stated goals for entering the program are all carefully reviewed. Committee members also look for evidence of leadership, interpersonal skills, entrepreneurial spirit, and good citizenship. International students must demonstrate competency in English through essays and interviews. Wharton offers three rounds of an admission each year; the first two rounds are equal with regard to a candidate's admissibility. The third round offers admission on a space-available basis and is generally more competitive.

FINANCIAL FACTS

Annual tuition	$44,480
Fees	$5,624
Cost of books	$1,763
Room & board	
(on-campus)	$21,398
% of students receiving aid	76
% of first-year students	
receiving aid	76
% of students receiving loans	66
% of students receiving grants	45
Average award package	$58,094
Average grant	$11,975
Average student loan debt	$76,748

ADMISSIONS

Admissions Selectivity Rating	99
# of applications received	7,328
% applicants accepted	16
% acceptees attending	69
Average GMAT	715
Range of GMAT	660–760
Average GPA	3.5
TOEFL required of	
international students	Yes
Application fee	$225
International application fee	$225
Application Deadline/Notification	
Round 1:	10/9 / 12/22
Round 2:	1/8 / 3/26
Round 3:	3/5 / 5/14
Early decision program?	No
Deferment available	Yes
Maximum length	
of deferment	case-by-case
Transfer students accepted	No
Non-fall admissions	No
Need-blind admissions	Yes

EMPLOYMENT PROFILE

Career Rating	99	**Grads Employed by Function% Avg. Salary**	
Percent employed at graduation	85	Marketing	7 NR
Percent employed 3 months		Operations	1 NR
after graduation	89	Consulting	28 $121,321
Average base starting salary	$112,186	Management	6 $109,603
Primary Source of Full-time Job Acceptances		Finance	55 NR
School-facilitated activities	459 (73%)	**Top Employers Hiring Grads**	
Graduate-facilitated activities	114 (18%)	McKinsey & Company (50), Boston Consulting	
Unknown	58 (9%)	Group (43), Bain & Company (36), Morgan Stanley (20)	

UNIVERSITY OF PITTSBURGH
JOSEPH M. KATZ GRADUATE SCHOOL OF BUSINESS

GENERAL INFORMATION
Type of school   Public
Academic calendar   August–April

SURVEY SAYS...
Students love Pittsburgh, PA
Smart classrooms
Solid preparation in:
Teamwork

STUDENTS
Enrollment of parent institution	35,394
Enrollment of MBA Program	784
% male/female	71/29
% out-of-state	23
% part-time	68
% minorities	11
% international	38
Average age at entry	27
Average years work experience at entry	3

ACADEMICS
Academic Experience Rating	85
Student/faculty ratio	10:1
Profs interesting rating	81
Profs accessible rating	82
% female faculty	21
% minority faculty	22

Joint Degrees
MBA/MS-Engineering in the following specialties in 20 months: Bioengineering, Chemical and Petroleum Engineering, Civil and Environmental Engineering, Electrical and Computer Engineering, Industrial Engineering, Materials Science and Engineering, Mechanical Engineering. MBA/MS-MIS in Management of Information Systems in 20 months; MBA/JD, Business and Law in 43 months; MBA/MPIA in Masters of Public and International Affairs in 20 months; MBA/MID in Masters of International Development in 20 months; MBA/MIB in Masters of International Business in 20 months.

Academics

Students are drawn to the University of Pittsburgh's Joseph M. Katz Graduate School of Business for its "value, location, course offerings, [and] study abroad program." In addition, many tout "the small class size, accessibility of the administration and faculty, and the collegial and collaborative environment, percent of matriculating students hailing from abroad." As one student says, "we have a very international class at Katz. In my first year, about 55 percent of the class hailed from outside the U.S., including China, Taiwan, India, and Europe." This is not surprising given the school's "dual-degree programs and international connections with universities abroad."

In 1960, Katz became the first business school to offer a one-year MBA program designed for students with a strong background in business or economics. Students continue to laud the "reputation of [the] finance department [and] reputation for placement in finance-related careers." In addition, the school offers a part-time program where working professionals can pursue an advanced degree in their field through evening classes. In the part-time program, "classes meet at night for three hours and some of the work can be a little tedious after you have put in a full day of work." The full-time, two-year MBA program focuses on providing students with a longer, more comprehensive introduction to all aspects of business management. The first-semester students "are focused on the core MBA classes." "Starting the second semester, students are able to start taking electives."

Overall, students say the faculty here "is adequate." Professors are "smart, engaged and come from diverse backgrounds—from prominent *Fortune* 500 companies to non-profits and start-up companies. They're generally very good at soft skills while maintaining a high level of skill in the more technical aspects of b-school." "The course offerings in certain departments are not extensive, particularly in marketing" and "adjunct professors are particularly weak." As is the case at many large research universities, others add a cautionary note saying, "professors are a mixed bag, ranging from excellent teachers who are extremely accessible, to...being so concerned with their research that they treat students like a nuisance." The administration however "is amazing." "I love the fact that the Dean knows students by name." "One can just walk into the Dean's office. The Dean and his staff at the MBA Programs Office interact with students all the time."

Career and Placement

In terms of job placement students here say, "the social networks...are priceless. I feel if I ever lost my current job, through my developed network I would be employed very quickly." In addition, "the network events and alumni database are particularly helpful." Most importantly, Katz has a long arm into the Pittsburgh community and the Pennsylvania region at large. However, students say "career services could be more involved in getting more companies on site for recruiting;" however they are quick to attribute any dip in recruiting opportunities to "the recession and difficult times as far as hiring and job availability in general."

In 2009, 38 percent of graduating Katz MBA students had received a job offer prior to graduation with a mean base salary of $59,048. Though by in large students accepted jobs in the surrounding Middle Atlantic region, an impressive 30.4 percent accepted jobs internationally. Financial services, manufacturing, consulting, and technology remain fields with big draws for Katz grads. Bayer, IBM, Deloitte & Touche, Crane Co., and Ford Motor Company were listed as the top five employers.

ADMISSIONS CONTACT: CLIFF McCORMICK, DIRECTOR
ADDRESS: 301 MERVIS HALL, ROBERTO CLEMENTE DRIVE PITTSBURGH, PA 15260
PHONE: 412-648-1700 • FAX: 412-648-1659
E-MAIL: MBA@KATZ.PITT.EDU • WEBSITE: WWW.BUSINESS.PITT.EDU/KATZ

Student Life and Environment

Katz students are "a very diverse group." There is "a large percentage of foreign students as well as a large female population. The students also have a wide variety of work backgrounds and they bring this to classroom conversations." Overall, students describe themselves as "active, intelligent, ambitious, a good group of individuals with good overall work ethic." Those directly out of undergraduate tend to be "young and fun-loving individuals with an excitement to learn the tools and acquire the expertise to advance their business careers." Part-time and returning students "generally have work and family lives outside of school" and "are able to bring their own life experiences to group and project work" which "enhances the learning experience."

Life on campus is "both exciting and stressful. There are always plenty of opportunities for various activities within professional and social realms." One student jokes, "There are too many different activities, lectures, clubs, etc. to choose from. Something is always going on." Working professionals note, "being a full-time employee and part-time student is difficult." However, "this school tries to tailor courses to meet the needs of busy adults while still catering to full-time students as well."

Admissions

Applicants to the Joseph M. Katz Graduate School of Business are evaluated on their demonstrated leadership skills, record of accomplishment, previous academic performance, and analytical skills as well as their future potential as leaders in business. The average GPA for the matriculating class of 2009 was 3.3 with an average GMAT of 602. While not a strict requirement for every prospective candidate, evaluative interviews are conducted regularly prior to the first application deadline. Last year, 97 percent of applicants to the full-time MBA program were interviewed. Interviews for part-time candidates are arranged by invitation and take place after the admissions committee's initial review of a candidate's application.

Prominent Alumni

Kevin Woods Sharer, Chair & CEO AMGEN, INC.; Raymond William Smith, Chairman Verizon Ventures; Louise Goeser, President & CEO, Siemans Mexico; Frank Gaoning Ning, CEO and Chairman of COFCO Ltd; Lewis F. Sutherland III, Executive Vice President and CFO, Aramark.

FINANCIAL FACTS

Annual tuition (in-state/ out-of-state)	$16,356/$23,674
Fees	$2,690
Cost of books	$1,050
Room & board (off-campus)	$12,175
Average grant	$13,000

ADMISSIONS

Admissions Selectivity Rating	87
# of applications received	649
% applicants accepted	48
% acceptees attending	50
Average GMAT	602
Range of GMAT	520–680
Average GPA	3.3
TOEFL required of international students	Yes
Minimum TOEFL (paper/computer)	600/250
Application fee	$50
International application fee	$50
Application Deadline/Notification	
Round 1:	10/15 / 12/01
Round 2:	12/1 / 2/1
Round 3:	2/01 / 4/01
Round 4:	4/01 / 5/14
Early decision program?	No
Deferment available	No
Transfer students accepted	Yes
Transfer application policy: Matching coursework, accepting up to 17 credits from an AACSB MBA program, provided that credits were not used to complete a previous MBA degree.	
Non-fall admissions	No
Need-blind admissions	Yes

EMPLOYMENT PROFILE

		Grads Employed by Function	% Avg. Salary
Career Rating	85		
Percent employed at graduation	38	Marketing	14 $62,185
Percent employed 3 months		Operations	11 $68,680
after graduation	62	Consulting	13 $51,910
Average base starting salary	$59,048	Finance	34 $54,399
Primary Source of Full-time Job Acceptances		MIS	9 $65,750
School-facilitated activities	17 (30%)	**Top 5 Employers Hiring Grads**	
Graduate-facilitated activities	20 (36%)	Bayer (6), IBM (5), Deloitte (4), Crane Co. (2),	
Unknown	19 (34%)	Ford Motor Company (2)	

UNIVERSITY OF PORTLAND
PAMPLIN SCHOOL OF BUSINESS ADMINISTRATION

GENERAL INFORMATION
Type of school	Private
Affiliation	Roman Catholic
Academic calendar	Semester

SURVEY SAYS...
Friendly students
Cutting-edge classes
Solid preparation in:
Marketing
Computer skills

STUDENTS
Enrollment of parent institution	3,600
Enrollment of MBA Program	128
% male/female	56/44
% out-of-state	30
% part-time	52
% minorities	15
% international	20
Average age at entry	29
Average years work experience at entry	5

ACADEMICS
Academic Experience Rating	74
Student/faculty ratio	13:1
Profs interesting rating	88
Profs accessible rating	97
% female faculty	33
% minority faculty	19

Prominent Alumni
Dr. Robert B. Pamplin. Jr., Philanthropist/Entreprenuer; Fidele Baccio, Co-Founder Bon Apetite.

Academics

The Pamplin MBA at the University of Portland is structured to suit the needs of its largely part-time student body. A flexible schedule built around evening classes accommodates a student body that typically is also part of the full-time work force of Portland. About 50 percent of the students here have full-time status.

The University of Portland MBA Program is a 36-39 hour program. It offers a solid, cross-disciplinary exposure to all key areas of management. The Pamplin MBA begins with a course in statistics and then offers a series of five core classes that cover economics, marketing, finance, and accounting and operations management. The mix of these five courses may vary depending on the experience and background of the student. In addition to statistics and the five core classes, students take a set of values classes; the values perspectives courses introduce students to issues of leadership, understanding cultural differences and developing multicultural skills, and the role of business in society. Students may use electives to establish a concentration in entrepreneurship, finance, health care, marketing, operations technology management, or sustainability. Alternatively, students may also choose electives from a variety of disciplines and graduate with a degree in general management.

Students praise the Pamplin School for its willingness to experiment and innovate. The school "has the flexibility to allow students to take classes in any area of business," writes one student, adding that she is "working on earning a CPA and CMA licenses in addition to my MBA. There were no other programs in this area that offered all of this!" Another student approvingly notes that "UP seems to always hire guest professors to offer new classes, such as special 'Summer only' classes in areas like real estate or nonprofit accounting and management." Participation in JEBNET, "a network of 30 universities nationwide," allows students who must relocate to complete their MBAs at another school without losing credits.

Portland business professors "are very good. They all have their doctorates, have decades of professional experience in their fields, know other professionals in their respective fields, and invite these professionals into class to give real-world examples of what we are learning." Students also value the school's "great local reputation." The program is "administered extremely well, with regular communications from the school, including schedules, a newsletter, etc. The same cannot be said for the university at large, unfortunately."

Career and Placement

The University of Portland's Office of Career Services provides career and placement services for the school's undergraduate students, graduate students, and alumni. Office staff maintain job and internship listings, company research, and lists of alumni contacts. The office also organizes resume-writing and interviewing workshops, job fairs, and networking events. Students feel that the office, like much of the university, "sees UP primarily as an undergraduate institution and provides services accordingly" and believe that the school "should network better with local companies to get them to recruit on campus." Employers that recruit on campus include Black and Veatch, Deloitte Touche Tohmatsu, Ernst & Young, KPMG, and PricewaterhouseCoopers.

ADMISSIONS CONTACT: MELISSA MCCARTHY, MBA PROGRAM DIRECTOR
ADDRESS: 5000 N. WILLAMETTE BLVD. PORTLAND, OR 97203
PHONE: 503-943-7225 • FAX: 503-943-8041
E-MAIL: MBA-UP@UP.EDU • WEBSITE: BUSINESS.UP.EDU

Student Life and Environment

"There are no real clubs on campus" for Pamplin MBAs, "and no one seems to care. Because of the scheduling—classes are from 4:00 P.M. to 7:00 P.M. or 7:00 P.M. to 10:00 P.M. Monday through Thursday—it is almost impossible to get out into the community and attend business-related events, or even most school events, since they are scheduled right during the middle of most of our classes." One student observes, "The University of Portland's MBA program is mostly attended by working professionals who are only on campus long enough to go to class and then go home to their families. While there is not really a sense of community with this group, there is a strong sense of pride that we are attending the best MBA program in the city, and one of the best in the Northwest."

The average Pamplin student "is about 29 years old. There are a few of us with a couple of years of work experience but the majority of the students have been out for four or five years and there are also others who have been out for eight to fifteen years." The program is "diverse both ethnically and financially, populated by people who are always willing to help while at the same time are very competitive."

The city of Portland is among the most appealing in the Pacific Northwest. An arts Mecca, the city also hosts numerous fine restaurants, great shopping, and major-league professional basketball. The city's location provides easy access to numerous locations ideal for outdoor activity.

Admissions

Applicants to the MBA program at the University of Portland must meet the following minimum requirements: an undergraduate GPA of at least 3.0; a GMAT score of at least 500; and an "admission index" of at least 1,100 under the formula [(undergraduate GPA x 200) + GMAT score]. Work experience, though strongly recommended, is not required; applicants with at least three years of post-baccalaureate professional experience are considered optimal candidates for the program. International students must score at least 570 on the TOEFL paper test or 230 on the computer-adaptive version of the TOEFL or a 7.0 on the IELTS exam. All applications to the University of Portland must include a completed application form, a resumé, a personal statement of goals, official transcripts for all postsecondary academic work, an official GMAT score report, and two letters of recommendation. International students must submit all of the above as well as an official TOEFL score report and a financial statement that indicates they will have adequate support throughout the duration of study. This is required before the I-20 form will be issued to them.

FINANCIAL FACTS

Annual tuition	$22,140
Fees	$945
Cost of books	$600
% of students receiving aid	55
% of first-year students receiving aid	25
% of students receiving loans	40
% of students receiving grants	43
Average award package	$11,531
Average grant	$6,741
Average student loan debt	$43,675

ADMISSIONS

Admissions Selectivity Rating	70
# of applications received	96
% applicants accepted	70
% acceptees attending	75
Average GMAT	530
Average GPA	3.3
TOEFL required of international students	Yes
Minimum TOEFL (paper/computer/internet)	570/230/88
Application fee	$50
International application fee	$50
Early decision program?	No
Deferment available	Yes
Maximum length of deferment	1 year
Transfer students accepted	Yes
Transfer application policy: 9 semester hours of transfer credit from AACSB accredited program, or all credits in the Jesuit Transfer Agreement	
Non-fall admissions	Yes
Need-blind admissions	Yes

UNIVERSITY OF RHODE ISLAND
COLLEGE OF BUSINESS ADMINISTRATION

GENERAL INFORMATION
Type of school	Public
Academic calendar	Semester

SURVEY SAYS...
Solid preparation in:
Accounting
General management

STUDENTS
Enrollment of parent institution	15,900
Enrollment of MBA Program	186
% male/female	58/42
% out-of-state	25
% part-time	87
% minorities	8
% international	21
Average age at entry	28

ACADEMICS
Academic Experience Rating	**76**
Profs interesting rating	87
Profs accessible rating	80

Joint Degrees
MBA/PharmD, 7 years;
MBA/Engineering, 5 years;
MBA/Master of Oceanography, 16 months.

Academics

Looking to fast track your MBA? Consider the one-year daytime program at University of Rhode Island's College of Business Administration, a small intensive program that combines a fully-equipped curriculum and an internship in a one year calendar. Not in so big a hurry? URI also has a part-time program designed with the needs of working professionals in mind. Both programs feature "small class sizes, which allow everyone to be involved in discussion and present their opinion" and "excellent professors."

URI's approach to business includes "a lot of case studies" but not, according to some, much in the way of quantitative work. Part-time students also bemoan the "recent abrupt and unannounced cancellation of the information technology concentration at a time when computers and money are so important to business." Full-time students at URI do not pursue concentrations.

In the asset column, part-time students praise "the ability to take graduate-level electives from any department in the university," and the convenience of the program's "evening schedule" and "multiple locations" for classes. Professors are "excellent," the sort of experts you "see on the local news all the time and in the Providence Journal newspapers." Part-timers appreciate the fact that "many schools with a day MBA program [treat] the non-traditional students that come along with [the part-time program] an afterthought. At URI, day and evening students have access to the same resources: professors, computer labs, advising." Of the disciplines offered here, students single out the marketing program as "excellent."

Career and Placement

Career and placement services are provided to URI MBAs by the university's Career Services Office, which serves the entire university population. All MBA students receive a RhodyNet account in order to access the university's online recruitment system. RhodyNet notifies students by e-mail when opportunities that fit their skill set are posted; it also enables students to monitor the on-campus interviewing schedule and to search a database of job postings. Other services available to grad students include one-on-one counseling; personal assessments; workshops on resume writing, interviewing, and job search skills; mock interviews; resume review; job and internship fairs; and networking events. Employers attending URI's Spring Career Fair include: Amica Mutual Insurance Company, FM Global, General Dynamics C4 Systems, Kent Hospital, Marketing Mentors, MetLife, Northwestern Mutual Financial Network—The Southern New England Group, Prudential, Sherwin Williams, Triumvirate Environmental, Vector Software, and Working Planet Marketing Group.

Student Life and Environment

URI's main campus in Kingston "artfully mixes history with technology," making "many building improvements and additions" to "modernize the look of the campus" without undercutting the effect of the "beautiful, large stone buildings and colonial houses" that define the campus' look. The school has updated where it counts; "When you enter the buildings you find state-of-the-art facilities: smart classrooms, computerized locks and plenty of computer labs," students report.

The same can't be said for the Providence campus where part-timers convene, unfortunately. There, "Classrooms lack technology: ...in-class TVs constantly broken, and professors have to sign up for projectors for laptops. Many times there aren't enough to go around and they have to steal from other classrooms from professors who are late."

URI's full-time program draws a mix of recent college grads and internationals, with a smattering of students with substantial professional experience; students have "extremely diverse backgrounds: theater to military, lots of engineers, and Chinese, Spanish, and German students." The part-time program is "95 percent people who work for companies in the area. The age range varies widely from 22 to 55." The part-time program draws students from the following employers: Banc of America Leasing & Capital LLC, Brown University, Camp, Dresser & McKee, Citizens Financial Group, Composites One LLC, CVS Caremark, Exchange City, Fidelity, GTECH, Hasbro Inc., Heartlab, Hexagon Metrology, Inc., ICF International, InVentiv Health, MetLife, Saint Elizabeth Place, Stryker Biotech, Taco Inc., Thomson Financial, URI, US Navy, and Veritude.

Admissions

URI offers many components of its application online and encourages applicants to submit materials online whenever possible. Students may provide all of the following materials via the Internet: a current resume, a personal statement of purpose, and letters of recommendation (applicants e-mail referees, who then send their recommendations directly to the school). Students must also provide the admissions office with official transcripts for all postsecondary academic work and an official score report for the GMAT (scores must be no more than five years old). International applicants must provide all the above plus an official TOEFL or IELTS score report (scores must be no more than two years old); the minimum required score for admission is 575 on the paper-based TOEFL, 91 on the Internet-based TOEFL, or 65 on the IELTS. The school notes that most successful applicants have an undergraduate GPA of at least 3.0 and GMAT scores ranked in at least the 50th percentile, but allows that grades and test scores are not the sole criteria for admission. The school seeks candidates with demonstrated strength in quantitative skills, work experience ("valued," but not required, according to university materials), leadership potential, motivation, and communication skills.

FINANCIAL FACTS

Annual tuition (in-state/ out-of-state)	$16,178/$40,520
Fees	$4,500
Cost of books	$4,500

ADMISSIONS

Admissions Selectivity Rating	**76**
# of applications received	97
% applicants accepted	75
% acceptees attending	75
Average GMAT	562
Average GPA	3.28
TOEFL required of international students	Yes
Minimum TOEFL (paper/computer)	575/233
Application fee	$65
International application fee	$65
Regular application deadline	4/15
Early decision program?	No
Deferment available	Yes
Maximum length of deferment	1 year
Transfer students accepted	Yes
Transfer application policy: Can take up to 20% of total credits from another AACSB accredited college/university.	
Non-fall admissions	Yes
Need-blind admissions	Yes

UNIVERSITY OF RICHMOND
ROBINS SCHOOL OF BUSINESS

GENERAL INFORMATION

Type of school	Private
Academic calendar	Semester

SURVEY SAYS...
Good peer network
Solid preparation in:
General management
Doing business in a global economy

STUDENTS

Enrollment of parent institution	4,322
Enrollment of MBA Program	148
% part-time	100
Average age at entry	28
Average years work experience at entry	5

ACADEMICS

Academic Experience Rating	**84**
Student/faculty ratio	2:1
Profs interesting rating	93
Profs accessible rating	87
% female faculty	20
% minority faculty	1

Joint Degrees
Juris Doctor/Master of Business Administration (3–4 years)

Prominent Alumni
David Beran, Senior Vice President, Philip Morris USA; Lyn McDermid, Chief Information Officer, Dominion Resources; Bruce Kay, VP, Markel Corp.

Academics

Discussion is the heart and soul of the Richmond MBA. At this small program, students are encouraged to put their opinions on the table, and "Classroom discussions drive a lot of the learning that takes place at the school." In the classroom, professors are excellent facilitators, ably "engaging students in an ongoing conversation instead of just lecturing to a captive audience." Classmates are another source of expertise; "Robins School doesn't separate the part-time students from the full-time students, so the younger students with only several years of experience can benefit from classroom discussion and debate with the more seasoned managers." A current student shares, "I have classes with senior managers in many different industries, and even a CEO." In the classroom, professors aren't afraid to tap into that vital resource, "allowing folks with experience in a particular issue to lead the discussion on some subjects." In addition to enhancing the learning experience, class discussion "familiarizes students with one another, and makes networking with each other much easier."

The Richmond MBA is comprised of eleven core courses and four elective courses, designed to emphasize analysis and decision-making skills. When they aren't overseeing discussions, professors are highly focused on student comprehension, and they "present the subject matter in a manner in which all of the students can grasp the concepts." Beyond the core, the Richmond MBA distinguishes itself through several special programs. The required International Residency gives students the opportunity to travel to another country "where they have to solve a real-world business case," for an international company. Closer to home, the "mandatory capstone projects" sends students to work on a live case with a local business, thus giving "the school visibility with top regional employers." On that note, University of Richmond's strong network in the local community is another strength of the program. On campus, you'll rub elbows with industry big wigs, as "professors have been leaders in business or have networked enough to bring C-Level executives into all of my classes." In addition, "Many projects in class are hands-on and involve interaction with local corporations and non-profits."

A student-friendly environment, Richmond professors are "always willing to provide additional instruction or assistance as requested." The administration is, likewise, very responsive to student concerns. On this small campus, "Administrators know everyone in the program," and they "are open to suggestions for new courses and clubs." In fact, "Dean Coughlan proactively engages the students on issues like planning the course offerings for future semesters." When it comes to the nuts and bolts, everything runs smoothly; administrators "are extremely communicative and keep everyone in the know."

Career and Placement

If you want to stay local after finishing your MBA, the city "Richmond is home to numerous headquarters of companies and their executives have great relationships with the University." If you've set your sights a bit farther, University of Richmond also maintains a "good business network in Midatlantic and Northeast regions." Alumni are active and involved; however, the best networking starts in the classroom. Over and over, students tell us that Richmond is "excellent for creating a network of students that I feel I can rely on throughout my career."

"Historically, most Robins School MBA candidates have had their companies paying for their educations," and therefore, there were "not a lot of career fairs or other opportunities outside of the classroom to pursue jobs or network with companies." Ever attentive to student needs, the school recently hired a Career Services director, who "has done a great job increasing assistance to students looking for a new career, as well as to provide opportunities for students to improve skills, such as interviewing." A student elaborates, "We're seeing more full-time students and career-changers, like me, and I think the trend will be more pronounced in the near future...I've had a lot of employer interest for internships and most of my leads have come from the efforts of the new Director of MBA services." Currently, Some of the school's top recruiters include Accenture, Citigroup, Deloitte & Touche, Dominion, Ernst & Young, Goldman Sachs, KPMG, Philip Morris, PricewaterhouseCoopers, Virginia Asset Management, and Wachovia.

Student Life and Environment

While the academic atmosphere is lively and collaborative, most "people are very busy juggling school, work and their personal lives." Therefore, many students only visit campus for class or to "use the library for school research and project meeting." Other students find a little time to hang out with their classmates; For example, "people arrive early and catch up in the atrium, or go to a local hangout after class to socialize." A student agrees, "The best social outing is getting together after class to grab a drink, some food and catch up with friends. Sometimes the guest speakers will join us as well—great networking opportunity!" In addition to casual gatherings, the school hosts, "at least one activity every week for MBA students to network, such as happy hours, super bowl parties, or bowling nights." As the number of fulltime students increases, "The professional organizations and clubs run by MBA students are increasing in number as well." In particular, "The MBA Leadership Council hosts activities, social, networking, and community service for MBA students (and when appropriate families) creating more opportunities for student interactions."

Admissions

At University of Richmond, classes start once a year, in August. There are no minimum admissions requirements with regards to GPA and GMAT scores; however, most entering students have a GMAT score of 600 or above. The average GPA for incoming students is 3.2. Applicants must have a minimum of two years of professional experience to be considered for the program; however, the average student has six years of work experience.

FINANCIAL FACTS

Annual tuition	$28,970
Cost of books	$4,780
Room & board (off-campus)	$9,360
% of students receiving aid	40
% of first-year students receiving aid	45
% of students receiving loans	24
% of students receiving grants	23
Average award package	$15,160
Average grant	$9,250
Average student loan debt	$43,170

ADMISSIONS

Admissions Selectivity Rating	77
# of applications received	83
% applicants accepted	77
% acceptees attending	73
Average GMAT	592
Range of GMAT	540–650
Average GPA	3.24
TOEFL required of international students	Yes
Minimum TOEFL (paper/computer)	600/250
Application fee	$50
International application fee	$50
Regular application deadline	5/1
Regular notification	6/1
Early decision program?	No
Deferment available	Yes
Maximum length of deferment	1 year
Transfer students accepted	Yes
Transfer application policy: Maximum of 12 hours of transfer credit accepted from other AACSB-accredited schools.	
Non-fall admissions	No
Need-blind admissions	Yes

UNIVERSITY OF ROCHESTER
WILLIAM E. SIMON GRADUATE SCHOOL OF BUSINESS ADMINISTRATION

GENERAL INFORMATION

Type of school	Private
Academic calendar	Quarter

SURVEY SAYS...
Helfpul alumni
Smart classrooms
Solid preparation in:
Finance
Teamwork
Quantitative skills

STUDENTS

Enrollment of parent institution	9,509
Enrollment of MBA Program	616
% male/female	71/29
% part-time	38
% minorities	9
% international	57
Average age at entry	25
Average years work experience at entry	4

ACADEMICS

Academic Experience Rating	**94**
Student/faculty ratio	10:1
Profs interesting rating	89
Profs accessible rating	87
% female faculty	16

Joint Degrees
MBA/Master of Public Health, 3 years; MD/MBA, 5 years.

Prominent Alumni
Karunas Chesonis, CEO/PAETEC; Jay Benet, CFO/The Travelers Companiesnds; Robert Keegan, CEO/Goodyear Tire Company; Mark Grier, Chairman, Prudential Insurance Co.; Mark Ain, Founder and CEO/Kronos Incorporated.

Academics

Founded in the 1960s under its already revered parent institution, the William E. Simon Graduate School of Business Administration is not only a "top school in the region," with "a strong faculty and course work and a solid reputation," it has gone on to stake its claim as a leading business school in the nation. Known for its "small size, economic-based academic framework, international diversity," "analytic curriculum," and "approachable faculty," "it is considered one of the best finance schools in the world."

Life at the Simon School "is very involved. Since the school is small, more responsibility is placed on students to fill leadership positions in clubs and student government. If somebody is looking to get involved both in[side] and out[side] the classroom, then Simon is definitely the place for them." Classes are "very intense." "Coupled with the clubs and job hunt, it can get overwhelming at times," says one overtaxed student. "Luckily we work in teams, so everyone is going through the same thing!" Others add, "Anyone who has been through the Simon MBA knows that what you receive in challenge and stress comes back two fold in confidence and business expertise."

Small class sizes at Simon "create phenomenal professor-student interaction." and are a consistent highlight for students. "By having a class of roughly 200 students you really have the opportunity to build relationships with all of your cohorts." Professors at Simon "are top-notch." Many operate on an "open-door policy, and even the most disguised professors are accessible." Others note, "The best teachers (tenured and otherwise) teach the core courses at Simon, which leaves us very well-prepared for our internships in the coming summer." In addition, the school boasts "three very well-reputed journals edited on campus (Journal of Financial Economics, the Journal of Monetary Economics, and the Journal of Accounting and Economics)."

The administration here "is 100 percent behind its students" and "is willing to do whatever is necessary to ensure all of its students are satisfied." "Our Dean [specifically] has impacted almost every student at our school. He is an amazing role model for all of the students and faculty." Succinctly put, "The overall academic experience is flawless at Simon; if you are seriously interested in receiving a top-notch education, I don't think you can consider any other university."

Career and Placement

Students say Simon's career center "has a great NYC recruiting program." Others feel "the school could do more to attract top employers." "Given that we are a small school, not many large firms are willing to devote a lot of resources to recruit on our campus." Alumni, however, "are very responsive." In fact, students feel that perhaps this provides an avenue which the school might tap into more heavily in the future; "I would like to see more alumni come to campus to share their experiences and help the school place talented students in great positions." Despite areas of needed improvement, students are quick to note that "it's a tough market right now"; "The career management office is still a work in progress—they need to diversify the job openings and provide international students more skills in networking and job search."

In 2009, 81.3 percent of full-time MBA graduates seeking employment received a job offer with a mean base salary of $74,752 for those who accepted positions within three months after graduation. The University of Rochester, Aurora Capital, Deloitte & Touche, Xerox Corporation, and Booz Allen Hamilton were the top five employers. Most students matriculated into the financial services, consulting, and consumer industries.

ADMISSIONS CONTACT: REBEKAH LEWIN, INTERIM EXECUTIVE DIRECTOR FOR ADMISSIONS
ADDRESS: 305 SCHLEGEL HALL ROCHESTER, NY 14627-0107
PHONE: 585-275-3533 • FAX: 585-271-3907
E-MAIL: ADMISSIONS@SIMON.ROCHESTER.EDU • WEBSITE: WWW.SIMON.ROCHESTER.EDU

FINANCIAL FACTS

Annual tuition	$40,980
Fees	$975
Cost of books	$1,875
Room & board	$14,760

ADMISSIONS

Admissions Selectivity Rating	**94**
# of applications received	1,048
% applicants accepted	31
% acceptees attending	37
Average GMAT	682
Range of GMAT	650–720
Average GPA	3.53
TOEFL required of international students	Yes
Application fee	$125
International application fee	$125
Application Deadline/Notification	
Round 1:	11/20 / 2/15
Round 2:	1/5 / 3/31
Round 3:	3/15 / 5/15
Round 4:	5/14 / 7/15
Early decision program?	Yes
ED Deadline/Notification	10/15 / 1/15
Deferment available	No
Transfer students accepted	Yes
Transfer application policy: No more than 9 credit hours, may not be core courses.	
Non-fall admissions	Yes
Need-blind admissions	Yes

Student Life and Environment

With over 50 percent of 2009's incoming class hailing from abroad, the student body at Simon is "very diverse, both in terms of work experience and ethnicity." "The culture mix is amazing, but also very rewarding to the b-school experience." Overall the student body reflects a mixture of younger students and returning executives which produces "a great bunch of students and professionals." With many students coming fresh out of undergraduate studies, "the mix is younger on average." The Executive MBA class "is close, and many socialize outside of class and study times. We have a wide variety of backgrounds, interests, ages, and cultures."

Overall, the atmosphere at Simon is "competitive yet very cooperative, [and] adaptive to the changing business environment." Although some may appear "to have a chip on their shoulder about attending Simon," [including] many wannabe investment bankers that have very little work experience," by in large students here are "intellectually curious, and very kind and helpful." Ambition and a hard-working attitude aren't hard to come by. Simon's students "are the most fascinating, motivated people you could hope to meet." "Every student is passionate about some area of business. I often find conversations taking place in the coffee shop about how what we are learning relates to the real world." "Many Simon students forgo the opportunity to have an internship over the summer and end up starting companies/practices with one another. It is a small school and the close-knit nature of the students reflects that."

Life at school is "extremely busy" with "lectures, study groups, assignments, networking, corporate presentations, alumni events, club activities, and recruitment events." In addition, "students are involved in clubs and activities and course work […] with a lot of team-based assignments, ensuring that we build communications, teamwork and leadership skills." The town of Rochester "is somewhat small, but people are friendly and there is plenty to do." The "beautiful Ivy League-looking campus" boasts an "amazing library and resources" and "separate graduate study areas both in the business school and the library."

Admissions

Admission to Simon is extremely competitive. Students with exceptional GPAs, applicable test scores, and relevant leadership experience (including post-baccalaureate work and extracurricular activities) rise to the top of the pool. Applicants to the school's MBA program must submit the following: an online application, three required essays, undergraduate transcripts, two letters of recommendation, a current resume, an official GMAT report, and interview (if requested by the Admissions Committee). International students for whom English is not a primary language must submit an official score report for the TOEFL. This requirement is waived if students have studied for at least one full year in a college or university where English is the language of instruction.

EMPLOYMENT PROFILE

		Grads Employed by Function	% Avg. Salary
Career Rating	92		
Percent employed at graduation	58	Marketing	27 $74,155
Percent employed 3 months		Operations	4 $77,333
after graduation	81	Consulting	20 $77,850
Average base starting salary	$74,752	Management	6 $56,800
Primary Source of Full-time Job Acceptances		Finance	40 $79,033
School-facilitated activities	51 (63%)	Other	4 $44,300
Graduate-facilitated activities	27 (33%)	**Top 5 Employers Hiring Grads**	
Unknown	3 (4%)	University of Rochester (7), Aurora Capital (6), Deloitte (5), Xerox Corporation (5), Booz Allen (3)	

UNIVERSITY OF SAN DIEGO
SCHOOL OF BUSINESS ADMINISTRATION

GENERAL INFORMATION
Type of school   Private
Affiliation   Roman Catholic
Academic calendar   Aug–May

SURVEY SAYS...
Students love San Diego, CA
Cutting-edge classes
Solid preparation in:
Teamwork
Doing business in a global economy

STUDENTS
Enrollment of parent institution	7,868
Enrollment of MBA Program	208
% male/female	73/27
% out-of-state	27
% minorities	18
% international	14
Average age at entry	26
Average years work experience at entry	4

ACADEMICS
Academic Experience Rating	85
Profs interesting rating	92
Profs accessible rating	88
% female faculty	32
% minority faculty	13

Joint Degrees
MBA/JD, 4 years; MBA/MSN, 3 years; MBA/MSRE 2.5 years; IMBA/JD, 4 years, 2 int'l dual degrees, 2 years.

Prominent Alumni
Lowell McAdam. President and CEO, Verizon Wireless; Robert Mac Kay, Vice President & General Auditor, PepsiCo, Inc.; Lorenzo Fertitta, Chief Executive Officer & Chairman, Zuffa, LLC, Gary Ridge, President & Chief Executive Officer, WD-40 Company.; Betsy Myers, Chief Operating Officer, Obama for America.

Academics

The relaxed Southern California atmosphere, intimate class size, and unique focus on ethics in business are among the most attractive aspects of a University of San Diego education. For established or budding professionals, USD's School of Business Administration offers several MBA options: the full-time MBA, the full-time International MBA, and the part-time evening MBA. Both the full-time MBA and the International MBA are two-year programs with the option to accelerate to 16 months, which begin with a cohort-based, lockstep curriculum in the first semester. Thereafter, full-time and IMBA students take required courses during the day and electives at night, along with part-time evening MBA students. Within the curriculum, students really like the fact that USD "emphasizes "soft" subjects like ethics in business and cultural sensitivity in addition to the core coursework in finance, economics, and general management." In fact, the school's "focus on corporate social responsibility" is "incorporated into just about every single class we take." Along the same lines, USD "is on the forefront of the green building movement and goes to great efforts to give us every opportunity to learn more about green practices." USD further distinguishes itself through its global focus and "opportunities for study abroad." Within the International MBA, "Classes are offered in four different continents" and include with a "required international consulting project."

Located in San Diego, the Southern California sunshine clearly influences campus culture. At USD, the "academic environment is very relaxed but very professional in nature." A current student attests, "I don't see many students that appear stressed, even in the MBA program." In addition, students benefit from "small class sizes" and "extremely personal attention from administration and faculty." A student agrees, "While many of the courses are rigorous, they are manageable, and I have found the professors to be very willing to help." On the whole, professors are "effective teachers with interesting backgrounds," who are "passionate about the subjects they teach." Collaboration is encouraged, and "there's a lot of group work in our classes, so you really get to know your fellow students." Like the faculty, some students note that the administration is "easily accessible" and "responsive to student needs." Others feel "the school's administration is improving but needs refinement."

Career and Placement

At USD, career planning begins long before graduation. During the MBA, "The administration is aggressive in securing internships and setting up events for business contacts" in the San Diego area. Through the Career Services offices, students may also be "assigned mentors from the local business community, so that's another great opportunity to network and help you learn more about your chosen industry." In fact, many students take advantage of the fact that, "after the first semester, we typically have night classes, so it opens up the potential for students to work or take on an internship." For one student, "Class work resulted in a new, higher-paying job even before finishing school."

University of San Diego's Career Services office has partnered with UC—San Diego and San Diego State to provide a large database of regional job opportunities. However, "Much of their efforts seem to be centered around the needs of undergraduate students," leaving graduate students with fewer resources than they need. Many graduate students feel they "must be self-driven to network and must create career opportunities for themselves." A student explains, "There should be partnerships and "feeder" programs in place, based on the reputation of the education, if nothing else. This is strongly lacking and one of the drawbacks to an otherwise fantastic program."

Student Life and Environment

In the school's full-time MBA programs, the cohort structure is a mainstay of the program. A current student enthuses, "My cohort provides me with a great blend of diversity from professional background to ethnicity and upbringing. I feel challenged and supported by them at the same time, which I feel adds more to my learning experience than I could have imagined." In addition to academic work, students say, "We try to socialize outside of class as often as possible." Fortunately, that goal is easily achieved as there is "a social event every almost weekend" at the business school, as well as a plethora of professional development activities on campus. A student agrees, "There are constantly social events on campus from speakers to panel discussions that support a fun lifestyle to reduce stress." Another adds, "There are so many more planned activities available to do than time to do them, and that does not even include unplanned or non-official activities."

Located in sunny Southern California, "the city of San Diego is vibrant and youthful and really embraces the students that attend universities." In addition, "USD has a beautiful campus," which "sits above Mission Bay in San Diego." While students complain that there is a pittance of parking and public transportation at USD, once on campus, the "food options are excellent, and it is easy to get around."

Admissions

To apply for admission to USD's MBA programs, prospective students must hold an undergraduate degree from an accredited college, with a GPA of B or better. For the most recent incoming class, students had a mean GMAT score of 669. The same year, International MBA candidates had an average GMAT score of 602, and evening MBA students averaged 601 on the GMAT. For all MBA programs, a minimum of two years of professional work experience is expected.

FINANCIAL FACTS

Annual tuition	$30,250
Fees	$164
Cost of books	$1,300
% of students receiving aid	98
% of first-year students receiving aid	98
% of students receiving grants	98
Average award package	$21,340
Average student loan debt	$16,376

ADMISSIONS

Admissions Selectivity Rating	86
# of applications received	114
% applicants accepted	66
% acceptees attending	29
Average GMAT	669
Range of GMAT	633–710
Average GPA	3.2
TOEFL required of international students	Yes
Minimum TOEFL (paper/computer/web)	580/237/92
Application fee	$80
International application fee	$80
Application Deadline/Notification	
Round 1:	12/15 / 2/15
Round 2:	2/1 / 4/1
Round 3:	4/1 / 5/1
Early decision program?	Yes
ED Deadline/Notification	NR / 2/15
Deferment available	Yes
Maximum length of deferment	1 year
Transfer students accepted	No
Non-fall admissions	Yes
Need-blind admissions	Yes

Applicants Also Look At
Pepperdine University, San Diego State University, Thunderbird, University of California—Irvine, University of California—San Diego, University of Southern California (Marshall)

EMPLOYMENT PROFILE

Career Rating	76	Grads Employed by Function	% Avg. Salary
Primary Source of Full-time Job Acceptances		Marketing	17 NR
School-facilitated activities	NR (25%)	Ops/Logistics	17 NR
Graduate-facilitated activities	NR (35%)	Finance	33 NR
Unknown	NR (40%)	General Management	17 NR

Top 5 Employers Hiring Grads
Northrop Gumman, Cricket Wireless, Life Technologies, Sony, SpaWar

UNIVERSITY OF SAN FRANCISCO
MASAGUNG GRADUATE SCHOOL OF MANAGEMENT

GENERAL INFORMATION

Type of school	Private
Affiliation	Jesuit
Academic calendar	Semesters

SURVEY SAYS...

Students love San Francisco, CA
Friendly students
Good social scene
Good peer network
Solid preparation in:
Teamwork
Doing business in a global economy
Entrepreneurial studies

STUDENTS

Enrollment of parent institution	8,772
Enrollment of MBA Program	372
% male/female	55/45
% out-of-state	5
% part-time	39
% minorities	28
% international	14
Average age at entry	30
Average years work experience at entry	4

ACADEMICS

Academic Experience Rating	**80**
Student/faculty ratio	5:1
Profs interesting rating	86
Profs accessible rating	86
% female faculty	30
% minority faculty	25

Joint Degrees

JD/MBA; MAPS/MBA (Asian Pacific Studies)MSEM/MBA (Master of Science in Environmental Management)MSFA/MBA, DDS/MBA (with UCSF Dental School)

Prominent Alumni

Gordon Smith, CEO, PG&E; Lip Bu-Tan, Founder, Walden International Investment Group; Mary Callanan, Retired Treasurer for the County/City of San Fran; Angela Alioto, Attorney, Political Leader; Pierre Salinger, Former Press Secretary to the U.S. President.

Academics

"A great emphasis on entrepreneurship and finance" is among the program strengths that draw MBAs to the University of San Francisco's School of Business and Professional Studies where a variety of MBA options to suit all needs is on offer. USF's MBA is available in six program formats: a traditional two-year, full-time MBA, an accelerated one-year MBA, a part-time MBA, an accelerated part-time MBA, a part-time MBA for those with fewer than two years' work experience (called the MBA Career Advantage Program), and an Executive MBA. Students in a hurry to receive their degrees laud the intensive programs, while those pursuing their degrees at a more leisurely pace appreciate their program's convenience.

In all programs, USF's "strong connections with venture capitalists in the area" as well as "the technology and innovation of the Silicon Valley" help make entrepreneurship "such a strength" of this MBA program. A "national business plan competition hosted by the school" further bolsters USF's status as a leader in entrepreneurship. The school's "international draw"—nearly 40 percent of students here are internationals—makes USF a great place for those interested in international business to learn and network. "I believe that anyone looking to get into international business would find USF a great fit," one student tells us. Each of USF's MBA programs maintains "small class sizes" that promote "personal relationships with professors," especially valuable since professors here "will get you business contacts." Each program embodies "the Jesuit approach toward a well-rounded education" and works at "ensuring ethics" throughout the curriculum.

Once core courses are completed, the USF curriculum is "taught in seven-week modules, which can be stressful. It's a tight workload within seven weeks, but it is also satisfying to have four classes done in seven weeks." The program places "an emphasis on group cooperation while nurturing individual growth."

Career and Placement

If you want to live and work in the Bay Area, USF will give you an edge in the local market. A staple in the community, USF has a strong alumni base and the school creates "good opportunities to network." Currently, USF graduates are employed at a range of prestigious companies, including Advanced Fibre Communications, Bank of the West, BioMarin Pharmaceutical, Inc., California Bank and Trust, Charles Schwab, Cisco Systems, EMQ Children & Family Services, Ernst & Young, LLP, IBM Global Services, Inverito, Inc., KPMG, LaRose Group, Lautze & Lautze, Live Capital, Marcus & Millichap, Marsh, Inc., Mervyn's, OPT Derivatives, Pacific Gas and Electric Company, Peat Marwick, Persona, International, Premier Accountants, Prudential, Salomon Smith Barney, Systron-Donner, Walden International Investment Group, and Wells Capital Management.

For those pursuing new positions after graduation, USF Career Services hosts career development workshops, special events, and recruiting activities. Career Services also keeps an up-to-date blog about careers and industries. Despite these services, students feel the office can do better. "The ability to bring in more big name companies or even jobs for the MBA students" is an area for improvement, one student writes, adding "I believe it is difficult because we have to compete with Stanford and Berkley, but USF MBA grads have a lot to offer and I believe being in San Francisco they should be marketing the MBA program much better to the job market."

Address: 2130 Fulton Street, Lone Mountain San Francisco, CA 94117-1045
Phone: 415-422-2221 • Fax: 415-358-9112 • E-mail: graduate@usfca.edu
Website: www.usfca.edu/mba

Student Life and Environment

USF's "wired campus" in "one of the most beautiful cities in the world" offers "good resources" to students. "We have easy access to study rooms, computers, technology, and food (very important)," one student reports. Students' involvement on campus depends on their program. Part timers here "are not very involved [with the program] outside the classroom," nor are students in the "intense" Executive MBA program, who happily report that the program "takes care of its students," a process that includes "catering all the food so you can concentrate on your classes."

Full timers, on the other hand, tell us that extracurricular life is "very active: a lot of clubs, good sport programs, a lot of speakers from Silicon Valley." There's also "Thirsty Thursday events, where students get together at local bars on Thursdays and have a drink" and "Hump Day Wednesday dinners at school." The event calendar is easy to track, as events "are summarized each week in an email from the VP of Marketing from the Graduate Business Association."

All here agree that San Francisco is an "excellent location" where there's "always something to do." There are "plenty of attractions nearby, including bars, parks, and museums. Students hang out with each other outside of school at these places." The MBA population is "a good mix of students in terms of background, gender, work experience" and include "many international students, students from across the U.S., married and single students, as well as students who come from all sorts of professional backgrounds."

Admissions

Admissions requirements vary among USF's various MBA programs. All require that applicants submit official transcripts for all post-secondary academic work. All but the MBA for Executives require a GMAT score. At least two years of professional business experience is required for all but the MBA Career Advancement Program; the MBA for Executives requires at least seven years of experience. Essays, letters of recommendation, and a current resume are required by all programs. International applicants may be required to demonstrate English proficiency through the TOEFL, IELTS, or PTE Academic. Those with non-English transcripts are required to have them translated by a recognized translation service. A Certification of Finances form is also required of all international students.

FINANCIAL FACTS

Annual tuition	$1,160 per credit
Fees	$70
Cost of books	$1,250
Room & board (on-campus)	$9,750
% of students receiving aid	55
% of first-year students receiving aid	57
% of students receiving loans	51
% of students receiving grants	9
Average award package	$22,069
Average grant	$12.372
Average student loan debt	$21,601

ADMISSIONS

Admissions Selectivity Rating	76
# of applications received	450
% applicants accepted	72
% acceptees attending	50
Average GMAT	600
Range of GMAT	550–730
Average GPA	3.1
TOEFL required of international students	Yes
Minimum TOEFL (paper/computer)	600/250
Application fee	$55
International application fee	$55
Application Deadline/Notification	
Round 1:	11/15 / 12/31
Round 2:	1/15 / 2/28
Round 3:	3/15 / 5/31
Round 4:	5/15 / 6/30
Early decision program?	No
Deferment available	Yes
Maximum length of deferment	1 year
Transfer students accepted	Yes
Transfer application policy	
Transfer up to 6 credits for students coming from another AACSB accredited program.	
Non-fall admissions	Yes
Need-blind admissions	Yes

Applicants Also Look At

Santa Clara University, University of California, Irvine, University of San Diego, Pepperdine University

EMPLOYMENT PROFILE

Career Rating	80	Grads Employed by Function	%	Avg. Salary
Average base starting salary	$68,000	Marketing	39	$70,000
		Consulting	4	$65,000
		Management	4	$59,000
		Finance	14	$72,000
		MIS	7	$63,000
		Nonprofit	1	$52,000

UNIVERSITY OF SCRANTON
KANIA SCHOOL OF MANAGEMENT

GENERAL INFORMATION
Type of school	Private
Affiliation	Roman Catholic/Jesuit

SURVEY SAYS...
Solid preparation in:
General management
Communication/interpersonal skills
Presentation skills

STUDENTS
Enrollment of parent institution	4,873
Enrollment of MBA Program	87
% male/female	67/33
% part-time	65
% minorities	1
% international	23
Average age at entry	27
Average years work experience at entry	2

ACADEMICS
Academic Experience Rating	**77**
Student/faculty ratio	12:1
Profs interesting rating	90
Profs accessible rating	85
% female faculty	36
% minority faculty	2

Academics

Jesuit values add a unique flavor to the graduate business programs at the University of Scranton, which emphasizes a contemporary approach to business while simultaneously exploring topics in ethics and social responsibility. University of Scranton's MBA is designed to ensure that every candidate gains valuable knowledge in a breadth of essential business areas. In addition to traditional academics, "the school's leadership is very in tune with the needs of the students, as well as focused on what will be required of a MBA graduate in today's market place." Therefore, the program puts particular weight on the integration of technology and business, and maintains "a strong focus on globalization" throughout the curriculum. Of particular note, the business school's building, Brennan Hall, is the university's most high-tech facility, including an auditorium (fully wired for audio-visual presentations), an executive center, simulated trading floor, well-equipped computer labs for student use, and a pleasant student lounge.

Jesuit philosophy influences the character of the business school community, inspiring a cooperative and supportive academic environment, which focuses attention on educating the whole individual. At the University of Scranton, it's not difficult to solicit extra help or a bit of advice, as "the professors are always available for questions, problems, or just to talk." A current student writes, "The administration and professors have all been very helpful. They are readily available for whatever you may need. They have made me feel very comfortable and reassured knowing that they are there for you." Likewise, teamwork and cooperation is encouraged between students, fostering "a very positive environment," which students liken to "a company where everyone works as a team." In summary, a student tells us, "The community at the University of Scranton is its greatest strength. The school would not be the same if I didn't feel at home every time I walked on campus."

Kania's MBA program can be completed on a part-time basis, and therefore, a majority of students work full time while enrolled in the program. Drawing hardworking professionals from the local community, Kania students are "diverse, friendly, and bring many real-world experiences that contribute in a positive way to discussions." Generally speaking, part-time students are well integrated into the MBA program. Some, however, say they would like more weekend classes, as well as a "wider range of courses and resources to graduate students who work full time during the day." For students who would like to attend the program full time, the school operates an "excellent graduate assistantship program," which can help offset the cost of education.

CAITLYN BEASLEY, ASSOCIATE DIRECTOR, GRADUATE ADMISSIONS
ADDRESS: THE UNIVERSITY OF SCRANTON, OFFICE OF ADMISSIONS,
800 LINDEN STREET SCRANTON, PA 18510-4631 •PHONE: 570-941-7600 • FAX: 570-941-5995
E-MAIL:CGCE@SCRANTON.EDU WEBSITE: SCRANTON.EDU/MBA

Career and Placement

From a career standpoint, University of Scranton's location has both pluses and minuses. On the one hand, Scranton is within striking distance of several major metropolitan centers on the East coast, putting students in the running for positions in Philadelphia, New York, or Pittsburg. However, because Scranton is a smaller city, there are fewer job and internship opportunities in the region. Fortunately, Scranton MBAs are first in line for local positions, as the school boasts "the best reputation among business schools in Northeastern PA."

The office of Career Services at the University of Scranton assists the school's undergraduate and graduate students in locating internships and full-time employment. Throughout the year, they hold workshops on various professional development topics and also maintain an online job database, which lists current vacancies. Students say they could use a bit more assistance from the Career Services center when it comes to looking for a job; however, they also point out that the "Jesuit tradition and help from other Jesuit schools is a big plus."

Student Life and Environment

The Kania School of Management is located on the university's "scenic," 58-acre campus in downtown Scranton. In addition to the beautiful and modern business facilities, students can take advantage of all the resources available through the larger campus, including numerous libraries and wide-ranging wireless Internet. The sense of community is among the most appealing aspects of the Scranton MBA program, and "life at the University of Scranton is very vibrant among the students." In fact, many students mention the school's unique, family-like atmosphere, which tends to attract "very diverse and extremely friendly" people.

Many graduate students commute to the University of Scranton in the evenings, and therefore "spend very little time on campus." However, there are also many students who play an active role in the student community. A case in point, a current student tells us, "I am heavily involved in activities in the business school. I am a graduate assistant, so I know most of the faculty pretty well. I am an officer of the MBA Club, and I coordinate socials and presentations for the MBA students and faculty to go to." For those who'd like to mingle with their classmates, the MBA Student Association "works to get all the MBA students involved outside of the classroom. They have socials and presentations a few times a semester in order to get the MBA student socializing."

Admissions

When evaluating applicants for admission, the University of Scranton evaluates candidates on four major factors: previous academic performance, standardized test scores, letters of recommendation, and previous work experience. While all these factors play a role in an admissions decision, academic performance and GMAT scores are the most heavily weighted.

FINANCIAL FACTS

Annual tuition	$837/credit
Fees	$2,500
Cost of books	$1,733
Room & board	
(on/off-campus)	$10,950/$14,495
% of students receiving aid	10
Average award package	$26,278

ADMISSIONS

Admissions Selectivity Rating	68
# of applications received	570
% applicants accepted	71
% acceptees attending	51
Average GMAT	510
Average GPA	3.3
TOEFL required of	
international students	Yes
Minimum TOEFL	
(paper/internet)	500/61
Early decision program?	No
Deferment available	Yes
Maximum length	
of deferment	2 years
Transfer students accepted	Yes
Transfer application policy:	
A full transfer from an AACSB-	
accredited school Jesuit school,	
otherwise 6 credits max.	
Non-fall admissions	Yes
Need-blind admissions	Yes

EMPLOYMENT PROFILE

Career Rating	82
Average base starting salary	$50,494

UNIVERSITY OF SOUTH CAROLINA
MOORE SCHOOL OF BUSINESS

GENERAL INFORMATION
Type of school   Public
Academic calendar   Semester

SURVEY SAYS...
Friendly students
Good social scene
Good peer network
Helfpul alumni
Solid preparation in:
Doing business in a global economy

STUDENTS
Enrollment of parent
  institution   28,000
Enrollment of MBA Program   550
% male/female   66/34
% out-of-state   68
% part-time   66
% minorities   6
% international   18
Average age at entry   27
Average years work experience
  at entry   3

ACADEMICS
Academic Experience Rating   **86**
Student/faculty ratio   30:1
Profs interesting rating   89
Profs accessible rating   88
% female faculty   22
% minority faculty   3

Joint Degrees
JD/IMBA (4 years); JD/MHR (3
years); JD/MACC (3 years);
JD/MAECON (4 years)

Prominent Alumni
Larry Wilson, CEO IT Company;
Shigeru Sekine, President, Nikko
Chemicals; Keilie Cooper Johnson,
Sr. Product Manager, Glazo Smith
Kline; Whitney MacEachern, VP
Latin American Affairs, Citigroup;
Larry Kellner, President, Continental
Airlines.

Academics

Widely considered "one of the top institutions to study international business," the Darla Moore School of Business at University of South Carolina offers an "alternative program to traditional business school" through its flagship international MBA (IMBA) program (although it does offer a professional MBA as well). The IMBA program exposes Moore's students to a combination of "international work experience, education, and opportunity to learn a new language while completing [an] MBA." The program's required core classes make lead to "well-rounded" students. In the IMBA program, "the first seven months are spent doing a year's worth of core classes. Students are very tightly woven to provide each other academic, mental, and social support. The next four (or 12) months are spent overseas learning another language...then a four to seven-month internship, internationally or domestically, followed by a year of electives (in Columbia or abroad)."

Supporting the unique structure of the program are the school's "extremely talented" and "stellar" professors who "truly bring a wealth of international experience into the classroom." These professors "teach worldwide and use cases, simulations, and other situations to help us get a better understanding of how our decisions interact instead of just reading text." They make "the most abstract material understandable." As a result, students develop "a deep understanding of business fundamentals." Particularly noteworthy is the Global Supply Chain and Operations Management department which "prepares students to manage supply chains in a global environment, and provides students with operations management knowledge and practical training that puts them at the same level [as] engineers currently working at *Fortune* 500 companies."

While generally pleased with the quality of their professors, students are a bit more critical of the business school's administration which "is new and has some kinks to work out." On a more positive note, students feel that the administration is "open to working with the students to improve the school community, which makes up for a lack of organization and gives students a chance to gain valuable leadership skills." One recent development that is generating a lot of excitement among the students is the new "green" "multimillion dollar business school building" which was designed with "input from everyone," including "undergrads, master's [students], PhD [students], [and] staff" and which all hope will "bring unbelievable opportunities for future students."

Career and Placement

The majority of students surveyed expressed the need to improve the Office of Career Management (OCM) which they suggested should "spend less time 'coaching' students and more time focusing on building relationships with employers" as well as "reach out to a more diverse company base including ones from a wider geographic range." They also point out that "the highly-touted internship experience has suffered in recent years—the result of a failure to maintain relationships with companies (specifically in Latin America)." Students realize that not all of the blame falls on the OCM and acknowledge that "classes are small and our alumni network is small as a result. We attract some *Fortune* 500 companies who recruit on campus, but because there aren't as many of us out there in leadership, sometimes it is harder for us to get our foot in the door with these companies and during the recession we were one of the first schools cut from recruiting trips as a result." One of the more optimistic students has hopes for a brighter future and observes, "The Office of Career Management has partnered this year with a new external company and I believe they are doing a good job at providing students with placement services in a difficult hiring environment."

ADMISSIONS CONTACT: REENA LICHTENFELD, GRADUATE PROGRAMS
ADDRESS: 1705 COLLEGE STREET COLUMBIA, SC 29208
PHONE: 803-777-4346 • FAX: 803-777-0414
E-MAIL: GRADINFO@MOORE.SC.EDU • WEBSITE: MOORESCHOOL.SC.EDU

Student Life and Environment

The city of Columbia "is small but the student population makes going out fun" and "football is king." Despite its "good bar scene and nightlife," many of the students are "too busy during the core to enjoy the Columbia area. During your second year you have more of a chance, but it is a challenge to become involved in the community outside of the business school." The school campus provides "a lot of social and cultural activities" and has "everything from the normal Finance Club to Net Impact and even a Wine Society. We organize plenty of intramural teams and usually open them up to most people in the class."

The school attracts "a diverse set of students from Peace Corps volunteers to *Fortune* 500 company employees," to "Mormons with families" who all form a "very close-knit community." One student offers the more general observation that "half the students are more conservative and half are more liberal." While coming from a diverse set of backgrounds and experiences, "all are interested in new adventures and experiences particularly those having to do with learning aspects of other cultures and how their business practices differ from U.S. standards." "Overall, everyone is friendly and the atmosphere was one more of cooperation than competition."

Admissions

Applicants must submit an application, an application fee, official transcripts of post-secondary academic work, personal essays, letters of recommendation, and an official GMAT score report. International students must also submit TOEFL or IELTS scores unless they are graduates of an American college or university. Strong preference is shown for applicants with at least two years of work experience.

FINANCIAL FACTS

Annual tuition (in-state/ out-of-state)	$35,000/$52,000
Fees	$525
Cost of books	$2,000
Room & board (on/off-campus)	$15,000/$18,000
Average award package	$12,000
Average grant	$14,000
Average student loan debt	$36,000

ADMISSIONS

Admissions Selectivity Rating	85
# of applications received	328
% applicants accepted	52
% acceptees attending	51
Average GMAT	650
Range of GMAT	610–690
Average GPA	3.3
TOEFL required of international students	Yes
Minimum TOEFL (paper/computer)	600/250
Application fee	$50
International application fee	$50
Application Deadline/Notification	
Round 1:	11/15 / 12/7
Round 2:	2/15 / 3/8
Round 3:	5/15 / 6/8
Early decision program?	Yes
ED Deadline/Notification	NR / 12/7
Deferment available	No
Transfer students accepted	Yes
Transfer application policy: Can transfer up to a maximum of 12 credit hours (4 courses).	
Non-fall admissions	Yes
Need-blind admissions	Yes

EMPLOYMENT PROFILE

		Grads Employed by Function	%	Avg. Salary
Career Rating	87			
Percent employed at graduation	67	Marketing	22	$68,800
Percent employed 3 months after graduation	86	Operations	12	$73,714
		Consulting	16	$92,714
Average base starting salary	$79,376	Management	9	$87,500
Primary Source of Full-time Job Acceptances		Finance	29	$82,206
School-facilitated activities	40 (60%)	HR	2	NR
Graduate-facilitated activities	30 (43%)	MIS	2	NR

UNIVERSITY OF SOUTH DAKOTA
BEACOM SCHOOL OF BUSINESS

GENERAL INFORMATION

Type of school	Public
Academic calendar	Semester

SURVEY SAYS...
Good peer network
Solid preparation in:
Finance
Communication/interpersonal skills
Quantitative skills

STUDENTS

Enrollment of parent institution	9,617
Enrollment of MBA Program	172
% male/female	35/65
% out-of-state	15
% part-time	75
% minorities	5
% international	10
Average age at entry	24

ACADEMICS

Academic Experience Rating	**72**
Student/faculty ratio	6:1
Profs interesting rating	84
Profs accessible rating	71
% female faculty	6
% minority faculty	6

Joint Degrees
JD/MBA, approximately 3 years of full-time study.

Prominent Alumni
John Thune, U.S. Senator from South Dakota;

Academics

Boasting both convenience and quality, University of South Dakota serves the local community with the only AACSB-accredited business program in the state. For South Dakotans, there is no better package than a USD MBA, as the "school is cheap, has small class sizes along with faculty that is always available to help out, is close to home, and has just as many opportunities as a bigger graduate school would have." Operating a full-time MBA program at the school's main campus in Vermillion, as well as a part-time face-to-face program at a satellite campus in Sioux Falls and a part-time online program, many students say the school's convenient location was one of the main factors in their decision to attend USD.

While this state school is low cost, it maintains high-quality academic programs. Drawing a team of experienced professors from across the nation, USD "faculty are overall very easy to talk to, are accessible outside of class, and are focused on learning." A student writes, "The professors seem very eager to help us learn. Often times I have asked many questions and they were willing to spend the time answering questions, even if it was not directly related to the coursework." When it comes to the administration, "it is easier to be in contact with the directors of the program, as well as the dean, because the school is small." A current student adds, "The way I look at it is, if a faculty member with a PhD is willing to stay at this school and teach here in this small town, there is more passion for educating students here than at some other schools."

While the program once required prerequisite courses in business essentials, as of May 2009 these foundation courses are now embedded in the program. Undergraduate business majors will easily meet these requirements; however, students coming to the program from other disciplines should expect to take introductory economics, accounting, statistics, and finance courses as they begin the MBA, or else be prepared to pass a challenge exam in these subjects. Once they have begun the advanced MBA curriculum, students will be versed in managerial and high-level business topics, with the option of specializing in health services administration, or simply pursuing a general MBA.

Throughout the MBA curriculum, students appreciate the fact that "classroom environments are small, making it easier to interact and get to know everyone at least on an acquaintance level." In both the daytime and evening programs, discussion is encouraged, and students learn a lot from their cohorts. While some have more limited career experiences, many others join the MBA program midway through careers as "software engineers, CFO, directors, and analysts." A student details, "My fellow students have great ideas and have great experiences to share with the class."

Career and Placement

The University of South Dakota Career Development Center offers a range of services to undergraduate and graduate students, including career and life coaching, resume review and cover letter assistance, and mock interviews. In addition, The Beacom School of Business has a separate Employment Center in house. Their full events calendar includes various career fairs and campus recruiting events. This year, recruiters from various companies visited the business school, including Wells Fargo Financial and Federated Insurance. In addition, you'll be able to accomplish some useful networking right on campus, because USD professors "have done their own research and teaching at other major universities as well as abroad. They have many contacts."

ADMISSIONS CONTACT: DR. ANGELINE LAVIN, MBA AND MPA PROGRAMS DIRECTOR
ADDRESS: 414 E. CLARK, SCHOOL OF BUSINESS VERMILLION, SD 57069
PHONE: 866-890-1622 • FAX: 605-677-5058
E-MAIL: MBA@USD.EDU • WEBSITE: WWW.USD.EDU/MBA

Student Life and Environment

University of South Dakota is a smaller state university with a friendly vibe and nice facilities. The full-time MBA program takes place on the school's main campus in Vermillion, where graduate students can take advantage of all the resources and facilities available at the school's peaceful, 200-acre campus. While the surrounding town of Vermillion isn't a hub of urban activity, there are plenty of outdoor activities in the surrounding area (and throughout the state) to satisfy your recreational needs.

The part-time program, on the other hand, is located in Sioux Falls. In this larger city environment, most students work full time and attend class in the evenings. As a result, the campus atmosphere is a bit more pared down, though students nonetheless report a friendly and collaborative environment. In and outside of classes, "everyone gets along for the most part, and their behavior is professional." MBA students "are all very outgoing; they understand when to have fun and when to get down to business." A part-time MBA program is also available online.

Admissions

To apply to the University of South Dakota, students must submit official GMAT scores and undergraduate transcripts, as well as two letters of recommendation, a statement of purpose, and a current resume. International applicants must have a TOEFL score of at least 550 (paper version) or 213 (computer version) as well as a score of at least 79 on the IBT or 6.0 on the IELTS. Qualified full-time students may also choose to apply for one of the competitive Graduate Assistantships, which helps offset the costs of the USD education.

FINANCIAL FACTS

Annual tuition (in-state/ out-of-state)	$4,587/$9,710
Fees	$5,661
Cost of books	$1,500
% of students receiving aid	57
% of first-year students receiving aid	56
% of students receiving loans	55
% of students receiving grants	18
Average award package	$16,134
Average grant	$988

ADMISSIONS

Admissions Selectivity Rating	68
# of applications received	52
% applicants accepted	96
% acceptees attending	74
Average GMAT	536
Average GPA	3.35
TOEFL required of international students	Yes
Minimum TOEFL (paper/computer)	550/213
Application fee	$35
International application fee	$35
Regular application deadline	6/1
Early decision program?	No
Deferment available	Yes
Maximum length of deferment	3 years
Transfer students accepted	Yes
Transfer application policy: Maximum of 9 credit hours from an accredited institution may be transferred.	
Non-fall admissions	Yes
Need-blind admissions	Yes

EMPLOYMENT PROFILE

Career Rating	86	Grads Employed by Function	% Avg. Salary
Percent employed 3 months after graduation	91	Operations	6 $30,000
		Consulting	6 NR
Average base starting salary	$54,566	Management	11 $100,000
Primary Source of Full-time Job Acceptances		Finance	38 $53,924
School-facilitated activities	3 (17%)	HR	6 $41,500
Graduate-facilitated activities	6 (28%)	MIS	6 $56,000
Unknown	13 (55%)	**Top 5 Employers Hiring Grads**	
		FDIC (3), Citi (1), McGladrey & Pullen (1), Sencore (1), First Dakota National Bank (1)	

UNIVERSITY OF SOUTHERN CALIFORNIA
MARSHALL SCHOOL OF BUSINESS

GENERAL INFORMATION
Type of school   Private
Academic calendar   Semester

SURVEY SAYS...
Good social scene
Good peer network
Helfpul alumni
Solid preparation in:
Doing business in a global economy

STUDENTS
Enrollment of parent institution	35,000
Enrollment of MBA Program	1,241
% male/female	69/31
% out-of-state	42
% part-time	63
% minorities	9
% international	26
Average age at entry	28
Average years work experience at entry	5

ACADEMICS
Academic Experience Rating	**92**
Student/faculty ratio	10:1
Profs interesting rating	75
Profs accessible rating	76
% female faculty	25
% minority faculty	5

Joint Degrees
Dual degree programs: Dental Surgery (MBA/DDS); East Asian Area Studies (MBA/MA); Gerontology (MSG/MBA); Industrial and Systems Engineering (MBA/MSISE); Jewish Communal Service (MBA/MA); Law (JD/MBA); Medicine (MD/MBA); Planning (MBA/MPL); Pharmacy (PharmD/MBA); Real Estate Development (MBA/MRED); Social Work (MBA/MSW); Education (MBA/EdD); Law and Business Taxation (JD/MBT).

Academics

Offering "international business learning opportunities not available elsewhere" as well as solid programs in entrepreneurship, real estate, marketing, and entertainment, the University of Southern California's Marshall School of Business excels in a broad range of areas. Best of all, perhaps, USC boasts "the most amazing alumni network in the nation," a huge asset when the time for job searches arrives. As one student explains, "I have never met another Trojan anywhere in the world who wasn't excited to meet another fellow Trojan!" "The Trojan Network is enormous and expansive, providing a lifetime equity of resources."

Marshall offers a two-year full-time program as well as a part-time evening MBA, an executive MBA, and a one-year international MBA (called the IBEAR MBA). The school "combines a rigorous curriculum" with "the personal attention of a private college." The MBA program here "has a strong emphasis on providing students an international perspective on business issues. It is more than just saying 'We think it is important that you consider other cultures.' At Marshall, it's mandatory that all students work on a consulting project for·a company overseas and travel to that region through the PRIME program. As a result of PRIME and other programs, I've had meaningful work, educational, and fun experiences in Singapore, Thailand, Vietnam, and in Western Europe."

Marshall professors "are outstanding. They bring new research into the classroom and encourage students to actively participate in class." The faculty represents "a mixture of academics and recent career switchers from their fields in business...they do a very good job giving us a base to learn from." Course work is demanding; one student warns, "Marshall is much more difficult than I expected. I have nine years of work experience and consider myself a fairly bright individual. If I put in a decent amount of work and keep up with the reading, I can get a B-plus in our classes with relative ease, but it really is difficult to break the A barrier." Administrators "are committed to growth and innovation as an institution." As a result, "Chaos is inherent when new programs and classes are initiated.... This is a leading school's greatest challenge, and USC Marshall does everything in its power to attend to students' individual needs as well as meet their own goals and expectations."

Career and Placement

Marshall's Career Resources Center "has already made incredible changes" since bringing on a new director five years ago. "The resources and energy the career coaches bring to the students are head and shoulders above what students at [another prominent area business school] have. While I'm sure the CRC will continue to improve and bring in more high-profile companies, it is already a premier organization." Students praise the center's one-week winter inter-term program for first-years, through which "students learn how to fine tune their resume and interview skills. Additionally, they learn about networking, discover their inner interests, and come up with a value proposition. I believe this gives Marshall students a leg up in recruiting."

Companies most likely to employ Marshall MBAs include: Deloitte Touche Tohmastu, Wells Fargo, Mattel, The Walt Disney Company, Warner Brothers, Bank of America, Countrywide, Neutrogena, JPMorgan Chase, Intel, Booz Allen Hamilton, McKinsey & Company, Ernst & Young, Nissan North America, and Goldman Sachs.

Student Life and Environment

Full-time students tell us that "there are numerous professional and social club opportunities in which to be involved at Marshall." Several point out that "being involved with the community is easy and fun due to the Challenge 4 Charity Club, which schedules regular volunteer days for junior achievement and hosts parties at popular LA night clubs where the entry fees are donated to the Special Olympics." One student adds, "With the numerous clubs and organizations, USC students are really only limited by the amount of time and energy they possess. Personally, I wanted to take a leadership role in the community, and have had the opportunity to do just that. That makes my schedule a little bit more hectic than normal, but that was a personal decision. Really, life at Marshall is as challenging as one has the ambition to make it." Throughout the program and the campus, students enjoy "a very communal atmosphere. Football season is amazing."

Los Angeles is a great hometown, "a fun and vibrant city" with "fabulous weather all year round." Students note that "living in LA requires a car" and tell us that there are "nice apartments by the ocean for a decent price" within a 20-minute commute of the campus. The city provides many opportunities "to spend time together outside of class." "There are parties or small get-togethers almost every weekend."

Admissions

The Marshall Admissions Office warns that its MBA programs are "highly selective," and that the Admissions Committee "carefully assesses each candidate on a number of dimensions, including prior academic, professional, and personal accomplishments." All applicants must provide the school with official transcripts for all postsecondary academic work, an official GMAT score report, an official TOEFL score report (for international students who have not previously attended an English-language undergraduate or graduate program), an online application, a current resume, three required essays (a fourth optional essay is available), and two letters of recommendation (at least one from a direct supervisor is preferred).

Prominent Alumni

Yang Ho Cho, Chairman & CEO, Korean Air Lines Co., Ltd.; Christopher DeWolfe, CEO, MySpace.com; Thomas O. Hicks, Chairman & CEO, Hicks Holdings LLC; William Schoen, Chairman, Health Management Associates; Robert L. Rodriguez, Principal & CEO First Pacific Advisors.

FINANCIAL FACTS

Annual tuition	$41,990
Fees	$2,879
Cost of books	$1,480
Room & board	$16,000

ADMISSIONS

Admissions Selectivity Rating	97
# of applications received	2,224
% applicants accepted	22
% acceptees attending	45
Average GMAT	690
Range of GMAT	670–720
Average GPA	3.3
TOEFL required of international students	Yes
Minimum TOEFL (paper/computer)	600/250
Application fee	$150
International application fee	$150
Application Deadline/Notification	
Round 1:	11/1 / 2/1
Round 2:	1/15 / 4/1
Round 3:	3/15 / 5/15
Early decision program?	No
Deferment available	No
Transfer students accepted	No
Non-fall admissions	No
Need-blind admissions	Yes

Applicants Also Look At

Columbia University, New York University, University of California—Berkeley, University of California—Los Angeles (Anderson), University of Michigan

EMPLOYMENT PROFILE

Career Rating	98	Grads Employed by Function	%	Avg. Salary
Percent employed at graduation	67	Marketing	26	$95,260
Percent employed 3 months after graduation	80	Operations	9	$86,643
		Consulting	15	$102,500
Average base starting salary	$93,886	Management	4	$89,834
Primary Source of Full-time Job Acceptances		Finance	32	$95,544
School-facilitated activities	NR (81%)	HR	4	$97,167
Graduate-facilitated activities	NR (14%)	Top 5 Employers Hiring Grads		
Unknown	NR (5%)	Cisco (5), Toyota (5), Deloitte (4), Morgan Stanley (4), Mattel (4)		

UNIVERSITY OF SOUTHERN MAINE
SCHOOL OF BUSINESS

GENERAL INFORMATION
Type of school	Public
Academic calendar	Semester

SURVEY SAYS...
Students love Portland, ME
Good social scene
Solid preparation in:
General management

STUDENTS
Enrollment of parent institution	10,478
Enrollment of MBA Program	136
% male/female	44/56
% out-of-state	25
% part-time	74
% minorities	5
% international	22
Average age at entry	30
Average years work experience at entry	5

ACADEMICS
Academic Experience Rating	**70**
Student/faculty ratio	20:1
Profs interesting rating	79
Profs accessible rating	70
% female faculty	21
% minority faculty	5

Joint Degrees
3–2 Master of Business Administration, 5 years, BS and MBA; MS in Nursing and MBA, 3–4 years; JD/MBA, 4–5 years.

Academics

The MBA program at the University of Southern Maine focuses its attention primarily on students "who wish to advance their careers and contribute to their companies." It serves a largely part-time student body whose members hold full-time jobs in the area and seek a degree that will help them "develop cross-functional business solutions to real-world problems [and] cultivate a broad critical perspective, interpersonal skills, and the analytical tools of management." USM's full-time student body is primarily enrolled in the 3-2 MBA program, which allows undergraduates to earn a bachelor's degree and an MBA in five years.

Part-time students can complete USM's 39-credit sequence in three years, although some take longer. The curriculum consists of 10 three-hour core courses and two three-hour electives. "All classes are held in the evening" so that working students can attend the MBA program, which students appreciate. One such student writes, "This school is well-located for part-time students and it caters well to them. The administration strongly supports the students." Optional concentrations are available in finance and taxation.

USM professors "are well-integrated into the local business community, opening up several great opportunities for enriching projects." Their quality as classroom instructors varies; "Some seem to teach to the lowest common denominator, but generally they are good to very strong," students tell us. They single out instructors in operations, accounting, and finance for their expertise and "ability to inspire learning in their students." Many agree the b-school facility "needs to be vastly improved," adding that "the school desperately needs a new building of their own with more modern, comfortable facilities."

Career and Placement

USM's website states: "Because many of our students are already employed in management positions, we do not have a formal placement service for MBA or MSA students." The site adds that "opportunities for employment often come to our attention," and these opportunities "are passed on to students for consideration." Students may also work with the Business School, which employs a career advisor to administer career assessments, counsel students in resume building and interviewing skills, and arrange networking opportunities.

Student Life and Environment

Because "the University of Southern Maine is mainly a commuter college," "there is really very little in the way of organized outside activities. We all have a local life outside of school which demands our time." One student observes, "There isn't a whole lot of school spirit and clubs like at other universities. The only club I've heard of for the MBA program is the MBA Association. Unfortunately, any clubs that students are asked to participate in have meetings when many students are in class. That also goes for most networking opportunities that are available." Extracurricular life isn't totally dead, though; according to one MBA, "The school does try to bring students together for occasional special events, and many professors hold off-campus gatherings on the last night of class that provide a good networking opportunity with other students."

ADMISSIONS CONTACT: ALICE B. CASH, ASSISTANT DEAN FOR STUDENT AFFAIRS
ADDRESS: 96 FALMOUTH STREET, P O BOX 9300 PORTLAND, ME 04104
PHONE: 207-780-4184 • FAX: 207-780-4662
E-MAIL: MBA@USM.MAINE.EDU • WEBSITE: WWW.USM.MAINE.EDU/SB

USM's MBA program is a small one, the majority of whose students attend part time. They are "good-natured, intelligent individuals" who are "motivated but not extremely driven in a business sense. They are hard-working and striving for knowledge," creating "a positive learning environment." The mix of "older students with families and substantial professional backgrounds and younger students with less work experience but more recent educational experience" is a "positive mix," students say. They also love that "the academic community is quiet and the scenery is wonderful, very relaxing."

Portland is home to the School of Business' main campus. With a population just under a quarter of a million, Portland is the largest city in Maine. It serves as the state's financial, business, and retail center; its major industries include tourism, telecommunications, technology, light manufacturing, and insurance.

Admissions

All applicants to the MBA program at USM must submit a completed application, two copies of official transcripts for all postsecondary work (including work at USM), GMAT scores, three letters of recommendation, a resume, and a personal essay. In addition, international students must also submit a certificate of finances and, if English is not their first language, TOEFL scores. Fully admitted students must have a formula score of 1,100 under the formula [(undergraduate GPA × 200) + GMAT score] and a minimum GMAT score of 500. The GMAT requirement is waived for students who have completed a terminal degree (e.g. PhD, JD, MD). The admissions office considers rigor of undergraduate field of study, reputation of undergraduate institution, potential, likelihood of enhancing the educational environment at USM, demonstrated leadership, evidence of creativity, and record of accomplishment in business in making its admissions decisions. All students must complete, or demonstrate competency in, the following 'foundation' areas: managing organizational behavior, economics, accounting, probability and statistics, finance. Students with deficiencies in these areas will be notified at the time of their admission.

FINANCIAL FACTS

Annual tuition (in-state/ out-of-state)	$4,860/$13,572
Fees	$561
Cost of books	$1,000
Room & board (on-campus)	$7,800
% of students receiving aid	68
% of first-year students receiving aid	47
% of students receiving loans	35
% of students receiving grants	47
Average award package	$8,779
Average grant	$5,479

ADMISSIONS

Admissions Selectivity Rating	**83**
# of applications received	53
% applicants accepted	55
% acceptees attending	79
Average GMAT	544
Range of GMAT	530–600
Average GPA	3.25
TOEFL required of international students	Yes
Minimum TOEFL (paper/computer)	550/213
Application fee	$50
International application fee	$50
Regular application deadline	8/1
Early decision program?	No
Deferment available	Yes
Maximum length of deferment	1 year
Transfer students accepted	Yes
Transfer application policy: A maximum of 9 semester hours of transfer credit may be accepted.	
Non-fall admissions	Yes
Need-blind admissions	Yes

THE UNIVERSITY OF TAMPA
JOHN H. SYKES COLLEGE OF BUSINESS

GENERAL INFORMATION

Type of school	Private
Academic calendar	Semester

SURVEY SAYS...

Students love Tampa, FL

STUDENTS

Enrollment of parent institution	5,800
Enrollment of MBA Program	380
% male/female	57/43
% out-of-state	6
% part-time	59
% minorities	14
% international	39
Average age at entry	30
Average years work experience at entry	6

ACADEMICS

Academic Experience Rating	85
Student/faculty ratio	15:1
Profs interesting rating	86
Profs accessible rating	85
% female faculty	31

Joint Degrees

MS-ACC/MBA, MS-FIN/MBA, MS-MKT/MBA, MSN/MBA, BS Chemistry/MBA.

Prominent Alumni

Dennis Zank, COO, Raymond James; John M. Barrett, President and CEO, First Citrus Bank; John Friedery, Senior VP, CFO, Ball Corporation; Karen Surplus, CFO, DNAprint Genomics, Inc.

Academics

The MBA program at the University of Tampa's John H. Sykes College of Business provides "a great, friendly place to study," with "small class sizes" that "enhance class interaction and active participation" and a "cheap tuition" that students can't help but appreciate. The school offers students three curricular options: a full-time program that can be completed in 16 months, a part-time program (with "a course schedule that is excellent for the working professional") that is typically completed in about three years, and a six-term Saturday pro MBA program for business leaders ("the only true Saturday program in the area," one student tells us). Roughly one-third of the student body attends full time.

In all programs, students tout the curriculum, which "is outlined with a lower core, integrated core, and principal concentration that involves four electives. The program is flexible with the electives if you wanted to do a general MBA concentration." "Most of the classes require heavy interaction instead of just the instructor speaking," one MBA writes, adding, "This leads to a lot of good insight and interesting conversations." Concentrations are available in innovation, entrepreneurship, finance, information systems management, international business, management, marketing, and nonprofit management.

MBAs are just as sanguine about their instructors. UT Professors "are willing to give their personal cell phone numbers and adapt to office hours at the students availability." Their only complaint is that they feel some instructors aren't utilized "to their full potential. For example, for finance courses, it would be cool if students got a field trip to a trading floor somewhere in either Tampa, or anywhere in the U.S. Other more hands on activities like that for other majors too would be good." Still, students generally concur that; overall, "The academic experience is excellent. The school has built an environment that pushes the students to talk to each other, and ask each other for support." Administrators "focus on teamwork and building an environment that puts very little stress on the student." Students also appreciate how the administration "strives to remain cutting edge by preparing students as leaders in this new global marketplace." One student sums up, "The University of Tampa does an excellent job preparing you for the business world."

Career and Placement

UT's Office of Career Services provides Sykes MBAs with a battery of services, including assessment tests, workshops in business etiquette and business dress, one-on-one counseling, and job fairs. Students here praise "the professors' desire to help students obtain careers after graduation." Attendees of a recent on-campus career fair included Becker Professional Review, the Department of Veteran Affairs, the Internal Revenue Services, State Farm Insurance, First Investors Corporation, KLH Capital, Northwestern Mutual, Red Frog Marketing, and Walgreens.

Student Life and Environment

UT students reap the benefits of "a beautiful campus and of course, warm weather and beaches" as well as a "business building that is top notch, with up-to-date facilities." MBAs enjoy access to "outstanding educational, professional and social events for future business leaders," including "numerous seminars in which well-known CEOs and entrepreneurs make presentations throughout the semester. This provides excellent networking opportunities." The MBA program hosts "numerous clubs and local activities advertised weekly," and students with the time to spare also enjoy "sporting events on and around campus."

Not all can. About one-third of students here attend full-time, and they generally reap the benefits of the gorgeous, lively campus. The rest are part-timers, typically working full time in addition to their class work; they have little time for anything other than school assignments. The school draws a diverse student body "with people from different cultures and countries" as well as different professional backgrounds. The school works hard to build cohorts that exploit these differences "so that everyone brings something to the table. We get along great and have in-depth discussions."

Students' wish list for quality of life improvements include more parking facilities. One writes, "Parking has always been an issue for this school. The student population is constantly growing, thereby requiring an increase in faculty and staff. Most of the area on campus is developed with various types of buildings (administrative, classrooms, residence halls, etc.) and although there are two parking garages it is sometimes difficult to find convenient parking." Some full-timers also feel that "Day care is needed as well as the introduction of family activities in order to get spouses and children more involved in students' lives. Many of us are so busy studying and doing assignments that our home life is highly affected."

Admissions

Admission to the full-time and part-time MBA programs at Sykes is based on undergraduate work; GMAT score (a minimum score of 500 is required); demonstration of proficiency in mathematics, computers, and written and oral communications skills; and professional experience. International students must demonstrate proficiency in English by scoring at least 577 on the written TOEFL, 230 on the computer-based TOEFL, 90 on the Internet-based TOEFL, or 7.0 on the IELTS. Admission to the Saturday MBA program requires relevant work experience; applicants are required to have five years of relevant work experience, including two years in a management position. Applicants to all programs must submit two letters of recommendation, a resume, and a personal statement.

FINANCIAL FACTS

Annual tuition	$7,552
Fees	$70
Cost of books	$659
Room & board (on/off-campus)	$7,978/$4,900
% of students receiving aid	45
% of first-year students receiving aid	26
% of students receiving loans	35
% of students receiving grants	24
Average award package	$12,424
Average grant	$8,258
Average student loan debt	$22,524

ADMISSIONS

Admissions Selectivity Rating	80
# of applications received	268
% applicants accepted	65
% acceptees attending	73
Average GMAT	539
Range of GMAT	490–590
Average GPA	3.37
TOEFL required of international students	Yes
Minimum TOEFL (paper/computer)	577/230
Application fee	$40
International application fee	$40
Regular application deadline	7/15
Early decision program?	Yes
ED Deadline/Notification	NR / 11/15
Deferment available	Yes
Maximum length of deferment	1 year
Transfer students accepted	Yes
Transfer application policy: Up to 9 hours. from an AACSB accredited school.	
Non-fall admissions	Yes
Need-blind admissions	Yes

EMPLOYMENT PROFILE

Career Rating		84	Grads Employed by Function	% Avg. Salary
Percent employed at graduation		33	Marketing	14 $55,000
Percent employed 3 months after graduation		44	Finance	62 $60,938
			HR	4 $82,500
Average base starting salary		$66,389	MIS	18 $85,500

Top 5 Employers Hiring Grads
Citigroup (4), T. Rowe Price (4), Southland Business Group (2), City of St. Petersburg, Chamber of Commerce (2)

THE UNIVERSITY OF TENNESSEE AT CHATTANOOGA
COLLEGE OF BUSINESS

GENERAL INFORMATION
Type of school	Public
Academic calendar	Semester

SURVEY SAYS...
Students love Chattanooga, TN
Solid preparation in:
Accounting
Computer skills

STUDENTS
Enrollment of parent institution	10,526
Enrollment of MBA Program	244
% male/female	61/39
% part-time	75
% minorities	6
% international	2
Average age at entry	28
Average years work experience at entry	4

ACADEMICS
Academic Experience Rating	**71**
Student/faculty ratio	23:1
Profs interesting rating	85
Profs accessible rating	84
% female faculty	46
% minority faculty	15

Prominent Alumni
General B.B. Bell, Four-Star General in U.S. Army

Academics

UT Chattanooga's College of Business offers an MBA program "geared to the working professional, with classes starting at 5:30 P.M." Students—a mix of regionally based recent undergrads and returning professionals—report that "UTC's MBA program is a great place for students to extend their base knowledge, especially if your undergraduate degree is not business-related." The focus here is on producing management generalists; no concentrations are offered.

CoB's academic strengths include an "entrepreneurial focus" in the curriculum and "great attention focused on international business." Students complain that MIS and finance and investment are underrepresented in the course catalog. Professors earn high marks for "real-world experience, motivation to teach, excitement about their areas of expertise, and the level of research each professor is involved in." One student notes "The majority of our professors not only teach the material, but also practice outside of the classroom. Our global management professor is a partner at a global management consulting firm, our business law professor is a former partner at a large law firm in Michigan, and the list goes on." Professors "also make themselves available for students, which is a great asset."

UTC offers an Executive MBA that "mainly meets on weekends" "every other week." The program "has its own room that is well equipped...[with] nice chairs, large work-spaces and multimedia." Students report "good camaraderie" and a "learning atmosphere conducive to enhancing the educational experience," but wish that "the projects could be established to promote more teamwork among students."

Career and Placement

UTC maintains a Career Resource Center for all students. The center houses a library of job-search related materials, including literature, annual reports, and job postings. The school's Placement and Student Employment Center also hosts on-campus recruitment interview sessions, one major annual career fair, and a number of special career fairs each year. Students and alumni may post their resumes online with the Placement Center. Students tell us that "the business school could improve with its internship program. They do not offer credits, nor push students to do summer internships." On the upside, they report that "alumni remain active within and around the university. They are always willing to help out in any way. The networking is great."

Student Life and Environment

"There are plenty of activities...to be involved in" on the UTC campus, which students describe as "medium-sized, accessible and located in the heart of the metropolitan area." As one MBA puts it, "UTC is the perfect size for a college. It is large enough to offer a diverse range of opportunities (lectures, concerts, extra learning opportunities) but not so large that you feel lost." Another adds, "The student population is large enough that you get the college experience yet small enough that you can easily get involved or receive extra help." But while students here observe "The campus seems to be very lively with lots of activities (recreational and social) in the evenings...when we are in class," most are "working professionals who have little time to spend on campus." These students "Sometimes work with other students on group projects" but otherwise spend minimal time, and even less of their leisure time, on extracurricular pursuits.

ADMISSIONS CONTACT: BONNY CLARK, GRADUATE PROGRAM LIAISON
ADDRESS: GRADUATE SCHOOL, DEPARTMENT 5305, 615 MCCALLIE AVENUE CHATTANOOGA, TN 37403
PHONE: 423-425-4667 • FAX: 423-425-5223
E-MAIL: BONNY-CLARK@UTC.EDU • WEBSITE: WWW.UTC.EDU/ACADEMIC/BUSINESS

Although they don't hang around long enough to enjoy it, students tell us that the UTC campus "is beautiful," "clean and well-kept," and "very green." "Most of the buildings are modern and those that are not are in the process of being renovated," one student notes. Those in student housing report that "UTC has some of the best housing in the Southeast."

When it comes to admitting students, "UTC focuses on getting a broad range of students rather than being exclusive like Vanderbilt or Harvard." Fortunately, "The workforce here in Chattanooga generally skews toward high-achieving people such as engineers, computer systems specialists, and financial experts." Still, some here feel that "UTC could raise its minimum requirements such as undergraduate GPA and GMAT scores for entry into the MBA program without hurting the total number of students enrolled." The student body is a mix of some "starting right after undergrad, so they are still college students" and "full-time workers [who] seem to be excited to be back on a campus and ambitious to meet a new challenge."

Admissions

Applicants to the MBA program at UTC must be admitted to the UTC Graduate School. Admittance is based on a minimum undergraduate GPA of 2.7. Students must also be admitted to the MBA program by the College of Business Admissions Committee with two official copies of transcripts for all academic work completed after high school and an official GMAT score report, or alternatively achieve a minimum score of 1000 on the GRE with at least a score of 400 on the verbal section and 500 on the quantitative section. All applicants must achieve a minimum score of 450 on the GMAT. Students who do not meet the above-mentioned qualifications may still earn conditional admission. International students whose first language is not English must submit an official score report for the TOEFL (minimum grade required: 550, paper-based; 213, computer-based; 79 Internet-based) or the IELTS (minimum score 6.0).

ADMISSIONS	
Admissions Selectivity Rating	**68**
# of applications received	150
% applicants accepted	87
% acceptees attending	50
Average GMAT	522
Range of GMAT	470–570
Average GPA	3.18
TOEFL required of international students	Yes
Minimum TOEFL (paper/computer)	550/213
Application fee	$30
International application fee	$35
Early decision program?	No
Deferment available	Yes
Maximum length of deferment	1 year
Transfer students accepted	Yes
Transfer application policy: Students can transfer up to six hours from an AACSB accredited school. All transfer courses are subject to departmant approval.	
Non-fall admissions	Yes
Need-blind admissions	Yes

EMPLOYMENT PROFILE		
Career Rating	73	**Top 5 Employers Hiring Grads**
		Blue Cross Blue Shield, Unum, TVA, CIGNA, Decosimo and Company

THE UNIVERSITY OF TENNESSEE AT KNOXVILLE
COLLEGE OF BUSINESS ADMINISTRATION

GENERAL INFORMATION
Type of school	Public
Academic calendar	Semester

SURVEY SAYS...
Good social scene
Cutting-edge classes
Happy students
Smart classrooms
Solid preparation in:
Teamwork
Presentation skills
Computer skills

STUDENTS
Enrollment of parent institution	27,107
Enrollment of MBA Program	177
% male/female	75/25
% out-of-state	32
% part-time	0
% minorities	7
% international	16
Average age at entry	26
Average years work experience at entry	3

ACADEMICS
Academic Experience Rating	**88**
Student/faculty ratio	5:1
Profs interesting rating	84
Profs accessible rating	87
% female faculty	37
% minority faculty	3

Joint Degrees
JD/MBA, 4years; MBA/Masters in Engineering, 2 years + 6 week summer session; MBA/MS Sport Managment, 2 years; MBA/ Masters in Agricultural Economics, 2 years.

Prominent Alumni
Ralph Heath, VP & COO, Lockheed Martin Aeronautics; Kiran Patel, CFO, Solectron; James M. Gower, CEO, Rigel Pharmaceuticals, Inc.; Kevin Clayton, President & CEO, Clayton Homes; Scott Parish, CFO, Alcon Entertainment.

Academics

At the University of Tennessee at Knoxville, the "intense 17-month program" crams a full MBA—including a required internship—into three semesters of hard work. In the first term, students follow an "integrated curriculum" of core course work, with a "focus on teamwork" and technical skills. This well-designed program provides a big-picture perspective on business, teaching students "how the entire supply chain is impacted by a single decision made in marketing, logistics, finance, and/or operations." With all the "latest technology" in the classroom, the MBA also "involves plenty of technical instruction," including "robust desktop modeling and Excel classes to enhance quantitative skills." While covering diverse topics, "the administration has done a good job working with the professors to make sure our classes do not overlap but are integrated across each department." Moreover, students laud UTK's "effort to teach about current and upcoming trends in the business world." A current student comments, "I have two large social media projects this term reflecting the continued commitment to stay relevant and teach up-to-date technologies in addition to traditional subject matter."

After completing the core curriculum, Knoxville students can tailor their education through the "in-depth study of a chosen concentration" or a dual master's degree in areas like engineering or sports management. Notably, UTK is ranked among "the top-10 business schools for [the] logistics field," offering lots of opportunities for students who are interested in supply chain management. In addition to logistics, students can choose an academic concentration in entrepreneurship and innovation, finance, operations management, and marketing. Each of these concentrations has unique electives and co-curricular offerings. For example, "The entrepreneurship program offers unique hands-on consultation projects as part of the course curriculum." Students may also choose a customized MBA concentration.

At UTK, "Professors are well-respected and experienced leaders" who join the Knoxville faculty after careers as "senior executives for *Fortune* 500 companies, the Federal Reserve, and others." Thanks to their star credentials, "the professors are able to integrate real-world experiences with academic teaching to add value to the learning experience." To augment the faculty's know-how, "numerous speakers and alumni are brought into classes to give [students] real-world opinions and views." In addition to sharing their expertise, "the majority of professors are willing to personally invest and mentor students." A student tells us, "Several of my professors have written letters of recommendation on my behalf, and helped facilitate internships in venture capital and investment banking." Similarly, the "administration listens to student needs and tailors classes to student preferences." In particular, "The Dean is very in touch and actively listens to the students."

Career and Placement

University of Tennessee at Knoxville maintains a "strong reputation in the Southeast," creating plenty of job prospects for those who want to stay in the region. By all accounts, "career services is outstanding," offering "training, critique, and practice for interviews [and] cover letters," as well as individual career counseling, job strategy course work, corporate recruiting events, and career fairs. Additionally, career services has "tons of information concerning corporate and alumni contacts," and the school's loyal graduates are "very willing and eager to help any of the students." A student exclaims, "I had a great summer internship lined up from a career fair the first month of school."

ADMISSIONS CONTACT: DONNA POTTS, DIRECTOR OF ADMISSIONS, MBA PROGRAM
ADDRESS: 504 HASLAM BUSINESS BUILDING KNOXVILLE, TN 37996-4150
PHONE: 865-974-5033 • FAX: 865-974-3826
E-MAIL: MBA@UTK.EDU • WEBSITE: MBA.UTK.EDU

In recent years, graduating UTK students reported a mean base salary of about $75,000, with a salary range between $33,000 and $100,000. Drawing on the school's strength in that area, almost 40 percent of students took jobs in logistics or operations. Half the class stayed in the South, with another 20 percent taking jobs in the Midwest.

Student Life and Environment

The MBA at UTKnoxville is definitely full-time. Here, MBA candidates "have class daily from roughly 8 a.m. until 12:30 p.m.," and the "afternoons are spent working on group assignments and individual readings or course work." To fill up your free time, there are "numerous extracurricular activities for students to get involved in, ranging from student-managed investment portfolios to intramural sports." While they spend most of the day on campus, UTK students are blessed with a brand-new business school building, which "is equipped with the latest technology in every classroom." There are "terrific finance resources" (including the Investment Learning Center, where students can earn Bloomberg certification), and even "the team rooms are very useful and all have 60-inch flat screens or projectors for presentation practice."

There's a surprisingly diverse crowd on UTK's small business school campus. The program draws students from "a broad range of ages, experiences, and undergraduate degrees." In addition to homegrown diversity, "Approximately 25 to 30 percent of the 2010 class [was] international students from Asia and Europe," whose unique perspectives are "incredibly valuable in class dialogue and group projects." No matter what their background, most students at UTK are "extremely hard workers and are truly interested in learning." A student attests, "In the hundreds of hours I have spent in team work, I have been impressed with the work ethic and interpersonal skills of my teammates." On this friendly campus, students are "outgoing" and "there is a strong social connection in our class." When they aren't hitting the books, students love the fact that "Tennessee has an incredible atmosphere, complete with major college athletics."

Admission

To apply for University of Tennessee at Knoxville's MBA program, students must submit a completed application form, undergraduate transcripts, a GMAT score report, two letters of recommendation, and four personal essays. A personal interview is also recommended. Students must have a minimum GPA of 2.7 to be eligible for the program. International candidates must have the equivalent GPA of 3.0 on a 4.0 scale. In recent years, incoming students had an average undergraduate GPA of 3.0, an average GMAT score of 606, and average work experience totaling almost three years.

FINANCIAL FACTS

Annual tuition (in-state/ out-of-state)	$18,017/$34,465
Fees	$1,000
Cost of books	$3,000
Room & board (on/off-campus)	$7,400/$12,500
% of students receiving aid	43
% of first-year students receiving aid	27
% of students receiving grants	8
Average award package	$17,784
Average grant	$7,038

ADMISSIONS

Admissions Selectivity Rating	85
# of applications received	260
% applicants accepted	54
% acceptees attending	61
Average GMAT	606
Range of GMAT	500–750
Average GPA	3.0
TOEFL required of international students	Yes
Minimum TOEFL (paper/computer)	600/250
Application fee	$35
International application fee	$35
Regular application deadline	2/1
Early decision program?	No
Deferment available	No
Transfer students accepted	No
Non-fall admissions	No
Need-blind admissions	Yes

EMPLOYMENT PROFILE

Career Rating	95	Grads Employed by Function	%	Avg. Salary
Average base starting salary	$75,000	Marketing	23	$72,333
		Logistics	44	$79,471
		Consulting	8	$81,667
		Finance	26	$62,400

THE UNIVERSITY OF TEXAS AT ARLINGTON
COLLEGE OF BUSINESS

GENERAL INFORMATION

Type of school	Public
Academic calendar	Semester

SURVEY SAYS...
Good peer network
Cutting-edge classes
Smart classrooms

STUDENTS

Enrollment of parent institution	28,085
Enrollment of MBA Program	929
% male/female	65/35
% part-time	66
% minorities	20
% international	39
Average age at entry	30
Average years work experience at entry	5

ACADEMICS

Academic Experience Rating	82
Student/faculty ratio	21:1
Profs interesting rating	89
Profs accessible rating	83
% female faculty	16
% minority faculty	5

Joint Degrees

May combine any two degrees (usually MBA and specialized program) or a business degree with others, such as Engineering, Architecture, Science, Nursing. Can obtain second degree with as few as 18 additional hours. May pursue MBA at UTA with MIM at Thunderbird, the American Graduate School, or international management, with reduced requirements.

Academics

Savvy business students looking for maximum return on investment say you'll get "a high-quality education for a reasonable price" at the University of Texas at Arlington. The school maintains an outstanding reputation in the Dallas-Fort Worth metropolitan area, and also attracts students for its unique fields of study, including an MBA concentration in real estate business and a rigorous master's program in quantitative finance. The accounting program also enjoys high repute, and "UT Arlington ranks in the top three schools in which the students pass all the sections of the CPA exam the first time around."

UT Arlington offers a number of MBA options for working professionals and for full-time students, both in Forth Worth and at the school's Arlington campus. In addition to the traditional MBA, which can be completed on a full-time or part-time basis, the school operates an accelerated 15-month Executive MBA for working professionals, and a full-time Cohort MBA, which offers a unique team-based approach to business study with a lockstep curriculum. You can even participate in a "wonderful" online MBA program through UT Arlington.

No matter if you are a full- or part-time student, you'll find yourself in classes with "a bright and disciplined group of folks," who are "focused on doing their best and contributing their part to the overall academic experience." Cohort students appreciate a particular sense of camaraderie, because "the lockstep program is crucial in getting to know [your] peers, and building and maintaining networks which can be used in future business endeavors." Of particular note, professional students feel that UT Arlington caters to their unique needs, helping them to balance the diverse challenges of work, school, and family life. At UT Arlington, both faculty and administrators "realize we have careers and lives, respect that, and work with us to make our learning experience the best it can be."

Academically, every professor has "an outstanding academic background, an impressive work history, and certifications in their field. Many are also authors, contributing to the advancement of their professions, while also putting their opinion out there to be criticized by their peers." In addition to full-time staff, "there is a good relationship between professors and companies around the DFW area; in many cases, executives have been invited as guest speakers." Although UT Arlington is a large public school, it isn't beleaguered by excessive administrative headaches. On the contrary, a current student attests, "Overall, I'm very pleased with the way the Business School is run. I haven't had any problems getting into the classes that I was interested in, and the professors have been very helpful."

Career and Placement

Thanks to the school's great regional reputation and the dedicated efforts of the career center, it's relatively easy to start a new career after finishing your MBA at UT Arlington. A current student praises, "The career services center in the College of Business provided me with resume preparation, mock interviews, and made it simple for me, through the electronic networking system, to set up on-campus interviews with industry leaders." In addition, "the school offers an employment fair that connects the school with other companies."

There are myriad opportunities in Dallas and Fort Worth, and "the school has established a very good rapport with businesses around the metroplex, who easily absorb fresh graduates!" Getting to know your business school instructors can also be a beneficial first step, as "professors also maintain a vast network of former students that proves helpful for current students when they begin their job hunt." An accounting graduate adds these positive comments: "I was heavily recruited by the Big 4 accounting firms, as well as small local firms, middle-market firms, and "industry" firms with accounting departments (which is every firm). The opportunity that I had with being placed with a company was extraordinary."

Student Life and Environment

On this diverse, metropolitan campus, "each student is different from the next." Representing a "wide cross-section of society," UT Arlington attracts students of "every race, a range of ages," and students who are "married, single, and with children." You'll also find "a large number of foreign students in this MBA program," which most see as an advantageous way to "globalize your Business School experience." The one uniting factor is that "most everyone works, and brings with him or her a breadth of knowledge and experience."

Despite the diversity, UT Arlington students can nonetheless be grouped into two major categories: "married working professionals working to improve themselves," and "students that entered the program shortly after obtaining an undergraduate degree." In both groups, most students commute to UT Arlington (keep in mind that "there is no public transportation [to Arlington], so we need cars"); however, students say there is still plenty of campus life, if you're looking for a more traditional college experience. In fact, a current MBA candidate insists, "The school overall is moving from a "commuter" school to a more traditional school. More students are living on campus [and] more activities and organizations are starting." In addition, the larger university is home to "many interdisciplinary groups that offer multiple activities on campus: theater, recitals, sports, and so forth." However, weekends quiet down around Arlington, so "be ready to commute to Fort Worth or Dallas to accommodate your night-life plans."

Admissions

UT Arlington carefully considers both quantitative and qualitative factors in every admissions decision. Admissions requirements vary by program; however, for the traditional, two-year program, the average GMAT score and GPA for students entering the MBA program was about 550 and 3.25, respectively in a recent academic year. Work experience is not a requirement, but 2–5 years is preferred. To be considered for admission, students must also submit test scores and transcripts, as well as a statement of purpose, recommendations, and a resume.

Prominent Alumni

Gen. Tommy Franks, U.S. Army (ret.); John Goolsby, President CEO (ret.), Howard Hughes Corporation; Roy Williams, Chief Scout Exec. (ret.), Boy Scouts America; Jerry Thomas, President & CEO, Decision Analyst, Inc.; Jackie Fouse, Sr. VP, CFO & Corp Strategy, Bunge, Ltd.; Dr. Roland Fryer, Professor of Economics, Harvard University.

FINANCIAL FACTS

Annual tuition (in-state/ out-of-state)	$8,400/$13,980
Fees (in-state/ out-of-state)	$2,058/$2,253
Cost of books	$1,000
Room & board (on/off-campus)	$6,097/$3,165
% of students receiving aid	43
Average award package	$11,339
Average grant	$2,531
Average student loan debt	$18,166

ADMISSIONS

Admissions Selectivity Rating	78
# of applications received	812
% applicants accepted	76
% acceptees attending	49
Average GMAT	514
Range of GMAT	310–720
Average GPA	3.49
TOEFL required of international students	Yes
Minimum TOEFL (paper/computer)	550/213
Application fee	$40
International application fee	$60
Regular application deadline	6/10
Early decision program?	Yes
ED Deadline/Notification	NR / 6/15
Deferment available	Yes
Maximum length of deferment	1 year
Transfer students accepted	Yes
Transfer application policy: Maximum number of transferable credits is nine. Grades B or better from an AACSB accredited university.	
Non-fall admissions	Yes
Need-blind admissions	Yes

THE UNIVERSITY OF TEXAS AT AUSTIN

McCOMBS SCHOOL OF BUSINESS

GENERAL INFORMATION

Type of school	Public
Academic calendar	Semester

SURVEY SAYS...

Students love Austin, TX
Good social scene
Solid preparation in:
Communication/interpersonal skills

STUDENTS

Enrollment of parent institution	50,995
Enrollment of MBA Program	1,000
% male/female	71/29
% out-of-state	35
% part-time	47
% minorities	11
% international	25
Average age at entry	28
Average years work experience at entry	5

ACADEMICS

Academic Experience Rating	**91**
Profs interesting rating	86
Profs accessible rating	93

Joint Degrees

MBA/Doctor of Jurisprudence, 116 semester hours; MBA/Master of Manufacturing and Decision Systems Engineering, 86 hours; MBA/Master of Science in Nursing, 82 hrs; MBA/Master of Arts in Public Affairs, 79 hours; MBA/Master of Arts with a Major in Advertising, 79–82 hours; MBA/Master of Arts with a Major in Asian Studies, 76–79 hours; MBA/Master of Arts with Major in Communication Studies, 79–82 hours; MBA/Master of Arts with a Major in Journalism, 79–82 hours; MBA/Master of Arts with a Major in Latin American Studies, 76–79 hours; MBA/Master of Arts with a Major in Middle Eastern Studies, 79 hours; MBA/Master of Arts with a Major in Radio-Television-Film, 79–82 hours; MBA/Master of Arts with a Major in Russian, East European, and Eurasian Studies, 79 hours.

Academics

The MBA program at the McCombs School of Business earns its stellar national reputation with "top-15 rankings in all the major concentrations" and excellent placement results, but it's the program's add-ons that have students here excited. McCombs students strive to do more than master their program's demanding curriculum; this school "attracts really driven and talented young professionals" anxious to "take advantage of all the MBA program has to offer, such as the MBA Investment Fund, Venture Fellows, MBA+ Leadership Program, MootCorp, the Austin Technology Incubator, etc."

McCombs' MBA+ Leadership Program "gets a lot of press" for "connecting students with their dream companies to work on consulting projects solving real business issues." One student reports that the program "enabled me to receive one-on-one professional coaching for teamwork, presentation skills, and interviewing. It has enabled me to do real projects with companies that I have always been curious about like REI. It has helped me get mergers and acquisition training that helped me learn the language prior to the interview season. It is a great way for me to branch out and build my exposure to new things." All these characteristics make MBA+ Program "very beneficial for career switchers," MBAs here agree.

Yet there are some here who insist that MBA+ Program "is not the crown jewel of the program." They point instead to several other programs, such as Venture Fellows, "a leadership and academic program that allows students the opportunity to learn more about the venture capital and private equity communities" through guest speakers and internships with local private equity and venture capital firms. They also trumpet the MBA Investment Fund, which "manages $15 million of all private dollars. No public or university money is managed here and the students have to report to private investors while managing the fund." Finally, there's the students' "widespread interest in global trips. With such a diverse student body and the importance of globalization, interest in international affairs is growing every day. Students can choose to study abroad for a semester and tons of students choose to participate in global trips--two-week excursions, part business/part culture—to large business development centers around the globe."

Students report strong offerings across the board, with pronounced strength in entrepreneurship, finance, and marketing. The faculty offers "both practitioners and academics that add to the overall learning experience," although they warn that "There are some incredible professors here, but those are the classes that are really hard to get into. If Texas can attract better teachers as opposed to just researchers (or develop them), it should be a top-ten school."

Career and Placement

McCombs' status as a high-ranking program ensures a robust recruitment season for MBAs. Students note that "the Texas MBA program offers one of the few specializations in energy finance and has considerable contacts in the energy industry, including major energy companies (ExxonMobil, Shell, El Paso, TXU, etc.). The MBA program also offers significant access to the major investment banks and their energy groups." Also, "The MBA alumni base is strong and supportive."

Top employers of McCombs MBAs include 3M, Accenture, Alliance Residential Co., Alvarez & Marsal, Bank of America Securities, Boston Consulting Group, Cambridge Associates, Capgemini U.S. LLC, Chase, Chevron, Citigroup, ConocoPhillips, Dell, Deloitte Consulting, AT&T, Dimensional Fund Advisors, Discover Financial, Eli Lilly & Co., Everest Group, Exxon Mobil Corp., Frito-Lay, Hewlett-Packard, Hoover's, IBM, J.P. Morgan, Johnson & Johnson International, KPMG, McKinsey & Co., Mercer Management

Consulting, Microsoft Corp., Progressive Insurance, USAA Real Estate Co., Wachovia Securities, and Walmart.

Student Life and Environment

The McCombs MBA program works hard to build community fast. As one student explains, "The Texas MBA program offers new students the opportunity to meet classmates before classes start through the McCombs Adventure Program. This summer students traveled to Morocco, Costa Rica, Chile, and Napa Valley." The trend continues through students' first semester. "At the beginning, classes are back to back with your own cohort," writes one student. "After the first semester, people do one core class and the rest electives. People are more united at the beginning of the MBA given the constant interaction. As semesters progress, people get to gather in groups and have classes with other graduate or undergraduate peers."

Life on the Austin campus provides "a good combination of work and play. The first semester is brutal and filled with busy work, but the rest of the semesters offer more options for classes and a better learning environment. Plenty of social and cultural events throughout the year offer the opportunity for networking and building up the strong community here at McCombs." In addition, "Austin is a vibrant city that is perfect for business school students. The attractive nightlife and social network of students make the transition from the professional world to business school very smooth."

Admissions

The McCombs School accepts online applications only. A completed application must include: a resume detailing work history (two years of post baccalaureate work experience is strongly recommended); personal essays; official copies of transcripts for all post-secondary academic work; letters of recommendation; an official score report for the GMAT or GRE; and, for international students whose first language is not English, an official score report for the TOEFL. Programs designed to increase minority and disadvantaged populations at McCombs include: Explore McCombs, a three-day preview of the school for qualified African-American, Hispanic-American, and Native-American applicants; participation in the Consortium for Graduate Study in Management, a 17-university alliance working to facilitate excellence in graduate business education for minority students; attending the annual conferences of the National Society for Hispanic MBAs (NSHMBA) and the National Black MBA; and Women's Forum, a three-day preview of the program for women considering an MBA. In addition to the full-time MBA program, McCombs also offers Working Professional MBA programs in Austin, Houston, and Dallas, and Executive MBA programs in Austin and Mexico City.

JA...
CEO/...
Johnson...
CEO/Heinz; ...
Secretary of Co...
Sara Martinez Tuck...
CEO/ Hispanic Scholars...
Gerard Arpey, Chairman, P...
& CEO/American Airlines.

FINANCIAL FACTS

Annual tuition (in-state/ out-of-state)	$26,450/$42,580
Cost of books	$1,504
Room & board (off-campus)	$15,040

ADMISSIONS

Admissions Selectivity Rating	97
# of applications received	2,284
% applicants accepted	23
% acceptees attending	49
Average GMAT	681
Range of GMAT	650–710
Average GPA	3.45
TOEFL required of international students	Yes
Minimum TOEFL (paper/computer)	620/260
Application fee	$175
International application fee	$175
Regular application deadline	4/1
Regular notification	5/1
Early decision program?	No
Deferment available	Yes
Maximum length of deferment	1 year
Transfer students accepted	No
Non-fall admissions	No
Need-blind admissions	Yes

EMPLOYMENT PROFILE

		Grads Employed by Function	% Avg. Salary
Career Rating	97		
Percent employed at graduation	69	Marketing	18 $96,576
Percent employed 3 months after graduation	78	Operations	4 $93,643
		Consulting	22 $111,555
Average base starting salary	$96,318	Management	12 $87,132
Primary Source of Full-time Job Acceptances		Finance	42 $90,344
School-facilitated activities	126 (65%)	MIS	2 $103,000
Graduate-facilitated activities	57 (30%)	**Top 5 Employers Hiring Grads**	
Unknown	10 (5%)	Bank of America (10), Dell (10), Deloitte Consulting (9), AT&T (6), Microsoft (4)	

...F TEXAS AT DALLAS

Prominent Alumni
...m Mulva, President &
...Conoco Phillips; William
... Chairman, President &
...Don Evans, former
...merce/U.S. Gov't,
..., President &
...ip Fund;
...resident

...emics

...matter what your age, background, or educational goals, UT Dallas is likely to offer ...MBA program that will be a good match for your objectives and lifestyle. The school ...s been conferring MBA degrees since the early 1980s, and currently offers a part-time ...ofessional MBA, an Executive MBA, and a Global Online MBA, as well as various PhD ...d MS programs. In addition, the school established a 16-month, Full-Time MBA ...ohort) Program in 1996. Through this program, "the school has an unbeatable value ...oposition for B-School students: 16 months, rigorous curriculum, excellent faculty and ...tuated in the heart of a vibrant commercial ecosystem."

While UTD's relatively new MBA programs have already garnered national attention for quality, you'll still enjoy the benefit of an atmosphere that is "young, dynamic, and open to change." A current student adds, "I am a professional student but when I go to school I feel that I am a high school kid again. The energy, enthusiasm and quest for knowledge makes me feel young and energetic." However, as the school ages, its reputation and rigorousness also seem to be on an upward trajectory. A student elaborates, "The school has really upped the ante, and the course work has double or tripled in recent years. The classes really demand that you learn the material and are able to demonstrate knowledge and fluency." At the helm of the academic experience is a fleet of talented, diverse, and "incredibly knowledgeable" faculty. A student details, "Many of the professors have a variety of life experiences to draw on when lecturing. I have had an Accounting instructor who used to design weapons for the military and a Marketing professor who has been an actor/talk show host. This variety brings a point of view that would never be found in a textbook."

Administration is smooth and efficient, and "even though UTD is a larger public university, it has a small-school feel in that you are not just a number. It would be quite difficult for a person to fall through the cracks." Nonetheless, UTD is a big school, so classes (especially in the evenings) can be uncomfortably over-stuffed with students. UT Dallas makes up for this unfortunate shortcoming through unmatched flexibility, offering students the ability "to complete your degree during the week, weekend, day, night, or online each semester as your life changes." The curriculum is likewise flexible and easy to tailor. After completing foundational courses, "the School of Management offers a broad array of electives, which allows the student to either specialize in a particular field or diversify and learn about several subjects."

Career and Placement

UTD business students have access to the university Career Center, as well as the SOM Career Management Center (CMC), which focuses exclusively on the business school. In addition to career workshops and counseling, the CMC hosts frequent panels and speaker sessions. At UTD, "almost every day it seems like some CEO is coming and speaking with the students in a panel. Placement is great at the Full-Time MBA (Cohort) Program."

Many prominent companies recruit on campus, including American Express, Boeing, Cisco Systems, Deloitte, McKesson, State Farm Insurance, and Texas Instruments Incorporated, among many others. However, students worry that the school's largely regional reputation doesn't do justice to its world-class graduates. A current student laments, "The business school is excellent at UTD and I don't think the majority of the country recognize how good the school is." Even so, most graduates are sitting pretty, with an average starting salary in excess of $65,000 in recent years.

Enrollment of parent institution	15,065
Enrollment of MBA Program	1,244
% male/female	64/36
% out-of-state	6
% part-time	62
% minorities	2
% international	44
Average age at entry	28
Average years work experience at entry	5

ACADEMICS

Academic Experience Rating	**88**
Student/faculty ratio	37:1
Profs interesting rating	84
Profs accessible rating	75
% female faculty	24
% minority faculty	4

Joint Degrees

Master of Science in Electrical Engineering/MBA, 3 years; Medical School/MBA, 4 years.

Prominent Alumni

Dr. Dipak Jain, Dean/Kellogg School of Management; Michael S. Gilliland, President, CEO/Sabre; Charles Davidson, President, CEO/Noble Oil; Linnet Deily, Former Ambassador/WTO; David Holmberg, President, CEO/Jo-Ann Stores Inc.

ADMISSIONS CONTACT: LISA SHATZ, DIRECTOR - FULL-TIME (COHORT) MBA PROGRAM
ADDRESS: UT DALLAS—SCHOOL OF MANAGEMENT, 800 WEST CAMPBELL ROAD, SM 21
RICHARDSON, TX 75080-3021 • PHONE: 972-883-6191 • FAX: 972-883-4095
E-MAIL: LISA.SHATZ@UTDALLAS.EDU • WEBSITE: SOM.UTDALLAS.EDU/GRADUATE/MBA/FULLTIMEMBA/

Student Life and Environment

UTD students share the drive and determination you'd expect to find at a top business program; however, they hail from a diverse cross-section of society. A student elaborates, "There is a huge mixture at UTD as far as work experience, cultural background, and gender. Some students are single, some are married with children, and others are just beginning their families." International students comprise 50 percent of the graduate population, a reflection of "the changes that are taking place in business due to globalization." Most students view their international classmates as yet another major advantage to the program, since students often have "the opportunity to share our diverse experiences and learn from each other" both in and out of the classroom.

For the many students who commute to UTD, campus life doesn't amount to much more than classes and library time. Still, the business school has a lively, hard-working atmosphere, and "the lounge areas are always bustling with students." On the larger university campus, there are "many clubs and organizations," and "from 24-hour gym facilities to a fantastic student union, where there is always something fun going on."

Admissions

UTD admissions standards are high. Currently, admission to the Full-Time MBA (Cohort) Program is particularly competitive, admitting just 25 percent of applicants. Admissions rates and requirements depend on the program to which you are applying. However, the entering class had an average GMAT score of 650 and an average undergraduate GPA of 3.5 on a 4.0 scale. In addition to transcripts and test scores, students are required to submit personal essays and recommendation letters.

FINANCIAL FACTS

Annual tuition (in-state/ out-of-state)	$13,777/$26,347
Fees	$2,700
Cost of books	$2,000
Room & board	$7,500
% of students receiving aid	94
% of first-year students receiving aid	75
% of students receiving grants	94
Average award package	$15,000
Average grant	$15,000

ADMISSIONS

Admissions Selectivity Rating	96
# of applications received	162
% applicants accepted	33
% acceptees attending	100
Average GMAT	650
Range of GMAT	600–730
Average GPA	3.5
TOEFL required of international students	Yes
Minimum TOEFL (paper/computer)	550/213
Application fee	$50
International application fee	$100
Regular application deadline	5/1
Regular notification	6/15
Application Deadline/Notification	
Round 1:	1/15 / 3/1
Round 2:	3/1 / 4/15
Round 3:	6/1 / 6/15
Early decision program?	No
Deferment available	Yes
Maximum length of deferment	1 year
Transfer students accepted	No
Non-fall admissions	No
Need-blind admissions	Yes

EMPLOYMENT PROFILE

Career Rating	88	**Grads Employed by Function% Avg. Salary**	
Percent employed at graduation	62	Marketing	4 NR
Percent employed 3 months		Operations	15 $69,500
after graduation	90	Consulting	19 $60,800
Average base starting salary	$65,857	Management	8 NR
Primary Source of Full-time Job Acceptances		Finance	46 $66,625
School-facilitated activities	19 (73%)	MIS	8 NR
Graduate-facilitated activities	7 (28%)	**Top 5 Employers Hiring Grads**	
		Blockbuster (3), Ernst & Young (2), Sabre (2),	
		Accenture (2), Corpus (2)	

THE UNIVERSITY OF TEXAS—PAN AMERICAN
COLLEGE OF BUSINESS ADMINISTRATION

GENERAL INFORMATION
Type of school	Public
Academic calendar	Semester

SURVEY SAYS...
Students love Edinburg, TX
Friendly students
Happy students

STUDENTS
Enrollment of parent institution	17,500
Enrollment of MBA Program	186
% male/female	68/32
% part-time	69
% minorities	75
% international	15
Average age at entry	31
Average years work experience at entry	2

ACADEMICS
Academic Experience Rating	**81**
Student/faculty ratio	27:1
Profs interesting rating	79
Profs accessible rating	86
% female faculty	30

Academics

The College of Business Administration at The University of Texas—Pan American offers both an evening Professional MBA program and an online MBA program. The college and the MBA program are accredited by the American Assembly of Collegiate Schools of Business (AACSB).

Students with an undergraduate background in business can complete UTPA's evening MBA program in two years. The program typically requires 36 credit hours, although students lacking academic background in some business-related areas are required to complete additional foundation courses that cover principles of accounting, economics, management, marketing, statistics, and finance. Students praise the program's "good study environment" with "very modern classrooms" as well as its diverse student population. One tells us that "UTPA is the University that educates most Mexican-Americans in the country, and it has a strong Hispanic MBA." They also appreciate that the program is "very affordable" and "has a great reputation" in the area. Students may develop an area of specialization by completing nine credit hours in one of the following disciplines: accounting, economics, finance, management, management information systems, or marketing. They may also choose to write a thesis instead of taking six of the nine hours of required electives; thesis topics must be approved by the academic committee.

The online MBA is administered jointly with seven other UT campuses (Arlington, Brownsville, Dallas, El Paso, Permian Basin, San Antonio, and Tyler). The online curriculum consists of 48 course hours. Students with sufficient backgrounds in business may have up to four core courses waived, reducing the number of required hours to 36.

UTPA professors "are genuinely interested in helping students in whatever is requested" and "will allow you the freedom to both learn as much as you want and explore your particular interests. The professors are all happy to be teaching you." Administrators are "making a concerted effort to improve the experience of the students" but "can be a bit slow to work with."

Career and Placement

Because UTPA's MBA program is relatively small, graduate students here share a career services office with business undergraduates. That office, called the Center for Advisement, Recruitment, Internships, and Retention (CARIR), provides career counseling services, job-related reference materials, and assistance in internship placements. The office participates in numerous regional and national online job databases, which students may access through their UTPA accounts. CARIR also organizes on-campus recruitment events each semester, although most of the recruitment is geared toward undergraduate students. Additionally, the office conducts career development workshops on topics such as networking, writing resume, developing leadership skills among others. organizations such as Boeing Ernest and Young, Proctor and Gamble, Texas Instruments and Northrop Grunman are among those who hire UTPA graduates.

Student Life and Environment

The typical UTPA MBA "works all day, goes to class half the night, and gets home just in time to put the kids to bed and have a late supper." He or she "is dedicated to the program and has the kind of work and world experience that high test scores can never make up for." There is "great diversity, especially culturally" here, as "most students speak Spanish as a second language and a high percent come from a variety of universities around the world. It is a great experience!" As one student explains, "Students' classroom comments often sound like a United Nations meeting! One of my classes has students from India, Mexico, Texas, China, Japan, Taiwan, Turkey, France, Romania, and I'm sure I've missed a couple others."

UTPA is a commuter school attended by part-time students with full time jobs, so "student life usually consists of a spouse and a child" when work and school aren't eating up their time. Those who can engage in extracurricular life praise "the new state-of-the-art gym," the "many mixers for students to attend," and "events from poker tournaments to trips to Europe."

UTPA is located in Edinburg, Texas, a city of nearly 58,000 in the southernmost section of the state. Students report that the location provides "great opportunities for those interested in a growing economy, proximity to the border, and industry." Education and health care are the area's major employment sectors; retail trade capitalizes on the city's location near the Mexico border.

Admissions

Applicants to University of Texas Pan American must submit all the following materials to the Admissions Committee: an application to the UTPA Graduate School; sealed copies of official transcripts for all previously attended post-secondary institutions; official GMAT scores sent directly to the Graduate Office from GMAC; current resume; three letters of recommendation; statement of purpose that answer five specific questions. in addition, international students whose first language is not English must submit a sealed copy of at least 1000 under the formula [(undergraduate GPA for the last 60 semester hours of academic work X200) + GMAT score] and have an undergraduate GPA of at least 3.0 and GMAT score of at least 400 in order to receive unconditional admission to the program. those required to take TOEFL must score at least 500.

FINANCIAL FACTS

Annual tuition (in-state/ out-of-state)	$2,797/$8,900
Fees (in-state/ out-of-state)	$314/$402
Cost of books	$1,500
Average grant	$10,000

ADMISSIONS

Admissions Selectivity Rating	73
# of applications received	78
% applicants accepted	47
% acceptees attending	73
Average GMAT	450
Range of GMAT	380–555
Average GPA	3
TOEFL required of international students	Yes
Minimum TOEFL (paper/computer)	500/173
Application fee	$50
International application fee	$50
Regular application deadline	8/1
Early decision program?	Yes
Deferment available	Yes
Maximum length of deferment	One Semester
Transfer students accepted	Yes
Transfer application policy: Accept max. 3 courses	
Non-fall admissions	Yes
Need-blind admissions	Yes

THE UNIVERSITY OF TEXAS AT SAN ANTONIO
COLLEGE OF BUSINESS

GENERAL INFORMATION

Type of school	Public
Academic calendar	Semester

SURVEY SAYS...
Students love San Antonio, TX
Solid preparation in:
Finance
Quantitative skills

STUDENTS

Enrollment of parent institution	28,955
Enrollment of MBA Program	256
% male/female	60/40
% part-time	72
% minorities	31
% international	6
Average age at entry	29
Average years work experience at entry	5

ACADEMICS

Academic Experience Rating	**79**
Student/faculty ratio	20:1
Profs interesting rating	88
Profs accessible rating	79
% female faculty	30
% minority faculty	38

Prominent Alumni
Gilbert Gonzalez, U.S. Depart Arg.
Undersecretary for Rural Dev;
Ernest Bromley, President & CEO of
Bromley & Associates; Jeanie
Wyatt, CEO of South Texas Money
Management.

Academics

The "affordable" University of Texas at San Antonio College of Business has a "solid" regional reputation" and it's "very accessible to working professionals." The "well-designed MBA program" here requires 36 hours of course work (beyond preparatory core courses). There's also a thesis option, which substitutes for six hours of electives. In addition to the general MBA, you can choose among 12 areas of concentration including business of health, accounting, marketing management, tourism destination development, and real estate finance. UTSA also offers an Executive MBA, a MBA in International Business, a PhD in business administration, and a bevy of full-time master's programs. Students brag that their "professors, curriculum, process, and flexibility far outweigh those of other programs in town." They also laud the "very hands-on" nature of the program. "The vast majority of students are completing their courses while working full time," explains one student, "so there is a very strong student-driven emphasis on practical skills, not only as they might apply in case studies, but as they apply in the actual work that is done by students."

There are "some very exceptional professors and some really lousy lecturers who do not seem to be qualified to teach" but, on the whole, professors are "engaging." "The quality of the faculty is probably the best kept secret in Texas," claims one happy student. Professors frequently bring substantial "real-world experience" to the classroom and they are "very attentive" once class is over. "They always emphasize office hours and promote asking for help," says one student. "It is encouraging to know that professors are always available and interested in helping students sort out individual problems or discuss research interests." Part-time students add that "professors will work with you if your job interferes with your school." A few students consider the administration "a bureaucratic nightmare" but most report that UTSA is "a well-oiled machine." The "efficient and helpful" staff is "ready and willing to help any time it is needed," they say. "There is a friendly atmosphere and supportive attitude permeating all levels."

Complaints among students at UTSA include the registration process. One student says the school "seems to be growing too fast and [is] not able to successfully catch up." "The library is awful." "Not enough places to study, not enough light, not enough books," gripes one student. Parking is also "a big issue" and the aesthetics around campus certainly are not the greatest. The architecture "can be best described as 'neo-brutalism' with its emphasis on concrete."

Career and Placement

MBA students at UTSA are really divided when it comes to the quality of Career Services. Satisfied students tell us that the staff "has been outstanding in directing students to potential employers, hosting information sessions, and providing on-campus interviews." They boast that "tons of recruiters" from Houston and other cities in Texas hire graduates. They say that career fairs bring "close to 100 companies each semester." They also note that "Valero, Ernst & Young, Deloitte, KPMG, and many other local and regional accounting firms" harvest many recruits here. Career Services does receive criticism from some students." "From my experience, there are few strong relationships between employers and our business school," laments one student. Unhappy students also charge that UTSA concentrates "only on San Antonio–based businesses."

ADMISSIONS CONTACT: MONICA RODRIGUEZ, MANAGER OF GRADUATE ADMISSIONS
ADDRESS: ONE UTSA CIRCLE SAN ANTONIO, TX 78249-0603
PHONE: 210-458-4330 • FAX: 210-458-4332
E-MAIL: GRADUATESTUDIES@UTSA.EDU • WEBSITE: BUSINESS.UTSA.EDU/GRADUATE

Student Life and Environment

Students say that the MBA program here is pretty heavily geared toward working professionals. It's possible to attend full time but the population is "largely part time" and "most students take longer than two years to get a degree." On one hand, "UTSA is a great place for part-time students" and it accommodates working students "very well." For example, courses are typically offered during the day at the school's downtown campus and during the evenings at the main UTSA campus. However, many full-timers feel overlooked and complain that "the school caters to part-time MBA students" too much.

Students at UTSA describe themselves as "very competitive, determined individuals" who are "looking to add extra education to their repertoire." They're also a very diverse group. "People from all around the world with different jobs, backgrounds, and home lives" attend UTSA. "Classes tend to be very diverse in terms of age, race, occupation, and virtually any other metric," explains one student. "The mixing of individuals in different fields adds a unique flavor to each classroom setting." You'll find some recent college grads here but many students are "older" and established in their careers. They "have families and jobs" and they attend UTSA because of its proximity to their homes and their existing places of employment. Consequently, "it's a commuter school." There's "not much social interaction between the students" and there are few activities outside of class hours beyond assigned group work. It's definitely possible to move here and make a rich social life for yourself, though. "Enchanting" San Antonio is reportedly "very welcoming for newcomers" and a "fiesta year round."

Admissions

Admitted students at the 25th percentile have GMAT scores in the upper 500s. Admitted students at the 75th percentile have GMAT scores in the low 600s. Work experience is not a requirement but it's certainly helpful. If your background and training isn't in business, you'll have to take some core courses (e.g., accounting, finance). If it's been seven years since you completed core courses, you may still have to take some core courses or you may be able to test out. It's a case-by-case decision. Also, be prepared to demonstrate competence with spreadsheets and commonly used business applications.

FINANCIAL FACTS
Annual tuition (in-state/ out-of-state) $8,422/$16,012

ADMISSIONS
Admissions Selectivity Rating	81
# of applications received	212
% applicants accepted	85
% acceptees attending	48
Average GMAT	600
Range of GMAT	530–710
Average GPA	3.11
TOEFL required of international students	Yes
Minimum TOEFL (paper/computer)	500/173
Application fee	$45
International application fee	$80
Regular application deadline	7/1
Early decision program?	No
Deferment available	Yes
Maximum length of deferment	2 terms
Transfer students accepted	Yes
Non-fall admissions	Yes
Need-blind admissions	Yes

EMPLOYMENT PROFILE
Career Rating	77	Grads Employed by Function	%	Avg. Salary
Percent employed at graduation	25	Marketing	13	$45,000
Percent employed 3 months after graduation	6	Management	25	$61,000
		Finance	25	$60,500
Average base starting salary	$55,375	Operations/Production	13	$55,000
Primary Source of Full-time Job Acceptances		Consulting	13	$55,000
School-facilitated activities	3 (30%)	Human Resources	13	$45,000
Graduate-facilitated activities	7 (70%)			

THE UNIVERSITY OF TOLEDO
COLLEGE OF BUSINESS ADMINISTRATION

GENERAL INFORMATION
Type of school   Public
Academic calendar   Semester

SURVEY SAYS...
Smart classrooms
Solid preparation in:
General management
Doing business in a global economy

STUDENTS
Enrollment of parent institution	19,374
Enrollment of MBA Program	302
% male/female	59/41
% out-of-state	39
% part-time	55
% minorities	62
% international	34
Average age at entry	28
Average years work experience at entry	5

ACADEMICS
Academic Experience Rating	76
Student/faculty ratio	10:1
Profs interesting rating	75
Profs accessible rating	73
% female faculty	30

Joint Degrees
JD/MBA, 3–4 years, MD/MBA, 4–5 years.

Prominent Alumni
Edward Kinsey, Co-Founder, Ariba, Inc.; Ora Alleman, VP, National City Bank; Michael Durik, Executive VP, The Limited Stores, Inc.; Marvin Herb, CEO Coca-Cola Bottling Company; Julie Higgins, Exective VP, The Trust Company of Toledo.

Academics

Offering a "good education at a very competitive price with convenient scheduling," the College of Business Administration at The University of Toledo fits the needs of area businesspeople in search of a quality MBA. One student explains, "The program is very accommodating toward people who work full-time. The majority of classes are taught at night, so I have been able to continue to work full-time while taking one or two classes at night." And, with a "low cost of living and low tuition fees when compared to other business schools," a UT MBA isn't a wallet buster.

UT distinguishes its MBA program with a number of cutting-edge concentrations. Students here may specialize in CRM and marketing intelligence, human resource management, information systems, operations and supply chain management, and professional sales as well as in the more traditional areas of administration, finance, international business, and marketing. Still, students warn that despite this apparent variety of choices, "The grad-level courses are fairly limited, [with] not enough variety/electives available to really customize our education. Classes are usually only offered once per semester at one specific time, so time conflicts between class and work schedules are quite common."

Students agree that "the greatest strengths of the UT MBA program come from its people. Overall, students are helpful, and it is easy to make connections through classmates. Professors follow a 40-40-20 rule with their time: 40 percent on research, 40 percent on preparing for classes, and 20 percent on advising students. This allows teachers to be student-centric." One student adds, "Receiving individual attention is a norm, be it in the Advising Office or from a professor."

Career and Placement

MBA students at Toledo may choose from an assortment of career support options. The school coordinates both academic graduate assistantships and corporate assistantships with employers like ProMedica Health System, Therma-Tru Doors, SSOE, Mercy Medical, Paramount Medical, and Goodwill. The school also sponsors regular networking events at which current students can meet and greet alumni. Finally, the Business Career Programs Office organizes on-campus recruiting, conducts mock interviews, performs resume reviews, provides counseling services, and manages a biannual Business Career Fair that brings more than 90 recruiters to campus.

Recent employers of UT MBAs include Calphalon, Chrysler, Dana Corp., DTE Energy, Ernst & Young, GM Powertrain, KeyBank, Heartland Information Systems, Hickory Farms, National City Corporation, Owens Corning, Owens Illinois, and Pilkington.

Student Life and Environment

"Life at UT is comfortable," students assure us. One praises, "Classrooms are clustered centrally so travel time between classes is quick. Most buildings have a computer lab, and the library has many quiet places to study. The fitness center is one of the largest I've seen for a college, and workouts are great. There aren't too many students crowding resources, so long lines are never a problem." If there's one area that needs help, students tell us it's the traffic and parking. One student warns, "There's an extreme lack of parking available.... On days/nights when a major event such as a basketball or football game is going on, the school allows outsiders (nonstudents) to park on campus for a fee. This usually keeps students from being able to go to class as there's so much spillover of vehicles sometimes that parking in grass or restricted areas is common. I've had to turn around and go home, missing class, due to not being able to park or to get through traffic in a timely manner to park." To top it off, "The traffic situation on campus is horrendous."

Most students attend UT's MBA program on a part-time basis, arriving after a full day of work. Consequently, they have little time or inclination to participate in activities other than classes and group projects. Full-time students tell us that "there are many organizations to be involved in if you choose to. There are also department social functions quite frequently that are highly advertised." As for evenings and weekends, they are "what you make of them. Most people settle for simply just going to house parties or campus bars, which grows old fast. The downtown area offers good times, but most of that area is dead."

Toledo MBAs "come from diverse backgrounds, including majors, universities, religions, and ethnicity." While they "are competitive in their pursuit of high-quality jobs," they also enjoy "an atmosphere of mutual respect and teamwork between students in the program. Students are very comfortable approaching other students for help in their studies. In exchange, it is expected that every student pulls his or her own weight on the many team-based assignments." About one in three students originates from outside the United States, "providing a unique and interesting perspective on major business topics of the day."

Admissions

Applicants to the MBA program at UT must submit the following materials: a completed application; official copies of transcripts from each undergraduate and graduate institution attended; three letters of recommendation (letters should speak to academic potential); and an official score report for the GMAT. In addition to the above, all international applicants must submit a financial statement and supporting documents. International applicants from countries in which English is not the primary language must submit an official score report for the TOEFL. Students are encouraged to complete their applications online.

FINANCIAL FACTS

Annual tuition (in-state/ out-of-state)	$12,096/$21,954
Fees	$1,150
Cost of books	$1,200
Room & board (off-campus)	$5,830
Average grant	$17,646

ADMISSIONS

Admissions Selectivity Rating	**72**
# of applications received	190
% applicants accepted	71
% acceptees attending	65
Average GMAT	525
Range of GMAT	450–780
Average GPA	3.2
TOEFL required of international students	Yes
Minimum TOEFL (paper/computer)	550/213
Application fee	$45
International application fee	$45
Early decision program?	No
Deferment available	Yes
Maximum length of deferment	1 semester
Transfer students accepted	Yes
Transfer application policy: Maximum 9 credit hours with at least a B from an AACSB-accredited school.	
Non-fall admissions	Yes
Need-blind admissions	Yes

THE UNIVERSITY OF TULSA

COLLINS COLLEGE OF BUSINESS

GENERAL INFORMATION

Type of school	Private
Academic calendar	Semester

SURVEY SAYS...
Solid preparation in:
Teamwork

STUDENTS

Enrollment of parent institution	4,165
Enrollment of MBA Program	121
% male/female	55/45
% out-of-state	36
% part-time	35
% minorities	13
% international	13
Average age at entry	24
Average years work experience at entry	2

ACADEMICS

Academic Experience Rating	84
Student/faculty ratio	9:1
Profs interesting rating	86
Profs accessible rating	88
% female faculty	22
% minority faculty	9

Joint Degrees

JD/MBA, 30 credit hours of business, 78 credit hours of law. JD/MTAX, 30 credit hours of TAX, 79 credit hours of law. Masters in JD/MSF 30 credit hours of business, 79 hours of law; MBA/MSF60 credit hours of business; MSF/MSAM 30 hours of business, 27 hours of mathematics; MBA/MSCS 30 credit hours of business, 24 credit hours of computer science.

Prominent Alumni

Doug McMillon, President and CEO, Wal-Mart International; David Kyle, Chairman, ONEOK; Robert E. Lorton, Chairman and CEO, World Publishing Co.; Debbie Fleming, VP and CFO, OGE Energy Corp.; Chet Cadieux, Charman and CEO, QuikTrip Corporation.

Academics

The University of Tulsa operates a rigorous and contemporary MBA program within the context of a small, friendly, private school environment. With a "low student-to-professor ratio," class sizes are uniformly small, and "you really get a chance to develop relationships with the faculty and other students." In the classroom, the teaching staff gets top marks for experience: "Many of them are leaders in their fields and have remained very current and relevant to the vast changes we are seeing economically and globally." They are also excellent educators, and "although classes are difficult and grades are competitive, the professors are able to drive home the overall picture of what we are studying and why." Most importantly, TU is a thoroughly supportive environment, so it's easy to stay on the right track academically. If a student needs extra help (or just wants to chat), "Professors are all readily available outside of class and genuinely interested in the well-being of each student." In addition, staff and advisors "work with students to ensure that we follow the right path, are able to do what we want and need to do, and succeed in all areas of our academic lives." A current student adds, "I have had a great experience in regards to the administration, especially the graduate advisor. She has been instrumental in helping me navigate course loads."

Although TU is a small school, the MBA program is constantly working to remain on the cutting edge. With an eye towards industry trends, administrators "recently revamped the course work to reflect what companies stated that they were looking for in MBA grads, and they also are constantly injecting anything current into the courses, seminars, and lectures." A current student observes, administrators "are constantly seeking outside input from various companies and individuals so that their students are as best prepared upon graduation as they can be." To offer one example, business ethics has been heavily introduced into the curriculum, which students say is "refreshing and relevant." In addition, the school recently redesigned the academic calendar from semesters to quarters. While they admit that, "the new MBA program still has some kinks to work out," students appreciate the fact that they can now "take a wider variety of courses." In addition to course work, TU students have the opportunity to participate in co-curricular activities on and off campus. A particularly popular offering, "the Friends of Finance organization, brings in CEOs, presidents of *Fortune* 500 companies, etc., to speak to the business students, and also offers a special session afterwards for students to ask the speaker questions one-on-one."

Career and Placement

With a "strong reputation in the energy industry" and a "prestigious reputation" in the area, TU students are well-positioned to find a choice position after graduating from the MBA program. For assistance with the career planning and placement process, "TU has a Business Career Development Center that is entirely focused on job placement for business students." Through the Career Development Center, students have access to myriad services, including resume and cover letter revisions, mock interviews, salary information, career workshops, and various online resources and job boards. In addition, "The events and workshops...allow students to have one-on-one time with executives of *Fortune* 500 companies." Recently, TU graduates have taken jobs at organizations including Bank of Oklahoma, ConocoPhillips, Deloitte Consulting, DHL, GE, Grant Thornton, Honeywell International, IBM, Level 3 Communications, PriceWaterhouseCoopers, Toyota, Trammel Crow, and the U.S. Government.

ADMISSIONS CONTACT: PATRICIA ZUMUALT, MARKETING AND RECRUITING
ADDRESS: 800 SOUTH TUCKER DRIVE, HELM 215 TULSA, OK 74104-9700
PHONE: 918-631-3660 • FAX: 918-631-2142
E-MAIL: GRADUATE-BUSINESS@UTULSA.EDU • WEBSITE: WWW.COLLINS.UTULSA.EDU/GRAD

Student Life and Environment

Drawing "a good mix of working professionals and recent graduates," TU students come from "a diverse background ethnically, academically, and professionally." Through group work and class discussions, "the diverse professional backgrounds of many of the students...lends itself to a very enriching atmosphere." Since the majority of students are "full-time working professionals or graduate student assistants that are taking classes part time," students admit that, "There isn't much time to take part in social or community activities." Nonetheless, the school offers plenty of opportunities for TU students to get together socially. For example, "graduate student luncheons take place every month where all graduate students are invited to eat and mingle." In addition, "there are many opportunities to meet other graduate students and employers at company panel sessions, etiquette dinners, and meet-and-greet times off campus."

Located on the edge of downtown Tulsa, "The campus is not large, but it is very beautiful and has all of the amenities of a larger university, just on a smaller scale." Looking to the future, the school's administration is "continually improving the campus;" For example, "Over the past three to four years they have built suite-style dormitories for student housing," in an effort to promote "a more united student body, and a better overall...experience." In addition, "The fitness facility is first class" and many students make use of the well-stocked library. The surrounding area is home to many students, and they "feel very safe walking to class in the evening."

Admissions

The Graduate Business Programs office at University of Tulsa accepts applications on a rolling basis. All students are automatically considered for merit-based scholarships (more than 80 percent of current students receive some form of merit-based aid). Students may also apply to the graduate assistantship program, through which they receive a full-tuition scholarship in exchange for 20 hours of work each week on campus. In recent years, the entering class had an average undergraduate GPA of 3.5 and an average of two years professional work experience before entering the program.

FINANCIAL FACTS

Annual tuition	$16,902
Fees	$72
Cost of books	$1,500
Room & board	$10,350

ADMISSIONS

Admissions Selectivity Rating	79
# of applications received	85
% applicants accepted	42
% acceptees attending	89
Average GMAT	610
Range of GMAT	560–700
Average GPA	3.5
TOEFL required of international students	Yes
Minimum TOEFL (paper/computer)	575/232
Application fee	$40
International application fee	$40
Early decision program?	No
Deferment available	Yes
Maximum length of deferment	1 year
Transfer students accepted	Yes
Transfer application policy: Maximum of 6 hours from an AACSB accredited institution.	
Non-fall admissions	Yes
Need-blind admissions	Yes

EMPLOYMENT PROFILE

Career Rating	91
Average base starting salary	$72,738

UNIVERSITY OF UTAH
DAVID ECCLES SCHOOL OF BUSINESS

GENERAL INFORMATION
Type of school	Public
Academic calendar	Semester

SURVEY SAYS...
Students love Salt Lake City, UT
Solid preparation in:
General management
Teamwork

STUDENTS
Enrollment of parent institution	30,000
Enrollment of MBA Program	304
% male/female	74/26
% out-of-state	30
% part-time	77
% minorities	7
% international	9
Average age at entry	28
Average years work experience at entry	4

ACADEMICS
Academic Experience Rating	87
Student/faculty ratio	4:1
Profs interesting rating	89
Profs accessible rating	82
% female faculty	28
% minority faculty	16

Joint Degrees
MBA/MS (Bioengineering, Mechanical Eng., Chemical Eng., Electrical Eng., Computer Science), 2 years; MBA/JD, 4 years; MBA/Master of Health Administration, 2 years; MBA/Master of Architecture, 3–4 years, depending on undergraduate degree.

Prominent Alumni
Pierre Lassonde, Co-Founder/Chairman, Franco-Nevada Mining; Spencer Kirk, Retired CEO, Megahertz Corp.; Robert McDonald, Vice-Chair Global Operations, Proctor & Gamble; Spencer Kirk, Co-Founder, Megahertz; President Extra Space Storage; Geoffrey Wooley, Founding Partner, Dominion Ventures.

Academics

Ask a Utahan about her state's flagship university and chances are good she'll pull from a litany of the school's selling points, including "a great medical school [known for] cancer research and the treatment center; a great business school; and strong athletics traditions." "An outstanding research school," the university's prestige is well known in the Beehive State and widely regarded as well-earned. Students in the Eccles MBA programs are no outliers in this regard; they enthusiastically praise both their program and the university that hosts it.

There are strong synergies between the Eccles School of Business and the university at large. The university's offerings in healthcare, international studies, and engineering all impact a business program that has "a strong reputation for innovation and technology commercialization" and provides "opportunities in the life science industry." Eccles' greatest strength is in entrepreneurship, with a program that creates "a great niche for entrepreneurs who want to team up with engineers and the life sciences." Highlights of the entrepreneurship program include the Utah Entrepreneur Challenge, which the university sponsors; the student-run Venture Development Fund; the Lassonde New Venture Center, a "great experience that allows business students to partner with researchers on campus to commercialize technology"; and Gangplank, "a club that connect[s] aspiring students to successful entrepreneurs."

Eccles offers a full-time MBA, a Professional MBA (part-time) that "caters to working professionals," and an Executive MBA; the last is "the top-ranked EMBA program in the region," with a student body numbering over 100. All programs benefit from "terrific professors" who "bring real-world experience and insight to class." The program is rigorous, with "material taught in class [that] is the same that is taught at Harvard, Georgetown, University of Chicago, etc., because that was where our professors were recruited from." Administrators are "very hands-on to ensure that the education is of quality and that the experience of the MBA courses is exciting and relevant."

Career and Placement

The Office of Career Services for Graduate Business Students works in conjunction with the university's Career Services Office to provide counseling and career placement services including career fairs and on-campus recruiting events. Student feedback on the service is mixed. Its harshest critics dismiss it as "poor, especially if you're not in accounting or finance." Others note that the office has "taken many steps this year to improve [services] for the future," but still has further to go. And others still report that with the arrival of a new dean in 2009, "alumni connections have been greatly improved" and the administration has grown more "supportive and informative, especially on career-related matters as well as courses offered at school. They are also very enthusiastic about connecting students with activities outside classrooms, such as company visits and networking events."

Employers who most frequently hire Utah MBAs include Comcast, ATK, GE Capital, Boart Longyear, Omniture, American Express, and the federal government. Nearly 40 percent of Eccles MBAs find work in finance and accounting after leaving the program.

ADMISSIONS CONTACT: MASTERS PROGRAMS & SERVICES,
ADDRESS: 1645 EAST CAMPUS CENTER DRIVE, ROOM 101 SALT LAKE CITY, UT 84112-9301
PHONE: 801-581-7785 • FAX: 801-581-3666
E-MAIL: INFORMATION@BUSINESS.UTAH.EDU • WEBSITE: WWW.BUSINESS.UTAH.EDU

Student Life and Environment

Eccles "is located on a hillside overlooking Salt Lake City" that is "located 15 minutes from world-class skiing (winter time) and mountain biking (summer time). The campus is in a great setting," and students try to take the opportunity to enjoy both the surroundings and campus life. UU fans are "rabid," one student informs us. "The school is confident and walks tall." In short, "the overall environment is excellent" at UU. "The school provides all the resources we need. The campus is excellent; the library is a really comfortable place to study; and most of [the] classrooms at DESB have outlets for every student, access to inter-net and technology needed to do presentations, etc."

The MBA program "is very supportive of students who have kids, and willing to help out any way they can. Once a month, the school hosts a 'Parent's Night Out' to watch students' children for free." Also, "there have been family-friendly tailgate parties where students can bring their families and mingle with alumni." The program also offers "some good activi-ties for single students as well as families," including sporting events, mixers, and outings.

Eccles "is making efforts to be more internationally diverse," but "the school needs to encourage more diversity of opinions as well. Utah is an extremely politically conservative state and the viewpoints within the classroom reflect [a range] from conservative to really, really conservative." While "most of the class is Mormon," there are plenty of students from other religious backgrounds here as well.

Admissions

The Eccles admissions committee requires applicants to provide the following: an under-graduate transcript demonstrating a GPA of at least 3.0 (students failing to meet this require-ment may gain entry based on evaluation of their performance during the final two years of undergraduate work); proof of successful completion of a college-level statistics course; GMAT scores (minimum 50th percentile score in math required); two recommendations, submitted online; responses to essay questions; and a resume. International students whose first language is not English must take the TOEFL. Two years of post-undergraduate profes-sional experience are strongly encouraged but not required. The school reports that it administers "several privately-donated scholarships reserved for underrepresented groups and [designed] to help us build the gender, ethnic, and geographic diversity of our student body."

FINANCIAL FACTS

Annual tuition (in-state/ out-of-state)	$15,500/$30,500
Fees	$800
Cost of books	$1,000
Room & board (on/off-campus)	$8,500/$11,000
% of students receiving aid	40
% of first-year students receiving aid	40
% of students receiving grants	40
Average award package	$21,000
Average grant	$21,000

ADMISSIONS

Admissions Selectivity Rating	81
# of applications received	223
% applicants accepted	61
% acceptees attending	52
Average GMAT	594
Range of GMAT	550–660
Average GPA	3.43
TOEFL required of international students	Yes
Minimum TOEFL (paper/computer)	600/250
Application fee	$55
International application fee	$65
Regular application deadline	2/15
Regular notification	3/15
Application Deadline/Notification	
Round 1:	1/15 / 2/15
Round 2:	2/15 / 3/15
Round 3:	3/15 / 4/1
Early decision program?	No
Deferment available	No
Transfer students accepted	Yes
Transfer application policy: In special circumstances, up to 6 credit hours may be transferred into the program from another AACSB program.	
Non-fall admissions	No
Need-blind admissions	Yes

EMPLOYMENT PROFILE

Career Rating	86	Grads Employed by Function	%	Avg. Salary
Percent employed at graduation	60	Operations	5	$61,383
Percent employed 3 months after graduation	85	Consulting	24	$60,000
		Management	14	$60,000
Average base starting salary	$69,875	Finance	10	$56,853
Primary Source of Full-time Job Acceptances		HR	29	$56,000
School-facilitated activities	12 (38%)	MIS	10	
Graduate-facilitated activities	17 (53%)	**Top 5 Employers Hiring Grads**		
Unknown	3 (9%)	L3 Communications (1), eBay (1), ATK (1), Zions Bancorporation (1), Intermountain Healthcare (1)		

THE UNIVERSITY OF VERMONT
SCHOOL OF BUSINESS ADMINISTRATION

GENERAL INFORMATION
Type of school	Public
Academic calendar	FA/SP

SURVEY SAYS...
Students love Burlington, VT
Solid preparation in:
Operations

STUDENTS
Enrollment of parent	
institution	12,800
Enrollment of MBA Program	55
% male/female	53/47
% out-of-state	47
% part-time	73
% minorities	11
% international	20
Average age at entry	29
Average years work experience	
at entry	5

ACADEMICS
Academic Experience Rating	80
Student/faculty ratio	5:1
Profs interesting rating	84
Profs accessible rating	84
% female faculty	31

Prominent Alumni
Doug Goldsmith, Earth Turbines, CFO & VP, Finance & Admin; Corp. Finance; Scottie Gim, IBM, VP, Microelectronics; Katherine B. Crosett, Kalex Enterprises, Principal; Mgmt cons, inter. exec svcs; tech wrtng; Alexander D. Crosett, III, Kalex Enterpr, Principal; Mgmt cons, inter. exec svcs; tech wrtng; Carrie Teffner, Sara Lee, SVP & CFO, Household and Body Care.

Academics

Small, friendly, and as "green" as the rolling hills of Vermont, UVM's business school offers a practical, stimulating, and balanced approach to business education. Bringing "a wealth of information and experience" to the classroom, UVM "professors are current and professionals in their area of study." With only 67 students in the MBA program, the teaching staff is "extremely accessible, and classes are a great small size." In fact, it's easy to receive one-on-one mentorship and guidance, as UVM's teaching staff is "accessible, supportive, willing to give constructive criticism and advice, both for school, work, and career questions." The pleasant vibe is echoed throughout the school community, where "advisors and staff are also very helpful and friendly."

The MBA curriculum at UVM begins with six core courses in organization and management, marketing, accounting, production and operations management, corporate finance, and the legal environment of business. After that, students take 10 advanced-level courses, tailoring their coursework to their individual interests. A feature of Vermont's MBA is "the ability to attain a general management concentration while being able to take classes in other colleges (Environment, Public Administration, Community Development) to meet electives." However, while the program's small size is certainly a benefit in the classroom, it limits the range of courses the business school is able to offer. "There is a definite finance/accounting slant" within the course selection, and students suggest that the university add more operations, entrepreneurship, and international business courses. Students would also like to see "more focus on technology, especially business applications, enterprise software, and use of collaboration tools (e.g., SharePoint) within the student body."

UVM offers a traditional MBA, which can be completed on a full-time or part-time basis, as well as an accelerated program. Working students really appreciate the fact that "most classes are at night to accommodate part-time commuters." Full-time students also benefit from the school's evening schedule, which allows them time to pursue internships. Fortunately, the surrounding town of "Burlington provides a lot of interesting and unique opportunities both inside and outside of business." With this progressive small city as a backdrop, UVM is highly "involved in green business," and "students are aware of sustainable business practices due to the university's emphasis on environmental studies." On the whole, students at UVM are "ambitious, analytical, [and] intellectual," and they "bring a lot to the table in terms of experience, insight, and determination." Encouraging participation and drawing on the experience of the student body, "classes are dynamic and discussion is facilitated well by the professors."

Career and Placement

The School of Business Career Services offers resume-building assistance, cover letter preparation, interview coaching, and a recruiting database, as well as an extensive library of books about job hunting, which all come in handy during the career fairs and a Spring Career Week. The UVM MBA is set up for working students, with all classes starting after 5 P.M. Therefore, most students in the MBA program are already employed and, consequently, students complain that "there are virtually no career services in place for graduate students." Some students also feel that the administration should encourage "much more interaction between the MBA program and area businesses." However, as the only AACSB-accredited program in the region, UVM has a corner on the local market.

Student Life and Environment

The laid-back Vermont lifestyle and "dynamic" university environment make UVM a highly appealing place to study. Maybe it's the calming effect of the Vermont's natural beauty, but the school attracts students who are "motivated to excel but lead a balanced lifestyle." A current student adds, "UVM feels like a second home. Class schedules are very comfortable, and there are a lot of options for spending time both on and off campus." However, "most students balance full-time jobs and part-time school responsibilities, and are very busy." As a result, "the social network is not very strong."

Despite the lack of a more formal graduate school culture, social relationships often form in the classroom because "the group/team activities build the strong bonds that exist between students. That organically grows into events outside of school and off campus." On top of that, "an MBA association has been restarted, and students go out once a month for drinks and to chat." A student offers, "MBA students at UVM are some of the friendliest people I've ever met. Everyone is more than willing to offer their opinions on classes and professors as well as potential career opportunities and contacts." When looking for a little recreation or down time, the beautiful town of "Burlington is a dream," offering plenty of outdoor activities as well as a lively, collegiate atmosphere.

Admissions

At the University of Vermont, there is no minimum GMAT score or undergraduate GPA required for admission; however, test scores and undergraduate record are considered in an admissions decision. Students are also evaluated on the quality of their undergraduate institution, perceived rigor of undergraduate coursework, quality and quantity of business experience, letters of recommendation, statement of purpose, and post-graduate work. The average GMAT for accepted students is 610 and the average GPA is 3.17.

FINANCIAL FACTS

Annual tuition (in-state/ out-of-state)	$11,712/$29,568
Fees	$1,812
Cost of books	$1,050
Room & board	$9,026
% of students receiving aid	17
% of first-year students receiving aid	31
% of students receiving loans	16
Average award package	$16,650
Average student loan debt	$22,167

ADMISSIONS

Admissions Selectivity Rating	**78**
# of applications received	32
% applicants accepted	75
% acceptees attending	50
Average GMAT	610
Range of GMAT	500–730
Average GPA	3.17
TOEFL required of international students	Yes
Minimum TOEFL (paper/computer)	550/213
Application fee	$40
International application fee	$40
Early decision program?	No
Deferment available	Yes
Maximum length of deferment	1 year
Transfer students accepted	Yes
Transfer application policy: Transfer credit is reviewed based upon each individual set of circumstances.	
Non-fall admissions	Yes
Need-blind admissions	Yes

EMPLOYMENT PROFILE

Career Rating	79	Grads Employed by Function	% Avg. Salary
Average base starting salary	$70,000	Consulting	9 $75,000
		Management	13 $83,000
		Finance	13 $70,000
		MIS	9 $60,000

Top 5 Employers Hiring Grads
University of Vermont (1), Husky Injection Molding (1), IBM (1), Duet-Pro (1), Business Financial Publications (1)

UNIVERSITY OF VIRGINIA
DARDEN GRADUATE SCHOOL OF BUSINESS ADMINISTRATION

GENERAL INFORMATION
Type of school   Public
Academic calendar   Semester

SURVEY SAYS...
Good peer network
Helpful alumni
Smart classrooms
Solid preparation in:
Finance
General management

STUDENTS
Enrollment of parent institution	20,643
Enrollment of MBA Program	642
% male/female	71/29
% part-time	0
% minorities	12
% international	22
Average age at entry	28
Average years work experience at entry	4

ACADEMICS
Academic Experience Rating	**99**
Student/faculty ratio	7:1
Profs interesting rating	77
Profs accessible rating	98
% female faculty	19
% minority faculty	7

Joint Degrees
MBA/JD, 4 years; MBA/MA in East Asian Studies, 3 years; MBA/MA in Government or Foreign Affairs, 3 years; MBA/ME, 3 years; MBA/MSN, 3 years; MBA/PhD, 4 years; MBA/MD; MBA/MPH.

Prominent Alumni
Ms. Susan Sobbott, President, Open-AMEX; Mr. William A. Hawkins, President and Chief Executive Officer, Medtronic; Mr. Douglas A. Scovanner, Executive Vice President and CFO, Target Group; Mr. Thomas J. Baltimore, Jr., President, RLJ Development, LLC; Mr. Henri Termeer, Chairman, President and Chief Executive Officer, Genzyme Corporation.

Academics

Offering a unique, challenging, and spirited MBA program, the Darden School of Business at the University of Virginia distinguishes itself through "the outstanding reputation of the faculty and students, the rigorous and exciting case method, and the broad focus on general management that the school offers." Hailed as "one of the toughest programs in the world," the hallmark of a Darden education is the case-based curriculum—an intensive, discussion-based teaching method with an emphasis "on experiential learning in a collaborative environment and through teamwork." Sounds fun, but students warn that "the first-year curriculum is rigorous, and the case method demands students be prepared and take leadership positions." Not to mention that curricular requirements are incredibly time consuming. First-year students typically spend the day at school: Classes run from 8:00 A.M. to 2:00 P.M. and related activities can run until 10:00 P.M.

It's a challenge, but a Darden education is well worth the effort as "you really gain mastery of the material." Encouraging a lively and interactive classroom environment, the school's savvy professors "are outstanding at leading a case conversation and covering all of the key learning points." A second-year student raves, "The faculty at Darden has revolutionized my life. They have challenged me to think differently, to go deeper to find solutions to complex problems and stimulate my mind each day." Darden really distinguishes itself in its commitment to the student experience: "Professors at Darden are there because they want to teach. Students are the priority, not research." A current student enthuses, "Professors have enormous levels of experience and are ridiculously available outside class. I've gone in unscheduled and been able to spend over an hour working on an issue—the professor just made the time."

Teamwork is integral to the Darden experience, and each new student is assigned to a learning team of five or six students with whom they prepare for class each day. Working together, students say that Darden's "intense and competitive" academic atmosphere is counterbalanced by the fact that "Darden has an extremely helpful and collegial environment." In this stimulating campus setting, "The common thread running through the student body is a general sense of appreciation for the atmosphere, enthusiasm toward the learning experience, and a desire to collaborate with the learning experience through student-led review sessions, informal help sessions, etc."

Career and Placement

Students say "the Career Development Center has improved to a great extent," bringing a "record number of recruiters and companies on grounds this [past] fall." The center offers a variety of services to MBA students, including Career Discovery Forums, individual career consultations, a professional development series, and workshops and special events. Through the Career Development Center, students also have access to the Darden Networking Partnership, a database of nearly 2,000 alumni who have volunteered to help fellow grads in career searches.

Last year, 85 percent of graduates seeking employment had received a job offer by graduation, and 91 percent had received a job offer within three months of graduation. Finance was the most popular career choice, drawing 43 percent of students; consulting drew 20 percent. Among the top recruiters were: A.T. Kearney, Booz Allen Hamilton, Deloitte Touche Tohmatsu, The Boston Consulting Group, Everest, General Mills, Johnson & Johnson, Kraft Foods, Bank of America, Citigroup, Merrill Lynch, McKinsey & Company, Bain and Company, Standard and Poor's, UTC, Progressive, Danaher Corp., Mass Mutual Financial Group, Goldman Sachs, DuPont, General Electric, JPMorgan Chase, The McGraw-Hill Companies, Centex, Target, Dell, EDS, Intel, and Sprint Nextel.

Student Life and Environment

For those who thrive under pressure, Darden is an ideal environment as "The rhythm is extremely hectic, but the atmosphere is jovial, and there is a real palpable energy and excitement about learning in the place." In fact, Darden students seem to take a masochistic pleasure in the hectic pace of life where "Sleep is a rare commodity." In the hearty words of one first-year student: "Although the workload seems unbearable at times, and I have to schedule phone calls with my spouse, I really wouldn't trade this experience for any other." While acknowledging the rigors of the workload, students continually emphasize the kindness of the Darden community, where "Everything from the computer services to the dining hall is done for the students and with their best interests at heart."

When it comes to extracurricular activities, students reassure us that "even with the demanding workload students are very active in clubs, social events, MBA case competitions, and the community." They also manage to sneak in a moment of socializing during the daily First Coffee, "a break between classes in which you can catch up with classmates in other sections, friends, or professors. Everyone in the Darden community comes by for a cup of joe (partners and children included at times)." When it's time to relax, "Saturdays during the fall are a time for attending football games, the Chili Cook-Off, or the International Food Festival." Another favorite is "the Thursday Night Drinking Club where the majority of students meet up at a different bar every Thursday." An ideal college town, "Charlottesville is a great place to live; it has a really low cost of living without sacrificing culture."

Admissions

Darden evaluates a student's readiness for business school in three broad areas: academics, professional experience, and personal qualities and characteristics. These competencies are measured through the applicant's undergraduate record, GMAT scores, resume and work experience, letters of recommendation, and admissions essays. In addition, interviews are required and are considered an important part of the application. While there are no minimum requirements for admission, last year's entering class had a mean GMAT of 701. The mean GPA was 3.38.

FINANCIAL FACTS

Annual tuition (in-state/ out-of-state)	$41,270/$46,270
Fees	$2,230
Cost of books	$2,800
Room & board	$17,700
% of students receiving aid	79
% of first-year students receiving aid	80
% of students receiving loans	77
% of students receiving grants	35
Average award package	$41,500
Average grant	$23,390
Average student loan debt	$66,272

ADMISSIONS

Admissions Selectivity Rating	97
# of applications received	2,690
% applicants accepted	25
% acceptees attending	45
Average GMAT	701
Average GPA	3.38
TOEFL required of international students	Yes
Minimum TOEFL (paper/computer)	650/270
Application fee	$200
International application fee	$200
Application Deadline/Notification	
Round 1:	10/28 / 1/28
Round 2:	1/07 / 3/26
Round 3:	3/31 / 5/12
Early decision program?	No
Deferment available	No
Transfer students accepted	No
Non-fall admissions	No
Need-blind admissions	Yes

EMPLOYMENT PROFILE

Career Rating	**99**	**Grads Employed by Function**	**% Avg.**	**Salary**
Percent employed at graduation	73	Marketing	14	$96,274
Percent employed 3 months after graduation	77	Consulting	31	$115,182
		Management	18	$90,808
Average base starting salary	$102,903	Finance	34	$98,680
Primary Source of Full-time Job Acceptances		**Top 5 Employers Hiring Grads**		
School-facilitated activities	176 (77%)	IBM Global Business Services (9); Bain &		
Graduate-facilitated activities	52 (23%)	Company, Inc. (8); Deloitte (8); Barclays (7);		
		Danaher Corporation (7)		

UNIVERSITY OF WASHINGTON
MICHAEL G. FOSTER SCHOOL OF BUSINESS

GENERAL INFORMATION
Type of school	Public
Academic calendar	Quarter

SURVEY SAYS...
Students love Seattle, WA
Good peer network
Helpful alumni
Solid preparation in:
Marketing
Finance
Teamwork

STUDENTS
Enrollment of parent institution	42,113
Enrollment of MBA Program	491
% male/female	62/38
% out-of-state	58
% part-time	54
% minorities	6
% international	25
Average age at entry	29
Average years work experience at entry	6

ACADEMICS
Academic Experience Rating	**93**
Student/faculty ratio	8:1
Profs interesting rating	88
Profs accessible rating	89
% female faculty	32
% minority faculty	8

Joint Degrees
JD/MBA, 4 years; MBA/MAIS, 3 years; MBA/MHA Health Administration, 3 years.

Prominent Alumni
William Ayer, CEO, Alaska Airlines; Dan Nordstrom, Former CEO, Nordstrom.com; Charles Lillis, Former CEO, Media One Group; Gary Neale, Chairman, Nisource; Yoshihiko Miyauchi, CEO, Orix.

Academics

The Foster School of Business at the University of Washington draws on its Seattle locale to inform the focus of its program. The curriculum emphasizes a global perspective (especially as it pertains to countries in the Pacific Rim), and there is an overall focus on technology reflecting UW's proximity to such tech heavyweights as Microsoft and Amazon ("Think tons of Microsoft alums"). There are also numerous opportunities to learn about entrepreneurship, in keeping with the city's relaxed and independent vibe. In fact, many students choose UW for its "entrepreneurship and technology focus." This plays out in case studies, projects, and real-world examples drawn from these areas during core courses, as well as in areas of concentration.

Those core courses comprise about half of the Foster MBA program. Foundation subjects such as accounting, finance, human resources, ethics, and marketing are included in the required core. Toward the end of the first year, each student selects three Advanced Core Electives, which allow closer exploration of areas available for concentration in the second year of the program. Students say, "All classes require a good bit of teamwork." "The level of involvement is left up to individuals, but most take part in a lot of the activities." Most students take an internship between their first and second years and return for the second year to specialize in fields such as entrepreneurship and innovation, international business, e-commerce, or marketing.

Washington's MBA students are happy with the quality of teaching, as well as the support from the university's administration. "UW has excellent professors who value teaching and helping students learn. That means everything!" The "mix of case and lecture method and small class size" also are helpful, as are professors who "go beyond to make sure that students get all the education they want." That same student adds, "I haven't met more dedicated professors than the professors at UW." Another MBA candidate says, "The core professors are superstars—far and away the best instructors I've ever had in my life." The evening MBA program is also well staffed: The "Evening program generally is taught by full-time established professors who are very good at their fields, and have made themselves available via e-mail if 'in person' is not convenient for working students."

Career and Placement

The Business Connections Center in the University of Washington program offers network events, career-evaluation tools, a mentorship program with local business leaders, an online jobs data base, and personal career counseling. They "excel at connecting students with alums and other business leaders in the community and elsewhere. They stress the importance of networking and help students to establish a network." The center boasts "great connections to the Seattle business community," and "relationships with world-class companies like Microsoft, Starbucks, [and] Amazon.com." "In most cases, students are extremely successful in landing desirable internships and jobs."

Students also say there's room for improvement: "UW could improve getting access to companies and jobs outside the Pacific Northwest," one student says, and others' comments echo his opinion. However, the career center now subsidizes travel to other regions for interviews.

AT&T Wireless, Alaska Airlines, Hewlett-Packard, Washington Mutual, Intel, Microsoft, Hitachi Consulting, Samsung, Starbucks, Tektronix, and Wells Fargo are among the companies that recruit on campus.

ADMISSIONS CONTACT: ERIN DENNETT, DIRECTOR OF ADMISSIONS
ADDRESS: 110 MACKENZIE HALL, BOX 353200 SEATTLE, WA 98195-3200
PHONE: 206-543-4661 • FAX: 206-616-7351
E-MAIL: MBA@U.WASHINGTON.EDU • WEBSITE: WWW.FOSTER.WASHINGTON.EDU/MBA

Student Life and Environment

Students find much to like about their classmates, the lifestyle, and the opportunities offered at the University of Washington. "UW has a collaborative, rigorous, and challenging academic environment, plus a sense of work/life balance that many schools do not have," says one student. "When I visited [before enrolling], I met several students, faculty, and staff, who all impressed me with their intelligence, enthusiasm, kindness, and humor. I knew that this was the type of community I wanted to be a part of."

"Smart people without the attitude," is how another MBA candidate described his classmates. Another says, "One of the greatest things about the MBA program is that there were activities and clubs for my wife. Some of these activities were social, while others were community-related." But improving the "quality of child care or providing child care for all students" is area that needs to be addressed, student agree.

Another issue is facilities. "The buildings are the ugliest ones on campus," one student complains. Another says, "UW is behind the curve for business school facilities. Another student adds, "The business school buildings are getting up there in terms of age and facilities. There is a plan to upgrade these, but it probably won't happen while I am a student there. Future students will certainly benefit from the improvements, though."Indeed, new state-of-the art-facilities will open in autumn 2010.

Admissions

Those making admissions decisions for the Foster MBA program look for leadership potential, academic strength, communicative ability, and intellectual ability. They evaluate quantitative and language skills through transcripts, GMAT scores, GPAs, and, if needed, TOEFL scores. UW does not have minimum GMAT score or GPA requirement. "If a student is lacking in one area but strong in others, he or she may still be admitted," the school says on its website. For the most recent class admitted, the average GMAT score was 682, and the average GPA was 3.38. These students averaged six and a half years of work experience.

FINANCIAL FACTS

Annual tuition (in-state/ out-of-state)	$21,782/$32,451
Fees	$552
Cost of books	$3,350
Room & board (on/off-campus)	$15,340/$15,780
% of students receiving aid	70
% of first-year students receiving aid	84
% of students receiving loans	68
% of students receiving grants	40
Average award package	$15,000
Average grant	$9,400
Average student loan debt	$24,000

ADMISSIONS

Admissions Selectivity Rating	97
# of applications received	651
% applicants accepted	31
% acceptees attending	52
Average GMAT	682
Range of GMAT	660–720
Average GPA	3.38
TOEFL required of international students	Yes
Minimum TOEFL (paper/computer)	600/250
Application fee	$65
International application fee	$65
Regular application deadline	1/15
Regular notification	3/27
Application Deadline/Notification	
Round 1:	10/15 / 12/12
Round 2:	11/15 / 1/16
Round 3:	1/15 / 3/27
Round 4:	3/15 / 5/8
Early decision program?	No
Deferment available	No
Transfer students accepted	Yes
Transfer application policy: Transfer applicants should apply as any other new student. The status of a transfer student is determined on a case-by-case basis, depending on the work completed at another school.	
Non-fall admissions	No
Need-blind admissions	Yes

EMPLOYMENT PROFILE

Career Rating	94	Grads Employed by Function	% Avg. Salary
Percent employed at graduation	67	Marketing	25 NR
Percent employed 3 months after graduation	97	Operations	4 NR
		Consulting	12 NR
Average base starting salary	$87,177	Management	9 NR
Primary Source of Full-time Job Acceptances		Finance	32 NR
School-facilitated activities	42 (57%)	MIS	8 NR
Graduate-facilitated activities	27 (36%)	Communications	1 NR
Unknown	5 (7%)	Entrepreneurship	3 NR
		Entrepreneurship	5 NR
		Internet	3 NR
		Nonprofit	1 NR
		Strategic	1 NR

Top 5 Employers Hiring Grads
Microsoft, Amazon.com, PricewaterhouseCoopers, T-Mobile, Intel

UNIVERSITY OF WEST GEORGIA
RICHARDS COLLEGE OF BUSINESS

GENERAL INFORMATION

Type of school	Public
Academic calendar	Semester

SURVEY SAYS...

Students love Carrollton, GA
Happy students
Smart classrooms
Solid preparation in:
General management

STUDENTS

Enrollment of parent institution	11,500
Enrollment of MBA Program	156
% male/female	56/44
% out-of-state	26
% part-time	72
% minorities	30
% international	19
Average age at entry	30

ACADEMICS

Academic Experience Rating	**82**
Student/faculty ratio	15:1
Profs interesting rating	87
Profs accessible rating	85
% female faculty	34
% minority faculty	18

Academics

The attractive blend of affordability, convenience, and quality defines the MBA program at the University of West Georgia. With strong academic programs and a low in-state tuition, the Richards College of Business is "very impressive for such an affordable school." UWG offers two campus programs at Carrollton and the Newnan Center, as well as a totally web-based MBA. Both campus programs cater to part-time students, with classes offered exclusively in the evenings. A current student tells us, "The part-time MBA program structure is the best I've been able to find for working professionals." On the other hand, for those who'd like to complete the program full-time, the MBA is both rapid and efficient, thereby minimizing the overall cost of attending a graduate school. As one student points out, "Tuition is a lot cheaper than other schools in the state of Georgia, and I could reasonably receive my MBA within one year." The UWG curriculum is comprised of 18 to 21 required credit hours in business essentials including managerial accounting, managerial economics, organizational theory and behavior, and marketing strategy. Students also complete four elective courses, working with the MBA director to develop a personal area of elective study. For those who do not have full-time jobs, MBA students can participate in the school's "Graduate Assistantship Program," which helps them offset the cost of the education.

University of West Georgia's MBA is efficient, but not pared down. You'll find fully supportive staff and an "outstanding" administration. In fact, "students are required to meet with an advisor regularly, and it's a huge help to ensure graduation within one-and-a-half to two years." Like the staff and administrators, teaching staff is open, friendly, and student-oriented. Students say the program is a "wonderful experience," praising "the teachers willingness to be available to help the students whenever they need it. Teachers really want the students to succeed." A student enthuses, "At UWG, the student comes first, and all the teachers abide by that." While you probably won't like every one of your classes, the academic programs are generally strong. A current student elaborates, "Like every school, there are some professors that are not as motivating and helpful as you would like, but on the whole West Georgia has some of the best teachers I have met." In particular, students say, "The Capstone teachers here are brilliant and will help a student more than any other."

With a low enrollment, the school "is small, which allows students to have access to abundance of one-on-one time with professors." The size also helps to forge bonds between students, and "typically everyone in every class knows one another. It's an extremely comfortable environment." While intimacy is one of the school's selling points, students also point out that, "the university and Carrollton are growing at a rapid rate, which is making it more attractive to go to school here." In fact, the program's enrollment recently doubled, bringing the head count to over 140. UWG draws both local and international students, resulting in a student body that is surprisingly varied. A student elaborates, "We have a large variety of foreign students, as well as an overall culture of working together to foster very good relationships within classes."

ADMISSIONS CONTACT: HOPE UDOMBON, ADMINISTRATIVE DIRECTOR OF GRADUATE PROGRAMS
ADDRESS: 1601 MAPLE STREET CARROLLTON, GA 30118-3000
PHONE: 678-839-5355 • FAX: 678-839-5040
E-MAIL: HUDOMBON@WESTGA.EDU • WEBSITE: WWW.WESTGA.EDU

Career and Placement

Many of University of West Georgia's MBA candidates already have jobs and aren't planning to make a career change. For those looking for a new position after graduation, the university's Career Services department hosts career fairs and campus recruiting events, as well as a range of career-related activities and seminars. These activities are open to both undergraduate and graduate students, though the Career Services website also maintains a page specifically dedicated to resources for MBA students. University of West Georgia maintains a strong regional reputation and ties to local companies. Notably, "The business school is named after the founder of Southwire company (North America's largest supplier of wire), and the company offers numerous opportunities for students and graduates from the business school." However, one student tells us, "I would like the school to try and get more big name companies recruiting."

Student Life and Environment

University of West Georgia MBA students are a friendly and close-knit bunch. A current student tells us, "I have a group of about 10+ friends throughout my business classes, and we all help each other out with difficult questions and strive to help everyone achieve." At this southern school, the student body is "somewhat conservative." Most students are also "hard-working, dedicated, and helpful individuals."

When they aren't studying, UWG students say their "classmates are very outgoing and sociable. Everyone likes to get together at least once or twice a week for dinner and drinks." A student enthuses, "Life in Carrollton at the University of West Georgia has been a myriad of incredible times, from the classes to the social life." Adds another (who also attended the school as an undergraduate), "I am very active on campus with intramurals and Greek life. Also, there are a large number of organizations just aimed at graduates." Located in Carroll County, Georgia, UWG's "campus is big and pretty," boasting a "a new $10 million gym," among other amenities. In the surrounding community, "all the places that you would need to go are close (Wal-mart, Target)."

Admissions

Students are considered for admission to UWG based on an admissions index number, which is calculated using a student's undergraduate GPA and GMAT scores. As such, these two items are the most important aspects of application package. At the same time, students are also evaluated based on their letters of recommendation (three are required), and a short personal statement. In some cases, a student with extensive business experience may be able to receive a GMAT waiver.

FINANCIAL FACTS

Annual tuition (in-state/ out-of-state)	$3,932/$15,736
Fees	$1,386
Cost of books	$1,545
Room & board (on-campus)	$8,304
% of students receiving aid	14
% of first-year students receiving aid	89
% of students receiving loans	12
% of students receiving grants	2
Average award package	$9,795
Average grant	$1,955
Average student loan debt	$16,091

ADMISSIONS

Admissions Selectivity Rating	77
# of applications received	98
% applicants accepted	50
% acceptees attending	96
Average GMAT	481
Range of GMAT	355–580
Average GPA	3.14
TOEFL required of international students	Yes
Minimum TOEFL (paper/computer)	550/213
Application fee	$30
International application fee	$30
Regular application deadline	7/17
Early decision program?	Yes
Deferment available	Yes
Maximum length of deferment	1 year without reapplying
Transfer students accepted	Yes
Transfer application policy: A maxium of 6 semester hours of graduate credit may be transferred from another accredited institution. See catalog for more information.	
Non-fall admissions	Yes
Need-blind admissions	Yes

UNIVERSITY OF WISCONSIN—MADISON

SCHOOL OF BUSINESS

GENERAL INFORMATION

Type of school	Public
Academic calendar	Semester

SURVEY SAYS...

Students love Madison, WI
Friendly students
Good social scene
Happy students
Smart classrooms
Solid preparation in:
Marketing

STUDENTS

Enrollment of parent institution	42,030
Enrollment of MBA Program	475
% male/female	70/30
% out-of-state	72
% part-time	51
% minorities	10
% international	18
Average age at entry	28
Average years work experience at entry	4

ACADEMICS

Academic Experience Rating	**95**
Student/faculty ratio	3:1
Profs interesting rating	86
Profs accessible rating	88
% female faculty	23
% minority faculty	1

Joint Degrees

JD/MBA, 4 years.

Prominent Alumni

Steve Bennett, Former CEO, Intuit; Glen Tellock, CEO, The Manitowoc Company; Tadashi Okamura, Chairman, Toshiba Corporation; Thomas J. Falk, Chairman of the Board & CEO, Kimberly Clark Corp.; John P. Morgridge, Chairman of the Board, Cisco Systems.

Academics

The University of Wisconsin—Madison offers a unique and challenging MBA program, well suited to highly-focused students with clear career goals. Whereas most MBA programs require a wide array of course work in general management topics, the Wisconsin MBA curriculum is designed around career specializations, through which students focus their studies on a single business area such as real estate, entrepreneurship, brand management, or marketing research. Through their career specialization, students work within the business school's Centers for Expertise, which "ensure that students have lots of exposure to alumni, specific industry news, and professionals at various levels." A current student explains, "I chose the University of Wisconsin because they have a specialized program in marketing research that would give me the specialized skill set to continue in this field."

While career specializations are the hallmark of the Wisconsin MBA curriculum, "The program emphasizes strong learning within a specific discipline while allowing flexibility to learn cross-functional skills." Before beginning their studies within a specific center, students must complete the general management core curriculum, which provides a solid foundation in management essentials. Even so, those looking for a more varied education will probably find a better match elsewhere. Students warn that "The specified 'center' does make it difficult at times to expand into other departments." Throughout the curriculum, applied learning is an important component of the Wisconsin MBA, and students participate in live business projects for a wide range of companies. For example, students may conduct market research for leading companies, manage stock portfolios, or manage a portfolio of real estate securities.

The business school draws a team of top-notch faculty "committed to up-to-date teaching styles and topics." Student input here is valued. "Feedback is taken from the students at the end of every semester and the recommended changes are implemented for the next incoming class," says one MBA. "It's a constantly evolving and improving program that is viewed as a collaborative effort between the administration and students." On the whole, "Wisconsin represents a culture of collaboration and teamwork," and students reassure us that "when students compete, there is a general collegiate respect for one another." Another major perk of a Wisconsin MBA education is its public school price tag, made better by the fact that through assistantships "The tuition is covered, benefits are covered, and you get a stipend." A student exclaims, "You might find it hard to catch your breath, but it's a great way to avoid loans."

Career and Placement

During the first semester at Wisconsin, students take a 6-week course to help them plan and initiate their internship search, including instruction on resume writing, interviewing, researching companies and more. After that, students have access to the Career Center's Internet database as well as one-on-one career advising with professional counselors. However, the program's unique in-depth focus is what really makes the difference in career placement. A current student explains, "Access to corporate recruiters is unprecedented since we have a program which consists of specializations, rather than a generic MBA. You get put on a niche career track right away, so recruiters know exactly what they're getting during interviews."

With strong ties in the region, 60 percent of students take jobs in the Midwest. However, for those looking to expand their horizons, students reassure us that "last year and the current year, we have been utilizing our alumni and board member connections to send a significant number of finance students out to New York for positions with bulge bracket firms." Currently, the top 15 recruiters at UW are: Proctor & Gamble, General Electric Company, Kraft Foods, Johnson & Johnson, Guidant, Abbott Laboratories, Nestlé, Best Buy, General Mills, SC Johnson, R.W. Baird, IBM, Cisco, UBS, and Starbucks.

Student Life and Environment

When they aren't hitting the books, Wisconsin MBA students say there are "plenty of activities to become involved in, such as fundraising events, guest lecturers and social get-togethers." Even if you aren't into extracurricular activities, it's easy to get to know your classmates, because "In addition to clubs, classes, and social events, most students are well connected with the other students in their centers." Most Wisconsin students maintain a balanced perspective on life, work, and studies. A current student elaborates, "The students in the business school are very serious about their studies and put in long, dedicated hours to get things done. Then they go party. It takes a mature kind of mindset to be able to effectively balance the two." Another chimes in, "It's not uncommon to work on group projects until two or three in the morning."

At this famous university, the business school is located "in the middle of campus with the 42,000 other students, so there is a constant buzz of activity." The consummate college town, students love Madison, "a city with a thriving arts and cultural scene, and plenty of opportunities for recreation and entertainment." And the school's downtown location means "you get the undergraduate as well as the professional demographic all within seven blocks." With so many entertainment options, it's no surprise that "most of the MBA students go out every Thursday night for a beverage—a great way to get to know everyone."

Admissions

The University of Wisconsin—Madison seeks students from diverse personal, professional, and cultural backgrounds, who have demonstrated success in business and management. Last year's class had an average GMAT score of 666 and average work experience of 4 years. In addition to their academic and professional achievements, Wisconsin looks for students who demonstrate intellectual curiosity, motivation, leadership, communication skills, and analytical ability. An applicant's fit with their chosen career specialization, academic record, standardized test scores, and work experience are among the most important factors in an admissions decision.

FINANCIAL FACTS

Annual tuition (in-state/ out-of-state)	$10,588/$25,678
Fees	$890
Cost of books	$990
Room & board (on-campus)	$10,972
% of students receiving aid	45
% of first-year students receiving aid	83
% of students receiving grants	27
Average award package	$18,149
Average grant	$19,283

ADMISSIONS

Admissions Selectivity Rating	95
# of applications received	508
% applicants accepted	33
% acceptees attending	74
Average GMAT	666
Range of GMAT	640–710
Average GPA	3.36
TOEFL required of international students	Yes
Minimum TOEFL (paper/computer)	600/250
Application fee	$56
International application fee	$56
Early decision program?	No
Deferment available	Yes
Maximum length of deferment	1 year
Transfer students accepted	No
Non-fall admissions	No
Need-blind admissions	Yes

EMPLOYMENT PROFILE

Career Rating	95	Grads Employed by Function	% Avg. Salary
Percent employed at graduation	83	Marketing	32 $87,817
Percent employed 3 months after graduation	94	Operations	9 $82,289
		Consulting	10 $82,000
Average base starting salary	$88,626	Management	4 $105,000
Primary Source of Full-time Job Acceptances		Finance	41 $90,333
School-facilitated activities	76 (78%)	HR	1 NR
Graduate-facilitated activities	21 (22%)	MIS	1 NR

Top 5 Employers Hiring Grads
Procter & Gamble (6), Kraft (4), HP (4), Bank of America (3), Kimberly-Clark (3)

UNIVERSITY OF WISCONSIN—MILWAUKEE
SHELDON B. LUBAR SCHOOL OF BUSINESS

GENERAL INFORMATION
Type of school   Public
Academic calendar   Semester

SURVEY SAYS...
Students love Milwaukee, WI

STUDENTS
Enrollment of parent institution	29,358
Enrollment of MBA Program	311
% male/female	62/38
% part-time	100
Average age at entry	27
Average years work experience at entry	5

ACADEMICS
Academic Experience Rating	**77**
Student/faculty ratio	4:1
Profs interesting rating	78
Profs accessible rating	77
% female faculty	30
% minority faculty	1

Joint Degrees
Master of Human Resources and Labor Relations, 2–7 years; Master Of Public Administration, Non-Profit Management, 2–7 years; MBA/MS Nursing, 3–7 years; MS-MIS/MBA, 3–7 years.

Prominent Alumni
Keith Nosbusch, CEO, Rockwell Automation; James Ziemer, President &CEO, Harley-Davidson Co.; Robert Probst, Exec VP, Tamarack Petroleum; Mary Ellen Stanek, Managing Director, Robert Baird & Co; Dennis Glaso, President & CEO, Jefferson Pilot Corporation.

Academics

The Lubar School of Business at University of Wisconsin-Milwaukee provides "a good core MBA program with many extra courses offered" to a student body as varied as the city it serves. Lubar MBA and MS programs can be completed on a full-time or part-time basis. The MBA degree can be completed at the main campus in Milwaukee, or at the campus in Waukesha. The MBA program at the Waukesha campus can be completed in 16 months. All classes meet in the evening, with a few courses scheduled on Saturdays or in a hybrid online format. The Executive MBA program meets on alternating Fridays and Saturdays for four semesters over a 22-month period.

Full-time students love the option of an "accelerated MBA program that allow you to complete your degree in 16 months," while part timers value the way the program "accommodates our needs" with a concentrated evening schedule. Everyone appreciates the convenience and affordability of the program. "It's the only decent business school in its price range in southeast Wisconsin," one student explains, alluding to the pricier cross-town program at Marquette. The Lubar MBA offers a number of "career focus concentrations," allowing students the option to develop a specialization in healthcare management, international business, managing change, or supply chain management. Students may also pursue an elective track in cost management and ERP, e-business, entrepreneurship, financial strategy, global strategy, HR management, IT management, innovation management, investment management, leadership, manufacturing and service operations, marketing, or nonprofit business.

"Most professors are great" at UWM, although "a few need to be weeded out," particularly those "who have little teaching experience." Students who can visit campus during the daytime praise "the availability of resources." One writes, "I've never had an issue talking with an adviser, career services staff, or a professor. It helps that it's encouraged to use these resources." Some evening students, on the other hand, would like to see more services.

Career and Placement

The Sheldon B. Lubar School of Business Career Services Center serves undergraduates, graduate students, and alumni of the UW Milwaukee business school. The staff includes two career advisors and a director of career services. The office schedules on-campus interviews online via the e-Recruiting system; coordinates internships; organizes career fairs; maintains a list of job postings; conducts workshops on resume writing, interviewing, and job-search skills; and hosts company information sessions. Employers of UWM MBAs include: Acuity, Bank One, Briggs & Stratton Corporation, Chortek & Gottschalk, Cobalt Corp., Deloitte & Touche, Ernst & Young, Extendicare Health Services, GE Healthcare, Generac Power Systems, Harley-Davidson, Komisar Brady & Co., KPMG, M&I Bank, Miller Brewing Company, Northwestern Mutual, PricewaterhouseCoopers, Quad/Graphics, Rockwell Automation, SC Johnson, Smith Barney, Stark Investments, UMB Fund Services, United Government Services, U.S. Bank, Virchow, Krause & Co., WE Energies, Wells Fargo, and Wipfli.

Student Life and Environment

UWM MBAs "are mostly in their upper 20s with a few years of work experience." They are "very focused and motivated, but also focused on personal lives as well. It's an evening program, so our class is focused on 'getting the job done' with class, but we have a good group where we enjoy each others company as well!" The population includes "mixed degree students, which allows for many different industry perspectives."

UWM faces the typical challenges of a "commuter school", with "very little networking or social activity, especially for graduate students." That's especially true for the majority who attend part-time in addition to working full-time and, often, attending to family obligations. There is only one graduate networking club, the Graduate Business Association. "Typically, I go to class and get the heck off campus when completed," a typical student reports. MBA classes are held in the evenings for the convenience of the majority. They appreciate it but warn that "there is definitely a lack of support[services] for evening classes." However, the Lubar School does have evening hours two nights per week for graduate students. Students report that "safety is a concern" around campus during the late evening hours and that the school "needs more parking for community students."

Students are much more bullish about Milwaukee, a city "with great public transportation." The life of Milwaukee is great to be surrounded by," one student tell us, noting also the presence of "plenty of employers" in the metropolitan region.

Admissions

Applicants to UW—Milwaukee's MBA program must apply to the university's Graduate School, which refers b-school applications to the School of Business Administration for review and recommendation. The Graduate School Admissions Office makes all final admissions decisions. All applicants must submit a completed application form, an official GMAT score, one official copy of transcripts for all undergraduate work, and a personal statement. Students must achieve a minimum undergraduate GPA of 2.75 and have a GMAT score "that indicates a high probability of success in graduate school" to be considered for "admission in good standing." Applicants who fail to meet these minimum requirements may be granted "admission on probation" status. International students must meet all of the above requirements and must also submit an official TOEFL score report (the minimum required score is 550 on the paper test, 213 on the computer test, and 79 on the internet-based test) or an official IELTS score of 6.5.

FINANCIAL FACTS

Annual tuition (in-state/ out-of-state)	$10,523/$28,188
Cost of books	$900
Room & board (on/off-campus)	$9,000/$10,000
% of students receiving aid	60
% of first-year students receiving aid	41
% of students receiving loans	52
% of students receiving grants	8
Average award package	$14,276
Average grant	$8,400
Average student loan debt	$20,369

ADMISSIONS

Admissions Selectivity Rating	80
# of applications received	223
% applicants accepted	54
% acceptees attending	69
Average GMAT	546
Range of GMAT	490–600
Average GPA	3.24
TOEFL required of international students	Yes
Minimum TOEFL (paper/computer)	550/213
Application fee	$45
International application fee	$85
Early decision program?	No
Deferment available	Yes
Maximum length of deferment	1 year
Transfer students accepted	Yes
Transfer application policy: The application process is the same for all applicants.	
Non-fall admissions	Yes
Need-blind admissions	Yes

EMPLOYMENT PROFILE

Career Rating	62	Grads Employed by Function	% Avg. Salary
		Marketing	2 $46,500
		Management	40 $63,845
		Finance	35 $57,091
		MIS	13 $69,750

Top 5 Employers Hiring Grads
US Bank, KPMG, Deloitte & Touche LLP, Northwestern Mutual, Quad/Graphics

UNIVERSITY OF WISCONSIN—WHITEWATER
COLLEGE OF BUSINESS AND ECONOMICS

GENERAL INFORMATION
Type of school	Public
Academic calendar	Semester

SURVEY SAYS...
Solid preparation in:
Marketing
General management
Communication/interpersonal skills
Computer skills
Doing business in a global economy

STUDENTS
Enrollment of parent institution	10,720
Enrollment of MBA Program	560
% male/female	45/55
% out-of-state	10
% part-time	85
% minorities	1
% international	28
Average age at entry	34
Average years work experience at entry	7

ACADEMICS
Academic Experience Rating	**71**
Student/faculty ratio	28:1
Profs interesting rating	85
Profs accessible rating	84
% female faculty	29
% minority faculty	22

Academics

University of Wisconsin—Whitewater's "well-regarded" and "inexpensive" MBA program is a two-sided affair, but you won't find any students complaining. The first side is its traditional classroom-based MBA program. The other side is its online MBA degree option, which students praise for its "quality of education and flexibility of hours." Classes are also offered "at a few remote locations," which students laud for its "convenience." "I've taken classes online, at Whitewater, and at their Madison, Wisconsin location," one student says. Another agrees: "They're ahead of the curve for implementing technologies to support the educational system. The system is designed for great convenience....I really like the fact that I can take courses in person or, if I choose, online." The option of fulfilling the requirements of your MBA according to your schedule is a huge draw, so much so that "There are even soldiers in Iraq who are taking UW—Whitewater courses online."

While the school "isn't as famous as UW—Madison," most students insist that its "reputation" in the "business field" more than makes up for it. Many appreciate that the Economics program is part of the Business school, allowing "multifunctional disciplines." UW—Whitewater offers "strong" programs in finance and accounting in a "safe environment." Students are equally positive about their "excellent" professors, who they believe to be "some of the most highly sought after in the nation." The "bright" faculty "strives to help students learn" and "most are available for students 100 percent of the time." Students also appreciate that the "teaching methods are very effective," meaning "you learn a lot quickly without sacrificing all of your time."

For those attending class via the World Wide Web, there are a few more shades of grey. "Some of the professors have been great and very interactive," one student explains. "Others have been phantom professors. After taking four classes, I'd say it is about 50–50. There really is no middle ground though. The professors have either been really good or really absent." A fellow online student has a sunnier view: 'I have been exceptionally satisfied with the amount of time and effort that the administration, professors, and dean have given to me personally. They are quick to respond to emails and call back in a timely manner. Since my program is online, I don't have any face-to-face conversations. However, they treat me as though I were in their office."

While most agree that "everything runs like butter," there are a few complaints. "Brand presence is lacking," one student notes. Others would like to see the school hire faculty with "real world" experience. I'd prefer experienced adjunct professors who are at the top of their field who work in an office environment so that we can get the true insight into what we need to learn," a student explains. On the technological front, "hiring a larger IT service force" would be welcomed due to some "server outages." However, the MBA program will take further prominence within the UW system once its "new business school" is completed. "It will be an excellent monument and addition to the Whitewater campus," one student says.

Career and Placement

UW—Whitewater's Career Services office offers a number of services to current students and alumni, including career counseling, career groups, a resource center and classes, workshops and presentations, career fairs, employer presentations, online job postings, on-campus interviews, and resume, cover letter, and interviewing advice. Few students

ADMISSIONS CONTACT: DONALD K. ZAHN, ASSOCIATE DEAN
ADDRESS: 800 WEST MAIN STREET WHITEWATER, WI 53190
PHONE: 262-472-1945 • FAX: 262-472-4863
E-MAIL: ZAHND@UWW.EDU • WEBSITE: WWW.UWW.EDU

had much to say about this area, most likely because of the large number of students who participate in the online MBA program, meaning they aren't on campus to take advantage of the career office. However, some who attend the school in person would like to see some improvement.

Student Life and Environment

Though some students find that "Whitewater is definitely not a popular vacation spot," the "hardworking," "dependable," and "diverse" students that populate it provide "a wide variety of experiences" to their MBA program peers. The student body is comprised of "many minorities and older returning students," along with a "handful" of younger students that came "directly after their undergraduate programs." "I am probably the youngest student at 23 years old," one student explains. "I would say most students in this program have been working for five+ years after undergraduate." Many are "very active in sports, arts, and, most importantly, participating in their education with a positive attitude." Students also always seem ready to lend a hand. "I have not in two years met anyone who does not pull their share of the workload during group projects, nor anyone who does not offer to take on more," one student says.

But what of those attending online? Well, it's about the same, really. "Since this is an online program, people often have other work or social commitments they must meet," one student explains. "The other students have been great to work with and very understanding of others' situations." As an online student, the campus is what you make of it, however many note that even though they can't experience Whitewater firsthand, it's clear there's no lack of things to do. As one student explains, "My campus email account is always getting filled up with all kinds of junk mail from the different campus groups."

Admissions

According to UW—Whitewater, applicants to the MBA program must have one of the following: a minimum GPA of 2.75 for all undergraduate work; a minimum GPA of 2.9 for at least half of all undergraduate work; or a Master's degree or higher from a regionally accredited school. In addition, applicants must submit GMAT scores with a minimum composite score of 1000 based on the formula [(GPA x 200) + GMAT], or a minimum composite score of 1050 based on the formula [(GPA from last half of undergrad program x 200) + GMAT]. Student who do not speak English as their native language are required to submit TOEFL scores of at least 550. However, the school does state that exceptions to these requirements may be made on a "case-by-case basis," so if you feel you have a convincing argument but lack the grades and test scores to back it up, it's worth stating your case to the admissions committee.

FINANCIAL FACTS

Annual tuition (in-state/ out-of-state)	$7,456/$18,092
Cost of books	$2,800
Room & board (on-campus)	$3,700
Average grant	$500

ADMISSIONS

Admissions Selectivity Rating	68
# of applications received	173
% applicants accepted	81
% acceptees attending	86
Average GMAT	479
Range of GMAT	300–700
Average GPA	3.2
TOEFL required of international students	Yes
Minimum TOEFL (paper/computer)	550/213
Application fee	$56
Early decision program?	No
Deferment available	Yes
Maximum length of deferment	1 year
Transfer students accepted	Yes
Transfer application policy: They must meet the same requirements as a non-transfer student. Nine credits may be transferred into the program.	
Non-fall admissions	Yes
Need-blind admissions	Yes

EMPLOYMENT PROFILE	
Career Rating	82
Average base starting salary	$54,000

VALPARAISO UNIVERSITY
GRADUATE SCHOOL OF BUSINESS

GENERAL INFORMATION
Type of school	Private
Affiliation	Lutheran

SURVEY SAYS...
Solid preparation in:
General management
Communication/interpersonal skills
Presentation skills

STUDENTS
Enrollment of MBA Program	69
% male/female	60/40
% part-time	60
% minorities	15
% international	1
Average age at entry	29
Average years work experience at entry	5

ACADEMICS
Academic Experience Rating	**86**
Student/faculty ratio	2:1
Profs interesting rating	85
Profs accessible rating	81
% female faculty	33
% minority faculty	19

Joint Degrees
Juris Doctorate/Master of Business Administration, 4 years; MSN/MBA

Academics

Lutheran-run Valparaiso University offers "strong academic programs with an emphasis on values-based leadership and sustainability," thereby creating MBAs who are "well-equipped to be the leaders of the future green economy," students report. It's a big deal; Valpo's "commitment to moral and ethical standing" is frequently cited by students when asked to explain why they chose to attend this northwest Indiana university. Convenience, especially for the part-time students who make up about half the MBA student body, is another factor. Valpo offers evening classes and "the integration of online class options," through which live on-campus classes are broadcast over the Internet (allowing those participating remotely to participate in class). Valpo's online software also allows students to collaborate on group projects remotely.

Valpo's MBA program is small and relatively new. It is also innovative, particularly in its scheduling. Valpo's eight-week bloc system creates six different entry dates during the academic year and allows a pick-and-choose approach that accommodates both fast-trackers and those who need take a little more time to complete the degree. The Valpo MBA entails 14 core courses and six elective, or "enhancement" courses; the latter run the gamut from business reporting to brand management to e-commerce. Students who lack adequate undergraduate training in business are required to complete a series of foundation courses in addition to their core and enhancement work.

The small size of the MBA program and a "low student-to-professor ratio" mean plenty of "individual attention from professors," which students appreciate. "Access to mentors and extra projects is excellent" here, and students report that "it's easy to get into the classes you want" (although class selection, due to the size of the program, is limited). Professors bring "real-world experience" to the classroom to "provide real-world examples that we can immediately implement at work." Administrators are "constantly looking to improve the available programs. They seek student input [on] topics [ranging from]...new courses offered to the overall strategic plan of the university."

Career and Placement

Valpo's MBA program is only a decade old. Students admit that "the word has not spread about Valpo," and the business community is just beginning to catch on to this new source of talented recruits. However, with the power of the Valparaiso name behind it and the strength of the MBA curriculum, students know it's just a matter of time before their program begins to draw its rightful share of attention from recruiters.

Many Valpo students are already employed when they begin their MBA and plan to continue at their current companies after graduation. However, those who are looking for new positions have access to the Valparaiso University Career Center. The Career Center serves the school's graduate and undergraduate community and offers a variety of professional development workshops and career counseling, an annual campus career fair, and a job search database.

ADMISSIONS CONTACT: CINDY A. SCANLAN, ASSISTANT DIRECTOR MBA
ADDRESS: 104 URSCHEL HALL, 1909 CHAPEL DRIVE VALPARAISO, IN 46383
PHONE: 800-599-0840 • FAX: 219-464-5789
E-MAIL: MBA@VALPO.EDU • WEBSITE: WWW.VALPO.EDU/MBA

Student Life and Environment

Valpo MBAs are a near-even mix of part-time and full-time students. Part-timers range from 22 to 54 years old and have, on average, almost seven years of professional experience coming into the program. They typically "exhibit strong leadership skills with an emphasis on integrity, fairness, honesty and trust." Full-timers tend to be younger, less experienced, and less likely to be valued class partners. "Those students who have been in the workforce following undergrad are good learning partners. Those straight from undergrad tend to be detrimental to the learning experience," one MBA opines. International students make up 10 percent of the part-time student body and 16 percent of the full-time population.

There is "little to do" in the small town of Valparaiso, so most students who live on campus "stay in on the weekends either to study or talk with friends." On campus, there are athletic events and multicultural events weekly for our enjoyment," and the program "encourages interaction with fellow students outside the classroom throughout the week." For those seeking big city entertainment, Chicago is only 50 miles to the northwest—you can't get much more "big city" than that! On the other hand, part-timers are typically too busy for any of that.

Admissions

Admissions decisions are made on a rolling basis with six different entry dates offered during the year (thanks to the program's eight-week course schedule). Valparaiso makes admissions decisions holistically, assessing a combination of undergraduate and postgraduate academic performance, applicable professional experience, letters of recommendation, GMAT scores (working professionals can apply for a GMAT waiver), and a one-page personal statement describing the applicant's goals in order to determine the candidate's potential to benefit, and to benefit from, a Valpo MBA. In addition to the qualifications listed above, international students whose first language is not English must submit an official score report for the TOEFL or IELTS. All international students must submit an Affidavit of Financial Support.

FINANCIAL FACTS

Cost of books	$1,000
% of students receiving aid	69
% of first-year students receiving aid	33
% of students receiving grants	69
Average student loan debt	$11,887

ADMISSIONS

Admissions Selectivity Rating	91
# of applications received	187
% applicants accepted	28
% acceptees attending	63
Average GMAT	600
Average GPA	3.22
TOEFL required of international students	Yes
Minimum TOEFL (paper/computer)	575/36
Application fee	$30
International application fee	$50
Early decision program?	No
Deferment available	Yes
Maximum length of deferment	1 year
Transfer students accepted	Yes
Transfer application policy: Students must meet admissions requirements and be in good standing at their current institution. Up to 6 credit hours may be transferred from an AA CSB accredited MBA program.	
Non-fall admissions	Yes
Need-blind admissions	Yes

VANDERBILT UNIVERSITY
OWEN GRADUATE SCHOOL OF MANAGEMENT

GENERAL INFORMATION

Type of school	Private
Academic calendar 7-week modules	

SURVEY SAYS...

Good social scene
Good peer network
Helpful alumni
Happy students
Solid preparation in:
Communication/interpersonal skills

STUDENTS

Enrollment of parent	
institution	12,514
Enrollment of MBA Program	362
% male/female	74/26
% out-of-state	78
% part-time	0
% minorities	13
% international	22
Average age at entry	28
Average years work experience	
at entry	5

ACADEMICS

Academic Experience Rating	**96**
Student/faculty ratio	10:1
Profs interesting rating	92
Profs accessible rating	98
% female faculty	15
% minority faculty	4

Joint Degrees

MBA/JD, 4 years; MBA/MD, 5 years; MBA/MALAS, 3 years; MBA/MDIV, 4 years; MBA/PhD Medicine or MBA/PhD Engineering, 3 years after the start of core courses at Owen; MBA/BA or MBA/BS, 5 years.

Prominent Alumni

David Farr, CEO, Emerson Electric; David Ingram, Chairman & President, Ingram Entertainment; Adena Friedman, NASDAQ, Chief Financial Officer; Doug Parker, Chairman, President & CEO, U.S. Airlines; Josue Gomes de Silva, President, Coteminas (Brazil).

Academics

Students are drawn to Vanderbilt University's Owen Graduate School of Management for its "outstanding reputation, world-class professors, impressive network of alumni, prestigious program, [and] competitive employment rates upon graduation." However, above and beyond the prestige of attending a top university, students universally cite the "small school size" as the "number one" draw. The tight-knit community "gives Owen a big advantage when it comes to administration and classes." As one student attests, "There has never been a class that I was not able to take, with the professor I wanted to take it with. Furthermore, it is very easy to get access to the world-class faculty here. I have great experiences working for hours one-on-one with celebrity professors [that] it might be impossible to even get into class with at a different institution. I was particularly impressed by the school's ability to have classes taught by Senators, Congressmen, and *Fortune* 500 CEOs."

Owen has a great reputation for energizing "a sense of camaraderie between the students as well as between the students and faculty." Though course work is "a very challenging and demanding experience," "students are very driven to excel, but do so while supporting one another." The academic atmosphere is "competitive, while maintaining a sense of camaraderie." All students "have a strong sense of honor." In essence, Owen "gives back a multiple of your effort." Due to the small class sizes, students benefit from individual attention. "You really get to know everyone in your class which helps to develop a strong network for your professional career." This sense of camaraderie pays off down the line when it comes to seeking out a career; "Given the small size of the student body, alumni are very receptive when you reach out for networking and advice."

Owens's MBA program "is known for its strong performance in the finance sector," as well as "one of the best healthcare MBA programs in the country." The school "is efficiently run, and the professors are accessible, social, and are willing to help in any way they can." Overall, the academic experience here "is extremely pleasant." Garnering equal praise as that attributed to professors, the school administrators are "fantastic and accessible." "Both the Dean and other administrators are more than willing to meet with students to address concerns."

Career and Placement

From the top brass to those working in career management, "the school is extremely well-organized and unfailingly prepared." Owen's Career Management Center "has beefed up efforts significantly given the recession." That said, students are always hoping to "increase the volume of on-campus recruiting." Others add, it's "easy to navigate a wide range of social and cultural activities balanced by dozens of neighboring market leaders in diverse industries that allows insights into career tracks and opportunities. The alumni community, stretched all over the world, is very generous with [its] time and insight, too."

In 2009, 81 percent of full-time MBA graduates seeking employment had received a job offer within three months of graduation. For those who accepted positions, the mean base salary was $91,569. Pharmaceutical/Biotechnology/Healthcare, Financial Services, and consumer products are the industries attracting the majority of recent Owen graduates with Bank of America, Deloitte & Touche, Exxon Mobil, Humana, and Johnson and Johnson listed as the top five employers in 2009.

Student Life and Environment

By in large, students at Owen embrace the age-old, "work hard, play hard approach." Students "are competitive academically but not to the point [that] they are unwilling to help or that they don't have a social life." The Owen culture "embraces diversity but we are collaborative in our social, personal, and professional discourse. We work hard and intelligently and moreover, [we] take advantage of Nashville-based social outlets to reduce stress and activate an intense sense of camaraderie." A nostalgic second year adds, "I have developed friendships in business school at Owen that are just as strong as the friendships I had in college. It's important to have such a welcoming atmosphere like the one at Owen so that you can balance your life as well as possible while in business school."

Nashville "is a great city." As one resident confesses, "I'm from the north and was very reticent to move below the Mason Dixon line. I'm convinced Nashville is a diamond in the [rough]—a city that has yet to be discovered and appreciated for its great food, live music, and expanding economy." Every Thursday night, "students...and the faculty mingle at a social for several hours. The relationships we are building with each other and the teachers are a vital part of our education." In addition, "the city has plenty of options for outdoor activities, music, food, bars, and sports." However, students lament, "there is no on-campus housing for post-graduate students," and a "bigger library with more study rooms would be great!"

Admissions

With an incoming class size of approximately 200 students each year, the Vanderbilt MBA program is one of the world's most selective. Admission to the full-time MBA program is highly competitive. Admissions officers seek out an "exceptionally talented and diverse group of students who are willing and able to grow, prosper, and contribute in an environment that is academically rigorous, professionally rewarding, and personally enriching." In selecting candidates for admission, incoming students are evaluated for their academic aptitude and interest, experience and goals, and personal qualities and potential. The class which entered in fall of 2009 had an average GPA of 3.3 and an average GMAT of 653.

FINANCIAL FACTS

Annual tuition	$41,792
Fees	$925
Cost of books	$1,720
Room & board (off-campus)	$9,170
% of students receiving aid	76
% of first-year students receiving aid	79
% of students receiving loans	57
% of students receiving grants	52
Average award package	$45,235
Average grant	$18,826
Average student loan debt	$76,957

ADMISSIONS

Admissions Selectivity Rating	91
# of applications received	916
% applicants accepted	37
% acceptees attending	55
Average GMAT	653
Range of GMAT	590–720
Average GPA	3.3
TOEFL required of international students	Yes
Minimum TOEFL (paper/computer)	600/250
Application fee	$125
International application fee	$125
Regular application deadline	3/1
Regular notification	4/15
Application Deadline/Notification	
Round 1:	10/12 / 11/16
Round 2:	11/16 / 1/11
Round 3:	1/11 / 3/1
Round 4:	3/1 / 4/16
Early decision program?	Yes
ED Deadline/Notification	NR / 11/20
Deferment available	Yes
Maximum length of deferment	1 year
Transfer students accepted	No
Non-fall admissions	No
Need-blind admissions	Yes

EMPLOYMENT PROFILE

Career Rating	94	Grads Employed by Function	%	Avg. Salary
Percent employed at graduation	54	Marketing	23	$86,558
Percent employed 3 months after graduation	73	Operations	6	$96,200
		Consulting	17	$99,067
Average base starting salary	$91,569	Management	15	$96,550
Primary Source of Full-time Job Acceptances		Finance	35	$92,242
School-facilitated activities	90 (67%)	HR	2	$72,333
Graduate-facilitated activities	36 (28%)	**Top 5 Employers Hiring Grads**		
Unknown	3 (5%)	Bank of America, Deloitte, ExxonMobil, Humana, Accretive Health		

VILLANOVA UNIVERSITY
SCHOOL OF BUSINESS

GENERAL INFORMATION
Type of school   Private
Affiliation   Roman Catholic
Academic calendar   Semester

SURVEY SAYS...
Good peer network
Cutting-edge classes

STUDENTS
Enrollment of parent
  institution   10,172
Enrollment of MBA Program   427
% part-time   92
% minorities   12
Average age at entry   29
Average years work experience
  at entry   6

ACADEMICS
Academic Experience Rating   **87**
Student/faculty ratio   5:1
Profs interesting rating   83
Profs accessible rating   84
% female faculty   26
% minority faculty   11

Joint Degrees
Two programs are offered jointly by
the Villanova School of Business
and the Villanova School of Law: 1)
Master of Taxation: 12–60 months
2) JD/MBA: 36–60 months

Prominent Alumni
James V. O'Donnell, CEO, American
Eagle Outfitters, Inc.; Sheila F.
Klehm, Executive Director, U.S.
Private Wealth Management
Division, Morgan Stanley; Robert F.
Moran, President and COO,
PetSmart; Robert J. McCarthy,
President, North American Lodging
Operations, Marriott International;
Daniel J. Brestle, Chief Operating
Officer, The Estee Lauder
Companies.

Academics

With "the best reputation in Philly (except for Wharton)," Villanova's School of Business offers "overall brand recognition" from "a well-respected and well-known school" with a "superb network of alumni up and down the East Coast." That suits the predominantly part-time student body here, which pursues graduate degrees either at the school's main campus in Philly's northwestern suburbs or at the "convenient Center City location" the school recently opened. Students report that "the facilities are excellent" at the new site and that "being located in Center City has advantages, not only from a proximity point of view, but we are also surrounded by the business world. It is easy to draw examples from business[es] that you can view outside your classroom window."

Villanova recently revamped its curriculum, renaming its PMBA (the part-time program) and FTE (the full-time program) MBA programs "Flex Track" and "Fast Track," respectively. The program has "changed by integrating some of the old core classes together and creating some new core classes." Course content was "changed to reflect the current trends in business" and provide opportunities to "analyze the current financial crisis." In addition, "the Fast Track program now includes additional course work and provides students with the opportunity to select a concentration," all of which students appreciate. Some, however, feel the programs were rolled out too quickly "before classes were fully designed," and as a result the school seems "unorganized." Most believe "this should improve as the new courses become set."

Villanova offers a "Catholic education" with "a strong focus on ethics" and "business practices that affect the global community. Ethics "[are] part of every class. I think this is especially important because people often check their ethics at the door when they go into work and do questionable things. Villanova teaches you to choose your ethical outlook and stick to it. This is especially important [in light] of the financial meltdown, and more businesses could do well to not only be corporately responsible but to focus on individual employee ethics." Within that framework, Villanova takes a "pragmatic approach to the program" with a "good mix of faculty that reside in the purely academic world and faculty that still work in private enterprise. The research interests and outside work of the faculty is also very impressive. In general they have been very helpful to the students and willing to join the networks of the students."

Career and Placement

Villanova's MBA candidates say the Career Services Office "isn't really a known resource to graduate students. The MBA program seems more for those who want to stay in their job, and doesn't have too much for those who want to change careers altogether." Reinforcing that perception is the fact that the school's website lists placement data for undergraduates only. While many in our survey feel that the office "is virtually no help," one student praises it for "bringing in companies that are relevant to the MBA program. Events are on campus and accessible even to evening students. In this down economy where candidates are a dime a dozen, career services provided the connections I needed to get my resume seriously considered. In addition, they worked with my current employer to get a better sense of the skills they were looking for to help develop a complimentary relationship."

ADMISSIONS CONTACT: RACHEL GARONZIK, DIRECTOR OF GRAD. RECRUITMENT AND MARKETING
ADDRESS: OFFICE OF GRADUATE AND EXECUTIVE PROGRAMS, VILLANOVA SCHOOL OF BUSINESS,
1074 BARTLEY HALL VILLANOVA, PA 19085 • PHONE: 610-519-4336 • FAX: 610-519-6273
E-MAIL: GRADBUSINESS@VILLANOVA.EDU • WEBSITE: WWW.GRADBUSINESS.VILLANOVA.EDU

Student Life and Environment

Most MBAs at Villanova tell us that "it is generally hard to participate in a lot of the activities that the business school sponsors, but it isn't due to a lack of sponsored events." Rather, it's because "most people have a full schedule between work, school, and life. It is a shame that [many of us] won't be able to experience as much as we would like to due to the work/life/school balance." These on-the-go students appreciate that "dining facilities are open for those of us coming in at night before class, and the business building is accessible on weekends for group meetings." In addition, students like that "the HUB (the Center City facility) has plenty of free soda, chips, and snacks…. Parties are catered…so when there is food, it's awesome." Students do occasionally find time to get together. "Once a month, the school and a student organization host a happy hour after class one night that is open to all grad students. The attendance is usually very high and [provides] an opportunity for people to mingle and network."

Villanova attracts "young executives…who are mainly looking to improve their position in their current company." They are "hard-working, career-driven individuals" who tend to be "very conservative" and "not very diverse culturally or geographically." Most students hail "from Pennsylvania or New Jersey and work in the suburbs at big corporate [headquarters]."

Admissions

Applicants to Villanova's MBA programs must submit an online application, official transcripts for all post-secondary academic work, an official GMAT score report, two personal essays (at a maximum of 600 words each), two letters of recommendation, and a professional resume. International students who earned undergraduate degrees in a country where English is not the first language must also submit an official TOEFL score report and an evaluation of their transcripts provided by an approved translation service.

FINANCIAL FACTS
Annual tuition	$10,850
Fees	$60
Cost of books	$800

ADMISSIONS
Admissions Selectivity Rating	82
# of applications received	340
% applicants accepted	65
% acceptees attending	85
Average GMAT	610
Range of GMAT	560–690
Average GPA	3.3
TOEFL required of international students	Yes
Minimum TOEFL (paper/computer)	550/213
Application fee	$50
International application fee	$50
Regular application deadline	6/30
Early decision program?	No
Deferment available	Yes
Maximum length of deferment	Up to 1 year
Transfer students accepted	Yes
Transfer application policy: Up to nine credits from AACSB accredited MBA Programs.	
Non-fall admissions	Yes
Need-blind admissions	Yes

Applicants Also Look At
University of Pennsylvania, Drexel University, Temple University, New York University, Pennsylvania State University, Saint Joseph's University

VIRGINIA COMMONWEALTH UNIVERSITY
SCHOOL OF BUSINESS

GENERAL INFORMATION

Type of school	Public
Academic calendar	Semester

SURVEY SAYS...

Smart classrooms
Solid preparation in:
General management

STUDENTS

Enrollment of parent institution	32,470
Enrollment of MBA Program	251
% male/female	70/30
% part-time	74
% international	12
Average age at entry	26
Average years work experience at entry	4

ACADEMICS

Academic Experience Rating	78
Student/faculty ratio	20:1
Profs interesting rating	77
Profs accessible rating	76
% female faculty	15
% minority faculty	5

Joint Degrees

5 year BS/Master of Accountancy (for entering undergraduate students); BS Engineering/MBA; PharmD/MBA; MBA/MSIS.

Academics

With a "low tuition rate," "flexibility in class choice and time," and a reputation as "an up-and-coming school," the School of Business at Virginia Commonwealth University has numerous assets with which to lure potential MBAs. One VCU student tells us that he "explored other local options, such as the University of Richmond, and found that the quality of faculty, reputation for excellent, well-balanced instruction and the reasonable cost made VCU the more attractive option." Most who choose the VCU MBA feel the same way.

VCU's Richmond location is a major asset, students agree. Richmond is home to a number of major corporate headquarters, and MBAs report that this creates excellent networking opportunities. VCU's solid reputation with regional employers helps translate those opportunities into positive results. Many of these same employers feed the VCU MBA program with young managers looking for a leg up in their careers, many of who plan to stay with their companies post-graduation (in fact, quite a few attend on their employer's dime). Several students cite "support of the community businesses and government" as one of VCU's main selling points.

The VCU MBA program offers "a wide variety of MBA concentrations," including business analytics, global business, human capital, managing innovation, real estate, and supply chain management. "Excellent" professors seek "to teach the students how to think outside of the box" and often succeed, according to the MBAs we surveyed. Administrators are "flexible...they're pretty good about allowing substitute courses, etc." They also have a vision for the future. As one student puts it, "the school's momentum is its strength. A great effort has been undergoing since the new [business school facility] was built." "Programs have been redesigned to [meet] the needs in today's economy and business world. The courses are actually based on everyday life...which adds both to the attractiveness of the courses and their usefulness also."

Career and Placement

The Career Center at the VCU School of Business serves all undergraduate and graduate students in the School of Business. The office provides a wide range of counseling, skills development, and placement services. Area businesses also contact the School of Business directly to post internship and career opportunities available to MBA students. Students can stay up-to-date on such notifications by subscribing to the School of Business Listserv. About 75 percent of VCU's MBA students attend part-time; nearly all work part-time or full-time, many for companies with whom they intend to remain after graduation. One student who sought, and found, a post-MBA position through the Center tells us that the "Career Services Center is excellent. I was given the opportunity to go to two career fairs on campus in the fall of 2009. I also took advantage of the bus ride to the MBA Career Quest career fair at the University at Maryland, College Park. The Career Services Center also got me two interviews on campus with federal government agencies. I was offered both positions!"

ADMISSIONS CONTACT: JANA P. MCQUAID, DIRECTOR, GRADUATE STUDIES IN BUSINESS
ADDRESS: 301 WEST MAIN STREET, PO BOX 844000 RICHMOND, VA 23284-4000
PHONE: 804-828-4622 • FAX: 804-828-7174
E-MAIL: GSIB@VCU.EDU • WEBSITE: WWW.BUSINESS.VCU.EDU/GRADUATE

Student Life and Environment

The VCU School of Business recently moved into a "state-of-the-art...newly built" facility that "provides a comfortable, well-designed environment, including all of the technological amenities one would expect of a top-tier business school." While many crow about "all the high technology installed" here, some are just as impressed that "the parking deck is located right next to [the] business school building." Despite the convenience, many students here tell us that "parking is quite the issue unless you purchase a parking pass."

VCU's "convenient" campus location is "equidistant from downtown Richmond and the more college-town environment of 'the Fan' district." Life on campus "is very diverse, with an established art school and up-and-coming business and engineering schools. The student life reflects the characteristics one might find in each of these three schools." The MBA program hosts "many clubs and organized meetings" that help "academic and social communication and activities occur seamlessly." Not everyone is fully engaged; "there is a very small group of students who are full-time and involved," with many others attending part-time while working at part-time or full-time jobs. The latter group has little time to participate in extracurriculars.

The VCU MBA program "is geared to part-time students, full-time employees. Most [students] are reimbursed for classes by their employers." These "friendly" and "professional" students "from diverse backgrounds" "take their academic studies seriously, as they are quite competitive. They're sociable and are very professional in their manners and their interactions with each other."

Admissions

Applicants to all MBA programs at VCU must submit a completed application, two copies of official transcripts for all post-secondary academic work, an official GMAT score report, a resume, a personal statement, and three letters of recommendation. International applicants whose first language is not English must also provide proof of English proficiency (the school accepts both the TOEFL and the IELTS and evidence of sufficient financial support to cover the cost of attending and expenses while at VCU. VCU admits students for the fall, spring, and summer semesters.

FINANCIAL FACTS

Annual tuition (in-state/ out-of-state)	$8,116/$16,871
Fees	$2,289
Cost of books	$2,500
Room & board (on/off-campus)	$6,000/$9,000

ADMISSIONS

Admissions Selectivity Rating	78
# of applications received	151
% applicants accepted	75
% acceptees attending	49
Average GMAT	560
Range of GMAT	490–640
Average GPA	3.2
TOEFL required of international students	Yes
Minimum TOEFL (paper/computer)	600/250
Application fee	$50
International application fee	$50
Regular application deadline	7/1
Regular notification	7/15
Early decision program?	No
Deferment available	Yes
Maximum length of deferment	1 year
Transfer students accepted	Yes
Transfer application policy: Students who were admitted to and completed coursework at other AACSB accredited institutions may apply to VCU and seek transfer of up to six Semester hours of work toward the VCU graduate degree. Students must have earned no less than a B in each class to be transferred. The decision to transfer courses is left to the discretion of the Director of Graduate Studies in Business.	
Non-fall admissions	Yes
Need-blind admissions	Yes

VIRGINIA POLYTECHNIC INSTITUTE AND STATE UNIVERSITY
PAMPLIN COLLEGE OF BUSINESS

GENERAL INFORMATION
Type of school   Public

SURVEY SAYS...
Students love Blacksburg, VA
Friendly students
Good social scene
Solid preparation in:
Finance
Communication/interpersonal skills

STUDENTS
Enrollment of parent institution	28,432
Enrollment of MBA Program	360
% male/female	71/29
% out-of-state	40
% part-time	29
% minorities	7
% international	47
Average age at entry	26
Average years work experience at entry	3

ACADEMICS
Academic Experience Rating	**88**
Student/faculty ratio	14:1
Profs interesting rating	87
Profs accessible rating	86
% female faculty	34
% minority faculty	30

Joint Degrees
MBA/Master of International Management (33 Semester hours in the Pamplin MBA Program and 30 trimester hours at Thunderbird). l'Institute National des Telecommunications (INT) in France.

Academics

A small business program within a large university, the Pamplin College of Business offers an appealing blend of academic excellence, affordable tuition, and an intimate student atmosphere. Depending on your needs and career experience, the school offers a number of MBA options, including a full-time MBA, a part-time MBA, and an executive MBA, each offered in a different Virginia location. All programs provide an advanced education in marketing, management, finance, and leadership. The full-time and part-time MBA offer the option of pursuing an area of concentration in a particular business field. The school also operates a dual-degree program with an international focus, offered jointly with Thunderbird School of Global Management in Arizona or Telecom Management SudParis in France. In addition, a number of special programs help add depth and distinctiveness to a Pamplin MBA. For example, the SEED program (Student-managed Endowment for Educational Development) allows business students to manage about $4 million of Virginia Tech's endowment through stock investment.

Thanks to its low graduate enrollment, Pamplin offers uniformly small class sizes and plenty of personal attention. In both full-time and part-time programs, "professors are more than willing to meet with students outside of class" and "are very knowledgeable, easily accessible and always ready to help." Despite their uniform accessibility, some of the teaching staff may have passed their prime. A student explains, "I have had some really inspiring professors, but I have also had the opposite, ones who have taught for so long that they just go through the motions." In addition to academics, the "school has great support functions, be it administration, HR, IT or any other department.... Everyone is on their toes to help and guide the students in all administrative affairs." The downside to the smaller student body is that the school cannot offer as diverse a course selection as larger schools. However, students point out that "the program is also willing to help create a concentration tailored toward the students' wants and goals through work-studies and outside courses." On that note, "the program [is] also very helpful in providing fellowships and assistantships," which can be an excellent way to offset the costs of the education while also providing valuable professional experience.

Career and Placement

Pamplin takes the job search seriously, offering personalized career counseling and placement assistance for students at every professional level. Through the MBA Program Office, students can participate in career talks and workshops, company field visits, mentoring programs, and alumni symposia, among many other useful offerings. During the first semester of their second year, full-time students are also required to take a one-unit course called Job Search Strategy.

Future students should be aware that this small program does not attract as many recruiters as other large graduate programs might, and for "people doing MBA in Finance there are no companies that come to campus." Many international students also complain that the school does not offer enough assistance for those seeking positions that will sponsor them for professional work visas. On the flip side, Pamplin students benefit from the fact that "the size of the school attracts many recruiters, despite a relatively small MBA program." MBA students can also augment Pamplin's career services by using the extensive services offered through the university's Career Services center.

ADMISSIONS CONTACT: MELANIE JOHNSTON, ASSOCIATE DIRECTOR
ADDRESS: 1044 PAMPLIN HALL, VIRGINIA TECH BLACKSBURG, VA 24061
PHONE: 540-231-6152 • FAX: 540-231-4487
E-MAIL: MBA_INFO@VT.EDU • WEBSITE: WWW.MBA.VT.EDU

Student Life and Environment

Pamplin offers a number of MBA programs in various Virginia locations, with the main campus located in Blacksburg. To each of these campuses, the school draws students from "a wide variety of different ethnicities, backgrounds, ages, and genders, which makes class much more interesting." A current student elaborates, "We have a diverse cohort made up of about 50 percent international students, mostly from India, China, and France." Despite diversity, everyone works together with ease, and "fellow students are very friendly and helpful…. No one faces any issues being in groups with anyone for the class assignments, and everyone is extremely polite." In fact, friendships quickly extend beyond the classroom as "most students venture outside their nationality and peer groups without hesitancy. Many have active social lives and make an effort to get to know the other students."

On that note, many Pamplin students are able to find some downtime amidst their busy schedule, enjoying "very social lives while working extremely hard at our school work." When they aren't hitting the books or preparing a presentation, "students get together out of class to hike on the Appalachian trail, bike, play golf, or just socialize at a pub/cafe." In the immediate area, the "Blue Ridge Mountains offer excellent hiking, trail running, rock climbing, kayaking, and mountain biking within close proximity to Blacksburg." While Blacksburg is a smaller city, you'll nonetheless find "a lot of good places to hang out and spend your Saturday nights." What's more, commuters and campus residents will like the fact that "Blacksburg has an excellent public transportation system and is pedestrian- and bicycle-friendly."

Admissions

Admissions criteria at Pamplin vary by program. For the full-time MBA, last year's entering class had an average GMAT score of 626. For part-time and professional MBA students, the average GMAT score was 600. Students in all programs submitted an average GPA of 3.49. During the admissions process, applicants may be contacted for a personal interview.

FINANCIAL FACTS

Annual tuition (in-state/out-of-state)	$14,120/$21,828
Fees	$3,900
Cost of books	$7,560
Room & board (off-campus)	$6,024
% of students receiving aid	87
% of first-year students receiving aid	97
% of students receiving loans	17
% of students receiving grants	59
Average award package	$19,765
Average grant	$12,156
Average student loan debt	$25,380

ADMISSIONS

Admissions Selectivity Rating	90
# of applications received	288
% applicants accepted	37
% acceptees attending	48
Average GMAT	626
Range of GMAT	570–680
Average GPA	3.49
TOEFL required of international students	Yes
Minimum TOEFL (paper/computer)	550/213
Application fee	$45
International application fee	$45
Early decision program?	Yes
Deferment available	Yes
Maximum length of deferment	1 year
Transfer students accepted	No
Non-fall admissions	No
Need-blind admissions	Yes

EMPLOYMENT PROFILE

Career Rating	83	Grads Employed by Function	% Avg. Salary
Percent employed at graduation	56	Marketing	8 $42,000
Percent employed 3 months after graduation	67	Operations	8 $55,000
		Consulting	8 $78,000
Average base starting salary	$61,681	Finance	50 $64,195
Primary Source of Full-time Job Acceptances		MIS	25 $60,000
School-facilitated activities	9 (75%)	**Top 5 Employers Hiring Grads**	
Graduate-facilitated activities	2 (17%)	Altria Client Services (2), IBM (1), Deloitte (1),	
Unknown	1 (8%)	FBI (1), Hershey Company (1)	

WAKE FOREST UNIVERSITY
SCHOOLS OF BUSINESS

GENERAL INFORMATION

Type of school	Private
Academic calendar	Semester

SURVEY SAYS...
Friendly students
Smart classrooms
Solid preparation in:
Finance
Teamwork
Quantitative skills

STUDENTS

Enrollment of parent institution	7,099
Enrollment of MBA Program	445
% male/female	82/18
% out-of-state	71
% part-time	0
% minorities	15
% international	15
Average age at entry	28
Average years work experience at entry	4

ACADEMICS

Academic Experience Rating	**87**
Profs interesting rating	85
Profs accessible rating	90
% female faculty	28
% minority faculty	13

Joint Degrees
JD/MBA (Law/MBA), 4 years;
MD/MBA (Medicine/MBA), 5 years;
PhD/MBA (Graduate School of Arts
& Sciences/MBA), 5 years;
MSA/MBA (Accountancy/MBA), 6
years.

Prominent Alumni
Charles W. Ergen, Founder,
Chairman, CEO, EchoStar
Corporation; Donald E. Flow,
Chairman & CEO of Flow
Automotive Companies; Warren A.
Stephens, Chairman, President &
CEO, Stephens Inc.; Eric Wiseman,
President & CEO of VF Corporation;
David Dupree, Managing Director &
CEO, The Halifax Group.

Academics

The Wake Forest University Schools of Business offers "a first-rate education delivered in a small school atmosphere that is conducive to high levels of interaction between students and the faculty." Students universally laud the "personal touch" the graduate business program employs with its "commitment to academic excellence, strong faculty, [and] small class size that enables plenty of interaction among students and faculty."

Academics at Wake Forest follow a holistic approach. The integrated curriculum helps students learn to analyze and solve problems by understanding the many components of a solution. Course content follows suit and is organized around a strong first-year core which includes essentials such as international business management, financial management, macroeconomics, operations management, and quantitative methods. In their second year students choose a career concentration within the broader areas of consulting/general management, finance, entrepreneurship, marketing, operations management, health, information technology management, or an individually-designed concentration. As one student attests, "The workload...is generally much more intense than what most students expect coming into the school and in comparison to students at similar schools. However, this intense and well-rounded education has already proven beneficial in my summer internship and in job interviews."

The administration is "easily accessible and from faculty to staff, everyone is friendly. Student voices can be heard." When it comes to professors, at Wake Forest it's a first name, open-door policy; "All of my professors are engaged in my success. The level of dedication is a defining factor that sets Wake Forest apart," says one student. In addition, "the new Dean has fantastic visions for the school." Dean of Business Steve Reinemund, former chairman and CEO of PepsiCo, believes that by developing passionate business leaders who are ready to succeed in the marketplace the School's overall goal—to impact the marketplace in positive ways and to get results with integrity—will be achieved.

Career and Placement

Wake Forest alumni "are very open to mentoring and helping with [students] job search." However, some current MBA students feel "Career Development needs to better prepare students for the internship and job search...clubs could have more activities that connect students with potential employers." In addition, current students would like to see more "diversity of companies that come to campus." Right now, "the focus is primarily on the Southeast, but they are taking strides to move to a more national scope." However, others note that the Career Management Center has already been making strides to improve; "For example, a dedicated mentoring program and alumni outreach program has been developed and is being implemented."

In 2009, 84 percent of full-time MBA students seeking employment received a job offer within three months after graduation with those accepting jobs averaging a mean base salary of $88,230. Bank of America, Hanesbrands, Inc., Altria, Wachovia, and PepsiCo were the top five employers of 2009 grads with financial services and consumer products being industries with the biggest draw.

ADMISSIONS CONTACT: STACY POINDEXTER OWEN, DIRECTOR OF GRADUATE BUSINESS ADMISSIONS
ADDRESS: 1834 WAKE FOREST RD., WORRELL PROFESSIONAL CENTER, ROOM 2119 WINSTON-
SALEM, NC 27106 UNITED STATES • PHONE: 336-758-5422 • FAX: 336-758-5830
E-MAIL: ADMISSIONS@MBA.WFU.EDU • WEBSITE: WWW.BUSINESS.WFU.EDU

Student Life and Environment

Wake Forest MBAs are "outgoing, dedicated, hard workers who are easy to get along with and fun to be around." There are countless student activities and the academic work is rigorous, but students love the atmosphere and enjoy getting together to debate key topics of the day or cheer on the Demon Deacons at a basketball game. "We are a tight-knit group. Everyone knows everyone for the most part. The week can get pretty busy, but a lot of us play intramurals or pickup games during the week." Fridays are the time "when we all go out and blow off some steam. Students, even ones on different teams, will help each other out."

Life on campus "is fast-paced and exciting." The workload is pretty demanding, but there is time for fun." "The student government "puts on lots of social events that bring most people out to socialize." There are "tons of clubs, activities, both athletic, cultural, and community oriented," and "the town of Winston-Salem also has plenty of dining venues." The typical day at Wake "ranges from all-nighter's in the study room with your learning team to happy-hour events in the courtyard where students cut loose, to Alive at 5 concerts in downtown. It very much is a work hard play hard atmosphere," which "prepares you well for the future." "Quality of life is part of what makes Wake Forest such a great place to be." In essence, Wake Forest's Full-Time MBA Program is full of "brilliant, type-A achievers you can get along with." There is "a prevailing atmosphere of collaboration and support."

Admissions

The Wake Forest University Schools of Business "seeks individuals who have demonstrated achievement through academic course work, professional experience, and community involvement." Admissions Counselors "look for leadership ability, motivation, focus, enthusiasm, strong values, and teamwork skills in its prospective students." Post-graduate work is extremely important to the admissions process. All full-time MBA applicants must have at least 24 months of full-time, post-graduate work experience prior to the August of their application year. Through the Wachovia Scholars Program, the Wake Forest University Schools of Business offer scholarships to full-time students from underrepresented minority groups. These scholarships include a full-tuition waiver, stipend and an international summer study trip. The average GPA for the 2009 entering class was 3.1 with a mean GMAT score of 658.

FINANCIAL FACTS

Annual tuition	$36,750
Fees	$616
Cost of books	$2,000
Room & board (off-campus)	$8,500
% of students receiving aid	89
% of first-year students receiving aid	91
% of students receiving loans	58
% of students receiving grants	66
Average award package	$38,902
Average grant	$26,277
Average student loan debt	$65,600

ADMISSIONS

Admissions Selectivity Rating	89
Average GMAT	658
Range of GMAT	630–690
Average GPA	3.1
TOEFL required of international students	Yes
Minimum TOEFL (paper/computer)	600/250
Application fee	$75
International application fee	$75
Regular application deadline	6/1
Early decision program?	Yes
ED Deadline/Notification	11/1 / 12/1
Deferment available	No
Transfer students accepted	No
Non-fall admissions	No
Need-blind admissions	Yes

Applicants Also Look At
Duke University, Indiana University, University of Maryland, University of North Carolina at Chapel Hill, University of Notre Dame, University of Virginia, Vanderbilt University

---

EMPLOYMENT PROFILE

Career Rating	91	Grads Employed by Function	% Avg. Salary
Average base starting salary	$88,230	Marketing	22 $91,427
Primary Source of Full-time Job Acceptances		Operations	16 $87,800
School-facilitated activities	35 (62%)	Consulting	8 $84,000
Graduate-facilitated activities	21 (38%)	Management	3 NR
		Finance	41 $86,581

Top 5 Employers Hiring Grads
Bank of America (10), Hanesbrands, Inc. (3), Altria (2), Wachovia (2), PepsiCo (1)

WASHBURN UNIVERSITY
SCHOOL OF BUSINESS

GENERAL INFORMATION
Type of school   Public
Academic calendar   Semester: Fall;
    Spring; Summer

SURVEY SAYS...
Good peer network
Solid preparation in:
General management
Communication/interpersonal skills

STUDENTS
Enrollment of parent institution	6,500
Enrollment of MBA Program	78
% male/female	75/25
% out-of-state	4
% part-time	96
% international	4
Average age at entry	31
Average years work experience at entry	7

ACADEMICS
Academic Experience Rating	73
Student/faculty ratio	15:1
Profs interesting rating	84
Profs accessible rating	84
% female faculty	10
% minority faculty	10

Joint Degrees
JD/MBA, 108 credit hours, approximately 8 semesters.

Prominent Alumni
Greg Brenneman, Chairman of CCMP Capital; Mayo Schmidt, CEO/President of Viterra; Dale C. Pond, Retired Former VP of Marketing Lowe's.

Academics

The Washburn School of Business "is a lovely place" to attend business school with "nice professors, nice people, a beautiful environment," and perhaps most importantly, a "reputable" program that "accommodates a working schedule." These many assets make Washburn an excellent choice for busy professionals in the Topeka area.

The Washburn MBA begins with a core-level curriculum covering quantitative methods, accounting, and other foundational subjects. After completing the core, students begin the upper-level curriculum, comprised of 30 semester hours in more specialized business topics. While eight courses in the upper-level curriculum are required, students may also take two or more electives in an area of special interest. However, be forewarned that elective offerings comprise a very small portion of Washburn's MBA program. One student explains that "There is a list of about 10 to 15 electives in the brochure, but the school can't offer all of them due to lack of professors to teach the course and funds." The program concludes with a 'closure experience,' during which students compile a portfolio of their best work for review by a faculty panel.

"Small classes" and "outstanding," "very accessible professors" help ease the rigors of the Washburn MBA experience. "It's a small program and in a lot of ways we are like family," one student writes. "In class we see many of the same faces." Small class sizes mean that "students are able to get one-on-one attention from professors," who represent "a good mix of tenured academic professors and persons from industry." "This provides a very good real-world perspective in many classes on business issues," and "also helps to forge contacts with businesses in the community."

Career and Placement

Many MBA students at Washburn are currently employed and plan to stay with their current company after graduation from the program. However, those looking for a new position can receive assistance through the Washburn University Career Services Office, which serves the undergraduate and graduate community at the school, as well as alumni. Though Career Services, students have access to numerous career fairs and interview days, interview and resume preparation assistance, and job search information. A number of prominent companies have offices in Topeka, including Payless ShoeSource, Blue Cross and Blue Shield Association, Burlington Northern & Santa Fe Railway, Hills Pet Foods, Southwestern Bell, Western Resources, Frito-Lay, Goodyear, and as well as a variety of smaller companies and medical resources. One student who has worked with the office reports "I have not had much luck with Career Services. Most of the jobs posted are minimum wage jobs geared towards undergrads looking for extra cash. There are not many opportunities to interview for positions aimed at MBA graduates."

Student Life and Environment

The Washburn campus is home to "a good mix of traditional and non-traditional students," with the MBA program made up mostly of "students attending part time [while] only taking a couple of classes per semester." Nearly all work full time and many also deal with family obligations. Presumably they also sleep occasionally (although one wonders when, exactly, that would be possible). Those who find time to relax on campus assure us that the school has excellent facilities. "The student recreation center has good hours, the student union has good hours," one student writes. An art museum and an observatory are just two of the other on-campus amenities. The surrounding capital city of Topeka is a low-cost, medium-sized city of about 150,000 inhabitants, and an excellent place to balance the rigors of work and school.

ADMISSIONS CONTACT: DR. ROBERT J. BONCELLA, MBA DIRECTOR
ADDRESS: SCHOOL OF BUSINESS, WASHBURN UNIVERSITY TOPEKA, KS 66621
PHONE: 785-670-1308 • FAX: 785-670-1063
E-MAIL: MBA@WASHBURN.EDU • WEBSITE: WWW.WASHBURN.EDU/BUSINESS/MBA

Within the MBA program, "Classes are small and students are tightly connected. Classes are fun because of the people," one student reports. Another notes that "the class sizes enable in-depth lecture and discussion." Group work is an important part of the Washburn MBA, giving students ample opportunity to meet and work with their classmates throughout the course of the program. Fortunately, they find their classmates "helpful, friendly, and willing to share their experiences." The student body includes "only a few direct from an undergraduate program. Most have three or more years of work experience." The program includes "a wide range of age, careers, marital status, and ethnicity." Students point out that "the advent of the student-run Washburn MBA Association allows more networking and fellowship among Washburn MBA students" than students in previous years had enjoyed.

Admissions

To be considered for admission to Washburn University's School of Business, students must submit official undergraduate transcripts (minimum GPA 2.75), a completed application form, official GMAT scores (minimum score 475), and two letters of recommendation from academicians, employers, or other sources who can attest to your ability to succeed in graduate school. Students with outstanding promise but incomplete applications may be considered for provisional admission to the program. International students make up 15 percent of the student population and, in addition to the preceding materials, must submit the International Student Application and TOEFL scores or IELTS scores. Students from all major fields are welcome at Washburn. Applications are accepted for the fall, spring, and summer terms, and are processed on a rolling basis.

FINANCIAL FACTS

Room & board (on-campus)	$11,500

ADMISSIONS

Admissions Selectivity Rating	62
# of applications received	28
% applicants accepted	100
% acceptees attending	82
Average GMAT	512
Range of GMAT	450–580
Average GPA	3.25
TOEFL required of international students	Yes
Minimum TOEFL (paper/computer)	550/213
Application fee	$40
International application fee	$110
Early decision program?	No
Deferment available	Yes
Maximum length of deferment	1 semester
Transfer students accepted	Yes
Transfer application policy: Meet WU MBA Admission Requirements and we will accept up to nine hours from an AACSB Accredited Graduate Program.	
Non-fall admissions	Yes
Need-blind admissions	Yes

EMPLOYMENT PROFILE

Career Rating	71	**Top 3 Employers Hiring Grads**
		Consolidated Brands (15), Security Benefit Companies (10), Westar Energy (8)

WASHINGTON STATE UNIVERSITY
COLLEGE OF BUSINESS

GENERAL INFORMATION

Type of school	Public
Academic calendar	Semester

SURVEY SAYS...
Friendly students
Smart classrooms

STUDENTS

Enrollment of parent institution	18,000
Enrollment of MBA Program	54
% male/female	73/27
% minorities	10
% international	19
Average age at entry	26
Average years work experience at entry	4

ACADEMICS

Academic Experience Rating	70
Student/faculty ratio	40:1
Profs interesting rating	70
Profs accessible rating	74

Joint Degrees
JD/MBA program with University of Idaho, 4 years.

Academics

Washington State's College of Business has gained a strong national reputation for its "fantastic" study environment and "relatively low tuition," but its many attributes are no secret to WSU undergrads. Many students like the school so much that they decide to remain Cougars. "I completed my undergrad at WSU and enjoyed the experience so much that I wanted to complete my graduate degree here as well," one student says.

The school offers classes at WSU's main campus in Pullman, and at its satellite campuses in Spokane, Vancouver, Washington, and the Tri-Cities area in the southeastern part of the state. Course work is offered in accounting, finance; insurance and real estate; information systems; management and operations; marketing; and hospitality business management. Master of Accounting, Master of Business Administration (MBA), and Doctor of Philosophy (in business administration) degrees are available. In addition, WSU offers an online MBA.

The recently revamped MBA program is "directed toward non-business undergraduate majors" and "accepts students with less than one year [of work] experience." Opinions of the intro-level courses are mixed: One student said his first semester was "a bit weak." Though difficult, it was "really just busywork." By all accounts, things pick up from there, with course work "designed around the issues and direction of the changing business world." There's an "emphasis on teamwork," and assignments are connected to "real-life experience." Professors are "highly experienced." One student says, "The quality of [the] faculty is by far the biggest asset." Professors maintain close contact with students through a "cohort system that allows for smaller classes and greater [student] teacher interaction." This can be a mixed blessing, however. While the faculty includes "some of the best research minds" in the field, some professors "don't know the first thing about teaching," one student says. Fortunately, "The program coordinators listen to and respect student feedback." The school's administrative staff is "on a first-name basis with all the students." They "will go out of their way to help you solve/remedy a problem," though their "speed of handling affairs" could improve.

Career and Placement

The Washington State MBA program is more than 50 years old and well-respected. The Associate Director works personally with full-time students on professional development, career coaching, resume writing, interviewing and placement. The "proud alumni base" is particularly helpful; many here believe that WSU's greatest strength is the "dedication to each other" shown by fellow Cougars. Some students, however, would like to see more direct "interaction with outside companies." Another student says the program is "so new [that] they do not have the reputation with employers that some other MBA programs have."

ADMISSIONS CONTACT: CHERYL OLIVER, CHERYL OLIVER
ADDRESS: PO BOX 644744 PULLMAN, WA 99164-4744
PHONE: 509-335-7617 • FAX: 509-335-4735
E-MAIL: MBA@WSU.EDU • WEBSITE: WWW.MBA.WSU.EDU

Student Life and Environment

Students at WSU hail from "extremely diverse backgrounds." However, as most students "lack real working experience," this diversity is generally of the cultural variety: "About half" the students in some years are foreign-born, and "All of the students are friendly and intelligent." Students describe their classmates as "mature individuals"—the average age at entry into the program is 26—"who are attending business school to better themselves for their future careers." They're "open-minded," perhaps to a fault: "They do not have very strong opinions about much in the world," one student reports. Many have part-time jobs on campus, and almost all are "willing to help others" with course work. While a few students believe that "the course load is usually too heavy to take part in extracurricular activities," "Most manage their time very well." Students say that because of the smaller groups in the cohort system, peers in the program "turn into lifelong friends."

There are two camps here. The first could be described as the nothing-to-do camp, which claims that life here "is just going to school for classes and returning home [to] study—there's not much entertainment in this city." The other camp says Pullman is a "wonderful college town," and that the campus is "very lively." The campus reportedly has a "perfect gym" that houses "great sports programs." Some students are "involved in organized sports and activities with [the] professors and administration." One student writes, "I am involved in two organizations on campus (MBA Association and Delta Sigma Pi business fraternity). I currently hold two jobs totaling 25 hours a week. I live with other MBA students so that we can do much [of] our homework together."

Admissions

WSU's MBA program accepts applications from those with a bachelor's degree from a regionally accredited undergraduate institution. All undergraduate fields of study are considered. To be qualified for regular admission, an applicant must have a GPA of 3.0 on a 4.0 scale for the final 60 hours of undergraduate course work, or for 12 or more credits of recognized graduate-level course work. International applicants also must have a score of 580 or better on the TOEFL. GMAT scores and three letters of recommendation are required of all applicants. In addition to the above requirements, to be qualified for regular admission to the Master of Accounting program, an applicant must have a bachelor's degree in business administration with a concentration in accounting.

FINANCIAL FACTS

Annual tuition (in-state/ out-of-state)	$11,894/$23,656
Fees	$794
Cost of books	$1,104
Room & board	$9,200
Average grant	$4,000

ADMISSIONS

Admissions Selectivity Rating	86
# of applications received	144
% applicants accepted	39
% acceptees attending	46
Average GMAT	560
Range of GMAT	410–590
Average GPA	3.88
TOEFL required of international students	Yes
Minimum TOEFL (paper/computer)	580/237
Application fee	$50
Regular application deadline	1/10
Regular notification	1/10
Early decision program?	No
Deferment available	No
Transfer students accepted	Yes
Transfer application policy: Transfer students will only be able to apply 6 credits of elective coursework to the WSU MBA on a case-by-case basis.	
Non-fall admissions	Yes
Need-blind admissions	Yes

EMPLOYMENT PROFILE

Career Rating	78
Percent employed at graduation	41
Percent employed 3 months after graduation	32
Average base starting salary	$70,666
Primary Source of Full-time Job Acceptances	
School-facilitated activities	2 (7%)
Graduate-facilitated activities	1 (4%)
Unknown	25 (90%)

WASHINGTON UNIVERSITY IN ST. LOUIS
JOHN M. OLIN SCHOOL OF BUSINESS

GENERAL INFORMATION

Type of school	Private
Academic calendar	Semester

SURVEY SAYS...
Good peer network
Happy students
Solid preparation in:
Accounting
Teamwork

STUDENTS

Enrollment of parent institution	13,749
Enrollment of MBA Program	658
% male/female	71/29
% part-time	58
% minorities	15
% international	32
Average age at entry	27
Average years work experience at entry	4

ACADEMICS

Academic Experience Rating	**93**
Profs interesting rating	89
Profs accessible rating	90
% female faculty	19
% minority faculty	7

Joint Degrees
MBA/MS Architecture (3 years); MBA/MA East Asian Studies (3 years); MBA/MS Social Work (3 years); 3 years; MBA/JD (4 years); MBA/MS BioMedical Engineering (3 years).

Prominent Alumni
David Peacock, MBA 2000, President, Anheuser-Busch; Edward A. Mueller, MBA 1988, Chairman & CEO, Qwest Communications; Jim Weddle, MBA 1977, Managing Partner, Edward Jones; W. Patrick McGinnis MBA 1972, President & CEO, Nestle Purina Pet Care; William J. Shaw MBA 1972, President & COO, Marriott International.

Academics

Offering the unbeatable combination of a strong reputation, small class sizes, and a dedicated and talented teaching staff, students at Washington University's Olin School of Business say theirs is the "best and most recognized business school in St. Louis." Get ready to hit the ground running: "Since the MBA program is front loaded with many classes," the first semester can be "very challenging." In fact, during the first semester, students complete all but two required core courses, which comprise a third of the required units for the MBA. After that, students can take advantage of the flexible curriculum to tailor their studies through ample elective course work, including a "strong program in international business and brand management."

Despite the "grueling schedule which doesn't seem to let up," Olin's decidedly "collaborative atmosphere" and consistently small class sizes make the experience both manageable and intimate. At Olin, students have "the ability to truly learn and get involved in the learning process, both from fellow classmates and the professors." As one current student explains, "After completing each class I can truly say that I have learned something new and useful, which makes the grueling schedule bearable." A diverse and talented faculty, Olin professors "each bring a unique perspective and personality to the classroom," teaching material that is "contemporary and relevant to the business world."

Boasting a student body that is "hardworking, competitive, driven, and opinionated," fellow students play a very large role in the Washington University experience, especially in the beginning of the program. Employing a cohort study system, "The first semester is based largely on loads of group work with a pre-selected group of four to five students." These groups are selected by the administration to ensure a diversity of background and experience amongst team members, which most students find extremely edifying.

At this small, private school "The entire program is very student-centered," and the "administration is extremely open to student suggestions." Program administrators even handle all the red tape, "taking pressure off students for items like financial aid, course selection, or other issues that may take away from time that can be used for course work." Even in the classroom student concerns are taken seriously, and "Teachers issue evaluation forms every six weeks so that they can adapt teaching styles midway through their courses if students feel it is needed."

Career and Placement

At Olin, the focus on career planning and placement begins in the first semester, during which all first-year students must take a course entitled Olin's Professional Development Program, which helps refine their career goals through expert panels, self-assessments, and instruction in "soft skills" like emotional intelligence. Thereafter, the Weston Career Center offers a host of resources, including an alumni and corporate database, advising by professional career counselors, skill-building activities, and workshops on topics such as interviews, evaluating offers, and cover letter and resume editing. Some feel "The school could bring more recruiters to campus" but appreciate the fact that "alumni are always happy to help and the Career Center does an excellent job making sure that [students] are positioned to talk to recruiters even if [they] have to go to their city."

In 2009, graduates from Washington University received a mean base salary of $87,802. Over half of students (56 percent) took positions in the Midwest. Jobs in healthcare, consumer products, and financial services drew the most students, at 30 percent, 15 percent, and 14 percent respectively. Top employers included Monsanto, ExxonMobil, Sigma-Aldrich, Emerson, and Essilor International.

ADMISSIONS CONTACT: EVAN BOUFFIDES, DIRECTOR OF MBA ADMISSIONS AND FINANCIAL AID
ADDRESS: 1 BROOKINGS DR., CAMPUS BOX 1133 ST. LOUIS, MO 63130
PHONE: 314-935-7301 • FAX: 314-935-6309 • E-MAIL: MBA@WUSTL.EDU
WEBSITE: WWW.OLIN.WUSTL.EDU

FINANCIAL FACTS

Annual tuition	$42,525
Fees	$1,086
Cost of books	$2,434
Room & board	$16,800

ADMISSIONS

Admissions Selectivity Rating	93
# of applications received	1,215
% applicants accepted	36
% acceptees attending	35
Average GMAT	686
Range of GMAT	650–710
Average GPA	3.42
TOEFL required of international students	Yes
Application fee	$100
International application fee	$100
Application Deadline/Notification	
Round 1:	11/2 / 1/22
Round 2:	1/4 / 4/6
Round 3:	3/1 / 5/21
Round 4:	4/18 / 6/18
Early decision program?	No
Deferment available	Yes
Maximum length of deferment If approved—1 year	
Transfer students accepted	Yes
Transfer application policy: With approval, up to 9 credits from an AACSB-accredited graduate program.	
Non-fall admissions	No
Need-blind admissions	Yes

Student Life and Environment

With a student body that is "friendly, eager to learn and approachable," it's easy to fit in at the Olin School of Business. A current student raves: "They're a great bunch, whether in class, in our cohort groups, or relaxing at the bar!" Despite the challenging course material, the average Olin student "works hard but realizes that every sane and normal person should put the books aside for a while to have some fun." A first-year student explains, "You could study here 24/7 if you wanted to but most students are able to find a nice balance." On weekends, business students enjoy a weekly get-together with free food and a keg, thanks to the school-sponsored "Friday Afternoon Clubs."

On campus, the environment is both pleasant and stimulating, as "The facilities are top-notch, and the school is always buzzing with activity, from conferences to club meetings." As one current student explains, "Our day actually starts when we get out of class as we meet with our groups, go to speaker events, company info sessions, club events, work on practicum projects, and much more." Located next to Forest Park in the center of St. Louis, Missouri, "There are tons of restaurants and bars very close by, and housing is VERY affordable in the area."

Admissions

Olin looks for self-directed, disciplined professionals who will be highly involved in the MBA community as demonstrated by their academic proficiency, leadership potential, communication skills, and history of participation in extracurricular activities. To apply to Olin, students must submit a completed application form (which includes several essays and a resume), official transcripts from college, two letters of recommendation, GMAT scores, and, for international students, TOEFL scores. Though there are no official minimums for entry into the program, last year's incoming class had an average GMAT score of 686 and an average GPA of 3.42. There is also no minimum work requirement, though the average work experience for students in last year's entering class was 4 years.

EMPLOYMENT PROFILE

Career Rating	96	Grads Employed by Function	% Avg. Salary
Percent employed at graduation	74	Marketing	25 $90,067
Percent employed 3 months after graduation	91	Operations	6 $83,400
		Consulting	24 $88,912
Average base starting salary	$87,802	Management	10 $85,833
Primary Source of Full-time Job Acceptances		Finance	25 $85,133
School-facilitated activities	52 (66%)	HR	1 NR
Graduate-facilitated activities	20 (25%)	Other	8 $91.250
Unknown	7 (9%)	**Top 5 Employers Hiring Grads**	
		Monsanto (7), ExxonMobil (4), Sigma-Aldrich (4), Emerson (3), Essilor International (3)	

WAYNE STATE UNIVERSITY
SCHOOL OF BUSINESS ADMINISTRATION

GENERAL INFORMATION
Type of school	Public
Academic calendar	Semester

SURVEY SAYS...
Solid preparation in:
Marketing
General management

STUDENTS
Enrollment of parent institution	33,240
Enrollment of MBA Program	1,255
% male/female	60/40
% part-time	89
Average age at entry	28
Average years work experience at entry	5

ACADEMICS
Academic Experience Rating	72
Student/faculty ratio	38:1
Profs interesting rating	83
Profs accessible rating	80
% female faculty	21
% minority faculty	33

Joint Degrees
JD/MBA, approximately 3 years to complete.

Prominent Alumni
Paul Glantz, President & CEO, Proctor Financial, Corp.; Honorable Jack Martin, CFO, U.S. Dept. of Education; Sandra E. Pierce, President & CEO, Charter One Bank MI & IN; James H. Vandenberghe, Vice Chairman, Lear Corp.

Academics

Asked why they chose the School of Business Administration at Wayne State, most MBAs cite the affordability and convenience of the program. The school offers classes at its 203-acre main campus in downtown Detroit, the Oakland Center in Farmington Hills and online; students extol these "convenient campus locations to choose from" and appreciate that "every MBA course can be taken at your choice of the two campuses or online." "Weekend and evening classes" and "a very flexible online class schedule" further help to facilitate the busy schedules of WSU MBAs, the great majority of whom work full-time while pursuing their degrees.

A "good finance" program and a strong local alumni network are among the other assets cited by students here. MBAs also point out that "WSU is an urban research-centered school," so "if you were interested in being a researcher, there are some great opportunities here." The downtown campus is "set in an urban environment" that "helps students get an education above and beyond classroom lectures," and because some adjunct "professors who teach the MBA classes work for local companies," participation in the program "is great for networking," not only with instructors but also with working classmates. Professors, students tell us, "have a nice mix of textbook-to-real world experience and knowledge... many published works and a few were either a CEO or high-ranking executive at a successful company. They challenge us to become better students but make themselves available to assist us in accomplishing our goals."

On the downside, some instructors have not yet figured out how to maximize the online course format even as it grows more popular with students. "Though some professors structure their in-class and online courses very, very well, this is not the norm at this school," one student explains. In many cases, "all we get are three to four-hour lectures, a talking head, and PowerPoint. The professors generally record their in-class lectures so we can't hear the students' questions," which students describe as "very annoying. It makes it hard to stay interested and focused." Some here also feel that the curriculum could use some revamping to place "more emphasis on core subjects and less on electives. Currently there is a 50/50 split."

Career and Placement

Dedicated solely to students in the School of Business Administration, the Career Planning and Placement Office offers career counseling and professional development assistance to undergraduate and graduate students, as well as alumni of Wayne State. The center hosts a variety of on-campus interviews, career days, and meet-and-greet events. The center also offers career counseling services and comprehensive online resources. The school is well-integrated into the Detroit community; "In the Detroit area Wayne State business, medical, and law school alumni can be found in all industries and are happy to help fellow Wayne State alumni," one student reports.

A vast majority of Wayne State students are already working in a full-time, professional capacity when they begin their MBA. In fact, 70 percent of Wayne State graduate students are receiving tuition reimbursement from their current company. Therefore, many students are more focused on progressing in their current job, rather than making a career change or finding new positions. Whether seeking a new career or continuing in their current job, 90 percent of Wayne State graduates stay in Michigan, most in the Detroit area.

ADMISSIONS CONTACT: LINDA S. ZADDACH, ASSISTANT DEAN OF STUDENT SERVICES
ADDRESS: OFFICE OF STUDENT SERVICES, 5201 CASS, ROOM 200 DETROIT, MI 48202
PHONE: 313-577-4505 • FAX: 313-577-5299
E-MAIL: L.S.ZADDACH@WAYNE.EDU • WEBSITE: WWW.BUSINESS.WAYNE.EDU

Student Life and Environment

WSU has an "urban Detroit campus" and so must live with "the city's poor reputation" for poverty-related crime. Public safety "is better on campus than the surrounding areas, but many people need to park or walk to surrounding areas and have issues." While "the school is not responsible" for the city's crime rate, some here feel that "perhaps it could take measures to make the campus area very safe. This could include more police, security, and surveillance cameras." However, the school does have its own police department. Others are philosophical on the matter. "Until the auto industry rebounds, this urban Detroit campus will always have problems with the occasional stranger on campus. They don't pose any immediate threat, however it can be an unnerving experience for some people," one student observes. Students also note that "there are not a lot of healthy eating options around campus, and the rest of the restaurants are hit or miss."

"There aren't a lot of graduate-targeted activities or clubs" at either of the two WSU MBA locations, but most students are much too busy for such endeavors anyway. The student body, which "has got to be one of the most diverse student populations in the country," is a "mixed group of working adults and international students, mostly aged 25 to 35." Students have "varying levels of work experience, although there are few who have management experience."

Admissions

Wayne State has one of the largest part-time MBA programs in the world, with over 1,250 students enrolled. Minimum qualifications for admission include a score of at least 450 on the GMAT and an undergraduate GPA of at least 2.5. The average entering student performs somewhat better: the median GMAT score among entering students is 510, while the median GPA is 3.15. The admissions committee also evaluates a student's leadership potential and professional experience when making an admissions decision. Students may apply for admission in the fall, spring, or summer semesters. International applicants must present an excellent academic record, demonstrate proficiency in English, and show sufficient means to cover tuition, supplies, and living expenses while enrolled in the program.

FINANCIAL FACTS

Annual tuition (in-state/ out-of-state)	$9,538/$19,538
Fees	$973
Cost of books	$1,500
Average grant	$5,500

ADMISSIONS

Admissions Selectivity Rating	71
# of applications received	351
% applicants accepted	72
% acceptees attending	69
Average GMAT	510
Average GPA	3.15
TOEFL required of international students	Yes
Minimum TOEFL (paper/computer)	550/213
Application fee	$50
International application fee	$50
Regular application deadline	8/1
Early decision program?	No
Deferment available	Yes
Maximum length of deferment	1 semester
Transfer students accepted	Yes
Transfer application policy: Meet admission standards.	
Non-fall admissions	Yes
Need-blind admissions	No

EMPLOYMENT PROFILE

Career Rating	83	Grads Employed by Function	%	Avg. Salary
Percent employed 3 months after graduation	98	Marketing	3	$53,500
		Operations	3	NR
Average base starting salary	$70,000	Management	7	$58,600
Primary Source of Full-time Job Acceptances		Finance	25	$75,900
School-facilitated activities	NR (75%)	HR	2	NR
		MIS	3	NR

WEBER STATE UNIVERSITY
JOHN B. GODDARD SCHOOL OF BUSINESS AND ECONOMICS

GENERAL INFORMATION
Type of school   Public

SURVEY SAYS...
Students love Ogden, UT
Happy students
Smart classrooms
Solid preparation in:
General management

STUDENTS
Enrollment of parent
  institution   23,003
Enrollment of MBA Program   205
% part-time   100
Average age at entry   30
Average years work experience
  at entry   4

ACADEMICS
Academic Experience Rating   **81**
Student/faculty ratio   27:1
Profs interesting rating   83
Profs accessible rating   80
% female faculty   14

Joint Degrees
MBA/Master of Health
Administration combined degree
program, length varies from 60–72
credit hours dependent upon undergraduate degree (business or non-
business).

Academics

Offering a "program [that] is geared toward the working professional," the Goddard School at Weber State University serves the needs of area professionals looking for an academically-sanctioned leg up. With "classes offered at night" on a "flexible schedule"—here you have "the freedom to take classes as your schedule permits rather than entering a program and being required to take courses in lock-step with the rest of the students who started at the same time"—Goddard facilitates "the ability to attend without leaving the workforce." "Affordability" and a "convenient location" further sweeten the deal, ensuring "great bang for your buck."

Goddard knows its customers and plans its curriculum "for working adults. It is designed to have input from many industries and companies, which is a great opportunity" to learn from potential (or present) employers. The scheduling also suits professionals; "classes are at night and are in an eight-week format, so you can finish two classes per semester even though you only take one class at a time. One class at a time only requires one night a week in class, which helps [to] not disrupt family life very much." As an added bonus, the nighttime-only scheduling means students "don't have to compete for attention with daytime students." An "online learning portion that is integrated perfectly with classroom time" (abetted by a "top-tier technology infrastructure") means students don't always have to be on campus to continue their academic work.

In a program like this, quality service is paramount. Goddard MBAs are happy to report that things run very smoothly here; administrators "are very easy to work with," with "very prompt" email responses, "good academic advising," and administrative staff who do "a good job helping students navigate the system, especially where there are differences in services at the university between undergrads and MBA students." The "very qualified and helpful" faculty earns even higher marks. Professors are typically "working professionals in their field and have given valuable advise using real world experiences." "Small class sizes" ensure that classes "are never too big so you just feel like a number."

Career and Placement

Within the Wattis Business Building, Goddard operates a Career Center exclusively for business students. Staff at the Career Center work with Human Resources Directors to place graduates in new positions, coordinate on-campus recruiting events and interviews, and host seminars, workshops, and provide personal counseling services to business students. Their annual career fair is the largest in the region. Though most students enroll at Weber State University while continuing to work in a professional capacity, those looking for a new position in 2009 reported an average starting salary of over $66,000 following graduation.

ADMISSIONS CONTACT: DR. MARK A. STEVENSON, MBA ENROLLMENT DIRECTOR
ADDRESS: 2750 N. UNIVERSITY PARK BLVD. MC102 LAYTON, UT 84041-9099
PHONE: 801-395-3519 • FAX: 801-395-3525
E-MAIL: MBA@WEBER.EDU • WEBSITE: WEBER.EDU/MBA

Student Life and Environment

The Goddard MBA is designed for working professionals who want to minimize their visits to campus and maximize their time while there. Most attend class only once a week. Under the circumstances one might assume that class cohesion is pretty much nonexistent. However, even though "we don't have a formal cohort," students are "strongly encouraged to work in teams and get to know the other students in the program. The secondary campus that houses the MBA program is very accessible and has lots of restaurants nearby, which is very convenient for study groups." That "secondary campus," by the way, is "a satellite facility for the university, which is about 15 miles away from the main Weber State campus." The facility includes a graduate-only computer lab, which students tell us is a nice convenience.

Those who go looking for a little something extra from the program report that "there are a lot of clubs and activities. Each week we get e-mails with a lot of activities for families and children." The school offers "a number of activities that are good for students with children. I've taken my five-year-old to see Santa, make Christmas ornaments, hunt for Easter eggs, watch movies, carve pumpkins and many others. It's nice to feel that they understand students tend not to have a lot of money so they have free activities to foster a sense of community."

The "career- and family-oriented" MBAs at Goddard are "working professionals with busy professional lives who are sacrificing a lot to go to school." Most "have families, work full time, and have a full class load." They also have "work experience that is easily applied in class." Most "are in their late twenties to early thirties and just starting to hit their stride in their careers."

Admissions

To apply to the John B. Goddard MBA Program, students must possess a bachelor's degree from an accredited university. The primary criteria for selection are the student's undergraduate record and GMAT performance. Current students have a median GMAT score of 570 and an average GPA of 3.45 on a 4.0 scale. Other factors, such as work experience and professional progression, are also considered by the admissions committee. Each application is evaluated individually for the applicant's ability to succeed, potential for success, and possible strengths to contribute to the program. International applicants whose first language is not English must demonstrate English proficiency through testing; they must also have their undergraduate transcripts translated by a recognized service. Applications should be submitted online.

FINANCIAL FACTS
Annual tuition (in-state/ out-of-state)	$8,202/$17,894
Fees	$458
Cost of books	$2,000
Room & board (on/off-campus)	$3,000/$4,000
% of students receiving grants	9
Average grant	$3,900

ADMISSIONS
Admissions Selectivity Rating	78
# of applications received	83
% applicants accepted	66
% acceptees attending	90
Average GMAT	569
Range of GMAT	500–710
Average GPA	3.3
TOEFL required of international students	Yes
Minimum TOEFL (paper/computer)	550/213
Application fee	$60
International application fee	$60
Regular application deadline	5/1
Regular notification	5/10
Early decision program?	No
Deferment available	Yes
Maximum length of deferment	1 year
Transfer students accepted	Yes
Transfer application policy: Transfer credits from AACSB-accredited programs accepted; from non-AACSB-accredited programs on a case-by-case basis.	
Non-fall admissions	Yes
Need-blind admissions	Yes

WEST VIRGINIA UNIVERSITY
COLLEGE OF BUSINESS AND ECONOMICS

GENERAL INFORMATION
Type of school   Public
Academic calendar   Semester

SURVEY SAYS...
Cutting-edge classes
Smart classrooms

STUDENTS
Enrollment of parent institution	28,113
Enrollment of MBA Program	53
% male/female	65/35
% out-of-state	11
% part-time	0
% minorities	33
% international	29
Average age at entry	25
Average years work experience at entry	5

ACADEMICS
Academic Experience Rating	**89**
Student/faculty ratio	17:1
Profs interesting rating	93
Profs accessible rating	87
% female faculty	18
% minority faculty	2

Joint Degrees
MBA/JD, 3 years.

Prominent Alumni
John Chambers, CEO, Cisco Systems; Glen Hiner, CEO, Owens Corning; Homer Hickam, Author; Ray Lane, Frm. Pres & COO, Oracle; Jerry West, GM, LA Lakers.

Academics

The College of Business and Economics at West Virginia University "has a well-known business program with top professors," and this earns it "prestige within the state," students in this growing MBA program tell us. Full-time students love the one-year accelerated program that gets them in and out quickly, while those in the Executive MBA program love the convenience of being able to attend in one of nine satellite sites scattered about the Mountain State.

Students in both programs praise "the curriculum design," noting that "the sequence of courses is good, giving a good foundation in business: economics, accounting, marketing, finance, and operations." They appreciate that the WVU MBA program "teaches skills instead of memorization" and that administrators are always looking for ways to improve the curriculum. "There have been some significant improvements to make the program have a more global focus on business education," one impressed student reports.

WVU's full-time MBA is a 48 credit-hour program presented over a 14-month period. All domestic students are required to participate in an international trip to China, Poland, Italy, German, or the Czech Republic. The curriculum interweaves business themes and skills, building toward culminating coursework in planning and strategy. Students in the full-time program do not specialize in an area of concentration; however, WVU also offers an MBA in Finance, which can be completed in 12 months by students with substantial academic or professional experience in the field and in two years by students lacking such experience. Students in the EMBA program tell us that the program "provides students with one of the most diverse faculty groups in the country" and that "The diverse background of each faculty member provides students with a unique view of real life business experiences." (Students in the full-time program share this assessment of the faculty.)

All students here point out that "Students not only focus on textbook examples, they get to participate in business experiences such as the Washington Campus and study-abroad programs to Italy, Czech Republic, Mexico, Germany, and China." These elements, they say, make for an "exceptional academic experience" and elevate the WVU MBA "a notch above the rest."

At the end of the day, the class sessions are very unique and productive based on multiple views from professionals working in various industries.

Career and Placement

The College of Business and Economics at WVU has its own dedicated Center for Career Development to serve business undergraduates and graduate students. The office provides counseling services, workshops, seminars, and on-campus recruiting events. Students tell us that the office seems geared mostly toward the needs of undergraduates. One writes that the office "is not geared well for MBA students. It is good for MSIR and MPA students. Even if they are for MBA students, the positions are only for entry level such as internships, leadership programs, etc." While students feel that "the career development center tries to give us information," they also feel that "it looks like they are working without any direction."

ADMISSIONS CONTACT: GERALD BLAKELY, DIRECTOR OF GRADUATE PROGRAMS
ADDRESS: P.O. BOX 6027 MORGANTOWN, WV 26506-6027
PHONE: 304-293-7932 • FAX: 304-293-8905
E-MAIL: MBA@WVU.EDU • WEBSITE: WWW.BE.WVU.EDU

Student Life and Environment

WVU's full-time MBA program is attended by "a mix of professionals going back for MBAs and current college students." The program calls for a lot of group work; students tell us that "Groups are very diverse, hardworking professionals that can appreciate the opinion of others…. The people in each group end up being the people you call for advice or to go out to dinner after class or on the weekend!" Some here, however, complain that the quality of students admitted to the full-time program needs to improve. One writes: "The class atmosphere is not that intellectually-motivating. Out of an entering class of 65 students, ten are very good and others are below average."

EMBA students may attend classes at the main campus in Morgantown or at any of nine satellite sites in Beckley, Charleston, Elkins, Keyser, Lewisburg, Martinsburg, Moorefield, Parkersburg, or Wheeling. One student calls these options "a blessing. The rural location where I live would not permit an economical pursuit of such a degree by traveling to the main campus for each class. The fact that classes are streamed to the distant location and the technology provides two-way communication and interaction is terrific!"

Admissions

Applicants to the MBA program must submit a completed application (paper or online), official transcripts for all postsecondary academic work, an official GMAT score report, and a resume. Letters of recommendation and a statement of purpose are optional. In addition, international students must submit an official TOEFL or IELTS score report (minimum score: 580, paper-and-pencil test; 237, computer-based test; 92, Internet-based test; or 6.5 IELTS). All students must have full use of a laptop PC that meets prescribed minimum software, memory, and processor-speed requirements; contact the school or visit the website for details. Applicants to the EMBA program must have at least two years of "significant work experience." For applicants with less than five years experience, GPA and GMAT figure most heavily in the admissions decision. Professional experience, especially managerial experience, is the greater factor for applicants with at least five years of experience.

FINANCIAL FACTS

Annual tuition (in-state/ out-of-state)	$11,776/$32,080
Cost of books	$1,800
Room & board	$9,080

ADMISSIONS

Admissions Selectivity Rating	85
# of applications received	171
% applicants accepted	31
% acceptees attending	100
Average GMAT	488
Range of GMAT	240–680
Average GPA	3.37
TOEFL required of international students	Yes
Minimum TOEFL (paper/computer)	580/237
Application fee	$50
International application fee	$50
Regular application deadline	3/1
Regular notification	3/15
Early decision program?	Yes
ED Deadline/ Notification	10/15 / 10/30
Deferment available	Yes
Maximum length of deferment	1 year
Transfer students accepted	Yes
Transfer application policy: Applicants request transfer credits, and the admission committee reviews the request.	
Non-fall admissions	Yes
Need-blind admissions	Yes

WESTERN CAROLINA UNIVERSITY
COLLEGE OF BUSINESS

GENERAL INFORMATION
Type of school	Public
Academic calendar	Semester

SURVEY SAYS...
Solid preparation in:
Finance
General management

STUDENTS
Enrollment of parent institution	9,050
Enrollment of MBA Program	107
% male/female	54/46
% out-of-state	4
% part-time	76
% minorities	8
% international	4
Average age at entry	29
Average years work experience at entry	4

ACADEMICS
Academic Experience Rating	76
Student/faculty ratio	12:1
Profs interesting rating	88
Profs accessible rating	77
% female faculty	29
% minority faculty	12

Prominent Alumni
Dr. David Ellis, Pardee Hospital; Carolyne Pelton, BB&T Corporate Banking, Senior Vice President; Wendy Cagle, Small Business Technology and Development Center; David Kemper, President, Kemper Strategies; Matthew Hutcherson, Regional Director for Mountain Bizworks.

Academics

Cullowhee, North Carolina isn't exactly a major business hub; the College of Business at Western Carolina University apparently recognizes this, offering a full slate of MBA classes in the nearby city of Asheville as well as on its main, rurally located campus. Area students appreciate the gesture; location and convenience are among their top reasons for choosing the WCU MBA.

Not that they have much choice, since the College of Business' MBA program is the only AACSB-accredited graduate business program in the area. Still, students don't seem to feel the lack of competition has hurt the program. On the contrary, they report positively that the program is "locally respected" and benefits from "excellent professors" as well as a "bucolic environment" that "provides relief from academic pressures." In 42 semester hours, students learn to manage and lead organizations. The program begins with management fundamentals, then progresses through the C-Suite: marketing, research and development, Information technology, operations, legal affairs, finance, and the Chief Executive Office. The program is a hands-on, integrative, interdisciplinary degree designed to create independent, lifelong learners who are Business-Ready to assume leadership positions. Students may also develop a specialization by completing concentrations in one of the following areas: entrepreneurship, health care administration, human resources, sales and marketing, or a certificate in project management.

MBAs here benefit from small classes; "I love the class sizes and the relationship created between student and teachers," one tells us, adding, "I speak with several of my professors even after I'm done with their classes on a weekly to monthly basis." Professors are "genuinely interested in each student's success both in class and in business," although some MBAs note a "huge degree of difference between the best and worst professors. The best have been really gifted teachers, even if they aren't luminaries in their field. The worst should be banned from teaching, tenure or not. Very few have current or continuing professional experience." Students also warn that the program's Internet-based programs need an upgrade; "Google groups offers better services for free than the university is paying for!" one student tells us. Reflecting Asheville's left-leaning, eco-friendly reputation, students here also wish the program placed a greater focus on green business issues.

Career and Placement

The Office of Career Services and Cooperative Education handles counseling and placement services for all undergraduate and graduate students at WCU. Services include a career library, co-op placement, one-on-one counseling, interviewing workshops, resume critiquing, online job listings, career-related personality assessment, career days, and on-campus recruitment events. Among the companies recruiting on campus in 2009: Kearfott Corporation, Nan Ya Plastics, Northwestern Mutual, Sherwin Williams, State Employees' Credit Union, and the U.S. Public Health Service. Students report that many here already have jobs and that their primary objective in pursuing the MBA is to advance their standing with their current employers.

ADMISSIONS CONTACT: DR. STEVE HENSON, DIRECTOR OF MBA PROGRAM
ADDRESS: 104D FORSYTH CULLOWHEE, NC 28723
PHONE: (828) 227-3227 • FAX: (828) 227-7414
E-MAIL: SHENSON@EMAIL.WCU.EDU • WEBSITE: WWW.WCU.EDU

Student Life and Environment

WCU's Cullowhee campus "isn't located within a city limit. It is a couple of miles from the small town of Sylva, NC." The campus provides easy access to "thousands and thousands of acres of public land (The Pisgah and Nantahala National Forests) where one can fish, hunt, hike, rock climb, mountain bike, take advantage of all-terrain vehicle trails, horseback ride, camp, etc." As one student puts it, "If someone prefers the hustle and bustle and traffic nightmares of a large city—which I don't—WCU might not be the place for them."

WCU also offers MBA classes in Asheville, a city with a population of more than 400,000. Asheville is well known throughout the region for its active arts community, its resorts, and a lively restaurant scene. Tourism, manufacturing, health care, and professional and business services drive the local economy. Top employers in the city include healthcare providers, the resort and tourism industries, and Eaton Corporation, a power management company.

WCU MBAs "come from different backgrounds. Some have just finished their undergraduate degree, some worked for a few years between undergraduate and graduate, and some have been out of school for a while." One student estimates the mix at "80 percent traditional students, 20 percent nontraditional." They tend to be "intelligent, friendly, and supportive." "We constantly are helping each other after classes to make sure everyone understands the material," one student reports. With only 110 students spread out over two campuses, this is a very small program in which students who attend classes together get to know each other quite well over the course of the program.

Admissions

Applicants to the MBA program at Western Carolina University must submit official copies of transcripts for all post-secondary academic work, an official score report for the GMAT, and two letters of recommendation. A minimum GMAT score of 450 and minimum undergraduate GPA of 3.0 are required. Graduates of institutions in which the language of instruction is not English must also submit official score reports for the TOEFL and achieve a minimum score of 79–80 on the Internet-based test, 550 on the paper test, or 213 on the computer test. International applications are due by April 1 for the fall semester and by September 1 for the spring semester.

FINANCIAL FACTS

Annual tuition (in-state/ out-of-state)	$2,372/$11,899
Fees	$2,118
Cost of books	$965
Room & board (on/off-campus)	$5,626/$7,468
% of students receiving aid	77
% of first-year students receiving aid	73
% of students receiving loans	58
% of students receiving grants	50
Average award package	$10,273
Average grant	$2,575
Average student loan debt	$6,853

ADMISSIONS

Admissions Selectivity Rating	**71**
# of applications received	50
% applicants accepted	80
% acceptees attending	93
Average GMAT	490
Range of GMAT	440–540
Average GPA	3.21
TOEFL required of international students	Yes
Minimum TOEFL (paper/computer)	550/213
Application fee	$40
International application fee	$40
Early decision program?	No
Deferment available	Yes
Maximum length of deferment	1 year
Transfer students accepted	Yes
Transfer application policy: Up to 6 hours of graduate credit may be transferred from an AACSB institution	
Non-fall admissions	Yes
Need-blind admissions	Yes

WICHITA STATE UNIVERSITY
BARTON SCHOOL OF BUSINESS

GENERAL INFORMATION
Type of school   Public
Academic calendar   Semester

SURVEY SAYS...
Friendly students
Happy students
Smart classrooms

STUDENTS
Enrollment of parent institution	15,000
Enrollment of MBA Program	220
% male/female	60/40
% part-time	91
% minorities	30
Average age at entry	27
Average years work experience at entry	3

ACADEMICS
Academic Experience Rating	80
Student/faculty ratio	4:1
Profs interesting rating	68
Profs accessible rating	68
% female faculty	3
% minority faculty	21

Joint Degrees
MBA/MS in Nursing: MBA, 30 hours: Nursing, 36 hours.

Academics

At the W. Frank Barton School of Business at Wichita State University, students benefit from a traditional, management-based MBA program that offers a broad range of course work in accounting, economics, finance, management, and marketing. Depending on a student's academic background (those who studied business as an undergraduate may be able to waive some requirements), the MBA is comprised of 36 to 48 credit hours, beginning with a core curriculum that covers business fundamentals. Throughout the core curriculum, particular attention is given to understanding the organization as an integrated system. Later, students may choose an area of concentration, taking up to 9 credit hours of electives in finance, marketing, entrepreneurship, technology and operations management, or health care administration.

The school offers a fast-paced executive MBA program for high-level professionals, as well as a traditional MBA program. Whether enrolled in the accelerated or traditional program, a majority of students work full-time while attending school in the evenings. In fact, "Most of them are professionals with aircraft industries in the Wichita area," which means a double dose of work and responsibility. However, the school is aware of its students' special needs and "is very adept at offering programs that fit the schedules of its students." On top of that, students reassure us that the workload is manageable—"substantial at times, but for the most part, the average workload is within the expected output of a graduate program."

Reporting on the great classroom experience, WSU students generally describe their professors as "candid, well-spoken, knowledgeable, prepared, and fun." Unfortunately, students admit that a few staff members don't deserve such rave reviews. "There are some professors' classes I wish I could get a refund on, simply because the professors seem to be there only to earn a paycheck or a boosted ego," grumbles one student. In addition to their professors, classmates form an essential part of the learning experience at WSU. Drawing "a mix of mid-career business people and young business students," Wichita State students enjoy the fact that "everyone is very opinionated, which makes for great class discussions."

The "only AACSB-accredited school in the Wichita area," WSU is an excellent match for those who work or wish to start a career in the region, and WSU promotes a great deal of "community involvement with local businesses and entrepreneurs." Students appreciate the fact that "the school brings in wonderful special speakers and has a good reputation in the community." For example, "Recently, the CEOs of Wal-Mart and PepsiCo visited the business school." Beyond Kansas, the school also runs an "international project with Berlin School of Economics, where students taking the advanced strategic management course go to Berlin, Germany for one week and do the project there in conjunction with Berlin students."

Career and Placement

The Career Services office at Wichita State University serves the school's undergraduate and graduate community, including the business school. Through Career Services, students have access to career counseling, an online job database, and an alumni database. The office also hosts several campus career fairs and on-campus interviews.

ADMISSIONS CONTACT: ANGELA R. JONES, DIRECTOR OF MBA PROGRAM
ADDRESS: 1845 FAIRMOUNT WICHITA, KS 67260-0048
PHONE: 316-978-3230 • FAX: 316-978-3767
E-MAIL: MBA@WICHITA.EDU • WEBSITE: WICHITA.EDU/MBA

At Wichita State, "Many students seem to be earning their MBAs in order to receive a raise or progress upward with their current employers," with a number of them also receiving tuition assistance. For those looking for a position with a new company after graduation, major employers in Wichita include Bank of America, Boeing, Bombardier Aerospace Learjet, Cargill Meat Solutions, Cessna Aircraft Company, The Coleman Company, Hawker Beechcraft, INTRUST Bank, Koch Industries, Spirit AeroSystems, Via Christi Health Systems, and York International.

Student Life and Environment

Those looking for a close-knit and community-oriented business school may be disappointed by "commuter-school" Wichita State. While they get a great business education, students admit that "the opportunities for networking are not particularly strong, as most students are too busy with work and families to attend mixers or be involved on campus." On the other hand, the atmosphere is pleasantly casual and friendly, and the community is "very diverse with local, national, and international students." A current student shares: "Even though we come from very different backgrounds and experiences, everyone seems to be incredibly open-minded and accepting to all students in the program."

The university provides plenty of extracurricular and recreational opportunities. In fact, students assure us that "if you want to do an activity and you look for one, you can find one." A case in point: One student who went from part-time to full-time status in his second year tells us, "I was surprised when I concentrated life to studies...I learned a lot that I missed when I was working in my first year." Off campus, Wichita is a pleasant, low-cost, medium-sized city with plenty of cultural, financial, shopping, performing arts, festivals, and entertainment options for graduate students.

Admissions

To be considered for admissions at Wichita State University, students must possess a four-year degree from an accredited college or university and be proficient in word processing, spreadsheet, and presentation software. Admissions decisions are made by evaluating the following: official GMAT scores, undergraduate transcript, an applicant's personal goals statement, two letters of recommendation, and a current resume. For the traditional MBA, career experience is a plus in an application package but is not required. Applicants to the executive MBA must have at least five years of relevant work experience. Students may apply for entry in the spring and fall semesters.

FINANCIAL FACTS
Cost of books	$1,200

ADMISSIONS
Admissions Selectivity Rating	83
# of applications received	92
% applicants accepted	64
% acceptees attending	97
Average GMAT	543
Average GPA	3.36
TOEFL required of international students	Yes
Minimum TOEFL (paper/computer)	570/230
Application fee	$50
International application fee	$65
Regular application deadline	7/1
Early decision program?	No
Deferment available	Yes
Maximum length of deferment	1 year
Transfer students accepted	Yes
Transfer application policy: Only AACSB accredited classes may be transferred in.	
Non-fall admissions	Yes
Need-blind admissions	Yes

WILFRID LAURIER UNIVERSITY
SCHOOL OF BUSINESS AND ECONOMICS

GENERAL INFORMATION
Type of school   Public

SURVEY SAYS...
Good peer network

STUDENTS
Enrollment of
business school   488
% male/female   70/30
% part-time   84
% international   5
Average age at entry   30
Average years work
experience at entry   7

ACADEMICS
Academic Experience Rating   61
Profs interesting rating   70
Profs accessible rating   70

Joint Degrees
MBA/CMA (Certified Management Accountant), MBA/CFA (Certified Financial Analyst), MBA/FCIP (Fellow Chartered Insurance Professional), 3.3 years part-time study.

Academics

As Canada's largest full classroom-contact MBA program, there is something for everyone at the School of Business and Economics at Wilfrid Laurier University. Whether you want to take courses during the week, during the weekend, during the day, at night, on a part-time basis, on a full-time basis, at the Waterloo campus, or at the satellite campus in Toronto, chances are there is going to be an MBA format option at Laurier that suits your needs. In addition, the school's many MBA options cater to students from all professional and academic backgrounds. At Laurier, business executives have the opportunity to get a high-speed degree though the school's accelerated MBA program, while students with no previous work experience may apply to the "co-op" program, designed to help business newcomers develop their managerial and organizational skills. In addition, many students come to Laurier because it offers "the ability to get a professional designation (i.e., CMA, CFA) along with the MBA" through several joint-degree programs.

No matter how, when, or where they pursue an MBA, Laurier students appreciate the school's commitment to the case-based learning method, which "requires that you understand both the theory and then apply them in real-world situations." Emphasizing practical competence over strict academic theory, "The Laurier experience builds your thinking skills and allows you to attack complex problems from many angles." Discussion and debate are fundamental to the program, and "Almost all courses include a group work component which promotes the teamwork abilities within each student." This interaction is an undeniable asset to the MBA education, since many "Students are already at the manager/director level in their careers." A current student praises the professors, saying, "Not only do they contribute to the learning experience due to their vast work experiences, but they are very willing to help out both within the classroom and outside of it (networking)."

The core curriculum takes an "integrated" approach to business topics, which "allows you to cement concepts since you are dealing with them in multiple courses at the same time." After completing the core, students can tailor their education through a concentration in a number of fields (such as finance, accounting, brand communication management, supply chain management, or international business to name a few) by completing at least four courses in that subject area. They may also add breadth to their education through one of the school's international programs in Europe and Asia, or through the school's ample list of special seminars.

At the top of their field, Laurier professors are an excellent "mix of tenured professors and recognized, practicing professionals." Most "are PhDs and have recent/relevant consulting or real business experience." Friendly, down to earth, and well run, administrators at Laurier "communicate frequently with students and have always responded to questions very quickly."

Career and Placement

Career Services for the School of Business and Economics Graduate Programs provides assistance to MBA and MABE students and alumni. Their services include one-on-one career counseling and specialized workshops on topics such as resume writing, networking, interviewing, and cocktail and dining etiquette. Career Services also hosts special events, such as executive recruiter panels.

MAUREEN FERRARO OR SUSAN MANNING-FABER, MBA MARKETING COORDINATOR'S
ADDRESS: 75 UNIVERSITY AVENUE WEST, WATERLOO, ON N2L3C5 CANADA
PHONE: 519-884-0710 • FAX: 519-886-6978
E-MAIL: MBAWLU@WLU.CA • WEBSITE: WWW.WLU.CA/MBA

Students agree that their school enjoys a great reputation in Canada, telling us that "employers love Laurier MBA students because they are much better educated and friendlier to work with." The following companies are among the extensive list of organizations recently recruiting Laurier MBAs: Accenture, American Express Canada, Bank of Canada, Canada Revenue Agency, CIBC World Markets, CPP Investment Board, Dell Canada, Deloitte Touche Tohmatsu, FedEx Canada, GE Canada, General Mills Canada, General Motors Canada, IBM Canada, The Loyalty Group, Managerial Design, Manulife Financial, National Bank Financial, Proctor & Gamble, Raytheon Canada, RLG International, Scotiabank Group, and TD Securities.

Student Life and Environment

With such a large and diverse student population, it's hard to summarize life at Laurier. Not surprisingly, there is something of a split between students who attend the program part-time and those who chose to pursue their studies full-time. There are two campuses in the Wilfrid Laurier University MBA program. One is on the Waterloo-based university campus and the other is a satellite campus right in downtown Toronto. Part-timers attending school at the Toronto MBA campus sometimes feel a little cut off from the main campus. However, Toronto students are required to participate in MBA events and competitions at the Waterloo campus.

In both locations, the majority of students are "mature with an established career and family life." For most, "Life happens off campus," and students admit that there isn't much enthusiasm for campus activities or after-hours socializing. "Social activities with the satellite or main campus are limited due to work/family commitments in addition to academic demands," explains a current MBA candidate.

With many personal and professional commitments, most students at Laurier are talented multitaskers, who "are very good at balancing personal, work, and school life." However, they warn that the many group assignments, homework, and classes can make it difficult to juggle your educational, professional, and personal life. A student laments, "You have to be tough skinned to do an MBA on a part-time basis at WLU."

Admissions

To be considered for admission to Wilfrid Laurier University's MBA program, students must possess a 4-year, undergraduate degree (in any field of study) with at least a B average in the last 10 half-credit courses taken. Except for the MBA with co-op option (for which no work experience is required), applicants must have at least 2 years of full-time work experience to apply for an MBA at Laurier. Students must also submit a GMAT score of at least 550. In addition to test scores and transcripts, students must send three letters of recommendation from professional and academic references.

FINANCIAL FACTS
Annual tuition (in-state/ out-of-state)	$17,100/$20,470
Cost of books	$5,120

ADMISSIONS
Admissions Selectivity Rating	60*
# of applications received	474
% applicants accepted	69
% acceptees attending	65
Average GMAT	600
Range of GMAT	550–710
Average GPA	3.3
TOEFL required of international students	Yes
Minimum TOEFL (paper/computer)	573/230
Application fee	$100
International application fee	$100
Regular application deadline	5/1
Regular notification	rolling
Deferment available	Yes
Maximum length of deferment	1 year, case-by-case
Non-fall admissions	Yes
Need-blind admissions	Yes

Applicants Also Look At
Brock University, McMaster University, Queen's University, University of Toronto, York University

WILLAMETTE UNIVERSITY
ATKINSON GRADUATE SCHOOL OF MANAGEMENT

GENERAL INFORMATION
Type of school   Private
Affiliation   Methodist
Academic calendar   Semester

SURVEY SAYS...
Cutting-edge classes
Solid preparation in:
Marketing
Teamwork
Presentation skills

STUDENTS
Enrollment of parent institution	2,663
Enrollment of MBA Program	291
% male/female	62/38
% out-of-state	67
% part-time	36
% minorities	8
% international	38
Average age at entry	24
Average years work experience at entry	1

ACADEMICS
Academic Experience Rating	**82**
Student/faculty ratio	8:1
Profs interesting rating	87
Profs accessible rating	87
% female faculty	29
% minority faculty	3

Joint Degrees
MBA/JD, Joint Degree in Management and Law, 4 years.

Prominent Alumni
Grace Crunican, Director, Seattle Dept. of Transportation; David Liu, Chairman & CEO, Longwell Technology International; Punit Renjen, CEO, Deloitte Consulting; Sandy Baruah, Senior Fellow, Council on Competitiveness; Marcus Robins, Owner, The Robins Group.

Academics

With a unique focus on young professionals, Willamette's friendly but rigorous MBA is a great way to get your feet wet in the business world. While most MBA programs require work experience before matriculation, this program is "specifically geared toward the early career or career change MBA." In fact, many Willamette students have never held a professional position. The focus on early career students does not mean that the curriculum is a cake walk. On the contrary, this "very fast-paced, intense program" is more like a crash course for future business leaders. "Active participation and discussion is strongly emphasized in most classes," and the "very well-thought out curriculum for first-year students," is augmented by excellent elective courses in the second year. Attracting a surprisingly "idealistic" business school crowd, many students also choose Willamette because of its unusual areas of concentration, especially it's "reputation for non-profit, government, and social entrepreneurship excellence." On the flip side, many note that, as the school does not offer a focus in information technology, "This school's weakest academic discipline is in fields of information technology and the use of computers to make business decisions." However, Willamette has hired new faculty in the area of 'operations, analysis and systems' and are building curriculum in that area.

While Willamette students may begin the program with very little career experience, they won't leave that way. Experiential learning is key to the curriculum, helping "students with all levels of experience gain that edge usually gained through lots of years in corporate jobs." For example, through Willamette's required Practical Application for Careers and Enterprises (PACE) program, students are "placed in a ten-person team for the year to do consulting work for an area non-profit organization." Practical applications take center stage in the classroom, as well. "Accomplished professionals" in their fields, professors "definitely bring expertise and know-how with a clear distinction between theory and real world practices." In addition to attending lectures, students "work on a lot of case studies," which prepare them "with the skills to analyze a situation from many different points of view." In addition, "There is also a lot of stress placed on teamwork and presentation skills," staples of a successful business career.

Bringing both warmth and enthusiasm to the classroom, "Most professors really make you love their courses, even if you're not an innate financier or marketer." With a clear focus on the student, "They are approachable and flexible if you require out of class time for assistance." A student agrees, "The learning environment at Willamette is incredibly unique in that it is more intimate than most business schools. Professors are very accessible and truly invested in helping students understand course material." Adds another, "Rarely do I write an e-mail to any of my professors without receiving a reply (and usually a solution to my problem) by the next day."

Career and Placement

In addition to the ample experiential education included in the Willamette curriculum, the Career Management Office offers recruiting programs, resume revisions and interview preparation services, company site visits, peer advisors, networking events, and career counseling. On the Willamette campus, "There are many activities and events that provide students with the opportunity to network with alumni and other professionals," though some would like to see those efforts expanded, especially when it comes to the alumni network. When it comes to career placement, one of the biggest obstacles is that "WU is still relatively unknown beyond the Northwest region"—though, fortunately, the school does enjoy an "incredible reputation in the Northwest" and strong ties in Portland and Salem.

In recent years, 70 to 80 percent of Willamette graduates had a job offer within three months of graduation, and 90 to 100 percent had received an offer within six months, with salaries ranging from about $36,000 to $100,000 annually. A third of graduates chose to pursue careers in non-profit or government organizations. Willamette graduates were hired by companies including Hewlett Packard Company, Americorps, U.S. Fish and Wildlife, SENTECH Inc, and LinkedIn.

Student Life and Environment

The life of a frazzled Willamette business student is comprised of "lots of classes, preparations, [and] project meetings, blended with a coffee mug at Bistro's (the university's student-managed coffee shop.)" With so much on their plates, "Free time can sometimes be scarce." Fortunately, "Social activities like Thursday Night Out, the small size of the class, along with the design of the class schedule, allow us not only to get to know all of our classmates but also to maintain the family atmosphere that characterizes Atkinson." Drawing a large international population, the MBA program is "extremely ethnically diverse and that brings a high level of intercultural experience to the students." For over-achievers (of which you'll meet a few), "There are many ways to be involved in more than just class: associations, peer advisor positions, TA positions, etc."

Set in Oregon, "The campus is gorgeous," with "a river crossing the university and many green areas." "Being in Oregon you always have things to do outside of the town like the beach, mountains, forests, trails, and hikes" and there are "lots of bars nearby" in downtown Salem. Savvy business students also point out that despite the private school tuition, "the low cost of living made Willamette University cheaper by thousands per year."

Admissions

While the GMAT is the typical exam required for business school entry, Willamette also accepts the General GRE. In recent years, the mean GMAT score and GPA for incoming Willamette students was 583 and 3.3, respectively. For the MBA for Career Change program, students must have at least two years of work experience, whereas there are no minimum work requirements for the Early Career MBA. All students must have a personal interview with the admissions staff.

FINANCIAL FACTS

Annual tuition	$28,500
Fees	$80
Cost of books	$1,200
Room & board (on/off-campus)	$12,000/$11,000
% of students receiving aid	89
% of first-year students receiving aid	89
% of students receiving loans	55
% of students receiving grants	75
Average award package	$29,652
Average grant	$11,000
Average student loan debt	$42,931

ADMISSIONS

Admissions Selectivity Rating	77
# of applications received	272
% applicants accepted	69
% acceptees attending	53
Average GMAT	583
Range of GMAT	540–620
Average GPA	3.3
TOEFL required of international students	Yes
Minimum TOEFL (paper/computer)	570/230
Application fee	$50
International application fee	$50
Regular application deadline	5/1
Application Deadline/Notification	
Round 1:	1/12 / NR
Round 2:	3/1 / NR
Round 3:	5/1 / NR
Early decision program?	No
Deferment available	Yes
Maximum length of deferment	1 year
Transfer students accepted	Yes
Transfer application policy: may transfer up to six semester credits of MBA course work from an AACSB accredited MBA program to the Willamette Early Career MBA or MBA for Career Change programs with the approval of the Dean.	
Non-fall admissions	No
Need-blind admissions	Yes

EMPLOYMENT PROFILE

Career Rating	83	Grads Employed by Function	% Avg. Salary
Percent employed at graduation	28	Marketing	42 $63,400
Percent employed 3 months after graduation	64	Operations	17 NR
		Finance	25 $48,233
Average base starting salary	$59,803	HR	8 NR
Primary Source of Full-time Job Acceptances		Nonprofit	8 NR
School-facilitated activities	25 (59%)	**Top 5 Employers Hiring Grads**	
Graduate-facilitated activities	16 (41%)	Oregon Department of Transportation (8), Hewlett Packard Company (1), Vestas (1), Johnson and Johnson (1)	

WILLIAM PATERSON UNIVERSITY
CHRISTOS M. COTSAKOS COLLEGE OF BUSINESS

GENERAL INFORMATION
Type of school   Public
Academic calendar   Semester

SURVEY SAYS...
Solid preparation in:
General management
Operations

ACADEMICS
Academic Experience Rating	**61**
Student/faculty ratio	4:1
Profs interesting rating	82
Profs accessible rating	79
% female faculty	20
% minority faculty	30

Academics

Located in Wayne, New Jersey, the Christos M. Cotsakos College of Business augments the traditional MBA curriculum with a number of experiential learning programs, which add depth and relevance to the academic experience. The MBA core curriculum is divided into two sections: lower core and upper core—though the former may be waived for those who majored in business as undergraduates. In addition to the core, students must take 15 credits of electives, including an international component, and may choose to pursue a concentration in accounting, finance, marketing or music management. Future record company executives take note: "William Paterson has one of the best reputations for music," and the school's "proximity to NY" makes it a particularly attractive choice for those interested in the music business. Other unique features of the business school are the mentoring program, the sales center facility, and the ETRADE Financial Learning Center, which hosts one of the few active trading rooms found in an academic institution.

In the classroom, the William Paterson experience is rewarding, spearheaded by "excellent professors who truly care about your success." Faculty is "accessible, helpful, challenging, and enlightening, and they all seem devoted to and knowledgeable in their subject area." In particular, practical instruction is incorporated into classroom lessons with ease because the "faculty has a lot of on-the-job experience and are able to incorporate case work very smoothly." A student enthuses, "I love the new challenges I must face with each class because what I am learning in the classroom, I use everyday in my profession." Like the teaching staff, the administration is "wonderful" and very responsive to student needs. In particular, "the MBA director is great to work with—he will solve any problem very quickly." If you have a question or concern, "it rarely takes more than a day to get a reply on an email, and most of the time it is within an hour of sending."

Most students at William Paterson graduated from college somewhat recently; however, you'll find a nice "mix of recent undergrads, 30-somethings who are professionally successful, and 40-plus-year-olds who want to improve their skill-sets." For full-time students who would like some professional experience while offsetting tuition costs, WPU offers "financial assistance in a form of Graduate Assistantship." However, even without financial assistance, this public school has an attractive price tag, which ensures a high "educational quality at a reasonable price."

Career and Placement

Located less than 20 miles from Manhattan, William Paterson's Wayne campus places students within striking distance of New York City jobs and internship opportunities. To help with the process, the Career Development and Gloria S. Williams Advisement Center serves undergraduate and graduate students, providing career decision-making and job-search assistance. The center also coordinates on-campus recruiting events. In addition, the MBA program maintains an online job resources center, which lists current vacancies and internship opportunities in some of the region's top business employers. Students can post their resume on the site, browse jobs, or search the large alumni database. This service is also open to William Paterson alumni and faculty.

ADMISSIONS CONTACT: TINU ADENIRAN, ASSISTANT DIRECTOR
ADDRESS: 300 POMPTON RD. WAYNE, NJ 07470 UNITED STATES
PHONE: 973-720-2237 • FAX: • E-MAIL: GRADUATE@WPUNJ.EDU • WEBSITE: WWW.WPUNJ.EDU/COB

Student Life and Environment

Christos M. Cotsakos College of Business is located on its own modern and "beautiful campus," separate from the school's main undergraduate school in Wayne. The Cotsakos building includes a "great library" and fabulous computer facilities as well as classrooms that incorporate the "latest technologies." In addition, William Paterson gets a thousand gold stars for this unusual advantage: "The parking there is exceptional; we do not have to deal with construction, traffic, or no parking. There is always a spot for you, due to the fact that we are located on our own campus."

"A warm, friendly environment for learning," WPU attracts students who are "very diverse from different age groups, but always willing to help." "The majority of B-school students commute" at WPU, so campus life is largely limited to classes. Most students are comfortable with this arrangement. However, some students would like the school to "offer more activities for graduate students to participate in…. Perhaps they could offer some classes during the day for individuals who may be able to attend class during the day and not just during evening hours."

Admissions

To be admitted to William Paterson University, students must submit a GMAT score of at least 500, or meet an admissions index criteria in which a lower GMAT score is balanced by a higher GPA. In some cases, students with a high undergraduate grade point average in a business field may be eligible to waive the GMAT requirement. All applicants must also submit two letters of recommendation and some applicants are also asked to interview. Fortunately, the school's administration is committed to making the application process straightforward and user-friendly. A new student explains, "The administration has worked with me from the time I applied, to before and after the GMAT, to the present day hiccups I may occasionally run into."

FINANCIAL FACTS

Cost of books	$600

ADMISSIONS

Admissions Selectivity Rating	60*
Average GMAT	507
Average GPA	3.2
TOEFL required of international students	Yes
Minimum TOEFL (paper/computer/web)	515/213/79
Application fee	$50
International application fee	$50
Deferment available	Yes
Maximum length of deferment	1 semester
Non-fall admissions	Yes

WORCESTER POLYTECHNIC INSTITUTE

SCHOOL OF BUSINESS

GENERAL INFORMATION

Type of school	Private
Academic calendar	Semester

SURVEY SAYS...

Cutting-edge classes
Solid preparation in:
General management
Operations
Doing business in a global economy

STUDENTS

Enrollment of parent institution	4,544
Enrollment of MBA Program	282
% male/female	52/48
% out-of-state	82
% part-time	76
% minorities	5
% international	63
Average age at entry	31
Average years work experience at entry	7

ACADEMICS

Academic Experience Rating	**87**
Student/faculty ratio	9:1
Profs interesting rating	89
Profs accessible rating	85
% female faculty	45
% minority faculty	3

Joint Degrees

Dual BS/MBA, 5 years.

Prominent Alumni

Paul Allaire, Chairman and CEO Xerox Corporation; Judith Nitsch, President, Judith Nitsch Engineering, Inc.; Windle Priem, President and CEO, Korn/Ferry International; Stephen Rubin, President and CEO, Intellution, Inc.; Ronald Zarella, President, GM North America.

Academics

Offering "more of a technical leadership program than a traditional MBA," the School of Business at the Worcester Polytechnic Institute unites a broad-based degree in business essentials with highly specialized instruction in technology and technology management to fit the needs of graduate-level biz-savvy technophiles. Students appreciate the value of this approach; "The technology focus is great, considering where the business world is headed," one MBA observes. Another explains that the program "works very well in the intersection of business and technology, teaching us how to create and extract maximum value" from that nexus.

WPI's 48-credit hour program features ten highly-integrated required courses; two major projects; and four electives. All coursework is taught from a technological perspective and practical applications to business theory are emphasized. Students tailor their education via electives in cutting-edge fields such as information security management, process design, or technological innovation. In addition to electives offered through the business school, WPI students can enroll in graduate-level electives in other departments, including computer science, biomedical engineering, and electrical engineering. Students may study on campus, online, or switch back and forth between the two formats, an arrangement they love. "You can take classes online or portions of it online in case you are away on business and can't make the class one night," creating a "high amount of schedule[ing] flexibility."

WPI is committed to keeping up with the Data Age, with "courses updated frequently" and online course delivery "allowing for larger numbers of students to take classes, so I have never been closed out of a class." It isn't just all-tech, all-the-time at WPI; professors "express strong concerns with teaching us the importance of ethics applied in business management." Course work, students warn, "is fairly extensive, averaging about three to six hours per week per credit for reading and homework," but "professors are fair in their grading and flexible to accommodate working student schedules," which helps. Administrators "operate the program seamlessly," another plus.

Career and Placement

A high percentage of WPI students work full time, many receiving tuition reimbursement from their current company while pursuing the MBA. Therefore, most will continue at the same company after completing the WPI program. However, those considering a career change can receive support and guidance through the university's Career Development Center, which serves the undergraduate, graduate, and alumni population. The CDC offers career counseling, workshops, and assessments, and maintains contact with regional employers and WPI alumni. The CDC also hosts several annual campus career fairs. Students appreciate "the way [WPI] fosters and enables networking opportunities and work with the students work toward their career goals."

Employers who most frequently hire WPI MBAs include: BAE Systems, EMC, Fidelity, GE, Intel, Raytheon, Staples, Teradyne, and Textron.

Student Life and Environment

WPI occupies "a small urban campus with excellent access," making it easy for busy part-time students to zip in and zip out for classes, group meetings, etc. Students tell us that the library and student center are excellent resources; both "are well-staffed, clean, and contain useful equipment and products to support the learning environment." The program "offers a variety of activities and events throughout the year. These events range from academic to social to career-driven to special interests." To the extent that time permits, students "are not only actively engaged in school-related activities, but also go out of their way to actively participate in building a better world for the future. From holding forums on solar energy to fundraising for the community, WPI is always active in working to improve life for everyone [else]." Even the program's many distance-learning-only participants are surprised by their level of engagement. "It is not what I expected...it is very interactive. I love chat sessions most."

WPI MBAs tend to be "technical people in the stage of their careers [where they are ready] to transit[ion] from [a] professional role to [a] managerial position." There are "multiple nationalities represented" among the students, most of whom "have a good comprehension of English."

Admissions

The MBA program at Worcester Polytechnic Institute accepts students whose academic and professional record demonstrates the ability to excel in a challenging, technology-focused graduate program. Students are analyzed on the basis of their academic and professional performance, as well as their career goals and personal statement. In addition, all applicants must have demonstrated capacity to succeed in a technology-driven management program; therefore, a minimum of three semesters of college-level math or two semesters of college-level calculus are a prerequisite of the program. To apply, students must submit undergraduate transcripts, official GMAT scores, three letters of recommendation, and a completed application form. Applicants whose native language is not English and who have not earned degrees from English-language institutions must submit an official score report for the TOEFL or IELTS. WPI recruits underrepresented minorities through the Society of Hispanic Professional Engineers and the Society of Women Engineers, and maintains offices of diversity to increase recruitment among these groups.

FINANCIAL FACTS

Annual tuition	$27,816
Fees	$85
Cost of books	$1,100
Room & board (off-campus)	$8,100
% of students receiving aid	65
% of first-year students receiving aid	75
% of students receiving loans	33
% of students receiving grants	65
Average award package	$4,800
Average grant	$35,000

ADMISSIONS

Admissions Selectivity Rating	85
# of applications received	212
% applicants accepted	72
% acceptees attending	49
Average GMAT	620
Range of GMAT	570–680
Average GPA	3.35
TOEFL required of international students	Yes
Minimum TOEFL (paper/computer)	550/213
Application fee	$70
International application fee	$70
Regular application deadline	8/1
Early decision program?	No
Deferment available	Yes
Maximum length of deferment	1 year
Transfer students accepted	Yes
Transfer application policy: Accepted transfer applicants may transfer in up to 9 prior graduate-level credits toward the WPI MBA, provided those credits were not applied toward another earned degree.	
Non-fall admissions	Yes
Need-blind admissions	Yes

EMPLOYMENT PROFILE

Career Rating	83	Grads Employed by Function	%	Avg. Salary
Percent employed at graduation	70	Marketing	15	$70,000
Percent employed 3 months after graduation	30	Consulting	40	$75,000
		Management	15	$78,000
Average base starting salary	$74,714	MIS	30	$80,000
Primary Source of Full-time Job Acceptances		Top 5 Employers Hiring Grads		
School-facilitated activities	5 (70%)	EMC, Fidelity, State Street, GE, Abbott (NR)		
Graduate-facilitated activities	2 (30%)			

WRIGHT STATE UNIVERSITY
RAJ SOIN COLLEGE OF BUSINESS

GENERAL INFORMATION

Type of school	Public
Academic calendar	Quarter

SURVEY SAYS...
Solid preparation in:
General management

STUDENTS

Enrollment of parent institution	18,786
Enrollment of MBA Program	447
% male/female	53/47
% part-time	90
% minorities	41
% international	17
Average age at entry	33
Average years work experience at entry	5

ACADEMICS

Academic Experience Rating	**79**
Student/faculty ratio	8:1
Profs interesting rating	85
Profs accessible rating	80
% female faculty	24
% minority faculty	1

Joint Degrees
MBA/MS Nursing (2–5 years); MBA/MS s/a Economics (2–5 years); MBA/MD (4 years).

Academics

Students come to Wright State University for its excellent blend of affordability, convenience, and local reputation. "Cost is competitively low for the MBA program, in comparison to other schools," yet Wright State students laud the university's "commitment to expand both regionally and globally thus strengthening the value of my MBA." A largely part-time program, the school caters to the needs of working professionals. As such, "Coursework is challenging, but sensitive to the time constraints of the full-time working students." Scheduling is specifically designed to meet the needs of professionals: classes start every quarter (including summer) and "night classes are a central portion of the curriculum." On top of that, students appreciate the ease of registering for classes, which are rarely impacted or unavailable. A current student explains, "I know there will always be a spot for me...I don't have to worry about anything besides attending class and making the grades."

Many part-time programs attempt to offer the same benefits as a fulltime MBA, but Wright State really delivers. Even the "international trips are planned during Spring Break," which makes it easier for part-time students to participate. A student elaborates, "I have been able to study abroad in Paris and China and meet with world renowned professors and business executives. When I tell people this, they are always surprised and were not aware this was an option in the part-time program." Academically, as well as logistically, Raj Soin caters to the needs of students at every stage in their career. While many students are working professionals, business newbies say the school offers "excellent survey courses in business classes for non-business undergraduates." On the other hand, for those with more experience, foundation coursework can be waived.

Wright State operates a "curriculum that is discussion-oriented not lecture-based," and many feel "The interaction within the classes is a major strength of the program." Learning, rather than grades, is the focus of the classroom experience, and "The faculty all seem really motivated to deliver value to the student." Open-minded, engaging, and "approachable," Raj Soin professors "entertain questions and are willing to discuss alternate points of view." In the classroom, "Students are encouraged to share present day experiences that relate to the material," enhancing the experience for everyone in the program. With lively discussions dominating the academic experience, Wright State "fosters creativity and innovation."

While there are no practicum or internship requirements within the curriculum, the Wright State MBA focuses on material that "applies to the real world business environment." "The classes are generally applicable to current events," and recently, many class topics have been "structured around the current economic downturn." With a faculty that boasts both academic and professional prowess, "Many of the professors bring real industry knowledge and experience to the classroom, which helps translate textbook terms into reality."

Career and Placement

Many Wright State students are already employed, with a number receiving tuition reimbursement from their current employer. As such, many MBA candidates are not looking for a new job after graduation. Even so, students benefit from ample networking opportunities through the school's well-connected faculty, alumni, and student body. In fact, your classmates will likely be your best business contacts in the future. A current student explains, "All of the students in my cohort have grown very close and I think we will have relationships that extend far beyond our graduation." In addition, there are more than 17,000 Wright State business school alumni.

ADMISSIONS CONTACT: MICHAEL EVANS, DIRECTOR, MBA PROGRAMS
ADDRESS: 100 RIKE HALL, 3640 COLONEL GLENN HIGHWAY DAYTON, OH 45435-0001
PHONE: 937-775-2437 • FAX: 937-775-3545
E-MAIL: MBA_DIRECTOR@WRIGHT.EDU • WEBSITE: WWW.WRIGHT.EDU/BUSINESS

For those looking to begin a new career after graduation, Raj Soin maintains a "well-known brand name in the local markets," and MBA students have access to the university Career Services center. The staff at Career Services can help with internship or co-op placements, and they host recruiting days and job fairs. Students say there are an "Array of employers coming in for recruiting" at Wright State, many from Dayton and the surrounding region.

Student Life and Environment

To accommodate the scheduling needs of working students, the bulk of Wright State classes are offered in the evenings. As a result, "The graduate program definitely seems to come alive at night, when everyone gets off work and comes in early to study before class." Students are happy to find comfortable and up-to-date facilities in the business school, including "very modern equipment in our classrooms." In addition, business students have access to all the amenities of the larger Wright State campus, which include "one of the best day care facilities in the city." While many say they only visit campus to attend classes, others come to "work in the computer lab and library, and use the gym." In fact, the "Library system is wonderful and connected to several organizations in the community."

For those who'd like to get involved in the student community, "There is a diverse array of student clubs and organizations for students to join, as well as events and festivals which take place throughout the year. There are both on-campus and off-campus professional groups for MBA students, as well as for undergraduate students at the college of business." Students also gather more informally. For example, a student tells us, "Our graduate cohort sometimes gets together after milestones such as end of projects, after tests, and at the end of the quarter."

Admissions

To apply to Wright State University, student must submit a graduate school application, official GMAT scores, official undergraduate transcripts, and the names and contact information for at least three references. Strong admissions candidates will have a high undergraduate GPA (or an upward trend in their undergraduate studies) and high GMAT scores.

FINANCIAL FACTS

Annual tuition (in-state/ out-of-state)	$10,500/$17,796
Cost of books	$1,300
Room & board (on/off-campus)	$12,000/$10,000
% of students receiving grants	35
Average award package	$10,500

ADMISSIONS

Admissions Selectivity Rating	74
# of applications received	600
% applicants accepted	68
% acceptees attending	100
Average GMAT	500
Average GPA	3.15
TOEFL required of international students	Yes
Minimum TOEFL (paper/computer)	550/213
Application fee	$25
International application fee	$25
Regular application deadline	8/1
Regular notification	8/15
Early decision program?	Yes
Deferment available	Yes
Maximum length of deferment	4 quarters
Transfer students accepted	Yes
Transfer application policy: They must meet WSU admissions requirements. Can transfer up to 3 classes, with faculty approval.	
Non-fall admissions	Yes
Need-blind admissions	Yes

XAVIER UNIVERSITY
WILLIAMS COLLEGE OF BUSINESS

GENERAL INFORMATION

Type of school	Private
Affiliation	Roman Catholic/Jesuit
Academic calendar	Semester

SURVEY SAYS...

Cutting-edge classes
Solid preparation in:
Finance
General management
Doing business in a global economy

STUDENTS

Enrollment of parent institution	6,966
Enrollment of MBA Program	1,049
% male/female	68/32
% out-of-state	4
% part-time	84
% minorities	16
% international	3
Average age at entry	29
Average years work experience at entry	7

ACADEMICS

Academic Experience Rating	84
Student/faculty ratio	26:1
Profs interesting rating	85
Profs accessible rating	86
% female faculty	37
% minority faculty	17

Joint Degrees

Master of Health Services Administration and Master of Business Administration Program Approximate Length, 3 years; Master of Science in Nursing and Master of Business Adminstration, approximate length, 3 years.

Prominent Alumni

George Schaefer, President/CEO Flfth Third Bancorp; Robert J. Kohlhepp, Vice Chairman, Cintas Corporation; John Lechleiter, President & CEO, Eli Lilly & Company; Carlos Alcantara, President/CEO Chalaco; Mary Jean Ryan, F.S.M. MEA., President and CEO SSM Health Care.

Academics

Garnering more prestige with every graduating class, Xavier University's practical MBA programs "have a very strong reputation among [members of] the business community in Cincinnati, and across the Midwest." Through the William's College of Business, Xavier offers several MBA options, specially designed for working professionals: the Evening MBA, the Weekend MBA, the Executive MBA, and two off-site programs. For most students, the "convenient class options" and "scheduling flexibility" are major advantages of this program, though the curriculum's "quality and reputation" are the number one reason they chose Xavier. No matter what your field, Xavier's core curriculum promotes a "holistic view of the business world," integrating business disciplines, from marketing strategy to finance. In addition, students must take a minimum of nine credit hours of electives, with the option of pursuing a concentration. Students praise Xavier's focus on the global business market (there are international trips offered over spring break in locations from China to Brazil), though some would like to see "more opportunities to learn about non-profit management and green business operations."

Xavier draws heavily on the local business community, and "Many professors are adjuncts that are pulled from the business community and bring in amazing real-life experience." A student elaborates, "Professors are either owners of very successful companies from a large amount of differing fields or well-known in their respective fields." In the classroom, the emphasis is on practice, not theory—perfect for those who want to boost their current career. A student raves, "Practical experience and engagement in case studies has enhanced my critical business thinking and allowed me to become a better thinker and leader." Although work experience is not a requirement of the program, Xavier's MBAs are best suited towards older students already in the workplace. An evening student says, "For an experienced manager like me, the academics are a good augmentation of the work I do today. I'm not convinced the younger students will have any idea of how to use what we are learning in their first job."

"One of the strengths of Xavier is that it is a smaller school," and this unique intimacy plays out in many positive ways. First of all, small class sizes assure that "You get a closer relationship with your classmates and faculty. These stronger relationships allow for an abundance of networking opportunities." On top of that, the staff is truly student-oriented; here, "professors really make you feel like the students are the highest priority, and getting published is a distant second." Likewise, "the administration bends over backwards to help with things like financial aid, and even military aid for veteran students." A student enthuses, "No matter what the question or concern, there is someone readily available to help...from scheduling questions, to tuition concerns, to library assistance. And everyone is always so pleasant and kind!"

Career and Placement

Ninety-five percent of Xavier's MBA candidates work full time and take classes in the evenings or on the weekends. A large percentage of those students are also receiving tuition assistance from their company, with the expectation that they will continue—with increased responsibilities—at the same company after graduation. As students tell us, "Cincinnati has a lot of big corporations (GE Aircraft, GE Finance, P&G, Kroger, Johnson & Johnson) and Xavier is the business school of choice for all these Cincinnati-based companies." Xavier alumni report that their salaries rose 29.5 percent after completing the MBA the program, and rose 66 percent within five years of graduation. Recent graduates had an average salary of $70,900, with a range between $65,000 and $170,000.

While many students aren't actively looking for a new job, the Williams' College of Business Professional Development Center is a full-service organization, which tailors its efforts to career starters, career changers, and those who want to advance their existing career. Among other offerings, the Professional Development Center offers one-on-one career counseling, a professional mentorship and internship program, resume and interview prep, and "excellent career and networking activities and talks."

Student Life and Environment

Xavier's pretty campus is "tucked away in the hills of Cincinnati" and dotted with "wonderful, ivy-covered, old European-looking buildings." In the business school, students are "impressed with the classrooms [and] library" as well as the "excellent student center with variety of eateries, game room, bookstore, movie theater, and hang-out spots." Throughout the business school, students can participate in "networking opportunities on campus with companies around Cincinnati," or attend "informative lectures and seminars" on business topics. Students admit that the school has recently outgrown its facilities; fortunately, "The administration recognized the need for a new business building and construction should be complete this year."

Most students at Xavier are working full-time, and therefore, they only come to campus for class and study groups. Even so, students are friendly and social with one another. For example, those in the Weekend MBA program "eat lunch together between classes, and perhaps play some racquetball." In addition to casual socializing, "There are a number of organizations solely within the MBA program that regularly go out for events, dinner, or drinks." While the school is ultra-accommodating to working students, those with families note, "There are no daycare or spouse resources."

Admission

To be considered for admission to Xavier's graduate programs, students must have a GPA of at least 2.5 from their undergraduate studies—though, on average, entering students had a 3.0 GPA, on a 4.0 scale. Students must also have a minimum GMAT score of 470. Letters of recommendation are optional, but are recommended for students whose test scores or GPA fall below the average applicant. Previous career experience is not a requirement of the program; however, it is highly recommended.

FINANCIAL FACTS

Annual tuition	$12,546
Cost of books	$900
% of students receiving aid	26
% of first-year students receiving aid	183
% of students receiving loans	21
% of students receiving grants	11
Average award package	$15,280
Average grant	$796
Average student loan debt	$31,280

ADMISSIONS

Admissions Selectivity Rating	83
# of applications received	355
% applicants accepted	63
% acceptees attending	87
Average GMAT	550
Range of GMAT	450–680
Average GPA	3.26
TOEFL required of international students	Yes
Minimum TOEFL (paper/computer)	550/213
Early decision program?	No
ED Deadline/Notification	
Deferment available	Yes
Maximum length of deferment	1 year
Transfer students accepted	Yes
Transfer application policy: 6 hours of core curriculum from AACSB accredited programs only. Up to 18 hours of core curriculum from AACSB accredited Jesuit MBA Network Schools.	
Non-fall admissions	Yes
Need-blind admissions	Yes

Applicants Also Look At
Ohio State University
University of Cincinnati
Miami University of Ohio

EMPLOYMENT PROFILE

Career Rating	85	Grads Employed by Function	% Avg. Salary
Percent employed at graduation	69	Marketing	18 $70,447
Percent employed 3 months after graduation	75	Operations	3 $47,500
		Consulting	1 $48,900
Average base starting salary	$76,869	Management	5 $58,000
		Finance	13 $67,695
		MIS	3 $67,700
		Communications	1 $62,500
		Entrepreneurship	1 NR
		Internet	3 NR
		Nonprofit	3 $48,500
		Strategic	1 $115,000

Top 5 Employers Hiring Grads
Procter & Gamble (7), Fidelity Investments (5), The Kroger Company (2), Fifth Third Bank (7), General Electric (5)

YALE UNIVERSITY
SCHOOL OF MANAGEMENT

GENERAL INFORMATION

Type of school — Private
Academic calendar — Semester

SURVEY SAYS...
Friendly students
Good social scene
Good peer network
Cutting-edge classes
Solid preparation in:
General management
Teamwork
Doing business in a global economy

STUDENTS
Enrollment of parent
institution — 11,416
Enrollment of MBA Program — 429
% male/female — 66/34
% minorities — 8
% international — 27
Average age at entry — 28
Average years work experience
at entry — 5

ACADEMICS
Academic Experience Rating — **98**
Profs interesting rating — 89
Profs accessible rating — 94
% female faculty — 18
% minority faculty — 2

Joint Degrees
MBA/JD with Yale Law School (4 years), Accelerated Integrated MBA/JD with Yale Law School (3 years), MBA/MD with Yale School of Medicine (5 years) MBA/MARCH with Yale School of Architecture (4 years), MBA/MFA with Yale School of Drama (4 years), MBA/MDIV or MAR with Yale Divinity School (3 years), MBA/MEM or MF with Yale School of Forestry and Environmental Studies (3 years), MBA/MPH with Yale School of Public Health (EPH) (3 years), MBA/PhD with Yale Graduate School of Arts and Sciences, MBA/MA International Relations, Eastern European Studies with Yale Graduate School of Arts and Sciences.

Academics

The Yale University School of Management boasts an innovative approach to management education. Students are drawn here for the unique "Yale brand" which includes an "outstanding curriculum," "small class size," "focus on socially-responsible business," "top-notch faculty," "collaborative environment," and "the culture of respect for nonprofit and public sector careers." In 2006, the program continued to develop its tradition of innovation with the development of the integrated MBA curriculum. Built around nine multidisciplinary courses called Organizational Perspectives, Yale's core curriculum is indeed cutting edge and employs the use of team teaching, especially in the core classes, where perspectives from multiple disciplines are deployed to help students better understand complex management challenges.

Yale SOM's small size "breeds a sense of community which is unparalleled by any other top MBA program." In addition, "the proximity to New York facilitates interaction with potential employers." Comprised of students who are "intellectually curious and unfailing passionate about what they're doing whether it's banking, education reform, consulting, or the environment," the variety of student interests and backgrounds "mitigates some of the competitiveness you see at many top programs, fostering a real sense of community." In addition, the school's "ethos of leadership for business and society is clearly visible;" "from pro-bono consulting for the New Haven community to raising funds for peers who intern in non-profit organizations."

Professors are "tremendously engaging." Students say there is "no prescribed teaching method here: each class varies a great deal and the mix of teaching styles is absolutely spot on." In addition, "the grading scheme encourages a collaborative working environment where risk-taking is encouraged." Due to the small class size, "students get a disproportionate amount of attention from the administration and faculty." "I feel I can go talk with almost anyone at any time." "Sharon Oster (our Dean) is fantastic, and the lower level-administration is great. In general, Yale offers a fantastic academic experience."

Career and Placement

The Career Development Office at Yale School of Management "is the anchor [of] an otherwise amazing program." Through the CDO, students have access to one-on-one career counseling, mock interviews, and special workshops on resume writing, career searches, networking, and negotiation. The CDO also hosts career fairs, company presentations, and on-campus interviews. In addition, students benefit from the "highly responsive and engaged alumni base," and the prestige of the Yale name.

In 2009, an impressive 92 percent of full-time MBA students seeking employment had received a job offer within three months after graduation with those accepting positions enjoying a mean base salary of $98,420. JP Morgan, Barclays, American Express, Bank of Americal/Merrill Lynch, PriceWaterhouse Coopers were among the top employers with financial services and consulting remaining top draw industries.

ADMISSIONS CONTACT: BRUCE DELMONICO, DIRECTOR OF ADMISSIONS
ADDRESS: 135 PROSPECT STREET , P.O. BOX 208200 NEW HAVEN, CT 06520-8200
PHONE: 203-432-5635 • E-MAIL: MBA.ADMISSIONS@YALE.EDU
WEBSITE: WWW.MBA.YALE.EDU

Student Life and Environment

Students at the Yale School of Management "are not the product of a cookie cutter." "There are people with all imaginable interests and talents—from financial engineers to Michael Jackson impersonators, a diversity which is amazing, given the size of the school." "Quirky might be a good word to describe your typical SOM student; more socially-oriented; very intelligent and impressive overachiever types with a heart." In sum, "a good mix of type-A's and Bs." When asked to reflect on their common traits, Yale MBAs themselves say, "It is hard to characterize such a diverse group of students. Some are quantitative finance experts who spend their time drinking and modeling, not necessarily in that order. Others are very socially conscious and are constantly looking for ways to help the less fortunate and to give back to the community. In general the students at Yale SOM are smart, driven, kind, helpful, and a lot of fun."

Intellectual curiosity at Yale is expressed by a desire "to make a positive impact on the world." "I never hear anyone talk about wanting to make a lot of money—people just want to learn as much as they can about business and then make a contribution, and be happy." Everyone on campus "is involved in multiple clubs." "There are always events going on—speakers or panels during the day, networking or happy hours in the evening." "The hockey team is quite popular since the ice rink is located across the street from school." As diverse in their extracurricular interests as they are in their studies, students are known to "throw impromptu jam sessions in our…student-run café," or "test out their business ideas in our student lounge area next to people using game theory to improve their job search." New Haven "is a small town," but the Yale campus "is just beautiful." Though some of the business facilities "are in need of updating," fortunately "a nice new building is on the way!"

Admissions

True to their innovative roots, Yale School of Management welcomes students who bring a diversity of backgrounds, experiences, and points of view to the classroom and community. In keeping with this tenet of inclusion and innovation, the school publishes no specific admissions standards. Admissions decisions are influenced by "academic potential, professional accomplishments, leadership qualities, entrepreneurial skills, and personal values and goals." That said, the average GPA for the matriculating class of 2009 was 3.5 with an average GMAT of 715.

Prominent Alumni

John Thornton, Former Co-COO & President, Goldman Sachs; Nancy Peretsman, Managing Director, Allen & Company; Indra Nooyi, Chairman and CEO, PepsiCo Inc.; Fred Terrell, Vice Chairman of Investment Banking, Credit Suisse; Timothy Collins, CEO & Senior Managing Director and CEO, Ripplewood Holding.

FINANCIAL FACTS

Annual tuition	$47,200
Fees	$1,000
Cost of books	$800
Room & board	$14,265
% of students receiving aid	76
% of first-year students receiving aid	80
% of students receiving loans	70
% of students receiving grants	28
Average award package	$43,647
Average grant	$23,147
Average student loan debt	$86,791

ADMISSIONS

Admissions Selectivity Rating	98
# of applications received	2,790
% applicants accepted	18
% acceptees attending	44
Average GMAT	715
Average GPA	3.5
TOEFL required of international students	Yes
Application fee	$220
Application Deadline/Notification	
Round 1:	10/8 / 12/18
Round 2:	1/7 / 4/2
Round 3:	3/10 / 5/7
Early decision program?	No
Deferment available	No
Transfer students accepted	No
Non-fall admissions	No
Need-blind admissions	Yes

EMPLOYMENT PROFILE

Career Rating	97	**Grads Employed by Function% Avg. Salary**	
Percent employed at graduation	69	Marketing	13 $90,981
Percent employed 3 months		Operations	1 NR
after graduation	85	Consulting	19 $116,245
Average base starting salary	$98,420	Management	20 $94,087
Primary Source of Full-time Job Acceptances		Finance	46 $96,903
School-facilitated activities	NR (66%)	MIS	1 NR
Graduate-facilitated activities	NR (31%)	**Top 5 Employers Hiring Grads**	
Unknown	NR (3%)	JP Morgan, Barclays, American Express, Bank of America/Merrill Lynch, PricewaterhouseCoopers	

Part III-B
Business School Data
Listings

ARKANSAS STATE UNIVERSITY
COLLEGE OF BUSINESS

ADMISSIONS CONTACT: DR. THOMAS WHEELER, DEAN, GRADUATE SCHOOL
ADDRESS: PO BOX 60, STATE UNIVERSITY, AR 72467
PHONE: 870-972-3029 • FAX: 870-972-3857
E-MAIL: GRADSCH@CHOCTAW.ASTATE.EDU
WEBSITE: BUSINESS.ASTATE.EDU

GENERAL INFORMATION
Type of school: Public **Academic calendar:** Semester

STUDENTS
Enrollment of MBA program: 104 **Average years work experience at entry:** 0

ACADEMICS
Student/raculty ratio: 25:1 **% female faculty:** 24 **% minority faculty:** 1

FINANCIAL FACTS
Annual tuition (in-state/out-of-state): $1,488/$3,744 **Books and supplies:** $2,100 **Room & board (on-campus):** $3,500 **Average grant:** $6,427

ADMISSIONS
Admissions Selectivity Rating: 60*

# of applications received: 53 **% applicants accepted:** 85 **% acceptees attending:** 80 **TOEFL required of international applicants?** Yes **Minimum TOEFL (computer):** 550

Early decision program? No **Deferment available?** No **Transfer students accepted?** No **Non-fall admissions?** No **Need-blind admissions?** No

ASIAN INSTITUTE OF MANAGEMENT (PHILIPPINES)
ASIAN INSTITUTE OF MANAGEMENT

ADMISSIONS CONTACT: MR. REY REYES, EXECUTIVE MANAGING DIRECTOR
ADDRESS: GROUND FLR. EUGENIO LOPEZ FOUNDATION BLDG., ASIAN INSTITUTE OF MANAGEMENT 123 PASEO DE ROXAS, MAKATI CITY, 1260 PHILIPPINES
PHONE: +63 2 8937631 • FAX: +63 2 8937631
E-MAIL: ADMISSIONS@AIM.EDU
WEBSITE: WWW.AIM.EDU

GENERAL INFORMATION
Type of school: Private **Academic calendar:** Sep to Dec of ff. year

STUDENTS
Enrollment of MBA program: 100 **% male/female:** 62/38 **% out-of-state:** 71 **% part-time:** 0 **% international:** 71 **Average age at entry:** 26 **Average years work experience at entry:** 3

ACADEMICS
Student/raculty ratio: 10:1
Joint degrees: None. **Prominent alumni:** Mr. Ashok Soota, Chairman and Managing Director, Mindtree Consulting; Hon. Jesli Lapus, Secretary, Philippine Department of Education; Hon. Angelo Reyes, Secretary, Philippine Department of Energy; Gen. Tan Sri Dato Seri Abdul Aziz, Chief of Defence Force, Malaysian Armed Forces; Tony Tan Caktiong, President, Jollibee Corp.

FINANCIAL FACTS
Annual tuition: $16,130 **Fees:** $7,870 **Books and supplies:** $8,000 **Room & board (on-campus):** $3,500

ADMISSIONS
Admissions Selectivity Rating: 60*

Average GMAT: 660 **TOEFL required of international applicants?** No

Early decision program? No **Deferment available?** Yes **Maximum length of deferment:** After one year **Transfer students accepted?** No **Non-fall admissions?** No **Need-blind admissions?** No

ASTON UNIVERSITY
ASTON BUSINESS SCHOOL

ADDRESS: ASTON TRIANGLE, BIRMINGHAM B4 7ET,
PHONE: 011-44 (0) 121 204 3100
E-MAIL: ABSPG@ASTON.AC.UK
WEBSITE: WWW.ABS.ASTON.AC.UK

GENERAL INFORMATION
Type of school: Private

STUDENTS
Average years work experience at entry: 0

FINANCIAL FACTS
Annual tuition: $35,608

ADMISSIONS
Admissions Selectivity Rating: 60*

TOEFL required of international applicants? No **Application deadline:** 7/1

Early decision program? No **Deferment available?** No **Transfer students accepted?** No **Non-fall admissions?** No **Need-blind admissions?** No

BALL STATE UNIVERSITY
MILLER COLLEGE OF BUSINESS

ADMISSIONS CONTACT: DR. JENNIFER BOTT, EXECUTIVE DIRECTOR OF MBA
ADDRESS: WB 147, MUNCIE, IN 47306
PHONE: 765-285-5329 • FAX: 765-285-8818
E-MAIL: MBA@BSU.EDU
WEBSITE: WWW.BSU.EDU/MBA

GENERAL INFORMATION
Type of school: Public **Academic calendar:** Semester

STUDENTS
Enrollment of parent institution: 18,161 **Enrollment of MBA program:** 189 **% male/female:** 89/11 **% out-of-state:** 4 **% part-time:** 72 **% minorities:** 1 **% international:** 4 **Average age at entry:** 28 **Average years work experience at entry:** 4

ACADEMICS

Student/raculty ratio: 30:1

FINANCIAL FACTS

Annual tuition (in-state/out-of-state): $9,406/$24,890 **Fees (in-state/out-of-state):** $1,343/$1,343 **Books and supplies:** $1,750 **Room & board (on/off-campus):** $9,000/$9,500

Average award package: $8,907

ADMISSIONS

Admissions Selectivity Rating: 60*

# of applications received: 62 % applicants accepted: 95 % acceptees attending: 93 **Average GMAT:** 535 **Range of GMAT:** 450-620 **Average GPA:** 3.27 **TOEFL required of international applicants?** Yes **Minimum TOEFL (computer):** 550 **Application fee:** $50 **International application fee:** $40

Early decision program? No **Deferment available?** Yes **Maximum length of deferment:** 2 years **Transfer students accepted?** Yes **Transfer application policy:** Up to 9 credit hours may be considered for transfer. **Non-fall admissions?** Yes **Need-blind admissions?** Yes

BILKENT UNIVERSITY
FACULTY OF BUSINESS ADMINISTRATION

ADMISSIONS CONTACT: ILHAM CIPIL, MBA COORDINATOR
ADDRESS: BILKENT UNIVERSITY FACULTY OF BUSINESS ADMINISTRATION, MA-209 TEL:+90 312 2902817 CANKAYA BILKENT, ANKARA, NA 06800 TURKEY
PHONE: +90 312 2902817 • FAX: +90 312 2664958
E-MAIL: MBACOORDINATOR@BILKENT.EDU.TR
WEBSITE: WWW.MAN.BILKENT.EDU.TR

GENERAL INFORMATION

Type of school: Private

STUDENTS

Enrollment of MBA program: 36 % male/female: 66/34 % international: 3 **Average age at entry:** 25 **Average years work experience at entry:** 27

FINANCIAL FACTS

% of students receiving aid: 15 % of first-year students receiving aid: 15 % of students receiving grants: 30

ADMISSIONS

Admissions Selectivity Rating: 60*

Average GMAT: 614 **TOEFL required of international applicants?** Yes **Minimum TOEFL (computer):** 213 **Application Deadline/Notification Round 1:** NR / 1/5 **Round 2:** 5/6 / NR

Early decision program? No **Deferment available?** No **Transfer students accepted?** Yes **Transfer application policy:** The transfer applicant should contact the MBA Coordinator for the required materials and deadlines. **Non-fall admissions?** No **Need-blind admissions?** Yes

BOISE STATE UNIVERSITY
COLLEGE OF BUSINESS AND ECONOMICS

ADMISSIONS CONTACT: J. RENEE ANCHUSTEGUI, PROGRAMS ADMINISTRATOR & ACADEMIC ADVISOR
ADDRESS: BUSINESS GRADUATE STUDIES, 1910 UNIVERSITY DRIVE B307, BOISE, ID 83725-1600
PHONE: 208-426-3116 • FAX: 208-426-1135
E-MAIL: GRADUATEBUSINESS@BOISESTATE.EDU
WEBSITE: COBE.BOISESTATE.EDU/GRADUATE

GENERAL INFORMATION

Type of school: Public **Academic calendar:** Semester

STUDENTS

Enrollment of parent institution: 18,447 **Enrollment of MBA program:** 190 % male/female: 74/26 % out-of-state: 20 % part-time: 34 % minorities: 4 % international: 7 **Average age at entry:** 35 **Average years work experience at entry:** 6

ACADEMICS

Student/raculty ratio: 23:1 % female faculty: 20 % minority faculty: 7

Prominent alumni: Jan Packwood, Retired President & COO, Idaho Power Co.; Ric Gale, VP Gov't Relations, Idaho Power Co; Steve Heyl, VP Strategic Planning, Arby's; Norm Schlachter, VP Finance, Micron Technology; Mary Schofield, Controller, Boise Division, Hewlett-Packard.

FINANCIAL FACTS

Annual tution: $8,576 **Fees:** $6,898 **Books and supplies:** $3,000 **Room & board (on/off-campus):** $6,800/$7,200

% of students receiving aid: 70 % of first-year students receiving aid: 23 % of students receiving loans: 48 % of students receiving grants: 22 **Average award package:** $16,700 **Average grant:** $19,492 **Average student loan debt:** $12,000

ADMISSIONS

Admissions Selectivity Rating: 60*

# of applications received: 130 % applicants accepted: 55 % acceptees attending: 66 **Average GMAT:** 579 **Range of GMAT:** 510–665 **Average GPA:** 3.32 **TOEFL required of international applicants?** Yes **Minimum TOEFL (paper/computer):** 587/240 **Application fee:** $55 **International application fee:** $55 **Application deadline:** 6/1 **Regular notification:** 7/15

Early decision program? Yes **ED deadline/notification:** NR / 3/31 **Deferment available?** Yes **Maximum length of deferment:** 1 year **Transfer students accepted?** Yes **Transfer application policy:** Limit of up to 1/3 of total credits required to completed the degree at Boise State. Must receive grade of B or above from an AACSB accredited institution for transfer consideration. **Non-fall admissions?** Yes **Need-blind admissions?** Yes

EMPLOYMENT PROFILE

% grads employed at graduation: 78

% grads employed within three
   months of graduation: 95

Average starting salary:...............$73,077

Primary Source of Full-time Job Acceptances

School-facilitated activities 3 (15%)

Graduate-facilitated activities 8 (40%)

Unknown 9 (45%)

Grads Employed by Industry:......% avg. salary:

Marketing 5 $70,000

Operations....................................10 $61,667

Consulting....................................5 $69,000

Management 15 $63,000

Finance 30 $48,000

HR..5 $53,000

MIS...10 $100,000

Top 5 Employers Hiring Grads (#)

Micron Technology (4), Northwest Mutual (2), Wells Fargo (2), Scentsy (2)

BRADLEY UNIVERSITY
FOSTER COLLEGE OF BUSINESS ADMINISTRATION

ADMISSIONS CONTACT: SUSANNAH GAWOR, ASSISTANT DIRECTOR OF GRADUATE PROGRAMS
ADDRESS: 1501 WEST BRADLEY AVENUE, PEORIA, IL 61625
PHONE: 309-677-2253 • FAX: 309-677-3374
E-MAIL: MBA@BRADLEY.EDU
WEBSITE: WWW.BRADLEY.EDU/FCBA

GENERAL INFORMATION

Type of school: Private **Academic calendar:** Semester

STUDENTS

Enrollment of parent institution: 5,873 **Enrollment of MBA program:** 175 % **part-time:** 74 **Average age at entry:** 27 **Average years work experience at entry:** 4

Prominent alumni: Ray LaHood, U.S. Secretary of Transportation; General John Shalikashvili, retired chairman of the Joint Chiefs of Staff; Rene C. Byer, winner of the Pulitzer Prize, senior photographer, Sacramento Bee; Richard Teerlink, retired chairman of Harley-Davidson, Inc.

FINANCIAL FACTS

Fees: $50 **Books and supplies:** $700

ADMISSIONS

Admissions Selectivity Rating: 60*

# of applications received: 59 % **applicants accepted:** 78 % **acceptees attending:** 67 **Average GMAT:** 540 **TOEFL required of international applicants?** Yes **Minimum TOEFL (paper/computer):** 550/213 **Application fee:** $40 **International application fee:** $50

Early decision program? No **Deferment available?** Yes **Maximum length of deferment:** 1 semester **Transfer students accepted?** Yes **Transfer application policy:** No more than 9 hours of credit from another AACSB-accredited school can transfer to Bradley MBA program **Non-fall admissions?** Yes **Need-blind admissions?** Yes

CALIFORNIA STATE UNIVERSITY— LOS ANGELES
COLLEGE OF BUSINESS AND ECONOMICS

ADMISSIONS CONTACT: JOAN WOOSLEY, ADMISSIONS OFFICER
ADDRESS: CSULA, ADMISSIONS OFFICE, 5151 STATE UNIVERSITY DRIVE, LOS ANGELES, CA 90032
PHONE: (323) 343-3901 • FAX: (323) 343-6306
E-MAIL: ADMISSION@CALSTATELA.EDU
WEBSITE: CBE.CALSTATELA.EDU

GENERAL INFORMATION

Type of school: Public

STUDENTS

Enrollment of MBA program: 121 % **male/female:** 41/59 % **out-of-state:** 0 % **part-time:** 72 % **minorities:** 15 % **international:** 56 **Average age at entry:** 27.6

ADMISSIONS

Admissions Selectivity Rating: 60*

# of applications received: 83 % **applicants accepted:** 40 % **acceptees attending:** 58 **Average GMAT:** 700 **Range of GMAT:** 630-740 **Average GPA:** 3.15 **TOEFL required of international applicants?** Yes **Minimum TOEFL (paper/computer):** 550/213 **Application fee:** $55 **International application fee:** $55 **Application deadline:** 3/1 **Regular notification:** 6/15

Early decision program? No **Deferment available?** No **Transfer students accepted?** Yes **Transfer application policy:** At most 13 units can be transfered. **Non-fall admissions?** No **Need-blind admissions?** No

CALIFORNIA STATE UNIVERSITY— SACRAMENTO
COLLEGE OF BUSINESS ADMINISTRATION

ADMISSIONS CONTACT: JEANIE WILLIAMS, GRADUATE PROGRAMS COORDINATOR
ADDRESS: 6000 J STREET, TAHOE HALL ROOM 1035, SACRAMENTO, CA 95819-6088
PHONE: 916-278-6772 • FAX: 916-278-4233
E-MAIL: CBAGRAD@CSUS.EDU
WEBSITE: WWW.CBA.CSUS.EDU

GENERAL INFORMATION

Type of school: Public **Academic calendar:** Semester

STUDENTS

Enrollment of parent institution: 23,280 **Enrollment of MBA program:** 492 **Average age at entry:** 27 **Average years work experience at entry:** 4

ACADEMICS

% female faculty: 33

Joint degrees: Masters of Business Administration and Juris Doctorate (MBA/JD) McGeorge School of Law: Full time; Approx. 4.5 years needed to complete combined program.

Prominent alumni: Carla Vasquez, Founder, President, and CEO of CV Logistics; Dennis Gardemeyer, Developer, CEO, and Co-Owner of Delta Bluegrass; Scott Syphax, President and CEO of Nehemiah Corporation; Dale Calsen, President of Sleep Train; Margo Murray, President, CEO/MMHA The Managers' Mentors Inc.

FINANCIAL FACTS

Annual tuition (in-state/out-of-state): $4,562/$10,664 **Books and supplies:** $1,700 **Room & board (on/off-campus):** $8,435/$8,435

ADMISSIONS

Admissions Selectivity Rating: 60*

# of applications received: 215 **% applicants accepted:** 52 % **acceptees attending:** 67 **Average GMAT:** 570 **Range of GMAT:** 440-740 **Average GPA:** 3.19 **TOEFL required of international applicants?** Yes **Minimum TOEFL (paper/computer):** 510/180 **Application fee:** $55 **International application fee:** $55 **Application deadline:** 4/1 **Regular notification:** 5/30

Early decision program? No **Deferment available?** No **Transfer students accepted?** Yes **Transfer application policy:** We accept up to 6 units of transfer coursework from other AACSB accredited institutions. **Non-fall admissions?** Yes **Need-blind admissions?** Yes

CANISIUS COLLEGE
RICHARD J. WEHLE SCHOOL OF BUSINESS

ADMISSIONS CONTACT: LAURA MCEWEN, DIRECTOR, GRADUATE BUSINESS PROGRAMS
ADDRESS: CANISIUS COLLEGE, 2001 MAIN ST, BAGEN HALL 201, BUFFALO, NY 14208-1098
PHONE: 716-888-2140 • FAX: 716-888-2145
E-MAIL: GRADUBUS@CANISIUS.EDU
WEBSITE: WWW.CANISIUS.EDU/MBA

GENERAL INFORMATION

Type of school: Private **Affiliation:** Roman Catholic-Jesuit **Academic calendar:** Semester

STUDENTS

Enrollment of parent institution: 4,979 **Enrollment of MBA program:** 261 **% male/female:** 51/49 **% out-of-state:** 0 **% part-time:** 74 **% minorities:** 9 **% international:** 9 **Average age at entry:** 28 **Average years work experience at entry:** 0

ACADEMICS

% female faculty: 13 **% minority faculty:** 8
Joint degrees: Bachelor and MBA, 5 years.

FINANCIAL FACTS

Annual tuition: $32,251 **Books and supplies:** $500 **Room & board (on/off-campus):** $8,300/$8,300

ADMISSIONS

Admissions Selectivity Rating: 60*

Average GMAT: 474 **Range of GMAT:** 410–550 **TOEFL required of international applicants?** Yes **Minimum TOEFL (paper/computer):** 500/200 **Application fee:** $25

Early decision program? No **Deferment available?** Yes **Maximum length of deferment:** 1 year **Transfer students accepted?** Yes

Transfer application policy: Case-by-case basis. **Non-fall admissions?** Yes **Need-blind admissions?** No

EMPLOYMENT PROFILE

Average starting salary:................$48,900

CLARION UNIVERSITY
COLLEGE OF BUSINESS ADMINISTRATION

ADMISSIONS CONTACT: DR. BRENDA PONSFORD, DIRECTOR OF MBA PROGRAM
ADDRESS: 302 STILL HALL, CLARION UNIVERSITY, 840 WOOD STREET, CLARION, PA 16214
PHONE: 814-393-2605 • FAX: 814-393-1910
E-MAIL: MBA@CLARION.EDU
WEBSITE: WWW.CLARION.EDU/MBA

GENERAL INFORMATION

Type of school: Public **Academic calendar:** Semester

STUDENTS

Enrollment of parent institution: 7,700 **Enrollment of MBA program:** 76 **% male/female:** 60/40 **% out-of-state:** 29 **% part-time:** 61% **minorities:** 30 **% international:** 9.6 **Average age at entry:** 31 **Average years work experience at entry:** 4

ACADEMICS

% female faculty: 18 **% minority faculty:** 23

FINANCIAL FACTS

Annual tuition (in-state/out-of-state): $6,430/$10,288 **Fees (in-state/out-of-state):** $1,958/$2,050 **Books and supplies:** $3,650 **Room & board (on/off-campus):** $5,246/$4,000

ADMISSIONS

Admissions Selectivity Rating: 60*

# of applications received: 33 **% applicants accepted:** 94 % **acceptees attending:** 245 **Average GMAT:** 495 **TOEFL required of international applicants?** Yes **Minimum TOEFL (paper/computer):** 550/213 **Application fee:** $30 **International application fee:** $30

Early decision program? No **Deferment available?** Yes **Maximum length of deferment:** 1 year **Transfer students accepted?** Yes **Transfer application policy:** May transfer up to six approved credits as electives. **Non-fall admissions?** Yes **Need-blind admissions?** Yes

CLARK ATLANTA UNIVERSITY
SCHOOL OF BUSINESS ADMINISTRATION

ADMISSIONS CONTACT: LORRI SADDLER RICE, DIRECTOR OF ADMISSIONS
ADDRESS: 223 JAMES P. BRAWLEY DRIVE, ATLANTA, GA 30314
PHONE: 404-880-8447 • FAX: 404-880-6159
E-MAIL: LRICE@CAU.EDU
WEBSITE: WWW.SBUS.CAU.EDU

GENERAL INFORMATION

Type of school: Private **Affiliation:** Methodist **Academic calendar:** Semester

STUDENTS

Enrollment of parent institution: 5,000 **Enrollment of MBA program:** 120 **% male/female:** 38/62 **% part-time:** 10 **% minorities:** 90 **% international:** 10 **Average age at entry:** 28 **Average years work experience at entry:** 5

ACADEMICS

Student/raculty ratio: 11:1 **% female faculty:** 39 **% minority faculty:** 92

FINANCIAL FACTS

Annual tuition: $19,127 **Fees:** $550 **Books and supplies:** $800 Room & board (off-campus): $4,875

% of students receiving aid: 95 **% of first-year students receiving aid:** 95 **% of students receiving loans:** 95 **% of students receiving grants:** 95 **Average award package:** $32,000 **Average grant:** $32,000 **Average student loan debt:** $65,000

ADMISSIONS

Admissions Selectivity Rating: 60*

# of applications received: 134 **% applicants accepted:** 67 **% acceptees attending:** 69 **Average GMAT:** 430 **Range of GMAT:** 340–520 **Average GPA:** 3 **TOEFL required of international applicants?** Yes **Minimum TOEFL (paper):** 175 **Application fee:** $40 **International application fee:** $55 **Application deadline:** 4/1 **Early decision program?** No **Deferment available?** Yes **Maximum length of deferment:** one year **Transfer students accepted?** Yes **Transfer application policy:** We will accept up to 6 credit hours earned while enrolled in an accredited MBA program. **Non-fall admissions?** No **Need-blind admissions?** No

EMPLOYMENT PROFILE

% grads employed at graduation: 25
% grads employed within three
   months of graduation: 2
Average starting salary:................$82,500
Primary Source of Full-time Job Acceptances
School-facilitated activities 7 (25%)
Graduate-facilitated activities 15 (50%)
Unknown..7 (25%)

Grads Employed by Industry:	......%	avg. salary:
Marketing	52	$80,000
Operations	7	$75,000
Finance	30	$82,000
HR	7	$75,000

Top 5 Employers Hiring Grads

Chevron/Texaco, Coca Cola, American Express, Union Pacific, Delta Airlines

CLEVELAND STATE UNIVERSITY
NANCE COLLEGE OF BUSINESS ADMINISTRATION

ADMISSIONS CONTACT: BRUCE M. GOTTSCHALK, MBA PROGRAMS ADMINISTRATOR
ADDRESS: 2121 EUCLID AVENUE, BU 219, CLEVELAND, OH 44115
PHONE: 216-687-3730 • FAX: 216-687-5311
E-MAIL: CBACSU@CSUOHIO.EDU
WEBSITE: WWW.CSUOHIO.EDU/BUSINESS/MBA/

GENERAL INFORMATION

Type of school: Public **Academic calendar:** Semester

STUDENTS

Enrollment of parent institution: 15,450 **Enrollment of MBA program:** 641 **% male/female:** 60/40 **% out-of-state:** 40 **% part-time:** 78 **% minorities:** 18 **% international:** 31 **Average age at entry:** 26 **Average years work experience at entry:** 5

ACADEMICS

Student/raculty ratio: 27:1 **% female faculty:** 22 **% minority faculty:** 15

Joint degrees: JD/MBA 4 years, MBA/MSN 3 years. **Prominent alumni:** Monte Ahuja, Chairman,President& CEO, Transtar Industries; Michael Berthelot, Chairman& CEO Transtechnolgy Corporation; Ted Hlavaty, Chairman & CEO, Neway Stamping&Manufacturing; Thomas Moore, President, Wolf Group; Stephen F. Kirk, President, Lubrizol Additives.

FINANCIAL FACTS

Annual tuition (in-state/out-of-state): $10,536/$20,016 **Fees (in-state/out-of-state):** $50/$50 **Books and supplies:** $1,300 **Room & board (on/off-campus):** $10,000/$12,000

% of students receiving aid: 4 **% of first-year students receiving aid:** 8 **% of students receiving loans:** 55 **% of students receiving grants:** 1 **Average award package:** $20,000

ADMISSIONS

Admissions Selectivity Rating: 60*

# of applications received: 464 **% applicants accepted:** 72 **% acceptees attending:** 60 **Average GMAT:** 500 **Range of GMAT:** 460–590 **Average GPA:** 3.14 **TOEFL required of international applicants?** Yes **Minimum TOEFL (paper/computer):** 550/213 **Application fee:** $30 **International application fee:** $30 **Application deadline:** 7/1 **Early decision program?** No **Deferment available?** Yes **Maximum length of deferment:** 12 months **Transfer students accepted?** Yes **Transfer application policy:** Must be in good academic standing **Non-fall admissions?** Yes **Need-blind admissions?** Yes

EMPLOYMENT PROFILE

% grads employed at graduation: 50
% grads employed within three
   months of graduation: 22
Average starting salary:................$60,900

Primary Source of Full-time Job Acceptances

School-facilitated activities 25 (45%)

Graduate-facilitated activities 12 (22%)

Unknown.......................................18 (33%)

Grads Employed by Industry:......% avg. salary:

Marketing 9 $64,500

Operations.....................................18 $62,500

Consulting.....................................5 $58,500

Management 11 $61,000

Finance 20 $62,500

HR..5 $58,500

MIS 5 $65,200

Nonprofit..5 $60,000

Top 5 Employers Hiring Grads (#)

Progressive Insurance (6), Cleveland Clinic (4), Key Bank (4), DFAS (2), Sherwin Williams (2)

COASTAL CAROLINA UNIVERSITY
WALL COLLEGE OF BUSINESS

ADMISSIONS CONTACT: DR. RICHARD L. JOHNSON, ASSOCIATE PROVOST FOR GRADUATE STUDIES
ADDRESS: P.O. BOX 261954, CONWAY, SC 29528-6054
PHONE: 843-349-2394 • FAX:
E-MAIL: GRADUATE@COASTAL.EDU
WEBSITE: WWW.COASTAL.EDU/BUSINESS

GENERAL INFORMATION

Type of school: Public

STUDENTS

Enrollment of parent institution: 8,360 **Enrollment of MBA program:** 53 **% male/female:** 57/43 **% out-of-state:** 40 **% part-time:** 34 **% minorities:** 0 **% international:** 9 **Average age at entry:** 25 **Average years work experience at entry:** 5

ACADEMICS

Student/raculty ratio: 7:1 **% female faculty:** 44 **% minority faculty:** 11

Joint degrees: None.

FINANCIAL FACTS

Annual tuition (in-state/out-of-state): $11,160/$12,480 **Fees (in-state/out-of-state):** $80/$80 **Books and supplies:** $2,948 Room & board (off-campus): $8,088

% of students receiving aid: 66 **% of first-year students receiving aid:** 70 **% of students receiving loans:** 54 **% of students receiving grants:** 43 **Average award package:** $18,701 **Average grant:** $9,456 **Average student loan debt:** $29,149

ADMISSIONS

Admissions Selectivity Rating: 77

# of applications received: 45 **% applicants accepted:** 67 **% acceptees attending:** 73 **Average GMAT:** 506 **Range of GMAT:** 470-550 **Average GPA:** 3.54 **TOEFL required of international applicants?** Yes Minimum TOEFL (paper): 575 **Application fee:** $45 **International application fee:** $45

Early decision program? No **Deferment available?** No **Transfer students accepted?** Yes **Transfer application policy:** All course work must be 3.0 or higher. 6 hours - maximum transfer. **Non-fall admissions?** Yes **Need-blind admissions?** Yes

COLORADO STATE UNIVERSITY—PUEBLO
MALIK AND SEEME HASAN SCHOOL OF BUSINESS

ADMISSIONS CONTACT: JOE MARSHALL, DIRECTOR OF ADMISSIONS
ADDRESS: 2200 BONFORTE BLVD, PUEBLO, CO 81001
PHONE: 719-549-2461 • FAX: 719-549-2419
E-MAIL: INFO@COLOSTATE-PUEBLO.EDU
WEBSITE: HSB.COLOSTATE-PUEBLO.EDU

GENERAL INFORMATION

Type of school: Public **Academic calendar:** students may begin at any time

STUDENTS

Enrollment of parent institution: 5,051 **Enrollment of MBA program:** 133 **% male/female:** 67/33 **% out-of-state:** 30 **% part-time:** 37 **% minorities:** 15 **% international:** 30 **Average age at entry:** 28

ACADEMICS

Student/raculty ratio: 8:1 **% female faculty:** 16 **% minority faculty:** 50

ADMISSIONS

Admissions Selectivity Rating: 61

# of applications received: 109 **% applicants accepted:** 100 **Average GMAT:** 440 **Range of GMAT:** 400-680 **Average GPA:** 3.3 **TOEFL required of international applicants?** Yes **Minimum TOEFL (paper/computer):** 550/213 **Application fee:** $35 **International application fee:** $35

Early decision program? No **Deferment available?** No **Transfer students accepted?** Yes **Transfer application policy:** Students may transfer up to 9 credit hours of approved graduate courses. **Non-fall admissions?** Yes **Need-blind admissions?** Yes

COLUMBUS STATE UNIVERSITY
TURNER COLLEGE OF BUSINESS

ADMISSIONS CONTACT: UNDERGRADUATE ADMISSIONS
ADDRESS: 4225 UNIVERSITY AVE., COLUMBUS, GA 31907
PHONE: 706-507-8800 • FAX:
WEBSITE: COB.COLSTATE.EDU/

GENERAL INFORMATION

Type of school: Public **Academic calendar:** Fall, Spring, Summer

STUDENTS

Enrollment of parent institution: 8,200 **Enrollment of MBA program:** 95 **% male/female:** 48/52 **% out-of-state:** 20 **% part-time:** 80 **% minorities:** 16 **% international:** 10 **Average age at entry:** 26 **Average years work experience at entry:** 4

ACADEMICS

Student/raculty ratio: 30:1 **% female faculty:** 30 **% minority faculty:** 10

FINANCIAL FACTS

Annual tuition (in-state/out-of-state): $1,706/$6,817 **Fees (in-state/out-of-state):** $337/$337 **Books and supplies:** $600

ADMISSIONS

Admissions Selectivity Rating: 80

# of applications received: 68 **% applicants accepted:** 65 **% acceptees attending:** 91 **Average GMAT:** 560 **Range of GMAT:** 430-650 **Average GPA:** 3.3 **TOEFL required of international applicants?** Yes **Minimum TOEFL (paper/computer):** 550/213 **Application fee:** $30 **International application fee:** $30 **Application deadline:** 7/1

Early decision program? No **Deferment available?** Yes **Maximum length of deferment:** 1 year **Transfer students accepted?** Yes **Transfer application policy:** No more than 6 semester hours may be transferred. **Non-fall admissions?** Yes **Need-blind admissions?** Yes

CRANFIELD UNIVERSITY
CRANFIELD SCHOOL OF MANAGEMENT

ADMISSIONS CONTACT: EILEEN FISHER, ADMISSIONS EXECUTIVE
ADDRESS: CRANFIELD SCHOOL OF MANAGEMENT, CRANFIELD, BEDFORD, MK43 0AL
PHONE: 0044-1234-754431 • FAX: 0044-1234-752439
E-MAIL: MBAADMISSIONS@CRANFIELD.AC.UK
WEBSITE: WWW.CRANFIELDMBA.INFO

GENERAL INFORMATION

Type of school: Public **Academic calendar:** Year Long

STUDENTS

Enrollment of MBA program: 236 **% male/female:** 79/21 **part-time:** 50 **% international:** 81 **Average age at entry:** 33 **Average years work experience at entry:** 8

ACADEMICS

Student/raculty ratio: 2:1 **% female faculty:** 25

. **Prominent alumni:** Ted Tuppen, CEO Enterprise Inns; Nigel Doughty, CEO Doughty Hanson; John McFarlane, CEO ANZ Banking Grp; Andy Bond, Chief Executive, Asda; Michael Wemms, Chairman House of Fraser.

FINANCIAL FACTS

Annual tuition (in-state/out-of-state): $39,500/$39,500 **Books and supplies:** $850 **Room & board (on-campus):** $7,900

% of students receiving aid: 75 **% of first-year students receiving aid:** 75 **% of students receiving grants:** 75 **Average grant:** $13,700

ADMISSIONS

Admissions Selectivity Rating: 60*

# of applications received: 532 **% applicants accepted:** 40 **% acceptees attending:** 55 **Average GMAT:** 660 **Range of GMAT:** 600–720 **TOEFL required of international applicants?** Yes **Minimum TOEFL (paper/computer):** 600/250

Early decision program? No **Deferment available?** Yes **Maximum length of deferment:** 2 years **Transfer students accepted?** No **Non-fall admissions?** No **Need-blind admissions?** Yes

EMPLOYMENT PROFILE

Average starting salary:...............$81,900

Primary Source of Full-time Job Acceptances

School-facilitated activities 30 (39%)
Graduate-facilitated activities 30 (38%)
Unknown......................................18 (23%)

Grads Employed by Industry:	......%	avg. salary:
Marketing	NR	$62,800
Operations	NR	$76,900
Consulting	NR	$74,700
Management	NR	$90,000
Finance	NR	$82,700
HR	NR	$104,400
MIS	NR	$55,100
Strategic	NR	$108,900

Top 5 Employers Hiring Grads (#)

Rolls Royce (3), Johnson & Johnson (3), AMEX (2), Capgemini (2), Arcelor Mittal (2)

CREIGHTON UNIVERSITY
COLLEGE OF BUSINESS ADMINISTRATION

ADMISSIONS CONTACT: GAIL HAFER, COORDINATOR OF GRADUATE BUSINESS PROGRAMS
ADDRESS: COLLEGE OF BUSINESS ADMINISTRATION, ROOM 212C, 2500 CALIFORNIA PLAZA, OMAHA, NE 68178
PHONE: 402-280-2853 • FAX: 402-280-2172
E-MAIL: COBAGRAD@CREIGHTON.EDU
WEBSITE: COBWEB.CREIGHTON.EDU

GENERAL INFORMATION

Type of school: Private **Affiliation:** Roman Catholic **Academic calendar:** 08-07

STUDENTS

Enrollment of parent institution: 6,723 **Enrollment of MBA program:** 118 **% male/female:** 58/42 **% part-time:** 84 **% minorities:** 1 **% international:** 31 **Average age at entry:** 25 **Average years work experience at entry:** 3

ACADEMICS

Student/raculty ratio: 2:1 **% female faculty:** 10

Joint degrees: Master of Business Administration/Juris Doctor (3 years); Master of Business Administration/Doctor of Pharmacy (4 years; Master of Business Administration/Master of International Relations (3 years); Master of Business Administration/Master of Science-Inf.

FINANCIAL FACTS

Annual tuition: $10,206 **Fees:** $764 **Books and supplies:** $1,600 **Room & board (on/off-campus):** $7,000/$6,000

% of students receiving aid: 15 **% of first-year students receiving aid:** 8 **Average award package:** $19,653

ADMISSIONS

Admissions Selectivity Rating: 60*

# of applications received: 24 **% applicants accepted:** 96 **% acceptees attending:** 78 **Average GMAT:** 570 **Average GPA:** 3.4 **TOEFL required of international applicants?** Yes **Minimum TOEFL (paper/computer):** 550/213 **Application fee:** $40 **International application fee:** $40

Early decision program? No **Deferment available?** Yes **Maximum length of deferment:** 1 year **Transfer students accepted?** Yes **Transfer application policy:** Maximum of 6 hours considered for transfer from AACSB accredited institution, unless student transferring from another AACSB accredited Jesuit institution in which case more than six hours may be considered for transfer. **Non-fall admissions?** Yes **Need-blind admissions?** No

DePaul University
Kellstadt Graduate School of Business

Admissions Contact: Robert Ryan, Assistant Dean
Address: 1 East Jackson Blvd, Suite 7900, Chicago, IL 60604
Phone: 312-362-8810 • Fax: 312-362-6677
E-mail: kgsb@depaul.edu
Website: kellstadt.depaul.edu

GENERAL INFORMATION

Type of school: Private **Affiliation:** Roman Catholic **Academic calendar:** quarter

STUDENTS

Enrollment of parent institution: 24,448 **Enrollment of MBA program:** 1,646 **% male/female:** 72/28 **% out-of-state:** 41 **% part-time:** 95 **% minorities:** 18 **% international:** 20 **Average age at entry:** 28 **Average years work experience at entry:** 5

ACADEMICS

Student/faculty ratio: 11:1 **% female faculty:** 24 **% minority faculty:** 23

Joint degrees: Master of Business Administration/Doctor of Jurisprudence (MBA/JD): Full-time, part-time; 140 total credits required; 2.8 to 3.8 years to complete program. Any of the concentrations listed for Evening MBA can be selected for this combined degree. **Prominent alumni:** Jim Jenness, CEO, Kellogg's; Richard Driehaus, President, Driehaus Capital Management; Edward Bosowski, President, USG Corporation; Daniel Ustian, Chairman, President and CEO, Navistar Internationa;

FINANCIAL FACTS

Annual tuition: $37,440 **Fees:** $200 **Books and supplies:** $1,500 **Room & board (on-campus):** $12,316

Average award package: $22,400 **Average grant:** $16,080 **Average student loan debt:** $38,500

ADMISSIONS

Admissions Selectivity Rating: 60*

# of applications received: 663 **% applicants accepted:** 64 **% acceptees attending:** 67 **Average GMAT:** 586.5 **Range of GMAT:** 540-630 **Average GPA:** 3.05 **TOEFL required of international applicants?** Yes **Minimum TOEFL (paper/computer):** 550/213

Application fee: $60 **International application fee:** $60 **Application deadline:** 7/1

Early decision program? No **Deferment available?** Yes **Maximum length of deferment:** One year **Transfer students accepted?** Yes **Transfer application policy:** Must apply like any other applicant. **Non-fall admissions?** Yes **Need-blind admissions?** Yes

EMPLOYMENT PROFILE

Average starting salary:................$73,546

Primary Source of Full-time Job Acceptances

School-facilitated activities 9 (50%)

Graduate-facilitated activities 9 (50%)

Grads Employed by Industry:......% avg. salary:

Marketing 25 $68,125

Consulting.....................................31 $83,500

Finance 38 $72,667

Top 5 Employers Hiring Grads

Grant Thornton, Motorola, Northern Trust, Morningstar

Drake University
College of Business and Public Administration

Admissions Contact: Danette Kenne, Director of Graduate Programs
Address: 2507 University Avenue, Aliber Hall, Suite 211, Des Moines, IA 50311
Phone: 515-271-2188 • Fax: 515-271-2187
E-mail: cbpa.gradprograms@drake.edu
Website: www.cbpa.drake.edu/aspx/programs/ProgramDetail.aspx?id=6

GENERAL INFORMATION

Type of school: Private **Academic calendar:** Semester

STUDENTS

Enrollment of parent institution: 5,617 **Enrollment of MBA program:** 167 **% male/female:** 20/80 **% part-time:** 97 **Average age at entry:** 28

ACADEMICS

Student/faculty ratio: 19:1 **% female faculty:** 19 **% minority faculty:** 5

Joint degrees: MBA/Pharm D 6 years, MBA/JD 3 years, MPA/JD 3 years, MPA/Pharm D 6 years. **Prominent alumni:** Robert D, Ray, Former Governor State of Iowa; Sherrill Milnes, Opera; Daniel Jorndt, Former Chairman/CEO Walgreen's; Dwight Opperman, Former CEO of West Publishing; Marie Wilson, President of MS Foundation for Women.

FINANCIAL FACTS

Annual tuition: $9,400 **Fees:** $412 **Books and supplies:** $800 **Room & board (on-campus):** $7,350

ADMISSIONS

Admissions Selectivity Rating: 60*

# of applications received: 98 **% applicants accepted:** 61 **% acceptees attending:** 65 **TOEFL required of international applicants?** Yes **Minimum TOEFL (paper/computer):** 550/213

Application fee: $25 International application fee: $25 Application deadline: 7/6

Early decision program? No Deferment available? Yes Maximum length of deferment: one term Transfer students accepted? Yes Transfer application policy: Case by case evaluation Non-fall admissions? Yes Need-blind admissions? Yes

EASTERN ILLINOIS UNIVERSITY
LUMPKIN COLLEGE OF BUSINESS AND APPLIED SCIENCES

ADMISSIONS CONTACT: DR. JOHN R. WILLEMS, COORDINATOR, GRADUATE BUSINESS STUDIES
ADDRESS: 600 LINCOLN AVENUE, 4025 LUMPKIN HALL, CHARLESTON, IL 61920-3099
PHONE: 217-581-3028 • FAX: 217-581-6642
E-MAIL: MBA@EIU.EDU
WEBSITE: WWW.EIU.EDU/~MBA

GENERAL INFORMATION
Type of school: Public Academic calendar: FA, SP, SU

STUDENTS
Enrollment of parent institution: 12,000 Enrollment of MBA program: 131 % male/female: 61/39 % out-of-state: 3 % part-time: 47 % minorities: 7 % international: 8 Average age at entry: 27 Average years work experience at entry: 5

ACADEMICS
Student/raculty ratio: 22:1 % female faculty: 27 % minority faculty: 23

FINANCIAL FACTS
Annual tuition (in-state/out-of-state): $7,194/$21,582 Fees (in-state/out-of-state): $2,312/$2,312 Books and supplies: $325 Room & board (on/off-campus): $7,298/$8,000

% of students receiving aid: 18 % of first-year students receiving aid: 30 % of students receiving grants: 18 Average grant: $7,560

ADMISSIONS
Admissions Selectivity Rating: 60*

# of applications received: 101 % applicants accepted: 79 % acceptees attending: 85 Average GMAT: 508 Range of GMAT: 450-543 Average GPA: 3.25 TOEFL required of international applicants? Yes Minimum TOEFL (paper/computer): 550/213 Application fee: $30 International application fee: $30

Early decision program? No Deferment available? Yes Maximum length of deferment: 1 academic year Transfer students accepted? Yes Transfer application policy: Maximum of 9 semester hours at grade of B or better. Non-fall admissions? Yes Need-blind admissions? Yes

EMPORIA STATE UNIVERSITY
EMPORIA STATE UNIVERSITY

ADMISSIONS CONTACT: MARY SEWELL, ADMINISTRATIVE SPECIALIST
ADDRESS: 1200 COMMERCIAL STREET, CAMPUS BOX 4003, EMPORIA, KS 66801
PHONE: 620-341-5403 • FAX: 620-341-5909
E-MAIL: MSEWELL@EMPORIA.EDU
WEBSITE: WWW.EMPORIA.EDU

GENERAL INFORMATION
Type of school: Public Academic calendar: Semester and Summer

STUDENTS
Enrollment of parent institution: 6,404 Enrollment of MBA program: 117 % male/female: 50/50 % out-of-state: 2 % part-time: 28 % minorities: 2 % international: 57 Average age at entry: 26

ACADEMICS
Student/raculty ratio: 7:1 % female faculty: 12.5 Prominent alumni: Yasunori Watanabe, TNT Express Worldwide, Inc.; Stephen V. Horner, Ph.D., Asst. Prof., Arkansas State Univ., Jonesboro; Shawn Keough, Ph.D., Assist. Prof., Univ. of Texas at Tyler; Doug Rymph, Ph.D., Asst. Prof., North Dakota State Univ.; Carl Ricketts, Vice President, Missouri Gas Energy,

FINANCIAL FACTS
Annual tuition (in-state/out-of-state): $3,976/$12,028 Fees (in-state/out-of-state): $842/$842 Books and supplies: $1,000 Room & board (on/off-campus): $7,090/$5,620

ADMISSIONS
Admissions Selectivity Rating: 60*

# of applications received: 70 % applicants accepted: 96 % acceptees attending: 60 Average GMAT: 526 Range of GMAT: 490-540 Average GPA: 3.42 TOEFL required of international applicants? No Minimum TOEFL (paper/computer): 550/213 Application fee: $40 International application fee: $75

Early decision program? No Deferment available? Yes Maximum length of deferment: One Year Transfer students accepted? Yes Non-fall admissions? Yes Need-blind admissions? Yes

EMPLOYMENT PROFILE
% grads employed at graduation: 29
% grads employed within three
  months of graduation: 54
Average starting salary:...............$42,500
Primary Source of Full-time Job Acceptances
School-facilitated activities 3 (23%)
Unknown.......................................10 (77%)

Grads Employed by Industry:	......%	avg. salary:
Management	4	NR
Finance	38	$40,000
MIS	4	$45,000
Strategic	4	NR

Top 5 Employers Hiring Grads ....#

Koch Industries (1), Grant Thornton (2), Emporia State University (2), BKD, LLP (1), CBIZ Accounting Tax & Advisory Services, LLC (1)

FAIRLEIGH DICKINSON UNIVERSITY
SILBERMAN COLLEGE OF BUSINESS

ADMISSIONS CONTACT: SUSAN BROOMAN, DIRECTOR OF GRADUATE RECRUITMENT & MARKETING
ADDRESS: FAIRLEIGH DICKINSON UNIVERSITY GRADUATE ADMISSIONS, COLLEGE AT FLORHAM 285 MADISON AVENUE (M-RIO-01), MADISON, NJ 07940
PHONE: 973-443-8905 • FAX: 973-443-8088
E-MAIL: GRAD@FDU.EDU
WEBSITE: WWW.FDU.EDU

GENERAL INFORMATION
Type of school: Private

ACADEMICS
Student/faculty ratio: 20:1 **% female faculty:** 22 **% minority faculty:** 41

Joint degrees: MBA in Management/MA in Corporate and Organizational Communications, 72 credit program. MBA in Human Resource Management/MA in Industrial/Organizational Psychology, 75 credit program. **Prominent alumni:** Cheryl Beebe, VP & CFO, Corn Products International, Inc.; Dennis Strigl, President & COO, Verizon Communications; Robert Huth, President & CEO, David's Bridal; Joseph Mahady, President, Wyeth Pharmaceuticals; John Legere, CEO, Global Crossing Ltd.

FINANCIAL FACTS
Annual tuition: $22,728 **Fees:** $648 **Books and supplies:** $2,000 **Room & board (on-campus):** $9,500
% of students receiving aid: 69 **% of students receiving loans:** 65 **% of students receiving grants:** 9 **Average award package:** $13,500 **Average grant:** $5,222

ADMISSIONS
Admissions Selectivity Rating: 77

TOEFL required of international applicants? Yes **Minimum TOEFL (paper/computer):** 550/213 **Application fee:** $40 **International application fee:** $40

Early decision program? No **Deferment available?** Yes **Maximum length of deferment:** N/A **Transfer students accepted?** Yes **Transfer application policy:** Core courses can be waived by meeting FDU waiver policy. 6 graduate level credits can be transferred from other AACSB schools. **Non-fall admissions?** Yes **Need-blind admissions?** Yes

EMPLOYMENT PROFILE
Average starting salary:................$70,000

Top 5 Employers Hiring Grads

Johnson & Johnson, ADP, Verizon, UBS, Deloitte

FU JEN CATHOLIC UNIVERSITY
COLLEGE OF MANAGEMENT, FU JEN CATHOLIC UNIVERSITY

ADMISSIONS CONTACT: MS. HSIU-HUA SHIH, SECRETARY OF THE COLLEGE
ADDRESS: 510, CHUNG-CHENG ROAD, HSINCHUANG, TAIPEI COUNTY, 242 TAIWAN
PHONE: 886+2-2905-2651 • FAX: 886+2-2905-2186
E-MAIL: 003856@MAIL.FJU.EDU.TW
WEBSITE: WWW.MANAGEMENT.FJU.EDU.TW/

GENERAL INFORMATION
Type of school: Private Affiliation: Catholic

ADMISSIONS
Admissions Selectivity Rating: 60*

TOEFL required of international applicants? No Minimum TOEFL (paper): 550 **Application deadline:** 3/1 **Regular notification:** 5/2

Early decision program? No **Deferment available?** No **Transfer students accepted?** No **Non-fall admissions?** No **Need-blind admissions?** Yes

GEORGE MASON UNIVERSITY
SCHOOL OF MANAGEMENT

ADMISSIONS CONTACT: ANGEL BURGOS, MBA DIRECTOR
ADDRESS: 4400 UNIVERSITY DRIVE, MSN 5A2, ENTERPRISE HALL, ROOM 28, FAIRFAX, VA 22030
PHONE: (703) 993-2136 • FAX: 703-993-1778
E-MAIL: MBA@GMU.EDU
WEBSITE: WWW.SOM.GMU.EDU

GENERAL INFORMATION
Type of school: Public **Academic calendar:** Semester

STUDENTS
Enrollment of parent institution: 30,714 **Enrollment of MBA program:** 342 **% male/female:** 54/46 **% part-time:** 88 **% international:** 28 **Average age at entry:** 29 **Average years work experience at entry:** 5

FINANCIAL FACTS
Annual tuition (in-state/out-of-state): $14,496/$26,112 **Books and supplies:** $1,000

ADMISSIONS
Admissions Selectivity Rating: 60*

# of applications received: 296 **% applicants accepted:** 49 **% acceptees attending:** 68 **Average GMAT:** 580 **Average GPA:** 3.2 **TOEFL required of international applicants?** Yes **Minimum TOEFL (paper/computer):** 650/250 **Application fee:** $60 **International application fee:** $60 **Application deadline:** 4/15 **Regular notification:** 5/15 **Application Deadline/Notification Round 1:** 3/15 / 4/15 **Round 2:** 4/15 / 5/15

Early decision program? No **Deferment available?** No **Transfer students accepted?** No **Non-fall admissions?** Yes **Need-blind admissions?** Yes

GEORGIA COLLEGE & STATE UNIVERSITY
THE J. WHITNEY BUNTING SCHOOL OF BUSINESS

ADMISSIONS CONTACT: MARYLLIS WOLFGANG, DIRECTOR OF GRADUATE ADMISSIONS
ADDRESS: GC&SU CAMPUS BOX 107, MILLEDGEVILLE, GA 31061
PHONE: 478-445-6289 • FAX: 478-445-1336
E-MAIL: MARYLLIS.WOLFGANG@GCSU.EDU
WEBSITE: WWW.GCSU.EDU

GENERAL INFORMATION
Type of school: Public **Academic calendar:** Semester

STUDENTS
Enrollment of parent institution: 6,506 **Enrollment of MBA program:** 153 **% male/female:** 57/43 **% out-of-state:** 16 **% part-time:** 76 **% minorities:** 29 **% international:** 11 **Average age at entry:** 27

ACADEMICS
Student/raculty ratio: 17:1 **% female faculty:** 14 **% minority faculty:** 11

. **Prominent alumni:** Tony Nicely, GEICO, President and CEO; Alex Gregory, YKK Corporation of America, President and CEO; Mike Garrett, Georgia Power Company, President and CEO.

FINANCIAL FACTS
Annual tuition (in-state/out-of-state): $3,942/$15,768 **Fees (in-state/out-of-state):** $930/$930 **Books and supplies:** $1,000 **Room & board (on/off-campus):** $7,048/$7,600

% of students receiving aid: 33 **% of first-year students receiving aid:** 38 **% of students receiving loans:** 22 **% of students receiving grants:** 8 **Average award package:** $8,623 **Average grant:** $4,056

ADMISSIONS
Admissions Selectivity Rating: 60*

# of applications received: 124 **% applicants accepted:** 65 **% acceptees attending:** 61 **Average GMAT:** 499 **Range of GMAT:** 440-550 **TOEFL required of international applicants?** Yes **Minimum TOEFL (paper/computer):** 500/173 **Application fee:** $35

Early decision program? No **Deferment available?** Yes **Maximum length of deferment:** One year **Transfer students accepted?** Yes **Transfer application policy:** Must meet regular admission requirements. Maximum of nine semester hours are transferable if equivalent to GC&SU curriculum. **Non-fall admissions?** Yes **Need-blind admissions?** No

GRENOBLE ECOLE DE MANAGEMENT (FRANCE)
ESC TOULOUSE GRADUATE SCHOOL OF MANAGEMENT

ADMISSIONS CONTACT: DIRECTOR ESC TOULOUSE
ADDRESS: 20, BD LASCROSSES - BP 7010, TOULOUSE, 31068 FRANCE
WEBSITE: WWW.ESC-TOULOUSE.FR

GENERAL INFORMATION
Type of school: Private **Academic calendar:** Trimester

STUDENTS
Enrollment of parent institution: 1,424 **Enrollment of MBA program:** 850 **% male/female:** 52/48 **% part-time:** 0 **% international:** 16 **Average age at entry:** 23 **Average years work experience at entry:** 0

ADMISSIONS
Admissions Selectivity Rating: 60*

# of applications received: 2,500 **% applicants accepted:** 20 **% acceptees attending:** 90 **TOEFL required of international applicants?** No **Application fee:** $99,999 **Application deadline:** 7/30
Early decision program? No **Deferment available?** Yes **Transfer students accepted?** No **Non-fall admissions?** No **Need-blind admissions?** No

EMPLOYMENT PROFILE
Average starting salary:................$175,000

HENDERSON STATE UNIVERSITY
SCHOOL OF BUSINESS ADMINISTRATION

ADMISSIONS CONTACT: MISSIE BELL, GRADUATE SCHOOL ADMINISTRATIVE ASSISTANT
ADDRESS: 1100 HENDERSON STREET, BOX 7802, ARKADELPHIA, AR 71999-0001
PHONE: (870) 230-5126 • FAX: (870) 230-5479
E-MAIL: GRAD@HSU.EDU
WEBSITE: WWW.HSU.EDU/SCHOOLOFBUSINESS/

GENERAL INFORMATION
Type of school: Public

STUDENTS
Enrollment of parent institution: 3,754 **Enrollment of MBA program:** 45 **% male/female:** 50/50 **% out-of-state:** 5 **% part-time:** 25 **% minorities:** 10 **% international:** 20 **Average years work experience at entry:** 0

ACADEMICS
Student/raculty ratio: 6:1 **% female faculty:** 38 .
Prominent alumni: Theresa Brown, Senior Systems Software Analyst; Junious Babbs, Assist. Superintendent of Little Rock School Dist.; Richard Hoover, NASA; Billy Hudson, Professor at Vanderbilt University; Bob Fisher, President of Belmont University.

FINANCIAL FACTS

Annual tuition (in-state/out-of-state): $2,916/$5,832 **Fees (in-state/out-of-state):** $411/$411 **Room & board (on/off-campus):** $3,874/$3,874

ADMISSIONS

Admissions Selectivity Rating: 60*

# of applications received: 19 **% applicants accepted:** 100 % **acceptees attending:** 32 **Average GMAT:** 450 **Range of GMAT:** 390-670 **Average GPA:** 3 **TOEFL required of international applicants?** Yes **Minimum TOEFL (paper/computer):** 550/213 **International application fee:** $40

Early decision program? No **Deferment available?** No **Transfer students accepted?** Yes **Transfer application policy:** 6 hours from an accredited university. **Non-fall admissions?** Yes **Need-blind admissions?** Yes

IE UNIVERSITY
IE BUSIENESS SCHOOL

ADMISSIONS CONTACT: JULIAN TRIGO, ADMISIONSS DIRECTOR
ADDRESS: MARÃ_A DE MOLINA, 11, 13, 15, MADRID, 28006 SPAIN
PHONE: 34915689610 • FAX:
E-MAIL: ADIMISIONSS@IE.EDU
WEBSITE: WWW.IE.EDU

GENERAL INFORMATION

Type of school: Private **Academic calendar:** November-December

STUDENTS

Enrollment of parent institution: 1,800 **Enrollment of MBA program:** 288 **% male/female:** 72/28 **% part-time:** 0 **% international:** 92 **Average age at entry:** 28 **Average years work experience at entry:** 6

ACADEMICS

% female faculty: 33

Joint degrees: Dual Degrees: Supply Chain Management with MIT International Diplomacy with Fletcher School of Law and Diplomacy.

FINANCIAL FACTS

Annual tuition: $62,250 **Fees:** $1,450 **Books and supplies:** $1,750 Room & board (off-campus): $18,000

% of students receiving aid: 30 **% of first-year students receiving aid:** 30 **% of students receiving loans:** 20 **% of students receiving grants:** 25

ADMISSIONS

Admissions Selectivity Rating: 60*

# of applications received: 1,643 **% applicants accepted:** 30 % **acceptees attending:** 58 **Average GMAT:** 680 **TOEFL required of international applicants?** Yes **Minimum TOEFL (paper/computer):** 600/250

Early decision program? No **Deferment available?** Yes **Maximum length of deferment:** 3 intakes **Transfer students accepted?** No **Non-fall admissions?** Yes **Need-blind admissions?** Yes

INCAE
GRADUATE PROGRAM

ADMISSIONS CONTACT: DEAN
ADDRESS: COSTA RICA
WEBSITE: WWW.INCAE.AC.CR

GENERAL INFORMATION

Type of school: Private **Academic calendar:** Trimester

STUDENTS

Enrollment of parent institution: 441 **Enrollment of MBA program:** 441 **% male/female:** 70/30 **% part-time:** 20 **Average age at entry:** 28

ACADEMICS

Student/raculty ratio: 15:1

FINANCIAL FACTS

Annual tuition: $11,500

% of students receiving aid: 3

ADMISSIONS

Admissions Selectivity Rating: 60*

# of applications received: 530 **% applicants accepted:** 60 % **acceptees attending:** 37 **TOEFL required of international applicants?** No **Application fee:** $50 **Application deadline:** 7/15

Early decision program? No **Deferment available?** Yes **Maximum length of deferment:** 9999 **Transfer students accepted?** No **Non-fall admissions?** No **Need-blind admissions?** No

EMPLOYMENT PROFILE

Average starting salary:................$53,000

INDIANA UNIVERSITY NORTHWEST
SCHOOL OF BUSINESS AND ECONOMICS

ADMISSIONS CONTACT: JOHN GIBSON, DIRECTOR, GRADUATE AND UNDERGRADUATE PROGRAMS IN BUSINESS
ADDRESS: 3400, BROADWAY, GARY, IN 46408-1197
PHONE: 219-980-6635 • FAX: 219-980-6916
E-MAIL: JAGIBSON@IUN.EDU
WEBSITE: WWW.IUN.EDU/~BUSNW

GENERAL INFORMATION

Type of school: Public **Academic calendar:** Semester

STUDENTS

Enrollment of parent institution: 4,300 **Enrollment of MBA program:** 115 **% male/female:** 100/0 **% out-of-state:** 0 **% part-time:** 99 **Average age at entry:** 35

ACADEMICS

Student/raculty ratio: 10:1 **% female faculty:** 26 **% minority faculty:** 37

FINANCIAL FACTS

Annual tuition (in-state/out-of-state): $4,300/$10,000 **Books and supplies:** $999

% of students receiving loans: 30 **% of students receiving grants:** 1

ADMISSIONS

Admissions Selectivity Rating: 64

# of applications received: 50 % **applicants accepted:** 70 % **acceptees attending:** 100 **Average GMAT:** 470 **TOEFL required of international applicants?** Yes **Minimum TOEFL (paper/computer):** 550/213 **Application fee:** $25 **International application fee:** $55 **Application Deadline/Notification Round 1:** 1/1 / 1/5 **Round 2:** 5/1 / 5/5 **Round 3:** 8/1 / 8/15

Early decision program? No **Deferment available?** Yes **Maximum length of deferment:** One year **Transfer students accepted?** Yes **Transfer application policy:** Must be a student in Good Standing from an accredtied institution. Up to six credit hours may transfer in if the grade is B or beter. **Non-fall admissions?** Yes **Need-blind admissions?** Yes

EMPLOYMENT PROFILE

Average starting salary:...............$60,000

Primary Source of Full-time Job Acceptances

School-facilitated activities ....NR (25%)

Graduate-facilitated activities ....NR (65%)

Unknown.......................................NR (10%)

INDIANA UNIVERSITY—PURDUE UNIVERSITY AT FORT WAYNE
SCHOOL OF BUSINESS AND MANAGEMENT

ADMISSIONS CONTACT: SANDY FRANKE, SECRETARY, MBA PROGRAM
ADDRESS: NEFF 366, 2101 COLISEUM BOULEVARD EAST, FORT WAYNE, IN 46805-1499
PHONE: 260-481-6498 • FAX:
E-MAIL: EMAIL@SCHOOL.EDU
WEBSITE: WWW.IPFW.EDU/BMS/MBA1.HTM

GENERAL INFORMATION

Type of school: Public **Academic calendar:** Semester

STUDENTS

Enrollment of parent institution: 10,749 **Enrollment of MBA program:** 191 **% male/female:** 65/35 **% part-time:** 91 **Average age at entry:** 32

ACADEMICS

Student/raculty ratio: 1:1

ADMISSIONS

Admissions Selectivity Rating: 60*

# of applications received: 45 % **applicants accepted:** 91 % **acceptees attending:** 95 **TOEFL required of international applicants?** No **Application fee:** $30 **Application deadline:** 7/15 **Regular notification:** 1/1

Early decision program? No **Deferment available?** Yes **Maximum length of deferment:** 1 **Transfer students accepted?** No **Non-fall admissions?** Yes **Need-blind admissions?** No

INSTITUTO TECNOLOGICO Y DE ESTUDIOS SUPERIORES DE MONTERREY (ITESM)
EGADE, MONTERREY CAMPUS

ADMISSIONS CONTACT: LIC. OLGA RENÉ DE LA TORRE, ACADEMIC SERVICES DIRECTOR
ADDRESS: AV. FUNDADORES Y RUFINO TAMAYO, COL. VALLE ORIENTE, SAN PEDRO GARZA GARCÃ_A, NL 66269 MEXICO
PHONE: 011-52-818-625-6204 • FAX: 818-625-6208
E-MAIL: ADMISIONES.EGADE@ITESM.MX
WEBSITE: WWW.EGADE.ITESM.MX

GENERAL INFORMATION

Type of school: Private **Academic calendar:** quarter

STUDENTS

Enrollment of parent institution: 19,358 **Enrollment of MBA program:** 597 **% male/female:** 79/21 **% part-time:** 90 **% international:** 66 **Average age at entry:** 28 **Average years work experience at entry:** 5

ACADEMICS

Student/raculty ratio: 14:1 **% female faculty:** 25

Joint degrees: Double Degree MBA (1 year more than the regular length). **Prominent alumni:** Eugenio Clariond Reyes-Retana, General Director of IMSA Group; Fernando Canales Clariond, Ministery of Economic Affairs, Mexico Government; Jose Antonio Rivero Larrea, President of Administration Board, Autlan Group; Jose Antonio Fernandez Carbajal, General Director of FEMSA Group; Luis Sada Gonzalez, General Director of John Deere Mexico.

FINANCIAL FACTS

Annual tuition: $17,500 **Books and supplies:** $780 **Room & board (on/off-campus):** $7,800/$6,400

% of students receiving aid: 26 **% of first-year students receiving aid:** 24 **% of students receiving loans:** 3 **% of students receiving grants:** 23 **Average grant:** $11,375

ADMISSIONS

Admissions Selectivity Rating: 82

# of applications received: 199 % **applicants accepted:** 73 % **acceptees attending:** 74 **Average GMAT:** 615 **Average GPA:** 3.5 **TOEFL required of international applicants?** No **Application fee:** $115 **International application fee:** $115 **Application deadline:** 5/1 **Regular notification:** 6/1

Early decision program? No **Deferment available?** Yes **Maximum length of deferment:** 1 year **Transfer students accepted?** Yes **Transfer application policy:** The applicant has to fulfill all of the admission requisites **Non-fall admissions?** Yes **Need-blind admissions?** No

EMPLOYMENT PROFILE

Grads Employed by Industry:......% avg. salary:

Marketing ....12 NR

Operations....................................25 NR

Finance ....38 NR

Strategic ....6 NR

IOWA STATE UNIVERSITY
COLLEGE OF BUSINESS

ADMISSIONS CONTACT: AMY HUTTER, DIRECTOR, MBA RECRUITMENT & MARKETING
ADDRESS: 1360 GERDIN BUSINESS BUILDING, AMES, IA 50011
PHONE: 515-294-8118 • FAX: 515-294-2446
E-MAIL: BUSGRAD@IASTATE.EDU
WEBSITE: WWW.BUS.IASTATE.EDU/MBA

GENERAL INFORMATION

Type of school: Public Academic calendar: Semester

STUDENTS

Enrollment of parent institution: 26,380 Enrollment of MBA program: 94 % male/female: 62/38 % out-of-state: 8 % part-time: 62 % international: 31 Average age at entry: 26 Average years work experience at entry: 3

ACADEMICS

Student/raculty ratio: 4:1 % female faculty: 9 % minority faculty: 12

Joint degrees: MBA/MS in Statistics, 72 cr. hrs., 3 years; MBA/MS in Community and Regional Planning, 73 cr. hrs., 3 years; MBA/BS in engineering, 5 years.

FINANCIAL FACTS

Annual tuition (in-state/out-of-state): $7,718/$18,132 Fees: $930 Books and supplies: $1,000 Room & board (on/off-campus): $10,200/$10,200

% of students receiving aid: 50 % of first-year students receiving aid: 50 Average award package: $8,120 Average grant: $1

ADMISSIONS

Admissions Selectivity Rating: 60*

# of applications received: 210 % applicants accepted: 69 % acceptees attending: 65 Average GMAT: 595 Average GPA: 3.41 TOEFL required of international applicants? Yes Minimum TOEFL (paper/computer): 600/250 Application fee: $30 International application fee: $70

Early decision program? No Deferment available? Yes Maximum length of deferment: One year Transfer students accepted? No Non-fall admissions? Yes Need-blind admissions? Yes

EMPLOYMENT PROFILE

% grads employed at graduation: 75

% grads employed within three

months of graduation: 94

Average starting salary:...............$57,848

Primary Source of Full-time Job Acceptances

School-facilitated activities 23 (69%)

Graduate-facilitated activities 12 (31%)

Unknown......................................35 (10%)

Grads Employed by Industry:......% avg. salary:

Marketing 11 $61,667

Operations....................................33 $53,000

Consulting....................................6 $68,000

Management 14 $43,500

Finance 21 $51,800

HR...3 NR

MIS 12 $74,500

JACKSON STATE UNIVERSITY
SCHOOL OF BUSINESS

ADMISSIONS CONTACT: JESSE PENNINGTON, DIRECTOR OF GRADUATE PROGRAMS
ADDRESS: PO BOX 18660, JACKSON, MI 39217
PHONE: 601-432-6315 • FAX: 601-987-4380
E-MAIL: GADMAPPL@CCAIX.JSUMS.EDU
WEBSITE: CCAIX.JSUMS.EDU/BUSINESS/

GENERAL INFORMATION

Type of school: Public Academic calendar: Semester

STUDENTS

Enrollment of parent institution: 6,292 Enrollment of MBA program: 1,104 Average years work experience at entry: 0

FINANCIAL FACTS

Annual tuition (in-state/out-of-state): $1,920/$2,378

% of students receiving aid: 8

ADMISSIONS

Admissions Selectivity Rating: 60*

# of applications received: 160 % applicants accepted: 77 % acceptees attending: 89 TOEFL required of international applicants? Yes Minimum TOEFL (paper): 525

Early decision program? No Deferment available? Yes Maximum length of deferment: text field Transfer students accepted? No Non-fall admissions? No Need-blind admissions? No

EMPLOYMENT PROFILE

Average starting salary:...............$30,000

JAMES MADISON UNIVERSITY
COLLEGE OF BUSINESS

ADMISSIONS CONTACT: KRISTA D. DOFFLEMYER, ADMINISTRATIVE ASSISTANT
ADDRESS: ZANE SHOWKER HALL, MSC 0206, ROOM 616, HARRISONBURG, VA 22807 • PHONE: 540-568-3253 • FAX: 540-568-3587
E-MAIL: MBA@JMU.EDU
WEBSITE: WWW.JMU.EDU/COB/MBA

GENERAL INFORMATION

Type of school: Public Academic calendar: Aug-July

STUDENTS

Enrollment of parent institution: 18,971 **Enrollment of MBA program:** 67 % male/female: 69/31 % out-of-state: 18 % part-time: 75 % international: 29 **Average age at entry:** 30 **Average years work experience at entry:** 7

ACADEMICS

Student/raculty ratio: 18:1 % female faculty: 25 % minority faculty: 25

Joint degrees: None. **Prominent alumni:** George Temidas, Director Security Division IBM; Marcus Cutts, Director Security Division Federal Reserve Bank Sy

FINANCIAL FACTS

Annual tuition (in-state/out-of-state): $7,320/$21,360 **Books and supplies:** $5,676

% of students receiving aid: 77 % of first-year students receiving aid: 90 % of students receiving loans: 46 % of students receiving grants: 44 **Average award package:** $5,456 **Average grant:** $5,330 **Average student loan debt:** $14,265

ADMISSIONS

Admissions Selectivity Rating: 60*

# of applications received: 35 % applicants accepted: 49 % acceptees attending: 76 **Average GMAT:** 550 **Range of GMAT:** 530–760 **Average GPA:** 3.3 **TOEFL required of international applicants?** Yes **Minimum TOEFL (paper/computer):** 550/100 **Application fee:** $55 **International application fee:** $55 **Application deadline:** 7/1

Early decision program? No **Deferment available?** Yes **Maximum length of deferment:** 1 year **Transfer students accepted?** Yes **Transfer application policy:** Can transfer up to 9 credit hours from another AACSB accredited MBA program. **Non-fall admissions?** No **Need-blind admissions?** No

EMPLOYMENT PROFILE

Average starting salary:...............$75,000

KANSAS STATE UNIVERSITY
COLLEGE OF BUSINESS ADMINISTRATION

ADMISSIONS CONTACT: LYNN WAUGH, GRADUATE STUDIES ASSISTANT
ADDRESS: 107 CALVIN HALL, MANHATTAN, KS 66506-0501
PHONE: 785-532-7190 • FAX: 785-532-7809
E-MAIL: LWAUGH@KSU.EDU
WEBSITE: WWW.CBA.KSU.EDU

GENERAL INFORMATION

Type of school: Public **Academic calendar:** Semesters

STUDENTS

Enrollment of MBA program: 91 % male/female: 70/30 % out-of-state: 4 % part-time: 18 % minorities: 9 % international: 22 **Average age at entry:** 24 **Average years work experience at entry:** 2

ACADEMICS

Student/raculty ratio: 5:1 % female faculty: 22 % minority faculty: 4

FINANCIAL FACTS

Annual tuition (in-state/out-of-state): $6,855/$19,340 **Fees (in-state/out-of-state):** $666/$666 **Books and supplies:** $1,000 **Room & board (on/off-campus):** $5,000/$6,000

% of students receiving aid: 18 % of first-year students receiving aid: 12 **Average grant:** $2,500

ADMISSIONS

Admissions Selectivity Rating: 60*

# of applications received: 86 % applicants accepted: 40 % acceptees attending: 100 **Average GMAT:** 548 **Range of GMAT:** 500–660 **Average GPA:** 3.4 **TOEFL required of international applicants?** Yes **Minimum TOEFL (paper/computer):** 550/213 **Application fee:** $60 **International application fee:** $60 **Application deadline:** 6/1 **Regular notification:** 7/15

Early decision program? No **Deferment available?** Yes **Maximum length of deferment:** 1 year **Transfer students accepted?** Yes **Transfer application policy:** KSU will accept up to 9 grad credit hours from an AACSB accredited institution **Non-fall admissions?** No **Need-blind admissions?** Yes

EMPLOYMENT PROFILE

Average starting salary:	$42,000
Grads Employed by Industry:	% avg. salary:
Marketing	8 $42,000
Consulting	22 $42,000
Finance	30 $46,000
HR	8 $52,000
MIS	8 $55,000
Communications	8 $57,000
Entrepreneurship	8 $38,000

LA SALLE UNIVERSITY
SCHOOL OF BUSINESS ADMINISTRATION

ADMISSIONS CONTACT: KATHY BAGNELL, DIRECTOR, MARKETING AND GRADUATE
  ENROLLMENT
ADDRESS: 1900 WEST OLNEY AVENUE, PHILADELPHIA, PA 19141
PHONE: 215-951-1057 • FAX: 215-951-1886
E-MAIL: EMAIL@SCHOOL.EDU
WEBSITE: WWW.LASALLE.EDU/ACADEM/SBA/GRAD/INDEX.SHTML

GENERAL INFORMATION

Type of school: Private **Academic calendar:** Trimester

STUDENTS

Enrollment of parent institution: 5,408 **Enrollment of MBA program:** 687 % male/female: 59/41 % part-time: 90 % minorities: 12 % international: 11 **Average age at entry:** 32

FINANCIAL FACTS

Annual tuition: $12,800 **Fees:** $85

ADMISSIONS

Admissions Selectivity Rating: 60*

# of applications received: 142 % applicants accepted: 85 %

acceptees attending: 89 **TOEFL required of international applicants?** Yes **Minimum TOEFL (paper):** 550 **Application fee:** $35 **Application deadline:** 8/14

Early decision program? No **Deferment available?** Yes **Maximum length of deferment:** 99999 **Transfer students accepted?** No **Non-fall admissions?** Yes **Need-blind admissions?** No

LEHIGH UNIVERSITY
COLLEGE OF BUSINESS AND ECONOMICS

ADMISSIONS CONTACT: CORINN MCBRIDE, DIRECTOR OF RECRUITMENT AND ADMISSIONS
ADDRESS: 621 TAYLOR STREET, BETHLEHEM, PA 18015
PHONE: 610-758-3418 • FAX: 610-758-5283
E-MAIL: MBA.ADMISSIONS@LEHIGH.EDU
WEBSITE: WWW.LEHIGH.EDU/MBA

GENERAL INFORMATION
Type of school: Private **Academic calendar:** Semester

STUDENTS
Enrollment of parent institution: 6,845 **Enrollment of MBA program:** 279 **% male/female:** 65/35 **% part-time:** 83 **% minorities:** 4 **% international:** 37 **Average age at entry:** 32 **Average years work experience at entry:** 7

ACADEMICS
Student/faculty ratio: 6:1 **% female faculty:** 20 **% minority faculty:** 27

Joint degrees: MBA & Engineering (MBA & E), 45 Credit Hours; MBA & Educational Leadership (MBA/MEd.), 45 Credit Hours. **Prominent alumni:** Dexter Baker, Ret. Chairman & CEO, Air Products & Chemicals; Stephen A. Riordan, Editor, Boston Globe; William H. Glenn, VP. Finance, CFO Dresser Rand Co; E. Joseph Hochreiter, Chairman and CEO M Cubed Technolgies, Inc; John E. McGlade, President & CEO, Air Products and Chemicals.

FINANCIAL FACTS
Annual tuition: $11,340 **Fees:** $300 **Books and supplies:** $1,300 Room & board (off-campus): $10,800

% of students receiving aid: 8 **% of first-year students receiving aid:** 15 **Average award package:** $24,260 **Average grant:** $11,000

ADMISSIONS
Admissions Selectivity Rating: 60*

# of applications received: 253 **% applicants accepted:** 61 % acceptees attending: 77 **Average GMAT:** 633 **Range of GMAT:** 590–670 **Average GPA:** 3.33 **TOEFL required of international applicants?** Yes **Minimum TOEFL (paper/computer):** 600/250 **Application fee:** $65 **International application fee:** $65 **Application deadline:** 5/1

Early decision program? No **Deferment available?** Yes **Maximum length of deferment:** one year **Transfer students accepted?** Yes **Transfer application policy:** Six credits from an AACSB accredited school **Non-fall admissions?** Yes **Need-blind admissions?** Yes

EMPLOYMENT PROFILE
% grads employed at graduation: 77

% grads employed within three months of graduation: 15
Average starting salary:...............$76,000
Primary Source of Full-time Job Acceptances
School-facilitated activities 4 (33%)
Graduate-facilitated activities 2 (17%)
Unknown.......................................6 (50%)
Grads Employed by Industry:.......% avg. salary:
Operations.....................................34 $75,666
Consulting.....................................8 NR
Finance 50 $82,600
Top 5 Employers Hiring Grads ....#
BlackRock (1), Bristol-Myers Squibb (1), CHEP (1), Procter & Gamble (1), MasterFoods (1)

LOUISIANA STATE UNIVERSITY— SHREVEPORT
COLLEGE OF BUSINESS ADMINISTRATION

ADMISSIONS CONTACT: SUSAN WOOD, MBA DIRECTOR
ADDRESS: ONE UNIVERSITY PLACE, SHREVEPORT, LA 71115
PHONE: 318-797-5213 • FAX: 318-797-5017
E-MAIL: SWOOD@PILOT.LSUS.EDU
WEBSITE: WWW.LSUS.EDU/BA/MBA/

GENERAL INFORMATION
Type of school: Public **Academic calendar:** Semester

STUDENTS
Enrollment of parent institution: 4,237 **Enrollment of MBA program:** 150 **% male/female:** 47/53 **% part-time:** 93 **% minorities:** 10 **% international:** 5 **Average years work experience at entry:** 0

ACADEMICS
Student/faculty ratio: 20:1

FINANCIAL FACTS
Annual tuition (in-state/out-of-state): $3,245/$9,420
% of students receiving aid: 60

ADMISSIONS
Admissions Selectivity Rating: 63

# of applications received: 70 **% applicants accepted:** 71 % acceptees attending: 80 **TOEFL required of international applicants?** Yes **Minimum TOEFL (paper):** 550 **Application fee:** $10 **Application deadline:** 6/30

Early decision program? No **Deferment available?** No **Transfer students accepted?** No **Non-fall admissions?** Yes **Need-blind admissions?** No

EMPLOYMENT PROFILE
Average starting salary:...............$40,000

Louisiana Tech University
College of Business

ADMISSIONS CONTACT: DR. DOUG AMYX, ASSOCIATE DEAN OF GRADUATE
STUDIES
ADDRESS: PO BOX 10318, RUSTON, LA 71272
PHONE: 318-257-4528 • FAX: 318-257-4253
E-MAIL: GSCHOOL@CAB.LATECH.EDU
WEBSITE: WWW.CAB.LATECH.EDU

GENERAL INFORMATION

Type of school: Public Academic calendar: quarter

STUDENTS

Enrollment of parent institution: 10,607 Enrollment of MBA program: 36 % male/female: 67/33 % minorities: 2 % international: 16

ACADEMICS

Student/raculty ratio: 25:1 % female faculty: 22

FINANCIAL FACTS

Annual tuition (in-state/out-of-state): $3,876/$7,456 Fees (in-state/out-of-state): $1,000/$1,000 Books and supplies: $1,000 Room & board (on-campus): $5,400

ADMISSIONS

Admissions Selectivity Rating: 60*

# of applications received: 26 % applicants accepted: 42 % acceptees attending: 73 Average GMAT: 490 Range of GMAT: 460–560 Average GPA: 3.19 TOEFL required of international applicants? Yes Minimum TOEFL (paper/computer): 550/213 Application fee: $30 International application fee: $40 Application deadline: 8/1

Early decision program? No Deferment available? Yes Maximum length of deferment: 1 year Transfer students accepted? Yes Transfer application policy: Can only transfer 6 graduate hours from the university in which you are coming from. Non-fall admissions? Yes Need-blind admissions? No

Marshall University
Lewis College of Business

ADMISSIONS CONTACT: DR. MICHAEL A. NEWSOME, MBA DIRECTOR
ADDRESS: CORBY HALL 217, 400 HAL GREER BOULEVARD, HUNTINGTON, WV
25755-2305
PHONE: 304-696-2613 • FAX: 304-696-3661
E-MAIL: EMAIL@SCHOOL.EDU
WEBSITE: LCOB.MARSHALL.EDU/

GENERAL INFORMATION

Type of school: Public Academic calendar: Semester

STUDENTS

Enrollment of MBA program: 80 % male/female: 40/60 % minorities: 15 % international: 30 Average years work experience at entry: 2

ACADEMICS

Student/raculty ratio: 5:1 % female faculty: 10 % minority faculty: 10

FINANCIAL FACTS

Annual tuition (in-state/out-of-state): $2,020/$5,653 Fees (in-state/out-of-state): $1,100/$1,250 Books and supplies: $1,000 Room & board (off-campus): $4,000

% of students receiving aid: 50 % of first-year students receiving aid: 50

ADMISSIONS

Admissions Selectivity Rating: 60*

# of applications received: 100 % applicants accepted: 84 % acceptees attending: 95 Average GMAT: 530 Average GPA: 3.5 TOEFL required of international applicants? Yes Minimum TOEFL (paper/computer): 525/195 Application fee: $30 International application fee: $25

Early decision program? No Deferment available? No Transfer students accepted? Yes Transfer application policy: When a student's Plan of Study is approved, credit may be transferred with the approval of the Graduate Dean. The work must have been completed at another regionally accredited graduate institution and must be appropriate to the student's program. Grades Non-fall admissions? Yes Need-blind admissions? No

EMPLOYMENT PROFILE

Average starting salary:............$50,000

McNeese State University
MBA Program

ADMISSIONS CONTACT: TAMMY PETTIS, UNIVERSITY ADMISSIONS
ADDRESS: BOX 92495, LAKE CHARLES, LA 70609-2495
PHONE: 337-475-5145 • FAX: 337-475-5189
E-MAIL: INFO@MCNEESE.EDU
WEBSITE: WWW.MCNEESE.EDU/COLLEGES/BUSINESS/MBA

GENERAL INFORMATION

Type of school: Public Academic calendar: Semester

STUDENTS

Enrollment of parent institution: 8,423 Enrollment of MBA program: 98 % male/female: 68/32 % out-of-state: 3 % part-time: 64 % minorities: 1 % international: 36 Average age at entry: 30

ACADEMICS

Student/raculty ratio: 16:1 % female faculty: 1 % minority faculty: 45

Joint degrees: None.

FINANCIAL FACTS

Annual tuition (in-state/out-of-state): $3,097/$9,163 Books and supplies: $1,200 Room & board (on/off-campus): $4,380/$3,600

ADMISSIONS

Admissions Selectivity Rating: 60*

# of applications received: 36 % applicants accepted: 97 % acceptees attending: 51 Average GMAT: 480 Range of GMAT:

250–690 **Average GPA:** 3.6 **TOEFL required of international applicants?** Yes **Minimum TOEFL (paper/computer):** 550/213
Application fee: $20 **International application fee:** $30

Early decision program? No **Deferment available?** Yes **Maximum length of deferment:** 1 year **Transfer students accepted?** Yes
Transfer application policy: No more than 6 hours from AACSB Accreditated School **Non-fall admissions?** Yes **Need-blind admissions?** Yes

MICHIGAN STATE UNIVERSITY
THE ELI BROAD GRADUATE SCHOOL OF MANAGEMENT

ADMISSIONS CONTACT: JEFF MCNISH, DIRECTOR, MBA ADMISSIONS
ADDRESS: FULL-TIME MBA PROGRAM, 215 EPPLEY CENTER, EAST LANSING, MI 48824-1121
PHONE: 517-355-7604 • FAX: 517-353-1649
E-MAIL: MBA@MSU.EDU
WEBSITE: MBA.MSU.EDU

GENERAL INFORMATION
Type of school: Public **Academic calendar:** Semester

STUDENTS
Enrollment of parent institution: 43,401 **Enrollment of MBA program:** 181 **% male/female:** 69/31 **% out-of-state:** 67 **% part-time:** 0 **% minorities:** 14 **% international:** 40 **Average age at entry:** 28 **Average years work experience at entry:** 5

ACADEMICS
Student/raculty ratio: 35:1 **% female faculty:** 20 **% minority faculty:** 5
Joint degrees: JD/MBA Program in conjunction with Michigan State University College of Law (4 year JD/MBA Program) and MBA/Masters in Global Management (MBA/M-GM Program) in conjuction with Thunderbird, School of Global Management. **Prominent alumni:** Matthew Barnhill, SVP, Market Research, BET; Susan Oaks, VP, A.T. Kearney, Inc.; Robert A. Olstein, Chairman, The Olstein Financial Alert Fund; Toichi Takenaka, President & CEO, Takenaka Corp.; Robert A. Chapek, President, Buena Vista Home Entertainment.

FINANCIAL FACTS
Annual tuition (in-state/out-of-state): $17,750/$24,850 **Fees (in-state/out-of-state):** $31/$31 **Books and supplies:** $1,700 **Room & board (on/off-campus):** $7,752/$7,752
% of students receiving aid: 87 **% of first-year students receiving aid:** 90 **% of students receiving loans:** 49 **% of students receiving grants:** 63 **Average award package:** $17,750 **Average grant:** $6,358 **Average student loan debt:** $36,997

ADMISSIONS
Admissions Selectivity Rating: 60*
# of applications received: 594 **% applicants accepted:** 33 **% acceptees attending:** 52 **Average GMAT:** 636 **Range of GMAT:** 580–700 **Average GPA:** 3.3 **TOEFL required of international applicants?** Yes **Minimum TOEFL (paper/computer):** 600/250
Application fee: $85 **International application fee:** $85 **Application**

Deadline/Notification Round 1: 11/1 / 12/18 **Round 2:** 1/9 / 2/23 Round 3: 2/20 / 3/30 Round 4: 4/10 / 5/11

Early decision program? No **Deferment available?** No **Transfer students accepted?** No **Non-fall admissions?** No **Need-blind admissions?** Yes

EMPLOYMENT PROFILE
% grads employed at graduation: 80
% grads employed within three months of graduation: 13
Average starting salary:................$83,588
Primary Source of Full-time Job Acceptances
School-facilitated activities 74 (83%)
Graduate-facilitated activities 15 (17%)
Grads Employed by Industry:.......% avg. salary:
Marketing 18 $82,467
Operations...................................29 $82,606
Consulting...................................15 $89,815
Management ....5 NR
Finance 27 $84,019
HR...3 $76,167
MIS 3 $85,333

Top 5 Employers Hiring Grads (#)
Cummins Inc. (4), Ford Mortor Company (4), Intel Corporation (4), Johnson & Johnson (4), Procter & Gamble (4)

MIDDLE TENNESSEE STATE UNIVERSITY
JENNINGS A. JONES COLLEGE OF BUSINESS

ADMISSIONS CONTACT: TROY A. FESTERVAND, DIRECTOR, GRADUATE BUSINESS STUDIES
ADDRESS: PO BOX 290 BAS N222, MURFREESBORO, TN 37132
PHONE: 615-898-2368 • FAX: 615-904-8491
E-MAIL: GBS@MTSU.EDU
WEBSITE: WWW.MTSU.EDU/~GRADUATE/PROGRAMS/BUAD.HTM

GENERAL INFORMATION
Type of school: Public

STUDENTS
Enrollment of MBA program: 383 **% male/female:** 77/23 **% minorities:** 12 **Average age at entry:** 26

ACADEMICS
Student/raculty ratio: 20:1

FINANCIAL FACTS
Annual tuition (in-state/out-of-state): $2,250/$6,100 **Fees (in-state/out-of-state):** $300/$300 **Books and supplies:** $1,000 **Room & board (on/off-campus):** $2,500/$2,500

ADMISSIONS
Admissions Selectivity Rating: 60*
# of applications received: 231 **% applicants accepted:** 82 %

acceptees attending: 106 **Average GMAT:** 490 **Average GPA:** 3.2 **TOEFL required of international applicants?** Yes **Minimum TOEFL (paper/computer):** 525/197 **Application fee:** $25 **International application fee:** $30 **Application deadline:** 7/1 **Regular notification:** 8/1

Early decision program? No **Deferment available?** Yes **Maximum length of deferment:** varies **Transfer students accepted?** Yes **Transfer application policy:** Depends on courses and programs **Non-fall admissions?** Yes **Need-blind admissions?** No

MISSISSIPPI STATE UNIVERSITY
COLLEGE OF BUSINESS

ADMISSIONS CONTACT: DR. BARBARA SPENCER, DIRECTOR OF GRADUATE STUDIES IN BUSINESS
ADDRESS: P.O.DRAWER 5288, MISSISSIPPI STATE, MS 39762
PHONE: 662-325-1891 • FAX: 662-325-8161
E-MAIL: GSB@COBILAN.MSSTATE.EDU
WEBSITE: WWW.BUSINESS.MSSTATE.EDU/GSB/

GENERAL INFORMATION
Type of school: Public **Academic calendar:** Semester

STUDENTS
Enrollment of parent institution: 17,824 **Enrollment of MBA program:** 75 **% male/female:** 71/29 **% out-of-state:** 26 **% part-time:** 44 **% minorities:** 10 **% international:** 10 **Average age at entry:** 27

ACADEMICS
Student/raculty ratio: 4:1 **% female faculty:** 28 **% minority faculty:** 13

Joint degrees: MBA in Project Management (12 months to 2 years). **Prominent alumni:** John Grisham, Best-selling author; James W. Bagley, Executive Chairman of Board of LAM Research Corporation; Marsha Blackburn, U. S. Congressman, Tennessee's 7th District; Richard C. Adkerson, President and CEO of Freeport McMoRan Copper & Gold, Inc.; John C. Stennis, former U. S. Senator.

FINANCIAL FACTS
Annual tuition (in-state/out-of-state): $7,726/$18,754 **Books and supplies:** $1,500 **Room & board (on/off-campus):** $14,073/$14,073 **% of students receiving aid:** 66 **% of first-year students receiving aid:** 75 **% of students receiving loans:** 32 **% of students receiving grants:** 47 **Average award package:** $15,793 **Average grant:** $3,880 **Average student loan debt:** $11,067

ADMISSIONS
Admissions Selectivity Rating: 60*

# of applications received: 156 **% applicants accepted:** 71 **% acceptees attending:** 68 **Average GMAT:** 521 **Range of GMAT:** 460–560 **Average GPA:** 3.42 **TOEFL required of international applicants?** Yes **Minimum TOEFL (paper/computer):** 575/233 **Application fee:** $30 **International application fee:** $30 **Application deadline:** 7/1

Early decision program? No **Deferment available?** Yes **Maximum length of deferment:** 1 year **Transfer students accepted?** Yes **Transfer application policy:** 6 hours of transfer credit from accredited institutions. **Non-fall admissions?** Yes **Need-blind admissions?** Yes

MORGAN STATE UNIVERSITY
EARL GRAVES SCHOOL OF BUSINESS AND MANAGEMENT

ADMISSIONS CONTACT: , DIRECTOR OF GRADUATE ADMISSIONS
ADDRESS: 1700 EAST COLD SPRING LANE, BALTIMORE, MD 21251
WEBSITE: WWW.MORGAN.EDU/ACADEMICS/SBM/ACADEMIC/SBM.HTM

GENERAL INFORMATION
Type of school: Public **Academic calendar:** Semester

STUDENTS
Enrollment of parent institution: 5,900 **Enrollment of MBA program:** 103 **% part-time:** 100 **Average years work experience at entry:** 0

ACADEMICS
Student/raculty ratio: 12:1

FINANCIAL FACTS
Room & board (on-campus): $2,990

ADMISSIONS
Admissions Selectivity Rating: 60*

TOEFL required of international applicants? Yes **Minimum TOEFL (paper):** 600 **Application fee:** $20

Early decision program? No **Deferment available?** Yes **Maximum length of deferment:** n/a **Transfer students accepted?** No **Non-fall admissions?** No **Need-blind admissions?** No

MURRAY STATE UNIVERSITY
COLLEGE OF BUSINESS AND PUBLIC AFFAIRS

ADMISSIONS CONTACT: DR. GERRY NKOMBO MUUKA, ASSISTANT DEAN AND MBA DIRECTOR
ADDRESS: 109 BUSINESS BUILDING, GRADUATE ADMISSIONS OFFICE, SPARKS HALL, MURRAY, KY 42071
PHONE: 270-762-6970 • FAX: 270-762-3482
E-MAIL: CBPA@MURRAYSTATE.EDU
WEBSITE: WWW.MURSUKY.EDU/QACD/CBPA/MBA/INDEX.HTM

GENERAL INFORMATION
Type of school: Public **Academic calendar:** Semester

STUDENTS
Enrollment of parent institution: 9,000 **Enrollment of MBA program:** 160 **% part-time:** 53 **Average age at entry:** 31

ACADEMICS
Student/raculty ratio: 20:1

FINANCIAL FACTS
Annual tuition (in-state/out-of-state): $4,185/$11,700 **Room & board (on-campus):** $3,800

ADMISSIONS
Admissions Selectivity Rating: 60*

# of applications received: 121 **% applicants accepted:** 75 **% acceptees attending:** 52 **TOEFL required of international applicants?** Yes **Minimum TOEFL (paper):** 525 **Application fee:** $25

Early decision program? No **Deferment available?** Yes **Maximum length of deferment: 000 Transfer students accepted?** Yes **Transfer application policy:** none **Non-fall admissions?** Yes **Need-blind admissions?** No

NANYANG TECHNOLOGICAL UNIVERSITY
NANYANG BUSINESS SCHOOL

ADMISSIONS CONTACT: ASSOCIATE PROFESSOR OOI LEE LEE, DIRECTOR (MBA)
ADDRESS: THE NANYANG MBA, NANYANG BUSINESS SCHOOL, NANYANG AVENUE, BLK S3, B3A, SINGAPORE, 639798 SINGAPORE
PHONE: 011-65-67906183 • FAX: 011-65-67913561
E-MAIL: NBSMBA@NTU.EDU.SG
WEBSITE: WWW.NANYANGMBA.NTU.EDU.SG

GENERAL INFORMATION
Type of school: Public

STUDENTS
Enrollment of parent institution: 28,949 **Enrollment of MBA program:** 282 **% male/female:** 72/28 **% part-time:** 34 **% international:** 81 **Average age at entry:** 31 **Average years work experience at entry:** 7

ACADEMICS
Student/faculty ratio: 2:1 **% female faculty:** 27
Joint degrees: NTU-Waseda Double MBA, full time, 12 months; NTU-St Gallen Double MBA, full time, 18 months; NTU-ESSEC Double MBA, full time, 18 months. **Prominent alumni:** Ms. Jill Lee, Senior Executive Vice President & CFO, Siemens Ltd; Mr. Yeo Tiong Eng, Sr Reg Financial Dir, Molex Far East South Mgt P/L; Ms. Elsie Sim, GM, Sales & Operations, Shell Eastern Petroleum; Mr. Terence Chan, CEO, CAD-IT Consultants (Asia) Pte Ltd; Mr. Chew Hong Gian, Executive VP & Head of Operations, S'pore Exchange.

FINANCIAL FACTS
Annual tuition: $19,000 **Books and supplies:** $5,000 **Room & board (on/off-campus):** $7,000/$10,000
% of students receiving grants: 9 **Average grant:** $17,300

ADMISSIONS
Admissions Selectivity Rating: 92
# of applications received: 904 **% applicants accepted:** 30 % **acceptees attending:** 62 **Average GMAT:** 652 **Range of GMAT:** 610-690 **TOEFL required of international applicants?** Yes **Minimum TOEFL (paper/computer):** 600/250 **Application fee:** $35 **International application fee:** $35 **Application deadline:** 3/31 **Regular notification:** 4/30
Early decision program? No **Deferment available?** Yes **Maximum length of deferment:** 1 year **Transfer students accepted?** Yes **Transfer application policy:** Reviewed on a case-by-case basis **Non-fall admissions?** Yes **Need-blind admissions?** No

EMPLOYMENT PROFILE
% grads employed at graduation: 51
% grads employed within three months of graduation: 40

Average starting salary:................$57,797
Primary Source of Full-time Job Acceptances
School-facilitated activities 45 (76%)
Graduate-facilitated activities 14 (24%)
Grads Employed by Industry:......% avg. salary:
Marketing ....15 NR
Operations....................................12 NR
Consulting....................................6 NR
Management ....4 NR
Finance ....57 NR
MIS..2 NR
Top 5 Employers Hiring Grads (#)
Cisco Systems (2), OCBC Bank (2), PricewaterhouseCoopers (2), ABN Amro Bank (1), Bain & Company (1)

NICHOLLS STATE UNIVERSITY
COLLEGE OF BUSINESS ADMINISTRATION

ADMISSIONS CONTACT: BECKY LEBLANC-DUROCHER, DIRECTOR OF ADMISSIONS
ADDRESS: PO BOX 2004, THIBODAUX, LA 70310
PHONE: 877-642-4655 • FAX: 985-448-4929
E-MAIL: ESAI-BL@NICHOLLS.EDU
WEBSITE: WWW.NICHOLLS.EDU

GENERAL INFORMATION
Type of school: Public **Academic calendar:** Semester

STUDENTS
Enrollment of parent institution: 7,482 **Enrollment of MBA program:** 116 **% male/female:** 49/51 **% out-of-state:** 1 **% part-time:** 59 **% minorities:** 6 **% international:** 12 **Average years work experience at entry:** 0

ACADEMICS
Student/faculty ratio: 15:1 **% female faculty:** 19
. **Prominent alumni:** Barry Melancon, President, AICPA; John Weimer, Justice, Louisiana Supreme Court; Billy Tauzin, U.S. Representative;

FINANCIAL FACTS
Annual tuition (in-state/out-of-state): $3,075/$8,523 **Books and supplies:** $2,000 **Room & board (on-campus):** $4,584
% of students receiving aid: 20 **Average grant:** $4,000

ADMISSIONS
Admissions Selectivity Rating: 60*
# of applications received: 70 **% applicants accepted:** 99 % **acceptees attending:** 57 **Average GMAT:** 486 **Average GPA:** 3.1 **TOEFL required of international applicants?** Yes **Minimum TOEFL (paper/computer):** 550/213 **Application fee:** $20 **International application fee:** $30 **Application deadline:** 7/1
Early decision program? No **Deferment available?** Yes **Maximum length of deferment:** 1 semester **Transfer students accepted?** Yes **Transfer application policy:** Maximum of 9 approved hours may be transferred from an accredited institution. **Non-fall admissions?** Yes **Need-blind admissions?** Yes

NORTH DAKOTA STATE UNIVERSITY
COLLEGE OF BUSINESS ADMINISTRATION

ADMISSIONS CONTACT: PAUL BROWN, MBA DIRECTOR
ADDRESS: PO BOX 5137, FARGO, ND 58018
PHONE: • FAX:
E-MAIL: PAUL.BROWN@NDSU.EDUX
WEBSITE: WWW.NDSU.EDU/CBA/

GENERAL INFORMATION
Type of school: Public

STUDENTS
Enrollment of MBA program: 537 **% male/female:** 60/40 **% part-time:** 89 **% international:** 8 **Average age at entry:** 29

ACADEMICS
Student/raculty ratio: 19:1
Joint degrees: MBA/JD, 105–127 credits (3.5 to 5 years).

FINANCIAL FACTS
Annual tuition (in-state/out-of-state): $4,600/$10,800 **Fees (in-state/out-of-state):** $340/$340

ADMISSIONS
Admissions Selectivity Rating: 60*
# of applications received: 162 **% applicants accepted:** 90 **% acceptees attending:** 80 **TOEFL required of international applicants?** Yes **Minimum TOEFL (paper):** 550 **Application fee:** $35 **Application deadline:** 7/15
Early decision program? No **Deferment available?** Yes **Transfer students accepted?** No **Non-fall admissions?** Yes **Need-blind admissions?** No

NORTHERN ILLINOIS UNIVERSITY, COLLEGE OF BUSINESS
MBA PROGRAMS

ADMISSIONS CONTACT: MONA SALMON, ASSISTANT DIRECTOR
ADDRESS: BARSEMA 203, DEKALB, IL 60115
PHONE: 866-648-6221 • FAX: 815-753-1668
E-MAIL: MBA@NIU.EDU
WEBSITE: WWW.COB.NIU.EDU/MBAPROGRAMS

GENERAL INFORMATION
Type of school: Public

STUDENTS
Enrollment of parent institution: 25,000 **Enrollment of MBA program:** 528 **% male/female:** 100/0 **% part-time:** 99 **Average age at entry:** 32 **Average years work experience at entry:** 9

ACADEMICS
Student/raculty ratio: 24:1 **% female faculty:** 19 **% minority faculty:** 4

FINANCIAL FACTS
Annual tuition (in-state/out-of-state): $8,154/$11,538 **Books and supplies:** $750

ADMISSIONS
Admissions Selectivity Rating: 60*
# of applications received: 262 **% applicants accepted:** 97 **% acceptees attending:** 70 **Average GMAT:** 550 **Average GPA:** 3.2 **TOEFL required of international applicants?** Yes **Minimum TOEFL (paper/computer):** 550/213 **Application fee:** $30 **Application deadline:** 6/1
Early decision program? No **Deferment available?** Yes **Maximum length of deferment:** 24 months **Transfer students accepted?** Yes **Transfer application policy:** For the Evening MBA a limit of 9-semester-hours accepted for phase two credit from AACSB-accredited schools only. **Non-fall admissions?** Yes **Need-blind admissions?** Yes

NYENRODE BUSINESS UNIVERSITEIT
NYENRODE BUSINESS UNIVERSITEIT

ADMISSIONS CONTACT: VICTORIA BRESSERS, HEAD OF ADMISSIONS
ADDRESS: P.O. BOX 130, BREUKELEN, 3620 AC, NETHERLANDS
PHONE: 00 31 346 291 291 • FAX: 00 31 346 291 450
E-MAIL: INFO@NYENRODE.NL
WEBSITE: WWW.NYENRODE.NL

GENERAL INFORMATION
Type of school: Private

STUDENTS
Enrollment of MBA program: 55 **% male/female:** 77/23 **% part-time:** 45 **% international:** 90 **Average age at entry:** 31 **Average years work experience at entry:** 7

ACADEMICS
Student/raculty ratio: 4:1 **% female faculty:** 16
Prominent alumni: Kai Jin, General Manager, Nokia, China; Pierro Overmars, Member of the Board ABN AMRO;

FINANCIAL FACTS
Annual tuition: $44,311 **Books and supplies:** $1,597 **Room & board (on-campus):** $15,000
% of first-year students receiving aid: 20

ADMISSIONS
Admissions Selectivity Rating: 60*
# of applications received: 103 **% applicants accepted:** 29 **Average GMAT:** 560 **TOEFL required of international applicants?** Yes **Minimum TOEFL (paper/computer):** 600/250 **Application fee:** $80 **Application deadline:** 8/31
Early decision program? No **Deferment available?** Yes **Maximum length of deferment:** 2 years **Transfer students accepted?** No **Non-fall admissions?** No **Need-blind admissions?** No

EMPLOYMENT PROFILE
Average starting salary:................$50,000

Primary Source of Full-time Job Acceptances

School-facilitated activities ....4 (NR%)

Unknown..18 (NR%)

Grads Employed by Industry:......% avg. salary:

Marketing ....15 NR

Consulting......................................31 NR

Management ....8 NR

Finance ....31 NR

HR...15 NR

Entrepreneurship............................23 NR

Entrepreneurship............................23 NR

Internet ....15 NR

Quantitative....................................8 NR

OAKLAND UNIVERSITY
SCHOOL OF BUSINESS ADMINSTRATION

*ADMISSIONS CONTACT: PAUL M. TRUMBULL, COORDINATOR OF GRADUATE
BUSINESS PROGRAMS*
ADDRESS: 238 ELLIOTT HALL, ROCHESTER, MI 48309-4493
PHONE: 248-370-3287 • FAX: 248-370-4964
E-MAIL: GBP@LISTS.OAKLAND.EDU
WEBSITE: WWW.SBA.OAKLAND.EDU

GENERAL INFORMATION

Type of school: Public **Academic calendar:** Semester

STUDENTS

Enrollment of parent institution: 18,920 **Enrollment of MBA program:** 387 **% male/female:** 68/32 **% out-of-state:** 5 **% minorities:** 15 **% international:** 5 **Average age at entry:** 28 **Average years work experience at entry:** 7

ACADEMICS

Student/raculty ratio: 19:1 **% female faculty:** 19 **% minority faculty:** 5

Joint degrees: Master of Business Administration/Juris Doctor in partnership with Cooley Law School (5–6 year time limit).

FINANCIAL FACTS

Annual tuition (in-state/out-of-state): $9,709/$16,749 **Books and supplies:** $1,136 **Room & board (on/off-campus):** $7,350/$8,400 **Average grant:** $4,500

ADMISSIONS

Admissions Selectivity Rating: 60*

Average GMAT: 535 **Average GPA:** 3.23 **TOEFL required of international applicants?** Yes **Minimum TOEFL (paper/computer):** 550/213 **Application deadline:** 8/1

Early decision program? No **Deferment available?** Yes **Maximum length of deferment:** 1 year **Transfer students accepted?** Yes **Transfer application policy:** Up to nine credits of relevant course work may be transfered(3.0 or better) **Non-fall admissions?** Yes **Need-blind admissions?** Yes

% grads employed within three months of graduation: 91

Average starting salary:................$78,625

OHIO UNIVERSITY
COLLEGE OF BUSINESS

ADMISSIONS CONTACT: JAN ROSS, ASSISTANT DEAN, GRADUATE PROGRAM
ADDRESS: 514 COPELAND HALL, ATHENS, OH 45701
PHONE: 740-593-4320 • FAX: 740-593-1388
E-MAIL: ROSSJ@OHIO.EDU
WEBSITE: WWW.COB.OHIOU.EDU/GRAD/

GENERAL INFORMATION

Type of school: Public **Academic calendar:** quarters

STUDENTS

Enrollment of parent institution: 19,000 **Enrollment of MBA program:** 119 **% male/female:** 68/32 **% out-of-state:** 67 **% part-time:** 64 **% minorities:** 12 **% international:** 16 **Average age at entry:** 25 **Average years work experience at entry:** 1.5

ACADEMICS

Student/raculty ratio: 4:1 **% female faculty:** 25 **% minority faculty:** 10

Joint degrees: MBA/MSp Ad, 24 months.

FINANCIAL FACTS

Annual tuition (in-state/out-of-state): $12,675/$25,995 **Fees:** $5,000 **Books and supplies:** $4,000 **Room & board (on/off-campus):** $10,000/$10,000

% of students receiving aid: 70 **% of first-year students receiving aid:** 70 **Average award package:** $15,000 **Average grant:** $8,000

ADMISSIONS

Admissions Selectivity Rating: 60*

# of applications received: 180 **% applicants accepted:** 32 **% acceptees attending:** 75 **Average GMAT:** 562 **Range of GMAT:** 480–670 **Average GPA:** 3.3 **TOEFL required of international applicants?** Yes **Minimum TOEFL (paper/computer):** 600/250 **Application fee:** $50 **International application fee:** $50 **Application deadline:** 2/1 **Regular notification:** 4/1

Early decision program? No **Deferment available?** Yes **Maximum length of deferment:** 1 year **Transfer students accepted?** No **Non-fall admissions?** Yes **Need-blind admissions?** Yes

EMPLOYMENT PROFILE

% grads employed at graduation: 58

Average starting salary:................$56,350

Primary Source of Full-time Job Acceptances

School-facilitated activities 13 (25%)

Graduate-facilitated activities 14 (25%)

Unknown..27 (50%)

Grads Employed by Industry:......% avg. salary:

Marketing 53 $56,350

Operations....................................14 $56,350

Consulting....................................3 $56,350

Management 19 $56,350

Finance 11 $56,350

Top 5 Employers Hiring Grads (#)

Deloitte & Touche (2), Ernst & Young (1), KPMG (1)

OKLAHOMA STATE UNIVERSITY
SPEARS SCHOOL OF BUSINESS

ADMISSIONS CONTACT: JANICE ANALLA, ASSISTANT DIRECTOR, GRADUATE PROGRAMS
ADDRESS: OKLAHOMA STATE UNIVERSITY, 102 GUNDERSEN HALL, STILLWATER, OK 74078-4022
PHONE: 405-744-2951 • FAX: 405-744-7474
E-MAIL: SPEARSMASTERS@OKSTATE.EDU
WEBSITE: SPEARS.OKSTATE.EDU/MBA/

GENERAL INFORMATION

Type of school: Public **Academic calendar:** Semester

STUDENTS

Enrollment of MBA program: 445 **% male/female:** 65/35 **% part-time:** 73 **% international:** 24 **Average age at entry:** 27

ACADEMICS

Student/raculty ratio: 25:1 **% female faculty:** 18 **% minority faculty:** 2

Joint degrees: MBA/MSTM - 68 credits (2.5 years) DO/MBA 36 credits (1.5 years/3 semesters), DVM/MBA 36 credits (1.5 years/3 semesters) Dental MBA 36 creditsEntrep.

FINANCIAL FACTS

Annual tuition (in-state/out-of-state): $4,026/$15,652 **Fees (in-state/out-of-state):** $2,466/$2,466 **Books and supplies:** $730 **Room & board (on-campus):** $7,650

ADMISSIONS

Admissions Selectivity Rating: 60*

# of applications received: 208 **% applicants accepted:** 77 **% acceptees attending:** 86 **Average GMAT:** 550 **Range of GMAT:** 490–610 **Average GPA:** 3.24 **TOEFL required of international applicants?** Yes **Minimum TOEFL (paper/computer):** 575/233 **Application fee:** $40 **International application fee:** $75 **Application deadline:** 7/1

Early decision program? No **Deferment available?** Yes **Maximum length of deferment:** 1 yr. **Transfer students accepted?** Yes **Transfer application policy:** They must be a student in good standing at an AACSB accredited university. **Non-fall admissions?** Yes **Need-blind admissions?** Yes

EMPLOYMENT PROFILE

% grads employed at graduation: 83

% grads employed within three

months of graduation: 17

Average starting salary:................$60,000

Primary Source of Full-time Job Acceptances

School-facilitated activities 11 (48%)

Graduate-facilitated activities 9 (39%)

Unknown...3 (13%)

Grads Employed by Industry:......% avg. salary:

Marketing 26 $46,500

Management 4 $50,000

Finance 44 $59,480

THE OPEN UNIVERSITY
THE OPEN UNIVERSITY BUSINESS SCHOOL

ADMISSIONS CONTACT: STUDENT REGISTRATION & ENQUIRY SERVICE,
ADDRESS: THE OPEN UNIVERSITY BUSINESS SCHOOL, THE OPEN UNIVERSITY / PO BOX 197, MILTON KEYNES, MK7 6BJ UNITED KINGDOM OF GREAT BRITAIN AND NORTHERN IRELAND
PHONE: +44 8700100311 • FAX: +44 1908 654806
E-MAIL: OUBS-ILGEN@OPEN.AC.UK
WEBSITE: WWW.OPEN.AC.UK/OUBS/

GENERAL INFORMATION

Type of school: Public **Academic calendar:** Rolling May & November intakes

STUDENTS

Enrollment of parent institution: 5,500 **Enrollment of MBA program:** 2,000 **% male/female:** 65/35 **% part-time:** 100 **Average age at entry:** 37 **Average years work experience at entry:** 14

ACADEMICS

Student/raculty ratio: 16:1

FINANCIAL FACTS

Annual tuition: $19,880

ADMISSIONS

Admissions Selectivity Rating: 60*

# of applications received: 2,000 **% applicants accepted:** 100 **% acceptees attending:** 100 **TOEFL required of international applicants?** No

Early decision program? No **Deferment available?** No **Transfer students accepted?** No **Non-fall admissions?** Yes **Need-blind admissions?** Yes

OREGON STATE UNIVERSITY
COLLEGE OF BUSINESS

ADMISSIONS CONTACT: JIM COAKLEY, MBA PROGRAM COORDINATOR
ADDRESS: 200 BEXELL HALL, COLLEGE OF BUSINESS, CORVALLIS, OR 97331
PHONE: 541-737-3716 • FAX: 541-737-6033
E-MAIL: OSUMBA@BUS.OREGONSTATE.EDU
WEBSITE: HTTP://WWW.BUS.OREGONSTATE.EDU/PROSPECTIVE/MBA.HTM

GENERAL INFORMATION

Type of school: Public **Academic calendar:** quarter

STUDENTS

Enrollment of parent institution: 21,100 **Enrollment of MBA program:** 85 **% male/female:** 62/38 **% out-of-state:** 10 **% part-time:** 35 **% minorities:** 5 **% international:** 19 **Average age at entry:** 27 **Average years work experience at entry:** 3

ACADEMICS

Student/faculty ratio: 3:1 **% female faculty:** 15 **% minority faculty:** 18

FINANCIAL FACTS

Annual tuition (in-state/out-of-state): $10,044/$16,281 **Fees (in-state/out-of-state):** $2,628/$2,628 **Books and supplies:** $1,527 **Room & board (on/off-campus):** $8,208/$8,208 **% of students receiving aid:** 40 **% of students receiving loans:** 25 **% of students receiving grants:** 30 **Average grant:** $822 **Average student loan debt:** $12,734

ADMISSIONS

Admissions Selectivity Rating: 60*

# of applications received: 115 **% applicants accepted:** 77 **% acceptees attending:** 98 **Average GMAT:** 565 **Range of GMAT:** 530–610 **Average GPA:** 3.33 **TOEFL required of international applicants?** Yes **Minimum TOEFL (paper/computer):** 575/233 **Application fee:** $55 **Application deadline:** 8/10

Early decision program? No **Deferment available?** Yes **Maximum length of deferment:** 99 **Transfer students accepted?** Yes **Transfer application policy:** Up to 15 credits of approved coursework (AACSB-accredited) **Non-fall admissions?** Yes **Need-blind admissions?** Yes

EMPLOYMENT PROFILE

% grads employed at graduation: 27

% grads employed within three
  months of graduation: 33

Average starting salary:................$55,000

Primary Source of Full-time Job Acceptances

Unknown..8 (100%)

Grads Employed by Industry:......**% avg. salary:**

Operations.....................................29 $53,000

Consulting.....................................14 $70,000

Management 43 $49,000

Finance 14 $50,000

PACE UNIVERSITY
LUBIN SCHOOL OF BUSINESS

ADMISSIONS CONTACT: SUSAN FORD-GOLDSCHEIN, ASSOCIATE DIRECTOR OF GRADUATE ADMISSION
ADDRESS: ONE PACE PLAZA, EXECUTIVE MBA, NEW YORK, NY 10038
PHONE: (212) 346-1531 • FAX: 212-346-1585
E-MAIL: GRADNYC@PACE.EDU
WEBSITE: WWW.PACE.EDU/LUBIN/

GENERAL INFORMATION

Type of school: Private **Academic calendar:** Semester

STUDENTS

Enrollment of parent institution: 12,704 **Enrollment of MBA program:** 731 **% male/female:** 54/46 **% out-of-state:** 11 **% part-time:** 73 **% minorities:** 9 **% international:** 43 **Average age at entry:** 26 **Average years work experience at entry:** 2

ACADEMICS

Student/faculty ratio: 21:1 **% female faculty:** 13 **% minority faculty:** 36

Joint degrees: Master of Business Administration/Doctor of Jurisprudence (MBA/JD). **Prominent alumni:** Ivan G. Seidenberg, Chairman and CEO Verizon Communications; Joseph R Ficalora, William C. Nelson, Chairman and CEO, Home Box Office; Mel Karmazin, CEO Sirius Satellite Radio Inc.; Marie J. Toulantis, CEO barnesandnoble.com.

FINANCIAL FACTS

Books and supplies: $3,450 **Room & board (on/off-campus):** $11,180/$19,427 **% of students receiving aid:** 59 **% of students receiving loans:** 36 **% of students receiving grants:** 40 **Average award package:** $17,184 **Average grant:** $6,765 **Average student loan debt:** $41,868

ADMISSIONS

Admissions Selectivity Rating: 60*

# of applications received: 988 **% applicants accepted:** 58 **% acceptees attending:** 36 **Average GMAT:** 554 **Range of GMAT:** 520–590 **Average GPA:** 3.21 **TOEFL required of international applicants?** Yes **Minimum TOEFL (paper/computer):** 570/230 **Application fee:** $65 **International application fee:** $65 **Application deadline:** 8/1

Early decision program? No **Deferment available?** No **Transfer students accepted?** Yes **Transfer application policy:** Maximum of 2 courses **Non-fall admissions?** Yes **Need-blind admissions?** Yes

EMPLOYMENT PROFILE

% grads employed at graduation: 32

% grads employed within three
  months of graduation: 6

Average starting salary:................$70,200

Primary Source of Full-time Job Acceptances

School-facilitated activities 47 (38%)

Graduate-facilitated activities 61 (48%)

Unknown..19 (14%)

Grads Employed by Industry:......**% avg. salary:**

Marketing ....9 NR

Operations.....................................3 NR

Consulting......................................2 NR

Management ....9 NR

Finance ....54 NR

HR...1 NR

MIS ....1 NR

Internet ....2 NR

Top 5 Employers Hiring Grads (#)

Pricewaterhouse Coopers (18), Deloitte Touche (5), Ernst & Young (7), KPMG (7), AIG (3)

PENNSYLVANIA STATE UNIVERSITY— GREAT VALLEY CAMPUS
SCHOOL OF GRADUATE PROFESSIONAL STUDIES

ADMISSIONS CONTACT: SUSAN HALDEMAN, GRADUATE ENROLLMENT COORDINATOR
ADDRESS: 30 EAST SWEDESFORD ROAD, MALVERN, PA 19355
PHONE: 610-648-3248 • FAX: 610-725-5296
E-MAIL: GVMBA@PSU.EDU
WEBSITE: WWW.GV.PSU.EDU

GENERAL INFORMATION
Type of school: Public **Academic calendar:** Semester

STUDENTS
Enrollment of parent institution: 2,000 **Enrollment of MBA program:** 340 **% part-time:** 97 **Average age at entry:** 31 **Average years work experience at entry:** 8

ACADEMICS
Student/raculty ratio: 18:1 **% female faculty:** 40 **% minority faculty:** 5

FINANCIAL FACTS
Annual tuition (in-state/out-of-state): $16,752/$27,312 **Fees (in-state/out-of-state):** $600/$600 **Books and supplies:** $4,872 Room & board (off-campus): $20,000

% of students receiving aid: 60 **% of first-year students receiving aid:** 50 **% of students receiving loans:** 60 **% of students receiving grants:** 1 **Average award package:** $4,500 **Average grant:** $15,000 **Average student loan debt:** $8,000

ADMISSIONS
Admissions Selectivity Rating: 72

# of applications received: 115 **% applicants accepted:** 72 **% acceptees attending:** 71 **Average GMAT:** 522 **Average GPA:** 3.23 **TOEFL required of international applicants?** Yes **Minimum TOEFL (paper/computer):** 550/230 **Application fee:** $60 **International application fee:** $60

Early decision program? No **Deferment available?** Yes **Maximum length of deferment:** one year **Transfer students accepted?** Yes **Transfer application policy:** Transfer applicants are encouraged and should submit all application materials, including official transcripts of courses already taken and course descriptions. **Non-fall admissions?** Yes **Need-blind admissions?** Yes

EMPLOYMENT PROFILE

Grads Employed by Industry:......% avg. salary:
Marketing ....6 NR
Operations.....................................8 NR
Consulting.....................................5 NR
Management ....10 NR
Finance ....10 NR
HR..4 NR
MIS...7 NR
Communications ....2 NR
Entrepreneurship............................5 NR
Entrepreneurship............................8 NR
Internet ....2 NR
Nonprofit...2 NR
Quantitative ....2 NR
Strategic ....5 NR
Strategic ....2 NR

PENNSYLVANIA STATE UNIVIVERSITY— HARRISBURG CAMPUS
SCHOOL OF BUSINESS ADMINISTRATION

ADMISSIONS CONTACT: DR. THOMAS STREVELER, DIRECTOR OF ENROLLMENT SERVICES
ADDRESS: 777 WEST HARRISBURG PIKE, UNIVERSITY PARK, PA 17057
PHONE: 717-948-6250 • FAX: 717-948-6325
E-MAIL: HBGADMIT@PSU.EDU
WEBSITE: WWW.HBG.PSU.EDU/SBUS

GENERAL INFORMATION
Type of school: Public **Academic calendar:** Semester

STUDENTS
Enrollment of parent institution: 3,239 **Enrollment of MBA program:** 207 **% male/female:** 64/36 **% out-of-state:** 5 **% part-time:** 88 **% minorities:** 7 **% international:** 5 **Average age at entry:** 27 **Average years work experience at entry:** 3

ACADEMICS
Student/raculty ratio: 12:1

FINANCIAL FACTS
Annual tuition (in-state/out-of-state): $12,000/$17,592 **Books and supplies:** $4,170 **Average grant:** $4,200

ADMISSIONS
Admissions Selectivity Rating: 60*

# of applications received: 76 **% applicants accepted:** 91 **% acceptees attending:** 90 **Average GMAT:** 520 **Average GPA:** 3 **TOEFL required of international applicants?** Yes **Minimum TOEFL (paper/computer):** 550/213 **Application fee:** $50 **International application fee:** $50 **Application deadline:** 7/18

Early decision program? No **Deferment available?** Yes **Maximum length of deferment:** 3 years **Transfer students accepted?** Yes **Transfer application policy:** 10 credits max will transfer **Non-fall admissions?** Yes **Need-blind admissions?** Yes

EMPLOYMENT PROFILE

Average starting salary:................$45,000

PURDUE UNIVERSITY CALUMET
SCHOOL OF MANAGEMENT

ADMISSIONS CONTACT: PAUL MCGRATH, COORDINATOR, GRADUATE MANAGEMENT PROGRAMS
ADDRESS: SCHOOL OF MANAGEMENT, PURDUE UNIVERSITY CALUMET, HAMMOND, IN 46323-2094
PHONE: 219-989-2425 • FAX: 219-989-3158
E-MAIL: PMCGRAT@CALUMET.PURDUE.EDU
WEBSITE: WWW.CALUMET.PURDUE.EDU

GENERAL INFORMATION

Type of school: Public **Academic calendar:** Semester

STUDENTS

Enrollment of parent institution: 9,500 **Enrollment of MBA program:** 213 **Average age at entry:** 28 **Average years work experience at entry:** 5

ACADEMICS

Student/faculty ratio: 10:1 **% female faculty:** 43 **% minority faculty:** 24

FINANCIAL FACTS

Annual tuition (in-state/out-of-state): $4,325/$9,322 **Books and supplies:** $6,000

ADMISSIONS

Admissions Selectivity Rating: 70

# of applications received: 102 **% applicants accepted:** 93 **% acceptees attending:** 98 **Average GMAT:** 538 **Average GPA:** 3.2 **TOEFL required of international applicants?** Yes **Minimum TOEFL (paper/computer):** 550/213 **Application fee:** $55 **International application fee:** $55 **Application deadline:** 8/1 **Regular notification:** 8/1

Early decision program? No **Deferment available?** Yes **Maximum length of deferment:** one year **Transfer students accepted?** Yes **Transfer application policy:** Six semester hours of B or better coursework, evaluated for equivalence by the Graduate Admissions Committee **Non-fall admissions?** Yes **Need-blind admissions?** Yes

EMPLOYMENT PROFILE

Average starting salary:................$37,000

RIDER UNIVERSITY
COLLEGE OF BUSINESS ADMINSTRATION

ADMISSIONS CONTACT: JAMIE MITCHELL, DIRECTOR, GRADUATE ADMISSIONS
ADDRESS: PJ CIAMBELLI HALL, 2083 LAWRENCEVILLE ROAD, LAWRENCEVILLE, NJ 08648-3099
PHONE: 609-896-5036 • FAX: 609-895-5680
E-MAIL: GRADADM@RIDER.EDU
WEBSITE: WWW.RIDER.EDU/CBA

GENERAL INFORMATION

Type of school: Private **Academic calendar:** Semester

STUDENTS

Enrollment of parent institution: 6,011 **Enrollment of MBA program:** 241 **% male/female:** 51/49 **% out-of-state:** 13 **% part-time:** 84 **% minorities:** 51 **% international:** 41 **Average age at entry:** 27

ACADEMICS

Student/faculty ratio: 10:1 **% female faculty:** 31 **% minority faculty:** 44

Joint degrees: BS/BA/MBA; BS/BA/MAcc Each are 5 year programs. **Prominent alumni:** Gregory Church Â'78, Â'82, Chairman, President and CEO, Church Capital Management; Clare Hart '86, Chair, Exec. VP, President, Dow Jones & Co. Inc.; Terry McEwen '98, Director, NJ State Dept. of Banking and Insurance; Steve Cosgrove '77, VP Corporate Controller, Johnson & Johnson Companies; Guy Del Grande Â'83, Â'90, CEO, President, Tekmark Global Solutions, Inc.

FINANCIAL FACTS

Books and supplies: $4,240

% of students receiving aid: 34 **% of first-year students receiving aid:** 43 **% of students receiving loans:** 22 **% of students receiving grants:** 15 **Average award package:** $11,385 **Average grant:** $6,143 **Average student loan debt:** $28,796

ADMISSIONS

Admissions Selectivity Rating: 60*

# of applications received: 101 **% applicants accepted:** 68 **% acceptees attending:** 75 **Average GMAT:** 484 **Range of GMAT:** 410-550 **Average GPA:** 3.33 **TOEFL required of international applicants?** Yes **Minimum TOEFL (paper/computer):** 585/240 **Application fee:** $50 **International application fee:** $50 **Application deadline:** 8/1 **Application Deadline/Notification Round 1:** 8/1 / NR **Round 2:** 12/1 / NR **Round 3:** 5/1 / NR

Early decision program? No **Deferment available?** Yes **Maximum length of deferment:** 1 year **Transfer students accepted?** Yes **Transfer application policy:** Each case is evaluated individually. No more than 24 transferred credits against 51 required maximum. Maximum of 6 credits against 30 in the advance portion. **Non-fall admissions?** Yes **Need-blind admissions?** Yes

Saint Mary's University of Minnesota

Schools of Graduate and Professional Programs

Admissions Contact: Yasin Alsaidi, Director of Admissions
Address: 2500 Park Avenue, Minneapolis, MN 55404-4403
Phone: 612-728-5100 • Fax: 612-728-5121
E-mail: TC-ADMISSION@SMUMN.EDU
Website: WWW.SMUMN.EDU/SectionGraduate.ASPX

GENERAL INFORMATION

Type of school: Private Affiliation: Roman Catholic

STUDENTS

Enrollment of parent institution: 5,565 Enrollment of MBA program: 210 % male/female: 44/56 % out-of-state: 0 % part-time: 80 % minorities: 30 % international: 22 Average age at entry: 32

FINANCIAL FACTS

Annual tuition: $9,480

ADMISSIONS

Admissions Selectivity Rating: 60*

# of applications received: 44 % applicants accepted: 98 % acceptees attending: 77 TOEFL required of international applicants? Yes Minimum TOEFL (paper/computer): 550/213 Application fee: $25

Early decision program? No Deferment available? Yes Maximum length of deferment: 1 year Transfer students accepted? Yes Transfer application policy: May transfer up to six graduate credits from another regionally accredited institution. Non-fall admissions? Yes Need-blind admissions? Yes

Saint Mary's University, Canada

Sobey School of Business

Admissions Contact: Leah Ray, Managing Director, MBA Program
Address: 923 Robie Street, Halifax, NS B3H 3C3 Canada
Phone: 902-420-5002 • Fax: 902-420-5119
E-mail: MBA@SMU.CA
Website: WWW.SOBEY.SMU.CA

GENERAL INFORMATION

Type of school: Private Academic calendar: Semester

STUDENTS

Enrollment of parent institution: 8,000 Enrollment of MBA program: 82 % male/female: 40/60 % out-of-state: 60 % part-time: 68 % international: 40 Average age at entry: 28 Average years work experience at entry: 6

ACADEMICS

Student/raculty ratio: 5:1

Joint degrees: MBA-CMA 28 months.

FINANCIAL FACTS

Annual tuition: $9,235 Fees: $480 Books and supplies: $1,000 % of students receiving aid: 20 % of first-year students receiving aid: 10 % of students receiving grants: 20 Average grant: $2,500

ADMISSIONS

Admissions Selectivity Rating: 60*

# of applications received: 114 % applicants accepted: 64 % acceptees attending: 78 Average GMAT: 610 Range of GMAT: 550–720 Average GPA: 3.3 TOEFL required of international applicants? Yes Minimum TOEFL (paper/computer): 580/237 Application fee: $70 International application fee: $70 Application deadline: 5/31

Early decision program? Yes ED deadline/notification: NR / 3/7 Deferment available? Yes Maximum length of deferment: 12 months Transfer students accepted? Yes Transfer application policy: Must submit full application & suppporting documents as we evaluate on a case by case basis. Non-fall admissions? No Need-blind admissions? Yes

Salisbury University

Franklin P. Perdue School of Business

Admissions Contact: , MBA Director
Address: 1101 Camden Avenue, Salisbury, MD 21801-6837
Phone: 410-548-5564 • Fax: 410-548-2908
E-mail: MBA@SALISBURY.EDU
Website: MBA.SALISBURY.EDU

GENERAL INFORMATION

Type of school: Public Academic calendar: Semester

STUDENTS

Enrollment of parent institution: 7,000 Enrollment of MBA program: 73 % male/female: 58/42 % part-time: 56 % minorities: 1 % international: 12 Average age at entry: 26 Average years work experience at entry: 1.5

ACADEMICS

Student/raculty ratio: 25:1 % female faculty: 4

FINANCIAL FACTS

Annual tuition (in-state/out-of-state): $9,180/$19,244 Fees (in-state/out-of-state): $1,870/$1,870 Books and supplies: $1,100 Room & board (off-campus): $8,500 Average grant: $9,680

ADMISSIONS

Admissions Selectivity Rating: 60*

# of applications received: 50 % applicants accepted: 70 % acceptees attending: 100 Average GMAT: 550 Range of GMAT: 490–750 Average GPA: 3.4 TOEFL required of international applicants? Yes Minimum TOEFL (paper): 550 Application fee: $45 International application fee: $45 Application deadline: 3/1 Regular notification: 4/1

Early decision program? No Deferment available? No Transfer students accepted? No Non-fall admissions? No Need-blind admissions? Yes

EMPLOYMENT PROFILE
% grads employed at graduation: 61

SAM HOUSTON STATE UNIVERSITY
COLLEGE OF BUSINESS ADMINISTRATION

ADMISSIONS CONTACT: DR. LEROY ASHORN, ASSOCIATE DEAN/COORDINATOR OF
GRADUATE STUDIES
ADDRESS: PO BOX 2056, HUNTSVILLE, TX 77341-2056
PHONE: 936-294-1239 • FAX: 936-294-3612
E-MAIL: BUSGRAD@SHSU.EDU
WEBSITE: COBA.SHSU.EDU/

GENERAL INFORMATION
Type of school: Public Academic calendar: September 1 to August 31

STUDENTS
Enrollment of MBA program: 164 % male/female: 49/51 % part-
time: 71 % minorities: 7 % international: 5 Average years work
experience at entry: 0

FINANCIAL FACTS
Annual tuition (in-state/out-of-state): $6,822/$11,466

ADMISSIONS
Admissions Selectivity Rating: 60*

# of applications received: 108 % applicants accepted: 71 %
acceptees attending: 53 Average GMAT: 504 Range of GMAT:
460–550 TOEFL required of international applicants? Yes
Minimum TOEFL (paper/computer): 550/213 Application fee: $20
International application fee: $20 Application deadline: 6/25

Early decision program? No Deferment available? Yes Maximum
length of deferment: One year Transfer students accepted? Yes
Transfer application policy: Accept up to six semester hours from
accredited universities Non-fall admissions? Yes Need-blind admissions? Yes

SAMFORD UNIVERSITY
SAMFORD UNIVERSITY BROCK SCHOOL OF
BUSINESS

ADMISSIONS CONTACT: MR. LARRON C. HARPER, DIRECTOR OF GRADUATE
PROGRAMS
ADDRESS: DBH 413, BROCK SCHOOL OF BUSINESS, 800 LAKESHORE DR.,
BIRMINGHAM, AL 35229
PHONE: 205-726-2040 • FAX: 205-726-2464
E-MAIL: LEPHILLI@SAMFORD.EDU
WEBSITE: WWW.SAMFORD.EDU/MBA

GENERAL INFORMATION
Type of school: Private Affiliation: Baptist Academic calendar: Two
16-week semesters, one 10-week

STUDENTS
Enrollment of parent institution: 4,416 Enrollment of MBA program: 131 % male/female: 100/0 % part-time: 100 % Average age
at entry: 26 Average years work experience at entry: 4

ACADEMICS
Student/faculty ratio: 12:1 % female faculty: 25 % minority faculty: 15

Joint degrees: Master of Business Administration/Master of
Accountancy (MBA/MAcc): part-time; 45–60 total credits required;
18 months to 7 years to complete program. Concentrations in management, accounting. Master of Business Administration/Juris
Doctor (MBA/JD): Full.

ADMISSIONS
Admissions Selectivity Rating: 60*

# of applications received: 71 % applicants accepted: 73 %
acceptees attending: 85 Average GMAT: 550 Range of GMAT:
470–670 TOEFL required of international applicants? No
Application fee: $25 International application fee: $25

Early decision program? No Deferment available? Yes Maximum
length of deferment: one year Transfer students accepted? Yes
Transfer application policy: must submit complete application and
meet admissions deadlines. Limited number of credits may transfer
Non-fall admissions? Yes Need-blind admissions? Yes

SHIPPENSBURG UNIVERSITY
JOHN L. GROVE COLLEGE OF BUSINESS

ADMISSIONS CONTACT: GRADUATE ADMISSIONS OFFICE,
ADDRESS: 1871 OLD MAIN DRIVE, SHIPPENSBURG, PA 17257
PHONE: (717) 477-1213 • FAX: (717)477-4016
E-MAIL: GRADUATE@SHIP.EDU
WEBSITE: WEBSPACE.SHIP.EDU/MBA/

GENERAL INFORMATION
Type of school: Public

STUDENTS
Average age at entry: 32 Average years work experience at entry:
5

FINANCIAL FACTS
Annual tuition (in-state/out-of-state): $3,024/$4,839 Fees (in-
state/out-of-state): $63/$94

ADMISSIONS
Admissions Selectivity Rating: 60*

TOEFL required of international applicants? No Minimum TOEFL
(paper/computer): 550/213 Application fee: $30 International
application fee: $30

Early decision program? No Deferment available? Yes Maximum
length of deferment: 1 year Transfer students accepted? Yes
Transfer application policy: Up to 9 credits may transfer Non-fall
admissions? Yes Need-blind admissions? No

SOUTHEASTERN LOUISIANA UNIVERSITY

COLLEGE OF BUSINESS

ADMISSIONS CONTACT: SANDRA MEYERS, GRADUATE ADMISSIONS ANALYST
ADDRESS: SLU 10752, HAMMOND, LA 70402
PHONE: 800-222-7358 • FAX: 985-549-5882
E-MAIL: SMEYERS@SELU.EDU
WEBSITE: WWW.SELU.EDU/ACAD_RESEARCH/COLLEGES/BUS

GENERAL INFORMATION

Type of school: Public **Academic calendar:** Semester

STUDENTS

Enrollment of parent institution: 15,160 **Enrollment of MBA program:** 143 **% male/female:** 43/57 **% out-of-state:** 2 **% part-time:** 29 **% minorities:** 17 **% international:** 16 **Average age at entry:** 25

ACADEMICS

Student/raculty ratio: 8:1 **% female faculty:** 13 **% minority faculty:** 27

.**Prominent alumni:** Robin Roberts, ESPN Sportscaster; Russell Carollo, Pulitzer Prize Winner; Harold Jackson, President (Retired) Sunsweet Products; James J. Brady, Former President, National Democratic Party; William Handal, Minister of Finance, EL Salvador.

FINANCIAL FACTS

Annual tuition (in-state/out-of-state): $3,086/$10,342 **Fees (in-state/out-of-state):** $1,195/$1,195 **Books and supplies:** $1,200 **Room & board (on/off-campus):** $6,450/$8,236

% of students receiving aid: 42 **% of first-year students receiving aid:** 10 **% of students receiving loans:** 36 **% of students receiving grants:** 2 **Average award package:** $10,954 **Average grant:** $4,156 **Average student loan debt:** $10,128

ADMISSIONS

Admissions Selectivity Rating: 60*

# of applications received: 44 **% applicants accepted:** 86 **% acceptees attending:** 55 **Average GMAT:** 464 **Range of GMAT:** 430–480 **Average GPA:** 3.42 **TOEFL required of international applicants?** Yes **Minimum TOEFL (paper/computer):** 525/195 **Application fee:** $20 **International application fee:** $30 **Application deadline:** 7/15

Early decision program? No **Deferment available?** Yes **Maximum length of deferment:** 1 year **Transfer students accepted?** Yes **Transfer application policy:** Must earn 12 hours of graduate credit at Southeastern before applying for any transfer credit from another university. That university must be an accredited institution that regularly grants the master's degree or an equivalent foreign institution. **Non-fall admissions?** Yes **Need-blind admissions?** Yes

SOUTHERN UTAH UNIVERSITY

SOUTHERN UTAH UNIVERSITY SCHOOL OF BUSINESS

ADMISSIONS CONTACT: CHRISTINE PROCTOR, ASSOCIATE DIRECTOR OF ADMISSIONS
ADDRESS: SOUTHERN UTAH UNIVERSITY, 351 W. UNIVERSITY BLVD., CEDAR CITY, UT 84720
PHONE: 435-586-7742 • FAX: 435-865-8223
E-MAIL: PROCTOR@SUU.EDU
WEBSITE: SUU.EDU/BUSINESS/

GENERAL INFORMATION

Type of school: Public **Academic calendar:** Semester

STUDENTS

Enrollment of MBA program: 88 **% male/female:** 75/25 **% part-time:** 33 **% minorities:** 8 **Average age at entry:** 26

ACADEMICS

Student/raculty ratio: 5.17:1 **% female faculty:** 17 **% minority faculty:** 8

Joint degrees: MBA/MAcc, 1.5 years or 4 semesters.

FINANCIAL FACTS

Annual tuition (in-state/out-of-state): $7,380/$24,358 **Fees (in-state/out-of-state):** $539/$539 **Books and supplies:** $1,200 **Room & board (on/off-campus):** $5,238/$3,248

% of students receiving aid: 59 **% of first-year students receiving aid:** 65 **% of students receiving loans:** 34 **% of students receiving grants:** 49 **Average grant:** $3,247

ADMISSIONS

Admissions Selectivity Rating: 60*

# of applications received: 82 **% applicants accepted:** 70 **% acceptees attending:** 88 **Average GMAT:** 538 **Range of GMAT:** 460–580 **Average GPA:** 3.51 **TOEFL required of international applicants?** Yes **Minimum TOEFL (paper/computer):** 500/173 **Application fee:** $50 **International application fee:** $50 **Application deadline:** 3/1

Early decision program? No **Deferment available?** Yes **Maximum length of deferment:** Two years **Transfer students accepted?** Yes **Non-fall admissions?** Yes **Need-blind admissions?** Yes

EMPLOYMENT PROFILE

% grads employed within three months of graduation: 86
Average starting salary: $39,647
Primary Source of Full-time Job Acceptances
Unknown.......................................41 (100%)

Grads Employed by Industry:	%	avg. salary:
Marketing	3	$55,000
Operations	6	$44,000
Management	27	$47,571
Finance	42	$41,143

Top 5 Employers Hiring Grads (#)

Southern Utah University (3), Brock & Associates (3), Skywest (3), Zions Bank (2), Hinton Burdick (2)

ST. CLOUD STATE UNIVERSITY
HERBERGER COLLEGE OF BUSINESS

ADMISSIONS CONTACT: GRADUATE STUDIES OFFICE—ANNETTE DAY, GRADUATE ADMISSIONS MANAGER
ADDRESS: 720 4TH AVE. SOUTH, AS-121, ST. CLOUD, MN 56301-4498
PHONE: 320-308-2112 • FAX: 320-308-3986
E-MAIL: GRADUATESTUDIES@STCLOUDSTATE.EDU
WEBSITE: WWW.STCLOUDSTATE.EDU/MBA/

GENERAL INFORMATION

Type of school: Public Academic calendar: Semester

STUDENTS

Enrollment of parent institution: 16,334 Enrollment of MBA program: 166 % male/female: 71/29 % out-of-state: 18 % part-time: 75 % minorities: 10 % international: 48 Average age at entry: 28 Average years work experience at entry: 5

ACADEMICS

Student/raculty ratio: 25:1 % female faculty: 27 % minority faculty: 20

FINANCIAL FACTS

Annual tuition (in-state/out-of-state): $14,292/$14,292 Fees (in-state/out-of-state): $165/$165 Books and supplies: $1,800

ADMISSIONS

Admissions Selectivity Rating: 60*

% acceptees attending: 48 Average GMAT: 525 Range of GMAT: 470-700 Average GPA: 3.3 TOEFL required of international applicants? Yes Minimum TOEFL (paper/computer): 550/213 Application fee: $35 International application fee: $35

Early decision program? Yes ED deadline/notification: NR / 1/1 Deferment available? Yes Maximum length of deferment: 2 years Transfer students accepted? No Non-fall admissions? Yes Need-blind admissions? No

EMPLOYMENT PROFILE

Average starting salary:...............$38,000

ST. JOHN FISHER COLLEGE
BITTNER SCHOOL OF BUSINESS

ADMISSIONS CONTACT: MR. JOSE PERALES, DIRECTOR OF TRANSFER/GRADUATE ADMISSIONS
ADDRESS: 3690 EAST AVENUE, KEARNEY BUILDING, ROCHESTER, NY 14618
PHONE: 585.385.8161 • FAX: 585.385.8344
E-MAIL: GRAD@SJFC.EDU
WEBSITE: WWW.SJFC.EDU/BITTNER/

GENERAL INFORMATION

Type of school: Private Academic calendar: Semester

STUDENTS

Enrollment of parent institution: 3,832 Enrollment of MBA program: 63 % male/female: 54/46 % out-of-state: 0 % part-time: 87 % minorities: 13 % international: 0 Average age at entry: 26

ACADEMICS

Student/raculty ratio: 14:1 % female faculty: 7 % minority faculty: 7

ADMISSIONS

Admissions Selectivity Rating: 60*

# of applications received: 31 % applicants accepted: 81 % acceptees attending: 60 Average GMAT: 475 Range of GMAT: 400-540 Average GPA: 3.22 TOEFL required of international applicants? Yes Minimum TOEFL (paper/computer): 575/233 Application fee: $30 International application fee: $30 Application deadline: 7/1

Early decision program? No Deferment available? Yes Maximum length of deferment: One Semester Transfer students accepted? Yes Transfer application policy: Students can request transfer credit for graduate course work taken at accredited institutions. These credits must have been taken in an appropriate graduate program related to MBA graduate program of study. Only courses with a grade of B or better. Non-fall admissions? Yes Need-blind admissions? Yes

STEPHEN F. AUSTIN STATE UNIVERSITY
NELSON RUSCHE COLLEGE OF BUSINESS

ADMISSIONS CONTACT: MICHAEL D. STROUP, MBA DIRECTOR
ADDRESS: PO BOX 13004, SFA STATION, STEPHEN F. AUSTIN STATE UNIVERSITY, NACOGDOCHES, TX 75962-3004
PHONE: 936-468-3101 • FAX: 936-468-1560
E-MAIL: MBA@SFASU.EDU
WEBSITE: WWW.COB.SFASU.EDU

GENERAL INFORMATION

Type of school: Public

STUDENTS

Enrollment of parent institution: 10,000 Enrollment of MBA program: 45 % male/female: 60/40 % out-of-state: 5 % part-time: 50 % minorities: 25 % international: 15 Average age at entry: 25 Average years work experience at entry: 3

ACADEMICS

Student/raculty ratio: 10:1 % female faculty: 30 % minority faculty: 10

Prominent alumni: Dr. Phil Stetz, Entrepreneurship; Dr. John Lewis, Finance; Dr. Dave Gundersen, Management.

FINANCIAL FACTS

Annual tuition (in-state/out-of-state): $1,134/$7,236 Fees (in-state/out-of-state): $126/$804 Books and supplies: $1,000 Room & board (on/off-campus): $5,000/$6,500

% of students receiving aid: 15 % of first-year students receiving aid: 5 % of students receiving loans: 5 % of students receiving grants: 0 Average award package: $3,500 Average grant: $3,500

ADMISSIONS

Admissions Selectivity Rating: 60*

# of applications received: 60 **Average GMAT:** 510 **Range of GMAT:** 290–660 **Average GPA:** 3 **TOEFL required of international applicants?** Yes **Minimum TOEFL (paper/computer):** 550/213 **Application fee:** $25 **International application fee:** $50 **Application deadline:** 8/1 **Regular notification:** 8/15

Early decision program? No **Deferment available?** Yes **Maximum length of deferment:** 1 year **Transfer students accepted?** Yes **Transfer application policy:** Applicant may transfer in 6 hours graduate credit from an AACSB International Accredited school. **Non-fall admissions?** Yes **Need-blind admissions?** Yes

EMPLOYMENT PROFILE

Average starting salary:...............$52,000

Grads Employed by Industry:.......% avg. salary:

Marketing 25 $45,000

Consulting......................................20 $45,000

Management 15 $65,000

TEL AVIV UNIVERSITY
LEON RECANATI GRADUATE SCHOOL OF BUSINESS ADMINISTATION

WEBSITE: WWW.TAU.AC.IL/GSBA

GENERAL INFORMATION

Type of school: Private **Academic calendar:** Semester

STUDENTS

Enrollment of parent institution: 26,000 **Enrollment of MBA program:** 2,196 **Average age at entry:** 29

ACADEMICS

Student/raculty ratio: 45:1

ADMISSIONS

Admissions Selectivity Rating: 60*

% acceptees attending: 100 **TOEFL required of international applicants?** No **Application fee:** $160 **Application deadline:** 2/1

Early decision program? No **Deferment available?** No **Transfer students accepted?** No **Non-fall admissions?** Yes **Need-blind admissions?** No

TENNESSEE STATE UNIVERSITY
TENNESSEE STATE UNIVERSITY

ADMISSIONS CONTACT: LISA SMITH, DIRECTOR OF PUBLIC SERVICE
ADDRESS: 330 10TH AVENUE NORTH, SUITE K, NASHVILLE, TN 37203
PHONE: 615-963-7137 • FAX: 615-963-7139
E-MAIL: LSMITH11@TNSTATE.EDU
WEBSITE: WWW.COB.TNSTATE.EDU

GENERAL INFORMATION

Type of school: Public

STUDENTS

Enrollment of MBA program: 100 **Average years work experience at entry:** 0

ACADEMICS

Student/raculty ratio: 12:1

Prominent alumni: Nicole Dunigan, Vice President, First Tennessee Bank; Thelma Harper, Senator, State of Tennessee; Kevin Williams, Vice President, General Motors; Karen Isabel, CEO, Dalmatian Creative Agency, Inc; Darren Johnson, Author, Entrepreneur.

FINANCIAL FACTS

Annual tuition (in-state/out-of-state): $2,569/$4,847 **Fees (in-state/out-of-state):** $428/$2,937 **Books and supplies:** $2,000 **Room & board (on/off-campus):** $3,160/$4,000

ADMISSIONS

Admissions Selectivity Rating: 60*

Average GMAT: 510 **Average GPA:** 3.2 **TOEFL required of international applicants?** Yes **Minimum TOEFL (paper):** 500 **Application fee:** $25 **Application deadline:** 1/1 **Regular notification:** 1/1

Early decision program? No **Deferment available?** Yes **Maximum length of deferment:** 1 **Transfer students accepted?** Yes **Transfer application policy:** 6 credits from - non AACGB 12 credits from AACGb college **Non-fall admissions?** No **Need-blind admissions?** Yes

TEXAS A&M UNIVERSITY— COMMERCE
COLLEGE OF BUSINESS AND TECHNOLOGY

ADMISSIONS CONTACT: VICKY TURNER, GRADUATE ADMISSIONS
ADDRESS: P O BOX 3011, COMMERCE, TX 75429
PHONE: 903-886-5167 • FAX: 903-886-5165
E-MAIL: GRADUATE_SCHOOL@TAMU-COMMERCE.EDU
WEBSITE: WWW.TAMU-COMMERCE.EDU/GRADUATEPROGRAMS

GENERAL INFORMATION

Type of school: Public **Academic calendar:** Semester

STUDENTS

Enrollment of parent institution: 8,875 **Enrollment of MBA program:** 489 **% male/female:** 56/44 **% part-time:** 61 **% minorities:** 53 **% international:** 23 **Average age at entry:** 22 **Average years work experience at entry:** 0

ACADEMICS

Student/raculty ratio: 27:1 **% female faculty:** 10 **% minority faculty:** 10

Joint degrees: BPA/MBA, emphasis: Accounting, 4 years + 1 year.

Prominent alumni: Sam Rayburn, Speaker of the House; Sheryl Leach, Creator of Barney; Durwood Merril, Baseball Umpire, Texas Baseball Hall of Fame; Duane Allen, Oak Ridge Boys- Lead Singer; Wade Wilson, Chicago Bears Quaterback Coach.

FINANCIAL FACTS

Annual tuition (in-state/out-of-state): $7,000/$18,000 **Books and supplies:** $1,000 **Room & board (on/off-campus):** $2,950/$2,200

ADMISSIONS

Admissions Selectivity Rating: 60*

# of applications received: 1,215 **% applicants accepted:** 60 **% acceptees attending:** 65 **Average GMAT:** 460 **Range of GMAT:** 380–620 **Average GPA:** 3 **TOEFL required of international applicants?** Yes **Minimum TOEFL (paper/computer):** 500/173 **Application fee:** $35 **International application fee:** $50 **Application deadline:** 6/1

Early decision program? No **Deferment available?** Yes **Maximum length of deferment:** 2 Semesters **Transfer students accepted?** Yes **Transfer application policy:** Students can transfer up to 9 SH for the 30-33 HR. **Non-fall admissions?** Yes **Need-blind admissions?** No

UNION GRADUATE COLLEGE
SCHOOL OF MANAGEMENT

ADMISSIONS CONTACT: RHONDA SHEEHAN, DIRECTOR OF ADMISSIONS, REGISTRAR
ADDRESS: 807 UNION STREET, LAMONT HOUSE, SCHENECTADY, NY 12308
PHONE: 518-388-6148 • FAX: 518-388-6686
E-MAIL: INFO@UNIONGRADUATECOLLEGE.EDU
WEBSITE: WWW.UNIONGRADUATECOLLEGE.EDU

GENERAL INFORMATION

Type of school: Private **Academic calendar:** July-June

STUDENTS

Enrollment of parent institution: 750 **Enrollment of MBA program:** 309 **% male/female:** 63/37 **% out-of-state:** 4 **% part-time:** 64 **% minorities:** 15 **% international:** 8 **Average age at entry:** 25 **Average years work experience at entry:** 2

ACADEMICS

Student/raculty ratio: 10:1 **% female faculty:** 17 **% minority faculty:** 13

Prominent alumni: Michael Keegan, Regional President, M&T Bank; Wayne McDougall, DFO MapInfo; James Mandall, President, Boston Children's Hospital; James Figge, Medical Director, CDPHP-HMO.

FINANCIAL FACTS

Annual tuition: $24,400 **Fees:** $125 **Books and supplies:** $1,200 Room & board (off-campus): $8,800

Average award package: $15,200 **Average grant:** $5,400

ADMISSIONS

Admissions Selectivity Rating: 60*

# of applications received: 137 **% applicants accepted:** 96 **% acceptees attending:** 84 **Average GMAT:** 545 **Range of GMAT:** 490–590 **Average GPA:** 3.34 **TOEFL required of international applicants?** Yes **Minimum TOEFL (paper/computer):** 550/213 **Application fee:** $60 **International application fee:** $60

Early decision program? No **Deferment available?** Yes **Maximum length of deferment:** 1 year **Transfer students accepted?** Yes **Transfer application policy:** Will accepted up to 8 transfer courses. **Non-fall admissions?** Yes **Need-blind admissions?** Yes

EMPLOYMENT PROFILE

% grads employed at graduation: 68

% grads employed within three months of graduation: 85

Average starting salary:................$58,250

Primary Source of Full-time Job Acceptances

Graduate-facilitated activities 10 (42%)

Grads Employed by Industry:......**% avg. salary:**

Marketing	6 NR
Operations	6 NR
Consulting	13 NR
Management	20 NR
Finance	23 NR
HR	6 NR

Top 5 Employers Hiring Grads

General Electric, Ayco

UNIVERSITÉ LAVAL
FACULTÉ DES SCIENCES DE L'ADMINISTRATION

ADDRESS: BUREAU DU REGISTRAIRE, PAVILLON JEAN-CHARLES-BONENFANT, 2345, ALLÉ DES BIBLIOTHÈQUES,LOCAL 2440, UNIVERSITÉ LAVAL, QUEBEC, QC G1V 0A6 CANADA
PHONE: 418-656-3080 • FAX: 418-656-5216
E-MAIL: REG@REG.ULAVAL.CA
WEBSITE: WWW.FSA.ULAVAL.CA

GENERAL INFORMATION

Type of school: Public **Academic calendar:** Semester

STUDENTS

Enrollment of parent institution: 37,181 **Enrollment of MBA program:** 936 **% male/female:** 60/40 **% out-of-state:** 36 **% part-time:** 70 **% international:** 50 **Average age at entry:** 28 **Average years work experience at entry:** 4

ACADEMICS

Student/raculty ratio: 25:1 **% female faculty:** 30

FINANCIAL FACTS

Annual tuition (in-state/out-of-state): $2,090/$10,488 **Books and supplies:** $17,307 **Room & board (on/off-campus):** $5,800/$9,200

ADMISSIONS

Admissions Selectivity Rating: 60*

# of applications received: 1,112 **% applicants accepted:** 65 **% acceptees attending:** 47 **Average GPA:** 3 **TOEFL required of international applicants?** Yes **Minimum TOEFL (paper/computer):** 550/213 **Application fee:** $30 **International application fee:** $30 **Application deadline:** 2/1

Early decision program? No **Deferment available?** Yes **Maximum length of deferment:** 1 year **Transfer students accepted?** No **Non-fall admissions?** Yes **Need-blind admissions?** No

EMPLOYMENT PROFILE

% grads employed at graduation: 48

% grads employed within three months of graduation: 72

Average starting salary:................$58,091

Primary Source of Full-time Job Acceptances

Grads Employed by Industry: ....% avg. salary:

Top 5 Employers Hiring Grads

Desjardins, Banque Laurentienne, Ranstad, Canadian government, Université Laval

UNIVERSITY COLLEGE DUBLIN
MICHAEL SMURFIT GRADUATE SCHOOL OF BUSINESS

ADMISSIONS CONTACT: ELAINE MCAREE, ADMISSIONS MANAGER
ADDRESS: CARYSFORT AVENUE, BLACKROCK, DUBLIN, IRELAND
PHONE: 00353 1 7168862 • FAX: 00353 1 7168981
E-MAIL: MBA@UCD.IE • WEBSITE: WWW.SMURFITSCHOOL.IE

GENERAL INFORMATION

Type of school: Public **Academic calendar:** Sept–Aug

STUDENTS

Enrollment of MBA program: 126 **% male/female:** 75/25 **% part-time:** 63 **% international:** 40

ACADEMICS

Student/raculty ratio: 1.5:1 **% female faculty:** 30

FINANCIAL FACTS

Fees (in-state/out-of-state): $29,500/$29,500 **Books and supplies:** $1,000 **Room & board (on/off-campus):** $5,000/$5,500 **Average award package:** $14,750

ADMISSIONS

Admissions Selectivity Rating: 60*

# of applications received: 363 **% applicants accepted:** 48 % **acceptees attending:** 73 **Average GMAT:** 630 **TOEFL required of international applicants?** Yes **Minimum TOEFL (paper/computer):** 600/250 **Application deadline:** 7/10 **Regular notification:** 7/20 **Application Deadline/Notification Round 1:** 3/27 / NR **Round 2:** 5/15 / NR **Round 3:** 7/10 / NR

Early decision program? No **Deferment available?** Yes **Maximum length of deferment:** 1 year **Transfer students accepted?** Yes **Transfer application policy:** Creditis may be awarded on the basis of ECTS (European Credit Transfer System) equivalency from accredited business schools only. **Non-fall admissions?** No **Need-blind admissions?** Yes

UNIVERSITY OF ALABAMA IN HUNTSVILLE
COLLEGE OF BUSINESS ADMINISTRATION

ADMISSIONS CONTACT: DR. J. DANIEL SHERMAN, ASSOCIATE DEAN
ADDRESS: BAB 126G, HUNTSVILLE, AL 35899
PHONE: 256-824-6681 • FAX: 256-890-7571
E-MAIL: GRADBIZ@UAH.EDU
WEBSITE: WWW.UAH.EDU

GENERAL INFORMATION

Type of school: Public **Academic calendar:** Semester

STUDENTS

Enrollment of MBA program: 101 **% male/female:** 54/46 **% part-time:** 67 **% minorities:** 9 **Average age at entry:** 29 **Average years work experience at entry:** 6

ACADEMICS

Student/raculty ratio: 8:1 **% female faculty:** 14 **% minority faculty:** 34

Prominent alumni: James L. Jennings, Deputy Director for Business Operations, John F. Kennedy Space Center; John W. Kilpatrick, Jr., Engineering Directorate, NASA/MSFC.; George P. Kappler, Jr., CEO, Kappler Safety Group; Stephen P. Zelnak, Jr., Chairman and CEO, Martin Marietta; Steven A. Glaza, General Manager-Storage Division, Vice President, Digital & Applied Imaging, Eastman Kodak Co.

FINANCIAL FACTS

Annual tuition (in-state/out-of-state): $6,296/$15,078 **Books and supplies:** $1,500 **Room & board (on-campus):** $8,424

ADMISSIONS

Admissions Selectivity Rating: 60*

# of applications received: 184 **% applicants accepted:** 65 % **acceptees attending:** 85 **Average GMAT:** 516 **Range of GMAT:** 470–585 **Average GPA:** 3.29 **TOEFL required of international applicants?** Yes **Minimum TOEFL (paper/computer):** 550/213 **Application fee:** $40 **International application fee:** $50 **Application deadline:** 8/1 **Regular notification:** 1/1

Early decision program? No **Deferment available?** No **Transfer students accepted?** Yes **Transfer application policy:** transfer credit evaluated by program advisor **Non-fall admissions?** Yes **Need-blind admissions?** Yes

EMPLOYMENT PROFILE

Average starting salary: $45,952

Grads Employed by Industry: ....% avg. salary:

Operations	NR	$55,000
Management	NR	$22,500
HR	NR	$37,500
MIS	NR	$57,500

University of Alaska—Anchorage
College of Business and Public Policy

Admissions Contact: Al Kastar, Director of Admissions
Address: PO Box 141629, Anchorage, AK 99514-1629
Phone: 907-786-1480 • Fax: 907-786-4888
E-mail: ayadmit@uaa.alaska.edu
Website: http://www.cbpp.uaa.alaska.edu/busadmin.asp

GENERAL INFORMATION
Type of school: Public **Academic calendar:** Sep-May

STUDENTS
Enrollment of MBA program: 100 **% male/female:** 65/35 **% out-of-state:** 17 **% part-time:** 40 **% minorities:** 30 **% international:** 26

ACADEMICS
Student/raculty ratio: 30:1 **% female faculty:** 13 **% minority faculty:** 38

FINANCIAL FACTS
Annual tuition (in-state/out-of-state): $5,418/$11,070 **Fees (in-state/out-of-state):** $560/$560 **Books and supplies:** $900 **Room & board (on-campus):** $8,350

ADMISSIONS
Admissions Selectivity Rating: 60*

# of applications received: 67 **% applicants accepted:** 85 **% acceptees attending:** 67 **Average GPA:** 3.1 **TOEFL required of international applicants?** Yes Minimum TOEFL (paper): 550 **Application fee:** $60

Early decision program? No **Deferment available?** Yes **Maximum length of deferment:** One year **Transfer students accepted?** Yes **Transfer application policy:** Applicants must meet all UAA and MBA admissions requirements. Up to 9 semester credits not previously used to obtain any other degree or certificate may be transferred to UAA from a regionally accredited institution and accepted toward a graduate degree **Non-fall admissions?** Yes **Need-blind admissions?** Yes

University of Alaska—Fairbanks
School of Management

Admissions Contact: Nancy Dix, Director
Address: P.O. Box 757480, Fairbanks, AK 99775
Phone: 907-474-7500 • Fax: 907-474-5379
E-mail: admissions@uaf.edu • Website: www.uafsom.com/gpmba.html

GENERAL INFORMATION
Type of school: Public

STUDENTS
Enrollment of parent institution: 5,025 **Enrollment of MBA program:** 30 **Average age at entry:** 32 **Average years work experience at entry:** 10

ACADEMICS
Student/raculty ratio: 3:1 **% female faculty:** 30 **% minority faculty:** 20

FINANCIAL FACTS
Annual tuition (in-state/out-of-state): $4,824/$9,846 **Fees (in-state/out-of-state):** $670/$670 **Books and supplies:** $1,076 **Room & board (on/off-campus):** $6,030/$10,413 **Average grant:** $16,928 **Average student loan debt:** $12,166

ADMISSIONS
Admissions Selectivity Rating: 60*

% acceptees attending: 92 **Average GMAT:** 547 **Average GPA:** 3.51 **TOEFL required of international applicants?** Yes **Minimum TOEFL (paper/computer):** 550/213 **Application fee:** $50 **International application fee:** $50 **Application deadline:** 8/1 **Regular notification:** 8/1 **Early decision program?** No **Deferment available?** Yes **Maximum length of deferment:** 1 year **Transfer students accepted?** Yes **Transfer application policy:** We take up to 3 courses. **Non-fall admissions?** Yes **Need-blind admissions?** Yes

University of Arkansas at Little Rock
College of Business

Admissions Contact: Dr. Ken Glachus, MBA Advisor
Address: 2801 South University Avenue, Little Rock, AR 72204
Phone: 501-569-3356 • Fax: 501-569-8898
Website: www.cba.ualr.edu

GENERAL INFORMATION
Type of school: Public **Academic calendar:** Semester

STUDENTS
Enrollment of parent institution: 9,925 **Enrollment of MBA program:** 225 **% male/female:** 58/42 **% out-of-state:** 1 **% part-time:** 87 **% minorities:** 8 **% international:** 15 **Average age at entry:** 29

FINANCIAL FACTS
Annual tuition: $30,500

ADMISSIONS
Admissions Selectivity Rating: 60*

# of applications received: 87 **% applicants accepted:** 66 **% acceptees attending:** 74 **TOEFL required of international applicants?** Yes Minimum TOEFL (paper): 550

Early decision program? No **Deferment available?** Yes **Maximum length of deferment:** text marker **Transfer students accepted?** No **Non-fall admissions?** No **Need-blind admissions?** No

EMPLOYMENT PROFILE
Average starting salary:................$40,000

UNIVERSITY OF BALTIMORE
MERRICK SCHOOL OF BUSINESS

ADMISSIONS CONTACT: DEAN DREIBELBIS, ASSISTANT DIRECTOR OF ADMISSIONS
ADDRESS: 1420 NORTH CHARLES STREET, BALTIMORE, MD 21201
PHONE: 888-664-0125 • FAX: 410-837-4774
E-MAIL: MBA@TOWSON.UBALT.EDU
WEBSITE: WWW.UBTOWSONMBA.COM

GENERAL INFORMATION

Type of school: Public **Academic calendar:** Semester

STUDENTS

Enrollment of parent institution: 5,240 **Enrollment of MBA program:** 518 **% male/female:** 58/42 **% out-of-state:** 17 **% part-time:** 77 **% minorities:** 15 **% international:** 37 **Average age at entry:** 30 **Average years work experience at entry:** 4

ACADEMICS

Student/raculty ratio: 15:1 **% female faculty:** 30 **% minority faculty:** 34

Joint degrees: MBA/JD with the University of Baltimore School of Law and the University of Maryland School of Law; MBA/MS in Nursing with the University of Maryland School of Nursing; MBA/PhD in Nursing with the University of Maryland School of Nursing. **Prominent alumni:** William Donald Schaeffer, Govenor, State of Maryland; Peter Angelos, Owner, Baltimore Orioles; Joseph Curran, Attorney General, State of Maryland; Vernon Wright, Vice Chairman, MBNA America Bank.

FINANCIAL FACTS

Books and supplies: $900

ADMISSIONS

Admissions Selectivity Rating: 60*

# of applications received: 434 **% applicants accepted:** 44 **% acceptees attending:** 81 **Average GMAT:** 525 **Range of GMAT:** 480–535 **Average GPA:** 3.15 **TOEFL required of international applicants?** Yes **Minimum TOEFL (paper/computer):** 550/213 **Application fee:** $30 **International application fee:** $30

Early decision program? No **Deferment available?** Yes **Maximum length of deferment:** 1 year **Transfer students accepted?** Yes **Transfer application policy:** Maximun 6 credits accepted in transfer. Must be from an AACSB accredited MBA program. **Non-fall admissions?** Yes **Need-blind admissions?** Yes

UNIVERSITY OF CENTRAL MISSOURI
HARMON COLLEGE OF BUSINESS ADMINISTRATION

ADMISSIONS CONTACT: LAURIE DELAP, ADMISSIONS EVALUATOR, GRADUATE SCHOOL
ADDRESS: WARD EDWARDS 1800, WARRENSBURG, MO 64093
PHONE: 660-543-4328 • FAX: 660-543-4778
E-MAIL: DELAP@UCMO.EDU
WEBSITE: WWW.UCMO.EDU/MBA

GENERAL INFORMATION

Type of school: Public **Academic calendar:** Semester

STUDENTS

Enrollment of parent institution: 10,711 **Enrollment of MBA program:** 79 **% male/female:** 57/43 **% out-of-state:** 35 **% part-time:** 30 **% minorities:** 9 **% international:** 25 **Average age at entry:** 25 **Average years work experience at entry:** 3

ACADEMICS

Student/raculty ratio: 2:1 **% female faculty:** 39 **% minority faculty:** 3

FINANCIAL FACTS

Annual tuition (in-state/out-of-state): $5,904/$11,808 **Fees (in-state/out-of-state):** $604/$726 **Books and supplies:** $1,200 **Room & board (on/off-campus):** $5,800/$5,800

% of students receiving grants: 50 **Average grant:** $4,500

ADMISSIONS

Admissions Selectivity Rating: 60*

# of applications received: 34 **% applicants accepted:** 74 **% acceptees attending:** 68 **Average GMAT:** 491 **Range of GMAT:** 455–528 **Average GPA:** 3.47 **TOEFL required of international applicants?** Yes **Minimum TOEFL (paper/computer):** 550/213 **Application fee:** $30 **International application fee:** $50

Early decision program? No **Deferment available?** Yes **Maximum length of deferment:** 2 semesters **Transfer students accepted?** Yes **Transfer application policy:** A maximum of 8 hours may be transferred and a B average or higher is required. **Non-fall admissions?** Yes **Need-blind admissions?** Yes

UNIVERSITY OF COLORADO AT BOULDER
LEEDS SCHOOL OF BUSINESS

ADMISSIONS CONTACT: ANNE SANDOE, DIRECTOR OF MBA PROGRAMS
ADDRESS: UCB 419, BOULDER, CO 80309
PHONE: 303-492-8397 • FAX: 303-492-1727
E-MAIL: LEEDSMBA@COLORADO.EDU
WEBSITE: LEEDS.COLORADO.EDU/MBA

GENERAL INFORMATION

Type of school: Public **Academic calendar:** Semester

STUDENTS

Enrollment of parent institution: 28,988 **Enrollment of MBA program:** 119 **% male/female:** 75/25 **% out-of-state:** 44 **% part-time:** 0 **% minorities:** 2 **% international:** 11 **Average age at entry:** 29 **Average years work experience at entry:** 5

ACADEMICS

% female faculty: 25

Joint degrees: JD/MBA, 4 years full time; MBA/MS in Telecommunications and/or Computer Science, 3–3.5 years full time; MBA/MA in Fine Arts, MBA/MA in Theatre and Dance, MBA/MA Germanic Languages, MBA/MS Environmental studies and MBA/MA in Anthropology all 3 years full.

FINANCIAL FACTS

Annual tuition (in-state/out-of-state): $13,536/$26,640 **Fees (in-state/out-of-state):** $1,515/$1,515 **Books and supplies:** $1,749 Room & board (off-campus): $17,047

% of students receiving aid: 46 **% of first-year students receiving aid:** 54 **% of students receiving grants:** 34 **Average grant:** $6,600 **Average student loan debt:** $33,430

ADMISSIONS

Admissions Selectivity Rating: 60*

# of applications received: 376 **% applicants accepted:** 18 **% acceptees attending:** 178 **Average GMAT:** 640 **Range of GMAT:** 600–680 **Average GPA:** 3.3 **TOEFL required of international applicants?** Yes **Minimum TOEFL (paper/computer):** 600/250 **Application fee:** $70 **International application fee:** $70 **Application deadline:** 4/1 **Regular notification:** 6/15 **Application Deadline/Notification Round 1:** 11/15 / 2/15 **Round 2:** 1/15 / 4/15 **Round 3:** 4/1 / 6/15

Early decision program? Yes **ED deadline/notification:** 11/15 / 2/15 **Deferment available?** Yes **Maximum length of deferment:** for one year **Transfer students accepted?** No **Non-fall admissions?** No **Need-blind admissions?** Yes

EMPLOYMENT PROFILE

% grads employed at graduation: 43

% grads employed within three
months of graduation: 69

Average starting salary:................$72,100

Primary Source of Full-time Job Acceptances

School-facilitated activities 12 (50%)

Graduate-facilitated activities 11 (46%)

Unknown...1 (4%)

Grads Employed by Industry:.......**% avg. salary:**

Marketing 33 $70,500

Operations.....................................11 $65,300

Consulting......................................8 $87,500

Management 20 $81,000

Finance 21 $71,200

Top 5 Employers Hiring Grads (#)

NREL (2), Tendril Networks (2), Colorado Altitude Training (2), KPMG Consulting (1), Prologis (1)

UNIVERSITY OF COLORADO AT COLORADO SPRINGS
GRADUATE SCHOOL OF BUSNIESS ADMINISTRATION

ADMISSIONS CONTACT: TAMARA MCCOLLOUGH, MBA ADMISSIONS COORDINATOR
ADDRESS: GRADUATE SCHOOL OF BUSINESS ADMINISTRATION, 1420 AUSTIN BLUFFS PKY, COLORADO SPRINGS, CO 80918
PHONE: 719-255-3122 • FAX: 719-255-3100
E-MAIL: MBACRED@UCCS.EDU
WEBSITE: WWW.UCCS.EDU/MBA

GENERAL INFORMATION

Type of school: Public **Academic calendar:** Semester

STUDENTS

Average age at entry: 30 **Average years work experience at entry:** 6

ADMISSIONS

Admissions Selectivity Rating: 60*

# of applications received: 126 **% applicants accepted:** 88 **Average GMAT:** 550 **Range of GMAT:** 500–570 **Average GPA:** 3.09 **TOEFL required of international applicants?** Yes **Minimum TOEFL (paper/computer):** 550/213 **Application fee:** $60 **International application fee:** $75 **Application Deadline/Notification Round 1:** 6/1 / NR **Round 2:** 11/1 / NR **Round 3:** 4/1 / NR

Early decision program? No **Deferment available?** Yes **Maximum length of deferment:** 1 year **Transfer students accepted?** Yes **Transfer application policy:** Students may transfer up to a maximum of 6 credit credit hours from another AACSB-accredited school. All potential transfer courses must be approved by the program director and members of the graduate faculty. **Non-fall admissions?** Yes **Need-blind admissions?** No

UNIVERSITY OF COLORADO— DENVER
BUSINESS SCHOOL

ADMISSIONS CONTACT: SHELLY TOWNLEY, DIRECTOR OF GRADUATE ADMISSIONS
ADDRESS: CAMPUS BOX 165, PO BOX 173364, DENVER, CO 80217-3364
PHONE: 303-315-8200 • FAX: 303-315-8199
E-MAIL: GRAD.BUSINESS@UCDENVER.EDU.
WEBSITE: WWW.BUSINESS.CUDENVER.EDU

GENERAL INFORMATION

Type of school: Public **Academic calendar:** Semester

STUDENTS

Enrollment of parent institution: 11,050 **Enrollment of MBA program:** 1,249 **% male/female:** 89/11 **% out-of-state:** 1 **% part-time:** 71 **% minorities:** 10 **% international:** 14 **Average age at entry:** 25 **Average years work experience at entry:** 0

ACADEMICS

Student/raculty ratio: 35:1

Joint degrees: Our MBA can be combined with any of our MS degree and students can complete in at little as three years and as long as seven years.

FINANCIAL FACTS

Annual tuition (in-state/out-of-state): $7,844/$18,638 **Fees (in-state/out-of-state):** $594/$594 **Books and supplies:** $1,700 **Room & board (on/off-campus):** $9,950/$8,110

% of students receiving aid: 61 **% of first-year students receiving aid:** 24 **% of students receiving loans:** 52 **% of students receiving grants:** 22 **Average award package:** $7,380 **Average grant:** $4,640 **Average student loan debt:** $33,815

ADMISSIONS

Admissions Selectivity Rating: 60*

# of applications received: 547 **% applicants accepted:** 74 **% acceptees attending:** 64 **TOEFL required of international applicants?** Yes **Minimum TOEFL (paper/computer):** 525/197 **Application fee:** $50 **International application fee:** $75 **Application deadline:** 6/1

Early decision program? No **Deferment available?** Yes **Maximum length of deferment:** 1 year **Transfer students accepted?** Yes **Transfer application policy:** Varies by student and program **Non-fall admissions?** Yes **Need-blind admissions?** Yes

EMPLOYMENT PROFILE

Average starting salary:	$57,903
Grads Employed by Industry:	**% avg. salary:**
Marketing	NR $61,250
Management	NR $62,143
Finance	NR $50,625
MIS	NR $59,285
Entrepreneurship	NR $75,000

UNIVERSITY OF DELAWARE
ALFRED LERNER COLLEGE OF BUSINESS & ECONOMICS

ADMISSIONS CONTACT: DENISE WATERS, DIRECTOR RECRUITMENT & ADMISSIONS
ADDRESS: 103 ALFRED LERNER HALL, NEWARK, DE 19716
PHONE: 302-831-2221 • FAX: 302-831-3329
E-MAIL: MBAPROGRAM@UDEL.EDU
WEBSITE: WWW.MBA.UDEL.EDU

GENERAL INFORMATION

Type of school: Public **Academic calendar:** Semester

STUDENTS

Enrollment of parent institution: 20,000 **Enrollment of MBA program:** 395 **% male/female:** 63/37 **% out-of-state:** 60 **% part-time:** 82 **% minorities:** 7 **% international:** 58 **Average age at entry:** 32 **Average years work experience at entry:** 5

ACADEMICS

Student/faculty ratio: 15:1 **% female faculty:** 16 **% minority faculty:** 19

Joint degrees: MA Economics/MBA, 57 credits; MBA/MS OEDC, 60 credits; MBA/MS ISTM, 60 credits; MBA/MS Engineering, 63 credits;

MBA/PhD Biotechnology, 33 MBA credits plus PhD. **Prominent alumni:** Thomas R. Carper, U.S.Pfizer Senator, Delaware; Thomas Oliver, COO, Next Proteins; Kenneth Whitney, Sr. Managing Director, Blackstone Group; Barry Niziolek, VP & Controller, DuPont; Dan Tipton, CEO, Tipton Communications.

FINANCIAL FACTS

Annual tuition (in-state/out-of-state): $10,462/$22,240 **Fees (in-state/out-of-state):** $850/$850 **Books and supplies:** $2,000 **Room & board (on/off-campus):** $9,500/$11,000

% of students receiving aid: 37 **% of first-year students receiving aid:** 30 **Average award package:** $29,495

ADMISSIONS

Admissions Selectivity Rating: 60*

# of applications received: 172 **% applicants accepted:** 72 **% acceptees attending:** 88 **Average GMAT:** 570 **Average GPA:** 3.1 **TOEFL required of international applicants?** Yes **Minimum TOEFL (paper/computer):** 600/260 **Application fee:** $70 **International application fee:** $70 **Application deadline:** 6/1

Early decision program? No **Deferment available?** Yes **Maximum length of deferment:** 1 academic year **Transfer students accepted?** Yes **Transfer application policy:** Up to nine semester hours of graduate credit earned at another AACSB accredited institution may be accepted toward the University of Delaware MBA degree. The courses must have completed with grades of B or better and within five years. **Non-fall admissions?** Yes **Need-blind admissions?** Yes

EMPLOYMENT PROFILE

% grads employed at graduation: 64

% grads employed within three months of graduation: 29

Average starting salary: $65,600

Primary Source of Full-time Job Acceptances

School-facilitated activities	4 (10%)
Graduate-facilitated activities	2 (5%)
Unknown	27 (66%)

Grads Employed by Industry:	**% avg. salary:**
Marketing	10 $73,000
Operations	5 $72,000
Consulting	2 $61,000
Finance	7 $58,000
HR	2 $70,000
MIS	2 $90,000

Top 5 Employers Hiring Grads (#)

AstraZeneca (1), J.P. Morgan (1), Barclay Card (1), GEICO (1), DuPont (1)

University of Detroit— Mercy
College of Business Administration

Admissions Contact: Tyra Rounds, Director of Recruiting
Address: 4001 W. McNichols, Detroit, MI 48221-3038
Phone: 313-993-1245 • Fax: 313-993-3326
E-mail: admissions@udmercy.edu • Website: www.business.udmercy.edu

GENERAL INFORMATION

Type of school: Private **Affiliation:** Roman Catholic **Academic calendar:** Semester

STUDENTS

Enrollment of parent institution: 5,550 **Enrollment of MBA program:** 126 **Average age at entry:** 24 **Average years work experience at entry:** 3

ACADEMICS

Student/raculty ratio: 30:1 **% female faculty:** 17 **% minority faculty:** 13 **Joint degrees:** JD/MBA, 3 years. **Prominent alumni:** Thomas Angott, Chairman of the Board, C.F. Burger Co.; Thomas Capo, Dollar Thrifty Automotive Group.

FINANCIAL FACTS

Annual tuition: $9,000 **Fees:** $570 **Books and supplies:** $1,200 **Room & board (on-campus):** $4,125 **Average grant:** $40,000

ADMISSIONS

Admissions Selectivity Rating: 60*

# of applications received: 79 **% applicants accepted:** 59 **% acceptees attending:** 81 **Average GMAT:** 541 **Range of GMAT:** 410–720 **Average GPA:** 3.35 **TOEFL required of international applicants?** No **Application fee:** $30 **International application fee:** $50 **Application Deadline/Notification Round 1:** 8/15 / NR **Round 2:** 12/15 / NR **Round 3:** 4/15 / NR **Round 4:** 5/15 / NR

Early decision program? No **Deferment available?** Yes **Maximum length of deferment:** 2 years **Transfer students accepted?** Yes **Transfer application policy:** Must submit transcripts and a GMAT for MBA program. GMAt can be waived. See website for conditions. **Non-fall admissions?** Yes **Need-blind admissions?** No

EMPLOYMENT PROFILE

Average starting salary:................$57,000

Top 5 Employers Hiring Grads

Daimler AG, Ford Motor, Bank One, Comerica

University of Hawaii at Manoa
Shidler College of Business

Admissions Contact: Jennifer Tutak, MBA Admissions Director
Address: 2404 Maile Way, G202, Honolulu, HI 96822
Phone: 808-956-8266 • Fax: 808-956-9890
E-mail: mba@hawaii.edu • Website: www.shidler.hawaii.edu

GENERAL INFORMATION

Type of school: Public **Academic calendar:** Semester

STUDENTS

Enrollment of parent institution: 50,000 **Enrollment of MBA program:** 75 **% male/female:** 69/31 **% out-of-state:** 56 **% part-time:** 40 **% minorities:** 58 **% international:** 18 **Average age at entry:** 28 **Average years work experience at entry:** 5

ACADEMICS

Student/raculty ratio: 25:1 **% female faculty:** 5 **% minority faculty:** 10 **Joint degrees:** MBA/JD, 122-128 credits, 4 years; MBA/Nursing, 3 years;. **Prominent alumni:** Robin Campaniano, Pres &CEO/AIG Insurance; Robert Clarke, Chairman, President & CEO, Hawaiian Electric Industries; Eric Yemen, CEO, Hawaiian Telcomm; Paul Higo, Managing Partner, Deloitte & Touche LLP; Richard Leung, Managing Director & Head of Wealth Management, UBS Securities Company Ltd.

FINANCIAL FACTS

Annual tuition (in-state/out-of-state): $6,456/$9,912 **Fees (in-state/out-of-state):** $300/$300 **Books and supplies:** $1,200 **Room & board (on/off-campus):** $13,517/$13,517

ADMISSIONS

Admissions Selectivity Rating: 60*

# of applications received: 224 **% applicants accepted:** 46 **% acceptees attending:** 73 **Average GMAT:** 628 **Range of GMAT:** 590–670 **Average GPA:** 3.3 **TOEFL required of international applicants?** Yes **Minimum TOEFL (paper/computer):** 600/250 **Application fee:** $60 **International application fee:** $60 **Application deadline:** 5/1 **Regular notification:** 7/1 **Application Deadline/Notification Round 1:** 11/15 / 1/15 **Round 2:** 1/15 / 3/15 **Round 3:** 3/1 / 5/1 **Round 4:** 5/1 / 7/1

Early decision program? Yes **Deferment available?** No **Transfer students accepted?** Yes **Transfer application policy:** Credits may be transferred into the Part-time MBA program from other AACSB-accredited business schools, from other University of Hawaii graduate programs, or by petition as follows: Nine credits of coursework may be transferred into the PT MBA program. T **Non-fall admissions?** No **Need-blind admissions?** Yes

University of Houston— Clear Lake
School of Business

Admissions Contact: Janice Saurwein, Interim Registrar/Director, Academic Records
Address: 2700 Bay Area Blvd, Houston, TX 77058-1098
Phone: 281-283-2500 • Fax: 281-283-2522
E-mail: admissions@uhcl.edu
Website: www.uhcl.edu

GENERAL INFORMATION

Type of school: Public **Academic calendar:** Semester

STUDENTS

Enrollment of parent institution: 7,288 **Enrollment of MBA program:** 368 **% male/female:** 55/45 **% out-of-state:** 10 **% part-time:** 62 **% minorities:** 23 **% international:** 15 **Average age at entry:** 30 **Average years work experience at entry:** 5

ACADEMICS

Student/raculty ratio: 18:1 % female faculty: 31 % minority faculty: 19

Joint degrees: Master of Healthcare Administration/MBA, 57 (3 years). Foundation courses may be required in addition to above hours and may lengthen time of program.

FINANCIAL FACTS

Annual tuition (in-state/out-of-state): $3,600/$13,608 Fees (in-state/out-of-state): $9,504/$10,116 Books and supplies: $1,800 Room & board (on/off-campus): $12,836/$12,836

% of students receiving aid: 20 Average award package: $8,300 Average grant: $1,000 Average student loan debt: $26,916

ADMISSIONS

Admissions Selectivity Rating: 60*

# of applications received: 148 % applicants accepted: 80 % acceptees attending: 42 Average GMAT: 507 Range of GMAT: 460–570 Average GPA: 2.86 TOEFL required of international applicants? Yes Minimum TOEFL (paper/computer): 550/213 Application fee: $35 International application fee: $75 Application deadline: 8/1 Early decision program? No Deferment available? Yes Maximum length of deferment: 12 months Transfer students accepted? Yes Transfer application policy: Final 24 semester hours earned at UHCL-BUS. Non-fall admissions? Yes Need-blind admissions? Yes

UNIVERSITY OF LONDON
LONDON BUSINESS SCHOOL

ADMISSIONS CONTACT: CAROLINE CHUKWUMA / NOEL CALISTE, CLIENT SERVICES OFFICER
ADDRESS: REGENT'S PARK, LONDON NW1 4SA, UNITED KINGDOM OF GREAT BRITAIN AND NORTHERN IRELAND
PHONE: +44 (0)20 7000 7500 • FAX: +44 (0)20 7000 7501
E-MAIL: MBAINFO@LONDON.EDU • WEBSITE: WWW.LONDON.EDU

GENERAL INFORMATION

Type of school: Public Academic calendar: August-July

STUDENTS

Average age at entry: 28.3

FINANCIAL FACTS

$62,675 Books and supplies: $345 Room & board (off-campus): $22,500

% of students receiving loans: 39 % of students receiving grants: 30 Average award package: $76,250 Average student loan debt: $65,500

ADMISSIONS

Admissions Selectivity Rating: 60*

# of applications received: 2,765 Average GMAT: 697 Range of GMAT: 600–790 TOEFL required of international applicants? Yes Application Deadline/Notification Round 1: 10/7 / 12/17 Round 2: 1/6 / 3/26 Round 3: 3/3 / 5/21 Round 4: 4/21 / 7/5

Early decision program? No Deferment available? No Transfer students accepted? No Non-fall admissions? No Need-blind admissions? Yes

EMPLOYMENT PROFILE

% grads employed within three
  months of graduation: 81
Average starting salary:............$108,212
Primary Source of Full-time Job Acceptances
School-facilitated activities ....NR (77%)
Graduate-facilitated activities ....NR (23%)
Top 5 Employers Hiring Grads (#)
McKinsey & Company (21), Credit Suisse (9), The Boston Consulting Group (10), Barclays Group (11), Booz & Company (7)

UNIVERSITY OF MAINE
MAINE BUSINESS SCHOOL

ADMISSIONS CONTACT: CINDY D'ANGELO, ADMINISTRATIVE ASSISTANT, BUSINESS GRADUATE PROGRAMS
ADDRESS: 5723 DP CORBETT BUSINESS BUILDING, ORONO, ME 04469-5723
PHONE: 207-581-1973 • FAX: 207-581-1930
E-MAIL: MBA@MAINE.EDU • WEBSITE: WWW.UMAINE.EDU/BUSINESS

GENERAL INFORMATION

Type of school: Public Academic calendar: Semester

STUDENTS

Enrollment of parent institution: 11,300 Enrollment of MBA program: 79 % male/female: 61/39 % out-of-state: 1 % part-time: 37 % minorities: 1 % international: 23 Average age at entry: 27 Average years work experience at entry: 6

ACADEMICS

Student/raculty ratio: 4:1 % female faculty: 40

Prominent alumni: Nick Heymann, Securities Analyst; Bernard Lown, Nobel Peace Prize winner.

FINANCIAL FACTS

Annual tuition (in-state/out-of-state): $5,328/$15,210 Fees (in-state/out-of-state): $644/$644 Books and supplies: $800 Room & board (on/off-campus): $7,150/$7,150 Average grant: $5,000

ADMISSIONS

Admissions Selectivity Rating: 60*

# of applications received: 42 % applicants accepted: 64 % acceptees attending: 56 Average GMAT: 576 Range of GMAT: 530–610 Average GPA: 3.47 TOEFL required of international applicants? Yes Minimum TOEFL (paper/computer): 550/213 Application fee: $50 Application deadline: 6/1 Regular notification: 7/1 Early decision program? No Deferment available? Yes Maximum length of deferment: 1 year Transfer students accepted? Yes Transfer application policy: A maximum of 6 hours accepted from accredited schools with approval. Non-fall admissions? Yes Need-blind admissions? Yes

UNIVERSITY OF MANITOBA
I.H. ASPER SCHOOL OF BUSINESS

ADMISSIONS CONTACT: EWA MORPHY, GRADUATE PROGRAM MANAGER
ADDRESS: 324 DRAKE CENTER, WINNIPEG, MB R3T 5V4 CANADA
PHONE: 204-474-8448 • FAX: 204-474-7544
E-MAIL: AsperMBA@UMANITOBA.CA • WEBSITE: WWW.UMANITOBA.CA/ASPER

GENERAL INFORMATION

Type of school: Public Academic calendar: Term based

STUDENTS

Enrollment of parent institution: 26,000 Enrollment of MBA program: 120 % male/female: 60/40 % part-time: 72 % international: 9 Average age at entry: 32 Average years work experience at entry: 10

ACADEMICS

Student/faculty ratio: 30:1 % female faculty: 18 % minority faculty: 32

Prominent alumni: F. Ross Johnson, Chairman/CEO RJM Group; Robert W. Pollock, Chairman, Drake International; Gerald W. Schwartz, Chair, President and CEO, Onyx Corp.

FINANCIAL FACTS

Annual tuition (in-state/out-of-state): $16,201/$16,201 Books and supplies: $2,543 Room & board (on/off-campus): $5,800/$10,174 % of first-year students receiving aid: 10 Average grant: $4,000

ADMISSIONS

Admissions Selectivity Rating: 60*

# of applications received: 67 % applicants accepted: 72 % acceptees attending: 63 Average GMAT: 566 Range of GMAT: 444–633 Average GPA: 3 TOEFL required of international applicants? Yes Minimum TOEFL (paper/computer): 550/213 Application fee: $75 International application fee: $90 Application deadline: 6/1 Early decision program? No Deferment available? No Transfer students accepted? Yes Transfer application policy: To earn an Asper MBA, at least half of the courses must be completed at Asper School of Business Non-fall admissions? Yes Need-blind admissions? No

EMPLOYMENT PROFILE

% grads employed at graduation: 71
% grads employed within three
  months of graduation: 12
Average starting salary: $75,000
Primary Source of Full-time Job Acceptances
School-facilitated activities 4 (15%)
Graduate-facilitated activities 14 (50%)
Unknown.......................................10 (35%)

Grads Employed by Industry:.......% avg. salary:
Marketing 5 $97,500
Management 36 $82,143
Finance 5 $62,500
Communications 5 $77,500
Internet 5 $102,500
Quantitative 24 $91,250

UNIVERSITY OF MINNESOTA
CARLSON SCHOOL OF MANAGEMENT

ADMISSIONS CONTACT: JEFF BIEGANEK, DIRECTOR OF ADMISSIONS
ADDRESS: 321 NINETEENTH AVENUE SOUTH, SUITE 1-110, MINNEAPOLIS, MN 55455
PHONE: 612-625-5555 • FAX: 612-626-7785
E-MAIL: FTMBA@UMN.EDU • WEBSITE: WWW.CARLSONSCHOOL.UMN.EDU

GENERAL INFORMATION

Type of school: Public Academic calendar: Semester

STUDENTS

Enrollment of parent institution: 51,690 Enrollment of MBA program: 2,073 % male/female: 64/36 % out-of-state: 34 % part-time: 90 % minorities: 11 % international: 19 Average age at entry: 28 Average years work experience at entry: 4

ACADEMICS

Student/faculty ratio: 15:1 % female faculty: 22 % minority faculty: 20

Joint degrees: JD/MBA, 4 years MHA/MBA, 3 years MD/MBA, 5 years. Prominent alumni: Charles W. Mooty, CEO, International Dairy Queen; William G. Van Dyke, Chairman, President & CEO, Donaldson Company, Inc.; Curtis C. Nelson, President & COO, Carlson Companies; Robert A. Kierlin, Chairman, Fastenal Company; Barbara J. Mowry, President & CEO, TMC Consulting.

FINANCIAL FACTS

Annual tuition (in-state/out-of-state): $21,300/$30,320 Fees (in-state/out-of-state): $2,500/$2,500 Books and supplies: $4,000 Room & board (on/off-campus): $13,000/$15,000 % of students receiving aid: 77 % of students receiving loans: 41 % of students receiving grants: 63 Average award package: $29,260 Average grant: $19,200 Average student loan debt: $41,877

ADMISSIONS

Admissions Selectivity Rating: 60*

# of applications received: 548 % applicants accepted: 41 % acceptees attending: 46 Average GMAT: 683 Range of GMAT: 650–713 Average GPA: 3.43 TOEFL required of international applicants? Yes Minimum TOEFL (paper/computer): 580/240 Application fee: $60 International application fee: $90 Application Deadline/Notification Round 1: 12/1 / 2/15 Round 2: 2/1 / 4/15 Round 3: 4/1 / 5/15

Early decision program? Yes Deferment available? Yes Maximum length of deferment: 1 year Transfer students accepted? No Non-fall admissions? No Need-blind admissions? Yes

EMPLOYMENT PROFILE

% grads employed at graduation: 88
% grads employed within three
  months of graduation: 97
Average starting salary: $82,436
Primary Source of Full-time Job Acceptances
School-facilitated activities 68 (77%)
Graduate-facilitated activities 20 (23%)

Grads Employed by Industry:.......% avg. salary:

Marketing 33 $80,574

Operations.....................................7 $75,417

Consulting.....................................12 $93,732

Management ....3 NR

Finance 24 $78,100

MIS ....1 NR

Top 5 Employers Hiring Grads (#)

Northwest Airlines (8), Best Buy Co., Inc. (7), Ecolab (6), Cargill (4), Deloitte (4)

UNIVERSITY OF MINNESOTA— DULUTH

LABOVITZ SCHOOL OF BUSINESS AND ECONOMICS

ADMISSIONS CONTACT: CANDY FURO, ASSOCIATE ADMINISTRATOR
ADDRESS: 111A LSBE, 1318 KIRBY DRIVE, DULUTH, MN 55812
PHONE: 218-726-8986 • FAX: 218-726-6789
E-MAIL: GRAD@D.UMN.EDU
WEBSITE: WWW.D.UMN.EDU/SBE/DEGREEPROGS/MBA/

GENERAL INFORMATION

Type of school: Public **Academic calendar:** Semester

STUDENTS

Enrollment of parent institution: 11,336 **Enrollment of MBA program:** 78 **% part-time:** 100 **Average age at entry:** 32 **Average years work experience at entry:** 8.5

ACADEMICS

Student/raculty ratio: 20:1 **% female faculty:** 23

Prominent alumni: Jon Gerlach, CFO; Chris Mahai, President/CEO; Elaine Hansen, Director; Jim Vizanko, CFO.

FINANCIAL FACTS

Books and supplies: $1,000 **Room & board (off-campus):** $6,000

ADMISSIONS

Admissions Selectivity Rating: 60*

# of applications received: 29 **% applicants accepted:** 90 **% acceptees attending:** 81 **Average GMAT:** 553 **Range of GMAT:** 470–680 **Average GPA:** 3.44 **TOEFL required of international applicants?** Yes **Minimum TOEFL (paper/computer):** 550/213. **Application fee:** $55 **International application fee:** $75 **Application deadline:** 7/15 **Regular notification:** 9/1 **Application Deadline/Notification Round 1:** 7/15 / 8/31 **Round 2:** 11/1 / 12/31 **Round 3:** 5/1 / 5/30

Early decision program? No **Deferment available?** Yes **Maximum length of deferment:** 1 year without reapp **Transfer students accepted?** Yes **Transfer application policy:** No more than 12 graduate credits can be transferred into program. **Non-fall admissions?** Yes **Need-blind admissions?** Yes

UNIVERSITY OF MONTANA— MISSOULA

SCHOOL OF BUSINESS ADMINISTRATION

ADMISSIONS CONTACT: ,
ADDRESS: 32 CAMPUS DRIVE, #6808, MISSOULA, MT 59812
PHONE: (406) 243-4983 • FAX: (406) 243-2086
WEBSITE: WWW.MBA-MACCT.UMT.EDU/

GENERAL INFORMATION

Type of school: Public

STUDENTS

Average years work experience at entry: 0

FINANCIAL FACTS

Annual tuition (in-state/out-of-state): $2,735/$7,117

ADMISSIONS

Admissions Selectivity Rating: 75

TOEFL required of international applicants? Yes **Application fee:** $45 **Application deadline:** 4/15

Early decision program? No **Deferment available?** No **Transfer students accepted?** No **Non-fall admissions?** No **Need-blind admissions?** No

UNIVERSITY OF NEBRASKA AT OMAHA

COLLEGE OF BUSINESS ADMINISTRATION

ADMISSIONS CONTACT: LEX KACZMAREK, DIRECTOR, MBA PROGRAM
ADDRESS: 6001 DODGE STREET, OMAHA, NE 68182-0048
PHONE: 402-554-2303 • FAX: 402-554-3747
E-MAIL: MBA@UNOMAHA.EDU
WEBSITE: CBA.UNOMAHA.EDU/MBA

GENERAL INFORMATION

Type of school: Public **Academic calendar:** Semester

STUDENTS

Enrollment of parent institution: 11,070 **Enrollment of MBA program:** 294 **% part-time:** 100 **Average age at entry:** 27 **Average years work experience at entry:** 5

ACADEMICS

Student/raculty ratio: 12:1 **% female faculty:** 28 **% minority faculty:** 3

Joint degrees: MBA/MS-MIS: 54 credits (18 mos to 10 years).

Prominent alumni: James R. Young, Pres. and COO, Union Pacific Railroad; R. Craig Hoenshell, Former CEO, Avis and American Express Internationa; Ronald J. Burns, Former Pres. and CEO, Union Pacific; Bernard R. Reznicek, Former Chairman, Pres. and CEO, Boston Edison Comp; Samuel G. Leftwich, Former Pres., K-Mart Corporation.

FINANCIAL FACTS

Room & board (on/off-campus): $8,000/$11,000

% of students receiving aid: 8 % of first-year students receiving aid: 2 % of students receiving grants: 3 Average award package: $14,232 Average grant: $6,763

ADMISSIONS

Admissions Selectivity Rating: 60*

# of applications received: 114 % applicants accepted: 75 % acceptees attending: 93 Average GMAT: 540 Range of GMAT: 500–600 Average GPA: 3.32 TOEFL required of international applicants? Yes Minimum TOEFL (paper/computer): 550/213 Application fee: $45 International application fee: $45 Application deadline: 7/1

Early decision program? No Deferment available? Yes Maximum length of deferment: one year Transfer students accepted? Yes Transfer application policy: A maximum of nine hours of transfer credit may be accepted from another accredited (AACSB) institution. Non-fall admissions? Yes Need-blind admissions? Yes

UNIVERSITY OF NEBRASKA— LINCOLN

COLLEGE OF BUSINESS ADMINISTRATION

ADMISSIONS CONTACT: JUDY SHUTTS, GRADUATE ADVISER
ADDRESS: CBA 125, LINCOLN, NE 68588-0405
PHONE: 402-472-2338 • FAX: 402-472-5997
E-MAIL: CGRADUATE@UNLNOTES.UNL.EDU
WEBSITE: WWW.CBA.UNL.EDU

GENERAL INFORMATION

Type of school: Public Academic calendar: Semester

STUDENTS

Enrollment of parent institution: 23,573 Enrollment of MBA program: 132 % male/female: 67/33 % out-of-state: 5 % part-time: 45 % minorities: 2 % international: 11 Average age at entry: 26 Average years work experience at entry: 4

ACADEMICS

Student/raculty ratio: 6:1 % female faculty: 17 % minority faculty: 13

Joint degrees: MBA/JD (4 years); MBA/Arch (3 years). Prominent alumni: Warren Buffet, Chairman, Berkshire Hathaway; W. Grant Gregory, Former Chrmn. Touche, Ross & Co.; Paul Hogan, Founder and CEO Home Instead Senior Care; Jim Davidson, Founder and Managing Director Silver Lake Partners; John Horner, CEO Arcadia Group.

FINANCIAL FACTS

Annual tuition (in-state/out-of-state): $5,393/$14,496 Fees (in-state/out-of-state): $810/$810 Books and supplies: $1,015 Room & board (on/off-campus): $8,370/$8,370

% of students receiving aid: 51 % of first-year students receiving aid: 69 % of students receiving loans: 27 % of students receiving grants: 38 Average award package: $15,000 Average grant: $9,179

ADMISSIONS

Admissions Selectivity Rating: 60*

# of applications received: 151 % applicants accepted: 36 % acceptees attending: 74 Average GMAT: 614 Range of GMAT: 580–640 Average GPA: 3.4 TOEFL required of international applicants? Yes Minimum TOEFL (paper/computer): 550/213 Application fee: $45 International application fee: $45 Application deadline: 6/15

Early decision program? No Deferment available? Yes Maximum length of deferment: one semester Transfer students accepted? Yes Transfer application policy: 12 credit hours may be accepted from an AACSB accredited institution if approved by the Graduate Committee Non-fall admissions? Yes Need-blind admissions? Yes

EMPLOYMENT PROFILE

% grads employed at graduation: 64

% grads employed within three
    months of graduation: 90

Average starting salary:................$60,275

Primary Source of Full-time Job Acceptances

School-facilitated activities 1 (6%)

Graduate-facilitated activities 2 (11%)

Unknown......................................15 (83%)

Grads Employed by Industry:.......% avg. salary:

Marketing 11 $70,000

Operations.....................................11 NR

Consulting......................................6 $75,000

Management 11 $52,000

Finance 28 $61,700

Communications ....5 NR

Entrepreneurship............................16 $60,000

Nonprofit..6 $40,000

Top 5 Employers Hiring Grads (#)

Gallup (2), TD Ameritrade (1), U.S. Bank (1), Bailey Lauerman (1), IRS Office of Chief Counsel (1)

UNIVERSITY OF NEW MEXICO

ROBERT O. ANDERSON GRADUATE SCHOOL OF MANAGEMENT

ADMISSIONS CONTACT: MEGAN CONNER, SENIOR ACADEMIC ADVISOR
ADDRESS: THE UNIVERSITY OF NEW MEXICO, MSC05 3090, 1 UNIVERSITY OF
NEW MEXICO, ALBUQUERQUE, NM 87131
PHONE: 505-277-3290 • FAX: 505-277-8436
E-MAIL: MCONNER@MGT.UNM.EDU
WEBSITE: WWW.MGT.UNM.EDU/

GENERAL INFORMATION

Type of school: Public Academic calendar: Semester

STUDENTS

Enrollment of parent institution: 34,674 Enrollment of MBA program: 329 % male/female: 49/51 % out-of-state: 4.3 % part-time:

43.2 % minorities: 40.6 % international: 9.6 **Average age at entry:** 25.92 **Average years work experience at entry:** 2

ACADEMICS

Student/raculty ratio: 24:1 **% female faculty:** 32

Joint degrees: MBA/MA in Latin American Studies, 57–72 credits (3 to 4 years); MBA/JD, 119 credits (4 years). **Prominent alumni:** Ann Rhoades, President, PeopleInk; Dr. Waneta Tuttle, President, Southwest Medical Ventures; Maria Griego-Raby, President, Contract Associates; Don Clampitt, Chairman & CEO, Clampitt Paper Co.; Dr. Ned Godshall, CEO, Altela, Inc.

FINANCIAL FACTS

Annual tuition (in-state/out-of-state): $5,929/$14,059 **Books and supplies:** $1,037 **Room & board (on/off-campus):** $18,630/$19,730 **% of students receiving aid:** 74 **% of first-year students receiving aid:** 76 **% of students receiving loans:** 48 **% of students receiving grants:** 46 **Average award package:** $11,518 **Average grant:** $4,978

ADMISSIONS

Admissions Selectivity Rating: 60*

# of applications received: 242 **% applicants accepted:** 60 **% acceptees attending:** 96 **Average GMAT:** 570.3 **Range of GMAT:** 530–610 **Average GPA:** 3.48 **TOEFL required of international applicants?** Yes **Minimum TOEFL (paper/computer):** 550/213 **Application fee:** $50 **International application fee:** $50 **Application deadline:** 4/1

Early decision program? No **Deferment available?** Yes **Maximum length of deferment:** 1 Year **Transfer students accepted?** Yes **Transfer application policy:** Up to 6 credit hours may transfer **Non-fall admissions?** Yes **Need-blind admissions?** Yes

EMPLOYMENT PROFILE

% grads employed at graduation: 13
Average starting salary:................$57,166
Grads Employed by Industry:.......% avg. salary:
Marketing 13 $40,000
Operations...................................13 $61,000
Finance 13 $50,000
MIS..38 $58,333

Top 5 Employers Hiring Grads (#)
Moss Adams (2), KPMG (1), REDW, Meyners & Co. (2)

UNIVERSITY OF NEW ORLEANS
COLLEGE OF BUSINESS ADMINSTRATION

ADMISSIONS CONTACT: ANDY BENOIT, DIRECTOR OF ADMISSIONS
ADDRESS: ADMIN BLDG RM 103, 2000 LAKESHORE DRIVE, NEW ORLEANS, LA 70148
PHONE: 504-280-6595 • FAX: 504-280-5522
E-MAIL: ADMISSIONS@UNO.EDU
WEBSITE: WWW.UNO.EDU

GENERAL INFORMATION

Type of school: Public **Academic calendar:** Semester

STUDENTS

Enrollment of parent institution: 17,360 **Enrollment of MBA program:** 810 **% male/female:** 51/49 **% out-of-state:** 30 **% part-time:** 46 **% minorities:** 25 **% international:** 26 **Average age at entry:** 30

ACADEMICS

Student/raculty ratio: 24:1

Prominent alumni: Dr. James Clark, Chairman of the Board, Netscape Communications; Michael Fitzpatrick, CEO, Rohm & Haas; Erving Johnson, Starting Center, Milwaukee Bucks; Mike Kettenring, President & General Manager, Gillett Broadcasting; Dr. Reuben Arminana, President, Sonoma State University.

FINANCIAL FACTS

Annual tuition (in-state/out-of-state): $3,300/$10,800 **Books and supplies:** $1,150 **Room & board (on/off-campus):** $4,122/$4,122 **Average grant:** $2,697

ADMISSIONS

Admissions Selectivity Rating: 60*

# of applications received: 575 **% applicants accepted:** 67 **% acceptees attending:** 63 **Average GMAT:** 459 **Range of GMAT:** 400–510 **Average GPA:** 3 **TOEFL required of international applicants?** Yes **Minimum TOEFL (paper/computer):** 550/213 **Application fee:** $40 **Application deadline:** 7/1 **Regular notification:** 9/1

Early decision program? No **Deferment available?** Yes **Maximum length of deferment:** 1 semester **Transfer students accepted?** Yes **Transfer application policy:** Maximum number of credit hours transferrable = 12. **Non-fall admissions?** Yes **Need-blind admissions?** Yes

THE UNIVERSITY OF NEW SOUTH WALES (UNSW)
AGSM MBA PROGRAMS

ADMISSIONS CONTACT: BRONWYN ALLAN, TEAM LEADER, ADMISSIONS
ADDRESS: AGSM BUILDING, UNSW, SYDNEY NSW, 2052 AUSTRALIA
PHONE: 0061 2 99319490 • FAX: 0061 2 99319205
E-MAIL: ADMISSIONS@AGSM.EDU.AU
WEBSITE: WWW.AGSM.EDU.AU

GENERAL INFORMATION

Type of school: Public **Academic calendar:** January

STUDENTS

% male/female: 81/19 **% part-time:** 0 **% international:** 56 **Average age at entry:** 29 **Average years work experience at entry:** 7

ACADEMICS

Student/raculty ratio: 4:1 **% female faculty:** 36

Joint degrees: MBA/LLM, 2 years.

FINANCIAL FACTS

Annual tuition (in-state/out-of-state): $48,930/$48,930 **Books and supplies:** $3,000 **Room & board (off-campus):** $20,000

ADMISSIONS

Admissions Selectivity Rating: 60*

# of applications received: 171 % applicants accepted: 63 % acceptees attending: 58 **Average GMAT:** 656 **Range of GMAT:** 620–700 **Average GPA:** 3 **TOEFL required of international applicants?** No **Minimum TOEFL (paper/computer):** 600/250 **Application fee:** $50 **International application fee:** $50 **Application deadline:** 10/15 **Application Deadline/Notification Round 1:** 9/1 / NR **Round 2:** 10/15 / NR

Early decision program? No **Deferment available?** Yes **Maximum length of deferment:** 1 year **Transfer students accepted?** Yes **Transfer application policy:** Transfer applicants must submit a completed application and meet all entry requirements; entry is January each year only; recognition of prior learning may be offered only for core courses correlations. **Non-fall admissions?** No **Need-blind admissions?** No

EMPLOYMENT PROFILE

% grads employed within three
  months of graduation: 3
Average starting salary:...............$116,411

Grads Employed by Industry:	%	avg. salary:
Marketing	9	$104,500
Consulting	35	$109,923
Management	13	$81,190
Finance	17	$92,821
Strategic	22	$85,662

Top 5 Employers Hiring Grads

ABN AMRO, American Express (Brazil), Australian Stock Exchange, Australian Campus Network, Bain & Company

UNIVERSITY OF NORTH TEXAS
COLLEGE OF BUSINESS

ADMISSIONS CONTACT: DENISE GALUBENSKI OR KONNI STUBBLEFIELD, GRADUATE ACADEMIC ADVISORS
ADDRESS: P.O. BOX 311160, DENTON, TX 76203
PHONE: 940-369-8977 • FAX: 940-369-8978
E-MAIL: MBA@COBAF.UNT.EDU
WEBSITE: WWW.COBA.UNT.EDU

GENERAL INFORMATION

Type of school: Public **Academic calendar:** Semester

STUDENTS

Enrollment of parent institution: 34,500 **Enrollment of MBA program:** 639 **% international:** 10 **Average age at entry:** 28 **Average years work experience at entry:** 5.85

ACADEMICS

Student/faculty ratio: 45:1 **% female faculty:** 22 **% minority faculty:** 17

Joint degrees: MBA Operations Management Science/MS Engineering Technology (48 hours); MBA (any professional field)/MS in Merchandising (54 hours); MBA (any professional field)/MS in Hospitality Management (54 hours). **Prominent alumni:** Laura Wright, CFO / Southwest Airlines; Noreen Henry, VP of Packaging & Hotels/ Travelocity; Brent Ryan, Owner of Ryan & Co.

FINANCIAL FACTS

Annual tuition (in-state/out-of-state): $1,898/$4,400 **Fees (in-state/out-of-state):** $639/$639 **Books and supplies:** $1,000 **Room & board (on/off-campus):** $6,000/$6,000

ADMISSIONS

Admissions Selectivity Rating: 60*

# of applications received: 343 % applicants accepted: 55 **Average GMAT:** 468 **Range of GMAT:** 410–530 **Average GPA:** 3 **TOEFL required of international applicants?** Yes **Minimum TOEFL (paper/computer):** 550/213 **Application fee:** $50 **International application fee:** $75 **Application deadline:** 7/15

Early decision program? No **Deferment available?** Yes **Maximum length of deferment:** Three semesters **Transfer students accepted?** Yes **Transfer application policy:** Transfer applicants must meet the same university application deadline. Only six to nine hours may transfer into our program. These hours will be determined by the departmental advisor. **Non-fall admissions?** Yes **Need-blind admissions?** Yes

UNIVERSITY OF QUEENSLAND
UQ BUSINESS SCHOOL

ADMISSIONS CONTACT: THE MANAGER, STUDENT ADMIN,
ADDRESS: UQ BUSINESS SCHOOL, THE UNIVERSITY OF QUEENSLAND, ST LUCIA, Q 4072 AUSTRALIA
PHONE: 011-617-3365 6475 • FAX: 011-617-3365 6988
E-MAIL: POSTGRAD_ENQUIRIES@BUSINESS.UQ.EDU.AU
WEBSITE: WWW.BUSINESS.UQ.EDU.AU

GENERAL INFORMATION

Type of school: Private

STUDENTS

Average years work experience at entry: 0

FINANCIAL FACTS

Annual tuition: $17,050

ADMISSIONS

Admissions Selectivity Rating: 60*

TOEFL required of international applicants? No **Application deadline:** 1/30 **Regular notification:** 1/30

Early decision program? No **Deferment available?** No **Transfer students accepted?** No **Non-fall admissions?** No **Need-blind admissions?** No

UNIVERSITY OF SOUTH ALABAMA
MITCHELL COLLEGE OF BUSINESS

ADMISSIONS CONTACT: OFFICE OF ADMISSIONS,
ADDRESS: MEISLER HALL SUITE 2500, MOBILE, AL 36688-0002
PHONE: 251-460-6141 • FAX: 251-460-7876
E-MAIL: ADMISS@USOUTHAL.EDU • WEBSITE: MCOB.SOUTHALABAMA.EDU/

GENERAL INFORMATION

Type of school: Public

STUDENTS

Enrollment of parent institution: 13,500 **Enrollment of MBA program:** 135 **% male/female:** 55/45 **% out-of-state:** 0 **% part-time:** 0 **% minorities:** 55 **% international:** 10 **Average age at entry:** 28

ACADEMICS

Student/faculty ratio: 31:1 **% female faculty:** 21 **% minority faculty:** 10

FINANCIAL FACTS

Annual tuition (in-state/out-of-state): $4,008/$8,016 **Fees (in-state/out-of-state):** $2,460/$2,460 **Books and supplies:** $1,200 **Room & board (on/off-campus):** $4,750/$7,200

ADMISSIONS

Admissions Selectivity Rating: 60*

# of applications received: 80 **% applicants accepted:** 78 **% acceptees attending:** 73 **Average GMAT:** 550 **Average GPA:** 3.4 **TOEFL required of international applicants?** Yes Minimum TOEFL (paper): 525 **Application fee:** $25 **International application fee:** $25 **Application deadline:** 7/15 **Regular notification:** 7/25

Early decision program? No **Deferment available?** No **Transfer students accepted?** Yes **Transfer application policy:** May transfer in up to 9 credits toward degeree. **Non-fall admissions?** No **Need-blind admissions?** Yes

UNIVERSITY OF SOUTH FLORIDA
COLLEGE OF BUSINESS

ADMISSIONS CONTACT: IRENE HURST, DIRECTOR OF MBA PROGRAMS
ADDRESS: 4202 E. FOWLER AVE. BSN 3403, LOC BSN 103, TAMPA, FL 33620
PHONE: 813-974-3335 • FAX: 813-974-4518
E-MAIL: MBA@COBA.USF.EDU
WEBSITE: WWW.COBA.USF.EDU

GENERAL INFORMATION

Type of school: Public **Academic calendar:** Semester

STUDENTS

Enrollment of parent institution: 40,267 **Enrollment of MBA program:** 269 **% male/female:** 68/32 **% out-of-state:** 8 **% part-time:** 62 **% minorities:** 18 **% international:** 14.5 **Average age at entry:** 27 **Average years work experience at entry:** 4.5

ACADEMICS

Student/faculty ratio: 5:1 **% female faculty:** 22 **% minority faculty:** 31

Joint degrees: All of the listed masters' program can be combined with each other. Most students do dual degree with MBA and another MS degree. They double count up to 9 credit hours. **Prominent alumni:** Rob Carter, Executive VP & CIO, Federal Express Corporation; Philip Singleton, President & COO (retired), AMC Entertainment; D. Beatty DÂ'Alessandro, Senior Vice President & CFO, Graybar Electric Co.; John Reich, FDIC Dir. of the U.S. Office of Thrift Supervision; Rear Admiral Adam Robinson, Jr., US Navy Commander & Chief, Nat'l Naval Med. Cntr.

FINANCIAL FACTS

Annual tuition (in-state/out-of-state): $7,963/$19,648 **Fees (in-state/out-of-state):** $184/$184 **Books and supplies:** $2,000 **Room & board (on/off-campus):** $9,660/$10,000 **Average grant:** $2,000

ADMISSIONS

Admissions Selectivity Rating: 60*

# of applications received: 335 **% applicants accepted:** 39 **% acceptees attending:** 57 **Average GMAT:** 538 **Range of GMAT:** 490–610 **Average GPA:** 3.2 **TOEFL required of international applicants?** Yes **Minimum TOEFL (paper/computer):** 550/213 **Application fee:** $30 **International application fee:** $30 **Application deadline:** 6/1 **Regular notification:** 6/1

Early decision program? No **Deferment available?** Yes **Maximum length of deferment:** 1 year **Transfer students accepted?** Yes **Transfer application policy:** 12 credits from an AACSB University. **Non-fall admissions?** Yes **Need-blind admissions?** Yes

EMPLOYMENT PROFILE

% grads employed at graduation: 35
% grads employed within three months of graduation: 41
Average starting salary:...............$53,000
Primary Source of Full-time Job Acceptances
School-facilitated activities 12 (36%)
Graduate-facilitated activities 12 (36%)
Unknown..9 (27%)

Grads Employed by Industry:	% avg. salary:
Marketing	20 $50,000
Operations	3 NR
Consulting	6 NR
Management	9 NR
Finance	54 $54,800
MIS	14 $48,000

UNIVERSITY OF SOUTH FLORIDA—ST. PETERSBURG
COLLEGE OF BUSINESS

ADMISSIONS CONTACT: ,
ADDRESS: 140 SEVENTH AVENUE SOUTH, BAY 104, ST. PETERSBURG, FL 33701
PHONE: 727-873-4142 • FAX: 727-873-4525
E-MAIL: ADMISSIONS@STPT.USF.EDU
WEBSITE: WWW.STPT.USF.EDU

GENERAL INFORMATION

Type of school: Public

STUDENTS

Enrollment of MBA program: 162 **% out-of-state:** 0 **% part-time:** 100 **% international:** 0 **Average age at entry:** 29 **Average years work experience at entry:** 4

ACADEMICS

Student/raculty ratio: 9:1 % female faculty: 39 % minority faculty: 6

ADMISSIONS

Admissions Selectivity Rating: 83

# of applications received: 75 % applicants accepted: 59 % acceptees attending: 82 Average GMAT: 568 Range of GMAT: 530–590 Average GPA: 3.44 TOEFL required of international applicants? No Minimum TOEFL (paper/computer): 550/213 Application fee: $30 International application fee: $30 Application deadline: 7/1 Regular notification: 7/8

Early decision program? No Deferment available? Yes Maximum length of deferment: 1 year Transfer students accepted? Yes Transfer application policy: Students who meet our admission criteria may import up to two courses (6 credit hours) from any AACSB accredit business school. Courses require MBA Director approval. Non-fall admissions? Yes Need-blind admissions? Yes

UNIVERSITY OF SOUTHERN INDIANA
COLLEGE OF BUSINESS

ADMISSIONS CONTACT: DR. PEGGY HARREL, DIRECTOR OF GRADUATE STUDIES
ADDRESS: 8600 UNIVERSITY BOULVARD, EVANSVILLE, IN 47712
PHONE: 812-465-7015 • FAX: 812-464-1956
E-MAIL: GSSR@USI.EDU
WEBSITE: BUSINESS.USI.EDU

GENERAL INFORMATION

Type of school: Public Academic calendar: Semester

STUDENTS

Enrollment of parent institution: 10,516 Enrollment of MBA program: 101 % male/female: 75/25 % out-of-state: 0 % part-time: 88 % international: 17 Average age at entry: 27 Average years work experience at entry: 7

ACADEMICS

Student/raculty ratio: 26:1 % female faculty: 17 % minority faculty: 17

FINANCIAL FACTS

Annual tuition (in-state/out-of-state): $4,592/$9,060 Fees (in-state/out-of-state): $200/$200 Books and supplies: $1,100 Room & board (on/off-campus): $6,700/$9,130

% of students receiving aid: 23 % of first-year students receiving aid: 36 % of students receiving loans: 8 % of students receiving grants: 10 Average award package: $9,107 Average grant: $1,912

ADMISSIONS

Admissions Selectivity Rating: 60*

# of applications received: 33 % applicants accepted: 91 % acceptees attending: 80 Average GMAT: 581 Range of GMAT: 530–640 Average GPA: 3.35 TOEFL required of international applicants? Yes Minimum TOEFL (paper/computer): 550/213 Application fee: $25 International application fee: $25

Early decision program? No Deferment available? No Transfer students accepted? Yes Transfer application policy: Twelve accepted hours can be transferred into the program Non-fall admissions? Yes Need-blind admissions? Yes

THE UNIVERSITY OF SOUTHERN MISSISSIPPI
COLLEGE OF BUSINESS

ADMISSIONS CONTACT: GABRIEL MCPHEARSON, ASSISTANT TO THE DIRECTOR
ADDRESS: 118 COLLEGE DRIVE #5096, HATTIESBURG, MS 39406-5096
PHONE: 601-266-4653 • FAX: 601-266-5814
E-MAIL: MBA@USM.EDU
WEBSITE: WWW.USM.EDU/MBA

GENERAL INFORMATION

Type of school: Public Academic calendar: Semester

STUDENTS

Enrollment of parent institution: 15,030 Enrollment of MBA program: 93 % male/female: 58/42 % out-of-state: 24 % part-time: 59 % minorities: 8 % international: 8 Average age at entry: 27

ACADEMICS

Student/raculty ratio: 30:1 % female faculty: 25 % minority faculty: 15

Joint degrees: MBA/MPH (Master of Public Health) - 69 credits (24 months to 6 years).

FINANCIAL FACTS

Annual tuition (in-state/out-of-state): $4,312/$4,312 $5,430 Books and supplies: $1,600 Room & board (on/off-campus): $5,800/$7,600

% of students receiving aid: 75 % of students receiving grants: 25 Average grant: $8,690

ADMISSIONS

Admissions Selectivity Rating: 60*

# of applications received: 73 % applicants accepted: 56 % acceptees attending: 76 Average GMAT: 508 Range of GMAT: 450–560 Average GPA: 3.36 TOEFL required of international applicants? Yes Minimum TOEFL (paper/computer): 550/213 Application fee: $25 International application fee: $25 Application deadline: 7/15

Early decision program? No Deferment available? Yes Maximum length of deferment: 2 semesters Transfer students accepted? Yes Transfer application policy: They must fully apply to the program and can only transfer a total of 6 hours of graduate courses from other accredited institutions. The coursework must be graded (i.e., not pass/fail). Non-fall admissions? Yes Need-blind admissions? Yes

EMPLOYMENT PROFILE

Average starting salary:...............$43,179

Primary Source of Full-time Job Acceptances

Unknown......................................13 (100%)

Grads Employed by Industry:.......% avg. salary:

Marketing 15 $35,000

Operations.....................................7 $48,600

Management 23 $37,301

Finance 15 $35,056

Top 5 Employers Hiring Grads

Cintas, Frito Lay, Walgreen's, Sherman Williams Co., AmSouth Bank

UNIVERSITY OF STRATHCLYDE, GLASGOW

UNIVERSITY OF STRATHCLYDE GRADUATE SCHOOL OF BUSINESS

ADMISSIONS CONTACT: 141-553- 6118, LUCY REYNOLDS
ADDRESS: 199 CATHEDRAL STREET, GLASGOW, G4 0QU
PHONE: 141-553-6118 • FAX: 141-553-6162
E-MAIL: ADMISSIONS@GSB.STRATH.AC.UK • WEBSITE: WWW.GSB.STRATH.AC.UK

GENERAL INFORMATION

Type of school: Private **Academic calendar:** 05/06

STUDENTS

Enrollment of MBA program: 107 **% male/female:** 86/14 **% part-time:** 37 **% minorities:** 88 **% international:** 84 **Average age at entry:** 32 **Average years work experience at entry:** 9

ACADEMICS

Student/raculty ratio: 4:1 **% female faculty:** 11

Joint degrees: MBA with a specialism in Leadership Studies, 2.5–3 years.

FINANCIAL FACTS

Fees: $31,600 **Books and supplies:** $150 **Room & board (on/off-campus):** $13,500/$15,300

ADMISSIONS

Admissions Selectivity Rating: 60*

# of applications received: 280 **% applicants accepted:** 90 **% acceptees attending:** 42 **Average GMAT:** 560 **Average GPA:** 3.4

TOEFL required of international applicants? Yes **Minimum TOEFL (paper/computer):** 600/250

Early decision program? No **Deferment available?** Yes **Maximum length of deferment:** 2 years **Transfer students accepted?** No **Non-fall admissions?** Yes **Need-blind admissions?** No

EMPLOYMENT PROFILE

Average starting salary:...............$124,000

Grads Employed by Industry:.......% avg. salary:

Marketing 5 $85,500

Consulting.....................................10 $142,000

Finance 13 $130,000

Entrepreneurship............................10

Internet 15 $114,000

Nonprofit..4 $66,500

Top 5 Employers Hiring Grads

Mott McDonald (4), BT (3), RBoS (1), Standard Life (1), Prince and Princess of Wales Hospice (1)

UNIVERSITY OF TENNESSEE AT MARTIN

COLLEGE OF BUSINESS AND PUBLIC AFFAIRS

ADMISSIONS CONTACT: KEVIN HAMMOND, COLLEGE OF BUSINESS & PUBLIC AFFAIRS GRADUATE PROG
ADDRESS: 109 BUSINESS ADMINISTRATION BUILDING, MARTIN, TN 38238-5015
PHONE: 731-881-7208 • FAX: 731-587-7241
E-MAIL: BAGRAD@UTM.EDU • WEBSITE: WWW.UTM.EDU/MBA

GENERAL INFORMATION

Type of school: Public **Academic calendar:** Semester

STUDENTS

Enrollment of parent institution: 7,000 **Enrollment of MBA program:** 53 **% male/female:** 73/27 **% out-of-state:** 0 **% part-time:** 79 **% minorities:** 9 **% international:** 36 **Average age at entry:** 26 **Average years work experience at entry:** 2

ACADEMICS

Student/raculty ratio: 3.5:1 **% female faculty:** 33 **% minority faculty:** 13

FINANCIAL FACTS

Annual tuition (in-state/out-of-state): $9,126/$25,089 **Books and supplies:** $1,000 **Room & board (on-campus):** $1,110

ADMISSIONS

Admissions Selectivity Rating: 60*

# of applications received: 20 **% applicants accepted:** 80 **% acceptees attending:** 94 **Average GMAT:** 493 **Range of GMAT:** 430–550 **Average GPA:** 3.4 **TOEFL required of international applicants?** Yes **Minimum TOEFL (paper):** 525 **Application fee:** $30

Early decision program? No **Deferment available?** Yes **Maximum length of deferment:** 99999 **Transfer students accepted?** Yes **Transfer application policy:** Transfer coursework must be from regionally accredited institution. See graduate section of the current catalog for further specifics. **Non-fall admissions?** Yes **Need-blind admissions?** No

THE UNIVERSITY OF TEXAS AT EL PASO

COLLEGE OF BUSINESS ADMINISTRATION

ADMISSIONS CONTACT: LAURA URIBARRI, DIRECTOR OF MBA PROGRAMS
ADDRESS: COLLEGE OF BUSINESS ADMINISTRATION,RM 102, 500 W UNIVERSITY AVENUE, EL PASO, TX 79968
PHONE: 915-747-5379 • FAX: 915-747-5147
E-MAIL: LMURIBARRI@UTEP.EDU. • WEBSITE: WWW.MBA.UTEP.EDU

GENERAL INFORMATION

Type of school: Public **Academic calendar:** Semester

STUDENTS

Enrollment of parent institution: 20,458 Enrollment of MBA program: 295 % male/female: 50/50 % out-of-state: 12 % part-time: 90 % minorities: 58 % international: 7 Average age at entry: 34 Average years work experience at entry: 7

ACADEMICS

Student/raculty ratio: 14:1 % female faculty: 20 % minority faculty: 25

Joint degrees: MBA/Master in Public Administration (MBA/MPA), 72 credits, 3 to 6 years.

FINANCIAL FACTS

Books and supplies: $3,512 Room & board (off-campus): $10,572 % of students receiving aid: 37 % of first-year students receiving aid: 7 % of students receiving loans: 29 % of students receiving grants: 10 Average award package: $10,810 Average grant: $3,704 Average student loan debt: $22,750

ADMISSIONS

Admissions Selectivity Rating: 60*

# of applications received: 99 Average GMAT: 460 Range of GMAT: 400–570 Average GPA: 3.19 TOEFL required of international applicants? Yes Minimum TOEFL (paper/computer): 600/250 Application fee: $45 International application fee: $80 Application deadline: 7/15

Early decision program? No Deferment available? Yes Maximum length of deferment: 1 yr for US Applicants Transfer students accepted? Yes Transfer application policy: Limited transfer credits allowed Non-fall admissions? Yes Need-blind admissions? Yes

EMPLOYMENT PROFILE

% grads employed at graduation: 100
% grads employed within three
  months of graduation: …………10
Average starting salary:……………$60,000
Top 5 Employers Hiring Grads
P&G, Lockheed Martin, Johnson & Johnson, ADP, Boeing

THE UNIVERSITY OF TEXAS AT TYLER
COLLEGE OF BUSINESS AND TECHNOLOGY

ADMISSIONS CONTACT: DR. MARY FISCHER, ASSOCIATE DEAN
ADDRESS: 3900 UNIVERSITY BOULEVARD, TYLER, TX 75799
PHONE: 903-566-7433 • FAX: 903-566-7372
E-MAIL: MFISCHER@UTTYLER.EDU
WEBSITE: WWW.UTTYLER.EDU/CBT

GENERAL INFORMATION

Type of school: Public Academic calendar: Semester

STUDENTS

Enrollment of parent institution: 6,150 Enrollment of MBA program: 189 % part-time: 99

ACADEMICS

Student/raculty ratio: 20:1 % female faculty: 45 % minority faculty: 33

Joint degrees: MSN/MBA 57 hours (2 to 6 years); MBA/MEng 57 hours (2 to 6 years).

FINANCIAL FACTS

/ Books and supplies: $975

ADMISSIONS

Admissions Selectivity Rating: 60*

# of applications received: 110 % applicants accepted: 76 % acceptees attending: 100 Average GMAT: 513 Average GPA: 3.11 TOEFL required of international applicants? Yes Minimum TOEFL (paper/computer): 550/213 Application fee: $25 International application fee: $50

Early decision program? No Deferment available? Yes Maximum length of deferment: 12 months Transfer students accepted? No Non-fall admissions? Yes Need-blind admissions? Yes

UNIVERSITY OF TORONTO
JOSEPH L. ROTMAN SCHOOL OF MANAGEMENT

ADMISSIONS CONTACT: CHERYL MILLINGTON, DIRECTOR OF MBA RECRUITING
  AND ADMISSIONS
ADDRESS: 105 ST. GEORGE STREET, TORONTO, ON M5S 3E6 CANADA
PHONE: 416-978-3499 • FAX: 416-978-5812
E-MAIL: MBA@ROTMAN.UTORONTO.CA
WEBSITE: WWW.ROTMAN.UTORONTO.CA

GENERAL INFORMATION

Type of school: Public Academic calendar: Sept–May

STUDENTS

Enrollment of parent institution: 70,000 Enrollment of MBA program: 366 % male/female: 72/28 % part-time: 28 % international: 37 Average age at entry: 27 Average years work experience at entry: 4.7

ACADEMICS

Student/raculty ratio: 7:1 % female faculty: 24

Joint degrees: BASC/MBA (5 years, 8 months) Collaborative Program in Asia-Pacific Studies (2+ years) Collaborative Program in Environmental Studies (2+ years). Prominent alumni: Joseph L. Rotman, Founder & Chairman, Clairvest Group Inc.; Bill Downe, President and Chief Executive Officer, BMO Financial Group; Don Morrison, COO, Research In Motion, Waterloo, Ont.; John Cassaday, President & CEO, Corus Entertainment; Richard Nesbitt, CEO, CIBC World Markets.

FINANCIAL FACTS

Annual tuition (in-state/out-of-state): $30,820/ Fees (in-state/out-of-state): $1,078/ Books and supplies: $5,000 Room & board (on/off-campus): $10,000/$10,000

% of students receiving aid: 70 % of first-year students receiving aid: 70 % of students receiving loans: 70 % of students receiving grants: 20 Average grant: $8,000

ADMISSIONS

Admissions Selectivity Rating: 60*

# of applications received: 1,100 **Average GMAT:** 660 **Range of GMAT:** 550–780 **Average GPA:** 3.4 **TOEFL required of international applicants?** Yes **Minimum TOEFL (paper/computer):** 600/250 **Application fee:** $150 **International application fee:** $150 **Application deadline:** 4/30 **Regular notification:** 7/1 **Application Deadline/Notification Round 1:** 11/15 / 1/15 **Round 2:** 1/15 / 3/15 **Round 3:** 4/30 / 7/1

Early decision program? Yes **Deferment available?** Yes **Maximum length of deferment:** one year **Transfer students accepted?** No **Non-fall admissions?** No **Need-blind admissions?** Yes

EMPLOYMENT PROFILE

% grads employed within three
months of graduation: 93
Average starting salary:................$83,067
Primary Source of Full-time Job Acceptances
School-facilitated activities ....NR (60%)
Graduate-facilitated activities ....NR (40%)
Grads Employed by Industry: ....% avg. salary:
Marketing 8 $78,000
Operations......................................2 $68,300
Consulting......................................23 $103,000
Management 10 $80,000
Finance 23 $77,600

Top 5 Employers Hiring Grads (#)
CIBC (19), RBC Financial Group (12), Deloitte (11), BMO Financial Group (9), Scotiabank (7)

UNIVERSITY OF WARWICK
WARWICK BUSINESS SCHOOL

ADMISSIONS CONTACT: HEATHER BROADBENT, MBA MARKETING & RECRUITMENT TEAM
ADDRESS: WARWICK BUSINESS SCHOOL, COVENTRY, CV4 7AL
PHONE: 011-44 (0)24 7652 4100 • FAX: 011-44 (0)24 7657 4400
E-MAIL: WARWICKMBA@WBS.AC.UK
WEBSITE: WWW.WBS.AC.UK

GENERAL INFORMATION
Type of school: Public **Academic calendar:** Trimester

STUDENTS
Enrollment of parent institution: 18,000 **Enrollment of MBA program:** 580 **% male/female:** 65/35 **% part-time:** 87 **% international:** 85 **Average age at entry:** 31 **Average years work experience at entry:** 7

ACADEMICS
Student/faculty ratio: 12:1
Prominent alumni: Svein Stokke, Director, Citigroup; Keith Bedell-Pearce, Chairman, Norwich & Peterborough Building Society; Mike O'Driscoll, President, Aston Martin, Jaguar, Land Rover; Steven Falk, Director of Financial Services, Manchester Utd FC; Roger Lovering, Head of Card Services, HSBC Bank plc.

FINANCIAL FACTS

Annual tuition (in-state/out-of-state): $28,532/$28,532 **Books and supplies:** $2,000 **Room & board (on/off-campus):** $11,000/$11,000 **% of students receiving aid:** 15 **% of students receiving grants:** 15 **Average award package:** $7,500 **Average grant:** $7,500

ADMISSIONS

Admissions Selectivity Rating: 60*

# of applications received: 268 **% applicants accepted:** 42 **% acceptees attending:** 65 **Average GMAT:** 610 **Range of GMAT:** 550–680 **TOEFL required of international applicants?** Yes **Minimum TOEFL (paper/computer):** 620/260 **Application fee:** $110 **International application fee:** $110

Early decision program? No **Deferment available?** Yes **Maximum length of deferment:** 12 months **Transfer students accepted?** No **Non-fall admissions?** No **Need-blind admissions?** No

EMPLOYMENT PROFILE

% grads employed within three
months of graduation: 88
Average starting salary:................$65,724
Primary Source of Full-time Job Acceptances
School-facilitated activities ....NR (30%)
Graduate-facilitated activities ....NR (70%)
Grads Employed by Industry:......% avg. salary:
Marketing ....17 NR
Operations......................................7 NR
Consulting.......................................14 NR
Management ....13 NR
Finance ....17 NR
MIS..3 NR
Entrepreneurship............................3 NR
Strategic ....14 NR

Top 5 Employers Hiring Grads
Deloitte, Cap Gemini, Johnson & Johnson, Pepsico, Proctor & Gamble

UNIVERSITY OF WEST FLORIDA
COLLEGE OF BUSINESS

ADMISSIONS CONTACT: GRADUATE ADMISSIONS OFFICE, GRADUATE ADMISSIONS OFFICERS
ADDRESS: 11000 UNIVERSITY PKWY, BLDG 18, PENSACOLA, FL 32514
PHONE: 850-474-2230 • FAX: 850-474-3360
E-MAIL: ADMISSIONS@UWF.EDU
WEBSITE: UWF.EDU/MBA

GENERAL INFORMATION
Type of school: Public

STUDENTS
Enrollment of MBA program: 178 **% male/female:** 60/40 **% out-of-state:** 80 **% part-time:** 90 **% international:** 80 **Average age at entry:** 29

ACADEMICS

Student/raculty ratio: 25:1 % female faculty: 13 % minority faculty: 13

Joint degrees: Joint MBA/Master of Science with Nyenrode University in the Netherlands. MBA is approximately 20 months; Master of Science is approximately 8-12 months.

FINANCIAL FACTS

Annual tuition (in-state/out-of-state): $8,325/$30,093 **Books and supplies:** $1,000 **Average grant:** $1,400

ADMISSIONS

Admissions Selectivity Rating: 60*

# of applications received: 71 % applicants accepted: 49 % acceptees attending: 80 Average GMAT: 537 Range of GMAT: 460–600 Average GPA: 3.36 TOEFL required of international applicants? Yes Minimum TOEFL (paper/computer): 550/213 Application fee: $30 International application fee: $30 Application deadline: 6/1

Early decision program? No Deferment available? Yes Maximum length of deferment: One year Transfer students accepted? Yes Transfer application policy: Student can transfer in no more than 6 credit hours from an AACSB Accredited School. Student must meet the minimum GMAT score of 450. Non-fall admissions? Yes Need-blind admissions? No

UNIVERSITY OF WISCONSIN— EAU CLAIRE
SCHOOL OF BUSINESS

ADMISSIONS CONTACT: MS. JAN STEWART, MBA PROGRAM ASSISTANT
ADDRESS: 105 GARFIELD AVENUE, EAU CLAIRE, WI 54702-4004
PHONE: 715-836-4733 • FAX: 715-836-2409
E-MAIL: ADMISSIONS@UWEC.EDU
WEBSITE: WWW.UWEC.EDU/COB/ACADEMICS/MBA/INDEX.HTM

GENERAL INFORMATION

Type of school: Public Academic calendar: Semester

STUDENTS

Enrollment of parent institution: 10,500 Enrollment of MBA program: 130 % male/female: 55/45 % out-of-state: 80 % part-time: 90 % minorities: 5 % international: 80 Average age at entry: 28 Average years work experience at entry: 7

ACADEMICS

Student/raculty ratio: 5:1 % female faculty: 30

Joint degrees: Partner in the University of Wisconsin Internet Consortium MBA Program. Students may combine online courses with on campus courses.

FINANCIAL FACTS

Annual tuition (in-state/out-of-state): $6,223/$16,833 **Books and supplies:** $1,000 **Room & board (on-campus):** $4,266

ADMISSIONS

Admissions Selectivity Rating: 60*

Average GMAT: 530 Average GPA: 3.2 TOEFL required of international applicants? Yes Minimum TOEFL (paper/computer): 550/213 Application fee: $45

Early decision program? No Deferment available? Yes Maximum length of deferment: 1 year Transfer students accepted? Yes Transfer application policy: Transfer credits are accepted from other AACSB accredited schools. Non-fall admissions? Yes Need-blind admissions? Yes

EMPLOYMENT PROFILE

Grads Employed by Industry:	%	avg. salary:
Marketing	20	NR
Operations	10	NR
Management	30	NR
MIS	10	NR
Entrepreneurship	10	NR

UNIVERSITY OF WISCONSIN— LA CROSSE
COLLEGE OF BUSINESS ADMINISTRATION

ADMISSIONS CONTACT: KATHY KIEFER, DIRECTOR
ADDRESS: 1725 STATE STREET, LA CROSSE, WI 54601
PHONE: 608-785-8939 • FAX: 608-785-6695
E-MAIL: ADMISSIONS@UWLAX.EDU
WEBSITE: WWW.UWLAX.EDU

GENERAL INFORMATION

Type of school: Public Academic calendar: Semester

STUDENTS

Enrollment of parent institution: 9,198 Enrollment of MBA program: 83 % international: 40 Average age at entry: 26 Average years work experience at entry: 3

ACADEMICS

Student/raculty ratio: 30:1 % female faculty: 28 % minority faculty: 22

FINANCIAL FACTS

Annual tuition (in-state/out-of-state): $8,450/$19,000 **Books and supplies:** $600 **Room & board (on/off-campus):** $8,000/$8,000

ADMISSIONS

Admissions Selectivity Rating: 60*

# of applications received: 56 % applicants accepted: 89 % acceptees attending: 78 Average GMAT: 510 Average GPA: 3.46 TOEFL required of international applicants? Yes Minimum TOEFL (paper/computer): 550/213 Application fee: $56

Early decision program? No Deferment available? Yes Maximum length of deferment: rolling Transfer students accepted? Yes Transfer application policy: Maximum of nine credits may be transferrable. Non-fall admissions? Yes Need-blind admissions? Yes

University of Wisconsin— Oshkosh

College of Business Adminstration

ADMISSIONS CONTACT: LYNN GRANCORBITZ, MBA PROGRAM ASSISTANT DIRECTOR AND ADVISOR
ADDRESS: 800 ALGOMA BLVD., OSHKOSH, WI 54901
PHONE: 800-633-1430 • FAX: 920-424-7413
E-MAIL: MBA@UWOSH.EDU
WEBSITE: WWW.UWOSH.EDU/COLLEGES/COBA/ASSETS/GRAD/INDEX.PHP

GENERAL INFORMATION

Type of school: Public **Academic calendar:** Semester

STUDENTS

Enrollment of parent institution: 10,528 **Enrollment of MBA program:** 525 **% male/female:** 55/45 **% out-of-state:** 2 **% part-time:** 95 **% minorities:** 2 **% international:** 3 **Average age at entry:** 32 **Average years work experience at entry:** 5

ACADEMICS

Student/raculty ratio: 11:1 **% female faculty:** 15 **% minority faculty:** 5

FINANCIAL FACTS

Annual tuition (in-state/out-of-state): $4,664/$13,622

% of students receiving aid: 5 **% of first-year students receiving aid:** 5 **% of students receiving loans:** 5 **% of students receiving grants:** 0

ADMISSIONS

Admissions Selectivity Rating: 60*

# of applications received: 115 **% applicants accepted:** 90 **% acceptees attending:** 93 **Average GMAT:** 540 **Range of GMAT:** 470–610 **Average GPA:** 3.1 **TOEFL required of international applicants?** Yes **Minimum TOEFL (paper):** 550 **Application fee:** $45 **International application fee:** $45 **Application deadline:** 7/1

Early decision program? No **Deferment available?** Yes **Maximum length of deferment:** 3 years **Transfer students accepted?** Yes **Transfer application policy:** Accept up to 9 credits from an AACSB accredited MBA program. **Non-fall admissions?** Yes **Need-blind admissions?** No

EMPLOYMENT PROFILE

% grads employed at graduation: 30

% grads employed within three months of graduation: 50

Primary Source of Full-time Job Acceptances
Graduate-facilitated activities 100 (100%)

University of Wisconsin— Parkside

School of Business and Technology

ADMISSIONS CONTACT: DIRK BALDWIN, ASSOCIATE DEAN
ADDRESS: 900 WOOD ROAD, BOX 2000, KENOSHA, WI 53141-2000
PHONE: 262-595-2046 • FAX: 262-595-2680
E-MAIL: GRADPROGRAMS.SBT@UWP.EDU
WEBSITE: WWW.UWP.EDU/DEPARTMENTS/BUSINESS

GENERAL INFORMATION

Type of school: Public **Academic calendar:** Semester

STUDENTS

Enrollment of parent institution: 5,000 **Enrollment of MBA program:** 82 **% male/female:** 64/36 **% out-of-state:** 57 **% part-time:** 83 **% minorities:** 21 **% international:** 57 **Average age at entry:** 28 **Average years work experience at entry:** 3

ACADEMICS

Student/raculty ratio: 6:1 **% female faculty:** 35 **% minority faculty:** 30

FINANCIAL FACTS

Annual tuition (in-state/out-of-state): $7,414/$17,759 **Fees (in-state/out-of-state):** $277/$277 **Books and supplies:** $600

ADMISSIONS

Admissions Selectivity Rating: 60*

# of applications received: 34 **% applicants accepted:** 94 **% acceptees attending:** 78 **Average GMAT:** 521 **Range of GMAT:** 440–615 **Average GPA:** 3.18 **TOEFL required of international applicants?** Yes **Minimum TOEFL (paper/computer):** 550/213 **Application fee:** $56 **International application fee:** $56 **Application deadline:** 8/1

Early decision program? No **Deferment available?** Yes **Maximum length of deferment:** 12 mo **Transfer students accepted?** Yes **Transfer application policy:** Must be accepted and max of 12 credits in transfer **Non-fall admissions?** Yes **Need-blind admissions?** Yes

University of Wyoming

College of Business

ADMISSIONS CONTACT: TERRI L. RITTENBURG, DIRECTOR OF MBA PROGRAM
ADDRESS: P.O. BOX 3275, LARAMIE, WY 82071
PHONE: 307-766-2449 • FAX: 307-766-4028
E-MAIL: MBA@UWYO.EDU
WEBSITE: BUSINESS.UWYO.EDU/MBA

GENERAL INFORMATION

Type of school: Public **Academic calendar:** Semester

STUDENTS

Enrollment of parent institution: 11,904 **Enrollment of MBA program:** 63 **% male/female:** 64/36 **% part-time:** 48 **% international:** 18 **Average age at entry:** 28

ACADEMICS

Student/raculty ratio: 3:1

FINANCIAL FACTS

Annual tuition (in-state/out-of-state): $2,988/$8,676 **Fees (in-state/out-of-state):** $246/$298 **Books and supplies:** $300 **Room & board (on-campus):** $6,212

% of students receiving loans: 34

ADMISSIONS

Admissions Selectivity Rating: 60*

Average GMAT: 558 **Average GPA:** 3.2 **TOEFL required of international applicants?** Yes **Minimum TOEFL (paper/computer):** 525/197 **Application fee:** $40 **Application deadline:** 2/1

Early decision program? No **Deferment available?** Yes **Maximum length of deferment:** 1 year **Transfer students accepted?** Yes **Transfer application policy:** Maximum number of transferable credits is nine with a minimum grade of B from an AACSB-accredited school. **Non-fall admissions?** No **Need-blind admissions?** Yes

EMPLOYMENT PROFILE

Average starting salary:................$38,878

UTAH STATE UNIVERSITY
JON M. HUNTSMAN SCHOOL OF BUSINESS

ADMISSIONS CONTACT: SCHOOL OF GRADUATE STUDIES, ADMISSIONS OFFICER
ADDRESS: 0900 OLD MAIN HILL, LOGAN, UT 84322-0900
PHONE: (435) 797-1189 • FAX: (435) 797-1192
E-MAIL: PETE.MORRIS@USU.EDU
WEBSITE: WWW.HUNTSMAN.USU.EDU

GENERAL INFORMATION

Type of school: Public **Academic calendar:** Semester

STUDENTS

Enrollment of parent institution: 23,925 **Enrollment of MBA program:** 206 **% male/female:** 82/18 **% out-of-state:** 5 **% part-time:** 78 **% international:** 24 **Average age at entry:** 28 **Average years work experience at entry:** 3.3

ACADEMICS

Student/raculty ratio: 4:1 **% female faculty:** 16 **% minority faculty:** 10 **Joint degrees:** MS/EE(Electrical Engineering) and MBA (2 years). **Prominent alumni:** Steve Milovich, Senior Vice President, Humas Resources, Disney/ABC Television Group; Crystal Maggelet, Co-owner Crystal Inns; James H. Quigley, CEO Deloitte Touche Tohmatsu; Charlie Denson, President Nike; Bradley K. Johnson, CFO REI.

FINANCIAL FACTS

Annual tuition (in-state/out-of-state): $10,756/$24,604 **Fees (in-state/out-of-state):** $859/$859 **Books and supplies:** $1,800 **Room & board (on/off-campus):** $4,580/$4,580

% of students receiving aid: 20 % of first-year students receiving aid: 20 % of students receiving grants: 20 Average award package: $6,000 Average grant: $2,800 Average student loan debt: $11,808

ADMISSIONS

Admissions Selectivity Rating: 60*

# of applications received: 217 **% applicants accepted:** 74 **% acceptees attending:** 69 **Average GMAT:** 571 **Range of GMAT:** 451–685 **Average GPA:** 3.52 **TOEFL required of international applicants?** Yes **Minimum TOEFL (paper/computer):** 550/213 **Application fee:** $55 **International application fee:** $55 **Application deadline:** 2/15 **Regular notification:** 3/15 **Application Deadline/Notification Round 1:** 12/1 / 1/15 **Round 2:** 2/1 / 3/1 Round 3: 3/1 / 4/1 Round 4: 4/1 / 5/1

Early decision program? Yes **ED deadline/notification:** NR / 1/15 **Deferment available?** Yes **Maximum length of deferment:** 1 year **Transfer students accepted?** Yes **Transfer application policy:** Classes to be transferred are reviewed and approved on an individual basis to ensure that equivalent course content is covered. **Non-fall admissions?** No **Need-blind admissions?** Yes

EMPLOYMENT PROFILE

% grads employed at graduation: 47

Average starting salary:................$54,533

Grads Employed by Industry:	% avg. salary:
Marketing	11 $46,000
Operations	5 NR
Consulting	5 $70,000
Management	16 $43,500
Finance	26 $44,000
MIS	11 $70,000

VALDOSTA STATE UNIVERSITY
LANGDALE COLLEGE OF BUSINESS ADMINISTRATION

ADMISSIONS CONTACT: JUDY TOMBERLIN, GRADUATE SCHOOL
ADDRESS: 903 N. PATTERSON STREET, VALDOSTA, GA 31698-0005
PHONE: (229) 333-5696 • FAX: (229) 245-3853
E-MAIL: MBA@VALDOSTA.EDU
WEBSITE: WWW.VALDOSTA.EDU/LCOBA/GRAD/

GENERAL INFORMATION

Type of school: Public **Academic calendar:** Semester

STUDENTS

Enrollment of parent institution: 10,500 **Enrollment of MBA program:** 31 **% male/female:** 50/50 **% part-time:** 100 **% international:** 8 **Average age at entry:** 30 **Average years work experience at entry:** 8

ACADEMICS

Student/raculty ratio: 3:1 **% female faculty:** 20

FINANCIAL FACTS

Annual tuition (in-state/out-of-state): $3,766/$12,544 **Fees (in-state/out-of-state):** $708/$708 **Books and supplies:** $800 **Room & board (on/off-campus):** $2,684/$2,684 **Average grant:** $1,000

ADMISSIONS

Admissions Selectivity Rating: 60*

# of applications received: 21 % applicants accepted: 48 % acceptees attending: 80 Average GMAT: 534 Range of GMAT: 500-640 Average GPA: 3.3 TOEFL required of international applicants? Yes Minimum TOEFL (paper/computer): 550/213 Application fee: $25

Early decision program? No Deferment available? Yes Maximum length of deferment: One semester Transfer students accepted? Yes Transfer application policy: Maximum of 6 hours transfered from AACSB institution. Non-fall admissions? Yes Need-blind admissions? Yes

VLERICK LEUVEN GENT MANAGEMENT SCHOOL
VLERICK LEUVEN GENT MANAGEMENT SCHOOL

ADMISSIONS CONTACT: YOLANDA HABETS, PROGRAMME MANAGER
ADDRESS: VLAMINGENSTRAAT 83, 3000 LEUVEN, BELGIUM., REEP 1, 9000 GENT, BELGIUM, LEUVEN, VB 3000 BELGIUM
PHONE: + 32 16 24 88 86 • FAX: + 32 16 24 88 11
E-MAIL: MBA@VLERICK.BE
WEBSITE: WWW.VLERICK.COM

GENERAL INFORMATION

Type of school: Public

STUDENTS

Enrollment of parent institution: 30,000 Enrollment of MBA program: 320 % male/female: 75/25 % out-of-state: 90 % part-time: 55 % international: 90 Average age at entry: 30 Average years work experience at entry: 6

ACADEMICS

Student/raculty ratio: 4:1 % female faculty: 25 % minority faculty: 100

Prominent alumni: Frank Meysman, CEO Sara Lee; Roger Chua, COO Banking; Bill Bygrave, Professor Author; Lutgart Van Den Berghe, Corporate Governance; Sophie Manigart, Entrepreneurial Finance.

FINANCIAL FACTS

Annual tuition (in-state/out-of-state): $42/$42 Room & board (on/off-campus): $12,000/$12,000

% of students receiving aid: 10 % of first-year students receiving aid: 10 % of students receiving grants: 10 Average grant: $15,000 Average student loan debt: $12,500

ADMISSIONS

Admissions Selectivity Rating: 60*

# of applications received: 600 % applicants accepted: 34 % acceptees attending: 43 Average GMAT: 660 Range of GMAT: 600–700 Average GPA: 3.5 TOEFL required of international applicants? Yes Minimum TOEFL (computer): 255 Application fee: $50 International application fee: $50 Application deadline: 6/30 Regular notification: 7/14 Application Deadline/Notification Round 1: 1/22 / 2/1 Round 2: 3/24 / 4/1 Round 3: 6/30 / 7/14

Early decision program? No Deferment available? Yes Maximum length of deferment: 1 year Transfer students accepted? No Non-fall admissions? No Need-blind admissions? Yes

EMPLOYMENT PROFILE

% grads employed at graduation: 50

% grads employed within three months of graduation: 90

Average starting salary:...............$120,000

Primary Source of Full-time Job Acceptances

School-facilitated activities ...,.......25 (45%)

Graduate-facilitated activities 15 (30%)

Unknown.......................................14 (25%)

Grads Employed by Industry:	.......%	avg. salary:
Marketing	10	$120,000
Consulting	15	$120,000
Management	10	$120,000
Finance	15	$120,000
Entrepreneurship	20	$120,000
Internet	5	$120,000
Nonprofit	5	$120,000
Strategic	5	$120,000
Strategic	5	$120,000

Top 5 Employers Hiring Grads (#)

Bechtel (1), Inbev (1), Belgacom (1), ING Bank (1), US Foreign Service (1)

WESTERN ILLINOIS UNIVERSITY
COLLEGE OF BUSINESS AND TECHNOLOGY

ADMISSIONS CONTACT: , DIRECTOR OF MBA PROGRAM
ADDRESS: 1 UNIVERSITY CIRCLE, 115 SHERMAN HALL, MACOMB, IL 61455
PHONE: 309-298-3157 • FAX: 309-298-3111
E-MAIL: ADMISSIONS@WIU.EDU
WEBSITE: WWW.WIU.EDU/USERS/MICOBTD/

GENERAL INFORMATION

Type of school: Public Academic calendar: Semester

STUDENTS

Enrollment of parent institution: 13,000 Enrollment of MBA program: 111 % male/female: 52/48 % part-time: 55 % minorities: 2 % international: 26

ACADEMICS

Student/raculty ratio: 24:1 % female faculty: 29 % minority faculty: 15

FINANCIAL FACTS

Annual tuition (in-state/out-of-state): $5,696/$11,392 Fees (in-state/out-of-state): $1,453/$1,453 Books and supplies: $1,150 Room & board (on/off-campus): $7,210/$9,000

% of students receiving aid: 17 % of first-year students receiving aid: 37 % of students receiving grants: 20 Average grant: $4,696

ADMISSIONS

Admissions Selectivity Rating: 60*

# of applications received: 47 **% applicants accepted:** 89 % **acceptees attending:** 64 **Average GMAT:** 549 **Range of GMAT:** 500–600 **Average GPA:** 3.26 **TOEFL required of international applicants?** Yes **Minimum TOEFL (paper):** 550 **Application fee:** $30

Early decision program? No **Deferment available?** Yes **Maximum length of deferment:** 1 **Transfer students accepted?** No **Non-fall admissions?** Yes **Need-blind admissions?** No

WESTERN MICHIGAN UNIVERSITY
HAWORTH COLLEGE OF BUSINESS

ADMISSIONS CONTACT: JACK RUHL, DIRECTOR, MBA PROGRAM
ADDRESS: 2320 SCHNEIDER HALL, MS #5480, KALAMAZOO, MI 49008-5480
PHONE: 269-387-5133 • FAX: 269-387-5045
E-MAIL: BUSINESS-ADV-OFFICE@WMICH.EDU
WEBSITE: WWW.WMICH.EDU/MBA

GENERAL INFORMATION

Type of school: Public **Academic calendar:** Semester

STUDENTS

Enrollment of parent institution: 24,576 **Enrollment of MBA program:** 397 **% male/female:** 64/36 **% out-of-state:** 2 **% part-time:** 37 **% minorities:** 6 **% international:** 14 **Average age at entry:** 29 **Average years work experience at entry:** 5

FINANCIAL FACTS

Annual tuition (in-state/out-of-state): $9,639/$20,415 **Fees (in-state/out-of-state):** $728/$728 **Books and supplies:** $5,268 **Room & board (on/off-campus):** $7,591/$7,544

% of students receiving aid: 60 **% of first-year students receiving aid:** 7 **% of students receiving loans:** 58 **% of students receiving grants:** 9 **Average award package:** $14,850 **Average grant:** $4,200 **Average student loan debt:** $15,800

ADMISSIONS

Admissions Selectivity Rating: 60*

# of applications received: 232 **% applicants accepted:** 56 % **acceptees attending:** 68 **Average GMAT:** 521 **Range of GMAT:** 480–568 **TOEFL required of international applicants?** Yes **Minimum TOEFL (paper/computer):** 550/217 **Application fee:** $40 **International application fee:** $100 **Application deadline:** 7/15 **Regular notification:** 8/1

Early decision program? No **Deferment available?** Yes **Maximum length of deferment:** Two Semesters **Transfer students accepted?** Yes **Transfer application policy:** Students transferring from an AACSB accredited MBA program that has the same admission requirements as WMU's MBA program may transfer six credit hours of work from their prior MBA program. **Non-fall admissions?** Yes **Need-blind admissions?** No

WESTERN WASHINGTON UNIVERSITY
COLLEGE OF BUSINESS AND ECONOMICS

ADMISSIONS CONTACT: DANIEL PURDY, MBA PROGRAM ASSOCIATE DIRECTOR
ADDRESS: 516 HIGH ST., PARKS HALL 419, BELLINGHAM, WA 98225-9072
PHONE: 360-650-3825 • FAX: 360-650-4844
E-MAIL: DANIEL.PURDY@WWU.EDU
WEBSITE: WWW.CBE.WWU.EDU/MBA

GENERAL INFORMATION

Type of school: Public **Academic calendar:** Quarter

STUDENTS

Enrollment of parent institution: 13,777 **Enrollment of MBA program:** 81 **% male/female:** 53/47 **% out-of-state:** 12 **% part-time:** 27 **% minorities:** 32 **% international:** 5 **Average age at entry:** 26 **Average years work experience at entry:** 6

ACADEMICS

Student/faculty ratio: 1.5:1 **% female faculty:** 21 **% minority faculty:** 20

FINANCIAL FACTS

Annual tuition (in-state/out-of-state): $7,329/$17,190 **Fees (in-state/out-of-state):** $846/$846 **Books and supplies:** $1,000 **Room & board (on-campus):** $11,000

% of students receiving aid: 31 **% of first-year students receiving aid:** 24 **% of students receiving grants:** 22 **Average award package:** $137,500 **Average grant:** $1,400

ADMISSIONS

Admissions Selectivity Rating: 60*

# of applications received: 83 **% applicants accepted:** 67 % **acceptees attending:** 82 **Average GMAT:** 569 **Range of GMAT:** 540–640 **Average GPA:** 3.32 **TOEFL required of international applicants?** Yes **Minimum TOEFL (paper/computer):** 567/227 **Application fee:** $50 **International application fee:** $50 **Application deadline:** 5/1

Early decision program? No **Deferment available?** Yes **Maximum length of deferment:** 1 year, fee required **Transfer students accepted?** Yes **Transfer application policy:** Transfer maximum of 9 quarter (six semester) credits; graded with a b, 3.0, or better; taken no more than three years prior to a student's quarter of admission; be acceptable to the granting institution for its master's degree; and meet the requirements a **Non-fall admissions?** Yes **Need-blind admissions?** Yes

WIDENER UNIVERSITY
SCHOOL OF BUSINESS ADMINISTRATION

ADMISSIONS CONTACT: ANN SELTZER, GRADUATE ENROLLMENT PROCESS ADMINISTRATOR
ADDRESS: 1 UNIVERSITY PLACE, CHESTER, PA 19013
PHONE: 610-499-4305 • FAX: 610-499-4615
E-MAIL: SBAGRADV@MAIL.WIDENER.EDU
WEBSITE: WWW.WIDENER.EDU

GENERAL INFORMATION

Type of school: Private **Academic calendar:** Semester

STUDENTS

Enrollment of MBA program: 105 **% male/female:** 40/60 **% part-time:** 90 **% international:** 10 **Average age at entry:** 29 **Average years work experience at entry:** 7

ACADEMICS

Student/raculty ratio: 6:1 **% female faculty:** 39 **% minority faculty:** 5

Joint degrees: MBA/Juris Doctor (3 years full-time, 4 years part-time), MBA/Master of Engineering (2 years full-time, 5 years part-time), MBA/Doctor of Clinical Psychology (5 years full-time), MBA in Health Care Management/Doctor of Clinical Psychology (5 years full-tim. **Prominent alumni:** Leslie C. Quick, founder, Quick & Reilly; H. Edward Hanway, CEO, Cigna Corp.; Paul Biederman, Chairman, Mellon Mid-Atlantic; Tiffany Tomasso, VP Sunrise Assisted Living.

FINANCIAL FACTS

Annual tuition: $21,600 **Fees:** $200 **Books and supplies:** $850 Room & board (off-campus): $7,650

% of students receiving aid: 9 **% of first-year students receiving aid:** 3 **% of students receiving loans:** 8 **% of students receiving grants:** 5 **Average award package:** $19,174 **Average grant:** $9,660

ADMISSIONS

Admissions Selectivity Rating: 60*

# of applications received: 130 **% applicants accepted:** 45 **% acceptees attending:** 85 **Average GMAT:** 533 **Range of GMAT:** 450–540 **Average GPA:** 3.2 **TOEFL required of international applicants?** Yes **Minimum TOEFL (paper/computer):** 550/213 **Application fee:** $25 **Application deadline:** 5/1

Early decision program? No **Deferment available?** Yes **Maximum length of deferment:** 1 year **Transfer students accepted?** Yes **Transfer application policy:** Students may transfer all foundation level courses from other institutions. Up to 6 credits of core or elective courses may be transferred from AACSB accredited programs. **Non-fall admissions?** Yes **Need-blind admissions?** Yes

WINTHROP UNIVERSITY
COLLEGE OF BUSINESS ADMINISTRATION

ADMISSIONS CONTACT: PEGGY HAGER, DIRECTOR OF GRADUATE PROGRAMS
ADDRESS: 213 THURMOND BUILDING, ROCK HILL, SC 29733
PHONE: 803-323-2409 • FAX: 803-323-2539
E-MAIL: MBAOFFICE@WINTHROP.EDU
WEBSITE: CBA.WINTHROP.EDU

GENERAL INFORMATION

Type of school: Public **Academic calendar:** Semester

STUDENTS

Enrollment of parent institution: 6,249 **Enrollment of MBA program:** 168 **% male/female:** 64/36 **% out-of-state:** 41 **% part-time:** 57 **% minorities:** 38 **% international:** 26 **Average age at entry:** 29 **Average years work experience at entry:** 5

ACADEMICS

Student/raculty ratio: 4:1 **% female faculty:** 40 **% minority faculty:** 12

FINANCIAL FACTS

Annual tuition (in-state/out-of-state): $5,325/$9,899 **Fees (in-state/out-of-state):** $50/$50 **Books and supplies:** $1,400 **Room & board (on-campus):** $8,000

ADMISSIONS

Admissions Selectivity Rating: 60*

# of applications received: 102 **% applicants accepted:** 90 **% acceptees attending:** 70 **Average GMAT:** 470 **Range of GMAT:** 400–550 **Average GPA:** 3.2 **TOEFL required of international applicants?** Yes **Minimum TOEFL (paper):** 550 **Application fee:** $50 **International application fee:** $50 **Application deadline:** 7/15

Early decision program? No **Deferment available?** Yes **Maximum length of deferment:** 1 year **Transfer students accepted?** Yes **Transfer application policy:** 9 graduate semester hours of approved coursework may be transferred **Non-fall admissions?** Yes **Need-blind admissions?** Yes

YOUNGSTOWN STATE UNIVERSITY
WILLIAMSON COLLEGE OF BUSINESS
ADMINISTRATION

ADMISSIONS CONTACT: SUE DAVIS, INTERIM DIRECTOR
ADDRESS: ONE UNIVERSITY PLAZA, YOUNGSTOWN, OH 44555
PHONE: 330-742-2000 • FAX: 330-742-1658
E-MAIL: ENROLL@YSU.EDU
WEBSITE: WWW.WCBA.YSU.EDU

GENERAL INFORMATION
Type of school: Public

STUDENTS
Average years work experience at entry: 0

FINANCIAL FACTS
Annual tuition (in-state/out-of-state): $5,670/$8,520

ADMISSIONS
Admissions Selectivity Rating: 60*

TOEFL required of international applicants? No

Early decision program? No **Deferment available?** No **Transfer students accepted?** No **Non-fall admissions?** No **Need-blind admissions?** No

SCHOOL SAYS . . .

In this section you'll find schools with extended listings describing Admissions, curriculum, internships, and much more. This is your chance to get in-depth information on programs that interest you. The Princeton Review charges each school a small fee to be listed, and the editorial responsibility is solely that of the university.

AMERICAN UNIVERSITY
Kogod School of Business

AT A GLANCE

American University's Kogod School of Business was established in 1955 as Washington, D.C.'s first university-level school of business. Kogod is recognized for program excellence and innovation by prestigious business and academic organizations worldwide.

Kogod is committed to offering interdisciplinary programs that give students the breadth and depth of knowledge necessary to succeed in a dynamic global business environment. Kogod's MBA program combines a high-quality business education with the top-rated programs of other American University professional schools to ensure a fully integrated learning experience.

CAMPUS AND LOCATION

The Kogod School of Business is situated on American University's beautiful, 84-acre campus in one of the most desirable residential neighborhoods of Northwest Washington, D.C. Getting to campus is simple; AU is located on the metro, along with several bus routes.

DEGREES OFFERED

MBA (full-time); MBA (part-time); MS in Taxation; MS in Accounting; MS in Finance; MS in Real Estate; LLM/MBA; JD/MBA; MBA/MA in International Studies; Graduate Business Certification

PROGRAMS AND CURRICULUM

Kogod's MBA program is built around an integrated core curriculum with a strong emphasis on global decision-making, quantitative analysis, and professional development.

At Kogod, education takes on real-world relevancy through close collaboration with corporations, nonprofits, and government organizations. This market-driven approach is reflected in our MBA hands-on consulting projects, co-curricular opportunities, scholarly research, and career development.

The MBA core curriculum consists of carefully sequenced and designed to build upon foundation coursework in economics, accounting, and quantitative methods. The program is balanced by elective courses that allow students the opportunity to concentrate coursework around a particular career path or take courses from the other AU graduate schools.

FACILITIES

Kogod recently opened a 21,000 square foot building expansion, with new student lounges, classrooms, break-out rooms, a Financial Services and Information Technology lab, a Behavioral Research lab, and computer lab.

COST AND EXPENSES

MBA degree program tuition (2009–2010 academic year):

Less than 12 credit hours: $1,111 per credit hour

12–17 credit hours: $14,536

Additional credits above 17 credit hours: $1,111 per credit hour

FACULTY

The Kogod faculty is composed of internationally recognized scholars, outstanding lecturers, researchers, and advisors, all of whom are committed to the highest standards of teaching. Most importantly, they bring real-world business challenges into the classroom for students to solve. Many faculty members are currently serving as consultants to major corporations and governments, or actively engaged in research.

STUDENTS

At Kogod we believe education should extend beyond the classroom. Hands-on experiences enhance leadership ability, communication skills, and self-confidence. K-LAB (Kogod Leadership and Applied Business) allows students to learn valuable professional skills in real-world settings and includes options to participate in graduate study abroad, the annual case competition, graduate clubs, and community volunteer programs.

ADMISSIONS

The application process for the Kogod School of Business is an electronic process. Complete the online application at http://kogod.american.edu/apply.

Kogod application requirements include the following:

• A bachelor's degree from a regionally accredited college or university.

• Official GMAT score.

• International Students: TOEFL paper-based score of 600 or Internet-based score of 100 (minimum) or IELTS score of 7 (minimum).

• Interview with a member of the Graduate Admissions Committee. (Interview invitations are extended to selected applicants after a preliminary review of the completed application).

SPECIAL PROGRAMS

Kogod offers an extensive set of interdisciplinary programs that include three dual-degree programs: LLM/MBA, JD/MBA, and the MA/MBA.

Kogod students are encouraged to have an international experience to broaden their perspectives and inform their decision-making. To facilitate this, Kogod offers quality short-term, summer, and semester abroad opportunities for graduate students.

The Kogod Center for Business Communication understands that all successful business people are by definition successful communicators. The Center helps students develop their academic and professional writing, public speaking, and team presentation skills. Through the Center, students receive individual coaching from season communications specialists.

Additional Information:
American University, Kogod School of Business
Attn: Graduate Admissions
4400 Massachusetts Avenue N.W.
Washington, DC 20016
Telephone: 202-885-1913
Fax: 202-885-1078
E-mail: kogodgrad@american.edu
Website: kogod.american.edu

CAREER SERVICES AND PLACEMENT

The Kogod Center for Career Development (KCCD) is committed to helping both students and employer partners meet their unique business goals, including transitioning to a new career or finding talented candidates for an organization.

KCCD's team of experience career development and employ relations professionals proactively partner with students to assess current strengths and employ creative strategies to reach future career goals.

Kogod's career development curriculum is led by KCCD and teaches students how to leverage their individual educational and professional backgrounds. Students learn how to apply project-management approach to career management process with plans, metrics, and benchmarks.

The career management team works with students in the classroom and individually on development of individual marketing and communications plans, strategies for effective networking, interviewing, and negotiation skills, cultivating offers, and productivity skills.

BABSON COLLEGE
F.W. Olin Graduate School of Business

AT A GLANCE

At the F.W. Olin Graduate School of Business at Babson College, we have a rich tradition of cultivating entrepreneurial thinking. While some of our graduates pursue start-up ventures, more of our graduates use their entrepreneurial training to succeed in the corporate environment. Here, entrepreneurship is a state of mind.

Babson features four unique programs that prepare students to become superior managers and meet the needs of progressive organizations.

Our Two-Year MBA program emphasizes the practical application of business ideas. The One-Year MBA Program is an accelerated, full-time MBA program for students with an undergraduate business degree. The Evening MBA program offers the flexibility and convenience to working professionals. The Fast Track MBA is a part-time program combining classroom instruction with Web-based, distance learning.

CAMPUS AND LOCATION

Babson College is located in Wellesley, Massachusetts, 12 miles from Boston. Babson's Fast Track MBA is also offered in Portland, Oregon, and San Francisco, California.

ACADEMIC PROGRAMS

All programs emphasize the global aspects of business and the value of the entrepreneurial spirit.

Our Two-Year MBA program features Babson's innovative modular approach and emphasizes the practical application of business ideas.

The accelerated One-Year MBA Program is for students with an undergraduate business degree. The One-Year program allows qualified students to earn an MBA in just 12 months, including an initial summer semester featuring Babson's innovative modular curriculum.

The Babson Evening MBA features the same modular learning approach used in our full-time programs.

The Fast Track MBA is a part-time program combining traditional classroom instruction with Web-based learning. Students earn a degree in just 24 months. Students attend classes on campus during intensive, two-day sessions approximately every six weeks. Convenience and flexibility make Fast Track the perfect choice for those balancing work and long-term career goals. Fast Track is offered in Wellesley, Massachusetts; Portland, Oregon; and San Francisco, California.

FACILITIES

Babson students have access to an extensive business collection through Horn Library, as well as professional staff to help them find the information they need.

Within Horn Library students may access a variety of electronic resources, such as Bloomberg, Reuters, Bridge, Compustat, and Morningstar, for economics, financial information, marketing, accounting, entrepreneurship, etc. Financial resources are showcased in the Stephen D. Cutler Investment Management Center in the library. Group study rooms linked to Babson's computer network provide space for team meetings and individual study.

EXPENSES AND FINANCIAL AID

Nine-month academic year cost estimates for 2010–2011 for the first year of the Two-Year MBA program are $46,000 for tuition, $1,200 for books and supplies, and approximately $21,778 for living expenses.

Twelve-month academic year cost estimates for 2010–2011 for the One-Year MBA program are $59,140 for tuition and fees, $2,220 for books and supplies, and approximately $28,740 for living expenses.

Fast Track tuition estimate for students enrolling in Spring 2010 is approximately $70,000.

Per-credit tuition for the Evening MBA program is $1,220.

FACULTY

Babson's faculty is an internationally and professionally diverse group. The faculty includes seasoned corporate executives, visionary entrepreneurs, and academic thought leaders.

STUDENTS

Students who started the Two-Year MBA class in 2009 are, on average, 28 years old and have about five years of work experience. The average GMAT score is 625, and women make up 32% of the class. Students come from diverse industries and represent 24 countries. International students compose 35% of the class. International students participate in an intensive Pre-MBA program, which includes familiarization with the campus and resources, basic introductions to economics, marketing, and the case method, recreational and social events.

ADMISSIONS

Students are admitted to the program based on a careful evaluation of academic records, professional qualifications, GMAT scores, and personal attributes. Interviews are required for admission to full-time MBA programs. International students must submit TOEFL results and official English translations of all academic documents. All candidates should have strong mathematics, computer, economics, and business writing skills.

Application deadlines for the Two-Year program are November 15, January 15, March 15, and April 15. Application deadlines and decision dates for all programs may be found at http://mba.babson.edu/admissions/applynow_timetable.aspx

For more information, contact:
Office of Graduate Admission, F. W. Olin Graduate School of Business
Babson Park, MA 02457
Telephone: 781-239-4317
800-488-4512 (toll-free within the U.S.)
Fax: 781-239-4194
E-mail: mbaadmission@babson.edu
Website: mba.babson.edu

SPECIAL PROGRAMS

The Global Management Program gives students the chance to work as project managers and consultants with more than 250 companies operating in 40 countries. This program is application-based and available to full-time MBA students and full-time Evening MBA students who have completed 30 credit hours.

Babson fosters the entrepreneurial spirit through a variety of activities, including electives, endowed chairs in entrepreneurship, induction of innovative business people into the Academy of Distinguished Entrepreneurs, the Douglass Foundation Entrepreneurial Prizes, and the Babson Entrepreneurial Exchange, a student-run network of current and future entrepreneurs.

Business partnerships are a major component of Babson's programs. First-year student teams consult with Boston-area organizations through the year-long Babson Consulting Alliance Program. The Management Consulting Field Experience offers a variety of second-year consulting projects.

CAREER SERVICES AND PLACEMENTS

The Center for Career Development's Relationship Management team will work with you in planning a career strategy.

BARRY UNIVERSITY

AT A GLANCE

With its beneficial South Florida locations and focus on early completion, the Andreas School of Business at Barry University prepares you to face the challenging, dynamic world of business. The Andreas School of Business is fully accredited by AACSB International, offering all the features you expect from a big business school, with the personal attention you can find only at Barry.

Small, interactive classes are led by scholarly, full-time faculty—more than 80 percent of whom hold doctoral degrees. Barry's faculty members bring real-world business experience to the classroom, having worked in firms such as Merrill Lynch, Deutsche Bank, Eastern Airlines, McDonald's, and Harris Corp. Teaching you strategies in leadership, decision-making, and collaboration, our professors help you to become an effective leader in today's marketplace.

CAMPUS AND LOCATION

Barry University's 122-acre, palm-tree lined main campus is in Miami Shores, Florida, just 5 miles from the ocean and a few minutes from the dynamic city of Miami. At the crossroads of the Americas, Miami has an enormous amount of cultural diversity. Here you'll find influences from Latin America, the Caribbean, Europe and more. It's also a hub for international business, with more than 1,000 multinational companies.

DEGREES OFFERED

Barry University's Andreas School of Business offers the Master of Business Administration (MBA) with concentrations in accounting, finance, health services administration, international business, management, and marketing; the Master of Science in Accounting (MSA); and the Master of Science in Management (MSM). Students may also pair the MBA with the Master of Science in Nursing or the Master of Science in Sport Management.

Programs offer flexible full-time and part-time options to suit your needs as a graduate student and working professional.

PROGRAMS AND CURRICULUM

Barry University's School of Business works to ensure that you're prepared to strive in today's exciting business climate. For students who require more undergraduate preparation, Barry University's School of Business sponsors subject-area workshops. And in addition to our high-quality academics, we offer a variety of student organizations that help you develop leadership skills, including the Accounting Association, American Marketing Association, Beta Gamma Sigma international honor society, and the Financial Management Association honor society.

FACILITIES

At Barry, you will find the facilities you need to enhance and support your studies. The Monsignor William Barry Memorial Library has over 950,000 items and is a member of various statewide library networks. There is on-campus wireless Internet access, and the campus' main computer lab is available to all students; overall there are 165 computer workstations available for use, including Windows-based computers, printers, and scanners. Campus facilities also include a fully equipped fitness center and outdoor sports and recreation complex, multimedia classrooms, and more.

EXPENSES AND FINANCIAL AID

The Andreas School of Business maintains a competitive tuition rate and participates in the full array of state and federal financial aid programs. The School also offers merit scholarships and graduate assistantships for both domestic and international students.

FACULTY

More than 80 percent of Barry's faculty holds a doctoral degree. Our professors bring real-world business experience to the classroom, having worked in firms such as Merrill Lynch, Deutsche Bank, Eastern Airlines, McDonald's, and Harris Corp. Barry business faculty also participate in the Barry Institute for Community Economic Development (BICED), lending their expertise to local small businesses, entrepreneurs, and nonprofit organizations.

STUDENTS

At Barry, you learn within a community of students representing all compass points, ethnicities, and faith perspectives. Princeton Review ranked the School of Business the No. 3 business school that offers the best opportunity for minority students, and *U.S. News & World Report* ranked Barry among the top 20 universities nationwide for campus diversity. Barry's student body includes more than 4,000 full-time undergraduate and 3,500 graduate students.

ADMISSIONS

The Andreas School of Business uses a composite of factors to determine admission. These include: GMAT score, college transcripts, recommendations, statement of purpose, writing skills, resume, and interview with the Admissions Committee.

The Admissions Committee also considers undergraduate preparation, including accounting proficiency, 6 credits in economics, and 3 credits in each of the following categories: finance, college algebra, probability/statistics, management, operations, and marketing.

Students can apply to start in the fall, spring, or summer.

Please note: The GMAT requirement may be waived for applicants with extensive managerial experience.

SPECIAL PROGRAMS

In supporting Barry University's Catholic heritage, the Andreas School of Business encourages service to the community. It sponsors the Barry Institute for Community Economic Development (BICED), providing information and skills development to small businesses, entrepreneurs, and nonprofit organizations in select local communities. It includes the Center for Social Entrepreneurship, Entrepreneurial Institute, and Center for Community Economies.

ADDITIONAL INFORMATION

Barry University is the second-largest private, Catholic university in the Southeast.

CAREER SERVICES AND PLACEMENT

Barry's Career Services staff is available to help you with all aspects of your professional development. We work closely with faculty, staff, and employers to make sure you're prepared for today's workforce. We offer career counseling and an employment database, sponsor on-campus career fairs, and help you navigate the world of job hunting and career planning. In other words, we empower you to achieve professional success.

BAYLOR UNIVERSITY
Hankamer School of Business

AT A GLANCE
Where you choose to attain your MBA is an important decision. Baylor University can be a valuable partner on your journey in achieving your highest personal and professional potential. Baylor offers MBA students the exceptional resources of a premier institution recognized worldwide for academic quality, superior teaching, and a reputation for graduating persons of both competence and character.

Small classes, hosted at the university's state-of-the-art Hankamer School of Business in Waco, Texas, set the stage for an integrated learning experience that balances leading-edge business theory with practical, hands-on, real-world challenges.

CAMPUS AND LOCATION
Chartered in 1845, Baylor University is the oldest institution of higher learning in continuous operation in Texas. Baylor has grown to a 735-acre campus with 14,000 students. With an area population of 208,000, Baylor is centrally located in Waco, Texas, within 150 miles of four major metropolitan cities: Dallas, Houston, Austin and San Antonio.

DEGREES OFFERED
Master of Business Administration (MBA)

Executive MBA Program in Dallas (EMBA)

Executive MBA Program in Austin (EMBA)

MBA/Master of Science in Information Systems (MBA/MSIS)

Juris Doctorate/MBA (JD/MBA)

MBA/Master of Engineering (MBA/ME)

Details are available at www.baylor.edu/mba/degreeoptions.

FACILITIES
The Hankamer School of Business features seminar-style classrooms, a 75-seat videoconferencing room, and the Graduate Center that maximizes discussion and interaction between students and faculty. With Baylor's wireless data network, AirBear, students can connect their notebook computers to the Internet from any location on campus, unencumbered by a physical network connection.

EXPENSES AND FINANCIAL AID
More than half of the MBA students receive some form of merit-based scholarships or graduate assistantship awards. Merit-based scholarships or assistantships are awarded ranging from 50 to 100 percent tuition remission. Additionally, students can earn a stipend in exchange for working 10 hours per week for a professor in the Business School.

Tuition and Fees for 2010–2011

$26,966 per academic year (fall and spring)

$844 per hour in the summer semester

Estimated student fees for an academic year are $3,000.

FACULTY
Baylor MBA students can expect a personalized and integrative educational experience administered by a highly supportive academic community. The MBA faculty is accessible, involved, and intent on your success. Your relationship with faculty members will help you sharpen your ambitions and form a solid basis upon which to develop the business acumen to succeed.

All professors teaching in the MBA programs hold doctorate degrees, are active in their professional fields, are business consultants, and are well published.

STUDENT BODY
MBA Student Profile—Fall 2009
Total number of full-time MBA students enrolled: 99
New in 2009: 50
Average GMAT: 614
Average age: 22–34
Percent male/female: 74/26
Average work experience: 2 years
Average class size: 15 students

ADMISSIONS
Admission to Baylor Business is competitive. We're looking for individuals with professional work experience, outstanding scholarship, a commitment to community service, and a motivation to pursue an intense graduate business program. MBA candidates should have strong analytical capabilities and communication skills.

SPECIAL PROGRAMS
The adage is true: The best way to learn something is through practice. It is the concept behind both the corporate-alliance practicum known as Focus Firm and the "Practicum in Portfolio Management" finance class.

In the Focus Firm project, students research, critically assess and recommend viable solutions to an identified business dilemma for an actual business.

In the portfolio management class, students manage a live fund valued at more than $4 million.

ADDITIONAL INFORMATION
Baylor Business—Our commitment to the personal as well as professional development of our students is distinctive. Values-based guidance of faculty mentors and innovative program design allow you to take your career—and your life—wherever you want to go. Baylor's graduate business programs provide the comprehensive learning experience you need to achieve your career objectives, within the context of greater personal development goals designed to serve you for life.

CAREER SERVICES AND PLACEMENT
MBA students take two career development courses that address critical areas such as self-assessment, job-search strategies and resume development, as well as provide valuable instruction on appropriate interviewing behavior, negotiating successfully and accepting a job offer in a professional manner.

A pivotal function of Career Management is matching our graduates with the perfect job opportunity. To accomplish this objective, each MBA develops a personalized plan of action based on his or her unique qualifications, talent, experience and vocational leanings.

Internships present opportunities to apply the management theory learned in the first year of your MBA program to the marketplace within a large or small corporation. At the same time, internship employers have an opportunity to discover an outstanding candidate with a proven record of expertise. Experience gained through internships aids both students and employers by providing each with what they need: the skills and expertise to get the job done.

All MBA students are required to participate in one off-campus educational experience in conjunction with their Career Development courses. Students will meet with corporate leaders of top financial companies to gain a greater understanding of how the financial services industry operates today. The one-week trip will be held in the fall semester only. Students will take the trip in the first fall semester of their MBA degree plan.

For additional information see www.baylor.edu/mba/careermanagement.

BELMONT UNIVERSITY

AT A GLANCE

The Jack C. Massey Graduate School of Business was founded in 1986 through a gift from one of the country's most successful entrepreneurs. Mr. Massey remains as the only U.S. businessperson to ever take three different private companies (i.e., Kentucky Fried Chicken, HCA, and Winners Corp.) public to the New York Stock Exchange. The School was created to offer graduate business programs to Nashville area working professionals and offers both the MBA and MACC degrees in a weeknight, evening format on the Belmont University campus. Belmont is the only private university in Tennessee to maintain AACSB International accreditation in business and accounting. Massey's part-time MBA program was 18th in *BusinessWeek's* most recent national ranking of part-time MBA programs, and *Fortune* magazine recently identified Belmont as one of the top five universities in the U.S. at which to study entrepreneurship.

CAMPUS AND LOCATION

As an academic unit within Belmont University, The Massey Graduate School is located in the heart of Nashville, Tennessee, a rare place combining big-city charisma and small-town charm. Known internationally as "music city," Nashville is also a hotbed for entrepreneurship, healthcare, and international trade. Belmont University, a host campus for the 2008 U.S. Presidential Debates, is located on a 62-acre campus and maintains a total enrollment of ~5,400 students.

Provide a URL to a page on your website where a prospective student can watch video of your campus: http://www.belmont.edu/interactivemap/index.html (building #37 on interactive map).

DEGREES OFFERED

The Massey Graduate School offers two degree programs:

The Master of Business Administration (MBA) degree requires 34 credits, with specialty tracks in accounting, entrepreneurship, finance, general business, healthcare management, marketing, and music business. The MBA is offered in two formats: (1) a part-time "Professional MBA" version designed for working professionals with prior business experience, and (2) a full-time "Accelerated MBA" version for individuals with little to no business work experience. Classes for both programs are offered Monday-Thursday evenings throughout the year.

The Master of Accountancy (MACC) degree requires 30 credits and is designed to prepare students to meet the 150-hour CPA requirement. MACC classes are also offered year-round, Monday–Thursday evenings.

PROGRAMS AND CURRICULUM

The Massey Graduate School resides within the College of Business Administration, which also includes the Center for Entrepreneurship, the Center for Business Ethics, Center for International Business, and the Scarlett Leadership Institute, each of which houses additional learning opportunities for students. A Summer Accounting Institute option for aspiring MACC students offers non-business undergraduates a fast-track opportunity to begin their graduate accounting course work.

All graduate students complete a brief study-abroad experience course as part of their degree requirements. Trips are scheduled between terms and typically last 8-10 days. Destination options for 2010–11 include Argentina, Belgium, China, Denmark, France, the Netherlands, South Africa, South Korea, Spain, Turkey and Vietnam.

The curriculum is designed with 2-credit hour courses instead of the traditional 3-credit format. This gives Massey students a greater breadth of curriculum in the core business/accounting offerings, while also assuring a greater number of electives for matching to a particular student career plan. All students also complete a required entrepreneurship course, as well as preparation in business ethics.

Massey alumni appreciate the existence of the "Massey Passport" program that provides a lifetime option for graduates to return to campus and attend graduate business classes for free on a space-available basis.

FACILITIES

All classes are held in the Jack C. Massey Business Center, which includes a variety of high-tech classrooms, computer labs, a finance trading center, and student support offices. Graduate students also have a separate computer lab workspace, as well as a well-equipped study area.

EXPENSES AND FINANCIAL AID

Tuition charges *per course* for 2010–11 are calculated at $2,425 for all MBA students and $1,875 for all MACC students. There are a limited number of scholarship opportunities (e.g., merit, financial need, minority status), as well as graduate assistant opportunities.

FACULTY

Over 90% of graduate faculty is doctorally-qualified and full-time professors, while the remaining minority are full-time business executives. Continuing faculty members are hired on the basis of their academic and professional preparation, as well as a demonstrated commitment to high-quality instruction.

STUDENTS

The typical Massey Professional MBA student has 6 years of business experience, is 29 years old, and works full-time, while completing the degree program in 2 years. The typical Accelerated MBA student has less than 2 years of business experience, is 23 years old, and is focused full-time on completing the degree program in 1 year. MACC students also tend to be somewhat younger as a group, with less business experience and are preparing to sit for the CPA exam. Many MACCs are full-time graduate students.

ADMISSIONS

All Professional MBA applicants are required to complete the GMAT test, submit a personal essay and two recommendations, submit transcripts from all undergraduate coursework, and have completed a minimum of two years of business experience. The experience requirement is waived for MACC and Accelerated MBA applicants. A personal interview is required of all graduate applicants.

SPECIAL PROGRAMS

Massey graduate students who complete elective coursework (2 courses) in business negotiation and mediation are eligible for certification as an "Approved Rule 31 Mediator" by the Supreme Court of the State of Tennessee.

CAREER SERVICES AND PLACEMENT

The Massey School has a dedicated Career Development Center that provides comprehensive career services to graduate business students and alumni. Career Services are a lifetime benefit for alumni of The Massey School.

CENTRAL MICHIGAN UNIVERSITY
College of Business Administration

AT A GLANCE

Central Michigan University's College of Business Administration, which is accredited by AACSB International, prepares future business leaders for positions in today's global economy. CMU's MBA curriculum receives constant review in light of emerging business trends and issues. It is tailored to develop managers both as leaders and team players and foster integrity, social responsibility, and a high degree of professionalism.

CAMPUS AND LOCATION

CMU's park-like 480-acre main campus, located in Mount Pleasant, Michigan, is a relaxing place to study, meet up with friends over a cup of coffee, or just enjoy the serene beauty of nature. Mount Pleasant feels like a classic college town, with a blend of natural features, exciting developments and small-town life. CMU also has more than 60 locations throughout the U.S., Canada and Mexico, along with offering classes online.

DEGREES OFFERED

CMU's MBA program requires a minimum of 30–31 credit hours and is tailored to meet the needs of every type of student:

• Full- and part-time MBA: Accelerated eight-week courses offered at CMU's Mount Pleasant campus and in Midland, Michigan, allow full-time students to complete the program in 12 or 18 months and part-time students to complete the program in two or three years. The program includes nine core two-credit-hour classes in one of the following concentrations: accounting, consulting, finance, general business, management information systems (also can include an emphasis in SAP), marketing and the value-driven organization. The program concludes with a four-credit hour integrative project. Learn more at http://www.cba.cmich.edu/mba/.

• Online MBA: CMU offers the only online MBA program with a management information systems concentration that includes an emphasis in SAP, the world's leading enterprise system. The online MBA is an accelerated program that can be completed within two years. All courses are delivered entirely online with the exception of an intensive two-week SAP Academy. All Online MBA programs are taught in a cohort format comprised of a group of students following a set schedule of courses together from start to finish, focusing on one of the following concentrations: management information systems with an emphasis in SAP or the value-driven organization. Learn more at http://www.cel.cmich.edu/onlinemba/.

FACILITIES

CMU offers top-level facilities and resources that are available for its MBA students. Among them are Park Library, which is located at the center of campus and provides state-of-the-art facilities for students, and its Off Campus Library Services, in which CMU excels as a leader.

TUITION AND FINANCIAL AID

CMU is dedicated to helping students of all financial backgrounds obtain a college degree. Approximately 80 percent of CMU on-campus students receive some form of financial assistance from federal, state, university and private agency sources. CMU has a wide variety of scholarships and grants available to all of its students.

MBA program costs differ between on-campus and online students. Visit the Web sites below to learn more about tuition, fees and financial aid for CMU's MBA programs.

Full- and Part-time MBA: http://www.registrars.cmich.edu/registration/tuitionfeesched.htm.

Online MBA: http://www.cel.cmich.edu/finances/graduate-tuition.html.

On-campus graduate students may apply for graduate assistantships and fellowships and may also be eligible for Legacy Tuition Awards, Neighboring Regions Tuition Awards or Out of State Merit Tuition Awards. Learn more at www.grad.cmich.edu.

FACULTY

The College of Business Administration faculty are highly renowned and dedicated to student success. Many are practicing and consulting members of the business community and conduct significant research. Several are Six Sigma Black Belt-certified and are well equipped to teach students the specialized concepts and methodologies of data-driven, decision-making skills.

STUDENT BODY

Students in the program come from a wide variety of academic, professional and personal backgrounds. The diversity of international and domestic students offers an engaging learning environment by adding a global perspective to teamwork situations.

ADMISSIONS

Applications are accepted from students who have earned a baccalaureate degree from an accredited university or college. To be admitted to the MBA program, a student must present an acceptable score on the Graduate Management Admission Test (GMAT) and an acceptable grade point average (GPA). The CMU College of Business Administration uses a set index formula to determine eligibility for admission. International students must submit a score of at least 79 (Internet-based test) or 550 (paper-based test) on the Test of English as a Foreign Language (TOEFL).

Learn more about admission requirements for the Full and Part-time MBA programs on campus at http://www.cba.cmich.edu/mba or www.grad.cmich.edu.

Learn more about admission requirements for CMU's online MBA program at http://www.cel.cmich.edu/onlinemba/admission.html.

SPECIAL PROGRAMS

Within CMU's Applied Business Studies Complex, the LaBelle Entrepreneurial Center helps small businesses reorganize and competitively reposition themselves and provides real-world connections between graduate students, corporations and small businesses.

CAREER SERVICES AND PLACEMENT

CMU provides a variety of career services, including on-campus interviews with potential employers. Students can register for e-recruiting services, resumes are critiqued, and mock interviews are provided to help you better prepare for real interviews. Career advising services are provided as well. Learn more at www.careers.cmich.edu/.

DREXEL UNIVERSITY

AT A GLANCE

Recognized by *Financial Times*, *U.S. News & World Report*, and *Entrepreneur*, Drexel University's LeBow College of Business empowers, enriches and inspires future business leaders through an innovative, strategic approach to business education defined by leadership and ethics, industry perspectives and technological orientation.

LeBow is accredited by AACSB International—The Association to Advance Collegiate Schools of Business—the top ranking available. Ranked by *U.S. News & World Report* as one of the best national doctoral universities, Drexel is one of fewer than 50 private universities classified by the Carnegie Foundation as Doctoral/Research Universities - Extensive.

CAMPUS AND LOCATION

Drexel University is located in Philadelphia in the Northeast business corridor, with close proximity to Baltimore, Boston, New York City, and Washington, D.C. Philadelphia is an ideal place to earn a graduate business degree as the Philadelphia business region is ranked ninth in the nation for the number of *Fortune* 500 companies and tenth for new business formations.

DEGREES OFFERED

LeBow offers a Master of Business Administration, Master of Science, and Doctor of Philosophy. One-Year, Two Year (full-time), Professional (part-time), LeBow Evening Accelerated Drexel (LEAD) MBA, MBA Anywhere (online), and Executive MBA degree programs are available.

Degrees are offered in Philadelphia; Malvern, PA; and Sacramento, CA.

All LeBow MBA degrees require the completion of 51 quarter credits.

In the Professional MBA program students take an initial series of integrated foundation courses followed by one or two areas of concentrations.

The Two Year MBA program provides students with the same concentration options as the Professional MBA. Courses in the Two Year program are daytime for the first two terms and then the students take evening courses to maximize their options and electives.

The One-Year MBA maximizes the quality, effectiveness and rigor of a comprehensive, full-time MBA program in an accelerated time frame and is designed for a select group of highly motivated students. The integrated curriculum explores the following areas: Entrepreneurship, International Business, Leadership, Managerial Finance, and Strategic Management.

The LEAD MBA and the MBA Anywhere program are accelerated programs requiring students to take two courses per term. Students are able to complete these lock-stepped and cohorted programs in two years.

The Drexel Executive MBA, ranked among the world's best and first in the nation for career progress by Financial Times, is designed for seasoned professionals who are looking to maximize their leadership potential.

The Pharma MBA is an online 51 credit MBA that provides specialized courses in the management of one of the region's largest industries – pharmaceuticals. This program is a cohorted, lockstepped program that takes two years to complete.

Students from all MBA programs who are seeking a high degree of specialization can complete the Master of Science degree in Accounting or Finance in two years taken independently or in one year after the completion of the MBA.

FACILITIES

MBA students take classes in the Leonard Pearlstein Business Learning Center—one of the nation's most technologically advanced academic business environments. Classes are taught in Web-enabled, simulated corporate boardrooms, equipped with the latest technology to allow teleconferencing and videoconferencing.

Drexel's W.W. Hagerty Library's strength lies in its extensive online collection, complete with electronic resources specializing in business information, which are accessible remotely. The Library houses 300,000 volumes including large collections in the fields of business and science. Hagerty Library offers one librarian dedicated solely to working with the faculty and students of the LeBow College of Business.

EXPENSES AND FINANCIAL AID

Tuition for the Professional MBA and the Two Year MBA program are billed on a per credit hour basis. For the 2009–2010 academic year, the cost is $915 per credit hour. Tuition for the cohorted programs 2009–2010 is $54,000.

Merit Scholarships and the Drexel Alumni-Trustee Endorsement Grant are available for students interested in the full-time or cohorted programs.

FACULTY

Drexel University's LeBow College of Business faculty is internationally recognized and globally focused. A large percentage of the LeBow faculty have lived, worked, studied, or taught internationally. As well as being experts in their fields, many of Drexel's professors are, or have been, executives or consultants with *Fortune* 500 companies, government agencies, and other organizations enabling them to blend theory with application. They offer a unique combination of theoretical knowledge and management practice that translates into the day-to-day practices needed to succeed professionally.

STUDENT BODY

Students represent widely diverse academic, professional, and international backgrounds and the student culture is enriched by the variety of their perspectives.

ADMISSIONS

All applicants must have received a four-year bachelor's degree from an accredited college or university. Degrees earned abroad will be evaluated and must be deemed equivalent. The admissions committee reviews applications based on undergraduate record, GMAT (Graduate Management Admission Test) score, quality and quantity of professional experience, clarity of career goals, professional references, a statement of purpose, and a professional resume. Students whose native language is not English and who do not hold a bachelor's degree from a U.S. institution are required to take and submit a score from the TOEFL (Test of English as a Foreign Language).

CAREER SERVICES AND PLACEMENT

LeBow's MBA Career Services offers students self-assessment resources, job search tools, and organized employer networking activities. Some of the resources include resume writing assistance, interviewing preparation and negotiation workshops.

LeBow also provides graduate students with a wide variety of networking opportunities on a weekly basis including having two companies per week attend Employer of the Week. At these events companies discuss the trends in their industries and how their company uses graduate educated employees.

Graduate Career Services provides a mentoring program for all full-time students.

FAIRFIELD UNIVERSITY
Dolan School of Business

AT A GLANCE

Fairfield University was founded in 1942 by the Jesuits, a Roman Catholic order renowned for its 450-year-old tradition of excellence in education and service to others. This Jesuit tradition inspires a commitment to educating the whole person for a life of leadership in a constantly changing world. Fairfield University welcomes students of all faiths and beliefs who value its mission of scholarship, truth, and justice, and it values the diversity their membership brings to the university community.

Faculty members are in the classroom at all times and are unusually accessible to students as mentors and advisors. The relationship between faculty and students leads to creative collaborations on independent study and hands-on research.

CAMPUS AND LOCATION

Set on 200 acres of woods and rolling lawns with views of the nearby Long Island Sound, Fairfield's campus is a beautiful setting for study and personal growth. Nearby, the beaches of the Sound offer recreation as well as research opportunities for marine biology and environmental science students, while the woods and trails of New England offer hiking, biking and other outdoor activity. Metro North railroad, also in town, takes students to New York City for all the diverse cultural and career opportunities available. Excursions to New York are frequently built into the class curriculum, as well as into social opportunities for students. Fairfield County itself is a Mecca for small and large corporations, with one of the largest concentrations of *Fortune* 500 companies in the nation.

PROGRAMS

An MBA program is meant to be a generalist degree, which covers all the relevant topical areas and gives a student the opportunity to specialize, but not major, in a functional area of business. The MBA program has three components: core courses, breadth courses, and specialization or concentration courses. The core courses are functional courses; they are designed to provide fundamental tools and functional area competencies for students who did not major in a business specialty as undergraduates, did not perform well academically as undergraduates, or took only a portion of the functional and tool courses that comprise the MBA core. This is called "leveling," i.e., everyone starts at the same level, or nearly so, before they go on to take advanced coursework. Therefore, the core courses are prerequisites to the breadth of the MBA program.

The full MBA program is comprised of the breadth courses and the specialization courses. The new AACSB accreditation standards require at least 30 semester hours of study beyond the core. The Dolan School of Business will limit the number of options that it offers in both the breadth and specialization courses to strengthen the program.

Core Courses - 18 credits

AC 400	Introduction to Accounting
FI 400	Principles of Finance
MG 400	Organizational Behavior
MK 400	Marketing Management
OM 400	Integrated Business Processes
QA 400	Applied Business Statistics

Breadth Courses - 18 credits

AC 500	Accounting for Decision-Making
FI 500	Shareholders Value
IS 500	Information Systems
MG 500	Managing People for Competitive Advantage
MG 503	Legal and Ethical Environment of Business
MK 500	Customer Value

Concentration Courses - 12 credits

Four concentration courses are required from the following concentrations (Accounting, Finance, Human Resource Management, ISOM, General Management, International Business, Marketing or Taxation).

Elective Course - 3 credits

Any 500-level free elective.

Capstone Course - 3 credits

| MG 584 | Global Competitive Strategy |

The Master of Science in Finance (30 credits)

The Master of Science in Finance provides unique opportunities for individuals who want to enhance their career opportunities in the areas of investments, corporate finance, or banking. The main program consists of ten 3-credit courses (7 required and 3 electives) and is especially useful for those who want to pursue advanced certification, such as the CFA, CFM, CFP. Applicants should hold an undergraduate or an MBA degree and have an adequate background in the areas of microeconomics, macroeconomics, financial accounting, and statistics.

Master of Science in Accounting (30 credits)

The M.S. in Accounting is designed to provide students with a Bachelor of Science degree in Accounting with an opportunity to complete the degree a 12 month period, based on undergraduate coursework, as well as fulfill the 150 hour criterion to sit for the uniform CPA examination, as passed in the State of Connecticut and most other jurisdictions. Students complete their studies over one or two summers and one academic year immediately following undergraduate commencement (May through the following May or August).

The Master of Science in Taxation (30 credits)

The M.S. in Taxation is designed to prepare students for careers in the field of taxation. Students will learn to use a variety of tax authorities (e.g., statutory, judicial, and administrative) and other resources to critically consider and resolve complex tax issues. The program consists of 10 three-credit courses (7 required and 3 electives) and it is especially useful for industry managers and executives, financial services and public accounting professionals, and others seeking a specialized education in taxation. Applicants must have a baccalaureate degree in accounting or finance or equivalent coursework prior to beginning the program. In addition, Federal Income Taxation I and II, or the equivalent are program prerequisites.

Certificate Programs for Advanced Study (15 credits)

The certificate program is designed to provide a complete integration to the theory and practice of contemporary business. The Certificate Programs for Advanced Study are suitable for working professionals who have already earned a graduate degree whose responsibilities are currently or expected to be in a particular specialty, and who desire greater depth of academic preparation in that subject area; or for individuals outside of the area who desire to understand multifunctional thinking in order to compete effectively in the marketplace.

FLORIDA INTERNATIONAL UNIVERSITY
Chapman Graduate School of Business

11200 SW 8th Street – CBC 200

Miami, Florida 33199

T: 305 348-7398

F: 305 348-7204

E: chapman@fiu.edu

W: http://business.fiu.edu/chapman

AT A GLANCE

Located in Miami, Florida, The Graduate School of Business is characterized by its rich active learning environment extending beyond the classroom, into the surrounding community, and across borders. Miami is recognized worldwide as the "Gateway to the Americas"; students enrolled in the programs are completely immersed in this world-class trade and commerce hub. The school has made significant investments over the past years in the fields of information technology, international business and entrepreneurship, helping it to gain national recognition in those strategic areas.

CAMPUS AND LOCATION

The Graduate School is located on the 344-acre campus of Florida International University, featuring lush tropical landscaping and impressive architecture. Strategically located in Miami, a truly global metropolis, Florida International University has the advantage of being at the center of it all. The school brings together people from all over the world with a diversity of backgrounds, experiences, and cultures to create a unique learning environment. Our tropical weather means students can enjoy year-round sporting and recreation activities from boating and water sports to tennis and golf.

PROGRAMS AND CURRICULUM

FIU's Graduate School of Business offers top-quality academic programs leading to an MBA:

• The one-year, full-time International MBA is completed in four quarters. Students complete all core courses, including a foreign language (Spanish, Portuguese, Chinese, or advanced business English) during the fall, winter, and spring quarters, leaving the summer quarter free to do a business internship, take specialization courses at FIU, or study abroad with academic partners in Latin America, Europe, and even China.

• The Executive MBA is designed for mid- to senior-level executives.

• The Professional MBA offers a lock-step program with classes held on Saturdays.

• The Evening MBA offers students a traditional program structure with classes meeting in the evenings.

• The Downtown MBA is designed to accommodate working professionals in the downtown Miami area.

In addition to the array of choices for an MBA, the school offers MS degrees in the areas of finance, human resource management, international business, international real estate, management information systems, and taxation; as well as a Master of Accounting and a PhD. Most programs are designed for the working professional with classes being held on weekends or in the evenings. With world-renowned faculty and business leaders sharing their expertise, students receive a top-notch education preparing them for an ever-changing, global business environment.

FACULTY

A dynamic force for excellence within Miami's only public, multi-campus research university. The dedicated, multicultural faculty of more than 100 in the College of Business Administration includes seven Eminent Scholars and a cadre of internationally distinguished experts in international business, information systems, operations research, knowledge management, e-commerce, international banking and trade, financial derivatives, consumer marketing and research, global marketing, human resource management, and corporate responsibility. The faculty brings a wealth of corporate and entrepreneur experiences to the classroom, combining practical knowledge with theory. As a result, this creates a dynamic and challenging learning experience for students.

ACCREDITATION AND RECOGNITION

The Chapman Graduate School is accredited by AACSB and and is consistently ranked as one of the top international business schools by *BusinessWeek*, *Financial Times*, *U.S.News & World Report*, *América Economia*, and *Hispanic Business*, among others.

ADMISSIONS

Particular program-specific requirements are listed on our program web sites, which are accessible at: http://business.fiu.edu/chapman. To be eligible for admission, prospective student must hold a Bachelor's degree or equivalent from an accredited institution and a minimum undergraduate GPA of 3.0 in upper division courses (last 60 credit hours). Official transcripts from all previously attended institutions are required to be submitted in a sealed university envelope. Applications and more information can be found online at http://gradschool.fiu.edu.

GEORGIA STATE UNIVERSITY

J. Mack Robinson College of Business, Global Partners MBA Program

Contact Information:
Global Partners MBA Program, Georgia State University
Tower Place 200, Ste. 400
3348 Peachtree Rd. NE, Atlanta, GA 30326
+1 404 413-7296
gpmba@gsu.edu
www.globalpartnersmba.com

AT A GLANCE
The Global Partners MBA is a unique 14-month, full-time dual-degree MBA experience on 4 continents. Robinson College of Business at Georgia State University (GSU) has teamed with recognized, world-class business schools in Paris—IAE the Graduate Business School at the Sorbonne, and Rio de Janeiro—the COPPEAD Graduate School of Business, Federal University of Rio de Janeiro—to offer an international MBA with a truly global immersion experience. A cohort program, you will study at each of the three partner institutions with residency stays in Atlanta, Rio de Janeiro and Paris respectively, and an intensive two-week field study in China. A diverse student group coupled with your different national cultural settings makes for a multi-cultural learning environment – both inside and outside the classroom. You will learn from faculty, nationally and internationally recognized for their field expertise, and research and teaching acumen. You will see first-hand how business is done with extensive company visits and access to senior level decision makers in Atlanta, Rio, Paris, and China, and side-trips to Washington, D.C., and Brussels for the program themes. The program culminates with a four-month international internship. Two program themes, Sustainable Leadership and Commercial Diplomacy, offer additional distinctiveness to the program and to your professional development.

CAMPUS AND LOCATION
The J. Mack Robinson College of Business is the 6th largest business school in the US and is located in the heart of Atlanta, one of the nation's most dynamic business communities. It provides students with opportunities that come only from being at the epicenter of business. Recognized as a leader in business education, the Robinson College has been ranked in the Top 10 Part-Time MBA program for the past 14 years by the *U.S. News and World Report*. Global Partners was ranked by the Aspen Institute & World Resources Institute's "Global Top 100" business schools in the world in 2009 for teaching & research in social, environmental, and ethical responsibility. QS, a leading business school education publication, has ranked the Global Partners MBA among the top full-time, MBA programs in the U.S. and Canada.

COPPEAD, our partner school in Rio de Janeiro is a center of excellence in business education and research. They are ranked in the top 100 by the *Financial Times*. IAE, the graduate business school of the Sorbonne University is located in the Latin Quarter in Paris and serves about 2,000 students primarily in executive education. Like Robinson, they have partners all around the world.

DEGREES OFFERED
Global Partners MBA students earn 2 degrees—an MBA from GSU and a Master's degree in Organizations with an emphasis in International Management from IAE—Sorbonne University.

PROGRAMS AND CURRICULUM
The Global Partners MBA is a cohort program. Courses are integrated across the partner schools offering a truly global perspective. The program incorporates two themes into the curriculum—Sustainable leadership and Commercial Diplomacy. Students interact with corporate and government leaders in each locale with business tours including extended company visits to China (3 cities), Washington, D.C., and Brussels. The coursework culmi-

nates with a 4-month international internship. Students live on 4 continents, earn 2 degrees, and have 1 global experience in 14 months.

FACILITIES
The Buckhead Education Center is located in the heart of Atlanta's Financial District. The facility contains three classrooms, four break-out rooms and administrative offices. Students have access to three libraries and a student recreation center. While abroad, the partner schools have dedicated classrooms.

EXPENSES AND FINANCIAL AID
Program fee is $55,000, covering:
• Tuition and Fees
• Required course materials
• Roundtrip airfare: Washington, D.C., Brazil, France, China. Transportation to Brussels.
• Accommodations: Washington, D.C., Brussels, China
Fees do not cover:
• Housing
• Personal Expenses: Visas, Insurance, Meals
Financial aid and merit-based partial scholarships are available.

FACULTY
The Global Partners MBA features internationally renowned faculty members with practical experience in their field. Please visit http://robinson.gsu.edu/gpmba/faculty/index.html for faculty biographies.

STUDENTS
Global Partners students come from around the world, making the classroom a micro United Nations. Countries represented by the program include Belgium, Brazil, Canada, Cameroon, China, Colombia, Congo, Ecuador, Estonia, Ethiopia, France, Honduras, India, Iran, Iraq, Jamaica, Kenya, Korea, Lebanon, Mexico, Nigeria, Oman, Pakistan, Poland, Russia, Taiwan, Togo, Turkey, United States, Venezuela. Languages spoken by candidates have included: Arabic, Amharic, Bengali, Cantonese, English, Estonian, Farsi, French, German, Hindi, Igbo, Italian, Japanese, Korean, Mandarin, Polish, Portuguese, Russian, Spanish, Swahili, Turkish, Yoruba.

ADMISSIONS
The program begins every October. The admissions application deadline is April 1. Admission requirements are:

• Bachelor's degree or equivalent
• Proficiency in a second language
• Two–three years' work experience preferred
• Graduate Masters Admission Test (GMAT)
• 2 Letters of Recommendation
• Essays

CAREER SERVICES AND PLACEMENT
The Global Partners MBA features a Global Career Curriculum that is integrated throughout the program. Class sessions include resume writing, job search strategies, leveraging social networking tools, and salary negotiation. Our dedicated career counselor and faculty director work one-on-one with the students. Personal career assessment tools include Culture Active, Career Leader, Myers-Briggs Type Indicator. Students have access to online job boards: Robinson Career Connections and QS Global Top MBA. Services include executive career coaching, mock interviews, individual counseling, and career fairs. More about the companies with whom we've worked are at www.globalpartnersmba.com.

GISMA BUSINESS SCHOOL

AT A GLANCE

GISMA Business School in Germany offers three accredited MBA programs in cooperation with Purdue University's Krannert School of Management, Indiana, USA and Leibniz Universität Hannover, Germany.

GISMA's highly international programs provide a combination of theory and business-related topics moving beyond typical lectures and exams to experiential learning exercises, computer simulations, student consulting projects and off-site trips. Study groups are diverse with regards to first academic degrees, cultural background, and work experience.

DEGREES OFFERED

GISMA offers three MBA programs: the 11-month full-time MBA starting in August, the 22-month Executive MBA starting in February and the 24-month Young Professional MBA starting in January.

PROGRAMS AND CURRICULUM

1. MBA program (full-time)

This 11-month AACSB-accredited full-time MBA program is offered uniquely in cooperation with Purdue University's Krannert School of Management, Indiana, USA and Leibniz Universität Hannover, Germany. It is aimed at young management professionals from around the world who hold a college degree and have already had some job experience. With its distinctly "real-world" approach, GISMA's full-time MBA program excels at preparing graduates for the challenges of an increasingly global, highly dynamic marketplace. The learning environment is characterized by a pronounced spirit of teamwork among young people from a great variety of cultural, educational and professional backgrounds. Graduates receive dual degrees from both Purdue University and Leibniz Universität Hannover.

2. Executive MBA program (part-time)

The "International Master's in Management Program" (IMM), offered in cooperation with Purdue University's Krannert School of Management in the United States,

TiasNimbas Business School in The Netherlands and CEU Business School in Budapest, Hungary, is designed for managerial professionals that have typically worked for an average of ten years. This MBA program (accredited by both AACSB and AMBA) is an "on-the-job" program with residencies at all four collaborating business schools and in China. Thanks to its concentrated phases of learning, the program is set up in such a way as to enable participants to strike a healthy balance between work, family and study. Graduates receive both the American MBA degree from Purdue University as well as a European MBA degree.

2. Weekend MBA for Young Professionals (part-time)

This 24-month accredited MBA program is aimed at young academics with first work experience and the potential to take on management responsibility within their companies. On 18 weekends a year (Friday and Saturday) as well as during phases of self-study, GISMA students are brought up to speed on the very latest management methods and problem-solving approaches for real-world challenges – with the added advantage of being able to immediately put their newly acquired knowledge to the test in their jobs. Graduates receive the GISMA MBA degree from Leibniz Universität Hannover.

EXPENSES AND FINANCIAL AID

GISMA Business School enables qualified applicants to participate in its full-time MBA program regardless of their financial means. Various forms of financial aid are available to cover tuition (EUR 30,000):

GISMA Education Fund:

Candidates can apply to the GISMA Education Fund for student loans. This enables students to finance up to 85 percent of their tuition without the need for parental sponsorship or bank guarantees.

GISMA Foundation scholarships:

The GISMA Foundation makes scholarships available to applicants with exceptional qualifications.

Scholarships by sponsoring firms:

Scholarships are also offered by firms supporting the GISMA cause.

FACULTY

A world-class team of instructors are the cornerstones of the academic program at GISMA Business School. In addition to helping students acquire the necessary skills and know-how to become tomorrow's business leaders, they are dedicated to providing a positive learning experience.

STUDENTS

"It's like meeting the whole world every day."

The student body at GISMA Business School consists of young professionals aged 28 on average. They come from all around the world and their linguistic and professional diversity culminate in a communicative, open-minded atmosphere.

Julia Gaydina from Russia (MBA 2007)

"I was a member of the Volkswagen consulting project team, which was one of the most popular in our class. Our team was made up of people from extremely diverse backgrounds, representing seven countries (Bosnia, Ecuador, Germany, Peru, Russia, Taiwan and the U.S.) on four continents. There was no doubt about it: Our team was every bit as international as GISMA itself!"

Christian Driemel from Germany (MBA 2007) on his internship in the "Silicon Valley" of India:

"For me, it was extremely gratifying to discover that what we had been learning at GISMA in just four short months could already be applied to real-world challenges. Even without prior business training, I was able to make proposals that ended up benefiting the company. It was also great to see that it's possible to work anywhere in the world."

ADMISSIONS

Student selection is based on a combination of individual academic performance, work experience, leadership potential, personal traits, international-mindedness and motivation to play an active role in an international student body.

The programs are open to all qualified individuals, regardless of their professional or cultural backgrounds. A previous degree in business or economics is not required.

CAREER SERVICES AND PLACEMENT

Besides its top-notch academic program, GISMA Business School also offers extensive career counseling and job-finding services to full-time students. Right from the start, professional coaches are there to help students target careers that are a close match for their individual wishes, abilities and strengths.

GISMA's 90 percent job placement rate within three months of graduation says a lot about the effectiveness of Career Center support in areas such as potential evaluation, interview coaching and assessment center training.

HONG KONG UNIVERSITY OF SCIENCE AND TECHNOLOGY
MBA Program, The HKUST Business School

AT A GLANCE

Established in 1991, HKUST carries a vision to be a leading university with strong local commitment and significant international impact. HKUST Business School is characterized by a genuine blend of East meeting West. We were the first in Asia to be awarded dual accreditation by AACSB in the U.S. and EQUIS in Europe and is one of the few business schools capable of studying issues specific to emerging markets of China with international research standards.

HKUST has also been ranked the region's premier business learning center and its MBA program has been consistently ranked no.1 in Asia by *The Economist* and world no. 9 by *Financial Times* in 2010.

CAMPUS AND LOCATION

The HKUST Business School is housed in the scenic HKUST Clearwater Bay Campus spreading over 60 hectares by the port shelter. Public transport is conveniently available with city center less than 30 minutes away.

DEGREES OFFERED

HKUST offers full-time, part-time and executive MBA programs to fit executives with different motivations at various professional development stages. The full-time program is 16-month incorporating internship opportunity in summer and a semester of international exchange program. Candidates with substantial work experience and international exposure may opt for an intensive 12-month study. The 2-year part-time program is offered both in Hong Kong and Shenzhen. The EMBA program jointly organized with Kellogg School of Management is catered for senior executives.

PROGRAMS AND CURRICULUM

HKUST is known for melting the best elements of western business education with Asian management philosophies. HKUST's expertise in China business offers students with close connections with Chinese practitioners and insights of the China market through popular China focus courses, field trips and wide range of cases.

Carrying a vision to train up responsible leader, a flagship core program on responsible leadership and ethics is offered to students. Apart from strong foundation built up in business essentials ranging from financial knowledge to management strategies through core courses, career-track electives on General Management in China, Finance, Consulting, Entrepreneurship and Family Business as well as Marketing help students to delve more deeply into the subjects that matter to their future most.

With cross-cultural teamwork along the program, students will be exposed to a lot of new views, perspectives and experiences with unique and rewarding learning opportunities. Partnering with other 56 leading business schools in 17 countries, HKUST further broadens students' international exposure through its exchange program.

FACILITIES

Students here enjoy benefits of a full-scale university campus within a relaxing environment. Student housing and amenities such as banks, medical clinics, a supermarket, a bookstore and catering outlets are conveniently located on campus. Other facilities include a five-story library with over 610,000 books and 100 electronic databases, computer barns, wireless Internet access, language learning center, swimming pools, fitness center, tennis courts, athletic track and soccer pitch.

EXPENSES AND FINANCIAL AID

Full-time Program fee for intake 2010: HK$420,000 (~US$53,900) (tuition fee on international exchange program inclusive). Students are advised to budget at least HK$126,000 for living expenses for 12-month study in Hong Kong and extra travel and living expenses for exchange program.

HKUST MBA Merit scholarship for top students: HK$50,000

HKUST MBA Need-based grant for students who demonstrate genuine financial needs: HK$25,000 to HK$150,000

FACULTY

Our faculty is one of the most internationalized and the strongest in research, ranked the world's no. 3 for its "international faculty" and world no. 10 for its "research rank" in the *Financial Times* Rankings 2010. Over 120 full-time faculty members from 15 countries, all PhD qualified, keep student up-to-date with the latest business thinking and developments. Top executives holding leading positions in multinational firms are invited to join the school as adjunct faculty to provide students with substantial industrial insights.

STUDENTS

Diversity is probably the best to describe our full-time cohort. We were ranked No. 6 in both "international students" and "international experience" in the *Financial Times* Rankings 2010. In small class size of around 120 students, over 85% come from outside Hong Kong in total 27 nationalities. They have 5 years of work experience on average. Kicking off with the residential and experiential learning program, HKUST MBA bonds students of different nationalities into a close connection.

ADMISSIONS

Full-time MBA applicants should meet following requirements:

- a strong bachelor degree
- a satisfactory GMAT score
- minimum 2-year post-degree full-time work experience
- Good TOEFL/IELTS result if undergraduate degree was not taught in English

Application period: September to March.

Application fee: HK$1,000 (~US$ 129)

Online Application link: www.mba.ust.hk/application

Short-listed candidates will be invited to either face-to-face or video-conferencing interview.

ADDITIONAL INFORMATION

HKUST Business School has representatives in Beijing, Shanghai, and Shenzhen to facilitate MBA alumni activities and student career services.

Field trips to different regions like Beijing, Shanghai, and Japan are organized to strengthen students' understanding of Asian business. We also sponsor 8 to 9 teams of full-time MBA students to take part in business case competitions worldwide annually to enrich their multi-dimensional experience.

Student-driven clubs, ranging from Energy Alliance and Finance club to China club, are strongly encouraged. They further enrich the academic experience, build leadership competencies and widen exposure beyond the classroom.

CAREER SERVICES AND PLACEMENT

Our dedicated Career team offers various resources, workshops and networking opportunities to support and enhance job search and career management skills of our full-time MBA students. Company presentation and recruitment talks are held regularly. One-on-one career coaching sessions on career development rendered by top business leaders are provided to students. Student consultancy service is initialized to enrich students' practical experience and exposure through working on paid-projects for organizations.

INDIANA UNIVERSITY OF PENNSYLVANIA
Eberly College of Business and Information Technology

AT A GLANCE

The Eberly College of Business and Information Technology MBA program (accredited by AACSB International), with its global strategy focus and highly international student and faculty composition, is designed to sharpen students' managerial, analytical, and decision-making skills so that they can compete in today's global environment. The Eberly MBA program has a long tradition of providing cost-effective preparation for a successful career in business. IUP is consistently ranked among the best institutions in the region for cost, and academic quality by a wide variety of sources such as *The Princeton Review's Best Colleges* publications; *Kiplinger's Personal Finance Magazine; Barron's Best Buys in College Education; The New York Times; Money* magazine; *Entrepreneur* magazine and *U.S. News & World Report*.

CAMPUS AND LOCATION

Indiana University of Pennsylvania enrolls 14,600 students from across the nation and around the globe. With 30,000 residents in the rolling foothills of the Allegheny Mountains, the community of Indiana has been commended in terms of safety. It is a place of tree-lined streets, pleasant neighborhoods, and friendly shops and restaurants. Pittsburgh is a short drive to the southwest from IUP. A variety of recreational activities are available year-round, such as skiing in the winter and swimming or baseball in the summer.

DEGREES OFFERED

Eberly College offers a full-time, on-campus MBA program for young professionals and recent college graduates that can be completed in 12 months. In addition, an executive MBA program for experienced working professionals is available at IUP's off-campus sites in the Pittsburgh area. A Master of Education in Business and Workforce Development (M.Ed.) is also offered. The college offers undergraduate bachelor's degrees in accounting, business education, business technology support, entrepreneurship and small business management, finance, general management, human resource management, supply chain management, international business, management information systems, and marketing.

THE MBA

The Eberly MBA is a 36-credit, integrated, general management program with an option to complete concentrations/specializations (nine additional credits) in *Entrepreneurship, Human Resource Management, International Business, Marketing, Professional Accountancy and Supply Chain Management*. The MBA courses focus on business applications and current analytical tools and techniques and strongly emphasize information technology utilization in managerial problem solving. A wide variety of elective courses are available in the concentration areas. Opportunities are available for internships with local, national, and international organizations.

FACILITIES

A state-of-the-art, $12-million facility houses the MBA classrooms. The Eberly complex is a beautiful, four-story facility that offer a spacious atrium for student interaction and studying, complete wireless access, a café, a 450-seat auditorium, and a 24-hour computing lab operation. Students of the Eberly College study in one of the most technologically advanced business schools in the country. The Eberly complex houses more than 600 computer workstations; more than 20 file servers; nine computing labs, including a financial trading room; digital production studio; wireless technology; and access to comprehensive online business periodicals and journals databases. The college also houses a Small Business Institute and a Small Business Incubator where MBA students can gain business consulting and entrepreneurship experience.

The Financial Trading Room in Eberly offers students databases and related software to conduct financial analysis and learn valuation techniques, arbitrage techniques, and portfolio risk-management strategies.

EXPENSES AND FINANCIAL AID

Tuition, Pennsylvania residents, 2009–2010; $3,333/semester

Tuition, non-Pennsylvania residents, 2009–2010: $5,333/semester

Miscellaneous fees are approximately $813/semester.

On-campus housing costs: from $2,065/semester (double) to $2,934/semester (single)

More than 30 percent of full-time MBA students receive graduate assistantships on a competitive basis that include a full- or partial-tuition waiver and stipend. International students are eligible to compete for partial-tuition waiver during the first semester of study.

FACULTY

Eberly MBA courses are taught by faculty members who have doctoral degrees in their fields of specialization and extensive research and publication track records. Their international backgrounds and/or exposure, experience in industry, and current research projects bring an ideal blend of theory and practice to the MBA courses. Eberly faculty members serve as editors on nine national/international journals.

STUDENTS

Eberly provides students with an opportunity to learn with a diverse group of individuals. More than half the students are from 27 countries other than the U.S., 26 percent have previous business work experience, and 6 percent are currently working full-time in professional careers. Eberly College takes great pride in the activities and initiatives of its College of Business Student Advisory Council and the members of its 14 student organizations. In addition to having the opportunity to serve on university-wide committees, students serve on Eberly College committees for strategic planning, technology, curriculum, outcomes assessment, student services, and programming.

ADMISSIONS

Requirements for admission include a completed undergraduate degree in any field with a superior academic track record from an accredited institution, GMAT scores, academic/professional letters of recommendation, and the applicant's career goal statement. The average GMAT score of admitted candidates range from 450–710 with an average GMAT of 517; the average undergraduate grade point average is 3.12. International applicants must also submit an official TOEFL score report with a minimum score of 76 (iBT Score) or IELTS minimum score of 6.0 and an affidavit of financial support indicating availability of sufficient funds to study in the U.S. For information and a complete application packet, visit www.iup.edu/mba; contact Dr. Krish Krishnan, Eberly College MBA Program, 301 Eberly College of Business and Information Technology, IUP, 664 Pratt Drive, Indiana, PA 15705; or e-mail iup-mba@iup.edu or Krishnan@iup.edu; Telephone: 1-724-357-2522 Fax: 1-724-357-6232.

CAREER PLACEMENT AND SERVICES

IUP assists MBA students with job placement through its recruiting programs, computerized job-search database, résumé referrals, individual counseling, workshops, and job fairs. Many major corporations recruit on the IUP campus, and recent MBA graduates have accepted positions with companies such as Accenture, BNY Mellon, BearingPoint, Citizens Bank, Coca-Cola, Deloitte & Touche, Deutsche Bank, Dow Chemical, Ernst & Young, GE, IBM, Merrill Lynch, MetLife, Novell, PPG, Renault, Rockwell International, Siemens, Symantec, Walt Disney, and World Bank. During 2009–10, the Eberly College held a "Business Day" that attracted more than 50 businesses and governmental agencies. Separately, 31 employers came to campus for one-on-one interviews.

LOYOLA UNIVERSITY—CHICAGO

AT A GLANCE

At Loyola, we provide an excellent faculty, a diversity of students, the resources of a great university, and individualized attention to create a superb learning environment. By studying with us, you will enhance your ability to think critically, solve problems, work in a team environment, think strategically about technology, and effectively communicate your ideas. Consistent with 450 years of Jesuit education, we emphasize the foundation necessary to make ethical decisions in today's complex business environment.

CAMPUS AND LOCATION

The Graduate School of Business campus is located adjacent to Chicago's Magnificent Mile. Chicago is home to the Chicago Board of Trade, Chicago Board Options Exchange, and Chicago Mercantile Exchange, making the city one of the largest financial trading centers in the world. Many national and multinational companies in a broad range of industries are headquartered in Chicago. As a result, job opportunities at major firms abound throughout the Chicago area, in fields as diverse as manufacturing, retailing, health care, and consulting.

On campus facilities include a student center, class rooms, computer labs, a library, conference rooms, and faculty and administrative offices. The Loyola Library system offers numerous computerized resources including the Internet, Lexis-Nexis, Legal Index, FirstSearch, and LUIS (the Loyola Library computerized catalog).

Career Management Services (CMS) assists Graduate School of Business students in making satisfying and informed career decisions, setting appropriate goals, and creating opportunities to help meet those goals. In addition, internship opportunities are available for full-time students needing to build their resumes and those considering a career change.

DEGREES OFFERED

- Masters of Business Administration (MBA)
- MBA Health Care Management (MBA-HCM)
- Masters of Science Accountancy (MSA)
- Masters of Science Finance (MSF)
- Masters of Science Human Resources (MSHR)
- Masters of Science Information Systems and Operations Management (MSISM)
- Masters of Science Integrated Marketing Communications (MSIMC)

Dual Degrees: MBA/MSISM, MBA/MSIMC, MBA/MSA, MBA/MSF, MBA/MSHR, MBA/MSN, and MBA/JD

ACADEMIC PROGRAMS

At Loyola, we help prepare you for the global demands of business by routinely including international considerations in all our courses and by offering courses that singularly focus on the international dimensions of a topic. Students whose career goals demand an intensive grounding in international business can take advantage of our innovative study abroad programs. We offer two-week courses at a number of international locations including our campuses in China and Rome. Each course focuses on topical international issues. Both part-time and full-time students have the opportunity to attend.

Additionally, MBA students can attend overseas programs through the AJCU (the Association of Jesuit Colleges and Universities).

TUITION AND FINANCIAL AID

Tuition for 2009–2010 is $3,498 per course for both full- and part-time students. A wide variety of housing is available both on and off campus. Many full-time students live within walking distance of the Graduate School of Business. Other students choose to live in housing located on the Water Tower Campus. The estimated cost of room and board for 12 months is $14,500.

FINANCIAL AID

Graduate scholarship positions, providing tuition support and monetary stipends, are available through the GSB. Merit scholarships are also available. All students are automatically considered for the merit scholarship upon admission.

FACULTY

The Loyola University Chicago faculty is strongly committed to teaching as well as research. Because 70 84 percent of the faculty members are full time and 95 percent of those have a PhD or equivalent degree, classes are taught by experienced, highly trained leaders in their fields. Loyola also augments the regular faculty with practicing managers and consultants who teach classes in special topics such as emerging technologies and negotiations.

As leaders in their fields, many faculty members have important industry and community ties in such areas as financial and policy studies, consulting, and marketing and communications. In the classroom, they offer a scholarly approach gained through research as well as practical business experience.

The faculty's dedication to research invigorates the MBA experience by developing new ideas that can be applied in the classroom. The faculty is involved in an impressive range of research projects in all major areas of business and is also widely published.

STUDENT ORGANIZATIONS AND ACTIVITIES

Being an active member of a student organization enriches your overall GSB experience with friendships, leadership experiences, professional growth, and industry-specific knowledge. It also helps potential employers see your commitment to the program and to a balance between your academic and social life.

Choose from: Economic Forum; The Association of Loyola Entrepreneurs; GSB Advisory Council; GSB Association; GSB International Club; Human Resource Student Association; Investment Banking & Financial Markets Club; ISOM Club; Marketing Club; Strategic Consulting Group.

For more information, visit http://www.luc.edu/gsb/gsb_student_orgs.shtml.

ADMISSIONS

Quarterly admission is available. Prospective students should apply well in advance of the quarter in which they plan to enter. Applications are accepted until July 1 for the fall quarter; September 1 for the winter quarter; December 1 for the spring quarter; and March 1 for the summer quarter.

Admission decisions are based on interest, aptitude, and capacity for business study as indicated by their previous academic record, achievement scores on the GMAT, recommendations, and professional experience. Our average student's undergraduate GPA is 3.2. The average GMAT score is 550, and average work experience of the entering students is three to five years.

Loyola welcomes applications from international students who have completed a four-year bachelor's degree or its equivalent.

LOYOLA UNIVERSITY—NEW ORLEANS

AT A GLANCE

The business environment of today, and surely that of tomorrow, is characterized as one of constant change, uncertainty, and greater connectivity through technology. Our MBA program has been designed to prepare individuals to thrive in this dynamic, global marketplace.

At Loyola University New Orleans, we provide a distinctive mix of faculty excellence and individualized attention to create a superb learning environment in which you can excel. By studying with us, you will enhance your ability to critically analyze business issues, work in a team environment, appropriately apply technology, and effectively communicate your ideas. Equally important is the emphasis we place on providing you the foundation necessary to make ethical decisions in today's complex society.

Loyola's MBA program is composed of 51 credit hours. However, students with an undergraduate degree from an AACSB-accredited business school may waive up to 15 credit hours of the foundation level classes. This program is ideal for business undergraduates and working professionals, but also works very well for students with non-business degrees. You decide how quickly you want to complete the program. Whether full-time or part-time, by attending evening classes, you have the opportunity to build your resume during the day through internships or participation in various organizations. Work experience is preferred, but not required, to support your application.

There are three key elements of the program: business ethics, leadership, and supply chain management, all taught with a global perspective. The average class size is 18 students, ensuring an interesting, interactive classroom experience.

CAMPUS AND LOCATION

Loyola University New Orleans is located in the heart of the old residential section of New Orleans. This gracious southern city is one of the most fascinating in the United States. The fascination with New Orleans has grown stronger since Hurricane Katrina. While many areas of New Orleans were greatly affected by the hurricane, The French Quarter, The Central Business District (CBD), and St. Charles Avenue, where Loyola is located, were spared from the flood. New Orleans is facing a long road to recovery from Hurricane Katrina, but New Orleans is a resilient city that will overcome the challenges that lie ahead.

Often described as more European than American in nature, it is known for its jazz, cuisine, the French Quarter, café au lait, the architecture, streetcars, riverboats, a bustling seaport, the history, the writers, and Mardi Gras. New Orleans offers world-class events and facilities such as the New Orleans Jazz and Heritage Festival, the Crescent City Classic, the Sugar Bowl, the Audubon Zoo, and the Aquarium of the Americas. Music weaves through every aspect of life in the Crescent City, from one of the oldest opera companies in the nation to jazz bands in street parades.

Our school is located five miles, by streetcar, from the Central Business District on a historic avenue in the heart of one of the most beautiful neighborhoods. Across the street you will find Audubon Park, a perfect place to enjoy jogging and picnicking among ancient oak trees or strolling past tranquil lagoons to the Audubon Zoo and the Mississippi River.

DEGREES OFFERED

Loyola University New Orleans offers a traditional MBA program that can be taken at a full-time or part-time basis. Additionally, we offer a JD/MBA program in coordination with the College of Law and a MBA/MPS program in coordination with Loyola's Institute for Ministry.

ACADEMIC PROGRAMS

Loyola's MBA program is an exceptionally flexible program. Students can choose to study part or full time; some students with business undergraduate degrees

are able to finish in one calendar year. Students who have heavy outside obligations may want to take only three or four courses a year. You decide how quickly you want to complete the program. Loyola's MBA Program is composed of 51 credit hours. However, students with an undergraduate degree from an AACSB-accredited business school may waive up to 15 credit hours of the foundation level classes. This program is ideal for business undergraduates and working professionals, but also works very well for students with non-business degrees. Whether full time or part time, by attending evening classes, students have the opportunity to build their resumes during the day either through internships or participating in various organizations. Work experience is preferred, but not required, to support this application.

There are three key elements of the program: business ethics, leadership, and supply chain management, all taught with a global perspective. The average class size is 18 students, ensuring an interesting, interactive classroom experience.

Classes begin each fall and spring. Classes are taught in the evening and occasionally on Saturday. This allows you to continue working full-time or it can allow you to participate in internships to add to your MBA experience.

FACILITIES

The College of Business offers wireless Internet connections throughout the building and has a computer lab dedicated for business students. Loyola's J. Edgar and Louise S. Monroe Library offers the latest in online technology, as well as traditional book and periodical references. Students and faculty have online computer network access at each table and study carrel, allowing more than 700 simultaneous computer links to millions of resources across the globe. It was named one of the ten best college libraries by Princeton Review in 2009.

EXPENSES AND FINANCIAL AID

Tuition for the 2009–2010 academic year is $855 per credit hour. For additional information about tuition and financial aid, please visit http://www.business.loyno.edu/mba/tuition-fees-financial-aid.

STUDENTS

Loyola's MBA program is a small evening program that allows the MBA students to develop a close-knit community and group of friends. The main student group is the MBA Association, which provides leadership opportunities to interested students; it also coordinates community-service projects and schedules special events.

ADMISSION

Loyola requires the following of applicants to its MBA program: official transcripts for all past postsecondary academic work; an official score report for the GMAT; two recommendation forms; a 400-word essay; and a resume. International students whose first language is not English must also submit TOEFL scores; all international students must provide an affidavit demonstrating sufficient financial resources to support themselves during their tenure at the university. Work experience, though not required, is strongly recommended.

CAREER SERVICES AND PLACEMENT

Loyola maintains a Career Development Center to serve all undergraduate and graduate students of the university. Services include self-assessment instruments, career counseling, internship and job placement services, and guidance in resume writing, interviewing, job search, and salary negotiation skills. The office organizes on-campus recruiting events. The MBA Association also contributes by organizing networking events.

In recent years, Loyola MBAs have been placed with Capital One, Entergy, Ernst & Young, LLP, Harrah's Entertainment, Ochsner Health System, Red Bull North America, Shell, and Whitney Bank.

NORTH CAROLINA STATE UNIVERSITY

AT A GLANCE

At NC State's Jenkins Graduate School of Management, we've created an MBA with focus. The NC State MBA Program will help you develop a keen understanding of general business and management principles. And your concentrated study of a technology-oriented business process or function will give you an edge in the marketplace.

The NC State MBA offers both a full-time program and part-time evening program.

Our focus on outstanding MBA education is illustrated by a reputation for excellence in technology management, an innovative faculty with cutting-edge teaching and research, quality students from diverse backgrounds, and unmatched value in management education.

CAMPUS AND LOCATION

NC State was founded in 1887 as a land-grant institution that has become one of the nation's leading research universities. Located in the Research Triangle, a world-renowned center of research, industry, and technology, the College of Management is housed on the 2,110-acre main campus of NC State, which lies just west of downtown Raleigh, the state capital. NC State comprises eleven colleges and schools, serving a total student population of over 30,000.

DEGREES OFFERED

MBA—Master of Business Administration

Full-time (56 credit hours) and part-time (47 credit hours) programs. Concentrations: Biosciences Management, Entrepreneurship & Technology Commercialization, Financial Management, Marketing Management, Product Innovation Management, Services Management, and Supply Chain Management

ACADEMIC PROGRAMS

The NC State MBA curriculum was designed to prepare students for management careers and to provide unique offerings of technology-oriented courses and concentrations. The curriculum is built around core classes in the basics of management, a specialized concentration and open electives.

Your MBA concentration will give you an opportunity to focus your studies on a specialized technology process or critical business function. Each concentration includes some required courses and a choice among electives in that field, and most require students to complete a semester-long team project by working closely with a corporate client to solve a relevant business problem.

No matter what your background, you will be surrounded by classmates with a wide range of experience. In some of the technical courses, you will work on projects with students from NC State's highly regarded graduate programs in computer science, engineering, design, and the sciences.

FACILITIES

The College of Management is located in Nelson Hall, which houses classrooms, computer labs, and the offices of the faculty members and students. Classrooms have been completely remodeled with tiered seating, laptop connections, and complete multimedia facilities. Nelson Hall is also wireless accessible.

EXPENSES AND FINANCIAL AID

The estimated annual tuition for the 2008–2009 school year is $13,818 for North Carolina residents in the full-time program and $8,701 for North Carolina residents in the part-time program. For non-residents, the estimated annual tuition for the 2008–2009 school year is $25,741 for students in the full-time program and $17,737 for students in the part-time program.

Graduate assistantships are available to full-time students. Graduate assistantships cover tuition, health insurance, and a monthly stipend. Grants and loan programs are available through the Graduate School and the University's Financial Aid Office.

FACULTY

The College of Management has built a faculty rich in technology-related business expertise, management experience and practical research. Our professors also have a passion for teaching and a commitment to working closely with industry to solve real-world problems. Our faculty excel in both traditional scholarly pursuits and practical, corporate-sponsored research. We are home to a number of extensively published scholars, and editors and editorial board members of prestigious research journals.

STUDENTS

Almost all MBA students have professional work experience, many in high-technology industries, such as telecommunications or software and others in industries, such as health care or financial services. A technical background is not essential for the MBA, but all students must be willing to learn about technology and the management challenges it creates.

The average full-time MBA student has four years of work experience. The age range of students is between 22 and 45. Women comprise approximately 35 percent of each entering class; members of minority groups, approximately eight percent; and international students, 32 percent.

ADMISSIONS

Admission to the MBA program is highly competitive. Applicants need to demonstrate the following personal accomplishments and attributes:

1. Strong intellectual performance and academic promise, evidenced by previous undergraduate and graduate work as well as GMAT scores

2. An employment history demonstrating management potential

3. Leadership skills, maturity, creativity, initiative and teamwork orientation

4. A desire and willingness to learn about technology and the management challenges it creates

MBA students must have a baccalaureate degree from an accredited college or university. Admissions decisions are based on previous academic performance, GMAT scores (610 average), essays, letters of reference, and previous work experience. Applicants whose native language is other than English, regardless of citizenship, must also submit TOEFL scores of at least 250 (computer-based test). Interviews are required for applicants for both the full-time and part-time MBA programs.

SPECIAL PROGRAMS

The NC State MBA Program now offers joint masters degrees in Microbial Biotechnology, Veterinary Medicine, Accounting, and Industrial Engineering.

CAREER SERVICES AND PLACEMENT

MBA students have access to a wide range of programs and services to enhance their marketability, including career counseling and workshops on resume writing, cover letters, interviewing, and job search strategies. In addition to on-campus recruiting for permanent jobs and internships, the Career Resource Center maintains an online resume referral and job posting service, hosts job fairs, and maintains a library of information about career opportunities with specific companies.

RICE UNIVERSITY

AT A GLANCE

Rice University aspires to path-breaking research, excellence in teaching and contributions to the enhancement of our world. As the university's business school, The Jesse H. Jones Graduate School of Business adheres to those same values to cultivate a diverse community of learning and discovery.

More specifically, the Jones School develops principled, innovative thought leaders in global communities. Through a combination of rigorous curriculum, elite faculty and impressive facilities, students receive an outstanding business school experience. The result is innovative leadership that engages the entrepreneurial spirit and impacts business on a global level.

The Jones School is one of the world's best teaching and research universities, offering Full-Time MBA, MBA for Executives, and MBA for Professionals programs. A Ph.D. program in debuted in 2009 and recently-introduced business concentrations highlight the school's strengths while allowing full-time MBA students to focus on areas of interest.

Additional information is available through our website at www.business.rice.edu.

CAMPUS AND LOCATION

Rice University is located on a beautiful wooded 300-acre campus in central Houston, minutes from the downtown business district and the city's world-class theater district. The campus is located across the street from the renowned Texas Medical Center and within walking distance to the museum district, Houston Zoological Gardens, and Hermann Park.

DEGREES OFFERED

The Jones School focuses all of its energy on graduate business education. A Rice MBA is available three distinct programs (Full-Time, MBA for Professionals and MBA for Executives) designed to accommodate students at every stage of their career. Also available are an MBA/Masters in Engineering in conjunction with the George R. Brown College of Engineering at Rice, and an MBA/MD in conjunction with Baylor College of Medicine. The Jones School also offers a Ph.D. in Management to develop business school faculty.

ACADEMIC PROGRAMS

Every course offers unparalleled opportunity to work one-on-one with an accessible, involved, and energetic faculty. The Jones School faculty maintains an important balance between teaching and research, believing that current industry knowledge is as critical as textbooks to your education.

A comprehensive core curriculum focuses on managerial and leadership skills, ethics, information technology, and communication skills in addition to the functional areas. Students take elective credit hours, which allow them to custom design their curriculum to suit career goals.

FACILITIES

McNair Hall is the 167,000-square-foot home of the Jones School. It offers a state-of-the-El Paso finance center; the Business Information Center (BIC); tiered classrooms; behavior research and observation room for marketing research and interviews; a 450-seat auditorium; and a career planning center. Fully loaded laptops are provided to all students, and the Jones School is equipped to make sophisticated use of electronic access.

EXPENSES AND FINANCIAL AID

Application fee: $125

Tuition: $40,000 for the 2009–2010 year.

Total estimated expenses: approximately $60,000 per year

Financial Aid: Over 80 percent of students attending the Jones School receive merit-based scholarships. Rice University's Office of Student Financial Services also administers a variety of federally and privately funded loan programs.

FACULTY

The Jones School's faculty is consistently recognized for their knowledge, research, teaching ability, and student focus. Each member of the Jones faculty maintains a balance between teaching and research, ensuring that students receive the most current, leading-edge education.

STUDENTS

The Jones School attracts students both nationally and internationally. In fact, 28 percent of first year students hail from outside the United States and nearly 20 percent are from outside of Texas. A variety of student organizations are available and many sponsor guest speakers, visit area businesses, and take on special projects. In addition, weekly corporate-sponsored "partios"—parties on the Jones School patio—provide relaxation and opportunities to network and bond with fellow students.

ADMISSIONS

The Jones School considers each aspect of the application when making admissions decision. The application requirements include: GMAT (GRE or MCAT for join candidates); TOEFL or PTE for some international applicants; transcripts from educational institutions; resume; confidential evaluations; essays; interview (invitation only); completed application form and application fee.

Academic Background: A four-year undergraduate degree from an accredited college or university is required for U.S. applicants. International applicants must have an undergraduate degree equivalent to a four-year U.S. degree. Undergraduate and graduate GPAs, GMAT scores (GRE or MCAT for joint candidates), choice of major, electives, course load, and grade patterns are all considered.

Leadership Potential: Demonstrated leadership and management experiences, both on the job and through extracurricular activities, will help us assess leadership potential. We look for individuals with at least two years of professional work experience.

Confidential Evaluations: Evaluations from employers provide perspective on potential student capabilities, enabling us to assess your qualifications more accurately.

Essays: Three essays articulating career goals, work experience, and reasons for choosing the Rice MBA program are a crucial component of the application process. These essays are designed to convey intangibles such as reasons for pursuing an MBA; benefits of academic, professional and personal opportunities; and personal expectations of the Jones School experience.

CAREER SERVICES

The Career Management Center (CMC) is housed within the Jones School building and works only with Rice MBA students and alumni. The CMC serves to support each student's development of a career plan throughout their two years at the Jones School. From day one of immersion to graduation, the CMC works individually with students to ensure they develop the strategy, job search skills, and networking opportunities that will help them succeed in the MBA job market.

UNIVERSITY OF CONNECTICUT
School of Business

AT A GLANCE
Educating business leaders for nearly 130 years, the University of Connecticut (UConn) is ranked among the top 3 percent of business schools worldwide according to *Business Week*, *Forbes*, and *U.S. News & World Report*. UConn's MBA Program offers a comprehensive state-of-the-art business education that empowers business leaders to anticipate and effectively manage the challenges within today's dynamic and complex world of business. The competitive edge that UConn's MBA Program offers is the integration of award-winning innovative experiential learning opportunities that radically challenge your intellect, enhance your skill set and prepare you for success in life as well as in the competitive world of business.

CAMPUS AND LOCATION
UConn has grown in recent years from a strong regional school to a prominent national academic institution with over 29,000 students and 190,000 alumni. The University's span of 4,300+ acres includes ten schools and colleges at its main campus in Storrs, separate Schools of Law and Social Work in Hartford, five regional campuses throughout the state and Schools of Medicine and Dental Medicine at the UConn Health Center in Farmington. Right in the middle of Fortune 500 territory, the state capital and metropolitan area of Hartford is 30 minutes away, Boston is a 90-minute drive, and New York City is a 3-hour drive.

DEGREES OFFERED
The UConn School of Business offers a traditional full-time MBA degree, as well as part-time and Executive MBA programs. UConn also offers an MS in Accounting degrees, as well as a variety of dual-degree programs including MBA/JD, MBA/MD, MBA/MA in International Studies, MBA/MS in Nursing, and MBA/MA of International Management (MIM). A post graduate Advance Business Certificate is also offered in various business disciplines.

ACADEMIC PROGRAMS
The full-time, 2-year MBA program at UConn offers students a practical, comprehensive business education that truly integrates basic business fundamentals with innovative experiential learning. This carefully blended curriculum is what yields the highly desirable real-world experience that today's global businesses demand.

The curriculum includes fundamental business courses, an Internship Milestone, experiential learning opportunities and focused concentrations which include Finance, Health Care Management & Insurance Studies, Marketing, Operations & Information Management, Real Estate, and Venture Consulting.

FACILITIES
UConn students study in state-of-the-art research and learning facilities. Classrooms and meeting spaces are outfitted with broad multimedia capability reflecting the School's commitment to meet the demands of the information era.

EXPENSES AND FINANCIAL AID
2009–2010 tuition and fees for the full-time MBA program for the academic year (two semesters) are $11,226 for Connecticut residents and $26,310 for non-residents. Housing and living costs vary among candidates, but are approximately $6,356 for graduate resident housing and $4,724 for meals. Additional costs include required health insurance, textbooks, mobile computer, laundry and incidentals.

Financial aid is available in the form of loans and scholarships. Most financial aid is awarded on the basis of established need, primarily determined through an analysis of an applicant's Free Application for Federal Student Aid (FAFSA). The School of Business also offers a limited number of merit-based graduate/teaching assistantships.

For further information, contact the University of Connecticut Financial Aid Office at 860-486-2819 or at www.financialaid.uconn.edu.

FACULTY
UConn's faculty offers a wealth of academic and business experience to students. Over 96% of them have earned a PhD or the highest degree in their field. Most are actively involved in scholarly activities that enable them to stay current in and contribute to their fields of knowledge, as well as to bring a balanced perspective between theory and practice into the classroom.

STUDENT BODY
UConn MBA students come from a wide variety of undergraduate institutions, both domestic and international. Their undergraduate degrees represent majors in many diverse areas—from engineering and English, sciences and fine arts, to business to economics. In a typical class of students, 35 percent are women, the average age is 28, and approximately 25–30 percent are international students. Friendliness and informality characterize student life at the main campus. Social and professional organizations, including the Graduate Business Association (GBA), offer a variety of activities to satisfy the needs of students.

ADMISSIONS
Admission to UConn's MBA Program is very competitive. The minimum requirements for admission include two years of postgraduate professional work experience; a minimum 3.0 GPA on a 4.0 scale, or the equivalent, from a four-year accredited institution; and a total GMAT score of at least 560. For international students whose native language is not English, a TOEFL score of at least 233 (computer-based) is required. The application deadline for international applicants is February 1 and for domestic applicants, March 1.

SPECIAL PROGRAMS
Essential to UConn's MBA Program curriculum is the incorporation of innovative experiential learning accelerators. These unique practice-based initiatives integrate traditional teaching and classroom instruction with high-profile practical applications to close the gap between theory and practice. UConn MBA experiential learning accelerators include the GE/UConn *edgelab*, SS&C Technologies Financial Accelerator, Innovation Accelerator, $2M Student Managed Fund, and SCOPE (sustainable community outreach and public engagement.)

ADDITIONAL INFORMATION
The UConn School of Business is nationally accredited by AACSB International – The Association to Advance Collegiate Schools of Business – and is a member of the Graduate Management Admissions Council (GMAC) and the European Foundation for Management Development (EFMD). UConn is also accredited by the New England Association of Schools & Colleges (NEASC).

CAREER SERVICES AND PLACEMENT
UConn's career planning activities begin during orientation and continue throughout the MBA. Primary recruiters include General Electric, CIGNA, Aetna, IBM, United Technologies Corp., Wachovia, Hartford Financial Services, PricewaterhouseCoopers, Gerber Technologies, ESPN, and UBS. For the class of 2008, the median salary was $89,000 with sign-on bonuses as high as $30,000.

UNIVERSITY OF ROCHESTER
Simon Graduate School of Business

AT A GLANCE

The William E. Simon Graduate School of Business Administration at the University of Rochester in Rochester, New York offers an integrated, cross-functional approach to management, which uses economics as both the framework and common language of business, and the skills to become an effective leader. Programs offered are full-time MBA and MS programs, Executive MBA and Part-Time MBA and MS programs.

The school is accredited by the AACSB—The International Association for Management Education since 1966. Simon: where thinkers become leaders.

CAMPUS AND LOCATION

The Simon School is situated on the River Campus of the University of Rochester, near the banks of the Genesee River, and three miles from downtown Rochester, New York. The Simon School is one of seven schools and colleges within the University of Rochester.

DEGREES OFFERED

Full-Time Study

The MBA degree requires 67 hours of study and a 3.0 grade-point average. There are two entrance dates, September or January. The degree requirements for the January entrance are the same as those for fall entry.

Part-Time Study

Applicants to the Part-Time MBA Program may matriculate in any quarter. They may also take up to seven classes before matriculating to the program. The part-time MBA degree requires 64 hours of study and a 3.0 grade-point average.

Executive MBA Programs

Offers candidates a fully accredited MBA degree without career interruption. Classes meet every other Friday/Saturday for two academic years in Rochester, New York; and Bern, Switzerland. (22 months).

MS Programs

Nine Master of Science in Business Administration programs are offered: Accountancy, Marketing, General Management, Medical Management, Manufacturing Management, Service Management, Information Systems Management, Technology Transfer and Commercialization and Finance.

Each M.S. degree is offered on a full-time or part-time basis.

Academic Programs General

The Simon School's MBA programs are designed to train individuals to solve management problems as team members in a study-team structure. It is a place where thinkers become leaders. The curriculum emphasizes learning the principles of economics and effective decision-making through a mix of lecture, case study, and project courses. Nine core courses are required. A three-credit course over two quarters in business communications is required of all full-time students. Eleven elective courses are required.

FACILITIES

The following is a description of Simon School facilities:

Schlegel Hall is a four-story classroom and student-services building. The building contains nine case-style classrooms, which seat 35 to 100 students, and 21 rooms for group study. Classrooms are equipped with state-of-the-art audio and visual technology.

Carol G. Simon Hall houses the school's administration, faculty and PhD students. Carol G. Simon Hall is linked to Schlegel and Gleason Halls by the Florescue-von Manstein Plaza and is also connected to it by a tunnel. The building contains more than 75 offices, several conference rooms, and a variety of lounge spaces for faculty and staff.

James S. Gleason Hall is the 38,000-square-foot classroom building linked to Schlegel Hall. Gleason Hall houses five new classrooms, up to 16 study rooms, and a significantly expanded Career Management Center suite, including eight dedicated interview rooms.

EXPENSES AND FINANCIAL AID

In addition to the $125 application fee, tuition is $1434 per credit hour, or $43,020 per year, for 2010–2011. The cost of books and supplies averages $1,500 a year, and living expenses (rent, food supplies, personal expenses, and health insurance) were estimated at less than $15,000 for the 2010–2011 academic year. Both U.S. and international applicants are eligible for merit awards.

STUDENT BODY

Each September approximately 160 students enter the Simon community. Another 60 students join their classmates in January. September entrants complete the first-year core courses during the fall, winter, and spring quarters; the majority of January entrants complete core courses during the winter, spring, and summer quarters. Within each cohort, students are assigned to a study team of 4 or 5 members. Each team always includes representatives from at least three countries.

In the class of 2011, 16 countries are represented. Prior full-time work experience averages 4.1 years, and the average age is 25. Women comprise 30 percent of the class. Nineteen percent of Simon students are members of American minority groups.

ADMISSIONS

A Simon School Admissions Committee reads each application individually and evaluates recommendations, teamwork and communication skills, the nature and scope of prior work experience, the undergraduate academic record, GMAT scores. All undergraduate majors are represented in the program.

SPECIAL PROGRAMS

During the two-week Orientation Program, students participate in self-assessment exercises, personal selling and communication skills instruction, corporate leadership training, and one-on-one career counseling. In addition, students participate in several VISION (the student-managed portion of a Simon MBA) modules designed to enhance leadership skills in the areas of team building, training in diversity issues, ethical decision making, and social responsibility.

ADDITIONAL INFORMATION

Year after year, the Simon School consistently ranks high on the lists of top b-school programs. These rankings include: *Business Week, U.S. News & World Report, Financial Times* of London and *Forbes*.

CAREER SERVICES AND PLACEMENT

The Career Management Center team works diligently to develop new and enhance existing corporate partnerships to provide a wide range of career opportunities for both summer internships and full-time career positions.

The Career Management Center's Counseling and Education staff offers targeted, personalized counseling to assist students in identifying, initiating, and implementing highly effective career plans.

THE UNIVERSITY OF TOLEDO

College of Business Administration

AT A GLANCE

The University of Toledo graduate programs in business feature affordability and flexibility that help you expand your skills and opportunities without interrupting your career. Our curriculum is designed to equip future leaders with relevant, real-world knowledge about the workings of every level of the enterprise: employees, customers, the firm itself, and all levels of the economy. The UT College of Business is accredited by AACSB and is a member of the prestigious Graduate Management Admissions Council.

CAMPUS AND LOCATION

The University of Toledo was established in 1872, became a member of the state university system in 1967, and merged with the former Medical University of Ohio in 2006. UT is a community built around 12 academic colleges and professional programs, an offering matched only by a handful of public universities nationwide. UT also has one of the largest distance learning programs in the country. The university's campus was named one of the 100 most beautifully landscaped university campuses in the country.

DEGREES OFFERED

The College of Business Administration offers the following degrees and programs: BBA (12 different fields); MBA (full-time and part-time); JD/MBA Dual Degree; MD/MBA Dual Degree; Executive MBA; Master of Science in Accountancy (MSA); PhD in Manufacturing and Technology Management; Post-Doctoral Bridge to Business Program

MBA Concentrations are available in: Administration; Finance; Human Resources; Information Systems; International Business; Leadership; Marketing (3 tracks): CRM and Marketing Intelligence; Marketing Management; Professional Sales; Operations and Supply Chain Management; Technological Entrepreneurship

ACADEMIC PROGRAMS GENERAL

You can earn an MBA program at UT in as little as one calendar year by completing 11 courses. Since we offer all of our core courses in the fall, spring, and summer, you will find that the UT MBA program is designed specifically for your busy schedule, allowing you to take the courses you need when you want to take them. Every UT MBA student is able to customize their MBA by taking their 9 credits of electives in one specific specialization. Many of our required courses are offered online.

The Executive MBA program is designed specifically for working professionals with three to five years of experience in a managerial role. EMBA students work in a cohort and complete the program in only 15 months working in weekend residencies on Friday nights and Saturdays.

The Master of Science in Accountancy (MSA) degree program is designed to meet the needs of the professional in accounting and to qualify candidates to sit for the CPA examination in Ohio. The UT MSA degree is a 30-semester-hour program and typically includes 21 semester hours of accounting classes and nine semester hours of diversification electives.

We also offer dual degree programs with the College of Law (JD/MBA) and the UT College of Medicine (MD/MBA).

FACILITIES

The College of Business Administration is fully equipped to instruct students in a cutting-edge learning environment that integrates technology into the curriculum. Over 100 laptop computers are available for students to check out on a daily basis. All of our laptops have integrated wireless network access, which allows students to get online in Stranahan Hall, the college's main building. The John Neff Stock Trading Floor is one of only 30 such facilities in the country and gives students real- and delayed-access to feeds from stock exchanges around the world. The College of Business also upgraded its physical facilities by opening a $15 million expansion in January 2010.

EXPENSES AND FINANCIAL AID

2009–2010 Academic Year Tuition and Fees (approximate, based on 6 credits per term)

Ohio residents: $6,000

Nonresidents: $12,000

Please visit the Bursar's Office webpage at http://www.utoledo.edu/offices/bursar/ for the most current information on tuition and fees. Federal Stafford loans, private educational loans and graduate assistantships are available to eligible students. Graduate students with residency in Hillsdale, Lenawee, Macomb, Monroe, Oakland, Washtenaw, and Wayne Counties in Michigan are eligible to attend UT graduate programs at the Ohio resident tuition rate.

ADMISSIONS

Admission to the MBA and MSA programs takes place in all three semesters: fall (August), spring (January), and summer (May).

The Admissions Committee requires the following documents in order to evaluate an application:

- Application for admission
- Application fee
- Three letters of recommendation
- One official transcript from each university attended
- GMAT results
- TOEFL results (if necessary)

Applicants are encouraged to apply as early as possible to ensure that their applications are processed and that they can be admitted for the term they want.

Since the Executive MBA is a cohort-based program, applicants can only enter the program in August of each calendar year. Applications are considered on a space-available basis. Admission to the PhD program takes place each fall as well. The Post-Doctoral Bridge program admits students each summer for the intensive residency-based program, which takes place over two months in June and July.

CAREER SERVICES AND PLACEMENT

The MBA program features special opportunities and resources to enhance your education and career. Through Corporate Graduate Assistantships, highly qualified students work 15–20 hours a week at a local company while pursuing an MBA full-time. MBA students can also utilize the resources of the Business Career Programs Office, which organizes on-campus recruiting, resume reviews, walk-in advising, mock interviews, and the biannual Business Career Fair, which attracts more than 90 companies.

UNIVERSITY OF TULSA
College of Business Administration

AT A GLANCE
The University of Tulsa's College of Business Administration has graduated skilled and inspired business professionals since 1935. In 2008, the college was renamed the Collins College of Business in honor of the visionary leadership of Tulsa businessman and Board of Trustees Chair, Fulton Collins. Today, as business evolves under the forces of globalization and technology, we pride ourselves on keeping pace with a variety of programs that prepare students for success in the business world.

CAMPUS AND LOCATION
Founded in 1894, The University of Tulsa is a private, doctoral-granting university located in Tulsa, OK. The university has an earned reputation for exceptional academics, with one in every ten undergraduate students being a National Merit Scholar. Student life abounds the campus of 4,100 students with over 40 Registered Student Organizations, 5 IFC fraternities and 6 NPC sororities. We are the nation's smallest university to participate in the NCAA's Division I-A, and one in ten students is participating in intercollegiate athletics. Located just 10 minutes from downtown Tulsa, students enjoy all of the amenities of the city.

DEGREES OFFERED
Master of Business Administration (MBA): Concentrations: Accounting, Finance, International Business, Management Information Systems, Taxation, Energy Management
Master of Science in Finance (MSF): Concentrations: Corporate Finance, Investments and Portfolio Management, Risk Management
Online Master of Taxation (MTAX)

The following dual programs are also available: MBA/MSF; MBA/MS Computer Science; MSF/MS Applied Mathematics; Juris Doctor/MBA; Juris Doctor/MSF; Juris Doctor/MTAX

PROGRAMS AND CURRICULUM
Student Investment Fund: Students are able to apply financial theories and models by making investment decisions and managing a real portfolio of financial assets in excess of $1.6M. Study Abroad: The Center for Global Education provides oversight for TU's academic programs abroad, managing 11 reciprocal exchange partnerships with universities in Austria, Australia, China, Finland, France, Germany, England, Switzerland and New Zealand.

Williams Risk Management Center: This learning laboratory allows students to participate in controlled financial scenarios where they make informed business decisions using Bloomberg terminals, extensive financial databases and computer software.

Governors Cup: The Donald W. Reynolds statewide Governor's Cup business plan competition is designed to encourage students to act upon their ideas and talents. Both our 2007 and 2008 teams earned top two finishes in the competition.

internships: Internships may be available to provide you with the relevant work experience you need to make the next step toward your ultimate career goal.

FACILITIES
The Williams Student Services Center, located in Helmerich Hall, home of the Collins College of Business, provides graduate students the ability to consult their academic advisor, enroll for classes, or research and strategize career opportunities with the Director of Business Career Development, all in the same suite.

Campus amenities include on-campus luxury apartments, wireless internet access, eateries, a post office, McFarlin Library, Collins Fitness Center and Case Tennis Center.

EXPENSES AND FINANCIAL AID
2010–11 Tuition is $939 per credit hour for all domestic and international students. Student fees are $4 per credit hour.

FACULTY
With an 11:1 student-to-faculty ratio, students are never a "number" to our professors. We have 30 full-time faculty members teaching at the graduate level. Passionate, approachable, and accessible, they are able to combine academic theory with real world experience.

ADMISSIONS
Students applying to a Collins College of Business Graduate Program must submit the following documents:
• Application (available online)
• $40.00 fee
• Transcripts from ALL institutions of higher education
• Acceptable GMAT score (*GRE acceptable for MSF programs ONLY*)
• Three professional reference letters
• Resumé
International Applicants must also submit:
• Acceptable TOEFL score (575 paper, 232 computer, 90 internet), or Acceptable IELTS score (6.5)
• Confirmation of Financial Resources

Application Deadlines:

Domestic Applicants: Fall—July 1; Spring—November 1; Summer—April 1

SPECIAL PROGRAMS
Friends of Finance: Friends of Finance is an organization of business professionals, TU constituents and students who network and share business perspectives. The organization hosts an Executive Speaker series of nationally prominent business and public leaders on campus.

Graduate Business Student Association: GBSA is a student-operated organization that promotes interaction among graduate students in order to develop networking opportunities with companies and business professionals.

International Business & EntrepreneurSHIP Institute: The IBEI is a gateway to international and entrepreneurial endeavors for students at TU.

ADDITIONAL INFORMATION
The Collins College of Business has been accredited by AACSB International since 1949. This accreditation is important to you because it provides assurance that the university and faculty are producing relevant research and remaining current with issues in business. Many companies are now requiring employees to attend AACSB accredited schools in order to participate in tuition reimbursement programs.

CAREER SERVICES AND PLACEMENT
Career services are an integral component of our graduate business programs; more than 200 companies turn to The University of Tulsa annually to hire our graduates. The Collins College of Business Director of Business Career Development works one-on-one with students to research and strategize career opportunities. These services are available to all business students and may include mentorship and internship opportunities.

WILLAMETTE UNIVERSITY
Atkinson Graduate School of Management

THE BASICS

Willamette's MBA programs build the knowledge and experience needed for careers in business, government and not-for-profit organizations.

Programs include the Early Career MBA for students seeking their first professional position; the MBA for Career Change for students seeking career change or advancement; and the MBA for Professionals for experienced students seeking career enhancement or advancement.

All Willamette MBA programs emphasize hands-on learning and are accredited by AACSB International—the global hallmark of excellence in business education.

ACADEMICS AND PROGRAMS

Early Career MBA and MBA for Career Change
The Early Career MBA and the MBA for Career Change are full-time MBA programs designed for students seeking career entry, change and advancement. In just 21 months, students learn the core principles of management, refine their career interests, develop an in-depth understanding of one or more career areas of interest, and build the portfolio of experience needed to succeed in a competitive job market

Faculty are excellent teachers committed to their students and to the educational model of "learning by doing." From the first day of class, students apply what they learn to real organizations. Class consulting projects with real clients, internships, in-depth case studies, innovative hands-on elective courses, and a complete program of career services offer powerful opportunities for professional development.

Areas of interest include accounting; entrepreneurship; finance; human resources; marketing; operations, analysis and systems; organizational analysis; sustainability management; and public and not-for-profit management.

Courses are taught on the Willamette University campus in Salem, Oregon. International exchange programs are available at Bordeaux Business School (France), Copenhagen Business School (Denmark) and E.M. Strasbourg Business School (France).

MBA for Professionals
Willamette's MBA for Professionals provides individuals with three or more years of work experience the opportunity to complete their MBA while employed. The program offers a quality AACSB International accredited MBA, experiential learning and convenient evening classes.

Students learn from professors who emphasize an integrated and practical approach to management concepts. The structure of the program helps students immediately apply what they learn to their job and accelerate their career in their organizations.

The MBA for Professionals is cohort based and can be completed in 24 months of evening study in Portland or Salem.

ADMISSIONS

Applicants interested in the Early Career MBA or the MBA for Career Change should visit http://www.willamette.edu/agsm/full-time/admission/ for information. Applicants interested in the MBA for Professionals program should visit http://www.willamette.edu/agsm/pmba/admission/ for information.

STUDENT BODY

Our students are described by their references as energetic, creative, ethical, exceptional, friendly, mature, hard working, insightful, professional, reliable, team-players and leaders.

Early Career and Career Change students come from around the world and across the U.S. The average student is 25 years of age, has zero to five

years of work experience, and is utilizing the MBA to prepare for career entry or career change.

MBA for Professionals students have three or more years of work experience and are preparing for career advancement and enhancement. The average student is 33 years of age and employed while completing their MBA. Students represent a wide variety of organizations from the Portland/Salem metropolitan areas (business, consulting, entrepreneurial ventures, government, not-for-profit).

CAMPUS LIFE AND FACILITIES

Location and lifestyle are two important benefits of the Willamette MBA experience. Our locations offer an excellent quality of life, friendly people, mild climate and the recreational resources of the beautiful Pacific Northwest. Professionally, the Portland-Salem area provides convenient access to a multitude of businesses (including Northwest legends Nike, Intel, and Tektronix) and hosts a number of government and not-for-profit organizations.

The MBA community participates in a variety of professional and social/recreational activities. Student professional organizations are available in accounting, consulting, finance, human resources, marketing, net-impact, project management, and the National Association of Women MBAs. Social organizations include the Atkinson student association, international graduate student association, golf association, and outdoor club. Barbecues, receptions, the international student dinner, community service projects, holiday celebrations, alumni activities, pizza nights, traditional Thursday Night Out events, and recreational activities balance the academic demands of the program.

The Salem campus includes two libraries, recreational and fitness facilities, dining centers, student center, concert hall, art museum, and more. The Portland Center is conveniently located in the Pearl District with easy access to public transportation and public parking. All facilities offer wireless access to the Internet, email, network software and printing services.

CAREERS

An outstanding program of career services supports the goals of Willamette MBA students. Services include the best practices of career management, workshops, internship programs, on-campus interviews, employment postings, databases, individual counseling, mentoring programs, career/networking fairs, peer advisors and student professional organizations.

Nearly 100 percent of Early Career/Career Change students participate in an internship. A sample of internship employers includes Columbia Sportswear, Hewlett Packard, Merrill Lynch, Microsoft, Nike, Tektronix, U.S. State Department and State of Oregon.

Eighty percent of Early Career/Career Change students generally receive a job offer for a professional position within three months of graduation. Typical employers include Nautilus, IBM, Mentor Graphics, KPMG, Hewlett Packard Company, Key Bank, Intel Corporation, State of Oregon, Tektronix and Providence Health Systems.

TUITION AND FINANCIAL AID

2009–10 tuition for Early Career MBA and MBA for Career Change programs is $29,900 for the two semester academic year. Merit-based scholarships, Federal Direct Stafford Loans and Federal Direct Graduate Plus Loans are available to eligible students.

2009–10 tuition for the MBA for Professionals is $49,480 (total cost) for the six-semester program. Tuition for the MBA for Professionals includes the cost of books and fees. Federal Direct Stafford Loans and Federal Direct Graduate Plus Loans are available to eligible students.

DECODING DEGREES

Many business programs offer a number of degrees, including joint- or combined-degree programs with other departments (or with other schools) that you can earn along with your MBA. You'll find the abbreviations for these degrees in the individual school profiles, but we thought we'd give you a little help in figuring out exactly what they are.

AGSIM	American Graduate School of International Management Social Service Administration		MA	Master of Arts
			MAB	Master of Agribusiness
APC	Advanced Professional Certificate		MAcc	Master of Accountancy (or Accounting)
BA	Bachelor of Arts		MAAE	Master of Arts in Applied Economics
BASC	Bachelor in Engineering		MAEcon	Master of Arts in Economics
BBA	Bachelor of Business Administration		MAg	Master of Agriculture
BPA	Bachelor of Public Affairs		MAIB	Master of Arts in International Business
BS	Bachelor of Science		MAIS	Master of Accounting and Information Systems
BSB	Bachelor of Science in Business			
BSBA	Bachelor of Science in Business Administration		MALL	Master of Arts in Language Learning
			MAPS	Master of Asian Pacific Studies
CIS	Computer Information Systems (or Sciences)		MAR	Master of Arts in Religion
			MArch	Master of Architecture
DBA	Doctor of Business Administration		MAS	Master of Actuarial Science
DDS	Doctor of Dental Surgery		MBA	Master of Business Administration
DMD	Doctor of Dental Medicine		MBE	Master of Business Education
DO	Doctor of Osteopathic Medicine		MBI	Master of Business Informatics
DPS	Doctor of Professional Studies		MBS	Master of Business Studies
EdD	Doctor of Education		MD	Doctor of Medicine
EDM	Executive Doctor of Management		MDIV	Master of Divinity
EMBA	Executive MBA		ME	Master of Engineering
EMIB	Executive Master of International Business		MECOM	Master of Electronic Commerce
EMPA	Executive Master of Public Administration		MEd	Master of Educational Leadership/ Master of Education
EMS	Executive Master of Science		MEM	Master of Engineering and Management
EMSM	Executive Master of Science in Management		MEng	Master of Engineering
EMSMOT	Executive Master of Science in Management of Technology		MF	Master of Forestry
			MFA	Master of Fine Arts
EMST	Executive Master of Science in Taxation		MHA	Master of Health Administration
GDPA	Graduate Diploma in Accounting		MHR	Master of Human Resources
GEMBA	Global Executive Master of Business Administration		MHRM	Master of Human Resources Management
HRIM	Hotel, Restaurants and Institutional Management		MIA	Master of International Affairs
			MIAS	Master of International and Area Studies
IAMBA	Information Age Master of Business Administration		MIB	Master of International Business
			MIE	Master of Industrial Engineering
IMBA	International MBA		MILR	Master of Industrial and Labor Relations
IPD	Interdisciplinary Product Development		MIM	Master of International Management
JD	Juris Doctorate		MIS	Management Information Systems
LLB	Bachelor of Law			

MISM	Master of Information Systems Management	MSIM	Master of Science in Industrial Management
MLAS	Master of Liberal Arts and Science	MSIMC	Master of Science in Integrated Marketing Communications
MMIS	Master of Management Information Systems	MSIR	Master of Science in Industrial Relations
MMR	Master of Marketing Research	MSIS	Master of Science in Information Systems
MMS	Master of Management Science	MSISE	Master of Science in Industrial and Systems Engineering
MNO	Master of Nonprofit Organizations		
MOD	Master of Science in Organizational Development	MSISM	Master of Science in Information Systems Management
MPA	Master of Public Administration	MSIT	Master of Science in Information Technology
MPAcc	Master of Professional Accounting	MSITM	Master of Science in Information Technology Management
MPH	Master of Public Health		
MPIA Affairs	Master of Public and International	MSM	Master of Science in Management
		MSMIS	Master of Science in Management Information Systems
MPL	Master of Planning		
MPP	Master of Public Policy	MSMOT	Master of Science in Management of Technology
MRED	Master of Real Estate Development		
MS	Master of Science	MSN	Master of Science in Nursing
MSA	Master of Science in Accountancy (or Accounting)	MSOD	Master of Science in Organization Development
MSAIS	Master of Science in Accounting Information Systems	MSpAd	Master of Sports Administration
		MSRE	Master of Science in Real Estate
MSAT	Master of Science in Accountancy, Taxation	MSS	Master of Social Science
		MSSA	Master of Science in Social Administration
MSB	Master of Science in Business	MST	Master of Science in Taxation
MSBA	Master of Science in Business Administration	MSTM	Master of Science in Telecommunications Management
MSE	Master of Science in Engineering		
MSEC	Master of Science in Electronic Commerce	MSW	Master of Social Work
		MTAX	Master of Taxation
MSF	Master of Science in Finance	MTLM	Master of Transportation and Logistics Management
MSFA	Master of Science in Financial Analysis		
MSFS	Master of Science in Foreign Services	NEMBA	National Executive Master of Business Administration
MSG	Master of Science in Gerontology		
MSGFA	Master of Science in Global Financial Analysis	PharmD	Doctor of Pharmacy
		PhD	Doctor of Philosophy
MSHA	Master of Science in Health Administration	SM	Master of Science
MSHFID	Master of Science in Human Factors in Information Design	TSM	Telecommunications Systems Management
MSIAM	Master of Science in Information Age Marketing	VMD	Doctor of Veterinary Medicine
MSIB Business	Master of Science in International		
MSIE	Master of Science in Industrial Engineering		

INDEX

ALPHABETICAL INDEX

INDEX BY LOCATION

INTERNATIONAL

INDEX BY COST

$15,000–$30,000

MORE THAN $30,000

INDEX BY MBA CONCENTRATION

HEALTHCARE ADMINISTRATION

HUMAN RESOURCES MANAGEMENT

NON-PROFIT MANAGEMENT

SUPPLY CHAIN MANAGEMENT

ABOUT THE AUTHOR

Nedda Gilbert is a graduate of the University of Pennsylvania and holds a master's degree from Columbia University. She has worked for The Princeton Review since 1985. In 1987, she created The Princeton Review corporate test preparation service, which provides Wall Street firms and premier companies tailored educational programs for their employees. She currently resides in New Jersey.

NOTES

NOTES

NOTES

NOTES

NOTES

NOTES

NOTES

Share your Princeton Review® success story with us!

Email **PrincetonReviewGuides@randomhouse.com** with your name, story, and the title of the guidebook that helped you crack a test or pick the perfect school.

By submitting your story, you agree to grant to Princeton Review a perpetual, non-exclusive, royalty-free, worldwide license to use your name and story, in whole or in part, in all media whether now known or hereinafter devised, on and in connetion with Princeton Review's publications and in the advertising and promotion thereof.

More expert advice from The Princeton Review

Increase your chances of getting into the business school of your choice with **The Princeton Review**. We can help you get higher test scores, make the most informed choices, and make the most of your experience once you get there. We can also help you make the career move that will let you use your skills and education to their best advantage.

Cracking the GMAT, 2011
978-0-375-42975-0
$22.99/C$26.99

1,012 GMAT Practice Questions
978-0-375-42927-9
$19.99/C$24.99

Verbal Workout for the GMAT, 2nd Edition
978-0-375-76462-2
$19.00/C$27.00

Math Workout for the GMAT, 3rd Edition
978-0-375-42985-9
$19.99/C$23.99

Cracking the GMAT with DVD, 2011
978-0-375-42976-7
$37.99/C$44.99

The Best 300 Business Schools, 2011
978-0-375-42790-9
$22.99/C$25.99

Word Smart for Business
978-0-679-78391-6
$12.95/C$19.95

The Anxious Test-Taker's Guide to Cracking Any Test
978-0-375-42935-4
$14.99/C$18.99

Available everywhere books are sold and at **PrincetonReviewBooks.com**